ADMIRALTY
AND
MARITIME LAW

VOLUME 1

ADMIRALTY
AND
MARITIME LAW

ROBERT FORCE
A.N. YIANNOPOULOS
MARTIN DAVIES

VOLUME 1

Beard Books
Washington, D.C.

CONTENTS

TABLE OF CASES

CHAPTER 1 — CARRIAGE OF GOODS

A. Carriage Under Bills of Lading

1. Historical Introduction

From the General Maritime Law to
the Carriage of Goods by Sea Act (COGSA)

During the eighteenth and nineteenth centuries, legislation and judicial practice in many countries in pursuit of "national" maritime policies displaced the venerable uniform "law of the sea" and gave rise to a sharp conflict of laws. By the end of the 19th century divergences in the regulation of sea-carriers' liability under contracts of affreightment evidenced by bills of lading had attracted attention and caused concern. The most spectacular conflict involved the question of the validity of "negligence" clauses, namely clauses designed to exonerate the carrier from liability for negligence in connection with damage to the cargo.

In some countries cargo interests prevailed and strict liability was imposed on carriers for loss or damage to the goods carried; in other countries hull interests prevailed, and carriers enjoyed an almost unlimited freedom of contract. Moreover, the national policy favoring either the shipper or the carrier was frequently extended through the adoption of choice of law rules designed to safeguard application of national law to bills of lading involving international contracts. Thus, due to varying substantive standards and conflicts rules, a negligence clause inserted in an international bill of lading could be valid in one country and invalid in another, and the liability of the carrier could differ with the forum. As a result, security in international transactions was endangered, the negotiability of bills of lading was imperiled, and world trade was seriously hampered.

Under the general maritime law of the United States as it existed until the middle of the 19th century, the contract of affreightment was generally enforceable according to its terms. Beginning in the 1880's, however, most state courts and federal courts consistently refused to enforce "unreasonable" stipulations inserted in domestic or international bills of lading. Soon it became "settled law" and "elementary doctrine" that exemptions limiting carriers from responsibility for the negligence of themselves or their servants were both "unjust and unreasonable, wanting in voluntary assent ... and in conflict with public policy." *See The Kensington*, 183 U.S. 263, 268, 22 S.Ct. 102, 46 L.Ed. 190 (1902). This legal regime did not successfully safeguard American cargo interests, because most cargo to or from the United States was carried in British ships, and it did not encourage the growth of American shipping industries. In order to attain these aims, the Harter Act (46 U.S.C.A. §§ 30702-30707, formerly 46 U.S.C. §§ 190-196) was passed in 1893.

It has been said that the Harter Act was enacted as a result of pressure from American carriers by water who "were naturally unhappy with the decisions prohibiting bills of lading 'negligence' clauses and holding them liable for the consequences of unseaworthiness, even when caused by no fault on their part" and "pressed for legislation entitling them to do what their British competitors were allowed to do under the English decisions, *i.e.*, contract away their liability for cargo loss, damage and delay caused by fault and unseaworthiness." HEALY AND SHARPE, CASES AND MATERIALS ON ADMIRALTY 300 (2d ed. 1986). However, it has been also said that it was the discontent of shippers of cargo, of their underwriters and bankers, who "forced a statutory solution of the problem, at least to the extent of legislating 'certain rules' agreed to by all interested parties and of forbidding certain other clauses, and of leaving the remaining field of free contract for further consideration by the courts." KNAUTH, THE AMERICAN LAW OF OCEAN BILLS OF LADING 116 (4th ed. 1953).

Whether the Harter Act was originally conceived as an instrument of international trade war or as a concession to American cargo interests, it was in fact a compromise between shippers' and carriers' interests. Under the Act, clauses relieving the shipowner from liability for negligence were declared "null and void and of no effect," but the shipowner was relieved from liability for negligence "in navigation or in the management" of the vessel if he used due diligence to make his vessel "seaworthy." Initially designed to apply only to foreign trade, the Harter Act was extended to cover domestic trade as well and was declared applicable to all shipments to and from the ports of the United States. This Act still plays an important role in the regulation of both the domestic and the international trade of the United States.

The United States, having succeeded in reaching this compromise between the conflicting interests of shippers and carriers, took the lead in urging a uniform international regulation of the sea-carriers' liabilities along similar lines. The need for such regulation was generally felt, and action was taken by interested business groups and international organizations, such as the International Law Association and the Comité Maritime International. After several decades of preparatory work and backstage negotiations, the International Law Association adopted at its Hague meeting in 1921 a body of rules known as "Hague Rules, 1921." The Hague Rules were drafted in the form of a uniform bill of lading in the hope that the great shipping companies would adopt them voluntarily and that smaller operators would follow suit. The carriers, however, were not prepared to give up their extensive immunities under the then existing laws of several countries, and it became apparent that legislative action was necessary to make the new rules a part of bills of lading. Introduction of uniform legislation by a number of contracting states in accordance with the provisions of an international convention seemed to be the proper way, and a tentative Draft Convention incorporating the Hague Rules was submitted by the Belgian Government to the Fifth Diplomatic Conference on Maritime Law (Brussels, October 1922). The original text of the Hague Rules was extensively discussed by the Conference in a number of sessions, and a final text was agreed upon. In the following year, the Rules were slightly amended by a committee appointed by the Conference, and finally, the movement for uniformity culminated in an International Convention for the Unification of Certain Rules of Law relating to Bills of Lading, signed in Brussels on August 25, 1924.

The Brussels Convention was not conceived as a comprehensive and self-sufficient code regulating the carriage of goods by sea; it was intended merely to unify certain rules relating to bills of lading, and only with regard to damages occurring to hull cargo (live animals excepted) between the time of loading and discharge. All bills of lading covered by the Convention were subject to certain standard clauses that define both the risks assumed by the carrier that cannot be altered by contrary agreement, and the immunities the carrier can enjoy unless the parties agree otherwise. In general, clauses relieving the carrier from liability for negligence in the loading, handling, stowing, keeping, carrying, and the discharge of the goods or diminishing his obligation to furnish a seaworthy vessel are declared null and void. The carrier is relieved from liability for negligence in "navigation or in the management" of the vessel and from the absolute warranty of seaworthiness. According to its Article X, the Convention applies to all bills of lading issued in any of the contracting States.

It was hoped that by balancing the conflicting policies of maritime nations and the interests of shippers and carriers, the Brussels Convention would standardize the liabilities of carriers on the international level. And it was expected that, as to matters regulated by the Convention, the outcome of litigation would be the same in the courts of any of the contracting states. The optimism that prevailed at the time the Convention was signed has largely been vindicated. Most of the maritime nations have ratified or adhered to the Brussels Convention; other countries, without formally adhering to the Convention, have enacted special legislation incorporating the rules agreed on in Brussels. In spite of this substantial formal uniformity of domestic legislation, however, problems in the determination of the carriers' liability and the validity of negligence clauses in bills of lading still persist. The very text of the Convention, as finally adopted, left the door open for subsequent variations to the prejudice of the desired uniformity. States adopted the rules with modifications and textual variations using various legislative methods; hence, conflicts among texts incorporating the uniform rules as well as conflicting interpretations are possible. Moreover, the area of application of the uniform rules and the choice of law applied to bills of lading outside the scope of the rules may differ from country to country. These divergences in domestic legislation and choice of law rules breed uncertainty. Depending on the place of litigation, the same bill of lading may or may not be subject to the uniform rules, even where the forum is a contracting country and the bill of lading involves contacts with another contracting nation. In certain cases the liability of the carrier may vary with the forum, and a negligence clause may be valid in one country and invalid in another, which is contrary to both the letter and spirit of the Brussels Convention.

In 1936 the United States enacted the Carriage of Goods by Sea Act (COGSA) (46 U.S.C. §§ 1300-1312), which adopted with some variation the text of Articles I to VIII of the Convention, and included provisions defining its area of application and its relation to other legislation of the United States. Less than a year after COGSA became effective, the United States deposited its ratification of the Brussels Convention (June 29, 1937). Textual variations between the Carriage of Goods by Sea Act and the Convention give rise to the question of the binding force of the latter on courts and individuals in the United States. Under the United States Constitution, an international treaty, if self-executing, is part of the law of the land. The Brussels Convention, however, was ratified subject to an "understanding" that, if the provisions of the Convention and the provisions of the Carriage of Goods by Sea Act should conflict, the Act shall prevail over the Convention. Thus, while a part of the law of the United States, the Convention is not directly binding upon courts and individuals; the law governing bills of lading is to be found in COGSA and related legislation.

---

2. Legislation

THE HARTER ACT
46 U.S.C.A. §§ 30702-30707

§ 30701. Definition

In this chapter, the term "carrier" means the owner, manager, charterer, agent, or master of a vessel.

§ 30702. Application

(a) In General—Except as otherwise provided, this chapter applies to a carrier engaged in the carriage of goods to or from any port in the United States.

(b) Live Animals—Sections 30703 and 30704 of this title do not apply to the carriage of live animals.

§ 30703. Bills of Lading

(a) Issuance—On demand of a shipper, the carrier shall issue a bill of lading or shipping document.

(b) Contents—The bill of lading or shipping document shall include a statement of—

(1) the marks necessary to identify the goods;

(2) the number of packages, or the quantity or weight, and whether it is carrier's or shipper's weight; and

(3) the apparent condition of the goods.

(c) Prima Facie Evidence of Receipt—A bill of lading or shipping document issued under this section is prima facie evidence of receipt of the goods described.

§ 30704. Loading, stowage, custody, care, and delivery

A carrier may not insert in a bill of lading or shipping document a provision avoiding its liability for loss or damage arising from negligence or fault in loading, stowage, custody, care, or proper delivery. Any such provision is void.

§ 30705. Seaworthiness

(a) Prohibition—A carrier may not insert in a bill of lading or shipping document a provision lessening or avoiding its obligation to exercise due diligence to—

(1) make the vessel seaworthy; and
(2) properly man, equip, and supply the vessel.

(b) Voidness—A provision described in subsection (a) is void.

§ 30706. Defenses

(a) Due Diligence—If a carrier has exercised due diligence to make the vessel in all respects seaworthy and to properly man, equip, and supply the vessel, the carrier and the vessel are not liable for loss or damage arising from an error in the navigation or management of the vessel.

(b) Other Defenses—A carrier and the vessel are not liable for loss or damage arising from—

(1) dangers of the sea or other navigable waters;
(2) acts of God;
(3) public enemies;
(4) seizure under legal process;
(5) inherent defect, quality, or vice of the goods;
(6) insufficiency of package;
(7) act or omission of the shipper or owner of the goods or their agent; or
(8) saving or attempting to save life or property at sea, including a deviation in rendering such a service.

§ 30707. Criminal Penalty

(a) In General—A carrier that violates this chapter shall be fined under title 18.

(b) Lien—The amount of the fine and costs for the violation constitute a lien on the vessel engaged in the carriage. A civil action *in rem* to enforce the lien may be brought in the district court of the United States for any district in which the vessel is found.

(c) Disposition of Fine—Half of the fine shall go to the person injured by the violation and half to the United States Government.

THE HARTER ACT, 1893

(Superseded Version)

46 App. U.S.C. 190, *et seq.*

§ 190. Stipulations relieving from liability for negligence

It shall not be lawful for the manager, agent, master, or owner of any vessels transporting merchandise or property from or between ports of the United States and foreign ports to insert in any bill of lading or shipping document any clause, covenant, or agreement whereby it, her, or they shall be relieved from liability for loss or damage arising from negligence, fault, or failure in proper loading, stowage, custody, care, or proper delivery of any and all lawful merchandise or property committed to its or their charge. Any and all words or clauses of such import inserted in bills of lading or shipping receipts shall be null and void and of no effect.

§ 191. Stipulations relieving from exercise of due diligence in equipping vessels

It shall not be lawful for any vessel transporting merchandise or property from or between ports of the United States of America and foreign ports, her owner, master, agent, or manager, to insert in any bill of lading or shipping document any covenant or agreement whereby the obligations of the owner or owners of said vessel to exercise due diligence [to] properly equip, man, provision, and outfit said vessel, and to make said vessel seaworthy and capable of performing her intended voyage, or whereby the obligations of the master, officers, agents, or servants to carefully handle and stow her cargo and to care for and properly deliver same, shall in any wise be lessened, weakened, or avoided.

§ 192. Limitation of liability for errors of navigation, dangers of the sea and acts of God

If the owner of any vessel transporting merchandise or property to or from any port in the United States of America shall exercise due diligence to make the said vessel in all respects seaworthy and properly manned, equipped, and supplied, neither the vessel, her owner or owners, agent, or charterers, shall become or be held responsible for damage or loss resulting from faults or errors in navigation or in the management of said vessel nor shall the vessel, her owner or owners, charterers, agent, or master be held liable for losses arising from dangers of the sea or other navigable waters, acts of God, or public enemies, or the inherent defect, quality, or vice of the thing carried, or from insufficiency of package, or seizure under legal process, or for loss resulting from any act or omission of the shipper or owner of the goods, his agent or representative, or from saving or attempting to save life or property at sea, or from any deviation in rendering such service.

§ 193. Bills of lading to be issued; contents

It shall be the duty of the owner or owners, masters, or agent of any vessel transporting merchandise or property from or between ports of the United States and foreign ports to issue to shippers of any lawful merchandise a bill of lading, or shipping document, stating, among other things, the marks necessary for identification, number of packages, or quantity, stating whether it be carrier's or shipper's weight, and apparent order or condition of such merchandise or property delivered to and received by the owner, master, or agent of the vessel for transportation, and such document shall be *prima facie* evidence of the receipt of the merchandise therein described.

§ 194. Penalties; lien; recovery

For a violation of any of the provisions of sections 190-193 of this title the agent, owner, or master of the vessel guilty of such violations, and who refuses to issue on demand the bill of lading provided for, shall be liable to a fine not exceeding $2,000. The amount of the fine and costs for such violation shall be a lien upon the vessel, whose agent, owner, or master is guilty of such violation, and such vessel may be libeled therefor in any district court of the

United States, within whose jurisdiction the vessel may be found. One-half of such penalty shall go to the party injured by such violation and the remainder to the Government of the United States.

§ 195. Certain provisions inapplicable to transportation of live animals

Sections 190 and 193 of this title shall not apply to the transportation of live animals.

§ 196. Certain laws unaffected

Sections 190-195 of this title shall not be held to modify or repeal sections 181, 182, and 183 of this title, or any other statute defining the liability of vessels, their owners, or representatives.

CARRIAGE OF GOODS BY SEA ACT[1]

46 U.S.C.A § 30701, Statutory Note

[Note]. Bills of lading subject to chapter

Every bill of lading or similar document of title which is evidence of a contract for the carriage of goods by sea to or from ports of the United States, in foreign trade, shall have effect subject to the provisions of this chapter.

§ 1. Definitions

When used in this chapter—

(a)   The term "carrier" includes the owner or the charterer who enters into a contract of carriage with a shipper.

(b)   The term "contract of carriage" applies only to contracts of carriage covered by a bill of lading or any similar document of title, insofar as such document relates to the carriage of goods by sea, including any bill of lading or any similar document as aforesaid issued under or pursuant to a charter party from the moment at which such bill of lading or similar document of title regulates the relations between a carrier and a holder of the same.

(c)   The term "goods" includes goods, wares, merchandise, and articles of every kind whatsoever except live animals and cargo which by the contract of carriage is stated as being carried on deck and is so carried.

(d)   The term "ship" means any vessel used for the carriage of goods by sea.

(e)   The term "carriage of goods" covers the period from the time when the goods are loaded on to the time when they are discharged from the ship.

* * *

§ 2. Duties and rights of carrier

Subject to the provisions of section 1306 of this title, under every contract of carriage of goods by sea, the carrier in relation to the loading, handling, stowage, carriage, custody, care, and discharge of such goods, shall be subject to the responsibilities and liabilities and entitled to the rights and immunities set forth in sections 1303 and 1304 of this title.

---

[1] The Carriage of Goods by Sea Act was formerly codified in Title 46 U.S.C. §§ 1300-1315. When Congress began to re-codify Title 46, COGSA was placed in an Appendix to that title but retained the same section numbers and substantive content. Congress has recently completed the re-codification which does not contain COGSA. COGSA was originally enacted by the 74th Congress as: the law of April 16, 1936 C. 229, 49 Stat. 1207.

§ 3. Responsibilities and liabilities of carrier and ship

Seaworthiness

(1) The carrier shall be bound, before and at the beginning of the voyage, to exercise due diligence to—

   (a) Make the ship seaworthy;
   (b) Properly man, equip, and supply the ship;
   (c) Make the holds, refrigerating and cooling chambers, and all other parts of the ship in which goods are carried, fit and safe for their reception, carriage, and preservation.

Cargo

(2) The carrier shall properly and carefully load, handle, stow, carry, keep, care for, and discharge the goods carried.

Contents of Bill

(3) After receiving the goods into his charge the carrier, or the master or agent of the carrier, shall, on demand of the shipper, issue to the shipper a bill of lading showing among other things—

   (a) The leading marks necessary for identification of the goods as the same are furnished in writing by the shipper before the loading of such goods, starts, provided such marks are stamped or otherwise shown clearly upon the goods if uncovered, or on the cases or coverings in which such goods are contained, in such a manner as should ordinarily remain legible until the end of the voyage.
   (b) Either the number of packages or pieces, or the quantity or weight, as the case may be, as furnished in writing by the shipper.
   (c) The apparent order and condition of the goods: *Provided*, That no carrier, master, or agent of the carrier, shall be bound to state or show in the bill of lading any marks, number, quantity, or weight which he has reasonable ground for suspecting not accurately to represent the goods actually received, or which he has had no reasonable means of checking.

Bill as Prima Facie Evidence

(4) Such a bill of lading shall be *prima facie* evidence of the receipt by the carrier of the goods as therein described in accordance with paragraphs (3) (a), (b), and (c), of this section: *Provided*, That nothing in this chapter shall be construed as repealing or limiting the application of any part of sections 81-124 of Title 49.
(The Pomerene Act.)

Guaranty of Statements

(5) The shipper shall be deemed to have guaranteed to the carrier the accuracy at the time of shipment of the marks, number, quantity, and weight, as furnished by him; and the shipper shall indemnify the carrier against all loss, damages, and expenses arising or resulting from inaccuracies in such particulars. The right of the carrier to such indemnity shall in no way limit his responsibility and liability under the contract of carriage to any person other than the shipper.

Notice of Loss or Damage; Limitation of Actions

(6) Unless notice of loss or damage and the general nature of such loss or damage be given in writing to the carrier or his agent at the port of discharge before or at the time of the removal of the goods into the custody of the person entitled to delivery thereof under the contract of carriage, such removal shall be *prima facie* evidence of the delivery by the carrier of the goods as described in the bill of lading. If the loss or damage is not apparent, the notice must be given within three days of the delivery.

   Said notice of loss or damage may be endorsed upon the receipt for the goods given by the person taking delivery thereof.

The notice in writing need not be given if the state of the goods has at the time of their receipt been the subject of joint survey or inspection.

In any event the carrier and the ship shall be discharged from all liability in respect of loss or damage unless suit is brought within one year after delivery of the goods or the date when the goods should have been delivered: *Provided,* That if a notice of loss or damage, either apparent or concealed, is not given as provided for in this section, that shall not affect or prejudice the right of the shipper to bring suit within one year after the delivery of the goods or the date when the goods should have been delivered.

In the case of any actual or apprehended loss or damage the carrier and receiver shall give all reasonable facilities to each other for inspecting and tallying the goods.

"Shipped" Bill of Lading

(7) After the goods are loaded the bill of lading to be issued by the carrier, master, or agent of the carrier to the shipper shall, if the shipper so demands, be a "shipped" bill of lading: *Provided,* That if the shipper shall have previously taken up any document of title to such goods, he shall surrender the same as against the issue of the "shipped" bill of lading, but at the option of the carrier such document of title may be noted at the port of shipment by the carrier, master, or agent with the name or names of the ship or ships upon which the goods have been shipped and the date or dates of shipment, and when so noted the same shall for the purpose of this section be deemed to constitute a "shipped" bill of lading.

Limitation of Liability for Negligence

(8) Any clause, covenant, or agreement in a contract of carriage relieving the carrier or the ship from liability for loss or damage to or in connection with the goods, arising from negligence, fault, or failure in the duties and obligations provided in this section, or lessening such liability otherwise than as provided in this chapter, shall be null and void and of no effect. A benefit of insurance in favor of the carrier, or similar clause, shall be deemed to be a clause relieving the carrier from liability.

§ 4. Rights and immunities of carrier and ship

Unseaworthiness

(1) Neither the carrier nor the ship shall be liable for loss or damage arising or resulting from unseaworthiness unless caused by want of due diligence on the part of the carrier to make the ship seaworthy, and to secure that the ship is properly manned, equipped, and supplied, and to make the holds, refrigerating and cool chambers, and all other parts of the ship in which goods are carried fit and safe for their reception, carriage, and preservation in accordance with the provisions of paragraph (1) of section 1303 of this title. Whenever loss or damage has resulted from unseaworthiness, the burden of proving the exercise of due diligence shall be on carrier or other persons claiming exemption under this section.

Uncontrollable Causes of Loss

(2) Neither the carrier nor the ship shall be responsible for loss or damage arising or resulting from—

- (a) Act, neglect, or default of the master, mariner, pilot, or the servants of the carrier in the navigation or in the management of the ship;
- (b) Fire, unless caused by the actual fault or privity of the carrier;
- (c) Perils, dangers, and accidents of the sea or other navigable water;
- (d) Act of God;
- (e) Act of war;
- (f) Act of public enemies;
- (g) Arrest or restraint of princes, rulers, or people, or seizure under legal process;
- (h) Quarantine restrictions;

(i)   Act or omission of the shipper or owner of the goods, his agent or representative;

(j)   Strikes or lockouts or stoppage or restraint of labor from whatever cause, whether partial or general: *Provided,* That nothing herein contained shall be construed to relieve a carrier from responsibility for the carrier's own acts;

(k)   Riots and civil commotions;

(l)   Saving or attempting to save life or property at sea;

(m) Wastage in bulk or weight or any other loss or damage arising from inherent defect, quality, or vice of the goods;

(n)   Insufficiency of packing;

(o)   Insufficiency or inadequacy of marks;

(p)   Latent defects not discoverable by due diligence; and

(q)   Any other cause arising without the actual fault and privity of the carrier and without the fault or neglect of the agents or servants of the carrier, but the burden of proof shall be on the person claiming the benefit of this exception to show that neither the actual fault or privity of the carrier nor the fault or neglect of the agents or servants of the carrier contributed to the loss or damage.

Freedom from Negligence

(3) The shipper shall not be responsible for loss or damage sustained by the carrier or the ship arising or resulting from any cause without the act, fault, or neglect of the shipper, his agents, or his servants.

Deviations

(4) Any deviation in saving or attempting to save life or property at sea, or any reasonable deviation shall not be deemed to be an infringement or breach of this chapter or of the contract of carriage, and the carrier shall not be liable for any loss or damage resulting therefrom: *Provided, however,* That if the deviation is for the purpose of loading or unloading cargo or passengers it shall, *prima facie,* be regarded as unreasonable.

Amount of Liability; Valuation of Cargo

(5) Neither the carrier nor the ship shall in any event be or become liable for any loss or damage to or in connection with the transportation of goods in an amount exceeding $500 per package lawful money of the United States, or in case of goods not shipped in packages, per customary freight unit, or the equivalent of that sum in other currency, unless the nature and value of such goods have been declared by the shipper before shipment and inserted in the bill of lading. This declaration, if embodied in the bill of lading, shall be *prima facie* evidence, but shall not be conclusive on the carrier.

By agreement between the carrier, master, or agent of the carrier, and the shipper another maximum amount than that mentioned in this paragraph may be fixed: *Provided,* That such maximum shall not be less than the figure above named. In no event shall the carrier be liable for more than the amount of damage actually sustained.

Neither the carrier nor the ship shall be responsible in any event for loss or damage to or in connection with the transportation of the goods if the nature or value thereof has been knowingly and fraudulently misstated by the shipper in the bill of lading.

Inflammable, Explosive, or Dangerous Cargo

(6) Goods of an inflammable, explosive, or dangerous nature to the shipment whereof the carrier, master or agent of the carrier, has not consented with knowledge of their nature and character, may at any time before discharge be landed at any place or destroyed or rendered innocuous by the carrier without compensation, and the shipper of such goods shall be liable for all damages and expenses directly or indirectly arising out of or resulting from such shipment. If any such goods shipped with such knowledge and consent shall become a danger to the ship or cargo, they may in like manner be landed at any place, or destroyed or rendered innocuous by the carrier without liability on the part of the carrier except to general average, if any.

§ 5. Surrender of rights; increase of liabilities; charter parties general average

A carrier shall be at liberty to surrender in whole or in part all or any of his rights and immunities or to increase any of his responsibilities and liabilities under this chapter, provided such surrender or increase shall be embodied in the bill of lading issued to the shipper.

The provisions of this chapter shall not be applicable to charter parties; but if bills of lading are issued in the case of a ship under a charter party, they shall comply with the terms of this chapter. Nothing in this chapter shall be held to prevent the insertion in a bill of lading of any lawful provision regarding general average.

§ 6. Special agreement as to particular goods

Notwithstanding the provisions of sections 1303-1305 of this title, a carrier, master or agent of the carrier, and a shipper shall, in regard to any particular goods be at liberty to enter into any agreement in any terms as to the responsibility and liability of the carrier for such goods, and as to the rights and immunities of the carrier in respect of such goods, or his obligation as to seaworthiness (so far as the stipulation regarding seaworthiness is not contrary to public policy), or the care or diligence of his servants or agents in regard to the loading, handling, stowage, carriage, custody, care, and discharge of the goods carried by sea: *Provided*, That in this case no bill of lading has been or shall be issued and that the terms agreed shall be embodied in a receipt which shall be a nonnegotiable document and shall be marked as such.

Any agreement so entered into shall have full legal effect: *Provided*, That this section shall not apply to ordinary commercial shipments made in the ordinary course of trade but only to other shipments where the character or condition of the property to be carried or the circumstances, terms, and conditions under which the carriage is to be performed are such as reasonably to justify a special agreement.

§ 7. Agreement as to liability prior to loading or after discharge

Nothing contained in this chapter shall prevent a carrier or a shipper from entering into any agreement, stipulation, condition, reservation, or exemption as to the responsibility and liability of the carrier or the ship for the loss or damage to or in connection with the custody and care and handling of goods prior to the loading on and subsequent to the discharge from the ship on which the goods are carried by sea.

§ 8. Rights and liabilities under other provisions of Title 46

The provisions of this chapter shall not affect the rights and obligations of the carrier under the provisions of the Shipping Act, 1916, or under the provisions of sections 175, 181-183, and 183b-188 of this title or of any amendments thereto; or under the provisions of any other enactment for the time being in force relating to the limitation of the liability of the owners of seagoing vessels.

§ 9. Discrimination between competing shippers

Nothing contained in this chapter shall be construed as permitting a common carrier by water to discriminate between competing shippers similarly placed in time and circumstances, either (a) with respect to their right to demand and receive bills of lading subject to the provisions of this chapter; or (b) when issuing such bills of lading, either in the surrender of any of the carrier's rights and immunities or in the increase of any of the carrier's rights and immunities or in the increase of any of the carrier's responsibilities and liabilities pursuant to section 1305 of this title; or (c) in any other way prohibited by the Shipping Act, 1916, as amended.

§ 10. Weight of bulk cargo

Where under the customs of any trade the weight of any bulk cargo inserted in the bill of lading is a weight ascertained or accepted by a third party other than the carrier or the shipper, and the fact that the weight is so ascertained or accepted is stated in the bill of lading, then, notwithstanding anything in this chapter, the bill of lading shall not be deemed to be prima facie evidence against the carrier of the receipt of goods of the weight so inserted in the bill of lading, and the accuracy thereof at the time of shipment shall not be deemed to have been guaranteed by the shipper.

§ 11. Liabilities before loading and after discharge; effect on other laws

Nothing in this chapter shall be construed as superseding any part of sections 190-196 of this title, or of any other law which would be applicable in the absence of this chapter, insofar as they relate to the duties, responsibilities, and liabilities of the ship or carrier prior to the time when the goods are loaded on or after the time they are discharged from the ship.

§ 12. Scope of Chapter; "United States; "foreign trade"

This chapter shall apply to all contracts for carriage of goods by sea to or from ports of the Unites States in foreign trade. As used in this chapter the term "United States" includes its districts, territories, and possessions. The term "foreign trade" means the transportation of goods between the ports of the United States and ports of foreign countries. Nothing in this chapter shall be held to apply to contracts for carriage of goods by sea between any port of the United States or its possessions, and any other port of the United States or its possessions: *Provided, however,* That any bill of lading or similar document of title which is evidence of a contract for the carriage of goods by sea between such ports, containing an express statement that it shall be subject to the provisions of this chapter, shall be subjected hereto as fully as if subject hereto by the express provisions of this chapter: *Provided further,* That every bill of lading or similar document of title which is evidence of a contract for the carriage of goods by sea from ports of the United States, in foreign trade, shall contain a statement that it shall have effect subject to the provisions of this chapter.

---

3. *Bills of Lading*

Introductory Note: Bills of Lading

Routine commercial activities often involve the formation of two kinds of contracts: sales contracts and transportation contracts. After having concluded a contract for the sale of goods either seller or purchaser may then enter into a contract of carriage, also referred to as a contract of affreightment, to provide for the transport of the goods to a particular place and delivery to a particular person. International sales transactions usually involve both sales and transportation contracts; interstate sales often do so as well. In such situations, not only must a seller sell goods to a purchaser, but the seller or the purchaser must arrange for someone to transport the goods to the purchaser or to the party who is ultimately to receive the goods.

Assume, for example, that Seller and Buyer have entered into a contract of sale and that the goods must be physically moved from Seller's place of business across a body of water, such as the Pacific Ocean, to Buyer's place of business. To this end, the services of a professional transporter are needed to accomplish this. Under the terms of this sales contract, Seller has the responsibility for arranging for transportation of the goods to Buyer. Seller has entered into a contract with a transporter, known as a "carrier," in which Carrier undertakes to deliver the goods on Seller's behalf to Buyer. This contract of carriage has given rise to new relationships. Seller who has arranged for the transport of the goods is no longer merely "the seller"; it has now also become "the shipper". Buyer is no longer just "the buyer"; it has now also become "the consignee". And a new party has entered the transaction, the company that has contracted to deliver the goods to the buyer-consignee is the "carrier".

In each aspect of the transaction, the participants have a variety of concerns. In the sales contract, Buyer wants the goods, title to the goods, and something like a bill of sale to show that it acquired the goods lawfully. Seller wants payment for the goods. The transportation contract raises a new set of concerns. Seller-as-shipper wants to assure that the goods will be delivered to the consignee or someone authorized to receive them— not anyone else. Buyer-as-consignee wants to assure that the goods will be released to it or its designee and to no one else. Carrier wants some method of identifying the buyer-consignee so that it can readily deliver the goods to the proper party. Carrier also wants to be paid for its services.

It is at this point that documents become an important factor in the transaction. How does the seller-shipper assure that it will be paid? How does the seller-shipper assure that the cargo will reach the consignee or its designee? How does the consignee lay proper claim to the cargo so the carrier will release it? How does the carrier assure itself that the person who claims the cargo has the right to receive it? The matter is made more complicated where buyer and seller have asked their respective banks to handle the payment and collection aspect of the sales transaction.

In these situations, a document, such as a bill of lading, may be used as a "link" between the sales part of the transaction and the transportation part of the transaction and may provide the assurances sought by the various parties. A bill of lading is a document issued by a carrier when goods have been received by it for transport from one port to another. Usually the shipper fills out the particulars on forms provided by the carrier. A bill of lading serves several purposes. It is a receipt which:

(1)   shows that the carrier received specific goods from the shipper;

(2)   evidences the contract of affreightment whereby the carrier agrees to transport shipper's goods from a specified place to another for a specified price;

(3)   is a document of delivery which allows the carrier to identify the party to whom it should deliver the cargo, and allows the person who possesses the bill of lading to have the goods released to it; and

(4)   may serve as a document of title, that is, by which it may prove ownership of the cargo.

After entering into the sales contract and promising to pay the sales price, Buyer notifies its bank, where it has established a line of credit, to expect a demand for payment from Seller's bank and, upon proper authorization, to pay the demand upon appropriate documentation from Seller's bank. Seller delivers goods to carrier and retains control of the goods by consigning the goods to itself. At Seller's request, Carrier issues a negotiable bill of lading to order of Seller. Seller then endorses the bill of lading in blank and gives the bill of lading to its bank to which is attached a document called a sight draft demanding payment. Seller's bank sends the bill of lading and draft to Buyer's bank which in turn notifies Buyer that it is in receipt of the bill of lading and draft. Buyer either pays the amount specified in the draft to its bank or through pre-arrangement with the bank authorizes the bank to debit its account in that amount. Buyer's bank then gives to Buyer the bill of lading and the draft. Buyer's bank forwards payment to Seller's bank which in turn deposits the amount in Seller's account or forwards the amount received to Seller depending on what arrangements have been made between Seller and its bank. Buyer gives Carrier the bill of lading and Carrier gives Buyer the goods, assuming that Carrier had been paid for transporting the goods.

Thus, in this transaction Seller is protected because the bill of lading will not be given to Buyer until the respective banks have assured that Seller will be paid the sales price. Carrier will not release the cargo to anyone except the person who presents the bill of lading. All parties are assured of delivery to the proper party, that is, the party who presents the bill of lading, because the transaction is structured so that only Buyer will have the bill of lading and then only after Seller has been assured of payment. Finally, inasmuch as Carrier has control of the goods, it can withhold delivery until it has been paid for its services. Of course, if freight (the charge for transporting the goods) has been pre-paid, there is no problem. If freight is to be paid by the buyer-consignee, then Carrier will insist on payment prior to releasing the cargo, for this right is invariably guaranteed in the bill of lading.

A carrier is not obliged to deliver the goods to any designated person but only to the person who presents the bill of lading. This makes it easy for the original buyer to transfer the bill to the person to whom it may have resold the goods, thereby enabling that party to receive them from the carrier. Some cargoes may be resold many times while in transit. Furthermore, banks which act as intermediaries are protected while they are in possession of the bill of lading. This is particularly important where a bank is extending credit to a buyer. Information contained in a bill of lading tells a bank that the cargo has been received by the carrier, loaded aboard a vessel and, the particulars about the cargo and its condition. Also, the bank can retain the bill of lading until the buyer has made satisfactory arrangements, if that had not been done beforehand.

There are alternatives to the use of negotiable bills of lading. The parties may use a straight (nonnegotiable) bill of lading or sea waybill to facilitate their transaction. Under these documents, the carrier delivers the goods to the person named in the document. Although it is not necessary for that person to produce a bill of lading, it will be necessary to produce proper identification. Likewise, a shipper may charter a vessel or part thereof in which case the charter party contract spells out the relations between shipper-charterer and the carrier.

FEDERAL BILLS OF LADING

49 U.S.C. §§ 80101-80116

(The Pomerene Act Recodified)

Text of the Statute appears on the Tulane Maritime Law Center website at www.tulanemaritimelaw.net/docs/pomerene

---

J.C.B. SALES, LTD. v. WALLENIUS LINES

124 F.3d 132, 1997 AMC 2705 (2d Cir. 1997)

VAN GRAAFEILAND, Circuit Judge:

M/V Seijin, *in rem*, and Wallenius Lines (Wallenius Lines North America, Inc.), the vessel's charterer, appeal from judgments of the United States District Court for the Southern District of New York (Pollack, J.) awarding damages to J.C.B. Sales Ltd., a British corporation, and Caterpillar, Inc., an Illinois corporation, for damage to machinery and equipment sustained during a voyage from Antwerp, Belgium and Southampton, England to Baltimore, Maryland. A third appellee, Land Rover Exports, Ltd., compromised its claim after the appeals against it were filed and is no longer a party. Liability has been stipulated. The only issue is the amount of the awards.

On February 28, 1995, Caterpillar delivered fifteen items of construction equipment to the M/V Seijin at Antwerp for carriage to Baltimore. The carrier, Wallenius, gave Caterpillar a Datafreight Receipt ("DFR"), which is prominently marked as non-negotiable and states that it:

is not a document of title to the goods [but] is deemed to be a contract of carriage which is subject to the exceptions, limitations, conditions and liberties ... set out in the Carrier's standard Terms and Conditions applicable to the voyage covered by this Datafreight Receipt and operative on its date of issue. Every reference in the Carrier's Standard Conditions of Carriage to the words "Bill of Lading" shall be read and construed as a reference to the words "Non-Negotiable Datafreight Receipt" and the terms and conditions thereof shall be read and construed accordingly.

Among the excerpts from the carrier's standard terms and conditions of carriage reproduced on the DFR is the following:

RESPONSIBILITY

11. Clause Paramount

(1) .... During any periods of carriage by water under this [DFR] the carriage shall be subject at all such times to

(a) The Hague Rules (meaning the provisions of the International Convention for the Unification of certain rules relating to Bills of Lading, dated Brussels the 25th August 1924) as enacted in the country of shipment, or if no such enactment is in force, as enacted in the country of destination, but in respect of shipments to which no such enactments are compulsorily applicable, the terms of the U.S. Carriage of Goods by Sea Act ... shall be considered incorporated herein as if set forth at length; or

(b) The Hague Visby Rules (meaning the Hague Rules as amended by the Protocol signed at Brussels on 23rd February 1968) in courts where they apply compulsorily.

After taking on Caterpillar's cargo, the M/V Seijin journeyed to Southampton where Wallenius and Caterpillar contracted to ship twenty-four additional items of construction equipment to Baltimore. Wallenius issued a second DFR, the terms of which are substantially the same as those of the Antwerp DFR. The Southampton DFR also states that it is non-negotiable and incorporates the "Carrier's Standard Conditions of Carriage applicable to the voyage," but recites from those standard conditions the following clause:

2. Responsibility.

The Hague Rules contained in the international convention for the unification of certain rules relating to bills of lading, dated Brussels the 25th August, 1924 as enacted in the country of shipment shall apply to this Contract. When no such enactment is in force in the country of shipment, the corresponding legislation of the country of destination shall apply, but in respect of shipments to which no such enactments are compulsory [sic] applicable, the terms of the said convention shall apply.

It also provides that the "Carrier's Standard Conditions of Carriage incorporate the Hague Rules contained in the Brussels Convention dated 25th August 1924 and any compulsorily applicable national enactment of these rules."

At Southampton, the M/V Seijin also took on for carriage to Baltimore eighty-one pieces of construction equipment from JCB for which it issued a DFR identical to Caterpillar's Southampton DFR. After a stop in Halifax, the M/V Seijin delivered the bulk of the cargo at Baltimore in seriously damaged condition. In the district court, the defendants sought unsuccessfully to limit their liability to $500 per package pursuant to the Carriage of Goods by Sea Act ("COGSA"), 46 U.S.C.App. §§ 1300 *et seq.*

COGSA represents the codification of the United States' obligations under the International Convention for the Unification of Certain Rules of Law Relating to Bills of Lading, August 25, 1924, 51 Stat. 233. This convention, which is also known as the Hague Rules, was the culmination of a multinational effort "to establish uniform ocean bills of lading to govern the rights and liabilities of carriers and shippers inter se in international trade." *Robert C. Herd & Co. v. Krawill Machinery Corp.*, 359 U.S. 297, 301, 79 S.Ct. 766, 768, 3 L.Ed.2d 820 (1959). Among the more prominent features of COGSA is its limitation of liability in the event of damage to or loss of cargo to "$500 per package ... or ... per customary freight unit ... unless the nature and value of such goods have been declared by the shipper before shipment and inserted in the bill of lading." 46 U.S.C.App. § 1304(5).

The Hague Rules, as enacted in COGSA, have remained the law in the United States since 1936 notwithstanding dramatic changes in the shipping industry. These changes prompted the convening of a diplomatic conference in 1968 which adopted a Protocol amending several provisions of the Hague Rules. Among other things, this Protocol, known as the Visby Amendments, increased the limitation on the carrier's liability to the higher of "the equivalent of 10,000 francs per package or unit or 30 francs per kilo of gross weight of the goods lost or damaged." Protocol to Amend the International Convention for the Unification of Certain Rules of Law Relating to Bills of Lading, Feb. 23, 1968, reprinted in 6 Benedict on Admiralty 1-25 to 1-29 (7th ed.1997). A subsequent 1979 Protocol further amended the limitation to provide for its calculation based on "special drawing rights," fluctuating units of account determined by the International Monetary Fund. Protocol Amending the International Convention for the Unification of Certain Rules of Law Relating to Bills of Lading, Dec. 21, 1979, reprinted in 6 BENEDICT, *supra*, at 1-32.2 to 1-32.5.

Because the United States ratified neither the Visby Amendments nor the 1979 Protocol, the $500 liability limitation controls in cases where COGSA applies. Both Belgium and the United Kingdom, however, employ the higher limitation set out in the 1979 Protocol. The difference in liability schemes is significant. If the $500 limitation of COGSA had been applied, defendants' liability to JCB would have been $18,061.84 rather than the $648,662.35 determined by the special drawing right. Similarly, defendants' liability to Caterpillar would have been $5,094.06 rather than the $128,141.36 pursuant to the special drawing right. The dispute in this case focuses primarily on whether the language in the DFRs expressing an intent to apply the "Hague Rules ... as enacted in the country of shipment" includes the Hague Rules as amended by the subsequent protocols.

In an opinion reported at 921 F.Supp. 1168 (S.D.N.Y.1996), Judge Pollack ruled that COGSA did not apply to the shippers' claims because the DFRs were not documents of title and therefore could not be bills of lading as that term is used in 46 U.S.C.App. § 1301(b). The district court went on to hold that the "as enacted" language of the DFRs evinced an intent to apply the Hague Rules that were in force in the countries of shipment, *i.e.* the Hague Rules as amended by the protocols.

Appellants contend that the district court made a number of errors. We turn first to Wallenius's contention that the district court erred in holding COGSA inapplicable on the ground that a DFR is not a "bill of lading or similar document of title" within the meaning of COGSA. COGSA applies to "all contracts for carriage of goods by sea to or from ports of the United States in foreign trade." *Id.* § 1312. However, the enacting clause of COGSA provides that it regulates rights and liabilities under "[e]very bill of lading or similar document of title which is evidence of a contract for the carriage of goods by sea to or from ports of the United States, in foreign trade." 46 U.S.C.App. § 1300. Section 1301(b) defines "contract of carriage" as applying "only to contracts of carriage covered by a bill of lading or any similar document of title, insofar as such document relates to the carriage of goods by sea."

Wallenius concedes that the DFRs are not documents of title, a concession compelled by the disclaimers appearing on the face of the documents. However, despite taking great pains to distance the DFRs from bills of lading, as evidenced by the provision that "[e]very reference" in the standard conditions of carriage to the phrase "bill of lading" is to "be read and construed as a reference to the words 'Non-Negotiable Datafreight Receipt,'" Wallenius contends that DFRs are forms of sea waybills and, as such, are the functional equivalent of non-negotiable straight bills of lading. There is ample authority, however, for the proposition that all bills of lading are documents of title. For example, section 1-201(15) of the Uniform Commercial Code states that " 'Document of title' includes bill of lading." See 1 RONALD ANDERSON, ANDERSON ON THE UNIFORM COMMERCIAL CODE 1-201 (3d ed. 1996) ("A bill of lading ... is a document of title."); see also WHARTON POOR, AMERICAN LAW OF CHARTER PARTIES AND OCEAN BILLS OF LADING § 59, at 134 (5th ed.1968); Stasia M. Williams, *Something Old, Something New: The Bill of Lading in the Days of EDI*, 1 TRANSNAT'L L. & CONTEMP. PROBS. 555, 560 (1991); *Associated Metals & Minerals Corp. v. S/S Jasmine*, 983 F.2d 410, 413 (2d Cir.1993); *Chase Manhattan Bank v. Nissho Pac. Corp.*, 22 A.D.2d 215, 224, 254 N.Y.S.2d 571 (N.Y.App.Div.1964), *aff'd*, 16 N.Y.2d 999, 265 N.Y.S.2d 660, 212 N.E.2d 897 (1965). An argument that, although a DFR is not a document of title, it is at the same time the functional equivalent of a non-negotiable bill of lading, which is by definition a document of title, is somewhat of an oxymoron.

In the final analysis, resolution of the issue whether the DFRs in the instant case are contracts of carriage under COGSA is not determinative of the issue of damages. Section 4(5) of COGSA, 46 U.S.C.App. § 1304(5), which contains the $500 maximum per package limitation, provides:

By agreement between the carrier, master, or agent of the carrier, and the shipper another maximum amount than that mentioned in this paragraph may be fixed: Provided, That such maximum shall not be less than the figure above named. In no event shall the carrier be liable for more than the amount of damage actually sustained.

If, as the district court held, the Hague Rules as modified by the Visby Amendments were incorporated into the contract of carriage, this constituted an agreement within the meaning of section 4(5). See *Francosteel Corp. v. M/V Deppe Europe*, No. 90 Civ. 1442, 1990 WL 121683, at *2 (S.D.N.Y. Aug. 10, 1990); *Daval Steel Prods. v. M/V Acadia Forest*, 683 F.Supp. 444, 1988 AMC 1669 (S.D.N.Y.1988).

COGSA elsewhere provides:

A carrier shall be at liberty to surrender in whole or in part all or any of his rights and immunities or to increase any of his responsibilities and liabilities under this chapter, provided such surrender or increase shall be embodied in the bill of lading issued to the shipper.

46 U.S.C.App. § 1305. Professors Gilmore and Black rely upon this latter section in their seminal treatise to support the proposition that COGSA:

allows a freedom of contracting out of its terms, but only in the direction of increasing the shipowner's liabilities, and never in the direction of diminishing them.

GILMORE & BLACK, THE LAW OF ADMIRALTY 145 (2d ed.1975). This proposition long has been accepted by the courts. *See, e.g.*, *Hanover Ins. Co. v. Shulman Transp. Enterprises, Inc.*, 581 F.2d 268, 273 & n. 8, 1979 A.M.C. 520 (1st Cir.1978); *Leather's Best, Inc. v. S.S. Mormaclynx*, 451 F.2d 800, 815, 1971 A.M.C. 2383, 15 Fed.R.Serv.2d 651 (2d Cir.1971); *Encyclopaedia Britannica, Inc. v. S.S. Hong Kong Producer*, 422 F.2d 7, 12 (2d Cir.1969), *cert. denied*, 397 U.S. 964, 90 S.Ct. 998, 25 L.Ed.2d 255 (1970). Thus, as the shippers contend, if we sustain the district court's finding that the parties intended to incorporate higher liability limitations into their contracts of carriage, it simply does not matter whether or not the DFRs are bills of lading covered by COGSA.

Because COGSA continues to exist, the provisions at issue herein are not governed by the Harter Act, 46 U.S.C.App. §§ 190 et seq., a backup contention of appellants. With the enactment of COGSA, Harter's coverage for damage occurring at sea was "superseded" or "repealed." Gilmore & Black, supra, at 147. Assuming for the argument that the parties herein could by agreement restore life to Harter, there is nothing in the record to indicate that they intended to do so. Indeed, the evidence is clear that the parties did not so intend.

As set out above, the DFRs state that they are to be governed by:

The Hague Rules contained in the international convention for the unification of certain rules relating to bills of lading, dated Brussels the 25th August, 1924 as enacted in the country of shipment....

The district court held that the language " 'as enacted in the country of shipment,' incorporates the Hague Rules in the manner that England has enacted them: to wit, including the Visby Amendments and the 1979 Protocol." 921 F.Supp. at 1171.

Influenced in substantial part by the titular word "Amendments," we agree with the district court's holding. See *People v. Sarver*, 102 Ill.App.3d 255, 57 Ill.Dec. 834, 429 N.E.2d 1108, 1109 (1981) ("An amendment is that which alters 'by modification, deletion, or addition.' ... By definition, an amendment is something which incorporates by reference some or all of a previously filed document.") (quoting BLACK'S LAW DICTIONARY 74 (5th ed.1979)); *Greenville Community Hotel Corp. v. Alexander Smith, Inc.*, 230 S.C. 239, 95 S.E.2d 262, 265 (1956) ("[T]he term 'amendment' by very definition connotes alteration, improvement or correction, and thus negates the idea of destruction or elimination of the original."). Thus, when a litigant appears before this Court asserting a constitutional right of due process, we recognize it as such despite the fact that it is contained in the Fifth Amendment.

The district court recognized that the Visby Amendments are drafted in such a way as to supplement the Hague Rules rather than supplant them. Article 6 of the Visby Amendments, for example, reads:

As between the Parties to [the Visby Amendments] the [Hague Rules] and the [Visby Amendments] shall be read and interpreted together as one single instrument.

Reprinted in 6 BENEDICT, *supra*, at 1-28.

In addition to the court below, three district courts have held that a document incorporating the law of the country of shipment, as in the instant case, adopted that country's interpretation of the Hague Rules, which treated the Rules and the Amendments together. *Ilva U.S.A., Inc. v. M/V Botic*, No. 92-717, 1992 WL 296562, at *2 (E.D.Pa. Oct.6, 1992), *aff'd mem.*, 998 F.2d 1003 (3d Cir.1993); *Associated Metals & Minerals Corp. v. M/V Arktis Sky*, No. 90 Civ. 4562, 1991 WL 51087, at *3 (S.D.N.Y. Apr.3, 1991); *A.T.I.C.A.M. v. Cast Europe (1983) Ltd.*, 662 F.Supp. 1443, 1448 (N.D.Ill.1987). Although there is some authority to the contrary, *see, e.g., Sunds Defibrator, Inc. v. M/V Atlantic Star*, 1986 AMC 368 (S.D.N.Y.1983), we find the reasoning in the three above-cited cases to be more persuasive.

Like the district court, we note a significant analogy in the English Carriage of Goods by Sea Act 1971, which, as the district court noted, reads as an amendment to existing law, i.e. the Hague Rules, and not as an independent statute. *See* 921 F.Supp. at 1171 (citing 43 HALSBURY'S LAWS OF ENGLAND 522- 23 (4th ed.1983)).

Contrary to appellants' assertions, the district court's interpretation of the DFRs does not contravene *Indussa Corp. v. S.S. Ranborg*, 377 F.2d 200, 203 (2d Cir.1967) (in banc). *Indussa*, recently overruled by *Vimar Seguros y Reaseguros, S.A. v. M/V Sky Reefer*, 515 U.S. 528, 115 S.Ct. 2322, 132 L.Ed.2d 462 (1995), held that forum selection clauses were invalid under COGSA because requiring "an American plaintiff to assert his claim only in a distant court lessens the liability of the carrier" in contravention of 46 U.S.C.App. 1303(8). 377 F.2d at 203. This was true not only because of the added expense of litigating abroad, but also because trial "in a foreign court would almost certainly lessen liability if the law which the court would apply was neither [COGSA] nor the Hague Rules." *Id.*

While application of the Visby Amendments might lessen a carrier's liability under COGSA in a general sense, see William Tetley, *Limitation, Non-Responsibility and Disclaimer Clauses*, 11 Mar. Law. 203, 225-26 (1986) (listing situations where use of Visby Amendments would operate to relieve carrier of liability in contravention of § 1303(8)), hypothetical examples have little relevance to the case before us. The sole issue in the instant case is whether the parties intended to apply the higher liability limitation of the Hague Rules as enacted in the countries of shipment. Giving effect to that intent does not offend § 1303(8) of COGSA.

The judgments of the district court are affirmed.

Notes

1. Professor Tetley in his text on Marine Cargo Claims (3d Ed. 1988) discusses the broad problem of "sea waybills" and specifically the situation in the United States as follows. After stating the argument made by some that inasmuch as sea waybills are not documents of title, they are not subject to the Hague or Hague-Visby Rules, Professor Tetley takes a contrary position.

> There is, however, another point of view which I wish to present. It is based on the public order nature of the Hague Rules and the fact that the only exceptions to the application of the Rules to contracts of carriage by sea are where non-negotiable receipts are issued under special circumstances contemplated in sec. 6 and where non-negotiable receipts are issued in the coasting trade in virtue of certain national legislation. (at 944).

* * *

> Sea waybills are now used extensively, especially in the container trades. It is my view that the Hague Rules or the Hague/Visby Rules apply to waybills by force of law, except in the coastal trade and except where the conditions in art. 6 are complied with. (at p. 1001).

As to the United States, he states:

> Non-negotiable receipts have not raised problems in the United States, perhaps because of the recognition of straight bills of lading in the Federal Bills of Lading Act, 1916, commonly known as the Pomerene Act. Upon reading the Pomerene Act one concludes that a straight bill of lading is a waybill strictly defined. (at p. 950).

* * *

> The application of the [Hague Rules] to straight bills of lading by force of law would seem to be less susceptible to challenge in the United States than in other jurisdictions because COGSA specifies at sect. 3(4) that it is not meant to limit in any way the operation of the Pomerene Act which, . . . , legislates in respect of both straight and order bills of lading. The Pomerene Act, however, applies only to straight bills of lading issued in the U.S. and not to waybills issued in other jurisdictions. (at p. *62*).

2. In *J.I. MacWilliam Co. Inc. v. Mediterranean Shipping Co. S.A. (The Rafaela S)* [2005] 1 Lloyd's Rep. 347, the English House of Lords held that a straight bill of lading is a "bill of lading" for the purposes of the Hague-Visby Rules, even though it is not negotiable. In *Voss v. A.P.L. Co. Pte Ltd* [2002] 2 Lloyd's Rep. 707, the Singapore Court of Appeal held that a straight bill of lading differs from a sea waybill because the named consignee must present the original straight bill of lading to the carrier in order to be entitled to delivery of the goods. Similarly, in *Porky Products, Inc. v. Nippon Express U.S.A. (Illinois), Inc.*, 1 F. Supp. 2d 227 (S.D.N.Y., 1997), the U.S. District Court for the Southern District of New York held that where a straight bill of lading contains a "surrender clause", which requires the document to be surrendered in return for the goods, the carrier is liable to the shipper for breach of contract, quite independently of the operation of the Pomerene Act, if it delivers to the named receiver without presentation of the original straight bill of lading.

3. The cases in note 2 disagree with the extract from Professor Tetley's book in note 1, by suggesting that there is indeed a difference between straight bills of lading and sea waybills. Several other types of shipping document are encountered in practice, including such documents as the DFRs (datafreight receipts) in *J.C.B. Sales, Ltd. v. Wallenius Lines*, 124 F.3d 132, 1997 AMC 2705 (2d Cir. 1997). Because it is not necessary to present an original sea waybill or DFR to take delivery of the goods, non-negotiable documents of this kind can easily be replaced by electronic documents. However, because it is necessary to present an original bill of lading in order to take delivery (even if it is a straight bill of lading), it proved more difficult to replace paper bills of lading with electronic equivalents. Thus, non-negotiable sea-carriage documents are increasingly in electronic form, but bills of lading are not.

---

4. Developments Since the Enactment of COGSA

THE VISBY AMENDMENTS

In 1968 the so-called Visby Amendments (The Brussels Protocol of Amendments to the Hague Rules) were signed at a Diplomatic Conference called by the Belgian government in response to a request by the Comité Maritime International (CMI). The occasion for the call of this conference was the widespread belief among nations that were party to the Hague Rules that the per unit limitation of liability (£100 sterling per package) provided by those rules had become inadequate. The Visby Amendments adjusted the limits to 30 franc Poincaré per kilogram ($.09 U.S. per pound) and 10,000 franc Poincaré per package ($662 U.S.). The franc Poincaré is a unit of account consisting of 65.5 milligrams of gold at a standard fineness of .00009.

Many shipping nations, including the United Kingdom, have adopted the Visby Amendments, which entered into force in 1977. By their terms (Art. X), they apply to (1) bills of lading issued in a contracting state, (2) carriage from a port in a contracting state, and (3) bills of lading incorporating the rules, "whatever may be the nationality of the ship, the carrier, the shipper, the consignee, or any interested person." The Visby Amendments have not been ratified by the United States.

The adoption and application of the Visby Rules was further complicated by the fact that in 1971, by international agreement and domestic legislation in the United States, gold lost its monetary functions and no longer has an official price. Thus the franc Poincaré became no longer convertible to a fixed dollars amount. For solutions in another context—aviation—and the enforcement of the Warsaw Convention's limits on liability for loss of cargo, *see Franklin Mint Corporation v. Trans-World Airlines*, 466 U.S. 243, 104 S.Ct. 1776, 80 L.Ed.2d 273, 1984 A.M.C. 1817 (1984).

In 1979, however, a protocol to the Visby Rules was adopted substituting the Special Drawing Right (SDR) for the franc Poincaré as a unit of account. An SDR is the unit of account used by the International Monetary Fund (IMF). Its value fluctuates and is published daily based on the weighted average of the values of a "basket" of key currencies. Since the value of an SDR is subject to daily fluctuations, many countries that have ratified both the Hague/Visby Rules or the Hague Rules only have adopted a "gold clause agreement" or other mechanism to fix the package limitation formula to a specific amount. Thus even among states that have ratified Visby, different limitations may apply.

The text of the Protocol amending the Hague Rules known as the Visby Amendments appears on the Tulane Maritime Law Center website at www.tulanemaritimelaw.net/docs/visby.

THE HAMBURG RULES AND UNCTAD

Unlike previous efforts to attain agreement on aspects of international shipping law, the most recent initiative for revision of the Brussels Conventions came from concerted action by the United Nations Conference for Trade and Development (UNCTAD) and the related United Nations Commission on Trade and Development (UNCITRAL). These forums were sought especially by developing countries who believed that organizations like the CMI did not suit their needs. The developing countries argued that the rules of international private maritime law had been written by traditional maritime states and were unfairly biased in favor of shipowners and carriers. UNCTAD has established a Permanent Committee on Shipping that has adopted as its mission a thoroughgoing review of virtually all the international conventions relating to shipping. This has created tension and disagreement with the more traditional organizations, the CMI and the International Maritime Organization (IMO), which consider themselves the guardians of the Brussels Conventions.

One of the first fruits of UNCTAD was the so-called Hamburg Rules, the United Nations Convention on the Carriage of Goods by Sea, 1978 (U.N. Doc. A/CONF. 89/13 (1978), reprinted in 17 INT'L LEGAL MATERIALS 603 (1978)). For a detailed history of the development of these rules, see *Sweeney, The UNCITRAL Draft Convention on*

Carriage of Goods By Sea, (Part I), 7 J. Mar. L. & Com 69 (1975); (Part II), 7 J. Mar. L. & Com. 327 (1976); (Part III), 7 J. Mar. L. & Com. 487 (1976); (Part IV), 7 J. Mar. L. & Com. 615 (1976).

The Hamburg Rules allocate shipment risks between carriers and shippers in a fundamentally different way than the Hague Rules/Visby Amendments. The system the Hamburg Rules establish is, therefore, controversial. On November 1, 1991, the International Convention was ratified by Zambia, the twentieth nation. Thus, in accordance with the International Convention, the Hamburg Rules entered into effect in those twenty countries that ratified the International Convention on November 1, 1992. The Committee on Carriage of Goods of the Maritime Law Association of the United States commented:

The list of 20 countries includes 15 countries in Africa, with the rest scattered about. Seven of the countries are landlocked states. Ten of the countries have never participated in any cargo convention before. That's not at all impressive. It represents a very small percentage of our foreign trade. It's an even smaller percentage of liner service trade into the United States. Thus, the opportunity for cargo subject to the Hamburg Rules, because it is in effect at the port of loading, to come here and thereby create a conflict with COGSA will be rare.

Fall 1991 Meeting of the MLA, *Proceedings* p. 9955 (1991).

Nevertheless, renewed activity to urge the United States Government to leapfrog the Visby Amendments and enact the Hamburg Rules into law is expected. The House Merchant Marine and Fisheries Committee has begun consideration of the Hamburg Rules. A key issue upon which there are differing views concerns the impact of the Hamburg Rules on marine insurance rates and practice. For a sympathetic view of this problem, *see* Selvig, *The Hamburg Rules, The Hague Rules and Marine Insurance Practice*, 12 J. Mar. L. & Com. 299 (1981). For an extensive commentary on the Hamburg Rules, *see* The Hamburg Rules on the Carriage of Goods by Sea (S. Mankabady ed. 1978). *See also Note, The Hamburg Rules Fault Concept and Common Carrier Liability under United States Law*, 19 Va. J. Int'l L. 433 (1979).

The Hamburg Rules introduce several new concepts, all of which tend to increase the liability of the carrier. First, in lieu of the "shopping list" of exceptions in the Hague Rules, there is a unitary concept of fault. The carrier is liable unless it proves that it took "all measures that could reasonably be required to avoid the occurrence and its consequences." Art. 5(1). This means that there is a continuing carrier duty for seaworthiness, and the exception to liability for negligence in the navigation and management of the ship in the Hague Rules is eliminated. Second, the fire exception is reduced, and the carrier will be liable for negligent acts of the crew in starting or fighting a fire. Art. 5(4)(a). Third, the carrier is liable for economic loss caused by delay in delivery up to a maximum of 2.5 times the freight charges on the shipment under that bill of lading. Arts. 5, 6(1)(b). Fourth, the liability limits are raised slightly above the Visby levels to 835 SDRs per package or 2.5 SDRs per kilogram, whichever is higher. Art. 6(1).

Note: MLA Proposed Compromise Between the Hague-Visby and the Hamburg Rules

The Maritime Law Association of the United States has proposed a compromise between advocates of the status quo (the Hague Rules), the Hague-Visby Rules and the Hamburg Rules. Final Report: Revising the Carriage of Goods by Sea Act, Feb. 19, 1996, approved by the MLA on May 3, 1996. MLA Document No. 724, May 3, 1996. The MLA compromise solution is now in the form of a Senate Staff Working Draft in the Transportation Committee of the U.S. Senate, dated September 24, 1999, which can be read at <http://tetley.law.mcgill.ca/cogsa99.htm>. The Draft has not progressed since 1999 and seems to have stalled completely. The MLA's efforts are now directed at work on a new international convention (see next note). See Force, A Comparison of the Hague, Hague-Visby, and Hamburg Rules: Much Ado About (?), 70 Tul.L.Rev. 2051 (1996).

The text of the Hamburg Rules appears on the Tulane Maritime Law Center website at www.tulanemaritimelaw.net/docs/hamburg

---

Note: Plans for a comprehensive new convention

Prompted by the fear that the United States might unilaterally adopt a non-uniform hybrid of the Hague, Hague-Visby and Hamburg Rules (see previous note), the Comite Maritime International (CMI) spent some years preparing a preliminary draft of a new international convention to replace the Hague, Hague-Visby and Hamburg Rules. The Final Draft Instrument prepared by CMI was handed over to the United Nations Commission on International Trade Law (UNCITRAL) on December 10th, 2001. In UNCITRAL's hands, the document is now called "Draft convention on the carriage of goods [wholly or partly] [by sea]". The latest draft (dated February 13th, 2007) can be read at: http://daccessdds.un.org/doc/UNDOC/LTD/VO7/807/35/PDF/VO780735.pdf?OpenElement.

---

5. *The Coverage of COGSA and the Multimodal and Container Revolution*

COGSA and the Hague Rules have been criticized because of limits on their coverage. Note that live animals and cargo "which by the contract of carriage is stated as being carried on deck and is so carried" are expressly excluded from COGSA. § 1(c). Does this exclusion allow the carrier to avoid COGSA by the single expedient of moving all the cargo it can on deck? What was the purpose of the exclusion? Is there any reason for this today in the age of containerized cargo?

COGSA also is limited in its application to foreign trade; however the parties can agree to COGSA coverage for coastwise trade between ports in the United States as well. § 12.

By its terms COGSA only applies "tackle to tackle," from the point of loading to the point of discharge. § 1(e). It is, however, common for a clause in the bill of lading to provide for COGSA coverage for the "entire time the goods are in the custody of the carrier" before the goods are loaded and after discharge to the point of delivery, and this will be enforced. *See Brown & Root, Inc. v. M/V Peisander,* 648 F.2d 415, 1982 AMC 929 (5th Cir. 1981). Why would this be desirable from the carrier's point of view?

Since COGSA expressly saves the Harter Act from repeal, the Harter Act applies to the coastwise trade and to the period of custody before loading and after discharge from the vessel up to the point of delivery (unless COGSA coverage is provided by the parties). However, the question of which act applies is of little importance because they both impose the same duties to the carrier (due diligence in providing a seaworthy vessel and in the handling of cargo) and "except for unimportant differences in phraseology, the two acts come down to much the same thing." *Gordon H. Mooney Ltd. v. Farrell Lines,* 616 F.2d 619, 623 n.6, 1980 AMC 505, n.6 (2d Cir. 1980) (*citing* Gilmore & Black.)

The introduction of containers and other new shipping technology have created new problems of coverage under COGSA and the Harter Act. For example, is a LASH (lighter aboard ship) barge that is designed to be off-and on-loaded upon a mother ship "cargo" or "ship" under COGSA? In *Wirth Ltd. v. S/S Acadia Forest,* 537 F.2d 1272, 1976 AMC 2178 (5th Cir. 1976), the court held that these barges are ships engaged in foreign commerce under COSGA. What would be the consequence of denying them "ship" status?

Additional problems arise from the fact that while COGSA and the Hague Rules were designed to cover one mode of transport, carriage by water, it is increasingly common with containers and other "piggy back" traffic to handle goods "door to door." Sea carriers are now becoming multimodal transport operators, and freight forwarders act as cargo consolidators, taking responsibility for an entire integrated transport system. Such operators have developed combined transport bills of lading for these shipments. The legal problems and conflicts arising from this development have not been definitively settled. In May, 1980, after long preparation, the United Nations adopted a Convention on International Multimodal Transport of Goods, U.N. Doc. TD/16 (1980). Only a few states have signed this convention, however, and a unified approach to multimodal transport lies in the future. For an analysis see Driscoll & Larsen, *The Convention on International Multimodal Transport of Goods,* 57 Tul. L. Rev. 193 (1982).

Both the MLA-drafted Senate Staff Working Draft of 1999 and the UNCITRAL Draft Convention (see Note 5 above) propose an extension of the period of the carrier's responsibility beyond the "tackle to tackle" period. Under the UNCITRAL Draft Convention, the carrier's responsibility covers the whole period from the time when the carrier has received the goods for carriage until the time when the goods are delivered to the consignee. Thus, if the carrier issues a combined transport bill, or even if it simply takes delivery of the goods before they are put onto the ship, its liability under the draft convention begins when it takes delivery of the goods.

When loss of or damage to cargo occurs within the United States on the land leg of an international multimodal carriage, the carrier's liability may be governed by the Carmack Amendment, 49 U.S.C. § 11706, which regulates the liability of land carriers, particularly in relation to limitation of liability. Federal circuits disagree about whether the Carmack Amendment applies to the land leg of a multimodal carriage governed by a single combined transport bill of lading. In *Altadis USA, Inc. v. Sea Star Line L.L.C.*, 458 F.3d 1288, 2006 AMC 1846 (11th Cir. 2006), the Eleventh Circuit held that the Carmack Amendment applies only where the land carrier issues a separate bill of lading governing the land leg of the voyage. In direct contrast, in *Sompo Japan Insurance Co. of America v. Union Pacific Railroad Co.*, 456 F.3d 54, AMC 1817 (2d Cir. 2006), the Second Circuit held that the Carmack Amendment applies to the land transport leg even though only a single multimodal bill of lading has been issued to govern the whole transit, including both ocean and land legs. Under the *Altadis* view, the rules and limits of liability of COGSA apply throughout a multimodal carriage, including on the land leg, if that is what the bill of lading so provides. Under the *Sompo* view, the ocean-carriage regimes of COGSA and the Harter Act cannot be extended by contract to govern the land leg of multimodal carriage because the Carmack Amendment applies by its own force to the land leg, no matter what the bill of lading purports to provide. The U.S. Supreme Court granted certiorari in *Altadis* to resolve this issue, but later dismissed the writ because the case had settled, thereby leaving the circuit split unresolved. *Altadis USA, Inc. v. Sea Star Line L.L.C.*, 458 F.3d 1288, 2006 AMC 1846 (11th Cir. 2006), *cert. granted* 127 S.Ct. 853 (2007) (Mem.), *cert. dismissed* 127 S.Ct. 1209 (2007) (Mem.).

* * *

---

6. Period of Responsibility

COGSA applies during "the period of time when the goods are loaded on to the time when they are discharged from the ship." This period is commonly referred to as "tackle to tackle", which Professor Tetley explains as follows:

> Tackle to tackle has traditionally meant from the moment when the ship's tackle is hooked on at the loading port until the moment when the ship's tackle is unhooked at discharge. If shore tackle is being used, that moment has traditionally been when the goods cross the ship's rail.

W. TETLEY, MARINE CARGO CLAIMS 14 (3d Ed. 1988).

Knauth suggests that COGSA "coverage … depends on physical acts at the ship's side or on her decks which can be seen and which are usually the occasion for a record, a tally and an inspection." A. KNAUTH, OCEAN BILLS OF LADING 144 (4th Ed. 1953). He offers the following explanation of "loading" and "discharge":

> The interpretation seems best satisfied by relating it to some physical act of possession associated with transfer of risk from a shore interest to a ship interest It would seem that the following points satisfy the requirements in the various usual situations:
>
> When cargo is hoisted by ship's gear and tackle, the loading on occurs when the ship's tackle is hooked onto the draft of cargo. When cargo is hoisted by a pier-side crane, or a floating derrick not controlled by the ship, the loading on occurs when the draft of cargo is first laid down at a point within the boundaries of the hull of the ship. When the cargo is rolled from the shore or lighter into the ship by a gangway, over the ship's rail or through a side door, the loading on occurs when the cargo passes over the ship's rail or through the ship's

side door. When the cargo flows through a chute or a pipe, the loading occurs at the ship's end of the chute or pipe; in handling liquids, this would be at the flange where the ship's piping or hose is connected to the shore or lighter pipe or hose.

As to the moment of "discharging from" the ship, there was a settled line of cases before 1936 to the effect that the carrier may terminate its carrier liability at the end of the ship's tackle. [citations omitted]

... There would seem to be various possibilities, depending on the method of discharge. If the ship's gear, booms and tackle are used, the moment of discharge from the ship seems to be generally accepted as the moment when the draft is laid down on a lighter or pier, and the hook of the tackle released. If shoreside cranes or floating derricks are used, the moment would seem to be when such apparatus lifts the draft from the ship's hold or deck. If a mechanical conveyor or shoveller is used, and is not furnished by the ship, the discharge would seem to occur when the item of cargo is picked up by the conveyor. And if the cargo flows through a pipe, it is delivered at the last flange supplied by the ship.

A. Knauth, Ocean Bills of Lading 145-146 (4th Ed. 1953).

As will be seen, COGSA provides a carrier with absolute defenses in some situations and limited liability in others. Therefore, it may be in a carrier's best interest to have COGSA applicable during the entire period for which the carrier may be legally responsible for the goods. It is not uncommon for carrier's to include a provision in its bill of lading which makes COGSA applicable from the time the carrier receives the goods until the time the carrier delivers the goods.

Suppose a bill of lading specified that Carrier would deliver the goods to the port of "X" and Carrier's vessel either because of insufficient draft or port congestion is unable to reach or enter the port. The cargo is then unloaded onto a lighter (smaller vessel) for which Carrier has contracted to bring the goods to the port of "X" and, as the lighter made its way to the port, the goods were damaged. Can Carrier invoke the benefits of COGSA? See, e.g., *U.S. v. Ultramar Shipping Co., Inc.*, 685 F. Supp. 887, 1988 AMC 527 (S.D.N.Y. 1987). Suppose some of the goods had been loaded on the lighter by means of the lighter's gear and as more of the goods were being lowered onto the lighter the operator of the gear prematurely released the goods which fell upon the goods which had already been unloaded onto the lighter. Damage resulted both to the goods dropped and the goods struck. Can Carrier invoke the benefits of COGSA as to either or both? *See, e.g., Hoegh Lines v. Green Truck Sales, Inc.*, 298 F.2d 240 (9th Cir. 1962).

The advent of multimodal transportation companies has complicated the question of when COGSA should apply. Multimodal transportation cargo companies and freight forwarders handle the entire transportation of the goods from point of inception to final destination, or from "door to door." It may involve transportation by water, land and air, all of which are often covered by one integrated bill of lading. This new method of transportation is largely due to the introduction of containers, which have become the fastest and most efficient way of moving cargo. Unfortunately, this new growth of technology has brought with it many problems as well.

One problem stemming from multimodal transportation is that often it is necessary to determine whether damage to goods occurred during the land-based or water-based leg of the trip. Liability may vary depending on which law is applied. Whether COGSA may be applied to the entire trip is yet another problem. Generally courts have agreed that COGSA may be applied to the entire trip if such intent is expressly provided for in the bill of lading, such as in a clause paramount. *See Taisho Marine & Fire Ins. Co., Ltd. v. Maersk Line, Inc.*, 796 F. Supp. 336, 1993 AMC 705 (N.D. Ill. 1992), *aff'd*, 7 F.3d 238, 1994 AMC 608 (7th Cir. 1993). Even if such intent is expressed, though, COGSA will only apply as a contractual term to the land-based portion of the trip, rather than by statutory force. Such contractual terms may be overcome if they conflict with applicable law. For a further discussion of COGSA and multimodal transportation, *see* Marva Jo Wyatt, *Contract Terms in Intermodal Transport: COGSA Comes Ashore*, 16 Tul. Mar. L.J. 177 (1991).

MANNESMAN DEMAG CORP. v. M/V CONCERT EXPRESS

225 F.3d 587, 2000 AMC 2935 (5th Cir. 2000)

This case arises from damage sustained to an oxygen compressor and instrument rack owned by Mannesman, which were transported from Bremerhaven, Germany, to Terre Haute, Indiana. Atlantic carried the goods from Bremerhaven to the Port of Baltimore, Maryland, aboard the M/V CONCERT EXPRESS. Trism carried the goods from Baltimore to Terre Haute. While en route from Baltimore to Terre Haute, the goods were damaged when Trism's trailer overturned.

There was only one bill of lading for the entire transportation, issued by Atlantic, reflecting an agreement to transport the goods from Bremerhaven, Germany, to the midwestern United States. The bill is what is called a "through bill of lading." Because the bill obligated the carrier to transport the cargo "through" the port to its ultimate destination, it is referred to as a "through bill." When the goods arrived at the Port of Baltimore, Atlantic hired Trism to transport them to Terre Haute.

A.

This case presents an issue of first impression regarding the applicability of federal maritime statutes to inland transport under a through bill of lading. The following excerpt describes the origin of this issue.

> Until the advent of the containerization of cargo, the cargo owner typically would enter into a new shipment contract with a new carrier each time the mode of transport changed. An inland carrier—a railroad, trucker or, in some cases, an inland barge operator—would carry the goods to a seaport under one contract of carriage. There someone, usually a "freight forwarder" acting on behalf of the cargo owner, would arrange to place the goods in the hands of a steamship line. Frequently it would be necessary to repack the goods for ocean shipment. The ocean carrier would transport them to a foreign seaport and release them there to the consignee or someone acting on the consignee's behalf.
>
> Different legal regimes arose to govern the parties' rights and liabilities, depending upon the mode of shipment.... If the railroad did the damage, then the rules of liability governing railroads would apply. If the steamship line was liable, then maritime law would govern. Along came intermodal shipping containers and everything changed. Now, the same steel cargo container can move freely between different modes of transport. Ocean carriers began to offer "door to door" service. Rail carriers, truckers or other transporters now contract, not with the owner of the goods, but as a subcontractor to the steamship line who has offered a complete transport package.
>
> Under United States law, a shipper or consignee may recover against non-ocean carriers for the loss of or damage to cargo subject to a "through bill of lading." The bill of lading may, if properly drafted, limit both the amount an owner may seek as well as the time in which recovery may be sought.

* * *

> The U.S. Carriage of Goods by Sea Act (COGSA) governs the liability of an ocean carrier on an international through bill of lading.... COGSA contains important benefits to the carrier. Inland carriers frequently attempt to take advantage of the benefits afforded by COGSA. One of COGSA's most important provisions limits a carrier's liability to five hundred dollars ($500 US) per package unless a higher value is declared by the shipper. COGSA also contains a one-year limitation for cargo claims.

* * *

> By its terms, COGSA applies "tackle-to-tackle" only; it does not extend to losses which occur prior to loading or subsequent to discharge from a vessel. A Period of Responsibility clause can be used to extend COGSA's application to the entire time the goods are within the carrier's custody.

Charles S. Donovan & Jill M. Haley, Who Done It and Who's Gonna Pay?—Rights of Shippers and Consignees Against Non-Ocean Carriers Performing Part of a Contract of Carriage Covered by a Through Bill of Lading, 7 J. INT'L L. & PRAC. 415, 415-17 (1998).

B.

The parties agree that the controlling contractual document is the single bill of lading issued by Atlantic, which provides:

3. CARRIER'S RESPONSIBILITY

(1) ... If and to the extent that the provisions of the Harter Act ... would otherwise be compulsorily applicable to regulate the Carrier's responsibility for the goods ... the Carrier's responsibility shall instead be subject to COGSA, but where COGSA is found not to be applicable such responsibility shall be determined by the provisions of 3(2) below....

* * *

(2) Save as is otherwise provided in this Bill of Lading, the Carrier shall be liable for loss of or damage to the goods occurring from the time that the goods are taken into his charge until the time of delivery to the extent set out below.

* * *

(B) Where the stage of carriage where the loss or damage occurred can be proved.

* * *

(ii) With respect to the transportation in the United States ... from the Port of Discharge, the responsibility of the Carrier shall be to procure transportation by carriers (one or more) and such transportation shall be subject to the inland carrier's contracts of carriage and tariffs and any law compulsorily applicable. The Carrier guarantees the fulfillment of such inland carriers' obligations under their contracts and tariffs.

* * *

6. PACKAGE/UNIT LIMITATION AND DECLARED VALUE

(1) Package or Unit Limitation

Where the Hague Rules or any legislation making such Rules compulsorily applicable (such as COGSA or COGWA) to this Bill of Lading apply, the Carrier shall not, unless a declared value has been noted ... be or become liable for any loss or damage to or in connection with the goods in an amount per package or unit in excess of the package or unit limitation as laid down by such Rules or legislation. Such limitation amount according to ... COGSA is U.S. $500....

* * *

7. TIME-BAR

... All liability whatsoever of the Carrier shall cease unless suit is brought within 12 months after delivery of the goods or the date when the goods should have been delivered.

* * *

III.

Atlantic contends that Mannesman waived argument regarding the Harter Act by failing to raise the issue in the district court. Mannesman moved for summary judgment, arguing that the inland carrier's tariff, not the COGSA $500 per package limitation, provided the applicable limitation of liability. Atlantic cross-moved for summary judgment, arguing that the limitation is the COGSA $500 per package amount and specifically averring that the Harter Act is compulsory applicable.

By granting Atlantic's cross-motion as to amount of liability, the court necessarily determined that the Harter Act was compulsorily applicable to the inland portion of carriage. This issue was therefore raised and considered by the district court and is properly before us.

IV.

We must determine, as a matter of first impression, whether the Harter Act is compulsorily applicable to the inland portion of carriage pursuant to a through bill of lading. We have decided a number of cases interpreting similar bills of lading and their reference to the Harter Act, but in none of those cases had the goods begun inland transport.

Atlantic's bill references two statutes, the Carriage of Goods by Sea Act ("COGSA"), 46 U.S.C. app. §§ 1300-1315, and the Harter Act, 46 U.S.C. app. §§ 190-196. Under COGSA, a carrier of goods in international commerce must "properly and carefully load, handle, stow, carry, keep, care for, and discharge the goods carried." 46 U.S.C. app. § 1303(2). The Harter Act imposes a duty of "proper loading, stowage, custody, care, [and] proper delivery." 46 U.S.C. app. § 190. Although the Harter Act's applicability to international commerce was partially superseded by COGSA, COGSA is applicable only from the time goods are loaded onto the ship until the time the cargo is released from the ship's tackle at port. See 46 U.S.C. app. § 1301(e); *Tapco,* 702 F.2d at 1255. Therefore, the Harter Act applies to the period between the discharge of the cargo from the vessel and "proper delivery." *See Tapco,* 702 F.2d at 1255.

Because the Harter Act does not define "proper delivery," courts have defined proper delivery as discharge of cargo "upon a fit and customary wharf". *Id.* Proper delivery also includes the general maritime law requirement that a carrier "unload the cargo onto a dock, segregate it by bill of lading and count, put it in a place of rest on the pier so that it is accessible to the consignee, and afford the consignee a reasonable opportunity to come and get it. These requirements of "proper delivery" are modified by "the custom, regulations, [and] law of the port." Thus, the critical question is "whether delivery was to persons charged by the law and the usage of the port with the duty to receive cargo and distribute it to the consignee." *Tapco,* 702 F.2d at 1257 (internal quotation marks omitted).

COGSA also refers to "delivery," which commences the running of a one-year limitations period. See 46 U.S.C. app. § 1303(6). In *Servicios- Expoarma, C.A. v. Industrial Maritime Carriers, Inc.,* 135 F.3d 984, 993 (5th Cir.1998), we determined that when such "delivery" occurs varies according to the custom and laws of a port but that "delivery" is not equivalent to receipt by the consignee. Thus, when an ocean carrier transferred its cargo to an authorized customs warehouse in the Venezuelan port of destination, delivery was completed regardless of the fact that the consignee had not yet received the goods. *See id.*

Atlantic's bill of lading provides that, to the extent the Harter Act is compulsorily applicable, the Carrier's "responsibility shall ... be subject to COGSA." It further states that "[w]here ... [COGSA] appl[ies], the Carrier shall not ... be or become liable for any loss or damage ... in an amount per package or unit in excess of ... $500." Therefore, if the Harter Act is compulsorily applicable to Trism's inland transport, the court correctly limited Atlantic's liability to $500 per package.

The same contractual provision extending COGSA to the limits of the Harter Act also states: "[B]ut where COGSA is found not to be applicable [the Carrier's] responsibility shall be determined by the provisions of 3(2) below." Paragraph 3(2)(B)(ii) provides that, where the occurrence of damage can be proved to occur during transportation "in the United States," "the responsibility of the Carrier shall be to procure transportation by carriers (one or more) and such transportation shall be subject to the inland carrier's contracts of carriage and tariffs and any law compulsorily applicable. The Carrier guarantees the fulfillment of such inland carrier's obligations under their contracts and tariffs."

Mannesman argues that Harter Act "proper delivery" occurred when Trism acquired control over the goods and began inland transportation. If this is correct, then at the time the goods were damaged, the Harter Act was not compulsorily applicable, in which case the Bill provides that Atlantic's liability is governed by Trism's contracts and tariffs. Atlantic counters that the through bill of lading provided for carriage from Germany to Terre Haute, inclusive, and therefore that Harter Act proper delivery had not yet occurred at the time the goods were damaged.

There is no precedent by any circuit court of appeals interpreting Harter Act proper delivery with respect to the inland portion of a through bill of lading. There is, however, a thorough and persuasive district court opinion, from another circuit, that has been followed by other district courts.

In *Jagenberg, Inc. v. Georgia Ports Auth.*, 882 F. Supp. 1065 (S.D.Ga.1995), the court considered an Atlantic bill of lading apparently identical to the one here. The court first cited a traditional definition of "proper delivery" found in *Wemhoener Pressen v. Ceres Marine Terminals, Inc.*, 5 F. 3d 734, 741- 42 (4th Cir.1993) as

> either actual or constructive delivery. Actual delivery consists of completely transferring the possession and control of the goods from the vessel to the consignee or his agent. Constructive delivery occurs where the goods are discharged from the ship upon a fit wharf and the consignee receives due and reasonable notice that the goods have been discharged and has a reasonable opportunity to remove the goods or put them under proper care and custody.

Jagenberg, 882 F.Supp. at 1076-77. The court then noted the complication raised by a through bill:

> [T]he contract was intermodal, meaning that [Atlantic] contracted with Jagenberg to transport the goods over sea from The Netherlands, and then over land to ... Macon, Georgia.... Macon was the place at which a consignee or its "agent" ... first encountered the cargo. Consequently, the Court must either extend the reach of the Harter Act—a maritime law—to the point of delivery in Macon, Georgia, or it must find some principled manner of deciding when a proper delivery occurred beforehand, despite the fact that, technically, no agent of Jagenberg had a reasonable opportunity to take the goods into "proper care and custody" before they reached Macon.

Id. at 1077. Based on the maritime nature of the Harter Act, the court held that inland transportation under a through bill occurs after Harter Act proper delivery:

> [T]he Harter Act is at its core a maritime law; the Court is unwilling to rule that simply because private parties enter an intermodal agreement federal maritime legislation is thus extended far beyond its congressionally intended bounds. The Harter Act is designed solely to regulate the liability of seagoing carriers. That said, the Court finds that the Harter Act does reach to the point at which goods are loaded onto the vehicles of an inland trucker, whether hired by the shipper or the carrier.

Id. at 1077-78 (internal citations omitted). Harter Act proper delivery, however, precedes that inland transport. *See id.* at 1077. The court concluded:

> In this age of "containerized" cargoes subject to "multimodal" bills of lading, it is often difficult to locate precisely the points of legal delivery. Increasing efficiency and integration in cargo transport continues to blur the lines separating sea carrier responsibilities from those of others. The Court finds it advisable to keep sea carriers to the standards imposed by the Harter Act until goods are in the hands of land carriers and actually leaving the maritime arena. With COGSA covering carriers' legal responsibilities through discharge, Harter fills a potential gap between discharge and inland transit in those situations where goods, though on the dock, are still within the control and responsibility of the sea carrier.

Id. at 1078-79. *Jagenberg* was adopted in *Colgate Palmolive Co. v. M/V ATLANTIC CONVEYOR*, 1997 AMC 1478, 1996 WL 742861, at *5 (S.D.N.Y. Dec. 31, 1996), which again concerned an Atlantic through bill of lading: "Proper delivery occurs when the cargo is ready for inland transport." The *Jagenberg* and *Colgate Palmolive* courts were not aware of a single case extending the Harter Act to all stages of a through bill of lading. The parties in the case *sub judice* cite no contrary authority.

We find these decisions persuasive and therefore conclude that the Harter Act was not compulsorily applicable at the time Mannesman's goods were damaged. This analysis not only avoids compulsory application of federal maritime law to non-maritime transportation, but has the benefit of not rendering superfluous the alternative liability provisions found at paragraph 3(2) of Atlantic's bill of lading

Our ruling is also consistent with *Servicios*'s interpretation of COGSA "delivery." As with COGSA, Congress could have, but chose not to, use "receipt" instead of "delivery." *See Servicios,* 135 F.3d at 989. Thus, Harter Act "delivery," like COGSA "delivery," is interpreted according to the "common law gloss" that "[d]elivery [is] not defined by receipt by the consignee, but rather occur[s] when the carrier ha[s] properly surrendered the goods in accordance with its contractual duties." *Servicios* did not interpret "delivery" in the context of a through bill of lading but made clear that delivery is governed by general maritime law obligations as modified by specific contractual provisions, not by receipt of the goods.

We do not preclude parties from contractually limiting liability during the entire time in which the carrier has custody or control over the cargo. We merely hold that where parties contractually tie such limitation to the extent that the Harter Act is compulsorily applicable, the limitation does not apply to inland transportation in through bills of lading. A contrary result extends the compulsory applicability of the Harter Act to transportation that Congress almost certainly did not intend to include within that act.

For all of the foregoing reasons, Harter Act proper delivery preceded the damage at issue, so we vacate the awards in favor of Mannesman and Atlantic. Because the record lacks evidence of, *inter alia,* the applicable tariff limitation and the extent of damage to the goods, we remand for further proceedings.

B. The Shipper's Prima Facie Case

According to controlling precedents in the United States, a person (shipper or consignee) who wishes to make a cargo claim against a carrier must make a *prima facie* case that the goods were damaged while in the carrier's custody. Plaintiff can make such a case by proving that the goods were delivered to the carrier in good condition and were damaged when they were delivered back to the shipper or consignee. *See Tenneco Resins, Inc. v. Davy International*, 881 F.2d 211, 1990 AMC 402 (5th Cir. 1989); *Blasser Brothers, Inc. v. Northern Pan-American Line*, 628 F.2d 376, 1982 AMC 84 (5th Cir. 1980). Plaintiff may prove his allegations by competent evidence, including inferences from established facts and other circumstantial evidence. Ordinarily, the carrier also introduces evidence tending to rebut the allegations of the plaintiff concerning the condition of the cargo when it was delivered to the carrier or when it was re-delivered to the shipper or consignee.

The bill of lading that was issued to the shipper may contain crucial information or may be determinative in the discharge of the plaintiff's burden of proof. *See* COGSA § 3(4). If the carrier issued a "clean" bill of lading, that is, one without exceptions as to the condition of the goods, the carrier may be estopped from denying the accuracy of the statements in the bill of lading. *See Trade Arbed, Inc. v. M/V Swallow*, 688 F. Supp. 1095, 1989 AMC 2218 (E.D. La. 1988). For what the carrier can do if there is a suspicion that false information has been given or if he is unable to verify the condition of the goods, *see* COGSA §§ 3(3)(c), 3(5), 10.

Bills of lading issued in the United States are subject to the Federal Bills of Lading Act, 49 U.S.C. § 1-24, known as the Pomerene Act. This law, passed in 1916 for the purpose of improving the negotiability of bills of lading, was expressly preserved by COGSA. Under 49 U.S.C. §§ 89, 90, the carrier is discharged by the delivery of the goods to the holder of the bill of lading. However, 49 U.S.C. § 102 provides that the carrier is liable to the holder of an "order" bill of lading for damages caused by non-receipt of all or part of the goods or by their failure to correspond with the description in the bill of lading. The holder of the bill is not required to prove that the misdescription was fraudulent, and full damages are recoverable because the Pomerene Act contains no provision limiting liability. *See Elgie & Co. v. Steamship Corporation of America*, 599 F.2d 1177, 1980 AMC 231 (2d Cir. 1979).

If the shipper or consignee fails to establish a *prima facie* case, the action is dismissed. If, however, he is successful, the carrier may escape liability by proving that "he exercised due diligence to prevent the damage or that the harm was occasioned by one of the excepted causes delineated in § 1304 (2)." *Blasser Brothers, Inc. v. Northern Pan-American Line*, 628 F.2d 376, 381, 1982 AMC 84 (5th Cir. 1980). If the carrier succeeds in proving due diligence or an excepted cause, the shipper or consignee may still recover on proof that the negligence of the carrier was a *concurrent* cause of the loss. The burden then rebounds to the carrier who has the difficult task of proving the part of the loss that was caused by the excepted cause. If the carrier is unable to carry this burden, he is liable for the entire loss. This is just a broad outline of the detailed and complex scheme governing liability and the burden of proof in cargo claims. Variations and refinements are found in the cases that follow.

PLASTIQUE TAGS, INC. v. ASIA TRANS LINE, INC.

83 F.3d 1367, 1996 AMC 2304 (11th Cir. 1996)

FAY, Senior Circuit Judge

This appeal arises from the District Court's order of summary judgment in favor of the defendants. The plaintiff, Plastique Tags, Inc., brought suit under the Carriage of Goods by Sea Act (COGSA), alleging that the defendant carriers were liable for the shortfall in a shipment of goods ordered by Plastique and transported by the defendants. Because Plastique's evidence is insufficient as a matter of law, we affirm.

I. BACKGROUND

In October, 1992, Defendant Asia Trans Line, Inc. contracted to transport one sealed container from Inter-Korea Corporation in Korea to Plastique in New York. Inter-Korea represented that the container held 4,437,500 plastic bags. Asia Trans then issued a bill of lading for the cargo, which stated: "'SHIPPER'S LOAD & COUNT' SAID TO CONTAIN: 5,600 boxes/4,437,500 ... plastic bags."

Asia then contracted with DSR Senator Lines to ship the container aboard the M/V Cho Yang World. Inter-Korea delivered the sealed container directly to Senator. Senator then issued another bill of lading, identical in all material terms to the Asia Trans bill of lading.

The M/V Cho Yang World delivered the container to New York, and Senator released the container with its seal intact to a trucking company. The trucking company transported the container to Gift Box Corporation of America, Plastique's client. Gift Box broke the seal, inventoried the container, and found 2,618,500 bags missing. Gift Box refused to pay Plastique for the shipment. Approximately one year later, in October of 1993, Plastique sent notice of the missing bags to an agent of Cho Yang.

Plastique subsequently brought suit against the carriers (but not Inter-Korea, the shipper). The District Court granted summary judgment for all the defendants, ruling as a matter of law that Plastique could not establish a claim under COGSA.

* ** *

III. ANALYSIS

To hold a carrier liable for missing or damaged goods under COGSA, a shipper must prove that the goods were damaged or lost while in the carrier's custody. *See Sony Magnetic Products Inc. v. Merivienti O/Y*, 863 F.2d 1537, 1539 (11th Cir.1989). The shipper can meet this burden by showing: 1) full delivery of the goods in good condition to the carrier, and 2) outturn by the carrier of the cargo with damaged or missing goods. *Id.*

Under COGSA, "a bill of lading shall be prima facie evidence of the receipt by the carrier of the goods as therein described ..." 46 U.S.C.App. § 1303(4) (1994). COGSA reflects the reality in international commerce that a buyer must often pay for goods sight unseen, relying only on the carrier's bill of lading. A clean bill of lading:

> is a fundamental and vital pillar of international trade and commerce, indispensable to the conduct and financing of business involving the sale and transportation of goods between parties located at a distance from one another. It constitutes an acknowledgment by a carrier that it has received the described goods for shipment.

Berisford Metals Corp. v. S/S Salvador, 779 F.2d 841, 845 (2d Cir.1985), *cert. denied*, 476 U.S. 1188, 106 S.Ct. 2928, 91 L.Ed.2d 556 (1986). As far back as 1895, the First Circuit recognized that the bill of lading had

> become so universal and necessary a factor in mercantile credits that the law should make good what the bill of lading thus holds out.

Pollard v. Reardon, 65 F. 848, 852 (1st Cir.1895).

Thus Plastique argues that the bills of lading issued in this case constitute prima facie proof that the defendants received full delivery of the goods, and that any other result would not only violate COGSA but also threaten the stability of international commerce. However, we must conclude that under the facts of this case, the bills of lading at issue are not clean. [FN1] In order for a bill of lading to constitute prima facie proof that the carrier received cargo consistent with the terms of the bill, it must either be without limiting language such as "shipper's load and count" or it must contain terms that the carrier can verify.

> FN1. The growth in shipping through the use of sealed containers has highlighted the importance of clarifying the difference between a clean bill of lading and a conditional or restricted bill of lading. When sealed containers are used it is normally impossible for the carrier to verify the stated contents. In this case, the parties have stipulated that the container was sealed when delivered to the carrier, and that the seal was intact when the container was delivered to Gift Box.

If a bill of lading contains no limiting language such as "shipper's load and count" then the bill of lading constitutes prima facie proof for each term. *See Nitram, Inc. v. Cretan Life*, 599 F.2d 1359 (5th Cir.1979) (though it was not possible for the carrier to actually count the goods loaded because of the rapidity of the loading process, where the carrier issued a bill of lading with no limiting language, the carrier was liable for a shortfall).

If the bill of lading does contain limiting language, but the terms at issue in the bill of lading are verifiable by the carrier, then the bill of lading may constitute prima facie proof for those terms. *Westway Coffee Corp. v. M.V. Netuno*, 675 F.2d 30 (2d Cir.1982) (the weight of a sealed container is verifiable by a carrier and so the bill of lading constituted prima facie proof of the weight at delivery to the carrier, despite limiting language in the bill of lading).

However, we agree with the conclusion of the Third Circuit that if the bill of lading contains limiting language, it does not constitute prima facie proof of terms not verifiable by the carrier. *See Bally, Inc. v. M.V. Zim America*, 22 F.3d 65 (2d Cir.1994) (while a bill of lading with limiting language constituted prima facie proof of the weight of a sealed container, it did not constitute prima facie proof of the number of items inside the sealed container).

These distinctions are based on COGSA. COGSA expressly states that a carrier shall not be bound to include in the bill of lading a term which he has no reasonable means of checking. 46 U.S.C.App. § 1303(3)(c) (1994). If the carrier includes such a term without limiting language, he is bound by the bill of lading whether or not he can verify the term. *See Nitram*, 599 F.2d at 1369-71 & n. 27. However, if the bill of lading does contain limiting language stating that a term was supplied by the shipper and not checked by the carrier, then the carrier is generally not bound. *See Bally*, 22 F.3d at 69. The only exception to this second rule is when the term is easily verifiable by the carrier; in that case he cannot avoid liability by simply including limiting language. *See Westway*, 675 F.2d at

This exception is necessary to prevent carriers from loading obviously empty containers or obviously inferior goods and avoiding liability by merely including limiting language.

In the instant case, (1) the bills of lading contained limiting language and (2) the amount of goods in the sealed container was not verifiable by the carrier. Thus the bills of lading do not constitute prima facie proof of delivery to the carrier of the full amount. Because Plastique presents no other proof of good delivery, it cannot show that the loss occurred while the cargo was in the carrier's custody, and its claim must fail.

IV. CONCLUSION

Because Plastique's proof is insufficient as a matter of law, the judgment of the District Court is hereby AFFIRMED.

Notes

1. *Bally, Inc. v. M/V ZIM AMERICA*, 22 F. 3d 65, 1994 AMC 2762, (2nd Cir. 1994) is a good combined example of the position outlined in *Plastique Tags* and *Westway Coffee*. There, a bill of lading marked "STC" (meaning "said to contain") was held to be prima facie evidence of the weight of the cargo, but not the number of cartons inside the container.

2. In *Fox and Associates, Inc. v. M/V HANJIN YOKOHAMA*, 977 F. Supp. 1022, 1028, 1998 AMC 1090, 48 Fed. R. Evid. Serv. 173 (C.D. Cal., 1997), the court refused to follow *Plastique Tags*, saying that in the Ninth Circuit, at least, a bill of lading marked "shipper's load stow and count" does *not* alter the effect of the bill as a clean bill for the goods listed:

> Hanjin argues that the bill of lading issued for the cargo is not a clean bill of lading and, thus, plaintiff has not established the first prong of its prima facie case. To support its position, Hanjin relies on *Plastique Tags Inc. v. Asia Trans Line Inc.*, 83 F. 3d 1367, 1996 AMC 2304 (11th Cir., 1996). Hanjin's reliance on *Plastique* is misplaced and its argument is without merit. In the Eleventh Circuit, unlike the Ninth Circuit, a bill of lading with a disclaimer such as "shipper's load and count" is not a "clean" bill of lading. This legal conclusion was the basis for the decision in *Plastique*, and it renders both the rationale of the decision and the decision itself inapplicable.
>
> Hanjin further argues, however, that because the cargo, here, was containerized and the bill of lading listed the number of cartons and weight of the cargo, which Hanjin could not verify, the bill of lading does not constitute prima facie evidence of receipt by the carrier of the goods described therein. There is no merit to this argument. First, under Section 3(3)(c) of COGSA, Hanjin could have refused to state the number of cartons and weight on the bill of lading. Second, Hanjin could have weighed the container in Manila, thereby verifying its weight; Hanjin chose not to do so.

TRANSATLANTIC MARINE CLAIMS AGENCY, INC. v. M/V "OOCL INSPIRATION"

137 F.3d 94, 1998 AMC 1327 (2d Cir. 1998)

CALABRESI, Circuit Judge:

This action is an appeal by defendants-appellants Orient Overseas Container Line (UK) Ltd. ("OOCL") and Sea-Land Services, Inc. ("Sea-Land") from a summary judgment entered in favor of plaintiff-appellee Transatlantic Marine Claims Agency, Inc. ("TMCA"). With the exception of its decision that Sea-Land's tariff (rather than OOCL's tariff) should limit the plaintiff's recovery, we affirm the judgment of the district court.

The plaintiff is the agent for an insurer with a subrogation interest in the claims of the shipper, Sibille Dalle, Inc., for damages to goods shipped by sea aboard the M/V OOCL Inspiration. (Despite her name, the Inspiration is part of Sea-Land's fleet, not OOCL's.) The action was brought under the Carriage of Goods by Sea Act ("COGSA"), 46 U.S.C. app. § 1300 *et seq.*

OOCL and the shipper executed a bill of lading to transport 367 rolls of printing paper from Stenay, France, to various points in the United States. The paper was shipped by container method; in other words, the rolls were carried in 26 sealed containers. OOCL, pursuant to a Space Charter and Sailing Agreement (the "VSAO Agreement") with Sea-Land, arranged for ocean transport of the containers from Antwerp to Charleston aboard one of Sea-Land's vessels, specifically, the Inspiration.

On March 25, 1994, OOCL received from the shipper the sealed containers at Stenay and issued a clean bill of lading.[3] OOCL, either by itself or through a third party (the record is unclear), transported the containers from Stenay to the port at Antwerp, Belgium. In Antwerp, the containers were loaded onto the Inspiration. The Inspiration promptly sailed (apparently stopping in England on the way) to Charleston, South Carolina. At Charleston, the containers were off-loaded and stored at port from April 7 to May 17. They were then sent by truck and/or rail to various final destinations in Tennessee. Upon arrival, 43 rolls of paper were discovered to have suffered "wetting," which experts for both the shipper and OOCL concluded resulted from sea water. The rolls were sold for salvage, and the cargo underwriter paid the shipper for the full loss. TMCA was then authorized to pursue the subrogation interest of the underwriter in this action.

The district court (Robert W. Sweet, Judge) concluded that TMCA had made out a prime facie case under COGSA that went unrebutted by either defendant. See Transatlantic Marine Claims Agency, Inc. v. M/V "OOCL Inspiration," 961 F.Supp. 55 (S.D.N.Y.1997). It also held that Sea-Land's tariff applied to the transport. It therefore entered summary judgment against defendants and denied their cross motions for summary judgment. Defendants now appeal these rulings on various grounds.

The COGSA Prima Facie Case

Appellants' first claim is that the district court erred in ruling that the plaintiff made out a prima facie case under COGSA. In a COGSA cause of action, a shipper "who wishes to recover against the carrier for damage to goods bears the initial burden of proving both delivery of goods to the carrier ... in good condition, and outturn by the carrier ... in damaged condition." Vana Trading, 556 F.2d at 104;[5] see also COGSA, 46 U.S.C. app. §§ 1303-04. Once the plaintiff has made out a prima facie case, however, the burden shifts to the defendant(s) to show that one of the statutory COGSA exceptions to liability exists. See Id. § 1304(2). COGSA's framework thus places the risk of non-explanation for mysterious maritime damage squarely on defendants:

Associated Metals & Minerals Corp. v. M/V Arktis Sky, 978 F.2d 47, 51 (2d Cir.1992) (quoting *Quaker Oats Co. v. M/V Torvanger*, 734 F.2d 238, 243 (5th Cir.1984) (citations omitted)) (alterations in original).[6]

In short, the statutory scheme, (1) clearly evinces an intent to hold carriers prima facially liable for damage to goods at sea, see Id. at 52 ("There should be little dispute that the purpose of COGSA is to place primary responsibility for the safety of the cargo upon the vessel, its operators and owners."), but under it, (2) the initial burden of persuasion falls on the plaintiff to make out a prima facie case that the goods were, indeed, damaged while in the defendant's care. There are, moreover, two general ways a plaintiff can make out such a prima facie case under COGSA.

First, the plaintiff may present direct evidence relating to the healthy condition of the goods at delivery and their damaged condition at outturn. In this respect, our caselaw and the statute itself have outlined various presumptions that may be relied upon by both plaintiffs and defendants. For example, the issuance of a clean bill of lading creates a presumption of delivery in good condition favorable to the plaintiff. See *supra* note 3. Conversely,

---

[3] Because the containers were pre-sealed, the clean bill was issued using the language "said to contain" good rolls of paper. Such bills establish "apparent good order and condition." *Vana Trading Co. v. S.S. "Mette Skou"*, 556 F.2d 100, 103 & n. 4 (2d Cir.1977) (resolving a heated debate about yam packaging). Although a clean bill of lading ordinarily establishes a presumption under COGSA of delivery in good condition, see *Caemint Food, Inc. v. Brasileiro*, 647 F.2d 347, 352 (2d Cir.1981), we have noted that "[c]lean on-board bills of lading of packaged goods ... merely attest to the apparent good condition of the cargo based upon external inspection." *Id.* at 353-54 n. 5 (emphasis added). Thus the clean-bill-of-lading presumption of delivery in good condition is qualified in containerization and other such cases where an inspection on issuance of the bill is necessarily limited.

[5] *Cf. Caemint Food*, 647 F.2d at 354 (Friendly, J.) ("It is fair to impose on the plaintiff the burden of showing the condition of packaged goods on delivery because the shipper has superior access to information as to the condition of the goods when delivered to the carrier, just as the carrier has superior access to information as to what happened thereafter.") (internal quotation marks and citations omitted).

To rebut the presumption of fault when relying upon its own reasonable care, the carrier must further prove that the damage was caused by something other than its own negligence. Once the shipper establishes a prima facie case, under "the policy of the law" the carrier must "explain what took place or suffer the consequences." "[T]he law casts upon [the carrier] the burden of the loss which he cannot explain or, explaining, bring within the exceptional case in which he is relieved from liability."

[6] If the defendant is able to show one of the COGSA exceptions, the burden returns to the plaintiff, where plaintiff may still prevail by showing exceptions to the exceptions—for example "concurrent causes" for loss. See *Vana Trading*, 556 F.2d at 105-06.

a consignee who does not give notice of damage within three days of receipt is burdened by a presumption of arrival in good condition. See 46 U.S.C. app. § 1303(6); *Bally, Inc. v. M.V. Zim*, 22 F.3d 65, 71 (2d Cir.1994).

Within this structure, second-order evidentiary disputes may take place (for example, whether notice was received on the third or fourth day) concerning the various COGSA presumptions. While different burdens with respect to these intermediate disputes are varyingly placed on the plaintiff and the defendant, in the end, the risk of non-persuasion remains on the plaintiff. This is so because "[t]he shipper has [the ultimate] burden on the issue whether the goods were damaged while in the carrier's custody." *Caemint Food*, 647 F.2d at 354 (internal quotation marks and citation omitted).

The second way a plaintiff may discharge its burden of making out a prima facie case under COGSA is to show that the characteristics of the damage suffered by the goods justify the conclusion that the harm occurred while the goods were in the defendant's custody. As we have made clear, "the consignee's burden does not mean that it must always introduce direct evidence that the cargo was in good condition when shipped. It may additionally meet its burden by showing, as was also done here, from the condition of the cargo as delivered or otherwise, that the damage was caused by the carrier's negligence and not by any inherent vice in the cargo." *Vana Trading*, 556 F.2d at 105 n. 8 (citing *Elia Salzman Tobacco Co. v. S.S. Mormacwind*, 371 F.2d 537, 539 (2d Cir.1967)) (emphasis added).

This second avenue is available because not infrequently a plaintiff who is unable to provide specific evidence as to the condition of the goods at delivery or outturn, can nonetheless show, by the nature of the damage, that the injury complained of happened to the cargo while it was in the carrier's custody. And the whole point of the prima facie requirements in COGSA, as our cases have repeatedly emphasized, is to establish that the damage to the goods occurred while under the supervision of the defendant. *See, e.g., Bally*, 22 F.3d at 69-70; *Caemint Food*, 647 F.2d at 354.

The applicability of this second avenue is the key to the case before us. And, to a large extent, appellants' various attacks on plaintiff's case miss the mark, because they are grounded in the erroneous assumption that the plaintiff is required to rely on the first approach, *i.e.*, on evidence directly pertaining to delivery and outturn, to make out its prima facie case. For example, appellants attack the bill of lading as establishing only "apparent" good condition at delivery, and argue that plaintiff cannot, on the facts before us, invoke the clean-bill-of-lading presumption. But, even if true, this would be beside the point. For the court below quite correctly found that the nature of the damage—seawater wetting—was of the sort that inexorably justified the conclusion that the injury occurred at sea.

Under the circumstances, we will not engage in fanciful assumptions that the harm might possibly have occurred outside the defendants' control. Suggestions of bizarre occurrences (for example, that the shipper paid to transport already damaged rolls of paper), and conjectures unsupported by evidence need not detain us. As a result, defendants' challenge to the condition of the cargo at delivery is not only inapposite, but unavailing. See *Arkwright Mut. Ins. Co. v. M.V. Oriental Fortune*, 745 F.Supp. 920, 923 (S.D.N.Y.1990) ("Indeed, the condition of the cargo upon outturn and the type of damage sustained can be such as to mandate a finding that the cargo was in good order upon shipment.") (citing, *inter alia, Caemint Food*, 647 F.2d at 351 (canned corn beef)).

For similar reasons, we reject the appellants' second attack on plaintiff's prima facie case. Appellants claim that plaintiff has failed to show outturn in damaged condition. They contend that because plaintiff's notice of damage was belated, COGSA's presumption of discharge in good condition governs. But even assuming, arguendo, that the good-outturn presumption applied against plaintiff, we would necessarily find that the presumption was rebutted by the nature of the damage to the goods—seawater wetting. Absent believable evidence to the contrary, such damage of itself establishes the fact that the goods were damaged during ocean transit and, hence, were not received unharmed. As a result, we need not become enmeshed in the intra-defendant wranglings over the scope of the bill of lading.[7] (And, similarly, the trial judge's erroneous reference to it as a "port-to-port" bill of lading is of no consequence.[8])

---

[7] Sea-Land contends, for the first time on appeal, that the bill of lading was house-to-house, and, thus, carried through all the way to the final destinations in Tennessee. At first blush, this seems most unusual—not only was this the position taken by plaintiff (unsuccessfully) at trial, but also, if correct, it would eliminate the claim that plaintiff's notice of damage was untimely. Sea-Land makes this argument, conceding "loss" on the

Appellants' final attack on the plaintiff's prima facie case also fails, but deserves some comment. Appellants contend that genuine issues of material fact render summary judgment inappropriate in this case. Because this argument, if valid, would be applicable to either type of prima facie case under COGSA, it is, in contrast to appellants' other contentions, apposite, though it too is ultimately unsuccessful.

The propriety of summary judgment in actions under COGSA has not received much attention in our circuit. A COGSA prima facie case, if unrebutted, compels judgment for the plaintiff. But what constitutes a "rebuttal" sufficient to avoid summary judgment? In fact, a defendant facing a summary judgment motion under COGSA can respond in three ways, each of which may or may not constitute an adequate answer.

First, in response to a plaintiff's motion for summary judgment, the defendant can do nothing, and simply argue that the plaintiff has not met its burden to make out a prima facie case. If the defendant takes this approach, however, and the court holds that the plaintiff's evidence does establish a prima facie case, the plaintiff would be entitled to summary judgment.

A second response would be to attack the plaintiff's evidence, and cast enough doubt on it to raise a genuine issue of material fact. For example, the defendant could raise questions about the plaintiff's witnesses' credibility. Or it could argue that the nature of the damage to the goods was not peculiarly maritime. While, strictly speaking, this would not be "rebutting" the COGSA prima facie case with affirmative evidence showing that the defendant fell under one of COGSA's specific exceptions, it is certainly a tactic that could, if enough of plaintiff's evidence were called into doubt, raise issues precluding summary judgment.

The third approach is to submit evidence (perhaps also in conjunction with an attack on the plaintiff's prima facie case) that the defendant meets one of the COGSA exceptions. (This is what the caselaw refers to when it speaks of a defendant's "rebuttal" of the prima facie case.) For example, the defendant could show that, notwithstanding the fact that the cargo sustained damage while the defendant had custody of it, the damage resulted from an act of God. *See* 46 U.S.C. app. § 1304(2)(d).

The interaction of a motion for summary judgment with these three responses is not complicated. In fact, the treatment of a summary judgment motion under COGSA is no different from the way similar motions are dealt with in any other litigation. For the establishment of a COGSA prima facie case—which is, after all, no more than a means of focusing attention on whether the cargo was damaged while in the custody of the defendant—entails no special considerations for summary judgment. As a result, a district court sitting in admiralty will, as courts regularly do, simply determine the existence of genuine issues of material fact.

Thus, if the defendant can show that plaintiff's prima facie case depends on resolution of disputed facts, then the court will set the matter for trial. *See, e.g., Seguros Banvenez, S.A. v. S/S Oliver Drescher,* 761 F.2d 855, 860 (2d Cir.1985) (reversing a district court's grant of summary judgment against a defendant because the question of whether defendant's agent acted outside the scope of its authority in preparing an allegedly

---

untimely notice point, in the hopes of achieving a different presumption, the so-called "last carrier" presumption. This rule presumes that the last carrier to transport cargo in a multi-staged voyage is responsible for damage to the shipped goods. *See* Madow Co. v. S.S. Liberty Exporter, 569 F.2d 1183, 1185 (2d Cir.1978). Even if we did not bar Sea-Land from taking this new position, we would find the result to which it would seem to lead—that the truckers who transported the containers from Charleston to Tennessee were liable for seawater wetting—to be both absurd and inapplicable. To the extent that the last carrier presumption is rebuttable, it would be rebutted in this case as a matter of law. Appellee engages in dry understatement when it states that "not a single case has been found in which a court held a railroad or a trucker liable for seawater wetting."

More to the point is OOCL's contention that the bill of lading only ran up to the time of discharge at Charleston harbor, and not for the six weeks of storage in port thereafter. The suggestion is, of course, that seawater could have damaged the goods while in port. There are, however, three problems with this argument. First, OOCL was ultimately responsible for arranging the truck transport to Tennessee, and it would be odd for there to be a "hiatus" in the bill of lading (or between two mini-bills of lading) during which the company with which the shipper transacted to move its goods was not responsible for custody and care. Second, the explicit instructions on the bill "To Hold at Charleston Port" countenanced delay in the transportation of the containers, from which it seems proper to conclude, absent any evidence to the contrary, that OOCL anticipated remaining in control of the goods for some time post-discharge. Finally, again in the absence of any evidence to the contrary (such as the warehouse's collapse into the sea or, perhaps, a freak tidal wave), we are unwilling to speculate that seawater damage occurred anywhere other than at sea.

[8] The bill of lading clearly states that the goods were to be picked up at Stenay, which is not a port. Therefore, the bill was house-to-house, or, possibly, "house-to-port" (if such a hybrid bill exists). *See supra* note 7.

negligent travel plan was an issue of fact for trial). And, if the defendant can show that the plaintiff's prima facie case has been rendered completely meritless by the defendant's response, the defendant may even win a dismissal. On the other hand, if the defendant's evidence is so weak that it inflicts no meaningful damage to the plaintiff's prima facie case, the defendant will have judgment entered against it. *See, e.g., Id.* at 859-60 (affirming summary judgment for plaintiff on the ground that "vague and conclusory references" did not create a factual dispute for trial concerning local stowage customs—which practices would have to be proven under COGSA to justify on-deck cargo stowage).

Before the district court, defendants in the instant case tried, albeit unsuccessfully, to employ a combination of the first and second approaches. They began by suggesting that the plaintiff had not made out a prima facie case at all, and then asserted that elements of the plaintiff's case rested on contested factual premises. On appeal, they make the same arguments.

They make reference to several "mysteries" in the case, and ask "questions" designed to cast doubt on plaintiff's prima facie case: How, if the containers were sealed and there was no pre-shipping inspection, did anyone know that the paper started out in good condition? What route did the containers take from Stenay to Antwerp? Why, if the damage was caused by "wicking,"[9] did containers not on the floor of the cargo hold suffer damage? And, if the damage occurred on board the Inspiration, how does it happen that there was neither a notation in the log of flooding nor evidence of "tide marks" on the containers? "This evidence," they insist, "creates, at the very least, a genuine issue of material fact as to whether the damage occurred while the cargo was in the defendants' custody."

We disagree, and think that the district court was quite right in its conclusion that:

[t]he Defendants have failed to raise a material issue of fact as to whether the damage was caused by their negligence. The question of precisely how, where and when the damage occurred is irrelevant in the absence of some credible evidence that the damage was caused by something other than Defendants' negligence.

While Defendants may have may have raised an issue of fact as to precisely when and where the damage occurred, that issue is not a material issue of fact, as required to defeat summary judgment.

Transatlantic Marine, 961 F.Supp. at 59 (citations omitted).

Indeed, when a defendant chooses to ground its attack in disparagement of the plaintiff's prima facie case (rather than, for example, offering affirmative evidence proving that the damage did not occur while in the defendant's custody, or indicating that the injury fell under one of COGSA's exceptions to liability), it runs a heavy risk. While it is true that the burden is on the plaintiff to establish a prima facie case under COGSA, a defendant must offer more than blanket assertions about mysterious possible causes if it is to survive a motion for summary judgment. The district court's judgment that plaintiff fulfilled its COGSA duty to create a prima facie case that the damage occurred to the goods while in the defendants' custody is without error and is, therefore, affirmed.

* * *

Conclusion

This case has presented this court with a number of challenges—an awkward and complex bill of lading, changing and contradictory positions by the co-defendants on the scope of the bill, a plaintiff who presented so little evidence that as to most types of damage to cargo it would almost certainly have lost a motion for summary judgment, co-defendants who adverted to numerous fanciful "possibilities" and "questions," but provided no evidence supporting any of them, and inapposite citations to federal statutes. Under the circumstances, though we

---

[9] We deduce from our investigation of the record that "wicking" refers to situations in which water passes through one substance onto an adjoining substance. Wicking damage is to be distinguished from damage caused directly by flooding or leaks.

affirm only in part, we cannot fault the district court for its handling of the matter. We AFFIRM the summary judgment for plaintiff-appellee on its prima facie case under COGSA.

* * *

_____

Notes

1. COGSA: Presumption of Good Delivery: § 3(6)

Section 3(6) of COGSA provides that the "removal of the goods into the custody of the person entitled to delivery thereof under the contract of carriage" is *prima facie* evidence of the delivery of the goods by the carrier as described in the bill of lading, unless notice of the loss or damage and the general nature of such loss or damage is given in writing to the carrier or his agent at the port of discharge before or at the time of the removal of the goods. This provision establishes what is known in practice as a *presumption of good delivery*. See *Pacific Employers Ins. Co. v. M/V Gloria*, 767 F.2d 229 (5th Cir. 1985). This presumption avails only in the absence of any other evidence on point. See *Socony Mobil Oil Co. v. Texas Coastal & International, Inc.*, 559 F.2d 1008, 1977 AMC. 2598 (5th Cir. 1977). When plaintiff provides sufficient evidence of the damage, the presumption disappears and the lack of notice "is accorded no special weight beyond that given other evidence concerning where the damage occurred." *Harbert International Establishment v. Power Shipping*, 635 F.2d 370, 373, 1983 AMC 785 (5th Cir. 1981).

2. Delivery under the Harter Act and COGSA

Under the Harter Act, the carrier is required to make "proper delivery" of the goods in order to be discharged of his responsibilities toward the shipper or consignee. 46 U.S.C.A. § 30704 (formerly 46 U.S.C. § 190).

The words "proper delivery" have not been defined by statute. According to the courts, as a general rule, proper delivery by the carrier contemplates "delivery of the cargo to the consignee or designee set forth in the bill of lading, at a fit and proper wharf, with the duty upon the carrier to give reasonable notice to the consignee that the cargo has arrived, with a reasonable opportunity to pick it up, and a duty on the consignee to receive the goods at the place of outturn." *Farrell Lines, Inc. v. Highlands Ins. Co.*, 532 F. Supp. 77, 1982 AMC 1430 (S.D.N.Y. 1982).

The general rule of proper delivery is subject to a well-recognized exception that a custom, regulation, or law at the port of discharge may provide otherwise. See *Black Sea & Baltic General Ins. Co. v. S.S. Hellenic Destiny*, 575 F. Supp. 685, 1984 AMC 1055 (S.D.N.Y. 1983). The court stated that it is the obligation of the carrier "to deliver the goods from wharf to wharf, notify the consignee of the vessel's arrival, and to protect the cargo until the consignee has a reasonable opportunity to remove it ... unless these obligations are modified by local port law, custom, or regulation." Placement of the goods on the dock and under the custody of the local institution has been held to be proper delivery. In *Allstate Insurance Co. v. Imparca Lines*, 646 F.2d 166, 1982 AMC 423 (5th Cir. 1981), a container was stolen after being placed on the dock at Puerto Cabello, Venezuela, in the custody of the Instituto Nacional de Puertos (INP), which was the entity charged by law with the duty of receiving the cargo and distributing it to the consignee. The court held that this "constitutes delivery in accordance with the bill of lading and the custom and usage of the port." 646 F.2d at 169.

For discussion of the question of whether a discharge of the goods into lighters constitutes proper delivery, see *A/S Dampskibselskabet Torm v. McDermott, Inc.*, 788 F.2d 1103 (5th Cir. 1986); *Caterpillar Overseas, S.A. v. Steamship Expeditor*, 318 F.2d 720, 1964 AMC 1662 (2d Cir. 1963). For the question of whether the discharge of the goods on a vessel is lighterage or transshipment, *see U.S. v. Ultramar Shipping Co.*, 685 F. Supp. 887, 1988 A.M.C. 527, 1988 AMC 984 (S.D.N.Y. 1988).

The Harter Act obligates the carrier to make proper delivery and holds the carrier liable for damage of or loss to cargo until proper delivery has been made. Delivery under COGSA, however, is important only because it marks the point at which the one year statute of limitation begins to run. The carrier's period of responsibility under COGSA is only from the time goods are loaded on the vessel until they are discharged. Nevertheless, the United States Court of Appeals for the Fifth Circuit has adopted the Harter Act rule of delivery for purposes of determining the point at which the COGSA limitation period begins to run. See, *Servicios-Expoarma, C.A. v. Industrial Maritime Carriers, Inc.*, 135 F.3d 984, 1998 AMC 1453 (5th Cir. 1998). Other courts have held to the contrary. See, *Lithotip, C.A. v. S.S. Guarico*, 569 F. Supp. 837, 1985 AMC 1813 (S.D.N.Y. 1983).

In *Mannesman Demag Corp. v. M/V CONCERT EXPRESS*, 225 F.3d 587, 2000 AMC 2935 (5th Cir., 2000), the court held that in the case of a "through" bill of lading for multimodal transport, "proper delivery" for Harter Act purposes took place when the goods were handed over to inland carrier. The Harter Act ceased to apply at that point, and the carriage thereafter was governed by the terms of the bill of lading and any law that might be compulsorily applicable to the land carriage. See *supra*, pp 3-4.

3. Non-delivery

When the goods are not delivered at all, or are delivered to the wrong person, the plaintiff's prima facie case is made out simply by showing delivery to the carrier and non-delivery to the intended receiver. The Harter Act prevents the carrier from excluding its liability for non-delivery or misdelivery by means of an exculpatory clause in the bill of lading. The carrier must establish one of the COGSA defenses to excuse non-delivery or misdelivery, or be held liable. See *Allied Chemical v. Companhia de Navegacao*, 775 F.2d 476, 482, 1986 AMC 826, 3 Fed.R.Serv.3d 1353 (2d Cir. 1988):

Lloyd contends that clauses 1 and 12 of the bill of lading absolve it from liability. Clause 1 provides that "[t]he Carrier shall not be liable in any capacity whatsoever for any delay, non-delivery or mis-delivery, or loss of or damage to the goods occurring while the goods are not in the actual custody of the Carrier." Clause 12 provides that "[t]he responsibility of the Carrier, in any capacity, shall altogether cease and the goods shall be considered to be delivered and at their own risk and expense in every respect when taken into the custody of customs or other authorities."

Lloyd's reliance on these clauses is unavailing because they are null and void...Although the enactment of COGSA sharply curtailed the applicability of the Harter Act, 46 U.S.C. § 190 *et seq.* to ocean bills of lading and matters of ocean carriers' liability, absent a valid agreement to the contrary, the Harter Act still governs prior to loading and after discharge of cargo until proper delivery is made...While a carrier and a shipper may specify by agreement what the responsibility of the carrier should be after the goods are discharged, the carrier may not simply disclaim all post-discharge responsibility.

C. Responsibilities of the Carrier

1. Due Diligence to Make Ship Seaworthy

46 U.S.C.A. § 30706 (formerly 46 U.S.C. § 192); COGSA § 3(1)(a)

UNITED STATES v. ULTRAMAR SHIPPING CO.

685 F. Supp. 887 , 1988 AMC 527 (S.D.N.Y.), *aff'd*, 854 F.2d 1315 (Table) (2d Cir. 1988)

BRIEANT, Chief Judge:

* * *

The carrier's duty of due diligence to make the vessel seaworthy is a condition precedent to its enjoyment of any of the Harter Act's** exemptions. *Isbrandtsen Co. v. Federal Ins. Co.*, 113 F. Supp. 357 (S.D.N.Y. 1952), *aff'd*, 205 F.2d 679 (2d Cir.), *cert. denied*, 346 U.S. 866, 74 S. Ct. 106, 98 L. Ed. 377 (1953). The duty to exercise due diligence is not *pro forma*; the carrier is held to a high standard of care. *Peter Paul, Inc. v. Rederi A/B Pulp*, 258 F.2d 901 (2d Cir. 1958), *cert. denied*, 359 U.S. 910, 79 S. Ct. 586, 3 L. Ed. 2d 574 (1959); *Gold Dust Corp. v. Munson S.S. Line*, 55 F.2d 900 (2d Cir. 1932). This duty relates specifically to the inception of the voyage and applies to each vessel participating in the carriage.

In the case of *The Silvia*, 171 U.S. 462, 464, 19 S. Ct. 7, 43 L. Ed. 241 (1898), the Supreme Court announced that "[t]he test of seaworthiness is whether the vessel is reasonably fit to carry the cargo which she has undertaken to transport." *Atlantic Banana Co. v. M/V "Calanca"*, 342 F. Supp. 447, 452 (S.D.N.Y. 1972). This commonly accepted definition of seaworthiness was later explained in *The Southwark*, 191 U.S. 1, 9, 24 S. Ct. 1, 3, 48 L. Ed. 65 (1903):

[S]eaworthiness is not an absolute but a relative term. It is to be considered in relation to the voyage undertaken, the cargo to be carried, and its stowage. Unless a vessel is reasonably fit to carry the cargo she has undertaken to transport, she is unseaworthy, but seaworthiness does not require perfection in a vessel.

Thus, a ship may be found seaworthy for lighterage but perhaps not fit for an ocean voyage, for lumber carriage but not for grain carriage, for summer travel but not for winter travel. *The Sagamore*, 300 F. 701 (2d Cir. 1924). Any doubt as to the seaworthiness of the vessel "must be resolved against the ship owner and in favor of the shipper." *The Southwark*, 191 U.S. at 24.

In an effort to establish the exercise of due diligence to render the CHERRY LAJU seaworthy, defendants introduced the testimony of naval architect Philip Kimball and Captains Edward P. Boyle and Scott Sammis of the National Cargo Bureau. These witnesses responded to plaintiff's claim that the CHERRY LAJU was rendered unsea-

---

** The Harter Act was applicable because the cargo had been properly "discharged" onto "lighters" one of which was the CHERRY LAJU, therefore, COGSA was no longer applicable and the Harter Act applied until "delivery." Eds.

worthy by her instability/improper stowage, unusable sailing directions, and broken fathometer. The Court finds that defendants failed to prove that they exercised the requisite diligence to make the CHERRY LAJU seaworthy.

Instability/Improper Stowage

Defendants failed to prove that the CHERRY LAJU complied with accepted safety rules for the carriage of bulk grain. The duty to make a vessel seaworthy requires that a vessel be safely loaded and properly stowed. *The Nidarholm*, 282 U.S. 681, 685, 51 S. Ct. 266, 268, 75 L. Ed. 614 (1931). "The law imposes upon owners of ships the duty of using due care to ascertain and consider the nature and characteristics of goods offered for shipment...." *The Poleric [Bank Line v. Porter]*, 25 F.2d 843, 845 (4th Cir. 1928). Section 1 of the Harter Act, 46 U.S.C. § 190, voids any provision in a bill of lading that attempts to relieve a carrier "from liability for loss or damage arising from negligence, fault, or failure in proper loading [or] stowage."

The rules and regulations of the National Cargo Bureau and SOLAS provide a measure of proper stowage. Even if these safety guidelines are not officially enforced as against vessels and voyages such as the CHERRY LAJU and her trip to Chalna, the Court must determine if the failure to abide by them was so dangerous or unreasonable under the circumstances as to be unacceptable. *The Silversandal [Bache v. Silver Line]*, 110 F.2d 60, 62 (2d Cir. 1940).

At trial, the National Cargo Bureau's current president, Captain Sammis, testified that he had participated in the drafting of the 1974 SOLAS requirements for grain carriage. Under these rules, a ship like the CHERRY LAJU was required to have shifting boards, to strap or lash down cargo in partly filled compartments such as the first hold, and to maintain throughout the voyage a minimum metacentric height ("GM"). Mr. Kimball testified that the SOLAS stability formula required the CHERRY LAJU to maintain a GM of 3.7 feet. (Kimball, Tr. 278; Ex. 23, 27, 27A, 33). Both he and Captain Boyle, Chief Deputy Surveyor of the National Cargo Bureau, conceded that the CHERRY LAJU's GM was well below that figure. The CHERRY LAJU had neither boards nor minimal stability and thereby exposed the cargo to undue risks.

Both Captain Sammis and Captain Boyle stated that the SOLAS regulations were not necessarily applicable to the CHERRY LAJU because she was engaged in a coastwise voyage and not an international voyage. (Sammis, Tr. 301; Ex. CC). However, Captain Boyle testified that during his career at sea he had never carried grain without shifting boards. (Tr. 272). He also testified that if the CHERRY LAJU had complied with the SOLAS regulations, the casualty would not have occurred. (Tr. 212). The Bangladesh Committee of Enquiry clearly considered the SOLAS guidelines applicable to the CHERRY LAJU. (Ex. 17). Similarly, plaintiff's witness, Captain Rajnikant Jadhav, a master experienced in the carriage of grain and familiar with the Bay of Bengal, testified that in such bad weather, typical of the monsoon season, he would never have made the voyage without equipping the grain holds with shifting boards and calculating the GM. (Tr. 323-324).

Notwithstanding the SOLAS stability requirements, an experienced seaman should have realized that the ship's GM was dangerously low. Mr. Kimball calculated it to range between 1.47 and 1.61 feet at the time the CHERRY LAJU broke ground, finally settling on the figure 1.49 feet. (Tr. 147-153, 186-188). Although he also testified that such a GM was "sufficient," the Court concludes from general maritime usage that such a low GM was not sufficient and rendered the CHERRY LAJU unseaworthy for the carriage of grain during the monsoon season. By ignoring the GM guidelines, the CHERRY LAJU failed to comport with the settled principle that a vessel must be able to withstand expectable action of the seas and expectable vicissitudes. *The Cypria [Ore Steamship Corp. v. D/S A/S Hasse]*, 137 F.2d 326 (2d Cir. 1943).

Similarly, defendants have not met their burden of proving that the vessel was seaworthy in the absence of shifting boards of greater diligence in stowing and securing the cargo. It is clear that both Captain Sobhan and Captain Guerrero were familiar with the expectable weather and sea conditions at the time of the 200 mile voyage and the evidence is clear that under these circumstances the failure to protect stowed grain from shifting rendered the vessel unseaworthy.

Broken Fathometer/Unusable Sailing Directions

Plaintiff argues that the lack of an operational fathometer aboard the CHERRY LAJU deprived her master and officers of the knowledge that the vessel had no clearance at all and thereby rendered her unseaworthy. Defendants respond that the presence or absence of a fathometer does not determine seaworthiness. They claim that a fathometer would be useful to warn a vessel that it was entering shallow water when it did not intend to do so, but that it would not be helpful once a ship reached shallow water in which the ship intended to navigate. Defendants' witness Captain Boyle testified that the depth soundings recorded by a fathometer are used primarily to compare with those noted on depth charts and thereby pinpoint the ship's location: "It is not a grounding avoiding device. It is a navigational device when you're coming in and you have the gradient at the bottom. It is one more confirmation of where you are." (Boyle, Tr. 255-257). Defendants claim that the absence of a functional fathometer will not render a vessel unseaworthy when the vessel has other equipment which will fix her position.

Plaintiff relies on the testimony of defendants' own witnesses in its assertion that a working fathometer is imperative to a ship's seaworthiness. Captain Ostromogilisky testified that a fathometer is required for American flag vessels in the CHERRY LAJU's class. (Tr. 63). Captain Boyle testified that amendments to the 1974 SOLAS convention, which went into effect September 1, 1984, shortly after the sinking of the CHERRY LAJU, require a fathometer on board ships such as the CHERRY LAJU. (Tr. 257-258). Plaintiff's witness Captain Jadhav explained that aside from fixing a ship's position, a fathometer would assist when there is a risk of grounding because "it also gives you an idea as to whether your depth is increasing or decreasing as you go along the depth of water under your keel and as you're going along when you start realizing that it is decreasing to an extent where it becomes dangerous...." (Tr. 310-311).

The Court is guided by the rule that a vessel must be supplied with the means by which she may be safely navigated. *The Southwark*, 191 U.S. at 8-9, 24 S. Ct. at 3. She must "have on board a reliable compass or compasses, sextants and sounding apparatus" and be "equipped with adequate charts, light books, pilot books, lists of radio beacons, and notices to marines." 2A Benedict on Admiralty § 67. The case law is mixed as to whether a fathometer is required. *Compare Hurst v. City of Virginia Beach*, 1972 AMC 2346 (E.D. Va. 1971), with *Indian Towing Co. v. United States*, 182 F. Supp. 264, 270 (E.D. La. 1959).

Over fifty years ago, when radios were not required on harbor tugs and were infrequently supplied, Judge Learned Hand addressed the issue of whether they nevertheless are a condition of seaworthiness. *The T.J. Hooper*, 60 F.2d 737, 740 (2d Cir. 1932). He stated that

> in most cases reasonable prudence is in fact common prudence; but strictly it is never its measure; a whole calling may have unduly lagged in the adoption of new and available devices. It never may set its own tests, however persuasive be its usages. Courts must in the end say what is required; there are precautions so imperative that even their universal disregard will not excuse their omission.

Judge Hand concluded that, even though "there was no custom at all as to receiving sets," failure to supply tugs with them constituted unseaworthiness. Regardless of whether Judge Hand's decision was correct at the time it was uttered, in the instant case there does appear to exist a custom favoring the use of fathometers. At the time of the sinking of the CHERRY LAJU, it was believed "prudent" to have one on board. (Boyle, Tr. 258). However, this custom does not necessarily dictate the seaworthiness of the CHERRY LAJU for the lighterage voyage she undertook in this case.

Under different circumstances, on a longer voyage, in a larger ship a fathometer might be deemed imperative. Here, the CHERRY LAJU was able to fix her position absent a working fathometer because of the presence of direction finders, compasses, navigational charts, radio bearings, and radar. (Boyle, Tr. 255). And the testimony is uniform that a fathometer is neither the ordinary means for determining depth, nor the most accurate, especially as it does not operate efficiently in very shallow water. The absence of a working fathometer under the facts in this case and standing alone, probably did not render the vessel unseaworthy.

Nor did the presence of unreadable sailing directions render the CHERRY LAJU unseaworthy. It is true that the sailing directions, if readable, would have informed Captain Guerrero that he should not attempt to cross the Chalna bar in a southwest monsoon unless he had at least four feet of water under the keel. However, according to the CHERRY LAJU's navigational and depth charts, at least that much of a margin was available to her. The Bangladesh Anticipated Drafts Chart (Ex. GG) indicated a tide of 29 feet 9 inches and the CHERRY LAJU's draft was 24 feet 6 inches. Under the circumstances of this case, a lighterage voyage in the Ganges River Delta, the instructions of the port's pilot would take precedence over any other sailing directions and thus, the absence of readable sailing directions standing alone, probably did not constitute unseaworthiness. However, as noted earlier, the CHERRY LAJU was unseaworthy due to her instability and improper stowage of cargo at the start of the voyage.

Because defendants have not established the seaworthiness of their vessel, the CHERRY LAJU, for the voyage she undertook in this case, they cannot avail themselves of the exceptions to liability under the Harter Act. They would rely on the Harter Act's exception for the damage or loss resulting from faults or errors in navigation or management of the vessel. 46 U.S.C. App. § 192. They blame the incident on the master's negligence and on the Bangladesh port authority's wrongful enticement of the CHERRY LAJU into a channel it should have known she could not navigate. However, in an Harter Act case, the faulty navigation exception is not available to unseaworthy vessels, regardless of whether the unseaworthy condition is related to the damage or loss. *The Isis*, 290 U.S. at 351, 54 S. Ct. at 167. Even if proof of a causal link were required, the unseaworthy condition in this case, the improper stowage of the cargo and the instability of the CHERRY LAJU, did proximately contribute to the loss.

* * *

Settle an appropriate judgment on five (5) days notice.

Note

The obligation of the carrier to exercise due diligence to make the ship seaworthy includes the duty of due care in the selection of the master and crew. If the master commits a navigational error that causes loss or damage to the goods, is there an inference of lack of due care in the selection of the master? See *In Re Ta Chi Navigation (Panama) Corp., S.A., as owner of the Steamship Eurybates*, 513 F. Supp. 148, 155, 1981 AMC 2350 (E.D. La. 1981).

Is the carrier responsible for assuring the due diligence of his servants or independent contractors to whom the ship is entrusted for repairs? Is the obligation imposed on the carrier by § 3(1) of COGSA delegable? See *Riverstone Meat Co. v. Lancashire Shipping Co. (The Muncaster Castle)*, [1961] 1 Lloyds' Rep. 57, 1961 AMC 1357 (House of Lords, 1960). In *The Muncaster Castle*, the House of Lords held that the obligation to exercise due diligence is "an inescapable personal" one; the carrier is responsible if any employee or agent, including an independent contractor, fails to exercise due diligence in making the ship seaworthy before and at the beginning of the voyage. *Compare: Fireman's Fund Ins. Co. v. The Vignes*, 794 F.2d 1552, 1987 AMC 291 (11th Cir. 1986). In this case, the court held that a shipowner did not breach his obligation to exercise due diligence to make the ship seaworthy when he delegated a particular test to a qualified and careful contractor.

However, delegation of inspection to a qualified contractor such as a classification society does not always amount to due diligence. *Nissan Fire & Marine Insurance Co. Ltd v. M/V HYUNDAI EXPLORER*, 93 F.3d 641, 1996 AMC 2409 (9th Cir. 1996).

---

2. Due Diligence in the Handling of the Goods

46 U.S.C.A. § 30705 (formerly 46 U.S.C. § 191); COGSA § 3(2)

The carrier's duty to "properly and carefully load, handle, stow, carry, keep, care for, and discharge the goods carried" under COGSA § 3(2) (formerly 46 U.S.C. § 1303(2)) is a distinct and distinguished obligation that the law imposes on the carrier. As a practical matter, however, the question of the discharge of this obligation by the carrier arises in connection with excepted causes. It is often difficult to determine whether the loss or damage to the goods was caused by the breach of the carrier's obligation under COGSA § 3(2) or by some excepted cause that exonerates the carrier from responsibility.

Carriers may contract with shippers or consignees with respect to the responsibility for and control of loading and stowage operations. *Caterpillar Overseas, S.A. v. S.S. Expeditor*, 318 F.2d 720 (2d Cir. 1963).

COGSA § 3(2) imposes on the carrier a non-delegable duty to load and stow the goods. Unlike the duty under § 3(1), this duty does not cease with commencement of the voyage, but continues through to completion of discharge.

Because the carrier's duty under § 3(2) is non-delegable, the carrier cannot simply say that it is not liable because it did not contract to load, stow or discharge the goods. For example, if the shipper agrees with the carrier on FIO (Free In and Out) or FIOS (Free In and Out, Stowed) terms, the shipper undertakes to arrange and be responsible for loading and discharging. Nevertheless, the carrier has a non-delegable duty under COGSA to load and stow (and discharge), and remains responsible for loading and stowing even if those operations are performed by stevedores engaged by the shipper. In order to avoid liability for damage caused during loading or by faulty stowing, the carrier must raise the defenses conferred by § 4(2)(i),(q) (see below) by *proving* that the damage was caused by the shipper's fault, or without fault on its own part. See *Associated Metals & Minerals Corp. v. M/V ARKTIS SKY*, 978 F. 2d 47, 1993 AMC 509 (2d Cir. 1992), reproduced *infra* at pp 107-109.

D. Immunities of the Carrier

1. Loss Caused by Unseaworthiness Despite the Exercise of Due Diligence

COGSA § 4(1) (formerly 46 U.S.C. § 1304(1))

COGSA imposes on the carrier "before and at the beginning of the voyage" the obligation to *exercise due diligence* to make the ship "seaworthy." Any damage caused to the goods as a result of the carrier's breach of this obligation is compensable under COGSA. Note, however, that if the carrier fulfills his obligation under § 3(1) of COGSA, § 4(1) of the Act relieves the carrier of liability for the loss caused to the goods by the unseaworthiness of the vessel. *See Complaint of Tecomar, S.A.*, 765 F. Supp. 1150, 1991 AMC 2432 (S.D.N.Y. 1991). Thus, the carrier is exonerated when he proves that, despite the exercise of due diligence to make the ship seaworthy, the loss or damage resulted from the unseaworthy condition of the vessel. Such a condition may result from *latent defects*, that is, defects not discoverable by the exercise of due diligence, or from *transitory unseaworthiness*, that is, a condition that arose after the ship broke ground.

For a case in which the carrier was exonerated from liability under § 4(1) because the defect was latent, *see Tata, Inc. v. Farrell Lines, Inc.*, 1987 AMC 1764 (S.D.N.Y. 1987):

> Cargo owner sought to recover the amount a salvor was paid for towing a disabled feeder vessel to a port of refuge.
>
> The cargo was loaded on board the feeder vessel at Tuticorin for final carriage and delivery at Calcutta. Within 72 hours of its departure, steering was lost because the "keeper" securing the locknut threaded to the rudder post broke off. As the nut backed off the rudder post, so did the rudder.
>
> The court found the loss due to latent defect and denied recovery. The court noted the ship was designed and maintained to Lloyd's standards and that all inspections required were done. Further, ... that the Master and Chief Engineer had conducted an appropriate pre-departure check of the steering mechanism....
>
> The only way to check the condition of the "keeper" would have required cutting away an inspection window in the rudder blade. The court held that defendant was clearly not obliged to perform such an inspection before each voyage. Thus, the case fell "within the narrow class of latent defects ... [for] which a carrier is relieved of liability for a vessel's unseaworthiness."

The carrier may be exonerated from liability, quite apart from "excused" unseaworthiness, when the cause of the loss or damage to the goods is an "error in management or navigation." *See* COGSA § 4(2)(a). What happens if the carrier does not show that he exercised due diligence to make the ship seaworthy but proves that the loss or damage was caused by an error in management or navigation? In this respect, there is an important difference between COGSA and the Harter Act. Under the Harter Act, a carrier may not claim immunity unless he has shown that he has exercised due diligence to make the ship seaworthy. A carrier who cannot show that he has exercised due diligence to make the ship seaworthy is, therefore, liable for loss or damage to the goods regardless of the cause of the loss or damage. The carrier cannot be exonerated from liability on proof that the cause of the loss or damage is an excepted peril. *See The Isis*, 290 U.S. 333, 54 S.Ct. 162, 78 L.Ed. 348, 1933 AMC 1565 (1933). It is different under COGSA. In a cargo claim, the liability of the carrier always rests on proof of causal connection between the loss or damage to the goods and the breach of the carrier's obligation to make the ship seaworthy before and at the commencement of the voyage. *See United States v. Ultramar Shipping Co., supra.*

---

2. Burden of proof in relation to other cases

For unseaworthiness claims, COGSA § 4(1) expressly provides that the carrier bears the burden of proving due diligence. For the other defenses in § 4(2), burden of proof issues are more complex because the burden can shift several times. The relevant principles were memorably likened to a ping-pong game in *Nitram, Inc. v. Cretan Life*, 599 F.2d 1359, 1373 (5th Cir. 1979):

> To enforce their respective rights under [COGSA], litigants must engage in the ping-pong game of burden-shifting mandated by [§§1303, 1304]. The plaintiff serves, and must establish a prima facie case by proving both delivery of the goods to the carrier in good condition and outturn by the carrier in damaged condition. The ball is now in the carrier's court; he bears the burden of showing that the loss or damage falls within one of the COGSA exceptions set forth in 46 U.S.C.A. § 1304(2). Once that burden is satisfied, the burden shifts back to the plaintiff to show that the carrier's negligence contributed to the damage or loss. Once again, and for the final time, the burden then shifts to the carrier to segregate the portion of the damage due to the excepted cause from that portion resulting from its own negligence. With the volley thus complete, the trial judge must ultimately apportion responsibility for the loss or damage so proven.

To add to the confusion, not all of the defenses follow this sequence. The burden of proof shifts differently under § 4(2)(b) (fire), § 4(2)(c) (perils of the sea) and (in some circuits at least), § 4(2)(m) (inherent vice). The "serve" and the first two shifts of the burden of proof in typical cases are illustrated in the case extracted next, *Lekas & Drivas, Inc. v. Goulandris*, 306 F.2d 426 (2d Cir. 1962), which is concerned with the "restraint of princes" defense in § 4(2)(g). The third shift occurs because of the rule in *Schnell v. The Vallescura*, 293 U.S. 296, 555 S. Ct. 194, 79 L. Ed. 373 (1934), which is reproduced after *Lekas & Drivas*. The defenses with a different shifting of the burden are considered separately below.

LEKAS & DRIVAS, INC. v. GOULANDRIS
306 F.2d 426 (2d Cir. 1962)

FRIENDLY, Circuit Judge:

Mussolini's unprovoked attack on Greece on October 28, 1940, touched off a modern Odyssey whose legal consequences have occupied the courts in this circuit for more than twenty years; hopefully, this decision may end the epic.

Having taken on cargo at Izmir, Cavalla and Salonica, principally tobacco, the SS. Ioannis P. Goulandris docked at Piraeus on October 26, 1940, before her intended voyage to the United States via Gibraltar, a crossing ordinarily taking 25 to 28 days. Two days later, Italy attacked. The Ioannis was first requisitioned by the Greek Government for a short military mission. Transit of the Mediterranean having become impracticable, she was then directed by her government to proceed to the United States via Suez and the Cape of Good Hope. She sailed from Piraeus on November 10, 1940; she arrived in the United States in May, 1941, her cargo badly damaged during the long, hot voyage.

We have previously affirmed Chief Judge Ryan's dismissal, 173 F.Supp. 140, of large claims for damage to the tobacco, 281 F.2d 179 (2 Cir. 1960). The instant appeals relate to much smaller claims allowed by the judge in the same opinion, 173 F.Supp. at 179-180, for damage to a shipment of 308 cases and 7 barrels of a soft cheese known as "Kefalotyr" by libelant Lekas & Drivas, Inc. as consignor and consignee, and of 500 and 350 drums of olive oil, respectively, consigned to libelants Victor Cory Company and Pompeian Olive Oil Corporation.

The voyage took place under the difficulties expectable in wartime. The Greek Government had ordered the Ioannis to sail in convoy to Port Said and thereafter to follow the instructions of the British Admiralty; because these orders were confidential, the vessel was unable throughout the voyage to communicate directly with her owners, although communication by way of an intermediary in London did occur during stops in ports along the way. On December 14, the convoy the Ioannis had finally joined, after waiting 16 days at Port Said and three days at Great Bitter Lake, reached Aden. The Ioannis, drawing water uncontrollably through her stern gland and suffering severe vibrations in her tail-shaft, dropped out for repairs. Due to the needs of the British Navy, drydock facilities were unavailable, so the tail-shaft had to be drawn for inspection while the ship was afloat. To facilitate this, much cargo, including the cheese here in question, had to be removed and stored on lighters, where it was covered with tarpaulins; according to the agreed summary of the master's deposition, "There were no warehouse facilities at Aden where the cargo could be taken." By the uncontradicted deposition of the chief officer, the cheese had not begun to spoil when it was so removed. Wartime conditions caused the repairs, normally taking some three days, to require 35. The chief officer observed that, when the cheese was reloaded, it was spoiling—"it was leaking though the cases and barrels and had begun to develop a certain odor." Thereafter the Ioannis stopped in Durban for 13 days to take on bunkers and to make some condenser repairs; later, after a fire in the tobacco, she was at Barbados for 23 days. The Ioannis finally arrived at Norfolk on May 3, 1941, and in New York on May 8. A surveyor found the cheese to be "Melted with a terrible stench, and worthless"; it was subsequently sold for about a sixth of what its sound value would have been. Seventeen drums of the Cory shipment of olive oil and five of the Pompeian were cut and leaking; also, the latter was one drum short.

* * *

On April 9, 1959, Chief Judge Ryan filed a comprehensive opinion, 173 F.Supp. 140, denying the tobacco owners' claims, action which we subsequently affirmed, 281 F.2d 179, and granting those regarding the cheese and the olive oil. After referral of the latter to a Commissioner and dispute over the interest to be awarded, a resettled final decree was filed on July 25, 1961. Lekas & Drivas, Inc. recovered $24,780.21, plus interest at 4 1/2% from May 7, 1945, amounting to $18,083.36. Pompeian Olive Oil Corp. was awarded $1,472.46, with interest, similarly computed, totalling $1,074.53. Victor Cory Co. was allowed $1,089.82, with interest of $795.30. Respondents appeal from these awards, alleging error both as to liability (save as to the one drum missing from the Pompeian consignment) and as to the award of 16 years' interest.

We find no error in the granting of the claims as to the olive oil. . . .

* * *

The cheese claim presents a more difficult problem. We have concluded that as to this we must reverse.

When the cheese was loaded at Salonica, all 7 barrels and 67 of the cases were stowed in the after part of the No. 4 hold, and the other 241 cases in the poop, along with 704 other cases belonging to parties not in the present litigation. The judge found, 173 F.Supp. at 156, that the cheese "had melted and spoiled due to the high temperatures experienced on the voyage," and, id. at 179, that the poop was an improper place to stow cheese. The latter finding, which was the predicate of liability, was cast in terms of the poop's not being "a fit and proper place for carriage of the cheese from Greece to New York via the Mediterranean-Gibraltar route . . ." The reasoning was that if the voyage had been made as contemplated, the cheese would nevertheless have spoiled; that the legal cause of that spoilage would have been the stowage in the poop; and that the vessel was therefore liable for the damage which in fact occurred.

Respondents vigorously attack the judge's conclusion that the poop was an unfit place to stow the cheese. They say that if the voyage had been made via Gibraltar as contemplated, air temperatures would have ranged between 53º and 65º Fahrenheit and that, although the poop had no permanent ventilators, adequate ventilation was had through an open hatch. We find it unnecessary to pass on this challenge, for reasons that will shortly appear.

It cannot be disputed that the voyage of the Ioannis was affected by "restraint of princes, rulers, or people" under § 4(2)(g) of COGSA. Indeed, there was a double restraint—the threat of attack by an enemy government on the planned voyage through the Mediterranean and the order of the Greek Government to proceed via Suez and the Cape of Good Hope. "'Restraints of princes, rulers, and peoples' covers any forcible interference with the voyage or adventure at the hands of the constituted government, or ruling power of any country, whether done by it as an enemy of the State to which the ship belongs, or not." CARVER'S CARRIAGE OF GOODS BY SEA (10 ed.), 129. This "restraint" altered the voyage from a four week trip of 5000 miles through the Mediterranean and North Atlantic, in cool November weather, to a trip of 13,000 miles and five months around Africa, with two crossings of the Equator. Outside temperatures repeatedly hit 100º and above. Even with perfect ventilation in the poop, or with stowage elsewhere under adequate ventilation, the cheese would therefore, unless it were refrigerated, have been subject to extremely high temperatures for a period of time long enough to cause it to spoil. Whether stowage of some of the cheese in the poop was improper for the Gibraltar voyage is thus immaterial; "if the accident would have happened without defendant's negligent act, then such is not the cause of it." 2 HARPER & JAMES, THE LAW OF TORTS (1956) § 20.2, at p. 1114 fn. 18, and cases there cited; American Law Institute, Restatement of Torts, § 432, comment b and illustrations 1 and 2.

We could stop here were it not for the episode at Aden. As to this libelant makes two claims. One is that keeping the cheese on lighters for a month was negligent since respondents should have placed it under refrigeration. The other is that, spoilage having begun, respondents should have sold the cheese rather than reloaded it. We could remand for further consideration of these claims by the district judge who, on his view of the case, did not reach them. However, all the evidence is before us, most of it was given by deposition, and we think it best to bring this long litigation to an end.

It will be convenient first to consider the claim as to the master's duty to sell. We do not doubt that circumstances may arise when the master of a ship has not merely the authority but, under § 3(2) of COGSA, the duty to sell cargo that is at risk of further deterioration, communicating with the owner if that is feasible but still having both the authority and duty if it is not. . . . This duty exists even if the cause of the deterioration is an excepted cause, GILMORE AND BLACK, ADMIRALTY (1957) 149. If the spoilage had been detected early in the Ioannis' stay at Aden, the master would thus have been bound to endeavor to communicate with the owners via London and, failing contrary instructions, to try to sell the cheese since, even if the price at Aden were well below what had been expected at New York, it still might substantially exceed what would be realized after further spoilage. On the other hand, if the spoilage was not detected until the reloading, it would be imposing a rather heavy burden to say, "now in the peace of a quiet chamber," 277 F.2d at 13, that the master was required further to postpone the already long postponed departure from Aden in order to achieve some possible mitigation of the damages on this relatively small part of the Ioannis' cargo, at the cost of perhaps enhancing the risk to the larger part. The only evidence as to the time of detection of the spoilage is the chief officer's deposition; although far from conclusive, this tends rather to the view that the spoilage was discovered only when the cheese was reloaded. Very likely the foregoing should be further qualified in the sense that the Ioannis was bound to maintain some surveillance while the cargo was on the lighters. As to this the evidence is simply that there were four watchmen on each lighter to see that the cargo was properly ventilated and protected from the elements; whether due diligence on their part would have detected the spoilage before the reloading, the evidence does not disclose.

Decision therefore turns, as it so ofter does in claims of this sort, upon the burden of proof. The classic statement, in *Clark v. Barnwell,* 12 How. 272, 280, 53 U.S. 272, 280, 13 L.Ed. 985 (1851), is that when a carrier has discharged the burden of showing the existence of an excepting cause, "in this stage and posture of the case, the burden is upon the plaintiff to establish the negligence, as the affirmative lies upon him." From this respondents could argue that, they having shown the "cause" of the loss to be the restraint of princes, the burden of proof shifted back to the libelant. However, libelant might be expected to counter with the statement, in *Schnell v. The Vallescura,* 293 U.S. 296, 306, 55 S.Ct. 194, 197, 79 L.Ed. 373 (1934), that "Where the state of the proof is such as to show that the damage is due either to an excepted peril or to the carrier's negligent care of the cargo, it is for him to bring himself within the exception or to show that he has not been negligent."

In fact, neither Supreme Court decision is directly in point. The respondents in *Clark v. Barnwell* had not only established a peril of the sea as a cause but had negated all others; libelants in that case not merely failed to sustain a burden, but no evidence of negligence "is found in the record," 12 How. 283, 13 L.Ed. 985. *Schnell v. The Vallescura,* decided under the Harter Act, was a case in which the ship proved an excepted cause to have been at work and the libelant showed that negligence was also operative; the decision was that the carrier then had to show how much of the damage resulted from the excepted cause or suffer the whole liability. Here respondents proved the restraint of princes to be a cause in the important practical sense that otherwise the stop at Aden and the hot voyage around Africa would not have occurred. However, it might be argued that the possibility that diligence with respect to the cargo at Aden would have reduced the loss is sufficient to cancel recognition of the restraint as the "legal" cause unless the carrier also proves that it discharged its duty, under § 3(2) of COGSA, "properly and carefully [to] load, handle, stow, carry, keep, care for, and discharge the goods carried,"—in other words, that the mere raising of the issue as to the carrier's duty to sell places the burden of persuasion back where the shipper's evidence of delivery in good condition and outturn in bad had put it originally. *See* Note, *Cargo Damage at Sea: The Ship's Liability,* 27 Tex.L.Rev. 525, 534 (1949).

Such a contention gives inadequate weight to the division, made in § 4(2) of COGSA, between the specifically excepted causes (a)-(p) and the "catch-all" (q), to wit, "Any other cause arising without the actual fault and privity of the carrier and without the fault or neglect of the agents or servants of the carrier, but the burden of proof shall be on the person claiming the benefit of this exception to show that neither the actual fault or privity of the carrier nor the fault or neglect of the agents or servants of the carrier contributed to the loss or damage." To hold that when a carrier has shown that the loss arose as a consequence of restraint of princes, § 4(2)(g), it still has the burden of negating any other fault or neglect of its agents or servants would be to read the qualification of (q) into (a)-(p), although Congress did not put it there. It follows that libelant had the burden of showing circumstances from which a trier of the facts could properly conclude that the master's failure to dispose of the cheese at Aden was a breach of § 3(2). Had libelant done this, we would have a parallel to *Schnell v. The Vallescura,* with one cause proved to be excepted and the other not, and the teaching of that case, which we assume to be applicable to COGSA in this respect, would then place upon respondents the burden of showing how much of the damages came from the excepted as distinguished from the unexcepted cause. However, libelant did not sustain the burden required to bring it to that stage.

The same analysis disposes of the claim with respect to failure to refrigerate during the stay at Aden, even if we were to assume in libelant's favor that this omission, since it contributed to the spoilage, could be a basis of liability when it was already inevitable that the cheese would spoil, from an excepted cause, on the hot voyage around Africa. *See Peaslee, Multiple Causation and Damage,* 47 Harv.L.Rev. 1127 (1934); 2 Harper & James, *supra,* at 1123; American Law Institute, Restatement of Torts Second, Tentative Draft No. 7, § 433B; compare *Schroeder Bros., Inc. v. The Saturnia,* 226 F.2d 147 (2 Cir. 1955). The only evidence that refrigeration might have been obtainable was general testimony of a witness for libelant, clearly referring to normal conditions, that "they have refrigeration at Aden." Even assuming that this sufficed to raise an issue of negligence, clearly, in the face of the master's deposition that no warehouse facilities of any kind were available at Aden when the Ioannis was there, it did not meet a burden of proof.

The decree in favor of libelants Pompeian Olive Oil Corporation and Victor Cory is affirmed; the decree in favor of libelant Lekas & Drivas, Inc. is reversed and the libel dismissed.

THE VALLESCURA

293 U.S. 296, 555 S. Ct. 194, 79 L. Ed. 373 (1934)

Mr. Justice STONE delivered the opinion of the Court.

Petitioners brought suit in admiralty in the district court for Southern New York, to recover damages for injury to a shipment of onions on respondent's S.S. "Vallescura" from Spain to New York City. The onions, receipt of which in apparent good condition was acknowledged by the bill of lading, were delivered in New York damaged by decay. The vessel pleaded as a defense an exception, in the bill of lading, from liability for damage by "decay" and "perils of the seas," and that the damage "was not due to any cause or event arising through any negligence on the part of the vessel, her master, owner or agents."

On the trial there was evidence that the decay was caused by improper ventilation of the cargo during the voyage, and that the failure to ventilate was due in part to closing of the hatches and ventilators made necessary by heavy weather, and in part to the neglect of the master and crew in failing to keep them open at night in fair weather. The district court entered an interlocutory decree, adjudging that the libelants recover the amount of the damage sustained by them, caused by closing the hatches and ventilators during good weather, and appointing a special commissioner to ascertain and compute the amount of damage.

The commissioner, after hearing evidence, found that it was impossible to ascertain how much of the damage was due to want of ventilation in fair weather and how much to want of it in bad. But, after comparing the periods during which the ventilators were negligently closed with those during which they were open or properly closed, he stated: "It would seem, therefore, that the greater part of the damage must have been due to improper shutting of the hatches and ventilators." He concluded that as the vessel had failed to show what part of the damage was due to bad weather, the petitioner should recover the full amount of the damage. The district court, accepting the report of the commissioner as presumably correct ... found no basis for rejecting its conclusions and gave judgment to libelants accordingly. The Court of Appeals for the Second Circuit reversed, 70 F.2d 261, holding that as the damage was within the clause of the bill of lading exempting the vessel from liability for decay, the burden was on petitioner to show what part of the damage was taken out of the exception, due to respondent's negligence.

* * *

The failure to ventilate the cargo was not a "fault or error in navigation or management" of the vessel, from the consequences of which it may be relieved by § 3 of the Harter Act of February 13, 1893, § 3, c. 105, 27 Stat. 445; § 192, Tit. 46, U.S.C. The management was of the cargo, within the meaning of §§ 1 and 2 of the Act, and not of the vessel, to which § 3 relates. *The Germanic*, 196 U.S. 589, 597; *Knott v. Botany Mills*, 179 U.S. 69, 73, 74; *The Jean Bart*, 197 Fed. 1002, 1006 (D.C.). Hence, we pass to the decisive question whether, in view of the presumptions which aid the shipper in establishing the vessel's liability under a contract for carriage by sea, it was necessary for the petitioners to offer further evidence in order to recover the damage which they have suffered....

In general the burden rests upon the carrier of goods by sea to bring himself within any exception relieving him from the liability which the law otherwise imposes on him. This is true at common law with respect to the exceptions which the law itself annexed to his undertaking, such as his immunity from liability for act of God or the public enemy. *See* Carver, *Carriage by Sea* (7th ed.) Chap. I. The rule applies equally with respect to other exceptions for which the law permits him to stipulate. The reason for the rule is apparent. He is a bailee entrusted with the shipper's goods, with respect to the care and safe delivery of which the law imposes upon him an extraordinary duty. Discharge of the duty is peculiarly within his control. All the facts and circumstances upon which he may rely to relieve him of that duty are peculiarly within his know-ledge and usually unknown to the shipper. In consequence, the law casts upon him the burden of the loss which he cannot explain or, explaining, bring within the exceptional case in which he is relieved from liability.

To such exceptions the law itself annexes a condition that they shall relieve the carrier from liability for loss from an excepted cause only if in the course of the voyage he has used due care to guard against it. This rule is recognized and continued in the first section of the Harter Act, which makes it unlawful to insert any clause in a bill of lading whereby the carrier shall be relieved of liability for negligence.

It is commonly said that when the carrier succeeds in establishing that the injury is from an excepted cause, the burden is then on the shipper to show that that cause would not have produced the injury but for the carrier's negligence in failing to guard against it. Such we may assume the rule to be, at least to the extent of requiring the shipper to give evidence of negligence where the carrier has sustained the burden of showing that the immediate cause of the loss or injury is an excepted peril.

But this is plainly not the case where the efficient cause of the injury for which the carrier is *prima facie* liable is not shown to be an excepted peril. If he delivers a cargo damaged by causes unknown or unexplained, which had been received in good condition, he is subject to the rule applicable to all bailees, that such evidence makes out a *prima facie* case of liability. It is sufficient, if the carrier fails to show that the damage is from an excepted cause, to cast on him the further burden of showing that the damage is not due to failure properly to stow or care for the cargo during the voyage.

Here the stipulation was for exemption from liability for a particular kind of injury, - decay. But the decay of a perishable cargo is not a cause; it is an effect. It may be the result of a number of causes, for some of which, such as the inherent defects of the cargo, or, under the contract, sea peril making it impossible to ventilate properly, the carrier is not liable. For others, such as negligent stowage, or failure to care for the cargo properly during the voyage, he is liable. The stipulation thus did not add to the causes of injury from which the carrier could claim immunity. It could not relieve him from liability for want of diligence in the stowage or care of the cargo.

It is unnecessary for us to consider whether the effect of the clause is to relieve the carrier from the necessity, in the first instance, of offering evidence of due diligence in caring for a cargo received in good condition, and delivered in a state of decay. For here want of diligence in providing proper ventilation is established and it is found that the failure to ventilate has caused the damage. It is enough that the clause plainly cannot be taken to relieve the vessel from bringing itself within the exception from liability for damage by sea peril where the shipper has carried the burden of showing that the decay is due either to sea peril, in that bad weather prevented ventilation, or to the vessel's negligence. Where the state of the proof is such as to show that the damage is due either to an excepted peril or to the carrier's negligent care of the cargo, it is for him to bring himself within the exception or to show that he has not been negligent.

Similarly, the carrier must bear the entire loss where it appears that the injury to cargo is due either to sea peril or negligent stowage, or both, and he fails to show what damage is attributable to sea peril.

The vessel in the present case is in no better position because, upon the evidence, it appears that some of the damage, in an amount not ascertainable, is due to sea peril. That does not remove the burden of showing facts relieving it from liability. If it remains liable for the whole amount of the damage because it is unable to show that sea peril was a cause of the loss, it must equally remain so if it cannot show what part of the loss is due to that cause.

Since the respondent has failed throughout to sustain the burden, which rested upon it at the outset, of showing to what extent sea peril was the effective cause of the damage, and as the petitioners are without fault, no question of apportionment or division of the damage arises.

Reversed.

3. Other defenses

a. Errors in Navigation or Management

COGSA § 4(2)(a)

i. Unseaworthiness v. Error in Management or Navigation

§§ 3(1)(a), 4 v. § 4(2)(a)

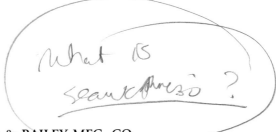

INTERNATIONAL NAV. CO. v. FARR & BAILEY MFG. CO.

481 U.S. 218, 21 S. Ct. 591, 45 L. Ed. 830 (1901)

Mr. Chief Justice FULLER, after stating the case as above, delivered the opinion of the court

Counsel for petitioner states that the question raised on this record is: "Was the Indiana unseaworthy at the time of beginning her voyage from Liverpool to Philadelphia, or was the failure to securely fasten the port covers and keep them fastened a fault or error in the management of the vessel under the exemption of the 'Harter Act?' "

The courts below concurred in the conclusion that the Indiana was unseaworthy when she sailed because of the condition of the port hole, but the District Judge on the re-argument felt constrained to yield his individual convictions to the rule he understood to have been laid down in *The Silvia*, 171 U.S. 462.

The Silvia was decided, as all these cases must be, upon its particular facts and circumstances. The case is thus stated by Mr. Justice Gray, who delivered the opinion of the court:

> The Silvia, with the sugar in her lower hold, sailed from Matanzas for Philadelphia on the morning of February 16, 1894. The compartment between decks next the forecastle had been fitted up to carry steerage passengers, but on this voyage contained only spare sails and ropes, and a small quantity of stores. This compartment had four round ports on each side, which were about eight or nine feet above the water line when the vessel was deep laden. Each port was eight inches in diameter, furnished with a cover of glass five eighths of an inch thick, set in a brass frame, as well as with an inner cover or dummy of iron. When the ship sailed, the weather was fair, and the glass covers were tightly closed, but the iron covers were left open in order to light the compartment should it become necessary to get anything from it, and the hatches were battened down, but could have been opened in two minutes by knocking out the wedges. In the afternoon of the day of sailing, the ship encountered rough weather, and the glass cover of one of the ports was broken—whether by the force of the seas or by floating timber or wreckage, was wholly a matter of conjecture—and the water came in through the port, and damaged the sugar.

And again:

> But the contention that the Silvia was unseaworthy when she sailed from Matanzas is unsupported by the facts. The test of seaworthiness is whether the vessel is reasonably fit to carry the cargo which she has undertaken to transport. The port holes of the compartment in question were furnished both with the usual glass covers and with the usual iron shutters or dead lights; and there is nothing in the case to justify an inference that there was any defect in the construction of either. When she began her voyage, the weather being fair, the glass covers only were shut, and the iron ones were left open for the purpose of lighting the compartment. Although the hatches were battened down they could have been taken off in two minutes, and no cargo was stowed against the ports so as to prevent or embarrass access to them in case a change of weather should make it necessary or proper to close the iron shutters. Had the cargo been so stowed as to require much time and labor to shift or remove it in order to get at the ports, the fact that the iron shutters were left open at the beginning of the voyage might have rendered the ship unseawor-

thy. *But as no cargo was so stowed, and the ports were in a place where these shutters would usually be left open for the admission of light, and could be speedily got at and closed if occasion should require, there is no ground for holding that the ship was unseaworthy at the time of sailing.*

In the present case the compartment in which the burlaps were stowed was used exclusively as a cargo hold; the glass and iron covers were intended to be securely closed before any cargo was received; the person whose duty it was to close them or see that they were closed, supposed that that had been properly done; and the hatches were battened down with no expectation that any more attention would be given to the port covers during the voyage; but in fact the port was not securely covered, and there was apparently nothing to prevent the influx of water, even under conditions not at all extraordinary, the port being only two or three feet above the water line.

But it is contended that in spite of the fact that the condition of the port hole rendered the ship unseaworthy when she sailed, the omission to securely cover it was a fault or error in management and within the exemption of the third section of the Harter Act ... .

We cannot accede to a view which so completely destroys the general rule that seaworthiness at the commencement of the voyage is a condition precedent, and that fault in management is no defence when there is lack of due diligence before the vessel breaks ground.

We do not think that a ship owner exercises due diligence within the meaning of the act by merely furnishing proper structure and equipment, for the diligence required is diligence to make the ship in all respects seaworthy, and that, in our judgment, means due diligence on the part of all the owners' servants in the use of the equipment before the commencement of the voyage and until it is actually commenced.

* * *

It is, of course, not to be understood as intimated that failure to close port holes necessarily creates unseaworthiness. That depends on circumstances, and we accept the finding of the District Court, and of the Court of Appeals, that it did so under the circumstances of this case.

* * *

Decree affirmed.

---

ii. Proper Care of the Cargo v. Error in Navigation

§ 3(2) v. § 4(2)(a)

KNOTT v. BOTANY WORSTED MILLS

179 U.S. 69, 21 S. Ct. 30, 45 L. Ed. 90 (1900)

Mr. Justice GRAY delivered the opinion of the court

The Botany Worsted Mills, a corporation of New Jersey, and Winter and Smillie, a firm of merchants in the city of New York, respectively owners of two separate lots of bales of wool, shipped at Buenos Aires for New York on board the steamship Portuguese Prince, severally filed libels in admiralty *in personam* in the District Court of the United States for the Southern District of New York, against James Knott, the owner of the vessel, to recover the damage caused to the wool by contact with drainage from wet sugar which also formed part of her cargo.

The Portuguese Prince was a British vessel, belonging to a line trading between New York and ports in the River Plata, Brazil, and the West Indies, loading and discharging cargo and having a resident agent at each port. The bills of lading of the wool, signed at Buenos Aires, December 21, 1894, gave her liberty to call at any port or ports to receive and discharge cargo, and for any other purpose whatever; and purported to exempt the carrier from liability for "negligence of masters or mariners;" "sweating, rust, natural decay, leakage or breakage, and all damage arising from the goods by stowage, or contact with, or by sweating, leakage, smell or evaporation from them;" "or any other peril of the seas, rivers, navigation, or of land transit, of whatsoever nature or kind; and whether any of the perils, causes or things above mentioned, or the loss or injury arising therefrom, be occasioned by the wrongful act, default, negligence, or error in judgment of the owners, masters, officers, mariners, crew, stevedores, engineers and other persons whomsoever in the service of the ship, whether employed on the said steamer or otherwise, and whether before, or after, or during the voyage, or for whose acts the shipowner would otherwise be liable; or by unseaworthiness of the ship at the beginning, or at any period of the voyage, provided all reasonable means have been taken to provide against such unseaworthiness."

The facts of the case are substantially undisputed. The bales of wool of the libelants were taken on board at Buenos Aires, December 21-24, 1894, and were stowed on end, with proper dunnage, between decks near the bow, and forward of a temporary wooden bulkhead, which was not tight. The vessel, after touching at other ports, touched on February 19, 1895, at Pernambuco, and there took on board two hundred tons of wet sugar, (from which there is always drainage,) which was stowed, with proper dunnage, between decks, aft of the wooden bulkhead. At that time the vessel was trimmed by the stern, and all drainage from the sugar, flowing aft, was carried off by the scuppers, which were sufficient for the purpose when the vessel was down by the stern, or on even keel in calm weather. There was no provision for carrying off the drainage in case it ran forward. She discharged other cargo at Para; and on March 10, when she left that port, she was two feet down by the head. She continued in this trim until she took on additional cargo at Port of Spain, where the error in trim was corrected, and she left that port on March 18, loaded one foot by the stern. It was agreed by the parties that there was no damage to the wool by sugar drainage until she was trimmed by the head at Para; that the wool was damaged, by sugar drainage finding its way through the bulkhead and reaching the wool, at Para, or between Para and Port of Spain, and not afterwards; that, after she was again trimmed by the stern at Port of Spain, none of the drainage from the sugar found its way forward; and that the court might draw inferences.

Upon the facts of this case, there can be no doubt that the ship was seaworthy, and that the damage to the wool was caused by drainage from the wet sugar through negligence of those in charge of the ship and cargo. The questions upon which the decision of the case turns are:

> Whether this damage to the wool was "loss or damage arising from negligence, fault or failure in proper loading, stowage, custody, care or proper delivery" of cargo, within the first section of the Harter Act; or was "damage or loss resulting from faults or errors in navigation or in the management of said vessel," within the third section of that act?

We fully concur with the courts below that the damage in question arose from negligence in loading or stowage of the cargo, and not from fault or error in the navigation or management of the ship—for the reasons stated by the District Judge, and approved by the Circuit Court of Appeals, as follows:

> The primary cause of the damage was negligence and inattention in the loading or stowage of the cargo, either regarded as a whole, or as respects the juxtaposition of wet sugar and wool bales placed far forward. The wool should not have been stowed forward of the wet sugar, unless care was taken in the other loading, and in all subsequent changes in the loading, to see that the ship should not get down by the head. There was no fault or defect in the vessel herself. She was constructed in the usual way, and was sufficient. But on sailing from Para she was a little down by the head, through inattention, during the changes in the loading, to the effect these changes made in the trim of the ship and in the flow of the sugar drainage. She was not down by the head more than frequently happens. It in no way affected her sea-going qualities; nor did the vessel herself cause any damage to the wool. The damage was caused by the drainage of the wet sugar alone. So that no question of the unseaworthiness of the ship arises. The ship herself was as seaworthy when she left Para, as when she sailed from Pernambuco. The negligence consisted in stowing the wool far forward, without taking care subsequently that

no changes of loading should bring the ship down by the head. I must, therefore, regard the question as solely a question of negligence in the stowage and disposition of cargo, and of damage consequent thereon, though brought about by the effect of these negligent changes in loading on the trim of the ship. "The change of trim was merely incidental, the mere negligent result of the changes in the loading, no attention being given to the effect on the ship's trim, or on the sugar drainage."

* * *

---

b. Perils of the sea

COGSA §4(2)(c) (formerly 46 app. U.S.C. § 1304(2)(c))

TAISHO MARINE & FIRE INS. CO., LTD. v. M/V SEA-LAND ENDURANCE

815 F.2d 1270, 1987 AMC 1730 (9th Cir. 1987)

BOOCHEVER, Circuit Judge:

Overview

Taisho Marine and Fire Insurance Company (Taisho) appeals the district court's judgment in favor of Sea-Land Service Incorporated (Sea-Land). The court held that the peril of the sea defense under the Carriage of Goods by Sea Act (COGSA), 46 U.S.C. App. § 1304(2)(c) (Supp. III 1985), prevented Taisho from recovering payments made to a shipper for cargo lost by Sea-Land. Taisho contends that the district court (1) reached a conclusion of law not supported by the facts, (2) improperly considered Taisho's status as an insurer, and (3) incorrectly placed the burden of proof on Taisho. We affirm.

Facts

In March 1984, a forty-foot aluminum cargo container packed with Sony stereo equipment was loaded aboard the M/V Sea-Land Endurance (Endurance) in Kobe, Japan. The container was stowed on the vessel's deck on the starboard side near her stern. The owner of the vessel, Sea-Land, issued bills of lading which are contracts of carriage subject to COGSA, 46 U.S.C. § 1300-1315. Sony insured the cargo with Taisho.

The vessel encountered adverse weather conditions en route to Long Beach, California. Between midnight and 9:00 A.M. on March 16, 1984, the cargo and the storage container were destroyed. Taisho paid the assured's claim for loss of cargo and brought this action as subrogee against the vessel Endurance and its owner, Sea-Land. The vessel was dismissed as Sea-Land agreed to be responsible for any liability imposed on the vessel.

The district court found that there was "no evidence of unseaworthiness on the part of the vessel or incompetent management of the ship by its Master." Further, the court concluded that Taisho did not fulfill its burden of proof to show that the loss of the cargo resulted from some fault of the crew or the vessel. The proof showed that the loss was caused by the weather alone. The court held that the peril of the sea defense, 46 U.S.C. § 1304(2)(c) was established by Sea-Land thereby exonerating Sea-Land from liability. The court wrote a Memorandum of Intended Decision and adopted Sea-Land's findings of fact and conclusions of law.

Taisho appeals.

Discussion

1) The Peril of the Sea Defense

Taisho argues that the district court's factual findings fail to meet the statutory requirements of the affirmative defense of peril of the sea provided by COGSA, 46 U.S.C. § 1304(2)(c). We review the court's determination of whether the established facts fall within the parameters of the peril of the sea defense under the deferential, clearly erroneous standard. *See United States v. McConney*, 728 F.2d 1195, 1202 (9th Cir.) (*en banc*), *cert. denied*, 469 U.S. 824, 83 L. Ed. 2d 46, 105 S. Ct. 101 (1984).

COGSA, 46 U.S.C. § 1304(2)(c) provides in pertinent part that "[n]either the carrier nor the ship shall be responsible for loss or damage arising or resulting from — ... (c) Perils, dangers, and accidents of the sea."

While "perils of the sea" is a term of art not uniformly defined, the generally accepted definition is "a fortuitous action of the elements at sea, of such force as to overcome the strength of a well-found ship or the usual precautions of good seamanship." G. Gilmore & C. Black, The Law of Admiralty, § 3-32 at 162 (2d ed. 1975); *States S.S. Co. v. United States*, 259 F.2d 458, 460-61 (9th Cir. 1958), *cert. denied*, 358 U.S. 933, 79 S. Ct. 316, 3 L. Ed. 2d 305 (1959); *R.T. Jones Lumber Co. v. Roen S.S. Co.*, 213 F.2d 370, 373 (7th Cir. 1954); *Philippine Sugar Centrals Agency v. Kokusai Kisen Kabushiki Kaisha*, 106 F.2d 32, 34-35 (2d Cir. 1939). Case law fails to set out a bright line test to determine whether cargo was lost by a peril of the sea. Rather, the cases indicate that the validity of the statutory defense depends on the nature and cause of the loss under the particular facts of a case.

Taisho cites *J. Gerber & Co. v. S.S. Sabine Howaldt*, 437 F.2d 580 (2d Cir. 1971), for the proposition that a series of factors must be established in order to use the peril of the sea affirmative defense. Taisho contends that the peril of the sea defense only exists upon proof of several of the following factors: (1) the extent of structural damage to the vessel, (2) the extent of any speed reduction, (3) the extent of any cross-seas, (4) how far the vessel was blown off course, and (5) to what extent other vessels in the same storm experienced cargo-related damage. Taisho fails to note that these factors are not the cumulative total of all the indicia that can be used to determine the existence of a peril of the sea.

In *Gerber*, the court stated that in deciding whether a case falls within the statutory purview of peril of the sea, the central inquiry is into the measure of the violence of the winds and tempestuousness of the sea. "These are matters of degree and not amenable to precise definition." *Id.* at 596. *Gerber* was a shipper seeking recovery for damage caused by sea water to cargo transported by the S.S. Sabine Howaldt. The court held that the vessel was seaworthy, there was no negligence on the part of the carrier, and that the damage was caused by hurricane force winds and resulting cross-seas which forced up hatch covers admitting sea water to the holds. The loss was from a peril of the sea and the vessel owner was exonerated from any liability.

Gerber states that a very important measure considered on the peril of the sea issue is the wind velocity on the Beaufort Scale because of direct relationship between wind velocity and the size and shape of the waves. *Id.* at 596. No Beaufort Scale index exists which divides cases into those qualifying for the peril of the sea exception and those which do not. Nevertheless, courts have almost always found a peril of the sea where the force has been 11 or greater and very few cases are found to qualify where the winds are force 9 or less. *Id.* Wind velocity, however, is only a rough measure and must be considered with other indicia such as nature and extent of damage to the ship, cross-seas and other factors.

> While the seaworthiness of a ship presupposes that she is designed, built and equipped to stand up under reasonably expectable conditions this means no more than the usual bad weather which is normal for a particular sea area at a particular time. It does not, however, include an unusual combination of the destructive forces of wind and sea which a skilled and experienced ship's master would not expect and which the ship encountered as a stroke of bad luck. Hurricane force winds and turbulent cross-seas generating unpredictable strains and pressures on a ship's hull are an example.

Id. (footnote omitted).

The district court found that the vessel Endurance encountered at least four waves in excess of 60 feet which rolled the vessel more than 40 degrees. A substantial number of waves between 40 and 60 feet in height battered the vessel. During the storm, between 0200 and 0900 hours, the sustained winds remained between Beaufort Force 10 (Whole Gale, 48-55 knots) and 12 (Hurricane force, 64-71 knots) with gusts in excess of 95 knots. Throughout this period, the master maintained a reduced speed of 17 knots (normal operating speed is 21.5 knots) to minimize the risk of damage to the vessel, cargo, and personnel while maintaining rudder control. The court found that only a few vessels in the area between 1946 and 1984 reported seas of equal or greater height and that the sustained winds of 65 knots were the highest ever recorded in the area.

On March 17, the crew noted that (1) the port gangway was washed overboard, (2) two firehoses and nozzles were missing, (3) the port lifeboat embarkation ladder was damaged, and (4) the starboard pilot ladder was damaged. In addition, containers at Hatch 10, portside and Hatch 11, starboard (the container in question) were lost overboard and eight other containers were found damaged, four severely and four slightly. Neither the stacking frame cargo system nor the locking devices used to secure the container were damaged or failed during the storm. Taisho does not dispute the validity of these findings or the finding that the vessel was seaworthy and that Sea-Land exercised due diligence to render the Endurance seaworthy.

Taisho's cited cases fail to support the contention that unless the district court finds several factors existed out of the five previously enumerated, the court cannot conclude that the peril of the sea defense exonerated Sea-Land. Taisho's cites the following cases in support of its proposition: *Virgin Island Corp. v. Merwin Lighterage Co.*, 251 F.2d 872 (3d Cir.), *cert. denied*, 357 U.S. 929, 78 S. Ct. 1369, 2 L. Ed. 2d 1372 (1958) (*No Peril*—Two barges next to each other, one with cargo lashed down—the other without its cargo lashed down, court said lashing could have saved cargo); *States S.S. Co.*, 259 F.2d 458 (*No Peril*—Beaufort Force 9, mountainous seas, inherent condition of the hull rather than the sea caused the sinking); *Ore S.S. Corp. v. D/S A/S Hassel*, 137 F.2d 326 (2d Cir. 1943) (*No Peril*—Beaufort Force 9-10 for 3 days, two windows knocked in, lifeboat damaged, reduced speed, rivet missing, *winds not extraordinary*); *Philippine Sugar*, 106 F.2d 32 (*Peril*—3 days at Beaufort Force 9-10, lifeboat crushed, steel superstructure broken or carried away, blown 160 miles off course); *American Int'l Ins. Co. v. S.S. Fortaleza*, 446 F. Supp. 221 (D.P.R.), *aff'd*, 585 F.2d 22 (1978) (*Peril*—Winds Beaufort Force 6-11 for 24 hours, vessel rolled 40 degrees and continued rolling 30-40 degrees, seas in excess of 40 feet, lost 30 trailers, foremast snapped off, railing and steel deck curbing destroyed); *Freedman & Slater Inc. v. M/V Tofevo*, 222 F. Supp. 964 (S.D.N.Y. 1963) (*No Peril*—Alteration in log book showing higher Beaufort Forces not supported by other evidence); *Palmer Distrib. Corp. v. S.S. American Counselor*, 158 F. Supp. 264 (S.D.N.Y. 1957) (*No Peril*—Beaufort Force 9-10 for 3 days, *not unusual weather for North Atlantic*, no structural damage, other cargo not damaged).

The district court's findings of unusually high winds and seas, the rolling of the ship, the damage to the ship, the loss and damage of other containers, and Sea-Land's due diligence in making the vessel and cargo system seaworthy support the conclusion that the cargo was lost because of a peril of the sea.

3) Burden of Proof

Taisho argues that the court placed the burden of proof as to the issue of negligence on the wrong party as the peril of the sea affirmative defense requires the showing of an absence of negligence. Sea-Land contends that once they have proved that the loss was from the sea alone, the burden then shifts to Taisho to show a concurrent act to defeat Sea-Land's peril of the sea affirmative defense. The selection of the appropriate burden of proof is a question of law reviewed *de novo*. See *McConney*, 728 F.2d at 1201-04.

Generally, under COGSA, a shipper establishes a *prima facie* case against the carrier by showing that the cargo was delivered in good condition to the carrier but was discharged in a damaged condition. 46 U.S.C. §§ 1302, 1303; *Gerber*, 437 F.2d at 584; Gilmore & Black, *supra*, § 3-43 at 183. The burden of proof then shifts to the vessel owner to establish that the loss came under a statutory exception to COGSA....

The burden then returns to the shipper to show, at a minimum, concurrent causes of loss in the fault and negligence of the carrier, unless it is a type of negligence excluded under COGSA. *Gerber*, 437 F.2d at 588; Gilmore & Black, *supra*, § 3-43 at 184. The carrier then has the burden of allocating the loss between (1) the loss caused by his fault and negligence and (2) the loss covered under the exception. *Vana Trading Co. v. S.S. Mette Skou*, 556 F.2d 100, 105 (2d Cir.), *cert. denied*, *Flota Mercante Grancolombiana, S.A. v. Vana Trading Co., Inc.*, 434 U.S. 892, 98 S. Ct. 267, 54 L. Ed. 2d 177 (1977). Failure of the carrier to do so results in the carrier bearing the full loss. *Gerber*, 437 F.2d at 588.

The burden of proof, however, alters when a carrier seeks exoneration under the peril of the sea exception. 46 U.S.C. § 1304(2)(c).

[I]n a sense, the absence of negligence as a concurring cause may be said to enter into the very definition of a sea peril, so that, in order to establish an exception under this clause, the ship would have to establish freedom from negligence.

Gilmore & Black, *supra*, § 3-32 at 162. Thus, under the peril of the sea exception, the carrier acquires the additional burden of showing freedom from negligence.

A prima facie case against Sea-Land was established by the stipulated facts that the cargo was delivered in good condition to the Endurance and never returned. The burden then shifted to Sea-Land to prove the loss fell under one of the statutory exceptions of COGSA. In choosing the peril of the sea defense, Sea-Land acquired the additional burden of proving freedom from negligence. The district court concluded that "[t]he proof establishes that the loss was caused by the weather alone." By finding that Sea-Land had established that the weather was the sole cause of the loss, the court inferredly found that Sea-Land had sustained its burden of proving that negligence was not a cause of the loss. At that point, the burden was placed on Taisho to show a concurrent cause of the loss. Taisho failed to meet this burden. We conclude that the district court correctly allocated the burdens of proof.

Conclusion

Taisho's argument that without proof of several enumerated factors there can be no peril of the sea defense is without merit. Taisho's second argument fails to show that the district court considered Taisho's rights as an insurer differently from that of a subrogee. Finally, Sea-Land sustained its burden of proving that the loss was caused solely by the perils of the sea and Taisho failed to rebut that evidence. Accordingly, we affirm the judgment of the district court.

AFFIRMED.

Note

1. There was no question in *Taisho Marine & Fire Ins. Co., Ltd. v. M/V Sea-Land Endurance, supra*, that the carrying ship was in seaworthy condition before it encountered the storm. In many cases, however, the ship's inability to carry the cargo safely through heavy weather raises questions about the ship's seaworthiness (or lack of it). For example, in *Edmond Weil, Inc. v. American West African Line, Inc.*, 147 F.2d 363, 1945 AMC 191 (2d Cir. 1945), cargo was damaged by water that entered the holds when "kick tubes" on the deck were broken off by deck cargo during a storm. The court said:

The first question is whether the ship was unseaworthy. *Arguendo*, we will assume that the "kick tubes" did not make her so if she had carried no deck cargo; and, perhaps also, even when she carried certain kinds of deck cargo. Indeed, we might go still further, and assume that she was seaworthy, just as she rode, for a summer voyage, for example in the Mediterranean. But she was to cross the Atlantic in January, ending in latitudes over 40 degrees; and the question is whether, with the deck cargo she actually did carry and the "kick tubes" in her deck, she was reasonably fitted for such a voyage… The case comes down to whether a ship proves that she is well found for a winter Atlantic voyage, when her stow breaks apart under such conditions. We do not see how less can be asked of her upon such a voyage, than that she shall successfully meet such weather, for surely gales—indeed even "whole gales"—are to be expected in such waters at such a season.

Some of the water that entered the holds had come through "goosenecks" on the bridge deck. The carrier would not have been liable for damage caused from that source. Nevertheless, the carrier was held to be liable in full, because of the *Vallescura rule*. The court continued:

[T]he seas which washed out the plugs [in the "goosenecks"] were either too strong to be resisted by ordinary means, or the plugs were driven home improperly; in either event the ship would be excused. Nevertheless the excuse will not serve her for several reasons. The greater part of the water which entered the bunker came over the sill of the open doorway from No. 4 'tween-deck [ie, from the "kick tubes"]; and for that the ship is liable in any event. How she could distinguish between the damage caused by that water, and the damage caused by the water which came from the storeroom [ie, from the "goosenecks"], it is impossible to imagine. Yet that would be her duty. *Schnell v. The Vallescura, supra.*

Questions

1. Compare the burden of proof on "negligence" allocated by the court in *Taisho Marine & Fire Ins. Co., Ltd. v. M/V Sea-Land Endurance, supra*, with that stated in *Complaint of Tecomar S.A.*, 765 F. Supp. 1150, 1175, 1991 AMC 2432 (S.D.N.Y. 1991):

Accordingly, the burdens of proof in this case are allocated as follows: Tecomar [carrier] must establish that the weather encountered by the ship constituted a peril of the sea and that the peril caused the loss. If Tecomar succeeds, the burden shifts to Claimants to establish that the vessel was unseaworthy and that the unseaworthiness was at least a concurrent cause of the loss. Even if this is proven, however, Tecomar can still avoid liability under COGSA if it shows that it exercised due diligence in attempting to make the *Tuxpan* seaworthy.

2. Suppose a court rejects a "perils of the sea" defense because the storm which the vessel encountered was of a magnitude that was common for that time of year. Should the shipowner prevail on an "errors in navigation" defense if the court finds that the master erred in his decision as to what action the vessel should take in response to the storm? *See, Yawata Iron & Steel Co., Ltd. v. Anthony Shipping Co., Ltd.*, 396 F. Supp. 619, 1975 AMC 1602, (S.D.N.Y. 1975), *aff'd*, 538 F.2d 317, 1976 AMC 2685 (2d Cir. 1976).

---

c. Other Immunities

In addition to the three immunities that have already been considered—errors in navigation or management, perils of the sea and restraint of princes—there are fourteen other carrier immunities specifically enumerated in COGSA § 4, all of which by the terms of the Act must be proved by the carrier. Most of these are self-explanatory and present little difficulty conceptually, although there are many overlaps among them.

Most of the carrier immunities can be grouped into three general categories: (1) overwhelming outside human forces (*i.e.*, acts of war; acts of public enemies; arrest or restraint of princes; quarantines; strikes or lockouts; and riots and civil commotions), (2) overwhelming natural forces (*i.e.*, perils of the sea and acts of God), and (3) faults of the shipper (*i.e.*, act or omission of the shipper or his agents; wastage in bulk or weight and losses due to inherent vice; insufficiency of packaging or marking; and latent defects). An important question is what is the effect of carrier contributory or concurrent fault here? This is a complex question and the answer depends upon the precise nature of the carrier fault involved. Logically there are three possible solutions: first, the carrier can be totally excused if the fault itself is immune as an error of navigation or management; second, the fault can completely prevent the application of the immunity if, as in act of God, the absence of human negligence is part of the definition of the immunity, third, the presence of concurrent carrier fault can make it incumbent on the carrier to prove which part of the loss was caused by the immunity as distinguished from the fault.

Of the remaining immunities, fire presents special problems and is treated separately below. Likewise saving or attempting to save life or property at sea is best thought of in the nature of a deviation, which is treated below.

The cases that follow discuss the catch-all immunity, the "(q) clause," and the troublesome question of "inherent vice."

---

i. Inherent Vice

COGSA § 4(2)(m)

UNITED STATES STEEL INTERNATIONAL, INC. v. M.T. GRANHEIM

540 F. Supp. 1326, 1982 AMC 2770 (S.D.N.Y. 1982)

CONNER, District Judge:

Plaintiff United States Steel International, Inc. ("USS") seeks to recover damages arising from the discoloration of a cargo of alpha methyl styrene ("AMS") during a voyage from Houston to Rotterdam. USS shipped 1,299.48 metric tons of AMS pursuant to a tanker voyage charter party with defendant Antilles Shipping Co., Ltd. ("Antilles"). Antilles was the time charterer of the chemical tanker M. T. Granheim, which is owned by defendant P.R. Granheim ("Granheim")....

Background

AMS is a colorless liquid that is produced as a by-product of the manufacture of other chemicals. AMS requires the presence of an inhibitor, which in this case was tertiary-butyl catechol ("TBC"). The manufacturing specification for the level of TBC that should be present in AMS is 10-20 parts per million ("ppm").

AMS has a color specification of 10 APHA, based on the American Society for Testing and Materials Standard ("ASTM"). An APHA rating of 10 or less is required for AMS because it otherwise imparts color to the final product. The APHA scale ranges from 0, or colorless, to 50, or yellow, in five-unit steps. To determine the APHA color, a sample of the AMS is visually compared to liquid color standards, superimposed on a light background.

USS produced the subject AMS in Haverhill, Ohio. When manufactured, the APHA color of AMS is usually less than five. In this case, the AMS was shipped in barges from the Haverhill plant to the GATX Terminal in Galena Park, Texas. When the first load of AMS was shipped to Texas on April 14, 1978, it had a color of less than 5, and the TBC was measured at 20 ppm. The shipment was stored in tank 12-6 at the GATX Terminal. On August 1, 1978, the contents of tank 12-6 were sampled and showed a color of less than 10 and an inhibitor level of 33 ppm. The tank's contents were again tested on August 8 to measure the inhibitor level, which was determined to be 33 ppm. On September 29, 1978, USS loaded another barge with AMS in Haverhill and sent the shipment to GATX, where it was added to the AMS previously stored in tank 12-6. At the time it was loaded in Haverhill, the second shipment of AMS had a color of less than 10 and an inhibitor level of 23.3 ppm. After discharge of the second shipment in late October of 1978, tests of the AMS in tank 12-6 showed a color of less than 10 and an inhibitor level of 22 ppm.

On November 12, 1978, preparations began for loading of the AMS aboard the M. T. Granheim. Superintendence Company, Inc. ("Superintendence"), which was retained by USS to inspect the AMS and supervise the loading procedures, inspected the vessel's tanks and issued a tank clean certificate indicating that the tanks were in good order and condition for receiving the cargo. After samples of the product in both the shoreline and the ship tanks were found satisfactory, loading was completed. Superintendence then conducted a composite analysis of the three ship tanks containing the AMS and found a color rating of less than 10 and an inhibitor concentration of 18.5 ppm. An ullage of several feet was left between the top of the cargo and the top of the tank.

A bill of lading dated November 12, 1978 was issued covering 1299.48 metric tons. The bill of lading incorporates by reference the terms and conditions of the October 28, 1978 charter party between USS and Antilles. The charter party specifically incorporates the Carriage of Goods by Sea Act ("COGSA"), 46 U.S.C. § 1300, *et seq.* Moreover, the charter party entered into between Antilles and Granheim includes a clause paramount requiring the charterer to issue bills of lading that incorporate COGSA.

The M. T. Granheim arrived in Rotterdam on December 14, 1978. Prior to discharge, a composite sample of the three tanks was taken and tested by Chemisch Technisch Expertise-bureau ("CTE"), which was hired by USS to perform the discharge analysis. The composite sample had a color of 15 and, seemingly inexplicably, a TBC level of 20 ppm. After these tests, prepumpings were conducted to test the vessel's discharge system. Because prepumpings serve to clean the ship's pump and lines, the prepumped AMS was stored in small mobile tank units commonly used for this purpose. The first three prepumpings were markedly off specification, showing color levels of 50-60, 50 and 30-40, respectively. At this time, it was decided that a fourth prepumping would be conducted, this time into a larger container so that greater force could be used to clear the line. A one-foot sample was pumped into shore tank 1419, after which the AMS being discharged appeared to be clear. Thereafter, the discharge was continued in tank 1420. The sample in tank 1419 showed a color of 20-35, but the decision was made to resume discharging AMS into tank 1419, thereby blending the prepumped material with the main stock. Tank 1419 showed a final color of 20; tank 1420 had a final color of 15-20. Tests run on the AMS after discharge failed to establish a conclusive reason for the discoloration. USS ultimately sold the AMS as off-specification material at a reduced price.

Discussion

The major task before the Court in deciding this dispute is to determine the cause of discoloration of the AMS. Given the conflicting evidence in this case, this is not an easy task. USS contends that the cargo was contaminated by foreign substances either in the M. T. Granheim's tanks or its pipelines. Granheim and Antilles argue that the discoloration, if any, was caused by an inherent vice of the cargo.

* * *

In the present case, USS introduced evidence showing that the AMS had a color of less than 10 after loading and a color of 15 before unloading in Rotterdam.[8] Plaintiff contends that this evidence alone establishes its *prima facie* case. Defendants hotly dispute this point, arguing (1) that ASTM reporting methods were not followed in rating the color and (2) that the color ratings of 10 and 15 are within the 7-unit range of reproducibility for the test and therefore no actual change in color was proved.

Defendants are correct that the ASTM reporting standards were not followed in rating the color of the AMS. The ASTM method provides that if the color of the sample lies in between two standards, as for example 5 and 10, the darker of the two standards should be reported. Thus in the present case, a rating of more than 5 but less than 10 should have been reported as 10. Even viewing the evidence in this light, however, there was still a five-unit change in color from the time the AMS was loaded in Houston to the time it reached Rotterdam.

* * *

The question whether USS has established a *prima facie* case, however, is complicated by Granheim's assertion that the discoloration of the cargo was caused by an inherent vice. "Whenever the defense of inherent vice is raised, and it appears that the damage arose internally, it self-evidently calls into question the good condition of the goods upon shipment." *American Tobacco Company v. The Katingo Hadjipatera*, 81 F. Supp. 438, 446 (S.D.N.Y. 1948), *modified on other grounds*, 194 F.2d 449 (2d Cir. 1951).

Granheim maintains that the increase in color was caused by properties of AMS which cause it to discolor over time.[9] An inherent vice is any existing defect, disease, decay or the inherent nature of the commodity which would cause it to deteriorate over a lapse of time. In this case, Granheim presented expert testimony that the oxidation of the inhibitor TBC will cause TBC to darken, thus imparting color to the AMS.

Dr. Frederick Eirich ("Dr. Eirich"), Granheim's expert witness, testified that TBC is added to AMS in order to prevent its oxidation. According to Dr. Eirich, AMS oxidizes easily and TBC is added to consume the oxygen before it can attack the AMS. As TBC becomes oxidized, however, it forms increasingly dark compounds that impart color to AMS. The amount by which the color of AMS increases depends upon the extent to which the TBC has oxidized and its own color deepened. Not surprisingly, agitation of the cargo causes TBC to oxidize more quickly, thus limiting its effective life and darkening its color.

Dr. Eirich testified that TBC at a level of 20 ppm, if oxidized substantially, can change the color of AMS. He estimated that 100 pounds of TBC had been added to the AMS in this case and testified that if half of that amount oxidized to the color of dark ink, it could raise the color of the AMS 8 to 10 points. Because of the danger that oxidized TBC will impart color to AMS, Dr. Eirich stated that lower levels of the inhibitor than those which are used in other styrenes should be maintained. He testified that 10 ppm is the safest level at which the TBC can prevent oxidation of the AMS without significant danger of discoloration. Dr. Eirich acknowledged that the agitation and resulting oxidation of the TBC during an ocean voyage would decrease the effectiveness of the inhibitor, but maintained that by increasing the TBC level the risk of discoloration is also increased.

---

[8] USS also had a clean bill of lading.

[9] One of USS's theories of contamination was that the tanks had not been sufficiently cleansed of their prior cargos. Granheim's expert conclusively established that six tons of ethyl acetate, which was previously stored in tank 6 center starboard, would have been necessary to discolor the AMS. It is beyond belief that 6 tons of ethyl acetate would have escaped the inspection by Superintendent before it issued the tank clean certificate. The two number 10 tanks contained hexane prior to receiving the AMS; the unrebutted expert testimony was that hexane would not affect AMS or TBC. Granheim also offered the testimony of Harold Solberg ("Solberg"), the first mate on the M. T. Granheim during the relevant voyage. Solberg explained the thorough cleaning procedures given the tanks and testified that nothing unusual happened during the voyage. Granheim also introduced the certificate issued by USS's surveyor which stated that the tanks were clean and suitable for the cargo.

Since the agitation of the cargo usually results in a drop of the inhibitor level, USS added extra TBC to the shipments of AMS before sending the barges from Haverhill to Houston, thereby increasing the TBC concentrations to 20-23 ppm. More TBC was added in Houston. Tank 12-6 at the GATX Terminal showed an inhibitor level in August of 33 ppm. When the AMS was loaded on the M. T. Granheim in November, the TBC level was 18.5 ppm.

Dr. Eirich believed that some color increase in the AMS had occurred before the vessel left Houston but that the increase was not reflected in the measurements because of the practice of reporting color only in 5-unit steps. He explained the increased discoloration reflected in the tests conducted in Rotterdam as the result of agitation of the cargo during the voyage. Moreover, Dr. Eirich stated that the passage of time allowed for increased interaction between the TBC and AMS.

*   *   *

Having presented the above evidence, Granheim contends that the burden of proof rests with USS to disprove the existence of an inherent vice. This argument, of course, assumes that USS established a *prima facie* case. Although USS offered into evidence documents showing that the AMS was on specification in Houston, there is a substantial question as to whether the carrier must prove inherent vice or whether the shipper must disprove inherent vice as a part of its showing that the cargo was in good condition upon delivery. *See Caemint Foods, Inc. v. Brasileiro, supra,* 647 F.2d at 356 (questioning whether carrier has burden of proving inherent vice exception) and cases cited therein; *Vana Trading Company, Inc. v. S. S. "Mette Skou,"* 556 F.2d 100, 105 n.9 (2d Cir.), *cert. denied,* 434 U.S. 892, 98 S. Ct. 267, 54 L. Ed. 2d 177 (1977); *Elia Salzman Tobacco Company v. S. S. Mormacwind,* 371 F.2d 537, 539 n.2 (2d Cir. 1967) (declining to decide whether carrier or shipper carries burden of proof on inherent vice). The older case law in this Circuit, however, has placed the burden of disproving inherent vice upon the shipper.* *See American Tobacco Company v. Goulandris,* 281 F.2d 179, 182 (2d Cir. 1960); *Hecht Lewis & Kahn, Inc. v. The S. S. President Buchanan,* 236 F.2d 627, 631 (2d Cir. 1956); *American Tobacco Company v. The Hadjipatera,* 81 F. Supp. 438, 446 (S.D.N.Y. 1948), *modified on other grounds,* 194 F.2d 449 (2d Cir. 1951).

In view of the clear holdings of these older Second Circuit cases which have never been overruled, this Court is bound to apply the burden of proof as stated therein. However, in this case, the question is purely academic because the Court finds that Granheim has established by a preponderance of the evidence that the discoloration was caused by an inherent vice.

*   *   *

Having failed to disprove or to rebut the preponderant evidence offered by defendant that AMS has an inherent vice that can cause it to discolor, USS alternatively could have sustained its burden by showing that defendants' negligence caused the damage. *See Caemint Foods v. Braseleiro, supra,* 647 F.2d at 355. In this case, however, USS did not come forward with actual proof of negligence in the handling of the main stock.

---

* *But see* footnote 3 in *Quaker Oats Co. v. M/V Torvanger, infra,* which shows that the Fifth Circuit takes a different view about the burden of proof in inherent vice cases: "The 'inherent defect' exception to a carrier's COGSA liability, § 1304(2)(m) was not proved by the testimony that the chemical has a natural tendency to form peroxides when exposed to oxygen. Here, the uncontradicted testimony was that the chemical was properly treated by an inhibitor and protected from oxygenization by a nitrogen blanket during shipment and, thus, should not have formed peroxides. In order to establish this exception to COGSA liability, the carrier must show (as it did not here) some defect, quality, or vice adhering to the individual cargo of the chemical in question." *Quaker Oats Co. v. M/V Torvanger,* 734 F.2d 238, 241 n.3 (5th Cir.1984), citing *Horn v. Cia de Navegacion Fruco, S.A.,* 404 F.2d 422, 435 (5th Cir. 1969).

ii. "Q" Clause

COGSA § 4(2)(q)

IN RE INTERCONTINENTAL PROPERTIES MANAGEMENT

604 F.2d 254, 1979 AMC 1680 (4th Cir. 1979)

James Dickson PHILLIPS, Circuit Judge:

* * *

I. Background

This litigation to decide whether the economic loss resulting from destruction of a ship's cargo shall be borne by the cargo owners or the shipowner grew out of a stark tragedy involving the destruction as well of several human lives.

The M/V Mimi sailed from Miami, Florida, at around 10:30 P.M., October 9, 1975, bound for ports of call in Venezuela and Guyana. Her cargo consisted of bagged fertilizer and other general cargo stowed below and containers of general cargo stowed on deck. A small vessel, just under 500 gross registered tons, the MIMI was owned at the time by the appellee-appellant International Properties Management, S.A., a Panamanian corporation (Shipowner) and was under time charter to two joint venturers, All-Caribbean, Inc. and High Watch Shipping Company, Ltd. (Charterers). She carried a complement of four German officers, four Indonesian seamen, and a Filipino cook. Among the seamen was one Gun Gun Supardi who had signed aboard five months before in Hamburg, Germany, and had since served continuously as a member of the crew.

During loading operations just before departure from Miami, Gun Gun Supardi was cut above one eye when a cable snapped and lashed him. He was taken to a hospital after the MIMI had left the dock, given four stitches and then returned to the vessel. The captain sent him to his cabin to rest and Supardi stayed there for about twenty-four hours. Shortly before midnight on October 10, having left his quarters he encountered the Chief Engineer in another part of the vessel. Words were exchanged, Supardi struck the officer with what he later described as an "iron," then knifed him. When another officer came to the rescue, Supardi knifed him. The berserk seaman then proceeded to seek out and knife in turn each of the other two officers. Those who survived the knife wounds were bludgeoned into submission. Supardi then awakened the sleeping crew members and forced them at knife-point to provision and lower a lifeboat. At some point in this process he shut down the engines and opened the sea-valves in the engine room. At about 4:00 A.M., October 11, 1975, while Supardi stood by in the lifeboat with his captive fellow crew members, the MIMI sank, carrying with it all its cargo and its already dead or incapacitated officers. Later that morning the lifeboat occupants were picked up by a passing ship, and at this point the author of the catastrophe passes from this factual account of the litigation's background.

* * *

Cargo's *prima facie* case of delivery and failure to return was stipulated. Similarly, the actual cause of loss was plain and undisputed: the ship was willfully scuttled by a member of its crew. Cargo adduced a great deal of evidence designed in various ways to establish that Shipowner had breached its obligation under § 3(1) to provide a seaworthy ship and that these breaches proximately caused the loss. This evidence went essentially to failures "properly [to] man" the ship, 46 U.S.C. § 1303(3)(1)(b), by pointing to carelessness in employing Gun Gun Supardi and in providing a crew adequate to have restrained him or otherwise prevented the scuttling. Shipowner countered with evidence designed to establish its § 4(1) "immunity" under the unseaworthiness theory by showing its "due diligence" in manning the ship in all the many respects challenged by Cargo and the lack of proximate causation between any of its acts or omissions respecting its "proper manning" obligation and the loss. The evidence of record supporting these opposing contentions respecting the unseaworthiness theory is voluminous, but its details need not be further described, for decision turns on whether or not shipowner successfully overcame by proof the *prima facie* imputation to it of fault in failing under § 3(2) "properly and carefully [to] carry, keep, care for, and discharge the goods carried."

As indicated in our general analysis of the proof scheme, this could only have been done by proof that established the cause of loss as one of those specifically excepted in § 4(2)(a)-(p), or as "[any] other cause arising without the actual fault ... of the carrier and without the fault or neglect of the agents or servants of the carrier," under § 4(2)(q) (the "Q-Clause"). In attempting to carry this burden, the Shipowner was of course constrained by indisputable evidence that the direct cause was the willful act of its seaman employee.

In summary, this was the proof laid before the district court and upon which it concluded that the Shipowner was entitled to exoneration. From that court's memorandum opinion it appears that although the parties argued and the court was advertent to the possible application of both theories of recovery, the court's legal conclusion of exoneration was related only to the unseaworthiness theory.

In attempting to exculpate itself from the breach of its general duty of care under § 3(2) that had been established *prima facie*, Shipowner expressly relied upon both § 4(2)(a) (errors in management) and § 4(2)(q) (the omnibus clause). The district court rightly rejected the "errors in management" exception and Shipowner has abandoned any reliance upon it on appeal. When the court then turned to the "Q-clause" omnibus exception, it revealed its critical misapprehension of the proper application of COGSA to the facts of the case, saying:

> The exception provided in § 1304(2)(q) appears to provide the same burden given in 46 U.S.C. § 1304(1), namely, that [Shipowner] prove that its fault, if any, did not contribute to or proximately cause the loss complained of. Thus, the one question before this Court is whether [Shipowner] has successfully proven that the cargo loss sustained from the sinking of the MIMI was not proximately caused by its negligence, if any.

The court then proceeded to analyze the evidence as it tended to prove or disprove proximate causal connection between the specific breaches of the seaworthiness obligation urged by Cargo and the loss. Finding no proximate cause, it held the Shipowner exonerated.

In this analysis, the district court wrongly equated the defensive proof requirements of §§ 4(1) and 4(2). While both do clearly relate to the question of Shipowner's fault, they are addressed, as our general analysis of COGSA has shown, to two distinctly different theories of recovery, and consequently have different substantive content. Specifically, the court's equating of the two led it completely to disregard the "Q-clause" requirement that the carrier prove not only that the identified cause of loss arose "without the actual fault and privity of the carrier" but also "without the fault or neglect of the agents or servants of the carrier" [emphasis supplied]. These dual requirements are plainly stated conjunctively in COGSA's "Q-clause."

Rightly applied to the undisputed facts of the case, COGSA posed a narrow question of law that the district court failed to identify as decisive. It is whether the loss of the MIMI's cargo by Supardi's act resulted from a cause "arising without the fault or neglect of the agents or servants of the carrier" within the meaning of the Q-clause, 46 U.S.C. § 1304(2)(q). Stated more abstractly, the question, apparently one of first impression under COGSA, is whether under the "Q-clause" a seaman's willful act of scuttling a ship is an excepted cause of cargo loss that exculpates the carrier/employer from liability.

Unless the plain language of the statute is to be disregarded, the answer seems equally plain: that it is not. Only one narrow interpretive problem may be thought left open by the quoted language. Applied to this case, it is whether Supardi, whose fault clearly caused the loss, was at the time of the scuttling an agent or servant of the Shipowner. That he was at the time employed by Shipowner is undisputed. He was therefore a "servant" of Shipowner unless there is to be read into the statute a "scope of employment" qualification outside whose reach his causative act fell.

Recognizing the problem posed for it by the literal language of this critical provision, Shipowner on this appeal argues that such a "scope of employment" qualification should be read into the Q-clause, citing an English case, *Leesh River Tea Co. v. British India Steam Navigation Co.*, [1966] 2 Q.B. 250 (C.A.), as persuasive authority for the proposition. Because the question is novel and because of the general policy favoring uniformity of interpretation of the various national counterparts to the Hague Rules, we have given careful consideration to the *Leesh River* decision.

We need neither adopt nor reject the *Leesh River* rule as one of general application in order to decide that Supardi's act in this case was that of a servant under the Q-clause, for his act lay within the scope of employment contemplated by *Leesh River* in any event. In *Leesh River* a carrier was sued for damage to cargo caused by seawater entering the hold of its ship. Stevedores employed by the carrier to transfer cargo had removed and stolen a brass plate from the hull, leaving a hole through which the water entered after the voyage resumed. Applying the English counterpart to pertinent provisions of COGSA, the *Leesh River* court held the carrier exculpated from liability under the Q-clause.

* * *

Obviously the very terms "agent and servant" imply at the minimum a temporal coincidence of general employment with causative act, and any rational interpretation of the Q-clause must start with that interpretation. *Leesh River* reads in only a modest further qualification: that the causative act shall have occurred at a place and time, and in respect of an object related to the general duties of the employment. It does not read in any further qualification related to the servant's culpability or state of mind, a qualification of the Q-clause that Shipowner here has contended for....

We are reinforced in this construction of the Q-clause by two other considerations than the plain meaning analysis. First, we think the result dictated by this construction conforms to the general policy that must underlie COGSA's careful allocation of proof burdens in respect of loss of goods at sea. In the proof scheme earlier analyzed appears a frequently used procedural device to force a preferred substantive result where proof is in equipoise or unavailable, or where only very specific exceptions to generally assumed liability are to be recognized. Where such a device is used it ordinarily reflects an intention that in the case where both parties are without direct fault but one must suffer the loss, it is ordinarily fairer that the loss shall fall upon the party in the better position to have controlled, and to produce evidence of, the operative facts. The device used is the evidentiary presumption (*prima facie case, res ipsa loquitur*) that casts the burden, hence the loss, on that disfavored party. That such a policy may well also cast the loss upon the disfavored party in some situations not precisely contemplated nor adequately described in a statute is itself likely to be an intended consequence. As between carrier and shipper of goods by sea, carrier is obviously the party more likely to be in control both of events and of evidence of events. So, we think is the result dictated by our construction of the Q-clause likely to conform to congressional policy in enacting COGSA.

Finally, the construction is suggested by considering Supardi's act as one of classic barratry. It meets the definition. *See, e.g., Carver's Carriage of Goods by Sea* § 185, at 159 (12th ed. R. Colinvaux 1971); and *see National Union Fire Insurance Co. v. Republic of China*, 254 F.2d 177, 182-84 (4th Cir. 1958) (insurance coverage). Before cargo damage law was codified, barratry was one of the exceptions to liability traditionally listed by the carrier in bills of lading. Many of these exceptions were carried into the specific exceptions in § 4(2) of COGSA. Barratry was not; and as perhaps the most obvious conceivable example of "fault" of a seaman servant, its intended inclusion within the general Q-Clause reference to servant fault seems a construction compelled by any common sense reading. From this, it would appear that barratry was simply not intended to be an exculpating cause of loss under COGSA. *See* Scrutton on Charter Parties art. 113, at 239 (18th ed. A. Mocatta, M. Mustill & S. Boyd 1974).

* * *

Vacated and remanded for further proceedings.

QUAKER OATS CO. v. M/V TORVANGER

734 F.2d 238, 1984 AMC 2943 (5th Cir. 1984), *cert. denied*, 469 U.S. 1189,
105 S. Ct. 959, 83 L.Ed.2d 965, 1985 AMC 2398 (1985)

TATE, Circuit Judge.

The plaintiff, the Quaker Oats Company ("Quaker Oats"), appeals from the district court's dismissal of its claim under the Carriage of Goods by Sea Act ("COGSA"), 46 U.S.C. § 1300-1315, for damages to a cargo of tetrahydrofuran, a white chemical, shipped aboard the M/V Torvanger, a vessel owned by Westfal Larsen and Company ("Westfal Larsen"), made defendants' herein. Quaker Oats contends that the district court erred as a matter of law in finding that Westfal Larsen, the defendant carrier, had successfully rebutted the shipper Quaker Oats' *prima facie* case, thus shifting the burden of proof back to Quaker Oats, without explaining the cause of the loss. Finding that the court did err in applying the COGSA burden-shifting scheme, we reverse.

Quaker Oats purchased approximately five hundred metric tons of tetrahydrofuran from Mitsubishi Corporation of Tokyo, Japan ("Mitsubishi"). Mitsubishi chartered the Torvanger to transport the tetrahydrofuran from Kobe, Japan to Houston, Texas. Analysis of a composite of samples of the tetrahydrofuran taken after the cargo had been loaded on the vessel in Kobe, Japan indicated that the peroxide content was well within commercially acceptable levels. Samples taken upon the Torvanger's arrival in Houston from the three tanks aboard the vessel in which the chemical was carried, however, revealed peroxide contamination in one of the tanks beyond commercially acceptable levels. Quaker Oats sued the Torvanger and Westfal Larsen, asserting rights under COGSA for recovery of expenses incurred in purging the peroxide from the tetrahydrofuran.

I

Both parties agree that this dispute is governed by COGSA, which regulates the rights and liabilities arising out of the carrier's issuance of a bill of lading with respect to cargo damage or loss. "To enforce their respective rights under the Act, litigants must engage in the ping-pong game of burden shifting mandated by Sections 3 and 4. [46 U.S.C. §§ 1303 and 1304]." *Nitram, Inc. v. Cretan Life*, 599 F.2d 1359, 1373 (5th Cir. 1979). The plaintiff establishes a *prima facie* case by proving that the cargo for which the bill of lading issued was "loaded in an undamaged condition, and discharged in a contaminated condition." *Socony Mobil Oil Company v. Texas Coastal and International, Inc.*, 559 F.2d 1008, 1010 (5th Cir. 1977). The "bill of lading shall be *prima facie* evidence of the receipt by the carrier of the goods as therein described." 46 U.S.C. § 1303(4).

Once the plaintiff has presented a *prima facie* case, "the carrier then has the burden of proving that it exercised due diligence to prevent the damage or that the harm was occasioned by one of the excepted causes delineated in 46 U.S.C. § 1304(2)." *Blasser Brothers, Inc. v. Northern Pan-American Line*, 628 F.2d 376, 381 (5th Cir. 1980); accord *Nitram, Inc. v. Cretan Life, supra*, 599 F.2d at 1373; *Socony Mobil Oil Company, supra*, 559 F.2d at 1010; *Nichimen Company, Inc. v. M/V Farland*, 462 F.2d 319, 325 (2nd Cir. 1972). *See also* 2A Benedict on Admiralty § 56 (7th ed. 1983).

If the carrier rebuts the plaintiff's *prima facie* case with proof of an excepted cause listed in § 4(2)(a)-(p) of COGSA, 46 U.S.C. § 1304(2)(a)-(p), the burden returns to the plaintiff to establish that the carrier's negligence contributed to the damage or loss. *Blasser Brothers, Inc. v. Northern Pan-American Line, supra*, 628 F.2d at 382; *cf. Lekas & Drivas, Inc. v. Goulandris*, 306 F.2d 426, 432 (2nd Cir. 1962). If the plaintiff is then able to establish that the carrier's negligence was a contributory cause of the damage, the burden shifts to the carrier "to segregate the portion of the damage due to the excepted cause from that portion resulting from [the carrier's] own negligence." *Nitram, Inc. v. Cretan Life, supra*, 599 F.2d at 1373.

In addition to rebuttal of the *prima facie* case by proof of one of the specific exception causes of cargo damage, 46 U.S.C. § 1304(2)(a)-(p), the carrier may also rebut the *prima facie* case by relying on the catch-all exception in § 1304(2)(q) of COGSA, which provides that the carrier may exonerate himself from loss from any cause other than those listed in § 4(2)(a)-(p) by proving that the loss or damage occurred "without the actual fault and privity of the carrier...." 46 U.S.C. § 1304(2)(q). The carrier's burden of establishing "his own freedom from contributing fault ... is no mere burden of going forward with evidence, but a real burden of persuasion, with the attendant risk of non-persuasion." GILMORE AND BLACK, THE LAW OF ADMIRALTY § 3-37 at p. 168; § 3-43 (2nd ed. 1975). Consequently, the burden of proof does not return to the plaintiff, but rather judgment must hinge upon the adequacy of the carrier's proof that he was free from any fault whatsoever contributing to the damage of the goods entrusted to his carriage. *Id.*

II

The district court in this case found that Quaker Oats had established a *prima facie* case by producing evidence that the tetrahydrofuran was "within purchase order specifications" upon delivery to the Torvanger and that "at least a portion of it was no longer in that condition when tendered to [Quaker Oats]" after shipment.

In rebuttal to that *prima facie* case, the carrier Westfal Larsen produced evidence by which peroxide formation could allegedly be considered an "inherent vice" of tetrahydrofuran, 46 U.S.C. § 1304(2)(m), and that due diligence was exercised by Westfal Larsen to avoid any other possible causes of peroxide formation. Though finding the evidence on the "inherent vice" exception to be "non-dispositive,"[3] the district court found that Westfal Larsen successfully rebutted Quaker Oats prima facie case by producing evidence of due diligence "with respect to the preparation of the loading and storage equipment, the loading of the cargo, and the care of the cargo during voyage ...," thus, "return[ing] to Quaker Oats the burden to show that the peroxide formation was caused at least in part by [Westfal Larsen's] negligence." Finding that the shipper Quaker Oats failed to carry the burden, the district court rendered judgment for Westfal Larsen, the defendant carrier.

III

Before explaining the error in the district court's application of the COGSA burden-shifting scheme, the nature of the chemical shipped and the reasons for its peroxide contamination should be noted.

Tetrahydrofuran ("the chemical") has a natural tendency to form peroxides, especially if exposed to oxygen, unless it is chemically inhibited. Here, before shipment, the seller had treated the chemical with an inhibitor, and in fact the two tanks fully filled with the shipped chemical arrived without contamination; only the third tank, partially filled, was found to be peroxide-contaminated upon arrival. As a further safeguard against exposure to oxygen, all tanks were injected with a "nitrogen blanket" of sufficient pressure, designed to insulate the chemical from oxygen during shipment. The vessel's officers inspected the "nitrogen blanket" periodically and with due diligence, the district court found, and a water content analysis performed upon the cargo's arrival in Texas indicated that the nitrogen blanket had been properly maintained.

We thus have the following situation: If we accept the testimony offered for the shipper Quaker Oats (as the district court did), the chemical was loaded and found after testing to be free of peroxide contamination when shipped and when the bill of lading was issued. If we accept the testimony offered for the defendant carrier, as the district court equally did, the vessel's officers performed with due diligence their duty of maintaining the protective nitrogen cover that should have made exposure to oxygen and peroxide contamination impossible during the period that the cargo was entrusted to the care of the shipper. Consequently, if all the evidence is true, the evidence shows no cause for the peroxide contamination. However, that contamination must have resulted either from some defect in the chemical or its processing for shipment, for which the carrier would not be responsible—which the evidence does not prove; or else that contamination must have resulted during shipment from some failure of the vessel's officers or of the vessel—which again is not proved.

* * *

---

[3] The "inherent defect" exception to a carrier's COGSA liability, § 1304(2)(m) was not proved by the testimony that the chemical has a natural tendency to form peroxides when exposed to oxygen. Here, the uncontradicted testimony was that the chemical was properly treated by an inhibitor and protected from oxygenization by a nitrogen blanket during shipment and, thus, should not have formed peroxides. In order to establish this exception to COGSA liability, the carrier must show (as it did not here) some defect, quality, or vice adhering to the individual cargo of the chemical in question. *Horn v. Cia de Navegacion Fruco, S.A.*, 404 F.2d 422, 435 (5th Cir. 1969).

IV

The district court held that the carrier's proof of due diligence in preparation of the cargo, its loading, and its care during the voyage "was sufficient to return to the Plaintiff the burden to show that the peroxide formation was caused at least in part by the Defendant's negligence." None of the specific excepting causes (including the "inherent defect" exception, *see* note 3 *supra*), 46 U.S.C. § 1304(2)(a)-(p), were proved by the carrier, so the burden did not shift back to the shipper to prove that carrier negligence contributed to the damage. Under COGSA, the carrier's proof of the remaining general catch-all exception to liability relied upon, § 1304(2)(q), is not shown by its simple and to be expected evidence that its crew did all it was supposed to do (although here, however, somewhat corroborated as to the nitrogen blanket by testing on arrival). The statute provides, more stringently, that the carrier shall prove that its fault did not contribute to the accident: "the burden of proof shall be on the person claiming the exception to show that neither the actual fault or privity of the carrier nor the fault or neglect of the agents or servants of the carrier contributed to the loss or damage." 46 U.S.C. § 1304(2)(q).

For purposes of this catch-all no-fault exception to liability, 46 U.S.C. § 1304(2)(q), the presumption of fault—resulting from the arrival of cargo, damage free when shipped under bill of lading, but contaminated on arrival—is thus not rebutted by simple proof of the carrier's own due diligence, evidence peculiarly within its knowledge and control during the period of the shipment of the cargo entrusted to its care. For the § 1304(2)(q) exception (*see* note 2, *supra*) to come into play, the carrier must first prove what that "other cause" was. *See*, W. Tetley, Marine Cargo Claims 245, 246 (1978). But the district court found that "no one knows what caused the cargo to form peroxide in the way it did" (R. 14) and indeed concluded that the cause of the damage was a "mystery" (R. 12).

To rebut the presumption of fault when relying upon its own reasonable care, the carrier must further prove that the damage was caused by something other than its own negligence. *Calmaquip Engineering West Hemisphere Corporation v. West Coast Carriers Ltd.*, 650 F.2d 633, 640-41 (5th Cir. 1981); *Socony Mobil Oil Company, supra*, 559 F.2d at 1013. Once the shipper establishes a *prima facie* case, under "the policy of the law" the carrier must "explain what took place or suffer the consequences." *Companie De Navigation, etc. v. Mondial United Corporation*, 316 F.2d 163, 170 (5th Cir. 1963); *see also* discussion of issue similar to the present in *Socony Mobil Oil Company, supra*, 559 F.2d at 111 [*sic*]. "[T]he law casts upon [the carrier] the burden of the loss which he cannot explain or, explaining, bring within the exceptional case in which he is relieved from liability." *The Vallescura*, 293 U.S. 296, 303, 55 S. Ct. 194, 196, 79 L. Ed. 373 (1934).

Here, contrary to the policy of the statutes, the trial court placed the burden upon the shipper, not the carrier, to explain the unexplained or unexplainable loss. Its judgment must therefore be reversed, and the case remanded for entry of judgment awarding the plaintiff the damages sustained.

Conclusion

For the reasons stated, the judgment dismissing the plaintiff's claim is REVERSED, and the case REMANDED for the award of damages.

---

iii. Fire

COGSA § 4(2)(b), 46 U.S.C. § 30504 (formerly 46 U.S.C. § 182)

COMPLAINT OF TA CHI NAVIGATION (PANAMA), CORP., S.A.

677 F.2d 225, 1982 AMC 1710 (2d Cir. 1982)

VAN GRAAFEILAND, Circuit Judge:

This is an appeal from an order of the United States District Court for the Southern District of New York, C.H. TENNEY, J., denying the petition of a shipowner for exoneration from or limitation of liability for cargo damage claims resulting from a shipboard explosion and fire. Because the district court erred in fixing the elements and burdens of proof, we reverse and remand for further proceedings.

Judge Tenney's opinion, reported at 504 F. Supp. 209, contains a comprehensive statement of the facts. A short summary will therefore suffice for our purpose. The stricken ship was the *S.S. Eurypylus*, owned by Ta Chi Navigation (Panama) Corp., and the fire occurred on November 10, 1975 while she was en route from Japan to Panama. The ship was gutted and sold for scrap, and most of her cargo was destroyed. The district court found that the fire began when acetylene gas escaping from a welding hose in the ship's engine room was ignited by a spark. Cylinders containing oxygen and acetylene, stored in a port tonnage alleyway near the engine room, two of which were feeding the torch, promptly exploded, and the fire was almost immediately out of control. The district court predicated its finding of liability upon the presence of the cylinders in the alleyway, and the propriety of such storage was the most vigorously contested issue on the trial.

Cargo claimants produced two expert witnesses in support of their contention that the storage was improper. The shipowner produced substantial evidence to the contrary. That evidence showed that the ship was built in Scotland in 1958 and carried a 100 A-1 classification with Lloyds Register of Shipping from the time it was built, indicating thereby that the ship was of the best quality. There was also testimony that a storage rack for the oxygen and acetylene cylinders was installed in the alleyway when the ship was built. From time to time thereafter, the ship was checked by representatives of Lloyds, and safety equipment certificates were issued in accordance with Safety of Life at Sea regulations [SOLAS], which were prepared under the auspices of the Intergovernmental Maritime Consultive Organization (IMCO).

* * *

It is in the light of this testimony that the district court's discussion of the elements and burdens of proof must be examined. The district judge said that "the [shipowner] is required to prove that the vessel was seaworthy at the commencement of the voyage." 504 F. Supp. at 229. He continued, "If the petitioner failed to use due and proper care, *i.e.*, due diligence, to provide a competent master and crew and to see that the ship was seaworthy at the commencement of the voyage, then any loss occurring by reason of fault or neglect in these particulars is within its privity, and it may not avail itself of the fire exemption statutes." *Id.* at 230. He went on:

In the instant case we are concerned with whether the carrier had exercised due diligence under § 1303 before and at the commencement of the voyage to make *S.S. Eurypylus* seaworthy, to properly man, equip, and supply her, and to make her holds fit and safe for the reception, carriage, and preservation of cargo. (*Id.*)

He then concluded that the storage of the oxyacetylene cylinders in the port tonnage alleyway rendered the *Eurypylus* unseaworthy at the commencement of the voyage. *Id.* at 233.

The district court's approach to the burden of proof is not as straightforward as we have presented it. It is clear, however, that the entire approach reflects a misunderstanding of the terms of the Fire Statute as they have been applied by the Supreme Court and the courts of this Circuit. The Fire Statute, 46 U.S.C. § 182, exonerates the shipowner from liability for fire damage to cargo unless the fire was caused by the "design or neglect" of the owner. "Neglect," as thus used, means negligence, not the breach of a non-delegable duty. *Consumers Import Co. v. Kabushiki Kaisha Kawasaki Zosenjo*, 320 U.S. 249, 252 (1943); *Earle & Stoddart, Inc. v. Ellerman's Wilson Line, Ltd.*, 287 U.S. 420, 427 (1932). "If the carrier shows that the damage was caused by fire, the shipper must prove that the carrier's negligence caused the damage." *Asbestos Corp. Ltd. v. Compagnie De Navigation Frais-Sinet Et Cyprien Fabre*, 480 F.2d 669, 673 (2d Cir. 1973).

* * *

The shipper can prove that the carrier caused the damage either by proving that a negligent act of the carrier caused the fire or that such an act prevented the fire's extinguishment. *Asbestos Corp. Ltd., supra*, 480 F.2d at 672.

This delineation of the carrier's liability did not change with the 1936 enactment of the Carriage of Goods by Sea Act (COGSA), ch. 229 § 1-16, 49 Stat. 1207 (current version at 46 U.S.C. §§ 1300-1315). Congress specifically provided that COGSA shall not affect the rights and obligations of the carrier under the Fire Statute. 46 U.S.C. § 1308. Congress also included in COGSA a provision that the carrier shall not be responsible for fire damage resulting from fire "unless caused by the actual fault or privity of the carrier." 46 U.S.C. § 1304(2) (b).

When COGSA was under consideration by the House Committee on Merchant Marine and Fisheries, the suggestion was made that "since this bill itself in section 8 disclaims all intent to modify the fire statute, and there is no apparent reason why it should be modified," the words "design or neglect of the carrier" as used in the Fire Statute be substituted for the words "fault or privity of the carrier" in the proposed Act. *Hearings on S. 1152 before the House Committee on Merchant Marine and Fisheries*, 74th Cong. 2d Sess. 13 (1936). However, it was pointed out that "the word 'fault' corresponds generally to the word 'neglect' and the word 'privity' to the word 'design,' " *id.* at 141, and the words "fault" and "privity" were retained in the statute.

We have adopted that reasoning in this Circuit and treat the COGSA fire exemption as being the same as that of the Fire Statute. *Asbestos Corp. Ltd. v. Compagnie De Navigation Frais-Sinet Et Cyprien Fabre, supra*, 480 F.2d at 672.

* * *

Unfortunately, the district court patterned its holding upon that of the Ninth Circuit in *Sunkist Growers, Inc. v. Adelaide Shipping Lines, Ltd.*, 603 F.2d 1327 (9th Cir. 1979), cert. denied, 444 U.S. 1012 (1980). In *Sunkist*, the Ninth Circuit held that the burden of proof is on the carrier to show that it exercised due diligence to provide a seaworthy ship in order to invoke the provisions of either section 1304(2) (b) or the Fire Statute. *Id.* at 1336. Commenting on this Court's holding in *Asbestos Corp. Ltd. v. Compagnie De Navigation, supra*, 480 F.2d 669, that the shipper must prove that the carrier's negligence caused the fire damage, the Ninth Circuit stated that the "use of this language was entirely unnecessary" and constituted a "casual treatment of the burden of proof by the author of the appellate court opinion." 603 F.2d at 1335. Strangely enough, the author of Sunkist did not fault the district court judge in *Asbestos* for holding that "[o]nce the defendant has sustained the burden of proving that it comes within the exemption of COGSA § 1304 (2) (b) or the Fire Statute the burden then shifts to the shipper to prove that the fire was caused by the 'design or neglect' or 'actual fault or privity' of the carrier". 345 F. Supp. 814, 821.

We disagree not only with *Sunkist's* unflattering characterization of Judge Timbers' opinion in *Asbestos*, an opinion that was concurred in by Judges Smith and Hayes, but also with the Ninth Circuit's interpretation of the interrelation between the Fire Statute and COGSA, an interpretation that is concurred in by no other Circuit. The "ping pong" effect of the shifting burden of proof under section 1304(2), *Nitram, Inc. v. Cretan Life*, 599 F.2d 1359, 1373 (5th Cir. 1979) did not receive its first recognition by this Court in *Asbestos Corp. v. Compagnie De Navigation Frais-Sinet Et Cyprien Fabre, supra*. In *American Tobacco Co. v. The Katingo Hadjipatera, supra*, decided twenty-two years prior to Asbestos Corp., Judge Frank, writing for himself, Judge Swan, and Judge Learned Hand, said that, once a shipowner established loss by fire, "[n]o liability could be imposed unless the owners of [cargo] carried the burden of proving that the fire was caused by the shipowner's design or negligence or the carriers' actual fault or privity." 194 F.2d at 450.

When Congress wanted to put the burden of proving freedom from fault on a shipowner claiming the benefit of an exemption, it specifically said so. *See* 46 U.S.C. § 1304(2)(q). The Sunkist court would read the language of subsection (q) into subsection (b), "although Congress did not put it there." *See Lekas & Drivas, Inc. v. Goulandris, supra*, 306 F.2d at 432. This Court has not put it there either. We adhere to our prior holdings that, if the carrier shows that the damage was caused by fire, the shipper must prove that the carrier's negligence caused the fire or prevented its extinguishment. If on remand the shipper fails to meet this burden, the action must be dismissed. Only if the shipper sustained the burden would the carrier have the obligation to establish what portion of the damage was not attributable to its fault.

* * *

Reversed and remanded.

———————

NISSAN FIRE & MARINE INS. CO., LTD. v. M/V HYUNDAI EXPLORER

93 F.3d 641, 1996 AMC 2409 (9th Cir. 1996)

D.W. NELSON, Circuit Judge:

I.

Introduction

This case arises out of an engine room fire aboard the M/V HYUNDAI EXPLORER (the "Vessel"), a Korean flag container cargo ship, on or about January 2, 1992. Defendant-appellant Hyundai Merchant Marine Co., Ltd. ("HMM"), the bareboat charterer[1] and operator of the Vessel when she experienced the fire, appeals the district court's grant of summary judgment for plaintiffs-appellees Nissan Fire & Marine Insurance Co., Ltd., Taiko Bussan Kaisha, Ltd., Fireman's Fund Insurance Co. and American Home Assurance Co., (collectively, "Cargo Interests"). Cargo Interests are the subrogated insurers or consignees of cargo that suffered damage because of the fire. We reverse the summary judgment for Cargo Interests and remand to the district court with instructions to enter judgment for HMM.

II.

Factual and Procedural Background

The parties stipulated to most of the relevant facts in their Agreed Statement of Facts, which they filed with the district court. During the voyage at issue, the Vessel loaded and discharged cargo at Long Beach, Oakland and Seattle. It departed Seattle for Pusan, Korea on December 22, 1991. During the cargo operations in the United States ports and on the voyage to Korea, both of the Vessel's generators operated with no apparent problems until a fire was discovered on the morning of January 2, 1992.

The Vessel has an automated control room and was therefore manned only between 0800 and 1730 hours. The Third Engineer, who was the duty officer on the night of January 1, noted nothing out of the ordinary when he visited the engine room at 2200 hours as part of his routine. At 0700 hours on January 2, however, an alarm alerted him to a fire in the engine room. Although the crew was able to extinguish the fire, the engine control room sustained significant damage, and the Vessel required a salvage tug to tow her to Pusan. While under tow, she was unable to provide refrigeration to the refrigerated ("reefer") cargo, and much of it spoiled.

The fire resulted from the failure of a compression coupling on a fuel oil line to the No. 2 generator fuel pressure alarm. When the coupling failed, the line separated from the main fuel line and sprayed oil, which ignited when it contacted the engine exhaust system. The line was not original, but had been replaced at some unknown time in the past. Inspection of the coupling indicated that it was not defective, but that it had been improperly fitted. Inspection also revealed that a rubber "O" ring and some thread sealing tape were attached to the coupling. Presumably, the ring and tape were used to repair a previous leak, but it is not known when they were applied.

Both parties' expert witnesses opined that the repair to the coupling was of the type normally performed by a crewmember and that the curves on the replacement line indicated that a crewmember, rather than a shipyard, most likely made the repair in question. None of the engineers aboard at the time of the fire, each of whom had joined the Vessel between March and August, 1991, fitted the coupling in question or had ever seen the coupling leak. Only the engine room log books and maintenance records might have reflected repairs made by prior crew members, and these were destroyed in the fire.

While assembled, the coupling completely concealed the "O" ring, sealing tape and its poor fit. Indeed, both experts agreed that the defective fitting would not have been visually apparent to even a trained engineer or surveyor while assembled. Moreover, Cargo Interests' expert testified that engineers and surveyors normally do not open compression

---

[1] A bareboat charterer is one who charters or leases a vessel without a crew. The charterer assumes full possession and control of the vessel and is deemed the owner of the vessel for purposes of the U.S. Carriage of Goods by Sea Act ("COGSA") during the period of the charter. 46 U.S.C.App. § 186.

couplings in an engine room for inspection purposes and that disassembly is not part of routine maintenance or inspection. These observations held true in this case as HMM's port engineer in charge of the Vessel's maintenance and repair failed to discover the defect in the coupling assembly before the Vessel departed on the voyage in issue.

In addition, official inspections of the Vessel had failed to discover the defective coupling if, in fact, it existed when they were performed. The Vessel is certified ("classed") by the Korean Register of Shipping ("KRS"), which inspects vessels' safety for governmental insurance purposes. In September, 1990, the KRS surveyed the Vessel's No. 2 generator and its safety devices and alarms and found them to be in order. The KRS made another hull/machinery survey in August, 1991 and issued a report stating that it had inspected the safety devices and alarms for the generators and again found them to be in order. The No. 2 generator was next due for survey in 1995.

Cargo Interests brought suit against the Vessel and HMM for damages they incurred due to the spoiled reefer cargo. This case originally was brought as two separate suits, each against HMM in personam as claimant to the Vessel and against the Vessel *in rem*. After the cases were consolidated, the district court heard the parties' cross motions for summary judgment. HMM moved for summary judgment on the basis of its assertion that the "fire defenses" insulated it from liability. The fire defenses are comprised of two statutes that limit a shipowner's liability for cargo damage caused by fire aboard a vessel: the "Fire Statute," 46 U.S.C.app. § 182,[2] and the COGSA Fire Exemption, 46 U.S.C.app. § 1304(2)(b).[3]

The court determined, and HMM concedes, that the defective coupling responsible for the fire was an unseaworthy condition. The court then ruled that under the law of this Circuit, HMM had the burden of proving it had exercised due diligence to make the Vessel seaworthy before it could invoke the fire defenses. Further, the district court held that HMM's duty of due diligence was "absolute or non-delegable" and that HMM had failed to meet its burden. We reverse.

* * *

[2] 46 U.S.C.App. § 182 [the Fire Statute], enacted as part of the original Limitation of Liability Act of 1851, provides:
No owner of any vessel shall be liable to answer for or make good to any person any loss or damage, which may happen to any merchandise whatsoever, which shall be shipped, taken in, or put on board any such vessel, by reason or by means of any fire happening to or on board the vessel, unless such fire is caused by the design or neglect of such owner.
[3] Congress enacted COGSA in 1936 to partially replace the Harter Act of 1893, 46 U.S.C.App. §§ 190-196, and to make the law more favorable to shipowners. See In re Damodar Bulk Carriers, Ltd., 903 F.2d 675, 684 (9th Cir.1990). 46 U.S.C.App. §§ 1303 and 1304, part of COGSA, provide in relevant part:
§ 1303. Responsibilities and liabilities of carrier and ship
Seaworthiness
(1)   The carrier shall be bound, before and at the beginning of the voyage, to exercise due diligence to -
(a)   Make the ship seaworthy;
(b)   Properly man, equip, and supply the ship;   * * *

§ 1304. Rights and immunities of carrier and ship
Unseaworthiness
(1)   Neither the carrier nor the ship shall be liable for loss or damage arising or resulting from unseaworthiness unless caused by want of due diligence on the part of the carrier to make the ship seaworthy, and to secure that the ship is properly manned, equipped, and supplied.... Whenever loss or damage has resulted from unseaworthiness, the burden of proving the exercise of due diligence shall be on the carrier or other persons claiming exemption under this section.
Uncontrollable causes of loss
(2)   Neither the carrier nor the ship shall be responsible for loss or damage arising or resulting from -
* * *
(b)   Fire, unless caused by the actual fault or privity of the carrier.

IV.

Discussion

A. Burden of proof on due diligence.

"Fire is the peril most dreaded by all mariners, and a peril most difficult to combat in a fully laden ship." *In re Liberty Shipping Corp.*, 509 F.2d 1249, 1250 (9th Cir.1975). That being so, the maritime law has developed unique provisions embodied in the fire defenses which govern a shipowner's liability in connection with a fire aboard his vessel. This court has held, however, that where unseaworthiness[4] caused the fire, a carrier[5] bears the burden of showing that it exercised due diligence to make the ship seaworthy before it can invoke the fire defenses to exonerate it from liability. *See Sunkist Growers, Inc. v. Adelaide Shipping Lines*, 603 F.2d 1327, 1340 (9th Cir.1979), *cert. denied*, 444 U.S. 1012, 100 S.Ct. 659, 62 L.Ed.2d 640 (1980); cf. *In re Damodar Bulk Carriers, Ltd.*, 903 F.2d 675, 686 (9th Cir.1990). Because the improperly fitted coupling on the Vessel was an unseaworthy condition, the district court correctly assigned to HMM the burden of proving its due diligence as a prerequisite to invoking the fire defenses.

B. The standard of due diligence under the fire defenses.

HMM contends that even if it bore the burden of showing that it acted with due diligence, the district court erred in holding that this duty was non-delegable.[6] Cargo Interests contend that the court imposed the proper standard and that HMM's duty of due diligence was in fact non-delegable.

This claim is without merit and manifests Cargo Interests' failure to recognize the different standards of due diligence that apply in the fire defenses and other COGSA exemptions. While the carrier's duty of due diligence is non-delegable for exoneration under the non-fire COGSA exemptions, a different standard of due diligence, one derived from the Fire Statute, governs fire cases and eliminates vicarious liability imputed to the carrier. Under the fire defenses, a carrier is liable only for "his personal negligence, or in case of a corporate owner, negligence of its managing officers and agents as distinguished from that of the master or subordinates." *Consumers Import Co. v. Kabushiki Kaisha*, 320 U.S. 249, 252, 64 S.Ct. 15, 16, 88 L.Ed. 30 (1943); *see also Earle & Stoddart v. Ellerman's Wilson Line*, 287 U.S. 420, 427, 53 S.Ct. 200, 201, 77 L.Ed. 403 (1932) ("The courts have been careful not to thwart the purpose of the fire statute by interpreting as 'neglect' of the owners the breach of what in other connections is held to be a non-delegable duty."); *Westinghouse Elec. Corp. v. M/V "LESLIE LYKES"*, 734 F.2d 199, 209 (5th Cir.), *cert. denied*, 469 U.S. 1077, 105 S.Ct. 577, 83 L.Ed.2d 516 (1984); *Hasbro Indus. v. M/S St. Constantine*, 705 F.2d 339, 342 (9th Cir.1983) (holding that the negligence of the "shipowner's supervisory or managing employees" was sufficient to find personal negligence); *In re Ta Chi Navigation Corp., S.A.*, 677 F.2d 225, 228 (2d Cir.1982) (" 'Neglect' ... means negligence, not the breach of a non-delegable duty."); *Sunkist*, 603 F.2d at 1336 (stating that " 'neglect of the owner' under the Fire Statute refers to 'the neglect of the managing officers and agents as distinguished from that of the master or other members of the crew' ") (quoting *Albina Engine & Machine Works v. Hershey Chocolate Corp.*, 295 F.2d 619, 621 (9th Cir.1961)); *In re Liberty Shipping Corp.*, 509 F.2d 1249, 1252 (9th Cir.1975); *Asbestos Corp. Ltd. v. Compagnie De Navigation Fraissinet et Cyprien Fabre et al.*, 480 F.2d 669, 673 n. 7 (2d Cir.1973).

---

[4] The legal test for seaworthiness is "whether the vessel is reasonably fit to carry the cargo which she has undertaken to transport." The Silvia, 171 U.S. 462, 464, 19 S.Ct. 7, 8, 43 L.Ed. 241 (1898). Courts have held that a broad range of conditions may render a vessel unseaworthy: crew error, a defect in the vessel's construction or equipment, improper loading or stowage of cargo and various sorts of dangerous conditions.

[5] "The term 'carrier' includes the owner or the charterer who enters into a contract of carriage with the [cargo] shipper." 46 U.S.C.App. § 1301(a). In this case, HMM is the carrier and Cargo Interests are the shippers.

[6] The court stated at the hearing on the cross motions for summary judgment:

> [T]he shipowner has this duty of putting the vessel in a seaworthy condition at the beginning of the voyage.
>
> So we do not really have an issue of whether the shipowner is being held vicariously liable for the act of the crew, as this was a condition of the vessel at the time that it embarked upon the voyage. And this was the duty of the shipowner.
>
> And whether one calls it ... absolute or nondelegable, or whatever term you use, it is a duty that the shipowner owed where I don't think it's entitled to step behind the, quote, no liability for the acts of the crew, close quote, principle.

* * *

Although a carrier generally is not liable for the negligence or lack of due diligence of its crew or other lower level employees, it still may be liable for the actions of an employee responsible for starting the fire or preventing its spread if the carrier was personally negligent, for example, by not adequately training the employee or by failing to provide sufficient fire fighting equipment. *See, e.g., Hasbro,* 705 F.2d at 342; *Asbestos Corp.,* 480 F.2d at 672. Under the facts of this case, however, there was nothing to implicate the crew's training, the Vessel's fire-fighting equipment, or any other personal duties of HMM. The district court improperly focused on the unseaworthy condition rather than assessing whether any personal negligence by HMM was responsible for that condition. As we have discussed above, however, the fire defenses impose a burden of personal due diligence. Because the district court applied the wrong standard of due diligence in determining whether HMM had carried its burden, the court erred in granting summary judgment for Cargo Interests.

C. Proving due diligence

Exoneration under the fire defenses is not voided by an unseaworthy condition, but rather by an "inexcusable" unseaworthy condition, i.e., one that existed because of the carrier's lack of due diligence. *See Hasbro,* 705 F.2d at 341; *Sunkist,* 603 F.2d at 1335 (quoting *Asbestos Corp.,* 480 F.2d at 672). To carry its burden of proving due diligence, HMM had to prove that it had done all that was "proper and reasonable" to make the Vessel seaworthy. *See Martin v. The Southwark,* 191 U.S. 1, 15-16, 24 S.Ct. 1, 5-6, 48 L.Ed. 65 (1903). All of the evidence indicates that a crewmember made the repair in question; indeed, Cargo Interests' expert witness agreed with that assessment. Because the facts do not suggest any theory under which the defective repair could be imputed to HMM personally, it is irrelevant whether HMM can identify the specific circumstances surrounding the repair.

The evidence also demonstrates that HMM inspected the Vessel and/or had it inspected regularly. We are aware that compliance with classification society requirements does not necessarily establish due diligence. *See Louis Dreyfus Corp. v. 27,946 Long Tons of Corn,* 830 F.2d 1321, 1327 (5th Cir.1987); *Fireman's Fund Ins. Cos. v. M/V VIGNES,* 794 F.2d 1552, 1556 (11th Cir.1986). Nevertheless, the testing of the Vessel in accordance with classification society requirements is a factor tending to prove due diligence. The failure of regular KRS surveys of the engine room and generators to reveal any problems with the coupling provides strong evidence of HMM's due diligence because it shows how difficult it would have been to detect the unseaworthy condition and that HMM was not on notice of any problem concerning the coupling. The undisputed evidence indicates that the coupling had functioned without leaking for at least the previous nine months and that the defective assembly was hidden from even a trained eye.

There is no evidence that the defect could have been discovered without disassembly of the coupling. Even the Cargo Interests' own expert testified that disassembly of the coupling is normally not a part of routine inspections. There is no credible evidence that could establish the personal lack of due diligence by HMM. Therefore, we hold that HMM carried its burden of proving due diligence and that the defectively repaired coupling was an excusable condition of unseaworthiness.

V.

Conclusion

The fire defenses do not hold shipowners or other carriers liable for an unseaworthy condition that contributed to a vessel fire unless that unseaworthy condition was preventable by the carrier in the exercise of due diligence. We are satisfied that HMM has carried its burden of proving its due diligence to make the Vessel seaworthy. Unfortunately for Cargo Interests, the defectively repaired coupling was the sort of rare condition that was not remedied despite the exercise of due diligence. For the foregoing reasons, we reverse the district court's grant of summary judgment for Cargo Interests and remand to the district court with instructions to enter judgment for HMM.

REVERSED and REMANDED.

Notes

1. The Fifth and Eleventh Circuits agree with the Second Circuit (and thus disagree with the Ninth Circuit) that the onus is on the cargo-owner to prove that the cause of the fire was due to the "actual fault or privity" of the carrier. *Westinghouse Elec. Corp. v. M/V Leslie Lykes*, 734 F.2d 199, 1985 AMC 247 (5th Cir. 1985); *Banana Services Inc. v. M/V Tasman Star*, 68 F. 3d 418, 1996 AMC 260 (11th Cir. 1995).

2. All circuits agree that the carrier only loses the right to rely on the fire defense if it itself was guilty of "actual fault or privity". In the case of corporate carriers, this involves consideration of whether the relevant fault was at a sufficiently high level in the corporate hierarchy to be regarded as the fault of the company itself, rather than one of its employees. For example, in *Westinghouse Elec. Corp. v. M/V Leslie Lykes*, 734 F.2d 199, 1985 AMC 247 (5th Cir. 1985), the fire was caused by poor stowage of cargo. The court held that the carrier was not liable for the ignition of the fire:

> [T]he burden of proof was on the cargo to show that this stowage decision was within the "design or neglect" of the "managing officers and agents as distinguished from the master or subordinates" of Lykes. Despite this burden, Cargo failed to present any evidence as to who within the layout department prepared this cargo plan and which, if any, supervisors checked and approved this person's work. There was no evidence of how many persons worked in this department, the various job categories and their corresponding spheres of authority, or the structure of the hierarchy leading from the layout personnel to the highest officers of the corporation… Without such evidence showing a broad range of corporate authority in a person involved in the stowage decision, the District Court could not properly conclude that the improper stowage was within the personal "design or neglect" of the corporate owner. The evidence was only that some employee or employees in the layout department designed the stowage in this case. This is not sufficient to defeat the Carrier's defense under the Fire Statute.

Problems: The Fire Exemption: A Theme With Variations

Facts: There was a shipment of goods on board the M/V Good Hope from Italy to the United States governed by the United States Carriage of Goods by Sea Act. In transit, a fire broke out. The goods carried were damaged. The shipper made his prima facie case.

1. In response to the shipper's claim, the carrier pleaded the fire exemption under COGSA § 4(2)(b). What should the carrier prove in order to be exonerated?

2. Suppose that the carrier proved that the loss resulted from the fire. Is this the end of the matter? Is there anything the shipper should do to prevent the carrier's exoneration?

3. Suppose that the shipper claimed that the carrier should not be allowed to assert the fire exemption, unless he proved first that he exercised due diligence to make the vessel seaworthy. How should the court rule?

4. Suppose that the shipper proved that the cause of the fire that damaged the goods was the *unseaworthiness of the vessel*. The shipper then claimed that the carrier should not be allowed to claim the fire exemption unless he first proved that he exercised due diligence to make the vessel seaworthy. How should the court rule?

5. *Variation*: Suppose the shipper proved that the vessel was unseaworthy and that the cause of the damage to the goods was the unseaworthiness of the vessel rather than the fire. Example: A fire broke out and fresh water was used to combat the fire. Bales of cotton untouched by the fire were found soaked in sea water. The carrier pleaded the fire exemption. What result?

6. *Variation*: Suppose that the shipper proved that the vessel was unseaworthy and that the unseaworthiness of the vessel was the cause of the fire. The carrier pleaded the fire statute and proved that the fire was the cause of the damage to the goods. Should the carrier be exonerated? Is there anything the shipper should do?

7. *Variation*: Suppose that the shipper proved that the vessel was unseaworthy and that the unseaworthiness of the vessel was the cause of the fire. The carrier pleaded the fire statute and proved that the fire was the cause of the damage and that he exercised due diligence to make the vessel seaworthy. The shipper claimed that, in order to be exonerated, the carrier must also prove that the fire had not been caused by the carrier' "actual fault or privity". How should the court rule?

8. What is "actual fault or privity" of the carrier?

9. Suppose that there is convincing evidence that the damage to the goods was caused by negligent fire fighting operations of the crew and master. Should the carrier be exonerated?

10. What happens when the cause of the fire is not established?

E. Damages and Limitation of Liability

Notes: Measure of Damages

1. Market value

SANTIAGO v. SEA-LAND SERVICE, INC.

366 F. Supp. 1309, 1974 AMC 673 (D.P.R. 1973)

* * *

In general, the measure of damages in cargo claims has been market value at the port of destination. . . . In the event goods are damaged rather than lost entirely, the measure would be the difference between sound market value at the port of destination and the market value of the goods in the damaged condition. . . . When cargo is wrongfully delayed rather than actually damaged, the proper measure of damages is the difference between the market value of the goods at the time and place they should have arrived and the market value of the goods when they arrived. This principle is very well illustrated by the case of *Atlantic Mutual Insurance Co. v. Poseidon Schiffahrt*, 313 F.2d 872 (7th Cir. 1963), *cert. den.* 375 U.S. 819, 84 S.Ct. 56, 11 L.Ed.2d 53 (1963), which discusses generally the measure of damages in all three situations, that is, loss, damage and delay.

* * *

An obvious exception arises where there exists no market value at the destination port for the commodity damaged. In such event the nearest market is often used with the addition of the cost of getting the goods to that market. In *Sanib Corp. v. United Fruit Co.*, 74 F. Supp. 64 (S.D.N.Y. 1947), there was damage to a shipment of banana powder upon its arrival at Tampa, Florida. The District Court found that there was no market value for banana powder at Tampa, so the court applied the New York market price with proper adjustment for the difference in freight and other necessary expenses.

Another rule is to apply when reconditioning of the damaged merchandise is feasible. Despite the fact that the market value of the commodity was decreased substantially by voyage damage, if restoration can be made at a modest cost so that the shipper realizes the market value of the product, the courts sometimes limit damages to such reconditioning costs. In *Weirton Steel Co. v. Isbrandtsen-Moller Co.*, 126 F.2d 593 (2nd Cir. 1942) tin plate was reconditioned for about 10% of its depreciation in value, and the shipper was able to use it for its intended purpose. Even though the tin plate was not completely restored in appearance, only the reconditioning costs were awarded as damages since the shipper was able to dispose of the merchandise without economical loss.

* * *

Various methods have been used to determine market value and the determination of said market value is not always a simple task for a judge or jury in a cargo claim. Thus, there is always the problem of proving market value prices at ports all over the world often on theoretical dates when goods should have arrived which can be the source of prolonged litigation. The solution to the problem is, of course the responsibility of the plaintiff, since he has the burden of proof as to the amount of the damages. . . . On occasions published listings for commodities such as sugar, grain, cotton or rubber constitute the best proof of market listings at the port of destination. On other occasions comparable sales are the best evidence of market value and in a large number of cases market value is actually determined by testimony of expert witnesses; the shipper himself which is familiar with the market, marine surveyors who have familiarized themselves with market conditions, etc. . . .

Whether the basis for market value set in a particular case is retail, wholesale, replacement, or even invoice value, it is not always susceptible of easy explanation. The courts usually select the value that is most in accord with basic principles of compensating or restoring the shipper, of making him whole. As a general provision, if goods are intended to be added to stock and no need exists for immediate replacement at retail costs or if no loss of sales at retail is shown the term market value would contemplate wholesale price. . . .

* * *

Retail values, including anticipated profits, have been awarded where it has been satisfactorily shown that these were in fact the sums lost. . . .

* * *

In addition to the actual loss of market value involved, there usually arise necessary expenses incidental to the loss sustained. These include survey fees (to determine the quantum of damage or to render expert assistance in restoration or salvage), necessary transportation, warehousing, and the like. *See Continental Distrib. Co. v. Reading Co.*, 168 F.2d 967 (3rd Cir. 1948). These charges are recoverable if they were reasonably considered necessary at the time they were incurred, although later developments indicate they were not really needed. . . .

Closely akin to the right to recover necessary incidental expenses is the obligation imposed upon the shipper to minimize his own damages. . . .

* * *

2. In *B.P. North American Petroleum v. Solar S/T*, 250 F.3d 307, 2001 AMC 1844 (5th Cir. 2001), the court held that in calculating the measure of damages, any price fluctuations or futures trading after discharge must be ignored. The court said:

> As we have noted, because of the applicability of the market value rule to this case, any futures trading by BP following the date of discharge does not affect a proper damages calculation. Because the market value rule considers the diminished value of the cargo on the date of discharge, later price fluctuations or changes in value beyond the date of discharge are irrelevant to the damages calculation. This principle was stated about as well as it can be said in 1878 by a California district court in *The Compta*, 6 F. Cas. 233, 234 (D. Cal. 1878) (No. 3070):
>
>> Where goods are delivered in a damaged condition, the damage sustained is the difference between their market value, if sound, and their market value in their unsound condition. Both values to be ascertained as of the time when the goods were, or should have been, delivered...If the shipper has seen fit to hold the goods for a better market, he has entered into a speculation the result of which can in no way affect the liability of the ship. If he has obtained a higher price than could have been realized at the time of the breach, the ship's liability is not thereby diminished. If he has sold them at a lower price, her liability is not increased.
>
> In sum, BP's futures trading is inapposite to a "market value" damages calculation in this case, and BP's damages should be calculated as the difference between the market value of sound oil on the date of discharge and an estimated valuation of the contaminated oil on the date of discharge.

250 F. 3d at 314; 2001 AMC at 1851.

————————

Notes:Package limitation

1. What is a "package" for limitation purposes?

(a) *Non-containerized Cargo: Fully Enclosed Goods*

The first step in determining what constitutes a COGSA package is to ascertain the intent of the parties. This is done by evaluating the contents of the bill of lading. *Seguros "Illimani" S.A. v. M/V Popi P*, 929 F.2d 89, 1991 AMC 1521 (2d Cir. 1991); *Binladen BSB Landscaping v. M/V Nedlloyd Rotterdam*, 759 F.2d 1006, 1985 AMC 2113 (2d Cir.), *cert. denied*, 474 U.S. 902, 106 S. Ct. 229, 88 L. Ed. 2d 229 (1985); *Fireman's Fund Insurance Co. v. Tropical Shipping and Construction Co. Ltd.*, 254 F.3d 987; 2001 AMC 2474 (11th Cir. 2001). It is only in the event of ambiguity in the bill of lading that it becomes necessary to look elsewhere. However, some courts begin their inquiry by asking whether the cargo was packaged or prepared for shipment in any way, regardless of what the bill of lading might say. If not, the goods are "not shipped in packages" for the purposes of § 4(5), and so the customary freight unit is used. *Aggreko Inc. v. L.E.P. International, Ltd*, 780 F. Supp. 429, 1992 AMC 1127 (S.D. Tex. 1991); *G.E. Power Systems Inc. v. Industrial Maritime Carriers (Bahamas), Inc.*, 89 F. Supp. 2d 782 (E.D. La. 2000) (both holding that a large unpackaged item did not constitute a "package" for limitation purposes, notwithstanding the entry "one" in the "number of packages or units" column on the bill of lading). This argument was unsuccessful in *Fireman's Fund, supra*.

When the bill of lading does not provide a solution, and the cargo is not containerized, the general rule is that cargo must be "sufficiently wrapped, bundled or tied" (*Mitsui & Co. v. American Export Lines, Inc.*, 636 F.2d 807, 822, 1981 AMC 331 (2d Cir. 1981)) in order to be a COGSA package. The cases indicate that when cargo is fully boxed or crated and the identity of the goods concealed, it is a package, regardless of its size, shape or weight. *Hartford Fire Insurance Co. v. Pacific Far East Line, Inc.*, 491 F.2d 960, 1974 AMC 1475 (9th Cir.), *cert. denied*, 419 U.S. 873, 955 S. Ct. 134, 42 L. Ed. 2d 112 (1974). The theory behind this rule is that carriers and their agents, for their own insurance purposes, need to know the nature and value of the cargo they carry and should not be required to guess the value of the cargo carried, when they have not been provided with an opportunity to examine the cargo themselves. In order to protect carriers who cannot confirm the value of the cargo, because it is concealed, the courts find that concealed cargo is a single COGSA package. *General Electric Co. v. Inter-Ocean Shipping*, 862 F. Supp. 166, 1995 AMC 871 (S.D. Tex. 1994).

(b) *Non-containerized Cargo: Partially Enclosed Goods*

The most difficult package cases are those in which the cargo is partially packaged. However, it is not clear how much packaging is required before the goods will be considered a COGSA "package". Generally, if goods are fully exposed to plain view they will not be a COGSA package, but, if goods are completely concealed, they will be considered a package. When faced with cases involving partially packaged goods, most courts rely heavily upon the expression of the parties in the bill of lading, but this is not always true.

In *Tamini v. Salen Dry Cargo AB*, 866 F.2d 741, 743, 1989 AMC 892 (5th Cir. 1989), it was held that a drilling rig was not a package because it was "for the most part fully exposed; no appurtenances or packaging were attached to facilitate its handling during transportation ... ." The Court noted that freight charges were calculated on a weight basis rather than per package and limited carrier's liability by reference to the customary freight unit.

In *Hartford Fire* the court held that an electric transformer on a skid was not a package. This decision is contrary to another court's finding that a toggle press on a skid *was* a package, *Aluminios Pozuelo Ltd. v. S.S. Navigator*, 407 F.2d 152, 1968 AMC 2532 (2d Cir. 1968). In *Hartford Fire*, the Court reasoned that an unpackaged transformer does not become a package simply because it is attached to a skid. By contrast, in *Aluminios* the Court relied heavily on the parties' description of the skid as a package in the bill of lading, but also stated that packaged cargo was "a class of cargo, irrespective of size, shape or weight, to which some packaging preparation for transportation has been made which facilities handling, but which does not necessarily conceal or completely enclose the goods." *Aluminos*, 407 F.2d at 155. Surprisingly, the Court did not comment on the contents of the bill of lading in *Hartford Fire*.

Pallets have also been held to be packages. *Standard Electrica, S.A. v. Hamburg Sudamerikanische Dampfschiffahrts-Gessellschaft*, 375 F.2d 943, 1967 AMC 881 (2d Cir.), *cert. denied*, 389 U.S. 831, 88 S.Ct. 97, 19 L.Ed. 2d 89 (1967). In *Standard Electrica*, the bill of lading, dock receipt, commercial invoice and claim letter, all indicated that the parties intended the pallets would be considered packages for the purpose of carriage. Although a container case, the court's decision in *Seguros "Illimani"* similarly advocates heavy reliance upon the unit listed in the "NO OF PKGS" column in the bill of lading in order to determine the parties' intentions.

(c) *Containerized Cargo*

MONICA TEXTILE CORPORATION v. S.S. TANA

952 F.2d 636, 1992 AMC 609 (2d Cir. 1991)

McLAUGHLIN, Circuit Judge:

We are (once again) presented with "the latest skirmish in the age old war between shippers and carriers over their respective rights and liabilities." *Matsushita Elec. Corp. v. S.S. Aegis Spirit*, 414 F. Supp. 894, 897 (W.D. Wash. 1976). This case requires us to revisit the issue whether a massive shipping container is a "package" for purposes of the $500 per-package limitation on liability of the Carriage of Goods by Sea Act ("COGSA"), 46 U.S.C. App. § 1304(5).

Holding that the single shipping container was the relevant COGSA package, the district court entered a $500 judgment for the shipper. We now reverse and hold that each of the 76 bales of cloth stowed inside the container is a separate package for COGSA purposes.

Background

Monica Textile Corporation ("Monica" or the "shipper") engaged the defendants-carriers to transport a single 20-foot shipping container from Africa to Savannah, Georgia. The parties' bill of lading disclosed that the container, which Monica had stuffed and sealed, held 76 bales of cotton cloth. The goods were damaged in transit and Monica brought suit in the District Court for the Southern District of New York (SAND, J.) to recover for the loss.

The carriers moved for partial summary judgment limiting their liability to $500 pursuant to COGSA's liability limitation provision, 46 U.S.C. App. § 1304(5). The district court initially denied the motion, holding "that where the bill of lading prepared by the carrier's agent discloses a specific number of identifiable units as the contents of the container, those units [the bales of cloth] constitute the package" for purposes of COGSA's limitation on liability. *Monica Textile Corp. v. S.S. Tana*, 731 F. Supp. 124, 127 (S.D.N.Y. 1990) ["*Monica I*"].

Shortly thereafter, this court decided *Seguros "Illimani" S.A. v. M/V Popi P*, 929 F.2d 89 (2d Cir. 1991), which held that for COGSA purposes the number of packages specified in the "No. of Pkgs." column of the bill of lading is generally controlling. *Id.* at 94. In the present case, though the "DESCRIPTION OF GOODS" column of the bill of lading stated that the contents of the container consisted of 76 bales of cotton cloth, the "No. of Pkgs." column of the bill of lading had the number "1" typed in, and a line labeled "Total Number of Packages or Units in Words (Total Column 19 [No. of Pkgs. column])," had the word "ONE" typed in. In light of these facts, Judge Sand permitted the carriers to renew their summary judgment motion to limit their liability to $500, and the district court reversed itself, holding that our intervening decision in Seguros compelled a finding that the single container, rather than the 76 bales stowed therein, was the relevant COGSA package. *See Monica Textile Corp. v. S.S. Tana*, 765 F. Supp. 1194, 1195-96 (S.D.N.Y. 1991) ["*Monica II*"]. Because the carriers conceded liability, the district court entered judgment for Monica in the amount of $500.

Monica appeals the judgment of the district court, maintaining that the 76 individual bales of cloth, not the solitary shipping container, were the appropriate COGSA packages. We agree and therefore reverse the judgment of the district court.

Discussion

The district court reversed itself in *Monica II* on the basis of *Seguros*, which it read

as establishing a bright-line rule for determining the number of COGSA packages from the bill of lading. The number of packages is the number appearing in the "No. of Pkgs." column of the bill, unless other evidence of the parties' intent plainly contradicts the applicability of that number, or unless the item referred to by that number is incapable of qualifying as a COGSA package.

Monica II, 765 F. Supp. at 1195-96. The district court's characterization of the *Seguros* rule is accurate, as far as it goes. *Seguros*, however, involved 600 separate steel-strapped bundles, each containing 15 tin ingots. The issue therefore was whether there were 600 "packages" or 9,000 (600 x 15) "packages". Most significantly, our *Seguros* decision did not purport to apply to containers, and the district court's application of the *Seguros* rule to the container context was erroneous. An understanding of the "container" cases is necessary to appreciate our present holding that *Seguros* should not be extended to containers.

The Container Cases

Long before COGSA was enacted, industrialized nations recognized the need to reconcile the desire of carriers to limit their potential liability with their vastly superior bargaining power over shippers. *See* H.R. Rep. No. 2218, 74th Cong., 2d Sess. 6-9 (1936); *Mitsui & Co. v. America Export Lines, Inc.*, 636 F.2d 807, 814-15 (2d Cir. 1981); *Comment, Containerization, the Per Package Limitation, and the Concept of "Fair Opportunity,"* 11 Mar. Law. 123, 124 (1986). The nations at the Brussels Convention of 1924 balanced these competing concerns with a per-package limitation on liability. *See* International Convention for the Unification of Certain Rules Relating to Bills of Lading, Aug. 25, 1924, 51 Stat. 233, 120 L.N.T.S. 155 (1931-32), *reprinted in* A. Knauth, The American Law of Ocean Bills of Lading 37-72 (4th ed. 1953); Note, *Defining "Package" in the Carriage of Goods by Sea Act*, 60 Tex. L. Rev. 961, 964-66 (1982). The principles established by the Brussels Convention became the template for COGSA. *See Robert C. Herd & Co. v. Krawill Mach. Corp.*, 359 U.S. 297, 301, 79 S. Ct. 766, 769, 3 L. Ed. 2d 820 (1959) ("[t]he legislative history of the Act shows that it was lifted almost bodily from the Hague Rules of 1921, as amended by the Brussels Convention of 1924").

Unhappily, neither the statute nor its legislative history provides any clue as to the meaning of "package" in the Act. *See Aluminios Pozuelo Ltd. v. S.S. Navigator*, 407 F.2d 152, 154 (2d Cir. 1968). Despite the difficulties this lack of guidance engendered,[1] courts managed to muddle through this oft-litigated issue by generally deferring to the intent of the contracting parties when that intent was both clear and reasonable. This intent-approach later became strained by technological advances in the shipping industry. Indeed, "[f]ew, if any, in 1936 could have foreseen the change in the optimum size of shipping units...." *Standard Electrica, S.A. v. Hamburg Sudamerikanische Dampfschifffahrts-Gesellschaft*, 375 F.2d 943, 945 (2d Cir.), *cert. denied*, 389 U.S. 831, 88 S. Ct. 97, 19 L. Ed. 2d 89 (1967).

We first addressed COGSA's application to shipping innovations in *Standard Electrica*, which required us to determine which was the relevant COGSA package: each 60-pound carton or the pallets on which the cartons were bound together. Divining the parties' intent, we held the pallet to be the relevant COGSA package. *See id.* at 946.

The so-called "container revolution", however, "added a new dimension to the problem." *Mitsui*, 636 F.2d at 816. *See generally* Schmeltzer & Peavy, *Prospects and Problems of the Container Revolution*, 1 J. Mar. L. & Com. 203 (1970). Shippers, carriers and industry commentators "speculated at the time whether the courts would adopt the analysis of *Standard Electrica* or fashion a new rule to apply to containers." Note, *The Shipping Container as a*

---

[1] *Compare, e.g., Hartford Fire Ins. Co. v. Pacific Far East Line, Inc.*, 491 F.2d 960, 965 (9th Cir.) (holding that 18-ton electrical transformer bolted to a skid was not a COGSA package), *cert. denied*, 419 U.S. 873, 95 S. Ct. 134, 42 L. Ed. 2d 112 (1974) with *Aluminios Pozuelo Ltd. v. S.S. Navigator*, 407 F.2d 152, 155 (2d Cir.1968) (holding that a 3-ton toggle press bolted to a skid was a COGSA package). *See generally id.* at 154-56 (discussing pre-container cases).

COGSA Package: The Functional Economics Test is Abandoned, 6 Mar. Law. 336, 340 n.16 (1981) (collecting citations). Our decision in *Leather's Best, Inc. v. S.S. Mormaclynx*, 451 F.2d 800 (2d Cir. 1971) (FRIENDLY, C.J.), settled the issue, distinguishing *Standard Electrica* and veering away from our pre-container cases because of our

> belief that the purpose of s 4(5) of COGSA was to set a reasonable figure below which the carrier should not be permitted to limit his liability and that "package" is thus more sensibly related to the unit in which the shipper packed the goods and described them than to a large metal object, functionally a part of the ship, in which the carrier caused them to be "contained."

Id. at 815 (footnote omitted). *Leather's Best* thus stood foursquare for the proposition " 'that a container rarely should be treated as a package.' " *Smythgreyhound v. M/V "Eurygenes"*, 666 F.2d 746, 748 n.5 (2d Cir. 1981) (quoting *Croft & Scully Co. v. M/V Skulptor Vuchetich*, 508 F. Supp. 670, 678 (S.D. Tex. 1981), *aff'd in relevant part*, 664 F.2d 1277 (5th Cir. 1982)).

Although other courts subsequently embraced *Leather's Best, see, e.g., Matsushita Elec. Corp. v. S.S. Aegis Spirit*, 414 F. Supp. 894, 907 (W.D. Wash. 1976), *cited with approval in Mitsui*, 636 F.2d at 819-20, we began to stray from it, in favor of a so-called "functional economics test." Whereas *Leather's Best* held that treating a container as a COGSA package is inconsistent with congressional intent and therefore strongly disfavored, *see Leather's Best*, 451 F.2d at 815; *accord Mitsui*, 636 F.2d at 820-21, the functional economics approach ignored congressional intent in favor of a "law and economics" analysis. *See, e.g., Royal Typewriter Co. v. M/V Kulmerland*, 483 F.2d 645, 648-49 (2d Cir. 1973) (container is presumptively the package where the units inside are not suitable for breakbulk shipment); *Cameco, Inc. v. S.S. American Legion*, 514 F.2d 1291, 1298-99 (2d Cir. 1974).

The reaction to our functional economics approach was swift and overwhelmingly negative, as courts and commentators roundly criticized us for it. *See Croft & Scully Co. v. M/V Skulptor Vuchetich*, 664 F.2d 1277, 1281 n.10 (5th Cir. 1982) (functional economics test "necessitated much judicial guessing work, and we are well rid of it"); *Allstate Ins. Co. v. Inversiones Navieras Imparca, C.A.*, 646 F.2d 169, 172 (5th Cir. Unit B May 1981) (test "was subject to severe criticism from all corners"); *Matsushita*, 414 F. Supp. at 906 (rejecting the test "as contrary to the statute, commercially impracticable and unwise"); DeOrchis, *The Container and the Package Limitation—The Search for Predictability*, 5 J. Mar. L. & Com. 251, 257 (1974); Simon, *The Law of Shipping Containers (pt. 1)*, 5 J. Mar. L. & Com. 507, 522 (1974).

Recognizing that the functional economics test was "basically inconsistent with the holding of *Leather's Best*," and acknowledging the criticism the new approach had drawn, we eventually abandoned it. *See Mitsui*, 636 F.2d at 818-21. Judge Friendly, who had earlier written *Leather's Best*, also authored the *Mitsui* decision, and circulated it to the entire court. *Mitsui* held that when a bill of lading discloses on its face what is inside the container, and those contents may reasonably be considered COGSA packages, then the container is not the COGSA package. *See id.*; *Smythgreyhound*, 666 F.2d at 753. Mitsui settled the law in container cases for this Circuit and has been steadfastly followed. *See, e.g., Binladen BSB Landscaping v. M.V. "Nedlloyd Rotterdam"*, 759 F.2d 1006, 1013 (2d Cir.), *cert. denied*, 474 U.S. 902, 106 S. Ct. 229, 88 L. Ed. 2d 229 (1985); *Smythgreyhound*, 666 F.2d at 753. *Mitsui* and its progeny, moreover, have been followed by courts in other circuits; *see* 2A E. Flynn & G. Raduazzo, Benedict on Admiralty § 167, at 16-34 (7th ed. 1991) ("the *Mitsui-Binladen* approach seems to be gaining favor in the rest of the country"); *see, e.g., Hayes-Leger Assocs., Inc. v. M/V Oriental Knight*, 765 F.2d 1076, 1080 (11th Cir. 1985); *Allstate Ins.*, 646 F.2d at 172; *International Adjusters, Inc. v. Korean Wonis-Son*, 682 F. Supp. 383, 385-86 (N.D. Ill. 1988); and it has been praised by courts and commentators. *See, e.g., Allstate Ins.*, 646 F.2d at 172 & n.1 ("we believe that the rule developed in *Mitsui* and *Leather's Best* is the best judicial solution, in the absence of a legislative solution"); 2A E. Flynn & G. Raduazzo, Benedict on Admiralty § 167, at 16-34 (7th ed. 1991) ("[a]mong other benefits, the *Mitsui-Binladen* approach is consistent with the position of the international community"); Note, *The Shipping Container as a COGSA Package: The Functional Economics Test is Abandoned*, 6 Mar. Law. 336, 345 (1981)

("In terms of predictability and judicial economy, the decision in *Mitsui* is a realistic approach in an area in desperate need of legislative reform.").

Although Mitsui was concerned with containers, a district court later extended it to pallets. *See Allied Int'l Am. Eagle Trading Corp. v. S.S. "Yang Ming"*, 519 F. Supp. 187, 190 (S.D.N.Y. 1981), *rev'd*, 672 F.2d 1055 (2d Cir. 1982). We reversed, holding that containers and pallets are quite different and that "*Standard Electrica* ... is still the law with regard to pallets." *Yang Ming*, 672 F.2d at 1061. In so doing, we methodically documented why our decisions in *Standard Electrica* and *Leather's Best* required distinct analyses for container and non-container cases. *See id.* at 1058-61. We explained:

> [T]he container cases involve factors not found in pallet cases. Because of their size and their function in the shipping industry, containers are ordinarily not considered "packages."
>
> * * *
>
> ... In *Mitsui* ... as in other container cases, the courts must look askance at an agreement which purports to define a container as a "package" because the results of such a limitation can be ludicrous.

Id. at 1061, 1062

We thus rejected any notion that container and non-container cases were interchangeable; they were then and remain now separate lines of authority. They had been uniformly so construed until the present case. *See, e.g., St. Paul Fire & Marine Ins. Co. v. Sea-Land Serv., Inc.*, 735 F. Supp. 129, 133 (S.D.N.Y. 1990) ("containers present different considerations than pallets"); E. Flynn & G. Raduazzo, Benedict on Admiralty § 167, at 16-28 (7th ed. 1991) ("These standards [for determining the relevant COGSA package] vary according to whether or not the cargo is shipped in a container, and the discussion here will therefore treat non-containerized and containerized shipments separately.").

Seguros "Illimani"

We now turn to *Monica II's* application of our *Seguros* decision. The dispute in *Seguros* was whether each bundle of 15 tin ingots, or each individual ingot, constituted the relevant COGSA package. *See Seguros "Illimani" S.A. v. M/V Popi P*, 929 F.2d 89, 92 (2d Cir. 1991). We therefore adopted the following test to settle such controversies:

> The number appearing under the heading "NO. OF PKGS." is our starting point for determining the number of packages for purposes of the COGSA per-package limitation, and unless the significance of that number is plainly contradicted by contrary evidence of the parties' intent, or unless the number refers to items that cannot qualify as "packages," it is also the ending point of our inquiry. "Package" is a term of art in the ocean shipping business, and parties to bills of lading should expect to be held to the number that appears under a column whose heading so unmistakably refers to the number of packages.

Seguros, 929 F.2d at 94.[2] As between bales, boxes, bundles, cartons, cases, crates and other COGSA packages, the *Seguros* rule is as sensible as it is straightforward. But all "packages" were not created equal, as our container cases make plain. Containers raise unique issues which we have addressed in a distinct line of case law.

In light of our significant container jurisprudence, the *Seguros* rule is inapposite in the container context. In *Seguros*, the parties disputed whether the ingots or the bundles containing the ingots should be considered the relevant COGSA packages. No one even questioned the district court's holding that "[i]t is clear that the container

---

[2] *Compare Smythgreyhound*, 666 F.2d at 748 n.4 & 751 ("on their face the bills of lading reflect the lack of agreement, insofar as they refer to both 'containers' and 'cartons'") *and Matsushita*, 414 F. Supp. at 906 (no mutual understanding with resect to what constitutes COGSA package where carrier and shipper had no direct or indirect dealings). Other container cases have accorded little or no weight to the number in the "number of packages" column. *See, e.g., Binladen*, 759 F.2d at 1009 & 1016 n.11; *Leather's Best*, 451 F.2d at 804.

is not the appropriate 'package' in this case." *Seguros "Illimani" S.A. v. M/V Popi P*, 735 F. Supp. 108, 111 (S.D.N.Y. 1990), *aff'd*, 929 F.2d 89 (2d Cir. 1991). Viewed in context, then, *Seguros* simply does not purport to apply when a container is alleged to be the relevant COGSA package. Indeed, that *Seguros* would, in dictum, overrule *sub silentio* a long line of Second Circuit precedent is inconceivable. Notwithstanding the insertion in the number-of-packages column(s) of the bill of lading of a number reflecting the number of containers, where the bill of lading discloses on its face what is inside the container(s) and those contents may reasonably be considered COGSA packages, the latter, not the container(s), are the COGSA packages. The district court's holding to the contrary in *Monica II* is erroneous.

Parties' Intent and Bill of Lading

We next consider the carriers' argument that the bill of lading manifests the parties' agreement that the container is the relevant COGSA package.

In non-container cases we have generally deferred to the parties' intent, as manifested by their bill of lading, in determining what unit is the relevant COGSA package. *See, e.g., Seguros*, 929 F.2d at 95; *Standard Electrica*, 375 F.2d at 946. Such deference to the parties' wishes permits commercial flexibility without offending the statute.

COGSA, however, requires that we view container cases through a different prism. Thus, in container cases we must " 'take a critical look' " at clauses purporting to define the container as the COGSA package, *Smythgreyhound*, 666 F.2d at 750 (quoting *Mitsui*, 636 F.2d at 815). Accordingly, we have consistently cast a jaundiced eye upon language purporting to embody such an agreement.

The reason for this skepticism is that such agreements run against the grain of COGSA. *See id.*; *Binladen*, 759 F.2d at 1012-13 ("classification of [the container] as a 'package' would violate the purpose of s 4(5) by permitting the carrier to limit its liability unduly"); *Yang Ming*, 672 F.2d at 1062 ("the courts must look askance at an agreement which purports to define a container as a 'package' "); *Mitsui*, 636 F.2d at 817 (*Leather's Best* "acknowledg[ed] that treating the containers as packages ... was precluded by the underlying purpose of [COGSA] § 4(5)"). Thus, "our repeatedly-expressed reluctance for sound reasons to treat a container as a package", *Binladen*, 759 F.2d at 1015, compels us to scrutinize the carriers' claim that they agreed with Monica to treat the container as the COGSA package.

The bill of lading in this case discloses on its face that 76 bales of cloth were stowed in the container. Even though that disclosure triggers *Mitsui's* presumption that the container is not the COGSA package, *see Mitsui*, 636 F.2d at 821; *see also Smythgreyhound*, 666 F.2d at 752 ("[*Mitsui*] adopted a general rule that where the bill of lading discloses the contents of the container, then the container is not the COGSA package.") (brackets in original), the carriers maintain that the bill of lading nevertheless discloses an agreement with Monica that the single container was the relevant package.

They emphasize two clauses appearing on the reverse of the carriers' standard bill of lading forms.[3] Clause 2 of the bill of lading provides, in relevant part:

The word "package" shall include each container where the container is stuffed and sealed by the Merchant or on his behalf, although the Shipper may have furnished in the Particulars herein the contents of such sealed container. (See Clause 11).

Clause 11 states:

Neither the Carrier nor the vessel shall in any event be or become liable for any loss or damage to or in connection with the transportation of goods in an amount exceeding U.S. $500 per package.... Where container(s) is stuffed by Shipper or on his behalf, and the container is sealed, the Carrier's liability will be limited to U.S.

---

[3] The district court was generous in its characterization of the typeface on the reverse of the bill of lading as "miniscule [sic]." *Monica I*, 731 F. Supp. at 126. Whereas standard typeface (like the body of this opinion) has six lines per inch, the carriers' boilerplate has sixteen lines per inch.

$500 with respect to the contents of each container, except when the Shipper declares value on the face hereof (Box 26) and pays additional charges on such declared value (Box 23). The freight charged on sealed containers when no higher valuation is declared by the Shipper is based on a value of U.S. $500 per container.

The carriers maintain that these clauses articulate an agreement between them and Monica to treat the container as the package.

The carriers' argument is premised on dicta in our container cases suggesting that parties to a bill of lading have the right to agree to treat a container as the relevant COGSA package. For example, in *Smythgreyhound*, we remarked in a footnote that parties may

agree between themselves that the container will be the COGSA "package," especially in cases where COGSA does not apply *ex proprio vigore*.... [W]e hold today that in the absence of clear and unambiguous language indicating agreement on the definition of "package," then we will conclusively presume that the container is not the package where the bill of lading discloses the container's contents.

Smythgreyhound, 666 F.2d at 753 n.20 (emphasis in original). Thus, the otherwise "clear rule that where the contents of the container are disclosed in the bill of lading then the container is not the COGSA package", *id.* at 753, seemingly has an exception: we will treat the container as the "package" if the bill of lading discloses that the parties have so agreed in terms that are explicit and unequivocal.

This supposed exception to the *Mitsui* rule, however, is more apparent than real. No appellate precedent has been found applying this exception to a bill of lading like the one before us now. And for good reason: our container cases recognize that when a bill of lading refers to both containers and other units susceptible of being COGSA packages, it is inherently ambiguous. In *Smythgreyhound*, we candidly admitted "that no shipper ever actually intends that its recovery will be limited to $500 per container, or that any carrier, in the absence of an express agreement, intends that the recovery should exceed $500 per container." *Smythgreyhound*, 666 F.2d at 748 n.4; *see also id.* at 751 ("on their face the bills of lading reflect the lack of agreement, insofar as they refer to both 'containers' and 'cartons' "); *Matsushita*, 414 F. Supp. at 906 ("it is clear that there was not and, realistically, could not have been any mutual understanding between [the shipper and carrier] with respect to the COGSA package"). *Mitsui* and its progeny resolve this ambiguity against the carriers. *See Mitsui*, 636 F.2d at 822-23.

It is not without significance that the two boilerplate clauses upon which the carriers rely have consistently failed to persuade us in the past that the container is intended to be the package. Clause 11, for example, is essentially the same one we ignored in *Leather's Best*, even though in *Leather's Best* the clause appeared on the front of the bill of lading in capital letters:

SHIPPER HEREBY AGREES THAT CARRIER'S LIABILITY IS LIMITED TO $500 WITH RESPECT TO THE ENTIRE CONTENTS OF EACH CONTAINER EXCEPT WHEN SHIPPER DECLARES A HIGHER VALUATION AND SHALL HAVE PAID ADDITIONAL FREIGHT ON SUCH DECLARED VALUATION PURSUANT TO APPROPRIATE RULE IN THE CONTINENTAL NORTH ATLANTIC WEST-BOUND FREIGHT CONFERENCE TARIFF.

Leather's Best, 451 F.2d at 804. *Compare Monica I*, 731 F. Supp. at 126 (similar clause "in miniscule [sic] type face" on reverse of bill of lading).

Similarly, Clause 2 is virtually indistinguishable from one rejected in *Matsushita* which provided:

where the cargo has been either packed into container(s) or unitized into similar article(s) of transport by or on behalf of the Merchant, it is expressly agreed that the number of such container(s) or similar article(s) of transport shown on the face hereof shall be considered as the number of the package(s) or unit(s) for the purpose of the application of the limitation of liability provided for herein.

Matsushita, 414 F. Supp. at 899;[4] *see also St. Paul Fire & Marine Ins.*, 735 F. Supp. at 132 ("Allowing the carrier ... to insert an essentially unbargained-for definition of 'package' in the bill of lading would effectively eliminate the protection COGSA was meant to afford shippers."); *Monica I*, 731 F. Supp. at 127 (*Mitsui* and its progeny "control [ ] despite the language of clause 11").

Because the bill of lading in this case is ambiguous on its face and Clauses 2 and 11 are unbargained-for boilerplate, we cannot say that Monica and the carriers unequivocally agreed to treat the container as the COGSA package. Thus, the exception to *Mitsui's* rule is not applicable; and the 76 bales, not the container, are the relevant units for determining the extent of the carriers' liability under the statute.

This conclusion is consistent with our longstanding recognition of what every shipper knows: that "bills of lading are contracts of adhesion ambiguities in which must be resolved against the carrier...." *Mitsui*, 636 F.2d at 822-23. Clauses 2 and 11, like others printed on the back of a form bill of lading, "carr[y] little weight toward establishing intent, being [ ] unilateral, self-serving declaration[s] by the carrier which w[ere] not negotiated by the parties and could scarcely be discerned by the unaided eye in the maze of microscopic and virtually illegible provisions on the back[ ] of the bill[ ] of lading." *Matsushita*, 414 F. Supp. at 906 n.52; *see also St. Paul Fire & Marine Ins. Co. v. Sea-Land Serv., Inc.*, 735 F. Supp. 129, 132 & n.4 (S.D.N.Y. 1990).

Conclusion

Seguros provides a bright-line rule in non-container cases that, "the more consistently it is followed, the more it should minimize disputes." *Seguros*, 929 F.2d at 94. Similarly, *Mitsui* and its progeny continue to provide a simple rule in container cases, a rule that is easily administered by the courts and readily amenable to *ex ante* application by contracting parties. Together, these rules foster predictability in this nettlesome area of the law. Applied faithfully and consistently, they should assist carriers, shippers and the courts to "avoid the pains of litigation." *Standard Electrica*, 375 F.2d at 945.

Monica I correctly construed and applied our continer jurisprudence; *Monica II* did not. Accordingly, the judgment of the district court in *Monica II* is reversed.

Note: Unpackaged items within containers.

In both *Alternative Glass Supplies v. M/V NOMZI*, 1999 AMC 1080 (S.D.N.Y. 1999) and *Orient Overseas Container Line (U.K.), Ltd. v. Sea-Land Service, Inc.*, 122 F. Supp. 2d 481, 2001 AMC 1005 (S.D.N.Y. 2000), it was held that the container was the "package" for limitation purposes because the contents of the container were unpackaged. Both cases focused on the following words used by the *Monica Textile* court: " when a bill of lading discloses on its face what is inside the container, *and those contents may reasonably be considered COGSA packages*, the container is not the COGSA package" (emphasis added). Although the bills of lading referred to the number of items inside the container, those items were not sufficiently "wrapped, bundled or tied" to be COGSA packages. As a result, the container itself was held to be the package in both cases.

---

[4] Judge Friendly praised *Matsushita* and adopted its reasoning in *Mitsui. See* 636 F.2d at 819-21 (quoting Judge Beeks' "outstanding" *Matsushita* opinion); *see also Smythgreyhound*, 666 F.2d at 750 n.11 (quoting *Matsushita* and repeating *Mitsui's* reference to Judge Beeks as " 'an experienced admiralty lawyer before his appointment to the bench'").

VISTAR, S.A. v. M/V SEALAND EXPRESS

680 F. Supp. 855, 1987 AMC 2881 (S.D. Tex. 1987)

DeANDA, United States District Judge:

* * *

The relevant facts are set forth in the Court's prior findings of fact and conclusions of law. This is a suit for damage to a varnishing machine sustained during transport from Le Havre, France, to Nuevo Laredo, Mexico. The varnishing machine was packed for transportation, presumably intact, in a single, large, wooden case. Defendant Sea-Land Service (Sea-Land) took delivery from the shipper in Le Havre and issued its bill of lading covering the movement to Nuevo Laredo. The case containing the varnishing machine was discharged from Sea-Land's vessel in Houston and delivered to Defendant Victory Transport Company, Inc. (Victory) under contract with Sea-Land, to complete the passage to Nuevo Laredo. Victory's driver took the wrong route and drove under a railroad bridge with inadequate vertical clearance. The package containing the varnishing machine struck the bridge and the machine was damaged. Plaintiff claims damages of $90,446.86.

At trial on the merits, Defendants contended that, by agreement of the parties, the terms of Carriage of Goods By Sea Act, 46 U.S.C. §§ 1300 *et seq.*, ("COGSA"), were applicable to the entire movement from Le Havre to Nuevo Laredo. Defendants contended that Plaintiff's loss was due to negligent navigation and thus excused by 46 U.S.C. § 1304(2)(a). In the alternative, Defendants argued that 46 U.S.C. § 1304(5) limited the liability of the carrier for cargo damage to $500.00 per package.

After a bench trial, the Court decided that Defendants had not committed an unreasonable deviation, and that the loss was due to negligence in navigation within the meaning of 46 U.S.C. § 1304(2)(a). The Court entered judgment that Plaintiff take nothing. The Court did not reach the damages question.

On appeal, the Fifth Circuit reversed this Court's holding that the loss was due to negligent navigation....The case was remanded for a determination of damages and entry of judgment consistent with the opinion on appeal.

At the trial, it was shown that Plaintiff's shipment consisted of one package. The bill of lading stated that in the event of damage of goods exceeding $500.00 per package, the value of the goods shall be deemed to be $500.00 per package or unit, unless the nature and higher value of the goods have been declared by the shipper and extra charge paid as provided in the carrier's tariff. [Plaintiff's Exhibit 10, at n.17]. COGSA provides that neither the carrier nor the ship shall become liable for any loss or damage to or in connection with the transportation of goods in an amount exceeding $500.00 per package, unless the nature and value of such goods have been declared by the shipper before shipment and inserted in the bill of lading. 46 U.S.C. § 1304(5). This provision of COGSA has been given effect repeatedly. *See, e.g., Gebr. Bellmer K.G. v. Terminal Services Houston, Inc.*, 711 F.2d 622 (5th Cir. 1983) (four crates loaded on container flat were four COGSA packages). *Wuerttembergische v. M/V Stuttgart Express*, 711 F.2d 621 (5th Cir. 1983) (winding block for nuclear reactor enclosed in crate was COGSA package); *Brown & Root, Inc. v. M/V Peisander*, 648 F.2d 415 (5th Cir. 1981) (crate of "machinery" was COGSA package).

* * *

In the alternative, Plaintiff argues that the varnishing machine was not a package within the meaning of COGSA. Plaintiff relies on *Allstate Ins. Co. v. Inversiones Navierras Imparca*, 646 F.2d 169 (5th Cir. 1981), in support of this proposition. *Allstate Insurance Co.*, involved 341 cartons of electronic equipment that were loaded into the carrier's container and described in the bill of lading as "one container with 341 cartons." The Court held that where the shipper placed goods in packages, as used in the ordinary sense of the word, and then loaded those packages into a container furnished by the carrier, and the number of packages in the container was disclosed to the carrier in the bill of lading, each package within the container constituted one "package" for the purposes of § 1304(5). 646 F.2d at 172-73. In the case at bar, Plaintiff packed the varnishing machine in its own case and delivered it to Defendant for carriage. The Court finds that this crate was a single package within the meaning of COGSA.

Plaintiff next asserts that inquiry as to the "customary freight unit" is called for in this case. This is necessary, however, only if the goods are not shipped in a package. 46 U.S.C. § 1304(5). Typical of cases in which the "customary freight unit" is the limitation unit are *Waterman S.S. Corp. v. United States S.R. & M. Co.*, 155 F.2d 687, 693 (5th Cir., 1946), *cert. denied*, 329 U.S. 761 (1946) (pieces of structural steel shipped unpackaged); *The Bill*, 55 F. Supp. 780 (D. Md. 1944), *aff'd.* 145 F.2d 470 (4th Cir. 1944) (bulk oil); and *Caterpillar Americas Company v. S. S. Sea Roads*, 231 F. Supp. 647 (S.D. Fla. 1964) (tractor delivered to vessel under its own power). The Court believes that none of these cases applies to the case at bar. Thus, Plaintiff's customary freight unit argument is without merit.

It is not unfair to limit Vistar's recovery to $500.00 because both the COGSA limitation provision and the bill-of-lading term provide that the $500.00 limitation is applicable only if the shipper has not declared a higher value. Defendant's bill of lading has a clear provision on its face for a declaration of higher value, and a plain warning as to the effect of not declaring such value. [Plaintiff's exhibit 10]. Defendant points out that the shipper chose not to declare a higher value, presumably to avoid the *ad valorem* freight charge. Plaintiff should not now be heard to complain of the application of the clear limitation terms of COGSA and the bill of lading.

Plaintiff, finally, argues that the provisions of the bill of lading are merely terms of the contract of carriage which, like other contractual terms, call out for judicial interpretation in case of dispute, citing *Croft & Skully Co. v. M/V Skulptor Vuchetich*, 664 F.2d 1277, 1280 (5th Cir. 1982). If this is the case, then straightforward contract analysis is called for in this action to determine the intent of the parties, and entries on the bill of lading are important evidence of the intent of the parties to the shipping contract. *Binladen BSB Landscaping v. M/V "NEDLLOYD ROTTERDAM"*, 759 F.2d 1006, 1012 (2d Cir. 1985), *cert. denied*, 106 S. Ct. 229 (1985). In determining the intent and mutual understanding of the parties, the Court is permitted to examine the documents indicating the intent of the parties to determine the meaning of the term "package." *Crispin Co. v. M/V Morning Park*, 578 F. Supp. 359, 360 (S.D. Tex. 1984).

In this action, the nature of goods being shipped is fully disclosed in a twenty-five word description in Spanish in the bill of lading. The word "caja" (meaning "box" or possibly "package") which precedes that twenty-five word description is significant. No where in the description is an attempt to declare higher value, escaping the COGSA package limitation.

Plaintiff at this point refers the Court to cases which have held that similar notations did not stand for "packages" for COGSA purposes, citing *Binladen BSB Landscaping* (where in bill of lading under column labeled "Number of Packages" were listed the number of containers shipped and total number of plants in each container, containers found not to be "COGSA packages."); *Bumblebee Seafoods v. S.S. KIKU MARU*, 1978 AMC 1586 (D. Md. 1978) (where under "Packages" column on bill of lading was the number 67,222, representing number of fish shipped, court holding that the number 67,222 did not constitute COGSA packages). The Court does not see these cases raise issues around facts where several units were packed within a container. This case involves a single, albeit an expensive, piece of machinery, packed intact in a single wooden box.

Plaintiff also refers the Court to cases involving large pieces of machinery where the machinery was not deemed to be a COGSA "package" and the Court made the determination of what was a customary freight unit, citing *Hartford Fire Insurance Co. v. Pacific Far East Line*, 491 F.2d 960, 965 (9th Cir. 1974) (transformer attached to wooden skid for purposes of protection and facilitation of movement not COGSA package); *Gulf Italia Co. v. American Export Lines*, 263 F.2d 135 (2d Cir. 1959) (tractor partially encased with wooden planks, partially covered with paper packing was not COGSA package); *Malloy v. Oregon Rainbow*, 1980 AMC 2183 (M.D. Fla. 1980) (yacht shipped in cradle was not COGSA package); *Eaton Corp. v. S.S. Galeona*, 474 F. Supp. 819 (S.D.N.Y. 1979) (unpackaged tractor was not COGSA package); *Kansas Packing Co. v. Atlantic Mutual Insurance*, 1984 AMC 277 (S.D.N.Y. 1983) (generator's loss estimated on basis of 1.5 ton "customary freight unit"). The Court finds none of these cases are applicable to the case at bar. The varnishing machine was encased in a single wooden box thus it was not a piece of machinery only partially packaged. No determination of a customary freight unit is then necessary based on this argument.

Plaintiff also pleads for $30,150.00 in attorney's fees in its original complaint. Although Congress undoubtedly could have explicitly provided for the award of attorney's fees to a party prevailing in a suit based upon COGSA, no such statutory authorization appears in the Act. *Noritake Co., Inc. v. M/V Hellenic Champion*, 627 F.2d 724, 730 (5th Cir. 1980). Nor is there any other federal statutory authorization for the award of attorney's fees in this type of admiralty proceeding. *See Dempsey & Associates, Inc. v. S.S. Sea Star*, 500 F.2d 409, 411 (2d Cir. 1974). Absent some statutory authorization, the prevailing party in an admiralty case is generally not entitled to an award of attorney's fees. *Sandoval v. Mitsui Sempaku K.K. Tokyo*, 460 F.2d 1163, 1171 (5th Cir. 1972); *American Union Transport Co. v. Aguadilla Terminal, Inc.*, 302 F.2d 394, 396 (1st Cir. 1962); *Compagnia Amonima Venezelana de Navegacion v. A. G. Solar & Co.*, 1977 AMC 1786, 1789 (S.D. Tex. 1977). *See also, Crispin Co. v. M/V Morning Park*, 578 F. Supp. 359 (S.D. Tex. 1984); *Platoro Ltd., Inc. v. Unidentified Remains, Etc.*, 695 F.2d 893, 905-06 (5th Cir. 1983), *cert. denied* 464 U.S. 818 (1983); *Brazosport Towing Co., Inc. v. Donjon Marine Co., Inc.*, 556 F. Supp. 640, 644 (S.D. Tex. 1983). Although there are some judicially created exceptions to this general rule, none are applicable here. On this basis, the Court

ORDERS that Defendant's motion for final judgment on mandate is GRANTED and Plaintiff's motion to amend final judgment is DENIED. Plaintiff shall take $500.00 in actual damages in accordance with the provisions of COGSA plus prejudgment interest thereon from three months following the date of shipment, June 6, 1982, to present at 7.00% per annum for a total of *$703.43*. Defendant is to pay all taxable costs, and post judgment interest at 7.00% per annum until judgment is paid.

This is a Final Judgment.

(d) Customary Freight Unit

1. *Introductory Note*

Carriers' liability for goods not shipped in packages is calculated by reference to the customary freight unit. COGSA provides that carriers' may limit their liability to $500 per customary freight unit. The customary freight unit is usually the actual unit of measurement which was used by the parties to calculate freight. The bill of lading and published tariff schedule should provide this information. However, if this information is not available, the usual unit of measurement used by the industry for cargo of that type will be applied. *Granite State Insurance Co. v. M/V Caraibe*, 825 F. Supp. 1113, 1994 AMC 680 (D. Puerto Rico 1993). In *Petition of Isbrandtsen Co.*, 201 F.2d 281, 286, 1953 AMC 86, 92 (2d Cir. 1953), the court held that uncrated locomotives were not packages, and applied the $500 per customary freight unit limitation. As freight for the shipment of 10 locomotives had been calculated at $10,000 per locomotive, the court limited the carrier's liability to $500 per locomotive. Total liability was $5,000.

Cargo which has been held not to have been shipped in packages includes cargo shipped: free standing and not enclosed in a box or crate, *Hartford Fire*, 491 F.2d 960, 1974 AMC 1475; without any packaging at all; *Binladen*, 759 F.2d 1006, 1985 AMC 2113 (2d Cir.), *cert. denied*, 474 U.S. 902, 106 S. Ct. 229 (1985); in its permanently enclosed condition, *Solar Turbines, Inc. v. S.S. "Al Shiadiah"*, 575 F. Supp. 939, 1984 AMC 2002 (S.D.N.Y. 1983); and cargo which is "for the most part fully exposed," *Tamini*, 866 F.2d 741, 743, 1989 AMC 892. Unboxed motor vehicles are not packages, *Aetna Ins. v. M/V Lash Italia*, 858 F.2d 190, 1989 AMC 135 (4th Cir. 1988); and neither are loose tractors, *Caterpillar Americas Co. v. S.S. Sea Roads*, 231 F. Supp. 647, 1964 AMC 2646 (S.D. Fla. 1964), *aff'd*, 364 F.2d 829, 1967 AMC 290 (5th Cir. 1966); nor are free standing locomotives, *Petition of Isbrandtsen Co.*, 201 F.2d at 286, 1953 AMC at 92.

2. *Application of the Customary Freight Unit*

In *Ulrich Ammann Building Equipment, Ltd. v. M/V Monsun*, 609 F. Supp. 87, 1985 AMC 1965 (S.D.N.Y. 1985), court had to decide how to apply the "customary freight unit" standard to 20 tractors that had been carried and lost.

* * *

The "guiding policy" of COGSA is "to limit liability of common carriers for damaged cargo where the value of the cargo is not known to the carrier." *THE MORMACOAK*, 451 F.2d 24, 26 (2d Cir. 1971). The statute was designed "to protect the shipping industry and to throw the burden to the shipper to declare the value of the goods and pay a higher tariff if he wished to have higher liability on the part of the carrier." *Caterpillar Americas Company v. Steamship Sea Roads*, 231 F. Supp. 647, 650 (S.D. Fla. 1964), *aff'd*, 364 F.2d 829 (5th Cir. 1966).

The words "customary freight unit," which describe the unit as to which the shipper's liability is limited to $500, refer not to the physical shipping unit but to the unit of cargo "customarily used as the basis for the calculation of the freight rate to be charged." *The*

MORMACOAK, supra, 451 F.2d at 25; *The Edmund Fanning*, 201 F.2d 281, 286 (2d Cir. 1953). Thus, where a freight charge is computed on a lump sum basis for each of several pieces of equipment, the relevant customary freight unit is each piece of equipment. *Caterpillar Americas Co., supra*, 231 F. Supp. at 650. If a freight charge is computed on a lump sum basis for an entire shipment, the relevant customary freight unit is the entire shipment.

In the case at hand, the parties agree that the tractors were shipped in an unpackaged form and are in a disagreement only as to the relevant customary freight unit. If the customary freight unit is held to be the entire shipment of thirty tractors, Ammann's recovery is limited to $500 under both COGSA and the terms of the bill of lading. Similarly, if the customary freight unit is held to be each piece of equipment shipped, Ammann's recovery is limited to $500 for each tractor. If, however, the customary freight unit is per measurement ton, as it would be if the ordinary tariff rates rather than the amended rates were held to control, Ammann would be entitled to recover $500 for each measurement ton shipped or approximately $65,000 per tractor.

The Ship Defendants assert that the parties agreed to a lump sum rate for the entire shipment of thirty scrapers on one or more vessels. They contend that there was no weight or measurement basis for the freight charge and that the customary freight unit agreed upon by the parties was instead the entire shipment. They point to both the filed amended tariff and the freight list, which states that the twenty tractors were shipped under a lump sum rate, as evidence of this agreement. They argue that Ammann took a calculated risk in agreeing to the lump sum freight basis because while it reduced the amount of COGSA coverage to which Ammann would be entitled, it also gave them a considerable savings on freight cost.

In response, Ammann asserts that the Ship Defendants have failed to prove that the customary freight unit to be applied was the special amended rate rather than the regular weight/measurement tariff. It claims that there is no evidence as to what the phrase "Freight as Agreed" was intended to mean. The thrust of Ammann's argument is that because the shipment in question was for twenty rather than thirty tractors, this court cannot assume that the shipment was covered by the rates listed in the amended tariff. It argues that while the lump sum rate was for thirty units, the bill of lading covers a shipment of only twenty units and that there is no actual evidence of the freight actually charged for the shipment. It also points to the fact that like the regular tariff, the bill of lading used kilograms and centimeters to describe the shipment, whereas the filed amended tariff used tons and feet.

Despite Ammann's contentions, the Ship Defendants have successfully met their burden of establishing that the shipment of twenty tractors was made on a lump sum basis. The amended tariff expressly lists the tractors as being on a lump sum rather than weight/measurement rate basis. *See The MORMACOAK, supra*, 327 F. Supp. at 669 (flat rate in filed amended tariff applied despite plaintiff's claim that missing bill of lading computed freight on weight basis). Ammann claims that because of the discrepancies in numbers the amended tariff pertaining to thirty tractors should not be applicable to a shipment of only twenty tractors. However, there is an express statement in the tariff that the tractors were to be shipped on one or two vessels. Furthermore, there is nothing on either the bill of lading or the freight list or in this record to suggest that the parties intended the shipment to be dealt with on a different basis than that listed in the amended tariff. The listing of weight and measurement and a measurement different from that on the tariff, does not obviate the implications of a lump sum payment. *See Freedman & Slater, Inc. v. M.V. TOFEVO*, 222 F. Supp. 964, 973 (S.D.N.Y. 1963). Courts have held that even where a lump sum rate is arrived at by using weight and measurement, the weight/measurement does not become the freight unit for the transaction. *See General Motors Corp. v. Moore-McCormack Lines, Inc.*, 451 F.2d 24, 25-26 (2d Cir. 1971); *Barth v. Atlantic container Line*, 597 F. Supp. 1254 (D. Md. 1984). In addition, there is no validity to Ammann's claim that a temporary rate cannot be a "customary" rate. A customary freight unit is one that is "known to the immediate parties." *Freedman & Slater, Inc. v. M/V TOFEVO*, 222 F. Supp. 964 (S.D.N.Y. 1963).

A tariff validly filed "is not a mere contract but is the law ..." *The Peisander*, 648 F.2d 415, 421 (5th Cir. 1981). Thus the rate basis listed in the amended tariff, which was in effect at the time of the shipment, must be applied. Because the freight charged for the shipment of twenty tractors was computed on a lump sum for the entire shipment rather than for each piece of equipment or on a weight/measurement basis, the relevant customary freight unit is the entire shipment. Ammann is therefore limited under both COGSA and the bill of lading to a recovery of $500. While this result seems harsh given the actual value of the cargo, it is consistent with the intent of the statute. Ammann could have paid a higher tariff if it wished to impose a higher liability on the carrier. *See Caterpillar Americas Co. v. Steamship Sea Roads, supra*, 231 F. Supp. at 650; *Petition of Isbrandtsen*, 201 F.2d 281 (2d Cir. 1953). Because the bill of lading contained language providing for limitation of liability and also incorporated COGSA, the burden is on Ammann to prove that an opportunity to declare a higher value did not exist. *Barth v. Atlantic Container Line, supra*, at 1257. Ammann has not met this burden.

* * *

2. The amount of the limit

(a) *The $500 Limitation*

COGSA § 4(5) provides that by agreement the carrier and the shipper may agree to *increase* (not decrease) the $500 limitation on liability. Presumably in this case a higher freight will be charged. Courts have declared that the shipper must be provided with a fair opportunity to declare a higher value. *See Komatsu, Ltd. v. States Steamship*, 674 F.2d 806, 1982 AMC 2152 (9th Cir. 1986). Recent cases have focused on the meaning of "fair opportunity." *See Couthino Caro and Co., Inc. v. M/V Sava*, 849 F.2d 166, 1988 AMC 2941 (5th Cir. 1988); *Sony Magnetic Products of America v. Merivienty O/Y*, 668 F. Supp. 1505, 1988 AMC 718 (S.D. Ala. 1987); *MacSteel International U.S.A. Corp. v. M/V Ibn Abdoun*, 154 F. Supp. 2d 826 (S.D.N.Y. 2001). See Note 3 below.

The "fair opportunity" requirement is discussed in Sturley, *The Fair Opportunity Requirement under COGSA Section 4(5): A Case Study in the Misinterpretation of the Carriage of Goods by Sea Act*, 19 J. Mar. L. & Com. 1 (pt. I), 157 (pt. II) (1988); Sturley, *The Future of the COGSA Fair Opportunity Requirement: Is There Life after Carman Tool and Chan?*, 20 J. Mar. L. & Com. 559 (1989).

Is there any liability under COGSA for the consequential damages of the carrier's breach?

COGSA does not preclude a carrier from offering to limit its liability in an amount in excess of $500. What happens when a bill of lading provides that the Visby Amendments to the Hague Rules apply? The Visby Amendments provide higher limits than the $500 per package limit contained in COGSA. Some courts have held that the Visby Amendments may be enforced because they are consistent with the provision of COGSA which permits a valuation in excess of $500 per package. *Francosteel Corp. v. M/V Pal Marinos*, 885 F. Supp. 86, 1995 AMC 2327 (S.D.N.Y. 1995); *Daval Steel Prods. v. M/V Acadia Forest*, 683 F. Supp. 444, 1988 AMC 1669 (S.D.N.Y. 1988); *J.C.B. Sales, Ltd., v. Wallenius Lines*, 124 F.3d 132, 1997 AMC 2705 (2d Cir. 1997). Others have refused to hold that incorporation of the Visby Amendments amounts to a voluntary increase of the carrier's liability, particularly if that incorporation is by way of a generally-worded Clause Paramount. *Acciai Speciali Terni U.S.A., Inc. v. M/V BERANE*, 182 F. Supp. 2d 503, 2002 AMC 519 (D. Md. 2002).

(b) *Fair Opportunity to Declare a Higher Value*

Suppose a seller-shipper is shipping an expensive piece of equipment worth $100,000 fully encased so that it qualifies as a COGSA package. Assuming that none of the § 4 defenses are available to the carrier, if the package is lost or its contents totally destroyed, its liability would be limited to $500 under COGSA. What are shipper's options? As a practical matter most shippers carry their own cargo insurance. Thus, shipper could collect $500 from carrier and the remainder from shipper's insurance company.

COGSA's limitation of liability provision, § 4(5) fixes the limit at $500 per package "unless the nature and value of such goods have been declared by the shipper before shipment and inserted in the bill of lading. This declaration, if embodied in the bill of lading, shall be *prima facie* evidence, but shall not be conclusive on the carrier." The latter provision has spawned the "fair opportunity" doctrine, whereby a carrier may not invoke the COGSA limitation provision unless the carrier has provided the shipper with a fair opportunity to declare the actual value of the goods, or at least, a value in excess of $500 per package. Of course, carriers are justified in changing a higher freight rate to reflect the increased risk, *i.e.*, the increased value of the goods beyond $500 per package. As a practical matter, it is cheaper for shippers to accept the COGSA $500 per package limitation and to procure their own insurance to cover the difference between that amount and the actual value of the goods, and this is what invariably occurs.

Nevertheless, a carrier who has failed to provide a shipper with a fair opportunity to declare a higher value on the goods will be precluded from invoking COGSA's $500 per package limit. Thus, a carrier must notify shipper that liability is limited under COGSA to $500 per package and provide shippers with an opportunity to opt out of the limitation. Courts seem generally in agreement with this proposition. The language in the bill of lading is crucial in establishing that a fair opportunity was provided. Courts, however, are not necessarily in complete agreement as to the specific provisions necessary to satisfy the requirement. Certainly a statement that the carriage is subject to the $500 per package limitation as provided in COGSA coupled with a statement that shipper may declare a higher value for a higher freight rate with space provided to insert the higher declared value would satisfy the requirement. *Nippon Fire & Marine Ins. Co. v. M/V Tourcoing*, 167 F.3d 99, 1999 AMC 913 (2d Cir. 1999).

Once the carrier has made a prima facie case that it has offered fair opportunity by pointing to bill of lading wording, the onus shifts to the shipper to show that fair opportunity did not in fact exist. In that context, the identity of the shipper may be relevant. In *Intercargo Ins. Co. v. Container Innovations, Inc.*, 100 F. Supp. 2d 198, 2000 AMC 2395 (S.D.N.Y. 2000), the shipper named on the bill of lading was Panalpina, one of the world's largest freight forwarders, a sophisticated party familiar with all the relevant statutes and international conventions. The court held that there was every reason to believe that Panalpina had knowledge of COGSA's actual liability limitation, and there was no evidence whatever to the contrary. See also *Vision Air Flight Service, Inc. v. M/V National Pride*, 155 F. 3d 1165, 1999 AMC 1168 (9th Cir. 1998) (sophisticated shipper could not be taken to say it had not had "fair opportunity" when it had bought cargo insurance).

The Third Circuit stands alone in rejecting the "fair opportunity" doctrine. In *Ferrostaal, Inc. v. M/V Sea Phoenix*, 447 F.3d 212, 2006 AMC 1217 (3d Cir. 2006), the Third Circuit held that the "fair opportunity" doctrine is not consistent with either the text or the underlying policies of COGSA and is not required by Supreme Court precedent. The court rejected the position taken in each of the seven sister circuits that have adopted some version of the doctrine.

---

3. The Harter Act and package limitation

In cases covered by the Harter Act, no limitation figure is specified, so the actual value rule would be applicable. If the contract contains a limitation of liability, courts will require such contractual limitations to be reasonable. *See Hanover Insurance Co. v. Shulman Transport Enterprise, Inc.*, 581 F.2d 268, 1979 AMC 520 (1st Cir. 1978) [$50 limit held violative of public policy and unenforceable]; *Gold Metal Trading Corp. v. Atlantic Overseas Corp.*, 580 F. Supp. 610, 1984 AMC 2052 (S.D.N.Y. 1984) [$500 per package limitation applied under Harter Act]. A crucial factor in these cases seems to be whether or not the shipper is given an opportunity to declare a higher value. Where a bill of lading provides for a "reduced" freight rate for goods which the shipper agrees to value at $50, one court held that this was a reasonable exchange for the lower rate. In this context, the contractual limitation was given effect. *Antilles Ins. Co. v. Transconex, Inc.*, 862 F.2d 391, 1989 AMC 984 (1st Cir. 1988). However, in *Colgate Palmolive v. S.S. Dart Canada*, 724 F.2d 313, 1984 AMC 305 (2d Cir. 1983), the bill of lading incorporated COGSA including the $500 limitation and made it applicable before loading and after discharge. The damage occurred before loading but while the carrier was in custody of the goods. The court held that the limitation was invalid under New Jersey law and that COGSA was not applicable by its own terms. Thus, the contractual incorporation of COGSA had to meet the standards of state law. The Harter Act was not discussed.

COMMONWEALTH PETROCHEMICALS, INC. v. S/S PUERTO RICO

607 F.2d 322, 1979 AMC 2772 (4th Cir. 1979)

James Dickson PHILLIPS, Circuit Judge:

En route from Baltimore, Maryland to San Juan, Puerto Rico, an electrical transformer aboard the S.S. Puerto Rico was damaged. The covering bill of lading incorporated the provisions of the Carriage of Goods by Sea Act (COGSA), 46 U.S.C. §§ 1300-1315, and limited the carrier's liability to $500 per package. The transformer was defined as being one package in the long form bill of lading that was incorporated by reference into the short form bill given to the shippers. The district court refused to give effect to this definition and held the carrier liable for the full amount of the damage to the transformer, $13,901.01.

On the carrier's appeal, three issues are presented for decision. May the parties to a domestic contract of ocean carriage incorporate the provisions of COGSA and at the same time define a term of that statute in a manner that may be inconsistent with the interpretation that has been placed upon it by the courts? If so, may this be done through the use of two bills of lading, a short form given to the shipper incorporating COGSA and a long form incorporated by reference in the short form which provides the possibly inconsistent definition? And finally, was this effectively done in the case at bar? We answer all three issues in the affirmative and reverse.

I

The pertinent facts and the proceeding below may be briefly stated. The transformer measured more than 10 feet in each dimension and weighed 47,700 pounds. It was bolted to an iron skid and then loaded, with a second such transformer, on a special flat-bed trailer for the land journey from Rome, Georgia to Baltimore. The iron skids were in turn bolted to the trailer and the transformers were further fixed in place with heavy chains. When it arrived in Baltimore, the trailer was loaded on the S.S. Puerto Rico and during the voyage to San Juan one of the transformers was damaged.

The shippers, Commonwealth Petrochemicals, Inc. and Fluor Engineers and Constructors, Inc., then brought this action against the S.S. Puerto Rico *in rem* and its owner *pro hac vice*, Puerto Rico Maritime Shipping Authority, *in personam* to recover for the damage. The carrier admitted liability and the case was submitted to the district court on the pleadings and a stipulated set of facts, the only issue for decision being the measure of damages. The carrier sought to limit recovery to $500 on the theory that the bill of lading and the Carriage of Goods by Sea Act incorporated by reference therein, permitted limitation to $500 per package and that the partially enclosed transformer had been defined as one package. The district court concluded that by incorporating COGSA, the parties had also incorporated the judicial construction of the term "package" as used in 46 U.S.C. § 1304(5), and that under those constructions the transformer did not constitute a package. *Commonwealth Petrochemicals, Inc. v. S/S Puerto Rico*, 455 F. Supp. 310 (D. Md. 1978). It therefore entered judgment in the full amount of the damage and this appeal followed.

* * *

Relying on the language that COGSA should apply to contacts of domestic carriage when incorporated therein "as fully as if subject hereto by the express provisions of this chapter," the district court reasoned that the transformer did not constitute a "package" within the meaning of § 1304(5) of COGSA and that to give effect to the contractual definition would lessen the carrier's liability in violation of 46 U.S.C. § 1303(8). In this we conclude the district court erred.

We have held that when COGSA does not apply of its own force but is incorporated into a maritime contract by reference, it does not have "statute rank"; rather, it is merely part of the contract, a term like any other. *United States v. M/V Marilena P*, 433 F.2d 164, 170 (4th Cir. 1969). In *Pannell v. United States Lines Co.*, 263 F.2d 497, 498 (2d Cir. 1959), the United States Court of Appeals for the Second Circuit held that when COGSA does not apply *ex proprio vigore*, effect should be given to the parties' definition of package even if that definition is contrary to that which would control if COGSA were directly applicable. We find *Pannell's* reasoning compelling.

This seems to be simply an application of the principle of construction applicable to ocean bills of lading that as between a general and a specific provision, effect is to be given to the more specific. *See, e.g., Farr v. Hain S.S. Co.*, 121 F.2d 940 (2d Cir. 1941) (L. HAND, J.) (Harter Act); *In re Petterson Lighterage & Towing Corp.*, 154 F. Supp. 461 (S.D.N.Y. 1957), *aff'd per curiam*, 253 F.2d 952 (2d Cir. 1958) (COGSA). The term "package" is not defined in COGSA except insofar as one may consider judicial construction of the term to be definition. That construction, furthermore, is not uniform with partially encased items such as the transformer involved here. 2A BENEDICT ON ADMIRALTY § 167 at 16-19 to -20 (7th ed. I. Hall, A. Sann & M. Katzman 1977) (collecting cases). Under this principle the COGSA usage would be deemed the more general and the specific contractual usage therefore controlling.

A number of lower courts, in opinions that are not officially published, have reached the same result as did the Second Circuit in *Pannell*.

* * *

The language in the *Pannell* bill of lading incorporating COGSA as well as the definition of package was in all pertinent parts identical to that of the long form bill of lading in the appeal before us. *Pannell* does differ from the case at bar, however, in one particular which shippers contend is critically distinguishing: it did not involve incorporation of COGSA into a contract of domestic carriage and therefore was not subject to the language of § 1312 that COGSA should apply "as fully as if subject hereto by the express provisions of this chapter." Likewise, none of the other cases reaching the same result were subject to § 1312's proviso; all involved incorporation of COGSA outside its statutory time frame, *see* 46 U.S.C. §§ 1307, 1311, or with respect to items that were not "goods" within the provisions of COGSA, *see* 46 U.S.C. § 1301(c).

As tenable as that distinction may appear at first blush, the weight of reported authority does not accept it. The Third Circuit has noted that COGSA can apply to domestic commerce "only as a matter of contract and only to the extent that the parties have manifested an intent that it should apply." *PPG Industries, Inc. v. Ashland Oil Co.— Thomas Petroleum Transit Division*, 527 F.2d 502, 507 (3d Cir. 1975) (footnote omitted). In a related context, the District Court for the District of Puerto Rico has expressly rejected such a distinction. *Empacadora Puertorriquena De Carnes, Inc. v. Alterman Transport Line, Inc.*, 303 F. Supp. 474, 479 n.10 (D.P.R. 1969).

The fact that Congress expressly provided for the incorporation of COGSA into domestic contracts of carriage to which it does not apply *ex proprio vigore* may be explained by the existence of the Harter Act. As noted earlier, Congress viewed the need for amendment of the Harter Act to present distinct problems for foreign and domestic commerce. The other mercantile nations were subscribing to the Hague Rules and to bring our law into uniformity with theirs Congress adopted our version of the Rules, COGSA. The need for uniformity was felt to be less strong with domestic trade, but Congress concluded that the option of following COGSA should be available to domestic carriers and shippers as well. Since the Harter Act was to be expressly preserved for the domestic trade, statutory authority for the incorporation of COGSA had to be provided and since the Harter Act and COGSA do differ in some particulars the language upon which the district court in the instant matter relied was used. As indicated, we do not believe that this merely authorizing language is properly read to alter the ordinary rules of contract interpretation when, pursuant to it, COGSA is incorporated.

III

Shippers argue that public policy precludes enforcement of a clause in a long form bill of lading when only the short form is actually given to the shipper and the clause is one that is not typically found in bills of lading.

The use of a long form bill of lading that is incorporated by reference into the short form given the shipper is specifically provided for in sections 2 and 5 of the Inter-coastal Shipping Act, 46 U.S.C. §§ 844, 845b. The long form must be posted in certain places and be available upon request, but no suggestion is made that that was not done in this case. The practice has received judicial approval, *e.g., Zifferer v. Atlantic Lines, Ltd.*, 278 F. Supp. 736 (D.P.R. 1968), and seems to be customary in the industry.

Several courts, however, have refused to give effect to provisions included in the long form when the provision was such that the shipper could not be expected to have anticipated its existence. *Encyclopaedia Britannica, Inc. v. SS Hong Kong Producer*, 422 F.2d 7 (2d Cir. 1969); *Caribbean Produce Exchange, Inc. v. Sea Land Service, Inc.*, 415 F. Supp. 88 (D.P.R. 1976). We do not think that the case at bar falls within this qualification to the permissible use of two bills of lading. As a leading commentator on ocean-carriage has stated, "[T]he key to determining what is a package or unit for purposes of limitation is the intention of the parties, particularly as declared on the bill of lading...." W. Tetley, Marine Cargo Claims 435 (2d ed. 1978) (emphasis omitted). A clause defining the term package should be expected. In fact the *Pannell* decision involved a definition of "package" in language essentially identical to that involved in this case.

IV

Remaining for determination is the question whether the provisions of the bill of lading in this case define the transformer as one package. The clause of the long form bill of lading which purports to limit liability to $500 per package, continues: "It is agreed that the meaning of the word 'package' includes animals, pieces and all articles of any description except goods shipped in bulk." That definition is for all practical purposes identical to that involved in *Pannell* where the Second Circuit held that a yacht shipped in a cradle was a package within its terms. The transformer involved here is also a package under that definition. We note, although it is not conclusive, *Nichimen v. M. V. Farland*, 462 F.2d 319, 335 (2d Cir. 1972), that in the space in the bill of lading entitled "No. of Pkgs." each transformer is designated as a separate package.

The shippers contend that to permit the incorporation of COGSA while at the same time allowing the carrier to redefine its provisions to limit its liability is unreasonable. When incorporated into a domestic contract of carriage, COGSA is just another term of the agreement. It must be construed, within reason, in harmony with the other provisions of the contract. The term involved here is clearly valid under the Harter Act, the statute applicable *ex proprio vigore, see Reid v. Fargo*, 241 U.S. 544, 551 (1916); *Venezuelan Meat Export Co. v. United States*, 12 F. Supp. 379, 387-88 (D. Md. 1935), so the danger posed by permitting the parties to supersede an Act of Congress by their agreement is not present. While more than minimal compliance with the Harter Act may be demanded in some circumstances, this is not one of them. Had shippers wanted to obtain greater coverage than that provided by the terms of the bill of lading, that bill permitted them to declare a greater value for their goods. They did not do so.

Finally, shippers suggest that the definition of "package" contained in the bill of lading is ambiguous, pointing to other places in the bill where assertedly the definition may not easily be transposed for the word it defines. An adequate response is that of Judge Learned Hand:

> [I]t is idle to invoke the canon against redundancy in the interpretation of such a maritime document as this. Courts have again and again observed the curious, often the fantastic, incongruities in charter parties, bills of lading and insurance policies, composed, as they so often are, of a motley patchwork of verbiage thrown together apparently at random, often in an unfamiliar diction three hundred years old. Particularly in a docu-

ment meant to do service in varying situations each word of such a discordant medley need not be made to count as we seek to make all the words count of carefully prepared contracts drawn for a particular occasion.

Farr v. Hain S.S. Co., 121 F.2d at 945. The definition is unambiguous in the context of the clause in which it was included and which alone is the subject of this litigation. It should be enforced, according to its plainly intended meaning there.

The judgment of the district court is reversed and the case is remanded for entry of judgment in favor of plaintiffs in the amount of $500.

REVERSED AND REMANDED.

Problems on the Applicability of Limitation of Liability

Two yachts and their equipment were shipped from Australia to the Untied States on the deck of the *M/V Prosperity* under a clean bill of lading that incorporated the United States Carriage of Goods by Sea Act. The yachts and equipment were damaged in transit due to the negligence of the carrier. The shipper/consignee filed suit in the United States District Court for the Southern District of New York seeking damages. *Cf. Sail America Foundation v. M/V T.S. Prosperity*, 778 F. Supp. 1282, 1992 AMC 1617 (S.D.N.Y. 1991)

1. The carrier admitted liability and claimed application of the $500 per package limitation under the United States Carriage of Goods by Sea Act. Does this act apply by its own force to the above shipment?
2. What is the effect of the incorporation of the United States Carriage of Goods by Sea Act into the bill of lading?
3. Does the Harter Act come into consideration as to the above shipment?
4. Should the carrier be entitled to the $500 per package limitation under the given facts? See *Enterprise, Inc. v. M/V Sam Houston*, 706 F. Supp. 451, 1988 AMC 2745 (E.D. La. 1988).
5. *Variation*: Suppose that the parties had agreed that the yachts and equipment would be carried on deck but the carrier stowed them under deck. Suppose, further, that the yachts and equipment were damaged by perils of the sea (*e.g.*, non-negligent stranding). Had the yachts and equipment been carried on deck, they would not have sustained any damage. Should the carrier be entitled to the $500 per package limitation?
6. *Variation*: Suppose that the bill of lading from Australia to the United States had provided for on deck carriage "at shipper's risk", that the yacht and equipment were carried on deck, and that they were damaged due to the carrier's negligence. Would the shipper be entitled to any recovery?

F. Who Is the COGSA Carrier?

Introductory Note on the COGSA Carrier

A shipowner which enters into a contract of carriage and issues a bill of lading to a shipper is a COGSA carrier. The shipowner may be liable *in personam* under COGSA for loss or damage to the goods. *Associated Metals & Minerals Corp. v. S.S. Portoria*, 484 F.2d 460, 1973 AMC 2095 (5th Cir. 1973). The shipowner's vessel may also be liable *in rem*. *Industria Nacional Del Papel, C.A. v. The Albert F*, 730 F.2d 622, 1985 AMC 1437 (11th Cir.), *cert. denied* 469 U.S. 1037 (1984); *Cavcar v. M/V SUZDAL*, 723 F.2d 1096, 1984 AMC 609 (3rd Cir. 1983).

A charterer (bareboat, time or voyage) which issues its own bill of lading to a consignee, will be regarded as a COGSA carrier and subject to *in personam* liability regardless of whether or not the shipowner might also be classified as a COGSA carrier. *Nitram, Inc. v. Cretan Life*, 599 F.2d 1359 (5th Cir. 1979); *Joo Seng Hong Kong Co., Ltd. v. S.S. Unibulkfir*, 483 F. Supp. 43 (S.D.N.Y. 1979); *Joseph L. Wilmotte & Co., Inc. v. Colbenfret Lines, S.P.R.L.*, 289 F. Supp. 601 (M.D. Fla. 1968).

Generally, when a shipowner carries goods for a person who has chartered its vessel for a voyage, the voyage charter party is the contract of carriage. Such contracts of carriage (voyage charter parties) are not subject to COGSA (unless the parties expressly agree to incorporate the terms of COGSA into the charter party). In voyage charter party situations, it is customary for the shipowner to issue a bill of lading to the shipper of the goods, whether or not that is the voyage charterer, so that the shipper may transfer the right to possession of the goods to the receiver by indorsing the bill of lading. As long as the bill of lading is in the hands of the charterer, it is regarded merely as a receipt and the charter party remains the contract of carriage which controls the legal relations between the shipowner and the charterer. Again, COGSA does not apply to contracts of carriage or "receipts" issued thereunder. *Vanol, U.S.A., Inc. v. M/T CORONADO*, 663 F. Supp. 79, 1988 AMC 560 (S.D.N.Y. 1987). If the charterer is the shipper and transfers or negotiates the bill of lading to a third party, such as a consignee, to whom the charterer may, for example, have sold the goods, the bill of lading is regarded not only as a receipt but also as a contract of carriage and the person to whom the bill has been transferred. Under these circumstances, the shipowner is regarded as the COGSA carrier and may be held liable in personam to the bill of lading holder.

In a charter party situation where the charterer (rather than the shipowner) has issued a bill of lading printed on its own form, the shipowner, nevertheless, may be liable *in personam* under agency principles to a consignee where the master signed the bill of lading as authorized or required by the terms of the charter party or where another person signed "for the master" as authorized by the terms of the charter party. *Instituto Cubano De Est. Del Azucar v. T/V GOLDEN WEST*, 246 F.2d 802 (2d Cir.) *cert. denied*, 355 U.S. 884 (1957); *Ross Industries v. M/V GRETKE OLDENVORFF*, 483 F. Supp. 195, 1980 AMC 1397 (E.D. Tex. 1980). This situation usually arises under a time charter party, by which the charterer charters the vessel for an agreed period of time (see Chapter 2 below). However, a consignee will not be able to prevail *in personam* against a vessel owner even where the bill of lading was signed by the master unless it introduces evidence that the master was authorized or required by the charter party to sign bills of lading and thereby bind the owner. *Sail America Foundation v. M/V T.S. PROSPERITY*, 778 F. Supp. 1282, 1992 AMC 1612 (S.D.N.Y. 1991); *Centennial Insurance Co. v. M/V CONSTELLATION ENTERPRISE*, 639 F. Supp. 1261, 1987 AMC 1155 (S.D.N.Y. 1986).

Ordinarily, liability *in rem* is grounded on the fiction that when the goods are loaded on board the vessel the shipowner has ratified the bill of lading. *Cf., Insurance Company of North America v. S.S. AM. ARGOSY*, 732 F.2d 299, 1984 AMC 1547 (2d Cir. 1984) where the court held that the "ratification" fiction would not apply to an unauthorized agreement of which the shipowner was unaware. In this case, the bill of lading had been issued by a freight forwarder.

A NVOCC (Non-Vessel Operating Common Carrier) or freight forwarder who issues a bill of lading whereby it undertakes the responsibilities of a carrier will be treated as a COGSA carrier. *Sabah Shipyard SDN, Bhd. v. M/V Harbel Tapper*, 178 F.3d 400, 2000 AMC 163 (5th Cir. 1999); *Fireman's Fund Amer. Ins. Cos. v. Puerto Rican For. Co., Inc.*, 492 F.2d 1294 (1st Cir. 1974); *M. Prusman Ltd. v. M/V Nathanel*, 670 F. Supp. 1141, 1988 AMC 296 (SDNY 1987).

PACIFIC EMPLOYERS INS. CO. v. M/V GLORIA

767 F.2d 229 (5th Cir. 1985)

THORNBERRY, Circuit Judge:

This case arises out of a shipment of bagged soybean meal from New Orleans, Louisiana, to Puerto Limon, Costa Rica. When the cargo arrived in Puerto Limon, tallies of the cargo showed that some of the bags were wet, some torn and slack, and some short-landed. Plaintiffs-appellees brought two admiralty actions under the Carriage of Goods by Sea Act, 46 U.S.C. § 1300, *et seq.* (West 1975) ("COGSA"), in which they sought to recover for the cargo damage, slackage, and shortage. The district court consolidated the two actions. The plaintiffs were: Cargill, Inc. ("Cargill"), the shipper of the cargo; Ternerina, S.A., Central Agricola De Cartago, S.A., Fabrica De Alimentos Para Animales, and Industria National De Alimentos Gibbons, S.A., the Costa Rican consignees and receivers of the cargo; and Pacific Employers Insurance, the cargo underwriter. Pursuant to a stipulation of the parties, Pacific Employers Insurance was subrogated to the rights of the owners of the cargo.

The plaintiffs sought recovery against the M/V GLORIA, Aquarius, Ltd., and Transportacion Maritima Mexicana, S.A. The defendant M/V GLORIA is a three-hatch bulk and general cargo vessel of Liberian registry owned by the defendant Aquarius, Ltd. ("Aquarius"). The GLORIA was under a long-term time charter to the defendant Transportacion Maritima Mexicana, S.A. ("TMM").

For the voyage in issue, TMM entered into a voyage charter with Greenwich Marine, Inc. ("Greenwich"), a subsidiary of plaintiff Cargill. Greenwich was not an original defendant in the action but was tendered as a party defendant by Aquarius and TMM pursuant to Fed.R Civ.P. 14(c). Aquarius and TMM also filed third-party actions against Greenwich seeking contribution and indemnity.

Cargill entered into contracts to sell soybean meal to certain parties in Costa Rica. Pursuant to these contracts Cargill engaged Greenwich to find a vessel to carry the soybean meal from New Orleans to Puerto Limon, Costa Rica. Greenwich then entered into a voyage charter of the M/V GLORIA for this purpose. Loading of the bagged soybean meal began in New Orleans on August 5, 1980. Rogers Terminal and Shipping Corp. ("Rogers Terminal") was responsible for bagging, clerking, tallying, and stowing the cargo. Rogers Terminal completed stowage on August 11, and seven bills of lading covering the cargo were issued by "ROGERS TERMINAL & SHIPPING

CORPORATION, AS AGENTS BY AUTHORITY OF THE MASTER." Each bill of
cargo was being shipped in apparent good order by Cargill, shipper's weight, quantity
Further, each bill of lading incorporated the terms of the voyage charter party and the prov
Goods by Sea Act. Cargill subsequently negotiated the bills of lading.

The GLORIA sailed from New Orleans on August 11 and arrived in Puerto Limon on *t*
cargo conducted by employees of the Puerto Limon Port Authority (the Japdeva) disclosed th
contained wet and torn bags and that the cargo was slack and short. Subsequently, the owne⌐ ⌐argo and the
cargo underwriter, as subrogee, brought this action to recover for the alleged damage, slackage, and shortage. Only
the cargo carried under bills of lading 1, 2, 3, 5, and 7 is at issue in this litigation.

The defendants-appellants, Aquarius and TMM, brought Greenwich into the action as a defendant to the main
demand and as a third-party defendant to their claims for contribution and indemnity. The district court ordered that the
third-party action by TMM against Greenwich be stayed pending arbitration as required by the voyage charter party. The
parties then agreed to submit the case to the district court on written briefs, depositions, exhibits, and proposed findings
of fact and conclusions of law. No oral evidence was taken.

On January 26, 1984, the district court entered judgment in favor of plaintiffs and against the GLORIA, *in
rem*, and Aquarius and TMM, *in personam*, in the amount of $59,540.24 plus legal interest from the date of judicial
demand. In a written opinion the district court found that the vessel, Aquarius, and TMM were carriers under
COGSA and that Greenwich was not a carrier. The court also found that plaintiffs established a *prima facie* case
against the carriers for recovery of the cargo damage, slackage, and shortage, and that defendants failed to rebut the
plaintiffs' evidence. On February 23, the district court entered an amended judgment dismissing the claims against
Greenwich. Aquarius and TMM appeal from the judgment and the amended judgment.

* * *

II. COGSA Carriers

Plaintiffs may recover under COGSA only from the "carriers" of the cargo. COGSA defines "carrier" to include
"the owner or the charterer who enters into a contract of carriage with a shipper." 46 U.S.C. § 1301(a). Accordingly,
the plaintiffs must establish that a party defendant executed a contract of carriage. *Associated Metals*, 484 F.2d at
462. COGSA defines a "contract of carriage" as follows:

> The term "contract of carriage" applies only to contracts of carriage covered by a bill of lading or any similar
> document of title, insofar as such document relates to the carriage of goods by sea, including any bill of lading
> or any similar document as aforesaid issued under or pursuant to a charter party from the moment at which
> such bill of lading or similar document of title regulates the relations between a carrier and a holder of the
> same.

46 U.S.C. § 1301(b). The district court found that TMM and Aquarius entered into a contract of carriage with
Cargill and thus were carriers under COGSA, and that Greenwich did not enter into a contract of carriage as defined
by the Act and thus was not a carrier.

* * *

TMM

The bills of lading were issued by Rogers Terminal and were signed: "ROGERS TERMINAL & SHIPPING CORPORATION,
AS AGENTS BY AUTHORITY OF THE MASTER." The district court found that in issuing the bills of lading, Rogers Terminal
acted as agent for TMM and therefore TMM entered into a contract of carriage. TMM contends that this finding
is clearly erroneous. We disagree and hold that there was sufficient evidence before the district court to support its
finding. The voyage charter party entered into by TMM and Greenwich was incorporated into the bills of lading
and provided, in part; that:

ners [TMM] to instruct their New York bank to advise Owners' agents at loading port immediately freight received by cable that freight payment has been received and Owners to instruct their agents to release Bill/s of Lading immediately on receipt of such advice. If release of Bill/s of Lading should be delayed, the Owners shall pay interest at one per cent over the New York Prime Rate on Bill/s of Lading date/s, on the cost and freight value of the cargo from the day on which the freight payment is received by the Owners' New York bank until the day on which the Bill/s of Lading are actually released by the Owners' agents.

The evidence before the district court did not clearly disclose for whom Rogers Terminal acted when it issued the bills of lading. Under the voyage charter party, Greenwich was obligated to appoint and employ stevedores at the loading port. Rogers Terminal performed stevedoring services in New Orleans. However, the National Cargo Bureau's Certificate of Loading, issued after loading of the GLORIA was completed, stated, "AGENT—ROGERS TERMINAL & SHIPPING CO.—T.M.M. CHARTERING." Moreover, the charter party states that TMM and/or its agents would be responsible for issuance of the bills of lading. The master of the GLORIA testified by deposition that he authorized Rogers Terminal to issue the bills of lading on his behalf. He also testified, however, that it was his belief that Rogers Terminal was acting on behalf of Greenwich.

The district court considered all of the evidence before it, and, relying primarily on the voyage charter party provision that TMM would issue the bills of lading upon payment of freight by Greenwich, the court found that the bills were issued by TMM through its agent, Rogers Terminal. The district court's finding, in light of the conflicting evidence, is not clearly erroneous and we Affirm the holding that TMM entered into a contract of carriage with respect to the soybean cargo and is thus a carrier under the provisions of COGSA.

Greenwich

The district court held that Greenwich was not a COGSA carrier because Greenwich did not issue the bills of lading and did not otherwise enter into a contract of carriage with Cargill. The court found that "Greenwich acted simply on behalf of the shipper in finding a vessel to carry the cargo and paying the appropriate freight." Greenwich did not enter into a contract that was "covered by a bill of lading or any similar document of title." *See* 46 U.S.C. § 1301(b).

In addition to contending that Greenwich issued the bills of lading, appellants argue that Greenwich is a COGSA carrier because the bills of lading were issued in connection with the voyage charter and because, under the voyage charter party, Greenwich was responsible for loading, stowage, and discharge—duties which COGSA places on the carrier. *See* 46 U.S.C. § 1303(2). First, we note that the voyage charter party merely states, "Charterers to appoint and employ stevedores at loading port/s," and "Charterers/Receivers Stevedores to be employed at discharging port/s." The charter party is not so explicit as appellants would have us believe. Moreover, even if Greenwich bore the responsibility under the voyage charter party for loading, stowage, and discharge, we do not believe this fact, alone, would make Greenwich a COGSA carrier. In *Dempsey & Associates v. S.S. SEA STAR*, 461 F.2d 1009 (2d Cir. 1972), the time charterer issued bills of lading in connection with a voyage charter. The court held that the time charterer was a COGSA carrier but that the voyage charterer was not. The court further held that the fact that the charter party required the voyage charterer to load, stow, and discharge the cargo created a duty running from the voyage charterer to the time charterer but did not affect the time charterer's obligations under COGSA and did not operate to make the voyage charterer a COGSA carrier. *Id.* at 1018-1019. We agree with the Second Circuit and we affirm the district court's finding that Greenwich is not a COGSA carrier.

Aquarius

Appellants also argue that the district court erred by finding that Aquarius is a COGSA carrier. Since appellees' causes of action were based on COGSA, there can be *in personam* liability against the vessel owner only if the owner is a carrier. *Associated Metals*, 484 F.2d at 462. Appellants contend that Aquarius did not enter into a contract of carriage and did not become bound by the bills of lading merely because they were signed "by authority of the master."

"A contract of carriage with an owner may either be direct between the parties, or by virtue of a charterer's authority to bind the owner by signing bills of lading 'for the master.'" *Matter of Intercontinental Properties Manage-*

ment, S.A., 604 F.2d 254, 258 n.3 (4th Cir. 1979) . Appellees argue that the bills of lading were issued by Rogers Terminal—TMM's agent—with the actual authority of the vessel owner and that Aquarius is therefore bound. The circumstances under which the vessel owner may be bound by the bills of lading were well-stated by the First Circuit in *EAC Timberlane v. Pisces, Ltd.,* 745 F.2d 715 (1st Cir. 1984):

> Generally, when a bill of lading is signed by the charterer or its agent "for the master" with the authority of the shipowner, this binds the shipowner and places the shipowner within the provisions of COGSA. *E.g., Gans S.S. Line v. Wilhelmsen (The Themis),* 2 Cir. 1921, 275 F. 254, 262; *Tube Products of India v. S.S. Rio Grande,* 1971, S.D.N.Y., 334 F. Supp. 1039, 1041; *see generally* Bauer, *Responsibilities of Owner and Charterer to Third Parties—Consequences Under Time and Voyage Charters,* 49 TUL. L. REV. 995, 997-1001 (1975). When, however, a bill of lading is signed by the charter or its agent "for the master" but without the authority of the shipowner, the shipowner is not personally bound and does not by virtue of the charterer's signature become a COGSA carrier. *E.g., Associated Metals and Minerals Corp. v. S.S. Portoria,* 5 Cir. 1973, 484 F.2d 460, 462; *Dempsey & Associates, Inc. v. S.S. Sea Star,* 2 Cir. 1972, 461 F.2d 1009, 1015.

Id. at 719. Aquarius' liability depends on the effect of the signature caption "by authority of the master." In order to determine the effect we must examine Rogers Terminal's authority to sign on behalf of the master and the master's authority to bind Aquarius. *See Yeramex International v. S.S. TENDO,* 595 F.2d 943, 946 (4th Cir. 1979).

The district court's finding that the master authorized Rogers Terminal to issue the bills of lading on his behalf is not clearly erroneous. The captain of the GLORIA testified by deposition that he "gave Rogers Terminal an undertaking that they should sign the bills of lading." Appellants presented no conflicting evidence. This case is therefore unlike those cited by appellants in which there was no evidence that the master authorized the charterer or its agent to sign on his behalf. *See Dempsey & Associates v. S.S. SEA STAR,* 461 F.2d 1009, 1012-15 (2d Cir. 1972); *Thyssen Steel Corp. v. S.S. ADONIS,* 364 F. Supp. 1332, 1335 (S.D.N.Y. 1973); *United Nations Children's Fund v. S/ S NORDSTERN,* 251 F. Supp. 833, 838 (S.D.N.Y. 1965).

We must next determine whether the master had actual authority to bind the vessel owner to the terms of the bills of lading. The charter party between Aquarius and TMM contained the following provisions:

> 8. [T]he Captain shall prosecute his voyages with the utmost despatch, and shall render all customary assistance with ship's crew and boats. The Captain (although appointed by the Owners), shall be under the orders and directions of the Charterers [TMM] as regards employment and agency; and Charterers are to load, stow, and trim and discharge the cargo at their expense under the supervision of the Captain, who is to sign Bills of Lading for cargo as presented, in conformity with Mate's or Tally Clerk's receipts.
>
> Rider 37. If required by Charterers and/or their Agents, Master to authorize Charterers or their Agents to sign Bills of Lading on his behalf in accordance with mates and/or tally clerks receipt without prejudice to this Charter Party.

We hold that Rider 37 to the charter party empowered the master to authorize TMM's agent to sign the bills of lading and thereby bind Aquarius. The case cited by appellants, *Yeramex International v. S.S. TENDO,* 595 F.2d 943 (4th Cir. 1979), is distinguishable. In *Yeramex* the charter party between the vessel owner and the time charterer contained a provision identical to clause 8 above. It also contained a provision that stated, in part: "Charterers shall indemnify Owners from all consequences arising out of Master or agents signing Bills of Lading in accordance with Charterers' instructions, or from complying with any orders or directions of Charterers in connection therewith." *Id.* at 947. The court in *Yeramex* found that under the provisions of the charter party the charterer assumed exclusive responsibility for handling of cargo and for issuance of bills of lading. The court further stated:

> In particular, we think all authority conferred by these provisions upon the vessels' masters for bills of lading issued by [time charterer] was authority which flowed, in fact, from [the time charterer] as principal to the

masters as its agents, rather than as authority granted to [the time charterer] from the masters as the traditional personal agents of the owner.... No authority in fact existed for [the time charterer] to bind the owner to the terms of the bill of lading as a contracting party, and no liability in personam under COGSA will lie against the owner in favor of third parties.

Id. at 948. The Aquarius/TTM charter party did not contain a provision requiring TMM to indemnify Aquarius from all consequences arising out of the master or agents signing bills of lading. Moreover, Rider 37 to the charter party contains an express authorization that was not present in the *Yeramex* charter party. The district court's findings that TMM was authorized to bind Aquarius to the terms of the bills of lading and that Aquarius is a COGSA carrier are not clearly erroneous.

* * *

CACTUS PIPE & SUPPLY CO., INC. v. M/V MONTMARTRE

756 F.2d 1103, 1985 AMC 2150 (5th Cir. 1985)

John R. BROWN, Circuit Judge:

This appeal arises from claims for damage to a cargo of steel tubing shipped aboard the M/V MONTMARTRE in July, 1979. Because we find that *in rem* jurisdiction was established in one case of this consolidated action, we reverse. We also reverse and remand for a determination of whether the vessel was liable *in rem*. We affirm the trial court's finding that appellee, vessel owner, was not liable as the carrier of cargo because there was no evidence that the vessel owner authorized issuance of the bills of lading either by actual or apparent authority.

How It All Began

Appellant Cactus Pipe & Supply Co., Inc. (Cactus), contracted with Corinth Pipeworks, S.A. (Corinth) to purchase steel tubing. Under this agreement, the trial court found that Corinth was to arrange for shipment from Corinth, Greece to Houston, Texas. The cargo was shipped aboard the M/V MONTMARTRE owned by appellee Orient Leasing Co., Ltd. (Orient).

Before the carriage of cargo in issue, Orient bareboat chartered the MONTMARTRE to Eternity Navigation Co., S.A. (Eternity), in September, 1976. Eternity, as bareboat charter owner, time chartered the vessel to Iino Kaiun Kaisha, Ltd. (Iino). Iino in turn time chartered the MONTMARTRE to Canadian Forest Navigation Co., Ltd. (Canadian) in June, 1979. In July, 1979, Canadian voyage chartered the MONTMARTRE to Seanav International Co. (Seanav). Seanav in turn voyage chartered the vessel to Corinth.

Nine bills of lading covering the cargo were issued on July 14, 1979, signed by Delpa Shipping and Transportation Co., Ltd. (Delpa) "For The Master." The vessel arrived in Houston in August, 1979, and surveyors observed damage in the hold before unloading. In addition to damage, appellant Cactus contends that portions of the cargo were never delivered.

Cactus, consignee of the cargo of steel tubing, instituted two causes of action seeking recovery of its damages. The First action (District Court No. H-80-1721) was brought in Cactus' name by its subrogated underwriter against the MONTMARTRE, Orient and Corinth. The Second action (District Court No. H-80-1769) was instituted by Cactus seeking recovery of the uninsured portion of its loss (approximately $10,000) against the vessel and against Orient, the vessel owner. The MONTMARTRE was never arrested. However, a claim of owner was filed by Orient in both actions. Subsequently the two cases were consolidated pending trial.

On July 6, 1983, the district court, after a bench trial, entered its opinion finding that the cargo was damaged and short upon delivery in Houston, Texas. It also found that Corinth, the voyage charterer and shipper, was liable as a carrier of the cargo and that Orient, the vessel owner, was not liable because it was not the COGSA carrier. The trial court found that the MONTMARTRE, although the carrying vessel, was not liable to Cactus because it was not liable for the acts or omissions of the charterer/shipper, Corinth. The district court entered judgment in favor of

Cactus and against Corinth for $28,673.51 plus interest. On August 11, 1983, the trial court issued amended conclusions of law determining that *in rem* jurisdiction over the vessel did not exist because the vessel was never arrested nor had any bond or letter of undertaking been filed in the court by the owner of the vessel. The court held that the claims of owner filed by the vessel owner, Orient, manifested only the vessel owner's interest in the vessel and did not establish *in rem* jurisdiction. The district court also determined that, although a voyage charterer such as Corinth may be liable as a carrier, the evidence was insufficient to hold Corinth liable as a carrier under the facts of this case. Accordingly, Cactus was awarded nothing.

* * *

Orient—Vessel Owner

Cactus asserts that the trial court erroneously refused to find *in personam* liability against Orient, the vessel owner. It does so on the basis that the bills of lading were issued with the apparent authority of the vessel owner and that Cactus relied on such apparent authority. The bills of lading were signed by Delpa "For The Master"—who technically was not the employee of Orient, the vessel owner. The trial court found that none of the parties to this case issued the bills of lading.

Cactus asserts that the apparent authority claim is based largely on the failure of the bills of lading to identify the carrier or the party who employed the Master or on whose behalf the agent was acting when the bills of lading were signed. In support of this claim it also argues that the bills of lading were on anonymous standard forms, and that the printed text of the bills of lading refer to "owner" and "shipowner." Cactus further argues that it and the holder of the bills of lading could reasonably believe that they were issued with the authority of the vessel owner. We conclude that this evidence alone did not justify Cactus in believing that the bills of lading were issued by an agent authorized to do so on behalf of Orient, the vessel owner.

Maritime law embraces the principles of agency. *West India Industries, Inc. v. Vance & Sons AMC-Jeep*, 671 F.2d 1384 (5th Cir. 1982). We initially point out that Cactus introduced no evidence of any actual authority of an agent to issue the bills of lading on behalf of the vessel owner. *See Associated Metals & Minerals Corp. v. SS PORTORIA*, 484 F.2d 460, 462, 1973 AMC 2095, 2096-97 (5th Cir. 1973). Nor was apparent authority established. Apparent authority is created as to a third person by conduct of the principal which, reasonably interpreted, causes the third person to believe that the principal consents to the act done on his behalf by the person purporting to act for him. RESTATEMENT (SECOND) OF AGENCY § 27. Apparent authority is distinguished from actual authority because it is the manifestation of the principal to the third party rather than to the agent that is controlling.

In this case there are no facts which could reasonably lead Cactus or the holder of the bills of lading to believe that they were issued on the vessel owner's behalf. Our analysis is based upon the premise that for apparent authority to exist there must be some manifestation (whether an act or an omission) of the principal that causes the third person to believe that the agent is authorized to act for him or the principal should realize that his conduct is likely to create such a belief. *See* RESTATEMENT (SECOND) OF AGENCY § 27 comment a. Cactus has not pointed to any facts sufficiently supporting some manifestation by the vessel owner to Cactus justifying reliance. Here, the bills of lading were issued by Delpa, the agent of Corinth or Iino.... Furthermore, there was no evidence that the vessel owner authorized Delpa to issue bills of lading or that the vessel owner approved the form or contents. An agent cannot confer authority upon himself. *Karavos Compania Naviera S.A. v. Atlantica Export Corp.*, 588 F.2d 1, 10, 1978 AMC 2634, 2647 (2d Cir. 1978). The court in *Karavos* quoted Judge Levet in *Dr. Beck & Co., GmbH. v. General Electric Co.*, 210 F. Supp. 86, 90 (S.D.N.Y. 1962), *aff'd*, 317 F.2d 538 (2d Cir. 1963) by an analysis which applies with equal force in this case:

> While agents are often successful in creating an appearance of authority by their own acts and statements, such an appearance does not create apparent authority (*quoting* MECHEM, AGENCY 61 (4th ed. 1952)), 588 F.2d at 10, 1978 AMC at 2647.

We thus can find no sufficient basis to conclude that Cactus or the holder of the bills of lading reasonably relied on some manifestation by Orient, the vessel owner, to justify a belief that the bills of lading were issued on Orient's behalf.

There was no basis, therefore for holding Orient liable *in personam*.

The Montmartre

Cactus nevertheless contends that the MONTMARTRE is itself liable *in rem* for damage to the cargo of steel tubing involved in the First suit (District Court No. 80-1721). A proceeding *in rem* in the admiralty is one against the vessel as the offending thing.[15] The vessel may be held liable even in the absence of the liability, *in personam*, of the vessel owner. *Canadian Aviator, Ltd. v. United States*, 324 U.S. 215, 224, 65 S. Ct. 639, 644, 89 L. Ed. 901, 908, 1945 AMC 265, 272 (1945); *Grigsby v. Coastal Marine Service*, 412 F.2d 1011, 1030-31, 1969 AMC 1513, 1539, (5th Cir. 1969), *cert. dismissed*, 396 U.S. 1033, 90 S. Ct. 612, 613, 24 L. Ed. 2d 531 (1970).[17]

In effect the arrangement between Corinth and the vessel was akin to special or private carriage as to which COGSA would not attach unless bills of lading are issued. COGSA, 46 U.S.C. § 1305. Although bills of lading were issued they were not issued either by the vessel owner, Orient, or by one acting with its authority. Therefore, as we have held above Orient has no liability *in personam*.

Nonetheless bills of lading were issued and the vessel sailed with the goods on board. Under those circumstances, Black Letter Law translates Cleirac's historic aphorism *"Le batel est oblige a la marchandise et la marchandise au batel" n.20* into the settled maritime principle that sweeps away as immaterial any question of the authority of the issuer of the bills of lading to hold the ship liable *in rem* for loss or damage to the cargo carried.

When cargo has been stowed on board the vessel and bills of lading are issued, the bills of lading become binding contracts of the vessel *in rem* upon the sailing of the vessel with the cargo. The sailing of the vessel constitutes a ratification of the bills of lading. *Compagnie De Navigation Fraissinet & Cyprien Fabre, S.A. v. Mondial United Corp.*, 316 F.2d 163, 173, 1963 AMC 946, 956 (5th Cir. 1963); *see Cavcar Co. v. M/V SUZDAL*, 723 F.2d 1096, 1101, 1984 AMC 609, 617 (3d Cir. 1983); *Demsey & Assoc. v. The S.S. SEA STAR*, 461 F.2d 1009, 1015, 1972 AMC 1440, 1447 (2d Cir. 1972); *cf. Insurance Co. of North America v. The S/S AMERICAN ARGOSY*, 732 F.2d 299, 303, 1984 AMC 1547, 1553 (2d Cir. 1984); *see also*, H. LONGLEY, COMMON CARRIAGE OF CARGO, § 3.05[1][b] at 26 (1967). This action gives rise to a maritime lien which is the basis of the *in rem* recovery. Even though the vessel is operating under charter parties, the lien against the vessel is not affected. *Demsey*, 461 F.2d at 1014, 1972 AMC at 1446. Therefore, the sailing of the MONTMARTRE with the cargo of steel pipes aboard constituted a ratification of the bills of lading.

* * *

---

[15] *But cf. Baker v. Raymond International, Inc.*, 656 F.2d 173, 184, 1982 AMC 2752, 2767 (5th Cir. 1981), *cert. denied*, 456 U.S. 983, 102 S. Ct. 2256, 72 L. Ed. 2d 861, 1982 AMC 2107 (1982). In *Baker*, Judge Rubin discussed the fiction of the vessel's personality. "[T]he fiction of ship's personality, according to Professors Gilmore and Black, 'has never been much more than a literary theme,' now fallen into disrepute." *Id.* Fiction or not, the notion still has vitality in those situations in which settled principles of maritime law recognizes the difference—indeed sometimes the absence—of *in personam* liability. *See e.g. Homer Ramsdell Transp. Co. v. La Compagnie Generale Transatlantique*, 182 U.S. 406, 21 S. Ct. 831, 45 L. Ed. 1155 (1981); *Associated Metals & Minerals Corp. v. S.S. PORTORIA*, 484 F.2d 460, 1973 AMC 2095 (5th Cir. 1973).

[17] In *Grigsby*, this court reasoned:

> Obviously of course, the absence of possession and control may well insulate the shipowner from a liability in personam in the absence of conduct which somehow implicates the remote owner in the deficiency. But on principles of *in rem* liability, or concepts akin to it, there seems to be no more reason for the physical absence of an owner's representative universally to insulate the vessel from accountability for personal injuries occasioned by unseaworthiness that there is to absolve the vessel from *in rem* liability for, say, other types of maritime torts including collision, even though the vessel, on this hypothesis, is wholly in the control of a demise charterer and, worse being conned by a compulsory pilot.

Note

Compare, *Yeramex International v. S.S. Tendo*, 595 F.2d 943, 1979 AMC 1282 (4th Cir. 1979) which held under its facts of the case, that only the time charterer and not the ship owner was liable *in personam*.

G. Extension of COGSA defenses, immunities and limitations to non-carriers

Note: The Himalaya Clause

A Himalaya Clause seeks to extend to non-carriers partial immunity or other protections afforded to the carrier by the bill of lading. *See* Healy, *Carriage of Goods by Sea: Application of the Himalaya Clause to Subdelegees of the Carrier*, 2 MAR. LAW. 91 (1977). Stevedores and others as bailees for hire owe a duty of reasonable care of the cargo and may also be held to a warranty of workman-like performance. *See*, for example, *Vitol Trading S.A., Inc. v. SGS Control Services, Inc.*, 680 F. Supp. 559, 1987 AMC 1995 (S.D.N.Y. 1987) [inspection company found in breach of warranty of workman-like performance because chemical analysis testing was deficient]. Absent contract, stevedores and terminal personnel are neither bound by the terms of a bill of lading nor regulated by contract. *ITT Rayonier, Inc. v. Southeastern Maritime Co.*, 620 F.2d 512, 1981 AMC 854 (5th Cir. 1980). A clear and unequivocal Himalaya Clause in the bill of lading, however, will be given effect to extend to the stevedore, who is the agent or subcontractor of the carrier, the benefit of the $500 limitation of liability. *See Miller Yacht Sales, Inc. v. M/V Vishva Shobha*, 494 F. Supp. 1005, 1981 AMC 2479 (S.D.N.Y. 1980).

Until recently, it was thought that Himalaya Clauses should be strictly construed. For example, it was held that where a clause applied by its terms to "agents and independent contractors" it did not extend to a trucker who was an agent or independent contractor of the consignee. *Taisho Marine & Fire Ins. Co. v. The Vessel Gladiolus*, 762 F.2d 1364, 1987 AMC 2047 (11th Cir. 1985). Also, where a stevedore was an agent of the shipper or consignee it was not covered by a clause that extended to agents of the carrier. *Ram Metals & Building Industries, Ltd. v. Zim Israel Navigation Company, Ltd.*, 732 F. Supp. 106, 1989 AMC 2215 (S.D. Fla. 1989).

However, in *Norfolk Southern Railway Co. v. Kirby*, 125 S. Ct. 385, 2004 AMC 2705 (2004), the Supreme Court recently held that there is no rule requiring especially strict interpretation of Himalaya clauses. The Court said:

> Kirby and ICC made a contract for the carriage of machinery from Sydney to Huntsville, and agreed to limit the liability of ICC and other parties who would participate in transporting the machinery. The bill's Himalaya Clause states:
>
> > These conditions [for limitations on liability] apply whenever claims relating to the performance of the contract evidenced by this [bill of lading] are made against *any servant, agent or other person (including any independent contractor) whose services have been used in order to perform the contract*. App. to Pet. for Cert. 59a, cl. 10.1 (emphasis added).

The question presented is whether the liability limitation in Kirby's and ICC's contract extends to Norfolk, which is ICC's sub-subcontractor. The Circuits have split in answering this question. Compare, *e.g., Akiyama Corp. of America v. M.V. Hanjin Marseilles*, 162 F.3d 571, 574 (C.A.9 1998) (privity of contract is not required in order to benefit from a Himalaya Clause), with *Mikinberg v. Baltic S.S. Co.*, 988 F.2d 327, 332 (C.A.2 1993) (a contractual relationship is required).

This is a simple question of contract interpretation. It turns only on whether the Eleventh Circuit correctly applied this Court's decision in *Robert C. Herd & Co. v. Krawill Machinery Corp.*, 359 U.S. 297, 79 S.Ct. 766, 3 L.Ed.2d 820 (1959). We conclude that it did not. In *Herd*, the bill of lading between a cargo owner and carrier said that, consistent with COGSA, "'the Carrier's liability, if any, shall be determined on the basis of $500 per package.'" *Id.*, at 302, 79 S.Ct. 766. The carrier then hired a stevedoring company to load the cargo onto the ship, and the stevedoring company damaged the goods. The Court held that the stevedoring company was not a beneficiary of the bill's liability limitation. Because it found no evidence in COGSA or its legislative history that Congress meant COGSA's liability limitation to extend automatically to a carrier's agents, like stevedores, the Court looked to the language of the bill of lading itself. It reasoned that a clause limiting "'the Carrier's liability'" did not "indicate that the contracting parties intended to limit the liability of stevedores or other agents.... If such had been a purpose of the contracting parties it must be presumed that they would in some way have expressed it in the contract." *Ibid.* The Court added that liability limitations must be "strictly construed and limited to intended beneficiaries." *Id.*, at 305, 79 S.Ct. 766.

The Eleventh Circuit, like respondents, made much of the *Herd* decision. Deriving a principle of narrow construction from *Herd*, the Court of Appeals concluded that the language of the ICC bill's Himalaya Clause is too vague to clearly include Norfolk. 300 F.3d, at 1308. Moreover, the lower court interpreted *Herd* to require privity between the carrier and the party seeking shelter under a Himalaya Clause. *Id.*, at 1308. But nothing in *Herd* requires the linguistic specificity or privity rules that the Eleventh Circuit attributes to it. The decision simply says that contracts for carriage of goods by sea must be construed like any other contracts: by their terms and consistent with the intent of the parties. If anything, *Herd* stands for the proposition that there is no special rule for Himalaya Clauses.

The Court of Appeals' ruling is not true to the contract language or to the intent of the parties. The plain language of the Himalaya Clause indicates an intent to extend the liability limitation broadly—to "*any* servant, agent or other person (including *any* independent contractor)" whose services contribute to performing the contract. App. to Pet. for Cert. 59a, cl. 10.1 (emphasis added). "Read naturally, the word 'any' has an expansive meaning, that is, 'one or some indiscriminately of whatever kind.'" *United States v. Gonzales*, 520 U.S. 1, 5, 117 S.Ct. 1032, 137 L.Ed.2d 132 (1997) (quoting Webster's Third New International Dictionary 97 (1976)). There is no reason to contravene the clause's obvious meaning. See *Green v. Biddle*, 8 Wheat. 1, 89-90, 5 L.Ed. 547 (1823) ("[W]here the words of a law, treaty, or contract, have a plain and obvious meaning, all construction, in hostility with such meaning, is excluded"). The expansive contract language corresponds to the fact that various modes of transportation would be involved in performing the contract. Kirby and ICC contracted for the transportation of machinery from Australia to Huntsville, Alabama, and, as the crow flies, Huntsville is some 366 miles inland from the port of discharge. See G. Fitzpatrick & M. Modlin, Direct-Line Distances 168 (1986). Thus, the parties must have anticipated that a land carrier's services would be necessary for the contract's performance. It is clear to us that a railroad like Norfolk was an intended beneficiary of the ICC bill's broadly written Himalaya Clause. Accordingly, Norfolk's liability is limited by the terms of that clause.

Norfolk Southern, 125 S. Ct. 385, 396-98 (2004).

GRACE LINE, INC. v. TODD SHIPYARDS CORPORATION

500 F.2d 361, 1974 AMC 1136 (9th Cir. 1974)

James M. CARTER, Circuit Judge:

This case arises out of a collision between a steamship and a drydock. We are presented with issues of negligence, the propriety of prejudgment interest, the scope of the United States Carriage of Goods by Sea Act, the interpretation and validity of so-called 'Himalaya' clauses in bills of lading, and laches. Notwithstanding the number and complexity of the legal issues and the number of parties involved, the facts are rather simple.

Facts

The Santa Ana is a 10,000-ton cargo steamship owned and operated by Grace Lines, Inc. (hereafter Grace). On December 8, 1967, the steamship arrived in San Francisco Bay laden with cargo of coffee, lumber, corned beef and quebracho. These goods were insured, respectively, by Home Insurance Company (hereafter Home), Atlantic Mutual Insurance Company (hereafter Atlantic Mutual), Royal Globe Insurance Co. (hereafter Royal Globe), and Commercial Insurance Company of Newark (hereafter Commercial).

During a voyage by a cargo steamship, it is customary for the vessel to enter a drydock for inspection and repair. With this purpose, the Santa Ana steamed into the Oakland Estuary where its intended drydock was located. This was Drydock No. 2, operated by Todd Shipyards Corporation (hereafter Todd).

Ordinarily, Captain Fillipow commanded the Santa Ana, but a special pilot named Carlier took the helm in order to perform the delicate operation of entering the drydock. Pilot Carlier was an employee of Shipowners & Merchants Towboat Company, Ltd. (hereafter S & M Towboat), which also supplied tugboats to assist in the maneuvers.

The Oakland Estuary runs generally east to west, and Drydock No. 2 is on the south shore. After heading east up the estuary until reaching the drydock, the steamship made a 90 degrees turn to the south and aimed towards the drydock's entry.

* * *

At the time Pilot Carlier proceeded to navigate the steamship into the submerged drydock, an eastward breeze and a flowing tide pushed against the vessel on the starboard (*i.e.*, right hand) side. No finding was made, and nobody can say for certain, whether this starboard pressure was what made the steamship enter the drydock as it did, off-center, towards the port (*i.e.*, left hand) side. The port side hull rammed into the unseen recessed wall, ripping a hole in the vessel beneath the water line. Besides damaging the steamship, the collision caused injury to the drydock and allowed flooding water to injure the cargo. The steamship, however, was ultimately drydocked and repaired by Todd.

Out of this accident arose four law suits. (1) Grace, the owner of the steamship sued Todd, the operator of the drydock, for the damages to the vessel and resultant damages. Todd filed a counterclaim against Grace for the damages to the drydock and for the money Todd had spent in repairing the ripped hull. Todd also filed a third-party complaint for the dock damage against S & M Towboat, which employed Pilot Carlier and the tugboats. (2) Two cargo insurers, Home and Atlantic Mutual, joined in suit against Grace, the Santa Ana itself, Todd and S & M Towboat for damage to the coffee and lumber. (3) Commercial brought a separate suit against the same defendants for damage to the quebracho. (4) Royal Globe likewise brought a separate suit against the same defendants for damage to the corned beef.

The suits were consolidated and tried to the district court. In its findings and conclusions, the court held that Todd was negligent and hence liable to Grace in the net amount of $17,265.03; that Todd, though negligent, was entitled to immunity against the cargo insurers; and that neither Grace nor S & M Towboat were negligent or liable to any party.

In the two appeals (by Todd and the cargo insurers) and the two cross-appeals (by Grace and Todd), we face the following questions:

(1) Did the trial court err in finding Todd negligent?
(2) Did the trial court err in finding that there was no negligence on the part of the Santa Ana, Grace or S & M Towboat?
(3) Did the trial court err in refusing to grant pre-judgment interest to Grace?
(4) Did the trial court err in holding that Todd is entitled to the same exemptions and immunities from and limitations of liability which Grace has against the cargo interests (these exemptions, immunities and limitations primarily being those that the United States Carriage of Goods by Sea Act provides specifically for carriers)?

As elaborated below, we answer questions (1), (2) and (3) in the negative, affirming the district court on those points. We conclude, however, that question (4) should be answered in the affirmative; we therefore reverse the district court's holding that Todd is entitled to immunity from liability to the cargo insurers.

* * *

IV. *The 'Himalaya' Clause and COGSA*

The district court held that Todd was entitled to the same exemptions and immunities from and limitations of liability which Grace had against the cargo insurers. We disagree, holding that Todd was entitled to some but not all, of the exemptions and immunities and limitations which Grace had, as detailed below.

A. *The Provisions of the 'Himalaya' Clause*

The bills of lading constituting the contract of carriage between Grace and the cargo interest contain a so-called 'Himalaya' clause, which reads in pertinent part as follows:

'The Carrier shall be discharged from all liability in respect of loss, damage and every claim whatsoever with respect to the goods unless suit is brought within one year after delivery of the goods or the date when the goods should have been delivered.... It is expressly agreed between the parties (the Carrier and the cargo owners) hereto that the master, officers, crew members, contractors, stevedores, longshoremen, agents, representatives, employees or others used, engaged or employed by the carrier in the performance of such work or services (undertaken in this contract), shall each be the beneficiaries of and shall be entitled to the same, but no further exemptions and immunities from and limitations of liability which the carrier has under this bill of lading, whether printed, written, stamped thereon or incorporated by reference.... Without limitation or restriction of the exemptions and immunities from and limitations of liability provided for (above), the persons and companies mentioned therein shall be entitled to the same, but no further, benefits which the carrier has under the U.S. Carriage of Goods by Sea Act, including but not limited to Sections 3(6), 4(1), 4(2)(a), 4(2)(q) and 4(5) of said Act.'

As will be further discussed below, the United States Carriage of Goods by Sea Act (hereafter COGSA), 49 Stat. 1207 (1936), 46 U.S.C. §§ 1300-1315, grants certain immunities, exemptions and limitations to carriers of cargo by sea. Although the Act does not itself extend these protections to non-carriers, the bills of lading purport to incorporate certain of COGSA's provisions into the contract and thereby protect certain non-carriers as well. As we discuss below. Todd was a contractor engaged in the performance of work undertaken in the bills of lading, and hence the following of COGSA's protections are purportedly extended to Todd contractually:

The one-year period of limitations for instituting suit and a notice-of-damage requirement (see COGSA, § 3(6), 46 U.S.C. § 1303(6)).

The immunity from liability for unseaworthiness of the vessel unless caused by want of due diligence (see COGSA, § 4(1), 46 U.S.C. § 1304(1));

The immunity from liability for negligent acts in the navigation or management of the ship (see COGSA, § 4(2)(a), 46 U.S.C. § 1304(2)(a));

The immunity from liability for damage caused by fire, unless caused by the actual fault or privity of the carrier (see COGSA, § 4(2)(b), 46 U.S.C. § 1304(2)(b));

The immunity from liability for damage arising from any cause without actual fault or privity (see COGSA, § 4(2)(q), 46 U.S.C. § 1304(2)(q)); and

The limited liability of $500 per package or freight unit unless the nature and value of the goods have been declared by the shipper before shipment and inserted in the bill of lading (see COGSA, § 4(5), 46 U.S.C. § 1304(5)).

The exemptions, immunities and limitations which are pertinent to the instant case are the complete exemption from liability (see COGSA, § 4(2)(a), 46 U.S.C. § 1304(2)(a)); the $500 limitation on liability (see COGSA, § 4(5), 46 U.S.C. § 1304(5)); and the one-year period of limitations for instituting suit (see COGSA, § 3(6), 46 U.S.C. § 1303(6)).

B. *The $500 Limitation on Amount of Liability*

In *Tessler Brothers (B.C.) Ltd. v. Italpacific Line and Matson Terminals, Inc.* (9 Cir. 1974) 494 F.2d 438, this court squarely faced the issue of whether a 'Himalaya' clause was valid which purported clearly and expressly to extend to a non-carrier to $500 limitation on liability which COGSA, § 4(5), 46 U.S.C. § 1304(5), provides for carriers. That clause was held valid, and Tessler Brothers is binding authority as regards the inclusion in bills of lading of limitations on amount of non-carrier's liability.

C. *The Complete Immunity from Liability for Negligence in Navigation and Management*

* * *

It will be noted that COGSA's provisions regulate the liability of carriers, but not non-carriers. Since the Act, in balance, is more protective than the common law, it is not surprising that noncarriers have nonetheless sought to place themselves under COGSA's shelter. This has been attempted by arguing in the courts that COGSA should be construed to protect parties other than carriers, despite the Act's language to the contrary; and since this argument has failed, the extension of COGSA has been attempted contractually, by providing in bills of lading that certain non-carriers would be subject to COGSA's protections.

In *Robert C. Herd & Co. v. Krawill Machinery Corp.*, 359 U.S. 297, 79 S.Ct. 766, 3 L.Ed.2d 820 (1959), the Supreme Court considered whether the provisions of COGSA should apply to a stevedore, either by virtue of the Act itself or by contractual extension in the bills of lading.

The Court held that nothing in the language, history, or environment of the Act showed a congressional intent to regulate by statute the liability of stevedores or other agents of the carrier.

The Court further noted that the bills of lading in that case did not expressly extend the provisions of COGSA to the stevedore.

In language of significance here, the Court stated as follows:

'This Court has several times held that an agent's only shield from liability 'for conduct harmful to the plaintiff ... is a constitutional rule of law that exonerates him.' ...Any such rule of law, being in derogation of the common law, must be strictly construed, for 'no statute is to be construed as altering the common law, farther than its words import. It is not to be construed as making any innovation upon the common law which it does not fairly express.' ...Similarly, contracts purporting to grant immunity from, or limitation of, liability must be strictly construed and limited to intended beneficiaries, for they 'are not to be applied to alter familiar rules visiting liability upon a tortfeasor for the consequences of his negligence, unless the clarity of the language used expresses such to be the understanding of the contracting parties."

The above quotation from the *Herd* opinion is of special import here. It suggests that the sole reason the Court refused to allow the contractual extension of COGSA's protections to stevedores was that the bill of lading in that case was not clear and express in its intent to make this extension; the *Herd* opinion might be interpreted to mean that a bill of lading, if it clearly and expressly extends a COGSA exemption, immunity or limitation to a non- carrier who is an agent of the carrier, is a valid derogation of the common law and will be given effect.

Thus the Court of Appeals for the Ninth Circuit in *Tessler Brothers, supra*, held on the basis of *Herd* that a bill of lading, if clear and express, was effective to extend the $500 limitation on the amount of liability, as provided in COGSA, § 4(5), 46 U.S.C. § 1304(5), to stevedores.

Our concern, however, is not with the contractual extension of the Act's limitation on amount of liability, but rather with an extension to non-carriers of the complete exemption from negligence in navigation and management as provided in COGSA, § 4(2)(a), 46 U.S.C. § 1304(2)(a).

3. Does the bill of lading clearly extend COGSA, § 4(2)(a), 46 U.S.C. § 1304(2) (a), to Todd? The bills of lading in our case expressly extended COGSA, § 4(2)(a), 46 U.S.C. § 1304(2)(a), to the master, officers, crewmembers, contractors, stevedores, longshoremen, agents, representatives, employees or others used, engaged or employed by the carrier in the performance of such work or services undertaken in the bills of lading. Although drydock operators were not expressly listed as persons covered, Todd would seem to be a 'contractor,' as the district court so held.

Less clear is whether Todd's services were part of the work or services undertaken in the bills of lading. The district court held that they were, and we are disposed to agree. The primary work undertaken in the bills of lading is the transporting of cargo. But implicit in the undertaking is the agreement to take reasonable steps to ensure the safety of the cargo in transport. Thus it is customary for cargo vessels to drydock in transit for routine inspections and repairs. The work performed by the drydock operator, although directly affecting the ship only, aids the carrier in safely transporting the cargo. We therefore hold that Todd was a contractor employed by Grace in performing the work undertaken in the bills of lading and hence was clearly intended by the parties thereto to be entitled to the immunities of COGSA, § 4(2)(a),46 U.S.C. § 1304(2)(a).

4. Was the 'Himalaya' clause an adhesion contract unenforceable against the cargo insurers? There is a general rule of contract law that when there is a gross disparity of bargaining power between two parties to a contract such that one party has no choice but to adhere to unfavorable and unfair terms, those terms will not be enforced against him unless he was given his understanding consent to be bound. See *Henningsen v. Bloomfield Motors*, 32 N.J. 358, 161 A.2d 69 (1960). The cargo insurers contend that the bills of lading are contracts of adhesion, see *Cabot Corp. v. S S. Mormacscan*, (2 Cir. 1971) 441 F.2d 476, 478, and that since they gave no 'understanding consent,' they are not bound.

We recognize, as said in *Tessler Brothers, supra*, p. 445, 'that the content of ocean bills of lading is for all practical purposes completely within the carrier's power, subject to the provisions of COGSA, and that contracts purporting to limit liability must be strictly construed.' But we are not persuaded that we should refuse to enforce the bills of lading simply because they are in this respect contracts of adhesion. The cases refusing to enforce contracts because they were contracts of adhesion have generally involved special circumstances, such as a grossly unfair bargain foisted by a noncompetitive industry upon the ordinary consumer on a 'take-it-or-leave-it' basis, with the terms often buried in fine print unlikely to be understood or even read by the consumer. *See, e.g., Henningsen, supra*. There is no binding authority for likewise refusing to enforce bills of lading. The shipper or insurer of cargo, while not equal in bargaining power to the carrier, is not in the position of the ordinary man facing an enormous, impersonal industry. Surely the cargo insurers were aware of the 'Himalaya' clauses. As a group they perhaps could muster the bargaining power necessary to alter the terms in the bills of lading. Therefore, although we might find the bills of lading sufficiently adhesive to warrant a strict construction against the carrier and his agents, we are not moved by their adhesive character to interfere with the freedom of contract to the extent of refusing entirely to give effect to the 'Himalaya' clause. *Cf. Tessler Brothers*, *supra*, p. 445.

5. Does COGSA, § 6, 46 U.S.C. § 1306, prohibit the extension of the Act to non-carriers? Section 6, 46 U.S.C. § 1306, provides that a carrier and a shipper may enter into any agreement in any terms as to the liability of the carrier's agents for negligence in respect to cargo, but may do so only if no bill of lading has been or shall be issued and the shipments are not ordinary commercial shipments made in the ordinary course of trade. Since in our case there is a bill of lading and the shipment is in ordinary commerce, § 6, 46 U.S.C. § 1306, does not apply.

But the cargo interests argue that § 6, 46 U.S.C. § 1306, prohibits by implication any agreement to which the Section does not apply. This argument was presented in *Tessler Brothers*, *supra*, p. 444, and found wanting. Although § 6, 46 U.S.C. § 1306, describes certain situations, none of which is present here, in which any exculpatory agreement is permissible, we see no implication in the Section that in all other situations, such as ours, no exculpatory agreement is permissible.

6. Does an extension of COGSA, § 4(2)(a), 46 U.S.C. § 1304(2)(a), to non-carriers impermissibly derogate a common law principle against exculpation? There is a controlling rule of the common law, stated in perhaps its clearest form in *United States v. Atlantic Mutual Insurance Co.*,343 U.S. 236, 72 S.Ct. 666, 69 L.Ed. 907 (1952), that 'without congressional authority (carriers) cannot stipulate against their own negligence or that of their agents or servants.' *Atlantic Mutual*, *supra*, at p. 242.

In COGSA, § 4(2)(a), 46 U.S.C. § 1304(2)(a), Congress has immunized carriers from liability for negligence in navigation or management. It has not, however, altered the common law rule as regards agents or servants. We must therefore inquire whether Todd was an 'agent' or 'servant' of the carrier. We have already held Todd to be a 'contractor' but that of course does not necessarily make Todd an 'agent.' Restatement (Second) of Agency § 14N, Comment b (1957). If Todd is an agent, we must further inquire whether cases such as *Herd* and *Tessler Brothers*, both decided after *Atlantic Mutual*, indicate a development in the common law such that it no longer forbids carriers from contractually exculpating their agents and servants from negligence.

"Agency" has been commonly defined as 'the fiduciary relation which results from the manifestation of consent by one person to another that the other shall act on his behalf and subject to his control, and consent by the other so to act.' Restatement (Second) of Agency § 1 (1957). The agent is the one who is to act. Restatement, *supra*.

From the facts of this case it is apparent that Todd was the carrier's agent within the meaning of the above definition. There was an agreement between the two that Todd should act on the carrier's behalf in maintaining the vessel in a seaworthy condition. Upon taking control of the vessel, Todd assuredly had a fiduciary duty to exercise skill and care in its work. This work, of course, would be subject to the ultimate control of the carrier as owner of the vessel.

As an 'agent,' Todd could not contractually be exculpated from its negligence, unless case law has modified the old common law rule. We do not think is has. *Herd* stands for the proposition that clear and express language in the contract is the *sine qua non* for altering the common law; but when that requirement is met, it is still left open for the courts to decide whether a particular alteration is repugnant to public policy. *Herd* did not imply that a contract, if clear and express in its intent, would be adequate to alter any familiar rule of tort liability whatsoever.

It is the holding of this court that a contract, no matter how clear and express, which purports wholly to immunize a non-carrier from liability for its negligence, is repugnant to traditional law and to sound policy. *Tessler Brothers*, which upheld the contractual monetary limitation of a non-carrier's (stevedore's) liability, is not inconsistent with our holding here, for as said in that case (at p. 443), 'This distinction between a limitation on liability and an exemption from liability is crucial. A limitation, unlike an exemption, does not induce negligence.'

Tessler Brothers, while stating that *Atlantic Mutual* was inapposite to a discussion of a 'Himalaya' clause that merely limits the amount of recovery for negligence, recognized that *Atlantic Mutual* '(invalidates) clauses that exempt carriers or their agents from liability for their negligence.' This language, of course, was not essential to the holding in *Tessler Brothers* and is therefore dictum; yet we believe it accurately states the law of *Atlantic Mutual*. Since the 'Himalaya' clause in this case purports to exempt non- carriers completely from any liability for negligence, and thereby strongly tends to induce negligence, the bill of lading is to that extent void.

7. Assuming that COGSA, § 4(2)(a), 46 U.S.C. § 1304(2)(a), could validly be extended to Todd, does the language of that provision apply to Todd's conduct? There is an alternate ground for holding that Todd is not immunized from liability—even if § 4(2)(a), 46 U.S.C. § 1304(2)(a), could validly be extended to protect non-carriers, its protection does not cover the sort of negligence of which Todd was culpable.

That section provides immunity only for 'Act, neglect, or default ... in the navigation or in the management of the ship....' A reading of the many cases giving content to the words 'navigation' and 'management' makes it evident that Todd was doing something else.

None of the cases actually gives a precise definition of the words, for the courts, eschewing abstractions, have been satisfied with determining on a case-to-case basis whether a particular act was or was not in 'navigation' or 'management.' Most of the cases have involved drawing the line between negligence in care of the cargo, for which there is liability, and negligence in navigation or management of the vessel, for which no liability attaches. Obviously, carelessness in navigating or managing a cargo-laden ship would simultaneously create a foreseeable danger to the cargo; hence, it is not easy to draw a distinct line. Yet read as a whole, the cases would seem to support this test: If the act in question has the primary purpose of affecting the ship, it is 'in navigation or in management'; but if the primary purpose is to affect the cargo, it is not 'in navigation or in management.'

This test can be applied to our case by rough analogy only, for Todd's negligence—a failure to maintain a safe drydock—was in omission, not commission, and hence had no primary purpose. But the omission-commission distinction presents no difficulty if we assume hypothetically that Todd, instead of omitting to make the drydock safe, had undertaken to repair it, and had performed the job negligently. If Todd had thereby caused damage to a ship that later used the facilities, then we would hold that such act of negligence would have the primary purpose of affecting the drydock, not of affecting the ship.

True, acts affecting the drydock would ultimately affect the ship, just as acts affecting a ship would indirectly affect the cargo inside, But we are not looking for ultimate and indirect effects when trying to determine whether an act is in navigation or management of the ship. What we are looking for is whether the act which is negligently done, or not done, is primarily directed at the ship itself, or at something else. It seems apparent that Todd's negligence was not primarily directed at the Santa Ana, for Todd had been negligent as regards the drydock long before the Santa Ana contracted to enter it. We therefore hold that Todd's negligent maintenance of the drydock was not 'in navigation or management' of the vessel and that § 4(2)(a), 46 U.S.C. § 1304(2) (a), has no relevance to this case.

D. *The Time Limitation Under COGSA, § 3(6), 46 U.S.C. § 1303(6)*

Tessler Brothers, *supra*, p. 443, stated that *Atlantic Mutual* while invalidating clauses that completely exempt the agents of carriers, is inapposite to clauses that merely limit the amount of liability. In a similar vein, we believe that *Atlantic Mutual* is inapposite to clauses merely limiting the time limit in which suit must be brought. We might hold differently if the time limit provided were so short that it created an unreasonable risk to the plaintiff that he would lose his cause of action. But such is not the case. COGSA indicates the congressional determination that one year is a reasonable time limit for instituting suit against a carrier, and we see no factors necessitating more time for suit against the carrier's agents.

Since the extension of § 3(6), 46 U.S.C. § 1303(6), to agents of the carriers is clear and express, and since it creates a reasonable limitation on the common law liability of agents, and since there is no binding authority for holding such clauses void, we uphold the validity of this portion of the bills of lading.

This necessarily moots the holding of the district court that Royal Globe's suit was barred by laches. Since Royal Globe commenced its suit well after the one-year limit of § 3(6), 46 U.S.C. § 1303(6), had passed, and was thus barred by that fixed period of limitations, there is no need to decide if laches provides an additional time-bar. We leave it for the district court to determine on remand whether any other plaintiffs are affected by § 3(6), 46 U.S.C. § 1303(6).

Affirmed in part, and reversed in part and remanded for further proceedings not inconsistent with this opinion.

H. Deviation

GENERAL ELECTRIC CO. v. STEAMSHIP "NANCY LYKES"

536 F. Supp. 687, 1982 AMC 1726 (S.D.N.Y. 1982), *aff'd*, 706 F.2d 80, 1983 AMC 1947 (2d Cir.), *cert. denied*, 464 U.S. 849, 104 S. Ct. 157, 78 L. Ed. 2d 145, 1984 AMC 2403 (1983)

LASKER, District Judge:

General Electric Company International Sales Division ("GE") sues to recover for two locomotive cabs which were shipped by Lykes Bros. Steamship Company ("Lykes") via its liner service aboard the vessel the S.S. Nancy Lykes from New Orleans, Louisiana, destination Keelung, Taiwan. The locomotives were lost at sea on May 5, 1978, when the vessel encountered gale winds and rough seas off the coast of California.

The relevant voyage of the Nancy Lykes commenced in Mobile, Alabama on April 10, 1978, and proceeded to New Orleans, its first port of call. The advertised itinerary for the vessel listed Yokohama, Japan ("Kobe") as the next port of call, with an estimated arrival date of May 11, 1978. Instead of proceeding directly to Kobe after passing through the Panama Canal, however, the vessel next went to San Pedro, California, to secure fuel (bunkers). San Pedro was not listed on the published itinerary of the voyage. Lykes candidly acknowledges that the stop was made to take advantage of the low fuel prices then available at San Pedro and that its operations department directed the master to make the stop while the vessel was still in the Gulf area.

I

GE contends that the bunkers call at San Pedro constituted an unreasonable deviation from the published itinerary of the vessel and that the deviation caused the vessel to encounter the gales which precipitated the loss of the locomotives. In addition, GE alleges that the locomotives, which were stowed on deck, were not properly secured.

* * *

II

Lykes contends that it is customary for liner services to stop for bunkers in ports that are not advertised in their published itineraries; that Lykes established a custom beginning in 1978 of using San Pedro as a bunkers only port; that the bill of lading liberty clause encompassed such a step; that the locomotives were properly secured on the deck of the Nancy Lykes; and that the diversion to San Pedro did not involve a substantial risk of encountering unfavorable weather.

* * *

III

GE has failed to establish that the locomotives were not properly secured on the deck of the Nancy Lykes. The only evidence presented on this point was Patterson's opinion that more chains should have secured the locomotives. This conclusion, however, is contradicted by the National Cargo Bureau Certificate of Inspection which followed an actual inspection of the locomotives on deck. It is undisputed that this Certificate is generally relied on in the maritime industry to establish proper stowage.

GE has established, however, that the decision to proceed to San Pedro for bunkers was unreasonable. It is undisputed that sufficient bunkers were available in the Gulf ports and in the Panama Canal ports to carry the vessel to Kobe. It is also clear that the ordinary and customary trade route from the Panama Canal to the Far East is within the area described by Raguso. This conclusion is confirmed by the testimony of Kaciak that, if he had been asked to route the vessel from the Panama Canal to Kobe, rather than from San Pedro to Kobe, he would have recommended a course on the northern portion of the area described by Raguso, at least for the first part of the voyage. Moreover, the evidence established that vessels on liner service ordinarily take bunkers at an advertised port of call. Most importantly, we are persuaded that the diversion to San Pedro created an increased risk that unfavorable weather would be encountered. Raguso and Kaciak agreed at least that the statistical probability of encountering gale or near gale winds, of whatever variety or designation, increases in the springtime in the region the more northerly one goes from a latitude of approximately 30 degrees. By leaving from San Pedro rather than the Panama Canal, the vessel was assured of passing through the region north of 30 degrees whatever routing was chosen from San Pedro. Furthermore, we accept Raguso's estimate that the statistical probability of gale winds during this time of year is approximately 5 or 6 percent off the coast of California since, in addition to the expert testimony of the weather routers, every mariner with experience on these seas who testified acknowledged that gale or near gale northerly winds are known among mariners to occur in the region in the winter and spring months. Accordingly, we find that whatever the precise percentage of increased probability of unfavorable weather, the decision to go to San Pedro created a significantly greater risk of encountering unfavorable weather. Indeed, the two prior Lykes' vessels which made the San Pedro stop prior to the Nancy Lykes both encountered such weather, one from Gulf of Tehuantepec winds, the other from winds off the coast after departing from San Pedro. At the least, this prior experience should have forewarned Lykes of the potential dangers in diverting to San Pedro.

Moreover, while it has not been demonstrated that the locomotives were improperly stowed on deck, the fact that such weighty cargo was being carried on deck should have been a significant consideration militating in favor of a route on the calmest seas possible. By directing the vessel to take on bunkers at San Pedro, Lykes foreclosed safer options and thrust the vessel into areas where the probability was increased that unfavorable weather would be encountered. This added risk of damage or loss to cargo solely for the benefit of the vessel must be deemed unreasonable. Indeed, there is no evidence that Lykes considered any factor other than its fuel cost savings in directing its vessels to take on bunkers at San Pedro.

Lykes' contention that the stop at San Pedro was not a deviation in light of the broad liberty clause contained in the bill of lading is unpersuasive. Paragraph III of the applicable bill of lading defines the permissible scope of the voyage as including "usual, customary or advertised ports, whether herein named or not, and ports in or out of the advertised, geographic or usual route or order...." In reference to a similarly broad liberties clause it has been noted that "[i]t would seem hard to 'deviate' from such a voyage." GILMORE & BLACK, THE LAW OF ADMIRALTY, 178 (2d Ed. 1975). Such a construction would undercut the policy and statutory provisions forbidding a carrier from contracting out of liability for his own wrongdoing and would be inconsistent with § 3(2) of the Carriage of Goods by Sea Act ("COGSA") which imposes upon the carrier a duty to " ... properly ... carry the goods." *Id.* at 178. Furthermore, § 4(4) of COGSA implies as clearly as possible that any unreasonable deviation is to be treated as a breach of the Act and the contract of carriage:

> Any deviation in saving or attempting to save life or property at sea, or any reasonable deviation shall not be deemed to be an infringement or breach of this Act or of the contract of carriage, and the carrier shall not be liable for any loss or damage resulting therefrom: Provided, however, That if the deviation is for the purpose of loading or unloading cargo or passengers it shall, *prima facie*, be regarded as unreasonable. [Emphasis supplied]

Indeed, § 4(4) confirms that a carrier may not define the voyage in such broad language as to render it impossible for any deviation to be found no matter how far the vessel wanders from the specified route. Lykes' proposed construction of the liberty clause is at odds with § 4(4)'s concept of reasonable and unreasonable deviations. The liberty clause must therefore be construed to permit only reasonable deviations from the anticipated journey. *Id.* at 179. Moreover, the reasonableness of the deviation may not be judged merely from the point of view of the carrier. As § 4(4)'s proviso suggests, the carrier may not justify a deviation merely because it was to his benefit. "The carrier, throughout the performance of the voyage, is always subject to the Section 3(2) duty to care for and carry the goods properly, and his decision on a route would seem to be improper and unreasonable whenever it is made in disregard of that duty." *Id; see Spartus Corp. v. S.S. Yafo*, 590 F.2d 1310 (5th Cir. 1979); *Encyclopedia Britannica Inc. v. S.S. Hong Kong Producer*, 422 F.2d 7, 18 (2d Cir. 1969), *cert. denied*, 397 U.S. 964, 90 S. Ct. 998, 25 L. Ed. 2d 255 (1970).

Nor are we persuaded that Lykes' prior stops at San Pedro rendered that practice "customary" so that the Nancy Lykes' stop was not a deviation or was a justified deviation. The evidence established that, at least for liner services, bunkers are ordinarily secured at one of the ports of call advertised in the Journal of Commerce. Indeed, Kohler, in his long experience as a bunkers broker, had never been asked by a liner operator to secure bunkers in a port that was not an advertised port of call. Despite GE's evidence of instances where such stops were made, it is clear that, at the least, such stops are extraordinary for liner service vessels.

Similarly, Lykes' contention that the stop at San Pedro was a customary one for vessels going to the Far East is without merit. Lykes relies on the facts that, prior to the Nancy Lykes, it had directed two other vessels to stop at San Pedro for bunkers and that it used San Pedro frequently in the years following, as did other lines. However, the critical element as to "custom" in the cases relied on by Lykes is the knowledge on the part of the shipper that a particular port was a customary port for the voyage. *See, e.g., W. R. Grace & Co. v. Toyo Kisen Kabushiki Kaisha*, 12 F.2d 519 (9th Cir. 1926); *The Frederick Luckenbach*, 15 F.2d 241 (S.D.N.Y. 1926); *The San Guiseppe*, 122 F.2d 579 (4th Cir. 1941). Of course, where the shipper has knowledge that a particular stop will be made and consents either explicitly or implicitly, as in the cited cases, the particular stop can hardly be labeled a deviation from the contemplated voyage. In such circumstances, the shipper is logically held to have consented to any greater risks to his cargo imposed by the additional stop. By contrast, in the present case there were only two such diversions before the voyage in question; regardless of the later practice of Lykes or other liner services, knowledge on the part of GE that Lykes would be bunkering at San Pedro cannot be inferred, and all the evidence indicates that GE did not in fact know that such a stop was planned. In these circumstances, GE cannot be held to have consented to whatever added risks that were occasioned by the San Pedro deviation. In addition, in light of the finding that liner services ordinarily only bunker at advertised ports of call and that the ordinary trade route to the Far East from the Panama Canal is significantly further south than San Pedro, it cannot be said, as in *The San Guiseppe, supra*, that the bunkering stop was merely ancillary to the contemplated voyage.

In sum, the stop of the Nancy Lykes at San Pedro for bunkers was a deviation from the ordinary route for a liner service vessel since San Pedro was not an advertised port of call and was not along the ordinary trade route from the Panama Canal to the Far East. In light of the fact that the deviation exposed the vessel to significantly greater risks of adverse weather, and was made solely for the benefit of the vessel, it was unreasonable. As an unreasonable deviation, the vessel is liable for any damage to cargo caused by the diversion and recovery is not limited to the $500 per package limitation contained in the Bill of Lading and in COGSA.

Accordingly, GE is entitled to recover the $1,709,000 it cost it to replace the locomotive cabs lost overboard. Submit judgment.

---

1. Consequences of deviation

The Second Circuit has led the way in holding that an unreasonable deviation from the contract of carriage deprives the carrier of the benefit of section 4(5)'s liability limitation. *See Sedco, Inc. v. S.S. Strathewe*, 800 F.2d 27, 1986 AMC 2801 (2d Cir. 1986). Both the Ninth and Fifth Circuits agree with this view. *See Nemeth v. General Steamship Corp.*, 694 F.2d 609, 1983 AMC 885 (9th Cir. 1982); *Vision Air Flight Service, Inc. v. M/V National Pride*, 155 F.3d 1165, 1999 AMC 1168 (9th Cir. 1998); *Spartus Corp. v. S/S Yafo*, 590 F.2d 1310, 1979 AMC 2294 (5th Cir. 1979). The Third and Eleventh Circuits have agreed with the Second, Fifth and Ninth Circuits in *dicta*. *S.P.M. Corp. v. M/V Ming Moon*, 965 F. 2d 1297, 1992 AMC 2409 (3d Cir. 1992); *Unimac Co., Inc. v. C.F. Ocean Service, Inc.*, 43 F.3d 1434, 1995 AMC 1484 (11th Cir. 1995). The Seventh Circuit, on the other hand, has concluded that the limitation applies regardless of whether there has been an unreasonable deviation. *Atlantic Mutual Insurance Co. v. Poseidon Schiffahrt*, 313 F.2d 872, 875, 1963 AMC 2697 (7th Cir. 1963). Which view is correct? The matter is analyzed in Friedell, *The Deviating Ship*, 32 Hast. L.J. 1535 (1981).

---

2. Basis for Liability

Historically, a geographic deviation from the agreed upon or customary route ousted the terms of the bill of lading and the carrier was liable as an insurer for the loss of goods. A deviation was considered to be a fundamental breach of the contract of carriage. The carrier was not allowed plead any of the exceptions in the bill of lading. These consequences were imposed on the carrier because a deviation revoked the shipper's insurance coverage, and, as a matter of fairness, the shipper was allowed to recover its loss from the carrier. COGSA, however, provides that "any reasonable deviation" shall not be an infringement of that statute or a breach of a contract of carriage, and that the carrier shall not be liable for any loss or damage resulting therefrom. It has been suggested that COGSA has thus abolished the strict insurer's liability. Furthermore, changes in insurance law lend support to this result because today "held covered" insurance clauses protect the cargo regardless of deviation. G. Gilmore & C. Black, The Law of Admiralty § 3-40 (2d Ed. 1975).

Although there is no doubt (except in the Third Circuit: see note 1 *supra*) that the doctrine of deviation still applies despite enactment of COGSA, the historic "deprived of insurance rationale" has fallen out of favor. In *Vision Air Flight Service, Inc. v. M/V National Pride*, 155 F.3d 1165, 1174 n.10, 1999 AMC 1168, (9th Cir. 1998), the U.S. Court of Appeals for the Ninth Circuit said:

> Another fundamental objection to expansion of the doctrine seems to be that the doctrine is outmoded because modern insurance contracts now cover losses resulting from deviation. *See, e.g.,* Black and Gilmore [sic], *supra* at 181-82. Yet, historically, application of the deviation doctrine did not turn on whether the goods were insured. *See* Steven F. Friedell, *The Deviating Ship*, 32 Hastings L.J. 1535, 1545 n. 45 (1981). Moreover, to the extent the deviation doctrine is concerned with providing an incentive for carriers not to undertake certain actions that impose unreasonable risks on cargo, insurance is irrelevant.

---

3. Causal Relationship

Must there be a causal relationship between deviation and the loss and if so, who has the burden of proving causal relationship or lack thereof? It appears that there must be some causal relationship between the deviation and the loss. Lack of causation seems to be treated as a defense which must be sustained by the carrier. *Hellenic Lines v. U.S.*, 512 F.2d 1196, 1975 AMC 697 (2d Cir. 1975); *Calmaquip Engineering West Hemisphere Corporation v. West Coast Carriers, Ltd.*, 650 F.2d 633, 1984 AMC 839 (5th Cir. 1981); *Mobil Sales & Supply Corp. v. M/V BANGLAR KAKOLI*, 588 F. Supp. 1134 (S.D.N.Y. 1984).

---

4. Quasi-Deviation

Originally, the doctrine of deviation was applied against the carrier only when it deviated geographically from the agreed upon route or the customary route. Some courts, however, found that when there were other fundamental breaches of the contract of carriage that these were analogous to deviation, hence, they characterize such breaches as "quasi-deviations." The effect of quasi-deviation has been to deprive a carrier of the benefit of a limitation of liability clause in its bill of lading and the $500 per package limitation of COGSA. *St. Johns N.F. Shipping Corp. v. S.A. Companhia Geral Commercial*, 263 U.S. 119, 44 S.Ct. 30, 68 L.Ed. 201 (1923) (stowage on deck despite clean bill of lading); *Encyclopaedia Britannica, Inc. v. S.S. Hong Kong Producer*, 422 F.2d 7 (2d Cir. 1969) *cert. denied*, 397 U.S. 964 (1970) (stowage on deck despite clean bill of lading); *Calmaquip Engineering West Hemisphere Corporation v. West Coast Carriers, Ltd.*, 650 F.2d 633, 1984 AMC 839 (5th Cir. 1981) (stowage on deck in contravention of shipper's express instruction to carry below deck).

More recently, however, some courts have begun to question the categorical conclusion that carrying cargo on deck constitutes a quasi-deviation in the face of a clean bill of lading. Courts have concluded that proof that goods were stowed in the customary manner for the particular trade precludes a finding of deviation and thereby makes an examination of the reasonableness of such stowage unnecessary. This is particularly significant in relation to cargo in containers, where carriage on the deck of a specially constructed container ship pursuant to a port or trade custom would not constitute a deviation. *Electro-Tec Corporation v. S.S. Dart Atlantica*, 598 F. Supp. 929, 1985 AMC 1606 (D. Md. 1984); *DuPont de Nemours International S.A. v. S.S. Mormacvega*, 367 F. Supp. 793, 1972 AMC 2366 *aff'd*. 493 F.2d 97, 1974 AMC 67 (2d Cir. 1974); *Konica Business Machines, Inc. v. Sea-Land Consumer, Vessel*, 153 F.3d 1076, 1998 AMC 2705, (9th Cir. 1998); *Vision Air Flight Service, Inc. v. M/V National Pride*, 155 F.3d 1165, 1172 n.8, 1999 AMC 1168 (9th Cir. 1998); *American Home Assurance Co. v. M/V Tabuk*, 170 F.Supp.2d 431, 2002 AMC 184 (S.D.N.Y. 2001) *aff'd* 45 Fed.Appx. 12 (2d Cir. 2002).

Moreover, the Second Circuit has also limited the doctrine of deviation to situations involving geographic deviation and unauthorized on-deck stowage of cargo (quasi-deviation), and has indicated that the doctrine should not be extended beyond these categories. "[M]ere negligence, lack of due diligence, or a failure to properly handle, stow, care, or deliver cargo never has constituted deviation" that would deprive a carrier of either a contractual or statutory limitation of liability. *Sedco, Inc. v. S.S. Strathewe*, 800 F.2d 27, 32, 1986 AMC 2801 (2d Cir. 1986). See also *Styling Plastics Co., Ltd. v. The Neptune Orient Lines, Ltd.*, 666 F. Supp. 1406, 1988 AMC 351 (N.D. Cal. 1987) and *C.A. Articulos Nacionales de Goma Gomaven v. M/V Aragua*, 756 F.2d 1156, 1986 AMC 2087 (5th Cir. 1985), where the court held that misdelivery of goods could not be considered an unreasonable deviation.

Although the doctrine of quasi-deviation is generally in retreat, another line of cases holds that a carrier who falsely issues a clean on-board bill of lading for goods that were never shipped, or who falsely issues a clean bill of lading for goods known to be shipped in damaged condition, is liable for misrepresentation and is precluded from limiting its liability under COGSA. *Berisford Metals Corporation v. S/S Salvadore*, 779 F.2d 841, 1986 AMC 874 (2d Cir. 1985) *cert. denied*, 476 U.S. 1188 (1986) (misrepresentation that cargo was loaded on ship); *Mitsui Marine Fire and Ins. Co. Ltd v. Direct Container Line, Inc.*, 119 F.Supp.2d 412, 416-17, 2002 AMC 190 (S.D.N.Y. 2000)(same); *Leather's Best Internat'l, Inc. v. M/V Lloyd Sergipe*, 760 F.Supp. 301, 311, 1991 AMC 1929 (S.D.N.Y. 1991)(same); *Condor Indus. Internat'l, Inc. v. M/V Am. Express*, 667 F.Supp. 99, 100, 1988 AMC 598 (S.D.N.Y. 1987)(clean bill of lading for cargo known to be damaged).

Authorized deck carriage is not governed by COGSA but it is governed by the Harter Act. COGSA does not apply to "cargo which by the contract of carriage is stated as being carried on deck and is so carried". COGSA § 1(c). Because COGSA does not apply to authorized deck carriage, § 3(8) of COGSA does not strike down a bill of lading clause that exonerates the carrier from liability for damage to cargo carried on deck, if the bill of lading states that the cargo is to be carried on deck or if it is obvious from the circumstances that it must be so carried. *Chester v. Maritima del Litoral, S.A.*, 586 F.Supp. 192, 198, 1985 AMC 2831 (E.D.Wis. 1984)("The plaintiffs'…argument that the use of a clause refusing liability for damage to goods carried on deck violates § 1303(8) of COGSA is circular. That provision prevents a carrier from relieving or lessening his liability for 'goods...as provided in this Act'. As explained above, § 1301(c) of COGSA explicitly excludes deck cargo from the category of 'goods' to which the Act's provisions apply, thereby neutralizing § 1303(8)".) However, the Harter Act strikes down such a clause to the extent that it purports to exonerate the carrier from liability for negligence. *Blanchard Lumber Co. v. S.S. Anthony II*, 259 F.Supp. 857 (S.D.N.Y. 1966). In this case, a shipment of lumber was agreed to be carried on deck and it was so carried from British Columbia to Providence, Rhode Island, under bills of lading providing that the shipment was "at shipper's risk." In an action by consignees against the carriers for damage caused to the cargo by negligent stowage, the court held that when shipments to or from ports of the United States in foreign trade are not covered by COGSA, the Harter Act applies during the entire voyage and exoneration clauses for negligence are invalid. Accordingly, because it had been agreed that the lumber would be carried on deck and it was so carried, it was not covered by the COGSA. Nevertheless, the Harter Act applied and the "at shipper's risk" clause in the bill of lading was null and void.

---

5. Land-Based Deviation

When the parties extend the application of COGSA to the entire transportation including the land portion does the doctrine of deviation apply? *See Asahi America, Inc. v. The M/V Arild Maersk*, 602 F. Supp. 25, 1986 AMC 53 (S.D.N.Y. 1985) where the court found a land-based deviation.

---

6. Statute of Limitations

An unreasonable course deviation does not oust COGSA's one year statute of limitation. *Mesocap Ind. Ltd. v. Torm Lines*, 194 F.3d 1342, 2000 AMC 370 (11th Cir. 1999).

I. Exoneration Clauses

Note: Exculpatory clauses and the Harter Act

In simplified form, the following was the situation before the enactment of the Harter Act. Assume that a shipper and carrier entered into a contract of affreightment and the goods were damaged because the vessel was unseaworthy. This unseaworthy condition was known both to the shipowner and the master. The shipper would have several options. First, it could allege a breach of the bailment contract which would subject the carrier to strict liability if it were a common carrier. Second, it could allege a breach of the warranty of seaworthiness which was implied in the contract of carriage. Third, it could allege that the carrier breached its duty to exercise due care for the cargo. Although all of these various contract and tort claims might not be available in all fact situations, a shipper ordinarily would have been in a reasonably good position to recover for loss or damage to cargo. It is significant to observe that some of the bases for liability are grounded grounded in strict liability while others are based on fault.

Carriers sought to counter such claims by introducing exculpatory clauses into the contract of carriage, namely the bill of lading. These clauses negated the warranty of seaworthiness and purported to relieve the carrier from any:

(1)   liability as bailee,
(2)   duty to exercise due diligence to provide a seaworthy vessel,
(3)   liability for loss caused by unseaworthiness,
(4)   duty to care for cargo, etc.

In essence, these exculpatory clauses purported to exculpate a carrier from liability for all damage and loss to cargo resulting from any cause—including the carrier's own negligence. These clauses placed the entire risk of loss and damage on the shipper.

If the principle of "freedom of contract" had held sway in the courts, the exculpatory clauses would have been upheld and carriers would have contracted their way out of liability. However, the courts in the United States, unlike others such as in England, held that it was against public policy to allow carriers to exempt themselves from liability for loss or damage caused by their own fault. The Harter Act was intended to prohibit such exculpatory clauses subject to certain exceptions and defenses which were concessions to keeping the United States fleet competitive with those of other countries, principally England. Thus, the Harter Act does not impose strict liability. It does not prohibit a carrier from contracting-out of strict liability. Generally, these statutes prohibit a carrier from contracting-out of liability for loss or damage caused by its negligence. However, the statute exonerates the carrier for damage or loss to cargo caused by "errors in navigation and management" of the vessel by master and crew, if the carrier exercised due diligence to make the vessel seaworthy.

ASSOCIATED METALS & MINERALS CORP. v. M/V ARKTIS SKY

978 F.2d 47, 1993 AMC 509 (2d Cir. 1992)

LAY, Senior Circuit Judge:

This appeal involves an action *in rem* brought in the district court by Associated Metals & Minerals Corp. against the vessel M/V Arktis Sky; its operator, Erhversinvestering K/S; as well as its owner, Elite Shipping I/S. Elite Shipping entered into a charter party agreement with Altos Hornos De Vizcaya, S.A., a non-party to this action, to ship a cargo of galvanized steel sheets in 398 coils from Bilbao, Spain to Port Elizabeth, New Jersey. The shipper/charterer, Altos Hornos, sold the coils to Associated Metals. Altos Hornos contracted with its own stevedore, Maritime Candida, to load and stow the coils aboard the vessel in Spain. After the cargo was loaded, the chief mate of the Arktis signed with the vessel's stamp a lashing statement which noted that the lash had been "performed under chief mate instructions and satisfactory."

When the vessel arrived in Port Elizabeth it was discovered that some of the cargo had shifted during the voyage. The coils were damaged in the sum of $249,629.76. Associated Metals brought an action against the vessel, its operator and its owner. Associated Metals moved for summary judgment. The district court granted summary judgment in favor of the defendants and dismissed the complaint. This appeal followed.

Both parties agree that the Carriage of Goods by Sea Act, 46 U.S.C. App. §§ 1300-1314 (1988) (COGSA), applies to the liability questions raised in this case. The district court found that the defendants (the vessel, the operator and owner) established as a matter of law two of the exceptions under COGSA and therefore were exonerated from any damage. We respectfully disagree with the court's analysis; we reverse and remand for further proceedings.

* * *

The district court started with the assumption that Associated Metals had established a prima facie case against the vessel under 46 U.S.C. App. § 1303(2) (1988), which obligates a carrier to "properly and carefully load, handle, stow, carry, keep, care for, and discharge the goods carried." Although this circuit has held that section 1303(2) creates a non-delegable duty on behalf of the vessel,[1] the district court found that these statements were dicta and that the better reasoned cases hold that an "FIOS" or "free in and out, stowed" clause in a bill of lading, binding on the parties, shifts liability to the shipper for improper stowage or discharge without violating COGSA. According to the defendants, the FIOS terms shift both the risk and expense of loading, stowing, and discharging cargo to the shipper and the consignee. The district court thus held that the carrier's duty to load and stow cargo properly and carefully under section 1303(2) is not genuinely non-delegable.

In so holding, the district court rejected the reasoning of *Nichimen Co. v. M.V. Farland*, 462 F.2d 319, 330 (2d Cir. 1972), and *Demsey & Assoc., Inc. v. S.S. Sea Star*, 461 F.2d 1009, 1014-15 (2d Cir. 1972), and followed the reasoning of two district court cases in *Sigri Carbon Corp. v. Lykes Bros. S.S. Co.*, 655 F. Supp. 1435 (W.D. Ky. 1987), and *Sumitomo Corp. of America v. M/V "Sie Kim"*, 632 F. Supp. 824 (S.D.N.Y. 1985). These cases construe COGSA to mean that vessels can be held liable for cargo damage only in cases where the vessel exercised control over the stowage or the stevedores. The district court quoted *Sigri Carbon* which held "[t]he inclusion of a FIOS term in a bill of lading should not be disregarded as inconsistent with COGSA so long as it is understood that the term in

---

[1] *See Nichimen Co. v. M.V. Farland*, 462 F.2d 319, 330 (2d Cir. 1972); *Demsey & Assoc., Inc. v. S.S. Sea Star*, 461 F.2d 1009, 1014-15 (2d Cir. 1972).

no way relieves the carrier of responsibility for its own acts or for the acts of others under its control." 655 F. Supp. at 1438. Thus, the district court held "that a carrier is not responsible for the consequences of improper stowage by agents of the shipper pursuant to an FIOS bill of lading."

We find this reasoning directly contrary to 46 U.S.C. App. § 1303(8) (1988):

> Any clause, covenant, or agreement in a contract of carriage relieving the carrier or the ship from liability for loss or damage to or in connection with the goods arising from negligence, fault, or failure in the duties and obligations provided in this section, or lessening such liability otherwise than as provided in this chapter, shall be null and void and of no effect.

In *Demsey*, this court observed:

> Under Sections 1303(1) and (2) of COGSA, the carrier is bound to exercise due diligence to make the ship seaworthy, to make the ship fit and safe for the reception, carriage and preservation of the cargo, and to properly load, handle, stow and discharge the goods being shipped. Every claim for cargo damage creates a maritime lien against the ship which may be enforced by a libel *in rem*. COGSA, Section 1303(8) prohibits a shipowner from contracting out of this liability. The fact that the [vessel] was operated under charter to [the charterer] does not affect the liability of the vessel.

Demsey, 461 F.2d at 1014 (citations omitted).

As in this lawsuit, the plaintiff in *Demsey* purchased steel coils that were damaged during shipping. In *Demsey*, the shipowner had arranged for the charterers "to load, stow, and trim the cargo at their expense under the supervision of the Captain...." 461 F.2d at 1012. A voyage charter stated that the "cargo was 'to be loaded, stowed and discharged free of risk and expense to the vessel.' " *Id.* This court held that these advance arrangements did not shield the vessel from liability because COGSA forbids a shipowner from contracting out of liability for improper stowage of cargo. *Id.* at 1014-15. The court did, however, give some effect to the agreements, ultimately determining that both the vessel owner and the time charterer should be indemnified by the voyage charterer. *Id.* at 1019.

Similarly, in *Nichimen*, the plaintiff sued a vessel owner and a charterer over damage to steel coils that occurred while the steel was in transit. 462 F.2d at 322. Examining the relationships between the parties, the district court rejected a factual assertion that the plaintiff's agent had stowed the cargo. *Id.* at 330. This court expressed its approval of the district court's factual finding and stated that "in any event, under § 3(2) of COGSA, the carrier's duty to 'properly and carefully load ... [and] stow ... the goods carried' is non-delegable." *Id.* As in *Demsey*, the court ultimately determined that the charterer must indemnify the vessel for cargo damage. *Id.* at 332-33.

We find *Nichimen* and *Demsey*'s statutory analysis to be persuasive. Under the district court's enforcement of the FIOS clause, 46 U.S.C. App. § 1303(8) would have no meaning. The plain language of section 1303(8) forbids enforcement of agreements to relieve carriers of liability for negligence in carrying out the duties set forth in section 3 of COGSA. *See* Anthony N. Zock, *Charter Parties in Relation to Cargo*, 45 TUL. L. REV. 733, 747-48 (1975) (stating that "any provision in the charter party or the bill of lading that stipulates for an obligation, liability, or exemption that conflicts with the terms of either COGSA or the Harter Act will have no effect"). One of the duties assigned to carriers is that of properly and carefully loading cargo. *See* 46 U.S.C. App. § 1303(2) (1988). Thus, an agreement such as the one in question here is "null and void" under the statute because it purports to relieve a carrier of liability for negligence in one of its duties, the stowing of cargo.[2] It is of no consequence that unlike in *Demsey* and *Nichimen*, indemnification for damages is not in issue here.

---

[2] In a recent opinion, the United States Court of Appeals for the First Circuit held that "parties are free ... to alter the general rule" that "the duty to load, stow, trim, and ultimately discharge a vessel's cargo generally falls on the shipowner who also bears the consequences of any failure." *Continental Grain Co. v. Puerto Rico Maritime Shipping Auth.*, 972 F.2d 426, 430 (1st Cir. 1992). This case involved a private carriage of goods, *see id.* at 430, and thus COGSA did not apply, *see* Zock, *supra*, at 738.

The defendants suggest an alternative reading of the statute. They suggest that 46 U.S.C. App. § 1303(8) "specifically permits a carrier to limit its liability for its statutory duties, so long as such a limitation is consistent with other provisions of COGSA." (Br. for Defs.-Appellees at 24). This argument is girded on the portion of 46 U.S.C. App. § 1303(8) which states carriers may not contractually lessen their liability "otherwise than as provided in this chapter...." Defendants contend this language suggests that the duties of section 1303 are limited by the immunities of section 1304(2). A more accurate reading of the phrase suggests that "otherwise than as provided in this chapter...." modifies the damage limitations ("lessening such liability") set forth in COGSA, which provides a $500 per package ceiling on damages. *See* 46 U.S.C. App. § 1304(5). The phrase does not affect the statute's prohibition on agreements relieving carriers of liability for negligence in carrying out their duties under the Act.

Section 1304(2)(i)

The district court held that the vessel had also established a second defense by carrying its burden of proof under section 1304(2)(i), which explicitly provides that a carrier shall not be liable for an act or omission of a shipper or owner of goods, his agent or representative.[3] The district court reasoned that its holding under the FIOS clause was consistent with this second defense. The result may be consistent but the analysis cannot be the same.

The liability provisions set forth in 46 U.S.C. App. § 1303(2) create a prima facie case against the vessel when a plaintiff (here a non-signator to the charter agreement) establishes that the carrier received the cargo in good condition and that the cargo arrived at its destination in a damaged condition. *See, e.g., Demsey,* 461 F.2d at 1014. Once a prima facie case is created, the burden shifts to the carrier to show, under section 1304(2)(i) and section 1304(2)(q), that the cargo loss or damage results from an act or omission of the shipper or owner of goods, his agent or representative; or if the loss or damage results from any other cause arising without the actual fault and privity of the carrier and without the fault or neglect of the agents or servants of the carrier. As previously discussed, this burden cannot be carried by contract terms or language of FIOS contained in a bill of lading. Both are barred by the non-delegable provisions of COGSA under section 1303(8).

* * *

There should be little dispute that the purpose of COGSA is to place primary responsibility for the safety of the cargo upon the vessel, its operators and owners. The parties cannot by private agreement circumvent the legislative purpose of the Act. 46 U.S.C. App. § 1303(8). The vessel may exonerate its responsibility by carrying its burden of proof that the damage did not occur because of its own acts. However, we find that the documentary proof and conflicting affidavits submitted in this case create a genuine dispute of material fact and that the defendants are not entitled at this stage of the proceeding to a judgment as a matter of law. Thus, we find the court has erred in granting a summary judgment in favor of the defendants.

The judgment is vacated and the case remanded for further proceedings in accord with this opinion.

Notes

1. In *Tubacex, Inc. v. M/V Risan,* 45 F.3d 951, 1995 AMC 1305 (5th Cir. 1995), cargo was damaged during unloading operations undertaken by stevedores hired by the shipper. In a suit by the shipper for recovery of damages, the carrier defended on the ground that the damage to the cargo was not caused by the negligence of the carrier but it was caused by the negligence of stevedores hired by and under the control of the shipper. The shipper argued, however, that Sections 1302(3) and 1303(8) of the Carriage of Goods by Sea Act preclude the defenses that the carrier made. The court of appeals, purporting to follow the *Arktis Sky* decision but in effect distinguishing it, affirmed a summary judgment in favor of the carrier. In the opinion of the court, there were no overreaching" bill of lading clauses and the carrier should be exonerated from liability because he met the burden of proof of the q clause defense.

---

[3] Section 1304(2)(i) reads:

Neither the carrier nor the ship shall be responsible for loss or damage arising or resulting from: (i) Act or omission of the shipper or owner of the goods, his agent or representative.

The *Arktis Sky* decision has been noticed by the United States Supreme Court. In *Vimar Seguros Y Reaseguros, S.A. v. M/V Sky Reefer*, 515 U.S. 528, 115 S.Ct. 2322, 2329, 132 L.Ed.2d 462, 1995 AMC 1817 (1995), the Court stated:

> The Japanese version of the Hague Rules, it is said, provides the carrier with a defense based on the acts or omissions of the stevedores hired by the shipper, Galaxie, see App. 112, Article 3(1), (carrier liable "when he or the persons employed by him" fail to take due care), while COGSA, according to petitioner, makes nondelegable the carrier's obligation to "properly and carefully . . . stow . . . the goods carried," COGSA § 3(2), 46 U.S.C.App. § 1303(2); see *Associated Metals & Minerals Corp. v. M/V Arktis Sky*, 978 F.2d 47, 50 (CA2 1992). But see COGSA § 4(2)(i), 46 U.S.C. § 1304(2)(i) ("[N]either the carrier nor the ship shall be responsible for loss or damage arising or resulting from . . . [a]ct or omission of the shipper or owner of the goods, his agent or representative"); COGSA § 3(8), 46 U.S.C.App. § 1303(8) (agreement may not relieve or lessen liability "otherwise than as provided in this chapter"); Hegarty, *A COGSA Carrier's Duty to Load and Stow Cargo is Nondelegable, or Is It?: Associated Metals & Minerals Corp. v. M/V Arktis Sky*, 18 Tul. Mar. L.J. 125 (1993).

British case law does not follow such a strict prohibition of private agreements shifting the primary responsibility for the safety of the cargo. *Pyrene Company, Ltd. v. Scindia Steam Navigation Company, Ltd.*, Q.B. 403 (1954), 2 All E.R. 158, acknowledges this fact.

> The extent to which the carrier has to undertake the loading of the vessel may depend not only upon the different systems of law but upon the custom and practice of the port and the nature of the cargo. It is difficult to believe that the Rules were intended to impose a universal rigidity in this respect, or to deny freedom of contract to the carrier. The carrier is practically bound to play some part in the loading and discharging, so that both operations are naturally included in those covered by the contract of carriage. But [there is] no reason why the Rules should not leave the parties free to determine by their own contract the part which each has to play. On this view the whole contract of carriage is subject to the Rules, but the extent to which loading and discharging are brought within the carrier's obligations is left to the parties themselves to decide.

[1954] 1 Ll.L.Rep. 321. *See also Jindal Iron & Steel Co. Ltd v. Islamic Solidarity Shipping Co. Jordan Inc. (The Jordan II)* [2004] UKHL 49, [2005] 1 All E.R. 175 (reaffirming British approach in preference to the American approach).

2. *Rust Clauses*

The Ninth Circuit, in *Tokio Marine & Fire Insurance Co. v. Retla Steamship Co.*, 426 F.2d 1372, 1970 AMC 1611 (9th Cir. 1970), approved the use of rust clauses which would explicitly relieve the carrier from delivering iron or steel goods in a rust-free condition. In *Sumitomo Corp. of America v. M/V Saint Venture*, 683 F. Supp. 1361 (M.D. Fla. 1988), the court disallowed the application of the "Retla rust clause" because the clause in question, unlike the clause in *Retla*, was buried in fine print on the bill of lading and did not offer to substitute an alternative bill of lading without the rust language. However, in *Acwoo Steel Corp. v. Toko Kaiun Kaisha, Ltd.*, 840 F.2d 1284, 1988 AMC 2922(6th Cir. 1988), the court upheld the use of a rust clause similar to the clause in *Sumitomo*.

3. *Lumber Clauses*

As to a Lumber Clause which is similar to the Rust Clause, *compare G.F. Co. v. Pan Ocean Shipping Co., Ltd.*, 23 F.3d 1498, 1994 AMC 1739 (9th Cir. 1994) *with Plywood Panels, Inc. v. M/V Sun Valley*, 804 F. Supp. 804, 1993 AMC 516 (E.D. Va. 1992).

Question

Can the carrier contract out of liability by getting the cargo-owner to agree that the carrier has exercised due care? What if the bill of lading for carriage of a bulk liquid cargo contains a clause stating "Vessel to clean tanks, lines and pumps to [cargo-owner's] surveyor's satisfaction" and the cargo-owner's surveyor inspects the tanks, lines and pumps and declares them to be suitable? If the cargo is contaminated during the voyage, can the carrier rely on the cargo-owner's surveyor's report to argue that its obligation under COGSA § 1303(2) was fulfilled? See *Jamaica Nutrition Holdings Ltd v. United Shipping Co. Ltd*, 643 F.2d 376, 1981 AMC 2883 (5th Cir. 1981).

J. Forum Selection Clauses

VIMAR SEGUROS Y REASEGUROS, S.A. v. M/V SKY REEFER

515 U.S. 528, 115 S. Ct. 2322, 132 L. Ed. 2d 462, 1995 AMC 1817 (1995)

Justice KENNEDY delivered the opinion of the Court.

This case requires us to interpret the Carriage of Goods by Sea Act (COGSA), 46 U.S.C. App. § 1300 *et seq.*, as it relates to a contract containing a clause requiring arbitration in a foreign country. The question is whether a foreign arbitration clause in a bill of lading is invalid under COGSA because it lessens liability in the sense that COGSA prohibits. Our holding that COGSA does not forbid selection of the foreign forum makes it unnecessary to resolve the further question whether the Federal Arbitration Act (FAA), 9 U.S.C. § 1 *et seq.* (1988 ed. and Supp. V), would override COGSA were it interpreted otherwise. In our view, the relevant provisions of COGSA and the FAA are in accord, not in conflict.

I

The contract at issue in this case is a standard form bill of lading to evidence the purchase of a shipload of Moroccan oranges and lemons. The purchaser was Bacchus Associates (Bacchus), a New York partnership that distributes fruit at wholesale throughout the Northeastern United States. Bacchus dealt with Galaxie Negoce, S.A. (Galaxie), a Moroccan fruit supplier. Bacchus contracted with Galaxie to purchase the shipload of fruit and chartered a ship to transport it from Morocco to Massachusetts. The ship was the M/V Sky Reefer, a refrigerated cargo ship owned by M.H. Maritima, S.A., a Panamanian company, and time-chartered to Nichiro Gyogyo Kaisha, Ltd., a Japanese company. Stevedores hired by Galaxie loaded and stowed the cargo. As is customary in these types of transactions, when it received the cargo from Galaxie, Nichiro as carrier issued a form bill of lading to Galaxie as shipper and consignee. Once the ship set sail from Morocco, Galaxie tendered the bill of lading to Bacchus according to the terms of a letter of credit posted in Galaxie's favor.

Among the rights and responsibilities set out in the bill of lading were arbitration and choice-of-law clauses. Clause 3, entitled "Governing Law and Arbitration," provided:

(1)   The contract evidenced by or contained in this Bill of Lading shall be governed by the Japanese law.

(2)   Any dispute arising from this Bill of Lading shall be referred to arbitration in Tokyo by the Tokyo Maritime Arbitration Commission (TOMAC) of The Japan Shipping Exchange, Inc., in accordance with the rules of TOMAC and any amendment thereto, and the award given by the arbitrators shall be final and binding on both parties. App. 49.

When the vessel's hatches were opened for discharge in Massachusetts, Bacchus discovered that thousands of boxes of oranges had shifted in the cargo holds, resulting in over $1 million damage. Bacchus received $733,442.90 compensation from petitioner Vimar Seguros y Reaseguros (Vimar Seguros), Bacchus' marine cargo insurer that became subrogated *pro tanto* to Bacchus' rights. Petitioner and Bacchus then brought suit against Maritima *in personam* and M/V Sky Reefer *in rem* in the District Court for the District of Massachusetts under the bill of lading. These defendants, respondents here, moved to stay the action and compel arbitration in Tokyo under clause 3 of the bill of lading and § 3 of the FAA, which requires courts to stay proceedings and enforce arbitration agreements covered by the Act. Petitioner and Bacchus opposed the motion, arguing the arbitration clause was unenforceable under the FAA both because it was a contract of adhesion and because it violated COGSA § 3(8). The premise of the latter argument was that the inconvenience and costs of proceeding in Japan would "lesse[n] ... liability" as those terms are used in COGSA.

The District Court rejected the adhesion argument, observing that Congress defined the arbitration agreements enforceable under the FAA to include maritime bills of lading, 9 U.S.C. § 1, and that petitioner was a sophisticated party familiar with the negotiation of maritime shipping transactions. It also rejected the argument that requiring the parties to submit to arbitration would lessen respondents' liability under COGSA § 3(8). The court granted the motion to stay judicial proceedings and to compel arbitration; it retained jurisdiction pending arbitration; and at petitioner's request, it certified for interlocutory appeal under 28 U.S.C. § 1292(b) its ruling to compel arbitration, stating that the controlling question of law was "whether [COGSA § 3(8)] nullifies an arbitration clause contained in a bill of lading governed by COGSA." Pet. for Cert. 30a.

The First Circuit affirmed the order to arbitrate. 29 F.3d 727 (1994). Although it expressed grave doubt whether a foreign arbitration clause lessened liability under COGSA § 3(8), 29 F.3d, at 730, the Court of Appeals assumed the clause was invalid under COGSA and resolved the conflict between the statutes in favor of the FAA, which it considered to be the later enacted and more specific statute, *id.*, at 731-733. We granted certiorari, 513 U.S. —, 115 S. Ct. 571, 130 L. Ed. 2d 488 (1994), to resolve a Circuit split on the enforceability of foreign arbitration clauses in maritime bills of lading. Compare the case below (enforcing foreign arbitration clause assuming *arguendo* it violated COGSA), with *State Establishment for Agricultural Product Trading v. M/V Wesermunde*, 838 F.2d 1576 (CA11) (declining to enforce foreign arbitration clause because that would violate COGSA), cert. denied, 488 U.S. 916, 109 S. Ct. 273, 102 L. Ed. 2d 262 (1988). We now affirm.

II

The parties devote much of their argument to the question whether COGSA or the FAA has priority. "[W]hen two statutes are capable of co-existence," however, "it is the duty of the courts, absent a clearly expressed congressional intention to the contrary, to regard each as effective." *Morton v. Mancari*, 417 U.S. 535, 551, 94 S. Ct. 2474, 2483, 41 L. Ed. 2d 290 (1974); *Pittsburgh & Lake Erie R. Co. v. Railway Labor Executives' Assn.*, 491 U.S. 490, 510, 109 S. Ct. 2584, 2596-2597, 105 L. Ed. 2d 415 (1989). There is no conflict unless COGSA by its own terms nullifies a foreign arbitration clause, and we choose to address that issue rather than assume nullification *arguendo*, as the Court of Appeals did. We consider the two arguments made by petitioner. The first is that a foreign arbitration clause lessens COGSA liability by increasing the transaction costs of obtaining relief. The second is that there is a risk foreign arbitrators will not apply COGSA.

A

The leading case for invalidation of a foreign forum selection clause is the opinion of the Court of Appeals for the Second Circuit in *Indussa Corp. v. S.S. Ranborg*, 377 F.2d 200 (1967) (en banc). The court there found that COGSA invalidated a clause designating a foreign judicial forum because it "puts 'a high hurdle' in the way of enforcing liability, and thus is an effective means for carriers to secure settlements lower than if cargo [owners] could sue in a convenient forum," *id.*, at 203 (citation omitted). The court observed "there could be no assurance that [the foreign court] would apply [COGSA] in the same way as would an American tribunal subject to the uniform control of the Supreme Court," *id.*, at 203-204. Following *Indussa*, the Courts of Appeals without exception have invalidated foreign forum selection clauses under § 3(8). See *Union Ins. Soc. of Canton, Ltd. v. S.S. Elikon*, 642 F.2d 721, 723-725 (CA4 1981); *Conklin & Garrett, Ltd v. M/V Finnrose*, 826 F.2d 1441, 1442-1444 (CA5 1987); *see also* G. Gilmore & C. Black, Law of Admiralty 145-146, n.23 (2d ed. 1975) (approving *Indussa* rule). As foreign arbitration clauses are but a subset of foreign forum selection clauses in general, *Scherk v. Alberto-Culver Co.*, 417 U.S. 506, 519, 94 S. Ct. 2449, 2457, 41 L. Ed. 2d 270 (1974), the *Indussa* holding has been extended to foreign arbitration clauses as well. See *State Establishment for Agricultural Product Trading, supra*, at 1580-1581; *cf. Vimar Seguros Y Reaseguros, supra*, at 730 (assuming *arguendo Indussa* applies). The logic of that extension would be quite defensible, but we cannot endorse the reasoning or the conclusion of the *Indussa* rule itself.

The determinative provision in COGSA, examined with care, does not support the arguments advanced first in *Indussa* and now by the petitioner. Section 3(8) of COGSA provides as follows:

Any clause, covenant, or agreement in a contract of carriage relieving the carrier or the ship from liability for loss or damage to or in connection with the goods, arising from negligence, fault, or failure in the duties or obligations provided in this section, or lessening such liability otherwise than as provided in this chapter, shall be null and void and of no effect. 46 U.S.C. App. § 1303(8).

The liability that may not be lessened is "liability for loss or damage ... arising from negligence, fault, or failure in the duties or obligations provided in this section." The statute thus addresses the lessening of the specific liability imposed by the Act, without addressing the separate question of the means and costs of enforcing that liability. The difference is that between explicit statutory guarantees and the procedure for enforcing them, between applicable liability principles and the forum in which they are to be vindicated.

The liability imposed on carriers under COGSA § 3 is defined by explicit standards of conduct, and it is designed to correct specific abuses by carriers. In the 19th century it was a prevalent practice for common carriers to insert clauses in bills of lading exempting themselves from liability for damage or loss, limiting the period in which plaintiffs had to present their notice of claim or bring suit, and capping any damages awards per package. *See* 2A M. Sturley, Benedict on Admiralty § 11, pp. 2-2 to 2-3 (1995); 2 T. Schoenbaum, Admiralty and Maritime Law § 10-13 (2d ed. 1994); Yancey, *The Carriage of Goods: Hague, COGSA, Visby, and Hamburg,* 57 Tulane L. Rev. 1238, 1239-1240 (1983). Thus, § 3, entitled "Responsibilities and liabilities of carrier and ship," requires that the carrier "exercise due diligence to ... [m]ake the ship seaworthy" and "[p]roperly man, equip, and supply the ship" before and at the beginning of the voyage, § 3(1), "properly and carefully load, handle, stow, carry, keep, care for, and discharge the goods carried," § 3(2), and issue a bill of lading with specified contents, § 3(3). 46 U.S.C. App. § 1303(1), (2), and (3). Section 3(6) allows the cargo owner to provide notice of loss or damage within three days and to bring suit within one year. These are the substantive obligations and particular procedures that § 3(8) prohibits a carrier from altering to its advantage in a bill of lading. Nothing in this section, however, suggests that the statute prevents the parties from agreeing to enforce these obligations in a particular forum. By its terms, it establishes certain duties and obligations, separate and apart from the mechanisms for their enforcement.

Petitioner's contrary reading of § 3(8) is undermined by the Court's construction of a similar statutory provision in *Carnival Cruise Lines, Inc. v. Shute,* 499 U.S. 585, 111 S. Ct. 1522, 113 L. Ed. 2d 622 (1991). There a number of Washington residents argued that a Florida forum selection clause contained in a cruise ticket should not be enforced because the expense and inconvenience of litigation in Florida would "caus[e] plaintiffs unreasonable hardship in asserting their rights," *id.*, at 596, 111 S. Ct., at 1528-1529, and therefore " 'lessen, weaken, or avoid the right of any claimant to a trial by court of competent jurisdiction on the question of liability for ... loss or injury, or the measure of damages therefor' " in violation of the Limitation of Vessel Owner's Liability Act, 499 U.S., at 595-596, 111 S. Ct., at 1528 (quoting 46 U.S.C. App. § 183(c). We observed that the clause "does not purport to limit petitioner's liability for negligence," *id.*, at 596-597, 111 S. Ct., at 1529, and enforced the agreement over the dissent's argument, based in part on the *Indussa* line of cases, that the cost and inconvenience of traveling thousands of miles "lessens or weakens [plaintiffs'] ability to recover." 499 U.S., at 603, 111 S. Ct., at 1532 (STEVENS, J., dissenting).

If the question whether a provision lessens liability were answered by reference to the costs and inconvenience to the cargo owner, there would be no principled basis for distinguishing national from foreign arbitration clauses. Even if it were reasonable to read § 3(8) to make a distinction based on travel time, airfare, and hotels bills, these factors are not susceptible of a simple and enforceable distinction between domestic and foreign forums. Requiring a Seattle cargo owner to arbitrate in New York likely imposes more costs and burdens than a foreign arbitration clause requiring it to arbitrate in Vancouver. It would be unwieldy and unsupported by the terms or policy of the statute to require courts to proceed case by case to tally the costs and burdens to particular plaintiffs in light of their means, the size of their claims, and the relative burden on the carrier.

Our reading of "lessening such liability" to exclude increases in the transaction costs of litigation also finds support in the goals of the Brussels Convention for the Unification of Certain Rules Relating to Bills of Lading, 51 Stat. 233 (1924) (Hague Rules), on which COGSA is modeled. Sixty-six countries, including the United States and Japan, are now parties to the Convention, *see* Department of State, Office of the Legal Adviser, Treaties in Force: A List of Treaties and Other International Agreements of the United States in Force on January 1, 1994, p. 367 (June 1994), and it appears that none has interpreted its enactment of § 3(8) of the Hague Rules to prohibit foreign forum selection clauses, *see* Sturley, *International Uniform Laws in National Courts: The Influence of Domestic Law in Con-*

flicts of Interpretation, 27 VA. J. INT'L L. 729, 776-796 (1987). The English courts long ago rejected the reasoning later adopted by the *Indussa* court. *See Maharani Woollen Mills Co. v. Anchor Line*, [1927] 29 LLOYD'S LIST L. REP. 169 (C.A.) (SCRUTTON, L.J.) ("[T]he liability of the carrier appears to me to remain exactly the same under the clause. The only difference is a question of procedure—where shall the law be enforced?—and I do not read any clause as to procedure as lessening liability"). And other countries that do not recognize foreign forum selection clauses rely on specific provisions to that effect in their domestic versions of the Hague Rules, *see, e.g.*, Sea-Carriage of Goods Act 1924, § 9(2) (Australia); Carriage of Goods by Sea Act, No. 1 of 1986, § 3 (South Africa). In light of the fact that COGSA is the culmination of a multilateral effort "to establish uniform ocean bills of lading to govern the rights and liabilities of carriers and shippers inter se in international trade," *Robert C. Herd & Co. v. Krawill Machinery Corp.*, 359 U.S. 297, 301, 79 S. Ct. 766, 769, 3 L. Ed. 2d 820 (1959), we decline to interpret our version of the Hague Rules in a manner contrary to every other nation to have addressed this issue. See Sturley, *supra*, at 736 (conflicts in the interpretation of the Hague Rules not only destroy aesthetic symmetry in the international legal order but impose real costs on the commercial system in the Rules govern).

It would also be out of keeping with the objects of the Convention for the courts of this country to interpret COGSA to disparage the authority or competence of international forums for dispute resolution. Petitioner's skepticism over the ability of foreign arbitrators to apply COGSA or the Hague Rules, and its reliance on this aspect of *Indussa*, *supra*, must give way to contemporary principles of international comity and commercial practice. As the Court observed in *The Bremen v. Zapata Off-Shore Co.*, 407 U.S. 1, 92 S. Ct. 1907, 32 L. Ed. 2d 513 (1972), when it enforced a foreign forum selection clause, the historical judicial resistance to foreign forum selection clauses "has little place in an era when ... businesses once essentially local now operate in world markets." *Id.*, at 12, 92 S. Ct., at 1914. "The expansion of American business and industry will hardly be encouraged," we explained, "if, notwithstanding solemn contracts, we insist on a parochial concept that all disputes must be resolved under our laws and in our courts." *Id.*, at 9, 92 S. Ct., at 1912. *See Mitsubishi Motors Corp. v. Soler Chrysler-Plymouth, Inc.*, 473 U.S. 614, 638, 105 S. Ct. 3346, 3359-3360, 87 L. Ed. 2d 444 (1985) (if international arbitral institutions "are to take a central place in the international legal order, national courts will need to 'shake off the old judicial hostility to arbitration,' and also their customary and understandable unwillingness to cede jurisdiction of a claim arising under domestic law to a foreign or transnational tribunal") (citation omitted); *Scherk v. Alberto-Culver Co.*, 417 U.S., at 516, 94 S. Ct., at 2456 ("A parochial refusal by the courts of one country to enforce an international arbitration agreement" would frustrate "the orderliness and predictability essential to any international business transaction"); *see also* Allison, *Arbitration of Private Antitrust Claims in International Trade: A Study in the Subordination of National Interests to the Demands of a World Market*, 18 N.Y.U. J. INT'L LAW & POLITICS 361, 439 (1986).

That the forum here is arbitration only heightens the irony of petitioner's argument, for the FAA is also based in part on an international convention, 9 U.S.C. § 201 *et seq.* (codifying the United Nations Convention on the Recognition and Enforcement of Foreign Arbitral Awards, June 10, 1958, [1970] 21 U.S.T. 2517), T.I.A.S. No. 6997, intended "to encourage the recognition and enforcement of commercial arbitration agreements in international contracts and to unify the standards by which agreements to arbitrate are observed and arbitral awards are enforced in the signatory countries," *Scherk*, *supra*, at 520, n.15, 94 S. Ct., at 2457, n.15. The FAA requires enforcement of arbitration agreements in contracts that involve interstate commerce, *see Allied-Bruce Terminix Cos. v. Dobson*, 513 U.S. ——, 115 S. Ct. 834, 130 L. Ed. 2d 753 (1995), and in maritime transactions, including bills of lading, *see* 9 U.S.C. §§ 1, 2, 201, 202, where there is no independent basis in law or equity for revocation. *Cf. Carnival Cruise Lines*, 499 U.S., at 595, 111 S. Ct., at 1528 ("forum-selection clauses contained in form passage contracts are subject to judicial scrutiny for fundamental fairness"). If the United States is to be able to gain the benefits of international accords and have a role as a trusted partner in multilateral endeavors, its courts should be most cautious before interpreting its domestic legislation in such manner as to violate international agreements. That concern counsels against construing COGSA to nullify foreign arbitration clauses because of inconvenience to the plaintiff or insular distrust of the ability of foreign arbitrators to apply the law.

B

Petitioner's second argument against enforcement of the Japanese arbitration clause is that there is no guarantee foreign arbitrators will apply COGSA. This objection raises a concern of substance. The central guarantee of § 3(8) is that the terms of a bill of landing may not relieve the carrier of the obligations or diminish the legal duties specified by the Act. The relevant question, therefore, is whether the substantive law to be applied will reduce the carrier's obligations to the cargo owner below what COGSA guarantees. See *Mitsubishi Motors, supra*, 473 U.S. at 637, n.19, 105 S. Ct., at 3359, n.19.

Petitioner argues that the arbitrators will follow the Japanese Hague Rules, which, petitioner contends, lessen respondents' liability in at least one significant respect. The Japanese version of the Hague Rules, it is said, provides the carrier with a defense based on the acts or omissions of the stevedores hired by the shipper, Galaxie, *see* App. 112, Article 3(1), (carrier liable "when he or the persons employed by him" fail to take due care), while COGSA, according to petitioner, makes nondelegable the carrier's obligation to "properly and carefully ... stow ... the goods carried," COGSA § 3(2), 46 U.S.C. App. § 1303(2); *see Associated Metals & Minerals Corp. v. M/V Arktis Sky*, 978 F.2d 47, 50 (CA2 1992). But see COGSA § 4(2)(i), 46 U.S.C. § 1304(2)(i) ("[N]either the carrier nor the ship shall be responsible for loss or damage arising or resulting from ... [a]ct or omission of the shipper or owner of the goods, his agent or representative"); COGSA § 3(8), 46 U.S.C. App. § 1303(8) (agreement may not relieve or lessen liability "otherwise than as provided in this chapter"); Hegarty, *A COGSA Carrier's Duty to Load and Stow Cargo is Nondelegable, or Is It?: Associated Metals & Minerals Corp. v. M/V Arktis Sky*, 18 Tulane Mar. L.J. 125 (1993).

Whatever the merits of petitioner's comparative reading of COGSA and its Japanese counterpart, its claim is premature. At this interlocutory stage it is not established what law the arbitrators will apply to petitioner's claims or that petitioner will receive diminished protection as a result. The arbitrators may conclude that COGSA applies of its own force or that Japanese law does not apply so that, under another clause of the bill of lading, COGSA controls. Respondents seek only to enforce the arbitration agreement. The district court has retained jurisdiction over the case and "will have the opportunity at the award-enforcement stage to ensure that the legitimate interest in the enforcement of the ... laws has been addressed." *Mitsubishi Motors*, 473 U.S., at 638, 105 S. Ct., at 3359; *cf.* 1 Restatement (Third) of Foreign Relations Law of the United States § 482(2)(d) (1986) ("A court in the United States need not recognize a judgment of the court of a foreign state if ... the judgment itself, is repugnant to the public policy of the United States"). Were there no subsequent opportunity for review and were we persuaded that "the choice-of-forum and choice-of-law clauses operated in tandem as a prospective waiver of a party's right to pursue statutory remedies ..., we would have little hesitation in condemning the agreement as against public policy." *Mitsubishi Motors, supra*, at 637, n.19, 105 S. Ct., at 3359, n.19. *Cf. Knott v. Botany Mills*, 179 U.S. 69, 21 S. Ct. 30, 45 L. Ed. 90 (1900) (nullifying choice-of-law provision under the Harter Act, the statutory precursor to COGSA, where British law would give effect to provision in bill of lading that purported to exempt carrier from liability for damage to goods caused by carrier's negligence in loading and stowage of cargo); *The Hollandia*, [1983] A.C. 565, 574-575 (H.L. 1982) (noting choice of forum clause "does not ex facie offend against article III, paragraph 8," but holding clause unenforceable where "the foreign court chosen as the exclusive forum would apply a domestic substantive law which would result in limiting the carrier's liability to the sum lower than that to which he would be entitled if [English COGSA] applied"). Under the circumstances of this case, however, the First Circuit was correct to reserve judgment on the choice-of-law question, 29 F.3d, at 729, n.3, as it must be decided in the first instance by the arbitrator, *cf. Mitsubishi Motors, supra*, 473 U.S., at 637, n.19, 105 S. Ct., at 3359, n.19. As the District Court has retained jurisdiction, mere speculation that the foreign arbitrators might apply Japanese law which, depending on the proper construction of COGSA, might reduce respondents' legal obligations, does not in and of itself lessen liability under COGSA § 3(8).

Because we hold that foreign arbitration clauses in bills of lading are not invalid under COGSA in all circumstances, both the FAA and COGSA may be given full effect. The judgment of the Court of Appeals is affirmed, and the case is remanded for further proceedings consistent with this opinion.

It is so ordered.

Justice BREYER took no part in the consideration or decision of this case.

Justice O'CONNOR, concurring in the judgment.

I agree with what I understand to be the two basic points made in the Court's opinion. First, I agree that the language of the Carriage of Goods by Sea Act (COGSA), 46 U.S.C. App. § 1300 *et seq.*, and our decision in *Carnival Cruise Lines, Inc. v. Shute*, 499 U.S. 585, 111 S. Ct. 1522, 113 L. Ed. 2d 622 (1991), preclude a holding that the increased cost of litigating in a distant forum, without more, can lessen liability within the meaning of COGSA § 3(8). *Ante*, at 2327-2328. Second, I agree that, because the District Court has retained jurisdiction over this case while the arbitration proceeds, any claim of lessening of liability that might arise out of the arbitrators' interpretation of the bill of lading's choice of law clause, or out of their ap-plication of COGSA, is premature. *Ante*, at 2329-2330. Those two points suffice to affirm the decision below.

Because the Court's opinion appears to do more, however, I concur only in the judgment. Foreign arbitration clauses of the kind presented here do not divest domestic courts of jurisdiction, unlike true foreign forum selection clauses such as that considered in *Indussa Corp. v. S.S. Ranborg*, 377 F.2d 200 (CA2 1967) (en banc). That difference is an important one—it is, after all, what leads the Court to dismiss much of petitioner's argument as premature—and we need not decide today whether *Indussa*, insofar as it relied on considerations other than the increased cost of litigating in a distant forum, retains any vitality in the context of true foreign forum selection clauses. Accordingly, I would not, without qualification, reject "the reasoning [and] the conclusion of the *Indussa* rule itself," *ante*, at 2326, nor would I wholeheartedly approve an English decision that "long ago rejected the reasoning later adopted by the *Indussa* court," *ante*, at 2328. As the Court notes, "[f]ollowing *Indussa*, the Court of Appeals without exception have invalidated foreign forum selection clauses under § 3(8)," *ante*, at 2326. I would prefer to disturb that unbroken line of authority only to the extent necessary to decide this case.

Justice STEVENS, dissenting

* * *

I

* * *

Thus, our interpretation of maritime law prior to the enactment of the Harter Act, our reading of that statute in *Knott*, and the federal courts' consistent interpretation of COGSA, buttressed by scholarly recognition of the commercial interest in uniformity, demonstrate that the clauses in the Japanese carrier's bill of lading purporting to require arbitration in Tokyo pursuant to Japanese law both would have been held invalid under COGSA prior to today.[7]

The foreign arbitration clause imposes potentially prohibitive costs on the shipper, who must travel—and bring his lawyers, witnesses and exhibits—to a distant country in order to seek redress. The shipper will therefore be inclined either to settle the claim at a discount or to forgo bringing the claim at all. The foreign-law clause leaves the shipper who does pursue his claim open to the application of unfamiliar and potentially disadvantageous legal standards, until he can obtain review (perhaps years later) in a domestic forum under the high standard applicable to vacation of arbitration awards.[8] *See Wilko v. Swan*, 346 U.S. 427, 436-437, 74 S. Ct. 182, 187-88, 98 L. Ed. 168 (1953). Accordingly, courts have always held that such clauses "lessen" or "relieve" the carrier's liability, *see, e.g., State*

---

[7] Of course, the objectionable feature in the instant bill of lading is a foreign arbitration clause, not a foreign forum selection clause. But this distinction is of little importance; in relevant respects, there is no difference between the two. Both impose substantial costs on shippers, and both should be held to lessen liability under COGSA. The majority's reasoning to the contrary thus presumably covers forum selection as well as arbitration. *See ante*, at 2326; *ante*, at 2330-2331 (O'CONNOR, J., concurring in judgment). The only ground on which one might distinguish the two types of clauses is that another federal statute, the Federal Arbitration Act, makes arbitration clauses enforceable, whereas no analogous federal statute exists for forum selection clauses. For the reasons expressed *infra*, at 2336-2337, this distinction is unpersuasive.

[8] I am assuming that the majority would not actually uphold the application of disadvantageous legal standards—these, even under the narrowest reading of COGSA, surely lessen liability. *See ante*, at 2329-330. Nonetheless, the majority is apparently willing to allow arbitration to proceed under

Establishment for Agricultural Product Trading v. M/V Wesermunde, 838 F.2d 1576, 1580-1582 (CA11), *cert. denied*, 488 U.S. 916, 109 S. Ct. 273, 102 L. Ed. 2d 262 (1988), and even the Court of Appeals in this case assumed as much, 29 F.3d 727, 730, 732, n.5 (CA1 1994). Yet this Court today holds that carriers may insert foreign-arbitration clauses into bills of lading, and it leaves in doubt the validity of choice-of-law clauses.

Although the policy undergirding the doctrine of *stare decisis* has its greatest value in preserving rules governing commercial transactions, particularly when their meaning is well understood and has been accepted for long periods of time,[9] the Court nevertheless has concluded that a change must be made. Its law-changing decision is supported by three arguments: (1) the statutory reference to "lessening such liability" has been misconstrued; (2) the prior understanding of the meaning of the statute has been "undermined" by the *Carnival Cruise* case; and (3) the new rule is supported by our obligation to honor the 1924 "Hague Rules." None of these arguments is persuasive.

II

The Court assumes that the words "lessening such liability" must be narrowly construed to refer only to the substantive rules that define the carrier's legal obligations. *Ante*, at 2327. Under this view, contractual provisions that lessen the amount of the consignee's net recovery, or that lessen the likelihood that it will make any recovery at all, are beyond the scope of the statute.

In my opinion, this view is flatly inconsistent with the purpose of COGSA § 3(8). That section responds to the inequality of bargaining power inherent in bills of lading and to carriers' historic tendency to exploit that inequality whenever possible to immunize themselves from liability for their own fault. A bill of lading is a form document prepared by the carrier, who presents it to the shipper on a take-it-or-leave-it basis. *See* Black, *The Bremen, COGSA and the Problem of Conflicting Interpretation*, 6 VAND. J. TRANSNAT'L L. 365, 368 (1973); *Liverpool Steam*, 129 U.S., at 441, 9 S. Ct., at 471-72. Characteristically, there is no arms-length negotiation over the bill's terms; the shipper must agree to the carrier's standard-form language, or else refrain from using the carrier's services. Accordingly, if courts were to enforce bills of lading as written, a carrier could slip in a clause relieving itself of all liability for fault, or limiting that liability to a fraction of the shipper's damages, and the shipper would have no recourse. COGSA represents Congress' most recent attempt to respond to this problem. By its terms, it invalidates any clause in a bill of lading "relieving" or "lessening" the "liability" of the carrier for negligence, fault, or dereliction of duty.

When one reads the statutory language in light of the policies behind COGSA's enactment, it is perfectly clear that a foreign forum selection or arbitration clause "relieves" or "lessens" the carrier's liability. The transaction costs associated with an arbitration in Japan will obviously exceed the potential recovery in a great many cargo disputes. As a practical matter, therefore, in such a case no matter how clear the carrier's formal legal liability may be, it would make no sense for the consignee or its subrogee to enforce that liability. It seems to me that a contractual provision that entirely protects the shipper from being held liable for anything should be construed either to have "lessened" its inability or to have "relieved" it of liability.

Even if the value of the shipper's claim is large enough to justify litigation in Asia, contractual provisions that impose unnecessary and unreasonable costs on the consignee will inevitably lessen its net recovery. If, as under the Court's reasoning, such provisions do not affect the carrier's legal liability, it would appear to be permissible to require the consignee to pay the costs of the arbitration, or perhaps the travel expenses and fees of the expert witnesses, interpreters, and lawyers employed by both parties. Judge Friendly and the many other wise judges who shared his opinion were surely correct in concluding that Congress could not have intended such a perverse reading of the statutory text.

---

foreign law, and to determine afterwards whether application of that law has actually lessened the carrier's formal liability. As I have discussed above, this regime creates serious problems of delay and uncertainty. Because the majority's holding in this case is limited to the enforceability of the foreign arbitration clause—it does not actually pass upon the validity of the foreign law clause—I will not discuss the foreign law clause further except to say that it is an unenforceable lessening of liability to the extent it gives an advantage to the carrier at the expense of the shipper.

[9] *See* Eskridge v. Frickey, *The Supreme Court 1993 Term—Foreword: Law as Equilibrium*, 108 HARV. L. REV. 26, 81 (1994).

More is at stake here than the allocation of rights and duties between shippers and carriers. A bill of lading, besides being a contract of carriage, is a negotiable instrument that controls possession of the goods being shipped. Accordingly, the bill of lading can be sold, traded, or used to obtain credit as though the bill were the cargo itself. Disuniformity in the interpretation of bills of lading will impair their negotiability. See *Union Ins. Soc. of Canton, Ltd. v. S.S. Elikon*, 642 F.2d, at 723, GILMORE & BLACK, LAW OF ADMIRALTY 146-147 (2d ed. 1975). Thus, if the security interests in some bills of lading are enforceable only through the courts of Japan, while others may be enforceable only in Liechtenstein, the negotiability of bills of lading will suffer from the uncertainty. COGSA recognizes that this negotiability depends in part upon the financial community's capacity to rely on the enforceability, in an accessible forum, of the bills' terms. Today's decision destroys that capacity.

* * *

I respectfully dissent.

Notes and Questions

1. How realistic is the Court's conclusion that the District Court may provide relief if the arbitration panel refuses to apply U.S. COGSA? Suppose the arbitrators simply announce their decision without explaining the legal basis for it. What should the District Court do? Suppose the goods had been shipped from Japan to the United States and that, under Japanese law, the law of the place where the cargo had been shipped controls the transaction. Also the bill of lading provided for the application of Japanese law. What law would you expect the arbitrator apply? If under those circumstances, the arbitrator applied Japanese law, what should the U.S. District Court do?

2. In *Central National-Gottesman, Inc. v. M/V GERTRUDE OLDENDORFF*, 204 F. Supp. 2d 675, 682, 2002 AMC 1477 (S.D.N.Y. 2002), the court refused to apply *Sky Reefer* to a clause providing for disputes to be resolved in a foreign *court*, citing the impossibility of the U.S. court retaining jurisdiction. The court said:

> An integral component of the Court's reasoning in *Sky Reefer* was that there existed a subsequent opportunity for the district court to review the foreign court's decision to ensure that it comported with the interest in enforcement of the laws in the United States and was not violative of public policy. *Sky Reefer*, 515 U.S at 540, 115 S. Ct. 2322. Absent this opportunity for review, it is readily apparent that the Court would have had a much harder time enforcing the forum selection clause and transferring the case to Japan. *See id.* ("Were there no subsequent opportunity for review [and foreign law operated to waive COGSA protection] ..., we would have little hesitation in condemning the agreement as against public policy.") (internal quotations omitted). However, this option of retaining jurisdiction is simply not available with respect to the dispute at hand. *Sky Reefer* involved a dispute over enforcement of a foreign arbitration clause. "The safeguard of retained jurisdiction is therefore not applicable here because this case involves a foreign jurisdiction clause". *In re Rationis Enterprises, Inc.*, No. 97 CV 9052, 1999 WL 6364 at *3 (S.D.N.Y. Jan. 7, 1999) ... Since this precaution, to which *Sky Reefer* accorded substantial weight, is missing here, the court is reluctant to enforce the forum selection clause and dismiss this action for improper venue.

See also, to similar effect, *Nippon Fire & Marine Ins. Co. v. M/V Spring Wave*, 92 F. Supp. 2d 574, 577, 2000 AMC 1717 (E.D. La. 2000).

3. Progeny of SKY REEFER

Following the *SKY REEFER* decision, courts have consistently upheld foreign arbitration clauses. Citing dicta from *SKY REEFER*, several courts have also upheld forum selection clauses reasoning that "foreign arbitration clauses are but a subset of foreign forum selection clauses in general...." *Mitsui & Co. (USA) Inc. v. MIRA M/V*, 111 F.3d 33, 36, 1997 AMC 2126 (5th Cir. 1997) (quoting *Vimar Seguros Y Reaseguros v. M/V SKY REEFER*, 515 U.S. 528, 533). See also *Talatala v. Nippon Yusen Kaisha Corp.*, 974 F. Supp. 1321, 1324 n. 4, 1997 AMC 1398 (D. Haw. 1997); *Pasztory v Croatia Line*, 918 F. Supp. 961, 965, 1996 AMC 1189 (E.D. Va. 1996); *Nippon Fire & Marine Ins. Co.v M/V EGASCO STAR*, 899 F. Supp. 164, 170 n. 8 (S.D.N.Y. 1995), *aff'd*, 104 F.3d 351 (2d Cir. 1996) (Table), all applying *Sky Reefer* to choice of court clauses. Compare, however, *In re Rationis Enterprises, Inc. of Panama*, 1999 AMC 889 (S.D.N.Y. 1999); *Nippon Fire & Marine Ins. Co. v. M/V Spring Wave*, 92 F. Supp. 2d 574, 577, 2000 AMC 1717 (E.D. La. 2000); *Central National-Gottesman, Inc. v. M/V GERTRUDE OLDENDORFF*, 204 F. Supp. 2d 675, 682, 2002 AMC 1477 (S.D.N.Y. 2002), all declining to dismiss on *Sky Reefer* grounds in cases involving choice of court clauses.

The Ninth Circuit even upheld a foreign forum selection clause that provided for litigation in Korea, despite findings that the plaintiff would be seriously inconvenienced and that *in rem* proceedings were not available under Korean law. *See Fireman's Fund Insurance Co. v. M.V. DSR ATLANTIC*, 131 F.3d 1336, 1338, 1998 AMC 583 (9th Cir. 1998). But compare *Union Steel America Co. v. M/V SANKO SPRUCE*, 14 F. Supp. 2d 682, 1999 AMC (D.N.J. 1998); *Allianz Ins. Co. of Canada v. Cho Yang Shipping Co., Ltd*, 131 F. Supp. 2d 787, 2000 AMC 2947 (E.D. Va. 2000), refusing to follow *DSR Atlantic*. For other cases applying the *SKY REEFER* rule, see *G.A. Pasztory v. Croatia Line*, 918 F. Supp 961 (E.D. Va. 1996) (upholding a clause selecting Croatia as the forum for the settlement of disputes despite arguments that Croatia was "politically unstable and jurisprudentially immature"); *Talatala v. Nippon Yusen Kaisha Corp.*, 974 F. Supp 1321, 1997 AMC 1398 (D. Hawaii 1997) (upholding a bill of lading provision that all actions be brought in Tokyo under the laws of Japan).

4. *Stipulation of the Applicable Law*

It is well settled that the provisions of the Harter Act and of the Carriage of Goods by Sea Act express the public policy of the United States and are mandatory. Accordingly, any clause in a bill of lading covered by these acts that purports to exonerate the carrier from liability for negligence or to lessen his liability otherwise than as provided by these acts is null and void. It is another question whether the same result may be achieved indirectly by a clause stipulating the application of a more favorable foreign law, granting exclusive jurisdiction to the courts of a foreign country, or providing for the settlement of disputes by arbitration in a foreign country.

Bills of lading issued in countries that have enacted the Visby Rules may incorporate these rules expressly or by implication. *See, e.g., Daval Steel Products v. The Acadia Forest*, 1988 AMC 1669 (S.D.N.Y 1988): *I.N.A. v. The Atlantic Corona*, 704 F. Supp. 528, 1989 AMC 875 (S.D.N.Y. 1989). When the Visby Rules are expressly incorporated in a bill of lading, the higher Visby limit of recovery ought to be allowed; there is no conflict with COGSA, because parties are free to increase the liabilities of the carrier. In the absence of an express incorporation of the Visby Rules, a question of contractual interpretation arises as to the intent of the parties. If the court concludes that the parties intended to adopt the higher Visby limits, their intent ought to be given effect. *See Francosteel Corp. v. The Deppe Europe*, 1990 AMC 2962 (S.D.N.Y. 1990) (higher limit allowed); *I.N.A. v. The Sealand Developer*, 1990 AMC 2967 (S.D.N.Y. 1989) (higher limit *not* allowed); *J.C.B. Sales, Ltd. v. Wallenius Lines*, 124 F.3d 132, 1997 AMC 2705 (2d Cir. 1997) (higher limit allowed). Compare *Acciai Speciali Terni U.S.A., Inc. v. M/V BERANE*, 182 F. Supp. 2d 503, 2002 AMC 519 (D.Md. 2002) (generally-worded Clause Paramount held not sufficient to give effect to higher limit).

Prior to the enactment of the Harter Act, contracts of affreightment involving foreign contacts were, in principle, governed by the law selected by the parties and, in absence of agreement, by the law of the place of contracting as impliedly intended. Nevertheless, unreasonable limitations of liability contained in contracts which were to be performed in part or in whole in the United States were considered contrary to public policy and of no effect, whether American or foreign law governed. Thus, it was held, not without good reason, that "the objections to the validity of stipulations exempting common carriers from responsibility for negligence ... apply precisely the same to a stipulation for the adoption of the law of another country.... That stipulation is plainly nothing but a further device." *The Energia*, 56 F. 124, 127 (S.D.N.Y. 1893), *aff'd*, 66 F. 604 (2d Cir. 1895). Similar results were reached much more readily after the enactment of the Harter Act, which included provisions defining its area of application. The act was thus declared applicable as a matter of law to all shipments to or from the ports of the United States, and party autonomy to select the applicable law was excluded.

Following the long-established precedent of the Harter Act, § 1312 (first paragraph) of the Carriage of Goods by Sea Act has been considered by certain decisions to be a rule of public policy that precludes any other choice of law for bills of lading coming under it. Thus a stipulation providing for application of foreign law to a bill of lading covered by the Carriage of Goods by Sea Act has been disregarded, and the liability of the carrier has been determined under the Act. *See, e.g., The Steel Inventor*, 35 F. Supp., 986, 997, 1941 AMC 169 (D. Md. 1940); *The Bill*, 47 F. Supp. 969, 975, 1942 AMC 1607 (D. Md. 1942). Ordinarily, the choice of law clause is coupled with a forum selection clause. *See, e.g., Conklin & Garrett Ltd. v. M/V Finnrose*, 826 F.2d 1441, 1988 AMC 318 (5th Cir. 1987) (clause providing that any disputes under the bill of lading "shall be decided in Finland under Finnish law"; *held*, this clause conflicts with 46 U.S.C. § 1303(8) and, therefore, is not enforceable).

According to consistent theory, private parties ought to have contractual freedom to choose the applicable law with respect to cases and matters not governed by the Harter Act or the Carriage of Goods by Sea Act. Contracts of affreightment lying outside the scope of these acts are generally governed by the conflicts of law rules that federal courts apply in maritime cases. It is thus with regard to matters and contracts not regulated by either act, such as carriage between foreign ports, carriage under charter-party rather than a bill of lading, or with regard to shipments of live animals or deck cargo, that resort to the general conflicts rules is made. Such contracts in the United States, as in all other countries, are primarily subject to the law selected by the parties. *See Teyseer Cement Co. v. Halla Maritime Corporation*, 583 F. Supp. 1268, 1985 AMC 356 (W.D. Wash. 1984) (shipment between foreign ports; choice of Korean law and forum upheld). For the enforceability for forum selection clauses in general and an elaboration on *The Bremen v. Zapata Off-Shore Co.*, 407 U.S. 1, 92 S.Ct. 1907, 32 L.Ed.2d 513, 1972 AMC 1407 (1972), *see Carnival Cruise Lines v. Shute*, 499 U.S. 585, 111 S. Ct. 1522, 113 L.Ed.2d 622, 1991 AMC 1697 (1991); *North River Insurance Co. v. Federal Sea/Federal Pacific Line*, 647 F.2d 985, 1982 AMC 2963 (9th Cir. 1981); *Sanko Steamship Co. v. Newfoundland Refining Co.*, 411 F. Supp. 285, 1976 AMC 417 (S.D.N.Y. 1976). The United States Supreme Court has indicated that "except as forbidden by some public policy, the tendency of the law is to apply in contract matters the law which the parties intended to apply". *Lauritzen v. Larsen*, 345 U.S. 571, 588, 73 S.Ct. 921, 97 L.Ed. 1254 (1953).

K. Statute of Limitations

Note

    COGSA provides for a one year statute of limitation that commences upon delivery for goods that have been damaged (for goods that are lost, the period runs from the date they should have been delivered). COGSA does not define the term "delivery". The Fifth Circuit has held that "'[d]elivery' occurs when the carrier places the cargo into the custody of whoever is legally entitled to receive it from the carrier." *Servicios-Expoarma, C.A. v. Industrial Maritime Carriers, Inc.*, 135 F.3d 984, 992, 1998 AMC 1453 (5th Cir. 1998). The court adopted the common definitions of delivery which courts have used to determine the meaning of term "delivery" under the Harter Act.

    General maritime law requires that a carrier "unload the cargo onto a dock, segregate it by bill of lading and count, put it into place of rest on the pier so that it is accessible to the consignee, and afford the cosignee a reasonable opportunity to come and get it." (at 993)

    There is an exception to this rule where customs or port regulations provide otherwise. Where a port regulation requires that cargo be delivered to an authorized customs warehouse, the carrier had "delivered" the cargo when it placed the goods in the hands of the customs officials. Some courts have held otherwise, *see, e.g., Lithotip, C.A. v. S.S. Guarico*, 569 F. Supp. 837, 1985 AMC 1813 (S.D.N.Y. 1983).

* * *

CHAPTER 2 — CHARTER PARTIES

A. Definitions and Introductory Note

1. Definitions

Charterparty: in medieval Latin, *carta partita*, an instrument written in duplicate on a single sheet and then divided by indented edges so that each part fitted the other (whence the term 'indenture'); only now used for this particular kind of shipping document.

STEWART BOYD, ANDREW BURROWS AND DAVID FOXTON, SCRUTTON ON CHARTERPARTIES AND BILLS OF LADING, 3 n.19 (20th ed. 1996).

There are several different types of charter party. The different types of contract have very different functions.

Voyage Charters. A voyage charter is a contract for the carriage of goods on a ship on a single voyage. Usually, the charterer charters the whole of the carrying capacity of the ship to carry a full cargo, but voyage charter parties for part cargoes are possible. The carrying ship is operated by the owner or disponent owner (a term that is explained further below) and not by the charterer. The charterer does not bear any of the ship's running costs directly. It simply pays freight to the owner for use of the ship to carry cargo.

Time Charters. A time charter is an agreement to divide responsibility for the navigational and commercial operations of the chartered ship. The shipowner (or disponent owner) remains responsible for the navigational operation of ship, along with its master and crew, without having to worry about finding commercial employment for it. The charterer finds commercial employment for the ship without having to worry about the technical and navigational aspects of running it, such as employing the master and crew. The charterer pays for the commercial use of the ship, and in return it is entitled to keep the freight paid by the cargo-owners for carriage of their goods on the ship. The shipowner is guaranteed payment for the use of the ship without having to find cargoes in the market; the charterer makes profits in the cargo market (the freights it receives from cargo-owners minus the hire it has to pay the shipowner) without having to run the ship itself.

Time and Voyage Charters Distinguished

Under a voyage charter the owner or disponent owner is using the vessel to trade for his own account. He decides and controls how he will exploit the earning capacity of the vessel, what trades he will compete in, what cargoes he will carry. He bears the full commercial risk and expense and enjoys the full benefit of the earnings of the vessel. A time charter is different. The owner still has to bear the expense of maintaining the ship and the crew. He still carries the risk of marine accidents and has to insure his interest in the vessel appropriately. But, in return for the payment of hire, he transfers the right to exploit the earning capacity of the vessel to the time charterer. The time charterer also agrees to provide and pay for the fuel consumed and to bear disbursements which arise from the trading of the vessel.

Whistler International Ltd v. Kawasaki Kisen Kaisha Ltd (The Hill Harmony) [2001] 1 App. Cas. 638, 652 (H.L.).

Demise or Bareboat Charters. Like a time charter, a demise charter is a contract for the use of a ship for a period of time. Unlike a time charterer, a demise charterer takes over possession of the ship in the legal sense. It becomes owner of the ship *pro hac vice*, the ship's disponent owner, rather than merely a hirer of the services of ship and crew. Because a demise charterer hires the ship without the services of master and crew, demise charters are also known as bareboat charters. Demise charter parties are not as commonly found as they were in the nineteenth century. In modern shipping practice, they are usually used as a vehicle for ship financing arrangements that split ownership of the ship as capital asset from entitlement to the stream of income it generates, for the purposes of avoiding tax.

All charterers of ships, by virtue of the charter party, have some control over the ship. Such control may relate only to a particular voyage; it may operate during a specified period. If the charter party is by way of demise, property in the ship temporarily passes to the charterer — for the duration of the charter. If possession, as well as some degree of control, passes to the charterer, then the property passes to the charterer and he is *pro tempore* the owner. But no property in the ship passes if possession is not given to the charterer by virtue of the terms of the charter. If the control of the master and crew in the navigation of the ship passes to the charterer he has possession. If, on the other hand, he acquires only a right to the use of the ship — a right to use her carrying capacity...there is no demise, but only a contract for services - *locatio operis vehendarum mercium.*

Australasian United Steam Navigation Co. Ltd v. Shipping Control Board, 71 C.L.R. 508, 521 (High Ct. Austl. 1945).

Although only a demise charterer can properly be called "disponent owner", that term is often used loosely to describe anyone who charters a ship to another. Thus, for example, a time charterer who sub-charters the ship to a voyage sub-charterer may be described as the "disponent owner," even though that is not strictly accurate to describe its rights over the ship.

Slot Charters. Slot charters are a relatively recent device for sharing the carrying capacity of a ship. They are commonly made between ocean carriers who form vessel-sharing alliances despite the fact that they are ostensibly competitors.

In such arrangements, two or more operators, usually of similarly sized vessels in a particular geographic trade, will agree to share space on one another's vessels. The attraction of such arrangements is evident. Space is utilized more efficiently and operating costs are reduced while service is expanded. Usually, space on all vessels in an alliance is shared among carriers in proportion to space contributed by each operator to the alliance. Each operator continues its own marketing efforts, booking cargo under its name. Each operator services its own customers, furnishing stuffing and lashing, and, depending on the terms of the arrangement, loading and discharging its own containers.

Vessel-sharing arrangements are implemented by charter parties known as slot charters, so named because space on container vessels is usually chartered by "slot," each slot representing the space required to accommodate one TEU [twenty-foot equivalent unit]. While members of an alliance may be parties to an overall operating agreement, the slot charter is the contract which governs the relationship on each voyage between only the Owner (i.e., the alliance member whose tonnage is performing the voyage) and the Slot Charterer (i.e., the alliance member who is chartering space from the Owner).

Mary T. Reilly, *Identity of the Carrier: Issues Under Slot Charters,* 25 Tul. Mar. L.J. 505, 506 (2001).

2. Introductory Note

In Chapter 1, you observed how various legal disputes involving loss and damage to goods carried by water are resolved by reference to the specific terms of the bill of lading and by the application of COGSA. In Chapter 2, you will see how legal relations between a shipowner and a charterer usually are controlled by the terms of the charter party. Because charter parties *per se* are excluded from the terms of COGSA, the principle of "freedom of contract" is generally applied by the courts. Under this principle the parties are free to strike their bargain in any terms mutually agreeable to them. This permits them to incorporate the terms of COGSA in the charter party. When that is done the various provisions of COGSA become terms of the charter party contract. In these situations the parties may modify or even exclude some provisions of COGSA. These modifications are permissible because the parties are not bound by COGSA in the first place.

There are circumstances in which COGSA is applicable to a transaction as a matter of law, notwithstanding the fact that the carrying vessel in under charter. These situations invariably involve the assertion of rights by a third party. Thus, if Owner charters its vessel for 10 years to "X" Shipping Company (Charterer) and "X" Shipping agrees to carry the goods of "Y" Products Company (Shipper) on the vessel to a designated port, any bill of lading which is issued to "Y" or its consignee is subject to the provisions of COGSA. In this situation, under COGSA either the charterer or the owner or both of them may be the COGSA carrier depending on the circumstances. Those circumstances include on whose form (letterhead) the bill of lading was issued, who is designated as the carrier in the bill, who signed the bill, on whose behalf was the form signed, etc. The legal relations between the owner and charterer are controlled by the charter party. The legal relations between the shipper or its consignee and the carrier, owner and/or charterer are controlled by the bill of lading and COGSA. Likewise where a shipper has entered into a voyage charter party with a shipowner to have its goods carried to a designated port, the legal relations between the owner and the charterer are governed by the charter party. Even if a bill of lading is also issued, it is regarded as a mere receipt as between those parties. But if that bill of lading is transferred to a third party such as a consignee, then the legal relations between the carrier, owner or charterer, and the third party are controlled by the terms of the bill of lading and COGSA. The cases in this section raise legal disputes mostly between vessel owners and charterers, consequently the terms of the charter party itself are usually controlling.

B. Demise Charters

1. Introductory Note

In *United States v. Shea,* 152 U.S. 178, 189-90, 14 S. Ct. 519, 522, 38 L. Ed. 403 (1894), the Supreme Court said:

> No technical words are necessary to create a demise. It is enough that the language used shows an intent to transfer the possession, command, and control…[T]he conduct of the parties in the execution of the contract removes all obscurity as to its scope and meaning. As the findings show, the vessel, the James Bowen, was furnished by petitioner, and was accepted and used by the defendants. During the time of its use it was under the exclusive management and control of the defendants. The very condition resulted which is the purpose and effect of a demise—the transfer of the exclusive possession, management, and control. The vessel was not, when injured, returned to the petitioner, but when the repairs were finished, "resumed work." It is insisted by the defendants that there was no demise because, as claimed, the petitioner did not contract to furnish one vessel for any length of time, and could, if he wished, change vessels. It is doubtful whether that is a correct interpretation of the instrument, and whether it was in the power of the petitioner, after a vessel had been tendered and accepted by the government, to substitute another therefor. But even if it were so, the substituted vessel would pass into the exclusive possession of the government, the same as the vessel for which it was substituted.

DANT & RUSSELL, INC. v. DILLINGHAM TUG & BARGE CORP.

895 F.2d 507, 1990 AMC 1372 (9th Cir. 1989)

Before SKOPIL, HALL and O'SCANNLAIN, Circuit Judges:

Per Curiam:

We are presented with the maritime law question of whether a vessel owner is liable to a cargo owner for damages in the absence of privity. We reverse the district court's finding that the vessel owner was negligent and its further finding that the vessel owner breached a warranty of seaworthiness. As a result, the district court's determination of damages owed by Pacific to Fireman's Fund cannot stand. We remand to the district court the issue of the barge's *in rem* liability to Dant & Russell.

Facts

In December 1981, appellant Pacific Hawaiian ("Pacific"), owner of the Barge Norton Sound, demise chartered the barge to Hvide Marine Transport, Inc. ("Hvide"). As demise charterer, Hvide assumed possession, control, and "temporary ownership" of the barge. Hvide then voyage chartered the barge to Terminal Steamship Co. ("Terminal"), a wholly-owned subsidiary of appellee Dant & Russell ("D & R"), to carry D & R's lumber from Astoria, Oregon to Florida. As voyage charterer, Terminal obtained the use of the barge for carriage, but responsibility and control remained with Hvide.

D & R insured the lumber with appellee Fireman's Fund Insurance Co. ("Fireman's Fund"). By endorsement, the policy named Hvide as an additional assured with waiver of subrogation. Hvide also added an endorsement to its own Protection and Indemnity ("P & I") policy to extend coverage to the barge during the voyage.

In accord with the terms of the demise charter which called for various inspections and surveys, the NORTON SOUND was dry-docked at Dillingham Ship Repair ("DSR") on Swan Island in Portland, Oregon, for repairs necessary to meet inspection standards. Pacific retained Hughes to consult with and assist Bartholomew, Hvide's representative at DSR. Bartholomew acted as port engineer and was authorized by Hvide to direct the repairs.

Both Hughes and Bartholomew knew that on previous voyages, a portable pump had been needed to suction water out of the cargo hold of the barge, and that major parts of the barge's bilge and ballast system did not work.

DSR tested the system, recommended substantial repairs, and gave Bartholomew and Hughes an estimate for the work. Bartholomew and Hughes then agreed, in a letter signed by Tennant, a Pacific vice-president, and by Santos, a vice-president of Hvide, to defer repairs until after the voyage.

The tug crew loaded and stowed the cargo of lumber under Hughes' instruction. Bartholomew then helped to ballast the barge, and the barge left Astoria. During the voyage, ballast water leaked through the ballast lines and into void tanks in the cargo hold. This caused the barge to list so that water washed over the open afterdeck and entered the deckhouse.

When the cargo was unloaded in Florida, ten to fifteen percent of the lumber was stained by water, oil, rust, and debris. Fireman's Fund paid D & R $169,981.23 under the policy. D & R absorbed the $25,000 deductible under the policy.

Litigation ensued between Hvide and D & R: Hvide sought to recover its voyage charter hire and D & R sought to recover for the cargo damage. That litigation ended with a settlement agreement under which, inter alia, the claims of each were waived and released.

D & R and Fireman's Fund then filed this action against Pacific and the barge. Upon motion, the trial court dismissed the barge *in rem*.

At trial, Pacific stipulated that the barge was unseaworthy when she left Portland, but contended as barge owner, it had exercised due diligence to make the barge seaworthy and that it did not know, or should it have known as a matter of law, of the unseaworthiness.

The district court entered summary judgment against Pacific for breach of warranty of seaworthiness. After trial on the issues of negligence and damages, the district court also found Pacific negligent and assessed damages. It held that Pacific was not relieved of liability by virtue of various indemnity and hold harmless agreements in the charters and the insurance policies. Pacific now appeals the district court's findings; D & R cross-appeals the dismissal of the barge and the district court's calculation of damages.

The parties agree there is no dispute of material fact. This court, therefore, reviews de novo the district court's application of law to facts. *Darring v. Kincheloe*, 783 F.2d 874, 876 (9th Cir.1986).

Discussion

I

The district court found that Hughes and Tennant were negligent for failing to have the bilge and ballast system repaired before the voyage when they knew or should have known the barge was unseaworthy. Since they were acting as agents of Pacific, their actions were imputed to Pacific. *W.R. Grace & Co. v. Western U.S. Indus., Inc.*, 608 F.2d 1214, 1218 (9th Cir.1979), *cert. denied*, 446 U.S. 953, 100 S.Ct. 2920, 64 L.Ed.2d 810 (1980).

Pacific contests the finding of liability, saying that it owed no duty to D & R. It argues that scant precedent exists for holding a vessel owner liable to a cargo owner for negligent conduct predating a chain of charters.

Even though the demise charter did not begin until Hvide took physical possession of the barge, Pacific is not liable to Hvide for the alleged negligence. Pacific's alleged negligence predated the charter term, but Hvide's vice-president waived Pacific's liability for any negligence by agreeing to defer repairs on the NORTON SOUND until after the voyage. It is true that one may not assume the risk for certain negligent torts. *See Prosser & Keeton on the Law of Torts* § 68, at 482-83 (5th ed. 1984). There is nothing in this rule, however, which precludes one from waiving another's liability for negligence after the allegedly negligent acts have occurred. In our view, the agreement to defer repairs operated as such a waiver. In short, Hvide decided to gamble that the barge would safely transport the lumber, and it lost; Pacific had no duty to pay the cost of Hvide's wager.

Therefore, the finding of negligence against Pacific is reversed.

II

The district court also found that Pacific had violated the warranty of seaworthiness. Pacific, however, claims waiver and points out that the warranty of seaworthiness is waived "where full inspection was made by those seeking to charter the vessels ... and the alleged defects or weaknesses were either patent or were especially called to such charterers' attention by the vessel owners." *Thomas Jordan, Inc. v. Mayronne Drilling Mud, Chem. & Eng'g Serv.*, 214 F.2d 410, 413 (5th Cir.1954) (quoting *Dempsey v. Downing*, 11 F.2d 15, 17 (4th Cir.1926)).

Here, Hvide, the demise charterer, supervised the inspection and took an active part in the repairs. Hvide had full knowledge of the vessel's unseaworthiness and assumed all risks. In similar cases, owners have been absolved of liability. *See id.*; *Nat G. Harrison Overseas Corp. v. American Tug Titan*, 516 F.2d 89, 96 (5th Cir.) (owner is not responsible for conditions which demise charter could have ascertained by reasonable inspection), *modified on other grounds*, 520 F.2d 1104 (5th Cir.1975). Hvide's conduct constitutes waiver of any warranty claims against Pacific.

Pacific cannot be held liable under a warranty theory for a second reason. The owner and the voyage charterer are not in privity and the owner does not owe a duty to the voyage charterer. *Martin v. Walk, Haydel & Assocs., Inc.*, 742 F.2d 246, 249 (5th Cir.1984) (since no demise charter, owner was held liable for unseaworthiness); *Kerr-McGee Corp. v. Law*, 479 F.2d 61, 63 (4th Cir.1973) (demise charterer liable for seaworthiness); *Uni-Petrol Gesellschaft Fur Mineraloel Produkte M.B.H. v. M/T Lotus Maru*, 615 F.Supp. 78, 81 (S.D.N.Y.1985). "'An owner who has demised his ship is not indeed liable to anyone but the demisee under his warranty of seaworthiness for any loss or injury suffered during the demise. Such liabilities sound in contract and he has not made any contract with anyone else.'" *M/T/ Lotus Maru*, 615 F.Supp. at 81 (quoting *Cannella v. Lykes Bros. S.S. Co.*, 174 F.2d 794, 796 (2d Cir.), *cert. denied*, 338 U.S. 859, 70 S.Ct. 102, 94 L.Ed. 526 (1949)).

The finding that Pacific was liable for breach of warranty must, therefore, also be reversed.

III

In their cross-appeal, D & R and Fireman's Fund argue that the district court improperly dismissed the NORTON SOUND from this action.

The original complaint was filed against the barge *in rem* as well as against Pacific in personam. Such a claim attempts to recover from Pacific's property if D & R cannot recover from Pacific personally. D & R's and Fireman's Fund's claim relies on the venerable dictum of *The Barnstable*, 181 U.S. 464, 467, 21 S.Ct. 684, 685, 45 L.Ed. 954 (1901), which held that "the law in this country is well settled, that the ship itself is to be treated in some sense as a principal, and as personally liable for the negligence of anyone who is lawfully in possession of her, whether as owner or charterer." *See* GILMORE & BLACK, THE LAW OF ADMIRALTY, 600 (2d ed. 1975).

By order, the district court held that a waiver of subrogation by Fireman's Fund to D & R also applied to the barge. The waiver clause provided that:

> no right of subrogation ... shall lie against any craft belonging in part or on [sic] whole to the Assured or a subsidiary and/or affiliated company of the Assured. This clause, however, does not extend to exclude recoveries that may be had under Protection and Indemnity Insurance.

An endorsement to the policy named Hvide as an additional assured, and waived Fireman's Fund's rights of subrogation against Hvide.

The district court reasoned that the barge was a "craft belonging" to Hvide under D & R's policy because a demise charterer is generally treated as the owner of the chartered vessel pro hac vice. *See, e.g., Marr Enters. v. Lewis Refrig. Co.*, 556 F.2d 951, 957-58 (9th Cir.1977). It therefore dismissed the barge as a defendant because D & R's policy with Fireman's Fund excluded rights of subrogation against vessels "belonging ... to the Assured."

However, the district court failed to note that this release did not operate against D & R, but only against Fireman's Fund. Therefore, with regard to the $25,000 deductible on the insurance policy, this clause is inoperative and does not prevent D & R's cross claim.

Fireman's Fund further argues that the exclusion in the policy with regard to protection and indemnity insurance should preclude the dismissal of the barge *in rem*. We are not persuaded that the exclusion precludes dismissal of the barge. At most, it allows Fireman's Fund to make a claim in personam against Hvide only if Hvide has protection and indemnity insurance. It does not give Fireman's Fund the right to make a claim against the barge *in rem*.

Fireman's Fund makes the further argument that even if the waiver of subrogation might have protected the NORTON SOUND, Hvide's non-disclosure of the unseaworthiness of the barge was a breach of good faith. Such a breach makes Hvide's coverage under the policy voidable. However, Hvide's breach of good faith should not be imputed to the barge which became a third party beneficiary by virtue of the waiver of subrogation. See *Everglades Marina, Inc. v. American Eastern Dev. Corp.*, 374 So.2d 517 (Fla.1979). Therefore, Fireman's Fund's claims against the NORTON SOUND, *in rem*, were properly dismissed.

Finally, D & R's claim for $25,000 may also be untenable. As Pacific notes, paragraph 21 of the voyage charter between Hvide and D & R provides:

> All privileges, rights, exemptions and defenses provided for the benefit of Owner herein ["Owner" being defined in this policy as Hvide] shall be equally available to and for the benefit of every vessel used in the transportation, including the named tug and any substitute tug, as well as the owners, operators, officers and crews thereof.

Thus, Pacific can claim any defenses for the barge that Hvide could claim for itself. If the settlement agreement in Florida between Hvide and D & R released Hvide from all liability, it will also have released the barge. We remand this issue to the district court to determine if D & R is barred from asserting any cause of action against Hvide because of the settlement. If so, this is fatal to D & R's claim against the barge.

Conclusion

Since we have found that Pacific neither was negligent nor breached a warranty of the barge's seaworthiness, we reverse the district court's findings on those issues and thereby reverse its finding on damages. We affirm the district court's dismissal of the barge *in rem* with regard to Fireman's Fund, but not with regard to D & R. We remand the issue of the barge's *in rem* liability to D & R to the district court.

AFFIRMED in part, REVERSED in part, and REMANDED.

The dissenting opinion of Judge Hall is omitted [eds.].

Notes

1. When a vessel has been demise chartered, the master and crew may remain on the vessel and operate the vessel for the charterer. Under the circumstances, the master and crew are subject to the orders of the charterer and are its employees. In some demise charters the owner turns over to the charterer its vessel without master and crew. These charters are frequently referred to as "bareboat" charters.

2. Can the owner of vessel which has been demise chartered be liable to a third party with whom it is not in privity for damages caused by the unseaworthiness of the vessel or its negligent operation? Compare; *American Commercial Lines, Inc. v. Valley Line Co.*, 529 F.2d 921, 1977 AMC 2265 (8th Cir. 1976) with *Dant & Russell, Inc. v. Dillingham Tug & Barge Corp.*, 895 F.2d 507, 1990 AMC 1372 (9th Cir. 1989). See also *Siderius v. M/V Amilla*, 880 F.2d 662, 665, 1989 AMC 2533 (2d Cir. 1989), where the U.S. Court of Appeals for the Second Circuit said:

> [W]e agree with the district court's determination that Siderius [the cargo owner] may recover directly from Amilla [the shipowner] given that the ship was unseaworthy. We have long held that "when the charterer of a ship is liable to a cargo owner", and that liability results because the vessel owner has violated its warranty of seaworthiness, the "cargo owner" may hold the shipowner on his warranty to the charterer". *New York Cent. R.R. v. New York, N.H. & H.R.R.*, 275 F.2d 865, 866 (2d Cir. 1960).

3. The demise, in practical effect and in important legal consequence, shifts the possession and control of the vessel from one person to another, just as the shoreside lease of real property shifts many of the incidents of ownership from lessor to lessee." Gilmore & Black, *supra*, Chapter IV, page 215. Then, the authors proceed to discuss typical characteristics of a demise or bareboat charterer. "The test is one of 'control', if the owner retains control over the vessel, merely carrying the goods furnished or designated by the charter, the charter is not a demisee." (Sec. 4-21). Put another way, "to create a demise the owner of the vessel must completely and exclusively relinquish 'possession, command and navigation' thereof to the demise" *Guzman v. Pichirilo*, 369 U.S. 698, 699 82 S. Ct. 1095, 1096, 8 L. Ed. 2d 205 (1962), and further "it is therefore tantamount to, though just short of, an outright transfer of ownership." 369 U.S. at 700, 82 S. Ct. at 1096. That case, moreover, states that "courts are reluctant to find a demise when the dealings between the parties are consistent with a lesser relationship." See *Reed v. United States*, 78 U.S. (11 Wall.) 591, 601, 20 L. Ed. 220 (1871). The words "demise" or "bareboat" are not used in the charter agreement in controversy, although no technical words are absolutely necessary to create a demise.

* * *

This Court is mindful that circumstances pertaining to a barge without an independent power source may differ from that of a vessel with its own means of propulsion. Some courts have indicated that charter of a barge without power is, in fact, a demise. See *R. Lenahan*, 48 F.2d 110 (2nd Cir., 1931); *Ira S. Bushey & Sons v. Hedger & Co.*, 40 F.2d 417 (2nd Cir., 1930); *The Nat E. Sutton*, 42 F.2d 229 (E.D.N.Y., 1930); *Moran Towing v. New York*, 36 F.2d 417 (S.D.N.Y. 1929); *Dailey v. Carroll*, 248 F. 466 (2nd Cir. 1917); *The Daniel Burns*, 52 F. 159 (S.D.N.Y., 1892). These cases and their holdings are noted in *The Doyle*, 105 F.2d 113, 114 (3rd Cir., 1939), but in the latter case which held a barge charterer to become the "owner pro hac vice", it was important that the charterer was a towing company with the right of and in the exercise of navigation of the barge, which caused damage to its cargo. (Its liability was held, however, to be less than the owners). *R.D. Wood Co. v. Phoenix Steel Corp.*, 211 F. Supp. 924, 927 (E.D. Pa., 1962) also comments on the latter aspect of Doyle, observing that "the towing company had clearly taken over *complete control of the vessel* and was, therefore, correctly treated as the owner." It was also observed, moreover, that there was "some indication that peculiar conditions at New York" required the second circuit rule pertaining to barge charters. It is concluded that whether or not the charter in controversy here is or is not a demise depends upon the facts of the case in light of effective control of the vessel and the charter provisions. *Leary v. United States*, 14 Wall. 607, 610, 20 L. Ed. 756 (1972). Where the charterer receives, in effect, only the *service* of a vessel (the word "use" is employed in *Leary*) without entire possession and control, it is less than a demise. *United States v. Shea*, 152 U.S. 178, 188, 14 S. Ct. 518, 38 L. Ed. 403 (1894).

* * *

Complaint of Cook Transp. System, Inc., 431 F. Supp 437, 443-44 (W.D. Tenn. 1976).

4. The liability of a charterer for damage to or loss of cargo is discussed in the Introductory Note to *Who is the COGSA Carrier?* in Chapter 1, section G.

5. Of course, a time charterer is liable to third persons for his own faults. However, in *Hasbro Industries, Inc. v. M/S St. Constantine*, 705 F.2d 339, 1983 AMC 1841 (9th Cir. 1983), the court found that charterers did not have a duty to exercise due diligence to make the ship seaworthy. In a similar vein, in *Haluapo v. Akashi Kaiun, K.K.*, 748 F.2d 1363, 1365, 1985 AMC 1107 (9th Cir. 1984), the court refused to hold a time charterer liable for injuries sustained by a longshoreman while unloading the vessel. The court distinguished other cases where liability had been extended either because the time charterer had hired a foreign stevedore and supervised its work and the charterer had actual control of the vessel. In the case at bar, the time charterer had "no involvement of the operation of the vessel or the loading of the cargo other than providing pilotage and tug boat service and arranging for the berthing of the vessel. The time charterer had neither knowledge of the defects on board the ship nor the ability to control the actions of the crew."

C. Time and Voyage Charters—Distinguished

E.A.S.T., INC. OF STAMFORD, CONN. v. M/V ALAIA

673 F. Supp. 796, 1988 AMC 1396 (E.D. La. 1987), *aff'd*, 876 F.2d 1168, 1989 AMC 2024 (5th Cir. 1989)

Charles SCHWARTZ, Jr., D.J.

East has come south to send everyone north before a vessel went west. Because the law on maritime liens should not wander in aimless directions, the Court believes a written explanation of that law as it pertains to this case is fit.

This matter is before the Court on the motion of claimant Advance Company, Inc. of Liberia (Advance) to release the vessel from seizure or alternatively to set the amount of security to be posted by claimant, and to set the amount of counter security to be posted by plaintiff. At the post-seizure hearing held October 26, 1987, the Court denied Advance's motion for immediate release of the vessel without bond, fixed security for the release at $175,000, fixed counter security at $100,000 and referred the parties to arbitration in London. The present Order & Reasons gives the reasons for these rulings.

The plaintiff, E.A.S.T., Inc. of Stamford, Connecticut (E.A.S.T.), argues that it had time chartered Advance's vessel, the M/V ALAIA, that Advance breached its warranty of seaworthiness and that E.A.S.T. is thus entitled to a maritime lien on the vessel. Advance naturally disagrees; it argues that the charter party either was never executed by Advance or was still executory at the time of the alleged breach and that no maritime lien was thus created. Because the Court believes Advance entered into a charter that was no longer executory at the time E.A.S.T. rejected the vessel for the alleged breach, the Court finds for the purpose of the preliminary, post-seizure hearing that the limited evidence brought out at the hearing supports E.A.S.T.'s claim for a maritime lien.

* * *

II.

* * *

A.

Advance points to the absence of its authorized signature on E.A.S.T.'s exhibits of the original charter and the fixture recap and argues that without such a signature Advance cannot be bound to the charter. The argument fails.

A charter party, such as the New York Produce Exchange time charter involved here, is merely a form of contract and is generally subject to the rules and principles of construction for ordinary commercial contracts. *See Marine Overseas Services, Inc. v. Crossocean Shipping Co.*, 791 F.2d 1227, 1234 (5th Cir. 1986). A charter comes into existence when the parties have a meeting of the minds on the essential terms of the charter. *E.g., Interocean Shipping Co. v. National Shipping & Trading Corp.*, 1975 AMC 1283, 1292, 523 F.2d 527, 534 (2d Cir. 1975), *cert. denied,*

423 U.S. 1054, 1976 AMC 1499 (1976). A charter does not have to be signed to be legally binding. *A/S Custodia v. Lessin International, Inc.*, 1974 AMC 865, 867, 503 F.2d 318, 320 (2d Cir. 1974); *see Valero Refining, Inc. v. M/ T Laubenhorn*, 1987 AMC 2100, 2105, 813 F.2d 60, 64 (5th Cir. 1987). Indeed, even an oral charter is valid and enforceable. *E.g.*, *St. Paul Fire & Marine Insurance Co. v. Vest Transportation Co.*, 1982 AMC 450, 459, 666 F.2d 932, 939 (5th Cir. 1982); *accord* Wilford, *supra* note 3, at 1 (on English law); *see Kossick v. United Fruit Co.*, 365 U.S. 731, 81 S. Ct. 886 (1961).

Mr. Dammers testified that both sides agreed to the essential terms of the charter and that the general shipping custom on fixture recaps did not require written confirmations to make these recaps binding. Advance offered no opposing testimony. Thus, based solely on the evidence presented so far, the Court finds that Advance is bound by the charter.[6]

* * *

In passing, Advance argues that commencement of the charter was conditioned on E.A.S.T.'s acceptance of the vessel. This argument must likewise fail. Not only does the charter not expressly state such a condition, but also it expressly states a specific time when the charter is to commence.... Binding authority squarely rejects Advance's argument. *See Eastern Marine Corp. v. Fukaya Trading Co.*, 1966 AMC 1959, 1963-64, 364 F.2d 80, 84 (5 Cir.) *cert. denied*, 385 U.S. 971 (1971) (concerning an NYPE46 time charter) ("the court will presume the formation of a contract upon execution of the document if all other standard contractual requirements, such as consideration and capacity, have been satisfied").

B.

* * *

The vast majority of cases addressing the executory contract doctrine have concerned contracts of affreightment evidenced by bills of lading and/or voyage charters; hardly any have concerned bareboat or time charters. *See* G. Gilmore & C. Black, *supra* note 1, at 635; *see also International Marine Towing*, 1985 AMC at 1914, 722 F.2d at 130 n.7. But Advance ignores this important distinction between these two categories of shipping contracts in contending that under the executory contract doctrine a maritime lien for breach of a time charter party arises only if cargo was loaded aboard. Though perhaps generally valid in the context of bills of lading or voyage charters, which were at issue in many of the cases cited by Advance, the proposition does not apply in the context of time charters, such as the NYPE46 form at issue here.

* * *

Some of the distinctions between the two forms of charters are explained in Scrutton on Charterparties and Bills of Lading 51 (19th ed. 1984) as follows:

Charterparties not by way of demise fall into two main categories: (1) time charters and (2) voyage charters. Under the ordinary form of time charter, the shipowner agrees with the time charterer to render services for a named period by his master and crew to carry goods put on board his ship by or on behalf of the time charterer. The shipowner's remuneration is usually termed "hire" and is generally calculated at a monthly rate on the tonnage of the ship.

A voyage charter differs from a time charter in many respects, but primarily in that it is a contract to carry specified goods on a defined voyage or voyages, the remuneration of the shipowner being a freight calculated according to the quantity of cargo loaded or carried, or sometimes lump sum freight. (footnotes omitted).

---

[6] The rule in *A/S Custodia* and *Valero* fully addresses and rejects Advance's objections to the charter party and recap.... Even considering these objections, however, Advance would still be bound by the charter in light of Mr. Dammers' oral testimony on a meeting of the minds.

See also O'Brien, *Freight and Hire*, 49 TULANE L. REV. 956 (1975). Other significant differences exist as well. Under a time charter, the charterer generally provides and pays for all fuel, port charges, pilotage, launch hire, tug assistance, consular charges, dock, harbor and tonnage dues at the ports of delivery, and redelivery and agency fees; whereas under a voyage charter, the owner generally absorbs all operating expenses, such as port charges, cost of bunkers, loading and discharging expenses and agency fees. *E.g.*, 1 J. BES, CHARTERING AND SHIPPING TERMS 69-71, 76-77 (10th ed. 1977). Thus, under a time charter, the time charterer begins his performance—well before cargo is, if ever, loaded on the vessel—by paying hire, appointing and funding a port agent, and arranging and paying for pilotage, tug assistance and line handlers and all else necessary to berth the vessel in order to load cargo; under a voyage charter, on the other hand, since the owner pays these operating expenses, the voyage charterer's performance does not begin until control of the cargo is transferred to the vessel owner. While a time charterer pays hire in advance for the use of the vessel, the voyage charterer does not pay until after cargo has been loaded and bills of lading signed or, in some cases, even later.

Before the vessel was arrested on October 21, 1987, E.A.S.T. had paid time charter hire, had appointed an agent to handle the vessel's needs in the Port of New Orleans, had forwarded $15,000 to the agent for payment of all port charges and had the New Orleans cargo on the dock ready for shipment. Under the terms of the charter, the vessel was delivered to E.A.S.T. when it arrived at the pilot station below New Orleans. *See* Exhibit Dammers 3, line 18. Through its agent, E.A.S.T. provided a pilot to bring the vessel upriver, tugs to maneuver it into berth at the Nashville Avenue Wharf and line handlers to make the vessel "all fast." There is no doubt that the vessel was delivered under the charter and that E.A.S.T. and Advance had commenced performance. In sum, the charter was not executory at the time of the arrest, and thus E.A.S.T. may properly assert a maritime lien for the alleged breach.

* * *

A voyage charter may constitute a contract of affreightment. *See, e.g., The Gracie D. Chambers*, 253 F. 182, 183 (2d Cir. 1918) (characterizing the payment to owner under a voyage charter as "freight," which is earned only upon delivery of cargo at destination), affirmed *sub nom. International Paper Co. v. The Gracie D. Chambers*, 248 U.S. 387, 39 S. Ct. 149 (1919). But a time charter should not be considered a contract of affreightment, for charter hire in a time charter is based on the period of the charter regardless of cargo carried. This basic distinction is discussed at length in O'Brien, *supra*, 49 TULANE L. REV. 956. *Cf., e.g., Clyde Commercial Steamship Co. v. West India Steamship Co.*, 169 F. 275 (2d Cir.) *cert. denied*, 214 U.S. 523 (1909) (no off-hire for a time charterer where the vessel was quarantined at a Texas harbor, for the charterer had the use of the vessel during the quarantine and could have sent the vessel elsewhere).

The requirement that a vessel take control over cargo before a charterer may assert a lien under a voyage charter is reasonable in light of the nature of the obligations of the parties: the owner is obliged to provide a vessel for carriage of a cargo to a destination, and the charterer is obliged to pay freight to the owner for delivery. With a time charter as in this case, it makes no sense to determine that the charter is executory until the loading of cargo. The charter itself provides a *time* when it commences. After that time, the charterer is responsible for charges as described above.

* * *

IV.

For those who may have found the foregoing a soporific dissertation, the Court summarizes the two main points of law discussed. First, a vessel owner may not deny the existence of a time charter merely because his signature does not appear on the written charter agreement, especially where he has already placed the vessel at the charterer's disposal and both have already begun performance under the charter. Second, once this performance has begun even if no cargo is ever loaded on the vessel, the charterer may assert a maritime lien on the vessel for breach of the warranty of seaworthiness to recover both the money already spent on the vessel and any contract damages.

Note: Review of charterparties and bills of lading

Understanding liability issues in charter party situations requires one to distinguish between those situations where the only parties involved in the transaction and ensuing dispute are the shipowner and the charterer from those where a third party, such as a shipper or consignee, is involved. In the two-party situation (involving only shipowner and charterer) legal relations between them are controlled by their contract—the charter party. COGSA is not applicable *ex proprio vigore*. The parties, nevertheless, may agree that COGSA or certain parts of COGSA shall apply to their transaction by incorporating the terms of COGSA into their charter party. This may be done by expressly including the text of COGSA in the charter party or by incorporating it by reference. In contrast, where a claim is made by a third-party shipper or consignee to whom a bill of lading has been transferred, COGSA usually will apply of its own force, regardless of whether or not it is incorporated by the charter party.

Charter party transactions do not in themselves fall within the ambit of COGSA. COGSA § 5; *Vanol, USA, Inc. v. M/T Coronado*, 663 F. Supp. 79, 1988 AMC 560 (S.D.N.Y. 1987). Where a shipowner enters into a demise or time charter with a charterer, the relationship is controlled by the terms of the charter party. Demise and time charters are not contracts of carriage but merely arrangements for the use of the carrying space on a vessel. In contrast to a contract of carriage, in a demise or time charter, the shipowner does not undertake to carry anyone's goods from one port to another; there is no third party such as a shipper, and, as no bill of lading or similar document is issued in these transactions, COGSA is not applicable.

Where a demise charterer uses the vessel to engage in the transportation business and enters into contracts of carriage with shippers, the vessel is not under the control of the shipowner. The charterer may issue bills of lading to a shipper and these will control the relationship between charterer-as-carrier and the shipper. Thus, COGSA may apply to cargo disputes between the charterer-carrier and shipper. However, because the shipowner has no contractual relationship with the shipper or its consignee, and has no control over the use of the vessel, the shipowner is not liable for acts of the charterer or its crew which result in loss of or damage to cargo.

The time charter party situation may be more complicated than explained above. Where a time charterer who enters into a contract of carriage with a shipper and issues to the shipper its own bill of lading signed by the charterer or its agent, the *charterer* is a COGSA carrier and the transaction is subject to COGSA. Under the facts as stated, however, the *shipowner* is not a COGSA carrier and is not personally liable for loss or damage to cargo. Neither it nor anyone acting on its behalf has issued a bill of lading. There is no contractual link between the shipowner and the shipper or its consignee.

In contrast to a demise charterer, however, a shipowner who time charters its vessel, has not given up control of its vessel. Although a demise charterer is regarded in law as owner *pro hac vice*, this is not so in the case of a time charterer. In a time charter, the shipowner and the charterer share responsibility for the operations of the vessel. In this respect, a charter party may contain a provision which purports to designate the master of the vessel as the agent of the charterer, at least with respect to cargo operations. This provision is often accompanied by another provision which obligates the master to sign bills of lading when requested by the charterer or which specifically authorizes the charterer or the charterer's agent to sign "for the master."

These provisions which are intended to insulate the shipowner from liability for cargo claims have not been given that effect by the courts. Thus, where a bill of lading obligates the master to sign bills of lading or authorizes the charterer or its agent to sign "for the master," the courts have generally held, in the absence of special circumstances, that the master still acts on behalf of the shipowner. *Pacific Emp. Ins. Co. v. M/V Gloria*, 767 F.2d 229 (5th Cir. 1985); *Insituto Cubano De Est. Del Azucar v. T/V Golden West*, 246 F.2d 802 (2d Cir.), *cert. denied*, 355 U.S. 884, 78 S. Ct. 152, 2 L. Ed. 2d 114 (1957). In such situations, the master is considered to be the shipowner's agent. Thus, if a shipowner has given its master authority to sign bills of lading at the request of the charterer and the master has, in fact, signed the bill of lading, the owner may be held liable *in personam* for damage or loss to cargo. Likewise, if a shipowner has given the charterer or charterer's agent authority to sign "for the master," the owner may be held liable. In these situations the bill of lading that has been signed by a person authorized by the shipowner to do so provides a contractual link between the shipowner and the shipper and its consignee.

A voyage charter party is different from the demise and time charters discussed above in that it is, in reality, a contract of carriage. In some contracts of carriage, a shipper contracts with a carrier for the carrier to transport the shippers goods from one place to another. Ordinarily, the selection of the carrying vessel, ports of destination, etc., are at the discretion of the carrier. By contrast, in a voyage charter party, the charterer contracts with the shipowner for space on board a vessel for the purpose of transporting a particular cargo on a particular voyage. The charter party may specify a named vessel and/or vessel characteristics. It may give the charterer the right to select from a range of loading and discharge ports, etc. In this respect, a voyage charter may give the charterer greater flexibility and control. It may also be more economically advantageous because a charterer may have greater negotiating strength than an ordinary shipper.

Notwithstanding the differences between voyage charters on the one hand and demise and time charters on the other, there is an important similarity among them: in two party situations, disputes between the shipowner and the voyage charterer will be resolved by the terms of their contract—the voyage charter party. COGSA specifically states that it is not applicable in such situations. COGSA § 5. Thus, in case of loss or of damage to cargo, the shipper-charterer's rights will be determined under the charter party. Of course, the parties may have elected to incorporate the terms of COGSA, but then COGSA is merely another provision of their contract. Even where shipowner has given to the shipper-charterer a document called a bill of lading, the rights of the shipper-charterer are determined under the charter party. The charter party is the contract of carriage—not the bill of lading. The bill of lading will be regarded as being merely a receipt which shows that the shipowner-carrier received the goods.

Suppose the following has occurred. Shipowner (Carrier) and Charterer (Shipper) have entered into a voyage charter party and Carrier has given Shipper a negotiable bill of lading. Shipper has sold the goods to Buyer and has transferred the bill of lading to Buyer. The goods arrived in damaged condition. What remedies does Buyer have? Buyer has no rights under the charter party because it is not a party to it. Buyer, however, is in possession of a bill of lading issued by Carrier which obligates Carrier to deliver the goods to the person in possession of the bill of lading. COGSA states it is applicable "to any bill of lading ... issued under or pursuant to a charter party from the moment at which such bill of lading ... regulates the relations between a carrier and a holder of the same." COGSA § 1(b). Buyer is entitled to invoke the provisions of COGSA against Carrier, which in this case is the shipowner. The charter party is irrelevant to the legal status of Buyer. Buyer would not have a COGSA action against Shipper (Charterer) because it is not a COGSA carrier. Owner has Charterer's (Shipper's) goods on its vessel, therefore, it is the carrier. Buyer, however, may have a breach of contract action against the seller, who in this situation is also the shipper-charterer, depending on which party to the contract of sale, seller or buyer, had the risk of loss.

Finally, under the law of the United States, vessels are "personified" and may be liable in an action *in rem*. Therefore, where goods are loaded aboard a vessel, this is considered a ratification of the contract of carriage by the vessel, and the vessel, itself, may be liable *in rem* if cargo is damaged or lost.

D. Contract Formalities

THE "JUNIOR K"

[1988] 2 Lloyd's Rep. 583.

Judgment

Mr. Justice STEYN:

In the context of an issue between the parties as to whether a binding charter-party was concluded, this case raises directly the question of the meaning and effect of a stipulation in telex exchanges that there is a fixture "subject to details". Since the decision in this case may affect the way in which negotiations for the chartering of vessels is conducted, I give this judgment in open Court.

The background to the dispute can be sketched relatively briefly. The plaintiffs in this case are the Star Steamship Society, a Lebanese concern which was the owner of the vessel *Junior K*. The defendants are Beogradska Plovidba, a Yugoslav corporation, and they were the proposed charterers. In the usual way negotiations took place through intermediaries. On the plaintiffs' side they were represented by their managers and London chartering brokers.

The defendants were represented by Rotterdam brokers. The negotiations for the chartering of the vessel by the plaintiffs to the defendants commenced on Oct. 1, 1985. The critical events took place on Oct 4. On that date there were various telex exchanges, and telephonic discussions, between the brokers who acted on behalf of the parties. The last exchange is a telex from the plaintiffs' brokers to the defendants' brokers which was timed at 19 27 hours on Oct 4. This telex is of considerable importance. It was in the usual brokers' shorthand to the following effect:

> Junior
> Confirm telcons here recap fixture *sub details*.
> Vessel as described before as per our earlier recap (tc) 2 Oct acct Beogradska Plovidba Beograd
> Min 6000 tons chopt up to full cargo of vessels capacity agprods stowed 55 cuft pmt
> Laycan Spot/7 Oct (vsl could ETA Mersin tomo pm)
> 1 sb Mersin aaaa/1 sb Bombay aaaa
> 650 tons per wwd shexeiu free in
> Disch cop free out
> Dem USD 2000 per hdwts loadport
> Frt USD 180,000 lsum FIO basis 6000 tons of cargo. Any additional cargo loaded to be settled at the
>   rate of USD 25 pmt FIO.

90 pct freight within 3 banking days of issuing and releasing bsl balance after right and true delivery latest within 7 days completion discharge.

Freight deemed earned on shipment discountless ship and or cargo lost or not lost

Taxes/dues and or fees on freight and vessel owners account

Taxes/dues and or fees on cargo including primage if any max 5 pct charterers account

For primage/freight tax calculations, authorities to be shown lumpsum freight as USD 120,000

Any overage premia chts account BS/l dated 30 Sept will be issued and delivered chasbe 3.75 pct

SUB DETS GENCON CP

It is common ground that there were no telephone conversations between the parties on Oct. 4 after the despatch and receipt of the "recap" telex. It is common ground that if a contract was concluded, it was concluded by the despatch and receipt of the "recap" telex. Turning back to the chronology, what happened was that on Oct. 5 the defendants indicated that they did not want to proceed with the negotiations. That was viewed as a repudiation of a concluded contract by the plaintiffs. On Oct. 7 they accepted that alleged repudiation, subject to their claim for damages. On Aug. 18, 1986 leave was granted to the plaintiffs to issue and serve proceedings against the defendants out of the jurisdiction. The defendants now apply to set aside that order and service pursuant to it.

A number of issues arise in this matter but I propose to address myself to one principal issue and that is whether a study of the contemporaneous documents reveals that a binding contract was concluded.

* * *

... [I]n negotiations parties are free to stipulate that no binding contract shall come into existence, despite agreement on all essentials, until agreement is reached on yet unmentioned and unconsidered detailed provisions. And the law should respect such a stipulation in commercial negotiations. That seems to me to be exactly what happened in this case. The Gencon charter-party is, of course, a detailed and well-known standard form. It is plain that the parties had in mind a contract on the Gencon form but that they had not yet considered the details of it. By the expression, "Subject to details of the Gencon charterparty" the owners made clear that they did not wish to commit themselves contractually until negotiations had taken place about the details of the charter-party. Such discussions might have covered a number of clauses. It does not follow that the owners were willing to accept all the detailed provisions of the standard form document. After all, it is a common occurrence for some of the detailed provisions of the Gencon form to be amended during the process of negotiation. In any event, the Gencon standard form contains within it alternative provisions which require a positive selection of the desired alternative.

* * *

The meaning of the words "subject to details" have also been discussed in a number of decisions. The first case to which I refer to is *The Solholt*, [1981] 2 Lloyd's Rep 574. In that case Mr. Justice Staughton made the following observation (at p. 576, col 2):

... Also on July 27 further employment for the vessel was arranged. She is described as having on that day been "fixed subject to details". That means that the main terms were agreed, but until the subsidiary terms and the details had also been agreed no contract existed.

It is right to add that his observation did not form part of the ratio decidendi of the case. Then there is another decision which is also of relevance. It is *The Nissos Samos*, [1985] 1 Lloyd's Rep 378. In that case Mr. Justice Leggatt referred to the expression "subject to details". He said (at p 385, col 2):

"Subject details" is a well-known expression in broking practice which is intended to entitle either party to resile from the contract if in good faith either party is not satisfied with any of the details as discussed between them.

I will return to the meaning of that passage in due course, but I only add at this stage that Mr Justice Leggatt's observation was also not part of the ratio decidendi of the case. These dicta do, however, reinforce my view as to the meaning of the relevant stipulation.

The plaintiffs rely on the way in which the matter has been approached in the United States, and I have been referred to four decisions of United States Courts and provided with transcripts of those decisions. These decisions are *Interocean v. National Shipping* 523 F 2d 527 (2d Circuit 1975); *Atlantic v. Steelmete* 565 F 2d 848 (2d Circuit 1977); *Pollux v. Dreyfus* 455 F. Supp 211 (S.D. NY 1978); and *Great Circle v Matheson* 681 F. 2d 121 (2d Circuit 1982). It was suggested that in the light of the decisions "the English approach" might be reconsidered.

It seems to me that it is only necessary to refer to the last case, *Great Circle v Matheson*, which is commonly referred to as *The Cluden*. That is so because it is the last of the four decisions; it considers the earlier decisions and it is noteworthy that it is a decision of the United States Court of Appeals 2nd Circuit.

* * *

It is clear that the issues were not placed before the United States Court in the way in which they arose in the present case, and the United States Court did not consider some of the matters discussed in this judgment. But there are a few comments that I would make about *The Cluden*. The suggestion which is made in *The Cluden* that details are unimportant and that one can simply go back to the printed form does not always work. That is classically illustrated by the present case, where one cannot solve the problem by simply going back to the printed form because the printed form contains alternatives. Moreover there is apparently no unanimity in the United States about this particular matter, and I draw attention to a report of a United States arbitration award which has been placed before me. It is arbitration award No. 1924 of the Society of Maritime Arbitrators of New York. In that particular case the tribunal, in accordance with the latitude allowed to United States arbitrators, declined to follow *The Cluden* and said:

> With all due respect to these rulings, I must uphold the basic understanding throughout the worldwide shipping markets that until all terms have been agreed no fixture has been concluded.

But the assertion in *The Cluden* that the details may not be important is also refuted in a dissenting opinion in an earlier United States arbitration award (Award No 1715 (1982)), which is quoted in an interesting article by Dr. Charles Debattista, *Charterparty Fixtures 'Subject details'—Further Reflections*, [1985] LMCLQ 241 at p. 251. The extract reads as follows:

> The need to agree on details and terms is as paramount as the need to agree on the freight rate. Indeed, until an owner is fully aware of all the possible financial consequences that may arise from the commitment to the charterparty details, he is not in a position to determine the anticipated results of the voyage; consequently he is unable to decide if the financial returns make that particular cargo desirable. It makes no commercial sense for either party to a negotiation to be obliged to accept all the terms submitted by the other one, if thereby financial risk may be involved.

But I return to *The Cluden* to point out that the United States Court referred to the English perception in the following terms (at p. 126 in the second column):

Finally Matheson argues that owing to its London situs its understanding of the terminology in use in the industry was different than that found by the trial court. Any lingering concern that the London-based owner of *The Cluden* might honestly have understood the phrase used to have a different meaning is dispelled by a leading treatise in this field published in London: J. BES, CHARTERING AND SHIPPING TERMS (9th ed, 1975). This context—considered a prominent international reference work on the shipping industry and one which has been translated into seven languages—reinforces the international scope of the industry's customs and usages. It discusses the function of the chartering brokers in much the same way as that found by the trial court, and defines a "fixing letter" (a condensed fixture) as a summary of the principal conditions of a charterparty. Under a listing of standard charterparties, it refers to the "time charterparty approved by the New York Produce Exchange. Hence, it may be surmised that the customs of the worldwide business were the same in London as in New York.

With the greatest deference, it does seem a little strange for a Court to base its decision as to what a "recap" telex "subject to details" means on a general dictionary definition of what such a document is.

To the extent the United States Court considered that the view which it upheld was consistent with the international perception of the meaning of "subject to details", it seems to me that the material before me convincingly demonstrates that that is not so. I refer to a bulletin by the Federation of National Associations of Shipbrokers and Agents, commonly called FONASBA, which in the relevant part reads as follows:

As we are all aware, several court decisions in the United States have recently determined that a fixture has resulted when the main terms have been agreed, despite the fact that it was still "subject to details". The US court's view is not shared by the rest of the shipping world and is being severely criticized by the entire market, including US shipowners, charterers and shipbrokers alike.

The bulletin then continues to give practical advice but I need not cite that.

Looking at the matter in the round, it does not seem to me that the suggested reappraisal of the English approach in the light of the United States decisions has any realistic prospect before an English Court. This Court has, of course, the greatest respect for the decisions of the United States Courts. Our Courts frequently gain assistance from United States decisions, notably in the field of international trade. On this occasion, I must say, that it is my clear impression that it is the United States Courts rather than the English Courts which are out of step with the way in which the shipping trade works. And, I would respectfully suggest, that it is in the interests of the chartering business that the Courts should recognize the efficacy of the maritime variant of the well-known "subject to contract". The expression "subject to details" enables owners and charterers to know where they are in negotiations and to regulate their business accordingly. It is a device which tends to avoid disputes and the assumption of those in the shipping trade that it is effective to make clear that there is no binding agreement at that stage ought to be respected.

My conclusion is, therefore, that no contract was concluded in this case.

Note

Although the decision in *The Cluden* (*Great Circle Lines, Ltd. v. Matheson & Co.*, 681 F.2d 121, 1982 AMC 2321 (2d Cir. 1982)) was criticized and not followed in *The Junior K*, it has been followed on several occasions in U.S. courts. *U.S. Titan, Inc. v. Guangzhou Zhen Hua Shipping Co., Ltd.*, 241 F.3d 135, 2001 AMC 2080 (2d Cir. 2001); *P.E.P. Shipping (Scandinavia) A.P.S. v. Noramco Shipping Corp.*, 1997 AMC 2933 (E.D. La. 1997); *Samsun Corp. v. Khozestan Marine Kar Co.*, 926 F. Supp. 436, 1996 AMC 1986 (S.D.N.Y. 1996); *In re Arbitration between Herlofson Management A/S and Ministry of Supply, Kingdom of Jordan*, 765 F. Supp. 78, 1991 AMC 2959 (S.D.N.Y. 1991). After the most recent of these decisions (*U.S. Titan*), an application for rehearing was filed, and the U.S. Court of Appeals for the Second Circuit panel issued an order on April 24th, 2001 directing the parties to brief whether the holding in *Great Circle* should be overruled and inviting amicus briefs from bar associations and trade industry groups on whether that holding is in accord with the law in other jurisdictions. No order for a rehearing was ultimately made, however.

E. Time Charters

1. *Failure of The Shipowner or Vessel to Comply With The Terms of The Charter Party: Misrepresentations, Conditions, Warranties, Etc.*

Introductory Note

What options, if any, does a charterer have when the statements made by the shipowner in a charter party do not comport with the true facts? For example, a charter party may state that the vessel will be delivered by a certain date and owner fails to do so. A vessel may be described as having a carrying capacity of so many tons, for example, and inspection by charterer's agent reveals that it has less than that capacity. Similarly, the charter party may state that the vessel can sail at certain speeds under normal conditions and during the voyage it is unable to maintain that speed. Finally suppose the vessel is unseaworthy when it is presented to charterer for acceptance or develops an unseaworthy condition during he voyage. In each of these situations, does charterer have the right to rescind, *i.e.*, cancel the charter party contract? Does charterer have the right to waive recission and recover damages for any losses it may have incurred as a result of the discrepancy? Are there situations where a charterer can both rescind and recover damages?"

In order for a discrepancy to create any rights in a charterer, it must be something more than *de minimis*. Unless an owner has absolutely guaranteed a specific fact, any negligible divergence from compliance will be disregarded by the courts. *Margaronis Navigation v. Peabody*, [1964] 2 Lloyd's Rep. 153. M. Wilford, T. Coglin, J. Kimball, Time Charters 86 (Lloyd's of London Press, 4th ed. 1995). Even where the discrepancy is substantial, the charterer's remedies may depend on whether the specific term is classified as a "condition" which would give rise to a right to rescind, or a "warranty" which creates a right to damages, or as "intermediate" or "inominate" terms where the right to either rescind or to recover damages depends on the circumstances of each cases. M. Wilford, T. Coglin, J. Kimball, Time Charters 88-96 (Lloyd's of London Press, 4th ed. 1995).

---

a. Size and Speed

GIANNELIS v. THE ATLANTA

82 F. Supp. 218, 1948 AMC 1769 (S.D. Ga. 1948)

* * *

The focal point of conflict in the litigation centers about the libel of Caravan Shipping Corporation as charterer of the "Atlanta" and Corinthian's cross-libel as owner. An amendment filed by Caravan alleges that the balance due it for cash advances, dry-docking costs, etc., is $8,585.72. During the course of the trial the elimination of certain items reduced this amount to $7696.03.

Corinthian Steamship Company claims, on the other hand, that, rather than being indebted to Caravan, the charterer is indebted to it in the amount of $16,884.15. This figure represents the charter hire from January 10, to March 31, 1948, when the ship was libelled, a total of $25,650, against which admitted credits to the charterer by way of cash advances and sums paid on account of charter hire are conceded to the extent of $9033.63, leaving a balance of $16,884.15 allegedly due Corinthian.

In this dispute two questions imperiously demand solution. They are:

(1) Was there a breach of the warranties (or representations) made in the time charter respecting the capacity of the ship and as to her approximate speed and fuel consumption?

(2) [The second question relating to agency is omitted. Eds.]

* * *

Breach of Warranties

(1) Capacity of Ship

The "Atlanta" was chartered for the purpose of moving steel pipe out of Tampico where Caravan had more than 2,000 tons which it desired to transport to Venezuela. Capacity of the vessel was important to the charterer. The charter provided: "Owners guarantee vessel to carry 550 gross tons of 4 to 12 inch mixed standard steel or iron pipe in lengths not exceeding 18 feet." Proctor for Corinthian has suggested that this was a most unusual provision. Nasios, the owner's representative, testified that he was not acquainted with the fact that it had been inserted in the charter, in fact had objected to its inclusion in the first instance. (Tr. of Evidence, p. 118.) However, we are not concerned with whether or not Georgaros made a bad bargain for his principal. The time charter which he signed for Corinthian is binding on the owner in all its terms and conditions, however onerous. It guaranteed a definite capacity. This provision constituted an express warranty. *Metropolitan Coal Co. v. Howard*, 2 Cir., 155 F.2d 780(4). A breach thereof permits the charterer to sue for damages. *Wood v. Sewall's Adm'rs*, D.C., 128 F. 141, *affirmed* 3 Cir., 135 F. 12, a case holding that a warranty of 3400 gross tons of iron pipe was not fulfilled by a shipment of 3258 tons. Or, at the election of the charterer, the breach of such a covenant may permit a rescission of the Charter Party. *Clydesdale Shipowners' Co. v. William W. Brauer Steamship Co.*, D.C., 120 F. 854.

The "Atlanta" carried 487 tons of pipe as loaded—a difference of some 63 tons from the capacity specified or approximately a 12% deficiency below the guarantee. The owner contends that the pipe was improperly loaded. It says that the pipe should have been "nested," that is, smaller pipes placed inside the larger ones. In this connection they rely, among other things, on "Modern Ship Stowage" published by the United States Department of Commerce where it is said (p. 382): "When a large quantity of cast iron pipes of varying sizes is shipped it is often possible to nest them by putting the smaller ones inside the larger, and so save considerable space."

The evidence as to this point is in sharp conflict. Captain Pantazopoulos himself was apparently uncertain whether it was proper procedure to nest or not to nest the pipe although he was of the opinion that the cargo was improperly loaded and that the stevedores were in "too much of a hurry." (Tr. of Evidence, p. 29, 32.)

As a matter of fact, about 1/3 to 1/2 of the pipe in the forward hold was nested. None was so loaded in the aft hatch. (Tr. of Evidence, p. 35, 136.) The exact reason why the stevedores stopped this method of stowage does not appear from the evidence. The Master testified that the pipes were slipping inside each other.

W. P. Jones testified for Caravan as an expert. He referred to the nesting of pipe as a "very abnormal practice." (Tr. of Evidence, p. 75.) On a ship with an aft hatch such as the "Atlanta" where the pipe had to be nested on the dock he thought such a procedure very unsafe. "The nesting of pipe is not good stowage; we never plan it," he said. From his personal examination of the aft hold of the "Atlanta" it would not have been possible under any conditions, he thought, to nest pipes in 18 foot lengths. (Tr. of Evidence, p. 146.)

Expert testimony on this subject was also produced by the owner. Mr. Martin Roberts testified that he would have nested the pipe in No. 2 hatch. However, the nesting there would have to have been done within the hatch, he said, as otherwise the pipe inside would slide out. Nesting is ordinary procedure "if you get in a jam for space." (Tr. of Evidence, p. 90.) However, he had never had any experience in discharging nested pipes and admitted that "it was not a normal stevedoring operation." He estimated that nesting pipes increases the time of labor about 20%. (Tr. of Evidence, p. 93.)

A diagram prepared by Mr. Jones shows that the stanchions in the aft hold of the "Atlanta" would have made it extremely difficult, if not impossible, to move 18 foot pipe therein for the purpose of nesting same. There was no space to swing the pipe. Mr. Nasios, the owner's representative, admitted that the vessel would not be seaworthy with pipe nested in the forward hatch and not in the aft hatch. (Tr. of Evidence, p. 137.) Captain Pantazopoulos also conceded that this was true. The fact was that when the "Atlanta" sailed from Tampico she was somewhat "down by the head." Some change of loading was made in order to trim her.

The question of fact involved is not an easy one. Certainly the "Atlanta" as loaded at Tampico did not comply with the owner's warranty as to capacity. The deficiency was a substantial and material one. In my opinion, a stevedore is not required to adopt out-of-the-ordinary methods of loading a ship, involving considerably more expense. There is nothing in the evidence suggesting that the stevedores were incompetent or that the "Atlanta" was not loaded according to the usual practices and standards prevailing at Tampico. The Agent under whom they operated was concededly one of the best. (Tr. of Evidence, p. 29.)

Clause 8 of the Charter Party provided that the charterers were to "load, stow and trim cargo at their expense under the supervision of the captain." Under such a charter the owner has a definite share of the responsibility and control as to the manner of loading. *Knohr & Burchard v. Pacific Creosoting Co., D.C.*, 181 F. 856; *The Giles Loring, D.C.*, 48 F. 463. Where the owner's guaranty of the ship's capacity is at stake the duty of the Master, even beyond precautions as to seaworthiness, is manifest. Captain Pantazopoulos and Nasios were present and observed the loading operations at Tampico. If they made any real objections to the manner of stowage the record fails to reflect them. Pantazopoulos says that he told the stevedores that the ship was being loaded "very badly." (Tr. of Evidence, p. 29.) But there his protests died though the charter definitely conferred upon him the right to do something about the situation. As I appraise the facts, I must and do hold that there was a breach of the warranty as to the "Atlanta's" capacity to lift cargo.

(2) Warranty as to Speed and Fuel Consumption.

The charter represented that the "Atlanta" was capable of steaming, fully laden, under good weather conditions at about 10 knots on a consumption of about 10 tons of the best grade fuel oil. Owners contend that such a statement is a representation and not a warranty, citing *The Beechpark (Denholm Shipping Co. v. W.E. Hedger Co. Inc.), D.C.*, 34 F.2d 572, 1929 A.M.C. 880. However, that was a District Court decision which was reversed on appeal. The Circuit Court of Appeals for the Second Circuit, in reversing the decision, held that where a steamer is described as being "capable of steaming about 11 knots to 12 knots an hour in good weather in smooth water on a consumption of about 32 to 34 tons best Welsh coal"—a warranty results rather than a representation, even though the statement is not expressly designated as a warranty. *Denholm Shipping Co., Ltd. v. W.E. Hedger Co., Inc.*, 2 Cir., 47 F.2d 213. The Beechpark was cited in *Romano v. West India Fruit & Steamship Co., Inc.*, 5 Cir., 151 F.2d 727 where the Court ruled in a decision by Judge Hutcheson that a charter representation that a ship has a speed of 9 knots per hour is a warranty and that it was breached when the vessel did not attain it between Cristobal and Miami.

The "Atlanta" had not been drydocked in about five months. She was admittedly foul, with some 5 feet of scale. Her speed was retarded as a result. Enroute to Tampico she averaged only 6 or 7 knots, steaming light. She arrived more than a day late at Tampico. Nasios testified that the ship did not try to make speed as her fuel was short and bad weather might arise. (Tr. of Evidence, p. 131.) But this is hardly a satisfactory explanation in view of the warranty that the ship would be at Tampico on January 8th at 4:00 P.M. If I should give credence to the testimony of Nasios in this respect it would tend to solve the troublesome question as to waiver of the warranty of speed by Caravan's accepting the ship knowing of the deficiency in her speed. But independently of Nasios' explanation I am of the opinion that under the peculiar circumstances of emergency confronting both charterer and owner at Tampico there was no waiver of the warranty by Caravan.

Undoubtedly the "Atlanta" was delayed by extremely bad weather out of Tampico. The log shows storm conditions prevailing for all except a few days of the voyage to Puerto Cabello. But I am satisfied that it was not the storm that kept the "Atlanta" from making 10 knots enroute to that port. She may have been prevented by it from making 7 or 8 knots but not 10 or even 9 knots as she was incapable of the latter, fully laden. Moreover the "Atlanta" consumed considerably more fuel than the owners warranted. She was burning up to 5 tons more fuel per day than had been stipulated.

The admissions of Georgaros and the owners are entitled to much weight in considering any question as to Corinthian's compliance with the warranties. Whether valid or not, the "Addendum'" is a deliberate admission by an agent authorized to deal with the charterer that there had been a breach as to capacity to lift cargo as well as in

---

ˑ On 8 February 1948 the time charter was drastically modified by a so-called Addendum. In the Addendum the owners conceded the failure of the vessel to measure up to the charter specifications as to lifting capacity, speed, and fuel oil consumption.

respect to speed and fuel oil consumption. On January 21st he writes Nasios telling him "The way the ship is now is no good at all." In his letter of February 17th to Nasseof, Georgaros goes into detail with respect to the "Atlanta's" failure to perform. On February 12th he had telegraphed the owners: "We guaranteed ship 10 knots on 10 tons of fuel and capacity minimum 550 tons. However ship did 6 knots on 15 tons and capacity is 480 tons." Nasios informed Georgaros: "The speed of the ship will be right after it goes to drydock." Neither Nasseof nor Nasios ever really challenged the assertions of Georgaros. Indeed, on February 16th the former clearly admitted the ship's inability to live up to the original specifications when he instructed Georgaros to reduce speed 8-9 knots on "new contracts" and to increase fuel "about 11-12."

To overcome the effect of such admissions is a large order. In the opinion of the Special Commissioner the owner has failed to do so. Aside from the admissions, however, the evidence shows a material breach of the charter provision as to a warranted speed of "about 10 knots" on "about 10 tons" of fuel. Under the circumstances Caravan was justified in rescinding the contract upon discharge of the ship at Puerto Cabello.

* * *

ROMANO v. WEST INDIA FRUIT & STEAMSHIP CO., INC.

151 F.2d 727, 1946 AMC 90 (5th Cir. 1945)

HUTCHESON, Circuit Judge

These appeals are from decrees entered in two admiralty suits consolidated for trial and appeal. Brought by the subcharterer, "West India," one against the charterer, "San Juan," the other against the ship, "Sonia II," they concern a cargo of bananas loaded at Cristobal, Panama, and discharged at Miami, instead of at West Palm Beach, Florida, as had been agreed.

The claim of the libels was: that the bananas had been loaded green at Cristobal, and if properly carried to destination as agreed would have arrived safely and been worth on arrival $13,025; that by reason of the breach by ship and charterer of the agreement that the ship would sail from Cristobal June 15th, and of the warranty that the vessel was of nine knot speed, and particularly by reason of the delivery of the cargo at Miami instead of at West Palm Beach, the cargo became a total loss.

The charterer denied that there was a breach of an agreement as to sailing time, and that there was a warranty of nine knot speed. Denying that the bananas had been loaded green, and that there was any unjustifiable deviation, it alleged that the bananas were ripe or semi-ripe when loaded and that because of their over ripe condition, they were already damaged when they arrived off Miami. There was a cross-libel for the freight, $6,975, and for $244.77 costs of handling the bananas in excess of their returns.

North Caribbean Transport Company, owner of the Sonia II, answering the libel against it, denied, as the charterer had done, that there was any breach of agreement as to sailing time, any warranty as to the vessel's speed, and that the bananas were loaded green. It alleged that they were loaded ripe or turning and had when they reached Miami, by reason of their inherent vice, already become a total loss.

The district judge heard the case on oral testimony. Of the opinion that carrying the bananas to Miami instead of West Palm Beach, was an unjustifiable deviation and that, because of it, the ship should be condemned to pay $13,025, the value of the bananas at West Palm Beach, Florida, if they had arrived in good condition, he passed without decision the other claims that the ship had failed to sail on time and that she had breached her warranty of speed. Concluding that San Juan should have judgment for the subcharter hire but not for the $244.77, net costs of disposing of the cargo, and that since the two suits were consolidated, one decree would suffice for both, he gave judgment condemning the ship to pay $13,025 and libelant's costs, $6,975, to the San Juan Shipping Company and $6,050 plus $140.38 costs to West India Fruit Company, libelant.

* * *

What, then, were the consequences of the deviation? The libelant claimed, and the district judge found, that they were the whole loss of value of the cargo. The respondent claimed that the preponderance of the evidence establishes that the bananas were already a total loss when the ship reached Miami and that if carried to West Palm Beach they would have been a total loss there. While the respondent was incorrect in its claim that the whole damage was done before the deviation occurred, we think it clear that the district judge was also wrong in finding that all of it occurred afterward and as a result thereof. The record leaves in no doubt that when the bananas were examined at Miami, after the ship had berthed there, a great part of them were, and had for some time been, in a bad condition, and that while the estimate of respondent's witnesses, that they were already then a total loss, is unreasonably high, the witnesses testifying most favorably for the libelant swore that not more than 50 to 75 per cent of them could be salvaged. In this state of the record, the district judge's finding that, as a result of the deviation, libelant sustained a total loss of the bananas, may not stand, and, if deviation were the sole fault, the judgment for libelant would have to be reduced accordingly. In addition to the fault of deviation, however, libelant has all along relied on (1) the lateness of the ship's sailing from Mayaguez to Cristobal, and (2) breach of warranty as to the vessel's speed. As to the claimed late sailing, the record will not support a finding that any of the damage was due to this cause. It is true that, in chartering the Sonia, "West India" did state, "It is understood the vessel now is in Mayaguez and is to sail not later than Thursday noon for Cristobal," and the proof shows that the Sonia did not sail on that day but a day or so later. But the sailing date was not warranted, the libelant was notified of the delay in ample time to have protected itself from a too early cutting of the bananas, and such damage, if any, as might have been caused by the too early cutting could not be said to be the proximate result of the delay. Besides there was no exception to the notation of the bill of lading that the bananas were loaded green, and we do not find that the damage suffered can be laid to the late sailing or to a too early cutting.

As to the speed of the vessel, however, the matter stands differently. The charter party contained this positive and unequivocal declaration: "Speed of nine knots per hours," and the evidence shows that she did not make this speed from Cristobal, with the result that she was many hours late, enough hours, indeed, in view of the condition of the bananas on arrival, to account, with the consequences of the deviation, for all the loss that occurred. If, then, this statement is a warranty, the judgment must be affirmed. The owner, agreeing that the speed of a vessel may be warranted, insists that the inserted clause was not a warranty at all because not expressly declared to be. But this will not stand up under the authorities. As *Denholm Shipping Co. v. W. E. Hedger Co.*, 2 Cir., 47 F.2d 213 points out, the failure to use the word 'warranty' in a statement of this kind is unimportant. What is important is whether the statement was positively and unequivocally made as a statement of fact and whether the natural tendency of its making was to induce the chartering of the ship. The charter showed that the trade for which the ship was engaged, that is that she was to run in, was between ports in Florida, the West Indies, Central America, the Caribbean Sea, Mexico, and certain ports in the northern part of South America. In subchartering, there was discussion of the speed of the vessel, and to support his assurance that she could and would make nine knots, the charterer drew to the subcharterer's attention the affirmation of the written charter that the vessel was of that speed. The statement was a warranty and the ship is liable for damages resulting from its breach.

The judgment is, therefore, affirmed.

b. *Seaworthiness*

Notes

1. *Implied warranty of seaworthiness*

In *Neubros Corporation v. Northwestern National Insurance Co.,* 359 F. Supp. 310, 1972 AMC 2443, 1973 AMC 511 (E.D.N.Y. 1972) owner sued Hull Underwriters and charterers for damage to chartered barge which it alleged had been overloaded by charterer. The defense was based on allegations that the owner had been aware of the purpose for which the barge was to be used and that the damage was caused by the unseaworthiness of barge, in that it was not fit for its intended purpose. The court upheld charterer's reliance on the "warranty" of seaworthiness.

* * *

The Warranty of Seaworthiness to the Charterer

The general rule is that every charter implies a warranty by the owner that the vessel is seaworthy unless the parties agree to the contrary. *The Caledonia,* 157 U.S. 124, 131, 15 S. Ct. 537, 540, 39 L. Ed. 644 (1895); *McAllister Lighterage Line, Inc. v. Insurance Co. of North America,* 244 F.2d 867, 871 (2d Cir. 1957); *Jordan, Inc. v. Mayronne Drilling Service,* 214 F.2d 410 (5th Cir. 1954), Gilmore and Black, *The Law of Admiralty,* p. 182. Knowledge by the charterer of an unseaworthy condition will not deny him the right to rely on the owner's implied warranty of seaworthiness. *Church Cooperage Co. v. Pinkney,* 170 F. 266 (2d Cir. 1909), *cert. denied,* 214 U.S. 526, 29 S. Ct. 704, 53 L. Ed. 1068. Agreements relieving the owner of obligation under the implied warranty of seaworthiness are not favored. *The Carib Prince,* 170 U.S. 655, 659, 18 S. Ct. 753, 755, 42 L. Ed. 1181 (1898). In the *Carib Prince* the Court said:

> ". . . clauses exempting the owner from the general obligation of furnishing a seaworthy vessel must be confined within strict limits, and were not to be extended by latitudinarian construction or forced implication so as to comprehend a state of unseaworthiness, whether patent or latent existing at the commencement of the voyage."

* * *

Seaworthiness

Seaworthiness is a relative term. "[It] expresses a relation between the state of the ship and the perils it has to meet in the situation it is in." 2 Arnould, Marine Insurance (14th Ed.), p. 630. It is the fitness in design, structure and condition to perform the task for which the vessel is chartered. *The Caledonia, supra,* 15 S.Ct. at p. 540; *McAllister Lighterage Lines, Inc. v. Insurance Company of North America, supra,* 244 F.2d at p. 870; 1 Carver, Carriage by Sea (12th Ed.), p. 98.

Neubros Corp. v. Northwestern Nat. Ins. Co., 359 F. Supp. 310, 316 (E.D.N.Y. 1972).

2. *Waiver of the Warranty of Seaworthiness*

In *A. Kemp Fisheries, Inc. v. Castle & Cooke, Inc.,* 852 F.2d 493, 1989 AMC 236 (9th Cir. 1988), the U.S. Court of Appeals for the Ninth Circuit said:

> After reviewing drafts of the agreement with Kemp's attorney, Bumble Bee sent the final bare boat Charter Agreement late in March. Louis Kemp, the charterer's president, found that the agreement differed from his understanding of the arrangement. Specifically, he understood that Bumble Bee had agreed that the engines would be in good working order and had represented orally that the freezing system would meet Kemp's specific needs. The agreement contained no such provisions and in fact, disclaimed all warranties, express or implied. Despite his reservations, Kemp signed it without voicing his concerns to Bumble Bee. He took the vessel in early April and sailed to Alaska for the May herring season.

> * * *

> Kemp argues that even if Bumble Bee did not expressly warrant the vessel's seaworthiness, the warranty is implied in every charter unless clearly and unequivocally waived. It claims that Bumble Bee failed to waive the implied warranty.

> California provides that waivers of warranties may be enforced if they "clearly communicate that a particular risk falls on the [charterer]." *Hauter v. Zogarts,* 120 Cal. Rptr. 681, 690 (Cal. S. Ct. 1975). Such waivers are construed strictly against the maker. *Zogarts, id.* Federal maritime law is similar. *See* Benedict at 3-9; and *In Compania De Navigacion La Flecha v. Brauer,* 168 U.S. 104, 118 (1897).

> Sub-paragraph 3E provides that after accepting delivery, Kemp "shall not be entitled to make or assert any claim against Owner on account of any representations or warranties, express or implied, with respect to the Vessel." Sub-paragraph 3F provides that Kemp's acceptance of the vessel is conclusive evidence that it inspected the vessel and "deemed" it seaworthy and suitable for its needs.

These clauses clearly and unequivocally communicate that the risk of unseaworthiness would fall on Kemp once it accepted the vessel. Similar disclaimers have been found to be clear and unequivocal and have been enforced in admiralty. *See, e.g., McAllister Lighterage Line v. Insurance Co.*, 244 F.2d 867, 871 (2d Cir.) *cert. denied sub nom.* 355 U.S. 871 (1957) ("The acceptance of said scow by charterer is to be conclusive evidence of the seaworthy condition of said scow at the commencement of this charter" is clear and unequivocal.) [Kemp] effectively waived the implied warranty of seaworthiness. The court erred in refusing to enforce its waiver.

3. *Remedies of charterer—English law*

A charter party which describes the vessel as, *inter alia*, "with hull, machinery and equipment in a thoroughly efficient state," is an undertaking of seaworthiness. A charter party may provide "that on delivery the ship is to be 'tight, staunch, strong and in every way fitted for the service.'" This is an undertaking that the vessel is seaworthy at the time of delivery. As Notes 1 & 2, *supra*, demonstrate, in absence of any of any express undertaking or waiver of the as to seaworthiness, an undertaking of seaworthiness will be implied. These undertakings are not on their own continuing obligations. However, if the charter party also contains terms to the affect that the ship will be "maintained in a thoroughly efficient state during service," then the undertaking will be considered as continuing one. M. WILFORD, T. COGLIN, J. KIMBALL, TIME CHARTERS 96-97 (Lloyd's of London Press, 4th ed. 1995).

The English cases seem to treat the "undertaking" of seaworthiness as an "intermediate" term and not as a condition. As such, charterer's right to rescind the contract depends on the facts and circumstances of the breach. The undertaking of seaworthiness is so far-reaching that it would be unreasonable for a minor breach in some trivial way to allow the charterer to terminate the charter. Charterers, however, need not accept an unseaworthy vessel, but they may require owner to correct the defect. If owner fails to do so, this could be considered a repudiation of the charter party which would give charterer the right to terminate. M. WILFORD, T. COGLIN, J. KIMBALL, TIME CHARTERS 97-99 (Lloyd's of London Press, 4th ed. 1995).

4. *Remedies of charterer—U.S. law*

The approach to discrepancies in the description of a ships characteristics in U.S. case law is not clear.

[S]tatements may be called 'representations", "warranties" or "conditions", although the term may not well dispose of the underlying issue of whether the ship's failure to comply entitles the charterer to treat the contact as terminated or merely to recover damages resulting from the breach. Rather than focus on the proper terminology, it is more useful to consider the inherent materiality of the representation or undertaking in question, the time at which a breach or default occurs, and the consequences thereof to the charter.

Under the American precedents, it is more important to distinguish between cases involving a misdescription determined prior to delivery of the vessel and one occurring after delivery. In the former a refusal to accept the vessel has been held justified even where the deviation from the represented characteristic is relatively small.

* * *

Once delivery of the vessel has been accepted, however, the charterer is entitled to refuse to perform the charter only if there is a material breach on the part of the owner which frustrates the essential purpose of the contract.

M. WILFORD, T. COGLIN, J. KIMBALL, TIME CHARTERS 108 (Lloyd's of London Press, 4th ed. 1995).

This is illustrated in *Aaby v. States Marine Corporation*, 181 F. 2d 383 (2d Cir.) *cert. denied*, 340 U.S. 829, 71 S. Ct. 66, 95 L. Ed. 609 (1950) where the court stated:

With respect to the undertaking of seaworthiness on the part of the owner of a vessel, it is usually said that it is a "warranty," implied in the absence of an express and unambiguous stipulation or a controlling statute to the contrary. Scrutton, however, speaks of it as being a "condition" similarly implied. CHARTERPARTIES AND BILLS OF LADING (12th ed.) p. 95. And it has sometimes been spoken of as simply a "covenant." *The Steel Navigator*, 2 Cir. 23 F.2d 590; *Franklin Fire Ins. Co. v. Royal Mail Steam Packet Co.*, 2 Cir. 58 F.2d 175, *certiorari denied* 287 U.S. 630, 53 S. Ct. 82, 77 L. Ed. 546; *Wilson v. Griswold*, C.C.S.D.N.Y., Fed. Cas. No. 17,806. Williston considers that "The basis of the undertaking of seaworthiness is the same as that of implied warranties in the sale of goods; the shipowner is in a position to know the condition of his ship and the charterer justifiably relies upon his judgment." 4 WILLISTON ON CONTRACTS § 1078. But this would not seem to explain the unquestioned line of authority that the undertaking of seaworthiness is absolute in the sense that the owner's exercise of due diligence to discover defects is immaterial. As Lord Blackburn, in *Steel v. State Line S. S. Co.*, (1887) 3 A.C. 72, 86, put it, the obligation is not merely that the owners "should do their best to make the ship fit," but that the ship should really be fit. The problem is not made any simpler when, as here, there is an express stipulation of seaworthiness but that stipulation is not made one of the express "conditions" to the contract, and is contained in the preliminary recital of agreements between the parties.

In the midst of this confusion, however, one thing rather clearly appears: that repudiation by a charterer is permissible only where the breach of the owner's undertaking of seaworthiness is so substantial as to defeat or frustrate the commercial purpose of the charter. The English authorities speak in these terms. *Tarrabochia v. Hickey*, (1856) 1 H. & N. 183, 156 Eng. Rep. 1168; *Tully v. Howling*, (1877) 2 Q.B.D. 182; *Stanton v. Richardson*, (1872) L.R. 7 C.P. 421, *aff'd*, (1875) L.R. 9 C.P. 390 (Exch), *aff'd* H.L., *see* (1875) 1 Q.B.D. 381; *see Scrutton*, *supra* at pp. 96, 103; Carver, *supra*, § 145. There are no American cases to the contrary. Thus, it has been said that "the stipulation of seaworthiness is not so far a condition precedent that the hirer is not liable in such case for any of the charter money. If he uses her, he must pay for the use to the extent to which it goes." *Work v. Leathers*, 97 U.S. 379, 380, 24 L.Ed. 1012; *The Toledo*, 2 Cir., 122 F.2d 255, 257, *certiorari denied Isbrandtsen-Moller Co. v. The Toledo*, 314 U.S. 689, 62 S. Ct. 302, 86 L. Ed. 551. The preliminary statement in a charter party as to the vessel's registered tonnage has been similarly treated, substantial compliance therewith being held sufficient, at least where the vessel has been designated by name and the kind and quantity of cargo has been specified. *Watts v. Camors*, 115 U.S. 353, 6 S. Ct. 91, 29 L. Ed. 406. Thus also, breach of a provision that the vessel shall sail with all convenient speed, "reasonable dispatch," or the like has been held not to justify repudiation unless delay has been so great as to frustrate the object of the charter. *Clipsham v. Vertue*, (1843) 6 Q.B. 265, 114 Eng. Rep. 1249; *see* 4 Williston on Contracts, § 1079.

We take it, then, that the undertaking of seaworthiness is to be treated like any other contractual undertaking not expressly made a condition precedent to a party's performance of his obligations: an insubstantial breach of it, not going to defeat the object of the contract, will not justify repudiation.

* * *

In *Aaby, supra,* the court concluded that charterer could not terminate the charter. The unseaworthy condition manifested itself shortly after the voyage commenced. The vessel returned to port where the condition was repaired. The vessel was ready to sail after a delay of two and one half days. The charter party which had just commenced was for a term of 12 months. Suppose the unseaworthy condition had been discovered during a joint inspection prior to charterer's acceptance of the vessel. Could charterer have rescinded the contract? If not, what remedy could charterer invoke.

---

2. Off Hire

a. Unseaworthiness—Off-Hire or Repudiation

UNITED STATES v. M/V MARILENA P

433 F. 2d 164, 1969 AMC 1155 (4th Cir. 1969)

Albert V. BRYAN, Circuit Judge

In admiralty asking damages, the United States complained of the M/V Marilena P [of Greek Registry] and her owner, Marilena Compania Naviera, S.A., for nullifying a charter party. The controversy grew out of the crew's refusal to sail.[*] As the ad-port was within the Viet Nam war theatre and the ship's lading was combat materials, they declined the voyage, either as too perilous or for some other reason not clearly recorded. The charterer argues that the ship thus became unseaworthy, in violation and dissolution of the charter. The shipowner, responding for itself and as the vessel's claimant, traversed the libel, and also counter-demanded damages upon the assertion that the Government had reneged on its agreement.

Appealing against a wholly adverse judgment, the shipowner persuades us to its view....

* * *

I. In our judgment no breach of the charter was committed by the respondent shipowner. The admiralty judge concluded that when presented to the charterer at Seattle on September 1, the Marilena P was unseaworthy because she was then "without a crew willing to sail the vessel to South Viet Nam". This determination, we think, is not altogether precise.

A few minutes past midnight of August 31-September 1 at Seattle she was an arrived ship. An MSTS[**] Deputy Operations Officer there boarded her, and with the first officer and a marine surveyor "made a thorough tour of the ship"—an on-hire survey. Thereafter, about 8 o'clock A.M. September 1, the Marilena P was accepted by the Government. She was then fueled by the charterer and, at its direction the vessel was moved to Tacoma.

---

[*] The members of the crew were Greek nationals. Eds.
[**] Military Sea Transportation Service of the United States. Eds.

At her new berth, loading commenced about 7:30 P.M. September 1. Neither before nor during that day did the crew protest the scheduled passage to South Viet Nam, although the log notes some grumblings. There was no cessation in the loading until between 2 and 3 o'clock on the afternoon of September 2nd. The record indicates no reluctance of the longshoremen to carry on the cargo.

Hence, MSTS can hardly be heard to say that the vessel was unseaworthy on September 1. The owner at that time had no warning or premonition of the group's recalcitrance. They had signed on for a definite period, including August and September 1965, without restriction of destination. It was not incumbent upon the owner or master to ask if they were willing to ship to Viet Nam. Their defiance was in violation of Greek law, and on return to Athens some of them were punished for their disobedience.

But, conceding arguendo the strike created unseaworthiness amounting to an infraction of the charter, no right of repudiation was automatically conferred upon the United States. The promises of seaworthiness in the charter were not made conditions, nor did the crew's inaction constitute a frustration of the hiring of the ship.[1] From the context of the contract it is plain that their breach did not give an election forthwith to the charterer to wind up the arrangement on account of this development.

The parties quite explicitly evidenced their understanding that a contingency of this kind should not, ex proprio vigore, end it. They foresaw the possibility and stipulated a remedy, at least for a temporary wait in the departure. This is the stipulation:

Article 17. Off-Hire.
(a) In the event of loss of time *from deficiency of men including but not limited to strikes* ... the payment of hire shall cease from the time thereby lost.... (Accent added)

This provision refutes the option claimed by the Government to withdraw immediately from its contract upon inception of a strike. The conclusively manifested intention of the parties was that a breach of this nature was not to be accompanied by such grave results. Consequently, we need not and do not decide the much debated question of when unseaworthiness or what degree thereof, without more, justifies renunciation by the charterer. *See Aaby v. States Marine Corporation*, 181 F.2d 383, 386 (2 Cir. 1950).

Of course, cancellation might have been imposed if the strike so plainly appeared unsolvable as to be a frustration, but that was not the appearance here. This, the United States acknowledged by indulging the owner additional time to obtain a full company. Tolerance in this respect is not uncommon; in the Government's charter of the Mormacrigel, 12 days waiting time was permitted. Further, nowhere in the charter was time declared of the essence. Indeed, it has not been stressed at any stage of the case. Overtopping all considerations, however, it must be recalled that the hindering event was not of the owner's making or neglect.

Finally, the assurance of seaworthiness was not absolute as it would be in the absence of qualification. Each assurance is modified in terms of due diligence. Therefore, the duty to maintain a crew was not unconditional. Once reasonable care was exerted, unseaworthiness non obstante was not a transgression of the charter. This understanding is punctuated by the following charter clauses:

Article 4. Delivery of the Vessel:
(b) ... Vessel on delivery shall be, *insofar as due diligence can make her so*, seaworthy, tight, staunch, strong, and in every way suitable and adequately fitted for and in all respects ready to receive and transport lawful cargo.... (Accent added)

---

[1] Frustration of a charter party is a change of conditions so radical that accomplishment of the commercial object of the charter is made impossible. *See* GILMORE & BLACK, ADMIRALTY at 198.

Article 18. Owner's Obligation:

   (a) ... The Owner shall use *due diligence* ... to keep the Vessel in a thoroughly efficient state in ... *personnel* ... relating to the seaworthiness of the Vessel.... (Accent added)

While the due diligence must be established by the shipowner, we think the proof here abrim in this demonstration. Nothing prior to presentation of the ship for service, as earlier noted, even remotely indicated intransigence of the crew. Vigilance in its discovery could not be expected without some prior clue of the men's dispositions. At once upon learning on September 4 of the revolt, respondent's port captain left Greece and went to Seattle. He offered the crew double pay. Ten replacements were recruited in Athens and the earliest available flight reservations for them obtained. Four more were secured in New York. The ship's company had consisted of 40, but the captain could not induce enough of the insubordinates to make up the requisite complement.

Furthermore, the Government cannot fairly charge lack of diligence. As heretofore stated, on September 3 the United States allowed the owner until September 8 to make good the deficiency of crew. Nevertheless, on September 4—within an hour or two after it issued this deadline—the Government arranged with the Mormacrigel to pick up the freight intended for the Marilena P. At that moment 400 tons of it were in her holds. On the same day, September 4, this laden was removed by the Government. Before September 8 the substitute vessel sailed away with the entire tonnage.

In *Aaby v. States Marine Corporation, supra*, 181 F.2d 383, 386, the Court refused to allow such impetuous action. Noting the differences among the authorities, at home and aboard, on the remedies for charter infringements or defaults, the opinion stated:

> in the midst of this confusion, however, one thing rather clearly appears; that repudiation by a charterer is permissible only where the breach of the owner's undertaking of seaworthiness is so substantial as to defeat or frustrate the commercial purpose of the charter. The English authorities speak in these terms.

In *Hong Kong Fir Shipping Co. v. Kawasaki Kisen Kaishe*, 1 All E.R. 474 (1962) the British Court of Appeal met and answered the questions here. There a time charter of December 26, 1956 let a vessel for 24 months to the charterer, with delivery at Liverpool. The agreement required the ship to be "in every way fitted for ordinary cargo service". On the day of delivery, February 13, 1957, she sailed for Newport News, Virginia to take on coal for Osaka. When accepted by the charterers at Liverpool, "her engineroom was undermanned and her engineroom staff incompetent". Because of this deficiency, her engines broke down and she lost several months of working time. Nevertheless, the charterer was denied the power to cancel the agreement.

Although the British courts may seem more lenient on this point than the American, the reasoning of the Court pertinently is notable. As a member of the unanimous Court, UPJOHN, L.J. observed:

> Yet with all respect to counsel's argument, it seems to me quite clear that the seaworthiness clause is *not in general treated as a condition* [accent added] for breach of which the charterer is at once entitled to repudiate. This is established by a number of authorities over a long period of years and I mention them without quoting from them.

* * *

Why is this apparently basic and underlying condition of seaworthiness not, in fact, treated as a condition? It is for the simple reason that the seaworthiness clause is breached by the slightest failure to be fitted 'in every way' for service. Thus, to take examples from the judgments in some of the cases I have mentioned above, if a nail is missing from one of the timbers of a wooden vessel, or if proper medical supplies or two anchors are not on board at the time of sailing, the owners are in breach of the seaworthiness stipulation. It is contrary to common sense to suppose that, in such circumstances, the parties contemplated that the charterer should at once be entitled to treat the contract as at an end for such trifling breaches.

1 All E.R. 474, 482-83 (1962).

In summary, on September 3 when the Government served its demand upon the owner to man the ship or be declared in default, and on September 4 when the loaded cargo was removed, the shipowner had not breached the contract. Consequently, the Government could not then terminate the agreement and cannot successfully claim, as it does in this action, damages for a breach at that time.

* * *

WINTER, Circuit Judge (dissenting):

* * *

From the scope of the undertaking, *i.e.*, to provide a ship to carry the cargo to Vietnam, it follows that the failure to do so, whether blameworthy or not, was a breach of the charter party. *Work v. Leathers*, 97 U.S. 379, 380, 24 L. Ed. 1012 (1878); *Davison v. Von Lingen*, 113 U.S. 40, 5 S. Ct. 346, 28 L. Ed. 885 (1885); *Pendleton v. Benner Line*, 246 U.S. 353, 357, 38 S. Ct. 330, 62 L. Ed. 770 (1918). *See also, Norrington v. Wright*, 115 U.S. 188, 203, 6 S. Ct. 12, 29 L. Ed. 366 (1885); *The March*, 25 F. 106 (D. Md. 1885); *Pedersen v. Pagenstecher*, 32 F. 841 (S.D.N.Y. 1887); *Dexter & Carpenter Co. v. United States*, 13 F.2d 498 (S.D.N.Y. 1926). The majority view notwithstanding, it is difficult to imagine a more substantial, basic default in a time charter than the failure to provide a crew, unless it be the failure to supply a ship and a crew. The entire purpose of the charter party was totally frustrated.

* * *

---

b. "Preventing the Working of the Vessel"

STEAMSHIP KNUTSFORD CO. v. BARBER & CO.

261 F. 866 (2d Cir. 1919), *cert. denied*, 252 U.S. 586, 40 S. Ct. 396, 64 L. Ed. 729 (1920)

Appeal from the District Court of the United States for the Southern District of New York.

Libel by the Steamship Knutsford Company, Limited, against Barber & Co., Incorporated. From a decree for respondent, libelant appeals. Modified, unless respondent should choose to take a reference.

The libel was by the owner of the steamship Knutsford upon a charter party entered into on March 11, 1915, by which the libelant let the Knutsford on a time charter for two round trips—the first to the United States, Atlantic Cost, then to the west coast of France not north of Havre; the second to the west coast of France, not north of Havre, returning direct to West Kingdom to be redelivered. The material portion of the charter party was article 16, which read as follows: "That in the event of loss of time from deficiency of men or stores, breakdown of machinery, stranding, or damage preventing the working of the vessel for more than twenty-four (24) consecutive hours, payment of hire shall cease until she shall be again in an efficient state to resume her service; but should the vessel be driven into port or to anchorage by stress of weather, or from any accident to cargo, such detention or loss of time shall be at the charterer's risk and expense."

... The third deduction was for 7 days and 12 hours, from 7 p.m. on July 16th to 7 a.m. on July 24th. The ground for this deduction was a fire which occurred on July 16th in the cargo stowed in hold 2 forward of the engine room. The fire broke out on July 16th at 7:10 p.m. and was put out at 4:40 a.m. on the 17th; but the hold remained flooded until 7 o'clock on the evening of the 17th. The 18th was Sunday and there is a dispute in the evidence as to whether the holds at that time were sufficiently dry to permit the discharge of the vessel. In any event, nothing was done until Monday, the 19th, when the captain began to shift the cargo from this hold. This was of five kinds—sugar in bags, carbon, cases of machinery, steel billets, and spelter. It did not appear how the cargo was stowed.

On Wednesday, the 21st, the sugar having been removed to the deck, the captain employed a surveyor to examine the hold. He found that in a part of the fore and aft steel bulkhead the steel plates had somewhat buckled, and that a wooden thwartship bulkhead that had been used to divide off a part of the hold for a reserve bunker had been burned and charred. He also found that some hatch covers had been destroyed, some of the battens burned, and the bilges, strainers, and suction pipes fouled and choked with melted sugar. He recommended that the wooden bulkhead be removed, the cargo battens be renewed, the charred portions of the ship's structure scraped clean, and the bilges, etc., that were fouled by melted sugar, cleared. This was done by the morning of the 23d, on which day the charterers, for their own purposes, built a magazine in the ship to carry explosives. The question was what portion of this time should be deducted in favor of the charterer.

The District Court ... allowed the third, [deduction of hire] upon the theory that during all the period after the fire the vessel had been damaged, so as to prevent her "working," within the language of article 16.

LEARNED HAND, District Judge (after stating the facts as above):

We quite agree with the learned District Court that within the language of article 16 it is not necessary that the damage should be "structural" in the sense that the frame of the ship must be injured, so as to prevent her "working." In this case the buckling of the fore and aft bulkhead was not such damage, and the charterer's right, under article 16 must rest upon the fact that the holds had to be cleaned before the ship was in seaworthy condition and that the charred bulkhead had to be removed. We further agree that the ship was not again in efficient state to resume her services until the morning of the 23d. Therefore, if article 16 had read that the charterer should not pay while the ship was in such a damaged condition as prevented her "working," we should have no difficulty in agreeing that during the whole of that period the hire ceased. However, in reaching such a result under the actual terms of this charter party, we should have to disregard the words, "in the event of loss of time," which were certainly intended to provide indemnity, if only partial indemnity, to the charterer. It follows that, if the cargo had been removed, not because of any damage to itself, but only to give access to the necessary repairs, then, as indeed Mr. Hickox admitted, all the time until July 23d would have been on the owner's account, but that, if the cargo had to be removed in any event for examination and restowage, the time taken for that purpose was not lost by reason of damage to the ship.

The evidence is far from clear, but it sufficiently appears that the sugar was taken out because it had to be. The hold had been flooded, and the charterer must examine and restow it before the ship could proceed. The same apparently was true of the cases of machinery, and possibly of the carbon, too, although the record is silent as to the last. But as regards the steel billets and the spelter it must be assumed that they were not injured. These being the circumstances, we think that the time necessary to examine and restow the sugar was not "loss of time" within the meaning of article 16, but that the charterer was using the ship at that time for a purpose which, though it necessarily delayed her, was still his own, and was not due to any "damage" to the ship. It seems to us that article 16 does not justify a deduction during that period, or until the charterer began to lose the use of the ship after he again wished to load her.

Had the spelter and billets been stowed at the bottom of the hold, in such wise that it had to be discharged before the bilges, limbers, etc., could be cleared, or the charred remains of the wooden bulkhead removed, then the ship would have gone off hire in our judgment from the time the discharge of the cargo had reached the spelter and billets. The rest of the time would have been lost only because it then became necessary to remove that portion of the cargo to gain access to the damaged parts. It would have been upon the owner's account. So far as we can gather from the somewhat fragmentary proof, the last day lost because of the removal of the sugar was the 21st, on which the repairs began. The only question that can arise, therefore, is of the 22d, for on the morning of the 23d a certificate was given to the ship, showing that she was again "in an efficient state to resume her service."

The only evidence of what was done by the charterer on the 22d is contained in the testimony of the master, who says that cases of machinery were taken out for examination on the 21st and 22d. If this is to be understood as meaning that the 22d as well as the 21st were necessary for the purpose of examining the cases of machinery—some of which were later taken off the ship—the ship would not have been off hire at all. It is impossible upon such a meager record to tell whether this was the reason, or whether the unloading of the cases had proceeded in a leisurely way because in any case the ship must be laid up for repairs on the 22d. The burden of proof to bring article 16 into operation is upon the charterer, and on this record it, strictly speaking, fails to sustain that burden. However, since the decree is to be modified, a reference may be taken, if the parties cannot agree, to ascertain at what time on the 21st the charterer had completed so much of the discharge of cargo as was necessary for its examination before proceeding to reload, had the ship then been in an efficient state to resume her service.

As we have already indicated, all the time after 9 o'clock on the morning of the 23d we charge to the charterer's account. As held in *Smailes & Son v. Evans & Reid* [1917] 2 K. B. 54, the clause does not provide full indemnity to the charterers, but only until such time as the vessel is in efficient condition for "working." We are in full accord with the judgment of Mr. Justice Bailhache in that case.

Finally, there is the question whether the ship's holds were clear of water by 7 p.m. on July 17th, or whether the failure of the stevedore to work on the 18th was because they were not so cleared. The master says the holds were cleared, with the exception of some water in the bilges. The stevedore, Spillane, says that he did not believe the men would have gone into the holds on Sunday, the 18th. Yet at most there were only 6 inches of water on his own statement, and such a condition scarcely supports his belief. We think that the respondent has not borne the issue on this point.

In *Hogarth v. Miller*, [1891] A.C. 48, it was held that, while the ship was being used for discharge, she was on hire though she was not in fact efficient to resume her service, because her machinery was broken down. There the ship had broken down at Las Palmas, and was towed from there to Harburg, her first port of discharge, where the charterer discharged her in part. The charterer was excused from paying hire during the period of the towage, and held during the period of discharge. The period of towage was not, indeed, lost time; certainly all of it was not; but the towage charge had been included as an expense in general average and was treated as a separate venture. We understand the case as meaning that the damage "prevented the working of the vessel," though possibly that is not wholly clear from the judgments delivered.

In *Lake Steam Shipping Co. v. Bacon* (D.C.) 129 Fed. 819, affirmed in this court without opinion in 145 Fed. 1022, 74 C.C.A. 476, the facts were substantially the same as in *Hogarth v. Miller*, except that the ship made port under her own steam in a crippled condition. The distinction regarding the towage charge above noted in *Hogarth v. Miller* seems not to have been observed, and it must be owned that the result is somewhat inconsistent in allowing a deduction for loss of time due to crippled power in steaming, while refusing to allow it for the period of discharge. Moreover, the allowance appears to us to be in face of the decision of the District Court here, which this court unanimously accepts, that the allowance is to be made only in case the breakdown prevents working of the vessel. However that may be, the allowance was refused during the period of discharge, and we see no distinction between that and the period of discharging the cargo for examination in the case at bar.

The Canadia, 241 Fed. 233, 154 C.C.A. 153 (C.C.A. 3d Cir.), squarely supports our ruling. In that case the vessel was held to be off hire during the period of a fire, but on hire while being discharged, though in an unseaworthy condition, being available for the purposes required by the charterer. We see no substantial difference between that form of expression and the one which we somewhat prefer; *i.e.*, that the charterer has lost no time because of the damage.

The ruling reported in the note to *The Santona* (C.C.) 152 Fed. 520, made by Judge Choate while acting as arbitrator, does not seem to us to bear out the libelant's contention that a damage such as the Knutsford suffered did not bring her within the breakdown clause. We understand the damage in that case to have been altogether to the cargo, except for some slight repairs, which could safely have been postponed. We do not regard the damage done to the Knutsford as of that class, for, in spite of the master's statement to the contrary, the surveyor clearly did not think her seaworthy without some repairs.

* * *

The decree will therefore be modified, by allowing the owner full hire, unless the charterer shall choose to take a reference as above indicated. Costs of this appeal to the appellant.

MANTON, Circuit Judge:

I dissent in part. I cannot agree with the prevailing opinion, in so far as it disagrees with the conclusions reached by the court below. The clause of the charter party which we are to consider provides:

That in the event of loss of time from deficiency of men or stores, breakdown of machinery, stranding, or damage preventing the working of the vessel for more than 24 consecutive hours, the payment of hire shall cease until she be again in an efficient state to resume her service.

On the voyage in question, the loading had been going on for several days, and prior to 1:30 p.m. on July 16th the hatches were closed down, as further cargo was not available. At 7:10 on July 16th fire was discovered in No. 2 hold, which had been loaded with steel billets and machinery in boxes and sugar. The fire was put out at 4:10 a.m. on July 17th. The hold, at this time, was flooded to a depth of 14 feet 6 inches. A salvage boat pumped the water out, and this work was completed at 7 p.m. on July 17th. No work was done on the two intervening days, but on July 19th the stevedores, assisted by the crew, took the damaged sugar out of No. 2 hold, and this work was completed on July 21st. An examination revealed that the wooden bulkhead which partitioned off the reserve bunker space, was burnt out. After a survey, it was recommended that the wooden bulkhead and the battens be renewed; also that repairs be made to the sounding pipe, and that the bilges be cleaned out where possible. The bilges and strainers had been made foul, due to the sugar water and syrup. The work was completed on July 22d. On the 23d of July the charterers built a power magazine in between decks, and on the 24th at 7 a.m. resumed the loading of the cargo.

The District Court held that the libelant could not recover for hire during the period after the fire in the vessel until reloading—that is, between July 16th, at 7 p.m. and the 24th, at 7 a.m.—and this because the damage caused prevented her working within article 16. During this period the ship was unfit for the service of receiving the cargo; that is, while the fire was raging, and until it was extinguished, the water removed, the hold repaired, and the pipes cleaned. We cannot read into this clause that the reason for the delay in loading cargo must be due to some damage of a structural character. Whether the damage was of a structural or nonstructural character is unimportant.

It is claimed, however, that the charterer's deduction of hire for the period referred to should be disallowed, upon the theory that during the period certain portions of the cargo were being shifted, and that the loss of time thus occurring was due to this cause, and not to damage preventing the working of the vessel, in the sense of the breakdown clause of the charter. This contention is untenable, because the interpretation of the charter party, upon which it rests, is irreconcilable, not only with the authorities, but it does not, when applied to the facts in the case, defeat the deduction of hire. Charter party provisions almost the same in effect—indeed, in haec verba—have been held to authorize a suspension of hire for the period within which the vessel was not in a condition fit to perform the service required of her, and this notwithstanding the fact that the charterer was able to and actually did make some use of the vessel during the period for the whole of which the deduction was sustained. To say that the loss of time here was due to cargo movements in which the charterer was interested, and not to the necessity for putting the vessel again in condition to resume her service, cannot be supported under the facts disclosed in this record. In the cases which are depended upon to support this claim, it will be found that the loss of time was due to other causes, and, in fact, there was not loss of time, or, at least, no loss covering the entire period for which the deduction was sustained. A controlling decision found in the English reports is *Hogarth v. Miller*, 60 L.J.P.C. 1, where the charter party provided:

In the event of loss of time from ... breakdown of machinery, want of repairs, or damage whereby the working of the vessel is stopped for more than 48 consecutive hours, the payment of the hire shall cease until she be again in an efficient state to resume her service.

In that case, the vessel put in at Las Palmas, owing to a breakdown in her engine. Thereafter a tug was sent out by the shipowners, under arrangement with the charterers, and the vessel proceeded with the aid of the tug, partly using her engines, to her destination, and there discharged her cargo. The Lord Ordinary held that the vessel was entitled to hire for the average period of the voyage from Las Palmas to the port of destination, and allowed a deduction only to the extent by which the duration of the voyage actually made with the assistance of the tug exceeded the duration of such average voyage. The House of Lords, however, held that the charterer was entitled to deduct the hire for the entire period of the voyage from Las Palmas to the destination. Lord Halsbury said:

> The test by which the payment for hire is to be resumed is the efficient state of the vessel to resume her service; so that each of those words, as it appears to me, has relation to that which both of the parties must be taken to have well understood—namely, the purpose for which the vessel was hired, the nature of the service to be performed by the vessel, and the efficiency of the vessel to perform such service as should be required of her in the course of the voyage.

* * *

We should not construe differently the same language in this charter party of later date. The vessel was not fit to receive cargo while she was afire, or while the fire was being extinguished, nor while the hold was flooded; and she was not in an efficient state to resume her service until the repairs found necessary were completed. To say that it is incumbent upon the charterer to remove the cargo, because that was damaged, is ignoring the effect of the *Hogarth v. Miller* and *Lake Steamship Co. v. Bacon Cases, supra.* Moreover, it appears that through the period while the fire was in progress, while it was being extinguished, and while the vessel was being repaired and the hold cleared in consequence thereof, there was a loss of time from damage preventing the working of the ship, and if, during part of the time, the charterer was in fact shifting cargo for his own account, the fire and its consequences were nevertheless, throughout the entire period, a concurring cause of the loss of time. Here the vessel itself was actually on fire. There is no evidence to bear out the suggestion, made upon the argument, that it originated in the cargo. A consequence was the flooding of the hold, that created the need for shifting the cargo, all being occasioned by the fire, and also the necessity for repairs after the fire.

So far as the undamaged part of the cargo which was removed is concerned, manifestly there was no occasion to shift that, except for that damaged condition of the ship, and for the purpose of enabling the owner to make the necessary repairs to the ship. The portion of the sugar which had been melted and drawn into the suction pipes in the operation of the pumps, or deposited, mixed with water, upon the limber boards, had ceased to be of any interest to the charterer and no longer existed as a cargo. It was a total loss so far as the charterer was concerned. The clearance of this sugar, as of any other obstruction in the pipes or hold, was the duty of the owner, not the charterer, and the ship was not fit to proceed to sea until this, as well as the repairs, whether classified as arising from structural or nonstructural damage, had been made. It appears that some of the sugar had only been partially damaged, and still had value as merchandise. It was necessary to be shifted, in order to preserve or recondition it. The master, however, was obliged to remove this from the hold—that is, the sound as well as the damaged cargo—in order to ascertain and repair the damage to the ship. Therefore all this work, including the movement of the cargo, was approximately caused by the fire, and the consequential damage by water, with its resulting damage to the ship. It seems clear to me, therefore, that the deduction of hire for this period was properly allowed by the District Court.

In reaching this conclusion, I do not overlook the decisions which have held that charter hire, after a period of suspension, begins to run again when the ship itself is fit for service, although certain consequences of the damage continue, involving actual loss of time to the charterer beyond the period during which the vessel itself is not fit for service. *Small & Sons v. Evans,* 2 K. B. 54, 33 T. L. R. 233.

Merely because one of the consequences of the unfitness is to require the charterer to perform some operation on his own account, it by no means follows that charter hire runs while the vessel is unfit. As in the case above referred to, the hire begins to run again because the vessel is "again in an efficient state to resume her service," not because the further period of delay is deemed not to be causally connected with the ship which suspended the accrual of hire.

For these reasons, I think the judgment of the court below is right, and should be affirmed.

---

c. *"Any Loss of Time"*

WOODS HOLE OCEANOGRAPHIC INST. v. UNITED STATES

677 F.2d 149, 1983 AMC 2324 (1st Cir. 1982)

WYZANSKI, Senior District Judge

Case 81-1239 involves appeals from two February 9, 1980 judgments of the district court. The first judgment allows Woods Hole Oceanographic Institution ["Woods Hole"] to recover from the United States government ["the government"] on its claim for a balance of unpaid charter hire for the use of R/V Alcoa Seaprobe ["Seaprobe"] during a period beginning August 2, 1977. The second judgment dismisses the government's counterclaim for breach of an implied warranty of seaworthiness. We vacate our opinion of December 14, 1981, and we consider, in turn, the claim and the counterclaim.

The Woods Hole Claim

[In August 1977, Captain Dinsmore, the negotiator for Woods Hole Oceanographic Institute ("Woods Hole"), and Worrall, the government's representative and principle negotiator, entered into a binding agreement whereby Woods Hole chartered the R/V Seaprobe for underwater research activities to the government for 38 days beginning on or about August 2, 1977 at $7,844.34 a day. Eds.]

* * *

On the same day the telex was sent—July 26—Woods Hole sent a letter which, so far as relevant, stated:

This responds to your request dated 26 July 1977 for a proposed charter for the R/V ALCOA SEAPROBE, August-September 1977, for NUSC, New London.
The Woods Hole Oceanographic Institution hereby proposes to operate the R/V ALCOA SEAPROBE in accordance with your request from 2 August 1977 to 9 September 1977 ... it is proposed to operate on a fixed daily charter rate of $7,844.34 per day....

* * *

On August 2, the actual charter began in New London.

* * *

Seven or eight days were spent outfitting Seaprobe and loading it with government equipment. The vessel left port on August 10 with government personnel aboard and, after at least five and probably six days' transit, reached the research site. On August 24 Seaprobe's starboard engine suffered a major breakdown which could not be repaired at sea and its other engine was working at only half capacity. At that time the government had not completed the research for which it planned to use Seaprobe.[2] On August 25 the master of the vessel directed the vessel back to port because of the severe engine casualty. Although the master informed the representatives of the government of his decision, they did not make that decision, and it is not suggested that the government had any power to control his decision. Without receiving any permission from any authorized representative of the government, the

---

[2] Robert F. LaPlante, the government's manager of the program for which Seaprobe was used, was on board Seaprobe when the breakdown occurred. He testified that "We were really in the middle of the business, and we had several more days of business to do." (A. 317).

master determined that the Seaprobe should proceed to the port of Woods Hole rather than to New London as contemplated by the charter.[3]

Thereupon Seaprobe departed leaving in the ocean government equipment valued at $3 million. En route to the port of Woods Hole Seaprobe had on an undisclosed date a rendezvous with a government LSD which had been at Bermuda and which took from Seaprobe "the transfer of a number of people who were on the vessel." On September 1 Seaprobe reached port at Woods Hole.

* * *

On October 30, 1979 the United States filed in the district court its answer denying liability as to the claim made by Woods Hole, and setting forth a counterclaim alleging that Woods Hole "By failing to furnish crew members who could operate the R/V SEAPROBE for the purposes for which she was chartered ... breached its implied warranty of seaworthiness which resulted in damages in the amount of $203,952.84," which the government seeks to recover.

* * *

Following a *de novo* trial, and in accordance with its December 29, 1980 opinion, findings and conclusions, the district court on February 9, 1981 entered judgment for Woods Hole on its claim for $39,221.70 and interest, for 5 days of charter hire.

From those two judgments the government appealed.

For the following reasons we reverse the judgment for Woods Hole on its claim of $39,221.70 (and interest).

It is undisputed that the district court correctly found that in August 1977 Woods Hole and the government entered into a binding agreement whereby Woods Hole chartered the Seaprobe to the government for 38 days beginning August 2, 1977 at $7,844.34 per day.... [W]e are of opinion that it is indisputable that the parties included in their binding agreement an *off-hire arrangement* "reasonably represented" by clause 13 of the MSC Form.*

* * *

We turn to the question whether as a matter of interpretation the off-hire clause relieves the government of an obligation to pay charter hire for the 7 days August 26 through September 1 when Seaprobe was en route from the research site to the port of Woods Hole. The essential words in the clause provide that "any loss of time ... by any cause whatsoever not due to the fault of the Government, preventing the full working of the Vessel, the payment of hire shall cease."

The evidence indisputably shows that the government suffered a "loss of time" from the moment when the master of Seaprobe, acting for Woods Hole and not for the government, directed the vessel to proceed from the research site to the port of Woods Hole. It was not for the government's purposes that Seaprobe left before the planned research was completed, and went to Woods Hole for repair. The voyage to Woods Hole was not on the government's time, but on the time of Woods Hole. The off-hire clause relieved that govern-

---

[3] We are not unmindful that Vernon P. Simmons, a naval officer who was aboard Seaprobe on August 25 but who was "not empowered to enter into any agreements" (A. 327) testified that the master "asked us if there would be any difficulty in the sense that originally the ship was supposed to go to New London to offload. And by going to Woods Hole, that modified our plan. We basically said we thought we could accommodate Woods Hole if it was better for him, and at that time the master directed the ship proceed to Woods Hole." (A. 332).

* Clause 13 of the MSC Form provided:

Any loss of time for deficiency of men or stores, fire, breakdown, or damages to hull, machinery, or equipment, collision, grounding, detention by average accidents to ship or cargo, dry-docking for the purpose of examination or painting bottom, or by any other cause whatsoever not due to the fault of the Government, preventing the full working of the Vessel, the payment of hire shall cease for the time thereby lost in excess of eight (8) hours, provided, however, that when the period of time lost to the Government on any one occasion exceeds twenty-four (24) consecutive hours, hire shall be reduced for the entire period, including the first eight (8) hours, provided further that where the Vessel is unable to perform due to failure of the Contractor to man the Vessel for continuous service, all time lost for this reason shall be without hire ....[Eds.]

ment from any *contractual* obligation to pay for the time Seaprobe was in the service of Woods Hole. A charterer is obligated to pay "for the use of the vessel *only* while she was in its service." [Emphasis added.] *Compania Bilbaina de Navegacion de Bilbao v. Spanish American Light & Power Co.*, 146 U.S. 483, 499, 13 S. Ct. 142, 148, 36 L. Ed. 1054 (1892). *Acc. Hogarth v. Miller*, [1891] A. C. 48; *Steamship Knutsford Co. v. Barber & Co.*, 261 F. 866, 870 (2nd Cir. 1919).

The facts do not support the argument of Woods Hole that the government was using in its service, in the sense of employing, Seaprobe from August 26 through September 1 to bring the vessel and the government's personnel to the port of Woods Hole. During those 7 days the government had no power to direct or control the vessel's movements. The master had in effect terminated the charter and, acting for the account of Woods Hole, was taking Seaprobe to the port of Woods Hole to be repaired. If the master, acting for Woods Hole employed Seaprobe in Woods Hole's service to confer an incidental benefit on the government by transporting its personnel to a rendezvous or elsewhere, this does not imply that the *government employed* Seaprobe in its service to realize that benefit. Charter hire is payable only if the *charterer* employs the vessel in its service, not if the *owner* employs the vessel in a way that incidentally benefits the charterer.

We need not decide whether if Woods Hole did employ Seaprobe on the return journey for the incidental benefit of the government, the government has a quasicontractual obligation to pay Woods Hole on a *quantum meruit* basis. The complaint in the instant case presents no such claim.

In short, the district court should have dismissed on its merits the complaint of Woods Hole because Seaprobe was not in the government's service during the 5 days for which recovery was sought.

---

3. Mutual Exceptions

CLYDE COMMERCIAL S.S. CO. v. WEST INDIA S.S. CO.

169 F. 275 (2d Cir. 1909)

WARD, Circuit Judge

This is a libel by the owner of the steamship Santona to recover deductions made by the charterer from the charter hire. The charter party contains the following provisions material to be considered:

The said owners agree to let and the said charterers agree to hire the said steamship from the time of delivery for six calendar months. Steamer to be placed at the disposal of the charterers at a safe U.S. Atlantic port.... It is understood that steamer is to come out in ballast ... being on her delivery ready to receive cargo and tight, staunch, strong and in every way fitted for the service ... (and with full complement of officers, seamen, engineers and firemen for a vessel of her tonnage) and to be so maintained during the continuation of this charter party.

(1)   That the owner shall provide and pay for all provisions, wages, and consular shipping and discharging fees of the captain, officers, engineers, firemen and crew ... also for all the cabin, deck, engineroom and other necessary stores and maintain her in a thoroughly efficient state in hull and machinery for and during the service.

(2)   That the charterers shall provide and pay for all the coals, fuel, port charges, pilotages, agencies, commissions, consular charges (except those pertaining to the captain, officers or crew) and all other charges whatsoever except those before stated.

(4)   "That the charterer shall pay for the use and hire of said vessel 962 pounds ten shillings per calendar month commencing on and from the date of her delivery," etc.

(6)   Payment of said hire to be made in cash semimonthly in advance at New York ... and in default of such payment or payments as herein specified the owner shall have the faculty of withdrawing said steamer from the service of the charterers without prejudice to any claim that the owners may otherwise have on the charterers in pursuance of this charter.

(9)   That the whole reach of the vessel's holds, decks, and usual places of loading and accommodation in the ship (not more than she can reasonably stow and carry) shall be at the charterers' disposal reserving only proper and sufficient space for ship's officers, crew, tackle, apparel, furniture, provisions, stores, and fuel.

(10) That the captain shall prosecute his voyages with the utmost dispatch....

(14) That the master shall use all diligence in caring for the ventilation of the cargo.

(15) That in the event of the loss of time from deficiency of men or stores, breakdown of machinery, stranding, fire or damage preventing the working of the vessel for more than twenty-four running hours the payment of hire shall cease until she be again in an efficient state to resume her service....

(17) The act of God, enemies, fire, restraint of princes, rulers and people and all dangers and accidents of the seas, rivers, machinery, boilers and steam navigation and errors of navigation throughout this charter party always mutually excepted.

(21) Steamer is to be docked, bottom cleaned when an opportunity occurs in U.S. north of Hatteras or in Europe and payment of the hire to be suspended until she is again in proper state for the service....

* * *

Irrespective of the special provisions and exceptions, there can be no doubt that, if the owner failed to perform any of its covenants, it would be responsible in damages to the charterer which might be measured in some cases by the charter hire and which in other cases might be more or less than the charter hire. If the charterer failed to perform its covenants, it would likewise be liable to the owner in damages, measured if the failure were in payment of the charter hire by the amount of hire unpaid with interest, or, if it were a failure to provide coals or pilots or pay port charges, measured by the amount of the damages so caused to the owner. The parties, however, did provide a series of exceptions in article 17 which are described as "mutual." We think this word cannot be construed in the sense of reciprocal in respect to the same broken engagement because the charter party contains no such reciprocal or interdependent covenants. The charterer makes no special covenant in consideration of the owner's undertaking to maintain the hull and machinery in good condition (1); to put the agreed space at the disposal of the charterer (9); to prosecute the voyage with dispatch (10); to ventilate the cargo (14); and to clean the ship's bottom (21). Its covenant to pay charter hire (4 and 6) is in consideration of the performance by the owner of all its covenants. Similarly the owner covenants nothing in special consideration of the charterer's undertaking to provide coals and pilotages and pay for port charges, etc. (2); all its covenants together being made in consideration of the charterer's single covenant to pay hire. By mutual we understand that the parties intended the exceptions to protect each from liability to the other whenever performance of any covenant was prevented or delayed by any exception. If the owner were prevented from maintaining the vessel in an efficient state or from giving the whole space contracted for or from prosecuting the voyage with dispatch or from properly ventilating the cargo or cleaning the ship's bottom by any of these exceptions, he would not be responsible to the charterer. On the other hand, if the charterer were so prevented from furnishing coals, paying port charges or furnishing pilots or from paying hire on the date fixed, it would be relieved from liability therefor to the owner, and, in the case of charter hire, the owner could not withdraw the steamer as provided in article 6.

If the causes enumerated in article 15 for which payment of hire is suspended were wholly different from the exceptions in article 17, it might be fairly contended that those exceptions applied to them, but they include many categories exactly alike. If hire is to be suspended for delay over 24 hours caused by breakdown of machinery, that delay is immediately excused by the exception of accidents to machinery in article 17. Suspension in case of stranding is immediately excused, whether the owner is at fault or not, by the exception of accidents of the sea or errors in navigation; suspension in case of fire by the exception of fire. This leads us to the conclusion that article 15 must be understood to state absolute categories in which the parties intended the hire to be suspended whether the owner was at fault or not, and therefore that article 17 does not apply to them at all.

Hard cases may be imagined, but the question is what does the contract, as written, mean, and by it the parties must abide whether the results are hard or not. The vessel was detained at Colon after she had discharged her cargo, and before she proceeded on her voyage, one day 18½ hours. The master wrote to the charterer at the time that he had to remain because the second and third engineers, having developed fever, were too weak to attend to their duties; "so I had to remain, but hope to get away to-morrow morning." The master having lost the time because he had not, or thought he had not, a sufficient crew to proceed with (though subsequent events showed he was wrong in this particular), the delay was due to a deficiency of men under article 15, and the charterer was entitled to deduct charter hire for that time. The vessel was subsequently delayed 10 days and 20 hours at Sabine because of the quarantine laws of the state of Texas. The proclamation of the Governor by authority vested in him by the laws of that state declared every vessel coming from a port south of 25 degrees north latitude to "be considered infected unless proof to the contrary be submitted to the state health officer and special exemption be granted to said places...." The Santona came from such a port, viz., Colon, and, as she was detained as infected, it is fair to assume that no such exemption had been granted to Colon. The proclamation further provided:

"Vessels from an infected place having had sickness or deaths en route, but having no sickness at the time of arrival, will be disinfected and held seven full days after disinfection under observation before being released and a longer time if considered necessary by the said health officer."

The Santona fell within this description, and her detention was prolonged after the first seven days because some new cases of fever appeared. The delay was not caused by a deficiency of men constructive or otherwise, as in the case of *Tweedie Trading Co. v. Emery*, 154 Fed. 472, 84 C.C.A. 253. In that case the crew were constructively deficient, just as the vessel in this case was constructively infected. There was, therefore, no deficiency of men within article 15.

Detention by quarantine authority is a restraint of princes or people. *The Progresso* (D.C.) 42 Fed. 229; *Id.*, 50 Fed. 835, 2 C.C.A. 45; *The Santona* (C.C.) 152 Fed. 516; Carver on Carriage of Goods by Sea, § 82. Accordingly this exception which prevented the owner from prosecuting his voyage with dispatch relieves him from liability to the charterer for the delay so caused. The case is to be treated as if no delay had occurred. On the other hand, the charterer is not protected by the exception from paying hire because it was not thereby prevented from paying hire and because it had the use of the vessel for which it was to pay notwithstanding the interruption. The case is not at all like that of *Northern Pacific Railway Co. v. American Trading Co.*, 195 U.S. 439, 25 Sup. Ct. 84, 49 L. Ed. 269, in which a deputy collector, through his mistaken understanding of the law, refused a clearance to a steamer unless a shipment of lead which was contraband of war during the Chinese-Japanese War were first discharged. In that case there was no statute of the United States nor any proclamation of the President requiring clearance to be refused to a vessel having on board articles contraband of war. Mr. Justice Peckham said:

Here there was no intervention of the government of the United States. The exportation of lead was never prohibited by the Treasury Department during the war between China and Japan. There was no change in the law or the policy of this government subsequently to the making of the contract by which its performance was excused. The exportation of the lead was legal when the contract was made and continued to be so after the execution of such contract, although the deputy collector mistakenly refused to grant the clearance unless the lead was taken off the vessel. Such mistaken decision did not render the original loading of the lead on the ship unlawful, nor would it have been unlawful for the ship to proceed with the lead on board provided the clearance had been had. It was not an act of the state, therefore, which prevented the sailing of the vessel within the true meaning of such a term, but a mistaken act of a subordinate official not justified by law, and not sufficient as an excuse for the nonperformance of the contract in question under the circumstances already detailed. If the bill of lading were regarded as applicable for this purpose, the refusal of the clearance did not constitute a 'restraint of princes, rulers or people,' within that clause of the bill.

The decree is reversed, and the court below directed to enter a decree for the libelant for the amount deducted from charter hire for delay at Sabine, with interest and one-half the costs of both courts.

---

4. Restraint of Princes—Frustration

THE CLAVERESK

264 F. 276 (2d Cir. 1920)

Libelant, a corporation of Pennsylvania, filed this libel *in rem* against the steamship Claveresk, and *in personam* against her owner—this respondent and a British corporation.

* * *

In 1913 respondent (hereafter called Sutherland) executed to libelant (hereafter called Earn Line) a charter of its steamship Claveresk for "about five years"; *i.e.*, until say April, 1918. The hiring was in the ordinary "government form" of time charter, which is not a demise; the use of the vessel was restricted to a part of the Atlantic and to Mediterranean waters. Earn Line could sublet, and the usual "break down" and "restraint of princes" clauses were embodied in the document.

On January 25, 1917, the Claveresk under this charter was on a voyage from Baltimore to Cuba, when Sutherland, at its home office in Newcastle, England, received a telegram from a division or bureau of the Admiralty, known as "Transports," stating that Claveresk was "required for government service after completion discharge in West Indies; form requisition follows." Two days later Sutherland received a "form requisitioning letter with the signature of the Secretary of the Admiralty."

Sutherland owned upwards of 20 steamers other than Claveresk; in January, 1917, all had been requisitioned except 3, and they were "running in special trades subject to approval of the government." Requisition was not objected to, and neither then nor down to trial (October 23, 1918) was effort made to obtain release of Claveresk. On February 1, 1917, the steamer was in a Cuban port, and the master was instructed by Sutherland to put himself under the orders of agents named by the Admiralty.

On February 10, 1917, her inward cargo having been discharged, Claveresk passed under control of the British Admiralty, which tendered Sutherland a formal charter at a rate much higher than that of Earn Line's contract, but much below the market. We find it proven that, following the general custom of owners of requisitioned bottoms, Sutherland declined to sign the Admiralty charter, but expected to get and did receive the rate of hire therein named. When Claveresk thus passed under control of British Admiralty, she seems to have been subchartered by Earn Line to Munson; and on the day for payment of charter hire next following February 10th. Earn Line tendered in writing to Sutherland's agents in New York the amount due under the original charter of 1913, and added: "Claveresk-Munson: We presume you will be collecting half month's hire to-day from Munson Line, and remit us in the usual way."

We infer from this that these agents (the house of Winchester & Co.) were acting for Earn Line in respect of the subcharter. Winchester replied, declining payment, adding: "The owners [of Claveresk] consider that the requisition of the steamer by the Admiralty has completely frustrated the adventure covered by the charter party."

From this we deduce the finding that, as of February 10, 1917, Sutherland took and stood on the position that the charter with Earn Line was then lawfully terminated, and that all rights or demands growing therefrom, including subcharters, ceased and determined; while Earn Line held, and in legal effect asserted, that the Admiralty requisition did not terminate the contractual relation either between Sutherland and itself, or itself and the subcharterer.

This exchange of views occurred February 16-17, 1917, but on February 10, 1917, this libel was filed, wherein the subtraction of the steamer from Earn Line's service was treated as a refusal by Sutherland to perform the charter party, and a repudication thereof. Damages for the breach are claimed in usual form; *i.e.*, the charter hire was £1,320 per month, the market rate at date of libel filed £18,500 per month, the charter party had still 14 months to run, wherefore libelant asserted its damages to be more than $1,250,000.

The answer substantially pleaded the requisition (1) as a restraint of princes; (2) as a frustration of the commercial adventure between the parties.

* * *

At trial respondent rested on the ambassador's certificate, or the legal effect of the facts therein set forth. Libelant showed the further facts hereinabove recited, and filed what is called a "replication"—in form a pleading wherein Earn Line (1) "denies that respondent was under any legal compulsion to withdraw the Claveresk," and asserts the vessel to have been "voluntarily withdrawn and relet" at a higher rate; and (2) alleges (in the event of legal compulsion on respondent being shown) that it as charterer is entitled to, and "respondent is bound to pay," all excess over the charter hire of 1913 which Sutherland in fact received from the Admiralty during so much of the period of requisition as coincided with the chartered period. This "replication" was filed over the respondent's "protest." In an opinion reported 254 Fed. 127, L. HAND, J., dismissed the libel; this appeal followed.

We here insert as findings of fact by us on this new trial: (1) Sutherland did not voluntarily—*i.e.*, did not seek to—withdraw Claveresk from libelant's service, nor ask nor induce government to requisition; (2) in January-February, 1917, having regard to the then violence of German submarine warfare on merchant vessels, and the success thereof, no reasonable man would have expected or even dared hope that the Claveresk, once taken into government service, would be released for any use contemplated by the charter of 1913, before the expiry of the term of that charter.

* * *

HOUGH, Circuit Judge....

That evidence shows that within the kingdom of England an order was given by the British Admiralty to the owner, requiring him on a day certain to place his vessel, then within (or soon to reach) the waters of the republic of Cuba, at the service of Admiralty agents, there to remain for an indefinite period. Thus the question is reached whether in obeying the order, Sutherland yielded to that restraint of princes excepted in the charter party.

* * *

On the question last stated appellant offers two propositions: (1) The clause refers merely to physical restraint of the ship; an order to the owner is not within its meaning. (2) The order was "ultra vires," meaning that it was not in accord with English municipal or constitutional law.

The first proposition is untenable. In times past, when a vessel left port, she disappeared from her owner's ken; there was no means of communicating with her, except by other ships like her, and electricity and steam did not keep owner and ship in constant touch. In such times force, governmental or other, was more swiftly and more usefully exerted on the ship than on the owner. Now it is more efficacious to act on the ship through the owner, and (so to speak) requisition or commandeer the owner, and through him his vessel, putting upon that owner the same necessity of obedience that in former days was exercised on the master wherever the ship might be. The theory has not changed, but the method of application has been modernized. The fundamental essential of a restraint of rulers is that the restraining act should be governmental. *Northern, etc., Co. v. American, etc., Co.*, 195 U.S. 467, 25 Sup. Ct. 84, 49 L. Ed. 269 *et seq.* That the restraint need not be physical was in effect held in *The Styria*, 186 U.S. 18, 22 Sup. Ct. 731, 46 L. Ed. 1027. And *see* cases cited in *The Athanasios*, 228 Fed. (D.C.) 558. The matter is fully covered by Lord Reading in *Sanday v. British, Etc., Co.*, [1915] 2 K.B. 802, in which case, on appeal to the House of Lords, it was said (in affirming the judgment) that "the circumstances that force was neither exerted nor present [is immaterial], for force is in reserve behind every state demand"; and it was added, in substance, that it would be "a strange law" which required one to resist, "till the hand of power was laid upon him, an order which it was his duty to obey. If it were an order which he was not bound to obey, and which he might have successfully resisted either by violence or by process of law, a question might arise...."

The evidence here is plain that resistance was impossible; all that Sutherland could have done would have been to say:

> I refuse to order my captain to report to the Admiralty agents; I prefer to leave my ship in the service of a neutral charterer.

The supposed case need not be pursued, to the probable and proper punishment of such an act. No citizen or subject is by lawful private contract either required to or justified in proceeding to such lengths in resisting or evading the compulsion of his government.

The second proposition is equally without support, even though we disregard the multiplied decisions, including our own, regarding the efficacy of the ambassadorial certificate. It is here proven, without any reference to that document, that the act commonly called "requisition" was governmental, and contained or expressed in a letter or order over the signature of the Secretary of the Admiralty. Further, that such letter or order was in assumed compliance with a proclamation dated August 3, 1914, and an Order in Council dated November 10, 1915. Whether in exercising this power the officers sending the telegram, signing letters, and issuing orders were acting in strict accord with the municipal and constitutional law of the United Kingdom, is a question with which we cannot be concerned; for there is plainly proven a governmental act done within British territory, and we entirely agree with the court below that it is settled law that the act of another sovereign within its own territory is for our purposes legal of necessity. *Hewitt v. Speyer*, 250 Fed. 370, 162 C.C.A. 437, and cases cited. The requisition of the Claveresk was a restraint of princes, lawful so far as we are concerned to inquire; what legal complaints the owner may seek to advance within the United Kingdom is not our business, nor that of the libelant.

It is next urged that "restraint of princes," etc., does not terminate the charter, nor dissolve the contractual bonds between the parties thereto. Within limits that is true; but no rule can be understood, unless it be measured by the reason for its existence.

Ordinarily that governmental pressure, which is restraint, is but temporary; and the usual restraint clause, such as we have before us, is drawn on that assumption. Thus in *Clyde, Etc., Co. v. West India, Etc., Co.*, 169 Fed. 279, 94 C.C.A. 551, we found a quarantine detention to be within the restraint clause, and held that such temporary delay did not even stop the daily hire due by charter, not only because the words of the clause did not provide for such stoppage, but because the charterer "had the use of the vessel for which it was to pay, notwithstanding the interruption."

Whether a given act suspends or dissolves a relation is, like most matters, a question of degree. It was well put arguendo by Lord Haldane, when he pointed to the restraint clause as an instance of providing for the "partial or temporary suspension of certain obligations" of a charter, yet said:

> To the extent to which the perils mentioned interfere with the fulfillment of [charter] obligations, the parties are exempted from liability for nonperformance. *Tamplin, Etc., Co. v. Anglo-Mexican, Etc., Co.*, [1916] 2 A.C. 397, at pages 406-409.

Evidently the interference may be total; it may amount to prevention.

The same kind of restraint, the same act of power, may at one time or in one instance produce but a temporary delay, changing the contractual obligations of no one, and at another time, or when operating on other attending circumstances, may so change the relation of parties as to destroy the contract itself.

* * *

The relief afforded by the restraint clause is also too slow; one party always demands, both parties ought to ask, and in the interest of the public the law insists on knowing: How does the contract stand eo instanti the ship is taken away? Is the private contract living or dead, and, if dead, what killed it? This question cannot be answered by reference to the restraint clause, or any other expressed term of the written contract; therefore another legal creation, and one underlying the words chosen by the parties, is appealed to, and we find that this charter party ended or died, and its obligations were forever dissolved, on February 10, 1917, because the commercial adventure was then frustrated.

This phrase is said to have been born in the judgment in *Jackson v. Union Marine Ins. Co.*, L.R. 10 C.P. 125 (*Bank Line v. Capel* [1919] 1 A.C. 457); it has been the subject of recent exhaustive discussion in the House of Lords (*Horlock v. Beal* [1916] 1 A.C. 486, and the *Tamplin & Bank Line* Cases, *supra*), and the doctrine was recently applied in *The Allanwilde*, 248 U.S. 377, 39 Sup. Ct. 147, 63 L. Ed. 312, 3 A.L.R. 15, and *Lewis v. Mowinckel*, 215 Fed. 710, 132 C.C.A. 88. It is so authoritatively held in the cases cited, and those on which they rely, that the doctrine of frustration applies to a variety of maritime contracts including time charters, that more than mention of the fact scarcely seems necessary. In our judgment the justification for the holdings is best expressed by Lord Sumner (*Bank Line* Case, at page 454), in saying:

> Rights ought not to be left in suspense or to hang on the changes of subsequent events. The contract binds or it does not bind, and the law ought to be that the parties can gather their fate then and there.

But since parties almost never agree about it, courts must ascertain fate for them, by (says Lord Loreburn, in *Tamplin Case* at page 404) inferring, "from the nature of the contract and the surrounding circumstances, that a condition not expressed was a foundation on which the parties contracted." It follows naturally that, when the foundation is removed the superincumbent contract falls and dies; it is killed by that malignant disease—a change of circumstances. It may also be accepted on authority that frustration of adventure and termination of contract may be the instant result of an act which may be properly described as "restraint of princes," etc. Bank Line Case, at page 442.

Applying these rules to the facts before us, it being true that government on February 10, 1917, made it impossible for either Sutherland, Earn Line, or any other private individual to use the Claveresk, and did this under circumstances clearly showing to any sensible man that such indefinite taking would almost certainly outlast the life of the charter, it further appearing that the boat was so retained far beyond the charter period, and indeed (by admission at bar) still is kept by government (*cf.* BANK LINE CASE, at page 454), it follows as a conclusion of law that the charter party was terminated by frustration on February 10, 1917.

Although this result has been worked out in the highest British court with an enormous expenditure of writing, an examination of the case law relied on shows that the doctrine of frustration as applied to time charters is regarded as a logical outcome of the *Union Marine Insurance* Case, *supra*, and *Geipel v. Smith*, L.R. 7 Q.B. 404, which are likewise the precedents forming the foundations of *The Styria*, *supra*, and kindred decisions.

Indeed, we cannot think the doctrine new except in phraseology and application; for it is elementary that among the ways in which any contract ends and is dissolved is the cessation of existence of some thing, condition, or state of things, upon the continued existence of which the contract was known to depend, provided such cessation of existence arises without fault in either contracting party. JENKS, DIG. ENGLISH CIVIL LAW, bk. 2, part 1, § 297, citing cases.

In the present instance, what ceased to exist was Sutherland's control of the Claveresk; that swept away the foundation of contract, as thoroughly as might a fire or shipwreck. All arguments leading to an opposite result, all suggestions that such charter as this survived February 10, 1917, make of the superior force that removed every reasonable chance of doing what both parties expected to do when they agreed together, no more than an option to cancel, to be exercised after a nice calculation of possible loss or gain, by owner or charterer as the case may be. Indeed, there seems nothing left to cancel but a chance of loss; for never is it admitted that any portion of the charter survived seizure except the chance of gain. No suggestion of sharing loss is admitted.

* * *

This libel was brought, and, after pleading a breach, could be brought, for libelant's damages only; what is now demanded is respondent's alleged profits. Profits are not damages, and Sutherland's gains are not Earn Line's losses. The first statement is elementary law; the second is a fact obvious from the evidence. Whether, after a contract is dissolved without fault in either party, there can therefrom arise or remain any contractual relation between the parties, except for matters preceding dissolution; whether, if such a demand as has been stated exists at all, it is legal or equitable (*cf. Agency, Etc., Co. v. American, Etc., Co., supra*); whether admiralty has any jurisdiction affording recovery either of the certain sum suggested by the "replication" or of a sum reachable only on accounting; whether Earn Line's demand is affected by the subcharter; and what are the rights of the subcharterer—are questions not before us on the pleadings, and matters on which the apostles are empty of sufficient evidence to justify findings, were they permissible.

We hold, then, only that no breach of charter party has been shown, wherefore no damages can be recovered, and damages only were demanded. Beyond this it is not necessary to go; if these findings are at variance with some of the reasoning of the learned court in *The Isle of Mull* (D.C.) 257 Fed. 798, we prefer the views above expressed; but we are not informed as to the pleadings in that case.

Decree affirmed, with costs.

Notes

1.' [F]rustration occurs whenever the law recognizes that without default of either party a contractual obligation has become incapable of being performed because the circumstances in which performance is called for would render it a thing radically different from that which was undertaken by the contract. *Non haec in foedera veni*—it was not that I promised to do.'
The Newa, [1981] 2 Lloyd's L. Rep. 239, 253.

2. *Transatlantic Financing Corporation v. United States*, 363 F.2d 312, 66 AMC 1455 (D.C. Cir. 1966) involved a voyage charter party entered into on October, 2, 1956, covering carriage of a cargo of wheat from a United States Gulf Port to a safe port in Iran. On October 29, 1956, Israel invaded Egypt. On October 31, 1956, Great Britain and France invaded the Suez Canal Zone. On November 2, 1956, the Egyptian Government obstructed the Suez Canal with sunken vessels and closed it to traffic. Although the Suez Canal was generally regarded as the customary route for the voyage, the charterer told the owner that it expected it to carry out its obligations under the charter. The owner made the voyage via the Cape of Good Hope. The use of this route entailed more expense for the owner. Owner sued charterer in *quantum meruit*. Its theory of recovery was that the original charter had been frustrated and that when it complied with charterers demand that the cargo be delivered it was entitled to additional compensation. The Court of Appeals affirmed the dismissal of the owner's claim.

The Court drew an analogy with and relied heavily on the rules used to decide ordinary land based contractual disputes, namely the doctrine of impossibility of contract.

When the issue is raised, the court is asked to construct a condition of performance based on the changed circumstances, a process which involves at least three reasonably definable steps. First, a contingency—something unexpected—must have occurred. Second, the risk of the unexpected occurrence must not have been allocated either by agreement or by custom. Finally, occurrence of the contingency must have rendered performance commercially impracticable. Unless the court finds these three requirements satisfied, the plea of impossibility must fail.

The first requirement was met here. It seems reasonable, where no route is mentioned in a contract, to assume the parties expected performance by the usual and customary route at the time of contract. Since the usual and customary route from Texas to Iran at the time of contract was through Suez, closure of the Canal made impossible the expected method of performance. But this unexpected development raises rather than resolves the impossibility issue, which turns additionally on whether the risk of the contingency's occurrence had been allocated and, if not, whether performance by alternative routes was rendered impracticable.

Proof that the risk of a contingency's occurrence has been allocated may be expressed in or implied from the agreement. Such proof may also be found in the surrounding circumstances, including custom and usages of the trade. The contract in this case does not expressly condition performance upon availability of the Suez route. Nor does it specify "via Suez" or on the other hand, "via Suez or Cape of Good Hope." Nor are there provisions in the contract from which we may properly imply that the continued availability of Suez was a condition of performance. Nor is there anything in custom or trade usage, or in the surrounding circumstances generally, which would support our constructing a condition of performance. The numerous cases requiring performance around the Cape when Suez was closed, *see e.g., Ocean Tramp Tankers Corp. v. V/O Sovfracht (The Eugenia)*, [1964] 2 Q.B. 226, and cases cited therein, indicate that the Cape route is generally regarded as an alternative means of performance. So the implied expectation that the route would be via Suez is hardly adequate proof of an allocation to the promisee of the risk of closure. In some cases, even an express expectation may not amount to a condition of performance.

The doctrine of deviation supports our assumption that parties normally expect performance by the usual and customary route, but it adds nothing beyond this that is probative of an allocation of the risk.

If anything, the circumstances surrounding this contract indicate that the risk of the Canal's closure may be deemed to have been allocated to Transatlantic. We know or may safely assume that the parties were aware, as were most commercial men with interests affected by the Suez situation, *see The Eugenia, supra,* that the Canal might become a dangerous area. No doubt the tension affected freight rates, and it is arguable that the risk of closure became part of the dickered terms. We do not deem the risk of closure so allocated, however. Foreseeability or even recognition of a risk does not necessarily prove its allocation. Parties to a contract are not always able to provide for all the possibilities of which they are aware, sometimes because they cannot agree, often simply because they are too busy. Moreover, that some abnormal risk was contemplated is probative but does not necessarily establish an allocation of the risk of the contingency which actually occurs. In this case, for example, nationalization by Egypt of the Canal Corporation and formation of the Suez Users Group did not necessarily indicate that the Canal would be blocked even if a confrontation resulted. The surrounding circumstances do indicate, however, a willingness by Transatlantic to assume abnormal risks, and this fact should legitimately cause us to judge the impracticability of performance by an alternative route in stricter terms than we would were the contingency unforeseen.

We turn then to the question whether occurrence of the contingency rendered performance commercially impracticable under the circumstances of this case. The goods shipped were not subject to harm from the longer, less temperate Southern route. The vessel and crew were fit to proceed around the Cape. Transatlantic was no less able than the United States to purchase insurance to cover the contingency's occurrence. If anything, it is more reasonable to expect owner-operators of vessels to insure against the hazards of war. They are in the best position to calculate the cost of performance by alternative routes (and therefore to estimate the amount of insurance required), and are undoubtedly sensitive to international troubles which uniquely affect the demand for and cost of their services. The only factor operating here in appellant's favor is the added expense, allegedly $43,972.00 above and beyond the contract price of $305,842.92, of extending a 10,000 mile voyage by approximately 3,000 miles. While it may be an overstatement to say that increased cost and difficulty of performance never constitute impracticability, to justify relief there must be more of a variation between expected cost and the cost of performing by an available alternative than is present in this case, where the promisor can legitimately be presumed to have accepted some degree of abnormal risk, and where impracticability is urged on the basis of added expense alone.

We conclude, therefore, as have most other courts considering related issues arising out of the Suez closure that performance of this contract was not rendered legally impossible. Even if we agreed with appellant, its theory of relief seems untenable. When performance of a contact is deemed impossible it is a nullity. In the case of a charter party involving carriage of goods, the carrier may return to an appropriate port and unload its cargo, *The Malcolm Baxter, Jr.,* 277 U.S. 323, 48 S. Ct. 516, 72 L. Ed. 901 (1928), subject of course to required steps to minimize damages. If the performance rendered has value, recovery in *quantum meruit* for the entire performance is proper. But here Transatlantic has collected its contract price, and now seeks *quantum meruit* relief for the additional expense of the trip around the Cape. If the contract is a nullity, Transatlantic's theory of relief should have been quantum meruit for the entire trip, rather than only for the extra expense. Transatlantic attempts to take its profit on the contract, and then force the Government to absorb the cost of the additional voyage. When impracticability without fault occurs, the law seeks an equitable solution, and *quantum meruit* is one of its potent devices to achieve this end. There is no interest in casting the entire burden of commercial disaster on one party in order to preserve the other's profit. Apparently the contract price in this case was advantageous enough to deter appellant from taking a stance on damages consistent with its theory of liability. In any event, there is no basis for relief.

Affirmed.

3. Depending on their duration, delays during the charter period may frustrate the charterparty contract. If the delay appears at the outset to be only temporary (unlike that in *The Claveresk, supra,* which appeared from the outset to be of indefinite duration), the question of whether the contract is frustrated depends on the probable length of delay, considered as a proportion of the time that the charter period has left to run. The delay must be of sufficient duration to deprive the parties of the commercial benefit of their original bargain. For example, many charterparties were frustrated by the outbreak of hostilities between Iran and Iraq in 1980, which trapped some 60 ships in the Shatt-al-Arab waterway leading to the port of Basrah. The outbreak of hostilities did not *ipso facto* frustrate time charterparties of the trapped ships, as initially it was possible that it might be of short duration only. The charterparties were frustrated only when it became clear that the conflict would continue for a sufficient period to bring an end to the contracts as commercial propositions. *International Sea Tankers Inc. v. Hemisphere Shipping Co. Ltd (The Wenjiang)(No. 2)* [1983] 2 Lloyd's Rep. 400; *Vinava Shipping Co. Ltd v. Finelvet A.G. (The Chrysalis)* [1983] 2 Lloyd's Rep. 503.

5. Redelivery*

a. Overlap and Underlap

PREBENSENS DAMPSKIBSSELSKABET A/S v. MUNSON S.S. LINE
258 F. 227 (2d Cir. 1919)

WARD, Circuit Judge

October 31, 1912, her owners chartered the steamer Falk to the Munson Line "for a period of about 36 calendar months (term of charter party to be understood to mean a month more or less)" from the time of delivery. The charter party was of the usual time charter form and contained the following articles:

4.   That the charterers shall pay for the use and hire of the said vessel nine hundred and fifty pounds British sterling (£950) per calendar month, commencing on and from the day of her delivery, as aforesaid, and at and after the same rate for any part of a month; hire to continue until her delivery, with clean holds to the owners (unless lost) at a port in the United Kingdom or on the continent between Bordeaux and Hamburg, both inclusive (Rouen excluded), at charterers' option.

5.   That should the steamer be on her voyage towards the port of return delivery at the time a payment of hire becomes due, said payment shall be made for such length of time as the owners or their agents and charterers or their agents may agree upon as the estimated time necessary to complete the voyage, and when the steamer is delivered to owner's agents any difference shall be refunded by steamer or paid by charterers, as the case may require.

January 20, 1913, the steamer was delivered to the charterer and redelivered by it to the owners March 1, 1916, to which date the charterer paid hire at the charter rate.

The owners contend that the term ended January 20, 1916, with a permissible overlap or underlap of one month, so that the charterer was liable until February 20, 1916, at the charter rate of freight, and for the 10 days thereafter until redelivery at the market rate of freight; the same amounting to about $9,000, to recover which this libel was filed. The charterer, on the other hand, contends that it is liable only at the charter rate of freight until the actual redelivery, March 1, 1916. Judge Mayer sustained the owner's contention and entered a decree for the libelant.

We think the construction of these articles is made clear by former decisions in this circuit. In the case of charters for a fixed time Judge Addison Brown held that the charterer was entitled to a reasonable overlap at the charter rate of freight. *Straits of Dover S.S. Co. v. Munson (D.C.)* 95 Fed. 690; *Anderson v. Munson (D.C.)* 104 Fed. 915. In the case of charters for "about" a named time, we have held that the charterer is entitled to a reasonable underlap as well as overlap. *The Rygja*, 161 Fed. 106, 88 C.C.A. 270; *Trechmann S.S. Co. v. Munson Line*, 203 Fed. 692, 121 C.C.A. 650.

* * *

But we construe the charter in this case as being for a term of 36 months, with a permitted underlap or overlap of 1 month. It is an "about" term charter, with the "about" period defined to be 1 month. Accordingly for any overlap beyond 37 months the charterer must pay at the market rate. The owners contend that the reasoning as to the difficulty of estimating the market rate of freight at a time of redelivery in the future is the same in this case as it was in the case of *Ropner v. S.S. Co.* But this subordinate consideration, which was consistent with the primary ground of decision in that case, must yield to the primary ground of decision in this case, with which it is not consistent. The charterer being liable to pay the market rate of freight after the expiration of the term of 36 months

---

* Redelivery problems occur in time and bareboat charter situations.

and the permitted overlap of 1 month, and the last installment falling due before the time of actual redelivery, the natural estimate as to the rate of freight would seem to have been the rate prevailing at the time the installment fell due. Both the estimated time and the estimated freight were to be corrected, if necessary, at the time of redelivery. The decree is affirmed.

BRITAIN S.S. CO. v. MUNSON S.S. LINE

31 F.2d 530 (2d Cir.), *cert. denied*, 280 U.S. 574, 50 S. Ct. 29, 74 L. Ed. 625 (1929)

From a decree in admiralty, awarding damages to the owner of the British steamship Putney for a redelivery of the vessels before the expiration of a time charter, and for a wrongful deduction from the charter hire of expenses of fumigation, the charterer has appealed. Modified.

By the terms of the charter party the Putney was let to the Munson Steamship Line "from the time of delivery, for about two (2) to about three (3) consecutive calendar months," to be employed between ports within specified geographical limits, and to be redelivered at a safe United States Atlantic port north of Cape Hatteras. The ship was delivered on March 20, 1925, at Matanzas, Cuba. She loaded there a cargo of sugar, discharged it at New York, and returned to Cuba for a second cargo, which she discharged at New York by May 7th. On that date, which was 13 days before the expiration of 2 months from the date of delivery, the charterer tendered redelivery of the vessel, which the owner accepted under protest. On May 9th a new charter was made between the parties, without prejudice to the rights of either, for one round trip from the United States to the West Indies, within limits as specified in the original charter, but at a lower rate of hire. Under this second charter the Putney was delivered May 13th, and made a voyage to Cuba and return. She was redelivered on June 23d, which was 3 months and 3 days after her original delivery on March 20th.

During the charterer's operation of the vessel in April, 1925, she was required by the quarantine officer at New York to under go fumigation. This was demanded under sections 102 and 103 of the Quarantine Laws and Regulations, because she had not been fumigated in nearly 2 years and had visited a Mediterranean port within the previous 4 months (before chartered to the appellant). The cost of fumigation and charter hire for the time it took were deducted by the charterer from the hire.

By a libel *in personam* the owner sought to recover these deductions for fumigation, as well as charter hire at the original rate from May 7 to June 23, less credit for hire paid under the second charter. On conflicting testimony the court found that a reasonable estimate of the time required for a voyage from New York to Cuba and return was 21 to 24 days. It was held that the redelivery on May 7th was premature, that hire at the original rate was payable until redelivery on June 23d, and that the expense of fumigation was upon the charterer. The opinion is reported in (D.C) 25 F.(2d) 868.

* * *

SWAN, Circuit Judge (after stating the facts as above):

When a charter party is for a term of "about six months," or other stated period, the use of the word "about" is interpreted as signifying an intention to allow the charterer a reasonable leeway in respect to the date on which the vessel shall be surrendered. It is a recognition, based on the necessities of practical business, that her voyages cannot be planned so accurately as to bring her home on an exact date, and that the parties have contemplated the possibility of a reasonable shortening or lengthening of the stated term. Hence, if a voyage terminates in a port of redelivery before the end of the stated term, the charterer may require the vessel to make another "reasonable" voyage, even though it is certain to overlap the stated term. If however, the time remaining before the end of the stated term is so short as to render another voyage "unreasonable," then the vessel may be surrendered by the charterer, or withdrawn by the owner, thus creating an underlap. These rules have been often stated by this court. *The Rygja* (C.C.A.) 161 F. 106; *Trechmann S.S. Co., Limited v. Munson S. S. Line* (C.C.A.) 203 F. 692; *Munson S.S. Line v. Elswick Steam*

Shipping Co., 207 F. 984 (D.C. N.Y), *affirmed* (C.C.A.) 214 F. 84 *Damp Skibs, Etc., v. Tropical Fruit Co.* (C.C.A.) 281 F. 749; *The Negus*, 298 F. 747 (D.C.N.Y.), *affirmed* (C.C.A.) 298 F. 752.

In the case at bar the District Court held that the phrase "for about two (2) to about three (3) consecutive calendar months" permitted no surrender of the vessel before May 20th; in other words, that there could be no underlap to the term of two months from her delivery. There is much force in the charterer's argument that the use of two "abouts" shows an intention to allow latitude at each end of the two to three month term, and that the court's construction gives no effect whatever to the first "about." But even if the charterer's construction be adopted, and it be conceded that an underlap would have been permissible under some circumstances, the option to surrender could be validly exercised on May 7th only if no "reasonable" voyage were then available. On conflicting evidence the court found that a reasonable estimate of the time required for a voyage from New York to Cuba and return was from 21 to 24 days. This finding is sufficiently supported to be accepted on appeal. It shows that the probable overlap from undertaking the voyage would be less than the 13-day underlap which would result from surrendering her on May 7th. Under such surrendering we think the voyage was reasonable in respect to its probable duration. So much is at least implied, if not decided, in *The Negus* and in *Trechmann v. Munson, supra.* That the voyage was commercially practicable and available to the charterer seems to be sufficiently demonstrated by the actual voyage under the charter of May 9th. Hence we agree with the court's conclusion that the redelivery on May 7th was premature and ineffective.

So we come to the question of damages. Where the charterer is privileged to make a voyage which will result in an overlap, and actually makes it, he must pay hire at the charter rate until redelivery. *Straits of Dover S.S. Co. v. Munson*, 95 F. 690 (D.C.) *affirmed* 100 F. 1005 (C.C.A. 2); *Anderson v. Munson*, 104 F. 913 (D.C.); *Ropner v. Inter-American S.S. Co.*, 243 F. 549 (C.C.A. 2). The instant case presents the problem of what hire is payable where an overlapping voyage is privileged, but is not made; for the voyage performed under the second charter was without prejudice. The owner argues that, where an overlapping voyage is permissible, it is compulsory.

It is true that, in *Munson S.S. Line v. Elswick Steam Shipping Co., Supra*, Judge Veeder says (page 991): "... If the voyage be reasonable its is compulsory; that is, the charter hire must be paid." And similar language, relying upon the *Elswick* Case, may be found in Judge Hough's opinion in *Dampskibs, etc., v. Tropical Fruit Co., supra*, at page 742. Both of these statements, however, were plain obiter, and it is clear that Judge Veeder's dictum cannot have the meaning ascribed to it by the appellee, because later in the same paragraph he adds: "... The owner either gets his vessel back if no such voyage is practicable, or, if it is practicable and not ordered by the charterer, his charter hire to the end of the specified term."

In affirming Judge Veeder's opinion, we expressly reserved a decision on this point. It was, however, decided in *Trechmann v. Munson, supra.* That case held that, where the charterer could have set out upon an overlapping voyage, but refused to do so, such refusal did not entitle the owner to hire during the assumed duration of such a voyage, but only to the date when the vessel could be legally redelivered. There a vessel chartered for "about 12 months" was surrendered 29 days before the expiration of the 12-month period. A voyage which would take 43 days was available to her. To reduce the loss, the parties made a second charter, without prejudice, at a lower rate. This voyage took 59 days. The owner claimed hire at the original charter rate for the full 59 days. The District Court allowed the original rate for 43 days. On appeal, the owner was awarded the original rate for only 29 days; that is, until the expiration of the stated term of the charter.

It is clear that the charterer is under no duty to the owner to employ the vessel; his full duty is performed by paying hire to the end of the term agreed upon. On May 20th, the charterer could have made a valid redelivery. The option which the charterer had to use her beyond May 20th cannot give the owner the right to insist that the charterer shall do so. To say that it does is to put the charterer's arrangements at the owner's mercy, which is precisely the opposite of what is intended by the charter. So the damages should be limited to the difference between the two charter hires until the expiration of two months; that is, until May 20th.

* * *

Note

The position taken by the parties in an overlap/underlap dispute is driven primarily by the relationship between the charterparty rate of hire and the prevailing market rate at the end of the charter period. In *Torvald Klaveness A/S v. Arni Maritime Corp. (The Gregos)* [1995] 1 Lloyd's Rep. 1, 4 (H.L.), Lord Mustill said:

> "Where the charter-party is for a period of time rather than a voyage, and the remuneration is calculated according to the time used rather than the service performed, the risk of delay is primarily on the charterer. For the shipowner, so long as he commits no breach and nothing puts the ship off-hire, his right to remuneration is unaffected by a disturbance of the charterer's plans. It is for the latter to choose between cautious planning, which may leave gaps between employments, and bolder scheduling with the risk of setting aims which cannot be realized in practice.
>
> This distribution of risk holds good during for most of the chartered service. As the time for redelivery approaches things become more complicated. (The word 'redelivery' is inaccurate, but it is convenient, and I will use it). If the market is rising, the charterer wants to have the use of the vessel at the chartered rate for as long as possible. Conversely, the shipowner must think ahead to the next employment, and if as is common he has made a forward fixture he will be in difficulties if the vessel is retained by the charterer longer than had been foreseen. This conflict of interest becomes particularly acute when there is time left for only one more voyage before the expiry of the charter, and disputes may arise if the charterer orders the ship to perform a service which the shipowner believes will extend beyond the date fixed for redelivery."

Conversely, if the market is falling, the charterer wants to redeliver the vessel as soon as possible so as to get out of the now disadvantageous charter rate and take advantage of the new, low, market rate. That is the sub-text that explains cases like *Britain S.S. Co. v. Munson S.S. Line*, supra.

---

6. Remedies: Damages—Withdrawal

DIANA CO. MARITIMA, S.A. OF PANAMA v. SUBFREIGHTS OF S.S. ADMIRALTY FLYER

280 F. Supp. 607 (S.D.N.Y. 1968)

Opinion

HERLANDS, District Judge

Petitioner, Diana Compania Maritima, S.A. of Panama [hereinafter "Owner"], owner of the S.S. Admiralty Flyer moves for (1) an order, pursuant to Section 9 of the Federal Arbitration Act, 9 U.S.C. § 9,[1] confirming an arbitration award rendered between the Owner and Admiralty Lines, Ltd. [hereinafter "Charterer"], and (2) an order releasing the subfreights of the Admiralty Flyer presently held by the Clerk of the United States District Court for the Southern District of New York.[2] The trustee in bankruptcy of the Charterer [hereinafter "Trustee"] objects to the release of the subfreights but does not object to the confirmation of the arbitration award. For the reasons hereinafter set forth, the Owner's motions are granted in all respects.

In order to place this motion in proper context, the Court will fully explicate the sequence of events leading to this motion as well as all facts material to its disposition. Many of these facts are either undisputed or have been conclusively determined.[3]

---

[1] Section 9 of the Arbitration Act pertinently provides:

> If the parties in their agreement have agreed that a judgment of the court shall be entered upon the award made pursuant to the arbitration, and shall specify the court, then at any time within one year after the award is made any party to the arbitration may apply to the court so specified for an order confirming the award, and thereupon the court must grant such an order unless the award is vacated, modified, or corrected as prescribed in sections 10 and 11 of this title. If no court is specified in the agreement of the parties, then such application may be made to the United States court in and for the district within which such award was made. Notice of the application shall be served upon the adverse party, and thereupon the court shall have jurisdiction of such party as though he had appeared generally in the proceeding.

[2] According to the Cashier of the Clerk of this Court, the fund presently amounts to $27,163.06.

[3] Many of the facts set forth have been found by the arbitrators and are, therefore, binding on the parties. *James Richardson & Sons, Ltd. v. W. E. Hedger Transp. Corp.*, 98 F.2d 55 (2nd Cir. 1938). See *South East Atlantic Shipping Ltd. v. Garnac Grain Company*, 356 F.2d 189, 191-192 (2nd Cir. 1966).

On May 4, 1965, the Charterer entered into a time charter party[4] with the Commercial Steamship Company, agents for the Owner of the Admiralty Flyer. The agreement provided that the Charterer would hire the vessel for a period of about 18 to 21 months, payment of hire to be made "monthly in advance". The vessel was presented to the Charterer on July 9, 1965, and proceeded on its voyage.

On November 9, 1965, the Charterer defaulted in payment of hire due on that date. At the time of default, the vessel was proceeding toward Capetown, South Africa, where an additional breach of the charter party occurred when the Charterer failed to supply fuel.

On November 23, 1965, the Owner sent a telegram to the Charterer, giving notice of withdrawal of the vessel. The telegram read:

"IN VIEW OF YOUR BREACH OF THE TIME CHARTER BY FAILURE TO PAY HIGHER (SIC) ON THE ADMIRALTY FLIER AND YOUR FAILURE TO SUPPLY THE VESSEL WITH BUNKERS YOU ARE HEREBY NOTIFIED THAT THE VESSEL IS WITHDRAWN BECAUSE OF YOUR BREACH AND OWNER IS TAKING STEPS TO MITIGATE DAMAGES OWNER HOLDS YOU RESPONSIBLE FOR ALL DIRECT AND CONSEQUENTIAL DAMAGES RESULTING FROM YOUR BREACH." (Charterer's Rebuttal Affidavit, Exhibit A)

The notice of withdrawal was given pursuant to clause 5 of the charter party.[5]

On November 29, 1965, the Owner filed a libel against the freights and subfreights of the Admiralty Flyer and attached certain subfreights in the hands of 14 cargo consignees.

Upon the arrival of the Admiralty Flyer at the United States Gulf Ports on December 25, 1965, the Owner retained possession of the cargo.

Upon motion of certain of the cargo consignees, this Court, on December 30, 1965, ordered the consignees to pay the freight due into court. This "Interim Order No. 1" provided that, upon payment, the Owner would release the cargo from the "possessory lien". The Court indicated that the purpose of the order was to serve as a method to substitute money deposits of freights due ... [for the asserted liens] in order to facilitate the release of said cargo and subfreights from the liens asserted....

In short, the order served as a practical method of releasing the cargoes and removing the consignees from a litigation in which they had neither an actual interest nor possible liability beyond the amount of the freights due.

Since the only persons legally interested in the fund being held by the Clerk of the Court were the Owner and the Charterer, this Court, on January 3, 1966, ordered the Owner and Charterer to proceed to arbitration in accordance with clause 17 of the charter party.[6] The Court retained jurisdiction to enter a decree upon the award.

After three arbitration hearings had been held, an involuntary bankruptcy petition was filed against the Charterer on February 4, 1966. On March 15, 1966, the Charterer was adjudicated a bankrupt.

---

[4] The time charter party is the standard government form of the New York Produce Exchange.

[5] The precise wording of the withdrawal clause is:

> ... otherwise failing the punctual and regular payment of the hire ... , or on any breach of this Charter Party, the Owners shall be at liberty to withdraw the vessel from the service of the Charterers, without prejudice to any claim they (the Owners) may otherwise have on the Charterers.

[6] The arbitration clause in the charter party provides:

> "That should *any dispute* arise between Owners and the Charterers, the matter in dispute shall be referred to three persons at New York, one to be appointed by each of the parties thereto, and the third by the two so chosen; their decision or that of any two of them, *shall be final*, and for the purpose of enforcing any award, this agreement may be made a rule of the Court. The Arbitrators shall be commercial men." (Emphasis added)

* * *

After the appointment of the Charterer's trustee in bankruptcy, a final arbitration hearing was held on May 10, 1967. The Trustee did not appear at this final hearing although prior written notice and a request to appear had been sent to the attorney for the Trustee. The "special admiralty counsel" to the attorney for the Trustee was also advised that he had 10 days to submit additional testimony; but he declined to do so.

The arbitration award, rendered on June 26, 1967, determined, *inter alia*, (1) that the Owner was entitled to withdraw the Admiralty Flyer; and (2) that the Owner sustained net damages of $40,605.95.

In opposition to the motion to release the subfreights to the Owner, the Trustee argues (1) that there is no maritime lien covering all the subfreights held by the Court; (2) that even if there is a valid maritime lien, transfer to the Owner of the funds held by the Court would run afoul of either Bankruptcy Act § 67(a), 11 U.S.C. § 107(a), or Bankruptcy Act § 60, 11 U.S.C. § 96; and (3) that an arbitration award rendered between the Owner and the Charterer cannot determine rights *in rem* in the subfreights held by the Court, and, therefore, cannot be adopted by an admiralty court as the basis of a judgment *in rem*.

I.

A shipowner's lien on earned subfreights due to a charterer is not created by general maritime law. Inclusion of an express lien clause in the charter of the vessel earning the subfreights is necessary. *Ocean Cargo Lines, Ltd. v. North Atlantic Marine Co.*, 227 F. Supp. 872 (S.D.N.Y. 1964); *In re North Atlantic and Gulf Steamship Co.*, 204 F. Supp. 899 (S.D.N.Y. 1962), and cases cited therein, affirmed *sub nom. Schilling v. A/S/D/S Dannebrog*, 320 F.2d 628 (2nd Cir. 1963); GILMORE AND BLACK, ADMIRALTY 517, n.103 (1957).

If an express lien clause is included in the charter, the shipowner has a maritime lien on the subfreights from the moment the cargo is loaded on the vessel. *Krauss Bros. Lumber Co. v. Dimon S.S. Corp.*, 290 U.S. 117, 121, 54 S. Ct. 105, 78 L. Ed. 216 (1933); *The Saturnus*, 250 F. 407, 412, 414 (2Nd Cir. 1918), *cert. denied sub nom. Midland Linseed Products Company v. The Steamship "Saturnus"*, 247 U.S. 521, 38 S. Ct. 583, 62 L. Ed. 1247 (1918); *In re North Atlantic and Gulf Steamship Co.*, 204 F. Supp. at 904; *In re Bauer Steamship Corporation*, 167 F. Supp. 909, 910 (S.D.N.Y. 1957).

In the instant case, the time charter contains a clause creating a lien on freights and subfreights. The clause provides:

18. That the Owners shall have a lien upon all cargoes, and all subfreights for any amounts due under this charter....

By this clause, the Charterer's lien against the consignees to secure the subfreights is made subject to the Owner's lien against cargoes and subfreights. *In re North Atlantic and Gulf S.S. Co., supra; In re Bauer S.S. Corp., supra.* Moreover, the Owner's lien was not relinquished by this Court's order directing payment of the subfreights into Court. The Trustee, however, argues that the maritime lien does not extend to all the funds held by this Court. It is his contention that the "present" language contained in the Owner's notice of withdrawal of November 23, 1965 and the resultant exercise of control over the Admiralty Flyer by the Owner show that withdrawal of the vessel took place on that date.

The effect of withdrawal of a vessel is to terminate the charter party. *Ocean Cargo Lines, Ltd. v. North Atlantic Marine Co.*, 227 F. Supp. at 881. There is no dispute that the Admiralty Flyer was withdrawn; the only question is *when* was the withdrawal "effective." The significance of the date when the withdrawal became effective is that the amount of the Owner's lien is computed as of that date.

The notice of withdrawal herein clearly speaks in "present" terms. It states that "... you are hereby notified that the vessel is withdrawn ... and owner is taking steps to mitigate damages." In addition, the arbitrators found:

6.   Owners in mitigation of damages, obtained additional cargo for the vessel at Walvis Bay, South Africa, for discharge at United States Gulf Ports and did pay all expenses incident to the loading carriage and discharge of said cargo including those which would properly have been the obligation of the Time Charterers.

It is this latter fact upon which the Trustee places chief reliance to support his assertion that the Charterer was deprived of control of the vessel on, or about, November 23, 1965, the date of the notice of withdrawal.

In the leading case of *Luckenbach v. Pierson*, 229 F. 130 (2nd Cir. 1915), the time charter provided that hire was to be paid semi-monthly in advance, with the shipowner having the "faculty of withdrawing the said steamer" upon default of such payment. Hire due on June 11, 1906 was already in arrears when the shipowner, on June 27, wrote the charterer that, if the arrears were not paid "... by four o'clock this afternoon, I *will withdraw* said steamer from your service...." At that time, the vessel was being loaded in port. However, the shipowner did not withdraw the vessel on that date. Instead, the vessel sailed; and, on June 30th, the shipowner informed the charterer that the vessel would be withdrawn at the end of the trip.

The Court held that the vessel was not withdrawn on June 27, the date of the notice of withdrawal, because the shipowner allowed the vessel to "proceed on her voyage, a proceeding entirely inconsistent with a then withdrawal" (229 F. at 132). The Court observed that the shipowner could have withdrawn the vessel on the date of the notice of withdrawal by relanding the cargo.

It should be noted that the notice of withdrawal in *Luckenbach* clearly contained "present language"; however, that fact was not deemed controlling. *Cf. Jebsen v. A Cargo of Hemp*, 228 F. 143, 149 (D. Mass. 1915) (date of withdrawal determined from owner's conduct controls despite contrary indication in notice of withdrawal).

Judge Ward, writing for the Court of Appeals for this Circuit in *Luckenbach*, stated the rule to be applied:
[The] withdrawal of a vessel from a charter party means that the owner shall deprive the charterer of any further enjoyment or use of the vessel and take it into his own exclusive possession. This can be presently done, even where the vessel is at sea, *provided she is light; but if there be any cargo on board no withdrawal can be made until the cargo be relanded if the vessel is at the loading port, or until it be discharged if she is at sea or at destination.* (229 F. at 132) (Emphasis added)

The rule of *Luckenbach v. Pierson* has recently been followed and approved in this circuit, *Ocean Cargo Lines, Ltd. v. North Atlantic Marine Co.*, 227 F. Supp. 872, 881 (S.D.N.Y. 1964), and in the Ninth Circuit, *Schirmer Stevedoring Co., Ltd. v. Seaboard Stevedoring Corp.*, 306 F.2d 188, 193 (9th Cir. 1962).[7]

Applying the rule of *Luckenbach v. Pierson* to the instant case, the Court holds that withdrawal of the Admiralty Flyer did not become effective until the cargoes were discharged at the United States Gulf ports in December of 1965. As *Luckenbach* makes clear, the language of the notice of withdrawal is not controlling. The Court rejects the Trustee's argument that the Owner assumed control of the Admiralty Flyer by loading additional cargo at Walvis Bay, South Africa because the Owner could not recharter the vessel until all of the cargo was discharged at the Gulf Ports. Since *Luckenbach v. Pierson* is based upon the assumption that a shipowner cannot have "exclusive possession" or control of his vessel while the charterer's cargo is aboard, obedience to that rule requires a holding that no withdrawal of the Admiralty Flyer became effective due merely to the loading of the additional cargo at Walvis Bay.

* * *

---

[7] The Trustee places some reliance on *Italian State Ry. v. Mavrogordatos*, [1919] 2 K.B. 305, which held that a withdrawal was effective immediately even though a vessel was on the high seas. *Italian State Ry.* represents the English rule as to when a notice of withdrawal is effective. *See* SCRUTTON, CHARTERPARTIES AND BILLS OF LADING (17th ed. 1964) 355; CARVER, CARRIAGE BY SEA (11th ed. Colinvaux 1963) 388. But the English rule is clearly contrary to that which is the law in the Second Circuit. Moreover, *Italian State Ry.* is factually distinguishable: the vessel had no cargo aboard and was proceeding toward the point of redelivery when the notice of withdrawal was sent.

Since this Court has determined that the withdrawal was effective at the time the cargo was discharged, the Owner has a lien on "any amounts due" under the charter as of that date. *See Luckenbach v. Pierson*, 229 F. at 133; *Freights of the Kate*, 63 F. 707, 722 (S.D.N.Y. 1894); *Ocean Cargo Lines, Ltd. v. North Atlantic Marine Co.*, 227 F. Supp. at 881. The lien on the subfreights presently held by this Court is, therefore, valid under maritime law.

* * *

Notes

1. In *Finora Co., Inc. v. Amitie Shipping, Ltd*, 54 F.3d 209, 212, 1995 AMC 2014 (4th Cir. 1995), the court said:

[T]o perfect liens on subfreights for unpaid charter hire, vessel owners must give *clear* notice to third parties *before* those parties pay subfreights to charterers. The notice should inform third-party obligors of the existence of the lien, the legal basis for the lien, and the fact that the lienholder intends to exercise it. If clear notice is not provided, the third party's obligations are discharged by payment to the charterer. [Emphasis in original.]

2. The key to understanding the parties' motivation in relation to withdrawal is consideration of the prevailing market rate of hire at the time the shipowner's right of withdrawal arises. In a rising market, the shipowner is keen to withdraw the vessel from the charterer's service as early as possible, to take advantage of the new, higher, market rate. In a falling market, the shipowner is reluctant to withdraw, preferring to keep the vessel at the charterer's service under the existing contract with its higher-than-market hire rate.

3. Under English law, withdrawal of a ship for non-payment of hire is effective immediately. If the ship is in the middle of a carrying voyage when withdrawal occurs (as it was in *Diana Co. Maritima*, supra), the charterer is left with little choice but to charter the vessel back from the shipowner at the new, higher, market rate, or even at a rate higher than the market. The English courts have refused to intervene in such cases, saying that there is no basis for equity to intervene to relieve commercial parties from the consequences of an unfavorable bargain. *Mardorf Peach & Co. Ltd v. Attica Sea Carriers Corp. of Liberia (The Laconia)* [1977] A.C. 850 (H.L.).

F. Safe Port—Safe Berth

ORDUNA S.A. v. ZEN-NOH GRAIN CORPORATION

913 F.2d 1149, 1991 AMC 346 (5th Cir. 1990)

W. Eugene Davis, Circuit Judge

While loading a ship, a loading arm fell from a grain elevator tower causing the ship damage. The district court found the elevator operator, the designer of the tower, and the ship's charterer liable for that damage. The various parties have filed multiple appeals and cross-appeals raising several issues. We affirm in part, reverse in part, and remand the case to the district court.

I. Facts

In March 1984, a steel loading arm fell from a grain elevator on the Mississippi River onto the deck of the M/V TREBIZOND which was loading cargo in the berth below. This incident damaged the ship and delayed its departure. The shipowners, Orduna, S.A. and Transglobal Maritime Corporation (collectively Orduna), sued its voyage charterers, Euro-Frachtkontor G.m.b.H. (Euro); the owner and operator of the grain elevator, Zen-Noh Grain Corporation (Zen-Noh); the design engineering firm of the collapsed structure, F & P Engineers, Inc. (collectively, with its insurers, F & P); and the loading arm manufacturer, Buhler-Miag, Inc. (Buhler). These defendants filed a flurry of cross-claims and third-party claims among themselves.

Following a bench trial, the district court found Zen-Noh and F & P jointly and severally liable to Orduna. The district court awarded Orduna $ 378,528.75 in damages with interest running from date of judgment. The court also found Euro liable to Orduna, but granted Euro full indemnification from Zen-Noh and F & P. The court apportioned fault between Zen-Noh and F & P at one-third and two-thirds respectively.

The parties raise several issues on appeal. Zen-Noh argues that the trial court erred in finding it negligent in not inspecting and maintaining its grain elevator properly. Zen-Noh also argues that the trial court should have found that the exculpatory clause of Zen-Noh's dock tariff relieved it from liability. Zen-Noh further argues that the trial court erred in failing to allow it to submit rebuttal testimony, and it questions the damages awarded to plaintiff.

F & P argues that because its inadequate design of the tower did not *cause* the accident, the judgment against it cannot stand. Euro argues that it should not be liable to Orduna based solely on the safe berth clause in the charter party. Orduna also challenges the district court's denial of prejudgment interest. We will address all these issues in turn.

* * *

V. Euro's Appeal

Euro, the vessel charterer, argues that the district court erred in imposing liability against it in the face of the finding that its conduct was unrelated to the tower's collapse. The district court predicated liability against Euro on the charter party between Euro and Orduna which contained a standard "safe berth" clause.[6] The trial court held that the clause made Euro the warrantor of the safety of the berth it selected for the vessel. Euro argues that at most this clause imposed upon it the obligation to use due diligence to select a safe berth.

In imposing liability against Euro, the trial court relied on three Second Circuit cases. These cases hold that a charterer warrants the safety of the berth it selects when the charter party includes a safe berth clause. *See Venore Transp. Co. v. Oswego Shipping Corp.*, 498 F.2d 469, 472-73 (2d Cir.), *cert. denied*, 419 U.S. 998, 95 S. Ct. 313, 42 L. Ed. 2d 272 (1974); *Ore Carriers of Liberia, Inc. v. Navigen Co.*, 435 F.2d 549, 550 (2d Cir. 1970) (per curiam); *Paragon Oil Co. v. Republic Tankers, S.A.*, 310 F.2d 169 (2d Cir. 1962), *cert. denied*, 372 U.S. 967, 83 S. Ct. 1092, 10 L. Ed. 2d 130 (1963). *But see Hastorf v. O'Brien*, 173 F. 346, 347 (2d Cir. 1909) (charterer held to reasonable man standard); *accord The TERNE*, 64 F.2d 502 (2d Cir.) (charterer not liable when ship caught in ice and damaged), *cert. denied*, 290 U.S. 635, 54 S. Ct. 53, 78 L. Ed. 552 (1933).

The commentators have strongly criticized these Second Circuit decisions which impose liability without fault on the charterer under a safe berth clause. Gilmore and Black argue that "these authorities go too far" for several reasons. G. GILMORE & C. BLACK, THE LAW OF ADMIRALTY § 4-4, at 204-06 (2d ed. 1975). First, the master on the scene, rather than a distant charterer, is in a better position to judge the safety of a particular berth. The master is an expert in navigation, knows the draft and trim of his vessel, and is on the spot. Conversely, the charterer, who is usually a merchant, may know nothing about navigation or the vessel and is ordinarily far from the scene. Moreover, the charterer customarily chooses ports and berths based on commercial as opposed to nautical grounds. *Id.*

Second, requiring negligence as a predicate for the charterer's liability does not increase the risk that the vessel will be exposed to an unsafe berth. The standard safe berth clause does not compel the master to take a vessel into an unsafe berth. *Id.* Because courts have interpreted safe berth clauses to free the master from any obligation to enter an unsafe port or berth, "it is by no means necessary that they be given the quite different meaning of creating an affirmative liability of charterer to ship, in case of mishap." *Id.* at 205; *see also* J. RAMBERG, UNSAFE PORTS AND BERTHS § 17, at 664 (1967) ("[A]n evaluation of the arguments *pro et contra* does not lead to a strict liability for the charterer."); Smith, *Time and Voyage Charters: Safe Port/Safe Berth*, 49 TUL. L. REV. 860, 868 (1975) ("[C]ourts are placing an undeserved burden on the charterer in holding him to a warrantor's liability.").

Moreover, Euro and the commentators (*see* G. Gilmore & C. Black, *supra*, § 4-4, at 205-06; Smith, *supra*, at 862-63) argue that a Supreme Court decision which has never been overruled or weakened supports their position. In *Atkins v. Fibre Disintegrating Co.*, 2 F. Cas. 78 (E.D.N.Y. 1868) (No. 601), *aff'd*, 85 U.S. (18 Wall.) 272, 21 L. Ed. 841 (1873), the district court confronted a claim for damages to a vessel that resulted when she entered an unsafe port. Judge Benedict held:

---

[6] The safe berth clause provided that the charterers should designate "safe discharging berths [the] vessel being always afloat."

[I]t is said that the master was induced to accept [the port] as within the terms of the contract by the representations of the charterers' agent that it was a safe port; and that his acceptance was a qualified acceptance, given upon representations which amounted to warranty.

I do not think it could be justly held ... that any thing said or done by the master was calculated to lead the charterers' agent to suppose that [the port] was not within the privilege given by the charter party, or to inform him that the charterer was to be held responsible in case the vessel received injury in using that port.

Id. at 79.

On appeal of a jurisdictional issue, the Supreme Court affirmed Judge Benedict's decision on the merits:

In regard to the merits—after a careful examination of the record—we have found no reason to dissent from the views of the learned district judge by whom the case was heard. However full might be our discussion, we should announce the same conclusions. They are clearly expressed and ably vindicated in his opinion. To go again through the process by which they were reached would be a matter rather of form than substance.

85 U.S. (18 Wall.) at 299 (citation omitted). Several district courts have at least in dicta expressed a preference for this view. *See In re Jubilant Voyager Corp. of Pan.* (The COCKROW), 1984 AMC 1725, 1726 (E.D. Va. 1983) (citing Gilmore and Black) (the proposition that a safe berth clause holds a charterer liable regardless of fault "may not be a sound one"); *California through Dep't of Transp. v. The S/T NORFOLK*, 435 F. Supp. 1039, 1047-49 (N.D. Cal. 1977) (charterer not liable to shipowner under safe berth clause when charterer exercised due diligence); *National Marine Serv., Inc. v. Gulf Oil Co.*, 433 F. Supp. 913, 917-18 (E.D. La. 1977) (quoting Gilmore and Black) (charterer not liable to shipowner under safe berth clause for shipowner's own negligence), *aff'd mem. per curiam*, 608 F.2d 522 (5th Cir. 1979); *see also International Tank Terminals, Ltd. v. M/V ACADIA FOREST*, 579 F.2d 964, 967 (5th Cir. 1978) (citing Gilmore and Black) (noting that use of safe berth clause "to impose liability upon the charter party who directs the vessel to a certain port ... has been under attack recently").

We agree with the commentators cited above that no legitimate legal or social policy is furthered by making the charterer warrant the safety of the berth it selects. Such a warranty could discourage the master on the scene from using his best judgment in determining the safety of the berth. Moreover, avoiding strict liability does not increase risks because the safe berth clause itself gives the master the freedom not to take his vessel into an unsafe port.

In conclusion, we hold that a charter party's safe berth clause does not make a charterer the warrantor of the safety of a berth. Instead the safe berth clause imposes upon the charterer a duty of due diligence to select a safe berth. Thus because the district court did not find Euro negligent, we must vacate the district court's judgment in favor of Orduna and against Euro.[7]

Note

Some time charterparties, such as Shelltime 4, expressly provide that the charterer's obligation in respect of the safety of the port or berth is only one of due diligence. Do you think that this supports the Second Circuit view in *Venore Transp. Co. v. Oswego Shipping Corp.*, 498 F.2d 469, 1974 AMC 827 (2d Cir. 1974), rejected in *Orduna*, namely that the position in the absence of such an express agreement is that the charterer absolutely warrants the safety of the port or berth? The position in the U.K. is the same as in *Venore*. *Reardon Smith Line, Ltd. v. Australian Wheat Board* (1955) 93 C.L.R. 577 (P.C.) (appeal taken from Australia).

---

[7] Euro also argues that the berth was "safe" at the time it directed the vessel to it and became "unsafe" only at a later time. Our disposition of this issue makes it unnecessary for us to reach this argument....

THE "EVIA" (NO. 2)

[1982] 2 Lloyd's Rep. 311.

LORD ROSKILL:...

My Lords, as a result of the outbreak of hostilities between Iran and Iraq in September, 1980, a large number of ships were trapped in the Shatt-al-Arab waterway. The appellants had the misfortune to be the owners of such a ship, *Evia*, registered in Liberia. The respondents were the time charterers of *Evia* under a time charter-party for a period of 18 months, two months more or less at the respondents' option, concluded in Greece and dated Nov. 12, 1979. This time charter-party was in the Baltime 1939 form as amended in 1950, that form being as is usual substantially amended and with a large number of typed clauses attached.

My Lords, disputes between the appellants thereupon arose as to their respective rights and obligations, as indeed they have done between many other shipowners and charterers who have found themselves in a similar predicament. The time charter-party contained a London arbitration clause (cl. 23). Pursuant to that clause the disputes were in due course referred to two arbitrators who appointed Mr. Basil Eckersley as umpire. Upon the disagreement of the arbitrators, it fell to Mr. Eckersley to decide the disputes, which he duly did on Mar. 20, 1981, attaching to his formal interim award some 35 pages containing 65 paragraphs of reasons expressed with admirable clarity.

* * *

With this brief introduction, I turn to consider the facts which give rise to this appeal. In March, 1980, the respondents ordered *Evia* to load a cargo of cement and other building materials for carriage from Cuba to Basrah which is on the west bank of the Shatt-al-Arab waterway. She left Cuba on May 28, 1980, passed through the Suez Canal on June 19/20, 1980, and arrived in the Shatt-al-Arab waterway on July 1. She there anchored in the river waiting for a berth her entry to which was delayed by congestion. She finally berthed on Aug. 20, 1980, and subject to some interruption, completed discharge at 10 00 hours on Sept. 22, 1980. In the ordinary course of events, she would then have sailed to continue her chartered service. Unhappily she could not do so. By that date, large-scale hostilities had broken out between Iran and Iraq, and the area around the Shatt-al-Arab waterway was in what the umpire called in par. 3 of his awards, "the thick of those hostilities". From Sept. 22, 1980, onwards, no ship of the many then in that area was able to escape. All were trapped. Gradually their crews in whole or in part left them. Only the master and a skeleton crew of about a dozen remained on board Evia after October 1, 1980, when the majority of that crew were repatriated. At the date of Mr. Eckersley's award Evia was still trapped. Some 16 months later your Lordships were told that she and the other ships were still there.

My Lords, in pars. 14 to 26 (inclusive) of his reasons, Mr. Eckersley set out the history, first down to and then after Sept. 23, 1980. No repetition is now required of that history. In par. 41 (vi), after considering the impact of that history upon the issues which he had to decide, Mr. Eckersley concluded:

Basrah was a safe port for the vessel both when she was ordered to proceed there and when she got there. It did not become unsafe until the 22nd September, and by then it was impossible for the vessel to leave....

My Lords, it is by reason of those findings that the principal issue on this appeal arises.

My Lords, Mr. Eckersley held, so far as is presently relevant, first that there was no breach of the charter-party by the respondents, secondly, that the charter-party was frustrated, and thirdly, that frustration took place on Oct. 4, 1980. He made a declaration accordingly. I ignore his conclusions on the question of war risk insurance premiums only because that issue is no longer relevant.

My Lords, in due course Mr. Justice Robert Goff, who had very properly given leave to appeal in view of the importance of this case, reversed that decision. He held that there was a breach of the charter-party by the respondents, and while agreeing with the umpire that apart from that breach the charter-party would have been frustrated, he held that the respondents were debarred from relying upon frustration as a defence to the claim for hire because of that breach since the case, as he said, was one of "self-induced" frustration. The respondents appealed to the Court of Appeal—Lord Denning, M.R., Lord Justice Ackner and Sir Sebag Shaw—who on Feb. 5, 1982, by a majority, Lord Justice Ackner dissenting, held that there was no breach of the charter-party by the respondents (*see* [1982] 1 Lloyd's Rep. 334). Mr. Eckersley's award was accordingly restored in the relevant respect.

* * *

My Lords, I propose to consider first the question which arises on cl. 2. It will be convenient to quote again those few words in that clause which are relevant—

The vessel to be employed ... between good and safe ports....

Learned Counsel were unable to offer any suggestion what in this context the word "good" added to the word "safe". Your Lordships are, I think, all of the like mind. So I will consider only the eight words "The vessel to be employed ... between ... safe ports....". The argument for the appellants is simple. The relevant restriction during her employment is to safe ports. Her employment took her to Basrah. Basrah, though safe when nominated, on Sept. 22, 1980, became and thereafter remained, unsafe. Evia was trapped. Those eight words applied. The respondents were therefore in breach.

It was this attractively simple answer which appealed to Mr. Justice Robert Goff. He said, at p. 620 of the report—

The relevant express term provides that the vessel is to be employed only between good and safe ports or places. I have to give those words their natural and ordinary meaning, unless the context otherwise requires; and I am bound to say that on their natural and ordinary meaning they comprise a warranty that any port or place to which the vessel is ordered shall be safe for the vessel throughout the period of the vessel's contractual service there. Furthermore, in my judgment this meaning of the provision is supported by authority. Here, unlike the umpire, I have the benefit of the analysis of the authorities by Mr. Justice Mustill in *Transoceanic Petroleum Carriers v. Cook Industries Inc. (The Mary Lou)*, [1981] 2 Lloyd's Rep. 272. With that analysis, I find myself respectfully in agreement; and I most gratefully adopt it.

The learned Judge also expressed his agreement with the earlier decisions on the same point which Mr. Justice Mustill had cited in that judgment. Put in other words, the learned Judge accepted the appellant's argument that there was an absolute continuing contractual promise that at no time during her chartered service would the ship find herself in any port which was or had become unsafe for her. Support for this view was said to be derived from a well-known passage in the judgment of Lord Justice Sellers in *Leeds Shipping Co. Ltd. v. Societe Francaise Bunge (The Eastern City)*, [1958] 2 Lloyd's Rep. 127 at p. 131; the learned Lord Justice had there said:

If it were said that a port will not be safe unless, in the relevant period of time, the particular ship can reach it, use it and return from it without, in the absence of some abnormal occurrence, being exposed to danger which cannot be avoided by good navigation and seamanship, it would probably meet all circumstances as a broad statement of the law.

* * *

... But the first question is whether, apart from authority, these words are to be construed in the manner suggested. In order to consider the scope of the contractual promise which these eight words impose upon a charterer, it must be determined how a charterer would exercise his undoubted right to require the shipowner to perform his contractual obligations to render services with his ship, his master, officers and crew, the consideration for the performance of their obligation being the charterer's regular payment of time-charter hire. The answer must be that a charterer will exercise that undoubted contractual right by giving the shipowner orders to go to a particular port or place of loading or discharge. It is clearly at that point of time when that order is given that that contractual promise by the charterer regarding the safety of that intended port or place must be fulfilled. But that contractual promise cannot mean that that port or place must be safe when that order is given, for were that so, a charterer could not legitimately give orders to go to an ice-bound port which he and the owner both knew in all human probability would be ice-free by the time that vessel reached it. Nor, were that the nature of the promise, could a charterer order the ship to a port or place the approaches to which were at the time of the order blocked as a result of a collision or by some submerged wreck or other obstacles even though such obstacles would in all human probability be out of the way before the ship required to enter. The charterer's contractual promise must, I think, relate to the characteristics of the port or place in question, and in my view, means that when the order is given that port or place is prospectively safe for the ship to get to, stay at, so far as necessary, and in due course, leave. But if those characteristics are such as to make that port or place prospectively safe in this way, I cannot think that if in spite of them, some unexpected and abnormal event thereafter suddenly occurs which creates conditions of unsafety where conditions of safety had previously existed and as a result the ship is delayed, damaged or destroyed, that contractual promise extends to making the charterer liable for any resulting loss or damage, physical or financial. So to hold would make the charterer the insurer of such unexpected and abnormal risks which in my view should properly fall upon the ship's insurers under the policies of insurance the effecting of which is the owner's responsibility under cl. 3 unless, of course, the owner chooses to be his own insurer in these respects.

* * *

My Lords, it follows that that passage of the judgment of Lord Justice Sellers in *The Eastern City* is no authority for construing those eight or other similar words as giving rise to an absolute continuing promise of safety by charterers after the order or nomination in question has been given subject only to the qualification of some subsequent unexpected and abnormal occurrence. It further follows from the concession properly made by learned Counsel for the appellants that there was no authority supporting the view accepted both by Mr. Justice Robert Goff in this case and by Mr. Justice Mustill in *The Mary Lou*, other than those recent first-instance cases which I have previously mentioned.

* * *

My Lords, on the view of the law which I take, since Basrah was prospectively safe at the time of nomination, and since the unsafety arose after her arrival and was due to an unexpected and abnormal event, there was at the former time no breach of cl. 2 by the respondents, and that is the first ground upon which I would dismiss this appeal.

* * *

... My Lords, unless there is something unusual in the relevant express language used in a particular charter-party, the charterer's obligation at the time of nomination which I have been discussing must, I think, apply equally to a voyage charterer as to a time charterer. But in considering whether there is any residual or remaining obligation after nomination it is necessary to have in mind one fundamental distinction between a time charterer and a voyage charterer. In the former case, the time charterer is in complete control of the employment of the ship. It is in his power by appropriate orders timeously given to change the ship's employment so as to prevent her proceeding to or remaining at a port initially safe which has since it was nominated become unsafe. But a voyage charterer may not have the same power. If there is a single loading or discharging port named in the voyage charter-party then, unless the charter-party specifically otherwise provides, a voyage charterer may not be able to order that ship elsewhere. If there is a range of loading or discharging ports named, once the voyage charterer has selected the contractual port or ports of loading or discharge, the voyage charter-party usually operates as if that port or those ports had originally been written into the charter-party, and the charterer then has no further right of nomination or renomination.

What, then, is the contractual obligation of such charterers whether for time or voyage if the nominated port becomes unsafe after it was nominated?

My Lords, in the case of a time charterer, I cannot bring myself to think that he has no further obligation to the owner even though for the reasons I have given earlier he is not the insurer of the risks arising from the unsafety of the nominated port. Suppose some event has occurred after nomination which has made or will or may make the nominated port unsafe. Is a time charterer obliged to do anything further? What is a voyage charterer to do in similar circumstances? My Lords, this problem seems never to have been judicially considered in any detail; indeed, as I have already stated, in *The Houston City* the Privy Council expressly declined to consider it.

In my opinion, while the primary obligation of a time charterer under cl. 2 of this charter-party is that which I have already stated, namely, to order the ship to go only to a port which, at the time when the order is given, is prospectively safe for her, there may be circumstances in which, by reason of a port, which was prospectively safe when the order to go to it was given, subsequently becoming unsafe, cl. 2, on its true construction, imposes a further and secondary obligation on the charterer.

In this connection two possible situations require to be considered. The first situation is where, after the time charter has performed his primary obligation by ordering the ship to go to a port which, at the time of such order, was prospectively safe for her, and while she is still proceeding towards such port in compliance with such order, new circumstances arise which render the port unsafe. The second situation is where, after the time charterer has performed his primary obligation by ordering the ship to go to a port which was, at the time of such order, prospectively safe for her, and she has proceeded to and entered such port in compliance with such order, new circumstances arise which render the port unsafe.

In the first situation it is my opinion that cl. 2, on its true construction, (unless the cause of the new unsafety be purely temporary in character) imposes on the time charterer a further and secondary obligation to cancel his original order and, assuming that he wishes to continue to trade the ship, to order her to go to another port which, at the time when such fresh order is given, is prospectively safe for her. This is because cl. 2 should be construed as requiring the time charterer to do all that he can effectively do to protect the ship from the new danger in the port which has arisen since his original order for her to go to it was given.

In the second situation the question whether cl. 2, on its true construction, imposes a further and secondary obligation on the time charterer will depend on whether, having regard to the nature and consequences of the new danger in the port which has arisen, it is possible for the ship to avoid such danger by leaving the port. If, on the one hand, it is not possible for the ship so to leave, then no further and secondary obligation is imposed on the time charterer. This is because cl. 2 should not be construed as requiring the time charterer to give orders with which it is not possible for the ship to comply, and which would for that reason be ineffective. If, on the other hand, it is possible for the ship to avoid the new danger in the port which has arisen by leaving, then a further and secondary obligation is imposed on the time charterer to order the ship to leave the port forthwith, whether she has completed loading or discharging or not, and, assuming that he wishes to continue to trade the ship, to order her to go to another port which, at the time when such fresh order is given, is prospectively safe for her. This is again because cl. 2 should be construed as requiring the time charterer to do all that he can effectively do to protect the ship from the new danger in the port which has arisen since his original order for her to go to it was given.

My Lords, what I have said with regard to these further and secondary obligations under cl. 2 of this charter-party will apply to any other similarly worded "safe port" clauses.

My Lords, for the reasons I have given I find it much more difficult to say what are the comparable obligations under a voyage charter-party at any rate where there is no express right to renominate. The well-known decision in *The Teutonia*, (1872) L.R. 4 P.C. 171—a case decided long before the doctrine of frustration assumed its modern form—has always presented difficulties and voyage charter-parties today almost invariably contain war and strike clauses which give the shipowners and their masters the right sometimes to require another nomination and sometimes an unfettered right in any event to proceed elsewhere.* I think, therefore, in a case where only a time charter-party is involved, it would be unwise for your Lordships to give further consideration to the problems which might

---

* For a discussion of the difference between time and voyage charters, *see E.A.S.T., Inc. of Stamford Conn. v. M/V Alia, supra.*

arise in the case of a voyage charter-party, and for my part, I would leave those problems for later consideration if and when they arise.

My Lords, on the basis that time charterers were potentially under the further and secondary obligations which I have held that cl. 2 may impose on them, it cannot avail the appellants against the respondents since the events giving rise to the unsafety did not occur until after *Evia* had entered Basrah, and an order to leave the port and proceed to another port could not have been effective.

My Lords, before leaving this part of the case, I would mention three further matters. First, with all respect to Sir Sebag Shaw, I cannot accept (still ignoring cl. 21) that cl. 2 only applies to physical unsafety. I think that both as a matter of construction and on the authorities, of which *Ogden v. Graham* is but an example, though an impressive one, it covers political unsafety as well. Secondly, it will have been observed that throughout this judgment I have eschewed the use of the phrases "safe port warranty" and "warranty of safety" though the word "warranty" is often used in the cases to which I have referred. As with the so-called warranty of seaworthiness, so with this so-called warranty, its use is historic but as well-known recent decisions have shown, inaccurate. So long as it is realized that it is used as a matter of convenience, and not an expression of the legal consequences of its breach and is not a definition of the character of the provision under consideration, that use may be convenient. But since your Lordships are here concerned with statements of principle, I have ventured, at the risk of accusations of pedantry, to call the obligation under discussion a contractual promise for in truth that is what it is rather than a warranty. Thirdly, if it be said that the imposition of these further and secondary obligations upon a time charterer may put him in difficulties with any sub time charterer or voyage charterer from him or under any bills of lading issued by him or at his behest, my answer is that a time charterer would be prudent to protect himself against the consequences of such possible inconsistencies by including suitable wording into whatever further contracts he chooses himself to make or into which the owners, the master or other agent of the owners, wish to enter.

Note

Negligence on the part of the master may relieve a charterer of its liability under the safe port provision. The master's negligence may permit the fact-finder to conclude either that the port was safe because peril could have been avoided by prudent seamanship, or, even where the port is found to be unsafe, the master's conduct may be regarded as supervening cause. But not every risk taken by the master will be considered to be a superseding cause. As explained in *American President Lines, Ltd. v. United States*, 208 F. Supp. 573, 577-78 (N.D. Cal. 1961):

> The decisions involving the so-called "safe-port" and "safe-berth" provisions in charter party agreements make it very clear that a charterer cannot escape liability for damage ultimately resulting from a directive that the chartered vessel go to an unsafe port or berth merely because the captain in attempting to comply, follows an obviously risky course of action in preference to an available alternative which might have avoided the damage. In most of the decisions finding liability on the part of the charterer there was a danger foreseeable to the captain and an available alternative.[1]
>
> The decisions recognize that when a charterer directs a vessel to a port the captain believes to be unsafe, he is confronted with a difficult dilemma. He may refuse to comply, thus thwarting the desires of the charterer and assuming the risk of an ultimate determination that the port was not in fact unsafe. Or, he may attempt to comply, and run the risk of making a miscalculation in seeking to avoid the danger to which the charterer's directive has subjected the vessel. When a captain has been placed in such a dilemma by a charterer's breach of contract in directing the vessel to an unsafe port, the entire burden of responsibility for the safety of the ship cannot legally be shifted to the captain. If the captain elects to attempt to comply with the charterer's directive, it would be inequitable to relieve the charterer of liability for harm caused by the peril which his wrongful demand created merely because the captain's choice of alternative courses, which give promise of avoiding such peril, proves to be incorrect. Thus, the applicable decisions have established the principle that the charterer is not relieved of legal responsibility for the consequences of his breach of contract unless the course followed by the captain is so imprudent that it can fairly be said to be an intervening act of negligence.[2] It is not enough that the course followed by the captain entails some foreseeable risk of harm. For, some risk

---

[1] *See e.g., Reardon Smith Line Ltd. v. Australian Wheat Board*, 1956 Appeal Cases 266; *Compania Naviera Maropan v. Bowaters*, 2 Q.B. 68 (1955); *G. W. Grace & Co., Ltd. v. General Steam Navigation Co., Ltd.*, 2 K.B. 383 (1950); *P. Dougherty Co. v. Bader Coal Co.*, 244 F. 267 (D.C. Mass. 1917); *The Northman*, 189 F. 33 (2 Cir. 1911).

[2] *Reardon Smith Line Ltd. v. Australian Wheat Board*, 1956 Appeal Cases 266; *Compania Naviera Maropan v. Bowaters*, 2 Q.B. 68 (1955); *G.W. Grace & Co., Ltd. v. General Steam Navigation Co., Ltd.* 2 K.B. 383 (1950).

is inherent in any attempt to proceed to an unsafe port. To constitute an intervening act of negligence, the course followed by the captain must entail an unreasonable risk.

In the present case the Board of Contract Appeals found that the Government breached the charter party agreement by directing the PRESIDENT ARTHUR to load at the unsafe port of Villa do Porto. The master of the PRESIDENT ARTHUR was initially unable to enter Villa do Porto because of the hazardous weather conditions. But, in an effort to comply with the Government's demand that cargo be loaded there, he followed the Port Captain's suggestion that he anchor in Sao Lourenco Bay to await an improvement in the weather. The Board of Contract Appeals found that this course entailed a foreseeable risk of harm because of the very weather conditions which made Villa do Porto an unsafe port. It also found that the master had an available alternative in that he might have skirted the island until the weather improved. It concluded that it necessarily followed that the damage suffered by the PRESIDENT ARTHUR at Sao Lourenco Bay was not the proximate result of the Government's demand that she load cargo at Villa do Porto. In so concluding, the Board committed an error of law. For the law, as established by the cited decisions, is that action taken by a master in an effort to comply with the demand of a charterer that he proceed to an unsafe port does not constitute an intervening act of negligence merely because the action taken entails some foreseeable risk. To break the chain of causation, the master's action must entail a risk that is unreasonable under all the circumstances.

G. Voyage Charters

1. Late Delivery—Cancellation

PAN CARGO SHIPPING CORP. v. UNITED STATES

234 F. Supp. 623, 1965 AMC 2649 (S.D.N.Y. 1964), *aff'd*, 373 F.2d 525 (2d Cir.),
cert. denied, 389 U.S. 836, 88 S. Ct. 51, 19 L. Ed. 2d 98 (1967)

[Libelant Pan Cargo Shipping Corporation (Pan Cargo) entered into a voyage charter party with the U.S. Navy on 3 December 1957. Under the charter party, Pan Cargo's tanker "National Peace" was to carry oil to a Far East port from one or more safe ports in the Persian Gulf to be determined by the charterer.

At the time the parties fixed the charter, a boycott by the Arab nations against ships that traded with Israel was in effect. Though aware of this situation, no one for the libelant advised the Navy that the Peace, under her former name of Memory I, had made a prior voyage to Israel. Libelant believed and hoped that because the name of the vessel had been changed since her prior visits to Israel that Arab authorities would not be aware of that voyage.

According to the terms of the charter party, the Navy notified the libelant that the Peace should load its oil cargo at the Saudi Arabian port of Ras Tanura. On 17 December 1957 the vessel docked at Ras Tanura and began discharging her water ballast in preparation for taking on cargo. At this point, the ship was not allowed to conduct any other activity with the shore of the foreign port until it obtained "free pratique", permission of the shore authorities.

Prior to completing the discharge of her ballast, an inspection of the ship's logs by a Saudi Arabian official revealed the prior voyage to Israel. Consequently, free pratique was denied and the Peace was immediately ordered to lay offshore where she remained.

The charter specified January 5, 1958 as the "canceling date" and included the following provision:

If the vessel is not ready to load by 4:00 p.m. (local time) on the canceling date named in the voyage order issued hereunder, the Charterer shall have the option of canceling the voyage order by giving the owner notice of such cancellation within twenty-for (24) hours after the canceling date;...

On 6 January 1958 the Navy gave libelant written notice that it was exercising this option and canceling the charter party, among other things, for failure of the National Peace to be "ready in all respects to load with clearances required of vessel by custom of loading port and laws of Saudi Arabia".

Libelant sues for $160,110.16 as damages for a claimed wrongful cancellation by Navy of the charter party.

[The issue is thus whether the consequences of the prohibition by the Saudi Arabian government against loading cargo are to be born by the libelant or by the Navy. Eds.]

* * *

Neither side is really at fault. The loss was occasioned by the refusal of Saudi Arabia to permit the cargo to be loaded.

As between the two parties thus situated, this loss should be borne by libelant, which knew the facts as to the voyage of Memory I to Israel and which deliberately took the risk thereby created. The loss should not be borne by respondent, which did not know the facts as to the voyage of Memory I to Israel and had no control over the events disabling Memory I from loading her cargo at Ras Tanura; respondent did not get the cargo carriage by the National Peace for which it had bargained.

It remains to be seen whether provisions of the charter party prevent a decision otherwise dictated by fairness and equity.

The charter plainly provides that the charterer may cancel if the vessel is not "ready to load" by January 5, 1958. The situation here was precisely covered by that provision.

It is obvious that the Peace was not "ready to load" at Ras Tanura. She had not obtained free pratique and never did obtain it. It was the responsibility of the vessel to secure free pratique. The reasons for its refusal are wholly irrelevant. The result is the same as if Asiatic cholera or some other contagious disease were rampant on board and on this account pratique had been refused. In that event, surely libelant could not claim the vessel as "ready to load". Here, the reason for refusing pratique was not, to our understanding, a reasonable one. But the reasons for the Saudi Arabian decision in this instance are beside the point. The fact is that pratique was refused, the ship was not an "arrived" ship, and did not have entry to the port. That lines were fast to the pier means nothing; no one was permitted to leave the ship; communication with the shore was refused. The vessel was promptly ordered away. She was never "ready to load".

* * *

It should be noted that the charter in suit requires that a notice of readiness be given; there is no option as to this. Whether any notice of readiness was given here is doubtful because the only such notice was addressed by the Master of the Peace to Aramco and not to the charterer. In any event, no effective notice of readiness could be given because the Peace was not in fact "ready to load". The leading case in this area is *Aktieselskabet Fido v. Lloyd Braziliero*, 283 F. 62 (2d Cir. 1922) where it was said (at 69):

A notice of readiness when a vessel is not actually ready has no effect. A notice is without legal effect, if the facts it states are untrue.

It is laid down in CARVER, CARRIAGE OF GOODS BY SEA (10th ed.), 861-62, as follows:

Before the lay days at the port of loading can begin to run against the charterer, he must have had notice of the ship's arrival, and of her readiness to receive cargo.

* * *

And such notice cannot be given until the ship is an 'arrived' ship, *i.e.*, has arrived at the stipulated place, and is, so far as she is concerned, ready to load.

* * *

The Austin Friars, 71 L.T. 27 (1894) is a decision of the President of the Probate, Divorce and Admiralty Division. The charterers had the option to cancel "if the ship does not arrive at port of loading and be ready to load on or before midnight of 10th Oct." The ship arrived at the loading port at 11 p.m. (2300) on October 10, "but no one could leave the ship or come on board until the doctor had visited her and pronounced her free from infection".

The doctor came on board next morning (October 11); the ship was given medical clearance but the charterers cancelled the charter for failure to be ready to load by midnight, October 10. The registrar had held that the ship was ready to load on arrival at 11 p.m. on October 10. This was specifically disapproved, the President stating:

> If the ship is not in fact ready to load by the specified time, they [the charterers] are to be entitled to cancel the charter party.

* * *

Settle decree or decrees on notice.

Notes

1. In *Pan Cargo Shipping Corp.*, *supra*, the ship never obtained free pratique and so could never give a valid notice of readiness (NOR). In ordinary circumstances, the granting of free pratique is a formality and the ship may give NOR before actually receiving the free pratique clearance. *Shipping Developments Corp. v. V/O Sojuznefexport: The Delian Spirit* [1972] 1 Q.B. 103; *Logs & Timber Products (Singapore) Pte Ltd v. Keeley Granite (Pty) Ltd (The Freijo)* [1978] 2 Lloyd's Rep. 1. This situation is equivalent to the opening of the ship's hatch covers. The ship is not literally ready to load or discharge until the hatch covers are open, but it may give NOR on arrival at the port, even if the hatch covers are still closed, as they will usually be if the ship has to wait for berth. Lord Justice Parker of the English Court of Appeal described the position as follows in *Antclizo Shipping Corp. v. Food Corp. of India (The Antclizo) (No. 2)* [1992] 1 Lloyd's Rep 558, 564:

> "When the notice is given, the situation must be such that at the earliest time that the charterers or consignees can be ready to perform their part in loading or discharging, the vessel will, barring accidents, be ready at once to perform her part in such operations."

The situation is different if the charterparty specifically provides that laytime cannot commence until the ship is granted free pratique: *See, e.g.*, *Sale Corp of Monrovia v Turkish Cargo Lines General Manager (The Amiral Fahri Engin)* [1993] 1 Lloyd's Rep. 75.

Since July 1st, 2004, when the International Ship and Port Facility Security Code (the ISPS Code) came into force, all ships must receive security clearance before entering port. Ships may be detained by the U.S. Coast Guard for inspection even if they are not actually in violation of the provisions of the Code: for example, if they are arriving from a port about which there are security concerns. Because the granting of security clearance under the ISPS Code is not routine, it may be a prerequisite to the giving of NOR unless the charterparty specifically provides that the ship can give NOR while waiting for clearance.

2. A charter party may provide that the charter has a right to cancel the charter if the vessel is not delivered by a specified date or within a specified period of time. This right, however, will be considered waived if the charterer agrees to an extension of time within which delivery may be made. *Fernales Shipping Co. v. Bonaire Petroleum Corp.*, 733 F.2d 381 (5th Cir. 1984). Where no date for delivery is specified the owner must tender the vessel "with reasonable dispatch." *Sanday v. United States Shipping Board Emergency Fleet Corporation*, 6 F.2d 384 (2d Cir.), *cert. denied*, 269 U.S. 556, 46 S. Ct. 19, 70 L. Ed. 409 (1925).

---

2. Laytime and Demurrage

Notes

1. Disputes about laytime and demurrage use a specialized vocabulary that can be confusing at times. Confusion can be compounded by the common habit of using abbreviations for terms that have technical meanings to begin with: for example, "WWDSSHEXUU", which means "weather working days, Saturdays, Sundays and holidays excluded, unless used". Interpretive assistance can be found in the Voyage Charter Party Laytime Interpretation Rules 1993 (known as Voylayrules 93), issued jointly by the Baltic and International Maritime Council (BIMCO), the Comité Maritime International (CMI), the Federation of National Associations of Ship Brokers and Agents (FONASBA) and the International Association of Dry Cargo Shipowners (INTERCARGO). The Voylayrules 93 are available on the Tulane Maritime Law Center website at www.tulanemaritimelaw.net/docs/volayrules. The Voylayrules definitions of "laytime" and "demurrage" themselves are as follows:

> "LAYTIME" shall mean the period of time agreed between the parties during which the owner will make and keep the vessel available for loading or discharging without payment additional to the freight.
> "DEMURRAGE" shall mean an agreed amount payable to the owner in respect of delay to the vessel beyond the laytime, for which the owner is not responsible. Demurrage shall not be subject to laytime exceptions.

2. "Demurrage" should be distinguished from "detention." As has been seen, demurrage is a charge imposed on the charterer for exceeding lay days or otherwise delaying the ultimate redelivery of the vessel to its owner. This should be distinguished from detention which is a penalty imposed on a charterer for a wrongful or unreasonable delay in redelivery of the vessel to its owner. A charter party may provide for demurrage for 10 days at $2,000 per day. If, however, the vessel is delayed beyond the specified 10 days, the owner may be entitled to *damages* for detention.

Also, where a charterer is able to expedite the redelivery to the owner such as by loading or unloading in less time than specified as laydays, the charter may be entitled to a financial credit or bonus called dispatch. *Government of Republic of Indonesia v. M/V Glapkos*, 553 F. Supp. 272, 1986 AMC 602 (E.D. La. 1982).

THE SHIPPING CORPORATION OF INDIA LTD. v. SUN OIL CO.

569 F. Supp. 1248, 1986 AMC 2752 (E.D. Pa. 1983)

Memorandum and Order

HUYETT, District Judge

This admiralty case arises out of a contractual dispute. The defendant, Sun Oil Company (charterer), twice chartered the MAHARSHI DAYANAND (vessel) owned by the plaintiff, the Shipping Corporation of India, Ltd. (owner), to carry two cargoes of crude oil. The dispute concerns the calculation of demurrage, which is liquidated damages for delay provided for in a charter party. Plaintiff brought this action to recover unpaid demurrage and all costs of this suit and attorneys' fees. Defendant has counterclaimed for $8,742.50 it alleges was erroneously paid as demurrage for a weather delay....

* * *

I

A. The Charter Forms

Plaintiff, the Shipping Corporation of India, and defendant, Sun Oil Company, entered into a contract of charter party dated January 9, 1979 (the first charter) and one dated December 10, 1979 (the second charter) under which the tanker MAHARSHI DAYANAND was to carry a port cargo of crude oil and/or dirty petroleum products. The charter form in each case was the ASBATANKVOY 1977 charter as modified by the parties. The ASBATANKVOY charter form is in all material respects identical to earlier versions entitled ESSONVOY and EXXONVOY 1969 charters. The key clauses in dispute are:

6. NOTICE OF READINESS. Upon arrival at customary anchorage at each port of loading or discharge, the Master or his agent shall give the Charterer or his agent notice by letter, telegraph, wireless or telephone that the Vessel is ready to load or discharge cargo, berth or no berth, and laytime, as hereinafter provided, shall commence upon the expiration of six (6) hours after receipt of such notice, or upon the Vessel's arrival in berth (*i.e.*, finished mooring when at a sealoading or discharging terminal and all fast when loading or discharging alongside a wharf), whichever first occurs. However, where delay is caused to Vessel getting into berth after giving notice of readiness for any reason over which Charterer has no control, such delay shall not count as used laytime.

7. HOURS FOR LOADING AND DISCHARGING. The number of running hours specified as laytime in Part I shall be permitted the Charterer as laytime for loading and discharging cargo; but any delay due to the Vessel's condition or breakdown or inability of the Vessel's facilities to load or discharge cargo within the time allowed shall not count as used laytime. If regulations of the Owner or port authorities prohibit loading or discharging of the cargo at night, time so lost shall not count as used laytime; if the Charterer, shipper or consignee prohibits loading or discharging at night, time so lost shall count as used laytime. Time consumed

by the vessel in moving from loading or discharge port anchorage to her loading or discharge berth, discharging ballast water or slops, will not count as used laytime.

8. DEMURRAGE. Charterer shall pay demurrage per running hour and pro rata for a part thereof at the rate specified in Part I for all time that loading and discharging and used laytime as elsewhere herein provided exceeds the allowed laytime elsewhere herein specified. If, however, demurrage shall be incurred at ports of loading and/or discharge by reason of fire, explosion, storm or by a strike, lockout, stoppage or restraint of labor or by breakdown of machinery or equipment in or about the plant of the Charterer, supplier, shipper or consignee of the cargo, the rate of demurrage shall be reduced one-half of the amount stated in Part I per running hour or pro rata for part of an hour for demurrage so incurred. The Charterer shall not be liable for any demurrage for delay caused by strike, lockout, stoppage or restraint of labor for Master, officers and crew of the Vessel or tugboat or pilots.

SUN LIGHTERING CLAUSE: If lightering is required to berth at a discharge port, it may be necessary to lighter the vessel while anchored at Anchorage. Laytime at anchorage (whether or not the vessel is on demurrage) shall begin six (6) hours after receipt of Notice of Readiness by Charterers or when first lighter barge arrives alongside, whichever occurs first, and shall end when vessel weighs anchor to proceed to a berth. Laytime shall begin again upon the vessel's arrival in berth (*i.e.*, all fast at the discharging wharf). Although the time used in such lightering shall count as laytime, such anchorage shall not be considered a second discharge port or second discharge berth and running time from anchorage to such discharge port or berth shall not count as laytime (whether or not the vessel is on demurrage).

* * *

[A variety of events and circumstances occurred during loading and discharging operations. The important fact is that the allowed laytime had been exhausted prior to the time the vessel began to load. Thus, the vessel was on demurrage prior to the commencement of the loading operation. Under the terms of the charter party, an all-inclusive number of hours stated as a total of 72 hours was available as laytime for both the loading and discharging operations, that is, the charterer had a grand total of 72 hours to complete both operations. The owner's position, simply stated, is that once laytime had been exhausted prior to loading, the vessel was on demurrage and *all* delays should be included in the calculation of demurrage. Eds.]

II.

A. Contractual Interpretation of Demurrage

Charterer contends that the six hour notice time[*] described in clause 6 and the time spent shifting and deballasting should not be included in a demurrage calculation because those activities are excluded or excepted from used laytime. Owner contends that once the ship is on demurrage the exclusions and exceptions to used laytime no longer apply. The language of the charter party must be interpreted in order to determine the proper outcome of this case.

* * *

The period of time used by a vessel at the loading and discharge ports is known generally as used laytime. 2B BENEDICT ON ADMIRALTY § 31, at 2-1 (7th ed. 1982). In this case, a certain amount of time at the loading and discharging port was designated "allowed laytime." It was agreed that allowed laytime constituted 72 running hours. The charter excludes from the used laytime calculation these 72 hours and certain other activities at port. *See* ASBATANKVOY charter, clause 7, *supra*.

After the allowed laytime has expired, the charterer is liable for delay according to an agreed daily or hourly rate of liquidated damages known as demurrage. *Id.* The vessel is then sometimes referred to as being "on demurrage," a

---

[*] *Six hours grace period of notice of readiness to discharge. Eds.*

term that has caused much confusion. Demurrage is intended to compensate the owner for freight it has lost because the vessel was not free when the parties agreed it would be. Shipowners rely on the maxim "once on demurrage, always on demurrage," to support the broadest and most inclusive calculation of demurrage. Although this maxim once received general acceptance, its strength has been eroded in recent years. *Id.* § 41, at 2-57. There are three instances in which the charterer is not liable for demurrage: (1) specific exonerating clauses in the charter party; (2) the delay being attributed to the fault of the shipowner or those for whom he is responsible; and (3) a *vis major* amounting to a sudden or unforeseen interruption or prevention of the act itself of loading or discharging, not occurring through the connivance or fault of the charterers. *United States v. Atlantic Refining Co.*, 112 F. Supp. 76 (D. N.J. 1951).

With respect to both charters, there is a dispute over how demurrage should be calculated.... The focus of this problem is the interpretation of the demurrage clause, clause 8, and whether the specific exonerating clauses in the charter party, clauses 6 & 7, remain in effect once the vessel is on demurrage. The controversial language extracted from clause 8 states:

Charterer shall pay demurrage per running hour and pro rata for a part thereof at the rate specified in Part I for all time loading and discharging and used laytime as elsewhere herein provided exceeds the allowed laytime elsewhere herein specified.

Plaintiffs argue that the maxim "once on demurrage, always on demurrage" is evidence of the absolute nature of demurrage and that once the allowed laytime has expired, then all time thereafter is time on demurrage. Furthermore, they argue that any clauses specifically excluding certain activities from used laytime are irrelevant once the vessel is on demurrage. Defendants argue that the time excluded from laytime by clauses 6 & 7 should not be included in a calculation of demurrage under the specific terms of the contract read as a whole.

B. Six Hour Notice Time

A number of arbitration panels have confronted the same issues as those presented in this case. The most frequent focus of this debate is the notice of readiness clause. *See* ASBATANKVOY charter, clause 6, *supra*. Upon arrival at anchorage at each port of loading or discharge, the vessel operator gives the charterer notice that the vessel is ready to load or discharge cargo. The effect is that laytime commences upon the expiration of six hours after receipt of this notice.

The arbitration panels are divided as to how the words of clause 8 should be interpreted. A number of arbitration panels found that the words "all time" in clause 8 simply mean that all time after a vessel is on demurrage should count in a demurrage calculation because all exceptions to used laytime are irrelevant once a vessel is on demurrage. [citations omitted] One of these panels reasoned that if the parties meant that demurrage was to be paid for all laytime used in excess of allowed laytime the charter would have contained the words "all laytime" rather than all time. *Rederi A/B Sally (Pegny) v. Amerada Hess Shipping Corporation*, S.M.A. 1015 (N.Y. Arb. 1976). Thus, these panels found that barring any language to the contrary, once the 72 hours of allowed laytime expired, the maxim "once on demurrage, always on demurrage" took effect with the result that exceptions to laytime were no longer applicable....

The panels in a second group of arbitration decisions interpreted the words "all time" differently and reached the conclusion that the charterer was not liable for the six hour notice time once the vessel went on demurrage. [citations omitted] The *Estreela* panel stated:

While it is an interesting play on words, the "all time" obviously modifies loading, discharging and used laytime. No other sensible meaning can be read into the clause. If "all time" does, in fact, mean any and all time, why would the drafter of the clause have exerted the effort of specifying the categories which they did? [*Estreela Tropica Navegacion, S.A. v. Golden Eagle Liberia Limited*, S.M.A. 1292 (N.Y. Arb. 1979)].

The *Estreela* panel thus concluded that the charterer was never liable for the six hour notice time.

Another panel that ruled in the charterer's favor interpreted the words of clause 8 as a whole instead of just focusing on the words "all time." The panel's interpretation was based upon the complete phrase "all time loading and discharging and used laytime as elsewhere herein provided exceeds the allowed laytime as elsewhere herein specified." *Carras (Hellas) Ltd., (M/T "Ioannis Carras") v. Amerada Hess Shipping Corporation*, S.M.A. 1544 (N.Y. Arb. 1981). The panel recognized that if the charterer had no right to any further laytime once allowed laytime has expired, then there could never be any "excess" laytime.... The *Carras* panel continued:

Since it is axiomatic that an excess of anything must be more of the same then it follows that the terms and conditions in the charter relative to the running of or exemptions from laytime must continue in force until the discharge is completed and the hoses disconnected. That is the only way that the total laytime can be determined and by deducting the allowed laytime, establish the "excess" laytime for which demurrage is paid.

Another group of arbitration panels held that the six hour notice of readiness did not count in a demurrage calculation by interpreting clauses 6 & 8 together. [Citations omitted] Since waiting at anchor is an activity that may use up laytime, the Atlantic Monarch panel began by asking when laytime actually commenced. [*Atlantic Monarch Shipping Company Limited v. Hess IL & Chemical Division Amerada Hess Corporation*, S.M.A. 939 (N.Y. Arb. 1975)]. Like clause 6 in this case, the clause under consideration in Atlantic Monarch provided that laytime commenced after the six hours or when the vessel reached the discharge berth.... Under a strict interpretation of the contract, a number of panels held that the charter was intended to provide the charterer with up to six hours of time waiting at anchorage at loading and discharging ports, whether or not the vessel was on demurrage because laytime does not commence until after the six hour time period has run.... An English case reached a contrary result and this decision is relied upon by the plaintiffs in this case to refute the Atlantic Monarch decision. *R. Pagnan & Fratelli v. Tradax Export, S.A.*, (1969) 2 Lloyd's Rep. 150 (Comm. Ct., Q.B. Div.). The Pagnan court held that since laytime is exhausted, there is no laytime left to begin and therefore the six hours should count as time on demurrage.

In addition to the contract arguments, there is an economic argument against including the six hour notice time in a demurrage calculation. *See Sun Shipping & Trading Co., (M/T Sunarussa) v. Joc Oil Ltd.*, S.M.A. 1205 (N.Y. Arb. 1978). The base rates of the World-Wide Tanker Nominal Freight Scale (World scale) have a built-in factor of 96 hours of port time while the charter provided only 72 hours of allowed laytime. The additional 24 hours, or 12 hours at each of the loading and discharge ports, are included in the base rates and are intended to compensate the owner for activities other than loading, discharging and other exceptions to used laytime. Two panels found that the six hour time fit into this category and to require charterer to pay for it simply because the vessel is on demurrage is to require him to pay twice for the same thing....

* * *

C. Shifting

In any charter, clauses are incorporated to stop the running of laytime during activities related to the navigation, maneuvering and management of the vessel. *See* ASBATANKVOY charter, clause 7, *supra*. These clauses stop the clock by providing that the activities should not count as used laytime. Shifting from anchorage to berth is one such activity. *Id.*

The arbitration decisions are generally divided on the issue of whether time spent shifting is included in demurrage calculations. Some panels which held that the six hours should count in a demurrage calculation, also held that shifting should not count in the same calculation.... Other panels held that shifting should count, whereas the six hours should not count....

One group of decisions included shifting in a demurrage calculation because those panels interpreted the words "all time" to include all time, regardless of any exceptions, once the vessel went on demurrage. [Citations omitted] Another interpretation of clause 8 is that since the clause did not expressly exclude shifting time from the meaning of demurrage, it should count as such. [Citation omitted] Another group of arbitration panels would not include shifting in a demurrage calculation because they found that the words "used laytime" had a significant and special meaning.... [Citations omitted] Because individual clauses exempt certain times and events from the category of "used laytime" these acts or events as are specifically treated in the charter party cannot be considered for demurrage calculation purposes regardless of whether the vessel has fully used its allowed laytime. The *Mammoth Bulk* panel further supported their decision with the rationale that the base rate allowed for 96 hours of port time although the laytime is fixed at 72 hours. Thus, to allow compensation for shifting would be to allow double compensation. [*Mammoth Bulk Carriers, Ltd., (M/T Viborg) v. Ilford Shipping and Trading, Bermuda*, S.M.A. 1062 (N.Y. Arb. 1976.]

Deballasting is another activity related to the navigation of the vessel. Four arbitration boards found that deballasting should not count as demurrage time because ballast is carried at the owner's discretion for the vessel's safety and stability. No board held that deballasting time should count as demurrage time. [Citations omitted].

III.

Mr. Justice Holmes stated, "It is one of the misfortunes of the law that ideas become encysted in phrases and thereafter for a long time cease to provide further analysis." *Hyde v. United States*, 225 U.S. 347, 391 (1912). I will not invoke the maxim "once on demurrage, always on demurrage" as a substitute for reasoning. The conflicting arbitration decisions establish the disagreement and lack of uniformity regarding the demurrage issue in the industry itself. I have reviewed the charter as a whole in order to determine the intention of the parties regarding the meaning of the words contained in clause 8.

Clause 8 specifies a number of contingencies exonerating the charterer from liability for demurrage or reducing the rate at which demurrage is payable. Plaintiff argues that once a ship is on demurrage, the six hour notice time and the shifting and deballasting exceptions are no longer applicable. Plaintiff further argues that Sun was well aware of this and Sun could have added language insuring that the exceptions would apply once the vessel was on demurrage. In support of this contention, owner points to the Sun Lightering Clause, inserted in the charter by Sun. The pertinent language of this clause reads:

> If lightering is required to berth at a discharge port, it may be necessary to lighter the vessel while anchored at anchorage. Laytime at anchorage (whether or not the vessel is on demurrage) shall begin six (6) hours after receipt of Notice of Readiness by Charterers or when first lighter barge arrives alongside, whichever occurs first, and shall end when vessel weighs anchor to proceed to berth.

Plaintiff argues that if clauses 6 and 7 can be read as if they contained the words "whether or not the vessel is on demurrage," then charterer would not have deemed it necessary to insert that language in the Sun Lightering Clause. The Sun Lightering Clause is Sun's own clause, whereas clauses 6 and 7 are standard clauses found in the ASBATANKVOY charter. Defendants argue that the Sun Lightering Clause is inserted in the charter and is adapted from a booklet written by a broker who is paid by the shipowner. Given the fact that the Sun Lightering Clause is an addition and not part of the ASBATANKVOY form, I do not believe that the incongruity of language between the Sun Lightering Clause and clauses 6, 7 and 8 is determinative of the parties' intention.

Clause 8 reads that charterer shall pay for "all time loading and discharging and used laytime as elsewhere herein provided exceeds the allowed laytime as elsewhere herein specified." (emphasis added). "All time loading and discharging" must mean all laytime, since the definition of laytime is that amount of time spent loading and discharging. Additionally, to follow the "all time" argument to its logical extension would require inclusion of voyage time, which the charterer is not required to pay.

The Notice of Readiness Clause (clause 6) states that laytime shall commence within six hours after receipt of the notice of readiness. Plaintiff argues that once allowed laytime has expired, there is no laytime to commence, thus all time, including the six hours, should count as time on demurrage. Clause 8 directs that in order to determine the amount of demurrage, the total amount of laytime used must first be determined. Thus, even though a vessel may be on demurrage, nevertheless laytime must always be calculated. Since laytime itself is still being calculated, it is fallacious to state that there is no laytime to commence once the vessel is on demurrage. The difference is that once the vessel is on demurrage, the laytime that will commence after the six hours has run is used laytime rather than allowed laytime. I conclude that the six hours after receipt of notice of readiness should not be included in a demurrage calculation.

The language of clause 8 which states "used laytime as elsewhere herein provided," requires that I must refer back to clause 7 in order to determine what are the exceptions to used laytime. Thus, the exceptions in clause 7 are applicable. Shifting and deballasting are specifically excepted from used laytime in a separate clause of the contract. Viewing the contract as a whole, shifting and deballasting should not be counted in a demurrage calculation because they remain exceptions to laytime.

Additionally, clause 8 states that "the charterer shall pay for all time loading and discharging [in other words, all laytime] and used laytime as elsewhere herein provided [in other words, excluding the shifting and deballasting exceptions in clause 7] exceeds the allowed laytime elsewhere herein specified [72 hours]." Thus, the charterer must pay for excess used laytime. Since an excess of something includes more of the same thing, it follows that at the end of the voyage, all laytime should be calculated and excepted used laytime should be subtracted along with the 72 hours of allowed laytime with the remainder constituting time on demurrage. This total would not include all activities specifically excluded from used laytime as well as the six hour port time. The six hour period is not included in demurrage under this theory because laytime does not commence until after the six hours. Therefore, the demurrage clause creates the following calculation: ALL LAYTIME ACTUALLY USED minus ALLOWED LAYTIME equals DEMURRAGE. Applying this equation to the present case, Sun Oil Company is not liable for damages for the six hour notice time and time spent shifting and deballasting.

IV.

The second issue in this case is a dispute whether bad weather interrupts laytime and the consequences to the parties in this case. Under the first charter, the parties agreed that the vessel was delayed by bad weather for 39 hours at the loading port. Once a vessel is on demurrage, clause 8 requires that the demurrage rate should be reduced by one-half if demurrage is incurred by fire, explosion, storms and other stated events. Sun argues that they, in error, paid demurrage at one-half the demurrage rate under the mistaken impression that the weather delay, which closed the port to all vessels, occurred after the 72 hours of allowed laytime had expired rather than before the vessel went on demurrage.

Clause 6 states, in part, "However, where delay is caused to vessel getting into berth after giving notice of readiness for any reason over which charterer has no control, such delay shall not count as used laytime." (emphasis added). This last sentence of clause 6 relieves charterer of responsibility for delays in berthing over which it has no control. [Citations omitted].

One panel held that weather delay interrupted the running of time and prevented laytime from commencing. Ore Sea Transport S.A. (M/V Siboto), S.M.A. 1469 (N.Y. Arb. 1980). Thus, in consideration of the foregoing discussion, I conclude that under clause 6, delays for which the charterer has no control are exceptions to used laytime and would generally remain exceptions throughout the voyage. However, clauses 6 & 8 must be interpreted together to determine the manifest intention of the parties. There is language in clause 8 which specifically addresses situations over which charterers have no control. This pertinent language, which follows the first sentence previously discussed in this opinion, states:

> If, however, demurrage shall be incurred at ports of loading and/or discharge by reason of fire, explosion, storm, or by a strike, lockout, stoppage or restraint of labor or by breakdown of machinery or equipment in or about the plant of the charterer, supplier, shipper or consignee of the cargo, the rate of demurrage shall be reduced one-half of the amount stated in Part I per running hour or pro rata for part of an hour for demurrage so incurred.

Since these events might accumulate a substantial amount of time, clause 8 addresses these specific risks and requires charterer to pay half the demurrage rate if the vessel is on demurrage once one of the stated events occurs, thereby carving out an exception to the general rule that these events would remain exceptions to laytime throughout the voyage. Defendants in this case contend that they are not liable for any demurrage when the bad weather delay occurred because the vessel was not yet on demurrage. They further argue that the owners would be unjustly enriched if allowed to keep the demurrage payment for the bad weather time.

* * *

Defendant argues that the owners would be unjustly enriched if they are allowed to keep the amount paid in respect to bad weather time. If one party is unjustly enriched, he should make repayment to the other. *Meehanv. Cheltenham Township*, 410 Pa. 446, 189 A.2d 593 (1963). No one should unjustly enrich himself at the expense of another by reason of an incorrect mistake of law or fact entertained by the parties. 13 WILLISTON ON CONTRACTS, § 1582 (3d ed. 1970). Money paid under a mistake of fact can be recovered. *Gulf Oil Corp. v. Lone Star Producing Co.*, 332 F.2d 28 (5th Cir. 1963).

I conclude that the Shipping Corporation of India was unjustly enriched because the vessel was not yet on demurrage when the bad weather delay occurred and Sun Oil Company is therefore not liable for half the demurrage rate during that period. Therefore, the Shipping Corporation of India will return the $8,742.50 to the Sun Oil Company.

* * *

Note

It is very doubtful whether this decision can be regarded as correct. The usual position is that charterparty clauses only interrupt the running of time on demurrage if they specifically so provide, and clauses interrupting the running of laytime have no effect once laytime has expired. The Voylayrules 93 (see *supra* p. 178), which reflect an international consensus, spell out that result in the definition of "demurrage":

"DEMURRAGE" shall mean an agreed amount payable to the owner in respect of delay to the vessel beyond the laytime, for which the owner is not responsible. *Demurrage shall not be subject to laytime exceptions.* [Emphasis added.]

ORIENT SHIPPING ROTTERDAM B.V. v. HUGO NEU & SONS, INC.

918 F. Supp. 806, 1996 AMC 1366 (S.D.N.Y. 1996)

HAIGHT, Senior District Judge:

Plaintiff Orient Shipping Rotterdam B.V., the disponent owner of the motor vessel Mastrogiorgis B, chartered her to defendant Hugo Neu & Sons, Inc. for a voyage from New York to Bombay, India, with a cargo of shredded scrap metal. The voyage having been completed, plaintiff sues for demurrage incurred at the discharging port. Defendant denies liability for demurrage and counterclaims for despatch.

Unlike most modern charterparties, this one did not contain an arbitration clause. The action, which falls within the admiralty and maritime jurisdiction, was tried to the Court. The following opinion constitutes the Court's findings of fact and conclusions of law pursuant to Rule 52(a), Fed.R.Civ.P.

I

The charterparty between plaintiff and defendant, dated June 19, 1992, called for the Mastrogiorgis B to load a full cargo of shredded scrap at New York and then proceed to one safe berth in Bombay.

The charterparty provided in clause 18:

Cargo is to be loaded, stowed, trimmed at the average rate of 10000 MT per weather working days of 24 consecutive hours, Saturdays after noon, Sundays and holidays excepted, even if used.

Cargo is to be discharged at the average rate of 1500 MT per weather working day of 24 consecutive hours, Saturdays, Sundays and holidays excepted, even if used.

Laytime is reversible.

The vessel loaded 21,262.8 metric tons of cargo at New York. She departed that port on June 25, 1992. On August 9, 1992, the vessel arrived at the port of Bombay.

The master tendered notice of readiness at 11:00 a.m. on August 9, which defendant's Bombay agent accepted on August 10. Upon arrival at the port, the Mastrogiorgis B anchored at the Bombay Floating Light. On August 21 the vessel shifted from the Bombay Floating Light to the anchorage. She was free of pratique on August 21. The vessel remained at the anchorage until August 25 when the port authorities ordered her to shift back to the Bombay floating light. The vessel did not berth until September 10, 1992, when discharging began.

The delay the Mastrogiorgis B encountered in berthing at Bombay resulted from port congestion. During the months of July and August, 1992, a total of eleven vessels with scrap cargoes arrived at the port. Seven scrap vessels arrived between July 13 and August 15. When the Mastrogiorgis B arrived at Bombay on August 9, there were three scrap vessels in berth and three earlier arriving vessels awaiting berth.

The Mastrogiorgis B was berthed in turn. Plaintiff does not contend otherwise.

Shredded scrap is a "direct delivery cargo" at Bombay. Discharge of such cargo is made directly from vessels into trucks for transportation inland. Scrap is not placed and stored on the pier. The trucks are obtained by the cargo receivers. The defendant at bar was the charterer of the vessel. It was not the receiver of the vessel's cargo. That was a third party.

The port authorities at Bombay control the use made of the various berths. Normally only two berths are allotted for the discharge of scrap vessels. Toward the end of July or early August, the port authorities allotted a third berth for the discharge of scrap. They were responding to appeals by cargo receivers to relieve the congestion and consequent waiting time incurred by scrap vessels at Bombay. But then shortages of trucks began to occur. On September 2, 1992, the port authorities reduced the allotted scrap discharging berths from three to two.

At midnight on June 30, 1992, an India-wide transporters' strike became effective. The strike ended on July 13. No trucks were available to receive scrap cargoes at Bombay during the strike and in point of fact, no scrap vessels discharged at the port during that time.

The parties dispute the effect, if any, of the transporters' strike on the delay encountered by the Mastrogiorgis B in obtaining a berth. I draw the logical inference that the strike, which made trucks unavailable to receive scrap cargoes, contributed to the number of vessels waiting in line to discharge when the Mastrogiorgis B arrived at Bombay. However, in the view I take of the case, that finding is not necessary to the decision.

II

The cargo receivers completed discharging the Mastrogiorgis B's cargo on October 4, 1992. The delay the vessel encountered in obtaining a berth caused her to exceed the reversible laytime for loading and discharging. Thus plaintiff asserts a claim for demurrage.

The liability of defendant charterer for demurrage turns upon the proper construction of clause 56 of the charterparty. That clause provides:

Should the delivery of cargo to the place of loading, or shipment or loading or discharging of cargo be prevented or interfered with by reason of war, blockade, revolutions, insurrections, mobilizations, strikes, lockouts of any class of workers, civil commotions, riots, acts of God, plague or other epidemics, the time by which loading/discharging shall be prevented or interfered with by any such cause or causes, or by other cause or causes whatsoever, whether or not of a nature or kind as enumerated above, which shall be beyond the Charterers/Receivers control, shall not count, and demurrage shall not accrue unless the vessel is already on demurrage.

This exception clause is drafted in the broadest possible language. While "strikes" is one of the several identified exceptions, the phrase "or by other cause or causes whatsoever" takes the clause out of the doctrine of ejusdem generis. Accordingly the exception clause relieves defendant from liability for demurrage resulting from port congestion, so long as that congestion was "beyond the Charterers/Receiver's control," clearly the case here.

I base these conclusions upon Steamship Rutherglen Co. Ltd. v. Howard Houlder & Partners, Inc., 203 F. 848 (2d Cir.1913). The charterparty in Rutherglen allowed a specified period of time for loading the cargo, and then provided: "The cargo to be discharged with all possible speed, according to the custom of the port of discharge." When the vessel arrived at the discharging port, "all berths where she could lie afloat were occupied or congested with freight, and neither the charterers' agents nor the master of the steamer were able to get a berth for her sooner." 203 Fed. at 851.

Reversing the district court, the Second Circuit held that the defendant charterer was not liable for demurrage. The first point of decision was that, given the circumstances just described, the charterer could not be charged "with any lack of reasonable diligence in discharging." Id. That holding is not squarely applicable to the case at bar, where the charterparty contained a specific daily discharging rate for the cargo.

However, the court of appeals' alternative ground for decision fully applies to the case at bar. The court said at 203 Fed. 852:

> Finally, we think that, if there was delay in discharging at Dalny, the charterers are relieved from liability therefor by the exceptions contained in the charter party, viz:
>
> > Any time lost in loading and/or discharging through riots, fire, frosts, floods, storms, strikes, lock-outs, accidents to mills or machinery, or any causes beyond the personal control of the said charterers not to be computed as part of the said laydays.
> >
> > The last words cover an independent category of causes not subject to the doctrine of ejusdem generis. It is quite clear that the vessel got the first vacant berth when she could lie afloat as loaded in accordance with the practice prevailing at Dalny. (citations omitted).

Plaintiff at bar seeks to distinguish the Rutherglen because the charterparty in that case provided only that the cargo was "to be discharged with all possible speed, according to the custom of the port of discharge," whereas the Mastrogiorgis B charterparty called for defendant to discharge the cargo at a specified average daily rate. But I think this is a distinction without a difference. All clauses of the charterparty must be read in harmony with each other to the extent possible, so that each may be given its meaning. The provisions in clause 56 that time "shall not count and demurrage shall not accrue" must be read to contemplate and embrace the provision in clause 18 for the rate of discharge. I can discern no principled basis for distinguishing the alternative holding in the Rutherglen from the case at bar. The port congestion at Bombay being beyond the control of defendant, the defendant is relieved from liability for the resulting delay, including liability for demurrage. The Second Circuit's holding in the Rutherglen is cited as the authority for the statement in the leading American text that an exception clause of this breadth "excused delay in discharging, owing to inability to obtain a berth." Poor, American Law of Charter Parties and Ocean Bills of Lading (1968) at 119.

* * *

Following the alternative holding of the Rutherglen, I conclude that in the case at bar, the parties agreed that demurrage would not accrue during delay occasioned by port congestion that was beyond the control of the defendant charterer.**

** As clause 56 specifically recognizes, defendant could not avail itself of its terms if the vessel was already on demurrage when she arrived at Bombay. "Once the lay-days have expired, and the ship is on demurrage, the demurrage days run continuously," notwithstanding the provisions of an exceptions clause. Poor, op. cit., at 120. But the Mastrogiorgis B was not on demurrage when she arrived at Bombay.

III

Given my construction of the exceptions clause in this charter party, I need not decide whether the congestion at Bombay resulted from the land transporters' strike. But it may be useful to recite my finding on that aspect of the case as well.

I find by a preponderance of the credible evidence that the transporters' strike, which made trucks unavailable to receive scrap cargoes at Bombay during the first two weeks in July, resulted in escalating congestion and delay.

Plaintiff's Ex. 58, a review of scrap imports and discharge operations at Bombay for the period April 1992--March 1993, published by the Steel Furnace Association of India (Western Region), contains an enlightening summary of scrap vessels dates of arrival, berthing and completing of discharge at the port. Prior to the transporters' strike, vessels discharging 20,000 metric ton cargoes got in and out of the port relatively quickly. Vessels arriving in early April had completed discharge in late April or early May. Vessels arriving in early May completed discharging in early June; vessels arriving in mid-May or late May completed discharging in mid or late June; but with vessel arrivals beginning in late June, significant slowdowns begin to appear. A vessel that did not make it to her discharging berth by early June was in trouble. P.Ex. 58 summarizes the activity on the part of Bombay's two scrap handling contractors. One of them completed the discharge on June 30 of a vessel that had arrived at the port on May 31 and was berthed on June 11. The other completed discharging a vessel on July 2 which had arrived at the port on May 22 and berthed on June 5. The next vessel handled by the first of these two contractors completed discharging on July 31, having arrived on June 21 and berthed on July 1. The next vessel handled by the second contractor completed discharging on July 24, having arrived on June 16 and berthed on June 23. These delays, which continued during the pertinent period of time, are entirely consistent with defendant's theory that a shortage of trucks during the first two weeks of July, which prevented the direct discharge of steel cargoes from vessels, contributed directly to port congestion and consequent delay in berthing scrap-carrying vessels. The experience of the Mastrogiorgis B was typical of those vessels arriving at the port of Bombay during this period of time.

The lingering effect upon the port of the transporters' strike, demonstrated by a preponderance of the evidence, is sufficient to bring the resulting delay of the Mastrogiorgis B in berthing within the strike exception in clause 56. That is the conclusion reached by Judge Learned Hand in The Nordhvalen, 1923 A.M.C. 398 (S.D.N.Y.1923) (not officially reported). Cargo at the discharge port in question had to be discharged into lighters. A strike of longshoreman had prevented the lighters from being discharged. The strike had been called off when the vessel arrived, but she had to wait for enough lighters to be discharged before her own cargo could be worked. Judge Hand held that the strike exception covered the case: "The Nordhvalen was as directly held up by the past strike as she might have been by a present one." 1923 A.M.C. at 399. In reaching that conclusion, Judge Hand cited and followed an English case, Leonis S.S. Co. v. Joseph Rank, Ltd., 11 Asp.M.C. 162. He regarded Leonis as "precisely in point," saying of it: "There the strike and insurrection had ended before the Leonis arrived at Bahia, but the harbor was filled with vessels with full hulls. The consequent delay was held to fall within a similar [strike] clause." Id.

In The Nordhvalen, Judge Hand distinguished a First Circuit case Niver v. Cheronea S.S. Co., 142 Fed. 402 (1st Cir.1905), where the cause of the crowded harbor was not a strike on wharves, but in the Pennsylvania mines (the charterparty was for the carriage of a cargo of coal). That general strike created a great demand for coal in New England, with the result that Boston Harbor was crowded by vessels beyond its capacity. Judge Hand held that the exception for strikes did not relieve the charterer from liability for demurrage, reasoning that "[a]s the strike had been on before the charter party was written it could not of course be regarded as an event not then in contemplation." 1923 A.M.C. at 399.

Plaintiff at bar seeks to bring itself within the Niver case by arguing that defendant, advised by its Bombay agents, should have foreseen the transporters' strike. But there is no substance to this argument. The charterparty of the Mastrogiorgis B was executed on June 19, 1992. The most that can be said from the trial evidence is that the possibility of a transporters' strike in India was known at that time, but there were widely held hopes for a settlement. There is a quantum difference between the possibility of a strike, which might yet be averted, and a strike in existence at the time the shipowner and charterer executed the charterparty. When the strike actually began, at midnight on June 30, the Mastrogiorgis B was at sea, bound for Bombay, having sailed from New York with her cargo on June 25.

IV

I must now deal with an argument that plaintiff makes to place liability for demurrage upon defendant, notwithstanding the existence of port congestion at Bombay, whether strike generated or not.

Clause 30 of the charterparty provides:

Charterers' privilege to load and unload from or into lighters at berths and/or anchorages. Lighterage and lightening, including fendering, if any, at either end, to be for Charterers' expense, time counting.

Plaintiff argues that in the light of this clause, defendant could and should have discharged the Mastrogiorgis B's cargo into lighters at the anchorage, so that it cannot be said that the delay was "beyond the Charterer's control" within the purview of the exceptions clause, clause 56.

I reject that contention. In the first place, the Second Circuit held in the Rutherglen that a comparable clause gave "the Charterers the privilege of requiring the vessel, if lightened, to go to a wharf where she could not lie afloat with all cargo aboard. They are not obligated to order her to such a berth." 203 Fed. at 852. The present parties' contemplation, as expressed in the charterparty, was that the vessel would proceed to a safe berth in Bombay to discharge. While defendant had the option to discharge into lighters at the anchorage, it was not obligated to do so.

In any event, the defendant cannot be taxed for failure to undertake a task that was not feasible. Discharge of the scrap cargo into lighters at the anchorage would have to be accomplished by the vessel's gear. But it appears to be common ground that the vessel's cargo handling gear could not operate sufficiently well to discharge this steel scrap cargo. That is presumably the reason why the cargo was discharged by shore cranes when the vessel finally reached her berth.

And even if that were not so, the testimony of plaintiff's own witness Pereira made it clear that in 1992, only a limited number of barges, less than ten, with a capacity of only 100 to 500 tons, were available for the lightening of scrap vessels at anchorage. Furthermore, only one daylight shift could be worked at the anchorage during the monsoon season, namely, July and August. The Mastrogiorgis B was loaded with more than 21,000 metric tons of scrap. Whatever the proper construction of clause 30, defendant did not have the practical option of discharging such a cargo into lighters at the anchorage.

* * *

VII

For the foregoing reasons, plaintiff's claim for demurrage fails and defendant's counterclaim for despatch succeeds.

* * *

It is SO ORDERED.

Notes

1. In *United States v. Atlantic Refining Co.*, 112 F. Supp. 76 (D.N.J. 1951) the court discussed the impact of strikes on the charterer's obligation to pay demurrage:

It is well recognized that demurrage is extended freight and that the risk of vissitudes which prevent the loading or discharge of cargo within the stipulated lay days lies unconditionally with the charterers. *Yone Suzuki v. Central Argentine Ry.*, 2 Cir., 27 F.2d 795; *The Marpesia*, 2 Cir., 292 F. 957. But, this absolute liability to pay demurrage is subject to three exceptions: (1) specific exonerating clauses in the charter party; (2) the delay being attributed to the fault of the shipowner or those for whom he is responsible; and (3) a vis major amounting to "a sudden or unforeseen interruption or prevention of the act itself of loading or discharging, not occurring throughout the connivance or fault of the charterers." *Crossman v. Burrill*, 179 U.S. 100, 21 S. Ct. 38, 42 L. Ed. 106; *see also, The Marpesia, supra.*

There is no question of vis major involved here for it can hardly be claimed that the strike referred to in the proof (particularly in view of the contention of respondent) was so unusual, extraordinary and unexpected a circumstance as to be equivalent to vis major.

Respondent contends, assuming arguendo, that the vessel required the assistance of tugboats in order to dock at the Fort Mifflin terminal, and was unable to obtain tugboat assistance because of a strike, the respondent would not be answerable for the resulting delay for the reason that Clause 20(a) of Part II, the general "strike exception" clause of the charter party is a complete and sufficient excuse. However, it does not appear that respondent's exculpation would be so justified particularly in the light of the specific limitations in the demurrage clause (10). In an analogous situation in the case of *Continental Grain Co. v. Armour Fertilizer Works*, D.C., 22 F. Supp. 49, 53, the court said:

> The general 'strike exception' clause in the charter party does not prevent the running of demurrage; some similar phrase is necessary in conjunction with the demurrage clause to free the charterer from the burden of paying demurrage when the delay is due to strikes, etc.

A review of the cases, wherein the courts have held that charterers were not liable for demurrage for delays due to strikes, reveals that, in addition to the general 'strike exception' clause, the charters also contained stipulations exonerating the charters from liability, for demurrage when the delay was due to strikes, riots, etc., said stipulations being incorporated in or appurtenant to the 'lay day' or 'demurrage' clauses of the charter parties. [Cases cited.] *See also Yone Suzuki v. Central Argentine Ry., supra.*

2. What effect, if any, on demurrage should it have when a vessel's crew goes out on strike? *See United States v. M/V Marelena P, supra*, which deals with the effect of a strike by the crew on the "off hire" clause.

3. *Vis major* may also result in frustration of a charter party.

---

a. Arrived Vessel

DEAN H.

Arbitration at New York, July 17, 1952.

1953 AMC 593

* * *

The Dispute

The owner claims demurrage in the sum of $9,792.00 from the charterer of the vessel on the ground that the total laytime at loading and discharging from the *Dean H* was 343 hours and 12 minutes over the 180 hours of total laytime provided for in the charters party.

The charterer denies liability for any demurrage. It contends that the owner did not properly compute the laytime. In addition, it contends that it is entitled to damages in the amount of $12,420.05, from the owner for breach of the charter party, on the ground that through the fault of the owner and its agents, the cargo of molasses was discharged at an inadequate rate and was "contaminated by the addition of water." It also alleges a breach of contract by the owner in placing a lien upon the cargo for freight in violation of the provision in the charter party that payment for freight was to be in New York.

The charter party dated March 24, 1950 and executed by the parties is the determinative document in this matter. Under this agreement the Steamship *Dean H* was chartered to transport 10,000 tons of Black Strap Molasses from Cuba to Greece commencing in April of 1950. The record shows that the molasses was loaded at the ports of Caibarien and Havana in Cuba between April 20th and 25th and that the ship arrived at Piraeus Roads on May 17, 1950. Because her draft was too deep it was necessary to lighter part of the molasses before the ship could proceed to the named port in Greece, Eleusis. Unloading was finally completed at Eleusis on May 27, 1950.

* * *

B. *Unloading at Piraeus.* With respect to the laytime for unloading, the chief dispute concerns the question whether the owner was justified under the charter party in commencing computation from the time the Steamship *Dean H* anchored at Pireaus Roads. The charter party provides, in part 1, as follows:

"Discharging Port(s): ONE (1) safe port in Greece, probably Eleusis (near Piraeus) Charterer's Option."

It is noted that the discharging port is designated as "probably" Eleusis. There is nothing the charter party definitely naming Eleusis as the port of discharge. On the other hand, the charter party is equally silent as to any desire on the charterer's part to name some other port. There is some colloquy between counsel in the minutes of the hearing before the arbitrators as to which of the parties was responsible for designating Eleusis as the discharging port in the new bills of lading, signed May 2, 1950 (*See* S.M. 71-72). Other than the fact that these bills of lading named Eleusis, and in that respect were perfectly consistent with the charter party, it is not at all clear who was responsible. Colloquy between counsel, of course, can hardly be regarded as proper evidence. Considering that under the charter party it was in the charterer's option to name the discharging port, that preference was indicated in the charter party to unload at Eleusis, and that there was no notice from the charterer to substitute another port in Greece, it was reasonable for the Steamship *Dean H* to regard Eleusis as the intended port of discharge, and proceed to act accordingly.

In addition, when the vessel's agent sent a letter to the charterer's agent and the receivers, on May 16th, requesting them to arrange to take part of the cargo "in the open sea of Piraeus Harbor to enable her" to pass through the Salamis Canal for Eleusis because her draft was between 27 feet and 28 feet, the charterer's agent in acknowledging, stated:

we have chartered the S/T *Leman* for partial discharge of the cargo of above mentioned tanker and consequently, we request you to proceed to the necessary formalities (Customs, etc.) for the carrying out of the above work.

There was nothing said in protest of Eleusis as the discharge port. Nor was there any stated desire of the charterer to change the discharge port to Piraeus or some other Greek port.

It is not disputed that no vessel with a draft exceeding 26 feet could reach Eleusis, because to reach the port it was necessary to pass through the Salamis Canal, and Greek Naval regulations prohibited vessels with a draft in excess of 26 feet from passing through the Canal. It is also beyond question that the charterer was on notice that the Steamship *Dean H's* loaded draft would exceed 26 feet. The description of the ship as contained in the charter party includes the following:

"Loaded draft of Vessel on assigned summer freeboard 27 ft. 7/8 in. in salt water."
"Capacity for cargo: 10,000 Tons (2240 lbs. each) of Molasses (10% more or less, Vessel's option)."
Furthermore, the cargo was designated in the charter party as:

BLACKSTRAP MOLASSES—TEN THOUSAND TONS (10,000) (2240 lbs.) MINIMUM/MAXIMUM Charterer's option.

In contending that the owner was in error in computing laytime from six hours after delivering its notice of readiness at the Piraeus anchorage, the charterer takes the position, *inter alia*, that, under the charter party, the Steamship *Dean H* could not be an "arrived ship" for purposes of unloading laytime, until she was inside the port of Eleusis. (*See* Exs. C and G attached to charterer's main brief). In other words, it argues that, under Clause 5 of the charter party, berth or no berth, laytime does not commence until the ship is within the port designated.

The charterer's argument, however, ignores or fails to consider the provisions of Clauses 1 (a) and 9 of the charter party. Clause 1 (a) states, in material part, as follows:

and being so loaded shall forthwith proceed, as ordered on signing Bills of Lading, to the Discharging Port(s), *or so near thereunto as she may safely get (always afloat) and deliver said cargo.* (emphasis added)

Clause 9 provides:

The Vessel shall load and discharge at any safe place or wharf, or alongside vessels or lighters reachable on her arrival, which shall be designated and procured by the Charterer, provided the Vessel can proceed thereto, lie at, and depart therefrom always safely afloat, any lighterage being at the expense, risk and peril of the Charterer. The Charterer shall have the right of shifting the Vessel at ports of loading and/or discharge from one safe berth to another on payment of all ... extra port charges and port expenses incurred by reason of using more than one berth. Time consumed on account of shifting shall count as used laytime except as otherwise provided in Clause 14.

That the anchorage at Pireaus was a safe place was never questioned by the charterer. Therefore, since the Steamship *Dean H* could not enter Eleusis "safely afloat," it was within the terms of the charter party for her to deliver the cargo at the Piraeus anchorage; and the notice of readiness to discharge was properly given.

Mencke vs. Cargo of Java Sugar, 187 U.S. 248, supports the owner's position here. There, the charter party provided, *inter alia*, as follows:

or at option of charterers to order vessels ... to discharge at New York ... or so near the port of discharge as she may safely get and deliver the same, always afloat....
all goods to be brought to and taken from alongside of the ship, always afloat, at the said charterers' risk and expense.... ; lighterage, if any, to reach the port of destination, or deliver the cargo at port of destination, remains for account of receivers,....

The vessel was ordered to discharge at New York at a refinery above Brooklyn Bridge, but was unable to proceed directly there because the height of her masts was such that she could not pass under the bridge. Consequently, the cargo was discharged into lighters at a dock below the bridge. In contending that the expense of lighterage was upon the owners, the receivers of the cargo argued that the lighterage clause of the charter party did not relieve the owners of the ship from their obligation to proceed to a designated dock above the bridge, and to there deliver the cargo. In rendering judgment in favor of the owners, however, the Court at pages 253-254, stated:

In such a condition of affairs we think that resort to lighterage was natural and reasonable and within the obvious and fair import of the terms of the charter party. The clause, which is claimed to give the charterers or their assigns the right to appoint the dock in which to discharge cargo contains conditions that the port must be safe, and that the vessel must discharge, always afloat, either at a safe port or so near the port of discharge as she can safely get.... A ship could not be said to be afloat, whether the obstacle encountered was a shoal or bar in the port over which she could not proceed, or a bridge under or through which she could not pass; nor could she be said to have safely reached a dock if required to mutilate her hull or her permanent masts.

In *The Gazelle and Cargo*, 128 U.S. 474, it was held that where a charter party provided for a voyage "to a safe, direct, Norwegian or Danish port, as ordered on signing bills of lading or as near thereunto as she can safely get and always lay and discharge afloat," it was the responsibility of the charterer to order the ship to a port which she could safely enter with her cargo, or which, at least, had a safe anchorage outside where she could lie and discharge afloat. In *The Edward T. Stotesbury*, 187 Fed. 111, the court ruled that, where by the terms of a charter party the charterer is to name the berth for discharging, he should be ready to receive the cargo when the vessel is ready to deliver, even if she cannot do so either because he has failed to name the berth, or because he has named a berth to which she cannot get, or to which she is prevented from getting through no fault of hers.

The charterer also contends that when the captain of the Steamship *Dean H* found that it was not safe to enter the port of Eleusis, he should have gone to the port of Piraeus instead of anchoring in Piraeus Roads. He cites *The Alhambra*, LR 6 Prob. Div. 68, in support of this contention. The case is distinguishable, however, for there the court held as inadmissible evidence sought to be presented of a custom of vessels which were too deep to enter the port in question to discharge a portion of their cargo in the roads outside, and that it could be done with reasonable safety. Therefore, according to the court, the vessel was justified in refusing to discharge at the unsafe port but in going to the nearest safe port. In the case at bar, as already noted, it is not disputed that the anchorage at Piraeus was a safe berth. That being so, the fact that the master did not take the more extreme step of discharging the entire cargo at some other port, rather than to lighten the ship by 1000 tons so he could unload the remaining 9000 tons at Eleusis as called for in the charter party and the bills of lading, cannot be regarded as a breach. Moreover, according to the Central Harbor Master of Piraeus, the anchorage in Piraeus Roads was considered to be within the legal and fiscal limits of the Port of Piraeus anyway.

C. *Unloading at Eleusis.* Charterer contends that the claim for demurrage must fail because of the inadequate rate of discharge of the cargo caused by, (1) inadequate facilities of the Steamship Dean H, (2) improper temperature, (3) insufficient pressure, and (4) neglect and default of the owner and its agents. The claim that the vessel's hose was inadequate because it was a 6 inch rather than an 8 inch hose, can be dismissed as being without merit. The charter party provides, in Special Provision #4, that the owner will furnish 130 feet of hose, but does not specify any particular dimension as being required. In the absence of a showing of a custom and practice to furnish hose of a minimum diameter of 8 inches, it cannot be said that the owner was bound to furnish any hose other than that which constituted the regular equipment of the vessel.

The evidence shows that when the Steamship Dean H anchored at Eleusis and prepared to discharge to the shore installations, it was discovered that an additional 50 feet of hose was needed. The required hose was furnished by the captain from the vessel's extra equipment in the absence, according to the captain, of any available hose on shore. The captain testified that the extra length of hose was furnished on the condition that neither he nor the ship, "would be responsible for any loss of cargo if the hose broke because I wasn't sure what shape it was in." (SM 21-22). He also testified that after the charterer's representative refused to confirm in writing the above condition, he wrote and gave to the representative the following letter:

> As you have stated you did not have any hose available to make the connection from the vessels (*sic*) stern to the shore line I have complied with your request and loaned you the use of one fifty foot length of six inch hose belonging to the vessel....
>
> As I informed you this hose is not new and I cannot guarantee it as to strength nor in any way at all but as you have requested that I loan you this hose under the circumstances as stated above I must also warn you that the vessel is not to be responsible for any loss of cargo or freight should this hose burst. I am complying with your request not to exceed 100 pounds pressure on the line also.
>
> The charterer admits receiving the letter in question.

Under the circumstances, any inadequacy in the rate of discharge attributable to the extra length of hose, which was admittedly not in good condition, cannot be made the responsibility of the owner. Clause 10 of the charter party providing that the risk and peril of pumping out operations was on the vessel applies "only so far as the Vessel's permanent connections" are involved.

* * *

YONE SUZUKI v. CENTRAL ARGENTINE RY.

27 F.2d 795 (2d Cir. 1928), *cert. denied*, 278 U.S. 652, 49 S. Ct. 178, 73 L. Ed. 563 (1929)

* * *

[The important clauses in each charter, all of which agreed "to freight on the said steamer ... to Beunos [sic] Aires, or as near thereunto as she may safely get and always lie afloat," were:

* * *

4. Lay days for loading...to commence from time steamer is ready to load (or within 96 hours after readiness to load if delayed awaiting turn at berth) and master has given notice in writing of such readiness to the party of the second part or his agent.

5. Lay days for discharging shall be as follows: Commencing from twenty-four (24) hours after arrival at or off discharging port whether steamer is in berth or not, cargo to be taken from alongside by the consignee named in the bill of lading at port of discharge as quickly as steamer can deliver, but in no case at less than 1,000 tons (of 2,240 pounds each) per running day, Sundays and legal holidays excepted, unless used.

* * *

15. Steamer to be discharged at such wharf as party of the second part or their agents may designate, where steamer may always safely lie afloat.]

* * *

AUGUSTUS HAND, Circuit Judge:

The most important contest is over the demurrage at the discharging port, for it affects all the vessels and represents by far the largest claims. It is said that the clause of the charter whereby the shipowners agreed "to freight on the said steamer ... to Beunos [*sic*] Aires or as near thereunto as she may safely get and always lie afloat and there deliver a full and complete cargo" is controlling, and that though clause 5 prescribed lay days for discharging as "commencing from twenty-four (24) hours after arrival at or off discharging port whether steamer is in berth or not," the effect of the two clauses was to require the vessels to reach their designated wharves before the lay days would begin. This argument is further pressed because clause 4 prescribed that lay days for loading should commence from a certain number of hours "after steamer is ready to load."

But we agree with the District Court that the clause as to lay days for discharging cannot be explained in any such way. The time when lay days for discharging are to commence is clearly stated to be the time when the vessel is "at or off discharging port whether vessel is in berth or not." The difference in the language from that governing lay days for loading was doubtless intended to give vessels the benefit of delays in reaching berth in calculating demurrage. Vessels at the time were in enormous demand and could exact charter provisions strongly in their favor. Lay days do not necessarily begin when a ship is at or off her berth, but their beginning depends on the terms of the charter provisions. The port is ordinarily the place where the port authorities are exercising jurisdiction. Such a place was Buenos Aires Roads. *Sailing Ship Garston Company v. Hickie*, [1884] 15 Q.B.D. 580. As the District Judge said:

No vessel can proceed beyond the roads without a permit. No permit is granted till an immediately available berth is designated. There is no stopping place between the roads and berths under ordinary circumstances. The roads are the place where vessels waiting for a berth usually lie. The time when the vessels arrived at the roads, therefore, must determine the beginning of lay days unless it was intended that they should not begin until after a vessel was actually in or at least off its berth.

The old Welsh form of coal charter, which had been used in the coal trade with Buenos Aires, provided that lay days at the discharging port should begin when the steamer is "ready to unload and written notice given, whether in berth or not." The Washington form of charter adopted by the Shipping Board was new and different, and plainly placed on the charterer and consignee the hazards of delay at the terminus of the voyage, which had theretofore been borne by the ship.

We think that such explicit language as "at or off" the "discharging port" made Buenos Aires Roads the place where the lay days began to run. The distance from the docks is not so extraordinarily great, and little, if any, greater than the distance from quarantine in New York Harbor to some of the uptown docks.

It is also significant that in one of the original answers it was admitted that the vessel "arrived at Buenos Aires Roads, which is at or off the port of Buenos Aires." *See, also,* answer in case of Sifuku Maru (folio 69).

* * *

In *Owners of Borg v. Darwen Paper Co.*, 8 Lloyd's List Law Reports, 49 (1921), the Court of King's Bench held that "at or off the port" did not mean arrival at the dock, and that those words fixed the time from which the vessel should be discharged at the rate of 400 tons per working day. The court, in holding that the 24-hour period began to run with the arrival of the ship at night off the port, said: "But, dock or no dock, the beginning of the discharge is to be reckoned from the time the ship arrived at or off the port, and I do not see how this letter affects it at all." (The letter was a notification that the vessel had reached her dock.)

Even if "readiness to discharge," and not arrival "at or off" the port, were the test of the beginning of the lay days, those days would begin when the vessel arrived at the port, and not when she arrived at or just off her berth. Such was the rule laid down by Judge Ward in *The Edward T. Stotesbury, supra,* who said:

> When ... the charterer is to name the berth, he should be ready to receive the cargo when the vessel is ready to deliver, even if she cannot do so, either because he has not named the berth, or because he has named a berth to which she cannot get, or to which she is prevented from getting through no fault of hers. *Carbon Slate Co. v. Ennis* (C.C.A.) 114 F. 260; *Roney v. Talbot & Co.* (C.C.A.) 161 F. 309; *The Lake Yelverton* (C.C.A.) 300 F. 47; *Pyman Bros. v. Dreyfus Bros. & Co.,* 24 Q.B.D. 152.

Even a case that goes as far as *Tharsis v. Morel,* [1891] 2 Q.B. 647, does not apply to a charter party which provides that lay days shall begin 24 hours after arrival "whether steamer is in berth or not." *W. K. Niver Coal Co. v. Cheronea S.S. Co.* (C.C.A.) 142 F. 402, 5 L.R.A. (N.S.) 126; *Northfield S.S. Co. v. Compagnie L'Union des Gaz,* [1911] 1 K.B. 434. In such cases the lay days begin when the vessel is in port, and not when at her berth.

* * *

Note: Notice of Readiness

Charterparties usually provide that the ship must give Notice of Readiness (NOR) before laytime can commence. They often also provide that NOR can be given "whether in berth or not" or (less commonly) "whether in port or not". These are commonly abbreviated to WIBON and WIPON. (Other variants can be found, such as WIFPON, "whether in free pratique or not", WCCON, "whether cleared Customs or not".) These provisions make it clear that the ship can give NOR before arriving at the designated berth and in particular, that it can give NOR and start the laytime clock running while waiting for berth. In effect, they shift the risk of waiting time from shipowner to charterer.

Note: Risk of Delay

In *Brennan Corporation v. United States*, 641 F. Supp. 245, 1987 AMC 1955 (D.D.C. 1986) the United States had contracted with Refinery to provide deballasting services for a vessel, the *Anatoli,* the United States had chartered. Refinery was negligent in providing these services. As a result the vessel became contaminated and could not load the cargo. Another vessel had to be substituted. Owner claimed demurrage for the time lost during the deballasting operation and the time expended in cleaning the contaminated vessel. The court upheld the vessel owner's claim.

> It is recognized under charter party and maritime law that after the Anatoli tendered a notice of readiness, the defendant assumed all risks for delays suffered by the plaintiff. *United States v. Atlantic Refining Co.,* 112 F. Supp. 76, 80 (D.N.J. 1951); *Compagnia di Navigazione Mauritius Rome v. Kulukundis,* 182 F. Supp. 258, 263 (E.D.N.Y. 1959), *aff'd,* 277 F.2d 161 (2d Cir. 1960). Once the Anatoli announced a readiness to accept the cargo, the defendant was required to provide a safe berth, to assist in loading the cargo and not to interfere with the Anatoli's efforts in the performance of the loading process. Likewise, the Refinery, acting at the behest of the Sealift Command, had a duty not to prevent the

Anatoli from completing the contract. When the Refinery caused the contamination of the Anatoli's ballast tanks, it interfered with the plaintiff's performance of the contract with Sealift Command.

* * *

The government's contention that it had a right to cancel the charter party contract because the Anatoli had contaminated tanks, irrespective of its origin, cannot be sustained. It should not have the right to cancel the agreement when the Refinery hired by the government to provide the cargo and to provide the deballasting facilities was the source of the contamination. "Charterers cannot, on the one hand, set up a barrier to the vessel's satisfying the charter party requirements for becoming an arrived ship and then seek to use this same barrier as a defense to avoid payment of demurrage. *Diamantis Gafos*, 1970 American Maritime Cases 945, 948 (Arb. N.Y. 1969).

---

b. Vis Major

CROSSMAN v. BURRILL

179 U.S. 100, 21 S. Ct. 38, 45 L. Ed. 106 (1900)

The libel alleged, in the fourth article, that the vessel was loaded with the cargo of lumber at Pensacola, and sailed thence for Rio Janeiro, where she arrived about August 30, 1893; and, in the fifth article, "that on September 4, 1893, notice in writing that the vessel was ready to discharge her said cargo was duly given by the master of said vessel or her duly authorized agents to the Companhia Industrial do Brazil, the agent of the respondents at said port of Rio, who received the said cargo;" but that the vessel did not complete the discharge until November 28, 1893, being a period of fifty-three days beyond the twenty-six days, Sundays exclusive, allowed for the discharge by the charter.

Third. "That when said vessel arrived at Rio Janeiro, the owners of said cargo used all reasonable diligence in and about receiving the cargo shipped upon the said vessel, and removing the same therefrom; that the libellants were prevented from discharging the same, and the respondents were prevented from receiving the same, any sooner than they did, by reason of the acts of the public enemy, to wit, certain vessels of war which were then in the harbor of Rio Janeiro, and were engaged in firing upon the forts in said harbor, and making war upon the government of Brazil, and that the firing between said vessels of war and the said forts made it impossible to discharge the said cargo or to receive it from the said vessel, any sooner than it was discharged or received; that the said cargo was delivered according to the custom of said port of Rio Janeiro, and that the detention alleged in the libel, if any such therebe, was caused by said acts of the public enemy, and not by any default of the respondents; that the captain of the said vessel and Messrs. Phipps Brothers & Co., the agents of the libellants, acquiesced in the said delay, and recognized the necessity therefor."

* * *

The libellants' claim for demurrage is based on the provisions of the charter-party by which, after the vessel is ready to discharge her cargo of lumber at the port of destination, and written notice thereof given to the charterers, they agree to discharge the lumber "at the average rate of not less than twenty thousand superficial feet per running day, Sundays excepted," and to pay a certain sum, by way of demurrage, "for each and every day's detention by default of" the charterers or their agents.

* * *

The other principal question is of the validity of the defense that the delay in discharging the cargo was caused by the acts of the public enemy, and not by any default of the charterers.

Upon this question, the courts below differed in opinion, the District Court holding that the defence pleaded was a good one, and the Circuit Court of Appeals holding that it was not.

This defence, as set up in the amended answer filed in the Circuit Court of Appeals, is that, when the vessel arrived at Rio Janeiro, the owners of the cargo used all reasonable diligence in and about receiving and removing it; that the ship owners were prevented from discharging the cargo, and the respondents were prevented from receiving it, any sooner than they did, "by reason of the acts of the public enemy, to wit, certain vessels of war which were then in the harbor of Rio Janeiro, and were engaged in firing upon the forts in said harbor, and making war upon the government of Brazil, and that the firing between said vessels of war and the said forts made it impossible to discharge the said cargo or to receive it from the said vessel, any sooner than it was discharged or received; that the said cargo was delivered according to the custom of said port of Rio Janeiro, and that the detention alleged in the libel, if any such there be, was caused by said acts of the public enemy and not by any default of the respondents."

We are of opinion that, under a charter-party expressed in such terms, the defence of vis major, as thus pleaded, affords a complete answer to the claim for demurrage.

It is to be remembered that by the terms of this charter party it is only for "detention by default of" the charterers or their agent, that they agree to pay the amount of demurrage specified in the charter.

A detention which is caused, not by any act of the ship owners or of the charterers, but wholly by the actual firing of guns from an enemy's ships of war upon the forts in the harbor, directly affecting the vessel and making the discharge of the cargo dangerous and impossible, cannot be considered as caused by "default" of the charterers, in any just sense of the word.

In *Towle v. Kettell*, (1849) 5 Cush. 18, the Supreme Judicial Court of Massachusetts, in an opinion delivered by Mr. Justice Fletcher, with the concurrence of Chief Justice Shaw and Justices Wilde and Dewey, held that, under a similar provision in a charter-party, the charterers were not liable for demurrage while the vessel was detained in quarantine by order of a foreign government.

The Circuit Court of Appeals, in support of the opposite conclusion, quoted from an opinion delivered by Mr. Justice Clifford, in the Circuit Court of the United States for the District of Massachusetts, the following passage:

The settled rule is that, where the contract of affreightment expressly stipulates that a given number of days shall be allowed for the discharge of the cargo, such a limitation is an express stipulation that the vessel shall in no event be detained longer for that purpose, and that if so detained it shall be considered as the delay of the freighter, even where it was not occasioned by his fault, but was inevitable. Where the contract is that the ship shall be unladen within a certain number of days, it is no defence to an action for demurrage that the overdelay was occasioned by the crowded state of the docks, or by port regulations or government restraints.

Davis v. Wallace, (1868) 3 Clifford, 123, 131. But in none of the authorities cited, either by the learned justice in that case, or by the Circuit Court of Appeals in this, in support of this general statement, was the liability of the charterers for demurrage restricted to the case of their default. In *Davis v. Wallace*, indeed, their liability was so restricted; but the defence was a crowded state of the docks, and no question of port regulations or government restraints was before the court.

In *Thatcher v. Boston Gas Light Co.*, (1875) 2 Lowell, 361, 363, Judge Lowell, while following that decision in a similar case, said that the decisions in *Towle v. Kettell*, and in *Davis v. Wallace* "are not inconsistent with each other; and they mean that the proviso intends to exonerate the charterer from delay occasioned by superior force acting directly upon the discharge of that cargo, and not from the indirect action of such force, which by its operation upon other vessels has caused a crowded state of the docks." And he distinctly recognized that a failure of contract on the part of the charterer, "caused by a direct and immediate vis major, or something like it," would not be a "default," within the meaning of the charter-party.

In *Davis v. Pendergast*, (1879) 16 Blatchford, 565, 567, Chief Justice Waite, speaking of a similar provision, said: "The respondents, in effect, agreed that no more than forty-five running days should be occupied in loading and discharging the cargo, unless it was occasioned by some fault of the vessel, or some unusual and extraordinary interruption that could not have been anticipated when the contract was made."

The case of *Nitrate of Soda*, (1894) 15 U.S. App. 369, in the Circuit Court of Appeals for the Ninth Circuit, upon which these libellants much rely, falls far short of supporting their claim. In that case, the clause in question was in the same words as in this case; the charterers sent the vessel, for the purpose of loading a cargo of nitrate of soda which they had purchased, to a port in Chili, during the existence of a civil war there, and while the port was in the possession of the insurgents; the sellers declined for a time to deliver the cargo, because they feared that if the export duty, which by the law of Chili [sic] was payable upon all such cargoes, was paid by them to the insurgents, they might remain liable for it to the rightful government. It was held that the charterers were liable for the stipulated demurrage during the delay so occasioned. The court, speaking of the word "default" in the charter, said: "The most that can be claimed for its effect is that it excludes liability of the charterers for delay in loading or discharging, if the delay result from a sudden or unforeseen interruption or prevention of the act itself of loading or discharging, not occurring through the connivance or fault of the charterers." "But there was no interference upon the part of the Chilian government, or upon the part of any armed force, to prevent their obtaining possession of the cargo, or handling or moving the same, or placing it within reach of the vessel's tackle." 15 U.S. App. 374, 376.

In the case at bar, the defence of vis major, as pleaded in the answer, was that the ship owners were prevented from discharging the cargo, and the charterers were prevented from receiving it, any sooner than they did, by reason of acts of the public enemy, to wit, certain vessels of war, then in the harbor of Rio Janeiro, were engaged in firing upon the forts in the harbor and in making war upon the government of Brazil; that the firing between those vessels and those forts made it impossible to discharge or to receive the cargo from the vessel any sooner than it was discharged or received; and that the detention alleged in the libel was caused by those acts of the public enemy, and not by any default of the charterers.

The *vis major*, so pleaded, was, in the words of opinions above cited, a "superior force, acting directly upon the discharge of the cargo;" "a direct and immediate vis major;" an "unusual and extraordinary interruption that could not have been anticipated when the contract was made;" "a sudden and unforeseen interruption or prevention of the act itself of loading or discharging, not occurring through the connivance or fault of the charterers," and an "interference on the part of an armed force, preventing the handling or moving of the cargo."

Upon principle, and according to the general current of authority, the detention alleged was not caused by default of the charterers, and did not render them responsible for demurrage, under this charter-party.

---

c. Cesser Clause

THE "AEGIS BRITANNIC"

Court of Appeal

[1987] 1 Lloyd's Rep. 119

Judgment

LORD JUSTICE DILLON: The Court has before it an application by charterers for leave to appeal against a decision of Mr. Justice Staughton given on June 7, 1985, in the Commercial Court....

* * *

As to the facts, by a charter-party in amended Synacomex form dated Apr. 23, 1980, owners chartered the vessel to charterers for the carriage of a cargo of rice from a United States Gulf port to Basrah in Iraq. During discharge by the stevedores, the cargo was partially damaged. In consequence, on Nov. 30, 1982, the owners were held liable to the cargo receivers by an Iraqi Court in Basrah in respect of that damage. In the arbitration, the owners claimed damages in so far as they had paid and an indemnity in so far as they had not yet paid from the charterers in respect of that liability. By his award of Dec. 4, 1984, the arbitrator, Mr. Bruce Harris, found the charterers liable to the owners. The question in the arbitration, in the hearing before Mr. Justice Staughton and in the appeal turns on whether the charterers can escape liability by the cesser clause in the charter-party. The argument has turned mainly on three clauses or parts of three clauses in the charter-party.

Firstly, there is cl. 5 which imposes the liability on the charterers in the first place. It provides as follows:

5. Cargo to be brought to, loaded, and stowed, respectively discharged at the expense and risk of Shippers Charterers respectively Receivers/Charterers.

Then there is cl. 20, the lien clause. It provides as follows:

20. Owners shall have a lien on the cargo for freight, deadfreight and demurrage. Charterers shall remain responsible for deadfrieght and demurrage incurred at loading port. Charterers shall also remain responsible for freight and demurrage incurred at discharge port.

Then there is the cesser clause, cl. 35, which is one of a number of typed additional clauses, starting with cl. 22, added to the printed form of the charter-party. Clause 35 provides as follows:

35. Charterers' liability under this charter-party to cease upon cargo being shipped except as regards payment of freight, deadfreight and demurrage incurred at both ends.

* * *

The Courts have long since considered cesser clauses. The leading authority is the decision of this Court in *Clink v. Radford & Co.*, [1891] 1 Q.B. 625. There it so happened that the difficulty of construction was concerned with how the lien clause and the cesser clause were to be read together. Lord Esher, it seems to me, put things on a more general basis. He said the following at p. 627:

It seems to me, without going through the cases that have been referred to, that certain rules have been laid down in them which will enable us to decide this particular case. In my opinion the main rule to be derived from the cases as to the interpretation of the cesser clause in a charter-party, is that the court will construe it as inapplicable to the particular breach complained of, if by construing it otherwise the shipowner would be left unprotected in respect of that particular breach, unless the cesser clause is expressed in terms that prohibit such a conclusion. In other words, it cannot be assumed that the shipowner without any mercantile reason would give up by the cesser clause rights which he had stipulated for in another part of the contract. If that be true, then the question in this particular case, as in every other case, will depend upon this, whether if we apply the cesser clause to the particular breach complained of, and so hold the charterer to be free, the shipowner has any remedy for his loss. If he has, we should construe the cesser clause in its fullest possible meaning, and say that the charterer is released: but if we find that by construing it, the shipowner would be left without any remedy whatever for the breach, then we should say that it could not have been the meaning of the parties that the cesser clause should apply to such a breach.

That language seems to me to be directly applicable to treating the liability of the charterers under cl. 5 as immediately discharged by the cesser clause, cl. 35. Lord Justice Bowen puts the matter similarly. He says, at p. 629, the following:

There is no doubt that parties may, if they choose, so frame the clause as to emancipate the charterer from any specified liability without providing for any terms of compensation to the shipowner; but such a contract would not be one we should expect to see in a commercial transaction. The cesser clauses as they generally come before the courts are clauses which couple or link the provisions for the cesser of the charterer's liability with a corresponding creation of a lien.

I interject that here the lien and the cesser clauses are separate from each other. I now continue the citation:

> ... There is a principle of reason which is obvious to commercial minds, and which should be borne in mind considering a cesser clause so framed, namely, that reasonable persons would regard the lien given as an equivalent for the release of responsibility which the cesser clause in its earlier part creates, and one would expect to find the lien commensurate with the release of liability. That is a sound principle of commercial reasoning which has been sanctioned by the courts in the cases cited to us, and which has been recognized in the chain of important and valuable judgments of the present Master of the Rolls. That being the principle of construction to apply, one would not expect to find a shipowner placing his ship and himself at the mercy of a charterer without some equivalent, or contracting on a given event to release the charterer from all liability unless there were some other mode of protecting himself against the act of the charterer.

Again, the wording is general and is not limited to find that the other remedy is given by the lien clause. This, as I see it, is all part of the normal process of construction in which all the various relevant clauses of the contract have to be read together, without taking the wording of one standing on its own and looking no further. The appellant's construction of the cesser clause in effect involves striking out the word "charterers" wherever it appears in the passage from cl. 5 which I have read, at any rate in relation to discharge.

It is submitted, very probably rightly by Mr. Priday for the charterers, that the references in that passage in cl. 5 to shippers and receivers, envisages that by adoption of clauses of the charter-party into the bills of lading, the owners will have protection against any claims of the receivers of the cargo for damage in discharge. In the present case, the clauses of the charter-party were, we are told, adopted into the bills of lading, but the Court in Iraq refused to give effect to those clauses and the arbitrator in his award has said that that is generally the case in Iraq. Hence the liability as held by the Iraqi Court of the owners to the receivers of the cargo. But where the question has arisen in a context of reconciling a cesser clause and a lien clause, the Court has held that the reconciliation is to be effected by holding that the cesser clause only applies in so far as the lien is effective. This was held first in *Hansen v. Harrold Brothers*, [1894] 1 Q.B. 612. In that case the charter-party permitted the charterers to recharter the ship. The effect of that was that the owners had a lien on the freight under the recharter, but for various reasons that came out as less than the freight payable under the charter-party and therefore it was not an adequate remedy.
Lord Esher, at p. 618, cited from the judgments of the Court in *Clink v. Radford & Co.* He said the following:

> It seems to me that this reasoning has not been and cannot be answered. Therefore the proposition is true that, where the provision for cesser of liability is accompanied by the stipulation as to lien, then the cesser of liability is not to apply in so far as the lien, which by the charterparty the charterers are enabled to create, is not equivalent to the liability of the charterers. Where, in such a case, the provisions of the charterparty enable the charterers to make such terms with the shippers that the lien which is created is not commensurate with the liability of the charterers under the charterparty, then the cesser clause will only apply so far as the lien which can be exercised by the shipowner is commensurate with such liability.

Similarly, in the case of *The Sinoe*, [1971] 1 Lloyd's Rep. 514—a decision of Mr. Justice Donaldson which was upheld by this Court in [1972] 1 Lloyd's Rep. 201—it was held that the cesser clause did not avail charterers where the owners had a lien on cargo which they could not enforce owing to local conditions. I find that reasoning directly applicable in the present case. If the owners had no alternative remedy against the receivers of the cargo or, for that matter anyone else, the cesser clause cannot be construed as immediately cutting out and extinguishing the charterers' primary liability under cl. 5. Accordingly, consistent with the principles in *The Antaios,* I would refuse leave to appeal

* * *

Notes

1. To what extent may a charterer rely on a cesser clause by disclaiming liability and by attempting to shift liability to a consignee of the goods to whom the charterer has transfered a bill of lading issued by the master of the vessel? This was addressed in *Crossman v. Burrill,* 179 U.S. 100, 21 S. Ct. 38, 45 L. Ed. 106 (1900). In this case owner sued charterer for demurrage. The charterer contended:

... That the charter-party referred to in the libel contained a clause providing that the vessel should have an absolute lien upon the cargo for freight and demurrage, and that the charterers' responsibility should cease upon the loading of the cargo and signing of the bills of lading; that said vessel was fully laden, as alleged in the fourth article of the libel, and that thereafter, and long prior to September 4, 1893, (the date upon which it is alleged in the fifth article of said libel that notice in writing was given to the agents of the respondents at Rio Janeiro that said vessel was ready to discharge her cargo,) bills of lading of similar tenor for the whole of said cargo were duly signed by the master of said vessel, a copy of which is annexed hereto, and made part hereof; and said bills of lading were duly assigned and delivered to the Companhia Industrial do Brazil, and by them assigned and delivered to Messrs. Manoel da Cruz & Filho, who thereby became the consignees of said cargo; and that thereupon all liability of these respondents to the owners of said vessel under said charter-party ceased, and it became the duty of the master and owner of said vessel, upon the failure, alleged in the fifth article of said libel, of the consignee of said cargo to discharge the same at the agreed rate per day, to notify said consignee of the amount of the demurrage claimed by reason of said failure, and to hold said cargo until the same should have been paid, in accordance with the terms of said charter party. The bills of lading (as appears by the copy annexed to the answer) state that the number had been shipped by the respondents, and was to be delivered "unto order or to their assigns, they paying freight for the said lumber as per charter party dated March 7, 1893, and average accustomed.

* * *

The libellants' claim for demurrage is based on the provisions of the charter-party by which, after the vessel is ready to discharge her cargo of lumber at the port of destination, and written notice thereof given to the charterers, they agree to discharge the lumber "at the average rate of not less than twenty thousand superficial feet per running day, Sundays excepted," and to pay a certain sum, by way of demurrage, "for each and every day's detention by default of" the charterers or their agents.

The charter-party further requires "the bills of lading to be signed as presented, without prejudice to this charter," and contains these clauses: "Vessel to have an absolute lien upon the cargo for all freight, dead freight and demurrage. Charterers' responsibility to cease when vessel is loaded and bills of lading are signed."

After the vessel had been loaded, bills of lading were duly signed by the master, by the terms of which the cargo was to be delivered to the charterers or their assigns, "they paying freight as per charter-party," "and average accustomed"—referring to the charter by its date, but not mentioning demurrage.

The first question to be considered is how far the claim of the ship owners against the charterers for demurrage is affected by what is commonly called the cesser clause in the charter party, "Charterers' responsibility to cease when vessel is loaded and bills of lading are signed."

The question here is how the clause providing that the charterers' responsibility shall cease when the vessel is loaded and bills of lading are signed is to be reconciled with the other provisions of the charter, which not only require the charterers to pay freight on delivery of the cargo, and demurrage for any delay in such delivery by fault of the charterers or their agent, but declare that the vessel is to have an absolute lien upon the cargo for both freight and demurrage.

* * *

...[I]n a charter-party which contains a clause for cesser of the liability of the charterers, coupled with a clause creating a lien in favor of the shipowner, the cesser clause is to be construed, if possible, as inapplicable to a liability with which the lien is not commensurate.

In the case at bar, the provision of the charter-party, which requires "the bills of lading to be signed as presented, without prejudice to this charter," while it obliges the master to sign bills of lading upon request of the charterers, does not mean that the bills of lading, or the consignee holding them, shall be subject to all the provisions of the charter; but only that the obligations of the charterers to the ship and her owners are not to be affected by the bill of lading so signed. *Gledstanes v. Allen,* (1852) 12 C.B. 202. The bills of lading, as already mentioned, provide only for "paying freight for said lumber as per charter-party dated 7th March, 1893, and average accustomed." They do not mention demurrage, or refer to any provisions of the charter, other than those concerning freight and average. It is well settled that a bills of lading in such a form does not subject an indorsee thereof, who receives the goods under it, to any of those other provisions of the charter. It does not give him notice of, or render him liable to, the specific provisions of the charter, which require a discharge of a certain quantity of lumber per day, or, in default thereof, the payment of a specific sum for a longer detention of the vessel; but he is entitled to take the goods within a reasonable time after arrival, and is liable to pay damages for undue delay in taking them, according to the ordinary rules of law which govern in the absence of specific agreement. *Chappel v. Comfort*, (1861) 10 C.B. (N.S.) 801; *Gray v. Carr*, (1871) L.R. 6 Q.B. 522; *Porteus v. Watney*, (1878) 3 Q.B.D. 534, 537; *Serraino v. Campbell*, (1891) 1 Q.B. 283; *Dayton v. Parke*, (1894) 142 N.Y. 391.

In *McLean v. Fleming*, (1871) L.R. 2 H.L. Sc. 128, on which the charterers relied at the argument in this court, the sole ground on which the endorsees of the bills of lading were held to be bound by the provisions of the charter-party was that they were the persons who had originally authorized the chartering of the ship. *See* L.R. 2 H.L. Sc. 133, 134, 136; S.C.L.R. 6 Q.B. 559, 560. No such fact was pleaded in the case at bar.

The only facts stated in the answer upon this point are that, after the vessel was fully laden, and long before the notice to the charterers that she was ready to discharge, bills of lading, acknowledging that the lumber had been shipped by the respondents, and was to be delivered to their order or assigns, "they paying freight for the said lumber as per charter-party," were signed by the master of the vessel, and "were duly assigned and delivered to the Companhia Industrial do Brazil, and by them assigned and delivered to" the partnership of da Cruz and Filho, "who thereby became consignees of the cargo."

Upon this state of facts, the rights of the ship owners against those consignees depended altogether on the contract created by the bills of lading, except so far as that contract referred to the charter-party. *Bags of Linseed*, (1861) 1 Black, 108. As observed by Mr. Justice Peckham, when delivering a judgment of the Court of Appeals of the State of New York, in regard to a bill of lading containing a clause exactly like that in the bills of lading in the case at bar, "It would be a wide stretch to hold that by this language of the bill of lading, which plainly referred only to the provisions of the charter-party as to the freight money, a consignee would become liable to demurrage if he accepted the cargo under such a bill." *Dayton v. Parke*, 142 N.Y. 391, 400.

The necessary consequence is that the responsibility of the charterers to the ship owners for demurrage according to the charter-party is not affected by the cesser clause.

2. To what extent may a consignee of goods claim the benefits of a cesser clause? In *Yone Suzuki v. Central Argentine Ry*, 27 F.2d 795 (2d Cir. 1928), *cert. denied*, 278 U.S. 652, 49 S. Ct. 178, 73 L. Ed. 563 (1929) the bill of lading which had been issued by the vessel to the charterer and then in turn to the consignee called "for delivery of the goods 'unto order or assigns, he or they paying freight for the same as per charter party' (described by date), 'all the terms and exceptions contained in which charter are herewith incorporated.' The bills of lading were stamped 'Freight Prepaid.' " The charterer had become insolvent and the carrier looked to the consignee for the payment of demurrage.

But the railway [Buyer-Consignee] relies on the cesser clause and says it discharged the charterer and therefore discharged it. There is a difficulty with this at the outset, ... for the charterer here was only discharged by the cesser clause as charterer, and was not discharged as consignor and owner of the goods, unless and until he parted with his title. A consignor, who was owner of the goods and holder of a bill of lading incorporating the conditions of the charter party, was held in *Gullischen v. Stewart Bros.*, 13 Q.B.D. 317, to obtain no exemption from liability by reason of the cesser clause. The court ... said:

> The contract by a bill of lading is different from a contract by a charter party, and the defendants are sued upon the contract contained in the bill of lading. It would be absurd to suppose that their liability upon the bills of lading would cease upon the loading of the cargo. What is their liability upon the bills of lading? It is to pay freight and other conditions 'as per charter party.' Upon the terms of the charter party the consignees were to pay demurrage at a certain rate; that is a condition which is incorporated in the bill of lading. But the clause as to the cesser of the charterers' liability is not incorporated.

Lord Bowen said:

> The bill of lading by its words incorporates the terms of the charter party; but these words must receive a reasonable construction. The result is that the bill of lading incorporates certain provisions of the charter party, but not the clause as to cesser of liability. The argument for the defendants would render the bill of lading a nullity; it would be a useless form except as an acknowledgment that the goods had been put on board.

To the same effect was the decision of Judge Putnam in *The Eliza Lines* (C.C.) 61 F. at pages 325, 326, who cites Carver, MacLachlan, and Abbott as reaching the same conclusion. Scrutton on Charter Parties, art. 19, at page 67, 11th Ed., says: "But the cesser clause ... will not be incorporated in the bill of lading." And Carver (6th Ed.) at page 227, says: "A cesser clause in the charter is not brought into the bill of lading, that being inconsistent with it." To the same effect is the dictum in *Repetto v. Millar's Karriet*, [1901] 2 K.B. at page 313.

* * *

Judge Putnam discussed the origin of the cesser clause in *The Eliza Lines*, *supra*, and said that it was first introduced to relieve agents who appeared as such in charter parties and was afterwards extended to charterers who were in fact agents, whether they appeared so or not. The cesser clause is in terms for the benefit of the charterer, and only affects him, and it is settled in this country and in England that an indorsee of a bill of lading incorporating the charter provisions, who receives the goods, is liable for demurrage and for other sums which may become due under the provisions in the charter party. The liability of the consignee is said to be based on an implied promise arising from his acceptance of the goods under a bill of lading that embraces the provisions. *Union Pacific R.R. Co. v. American Smelting & Refining Co. (C.C.A.)* 202 F. 720. The American decisions as to the liability of the consignee are collected in *Yone Sukuzi v. Central Argentine Ry. Co. (D.C.)* 275 F. 54, and some of the English decisions are referred to in *Gullischen v. Stewart Bros.*, 11 Q.B.D. 186, *affirmed* 13 Q.B.D. 317. The *Eliza Lines, supra*, also involved the liability of the consignee, irrespective of the cesser clause.

* * *

It is contended on behalf of the railway company that it only became bound by an implied contract (arising upon acceptance of the goods in the Argentine) to pay according to the terms of a bill of lading issued to the consignor in America, and that, while the bill of lading did not incorporate the cesser clause under our laws, it did do so in the Argentine, where the liability of the railway came into being. But this seems an untenable view, for the implied contract was to perform the obligations of the existing contract of carriage that had been executed in America. By its terms the holder of the bill of lading agreed to pay demurrage, and by the American law the cesser clause was not incorporated in it. The railway stood precisely in the position of the consignors, if they had never transferred the bills of lading to the railway. To say that the implied contract, though based upon the terms of the bills of lading and arising through transfer thereof, embraces provisions of the charter party which were never incorporated in the bill of lading as between the parties thereto, would involve implications unwarranted by the facts and would take from the libelants all right to enforce their contracts. We therefore hold that the libelants were rightly adjudged entitled to recover any demurrage that occurred at the discharging port, unless it was occasioned by their fault or covered by some exception in the bill of lading.

* * *

CHAPTER 3 — PERSONAL INJURY AND DEATH CLAIMS

Section I. Remedies of Seamen

Part 1. Maintenance, Cure, and Wages: Cases and Notes

A. Recognition of Cause of Action

COX v. DRAVO CORP.

517 F.2d 620 (3d Cir. 1975), *cert. denied* 423 U.S. 1020, 96 S. Ct. 475, 46 L. Ed. 2d 392.

GIBBONS, Circuit Judge:

The obligation of the vessel to provide maintenance and cure first appeared in American maritime law in *Harden v. Gordon*, 11 F. Cas. 480 (No. 6,047) (C.C.D. Me. 1823). In that well-known decision Justice Story wrote:

My opinion is that if the plaintiff is entitled to be cured at the expense of the ship, it is a claim in the nature of additional wages during the period of sickness, and is just as proper for a suit [in admiralty], as a claim for additional pay, while in port, or for subsistence in port, where that has been unjustly withheld. It stands upon the same analogy, as the compensation allowed by our laws in cases of short allowance of provisions and water, where it is expressly provided, that the amount shall be recoverable in the same manner as wages.... *Id.* at 482.

B. Elements of Cause of Action

WARREN v. UNITED STATES

340 U.S. 523, 71 S. Ct. 432, 95 L. Ed. 503, 1951 AMC 416 (1951)

Mr. Justice DOUGLAS delivered the opinion of the Court.

Petitioner seeks in this suit maintenance and cure from the United States, as owner of *S.S. Anna Howard Shaw.* Petitioner was a messman who went ashore on leave while the vessel was at Naples in 1944. He and two other members of the crew first did some sightseeing. Then the three of them drank one bottle of wine and went to a dance hall, where they stayed an hour and a half, dancing. There was a room adjoining the dance hall that over looked the ocean. French doors opened onto an unprotected ledge which extended out from the building a few feet. Petitioner stepped to within 6 inches of the edge and leaned over to take a look. As he did so, he took hold of an iron rod which seemed to be attached to the building. The rod came off and petitioner lost his balance and fell, breaking a leg.

The District Court awarded maintenance. 75 F. Supp. 210, 76 F. Supp 735. The Court of Appeals disallowed it. 179 F.2d 919. The case is here on certiorari.

* * *

The Shipowner's Liability Convention, proclaimed by the President Sept. 29, 1939, 54 Stat. 1693, provides in Art. 2:

1. The shipowner shall be liable in respect of—
    (a) sickness and injury occurring between the date specified in the articles of agreement for reporting for duty and the termination of the engagement;
    (b) death resulting from such sickness or injury.

2. Provided that national laws or regulations may make exceptions in respect of:
    (a) injury incurred otherwise than in the service of the ship;
    (b) injury or sickness due to the wilful act, default or misbehavior of the sick, injured or deceased person;
    (c) sickness or infirmity intentionally concealed when the engagement is entered into.

Petitioner's argument is twofold. He maintains first that under paragraph 1 a shipowner's duty to provide maintenance and cure is absolute and that the exceptions specified in paragraph 2 are not operative until a statute is enacted which puts them in force. He argues in the second place that, even if paragraph 2 is operative without an Act of Congress, his conduct was not due to a "wilful act, default or misbehavior" within the meaning of that paragraph. An amicus curiae argues that the injury was not received "in the service of the ship" within the meaning of Paragraph 2(a) of Art. 2.

There is support for petitioner's first point in the concurring opinion of Chief Justice Stone in *Waterman Steamship Corp. v. Jones*, 318 U.S. 724, 738. But we think the preferred view is opposed. Our conclusion is that the exceptions permitted by paragraph 2 are operative by virtue of the general maritime law and that no Act of Congress is necessary to give them force.

* * *

The District Court held that petitioner's degree of fault did not bar a recovery for maintenance and cure. The Court of Appeals thought otherwise. The question is whether the injury was "due to the wilful act, default or misbehavior" of petitioner within the meaning of Art. 2, paragraph 2 (b) of the Convention. The standard prescribed is not negligence but wilful misbehavior. In the maritime law it has long been held that while fault of the seamen will forfeit the right to maintenance and cure, it must be "some positively vicious conduct—such as gross negligence or willful disobedience of orders." *The Chandos*, 6 Sawy, 544, 549-550; *The City of Carlisle*, 39 F. 807, 813; *The Ben Flint*, 1 Bliss 562, 566. And *see Reed v. Canfield*, 1 Sumn. 195, 206. In *Aguilar v. Standard Oil Co.*, 318 U.S. 724, 731, we stated the rule as follows: "Conceptions of contributory negligence, the fellow-servant doctrine, and assumption of risk have no place in the liability or defense against it. Only some wilful misbehavior or deliberate act of indiscretion suffices to deprive the seaman of his protection."

The exception which some cases have made for injuries resulting from intoxication (*see, Aguilar v. Standard Oil Co., supra*, p. 731) has no place in this case. As the District Judge rules, the amount of wine consumed hardly permits a finding of intoxication. Petitioner was plainly negligent. Yet we should have to strain to find the element of wilfulness or its equivalent. He sought to use some care when he looked down from the small balcony, as evidenced by his seizure of the iron bar for a handhold. His conduct did not measure up to a standard of due care under the circumstances. But we agree with the District Court that it was not wilful misbehavior within the meaning of the Convention.

Finally it is suggested that the injury did not occur "in the service of the ship," as that term is used in paragraph 2 (a) of Art. 2 of the Convention. We held in *Aguilar v. Standard Oil Co., supra*, that maintenance and cure extends to injuries occurring while the seaman is departing on or returning from shore leave though he has at the time no duty to perform for the ship. It is contended that the doctrine of that case should not be extended to injuries received during the diversions of the seaman after he has reached the shore. Mr. Justice Rutledge, speaking for the

Court in the *Aguilar* case, stated the reasons for extending maintenance and cure to shore leave cases as follows (pp. 733-734):

> To relieve the shipowner of his obligation in the case of injuries incurred on shore leave would cast upon the seaman hazards encountered only by reason of the voyage. The assumption is hardly sound that the normal uses and purposes of shore leave are 'exclusively personal' and have no relation to the vessel's business. Men cannot live for long cooped up aboard ship without substantial impairment of their efficiency, if not also serious danger to discipline. Relaxation beyond the confines of the ship is necessary if the work is to go on, more so that it may move smoothly. No master would take a crew to sea if he could not grant shore leave, and no crew would be taken if it could never obtain it.*** In short, shore leave is an elemental necessity in the sailing of ships, a part of the business as old as the art, not merely a personal diversion.
>
> The voyage creates not only the need for relaxation ashore, but the necessity that it be satisfied in distant and unfamiliar ports. If, in those surroundings, the seaman, without disqualifying misconduct, contracts disease or incurs injury, it is because of the voyage, the shipowner's business has separated him from his usual places of association. By adding this separation to the restrictions of living as well as working abroad, it forges dual and unique compulsions for seeking relief wherever it may be found. In sum, it is the ship's business which subjects the seaman to the risks attending hours of relaxation in strange surroundings. Accordingly, it is but reasonable that the business extend the same protections against injury from them as it gives for other risks of the employment.

This reasoning is as applicable to injuries received during the period of relaxation while on shore as it is to those received while reaching it. To restrict the liability along the lines suggested would be to whittle it down "by restrictive and artificial distinctions" as attempted in the *Aguilar* case. We repeat what we said there, "If leeway is to be given in either direction, all the considerations which brought the liability into being dictate it should be in the sailor's behalf." 318 U.S. at 735.

Reversed.

Note: Fraud or Willful Misconduct as a Defense

Maintenance and cure must be paid regardless of fault or contributory negligence of the seaman. *Warren v. United States*, 340 U.S. 523, 71 S.Ct. 432, 95 L.Ed. 503 (1951). However, willful misconduct or fraudulent concealment of a pre-existing condition is a defense, *see Lancaster Towing, Inc. v. Davis*, 681 F. Supp 387 (N.D. Mass. 1987).

ARCHER v. TRANS/AMERICAN SERVICES, LTD.

834 F.2d 1570 (11th Cir. 1988)

HATCHETT, Circuit Judge:

We are called upon to determine whether the district court properly ruled that a person was a seaman "in the service of the ship" at the time the person suffered an injury on shore entitling the person to maintenance and cure as well as wages. Finding the district court's ruling proper, we affirm.

Facts

Trans/American Services, Ltd. (Trans/American) is a catering concessionaire that provides food and beverage service, with attendant personnel, to cruise ships. It had a contract with Scandinavian World Cruises (Bahamas), Ltd., (Scandinavian) the owner and operator of the M/V Scandinavian Sun. In February, 1982, Trans/American's recruiting agent in Jamaica hired Devon Archer, the appellee. Archer worked as an assistant pantryman and lived aboard the vessel until January, 1984, except for brief vacations.

In April, 1983, Archer signed his second contract of employment with Trans/American for a one-year term beginning May 11, 1983, and expiring May 11, 1984. In January, 1984, the need for maintenance and repairs required that the M/V Scandinavian Sun be placed in dry dock for two weeks. Although Archer's contract term had not expired, he was required to vacate the ship during dry docking, but was invited to sign a new contract of employment for a one-year term beginning January 23, 1984. Archer signed the new contract and then left on a two-week unpaid vacation to Jamaica, his homeland.

Although the ship was not scheduled to depart until January 23, 1984, the new employment contract required that Archer report to Trans/American's offices in Miami on January 21, 1984. On January 21, 1984, as required, Archer returned from Jamaica and upon reporting in at the Trans/American office, company officials instructed Archer to report to the ship on January 23, 1984. As to the instructions, the district court found: "They informed him that in the interim he would have no specifically assigned duties and he was free to do as he pleased until the time of departure." The following day, Archer was injured while a passenger in a friend's automobile on a personal pleasure trip.

Archer filed a three-count complaint against Trans/American and Scandinavian for recovery under the Jones Act, recovery of maintenance and cure under the general maritime law, and recovery of punitive damages and attorney's fees. Because the essential facts pertaining to Archer's claims were not in dispute, the parties submitted cross-motions for summary judgment. The district court granted Archer's motion for summary judgment and awarded him general damages, but denied his requests for attorney's fees and punitive damages. Trans/American Services appeals the award.

Issues

Trans/American presents four issues in this appeal: (1) whether Trans/American was acting as an agent for the vessel; (2) whether Archer was "in the service of the ship" while awaiting its departure; (3) whether he is entitled to maintenance and cure; and (4) whether he is entitled to wages for the one-year period during which he was recovering from his injuries.

* * *

In this case, an agency relationship exists between Trans/American and Scandinavian. Trans/American independent contractor status does not render the agency finding clearly erroneous or improper as a matter of law.

If the law were to recognize this contractual arrangement as something other than an agency relationship, the result would be anomalous. In this case, a cruise ship has contracted for its entire food and beverage service, thus, completely insulating itself from any and all liability which might arise from that service. If the ship owner or operator can contract for its food and beverage service, then it may also contract for its crew members, its engineers, its maintenance, housekeeping, and hospitality staffs. The logical extension of this notion is that the ship owner or operator could contract for its entire operation. In such a manner, the ship owner or operator would escape all accountability for the ship's condition and the conduct of those working abroad. In every instance in which the ship owner or operator has historically been held accountable, an independent contractor allegedly unrelated to the ship would be the responsible party.

2. Archer's Status

The district court also found that Archer attained seaman status at the time he checked in at Trans/American's Miami office and was "in the service of the ship." Trans/American contends that this finding is clearly erroneous, arguing that Archer was on leave until January 23, 1984, that he had signed off the ship's articles before going on leave, and that he had not yet signed back on the ship's articles when he was injured.

We conclude that Archer was "in the service of the ship." We arrive at this conclusion by recognizing that Trans/American was acting as the ship's agent in hiring the personnel to handle the food and beverage concession. In order to efficiently provide its services, Trans/American had to marshal its personnel prior to the ship's departure date. Consequently, Trans/American required Archer to check in at the Miami office on January 21, 1984, to commence his employment which resulted in his assignment to ship board duty on January 23, 1984. Archer's compliance, therefore, was in the "course of his employment" and inured to Trans/American's benefit. *See Vincent v. Harvey Well Service*, 441 F.2d 146 (5th Cir. 1971).

Trans/American argues that Archer's scheduled leave of absence was not to end until January 23, 1984, when the ship was scheduled to depart from Miami. It is important to recognize, however, that Archer's leave of absence was effectively terminated by the requirement that he make an appearance in Miami prior to that date. Furthermore, the new employment contract stated that Immigration officials had been instructed by Trans/American to refuse Archer admittance if he failed to arrive on January 21, 1984. It was necessary, therefore, that Archer return from Jamaica two days before the scheduled departure of the M/V Scandinavian Sun not only to secure his employment, but also to ensure his entry into this country. Finally, the fact that Archer was not performing duties aboard the ship for Trans/American at the time of injury does not deprive him of seaman status. *Braen v. Pfeifer Oil Transp. Co.*, 361 U.S. 129, 80 S. Ct. 247, 4 L. Ed. 2d 919 (1959); *Magnolia Towing Co. v. Pace*, 378 F.2d 12 (5th Cir. 1967). Because Trans/American made Archer's return to Miami a prerequisite to commencing work aboard ship, we find that the district court correctly concluded that Archer had seaman status when he was injured.

B. Legal Conclusions—Standard of Review

* * *

The law provides that blue water seamen may recover for injuries suffered during shore leave while on personal business. *Liner v. J.B. Talley and Co., Inc.*, 618 F.2d 327 (5th Cir. 1980). Archer was a blue water seaman. He lived aboard the M/V Scandinavian Sun from February, 1982, until the time of his accident, except during a few brief vacations over that two-year period. Had he not been injured, he would have boarded the M/V Scandinavian Sun on January 23, 1984, and again resided on the ship for the duration of his twelve-month employment contract. Archer was essentially a blue water seaman on shore leave. He was neither at this home in Jamaica, nor on the ship where he resides. The purpose for his presence in Miami on the date of the accident was solely to serve Trans/American's interest in marshaling personnel to meet its contractual obligation. Once he arrived in Miami and signed in with Trans/American's office, he was a member of the ship's crew. The two-day wait in Miami was the equivalent of shore leave in a foreign port. We conclude that, as a blue water seaman, Archer was in the same position during his two days in Miami as he would have been had he been on leave in some other port during a cruise.

2. Wages

* * *

As for Archer's entitlement to an award of wages, it is settled law that wages is a basic component of an award of maintenance and cure. *See Vickers v. Tumey*, 290 F.2d 426 (5th Cir. 1961). Because we conclude that Archer, as a blue water seaman in a foreign port, is entitled to maintenance and cure under governing principles of maritime law, he is also entitled to his wages.

With regard to the appropriate time period for calculating an award of wages, the law is also clear in this circuit. A seaman under contract for a year can collect a year's lost wages as part of maintenance. *Nichols v. Barwick*, 792 F.2d 1520, 1524 (11th Cir. 1986). We concur with the law of our predecessor circuit. In *Vickers v. Tumey*, 290 F.2d 426, 434 (5th Cir. 1961), the Fifth Circuit stated: "If employment is for a period other than the voyage, such as coastwise articles for six months or for a definite time, the end of the voyage concept does not apply and wages are due him for the period of employment." Archer's employment contract with Trans/American was for the one-year period from January 23, 1984, to January 23, 1985. He is entitled not only to maintenance and cure, but also to his lost wages for the full term of his contract.

Accordingly, the district court's judgment is affirmed.

HODGES, Chief District Judge, dissenting:

... Although the issue is both novel and difficult, I do not believe that the "shore leave" analogy is appropriate in this case.

* * *

In my view, therefore, it cannot fairly be said that on these facts that Archer was on "shore leave" at any time between January 9 and January 23. The vessel was not on a voyage calling in a distant or foreign port; it was between voyages and was due to reenter service in its home port. Archer had signed off the ship and never signed back on. Indeed, he could have been assigned prior to January 23 to work on a entirely different vessel. He may well have been an employee of Trans/American for some purposes during that crucial period given his contract of employment and the requirement that he check in on January 21, but he was not in the service of the ship.

Note

In *Gheorghita v. Royal Caribbean Cruises, Ltd.*, 93 F. Supp. 2d 1237, 1244 n.12, 2001 AMC 1187, 1194 n.12 (S.D. Fla. 2000), the court questioned whether *Archer* had been correctly decided, because the lower court's case file showed that the employment contract allowed for seven days' notice on either side, despite the fact that it was for one year's duration. The court pointed out that the duration of the wages obligation (until the end of the contract) is different from the duration of the maintenance and cure obligation (until "maximum possible cure"). Unless the contract is for a fixed duration, wages are payable only to the end of the voyage. A contract with a notice period, like the one in *Gheorghita*, is not a fixed-term contract, so the court held that wages were payable only to the end of the voyage.

Note: Persons Liable to Pay Maintenance and Cure

Responsibility for maintenance and cure ordinarily lies with the vessel owner who is usually the seaman's employer. Charterers are normally not liable for maintenance and cure unless the plaintiff establishes the existence of a demise charter. A demise charterer assumes not only full control over the vessel, but also the owner's responsibility for maintenance and cure. *Matute v. Lloyd Bermuda Lines, Ltd.*, 931 F.2d 231, 235, 1991 AMC 1830 (3d Cir. 1991).

Where a seaman is employed by one person and the vessel on which he is employed is owned by another, his employer is liable as employer and the vessel owner may be liable on an agency theory. *See Archer v. Trans/American Services, Ltd.*, *supra*. In any event the vessel is liable *in rem*. *Solet v. M/V Captain H.V. Dufrene*, 303 F. Supp. 980, 1970 AMC 571 (E.D. La. 1969).

Notes on Injuries on Land and "Service of the Ship"

1. *Blue Water Seaman: Shore Leave or Vacation*

"Shore Leave consisting of brief periods ashore in home or foreign ports in the course of a voyage, or perhaps even before a voyage begins or after it has terminated, is no doubt, a usual, traditional, and perhaps essential incident of a seaman's employment. Furthermore, during such leave the seaman in a sense is in the service of his ship, for, we suppose he could be called back on board, if he could be found, to cope with any shipboard emergency which might arise in port. But protracted vacations are not of 'elemental necessity in the sailing of ships, a part of the business as old as the art.' They are not traditional in maritime employment; they are the product of modern collective bargaining agreements now generally common both to sea and ashore. And, during vacation periods we cannot assume that the seaman is answerable to the call of duty; and hence in a sense is in the service of the ship." *Haskell v. Socony Mobil Oil Co.*, 237 F.2d 707, 710 (1st Cir. 1956).

2. *Commuter Seaman*

Gilmore & Black in THE LAW OF ADMIRALTY 292 (2d ed. 1975) have observed that the extension of the maintenance and cure remedy to shore leave raises questions in cases involving "'commuter seamen'", those who live at home and commute to work or who serve for a fixed period of time on a vessel and are then on shore for a period of time fixed or otherwise. An example of the former would be a seaman employed on a ferry boat that crossed the Mississippi River going back and forth between the east bank of New Orleans to the west bank—a voyage that took but a few minutes. The latter are illustrated by off-shore workers who often work a 7 day shift on a drilling platform and then are on shore for their seven days off, or persons who work rotating shifts, that is they work a shift on a vessel until a particular job is finished and then they are on shore until their turn comes up to work another shift.

The Fifth Circuit has stated that there are two factors to be considered in the "commuter seaman" situation: (1) whether or not the seaman was on authorized shore leave when injured, and (2) whether or not the seaman was answerable to the call of duty. Shore leave status in the traditional sense refers to the seaman "who, as a necessary incident of irregular shipboard employment, was authorized to go ashore from time to time and place to place for diversion and relax from the routine of the ship.... [N]ot only did the shipowner's business separate such a seaman from his usual places of association, but also, since he was not replaced while he was ashore, he remained at all times subject to his shipping articles and recallable at the will of his master.... Not so for this off-shore worker in the oil industry. Sellers employment was arranged into definite, equal periods on shore and on the rig. He was subjected to no foreign or irregular accommodations. Such a worker was to a large extent able to maintain the home life of ordinary shore dwellers. A separate crewman regularly replaced him and recall was not contemplated under any ordinary circumstances." *Sellers v. Dixilyn Corporation*, 433 F.2d 446, 448, 1971 AMC 425 (5th Cir. 1970)

In another case the Fifth Circuit discussed in some detail the meaning of "in the service of the ship" the context of a land based injury: "The determination of whether a seaman is 'in the service of the vessel' and 'answerable to the call of duty' at the time of the accident depends on the particular facts and circumstances of each case. Nevertheless, it is clear as a matter of law that the seaman's answerability to the 'call of duty' imports at the very least some binding obligations on the part of the seaman to serve.... The fact that a seaman is 'answerable to the call of duty' imports a legal obligation both on the part of the seaman, enforceable by the shipowner, and on the part of the vessel, to pay him and provide maintenance and cure in terms of illness or injury, enforceable by the seaman in courts of admiralty. It is because the seaman remains bound to the vessel that the vessel and the shipowner are correspondingly obligated to him for maintenance and cure in case of injury. These reciprocal obligations determine an individual's status as a seaman, and whether the seaman is in the service of his vessel." *Baker v. Ocean Systems, Inc.*, 454 F.2d 379, 384-85 (5th Cir. 1972). The court found that an employee who worked a rotating shift was not "answerable to the call of duty" during the periods when he was "off shift."

C. Amount of Maintenance

RITCHIE v. GRIMM

724 F. Supp. 59, 1989 AMC 2948 (E.D.N.Y. 1989)

WEXLER, District Judge:

In this lawsuit plaintiffs seek compensation for injuries allegedly sustained by Bart Ritchie ("Ritchie") while he was employed on a commercial fishing vessel. Presently before the Court is Ritchie's request for maintenance and cure payments. For the reasons set forth below, defendant Grimm is ordered to pay all medical bills that have been incurred in connection with Ritchie's accident. Maintenance payments in the amount of $381 per week must also be paid to Ritchie. Finally, plaintiff's counsel is awarded $5,000 in attorneys fees.

I. Background

As noted above, Ritchie seeks compensation for injuries sustained while working aboard a commercial fishing vessel. The owner of that vessel, Ritchie's employer, was defendant William Grimm ("Grimm"). Plaintiffs' testimony revealed that immediately following the accident, Grimm's insurer began making payments of $555 per week to plaintiffs. One hundred and five dollars of this amount was designated as a maintenance payment while the remainder was designated to be a "disability" payment. In addition, all of Ritchie's medical bills were promptly paid. Unfortunately, according to the Ritchies, these payments did not continue. Medical bills went unpaid and maintenance payments were cut. According to plaintiffs, the payments to Ritchie lagged when plaintiffs commenced this lawsuit. Ultimately, the non-payment of medical and maintenance payments led plaintiffs to bring an order to show cause aimed at amending their complaint to add a cause of action for maintenance and cure and seeking an immediate trial on those issues.

On October 30, 1989 this Court held a hearing to determine the merits of plaintiffs' claim. At the hearing defense counsel repeatedly assured the Court that all medical expenses incurred by Ritchie would be paid by Grimm. While counsel's concession mooted the issue of cure, the issue of the proper maintenance was hotly debated. According to Grimm, maintenance payments are to be calculated solely with reference to the seaman's accommodations while at sea. Thus, Grimm argues that Ritchie's actual living expenses while recuperating at home with his wife and son are irrelevant to the issue of the proper amount of maintenance. Plaintiffs argue, on the other hand, that the proper amount of maintenance is to be calculated solely with reference to plaintiffs actual living expenses including such items as the cost of day care for plaintiffs' son and meals eaten by Ritchie's wife while visiting Ritchie in the hospital.

II. Maintenance

Although the law of the proper amount of maintenance an injured seaman may collect is anything but crystal clear, the Court holds that the proper application of the law falls somewhere between the parties' contentions.

The law of maintenance is of ancient origin. One Court has traced the law back to the ancient Laws of Oleron, a code of maritime law published in the twelfth century. According to ancient law, when "sickness seizes on any one of the mariners, while in the service of the ship, the master ought to set him ashore, to provide lodging and candlelight for him, and also spare him one of the ship-boys, or hire a woman to attend him...." Article VII of the Laws of Oleron quoted in *McWilliams v. Texaco, Inc.*, 781 F.2d 514, 517 n.7 (5th Cir. 1986).

Although the Laws of Oleron state that a seaman is entitled only to "so much as he had on shipboard in his health," *id.*, modern day Courts have not hesitated to award seamen their actual living expenses while on shore. For example, in *Incandela v. American Dredging Corp.*, 659 F.2d 11 (2d Cir. 1981), the Court of Appeals for the Second Circuit awarded an injured seaman maintenance payments sufficient to cover the cost of his actual living expenses on shore. There, the Court noted that a seaman makes out a "prima facie case on the maintenance rate question when he proves the actual living expenditures which he found it necessary to incur during his convalescence." *Id.* at 14.

Grimm relies heavily on *Harper v. Zapata Off-Shore Co.*, 741 F.2d 87 (5th Cir. 1984), in support of the claim that an injured seaman's maintenance payments may not include the cost of lodging for the seaman's wife and child. Grimm, however, reads too much into *Harper*. There, the Court held only that the jury's award of maintenance payments could not be upheld because no record evidence supported the claim that any expenses were incurred. *See Harper*, 741 F.2d at 91. For similar reasons the Court rejects Grimm's reliance on *Johnson v. United States*, 333 U.S. 46, 92 L. Ed. 468, 68 S. Ct. 391 (1948). That case, like *Zapata*, held only that no maintenance payments were owed where no lodging costs were incurred.

Here, as in *Incandela*, the Court notes that Ritchie, like the seaman in *Incandela*, made out a prima facie case when he and his wife testified as to the actual costs of such items as food and rent. Having done so, the burden shifted to Grimm to produce some evidence in rebuttal. On this issue, however, Grimm produced neither a single witness nor document. Under these circumstances, the Court might be justified in awarding plaintiffs the full amount requested—an amount in excess of $600 per week. In the Court's view, however, the making of such an award would stretch the law of maintenance to a point that does not appear to be warranted by the Second Circuit opinion in *Incandela*. Instead, the Court holds that the proper amount of maintenance should include the total cost of rent for Ritchie's apartment as well as his share of food and other costs testified to at the October 30 hearing. Specifically, the Court holds that Ritchie is entitled to receive $125 per week for rent,[1] $47 per week for food (Ritchie's share of the weekly food expenses) and $209 per week for other expenses (Ritchie's share of all other expenses testified to). *See Macedo v. F/V Paul & Michelle*, 868 F.2d 519, 522 (1st Cir. 1989) (maintenance payments should not include expenses attributable to seaman's family). Thus, the total amount of maintenance to which Ritchie is entitled is fixed at $381 per week.

III. Attorney's Fees

Plaintiffs claim that Grimm's conduct was so callous as to entitle them to counsel fees and punitive damages. Although the Court agrees that an award of counsel fees is appropriate, the Court notes that punitive damages are not available in a maintenance action. *See Kraljic v. Berman Enterprises, Inc.*, 575 F.2d 412, 416 (2d Cir. 1978).

Counsel fees are available in a maintenance case only where the employer was "callous" or "recalcitrant." *Incandela*, 659 F.2d at 15, quoting *Roberts v. S.S. Argentina*, 359 F.2d 430 (2d Cir. 1966). Although Grimm paid Ritchie maintenance immediately following the accident, those payments stopped as did the payment of Ritchie's medical bills. The interruption of the payments coincided with the filing of this lawsuit and payments were not reinstated until plaintiffs brought an order to show cause. Under these circumstances, the Court holds that an award of

---

[1] The payment of $125 is based upon the $500 monthly rental payment testified to by Mrs. Ritchie. Although the Court notes that Ritchie resides in the apartment with his wife and child, the Court holds that it is reasonable to award Ritchie the full monthly payment since it is likely that Ritchie would pay the same amount in rent even if he alone resided in the apartment.

reasonable counsel fees is warranted. *See Incandela*, 659 F.2d at 15 (necessity of bringing suit to recover maintenance payments warrants award of counsel fees).

Plaintiffs' attorney claims to have spent fifty hours working on this case. He also claims that his normal billing rate is $200 per hour. When considering the difficulty of the issues presented, the Court holds that it is reasonable to award plaintiffs' counsel a fee of $100 per hour for the fifty hours worked. Accordingly, plaintiffs' counsel is awarded a fee of $5,000.

* * *

Notes

1. *Amount of Maintenance*

The amount of maintenance awarded will be determined by the court based on the evidence presented by the seaman. The seaman has the burden to prove the amount necessary, but the court may take into account the ordinary "costs of food and lodging in a particular area comparable to that received on board the vessel." *See Castro v. M/V Ambassador*, 657 F. Supp 886, 1989 AMC 128 (E.D. La. 1987). *See also Incandela v. American Dredging Co.*, 659 F.2d 11, 14, 1981 AMC 2401, 2404 (2d Cir. 1981):

> To fulfill its purpose, the maintenance rate should be set at a level which will "provide a seaman with food and lodging when he becomes sick or injured in the ship's service." *Vaughn v. Atkinson*, 369 U.S. 527, 531 (1962). Nevertheless, since at least the early 1950's many courts have fallen into the habit of awarding maintenance at the fixed rate of $8.00 per day, regardless of the gradual erosion of the purchasing power which the amount represents. 1B Benedict on Admiralty § 51 (1980); G. Gilmore & C. Black, The Law of Admiralty 307 (2d ed. 1975). On the other hand, some courts have awarded higher maintenance rates after seamen have introduced evidence of higher living costs.

* * *

> In this case, plaintiff's uncontradicted testimony that he spent between $175 and $200 per week on maintenance costs made out a prima facie case for an award of $26.80 per day (one-seventh of $187.50, the mid-point between the two estimates). Defendant made no attempt to introduce rebuttal evidence on this point, and would have faced an uphill battle if it had tried; it was conceded at oral argument that the cheapest room at the Seamen's Institute in New York City now costs $18.00 per night. Therefore it was error for the district court to have refused to allow the jury to utilize the $26.80 figure in calculaing the maintenance owed to plaintiff.
>
> Once plaintiff's testimony was in the record, a *prima facie* case was made out and the burden shifted to the defendant to demonstrate that plaintiff's actual expenditures were excessive, in light of any realistic alternatives for room and board available to him in New York. Since the $26.80 figure was not disputed and was reasonable in view of living costs in New York the $13.50 figure merely represented defendant's arbitrary decision to pay plaintiff half of his regular salary, and was not intended to reflect in any way the cost of housing and food in New York. It was not rebuttal evidence on the issue of maintenance and can therefore be disregarded. Incandela is therefore entitled to a maintenance award calculated at the rate of $26.80 per day.

In *Hall v. Noble Drilling (U.S.), Inc.*, 242 F.3d 582, 2001 AMC 1099 (5th Cir. 2001) the Fifth Circuit held that a seaman who pays the rent or mortgage of a home he shares with his family may recover the full amount of the rent or mortgage for purposes of calculation of a maintenance award, not a prorated amount. However, the costs of heat, electricity and water may be prorated.

2. *Damages for Failure to Pay Maintenance and Cure*

In most circuits, an employer's refusal or failure to pay maintenance and cure will give a seaman an independent cause of action for compensatory damages, attorney's fees and possibly punitive damages. *See Harper v. Zapata Off-Shore Co.*, 741 F.2d 87, 1985 AMC 979 (5th Cir. 1984). However, courts have struggled to define a clear legal standard for damage awards. In *Morales v. Garijak, Inc.*, 829 F.2d 1355, 1988 AMC 1075 (5th Cir. 1987), the court explained that only *unreasonable* behavior, would be enough for a recovery of compensatory damages.

3. *Punitive Damages*

Since *Miles v. Apex Marine Corp.*, 498 U.S. 19, 111 S. Ct. 317, 112 L. Ed. 2d 275, 1991 AMC 1 (1990), punitive damages in maintenance and cure actions have been denied in the Fifth and Ninth Circuits. *Guevara v. Maritime Overseas Corporation*, 59 F.3d 1496, 1995 AMC 2409 (5th Cir. 1995), *cert. denied*, 116 S. Ct. 706 (1996); and *Glynn v. Roy Al Boat Management Corp.*, 57 F.3d 1395, 1995 AMC 2022 (9th Cir. 1995), *cert denied*, 516 U.S. 1046, 116 S. Ct. 708 (1996).

D. Preexisting Injury

GAUTHIER v. CROSBY MARINE SERVICE, INC.

499 F. Supp. 295, 1981 AMC 1170 (E.D. La. 1980), *aff'd*, 752 F.2d 1085, 1985 A.M.C. 2477.

CASSIBRY, District Judge:

* * *

A vessel owner is obligated to furnish a seaman with maintenance and cure benefits with respect to an injury or illness that occurs or manifests itself while the seaman is in the service of the vessel. The origin or cause of the disability, the fact that it pre-existed the voyage, originated on another vessel, or even was due to the fault of another vessel are all irrelevant. *Meade v. Skip Fisheries, Inc.*, 385 F. Supp. 725 (D. Mass. 1974) and cases cited therein. As long as a seaman believes in good faith that he is fit for duty, he is entitled to maintenance and cure from his present employer notwithstanding that he falls ill from a pre-existing illness. *Gooden v. Sinclair Refining Co.*, 378 F.2d 576 (3rd Cir. 1967);.... In fact, at least two courts would hold the present employer solely liable for all maintenance and cure under the "last ship" rule. *Meade*, 385 F. Supp. 725, 728, (D. Mass. 1974) (ALDRICH, J.); *Diaz*, 237 F. Supp. 261 (FEINBERG, J.). Mr. Gauthier, in the instant case, had a reasonable, good faith belief on September 22, 1978 that he was fit for duty with Griffin. Griffin was therefore liable to plaintiff for maintenance and cure for the hydrocele and the heart condition after plaintiff's groin symptoms recurred on September 25, *see Gooden*, 378 F.2d at 578 (prior injuries "heightened" on later ship although not involved in any other accidents), and the heart condition was subsequently discovered. Griffin was further liable for maintenance and cure during the period plaintiff was convalescing and he contracted hepatitis, continuing to the date of maximum cure. *Brahms v. Moore McCormack Lines, Inc.*, 133 F. Supp. 283 (S.D.N.Y. 1955) (new illness part of the progressive manifestation of plaintiff's present inability to care for himself which began aboard ship).

* * *

The testimony also established that plaintiff's heart condition was the result of many years of accumulation of fatty deposits and cholesterol in the arteries. Both these conditions afflicted plaintiff while he was in the employ of Crosby, and it is only fair that Crosby share the burden of maintenance and cure for them. Because the hepatitis was totally divorced from plaintiff's service for Crosby, Crosby is not liable for maintenance and cure associated with that illness.

I agree with my brethren who espouse the last ship rule that a seaman should not be required to ascertain, seek out, and pursue the proper employer to get his award. *See Meade*, 385 F. Supp. at 728; *Diaz*, 237 F. Supp. at 266. Yet both potentially liable employers are before me here, and it would be inequitable to force one or the other to shoulder the entire burden. I will therefore follow the Third Circuit and apportion liability equally between the two ostensibly innocent employers. *Gooden*, 378 F.2d 576. Of course, if Crosby is later found to be culpable for negligence or unseaworthiness, it will be liable for all of the maintenance and cure attributable to the groin injury. ... Because the heart condition would have needed immediate attention eventually, and its discovery in connection with the groin injury was coincidental (although apparently quite fortunate for Mr. Gauthier), those expenses will be shared equally regardless of the findings of the jury on the other causes of action.

Note

In *Howard v. A.S.W. Well Service, Inc.*, 1992 AMC 2041, 2044 (W.D. La., 1992), where the seaman had sustained a back injury while at work, the court said:

[A] seaman who intentionally misrepresents or conceals material medical facts in a pre-hiring examination is not entitled to an award of maintenance and cure. A critical limitation on this rule, however, immediately follows: the defense will not prevail unless there is a causal link between the pre-existing disability that was concealed and the disability incurred during the voyage. Absent a causal link, plaintiff is entitled to maintenance and cure. While it is certainly possible that plaintiff's chronic alcoholism, along with its accompanying physical symptoms, and his acute alcoholic intake just prior to reporting to work could certainly have contributed to or even caused the injury, there is no evidentiary link joining the events. The same holds true for plaintiff's previous foot injury: Sundowner has presented no evidentiary basis of a causal link between the foot injury and the accident and/or injury at issue.

E. Contribution/Indemnity

BLACK v. RED STAR TOWING & TRANSP. CO., INC.

860 F.2d 30, 1989 AMC 1 (2d Cir. 1988)

On Rehearing in banc

MINER, Circuit Judge:

Plaintiff Andrew G. Black, a marine engineer employed by Red Star Towing & Transportation Co., Inc., brought this action to recover for personal injuries sustained in a maritime accident at Port Mobil, a facility owned and operated by defendant Mobil Oil Corporation at Staten Island, New York. Following a jury trial in the United States District Court for the Southern District of New York (TURRENTINE, J.), judgment was entered dismissing the Jones Act and unseaworthiness claims asserted by Black against Red Star, and apportioning liability between Mobil (10%) and Black (90%) on the negligence claim pleaded against Mobil. By order filed after the entry of judgment, the District Court determined that Red Star was not entitled to be indemnified by Mobil for the maintenance and cure it had provided to Black or for the counsel fees it expended in defense of the action.

On appeal by plaintiff Black and cross-appeal by defendant Red Star, a panel of this Court affirmed the judgment and order of the District Court. 838 F.2d 1202 (2d Cir. 1987). Following Red Star's suggestion for rehearing in banc, a majority of the judges in regular active service voted to reconsider the cross-appeal and directed the parties to file additional briefs "focus[ing] on the issue of whether a shipowner has a right of indemnity against a third-party tortfeasor for maintenance and cure paid to an injured seaman." Order dated February 1, 1988. The case was submitted without oral argument. Upon reconsideration, we conclude that a shipowner has such a right, overrule The Federal No. 2, 21 F.2d 313 (2d Cir. 1927), and direct the District Court to enter judgment in favor of Red Star and against Mobil in proportion to Mobil's fault for the accident in which Black was injured.

Background

The accident giving rise to this action occurred on February 27, 1985, while Red Star's tug CRUSADER was tied up to the Mobil dock to take on lube oil. A deckhand placed a wooden ladder on the tug's deck to provide access from the vessel to the pier above. As the vessel's engineer, Black was responsible for arranging to purchase the oil and transfer it to the tug. In the course of discharging those responsibilities, including assisting the dockman with the hose connections, Black ascended and descended the ladder on several occasions. He testified that "the ladder was moving up and down and also in and out" and "seem[ed] to be wobbly" because of high winds and choppy seas. Jt. App. at 57-58.

Apparently concerned about the instability of the wooden ladder, Black began to use a steel access ladder affixed to a recess in the Mobil dock and running from below the water line to the pier. He descended the steel ladder once and ascended it once without incident. On his second descent, the left side of one of the ladder's rungs gave way from under his feet. Black then fell to the broken rung, which became imbedded in his buttocks, pinning him between the lower rungs of the ladder and the dock. This action was brought to recover for various injuries sustained in that accident, including severe contusions of the sciatic nerve.

The parties agreed that Black sustained damages in the sum of $500,000, and only the issues of liability and apportionment were presented to the jury. In response to specific interrogatories propounded by the Court, the jury determined (1) that Red Star was not negligent; (2) that the vessel CRUSADER not unseaworthy; (3) that Mobil was negligent; (4) that Mobil's negligence was a legal cause of damage and injury to Black; (5) that Black was contributorily negligent; and (6) that his negligence was a legal cause of his injury and damage. In response to the interrogatory requiring it to "[s]tate as a percentage the part, if any, that each party's negligence contributed to plaintiff's injury," the jury apportioned 90% to Black, 10% to Mobil and 0% to Red Star. Judgment was entered on May 27, 1987, apportioning liability in accordance with the verdict and dismissing the complaint against Red Star. Pursuant to the agreement between the parties, Mobil thereupon became obligated to pay Black the sum of $50,000 (10% x $500,000).

By means of a motion made after the entry of judgment, Red Star sought indemnity from Mobil for the maintenance and cure payments it voluntarily had made to Black, together with the counsel fees incurred in defending the action. The parties to the motion stipulated that the maintenance and cure payments amounted to $34,000 and that counsel fees of $41,000 were incurred. In an order filed on May 29, 1987, the District Court denied the relief sought. Recognizing that the rule to be followed is not universally recognized, the Court nevertheless wrote as follows: "In this Circuit, a shipowner is not entitled to indemnity for maintenance and cure from a negligent third party. The Federal No. 2, 21 F.2d 313 (2d Cir. 1927)." Jt. App. at 505. Finding no bad faith and no vexatious, wanton or oppressive conduct on the part of Mobil, the District Court "in its discretion" denied the motion for attorneys fees.

In the summary order filed by a panel of this Court on December 4, 1987, affirming the judgment and order of the District Court, Red Star's indemnity claim against Mobil was disposed of as follows:

> Red Star's claim for indemnity or contribution from Mobil for maintenance and cure must fail. The rule established in The Federal No. 2 ... remains the law of the circuit, and we decline to overrule it here. Red Star's alternative argument that it be allowed to recover against Mobil for a breach of the implied warranty of workmanlike performance is meritless. The warranty cannot be implied in the absence of a more extensive relationship than the single transaction between Mobil and Red Star.

Summary Order at 3. It is this disposition that we now address.

Discussion

The right of a seaman injured in the service of a ship to recover maintenance and cure benefits without regard to fault is considered to be "[a]mong the most pervasive incidents of the responsibility anciently imposed upon a shipowner." *Aguilar v. Standard Oil Co.*, 318 U.S. 724, 730 (1943). Because of his employer's unqualified obligation to pay a stipend for living expenses as well as the expenses of medical treatment, an injured seaman is "the beneficiary of a system of accident and health insurance at shipowner's expense more comprehensive than anything yet achieved by shorebound workers." G. GILMORE & C. BLACK, THE LAW OF ADMIRALTY § 6-6, at 282 (2d ed. 1975) [hereinafter Gilmore & Black]. Whether an employer may shift its obligation to one directly responsible for the seaman's injuries in an action for indemnity is an issue over which the courts have differed.

In *The Federal No. 2, supra*, a seaman working on a barge was injured solely as the result of a tugboat's negligence. The barge owner voluntarily paid maintenance and cure to the injured employee and then sought indemnity for the payments in an action brought against the tortfeasor. We denied recovery, distinguishing the "social condition" that permits a parent to recover for a child's medical expenses and one spouse to recover for the loss of services of another. We held that

> this social condition does not exist in the relationship of a seaman and his employer. It is a contract obligation, which he must perform, that imposes this responsibility, even though it be a special damage he suffers from a tortiousact. The cause of the responsibility is the contract; the tort is the remote occasion.

Id. at 314.

According to this analysis, a tortfeasor is not "expected to recognize" that the employer's payment of a seaman's maintenance and cure is "the natural and probable consequence[s] of his act." *Id.*

Shortly after our decision in *The Federal No. 2*, we were confronted with a case in which an injured seaman's claim for damages, including maintenance and cure, was asserted in a single action brought against the seaman's employer and the tortfeasor whose negligence was responsible for his injuries. *Seely v. City of New York*, 24 F.2d 412 (2d Cir. 1928) (per curiam). In that case, we had no difficulty in deciding that primary liability for all the damages sustained by the seaman should fall on the tortfeasor, and that the shipowner would be responsible for maintenance and cure only in the event of the tortfeasor's failure to pay. *Id.*; *see also The Jefferson Myers*, 45 F.2d 162 (2d Cir. 1930) (per curiam). For the past sixty years, we have continued the distinction between Seely-type actions and actions by shipowners seeking indemnity for maintenance and cure payments, shifting primary responsibility for such payments to third-party tortfeasors in the former but not in the latter. Contrary to the maritime law policy that calls for prompt and voluntary payment of maintenance and cure, *Vaughan v. Atkinson*, 369 U.S. 527, 533 (1962), this distinction encourages employers to withhold payments pending the outcome of actions by seamen against primarily responsible tortfeasors.

Our rule has not been without criticism, both in this circuit and elsewhere. In *Jones v. Waterman Steamship Corp.*, 155 F.2d 992 (3d Cir. 1946), the Third Circuit allowed a shipowner sued for maintenance and cure to implead a third party allegedly responsible for the injuries sustained by the seaman plaintiff. Applying state common law, rather than maritime law, the court found the shipowner-seaman relationship analogous to the parent-child relationship and therefore worthy of "a status or a 'social condition' in excess of that given under the ruling in *The Federal No. 2*." *Id.* at 1000-01; *see also Gore v. Clearwater Shipping Corp.*, 378 F.2d 584 (3d Cir. 1967); *Gooden v. Sinclair Refining Co.*, 378 F.2d 576 (3d Cir. 1967). In the Fifth Circuit, it has been "well established ... that an innocent employer is entitled to indemnification from a negligent third party for payments made to an employee." *Savoie v. LaFourche Boat Rentals, Inc.*, 627 F.2d 722, 723 (5th Cir. Unit A 1980) (per curiam); *see also Richardson v. St. Charles-St. John the Baptist Bridge & Ferry Authority*, 284 F. Supp. 709, 716 (E.D. La. 1968) ("[T]he result reached in *The Federal No. 2* is a poor one from the standpoint of policy."). We have "question[ed] the continued validity of The Federal No. 2," *Mahramas v. American Export Isbrandtsen Lines, Inc.*, 475 F.2d 165, 170 n.7 (2d Cir. 1973), the authors of a leading admiralty law treatise have criticized it, *see* Gilmore & Black § 6-18, at 319, and at least one commentator has urged its reexamination, *see* Edelman, *Time for Change in Indemnity Rulings*, N.Y.L.J., Jan. 8, 1988, at 1, col. 1.

Our rule has been undercut by the cases that have allowed employers of injured seamen to be indemnified by negligent third parties for maintenance and cure payments where there is a contractual relationship between shipowner and tortfeasor. The warranty of workmanlike performance implied in the contract between shipowner and stevedore, *Ryan Stevedoring Co., Inc. v. Pan-Atlantic Steamship Corp.*, 350 U.S. 124 (1956), has been extended to contracts for vessel towing, *United States v. Tug Manzanillo*, 310 F.2d 220 (9th Cir. 1962); *Rogers v. New Jersey Barging Corp.*, 567 F. Supp. 822, 827 (S.D.N.Y. 1983) ("While *The Federal No. 2* has never been expressly overruled, it undoubtedly retains little, if any, vitality in light of Ryan and its progeny."), and imposed on the operator of a launch service, *Flunker v. United States*, 528 F.2d 239, 242 n.1 (9th Cir. 1975) ("We are aware that *The Federal No. 2* does not sail in untroubled waters."), to allow employers to recover their maintenance and cure costs when the warranty is breached. Indeed, it may be that "[g]iven the contractual arrangement between the owner of the barge ... and the owner of the tug, *The Federal No. 2*, on its own facts, would not be followed anywhere today." Gilmore & Black § 6-15, at 317 n.78.

In the case at bar, however, there was no preexisting contractual relationship between the shipowner-employer, Red Star, and the third-party tortfeasor, Mobil. We therefore reject the contractual basis for recovery asserted here for the same reason given in the summary order disposing of the original appeal: "The warranty [of workmanlike performance] cannot be implied in the absence of a more extensive relationship than the single transaction between Mobil and Red Star." Summary Order at 3.

We nonetheless conclude that equity, which "is no stranger in admiralty," *Vaughan*, 369 U.S. at 530, requires Mobil to reimburse Red Star for the maintenance and cure it provided to Black. For the reasons given below, we limit that reimbursement to Mobil's proportionate share of fault for the accident in which Black was injured. We hold that this type of claim, whether the subject of an independent action, a third-party action or a cross-claim in a pending action, may be pursued as a matter of general maritime law. *See* Gilmore & Black § 6-18, at 319. Accordingly, after sailing in Second Circuit waters for six decades, *The Federal No. 2* formally is abandoned.

When a contributorily negligent seaman is paid maintenance and cure by a non-negligent shipowner, equity dictates that a third-party tortfeasor should not bear liability in excess of its proportionate share of fault. There is authority to the contrary, predicated on the notion that the entire burden of maintenance and cure should be shouldered by the third-party tortfeasor rather than the negligent seaman's innocent employer. *Savoie*, 627 F.2d at 722-23. Even in the Fifth Circuit, however, a *negligent* shipowner can secure from a third-party tortfeasor contribution for maintenance and cure paid to a contributorily negligent seaman only to the extent of the third-party's proportionate share of fault. *Adams v. Texaco, Inc.*, 640 F.2d 618, 621 (5th Cir. Unit A Mar. 1981) ("Under the 'commonsense principle' that a party whose neglect has in part contributed to the need for maintenance and cure payments, that party should reimburse the costs of those payments to the extent occasioned by its fault.") We think that equity, as well as good sense, should serve to limit the liability of a third-party tortfeasor to its proportionate share of fault in *all* cases where reimbursement is sought for maintenance and cure. This sort of claim for reimbursement is nothing more than a claim for contribution under well-settled admiralty principles. *See id.* Of course, total contribution, often called *indemnity*, is owed to the shipowner-employer where a third-party tortfeasor is entirely at fault.

The district court's order denying to Red Star any reimbursement from Mobil for counsel fees incurred in defending the action is affirmed. There was no contractual basis for such an award, and we decline to require contribution for attorney's fees in a situation such as that presented here. We also would deny reimbursement for counsel fees expended in seeking contribution for maintenance and cure.

Reversed and remanded to the district court, with instructions to enter judgment in favor of Red Star Towing and Transportation Co., Inc. against Mobil Oil Corp. in the sum of $3,400, representing that portion of the maintenance and cure paid by Red Star that is proportionate to Mobil's share of the damages sustained by the plaintiff, Andrew G. Black.

Notes

1. *Contracts for Maintenance and Cure*

What effect, if any, should a court give to the rate of maintenance which has been fixed in a collective bargaining agreement between a seaman's union and a shipowner? The Ninth Circuit has held that the rate is binding on the seaman despite the district court's determination that the amount is inadequate to obtain food and lodging. *Gardiner v. Sea-Land Service, Inc.*, 786 F.2d 943, 1986 AMC 1521 (9th Cir.), *cert. denied*, 479 U.S. 924, 107 S.Ct. 331 (1986). This approach was followed in *Macedo v. F/V Paul & Michelle*, 868 F.2d 519, 1990 AMC 1368 (1st Cir.) 1989), *Al-Zawkari v. American Steamship Co.*, 871 F.2d 585, 1990 AMC 1312 (6th Cir. 1989); *Baldassaro v. United States*, 64 F.3d 206, 1995 AMC 2947 (5th Cir. 1995) and *Frederick v. Kirby Tankships, Inc.*, 205 F.3d 1277, 2000 AMC 1839 (11th Cir. 2000). In contrast the Third Circuit has held that a seaman may challenge the rate stipulated in the collective bargaining agreement. *Barnes v. Andover Co., L.P.*, 900 F.2d 630, 1990 AMC 1265 (3rd Cir. 1990).

There were several decisions at District Court level in the Second Circuit agreeing with *Barnes* - see *Gilliken v. United States*, 764 F. Supp 261, 1992 AMC 111 (E.D.N.Y. 1991); *Brown v. United States*, 882 F. Supp. 1424, 1995 AMC 1801 (S.D.N.Y. 1995); *McMillan v. Tug Jane A. Bouchard*, 885 F. Supp. 452 (E.D.N.Y. 1995); *Covella v. Buchanan Marine, Inc.*, 1997 AMC 1192 (S.D.N.Y. 1996); *Durfor v. K-Sea Transportation Corp.*, 2001 AMC 2390 (S.D.N.Y. 2001) – but in *Ammar v. U.S.*, 342 F.3d 133, 1995 AMC 1801 (2d Cir. 2003), the U.S. Court of Appeals for the Second Circuit joined the Ninth Circuit in holding that the rate of maintenance should be limited to the amount fixed in the collective bargaining agreement.

In contrast, several state courts have sided with *Barnes* in holding that the collective bargaining agreement cannot abrogate the seaman's right to adequate maintenance and cure. *See Lundborg v. Keystone Shipping Co.*, 981 P.2d 854, 1999 AMC 2635 (Wash. 1999), *Daniels v. Standard Marine Transport Service, Inc.*, 680 N.Y.S.2d 41, 1999 AMC 2889 (C.A.N.Y. 1998). Some state courts apply the collective bargaining rate: *Jordan v. Intercontinental Bulktank Corp.*, 621 So. 2d 1141 (La. App., 1st Cir. 1993).

2. *Disability and Health Care Plans*

Does an employer satisfy its legal obligation to pay maintenance when it establishes a disability plan pursuant to a collective bargaining agreement? The answer seems to depend upon whether the "benefits" are regarded as a form of "deferred compensation," *Shaw v. Ohio River*

Company, 526 F.2d 193, 200, 1976 AMC 1164 (1975), or as substitute for maintenance, *Thomas v. Humble Oil & Refining Company*, 420 F.2d 793, 794, 1970 AMC 25 (4th Cir. 1970) (where the collective bargaining agreement clearly provided that: "Maintenance shall not be paid concurrently with payments under the Disability Benefits Plan, ...") Benefits which are regarded as "deferred compensation are not considered to be the payment of maintenance.

As to cure, it appears that an employer incurs no further obligation to pay for medical treatment which has already been paid by a welfare plan or by health insurance such as Blue Cross, pursuant to a collective bargaining agreement. The courts seem to have distinguished Jones Act and similar actions and rejected the application of the so-called "collateral source" rule. "[A] vessel owner's duty to provide maintenance and cure arises independently of any considerations of fault and without regard to whether or not the seaman's disability is causally related to his employment. Whatever justification there may be for the collateral source rule in situations where liability is based on fault, there is no perceivable basis for applying it to the no-fault obligation to furnish maintenances and cure. *Shaw v. Ohio River Company*, 526 F.2d 193, 201, 1976 AMC 1164 (3d Cir. 1975). *See also, Al Zawkari v. American S.S. Co.*, 871 F.2d 585, 1990 AMC 1312 (6th Cir. 1989).

3. *Public Health Hospitals*

In 1981, Congress enacted the Omnibus Budget Reconciliation Act, Pub. L. No 97-35, 95 Stat. 357 (1981), a comprehensive appropriations bill that adjusted the eligibility requirements and amounts budgeted for a large number of federal programs. Among its other provisions, the Act ordered the closure and transfer to nonfederal control of the Public Health hospitals and clinics. Section 986 of the Act terminated the right of outpatient seamen to obtain free medical care in the facilities after October 1, 1981, while Section 988 allowed continued free care for a maximum of one additional year for in-patient seamen hospitalized prior to October 1, 1981. In *Jones v. Reagan*, 748 F.2d 1331, 1985 AMC 944 (9th Cir. 1984), permanently disabled seamen filed suit challenging the validity of the sections of the Omnibus Budget Reconciliation Act of 1981 that terminated a seaman's right to free medical care in governmental facilities. The court held that the Act did not unconstitutionally deprive seamen of any right. A summary judgment for the government was affirmed on appeal.

4. *Medicare*

Several courts have held that the availability of free medical care to an injured seaman under the Medicaid Program satisfies the vessel owners obligation to furnish cure. *Moran Towing & Transportation Co. v. Lombas*, 58 F.3d 24, 1995 AMC 2113 (2d Cir. 1995). See *Blige v. M/V GEECHEE GIRL*, 180 F. Supp. 2d 1349, 1355, 2001 AMC 2425, 2431-32 (S.D. Ga. 2001), the court said:

> Historically, the availability of cost-free cure at the United States Public Health Services marine hospitals satisfied the shipowner's cure obligation. Today, the shipowner's cure obligation is satisfied by Medicare/Medicaid, since it is the functional equivalent of the previously available free treatment at Public Heath Services hospitals…Thus, the shipowner is not liable for medical expenses paid by Medicaid, although it remains liable for out of pocket expenses, such as premiums or co-payments.

5. *Distinction Between Maintenance & Cure and "Found"*

Occasionally, a claim for "found" is made. In *Youn v. Maritime Overseas Corp.*, 623 So. 2d 1257, 1261 (La. 1993), plaintiff's injury was such that he was unable to work on his employers vessels. The Louisiana Supreme Court upheld an award for "found" in the amount of $10 per day for loss of past and future found. The court stated:

> 'Found' is an admiralty term which describes the element of damages representing the value of the living expenses provided to a seaman by his employer as a condition of employment while aboard ship. Found generally includes expenses for food, lodging and clothing. Frank L. Maraist, Admiralty in a Nutshell 194 (2d ed. 1988).

> Plaintiff clearly suffered this loss, inasmuch as he will never again receive these sums from his employer while aboard ship. The only issue is the precise value of the loss.

F. Duration of the Obligation

FARRELL v. UNITED STATES

336 U.S. 511, 69 S. Ct. 707, 93 L. Ed. 850 (1949)

Mr. Justice JACKSON delivered the opinion of the Court.

Petitioner, a seaman, brought suit in admiralty to recover damages under the Jones Act, 41 Stat. 1007, 46 U.S.C. § 688, and maintenance, cure and wages under maritime law. The issue of negligence was decided against him by both courts below and the claim is abandoned here. Petition for certiorari to review other issues was granted. 335 U.S. 869.

I. Maintenance and Cure

The facts which occasion maintenance and cure for this seaman are not in dispute. The claimant, 22 years of age and in good health, was a member of the Merchant Marine. He was in the service of the *S.S. James E. Haviland,* a merchant vessel owned and operated by the United States as a cargo and troop ship. On February 5, 1944, she was docked at Palermo, Sicily, and Farrell was granted shore leave which required his return to the ship by 6 p.m. of the same day. He overstayed his leave and about eight o'clock began, in rain and darkness, to make his way to the ship. He became lost and was misdirected to the wrong gate, by which he entered the shore-front area about a mile from where the ship lay moored. The area generally was blacked out but petitioner's companion, forty or fifty feet away, saw him fall over a guard chain into a drydock which was lighted sufficiently for night work then in progress. Farrell was grievously injured.

He was treated without expense to himself in various government hospitals until June 30, 1944, when he was discharged at Norfolk, Virginia, as completely disabled. He is totally and permanently blind and suffers posttraumatic convulsions which probably will become more frequent and are without possibility of further cure. From time to time he will require some medical care to ease attacks of headaches and epileptic convulsions. The court below concluded that the duty of a shipowner to furnish maintenance and cure does not extend beyond the time when the maximum cure possible has been effected. Petitioner contends that he is entitled to maintenance as long as he is disabled, which in this case is for life.

Admittedly there is no authority in any statute or American admiralty decisions for the proposition that he is entitled to maintenance for life. But an argument is based upon the ancient authority of Cleirac, *Jugmens d'Oleron,* Arts. 6 and 7 and notes by Cleirac; *Consolato del Mare,* cc. 182, 137; 2 Pard Coll. Mar. 152; to which American authorities have paid considerable respect. *See* Story, Circuit Justice, in *Reed v. Canfield,* Fed. Cas. No. 11,641, p. 429. A translation of the note relied upon reads:

> If in defending himself, or fighting against an enemy or corsairs, a mariner is maimed, or disabled to serve on board a ship for the rest of his life, besides the charge of his cure, he shall be maintained as long as he lives at the cost of the ship and cargo. Vide the Hanseatic law, art. 35. 1 Peters' Admiralty Decisions (1807), Appendix, p. xv.

Article 35 of the Laws of the Hanse Towns referred to reads:

> ART. XXXV. The seamen are obliged to defend their ship against rovers, on pain of losing their wages; and if they are wounded, they shall be healed and cured at the general charge of the concerned in a common average. If anyone of them is maimed and disabled, he shall be maintained as long as he lives by a like average. *Ibid.,* p. civ.

We need not elaborate upon the meanings or weight to be given to these medieval pronouncements of maritime law. As they show, they were written when pirates were not operatic characters but were real-life perils of the sea. When they bore down on a ship, all was lost unless the seaman would hazard life and limb in desperate defense. If they saved the ship and cargo, it was something in the nature of salvage and for their sacrifice in the effort a contribution on principles of average may have been justly due. Perhaps more than humanitarian considerations, inducement to stand by the ship generated the doctrine that saving the ship and her cargo from pirates entitles the seaman to lifelong maintenance if he is disabled in the struggle.

But construe the old-time law with what liberality we will, it cannot be made to cover the facts of this case. This ship was not beset but was snug at berth in a harbor that had capitulated to the United States and her allied forces six months before. No sea rovers, pirates or corsairs appeared to have menaced her. It is true that the ship was engaged in warlike operations and was a legitimate target for enemy aircraft or naval vessels, which made her service a war risk, but at that time and place no enemy attack was in progress or imminent. Even if we pass all this and assume the ship always to have been in potential danger and in need of defense, this seaman at the time of his injury had taken leave of her and he is in no position to claim that he was a sacrifice to her salvation. Far from helping to man the ship at the moment, he was unable to find her; he was lost ashore and not able adequately to take care of himself. However patriotic his motive in enlisting in the service and however ready he may have been to risk himself for his country, we can find no rational basis for awarding lifetime maintenance against the ship on the theory that he was wounded or maimed while defending her against enemies.

It is claimed, however, even if the basis for a lifetime award does not exist, that he is entitled to maintenance and cure beyond the period allowed by the courts below. This is based largely upon statements in the opinion of the Court in *Calmar Steamship Corp. v. Taylor*, 303 U.S. 525. There the question as stated by the Court was whether the duty of a shipowner to provide maintenance and cure for a seaman falling ill of an incurable disease while in its employ, extends to the payment of a lump-sum award sufficient to defray the cost of maintenance and cure for the remainder of his life. The Court laid aside cases where incapacity is caused by the employment and said, "We can find no basis for saying that, if the disease proves to be incurable, the duty extends beyond a fair time after the voyage in which to effect such improvement in the seaman's condition as reasonably may be expected to result from nursing, care, and medical treatment. This would satisfy such demands of policy as underlie the imposition of the obligation. Beyond this we think there is no duty, at least where the illness is not caused by the seaman's service."

It is claimed that when the Court reserved or disclaimed any judgment as to cases where the incapacity is caused "by the employment" or "by the seaman's service" it recognized or created such cases as a separate class for a different measure of maintenance and cure. We think no such distinction exists or was premised in the *Calmar* case. In *Aguilar v. Standard Oil Co.*, 318 U.S. 724, the Court pointed out that logically and historically the duty of maintenance and cure derives from a seaman's dependence on his ship, not from his individual deserts, and arises from his disability, not from anyone's fault. We there refused to look to the personal nature of the seaman's activity at the moment of injury to determine his right to award. Aside from gross misconduct or insubordination, what the seaman is doing and why and how he sustains injury does not affect his right to maintenance and cure, however decisive it may be as to claims for indemnity or for damages for negligence. He must, of course, at the time be "in the service of the ship," by which is meant that he must be generally answerable to its call to duty rather than actually in performance of routine tasks or specific orders.

It has been the merit of the seaman's right to maintenance and cure that it is so inclusive as to be relatively simple, and can be understood and administered without technical considerations. It has few exceptions or conditions to stir contentions, cause delays, and invite litigations. The seaman could forfeit the right only by conduct whose wrongful quality even simple men of the calling would recognize—insubordination, disobedience to orders, and gross misconduct. On the other hand, the master knew he must maintain and care for even the erring and careless seaman, much as a parent would a child. For any purpose to introduce a graduation of rights and duties based on some relative proximity of the activity at time of injury to the "employment" or the "service of the ship," would alter the basis and be out of harmony with the spirit and function of the doctrine and would open the door to the litigiousness which has made the landman's remedy so often a promise to the ear to be broken to the hope.

Nor is it at all clear to us what this particular litigant could gain from introduction of the distinction for which contention is made. If we should concede that larger measure of maintenance is due those whose injury is caused by the nature of their employment, it would seem farfetched to hold it applicable here. Claimant was disobedient to his orders and for his personal purposes overstayed his shore leave. His fall into a drydock that was sufficiently lighted for workmen to be carrying on repairs to a ship therein was due to no negligence but his own. These matters have not been invoked to forfeit or reduce his usual seaman's right, but it is difficult to see how such circumstances would warrant enlargement of it. We hold that he is entitled to the usual measure of maintenance and cure at the ship's expense, no less and no more, and turn to ascertainment of its bounds.

The law of the sea is in a peculiar sense an international law, but application of its specific rules depends upon acceptance by the United States. The problem of the sick or injured seaman has concerned every maritime country and, in 1936, the General Conference of the International Labor Organization at Geneva submitted a draft convention to the United States and other states. It was ratified by the Senate and was proclaimed by the President as effective for the United States on October 29, 1939. 54 Stat. 1693. Article 4, paragraph 1, thereof, provides: "The shipowner shall be liable to defray the expense of medical care and maintenance until the sick or injured person has been cured, or until the sickness or incapacity has been declared of a permanent character."

While enactment of this general rule by Congress would seem controlling, it is not amiss to point out that the limitation thus imposed was in accordance with the understanding of those familiar with the laws of the sea and sympathetic with the seaman's problems.

The Department of Labor issued a summary of the Convention containing the following on this subject: "The shipowner is required to furnish medical care and maintenance, including board and lodging, until the disabled person has been cured or the disability has been declared permanent." ROBINSON, ADMIRALTY, p. 300.

Representatives of the organized seamen have recognized and advised Congress of this traditional limitation on maintenance and cure. When Congress has had under consideration substitution of a system of workmen's compensation on the principles of the Longshoremen's and Harbor Workers' Compensation Act, 44 Stat. 1424, as amended, 33 U.S.C. §§ 901-950, organized seamen, as we have heretofore noted, have steadfastly opposed the change. *Hust v. Moore-McCormack Lines*, 328 U.S. 707, 715. In doing so the legal representative of one maritime union advised the Committee on Merchant Marine of the House of Representatives that maintenance extended during "(a) the period that a seaman receives treatment at a hospital either as an in-patient or an out-patient; and (b) during a period of convalescence, and until the maximum cure is obtained." Another representative, after defining it to include hospitalization, said, "In addition a seaman is entitled to recover maintenance while outside of the hospital until his physical condition becomes fixed."

That the duty of the ship to maintain and care for the seaman after the end of the voyage only until he was so far cured as possible, seems to have been the doctrine of the American admiralty courts prior to the adoption of the Convention by Congress, despite occasional ambiguity of language or reservation as to possible situations not before the court. It has been the rule of admiralty courts since the Convention.

Maintenance and cure is not the only recourse of the injured seaman. In an appropriate case he may obtain indemnity or compensation for injury due to negligence or unseaworthiness and may recover, by trial before court and jury, damages for partial or total disability. But maintenance and cure is more certain if more limited in its benefits. It does not hold a ship to permanent liability for a pension, neither does it give a lump-sum payment to offset disability based on some conception of expectancy of life. Indeed the custom of providing maintenance and cure in kind and concurrently with its need has had the advantage of removing its benefits from danger of being wasted by the proverbial improvidence of its beneficiaries. The Government does not contend that if Farrell receives future treatment of a curative nature he may not recover in a new proceeding the amount expended for such treatment and for maintenance while receiving it.

The need of this seaman for permanent help is great and his plight most unfortunate. But as the evidence has afforded no basis for supplying that need by finding negligence, neither does the case afford a basis for distortion of the doctrine of maintenance and cure. This seaman was in the service of the United States and extraordinary measures of relief while not impossible are not properly addressed to the courts.

II. Wages

The two courts below have held the petitioner entitled to wages until the completion of the voyage at the port of New York on March 28, 1944. The petitioner contends that he has a right to wages for twelve months from December 16, 1943, the date he joined the vessel. The articles of the *Haviland*, signed by petitioner, were on a printed form which left a vacant space subject to the following footnote: "Here the voyage is to be described, and the places named at which the ship is to touch; or, if that cannot be done, the general nature and probable length of the voyage is to be stated, and the port or country at which the voyage is to terminate." The *Haviland's* articles, for security reasons during the war, did not describe the voyage in such terms but provided, "from the Port of Philadelphia, to A point in the Atlantic Ocean to the eastward of Phila. and thence to such ports and places in any part of the world as the Master may direct or as may be ordered or directed by the United States Government or any department, commission or agency thereof ... and back to a final port of discharge in the United States, for a term of time not exceeding 12 (Twelve) calendar months." It is not questioned that the general custom in ships, other than the coastwise trade, is to sign on for a voyage rather than for a fixed period. But it is contended that the last clause of this contract obligated the petitioner to serve for twelve calendar months, irrespective of the termination of the voyage, and therefore gave him the right to wages for a similar period. The contract is not an uncommon form and complied with war-time requirements as to voyage contracts. We think, in the light of the custom of the industry and the condition of the times, there is nothing ambiguous about it and that it obligated the petitioner only for the voyage on which the ship was engaged when he signed on and that, when it terminated at a port of discharge in the United States, he could not have been required to reembark for a second voyage. The twelve-month period appears as a limitation upon the duration of the voyage and not as a stated period of employment. We think the court below made no error in determining the wages.

For the reasons set forth, the judgment is
Affirmed.

* * *

VELLA v. FORD MOTOR CO.

421 U.S. 1, 95 S. Ct. 1381, 43 L. Ed. 2d 682, 1975 AMC 563 (1974)

Mr. Justice BRENNAN delivered the opinion of the Court.

We granted certiorari in this case limited to the question whether a shipowner's duty to furnish an injured seaman maintenance and cure continues from the date the seaman leaves the ship to the date when a medical diagnosis is made that the seaman's injury was permanent immediately after his accident and therefore incurable. 419 U.S. 894 (1974).

Petitioner was a seaman aboard respondent's Great Lakes vessel, S.S. Robert S. McNamara. He was discharged and left the ship on June 29, 1968. Thereafter he filed this suit in the District Court for the Eastern District of Michigan, Southern Division, based on a claim that on April 4, 1968, while replacing a lower engineroom deck plate, he slipped and fell on the oily floor plate causing his head to suffer a severe blow when it struck an electrical box. The complaint included a count, among others, for maintenance and cure. The medical testimony at the trial was that petitioner suffered from a vestibular disorder defined as damage to the balancing mechanism of the inner ear. The testimony of respondent's medical witness, Dr. Heil, an otolaryngologist, supplied the only medical diagnosis as to the time when the disorder became permanent and not susceptible of curative treatment. Dr. Heil testified on April 27, 1972, that he had recently examined petitioner. He conceded that a severe blow to the head, such as alleged by petitioner, could have caused the disorder. He said, however, that the disorder is not a condition that can be cured by treatment. The jury awarded petitioner maintenance and cure in the amount of $5,848. Respondent moved for a judgment notwithstanding the verdict on the ground that the award was not within the permissible scope of maintenance and cure. The District Court denied the motion and stated: "While it is true that maintenance and cure is not available for a sickness declared to be permanent, it is also true that maintenance and cure continues until such time as the incapacity is declared to be permanent." App. 20a. The Court of Appeals for the Sixth Circuit reversed without a published opinion, 495 F.2d 1374 (1974). The Court of Appeals held that "once the seaman reaches 'maximum medical recovery,' the shipowner's obligation to provide maintenance and cure ceases," App. 28a, and since "[t]he record in this case does not permit an inference other than that [petitioner's] condition was permanent immediately after the accident," *id.*, at 29a, the District Court's holding impermissibly extended the shipowner's obligation.

We disagree with the Court of Appeals and therefore reverse. The shipowner's ancient duty to provide maintenance and cure for the seaman who becomes ill or is injured while in the service of the ship derives from the "unique hazards [which] attend the work of seamen," and fosters the "combined object of encouraging marine commerce and assuring the well-being of seamen." *Aguilar v. Standard Oil Co.*, 318 U.S. 724, 727 (1943). To further that "combined object" we have held that the duty arises irrespective of the absence of shipowner negligence and indeed irrespective of whether the illness or injury is suffered in the course of the seaman's employment. *Calmar S.S. Corp. v. Taylor*, 303 U.S. 525, 527 (1938). And, "[s]o broad is the shipowner's obligation, ... negligence or acts short of culpable misconduct on the seaman's part will not relieve [the shipowner] of the responsibility." *Aguilar v. Standard Oil Co.*, *supra*, at 730-731. Thus, the breadth and inclusiveness of the shipowner's duty assure its easy and ready administration for "[i]t has few exceptions or conditions to stir contentions, cause delays, and invite litigations." *Farrell v. United States*, 336 U.S. 511, 516 (1949).

Denial of maintenance and cure when the seaman's injury, though in fact permanent immediately after the accident, is not medically diagnosed as permanent until long after its occurrence would obviously diserve and frustrate the "combined object of encouraging marine commerce and assuring the well-being of seamen." A shipowner might withhold vitally necessary maintenance and cure on the belief, however well or poorly founded, that the seaman's injury is permanent and incurable. Or the seaman, if paid maintenance and cure by the shipowner, might be required to reimburse the payments, if it is later determined that the injury was permanent immediately after the accident. Thus uncertainty would displace the essential certainty of protection against the ravages of illness and injury that encourages seamen to undertake their hazardous calling. Moreover, easy and ready administration of the shipowner's duty would seriously suffer from the introduction of complexities and uncertainty that could "stir contentions, cause delays, and invite litigations."

The Shipowners' Liability Convention, made effective for the United States on October 29, 1939, *Farrell v. United States*, *supra*, at 517, buttresses our conclusion that the District Court correctly held that "maintenance and cure continues until such time as the incapacity is declared to be permanent."[4] That holding tracks the wording of Art. 4, P. 1, of the Convention which provides: "The shipowner shall be liable to defray the expense of medical care and maintenance until the sick or injured person has been cured, or until the sickness or incapacity has been declared of a permanent character." 54 Stat. 1696. (Emphasis supplied.) The aim of the Convention "was not to change materially American standards but to equalize operating costs by raising the standards of member nations to the American level." *Warren v. United States*, 340 U.S. 523, 527 (1951). Thus Art. 4, P. 1, is declaratory of a longstanding tradition respecting the scope of the shipowner's duty to furnish injured seamen maintenance and cure, *Farrell v. United States*, *supra*, at 518, and therefore the District Court's interpretation was correct.

The judgment of the Court of Appeals is reversed, and the case is remanded for further proceedings consistent with this opinion.

So ordered.

---

[4] On this record maintenance and cure could have been claimed to continue from June 29, 1968, the date petitioner left the vessel, to April 27, 1972, the date Dr. Heil testified that the vestibular disorder was permanent immediately after the accident and not susceptible of curative treatment. The jury, however, awarded petitioner maintenance and cure at $8 per day only for the period from June 29, 1968, to June 29, 1970. Petitioner's appeal to the Court of Appeals did not, however, draw into question a claim of entitlement to maintenance and cure for the longer period sought by him in this Court, Brief for Petitioner 19. *See Le Tulle v. Scofield*, 308 U.S. 415, 421-422 (1940). Moreover, in light of our holding that the shipowner's duty continued until Dr. Heil's testimony, it is not necessary to address the question whether the jury award might also be sustained on the ground that the shipowner's duty in any event obliged him to provide palliative medical care to arrest further progress of the condition or to reduce pain, and we intimate no view whatever upon the shipowner's duty in that regard. *Compare Ward v. Union Barge Line Corp.*, 443 F.2d 565, 572 (CA3 1971), with the opinion of the Court of Appeals in this case. App. 29a n.1. Nor do we express any view whether a seaman may forfeit his right to maintenance and cure by not reporting a known injury or malady, or by refusing from the outset to allow proper medical examination, or by discontinuing medical care made available.

Note: Duration of the Obligation

In *Cox v. Dravo Corp.*, 517 F.2d 620 (3d Cir. 1975), the court held that an award of maintenance and cure cannot be sustained on the ground of a shipowner's duty to provide medical care that can serve only to reduce pain. Further, the court announced that there is no duty to provide treatment that arrests the progress of a deteriorating condition. The plaintiff, relying on language in the *Vella* case, argued that the duty to provide maintenance and cure inevitably continues until such time as there has been a judicial determination of the permanency of the injury. The court declared (517 F.2d at 627):

> We can imagine a factual dispute as to when a diagnosis of permanency was made. If there is such a dispute it must be resolved by the trier of fact. When it is so resolved the date of diagnosis so determined, not the date of the judicial determination, defines the end of the vessel's maintenance and cure obligation.

For a discussion of the case, *see,* Note, 17 B.C. Ind. & Com. L. Rev. 648 *(1976).*

What about a seaman who suffered a renal failure? The condition of his kidneys cannot be improved, *i.e.*, cannot be cured, but without regular dialisis treatment or a kidney transplant, he will die. Does this situation suggest that there is a type of therapeutic treatment that falls somewhere in between "cure" and mere "palliative treatment" which should qualify for an award of maintenance and cure? *See Costa Crociere, S.p.A. v. Rose*, 939 F. Supp. 1538, 1996 AMC 2797 (S.D. Fla. 1996).

G. Wage Penalties

GRIFFIN v. OCEANIC CONTRACTORS, INC.

458 U.S. 564, 102 S. Ct. 3245, 73 L. Ed. 2d 973, 1982 AMC 2377 (1982)

Justice REHNQUIST delivered the opinion of the Court.

This case concerns the application of 46 U.S.C. § 596, which requires certain masters and vessel owners to pay seamen promptly after their discharge and authorizes seamen to recover double wages for each day that payment is delayed without sufficient cause. The question is whether the district courts, in the exercise of discretion, may limit the period during which this wage penalty is assessed, or whether imposition of the penalty is mandatory for each day that payment is withheld in violation of the statute.

I.

On February 18, 1976, petitioner signed an employment contract with respondent in New Orleans, agreeing to work as a senior pipeline welder on board vessels operated by respondent in the North Sea. The contract specified that petitioner's employment would extend "until December 15, 1976 or until Oceanic's 1976 pipeline committal in the North Sea is fulfilled, whichever shall occur first." The contract also provided that respondent would pay for transportation to and from the work site, but that if petitioner quit the job prior to its termination date, or if his services were terminated for cause, he would be charged with the cost of transportation back to the United States. Respondent reserved the right to withhold $137.50 from each of petitioner's first four paychecks "as a cash deposit for the payment of your return transportation in the event you should become obligated for its payment." On March 6, 1976, petitioner flew from the United States to Antwerp, Belgium, where he reported to work at respondent's vessel, the "Lay Barge 27," berthed in the Antwerp harbor for repairs.

On April 1, 1976, petitioner suffered an injury while working on the deck of the vessel readying it for sea. Two days later he underwent emergency surgery in Antwerp. On April 5, petitioner was discharged from the hospital and went to respondent's Antwerp office, where he spoke with Jesse Williams, the welding superintendent, and provided a physician's statement that he was not fit for duty. Williams refused to acknowledge that petitioner's injury was work-related and denied that respondent was liable for medical and hospital expenses, maintenance, or unearned wages. Williams also refused to furnish transportation back to the United States, and continued to retain $412.50 in earned wages that had been deducted from petitioner's first three paychecks for that purpose. Petitioner returned to his home in Houston, Texas, the next day at his own expense. He was examined there by a physician who determined that he would be able to resume work on May 3, 1976. On May 5, petitioner began working as a welder for another company operating in the North Sea.

In 1978 he brought suit against respondent under the Jones Act, 38 Stat. 1185, as amended, 46 U.S.C. § 688, and under general maritime law, seeking damages for respondent's failure to pay maintenance, cure, unearned wages, repatriation expenses, and the value of certain personal effects lost on board respondent's vessel. Petitioner also sought penalty wages under Rev. Stat. § 4529, as amended, 46 U.S.C. § 596, for respondent's failure to pay over the $412.50 in earned wages allegedly due upon discharge. The District Court found for petitioner and awarded damages totalling $23,670.40.

Several findings made by that court are particularly relevant to this appeal. First, the court found that petitioner's injury was proximately caused by an unseaworthy condition of respondent's vessel. Second, the court found that petitioner was discharged from respondent's employ on the day of the injury, and that the termination of his employment was caused solely by that injury. Third, it found that respondent's failure to pay petitioner the $412.50 in earned wages was "without sufficient cause." Finally, the court found that petitioner had exercised due diligence in attempting to collect those wages.

In assessing penalty wages under 46 U.S.C. § 596, the court held that "[t]he period during which the penalty runs is to be determined by the sound discretion of the district court and depends on the equities of the case." It determined that the appropriate period for imposition of the penalty was from the date of discharge, April 1, 1976, through the date of petitioner's reemployment, May 5, 1976, a period of 34 days. Applying the statute, it computed a penalty of $6,881.60. Petitioner appealed the award of damages as inadequate.

The Court of Appeals for the Fifth Circuit affirmed. 664 F.2d 36 (1981). That court concluded, *inter alia*, that the District Court had not erred in limiting assessment of the penalty provided by 46 U.S.C. § 596 to the period beginning April 1 and ending May 5. The court recognized that the statute required payment of a penalty for each day during which wages were withheld until the date they were actually paid, which in this case did not occur until September 17, 1980, when respondent satisfied the judgment of the District Court. Nevertheless, the court believed itself bound by prior decisions within the circuit, which left calculation of the penalty period to the sound discretion of the district courts. It concluded that the District Court in this cade had not abused its discretion by assessing a penalty only for the period during which petitioner was unemployed.

We granted certiorari to resolve a conflict among the Circuits regarding the proper application of the wage penalty statute.

* * *

The District Court found that respondent had refused to pay petitioner the balance of earned wages promptly after discharge, and that its refusal was "without sufficient cause." Respondent challenges neither of these findings. Although the two statutory conditions were satisfied, however, the District Court obviously did not assess double wages "for each and every day" during which payment was delayed, but instead limited the assessment to the period of petitioner's unemployment. Nothing in the language of the statute vests the courts with the discretion to set such a limitation.

It is highly probable that respondents are correct in their contention that a recovery in excess of $300,000 in this case greatly exceeds any actual injury suffered by petitioner as a result of respondent's delay in paying his wages. But this Court has previously recognized that awards made under this statute were not intended to be merely compensatory:

"We think the use of this language indicates a purpose to protect seamen from delayed payments of wages by the imposition of a liability which is not exclusively compensatory, but designed to prevent, by its coercive effect, arbitrary refusals to pay wages, and to induce prompt payment when payment is possible." *Collis v. Fergusson*, 281 U.S. 52, 55-56 (1930).

* * *

... Under the plain language of the statute, therefore, its decision to limit the penalty period was error. The judgment of the Court of Appeals affirming that decision accordingly is reversed and the case is remanded for proceedings consistent with this opinion.

It is so ordered.

[Dissenting opinion of JUSTICE STEVENS, with whom JUSTICE BLACKMUN joins, is omitted.]

Notes

1. What can an employer do if it believes that it has a defense to the wage claim? Can it pay the funds representing the disputed claims into the court registry? *See Mateo v. M/S Kiso* 805 F. Supp. 761, 1993 AMC 2278 (N.D. Cal. 1991). Also, *see Cohen v. S/S Consumer*, 746 F.2d 1069, 1985 AMC 1686 (5th Cir. 1985) for a discussion of the purpose of the penalty provision.

2. The penalty wage statute is now 46 U.S.C. § 10313(g).

3. In *Governor and Co. of Bank of Scotland v. Sabay*, 211 F.3d 261, 2000 AMC 1532 (5th Cir. 2000) *rehearing and rehearing en banc denied* 218 F.3d 745 (5th Cir. 2000), it was held that the penalty wages action lies directly against the owner (and master) *in personam*. Thus, the seamen's preferred maritime lien for penalty wages could only be enforced against vessel sale proceeds in which the owner had an interest. Because there was a secured mortgagee whose claim exceeded the sale proceeds, the owner no longer had any interest to which the penalty wages lien could attach.

Part 2. Action for Negligence—The Jones Act

Injury But No Death: Cases and Notes

THE OSCEOLA

189 U.S. 158, 23 S. Ct. 483, 47 L. Ed. 760 (1903)

This was a libel *in rem* filed in the District Court for the Eastern District of Wisconsin, in admiralty, against the propeller Osceola, to recover damages for a personal injury sustained by one Patrick Shea, a seaman on board the vessel, through the negligence of the master.

Upon a full review ... of English and American authorities, we think the law may be considered as settled upon the following propositions:

(1) That a vessel and her owners are liable, in case a seaman falls sick or is wounded in the service of the ship, to the extent of his maintenance and cure, and to his wages, at least so long as the voyage is continued.

(2) That the vessel and her owners are, both by English and American law, liable to an indemnity for injuries received by seamen in consequence of the unseaworthiness of the ship, or a failure to supply and keep in order the proper appliances appurtenant to such ship.

(3) That all the members of the crew, except perhaps the master, are, as between themselves, fellow servants, and hence seamen cannot recover for injuries sustained through the negligence of another member of the crew beyond the expense of their maintenance and cure.

(4) That the seaman is not allowed to recover an indemnity for the negligence of the master, or any member of the crew, but is entitled to maintenance and cure, whether the injuries were received from negligence or accident.

It will be observed in these cases that a departure has been made from the Continental codes in allowing an indemnity beyond the expense of maintenance and cure in cases arising from unseaworthiness. This departure originated in England in the Merchants' Shipping Act of 1876, ... and in this country, in a general consensus of opinion among the Circuit and District Courts, that an exception should be made from the general principle before obtaining, in favor of seamen suffering injury through the unseaworthiness of the vessel. We are not disposed to disturb so wholesome a doctrine by any contrary decision of our own.

Note

In suits against persons other than his employer, a seaman has the same rights against negligent third parties as anyone else. If a seaman is aboard his employers' vessel and is injured when another vessel negligently collides with the one on which he is aboard, he may bring an action for negligence under the general maritime law which has always provided a remedy in case of collision. The action may be brought in federal court in admiralty or at law if there is diversity of citizenship. It may be brought in state court under saving to suitors. Damages recoverable are those permitted under general maritime law and are enumerated in the discussion of unseaworthiness, *infra*.

A. The Statutes

THE JONES ACT

46 U.S.C.A. §§ 30104-5

§ 30104. Personal injury to or death of seamen

(a) Cause of Action—A seaman injured in the course of employment or, if the seaman dies from the injury, the personal representative of the seaman may elect to bring a civil action at law, with the right of trial by jury, against the employer. Laws of the United States regulating recovery for personal injury to, or death of, a railway employee apply to an action under this section.

(b) Venue—An action under this section shall be brought in the judicial district in which the employer resides or the employer's principal office is located.

§ 30105. Restriction on recovery by non-citizens and non-resident aliens for incidents in waters of other countries.

(a) Definition—In this section, the term "continental shelf" has the meaning given that term in article I of the 1958 Convention on the Continental Shelf.

(b) Restriction—Except as provided in subsection (c), a civil action for maintenance and cure or for damages for personal injury or death may not be brought under a maritime law of the United States if —

  (1) the individual suffering the injury or death was not a citizen or permanent resident alien of the United States at the time of the incident giving rise to the action;

  (2) the incident occurred in the territorial waters or waters overlaying the continental shelf of a country other than the United States; and

  (3) the individual suffering the injury or death was employed at the time of the incident by a person engaged in the exploration, development, or production of offshore mineral or energy resources, including drilling, mapping, surveying, diving, pipelaying, maintaining, repairing, constructing, or transporting supplies, equipment, or personnel, but not including transporting those resources by a vessel constructed or adapted primarily to carry oil in bulk in the cargo spaces.

(c) Nonapplication—Subsection (b) does not apply if the individual bringing the action establishes that a remedy is not available under the laws of—

(1) the country asserting jurisdiction over the area in which the incident occurred; or

(2) the country in which the individual suffering the injury or death maintained citizenship or residency at the time of the incident.

Also relevant is 46 U.S.C.A. § 30510 (formerly 46 app. U.S.C. § 183):

§ 30510. Vicarious liability formedical malpractice with regard to crew

In a civil action by any person in which the owner or operator of a vessel or employer of a crewmember is claimed to have vicarious liability for medical malpractice with regard to a crewmember occurring at a shoreside facility, and to the extent the damages resulted from the conduct of any shoreside doctor, hospital, medical facility, or other health care provider, the owner, operator, or employer is entitled to rely on any statutory limitations of liability applicable to the doctor, hospital, medical facility, or other health care provider in the State of the United States in which the shoreside medical care was provided.

THE JONES ACT
(Superseded Version)
46 U.S.C. app.

§ 688. Recovery for injury to or death of seaman

(a) Application of railway employee statutes; jurisdiction

Any seaman who shall suffer personal injury in the course of his employment may, at his election, maintain an action for damages at law, with the right of trial by jury, and in such action all statutes of the United States modifying or extending the common-law right or remedy in cases of personal injury to railway employees shall apply; and in case of the death of any seaman as a result of any such personal injury the personal representative of such seaman may maintain an action for damages at law with the right of trial by jury, and in such action all statutes of the United States conferring or regulating the right of action for death in the case of railway employees shall be applicable. Jurisdiction in such actions shall be under the court of the district in which the defendant employer resides or in which his principal office is located.

(b) Limitation for certain aliens; applicability in lieu of other remedy

(1) No action may be maintained under subsection (a) of this section or under any other maritime law of the United States for maintenance and cure or for damages for the injury or death of a person who was not a citizen or permanent resident alien of the United States at the time of the incident giving rise to the action if the incident occurred—

   (A) while that person was in the employ of an enterprise engaged in the exploration, development, or production of off-shore mineral or energy resources—including but not limited to drilling, mapping, surveying, diving, pipelaying, maintaining, repairing, constructing, or transporting supplies, equipment or personnel, but not including transporting those resources by a vessel constructed or adapted primarily to carry oil in bulk in the cargo spaces; and

   (B) in the territorial waters or waters overlaying the continental shelf of a nation other than the United States, its territories, or possessions. As used in this paragraph, the term "continental shelf" has the meaning stated in article I of the 1958 Convention on the Continental Shelf.

(2) The provisions of paragraph (1) of this subsection shall not be applicable if the person bringing the action establishes that no remedy was available to that person—

(A) under the laws of the nation asserting jurisdiction over the area in which the incident occurred; or

(B) under the laws of the nation in which, at the time of the incident, the person for whose injury or death a remedy is sought maintained citizenship or residency.

Federal Employers' Liability Act

45 U.S.C. § 51, *et seq.*

§ 51. Liability of common carriers by railroad, in interstate or foreign commerce, for injuries to employees from negligence; employee defined

Every common carrier by railroad while engaging in commerce between any of the several States or Territories, or between any of the States and Territories, or between the District of Columbia and any of the States or Territories, or between the District of Columbia or any of the States or any of the States or Territories and any foreign nation or nations, shall be liable in damages to any person suffering injury while he is employed by such carrier in such commerce, or, in case of the death of such employee, to his or her personal representative, for the benefit of the surviving widow or husband and children of such employee; and, if none, then of such employee's parents; and, if none, then of the next of kin dependent upon such employee, for such injury or death resulting in whole or in part from the negligence of any of the officers, agents, or employees of such carrier, or by reason of any defect or insufficiency, due to its negligence, in its cars, engines, appliances, machinery, track, roadbed, works, boats, wharves, or other equipment.

Any employee of a carrier, any part of whose duties as such employee shall be the furtherance of interstate or foreign commerce; or shall, in any way directly or closely and substantially, affect such commerce as above set forth shall, for the purposes of this chapter, be considered as being employed by such carrier in such commerce and shall be considered as entitled to the benefits of this chapter.

* * *

§ 53. Contributory negligence; diminution of damages

In all actions on and after April 22, 1908 brought against any such common carrier by railroad under or by virtue of any of the provisions of this chapter to recover damages for personal injuries to an employee, or where such injuries have resulted in his death, the fact that the employee may have been guilty of contributory negligence shall not bar a recovery, but the damages shall be diminished by the jury in proportion to the amount of negligence attributable to such employee: *Provided*, That no such employee who may be injured or killed shall be held to have been guilty of contributory negligence in any case where the violation by such common carrier of any statute enacted for the safety of employees contributed to the injury or death of such employee.

§ 54. Assumption of risks of employment

In any action brought against any common carrier under or by virtue of any of the provisions of this chapter to recover damages for injuries to, or the death of, any of its employees, such employee shall not be held to have assumed the risks of his employment in any case where such injury or death resulted in whole or in part from the negligence of any of the officers, agents, or employees of such carrier; and no employee shall be held to have assumed the risks of his employment in any case where the violation by such common carrier of any statute enacted for the safety of employees contributed to the injury or death of such employee.

§ 55. Contract, rule, regulation, or device exempting from liability; set-off

Any contract, rule, regulation, or device whatsoever, the purpose or intent of which shall be to enable any common carrier to exempt itself from any liability created by this chapter, shall to that extent be void: *Provided*, That in any action brought against any such common carrier under or by virtue of any of the provisions of this chapter, such common carrier may set off therein any sum it has contributed or paid to any insurance, relief benefit, or indemnity that may have been paid to the injured employee or the person entitled thereto on account of the injury or death for which said action was brought.

§ 56. Actions; limitations; concurrent jurisdiction of courts

No action shall be maintained under this chapter unless commenced within three years from the day the cause of action accrued.

Under this chapter an action may be brought in a district court of the United States, in the district of the residence of the defendant, or in which the cause of action arose, or in which the defendant shall be doing business at the time of commencing such action. The jurisdiction of the courts of the United States under this chapter shall be concurrent with that of the courts of the several States.

* * *

§ 59. Survival of right of action of person injured

Any right of action given by this chapter to a person suffering injury shall survive to his or her personal representative, for the benefit of the surviving widow or husband and children of such employee, and, if none, then of such employee's parents; and, if none, then of the next of kin dependent upon such employee, but in such cases there shall be only one recovery for the same injury.

Note

The constitutionality of the Jones Act was upheld in *Panama Railroad Co. v. Johnson*, 264 U.S. 375, 44 S.Ct. 391, 68 L.Ed. 748, 1924 AMC 551 (1924). In that case, the Supreme Court held that the word "jurisdiction" in the last sentence of the Jones Act means "venue"; the words "at his election" in the first sentence of the same statute do not accord a choice to an injured seaman to seek relief under a nonmaritime system of law; and that these words allow any injured seaman to seek relief, either on the side of the court with a jury or in admiralty without a jury, under the rules of substantive maritime law as modified by the statute.

In *Plamals v. The Pinar Del Rio*, 277 U.S. 151, 48 S.Ct. 457, 72 L.Ed. 827, 1928 AMC 932 (1928), the Supreme Court held that the Jones Act does not give rise to a maritime lien in favor of an injured seaman. Plaintiff, accordingly, may not proceed *in rem* in a Jones Act suit; he must proceed *in personam* against his employer. He may proceed in admiralty though without jury trial. The employer, however, need not to be owner or operator of a vessel to be liable under the Jones Act. *Barrios v. Louisiana Construction Materials Co.*, 465 F.2d 1157, 1972 AMC 2659 (5th Cir. 1972).

If a Jones Act suit is commenced in a state court, it is not removable to the federal court. *See Pate v. Standard Dredging Co.*, 193 F.2d 498 (5th Cir. 1952). This is so even in the presence of complete diversity between the parties.

In 1980, Congress established a uniform national statute of limitations of three years for suits "for recovery of damages for personal injury or death, or both, arising out of a maritime tort." 46 U.S.C.A. § 30106 (formerly 46 U.S.C. § 763a.)

---

1. Coverage: "Any Seaman..."

a. Status

McDERMOTT INTERN., INC. v. WILANDER

498 U.S. 337, 111 S. Ct. 807, 112 L. Ed. 2d 866, 1991 AMC 913 (1991)

Justice O'CONNOR delivered the opinion of the Court.

The question in this case is whether one must aid in the navigation of a vessel in order to qualify as a "seaman" under the Jones Act, 46 U.S.C. App. § 688.

I.

Jon Wilander worked for McDermott International as a paint foreman. His duties consisted primarily of supervising the sandblasting and painting of various fixtures and piping located on oil drilling platforms in the Persian Gulf. On July 4, 1983, Wilander was inspecting a pipe on one such platform when a bolt serving as a plug in the pipe blew out under pressure, striking Wilander in the head. At the time, Wilander was assigned to the American flag vessel M/V *Gates Tide*, a "paint boat" chartered to McDermott that contained equipment used in sandblasting and painting the platforms.

Wilander sued McDermott in the United States District Court for the Western District of Louisiana, seeking recovery under the Jones Act for McDermott's negligence related to the accident. McDermott moved for summary judgment, alleging that, as a matter of law, Wilander was not a "seaman" under the Jones Act, and therefore not entitled to recovery. The District Court denied the motion. App. 19. In a bifurcated trial, the jury first determined Wilander's status as a seaman. By special interrogatory, the jury found that Wilander was either permanently assigned to, or performed a substantial amount of work aboard, the *Gates Tide*, and that the performance of his duties contributed to the function of the *Gates Tide* or to the accomplishment of its mission, thereby satisfying the test for seaman status established in *Offshore Co. v. Robison*, 266 F.2d 769 (CA5 1959). *App. to Pet. for Cert.* 16-17. The District Court denied McDermott's motion for judgment based on the jury findings. *Id.*, at 10-16.

The case then proceeded to trial on the issues of liability and damages. The jury found that McDermott's negligence was the primary cause of Wilander's injuries, but that Wilander had been 25% contributorily negligent. The jury awarded Wilander $337,500. The District Court denied McDermott's motion for judgment notwithstanding the verdict, *id.*, at 19-21, and both parties appealed.

The United States Court of Appeals for the Fifth Circuit affirmed the determination of seaman status, finding sufficient evidence to support the jury's finding under the *Robison* test. 887 F.2d 88, 90 (1989). McDermott asked the court to reject the *Robison* requirement that a seaman "contribute to the function of the vessel or to the accomplishment of its mission," *Robison*, *supra*, at 779, in favor of the more stringent requirement of *Johnson v. John F. Beasley Construction Co.*, 742 F.2d 1054 (CA7 1984). In that case, the Court of Appeals for the Seventh Circuit—relying on cases from this Court requiring that a seaman aid in the navigation of a vessel—held that seaman status under the Jones Act may be conferred only on employees who make "a significant contribution to the maintenance, operation, or welfare of the *transportation* function of the vessel." *Id.*, at 1063 (emphasis added).

The Fifth Circuit here concluded that Wilander would not meet the requirements of the *Johnson* test, but reaffirmed the rule in *Robison* and held that Wilander was a "seaman" under the Jones Act. 887 F.2d, at 90-91. We granted certiorari, 496 U.S. —, 110 S. Ct. 3212, 110 L. Ed. 2d 660 (1990), to resolve the conflict between the *Robison* and *Johnson* tests on the issue of the transportation/navigation function requirement, and now affirm.

II.

A.

* * *

The Jones Act does not define "seaman."

* * *

In the absence of contrary indication, we assume that when a statute uses such a term, Congress intended it to have its established meaning. *See Morissette v. United States,* 342 U.S. 246, 263 (1952); *Gilbert v. United States,* 370 U.S. 650, 658 (1962). Our first task, therefore, is to determine who was a seaman under the general maritime law when Congress passed the Jones Act.

B.

Since the first Judiciary Act, federal courts have determined who is eligible for various seamen's benefits under general maritime law. Prior to the Jones Act, these benefits included the tort remedies outlined in The Osceola and a lien against the ship for wages. See generally Gilmore & Black, supra, at 35-36, 281; The John G. Stevens, 170 U.S. 113, 119 (1898); *The Osceola, supra,* at 175. Certain early cases limited seaman status to those who aided in the navigation of the ship. The narrow rule was that a seaman—sometimes referred to as a mariner—must actually navigate: "[T]he persons engaged on board of her must have been possessed of some skill in navigation. They must have been able to 'hand, reef and steer,' the ordinary test of seamanship." *The Canton,* 5 F. Cas. 29, 30 (No. 2,388) (D Mass. 1858). *See also Gurney v. Crockett,* 11 F. Cas. 123, 124 (No. 5,874) (SDNY 1849).

Notwithstanding the aid in navigation doctrine, federal courts throughout the last century consistently awarded seamen's benefits to those whose work on board ship did not direct the vessel. Firemen, engineers, carpenters, and cooks all were considered seamen. *See, e.g., Wilson v. The Ohio,* 30 F. Cas. 149 (No. 17,825) (ED Pa. 1834) (firemen); *Allen v. Hallet,* 1 F. Cas. 472 (No. 223) (SDNY 1849) (cook); *Sageman v. The Brandywine,* 21 F. Cas. 149 (No. 12,216) (D Mich. 1852) (female cook); *The Sultana,* 23 F. Cas. 379 (No. 13,602) (D Mich. 1857) (clerk). *See generally* M. NORRIS, THE LAW OF SEAMEN § 2.3 (4th ed. 1985); Engerrand & Bale, *Seaman Status Reconsidered,* 24 S. TEX. L. J. 431, 432-433 (1983).

Some courts attempted to classify these seamen under a broad conception of aid in navigation that included those who aided in navigation indirectly by supporting those responsible for moving the vessel: "The services rendered must be necessary, or, at least, contribute to the preservation of the vessel, or of those whose labour and skill are employed to navigate her." *Trainor v. The Superior,* 24 F. Cas. 130, 131 (No. 14,136) (ED Pa. 1834). This fiction worked for cooks and carpenters—who fed those who navigated and kept the ship in repair—but what of a cooper whose job it was to make barrels to aid in whaling? As early as 1832, Justice Story, sitting on circuit, held that "[a] 'cooper' is a seaman in contemplation of law, although he has peculiar duties on board of the ship." *United States v. Thompson,* 28 F. Cas. 102 (No. 16,492) (CCD Mass.). Justice Story made no reference to navigation in declaring it established that: "A cook and steward are seamen in the sense of the maritime law, although they have peculiar duties assigned them. So a pilot, a surgeon, a ship-carpenter, and a boatswain, are deemed seamen, entitled to sue in the admiralty." *Ibid.*

By the middle of the 19th century, the leading admiralty treatise noted the wide variety of those eligible for seamen's benefits: "Masters, mates, sailors, surveyors, carpenters, coopers, stewards, cooks, cabin boys, kitchen boys, engineers, pilots, firemen, deck hands, waiters,—women as well as men,—are mariners." E. BENEDICT, THE AMERICAN ADMIRALTY § 278, p. 158 (1850). Benedict concluded that American admiralty courts did not require that seamen have a connection to navigation. "The term mariner includes all persons employed on board ships and vessels during the voyage to assist in their navigation and preservation, *or to promote the purposes of the voyage.*" *Ibid.* (emphasis added). Moreover, Benedict explained, this was the better rule; admiralty courts throughout the world had long recognized that seamen's benefits were properly extended to all those who worked on board vessels in furtherance of the myriad purposes for which ships set to sea:

It is universally conceded that the general principles of law must be applied to new kinds of property, as they spring into existence in the progress of society, according to their nature and incidents, and the common sense of the community. In the early periods of maritime commerce, when the oar was the great agent of propulsion, vessels were entirely unlike those of modern times—and each nation and period has had its peculiar agents of commerce and navigation adapted to its own wants and its own waters, and the names and descriptions of ships and vessels are without number. Under the class of mariners in the armed ship are embraced the officers and privates of a little army. In the whale ship, the sealing vessel—the codfishing and herring fishing vessel—the lumber vessel—the freighting vessel—the passenger vessel—there are other functions besides these of mere navigation, and they are performed by men who know nothing of seamanship—and in the great invention of modern times, the steamboat, an entirely new set of operatives, are employed, yet at all times and in all countries, all the persons who have been necessarily or properly employed in a vessel as co-labourers to the great purpose of the voyage, have, by the law, been clothed with the legal rights of mariners—no matter what might be their sex, character, station or profession. *Id.*, § 241, pp. 133-134.

By the late 19th and early 20th centuries, federal courts abandoned the navigation test altogether, including in the class of seamen those who worked on board and maintained allegiance to the ship, but who performed more specialized functions having no relation to navigation. The crucial element in these cases was something akin to Benedict's "great purpose of the voyage." Thus, in holding that a fisherman, a chambermaid, and a waiter were all entitled to seamen's benefits, then-Judge Brown, later the author of *The Osceola*, eschewed reference to navigation: "[A]ll hands employed upon a vessel, except the master, are entitled to a [seaman's lien for wages] if their services are in furtherance of the main object of the enterprise in which she is engaged." *The Minna*, 11 F. 759, 760 (ED Mich. 1882). Judge Learned Hand rejected a navigation test explicitly in awarding seamen's benefits to a bartender: "As I can see in principle no reason why there should be an artificial limitation of rights to those engaged in the navigation of the ship, to the exclusion of others who equally further the purposes of her voyage, ... I shall decide that the libelant has a lien for his wages as bartender." *The J.S. Warden*, 175 F. 314, 315 (SDNY 1910). In *Miller v. The Maggie P.*, 32 F. 300, 301 (ED Mo. 1887), the court explained that the rule that maritime employment must be tied to navigation had been "pronounced to be inadmissible and indecisive by later decisions." See also *The Ocean Spray*, 18 F. Cas. 558, 560-561 (No. 10,412) (D Ore. 1876) (sealers and interpreters; citing Benedict, *supra*); *The Carrier Dove*, 97 F. 111, 112 (CA1 1899) (fisherman); *United States v. Atlantic Transport Co.*, 188 F. 42 (CA2 1911) (horseman); *The Virginia Belle*, 204 F. 692, 693-694 (ED Va. 1913) (engineer who assisted in fishing); *The Baron Napier*, 249 F. 126 (CA41918) (muleteer). *See generally* Norris, The Law of Seamen § 2.3; Engerrand & Bale, 24 S. Tex. L.J., at 434-435, and nn. 29-30. An 1883 treatise declared, "[a]ll persons employed on a vessel to assist in the main purpose of the voyage are mariners, and included under the name of seamen." M. Cohen, Admiralty 239.

We believe it settled at the time of *The Osceola* and the passage of the Jones Act that general maritime law did not require that a seaman aid in navigation. It was only necessary that a person be employed on board a vessel in furtherance of its purpose. We conclude therefore that, at the time of its passage, the Jones Act established no requirement that a seaman aid in navigation. Our voyage is not over, however.

C.

As had the lower federal courts before the Jones Act, this Court continued to construe "seaman" broadly after the Jones Act. In *International Stevedoring Co. v. Haverty*, 272 U.S. 50 (1926), the Court held that a stevedore is a "seaman" covered under the Act when engaged in maritime employment. Haverty was a longshore worker injured while stowing freight in the hold of a docked vessel. The Court recognized that "as the word is commonly used, stevedores are not 'seamen.'" *Id.*, at 52. "But words are flexible.... We cannot believe that Congress willingly would have allowed the protection to men engaged upon the same maritime duties to vary with the accident of their being employed by a stevedore rather than by the ship." *Ibid.*

Congress would, and did, however. Within six months of the decision in *Haverty*, Congress passed the Longshore and Harbor Workers' Compensation Act (LHWCA), 44 Stat. (part 2) 1424, as amended, 33 U.S.C. §§ 901-950. The Act provides recovery for injury to a broad range of land-based maritime workers, but explicitly excludes from its coverage "a master or member of a crew of any vessel." 33 U.S.C. § 902(3)(G). This Court recognized the distinction, albeit belatedly, in *Swanson v. Marra Brothers, Inc.*, 328 U.S. 1 (1946), concluding that the Jones Act and the LHWCA are mutually exclusive. The LHWCA provides relief for land-based maritime workers, and the Jones Act is restricted to "a master or member of a crew of any vessel": "We must take it that the effect of these provisions of the [LHWCA] is to confine the benefits of the Jones Act to the members of the crew of a vessel plying in navigable waters and to substitute for the right of recovery recognized by the Haverty case only such rights to compensation as are given by the [LHWCA]." *Id.,* at 7. "Master or member of a crew" is a refinement of the term "seaman" in the Jones Act; it excludes from LHWCA coverage those properly covered under the Jones Act. Thus, it is odd but true that the key requirement for Jones Act coverage now appears in another statute.

With the passage of the LHWCA, Congress established a clear distinction between land-based and sea-based maritime workers. The latter, who owe their allegiance to a vessel and not solely to a land-based employer, are seamen. Ironically, on the same day that the Court decided Swanson it handed down *Seas Shipping Co. v. Sieracki*, 328 U.S. 85 (1946). With reasoning remarkably similar to that in *Haverty*, the Court extended to a stevedore the traditional seamen's remedy of unseaworthiness in those cases where the stevedore "is doing a seaman's work and incurring a seaman's hazards." *Id.,* at 99. It took Congress a bit longer to react this time. In 1972, Congress amended the LHWCA to bar longshore and harbor workers from recovery for breach of the duty of seaworthiness. *See* 86 Stat. 1263, 33 U.S.C. § 905(b); *Miles v. Apex Marine Corp.*, 498 U.S. 19, —, 111 S. Ct. 317 —, 112 L. Ed. 2d 275, 1991 AMC 1 (1990). Whether under the Jones Act or general maritime law, seamen do not include land-based workers.

The LHWCA does not change the rule that a seaman need not aid in navigation. "Member of a crew" and "seaman" are closely related terms. Indeed, the two were often used interchangeably in general maritime cases. *See, e.g., The Osceola,* 189 U.S., at 175; *The Buena Ventura,* 243 F. 797, 799 (SDNY 1916). There is nothing in these cases, or the LHWCA, to indicate that members of a crew are required to navigate. The "member of a crew" exception in the LHWCA overrules *Haverty*; "master or member of a crew" restates who a "seaman" under the Jones Act is supposed to be: a sea-based maritime employee.

III.

The source of the conflict we resolve today is this Court's inconsistent use of an aid in navigation requirement. The inconsistency arose during the 19 years that passed between the enactment of the LHWCA in 1927 and the decision in *Swanson* in 1946—19 years during which the Court did not recognize the mutual exclusivity of the LHWCA and the Jones Act.

* * *

IV.

We think the time has come to jettison the aid in navigation language. That language, which had long been rejected by admiralty courts under general maritime law, and by this Court in *Warner*, a Jones Act case, slipped back in through an interpretation of the LHWCA at a time when the LHWCA had nothing to do with the Jones Act.

We now recognize that the LHWCA is one of a pair of mutually exclusive remedial statutes that distinguish between land-based and sea-based maritime employees. The LHWCA restricted the definition of "seaman" in the Jones Act only to the extent that "seaman" had been taken to include land-based employees. There is no indication in the Jones Act, the LHWCA, or elsewhere, that Congress has excluded from Jones Act remedies those traditional seamen who owe allegiance to a vessel at sea, but who do not aid in navigation.

In his dissent in *Sieracki*, Chief Justice Stone chastised the Court for failing to recognize the distinct nature of land-based and sea-based employment. Traditional seamen's remedies, he explained, have been "universally recognized as ... growing out of the status of the seaman and his peculiar relationship to the vessel, and as a feature of the maritime law compensating or offsetting the special hazards and disadvantages to which they who go down to sea in ships are subjected." 328 U.S., at 104. It is this distinction that Congress recognized in the LHWCA and the Jones Act. *See id.*, at 106; *Swanson v. Marra Brothers, Inc.*, 328 U.S. 1 (1946). It also explains why all those with that "peculiar relationship to the vessel" are covered under the Jones Act, regardless of the particular job they perform.

We believe the better rule is to define "master or member of a crew" under the LHWCA, and therefore "seaman" under the Jones Act, solely in terms of the employee's connection to a vessel in navigation. This rule best explains our case law, and is consistent with the pre-Jones Act interpretation of "seaman" and Congress' land-based/sea-based distinction. All who work at sea in the service of a ship face those particular perils to which the protection of maritime law, statutory as well as decisional, is directed. *See generally* Robertson, *A New Approach to Determining Seaman Status*, 64 Texas L. Rev. 79 (1985). It is not the employee's particular job that is determinative, but the employee's connection to a vessel.

Shortly after *Butler*, our last decision in this area, the Court of Appeals for the Fifth Circuit attempted to decipher this Court's seaman status cases. *See Offshore Co. v. Robison*, 266 F.2d 769 (CA5 1959). The Fifth Circuit correctly determined that, regardless of its language, this Court was no longer requiring that seamen aid in navigation. *Id.*, at 776. As part of its test for seaman status, *Robison* requires that a seaman's duties "contribute to the function of the vessel or to the accomplishment of its mission." *Id.*, at 779.

The key to seaman status is employment-related connection to a vessel in navigation. We are not called upon here to define this connection in all details, but we hold that a necessary element of the connection is that a seaman perform the work of a vessel. *See Maryland Casualty Co. v. Lawson*, 94 F.2d 190, 192 (CA5 1938) ("There is implied a definite and permanent connection with the vessel, an obligation to forward her enterprise"), cited approvingly in *Norton*, 321 U.S., at 573. In this regard, we believe the requirement that an employee's duties must "contribute to the function of the vessel or to the accomplishment of its mission" captures well an important requirement of seaman status. It is not necessary that a seaman aid in navigation or contribute to the transportation of the vessel, but a seaman must be doing the ship's work.

V.

Jon Wilander was injured while assigned to the *Gates Tide* as a paint foreman. He did not aid in the navigation or transportation of the vessel. The jury found, however, that Wilander contributed to the more general function or mission of the *Gates Tide*, and subsequently found that he was a "seaman" under the Jones Act. McDermott argues that the question should not have been given to the jury. The company contends that, as a matter of law, Wilander is not entitled to Jones Act protection because he did not aid in navigation by furthering the transportation of the *Gates Tide*.

We have said that seaman status under the Jones Act is a question of fact for the jury. In Bassett, an LHWCA case, the Court held that Congress had given to the deputy commissioner, an administrative officer, the authority to determine who is a "member of a crew" under the LHWCA. 309 U.S., at 257-258. If there is evidence to support the deputy commissioner's finding, it is conclusive. *Ibid.* In *Senko*, we applied the same rule to findings by the jury in Jones Act cases. 352 U.S., at 374. "[A] jury's decision is final if it has a reasonable basis." *Ibid.* We are not asked here to reconsider this rule, but we note that the question of who is a "member of crew," and therefore who is a "seaman," is better characterized as a mixed question of law and fact. When the underlying facts are established, and the rule of law is undisputed, the issue is whether the facts meet the statutory standard. *See Pullman-Standard v. Swint*, 456 U.S. 273, 289, n.19 (1982) (defining a mixed question).

It is for the court to define the statutory standard. "Member of a crew" and "seaman" are statutory terms; their interpretation is a question of law. The jury finds the facts and, in these cases, applies the legal standard, but the court must not abdicate its duty to determine if there is a reasonable basis to support the jury's conclusion. If reasonable persons, applying the proper legal standard, could differ as to whether the employee was a "member of a crew," it is a question for the jury. *See Anderson v. Liberty Lobby, Inc.*, 477 U.S. 242, 250-251 (1986). In many cases, this will be true. The inquiry into seaman status is of necessity fact-specific; it will depend on the nature of the vessel, and the employee's precise relation to it. *See Desper v. Starved Rock Ferry Co.*, 342 U.S. 187, 190 (1952) ("The many cases turning upon the question whether an individual was a "seaman" demonstrate that the matter depends largely on the facts of the particular case and the activity in which he was engaged at the time of injury"). Nonetheless, summary judgment or a directed verdict is mandated where the facts and the law will reasonably support only one conclusion. *Anderson, supra,* at 248, 250-251.

The question presented here is narrow. We are not asked to determine if the jury could reasonably have found that Wilander had a sufficient connection to the *Gates Tide* to be a "seaman" under the Jones Act. We are not even asked whether the jury reasonably found that Wilander advanced the function or mission of the *Gates Tide*. We are asked only if Wilander should be precluded from seaman status because he did not perform transportation-related functions on board the Gates Tide. Our answer is no. Accordingly, the judgment of the Court of Appeals is
Affirmed.

CHANDRIS, INC. v. LATSIS

515 U.S. 347, 115 S. Ct. 2172, 132 L. Ed. 2d 314, 1995 AMC 1840 (1995)

Justice O'CONNOR delivered the opinion of the Court

This case asks us to clarify what "employment-related connection to a vessel in navigation," *McDermott International, Inc. v. Wilander*, 498 U.S. 337, 355, 111 S. Ct. 807, 817, 112 L. Ed. 2d 866 (1991), is necessary for a maritime worker to qualify as a seaman under the Jones Act, 46 U.S.C. App. § 688(a). In *Wilander*, we addressed the type of activities that a seaman must perform and held that, under the Jones Act, a seaman's job need not be limited to transportation-related functions that directly aid in the vessel's navigation. We now determine what relationship a worker must have to the vessel, regardless of the specific tasks the worker undertakes, in order to obtain seaman status.

I

In May 1989, respondent Antonios Latsis was employed by petitioner Chandris, Inc., as a salaried superintendent engineer. Latsis was responsible for maintaining and updating the electronic and communications equipment on Chandris' fleet of vessels, which consisted of six passenger cruise ships. Each ship in the Chandris fleet carried between 12 and 14 engineers who were assigned permanently to that vessel. Latsis, on the other hand, was one of two supervising engineers based at Chandris' Miami office; his duties ran to the entire fleet and included not only overseeing the vessels' engineering departments, which required him to take a number of voyages, but also planning and directing ship maintenance from the shore. Latsis claimed at trial that he spent 72 percent of his time at sea, his immediate supervisor testified that the appropriate figure was closer to 10 percent.

On May 14, 1989, Latsis sailed for Bermuda aboard the S.S. Galileo to plan for an upcoming renovation of the ship, which was one of the older vessels in the Chandris fleet. Latsis developed a problem with his right eye on the day of departure, and he saw the ship's doctor as the Galileo left port. The doctor diagnosed a suspected detached retina but failed to follow standard medical procedure, which would have been to direct Latsis to see an ophthalmologist on an emergency basis. Instead, the ship's doctor recommended that Latsis relax until he could see an eye specialist when the Galileo arrived in Bermuda two days later. No attempt was made to transport Latsis ashore for prompt medical care by means of a pilot vessel or helicopter during the 11 hours it took the ship to reach the open sea from Baltimore, and Latsis received no further medical care until after the ship arrived in Bermuda. In Bermuda, a doctor diagnosed a detached retina and recommended immediate hospitalization and surgery. Although the operation was a partial success, Latsis lost 75 percent of his vision in his right eye.

Following his recuperation, which lasted approximately six weeks, Latsis resumed his duties with Chandris. On September 30, 1989, he sailed with the Galileo to Bremerhaven, Germany, where the vessel was placed in drydock for a 6-month refurbishment. After the conversion, the company renamed the vessel the S.S. Meridian. Latsis, who had been with the ship the entire time it was in drydock in Bremerhaven, sailed back to the United States on board the Meridian and continued to work for Chandris until November 1990, when his employment was terminated for reasons that are not clear from the record.

In October 1991, Latsis filed suit in the United States District Court for the Southern District of New York seeking compensatory damages under the Jones Act, 46 U.S.C. App. § 688, for the negligence of the ship's doctor that resulted in the significant loss of sight in Latsis' right eye.... The District Court instructed the jury that it could conclude that Latsis was a seaman within the meaning of the statute if it found as follows: "[T]he plaintiff was either permanently assigned to the vessel or performed a substantial part of his work on the vessel. In determining whether Mr. Latsis performed a substantial part of his work on the vessel, you may not consider the period of time the Galileo was in drydock in Germany, because during that time period she was out of navigation. You may, however, consider the time spent sailing to and from Germany for the conversion. Also, on this first element of being a seaman, seamen do not include land-based workers." The parties stipulated to the District Court's second requirement for Jones Act coverage—that Latsis' duties contributed to the accomplishment of the missions of the Chandris vessels.... The jury returned a verdict in favor of Chandris solely on the issue of Latsis' status as a seaman under the Jones Act.

Respondent appealed to the Court of Appeals for the Second Circuit, which vacated the judgment and remanded the case for a new trial. 20 F.3d 45 (1994). The court emphasized that its longstanding test for seaman status under the Jones Act required "'a more or less permanent connection with the ship,'" a connection that need not be limited to time spent on the vessel but could also be established by the nature of the work performed. The court thought that the alternate formulation employed by the District Court (permanent assignment to the vessel or performance of a substantial part of his work on the vessel), which was derived from *Offshore Co. v. Robison*, 266 F.2d 769, 779 (CA5 1959), improperly framed the issue for the jury primarily, if not solely, in terms of Latsis' temporal relationship to the vessel. With that understanding of what the language of the Robison test implied, the court concluded that the District Court's seaman status jury instructions constituted plain error under established circuit precedent. The court then took this case as an opportunity to clarify its seaman status requirements, directing the District Court that the jury should be instructed on remand as follows: "[T]he test of seaman status under the Jones Act is an employment-related connection to a vessel in navigation. The test will be met where a jury finds that (1) the plaintiff contributed to the function of or helped accomplish the mission of, a vessel; (2) the plaintiff's contribution was limited to a particular vessel or identifiable group of vessels; (3) the plaintiff's contribution was substantial in terms of its (a) duration or (b) nature; and (4) the course of the plaintiff's employment regularly exposed the plaintiff to the hazards of the sea." 20 F.3d, at 57. Elsewhere on the same page, however, the court phrased the third prong as requiring a substantial connection in terms of both duration and nature. Finally, the Court of Appeals held that the District Court erred in instructing the jury that the time Latsis spent with the ship while it was in drydock could not count in the substantial connection equation.

We granted certiorari, 513 U.S. ——, 115 S. Ct. 354, 130 L. Ed. 2d 309 (1994), to resolve the continuing conflict among the Courts of Appeals regarding the appropriate requirements for seaman status under the Jones Act.

II

* * *

A

In *Wilander*, decided in 1991, the Court attempted for the first time in 33 years to clarify the definition of a "seaman" under the Jones Act....

* * *

Beyond dispensing with the "aid to navigation" requirement, however, Wilander did not consider the requisite connection to a vessel in any detail and therefore failed to end the prevailing confusion regarding seaman status.

B

Respondent urges us to find our way out of the Jones Act "labyrinth" by focusing on the seemingly activity-based policy underlying the statute (the protection of those who are exposed to the perils of the sea), and to conclude that anyone working on board a vessel for the duration of a "voyage" in furtherance of the vessel's mission has the necessary employment-related connection to qualify as a seaman. Such an approach, however, would run counter to our prior decisions and our understanding of the remedial scheme Congress has established for injured maritime workers. A brief survey of the Jones Act's tortured history makes clear that we must reject the initial appeal of such a "voyage" test and undertake the more difficult task of developing a status-based standard that, although it determines Jones Act coverage without regard to the precise activity in which the worker is engaged at the time of the injury, nevertheless best furthers the Jones Act's remedial goals.

Our Jones Act cases establish several basic principles regarding the definition of a seaman. First, "[w]hether under the Jones Act or general maritime law, seamen do not include land-based workers." *Wilander, supra,* at 348, *see also* Allbritton, *Seaman Status in Wilander's Wake,* 68 TULANE L. REV. 373, 387 (1994)....

In addition to recognizing a fundamental distinction between land-based and sea-based maritime employees, our cases also emphasize that Jones Act coverage, like the jurisdiction of admiralty over causes of action for maintenance and cure for injuries received in the course of a seamen's employment, depends "not on the place where the injury is inflicted ... but on the nature of the seaman's service, his status as a member of the vessel, and his relationship as such to the vessel and its operation in navigable waters." Thus, maritime workers who obtain seaman status do not lose that protection automatically when on shore and may recover under the Jones Act whenever they are injured in the service of a vessel, regardless of whether the injury occurs on or off the ship....

Our LHWCA cases also recognize the converse: land-based maritime workers injured while on a vessel in navigation remain covered by the LHWCA, which expressly provides compensation for injuries to certain workers engaged in "maritime employment" that are incurred "upon the navigable waters of the United States," 33 U.S.C. § 903(a). Thus, in *Director, OWCP v. Perini North River Associates,* 459 U.S. 297, 103 S. Ct. 634, 74 L. Ed. 2d 465 (1983), we held that a worker injured while "working on a barge in actual navigable waters" of the Hudson River, could be compensated under the LHWCA....

* * *

We believe it is important to avoid "'engrafting upon the statutory classification of a "seaman" a judicial gloss so protean, elusive, or arbitrary as to permit a worker to walk into and out of coverage in the course of his regular duties.'" *Barrett v. Chevron, U.S.A., Inc.,* 781 F.2d 1067, 1075 (CA5 1986) (en banc) (quoting *Longmire v. Sea Drilling Corp.,* 610 F.2d 1342, 1347, n.6 (CA5 1980)). In evaluating the employment-related connection of a maritime worker to a vessel in navigation, courts should not employ "a 'snapshot' test for seaman status, inspecting only the situation as it exists at the instant of injury; a more enduring relationship is contemplated in the jurisprudence." Thus, a worker may not oscillate back and forth between Jones Act coverage and other remedies depending on the activity in which the worker was engaged while injured. Unlike Justice STEVENS, we do not believe that any maritime worker on a ship at sea as part of his employment is automatically a member of the crew of the vessel within the meaning of the statutory terms. Our rejection of the voyage test is also consistent with the interests of employers and maritime workers alike in being able to predict who will be covered by the Jones Act (and, perhaps more importantly for purposes of the employers' workers' compensation obligations, who will be covered by the LHWCA) before a particular work day begins.

To say that our cases have recognized a distinction between land-based and sea-based maritime workers that precludes application of a voyage test for seaman status, however, is not to say that a maritime employee must work only on board a vessel to qualify as a seaman under the Jones Act. In *Southwest Marine, Inc. v. Gizoni,* 502 U.S. 81, 112 S. Ct. 486, 116 L. Ed. 2d 405 (1991), decided only a few months after *Wilander,* we concluded that a worker's status as a ship repairman, one of the enumerated occupations encompassed within the term "employee" under the

LHWCA, 33 U.S.C. § 902(3), did not necessarily restrict the worker to a remedy under that statute. We explained that, "[w]hile in some cases a ship repairman may lack the requisite connection to a vessel in navigation to qualify for seaman status, ... not all ship repairmen lack the requisite connection as a matter of law. This is so because '[i]t is not the employee's particular job that is determinative, but the employee's connection to a vessel.'" Gizoni, *supra*, at 89, 112 S. Ct., at 492 (quoting *Wilander*, 498 U.S., at 354, 111 S. Ct., at 817) (footnote omitted). Thus, we concluded, the Jones Act remedy may be available to maritime workers who are employed by a shipyard and who spend a portion of their time working on shore but spend the rest of their time at sea.

Beyond these basic themes, which are sufficient to foreclose respondent's principal argument, our cases are largely silent as to the precise relationship a maritime worker must bear to a vessel in order to come within the Jones Act's ambit. We have, until now, left to the lower federal courts the task of developing appropriate criteria to distinguish the "ship's company" from those members of the maritime community whose employment is essentially land-based.

C

The Court of Appeals for the First Circuit was apparently the first to develop a generally applicable test for seaman status. In *Carumbo v. Cape Cod S.S. Co.*, 123 F.2d 991 (CA1 1941), the court retained the pre-Swanson view that "the word 'seaman' under the Jones Act did not mean the same thing as 'member of a crew' under the [LHWCA]," *id.*, at 994. It concluded that "one who does any sort of work aboard a ship in navigation is a 'seaman' within the meaning of the Jones Act." The phrase "member of a crew," on the other hand, the court gave a more restrictive meaning. The court adopted three elements to define the phrase that had been used at various times in prior cases, holding that "[t]he requirements that the ship be in navigation; that there be a more or less permanent connection with the ship; and that the worker be aboard primarily to aid in navigation appear to us to be the essential and decisive elements of the definition of a 'member of a crew.'" Once it became clear that the phrase "master or member of a crew" from the LHWCA is coextensive with the term "seaman" in the Jones Act, courts accepted the Carumbo formulation of master or member of a crew in the Jones Act context. The Court of Appeals for the Second Circuit initially was among the jurisdictions to adopt the Carumbo formulation as the basis of its seaman status inquiry, *see Salgado v. M.J. Rudolph Corp.*, 514 F.2d, at 755, but that court took the instant case as an opportunity to modify the traditional test somewhat (replacing the "more or less permanent connection" prong with a requirement that the connection be "substantial in terms of its (a) duration and (b) nature"), 20 F.3d, at 57.

The second major body of seaman status law developed in the Court of Appeals for the Fifth Circuit, which has a substantial Jones Act caseload, in the wake of *Offshore Co. v. Robison*, 266 F.2d 769 (CA5 1959). At the time of his injury, Robison was an oil worker permanently assigned to a drilling rig mounted on a barge in the Gulf of Mexico. In sustaining the jury's award of damages to Robison under the Jones Act, the court abandoned the aid in navigation requirement of the traditional test and held as follows: "[T]here is an evidentiary basis for a Jones Act case to go to the jury: (1) if there is evidence that the injured workman was assigned permanently to a vessel ... or performed a substantial part of his work on the vessel; and (2) if the capacity in which he was employed or the duties which he performed contributed to the function of the vessel or the accomplishment of its mission, or to the operation or welfare of the vessel in terms of its maintenance during its movement or during anchorage for its future trips." Soon after Robison, the Fifth Circuit modified the test to allow seaman status for those workers who had the requisite connection with an "identifiable fleet" of vessels, a finite group of vessels under common ownership or control. *Braniff v. Jackson Avenue-Gretna Ferry, Inc.*, 280 F.2d 523, 528 (1960). *See also Barrett*, 781 F.2d, at 1074; *Bertrand v. International Mooring & Marine, Inc.*, 700 F.2d 240 (CA 5 1983), *cert. denied*, 464 U.S. 1069, 104 S. Ct. 974, 79 L. Ed. 2d 212 (1984). The modified Robison formulation, which replaced the Carumbo version as the definitive test for seaman status in the Fifth Circuit, has been highly influential in other courts as well. *See* Robertson 95; *Miller v. Patton-Tully Transp. Co.*, 851 F.2d 202, 204 (CA 8 1988); *Caruso v. Sterling Yacht & Shipbuilders, Inc.*, 828 F.2d 14, 15 (CA 11 1987); *Bennett v. Perini Corp.*, 510 F.2d 114, 115 (CA 1 1975).

While the Carumbo and Robison approaches may not seem all that different at first glance, subsequent developments in the Fifth Circuit's Jones Act jurisprudence added a strictly temporal gloss to the Jones Act inquiry. Under *Barrett v. Chevron, U.S.A., Inc., supra*, if an employee's regular duties require him to divide his time between vessel and land, his status as a crew member is determined "in the context of his entire employment" with his current employer. In Barrett, the court noted that the worker "performed seventy to eighty percent of his work on platforms and no more than twenty to thirty percent of his work on vessels" and then concluded that, "[b]ecause he did not perform a substantial portion of his work aboard a vessel or fleet of vessels, he failed to establish that he was a member of the crew of a vessel." 781 F.2d, at 1076. Since Barrett, the Fifth Circuit consistently has analyzed the problem in terms of the percentage of work performed on vessels for the employer in question—and has declined to find seaman status where the employee spent less than 30 percent of his time aboard ship. *See, e.g., Palmer v. Fayard Moving & Transp. Corp.*, 930 F.2d 437, 439 (CA5 1991); *Lormand v. Superior Oil Co.*, 845 F.2d 536, 541 (CA5 1987), *cert. denied*, 484 U.S. 1031, 108 S. Ct. 739, 98 L. Ed. 2d 774 (1988); *cf. Leonard v. Dixie Well Service & Supply, Inc.*, 828 F.2d 291, 295 (CA5 1987); *Pickle v. International Oilfield Divers, Inc.*, 791 F.2d 1237, 1240 (CA5 1986), *cert. denied*, 479 U.S. 1059, 107 S. Ct. 939, 93 L. Ed. 2d 989 (1987).

Although some courts of appeals have varied the applicable tests to some degree, *see, e.g., Johnson v. John F. Beasley Constr. Co.*, 742 F.2d, at 1062-1063, the traditional Carumbo seaman status formulation and the subsequent Robison modification are universally recognized, and one or the other is applied in every federal circuit to have considered the issue. *See* Bull, *Seaman Status Revisited: A Practical Guide To Status Determination*, 6 U.S. F. MAR. L.J. 547, 562-572 (1994) (collecting cases). The federal courts generally require at least a significant connection to a vessel in navigation (or to an identifiable fleet of vessels) for a maritime worker to qualify as a seaman under the Jones Act. Although the traditional test requires a "more or less permanent connection" and the Robison formulation calls for "substantial" work aboard a vessel, "this general requirement varies little, if at all, from one jurisdiction to another," *id.*, at 587, and "[t]he courts have repeatedly held that the relationship creating seaman status must be substantial in point of time and work, and not merely sporadic," *id.*, at 587-588.

D

... [W]e think that the essential requirements for seaman status are twofold. First, as we emphasized in *Wilander*, "an employee's duties must 'contribut[e] to the function of the vessel or to the accomplishment of its mission.'" 498 U.S., at 355, 111 S. Ct., at 817 (quoting Robison, 266 F.2d, at 779). The Jones Act's protections, like the other admiralty protections for seamen, only extend to those maritime employees who do the ship's work. But this threshold requirement is very broad: "[a]ll who work at sea in the service of a ship" are eligible for seaman status. 498 U.S., at 354, 111 S. Ct., at 817.

Second, and most important for our purposes here, a seaman must have a connection to a vessel in navigation (or to an identifiable group of such vessels) that is substantial in terms of both its duration and its nature. The fundamental purpose of this substantial connection requirement is to give full effect to the remedial scheme created by Congress and to separate the sea-based maritime employees who are entitled to Jones Act protection from those land-based workers who have only a transitory or sporadic connection to a vessel in navigation, and therefore whose employment does not regularly expose them to the perils of the sea. *See* 1B A. JENNER, BENEDICT ON ADMIRALTY, § 11a, pp. 2-10.1 to 2-11 (7th ed. 1994) ("If it can be shown that the employee performed a significant part of his work on board the vessel on which he was injured, with at least some degree of regularity and continuity, the test for seaman status will be satisfied" (footnote omitted)). This requirement therefore determines which maritime employees in *Wilander's* broad category of persons eligible for seaman status because they are "doing the ship's work," 498 U.S., at 355, 111 S. Ct., at 817, are in fact entitled to the benefits conferred upon seamen by the Jones Act because they have the requisite employment-related connection to a vessel in navigation.

It is important to recall that the question of who is a "member of a crew," and therefore who is a "seaman," is a mixed question of law and fact. Because statutory terms are at issue, their interpretation is a question of law and it is the court's duty to define the appropriate standard. On the other hand, "[i]f reasonable persons, applying the proper legal standard, could differ as to whether the employee was a 'member of a crew,' it is a question for the jury." The jury should be permitted, when determining whether a maritime employee has the requisite employment-related connection to a vessel in navigation to qualify as a member of the vessel's crew, to consider all relevant circumstances bearing on the two elements outlined above.

In defining the prerequisites for Jones Act coverage, we think it preferable to focus upon the essence of what it means to be a seaman and to eschew the temptation to create detailed tests to effectuate the congressional purpose, tests that tend to become ends in and of themselves. The principal formulations employed by the Courts of Appeals—"more or less permanent assignment" or "connection to a vessel that is substantial in terms of its duration and nature"—are simply different ways of getting at the same basic point: the Jones Act remedy is reserved for sea-based maritime employees whose work regularly exposes them to "the special hazards and disadvantages to which they who go down to sea in ships are subjected." *Sieracki*, 328 U.S., at 104, 66 S. Ct., at 882 (STONE, C.J., dissenting). Indeed, it is difficult to discern major substantive differences in the language of the two phrases. In our view, "the total circumstances of an individual's employment must be weighed to determine whether he had a sufficient relation to the navigation of vessels and the perils attendant thereon." *Wallace v. Oceaneering Int'l*, 727 F.2d 427, 432 (CA5 1984). The duration of a worker's connection to a vessel and the nature of the worker's activities, taken together, determine whether a maritime employee is a seaman because the ultimate inquiry is whether the worker in question is a member of the vessel's crew or simply a land-based employee who happens to be working on the vessel at a given time.

Although we adopt the centerpiece of the formulation used by the Court of Appeals in this case—that a seaman must have a connection with a vessel in navigation that is substantial in both duration and nature—we should point out how our understanding of the import of that language may be different in some respects from that of the court below. The Court of Appeals suggested that its test for seaman status "does not unequivocally require a Jones Act seaman to be substantially connected to a vessel" in terms of time if the worker performs important work on board on a steady, although not necessarily on a temporally significant, basis. 20 F.3d, at 53. Perhaps giving effect to this intuition, or perhaps reacting to the temporal gloss placed on the Robison language by later Fifth Circuit decisions, the court phrased its standard at one point as requiring a jury to find that a Jones Act plaintiff's contribution to the function of the vessel was substantial in terms of its duration or nature. *Id.*, at 57. It is not clear which version ("duration or nature" as opposed to "duration and nature") the Court of Appeals intended to adopt for the substantial connection requirement—or indeed whether the court saw a significant difference between the two. Nevertheless, we think it is important that a seaman's connection to a vessel in fact be substantial in both respects.

We agree with the Court of Appeals that seaman status is not merely a temporal concept, but we also believe that it necessarily includes a temporal element. A maritime worker who spends only a small fraction of his working time on board a vessel is fundamentally land-based and therefore not a member of the vessel's crew, regardless of what his duties are. Naturally, substantiality in this context is determined by reference to the period covered by the Jones Act plaintiff's maritime employment, rather than by some absolute measure. Generally, the Fifth Circuit seems to have identified an appropriate rule of thumb for the ordinary case: a worker who spends less than about 30 percent of his time in the service of a vessel in navigation should not qualify as a seaman under the Jones Act. This figure of course serves as no more than a guideline established by years of experience, and departure from it will certainly be justified in appropriate cases. As we have said, "[t]he inquiry into seaman status is of necessity fact specific; it will depend on the nature of the vessel and the employee's precise relation to it." *Wilander*, 498 U.S., at 356, 111 S. Ct., at 818. Nevertheless, we believe that courts, employers, and maritime workers can all benefit from reference to these general principles. And where undisputed facts reveal that a maritime worker has a clearly inadequate temporal connection to vessels in navigation, the court may take the question from the jury by granting summary judgment or a directed verdict. *See, e.g., Palmer*, 930 F.2d, at 439.

On the other hand, we see no reason to limit the seaman status inquiry, as petitioners contend, exclusively to an examination of the overall course of a worker's service with a particular employer. When a maritime worker's basic assignment changes, his seaman status may change as well. See Barrett, 781 F.2d, at 1077 (RUBIN, J., dissenting)

("An assignment to work as a crew member, like the voyage of a vessel, may be brief, and the Robison test is applicable in deciding the worker's status during any such employment"); Longmire, 610 F.2d, at 1347, n.6. For example, we can imagine situations in which someone who had worked for years in an employer's shoreside head-quarters is then reassigned to a ship in a classic seaman's job that involves a regular and continuous, rather than intermittent, commitment of the worker's labor to the function of a vessel. Such a person should not be denied seaman status if injured shortly after the reassignment, just as someone actually transferred to a desk job in the company's office and injured in the hallway should not be entitled to claim seaman status on the basis of prior service at sea. If a maritime employee receives a new work assignment in which his essential duties are changed, he is entitled to have the assessment of the substantiality of his vessel-related work made on the basis of his activities in his new position. *See* Cheavens, 64 Tulane L. Rev., at 389-390. Thus, nothing in our opinion forecloses Jones Act coverage, in appropriate cases, for Justice STEVENS' paradigmatic maritime worker injured while reassigned to "a lengthy voyage on the high seas," post, at 2198. While our approach maintains the status-based inquiry this Court's earlier cases contemplate, we recognize that seaman status also should not be some immutable characteristic that maritime workers who spend only a portion of their time at sea can never attain.

III

One final issue remains for our determination: whether the District Court erred in instructing the jurors that, "[i]n determining whether Mr. Latsis performed a substantial part of his work on the vessel, [they could] not consider the period of time the Galileo was in drydock in Germany, because during that time period she was out of navigation." We agree with the Court of Appeals that it did.

The foregoing discussion establishes that, to qualify as a seaman under the Jones Act, a maritime employee must have a substantial employment-related connection to a vessel in navigation. Of course, any time Latsis spent with the Galileo while the ship was out of navigation could not count as time spent at sea for purposes of that inquiry, and it would have been appropriate for the District Court to make this clear to the jury. Yet the underlying inquiry whether a vessel is or is not "in navigation" for Jones Act purposes is a fact-intensive question that is normally for the jury and not the court to decide.... Based upon the record before us, we think the court failed adequately to justify its decision to remove the question whether the Galileo was "in navigation" while in Bremerhaven from the jury.

Under our precedent and the law prevailing in the circuits, it is generally accepted that "a vessel does not cease to be a vessel when she is not voyaging, but is at anchor, berthed, or at dockside," even when the vessel is undergoing repairs. At some point, however, repairs become sufficiently significant that the vessel can no longer be considered in navigation. In *West v. United States*, 361 U.S. 118, 80 S. Ct. 189, 4 L. Ed. 2d 161 (1959), we held that a shoreside worker was not entitled to recover for unseaworthiness because the vessel on which he was injured was undergoing an overhaul for the purpose of making her seaworthy and therefore had been withdrawn from navigation. We explained that, in such cases, "the focus should be upon the status of the ship, the pattern of the repairs, and the extensive nature of the work contracted to be done." The general rule among the Courts of Appeals is that vessels undergoing repairs or spending a relatively short period of time in drydock are still considered to be "in navigation" whereas ships being transformed through "major" overhauls or renovations are not. *See* Bull, 6 U.S. F. Mar. L.J., at 582-584 (collecting cases).

... Our review of the record in this case uncovered relatively little evidence bearing on the Galileo's status during the repairs, and even less discussion of the question by the District Court. On the one hand, the work on the Chandris vessel took only about six months, which seems to be a relatively short period of time for important repairs on oceangoing vessels. On the other hand, Latsis' own description of the work performed suggests that the modifications to the vessel were actually quite significant, including the removal of the ship's bottom plates and propellers, the addition of bow thrusters, overhaul of the main engines, reconstruction of the boilers, and renovations of the cabins and other passenger areas of the ship. On these facts ... it is possible that Chandris could be entitled to partial summary judgment or a directed verdict concerning whether the Galileo remained in navigation while in drydock; the record, however, contains no stipulations or findings by the District Court to justify its conclusion that the modifications to the Galileo were sufficiently extensive to remove the vessel from navigation as a matter of law. On that basis, we agree with the Court of Appeals that the District Court's drydock instruction was erroneous.

* * *

IV

* * *

On remand, the District Court should charge the jury in a manner consistent with our holding that the "employment-related connection to a vessel in navigation" necessary to qualify as a seaman under the Jones Act, *id.*, at 355, 111 S. Ct., at 817, comprises two basic elements: the worker's duties must contribute to the function of the vessel or to the accomplishment of its mission, and the worker must have a connection to a vessel in navigation (or an identifiable group of vessels) that is substantial in terms of both its duration and its nature. As to the latter point, the court should emphasize that the Jones Act was intended to protect sea-based maritime workers, who owe their allegiance to a vessel, and not land-based employees, who do not. By instructing juries in Jones Act cases accordingly, courts can give proper effect to the remedial scheme Congress has created for injured maritime workers.

It is so ordered.

Justice STEVENS, with whom Justice THOMAS and Justice BREYER join, concurring in the judgment.

The majority has reached the odd conclusion that a maritime engineer, injured aboard ship on the high seas while performing his duties as an employee of the ship, might not be a "seaman" within the meaning of the Jones Act. This decision is unprecedented. It ignores the critical distinction between work performed aboard ship during a voyage—when the members of the crew encounter "the perils of the sea"—and maritime work performed on a vessel moored to a dock in a safe harbor. In my judgment, an employee of the ship who is injured at sea in the course of his employment is always a "seaman." I would leave more ambiguous, shore-bound cases for another day. Accordingly, though I concur in the Court's disposition of this case, returning it to the District Court for a new trial, I disagree with the standard this Court directs the trial court to apply on remand.

* * *

II

Despite the language, history, and purpose of the Jones Act, the Court today holds that seaman status may require more than a single ocean voyage. The Court's opinion thus obscures, if it does not ignore, the distinction between the perils of the sea and the risks faced by maritime workers when a ship is moored to a dock. The test that the Court formulates may be appropriate for the resolution of cases in the latter category. The Court fails, however, to explain why the member of the crew of a vessel at sea is not always a seaman.

Respondent's argument, "that any worker who is assigned to a vessel for the duration of a voyage and whose duties contribute to the vessel's mission must be classified as a seaman respecting injuries incurred on that voyage," Brief for Respondent 14, is not inconsistent with the Court's view, *ante*, at 2185-2186, that an employee must occupy a certain status in order to qualify as a seaman. It merely recognizes that all members of a ship's crew have that status while the vessel is at sea. In contrast, when the ship is in a harbor, further inquiry may be necessary to separate land-based from sea-based maritime employees. The Court is therefore simply wrong when it states that a "'voyage test' would conflict with our prior understanding of the Jones Act as fundamentally status-based, granting the negligence cause of action to those maritime workers who form the ship's company," *ante*, at 2186. The "ship's company" is readily identifiable when the ship is at sea; the fact that it may be less so when the ship is in port is not an acceptable reason for refusing to rely on the voyage test in a case like this one.

The Court is also quite wrong to suggest that our prior cases "indicate that a maritime worker does not become a 'member of a crew' as soon as a vessel leaves the dock," *ante*, at 2186. In neither of the two cases on which it relies to support this conclusion did the injured workman even claim the status of a seaman. In *Director, Office of Workers'*

Compensation Programs v. Perini North River Associates, 459 U.S. 297, 103 S. Ct. 634, 74 L. Ed. 2d 465 (1983), we held that an employee of a firm that was building the foundation of a sewage treatment plant, which extended over the Hudson River adjacent to Manhattan, was covered by the LHWCA because he was injured while working on a barge in navigable waters. The Court of Appeals had denied coverage on the ground that this worker was not engaged in maritime employment. Thus, *Perini* had nothing to do with any possible overlap between the Jones Act and the LHWCA; this Court's reversal merely found a sufficient maritime connection to support LHWCA coverage of an admittedly shore-based worker.

The other case that the Court cites, *Parker v. Motor Boat Sales, Inc.*, 314 U.S. 244, 62 S. Ct. 221, 86 L. Ed. 184 (1941), involved a janitor who had drowned while riding in a motor boat on the James River near Richmond. The Court of Appeals had held that his widow was not entitled to compensation under the LHWCA on the alternative grounds (1) that the janitor was not acting in the course of his employment when the boat capsized, and (2) that the LHWCA did not apply because Virginia law could provide compensation. *See id.*, at 245, 62 S. Ct., at 222-223. As in *Perini*, our opinion reversing that decision did not discuss the Jones Act, because no one had even mentioned the possibility that the janitor might be a "seaman."...

The Court's only other justification for refusing to apply a voyage test is its purported concern about a worker who might "walk into and out of coverage in the course of his regular duties." *Ante* at 2187 (internal quotation marks omitted). Because the only way that a seaman could walk out of Jones Act coverage during a voyage would be to quit his job and become a passenger (or possibly jump overboard), I take the majority's argument to mean that a single voyage is not a long enough time to establish seaman status. I simply do not understand this argument. Surely a voyage is sufficient time to establish an employment-related, status-based connection to a vessel in navigation that exposes the employee to the perils of the sea. The majority cannot explain why an employee who signs on for a single journey is any less a "seaman" or "member of a crew" if he intends to become an insurance agent after the voyage than if he intends to remain with the ship. What is important is the employee's status at the time of the injury, not his status a day, a month, or a year beforehand or afterward.

Apparently, the majority's real concern about walking in and out of coverage is that an employer will be unable to predict which of his employees will be covered by the Jones Act, and which by the LHWCA, on any given day. I think it is a novel construction of the Jones Act to read it as a scheme to protect employers. But even if Congress had shared the Court's concern, this case does not implicate it in the least. We are talking here about a lengthy voyage on the high seas. The employer controls who goes on that voyage; he knows, more or less, when that voyage will begin and when it will end. And, but for the majority's decision today, he would know that while the ship is at sea, all his employees thereon would be covered by the Jones Act and not by the LHWCA. Thus, no one is walking out of Jones Act coverage and into LHWCA coverage (or vice versa) without the employer's knowledge and control. Once again, the majority's concern—and its method of determining seaman status—is properly directed at injuries occurring while the ship is at port.

* * *

HARBOR TUG AND BARGE COMPANY v. PAPAI

520 U.S. 548, 117 S. Ct. 1535, 137 L. Ed. 3d 80, 1999 AMC 1817 (1997)

Justice KENNEDY delivered the opinion of the Court.

* * *

On the question of seaman status, there is an issue of significance beyond the facts of this case. Our statement in an earlier case that a worker may establish seaman status based on the substantiality of his connection to "an identifiable group of ... vessels" in navigation, *see Chandris, Inc. v. Latsis*, 515 U.S. 347, 368, 115 S.Ct. 2172, 2179, 132 L.Ed.2d 314 (1995), has been subject to differing interpretations, and we seek to provide clarification.

I

Respondent John Papai was painting the housing structure of the tug Pt. Barrow when a ladder he was on moved, he alleges, causing him to fall and injure his knee. Petitioner Harbor Tug & Barge Co., the tug's operator, had hired Papai to do the painting work. A prime coat of paint had been applied and it was Papai's task to apply the finish coat. There was no vessel captain on board and Papai reported to the port captain, who had a dockside office. The employment was expected to begin and end the same day, and Papai was not going to sail with the vessel after he finished painting. Papai had been employed by Harbor Tug on 12 previous occasions in the 2 1/2 months before his injury.

Papai received his jobs with Harbor Tug through the Inland Boatman's Union (IBU) hiring hall. He had been getting jobs with various vessels through the hiring hall for about 2 1/4 years. All the jobs were short term. The longest lasted about 40 days and most were for three days or under. In a deposition, Papai described the work as coming under three headings: maintenance, longshoring, and deckhand. Papai said maintenance work involved chipping rust and painting aboard docked vessels. Longshoring work required helping to discharge vessels. Deckhand work involved manning the lines on- and off-board vessels while they docked or undocked. As for the assignments he obtained through the hiring hall over 2¼ years, most of them, says Papai, involved deckhand work.

After his alleged injury aboard the Pt. Barrow, Papai sued Harbor Tug in the United States District Court for the Northern District of California, claiming negligence under the Jones Act and unseaworthiness under general maritime law, in addition to other causes of action. His wife joined as a plaintiff, claiming loss of consortium. Harbor Tug sought summary judgment on Papai's Jones Act and unseaworthiness claims, contending he was not a seaman and so could not prevail on either claim. The District Court granted Harbor Tug's motion and later denied Papai's motion for reconsideration. After our decisions in McDermott International, Inc. v. Wilander, 498 U.S. 337, 111 S.Ct. 807, 112 L.Ed.2d 866 (1991), and Southwest Marine, Inc. v. Gizoni, 502 U.S. 81, 112 S.Ct. 486, 116 L.Ed.2d 405 (1991), the District Court granted a motion by Harbor Tug "to confirm" the earlier summary adjudication of Papai's non-seaman status. The District Court reasoned, under a test since superseded, see Chandris, supra, that Papai was not a seaman within the meaning of the Jones Act or the general maritime law, because "he did not have a 'more or less permanent connection' with the vessel on which he was injured nor did he perform substantial work on the vessel sufficient for seaman status."

The Court of Appeals for the Ninth Circuit reversed and remanded for a trial of Papai's seaman status and his corresponding Jones Act and unseaworthiness claims. Based on our decision in Chandris, the court described the relevant inquiry as "not whether plaintiff had a permanent connection with the vessel [but] whether plaintiff's relationship with a vessel (or a group of vessels) was substantial in terms of duration and nature, which requires consideration of the total circumstances of his employment." 67 F.3d 203, 206 (1995). A majority of the panel believed it would be reasonable for a jury to conclude the employee satisfied that test. In the majority's view, "[i]f the type of work a maritime worker customarily performs would entitle him to seaman status if performed for a single employer, the worker should not be deprived of that status simply because the industry operates under a daily assignment rather than a permanent employment system." Ibid. The majority also said the "circumstance" that Papai had worked for Harbor Tug on 12 occasions during the 2½ months before his injury "may in itself provide a sufficient connection" to Harbor Tug's vessels to establish seaman status.

* * *

We granted certiorari, 519 U.S. —, 117 S.Ct. 36, 135 L.Ed.2d 1127 (1996), and now reverse.

II

The LHWCA, a maritime workers' compensation scheme, excludes from its coverage "a master or member of a crew of any vessel," 33 U.S.C. § 902(3)(G). These masters and crewmembers are the seamen entitled to sue for damages under the Jones Act. Chandris, 515 U.S., at 355-358, 115 S.Ct., at 2183. In other words, the LHWCA and the Jones Act are "mutually exclusive."

Our recent cases explain the proper inquiry to determine seaman status. We need not restate that doctrinal development ... . It suffices to cite Chandris, which held, in pertinent part:

> [T]he essential requirements for seaman status are twofold. First ... an employee's duties must contribute to the function of the vessel or to the accomplishment of its mission. ...
> Second, and most important for our purposes here, a seaman must have a connection to a vessel in navigation (or to an identifiable group of such vessels) that is substantial in terms of both its duration and its nature.

* * *

Harbor Tug does not dispute that it would reasonable for a jury to conclude Papai's duties aboard the Pt. Barrow (or any other vessel he worked on through the IBU hiring hall) contributed to the function of the vessel or the accomplishment of its mission, satisfying Chandris' first standard. Nor does Harbor Tug dispute that a reasonable jury could conclude that the Pt. Barrow or other vessels Papai worked on were in navigation. The result, as will often be the case, is that seaman status turns on the part of Chandris' second standard which requires the employee to show "a connection to a vessel in navigation (or to an identifiable group of such vessels) that is substantial in terms of both its duration and its nature." We explained the rule as follows:

"The fundamental purpose of th[e] ... substantial connection requirement is to give full effect to the remedial scheme created by Congress and to separate the sea-based maritime employees who are entitled to Jones Act protection from those landbased workers who have only a transitory or sporadic connection with a vessel in navigation, and therefore whose employment does not regularly expose them to the perils of the sea."

For the substantial connection requirement to serve its purpose, the inquiry into the nature of the employee's connection to the vessel must concentrate on whether the employee's duties take him to sea. This will give substance to the inquiry both as to the duration and nature of the employee's connection to the vessel and be helpful in distinguishing land-based from sea- based employees.

Papai argues, and the Court of Appeals majority held, that Papai meets Chandris' second test based on his employments with the various vessels he worked on through the IBU hiring hall in the 2 1/4 years before his injury, vessels owned, it appears, by three different employers not linked by any common ownership or control. He also did longshoring work through the hiring hall, id., at 31, and it appears this was for still other employers. As noted above, Papai testified at his deposition that the majority of his work during this period was deckhand work. According to Papai, this satisfies Chandris because the group of vessels Papai worked on through the IBU hiring hall constitutes "an identifiable group of ... vessels" to which he has a "substantial connection."

The Court of Appeals for the Fifth Circuit was the first to hold that a worker could qualify as a seaman based on his connection to a group of vessels rather than a particular one. In Braniff v. Jackson Ave.-Gretna Ferry, Inc., 280 F.2d 523 (5th Cir. 1960), the court held the employer was not entitled to summary judgment on the seaman-status question where an employee's job was to perform maintenance work on the employer's fleet of ferry boats, often while the boats were running: "The usual thing, of course, is for a person to have a Jones Act seaman status in relation to a particular vessel. But there is nothing about this ... concept to limit it mechanically to a single ship." There is "no insurmountable difficulty," the court explained, in finding seaman status based on the employee's relationship to "several specific vessels"—"an identifiable fleet"—as opposed to a single one.

We, in turn, adverted to the group of vessels concept in Chandris. We described it as a rule "allow[ing] seaman status for those workers who had the requisite connection with an 'identifiable fleet' of vessels, a finite group of vessels under common ownership or control." The majority in the Court of Appeals did not discuss our description of the group of vessels concept as requiring common ownership or control, nor did it discuss other Courts of Appeals cases applying the concept, see, e.g., Reeves v. Mobile Dredging & Pumping Co., 26 F.3d, at 1258. The court pointed to this statement from Chandris: "[W]e see no reason to limit the seaman status inquiry ... exclusively to an examination of the overall course of a worker's service with a particular employer." It interpreted this to mean "it may be necessary to examine the work performed by the employee while employed by different employers during the relevant time period." 67 F.3d, at 206. The court did not define what it meant by "the relevant time period." In any event, the context of our statement in Chandris makes clear our meaning, which is that the employee's prior work history with a particular employer may not affect the seaman inquiry if the employee was injured on a new assignment with the same employer, an assignment with different "essential duties" than his previous ones. In Chandris, the words "particular employer" give emphasis to the point that the inquiry into the nature of the employee's duties for seaman-status purposes may concentrate on a narrower, not broader, period than the employee's entire course of employment with his current employer. There was no suggestion of a need to examine the nature of an employee's duties with prior employers. ("Since Barrett [v. Chevron, U.S.A., Inc., 781 F.2d 1067 (5th Cir. 1986) (en banc)], the Fifth Circuit consistently has analyzed the problem [of determining seaman status] in terms of the percentage of work performed on vessels for the employer in question"). The Court of Appeals majority interpreted the words "particular employer" outside the limited discussion in which we used them and, as a result, gave the phrase a meaning opposite from what the context requires.

The Court of Appeals stressed that various of Papai's employers had "join[ed] together to obtain a common labor pool on which they draw by means of a union hiring hall." (suggesting that this case involves a "group of vessels [that] have collectively agreed to obtain employees" from a hiring hall). There is no evidence in the record that the contract Harbor Tug had with the IBU about employing deckhands (IBU Deckhands Agreement) was negotiated by a multiemployer bargaining group, and, even if it had been, that would not affect the result here. There was no showing that the group of vessels the court sought to identify were subject to unitary ownership or control in any aspect of their business or operation. So far as the record shows, each employer was free to hire, assign, and direct workers for whatever tasks and time period they each determined, limited, at most, by the IBU Deckhands Agreement. In deciding whether there is an identifiable group of vessels of relevance for a Jones Act seaman status determination, the question is whether the vessels are subject to common ownership or control. The requisite link is not established by the mere use of the same hiring hall which draws from the same pool of employees.

Considering prior employments with independent employers in making the seaman status inquiry would undermine "the interests of employers and maritime workers alike in being able to predict who will be covered by the Jones Act (and, perhaps more importantly for purposes of the employers' workers' compensation obligations, who will be covered by the LHWCA) before a particular work day begins." Chandris, supra, at 363, 115 S.Ct., at 2187. There would be no principled basis for limiting which prior employments are considered for determining seaman status. The Court of Appeals spoke of a "relevant time period" but, as noted above, it did not define this term. Since the substantial connection standard is often, as here, the determinative element of the seaman inquiry, it must be given workable and practical confines. When the inquiry further turns on whether the employee has a substantial connection to an identifiable group of vessels, common ownership or control is essential for this purpose.

Papai contends his various employers through the hiring hall would have been able to predict his status as a seaman under the Jones Act based on the seagoing nature of some of the duties he could have been hired to perform consistent with his classification as a "qualified deckhand" under the IBU Deckhands Agreement. By the terms of the Agreement, Papai was qualified as a "satisfactory helmsman and lookout," for example, and he could have been hired to serve a vessel while it was underway, in which case his duties would have included "conduct[ing] a check of the engine room status a minimum of two (2) times each watch ... for vessel safety reasons." In South Chicago Coal & Dock Co. v. Bassett, 309 U.S. 251, 60 S.Ct. 544, 84 L.Ed. 732 (1940), we rejected a claim to seaman status grounded on the employee's job title, which also happened to be "deckhand." "The question," we said, "concerns his actual duties." See also Northeast Marine Terminal Co. v. Caputo, 432 U.S. 249, 268, n. 30, 97 S.Ct. 2348, 2359, 53 L.Ed.2d 320 (1977) (reasoning that employee's membership in longshoremen's union was, in itself, irrelevant to whether employee was covered by the LHWCA, as fact of union membership was unrelated to the purposes of the LHWCA's coverage provisions). The question is what connection the employee had in actual fact to vessel operations, not what a union agreement says. Papai was qualified under the IBU Deckhands Agreement to perform non-seagoing work in addition to the seagoing duties described above. His actual duty on the Pt. Barrow throughout the employment in question did not include any seagoing activity; he was hired for one day to paint the vessel at dockside and he was not going to sail with the vessel after he finished painting it. This is not a case where the employee was hired to perform seagoing work during the employment in question, however brief, and we need not consider here the consequences of such an employment. The IBU Deckhands Agreement gives no reason to assume that any particular percentage of Papai's work would be of a seagoing nature, subjecting him to the perils of the sea. In these circumstances, the union agreement does not advance the accuracy of the seaman status inquiry.

Papai argues he qualifies as a seaman if we consider his 12 prior employments with Harbor Tug over the 2 1/2 months before his injury. Papai testified at his deposition that he worked aboard the Pt. Barrow on three or four occasions before the day he was injured, the most recent of which was more than a week earlier. Each of these engagements involved only maintenance work while the tug was docked. The nature of Papai's connection to the Pt. Barrow was no more substantial for seaman-status purposes by virtue of these engagements than the one during which he was injured. Papai does not identify with specificity what he did for Harbor Tug the other eight or nine times he worked for the company in the 2 1/2 months before his injury. The closest he comes is his deposition testimony that 70 percent of his work over the 2 1/4 years before his injury was deckhand work. Coupled with the fact that none of Papai's work aboard the Pt. Barrow was of a seagoing nature, it would not be reasonable to infer from Papai's testimony that his recent engagements with Harbor Tug involved work of a seagoing nature. In any event, these discrete engagements were separate from the one in question, which was the sort of "transitory or sporadic" connection to a vessel or group of vessels that, as we explained in Chandris, does not qualify one for seaman status.

Jones Act coverage is confined to seamen, those workers who face regular exposure to the perils of the sea. An important part of the test for determining who is a seaman is whether the injured worker seeking coverage has a substantial connection to a vessel or a fleet of vessels, and the latter concept requires a requisite degree of common ownership or control. The substantial connection test is important in distinguishing between sea- and land-based employment, for land-based employment is inconsistent with Jones Act coverage. This was the holding in Chandris, and we adhere to it here. The only connection a reasonable jury could identify among the vessels Papai worked aboard is that each hired some of its employees from the same union hiring hall where it hired him. That is not sufficient to establish seaman status under the group of vessels concept. Papai had the burden at summary judgment to "set forth specific facts showing that there is a genuine issue for trial." Fed. Rule Civ. Proc. 56(e). He failed to meet it. The Court of Appeals erred in holding otherwise. Its judgment is reversed.

It is so ordered.

Justice STEVENS, with whom Justice GINSBURG and Justice BREYER join, dissenting.

* * *

[The dissenting opinion is omitted.]

Notes

1. *Pilots*

In *Bach v. Trident Steamship Co.*, 920 F.2d 322, 1991 AMC 928, *vacated & remanded*, 500 U.S. 949, *aff'd.*, 947 F.2d 1290 (1991), *cert. denied*, 504 U.S. 931, 112 S. Ct. 199 (1992), the Fifth Circuit refused to grant "seaman" status to a compulsory river pilot.

Eugene G. Bach, Jr., a compulsory river pilot between New Orleans and Pilottown, suffered a fatal heart attack shortly after boarding the M/V JAYMAT TRIDENT, a small pilot boat. His survivors brought suit under the Jones Act, the LHWCA and the general maritime law. The court, reciting the two-prong test for seaman status—permanent attachment to a vessel or fleet of vessels and contribution to the function or mission of a vessel or fleet of vessels—concluded that Bach had failed to meet the first prong requiring attachment. Bach's survivors argued that since the total of the vessels that he piloted and controlled, including the M/V JAYMAT TRIDENT, constituted a fleet in their aggregate, he fulfilled the required connection. The court rejected this argument stating that a fleet is more than a "group of vessels an employee happened to work aboard." 920 F.2d at 324. Rather, a fleet is an identifiable group of vessels under one common ownership.

The court considered whether an exception for the attachment to a vessel test should be made for workers who perform traditional maritime work onboard various unconnected vessels. They answered this question in the negative:

[T]o create an exception for a worker such as Bach who has the duties and faces the risks of a traditional seaman but who lacks requisite vessel connection would include all sorts of workers we have previously excluded, would widen the divergence of views between our circuit and others, and would make our seaman test unnecessarily uncertain and ambiguous. We therefore decline to make such a radical change in this circuit's test for Jones Act coverage.

920 F.2d at 326.

Judge Brown, in his dissent, argued that it was "simply inconceivable that Congress ... would exclude from the broad term 'seaman' one so vital, so indispensable, so legislatively recognized as a compulsory pilot," Calling the compulsory pilot "the very essence of maritime commerce," 920 F.2d at 332, Brown concluded that compulsory pilots should not be excluded from Jones Act protection while aboard and directing the navigation of a vessel. 920 F.2d at 332.

Bach was appealed to the Supreme Court, which granted certiorari, vacated the judgment and remanded to the Fifth Circuit for reconsideration in light of the *Wilander* decision. *Bach v. Trident S.S. Co.*, 11 S. Ct. 2253 (1991). On remand, the Fifth Circuit noted that the holding in *Wilander* was that a maritime worker need not aid in the navigation of the vessel to be a seaman. The court held that since its original decision was not based upon whether *Bach* aided in the navigation of the vessel but upon his lack of a permanent relationship to any vessel or fleet of vessels, the *Wilander* decision did not affect the conclusion originally reached by the court in Bach. The Fifth Circuit therefore reinstated its earlier judgment. *Bach v. Trident S.S. Co.*, 947 F.2d 1290, 1992 AMC 643 (5th Cir. 1991), and certiorari was denied, 504 U.S. 931, 112 S. Ct. 1996, 118 L. Ed. 2d 592 (1992).

2. *Divers*

In *Wisner v. Professional Divers of New Orleans*, 731 So. 2d 200, 1999 AMC 1189 (La. 1999), *cert. denied*, 120 S. Ct. 285, 145 L. Ed. 2d 238 (1999), the Supreme Court of Louisiana held that a diver doing 90% of his work at sea from different vessels was entitled to Jones Act remedies from his employer. Is this consistent with the Supreme Court's *Wilander/Chandris/Papai* trilogy?

3. *Who is the Employer?*

For determination of the question of who is the employer of an injured seaman, see *Wheatley v. Gladden*, 660 F.2d 1024, 1982 AMC 618 (4th Cir. 1981):

> The trial court also held that Wheatley could not recover on his Jones Act claim and his "maintenance and cure" claim against Gladden because each required an employer/employee relationship which was absent in this case as a matter of law.
>
> It is true that an employer/employee relationship is a necessary antecedent to a Jones Act negligence claim. *Cosmopolitan Shipping Co. v. McAllister*, 337 U.S. 783 (1949), and to a "maintenance and cure" claim, *Cortes v. Baltimore Insular Line*, 287 U.S. 367, 371 (1932). The existence of such an employer/employee relationship must be determined under maritime law, *United States v. Webb, Inc.*, 397 U.S. 179 (1970), and the burden of proof is on the seaman to establish the employment relationship. Among the factors to be considered in determining whether a party is an employer are the degree of control exercised over the details of the operation, the amount of supervision, the amount of investment in the operation, the method of payment and the parties' understanding of the relationship. *United States v. Webb, Inc. supra; Kirkconnell v. United States*, 347 F.2d 260, 171 Ct. Cl. 43 (1965). The resolution of the issue is normally a factual one within the province of a jury. *The Norland*, 101 F.2d 967, 9 Alaska 471 (9th Cir. 1939); *Claussen v. Gulf Oil Corp.*, 136 F. Supp. 110 (W.D. Pa. 1955); 2 M. NORRIS, THE LAW OF SEAMEN § 670 (3d ed. 1970).

* * *

> A boat owner may retain sufficient control over his property to be charged with the duties of an employer even though another party actually is in charge of the vessel's operation.

Because an employer/employee relationship is a necessary antecedent to a Jones Act claim, "only one person, firm, or corporation can be sued as employer". *Cosmopolitan Shipping Co. v McAllister*, 337 U.S. 783, 791, 69 S. Ct. 1317, 1322 (1949).

4. *Borrowed Servant Doctrine*

A person may be a member of the crew of a vessel, and, therefore, a Jones Act seaman even though he is employed by an independent contractor rather than the shipowner. In such a case, the seaman is a *borrowed servant* of the shipowner and the shipowner occupies the position of an employer under the Jones Act. In *Ruis v. Shell Oil*, 413 F.2d 310, 312-13 (5th Cir. 1969), the court said that the crucial element is "control" and suggested several factors that were helpful in determining who had control. These are:

1) who has control over the employee and work he is performing, beyond mere suggestion of details or cooperation?
2) whose work is being performed?

3)   was there an agreement, understanding or meeting of the minds between the original employer and the subsequent person for whom the employee performed services?

4)   did the employee acquiesce in the new work situation?

5)   did the original employer terminate his relationship with the employee?

6)   who furnished the tools and place for performance?

7)   was the new employment over a period of time?

8)   who had the right to discharge the employee?

9)   who had the obligation to pay the employee?

The borrowed servant doctrine is also important for purposes of LHWCA. *See West v. Kerr-McGee Corporation*, 765 F.2d 526, 1986 AMC 150 (5th Cir. 1985).

5. Substantiality—Length of Employment

The requirements formulated in *Chandris* that a person have "a connection to a vessel in navigation (or to an identifiable group of such vessels) that is substantial in terms of both its duration and nature" presents particular difficulties in light of current employment practices.

How should courts apply the durational test to an employee who is injured within a relatively short time after commencing his duties on the vessel?

Because it found that Rig 3 was not a vessel as a matter of law, the district court did not consider whether Manuel satisfied the other requisite for seaman status—a substantial employment-related connection to a vessel in navigation. *Chandris*, 515 U.S. at 368, 115 S. Ct. at 2189. Ordinarily, seaman status is a fact-specific inquiry better left to the province of the jury. *Ducote*, 953 F.2d at 1002; *see also Offshore Co. v. Robiso*, 266 F.2d 769, 779-80 (5th Cir.1959). However, "[w]hen the underlying facts are established, and the rule of law is undisputed, the issue is whether the facts meet the statutory standard." *McDermott Int'l. v. Wilander*, 498 U.S. 337, 356, 111 S. Ct. 807, 817, 112 L. Ed.2d 866 (1991).

The summary judgment evidence established that Manuel was assigned to and worked aboard Rig 3 the entire two months he worked for P.A.W. Also, it is undisputed that Manuel's duties contributed to the function of Rig 3. P.A.W.'s argument that Manuel does not have the requisite connection to a vessel is limited to the assertion that the possibility that Manuel could have been assigned to other work locations renders his assignment to Rig 3 less than permanent. This argument is seriously flawed. In *Chandris*, the Supreme Court makes it clear that the adequacy of the plaintiff's connection to a vessel is properly assessed on the basis of his work assignment at the time of his injury:

> Such a person should not be denied seaman status if injured shortly after the reassignment [to a vessel], just as someone actually transferred to a desk job in the company's office and injured in the hallway should not be entitled to claim seaman status on the basis of prior service at sea.

Chandris, 515 U.S. at 372, 115 S. Ct. at 2191. At the time of his injury, Manuel was assigned to work aboard a vessel in navigation. The fact that Manuel was subject to reassignment by P.A.W. at some later time is of no moment. As the Supreme Court pointed out in *Chandris*, "[w]hen a maritime worker's basic assignment changes, his seaman status may change as well." *Chandris*, 515 U.S. at 372, 115 S. Ct. at 2191. Manuel's basic assignment never changed; he remained assigned to Rig 3 for the entire two months leading up to his injury. Therefore, we conclude that Manuel satisfies *Chandris*' two-prong test for seaman status as a matter of law.

* * *

Manuel v. P.A.W. Drilling & Well Service, 135 F.3d 344, 1988 AMC 1390 (5th Cir. 1998).

How should courts apply the durational test to an employee whose work is clearly seaman's work, but whose employment on that job is of a relatively short duration?

In *Foulk v. Donjon Marine Co., Inc.*, 144 F.3d 252, 1998 AMC 2926 (3d Cir. 1998) the court reversed the grant of summary judgment which had held that a person hired to work on a project for ten days, as a matter of law, could not satisfy the durational test. The appellate court concluded "that the durational element cannot be answered by an absolute measure. It is the temporal element and the nature of the activities performed that, taken together, determine seaman status." 144 F.3d 259. Specifically that court found that it was "inappropriate to determine the minimum durational element by an absolute number, such as 10 days." *Id.*

How should courts apply the durational test to an employee whose employer owns no vessels but who assigns the employee to work on vessels owned by other persons where those vessels are not under common ownership, control, or operation?

See, Wisner v. Professional Divers of New Orleans, 731 So. 2d 200 (La. 1999), *cert. denied*, 120 S. Ct. 285, 145 L. Ed. 2d 238 (1999), where the Louisiana Supreme Court held that a diver whose employment placed him on vessels for ninety percent of his work life, qualified as a Jones Act seaman.

How should courts apply the durational test to an employee who initially worked for employer X, then left to work for employer Y, and finally, returned to work for the original employer, X, at which time he sustained an injury?

One court has held "that evidence of an employee's prior assignment with the same employer is not admissible under the Fleet Seaman Doctrine if those assignments were not part of a continuous employment relationship between the employer and employee." *Shade v. Great Lakes Dredge & Dock Co.*, 154 F.3d 143, 154 (3d Cir. 1998).

---

b. Vessel in Navigation

DESPER v. STARVED ROCK FERRY CO.

342 U.S. 187, 72 S. Ct. 216, 96 L. Ed. 205, 1952 AMC 12 (1951)

Mr. Justice JACKSON delivered the opinion of the Court.

Petitioner brought suit under the Jones Act to recover damages for the death of her intestate son from injuries sustained during the course of his employment by respondent. The Court of Appeals for the Seventh Circuit reversed the judgment of the District Court entered on a jury's verdict in petitioner's favor. This Court granted certiorari.

Respondent operates a small fleet of sightseeing motorboats on the Illinois River in the vicinity of Starved Rock. The boats are navigated under Coast Guard regulations by personnel licensed by the Department of Commerce. Operations are necessarily restricted to summer months. Each fall the boats are beached and put up on blocks for the winter. In the spring each is overhauled before being launched for the season. The decedent, Thomas J. Desper, Jr., was first employed by respondent in April, 1947, to help prepare the boats for their seasonal launching. In June of the same year he acquired the necessary operator's license from the Department of Commerce and, for the remainder of that season, he was employed as a boat operator. When the season closed, he helped take the boats out of the water and block them up for the winter. His employment terminated December 19, 1947.

Desper was re-employed March 15, 1948. There was testimony that he was then engaged for the season and was to resume his operator's duties when the boats were back in the water. For the time being, however, he was put to cleaning, painting, and waterproofing the boats, preparing them for navigation. On the date of the accident, April 26th, the boats were still blocked up on land. Several men, Desper among them, were on board a moored barge, maintained by respondent as a machine shop, warehouse, waiting room and ticket office, engaged in painting life preservers for use on the boats. One man was working on a fire extinguisher. It exploded, killing him and Desper.

The Jones Act confers a cause of action on "any seaman." In opposition to petitioner's suit under the Act, respondent contended that Desper, at the time of his death, was not a "seaman" within the meaning of the Act. Whether he was such a "seaman" is the critical issue in the case which reached this Court.

* * *

The ... question is whether, ... decedent was a "seaman" at the time of his death. The many cases turning upon the question whether an individual was a "seaman" demonstrate that the matter depends largely on the facts of the particular case and the activity in which he was engaged at the time of injury. The facts in this case are unique. The work in which the decedent was engaged at the time of his death quite clearly was not that usually done by a "seaman." The boats were not afloat and had neither captain nor crew. They were undergoing seasonal repairs, the work being of the kind that, in the case of larger vessels, would customarily be done by exclusively shore-based personnel. For a number of reasons the ships might not be launched, or he might not operate one. To be sure, he was a probable navigator in the near future, but the law does not cover probable or expectant seamen but seamen in being. It is our conclusion that while engaged in such seasonal repair work Desper was not a "seaman" within the purview of the Jones Act. The distinct nature of the work is emphasized by the fact that there was no vessel engaged in navigation at the time of the decedent's death. All had been "laid up for the winter." *Hawn v. American S. S. Co.*, 107 F.2d 999, 1000 (2d Cir.); *cf. Seneca Washed Gravel Corp. v. McManigal*, 65 F.2d 779, 780 (2d Cir.). In the words of the court in *Antus v. Interocean S. S. Co.*, 108 F.2d 185, 187 (6th Cir.), where it was held that one who had been a member of a ship's crew and was injured while preparing it for winter quarters could not maintain a Jones Act suit for his injuries: "The fact that he had been, or expected in the future to be, a seaman does not render maritime work which was not maritime in its nature."...

We think the court below properly disposed of the question presented. Accordingly, its judgment is Affirmed.

WIXOM v. BOLAND MARINE & MFG. CO., INC.

614 F.2d 956, 1950 AMC 2992 (5th Cir. 1980)

GODBOLD, Circuit Judge:

Wixom brought this suit against his employer, Boland Marine & Manufacturing Company, invoking general maritime jurisdiction. He alleges that on March 5, 1976, he fell to the deck of the U.S.S. KING from the scaffold on which he was working and sustained serious injuries. He claims general damages under both the Jones Act and the doctrine of unseaworthiness, and also maintenance and cure. The district court granted Boland's motion for summary judgment because, under the material undisputed facts, the vessel on which Wixom was working was not in navigation and he was not a member of the vessel's crew contributing to its mission or the accomplishment of the vessel's function. Wixom appealed. We affirm.

Only "seamen" can recover damages under the Jones Act. This court has previously set forth a threepart test for "seaman" status, one requirement of which is that the vessel must have been "in navigation" at the time the claimant was injured. *Williams v. Avondale Shipyards, Inc.*, 452 F.2d 955, 958 (5th Cir. 1971); *Bodden v. Coordinated Caribbean Transport, Inc.*, 369 F.2d 273, 274 (5th Cir. 1966). In determining whether a ship under repair is still in navigation, the court should look at the extent and nature of the repair operations and who controls them.

Here, Boland accepted custody of the U.S.S. KING on April 24, 1974, and did not return the ship to the Navy until March 8, 1977, almost three years later. During this period the ship's captain and crew were not aboard the vessel, and responsibility for the ship was vested entirely in Boland. The work performed on the vessel included major structural changes such as the addition of a section to the deckhouse and of a forward mast. The bill for repair exceed 25 million dollars. For at least some of the time, the ship's engine and propellers were inoperable. On these facts, the district court was entitled to conclude that, at the time of Wixom's fall, the U.S.S. KING was not "in navigation" as a matter of law. Compare *Hodges, supra*, with *Waganer v. Sea-Land Service, Inc.*, 486 F.2d 955, 958-59 (5th Cir. 1973).

Wixom claims that because 90% of his past employment had taken place on ships that were clearly in navigation, he was a seaman for purposes of Jones Act coverage even if the U.S.S. KING was not itself in navigation. The appellant has not cited cases that support his position and we find none. The appellant's argument that he should be covered because the Jones Act is meant to be read expansively is not persuasive.

* * *

Affirmed.

Notes

1. *Vessels Undergoing Repairs*

As to vessel status, the Supreme Court adopted the general rule in the lower court that "vessels undergoing repairs or spending a relatively short period of time in dry dock are still considered to be 'in navigation' whereas ships being transformed through 'major' overhauls or renovation are not." *Chandris, Inc. v. Latsis*, 515 U.S. 347, 115 S. Ct. 2172, 132 L. Ed. 2d 314, 1995 AMC 1840 (1995).

2. *Vessel in Navigation*

In a Jones Act action, the question of whether a vessel has been *withdrawn* from navigation is, ordinarily, one of fact. *See Abshire v. Seacoast Products, Inc.*, 668 F.2d 832 (5th Cir. 1982). Likewise, the question of whether a floating structure has acquired the status of a vessel in navigation for purposes of a Jones Act action is ordinarily one of fact. *Cf. Garrett v. Dean Shank Drilling Co.*, 719 F.2d 1009 (5th Cir. 1986). In this case, a drilling barge was launched on navigable waters and delivered to its owner. However, before the barge could operate as a drilling rig, it required the addition of living quarters for the crew, a derrick, navigational lights, and other accoutrements. While these additions were being made, a worker was injured on the barge. In due course, the injured worker filed a Jones Act action against the owner of the barge rather than his employer, the shipbuilder. The jury found the plaintiff to be a Jones Act seaman. The Court of Appeal conceded that the question of whether a vessel is in navigation is one of fact but reversed on the ground that the matter here should be determined as a question of law: a structure that is being outfitted for its intended purpose cannot be a vessel in navigation. *See also Reynolds v. Ingalls Shipbuilding Division, Litton Systems, Inc.*, 788 F.2d 264, 1986 AMC 2839 (5th Cir. 1986), in which the court held that "a ship undergoing sea trials is not 'in navigation' for purposes of the Jones Act." For the question whether a floating structure is a vessel in navigation for purposes of LHWCA, *see Stewart v. Dutra Construction Co.* 543 U.S. 481, 125 S.Ct. 1118, 2005 WL 405475 (2005), *infra*.

---

c. *Vessel or Work Platform*

STEWART v. DUTRA CONSTRUCTION CO.

543 U.S. 481, 125 S. Ct. 1118, 2005 WL 405475 (2005)

Justice THOMAS delivered the opinion of the Court.

I

As part of Boston's Central Artery/Tunnel Project, or "Big Dig," the Commonwealth of Massachusetts undertook to extend the Massachusetts Turnpike through a tunnel running beneath South Boston and Boston Harbor to Logan Airport. The Commonwealth employed respondent Dutra Construction Company to assist in that undertaking. At the time, Dutra owned the world's largest dredge, the *Super Scoop*, which was capable of digging the 50-foot-deep, 100-foot-wide, three-quarter-mile-long trench beneath Boston Harbor that is now the Ted Williams Tunnel.

The *Super Scoop* is a massive floating platform from which a clamshell bucket is suspended beneath the water. The bucket removes silt from the ocean floor and dumps the sediment onto one of two scows that float alongside the dredge. The *Super Scoop* has certain characteristics common to seagoing vessels, such as a captain and crew, navigational lights, ballast tanks, and a crew dining area. But it lacks others. Most conspicuously, the *Super Scoop* has only limited means of self-propulsion. It is moved long distances by tugboat. (To work on the Big Dig, it was towed from its home base in California through the Panama Canal and up the eastern seaboard to Boston Harbor.) It navigates short distances by manipulating its anchors and cables. When dredging the Boston Harbor trench, it typically moved in this way once every couple of hours, covering a distance of 30-to-50 feet each time.

Dutra hired petitioner Willard Stewart, a marine engineer, to maintain the mechanical systems on the *Super Scoop* during its dredging of the harbor. At the time of Stewart's accident, the *Super Scoop* lay idle because one of its scows, Scow No. 4, had suffered an engine malfunction and the other was at sea. Stewart was on board Scow No. 4, feeding wires through an open hatch located about 10 feet above the engine area. While Stewart was perched beside the hatch, the *Super Scoop* used its bucket to move the scow. In the process, the scow collided with the *Super Scoop*, causing a jolt that plunged Stewart headfirst through the hatch to the deck below. He was seriously injured.

Stewart sued Dutra in the United States District Court for the District of Massachusetts under the Jones Act, 38 Stat. 1185, 46 U.S.C.App. § 688(a), alleging that he was a seaman injured by Dutra's negligence. He also filed an alternative claim under § 5(b) of the LHWCA, 33 U.S.C. § 905(b), which authorizes covered employees to sue a "vessel" owner as a third party for an injury caused by the owner's negligence.

Dutra moved for summary judgment on the Jones Act claim, arguing that Stewart was not a seaman. The company acknowledged that Stewart was "a member of the [*Super Scoop's*] crew," 230 F.3d 461, 466 (1st Cir. 2000); that he spent "[n]inety-nine percent of his time while on the job" aboard the *Super Scoop*, App. 20 (Defendant's

Memorandum in Support of Summary Judgment); and that his "duties contributed to the function" of the *Super Scoop*, *id.*, at 32. Dutra argued only that the *Super Scoop* was not a vessel for purposes of the Jones Act. Dutra pointed to the Court of Appeals' en banc decision in *DiGiovanni v. Traylor Brothers, Inc.*, 959 F.2d 1119 (1ˢᵗ Cir. 1992), which held that "if a barge ... or other float's purpose or primary business is *not* navigation or commerce, then workers assigned thereto for its shore enterprise are to be considered seamen only when it is in actual navigation or transit" at the time of the plaintiff's injury. *Id.*, at 1123 (internal quotation marks omitted). The District Court granted summary judgment to Dutra, because the *Super Scoop's* primary purpose was dredging rather than transportation and because it was stationary at the time of Stewart's injury.

On interlocutory appeal, the Court of Appeals affirmed, concluding that it too was bound by *DiGiovanni.* 230 F.3d, at 467-468. The court reasoned that the *Super Scoop's* primary function was construction and that "[a]ny navigation or transportation that may be required is incidental to this primary function." *Id.*, at 468. The court also concluded that the scow's movement at the time of the accident did not help Stewart, because his status as a seaman depended on the movement of the *Super Scoop* (which was stationary) rather than the scow. *Id.*, at 469.

On remand, the District Court granted summary judgment in favor of Dutra on Stewart's alternative claim that Dutra was liable for negligence as an owner of a "vessel" under the LHWCA, 33 U.S.C. § 905(b). The Court of Appeals again affirmed. It noted that Dutra had conceded that the *Super Scoop* was a "vessel" for purposes of § 905(b), explaining that "the LHWCA's definition of 'vessel' is 'significantly more inclusive than that used for evaluating seaman status under the Jones Act.' " 343 F.3d 10, 13 (1ˢᵗ Cir. 2003) (quoting *Morehead v. Atkinson-Kiewit*, 97 F.3d 603, 607 (1ˢᵗ Cir. 1996) (en banc)). The Court of Appeals nonetheless agreed with the District Court's conclusion that Dutra's alleged negligence was committed in its capacity as an employer rather than as owner of the vessel under § 905(b).

We granted certiorari to resolve confusion over how to determine whether a watercraft is a "vessel" for purposes of the LHWCA. 540 U.S. 1177, 124 S.Ct. 1414, 158 L.Ed.2d 76 (2004).

II

Prior to the passage of the Jones Act, general maritime law usually entitled a seaman who fell sick or was injured both to maintenance and cure (or the right to be cared for and paid wages during the voyage, see, *e.g., Harden v. Gordon,* 11 F. Cas. 480, 482-483 (No. 6,047) (CC Me. 1823) (Story, J.)), and to damages for any "injuries received ... in consequence of the unseaworthiness of the ship," *The Osceola,* 189 U.S. 158, 175, 23 S.Ct. 483, 47 L.Ed. 760 (1903). Suits against shipowners for negligence, however, were barred. Courts presumed that the seaman, in signing articles of employment for the voyage, had assumed the risks of his occupation; thus a seaman was "not allowed to recover an indemnity for the negligence of the master, or any member of the crew." *Ibid.*

Congress enacted the Jones Act in 1920 to remove this bar to negligence suits by seamen. See *Chandris, Inc. v. Latsis,* 515 U.S. 347, 354, 115 S.Ct. 2172, 132 L.Ed.2d 314 (1995). Specifically, the Jones Act provides:

"Any seaman who shall suffer personal injury in the course of his employment may, at his election, maintain an action for damages at law, with the right of trial by jury, and in such action all statutes of the United States modifying or extending the common-law right or remedy in cases of personal injury to railway employees shall apply." 46 U.S.C.App. § 688(a).

Although the statute is silent on who is a "seaman," both the maritime law backdrop against which Congress enacted the Jones Act and Congress' subsequent enactments provide some guidance.

First, "seaman" is a term of art that had an established meaning under general maritime law. We have thus presumed that when the Jones Act made available negligence remedies to "[a]ny seaman who shall suffer personal injury in the course of his employment," Congress took the term "seaman" as the general maritime law found it. *Chandris, supra,* at 355, 115 S.Ct. 2172 (citing *Warner v. Goltra,* 293 U.S. 155, 159, 55 S.Ct. 46, 79 L.Ed. 254 (1934)); G. Gilmore & C. Black, Law of Admiralty § 6-21, pp. 328-329 (2d ed.1975).

Second, Congress provided further guidance in 1927 when it enacted the LHWCA, which provides scheduled compensation to land-based maritime workers but which also excepts from its coverage "a master or member of a crew of any vessel." 33 U.S.C. § 902(3)(G). This exception is simply "a refinement of the term 'seaman' in the Jones Act." *McDermott Int'l, Inc. v. Wilander,* 498 U.S. 337, 347, 111 S.Ct. 807, 112 L.Ed.2d 866 (1991). Thus the Jones Act and the LHWCA are complementary regimes that work in tandem: The Jones Act provides tort remedies to *sea*-based maritime workers, while the LHWCA provides workers' compensation to *land*-based maritime employees. *Ibid.; Swanson v. Marra Bros., Inc.,* 328 U.S. 1, 6-7, 66 S.Ct. 869, 90 L.Ed. 1045 (1946).

Still, discerning the contours of "seaman" status, even with the general maritime law and the LHWCA's language as aids to interpretation, has not been easy. See *Chandris, supra,* at 356, 115 S.Ct. 2172. We began clarifying the definition of "seaman" in a pair of cases, *McDermott Int'l, Inc. v. Wilander, supra,* and *Chandris, supra,* that addressed the relationship a worker must have to a vessel in order to be a "master or member" of its crew. We now turn to the other half of the LHWCA's equation: how to determine whether a watercraft is a "vessel."

A

Just as Congress did not define the term "seaman" in the Jones Act,[1] it did not define the term "vessel" in the LHWCA itself.[2] However, Congress provided a definition elsewhere. At the time of the LHWCA's enactment, §§ 1 and 3 of the Revised Statutes of 1873 specified:

"In determining the meaning of the revised statutes, or of any act or resolution of Congress passed subsequent to February twenty-fifth, eighteen hundred and seventy-one, ... [t]he word 'vessel' includes every description of water-craft or other artificial contrivance used, or capable of being used, as a means of transportation on water."[3] 18 Stat., pt. 1, p. 1.

Sections 1 and 3 show that, because the LHWCA is an Act of Congress passed after February 25, 1871, the LHWCA's use of the term "vessel" "includes every description of water-craft or other artificial contrivance used, or capable of being used, as a means of transportation on water." *Ibid.*

Section 3's definition, repealed and recodified in 1947 as part of the Rules of Construction Act, 1 U.S.C. § 3, has remained virtually unchanged from 1873 to the present.[4] Even now, § 3 continues to supply the default definition of "vessel" throughout the U.S.Code, "unless the context indicates otherwise." 1 U.S.C. § 1. The context surrounding the LHWCA's enactment indicates that § 3 defines the term "vessel" for purposes of the LHWCA.

Section 3 merely codified the meaning that the term "vessel" had acquired in general maritime law. See 1 S. Friedell, Benedict on Admiralty § 165 (rev. 7th ed.2004). In the decades following its enactment, § 3 was regularly used to define the term "vessel" in maritime jurisprudence. Taking only the issue presented here—whether a dredge

---

[1] The Shipping Act of 1916 defines the term "vessel" for purposes of the Jones Act. See 46 U.S.C.App. § 801. However, the provision of the Jones Act at issue here, § 688(a), speaks not of "vessels," but of "seamen." In any event, because we have identified a Jones Act "seaman" with reference to the LHWCA's exclusion, see 33 U.S.C. § 902(3)(G) ("a master or member of a crew of any vessel"), it is the LHWCA's use of the term "vessel" that matters. And, as we explain, the context surrounding Congress' enactment of the LHWCA suggests that Rev. Stat. § 3, now 1 U.S.C. § 3, provides the controlling definition of the term "vessel" in the LHWCA.

[2] As part of its 1972 Amendments to the LHWCA, Congress amended the Act with what appears at first blush to be a definition of the term "vessel": "Unless the context requires otherwise, the term 'vessel' means any vessel upon which or in connection with which any person entitled to benefits under this chapter suffers injury or death arising out of or in the course of his employment, and said vessel's owner, owner pro hac vice, agent, operator, charter or bare boat charterer, master, officer, or crew member." 33 U.S.C. § 902(21). However, Congress enacted this definition in conjunction with the third-party vessel owner provision of § 905(b). Rather than specifying the characteristics of a vessel, § 902(21) instead lists the parties liable for the negligent operation of a vessel. See *McCarthy v. The Bark Peking,* 716 F.2d 130, 133 (C.A.2 1983) (§ 902(21) is "circular" and "does not provide precise guidance as to what is included within the term 'vessel' ").

[3] Congress had used substantially the same definition before, first in an 1866 antismuggling statute, see § 1, 14 Stat. 178, and then in an 1870 statute "provid[ing] for the Relief of sick and disabled Seamen," § 7, 16 Stat. 170.

[4] During the 1947 codification, the hyphen was removed from the word "watercraft." § 3, 61 Stat. 633.

is a vessel—prior to passage of the Jones Act and the LHWCA, courts often used § 3's definition to conclude that dredges were vessels.[5]

From the very beginning, these courts understood the differences between dredges and more traditional seagoing vessels. Though smaller, the dredges at issue in the earliest cases were essentially the same as the *Super Scoop* here. For instance, the court could have been speaking equally of the *Super Scoop* as of *The Alabama* when it declared:

> "The dredge and scows have no means of propulsion of their own except that the dredge, by use of anchors, windlass, and rope, is moved for short distances, as required in carrying on the business of dredging. Both the dredge and the scows are moved from place to place where they may be employed by being towed, and some of the tows have been for long distances and upon the high seas. The dredge and scows are not made for or adapted to the carriage of freight or passengers, and the evidence does not show that, in point of fact, this dredge and scows had ever been so used and employed." *The Alabama*, 19 F. 544, 545 (S.D.Ala.1884).

See also *Huismann v. The Pioneer*, 30 F. 206 (E.D.N.Y.1886). None of this prevented the court from recognizing that dredges are vessels because they are watercraft with "the capacity to be navigated in and upon the waters." *The Alabama, supra,* at 546; see also *The Pioneer, supra,* at 207; *The International,* 89 F. 484, 485 (C.A.3 1898).

This Court also treated dredges as vessels prior to the passage of the Jones Act and the LHWCA. It did so in a pair of cases, first implicitly in *The "Virginia Ehrman" and the "Agnese,"* 97 U.S. 309, 24 L.Ed. 890 (1878), and then explicitly in *Ellis v. United States,* 206 U.S. 246, 27 S.Ct. 600, 51 L.Ed. 1047 (1907). In *Ellis,* this Court considered, *inter alia,* whether workers aboard various dredges and scows were covered by a federal labor law. Just as in the present case, one of the *Ellis* appellants argued that the dredges at issue were "vessels" within the meaning of Rev. Stat. § 3, now 1 U.S.C. § 3. 206 U.S., at 249, 27 S.Ct. 600. The United States responded that dredges were only vessels, if at all, when in actual navigation as they were "towed from port to port." *Id.,* at 253, 27 S.Ct. 600. Citing § 3, Justice Holmes rejected the Government's argument, stating that "[t]he scows and floating dredges were vessels" that "were within the admiralty jurisdiction of the United States." *Id.,* at 259, 27 S.Ct. 600.

These early cases show that at the time Congress enacted the Jones Act and the LHWCA in the 1920's, it was settled that § 3 defined the term "vessel" for purposes of those statutes. It was also settled that a structure's status as a vessel under § 3 depended on whether the structure was a means of maritime transportation. See R. Hughes, Handbook of Admiralty Law § 5, p. 14 (2d ed.1920). For then, as now, dredges served a waterborne transportation function, since in performing their work they carried machinery, equipment, and crew over water. See, *e.g., Butler v. Ellis,* 45 F.2d 951, 955 (C.A.4 1930) (finding the vessel status of dredges "sustained by the overwhelming weight of authority"); *The Hurricane,* 2 F.2d 70, 72 (E.D.Pa.1924) (expressing "no doubt" that dredges are vessels), *aff'd,* 9 F.2d 396 (C.A.3 1925).

This Court's cases have continued to treat § 3 as defining the term "vessel" in the LHWCA, and they have continued to construe § 3's definition in light of the term's established meaning in general maritime law. For instance, in *Norton v. Warner Co.,* 321 U.S. 565, 64 S.Ct. 747, 88 L.Ed. 931 (1944), the Court considered whether a worker on a harbor barge was "a master or member of a crew of any vessel" under the LHWCA, 33 U.S.C. § 902(3)(G). In finding that the "barge [was] a vessel within the meaning of the Act," the Court not only quoted § 3's definition of the term "vessel," but it also cited in support of its holding several earlier cases that had held dredges to be vessels based on the general maritime law. 321 U.S., at 571, and n. 4, 64 S.Ct. 747. This Court therefore confirmed in *Norton* that § 3 defines the term

---

[5] See, *e.g., The Alabama,* 19 F. 544, 546 (S.D.Ala.1884) (dredge was a vessel and subject to maritime liens); *Huismann v. The Pioneer,* 30 F. 206, 207 (E.D.N.Y.1886) (dredge was a vessel under § 3); *Saylor v. Taylor,* 77 F. 476, 477 (C.A.4 1896) (dredge was a vessel under § 3, and its workers were seamen); *The International,* 89 F. 484, 484-485 (C.A.3 1898) (dredge was a vessel under § 3); *Eastern S.S. Corp. v. Great Lakes Dredge & Dock Co.,* 256 F. 497, 500-501 (C.A.1 1919) (type of dredge called a "drillboat" was a vessel under § 3); *Los Angeles v. United Dredging Co.,* 14 F.2d 364, 365-366 (C.A.9 1926) (dredge was a vessel under § 3 and its engineers were seamen).

"vessel" in the LHWCA and that § 3 should be construed consistently with the general maritime law. Since *Norton*, this Court has often said that dredges and comparable watercraft qualify as vessels under the Jones Act and the LHWCA.[6]

B

Despite this Court's reliance on § 3 in cases like *Ellis* and *Norton*, Dutra argues that the Court has implicitly narrowed § 3's definition. Section 3 says that a "vessel" must be "used, or capable of being used, as a means of transportation on water." 18 Stat., pt. 1, p. 1. In a pair of cases, the Court held that a drydock, *Cope v. Vallette Dry-Dock Co.*, 119 U.S. 625, 630, 7 S.Ct. 336, 30 L.Ed. 501 (1887), and a wharfboat attached to the mainland, *Evansville & Bowling Green Packet Co. v. Chero Cola Bottling Co.*, 271 U.S. 19, 22, 46 S.Ct. 379, 70 L.Ed. 805 (1926), were not vessels under § 3, because they were not *practically* capable of being used to transport people, freight, or cargo from place to place. According to Dutra, *Cope* and *Evansville* adopted a definition of "vessel" narrower than § 3's text.

Dutra misreads *Cope* and *Evansville*. In *Cope*, the plaintiff sought a salvage award for having prevented a drydock from sinking after a steamship collided with it. 119 U.S., at 625-626, 7 S.Ct. 336. At the time of the accident, the drydock, a floating dock used for repairing vessels, was "moored and lying at [the] usual place" it had occupied for the past 20 years. *Id.*, at 626, 7 S.Ct. 336. In those circumstances, the drydock was a "fixed structure" that had been "permanently moored," rather than a vessel that had been temporarily anchored. *Id.*, at 627, 7 S.Ct. 336. *Evansville* involved a wharfboat secured by cables to the mainland. Local water, electricity, and telephone lines all ran from shore to the wharfboat, evincing a "permanent location." 271 U.S., at 22, 46 S.Ct. 379. And the wharfboat, like the drydock in *Cope*, was neither "taken from place to place" nor "used to carry freight from one place to another." 271 U.S., at 22, 46 S.Ct. 379. As in *Cope*, the Court concluded that the wharfboat "was not practically capable of being used as a means of transportation." 271 U.S., at 22, 46 S.Ct. 379.

Cope and *Evansville* did no more than construe § 3 in light of the distinction drawn by the general maritime law between watercraft temporarily stationed in a particular location and those permanently affixed to shore or resting on the ocean floor. See, *e.g.*, *The Alabama*, 19 F., at 546 (noting that vessels possess "mobility and [the] capacity to navigate," as distinct from fixed structures like wharves, drydocks, and bridges). Simply put, a watercraft is not "capable of being used" for maritime transport in any meaningful sense if it has been permanently moored or otherwise rendered practically incapable of transportation or movement.

This distinction is sensible: A ship and its crew do not move in and out of Jones Act coverage depending on whether the ship is at anchor, docked for loading or unloading, or berthed for minor repairs, in the same way that ships taken permanently out of the water as a practical matter do not remain vessels merely because of the remote possibility that they may one day sail again. See *Pavone v. Mississippi Riverboat Amusement Corp.*, 52 F.3d 560, 570 (C.A.5 1995) (floating casino was no longer a vessel where it "was moored to the shore in a semi-permanent or indefinite manner"); *Kathriner v. UNISEA, Inc.*, 975 F.2d 657, 660 (C.A.9 1992) (floating processing plant was no longer a vessel where a "large opening [had been] cut into her hull," rendering her incapable of moving over the water). Even if the general maritime law had not informed the meaning of § 3, its definition would not sweep within its reach an array of fixed structures not commonly thought of as capable of being used for water transport. See, *e.g.*, *Leocal v. Ashcroft*, 543 U.S. —, —, 125 S.Ct. 377, 382, 160 L.Ed.2d 271 (2004) ("When interpreting a statute, we must give words their 'ordinary or natural' meaning" (quoting *Smith v. United States*, 508 U.S. 223, 228, 113 S.Ct. 2050, 124 L.Ed.2d 138 (1993))).

---

[6] See, *e.g.*, *Jerome B. Grubart, Inc. v. Great Lakes Dredge & Dock Co.*, 513 U.S. 527, 535, and n. 1, 115 S.Ct. 1043, 130 L.Ed.2d 1024 (1995) (indicating that a stationary crane barge was a "vessel" under the Extension of Admiralty Jurisdiction Act); *Southwest Marine, Inc. v. Gizoni*, 502 U.S. 81, 92, 112 S.Ct. 486, 116 L.Ed.2d 405 (1991) (holding that a jury could reasonably find that floating platforms were "vessels in navigation" under the Jones Act); *Jones & Laughlin Steel Corp. v. Pfeifer*, 462 U.S. 523, 528-530, 103 S.Ct. 2541, 76 L.Ed.2d 768 (1983) (treating coal barge as a "vessel" under the LHWCA, 33 U.S.C. § 905(b)); cf. *Senko v. LaCrosse Dredging Corp.*, 352 U.S. 370, 372, 77 S.Ct. 415, 1 L.Ed.2d 404 (1957) (assuming that a dredge was a Jones Act vessel); *id.*, at 375, n. 1, 77 S.Ct. 415 (Harlan, J., dissenting) (same).

Applying § 3 brings within the purview of the Jones Act the sorts of watercraft considered vessels at the time Congress passed the Act. By including special-purpose vessels like dredges, § 3 sweeps broadly, but the other prerequisites to qualifying for seaman status under the Jones Act provide some limits, notwithstanding § 3's breadth. A maritime worker seeking Jones Act seaman status must also prove that his duties contributed to the vessel's function or mission, and that his connection to the vessel was substantial both in nature and duration. *Chandris,* 515 U.S., at 376, 115 S.Ct. 2172. Thus, even though the *Super Scoop* is a "vessel," workers injured aboard the *Super Scoop* are eligible for seaman status only if they are "master[s] or member[s]" of its crew.

C

The Court of Appeals, relying on its previous en banc decision in *DiGiovanni v. Traylor Brothers, Inc.,* 959 F.2d 1119 (1ˢᵗ Cir. 1992), held that the *Super Scoop* is not a "vessel," because its primary purpose is not navigation or commerce and because it was not in actual transit at the time of Stewart's injury. 230 F.3d, at 468-469. Neither prong of the Court of Appeals' test is consistent with the text of § 3 or the established meaning of the term "vessel" in general maritime law.

Section 3 requires only that a watercraft be "used, or capable of being used, as a means of transportation on water" to qualify as a vessel. It does not require that a watercraft be used *primarily* for that purpose. See *The Alabama, supra,* at 546; *The International,* 89 F., at 485. As the Court of Appeals recognized, the *Super Scoop's* "function was to move through Boston Harbor, ... digging the ocean bottom as it moved." 343 F.3d, at 12. In other words, the *Super Scoop* was not only "capable of being used" to transport equipment and workers over water—it *was* used to transport those things. Indeed, it could not have dug the Ted Williams Tunnel had it been unable to traverse the Boston Harbor, carrying with it workers like Stewart.

Also, a watercraft need not be in motion to qualify as a vessel under § 3. Looking to whether a watercraft is motionless or moving is the sort of "snapshot" test that we rejected in *Chandris.* Just as a worker does not "oscillate back and forth between Jones Act coverage and other remedies depending on the activity in which the worker was engaged while injured," *Chandris,* 515 U.S., at 363, 115 S.Ct. 2172, neither does a watercraft pass in and out of Jones Act coverage depending on whether it was moving at the time of the accident.

Granted, the Court has sometimes spoken of the requirement that a vessel be "in navigation," *id.,* at 373-374, 115 S.Ct. 2172, but never to indicate that a structure's locomotion at any given moment mattered. Rather, the point was that structures may lose their character as vessels if they have been withdrawn from the water for extended periods of time. *Ibid.; Roper v. United States,* 368 U.S. 20, 21, 23, 82 S.Ct. 5, 7 L.Ed.2d 1 (1961); *West v. United States,* 361 U.S. 118, 122, 80 S.Ct. 189, 4 L.Ed.2d 161 (1959). The Court did not mean that the "in navigation" requirement stood apart from § 3, such that a "vessel" for purposes of § 3 might nevertheless not be a "vessel in navigation" for purposes of the Jones Act or the LHWCA. See, *e.g., United States v. Templeton,* 378 F.3d 845, 851 (C.A.8 2004) ("[T]he definition of 'vessel in navigation' under the Jones Act is not as expansive as the general definition of 'vessel' " (citations omitted)).

Instead, the "in navigation" requirement is an element of the vessel status of a watercraft. It is relevant to whether the craft is "used, or capable of being used" for maritime transportation. A ship long lodged in a drydock or shipyard can again be put to sea, no less than one permanently moored to shore or the ocean floor can be cut loose and made to sail. The question remains in all cases whether the watercraft's use "as a means of transportation on water" is a practical possibility or merely a theoretical one. *Supra,* at — - — 11-12. In some cases that inquiry may involve factual issues for the jury, *Chandris, supra,* at 373, 115 S.Ct. 2172, but here no relevant facts were in dispute. Dutra conceded that the *Super Scoop* was only temporarily stationary while Stewart and others were repairing the scow; the *Super Scoop* had not been taken out of service, permanently anchored, or otherwise rendered practically incapable of maritime transport.

Finally, although Dutra argues that the *Super Scoop* is not a "vessel" under § 902(3)(G), which is the LHWCA provision that excludes seamen from the Act's coverage, Dutra conceded below that the *Super Scoop is* a "vessel" under § 905(b), which is the LHWCA provision that imposes liability on vessel owners for negligence to longshoremen. The concession was necessary because the Court of Appeals had previously held that § 905(b)'s use of the term "vessel" is " 'significantly more inclusive than that used for evaluating seaman status under the Jones Act.' " 343 F.3d, at 13 (quoting *Morehead v. Atkinson-Kiewit,* 97 F.3d, at 607). The Court of Appeals' approach is no longer tenable. The LHWCA does not meaningfully define the term "vessel" as it appears in either § 902(3)(G) or § 905(b), see n. 2, *supra,* and 1 U.S.C. § 3 defines the term "vessel" throughout the LHWCA.

III

At the time that Congress enacted the LHWCA and since, Rev. Stat. § 3, now 1 U.S.C. § 3, has defined the term "vessel" in the LHWCA. Under § 3, a "vessel" is any watercraft practically capable of maritime transportation, regardless of its primary purpose or state of transit at a particular moment. Because the *Super Scoop* was engaged in maritime transportation at the time of Stewart's injury, it was a vessel within the meaning of 1 U.S.C. § 3. Despite the seeming incongruity of grouping dredges alongside more traditional seafaring vessels under the maritime statutes, Congress and the courts have long done precisely that:

> "[I]t seems a stretch of the imagination to class the deck hands of a mud dredge in the quiet waters of a Potomac creek with the bold and skillful mariners who breast the angry waves of the Atlantic; but such and so far-reaching are the principles which underlie the jurisdiction of the courts of admiralty that they adapt themselves to all the new kinds of property and new sets of operatives and new conditions which are brought into existence in the progress of the world." *Saylor v. Taylor,* 77 F. 476, 479 (C.A.4 1896).

The judgment of the Court of Appeals is reversed, and the case is remanded for further proceedings consistent with this opinion.

It is so ordered.

THE CHIEF JUSTICE took no part in the decision of this case.

Notes

1. *Pre-Dutra cases*

Before *Stewart v. Dutra Construction Co., supra,* the broad definition of "vessel" in 1 U.S.C. § 3 was applied to actions for recovery under the Jones Act and quite a few special purpose structures have been found to be vessels. *See Colomb v. Texaco,* 736 F.2d 218 (5th Cir. 1984) (a submersible drilling barge); *Hicks v. ODECO,* 512 F. 2d 817, 1975 AMC 1378 (5th Cir. 1975) (a submersible oil storage facility); *Marathon Pipe Line Co. v. Drilling Rig ROWAN/ODESSA,* 761 F.2d 229, 1986 AMC 2343 (5th Cir. 1985) (a jack-up rig). Certain courts, however, sought to narrow this definition. *See Bernard v. Binnings Constr. Co., Inc.,* 741 F.2d 824, 1985 AMC 784 (5th Cir. 1984) (finding a work punt not to be a vessel); *Barger Petroleum Helicopters, Inc.,* 692 F.2d 337, 1983 AMC 2854 (5th Cir. 1982) (holding that a helicopter, though equipped with floaters and serving in the Gulf of Mexico, is not a vessel for Jones Act purposes); *Cook v. Beldon Concrete Products, Inc.,* 472 F.2d 999, 1973 AMC 285 (5th Cir. 1973) (finding that a floating construction platform was not a vessel).

In *Manuel v. P.A.W. Drilling & Well Service, Inc.,* 135 F.3d 344, 1998 AMC 1390 (5th Cir. 1998), the court engaged in an extensive examination of the prior jurisprudence, contrasting "special purpose vessel" cases with "work platform" cases. The Fifth Circuit view was that vessels were required to have some transportation function or at least be in navigation at the time of injury. *Michel v. Total Transportation, Inc.,* 957 F.2d 186, 189, 1993 AMC 2406 (5th Cir. 1992), 1993 AMC 2406 and *Manuel v. P.A.W. Drilling & Well Service, Inc.,* 135 F.3d 344, 1998 AMC 1390 (5th Cir. 1998). In contrast, the Ninth Circuit in *Gizoni v. Southwest Marine Incorporated,* 56 F.3d 1138, 1995 AMC 2093 (9th Cir.), *cert. denied,* 516 U.S. 944, 116 S. Ct. 381 (1995) held that "unusual-looking crafts whose purpose is not the transportation of persons or things can be considered vessels under the Jones Act".

2. *Transportation Function*

In *Fields v. Pool Offshore, Inc.,* 182 F.3d 353, 357-59 (5th Cir. 1999), the Fifth Circuit elaborated further on its approach to the work platform issue.

Courts have long recognized a distinction between "work platforms" that are designed for primarily stationary residence and true vessels. . . Looking to the language of the statute, we have consistently defined vessel status in reference to the importance of transportation as the craft's purpose. . . . In particular, we have focused on three factors when trying to determine whether a structure is a work platform beyond the realm of the Jones Act. First, we ask whether the structure was constructed to serve primarily as a work platform. Second, we look to whether or not the structure was moored or otherwise secured at the time of the accident. Lastly, we attempt to ascertain whether the transportation function of the structure went beyond theoretical mobility and occasional incidental movement. . . .

In applying the three-factor test of work-platform status to the Neptune Spar, it becomes apparent that it cannot be a vessel. As the defendants' affidavits indicated, there are no plans to even consider moving the Neptune Spar until the current field is exhausted. While nothing can ever be certain in the petroleum industry, the unchallenged prediction of defendants is that the field will remain productive for the next fifteen years. This distinguishes the Neptune Spar from the types of specialized mobile drilling craft that we have previously classified as vessels. As we have taken care to point out, while such drilling craft may stay on a particular site, they always move on to the next location when their work is done. *See Manuel,* 135 F.3d at 346 (noting that drilling vessel had been deployed at nineteen different sites over the course of two years); *Colomb v. Texaco, Inc.,* 736 F.2d 218, 221 (5th Cir. 1984) ("highly mobile" submersible drilling barge was "routinely" refloated and moved to the next location). *See also Blanchard v. Engine and Gas Compressor Services, Inc.,* 575 F.2d 1140, 1143 (5th Cir. 1978) (distinguishing work platform from drilling barge rigs because there was no intention to move structures "on a regular basis, as is done with submersible drilling rigs"). Unlike these vessels, the Neptune Spar is designed not only to discover and open a field, but also to exploit it—a goal that requires considerably greater commitment to a particular location. Given these undisputed facts, it would seem readily apparent that the primary, indeed only, purpose of the Neptune Spar is to serve as a work platform in a specific, fixed location for the foreseeable future.

The work platform status of the Neptune Spar is reinforced by reference to the second factor. The Neptune Spar was not only secured to the ocean floor at the time of the accident, it was secured using an elaborate system that guarantees movement will be a difficult and expensive undertaking. We are not talking about a case in which a structure merely rests on the bottom or is secured by a run-of-the-mill anchor. Here, the defendants have at presumably considerable expense sunk massive (180 foot) pilings into the ocean floor, and attached the spar to these pilings by means of similarly impressive chain lines. And like its sibling conventional fixed production platforms, the Neptune Spar is further anchored in position by the underwater infrastructure of extraction and exportation pipes that transport the petroleum from wellhead to the platform and from the platform to the shore. In this case, the infrastructure consists of two eight-inch pipelines and seven nine-and-a-half- inch casing risers. This distinguishes it from other structures whose commitment to a particular location is less firmly evidenced by the strength of their physical attachment. *Cf. Hicks v. Ocean Drilling and Exploration Co.,* 512 F.2d 817, 823-24 (5th Cir. 1975) (evidence sufficient to sustain jury finding that submersible petroleum storage barge sunk to the bottom and then connected to nearby platform by pipe and catwalk, but not in any way affixed into seabed, was a vessel) with *Blanchard,* 575 F.2d at 1143 (5th Cir. 1978) (compressor building mounted on submersible barge was distinguishable from structure in *Hicks* because barge was anchored with steel cables attached to fixed pilings); *Hemba v. Freeport McMoran Energy Partners, Ltd.,* 811 F.2d 276, 278 (5th Cir. 1987) (rig attached by pilings driven two hundred feet into the seabed was not a vessel).

Any lingering doubt would seemingly be eradicated by examination of the third factor. While the Neptune Spar remains in its current position, it will have extremely limited and purely incidental mobility. According to the defendants' unchallenged affidavits, the Neptune Spar can be moved by tightening and slackening the chain lines connected to the pilings. This procedure is used to place the structure over one of the site's seven closely packed wellheads to perform needed work. Because of the location of the pilings, however, this movement is limited to 250 feet in any direction. This tightly-constrained range of motion is not inconsistent with work platform status. *See Burchett,* 48 F.3d at 177-78 (loading barge was a work platform despite the fact it was regularly moved to align itself with boat receiving goods); *Cook v. Belden Concrete Products, Inc.,* 472 F.2d 999, 1002 (5th Cir. 1973) (construction barge that was regularly towed into open water to launch completed craft was not a vessel). While there remains some theoretical possibility of more lengthy movement when the current field is exhausted, the mere possibility of movement so many years hence cannot render irrelevant the structure's current and long-term immobility. [some citations omitted.]

3. Oceanographic Research Vessel

The Oceanographic Research Vessels Act (formerly 46 U.S.C. app. § 444) provided that scientific personnel on oceanographic research vessels shall not be considered seamen under the provisions of the merchant seamen statutes. This section was removed because scientific personnel are excluded from the definition of "seamen" by operation of 46 U.S.C.A. § 10101(3). In *Presley v. Carribean Seal,* 709 F.2d 406, 1984 AMC 2307 (5th Cir. 1983), 1984 AMC 2307, the court held that the Oceanographic Research Vessels Act did not prevent plaintiff, a member of the scientific personnel of an oceanographic vessel, from being considered a seaman under the general maritime law but the Act prevented him from being considered a seaman under the provisions of the Jones Act. *Cf., Sennet v. Shell Oil Co.,* 325 F. Supp. 1, 1972 AMC 1346 (E.D. La. 1971).

4. *Gambling Structures*

Many different kinds of structures are currently placed in navigable waters to function as gambling casinos. Some of these structures regularly sail on gambling cruises, others never sail and some sail only infrequently or sporadically. Furthermore, some of these structures are incapable of independent movement in the water and some may not be capable of moving even with the assistance of a vessel. The issue as to whether or not these structures are "vessels" is discussed in *Pavone v. Miss. Riverboat Amusement Corp.*, 52 F.3d 560, 1995 AMC 2038 (5th Cir. 1995). The recent trend has been to hold that permanently moored riverboat casinos are not "vessels in navigation" for the purposes of the Jones Act, even if they were originally built as vessels and are capable of sailing. *Martin v. Boyd Gaming Corp.*, 374 F.3d 375, 2004 AMC 1944 (5th Cir. 2004); *Howard v. Southern Ill. Riverboat Casino Cruises, Inc.*, 364 F.3d 854, 2004 AMC 956 (7th Cir. 2004); *De La Rosa v. St. Charles Gaming Co.*, 474 F.3d 185, 2006 AMC 2997 (5th Cir. 2006).

---

d. *"In the Course of His Employment"*

HOPSON v. TEXACO, INC.

383 U.S. 262, 86 S. Ct. 756, 15 L. Ed. 2d 740, 1966 AMC 281 (1966)

Per Curiam

These actions were brought under the Jones Act, as amended (41 Stat. 1007, 46 U.S.C. § 688 (1964 ed.)), to recover damages for injuries sustained by one seaman, and for the death of another, as a result of an automobile accident on the island of Trinidad. Judgment on the jury's verdict was entered in United States District Court in favor of the plaintiffs, but the Court of Appeals reversed. 351 F.2d 415. We grant the petition for a writ of certiorari and reverse.

The facts are not in dispute. The two seamen were members of the crew of respondent's tanker which was docked at respondent's refinery at Pointe-a-Pierre on the island of Trinidad. Both fell ill and it was determined that they would be unable to continue the voyage. In order to discharge an incapacitated seaman in a foreign port, federal law requires that he be taken to a United States Consul where arrangements for his return to the United States can be made. The United States Consul's Office was located in Port of Spain, some 38 miles distant. Although respondent had a fleet of motor vehicles used for transportation in the immediate vicinity of the refinery and docking area, its practice was to utilize either of two local taxi companies for journeys to more distant points. The ship's Master procured one of these cabs which set out for Port of Spain with the two ill seamen. En route, the taxi collided with a truck, killing the Master and one of the seamen; the other seaman was seriously injured. The jury found that the taxi driver had been negligent—a finding challenged neither in the Court of Appeals nor here. The Court of Appeals reversed the District Court's determination that respondent is liable to petitioners for this negligence of the taxi operator.

The Jones Act incorporates the standards of the Federal Employers' Liability Act, as amended, which renders an employer liable for the injuries negligently inflicted on its employees by its "officers, agents, or employees." We noted in *Sinkler v. Missouri Pac. R. Co.*, 356 U.S. 326, that the latter Act was "an avowed departure from the rules of the common law" (*id.*, at 329), which, recognizing "[t]he cost of human injury, an inescapable expense of railroading," undertook to "adjust that expense equitably between the worker and the carrier." *Ibid.* In order to give "an accommodating scope ... to the word 'agents'" (*id.*, at 330-331), we concluded that "when [an] ... employee's injury is caused in whole or in part by the fault of others performing, under contract, operational activities of his employer, such others are 'agents' of the employer within the meaning of § 1 of FELA." (*Id.*, at 331-332).

We think those principles apply with equal force here. These seamen were in the service of the ship and the ill-fated journey to Port of Spain was a vital part of the ship's total operations. The ship could not sail with these two men, nor could it lawfully discharge them without taking them to the United States Consul. Indeed, to have abandoned them would have breached the statutory duty to arrange for their return to the United States. Getting these two ill seamen to the United States Consul's office was, therefore, the duty of respondent. And it was respondent—not the seamen—which selected, as it had done many times before, the taxi service. Respondent—the law says—should bear the responsibility for the negligence of the driver which it chose. This is so because, as we said in *Sinkler*, "justice demands that one who gives his labor to the furtherance of the enterprise should be assured that all combining their exertions with him in the common pursuit will conduct themselves in all respects with sufficient care that his safety while doing his part will not be endangered." 356 U.S., at 330.

Reversed.

Note

When does the Jones Act coverage commence? When the seaman signs a contract of employment? When he reports for service on board the ship? When he signs articles and commences to serve? Does it make any difference if the master has the right to reject the seaman? What if the employer furnishes transportation to the seaman from his home city to the ship? *See Vincent v. Harvey Well Service*, 441 F.2d 146, 1971 AMC 2541 (5th Cir. 1971).

In *Mounteer v. Marine Transport Lines, Inc.*, 463 F. Supp. 715, 1979 AMC 313 (S.D.N.Y. 1979), plaintiff, a Third Assistant Marine Engineer, was being transported from Cairo to Port Said, Egypt, at the expense of the defendant, to serve on defendant's vessel. Plaintiff was injured in an accident caused by the negligence of the taxi driver who was driving plaintiff across the desert. Plaintiff brought a Jones Act claim for his injuries, loss of wages and maintenance and cure. Defendant argued that the plaintiff was not "in the service of the vessel," because his employment with the defendant had not yet begun. Relying on the Supreme Court's decision in *Hopson v. Texaco*, the court held that the defendant's transportation of the plaintiff across the Egyptian desert to join its stranded vessel (which could not leave port without the plaintiff on board) was for the service of the vessel from the defendant's standpoint.

---

2. Standard of Care and Causation

GAUTREAUX v. SCURLOCK MARINE, INC.

107 F.3d 331, 1997 AMC 1521 (5th Cir. 1997)

DUHE, Circuit Judge:

Defendant-Appellant Scurlock Marine, Inc. moves this En Banc Court to consider whether seamen, in Jones Act negligence cases, are bound to a standard of ordinary prudence in the exercise of care for their own safety, or whether they are bound to a lesser duty of slight care. On appeal to a panel of this Court, Scurlock Marine had assigned as error, *inter alia*, the district court's instructions to the jury charging that seamen were bound only to a duty of slight care for their own safety. The panel denied Scurlock Marine relief on this point because the jury instructions were consistent with what the panel considered was the settled law of this Circuit. *Gautreaux v. Scurlock Marine, Inc.*, 84 F.3d 776, 780-81 (5th Cir.1996). A review of our Jones Act case law reveals, however, that this "settled law" obtains from doubtful parentage. We thus now overrule cases contrary to the principles embraced in this opinion and AFFIRM in part, VACATE in part and REMAND for further proceedings as to comparative fault consistent with our decision today.

Background

Archie Scurlock, as President and owner of Scurlock Marine, Inc., ("Scurlock Marine") purchased the M/V BROOKE LYNN in May, 1993, and retained Lance Orgeron as her first and permanent captain. Scurlock hired Charles Gautreaux as the BROOKE LYNN's relief captain in October, 1993. Gautreaux was qualified for the position, having worked as a tanker man since the early 1980s and having recently earned a United States Coast Guard master's license.

The BROOKE LYNN is a standard inland push boat, equipped with two towing winches on her bow, which are used to secure lines joining the BROOKE LYNN to the barges in her tow. The starboard side winch is hydraulic, and the port side winch is electric. Upon being hired, Gautreaux was taken to the BROOKE LYNN and instructed on her operation by Archie Scurlock. Orgeron took Gautreaux on a tour of the vessel, showing him her layout and familiarizing him with her equipment. Orgeron showed Gautreaux the manual crank handle that accompanied the port side electric winch and told him that it was to be used to override the electric switches on the winch if they failed. Orgeron explained that, if the winch became "bound up" and failed to engage by use of the electric ignition switch, the manual crank should be attached to the winch motor and turned a few times to "unbind" the winch, and then the electric ignition switch should be used to try to engage the winch. Neither Scurlock nor Orgeron told Gautreaux that if he needed to use the manual crank handle to unbind the winch, he should not leave it on the winch motor when attempting to engage the winch by use of the electric ignition switch.

About four months after he was hired, Gautreaux, serving as captain of the BROOKE LYNN, relieved the tanker man on duty and began off loading of the barge in tow. As the barge discharged its cargo, it began to rise in the water, eventually causing the towing wires to become taut. Noticing this, Gautreaux attempted to relieve the tension in the wires by unwinding them from the winches. He released the starboard wire first, which caused that side of the BROOKE LYNN to drop and the port side towing wire to become even tighter. Gautreaux then attempted to release the port side wire, but the electric winch would not work. He attached the manual crank to the winch motor, and began turning the crank while simultaneously pressing the electric ignition switch. When the motor started, the manual crank handle flew off and struck Gautreaux on the right side of his face, crushing his right eye and inflicting other severe injuries.

Gautreaux sued Scurlock Marine, alleging that his injuries were caused by its negligence and the unseaworthiness of the BROOKE LYNN. Gautreaux's primary complaint was that Scurlock Marine failed to properly train him in the use and operation of the electric towing winch and its manual crank handle, thereby not providing him a safe place to work. Scurlock Marine answered and sought exoneration from or limitation of its liability. After a two-day trial, the jury returned a verdict in favor of Gautreaux on his Jones Act negligence claim, but found the BROOKE LYNN seaworthy. The jury apportioned fault 95% to Scurlock Marine and 5% to Gautreaux and awarded a total of $854,000 in damages.

* * *

On appeal to this Court, Scurlock Marine argued, *inter alia*, that in its instructions regarding contributory negligence, the district court erred by charging the jury that a Jones Act seaman need exercise only "slight care" for his own safety. Scurlock Marine maintained that the standard to which Gautreaux, and all seamen, should be held is that of a reasonably prudent person exercising ordinary or due care under like circumstances. Accordingly, Scurlock Marine urged this Court to abandon the slight care standard in Jones Act cases, contending the standard "has evolved from this Court's blind adherence to an incorrect statement of the law." *Gautreaux*, 84 F.3d at 781 n. 7. The panel acknowledged that the viability of the slight care standard has recently been questioned but considered it the settled law of this Circuit. It thus refused to hold that the district court erred in giving the "slight care" instruction, noting that "settled law of this Circuit, such as the slight care standard in a Jones Act case, can only be changed, absent action by the United States Supreme Court, by this Court sitting en banc." *Id.* The panel accordingly affirmed the district court's judgment and this en banc rehearing followed.

* * *

Discussion

The district court's instruction, consistent with the Fifth Circuit's Pattern Jury Instructions, informed the jurors that "[i]n determining whether the plaintiff was contributorily negligent, you must bear in mind that a Jones Act seaman does not have a duty to use ordinary care under the circumstances for his own safety. A Jones Act seaman is obliged to exercise only slight care under the circumstances for his own safety at the time of the accident." Scurlock Marine asserts that this charge is defective, maintaining that historically, Jones Act seamen had been expressly bound to a standard of ordinary prudence under like circumstances. In support of its contention, Scurlock Marine cites early Supreme Court opinions to illustrate that the phrase "slight negligence" or "slight care" stood not for the duty of care owed by employers and employees, as the phrase is now understood, but for that quantum of evidence necessary to sustain a jury verdict on review. The duty of care owed by both parties, Scurlock Marine contends, had always been, and should remain, that of the reasonable person.

We acknowledge there is much confusion in this Circuit as to the proper standard of care by which juries should measure a plaintiff's duty under the Jones Act to protect himself. While some courts have instructed juries that a plaintiff's duty is only one of slight care, as did the district court in the instant case, others charge that the duty is one of ordinary prudence. Admittedly, this Court has been less than clear in its articulation of the proper standard of care to which seamen are bound. We granted this *en banc* rehearing to eliminate the uncertainty and to consider returning, as Scurlock Marine requests, to the reasonable person standard.

A. The Development of the Slight Care, or Slight Negligence, Standard

The language chosen by Congress to determine the responsibility of both employers and employees under the Jones Act is simple and direct. Nothing in the statute indicates Congress's intention to hold Jones Act employees to a standard of slight duty of care in the exercise of concern for their own safety. Below, we explain the statutory scheme and Supreme Court precedent interpreting it before we illustrate our departure from their clear mandates.

1. The Statutory Scheme and Supreme Court Precedent

Under the Jones Act, seamen are afforded rights parallel to those of railway employees under the Federal Employers' Liability Act ("FELA"). 46 U.S.C. § 688. Section 51 of the FELA provides, in pertinent part, that "[e]very common carrier by railroad ... shall be liable in damages ... for such injury or death *resulting in whole or in part* from the negligence of any of the officers, agents, or employees of such carrier." 45 U.S.C. § 51 (emphasis added). A seaman is entitled to recovery under the Jones Act, therefore, if his employer's negligence is the cause, in whole or in part, of his injury. In their earlier articulations of § 51 liability, courts had replaced the phrase "in whole or in part" with the adjective "slightest." In *Rogers v. Missouri Pacific R. Co.*, 352 U.S. 500, 506, 77 S.Ct. 443, 448, 1 L.Ed.2d 493 (1957), the Supreme Court used the term "slightest" to describe the reduced standard of causation between the employer's negligence and the employee's injury in FELA § 51 cases. In *Ferguson v. Moore-McCormack Lines, Inc.*, 352 U.S. 521, 523, 77 S.Ct. 457, 458, 1 L.Ed.2d 511 (1957), the Court applied the same standard to a Jones Act case, writing, "'Under this statute the test of a jury case is simply whether the proofs justify with reason the conclusion that employer negligence played any part, even the slightest, in producing the injury or death for which damages are sought.'" (quoting *Rogers*, 352 U.S. at 506, 77 S.Ct. at 448).

Nothing in these cases, then, supports the proposition that the duty of care owed is slight. Rather, the phrase "in whole or in part" as set forth in the statute, or, as it has come to be known, "slightest," modifies only the causation prong of the inquiry. The phrase does not also modify the word "negligence." The duty of care owed, therefore, under normal rules of statutory construction, retains the usual and familiar definition of ordinary prudence. See *Texas Food Indus. Assoc. v. United States Dept. of Agriculture*, 81 F.3d 578, 582 (5th Cir.1996) (stating it is a "cardinal canon of statutory construction ... that [in interpreting a statute,] the words of a statute will be given their plain meaning").

Despite the clarity of the Supreme Court's decisions, the word "slightest," used initially to refer to the quantum of evidence of an employer's breach of duty necessary to sustain a jury verdict, soon took on a different referent. Once the Supreme Court had reduced the statutory language "in whole or in part" to "any part, even the slightest," it was not long before our court further reduced the phrase "any part, even the slightest" to a shorthand expression of "slight negligence" or "slight evidence of negligence." Thereafter we used the phrase "slight negligence" uncritically. Justice Frankfurter's comment on the (mis)use of the phrase "assumption of the risk" in FELA actions aptly applies to our discussion today: "A phrase begins life as a literary expression; its felicity leads to its lazy repetition; and repetition soon establishes it as a legal formula, undiscriminatingly used to express different and sometimes contradictory ideas." *Tiller v. Atlantic Coast Line R. Co.*, 318 U.S. 54, 68, 63 S.Ct. 444, 452, 87 L.Ed. 610 (1943) (Frankfurter, J., concurring). The same holds true of our use of the phrase "slight negligence" or "slight care" in Jones Act negligence cases.

Guided by the Supreme Court, we initially employed the phrase "slight negligence" as a shorthand expression for the standard by which we measure, in our review of a jury verdict, the sufficiency of evidence to establish a causal link between an employer's negligence and a seaman's injury. Significantly, an employer's duty of care always remained that of *ordinary* negligence. Soon, however, we began using the phrase "slight negligence" to refer not only to the sufficiency of the evidence inquiry but also to that duty of care Jones Act employers owed to their employees. A plaintiff, therefore, could now reach the jury not only with "slight evidence" of his employer's negligence, but also with slight evidence of his employer having been only "slightly negligent." Once we had characterized the phrase "slight negligence" as shorthand to depict a duty of care owed by an employer to its employee, it was not long before we also used the phrase to represent the plaintiff's duty of care to protect himself from work-related injuries. We did so by rephrasing "slight negligence" to "slight care."

Historically, then, Jones Act employers and seamen were expressly bound to a standard of ordinary prudence; when the phrase "slight negligence" came to stand for the duty of care owed by employers and employees, however, employers were understood to be held to a higher degree of personal responsibility as to their employees, and plaintiff-seamen were understood to be held to a lower degree of personal responsibility for themselves. We hold that the historical interpretation always should have been, and should now be, applied in this Circuit. We offer the following survey of our case law, however, to illustrate just how we devolved from the Supreme Court's pronouncements in *Rogers* and *Ferguson* to our "settled law" today.

2. Our Departure from the Standard of Reasonable Care

In *Page v. St. Louis Southwestern Railway Co.*, 349 F.2d 820, 823 (5th Cir.1965), we kept the standards for determining duty of care and causation distinct when we clarified that in FELA cases, the traditional standard for determining negligence applied:

> As to both attack or defense, there are two common elements, (1) negligence, i.e., the standard of care, and (2) causation, i.e., the relation of the negligence to the injury. So far as negligence is concerned, that standard is the same—ordinary prudence—for both Employee and Railroad alike.

In *Boeing Co. v. Shipman*, 411 F.2d 365 (5th Cir.1969) (en banc), however, the standards became more nebulous. We misinterpreted *Rogers*'s "any part, even the slightest" language to refer not to the evidence necessary to support a jury verdict, but to an employer's duty of care. We concluded that "[s]light negligence, necessary to support an [sic] FELA action, is defined as 'a failure to exercise *great* care,' and that burden of proof, obviously, is much less than the burden required to sustain recovery in ordinary negligence actions." *Id.* at 371. Thus, in *Boeing*, we broadened the scope of a FELA—and by implication Jones Act—action insofar as we exposed employers to a higher degree of care and thus more liability than they otherwise would be exposed to in ordinary negligence actions.

In the following years, we vacillated considerably in our pronunciations of the proper standard of care.

* * *

B. Ordinary Prudence

The above survey of our decisions shows the confused start and the diverted path leading to the "settled law" in this Circuit that a Jones Act employer is bound by a greater-than-ordinary standard of care towards its employees and that a seaman owes only a slight duty to look after his own safety. We agree with the Third Circuit that nothing in the text or structure of the FELA-Jones Act legislation suggests that the standard of care to be attributed to either an employer or an employee is anything different than ordinary prudence under the circumstances. *Fashauer v. New Jersey Transit Rail Operations, Inc.*, 57 F.3d 1269, 1283 (3d Cir.1995). In addressing a seaman's duty to act with reasonable care, the Third Circuit reasoned:

> By its very terms, the FELA provides that "the damages shall be diminished by the jury in proportion to the amount of negligence attributable to such employee." 45 U.S.C. § 53. The statute does not distinguish between degrees of negligence; the statute does not say that the plaintiff only has a slight duty of care. Under the statute, a plaintiff's recovery is reduced to the extent that he is negligent and that such negligence is responsible for the injury. In such a situation, one must assume that Congress intended its words to mean what they ordinarily are

taken to mean—a person is negligent if he or she fails to act as an ordinarily prudent person would act in similar circumstances. Such a reading also is in accord with the FELA's pure comparative negligence scheme; and to adopt [plaintiff's] argument would be to abandon the clear dictate of the statute in favor of a policy decision to favor employees over employers.

Id.; *see also Tiller v. Atlantic Coast Line R. Co.*, 318 U.S. 54, 67, 63 S.Ct. 444, 451, 87 L.Ed. 610 (1943) (holding that "the employer's liability is to be determined under the general rule which defines negligence as the lack of due care under the circumstances; or the failure to do what a reasonable and prudent man would ordinarily have done under the circumstances of the situation"). Our sister circuits have similarly held. *See, e.g., Smith v. Tow Boat Serv. & Management, Inc.*, 66 F.3d 336 (9th Cir.1995) (unpublished) (rejecting "slight care" standard); *see also Karvelis v. Constellation Lines, S.A.*, 806 F.2d 49, 52-53 & n. 2 (2d Cir.1986), *cert. denied*, 481 U.S. 1015, 107 S.Ct. 1891, 95 L.Ed.2d 498 (1987), (approving jury instruction informing that both employer and employee under Jones Act are charged with duty of reasonable care under the circumstances); *Ybarra v. Burlington N., Inc.*, 689 F.2d 147, 150 (8th Cir.1982) (approving jury instruction that railroad has duty to exercise reasonable care for protection of employees); *Joyce v. Atlantic Richfield Co.*, 651 F.2d 676, 681 (10th Cir.1981) (defining negligence as failure to use reasonable care).

We find further support for our position in Supreme Court precedent. In *Urie v. Thompson*, 337 U.S. 163, 174, 69 S.Ct. 1018, 1027, 93 L.Ed. 1282 (1949), the Court emphasized that the term "negligence" is to be defined "by the common law principles as established and applied in the federal courts." (internal quotations and citation omitted). Although the Court's discussion refers specifically to § 51 "negligence," it would defy logic not to extend this reasoning to the term as used in § 53, which discusses a plaintiff's contributory negligence. *See also Consolidated Rail Corp. v. Gottshall*, 512 U.S. 532, —, 114 S.Ct. 2396, 2404, 129 L.Ed.2d 427 (1994) (holding that common law principles are entitled to great weight in FELA analysis unless expressly rejected in text of statute).

A seaman, then, is obligated under the Jones Act to act with ordinary prudence under the circumstances. The circumstances of a seaman's employment include not only his reliance on his employer to provide a safe work environment but also his own experience, training, or education. The reasonable person standard, therefore, under the Jones Act becomes one of the reasonable *seaman* in like circumstances. To hold otherwise would unjustly reward unreasonable conduct and would fault seamen only for their gross negligence, which was not the contemplation of Congress. *See* Robert Force, Allocation of Risk and Standard of Care Under the Jones Act: "Slight Negligence," "Slight Care"?, 25 J. Mar. L. & Com. 1, 31 (1994).

By ascribing to seamen a slight duty of care to protect themselves from the negligence of their employers, *Spinks* and its progeny, specifically *Brooks*, are repugnant to the principles we espouse today and are therefore overruled. Moreover, by attributing to Jones Act employers a higher duty of care than that required under ordinary negligence, *Allen* and its progeny repudiate the reasonable person standard and are also overruled.

Conclusion

In light of the foregoing discussion about the appropriate standards of care that should guide employers and employees under the Jones Act, we hold that the jurors in the instant case were improperly instructed as to Gautreaux's duty to exercise care for his own safety. We, however, express no opinion as to the proper apportionment of fault between the two parties. We accordingly AFFIRM the district court's determination of the amount of damages, VACATE the district court's judgment as to comparative fault and REMAND for proceedings to determine the comparative fault (if any) of the plaintiff and apportionment of the damages consistent with this opinion. In all other respects, we reinstate the panel's opinion.

AFFIRMED IN PART, VACATED IN PART, and REMANDED.

Notes

1. The doctrine of negligence is utilized in many areas of the law. Maritime law is no exception. As a general proposition "negligence is negligence" whether the doctrine is being applied in tort law, contract law, etc. or whether it is being applied as a matter of land based law or maritime law. Also, as a general proposition, with a few exceptions, American law does not distinguish among "degrees" of negligence. Thus, in tort law, for example, usually it does not matter whether or not defendant's negligence was only "slight" or whether it was "ordinary" or whether it was "great". It is in this sense that one may say "negligence is negligence." All negligence, regardless of the context in which the doctrine is being applied, is premised on a finding of a breach of a duty to act as reasonable person under the circumstances. A finding of a breach of duty is generally insufficient to justify recovery unless it is also found that the breach of duty contributed to the injury or damage in question. The "standard of care" required in maritime law can be stated generically as being that of a reasonable person under the circumstances.

Under the Jones Act, however, the courts have often characterized the seaman-plaintiff's burden of proof as "featherweight". The language of "slight" negligence is only appropriate when referring to the quantum of proof plaintiff needs to adduce to withstand defendant's motion for judgment as a matter of law (formerly known as motion for directed verdict and motion for judgment notwithstanding the verdict).

> As this Court has held in countless cases presenting the Jones Act "featherweight" burden, directed verdict is justified "[o]nly when there is a complete absence of probative facts to support the verdict." *Thornton v. Gulf Fleet Marine Corp.*, 752 F.2d 1074, 1076 (5th Cir. 1985) (quoting *Lavender v. Kurn*, 327 U.S. 645, 652, 66 S. Ct. 740, 743, 90 L. Ed. 916, 922 (1946)); *see also Comeaux v. T.L. James & Co.*, 702 F.2d 1023, 1024 (5th Cir. 1983), modifying 666 F.2d 294 (5th Cir. 1982); *Alvarez v. J. Ray McDermott & Co.*, 674 F.2d 1037, 1042 (5th Cir. 1982). The jury's verdict must be allowed to stand unless the plaintiff failed to put forth at least a marginal claim for relief. *See id.*; *Holmes v. J. Ray McDermott & Co.*, 734 F.2d 1110, 1120 (5th Cir. 1984); *Leonard v. Exxon Corp.*, 581 F.2d 522, 524 (5th Cir.), *cert. denied*, 411 U.S. 923, 99 S. Ct. 2032, 60 L. Ed. 2d 397 (1979). Like the trial court, we review all evidence in the light most favorable to the party (*Bommarito*) opposing the motion. *Day v. South Park Independent School Dist.*, 768 F.2d 696, 699-700 (5th Cir. 1985); *Brewer v. Blackwell*, 692 F.2d 387, 391 (5th Cir. 1982).

Bommarito v. Penrod Drilling Corp., 929 F.2d 186, 188 (5th Cir. 1991).

Thus, even in a Jones Act case it is necessary for the seaman-plaintiff to introduce some evidence from which a jury could find that his employer's conduct fell below the standard of care that a reasonable employer would have used under the circumstances. However, the introduction of virtually any evidence regardless of how slight is sufficient to have the jury resolve the issue of negligence. Stated otherwise, the introduction of even the slightest evidence that the employer's conduct fell below the reasonable person standard precludes the trial judge from taking the case away from the jury or from setting aside a plaintiff's verdict.

Likewise, courts have often referred to plaintiff's burden of proving causation as being "featherweight" because FELA and the Jones Act only require a seaman to prove that his employer's negligence was *a* cause, sometimes referred to as the "producing cause", and not *the* cause of his injury. *Landry v. Oceanic Contractors, Inc.*, 731 F.2d 299, 1986 AMC 865 (5th Cir. 1984). In *Norfolk Southern Ry. Co. v. Sorrell*, 127 S.Ct. 799, 2007 AMC 192 (2007), a FELA case, the Supreme Court held that the same causation standard should be applied to both employer and employee, but declined to consider what that causation standard should be. The Court said:

> Sorrell argues that FELA does contain an explicit statutory alteration from the common-law rule: Section 1 of FELA — addressing railroad negligence — uses the language "in whole or in part," 45 U.S.C. § 51, while Section 3 — covering employee contributory negligence — does not, § 53. This, Sorrell contends, evinces an intent to depart from the common-law causation standard with respect to railroad negligence under Section 1, but not with respect to any employee contributory negligence under Section 3.
>
> The inclusion of this language in one section and not the other does not alone justify a departure from the common-law practice of applying a single standard of causation. It would have made little sense to include the "in whole or in part" language in Section 3, because if the employee's contributory negligence contributed "in whole" to his injury, there would be no recovery against the railroad in the first place. The language made sense in Section 1, however, to make clear that there could be recovery against the railroad even if it were only partially negligent.

Norfolk Southern Ry. Co. v. Sorrell, 127 S.Ct. 799, 808 (2007).

Thus, the effect of *Sorrell* in conjunction with such decisions as *Landry* is presumably that both employee and employer need only prove that the other's fault was a "producing cause".

FERGUSON v. MOORE-McCORMACK LINES, INC.

352 U.S. 521, 77 S. Ct. 457, 1 L. Ed. 2d 511, 1957 AMC 647 (1957)

Mr. Justice Douglas announced the judgment of the Court and an opinion in which The Chief Justice, Mr. Justice CLARK and Mr. Justice BRENNAN join.

Petitioner was injured in 1950 while serving as a second baker on respondent's passenger ship *Brazil*. Among his duties, he was required to fill orders of the ship's waiters for ice cream. On the day of the accident, he had received an order from a ship's waiter for 12 portions of ice cream. When he got half way down in the two-and-one-half-gallon ice-cream container from which he was filling these orders, the ice cream was so hard that it could not be removed with the hemispherical scoop with which he had been furnished. Petitioner undertook to remove the ice cream with a sharp butcher knife kept nearby, grasping the handle and chipping at the hard ice cream. The knife struck a spot in the ice cream which was so hard that his hand slipped down onto the blade of the knife, resulting in the loss of two fingers of his right hand.

Petitioner brought this suit under the Jones Act, 41 Stat. 1007, 46 U.S.C. § 688, to recover for his injuries, which were alleged to be the result of respondent's negligence. At the close of petitioner's case, respondent's motion for a directed verdict was denied. Respondent offered no evidence. After the jury returned a verdict of $17,500 for the petitioner, respondent moved to set aside the verdict. This motion was also denied and judgment entered for the petitioner in accordance with the jury verdict. The Court of Appeals reversed, holding that it was "not within the realm of reasonable foreseeability" that petitioner would use the knife to chip the frozen ice cream. 228 F.2d 891, 892. We granted certiorari. 351 U.S. 936.

We conclude that there was sufficient evidence to take to the jury the question whether respondent was negligent in failing to furnish petitioner with an adequate tool with which to perform his task.

Petitioner testified that the hard ice cream could have been loosened safely with an ice chipper. He had used such an instrument for that purpose on other ships. He was not, however, furnished such an instrument. There was evidence that the scoop with which he had been furnished was totally inadequate to remove ice cream of the consistency of that which he had to serve. And, there was evidence that its extremely hard consistency was produced by the failure of another member of the crew to transfer it from the deep freeze to a tempering chest in sufficient time to allow all of it to become disposable by means of the scoop when the time came for it to be served. There was no showing that any device was close at hand which would have safely performed the task. Finally, there was evidence that petitioner had been instructed to give the waiters prompt service.

Respondent urges that it was not reasonably foreseeable that petitioner would utilize the knife to loosen the ice cream. But the jury, which plays a pre-eminent role in these Jones Act cases (*Jacob v. New York City*, 315 U.S. 752; *Schulz v. Pennsylvania R. Co.*, 350 U.S. 523), could conclude that petitioner had been furnished no safe tool to perform his task. It was not necessary that respondent be in a position to foresee the exact chain of circumstances which actually led to the accident. The jury was instructed that it might consider whether respondent could have anticipated that a knife would be used to get out the ice cream. On this record, fairminded men could conclude that respondent should have foreseen that petitioner might be tempted to use a knife to perform his task with dispatch, since no adequate implement was furnished him. See *Schulz v. Pennsylvania R. Co.*, 350 U.S. 523, 526. Since the standard of liability under the Jones Act is that established by Congress under the Federal Employers' Liability Act, what we said in *Rogers v. Missouri Pacific R. Co.*, ante, p. 500, decided this day, is relevant here:

Under this statute the test of a jury case is simply whether the proofs justify with reason the conclusion that employer negligence *played any part, even the slightest*, in producing the injury or death for which damages are sought.

Because the jury could have so concluded, the Court of Appeals erred in holding that respondent's motion for a directed verdict should have been granted. "Courts should not assume that in determining these questions of negligence juries will fall short of a fair performance of their constitutional function." *Wilkerson v. McCarthy*, 336 U.S. 53, 62.

Reversed.

KERNAN v. AMERICAN DREDGING CO.

355 U.S. 426, 78 S. Ct. 394, 2 L. Ed. 2d 382, 1958 AMC 251 (1958)

Mr. Justice BRENNAN delivered the opinion of the Court.

In this ... proceeding ... the District Court for the Eastern District of Pennsylvania denied the petitioner's claim for damages filed on behalf of the widow and other dependents of a seaman who lost his life on respondent's tug in a fire caused by the violation of a navigation rule. 141 F. Supp. 582. The Court of Appeals for the Third Circuit affirmed. 235 F.2d 618, rehearing denied, 235 F.2d 619. We granted certiorari. 352 U.S. 965.

The seaman lost his life on the tug *Arthur N. Herron*, which, on the night of November 18, 1952, while towing a scow on the Schuylkill River in Philadelphia, caught fire when an open-flame kerosene lamp on the deck of the scow ignited highly inflammable vapors lying above an extensive accumulation of petroleum products spread over the surface of the river. Several oil refineries and facilities for oil storage, and for loading and unloading petroleum products, are located along the banks of the Schuylkill River. The trial court found that the lamp was not more than three feet above the water. Maintaining the lamp at a height of less than eight feet violated a navigation rule promulgated by the Commandant of the United States Coast Guard. The trial court found that the vapor would not have been ignited if the lamp had been carried at the required height.

The District Court held that the violation of the rule, "whether ... [it] be called negligence or be said to make the flotilla unseaworthy," did not impose liability because "the Coast Guard regulation had to do solely with navigation and was intended for the prevention of collisions, and for no other purpose. In the present case there was no collision and no fault of navigation. True, the origin of the fire can be traced to the violation of the regulation, but the question is not causation but whether the violation of the regulation, of itself, imposes liability." 141 F. Supp., at 585.

* * *

The petitioner also urges that, since the violation of the rule requiring the lights to be eight feet above the water resulted in a defect or insufficiency in the flotilla's lighting equipment which in fact caused the seaman's death, liability was created without regard to negligence under the line of decisions of this Court in actions under the FELA based upon violations of either the Safety Appliance Acts or the Boiler Inspection Act. That line of decisions interpreted the clause of § 1 of the FELA, 45 U.S.C. § 51, which imposes liability on the employer "by reason of any defect or insufficiency, due to its negligence, in its cars, engines, appliances, machinery, track, roadbed, works, boats, wharves, or other equipment." The cases hold that under this clause, a defect resulting from a violation of either statute which causes the injury or death of an employee creates liability without regard to negligence. *San Antonio & A.P.R. Co. v. Wagner*, 241 U.S. 476, 484. Here the defect or insufficiency in the flotilla's lighting equipment due to a violation of the statute resulted in the death of the seaman. The question for our decision is whether, in the absence of any showing of negligence, the Jones Act—which in terms incorporates the provisions of the FELA—permits recovery for the death of a seaman resulting from a violation of a statutory duty. We hold that it does.

In denying the claim the lower courts relied upon their views of general tort doctrine.... In the railroad and shipping industries, however, the FELA and Jones Act provide the framework for determining liability for industrial accidents. But instead of a detailed statute codifying common-law principles, Congress saw fit to enact a statute of the most general terms, thus leaving in large measure to the courts the duty of fashioning remedies for injured employees in a manner analogous to the development of tort remedies at common law. But it is clear that the general congressional intent was to provide liberal recovery for injured workers, *Rogers v. Missouri Pacific R. Co.*, 352 U.S. 500, 508-510, and it is also clear that Congress intended the creation of no static remedy, but one which would be developed and enlarged to meet changing conditions and changing concepts of industry's duty toward its workers.

The FELA and the Jones Act impose upon the employer the duty of paying damages when injury to the worker is caused, in whole or in part, by the employer's fault. This fault may consist of a breach of the duty of care, analogous but by no means identical to the general common-law duty, or of a breach of some statutory duty. The tort doctrine which the lower courts applied imposes liability for violation of a statutory duty only where the injury is one which the statute was designed to prevent. However, this Court has repeatedly refused to apply such a limiting doctrine in FELA cases. In FELA cases based upon violations of the Safety Appliance Acts or the Boiler Inspection Act, the Court has held that a violation of either statute creates liability under FELA if the resulting defect or insufficiency in equipment contributes in fact to the death or injury in suit, without regard to whether the injury flowing from the breach was the injury the statute sought to prevent. Since it appears in this case that the defect or insufficiency of the flotilla's lighting equipment resulting from the violation of 33 U.S.C. § 157 actually caused the seaman's death, this principle governs and compels a result in favor of the petitioner's claim.

* * *

The decisive question in this case, then, is whether the principles developed in this line of FELA cases permit recovery for violation of this navigation statute or are limited, as the dissenting opinion would have it, to cases involving the Safety Appliance and Boiler Inspection Acts. Our attention is directed to the provisions of § 4 of the FELA, which makes reference to "any statute enacted for the safety of employees ... ," and it is urged that this phrase, in some unexplained manner, creates a special relationship between the FELA and the Safety Appliance and Boiler Inspection Acts. Several answers may be given to this contention.

First, § 4 relates entirely to the defense of assumption of risk, abolishing this defense where the injury was caused by the employer's negligence or by "violation ... of any statute enacted for the safety of employees...." It is § 1 of the FELA which creates the cause of action and this section, on its face, is barren of any suggestion that injuries caused by violation of *any* statute are to be treated specially. In formulating the rule that violation of the Safety Appliance and Boiler Inspection Acts creates liability for resulting injuries without proof of negligence, the Court relied on judicially evolved principles designed to carry out the general congressional purpose of providing appropriate remedies for injuries incurred by railroad employees. For Congress, in 1908, did not crystallize the application of the Act by enacting specific rules to guide the courts. Rather, by using generalized language, it created only a framework within which the courts were left to evolve, much in the manner of the common law, a system of principles providing compensation for injuries to employees consistent with the changing realities of employment in the railroad industry.

Second, it is argued that the Safety Appliance and Boiler Inspection Acts are special safety statutes and thus may easily be assimilated to the FELA under general common-law principles. But there is no magic in the word "safety." In the cases we have discussed it was regarded as irrelevant that the defects in the appliances did not disable them from performing their intended safety function. For instance, in *Gotschall* the coupling defect parting the cars resulted in the automatic setting of the emergency brakes as a safety measure. In *Coray* the train stopped due to the operation of the very safety mechanism required by the statute. In *Urie* the defect in the sanders which caused sand to come into the locomotive cabs in no wise impaired the designed safety function of the sanders—to provide sand for traction. We think that the irrelevance of the safety aspect in these cases demonstrates that the basis of liability is a violation of statutory duty without regard to whether the injury flowing from the violation was the injury the statute sought to guard against. It must therefore be concluded that the nature of the Acts violated is not a controlling consideration; the basis of liability is the FELA.

The courts, in developing the FELA with a view to adjusting equitably between the worker and his corporate employer the risks inherent in the railroad industry, have plainly rejected many of the refined distinctions necessary in common-law tort doctrine for the purpose of allocating risks between persons who are more nearly on an equal footing as to financial capacity and ability to avoid the hazards involved. Among the refinements developed by the common law for the purpose of limiting the risk of liability arising from wrongful conduct is the rule that violation of a statutory duty creates liability only when the statute was intended to protect those in the position of the plaintiff from the type of injury in fact incurred. This limiting approach has long been discarded from the FELA. Instead, the theory of the FELA is that where the employer's conduct falls short of the high standard required of him by this Act, and his fault, in whole or in part, causes injury, liability ensues. And this result follows whether the fault is a violation of a statutory duty or the more general duty of acting with care, for the employer owes the employee, as much as the duty of acting with care, the duty of complying with his statutory obligations.

We find no difficulty in applying these principles, developed under the FELA, to the present action under the Jones Act, for the latter Act expressly provides for seamen the cause of action—and consequently the entire judicially developed doctrine of liability—granted to railroad workers by the FELA. The deceased seaman here was in a position perfectly analogous to that of the railroad workers allowed recovery in the line of cases we have discussed, and the principles governing those cases clearly should apply here.

The judgment of the Court of Appeals is reversed with direction to remand to the District Court for further proceedings not inconsistent with this opinion.

Reversed.

Mr. Justice HARLAN, whom Mr. Justice FRANKFURTER, Mr. Justice BURTON, and Mr. Justice WHITTAKER join, dissenting.

* * *

The District Court granted exoneration to respondent upon findings that the accident was not attributable to negligence of any kind on its part, and in particular that respondent was not negligent in carrying the kerosene signal lantern, which ignited the fumes from the petroleum products on the surface of the river, at a height of three feet in a part of the river which had never been considered a danger area. Although the District Court found that the accident was traceable in fact to respondent's violation of a Coast Guard regulation, 33 CFR § 80.16(h), which required a white light to be carried at a minimum height of eight feet above the water, the court held that this violation did not of itself give rise to liability in negligence because the sole purpose of the statute authorizing the regulation, 30 Stat. 102, as amended, 33 U.S.C. § 157, was to guard against collisions and not to prevent the type of accident which here resulted.

This holding, as the Court seems to recognize, was in accord with the familiar principle in the common law of negligence that injuries resulting from violations of a statutory duty do not give rise to liability unless of the kind the statute was designed to prevent. Indeed that principle, which is but an aspect of the general rule of negligence law that injuries in order to be actionable must be within the risk of harm which a defendant's conduct has created....

The Court neither casts doubt on the District Court's finding that respondent was not negligent in carrying the tug's lantern at three feet above the water surface nor disputes that the sole purpose of the Coast Guard regulation was to guard against the risk of collision, but it nevertheless decides that violation of the regulation in and of itself rendered the respondent liable for all injuries flowing from it. This holding is said to follow from the decisions of this Court in a series of FELA cases based on violations of the Safety Appliance Act, 27 Stat. 531, as amended, 45 U.S.C. §§ 1-16, and the Boiler Inspection Act, 36 Stat. 913, as amended, 45 U.S.C. §§ 22-34. These decisions, as the Court here properly states, have created under the FELA an absolute liability—that is, a liability "without regard to negligence"—for injuries resulting from violations of the other Acts. From this, the Court concludes that there is no reason not to extend this absolute liability to cases based on the violation of a statutory duty which are brought under the Jones Act.

This conclusion I cannot share. A reading of the cases relied upon by the Court demonstrates beyond dispute that the reasons underlying those decisions have no application in the context of this Coast Guard regulation and the Jones Act. It follows that liability can be impressed on respondent only because of negligence, the theory upon which the Jones Act is founded.

Notes

1. *Kernan* was distinguished by the Second Circuit in *Jones v. Spentonbush-Red Star Co.*, 155 F.3d 587, 1999 AMC 324 (2d Cir. 1998), where the court refused to regard a breach of an Occupational Safety and Health Act (OSHA) regulation as establishing negligence *per se* for Jones Act purposes, even though the regulation was a safety one, requiring a grinding wheel to have a guard.

In contrast to the defendants in *Kernan* ... however, Spentonbush did not violate a Coast Guard regulation or maritime statute. Instead, it violated an OSHA regulation. This distinction in the source of defendant's statutory duty is key to this appeal. Unlike Coast Guard regulations and maritime statutes that are specifically aimed at shipping activities, Jones relies on a general workplace safety regulation to attain the same results in a maritime context. We do not think it was Congress' purpose for the Occupational Safety and Health Act (the Act) to have such an all- encompassing effect. ... Congress provides the following limitation to the Act's applicability:

> Nothing in this chapter shall be construed to supersede or in any manner affect any workmen's compensation law or *to enlarge or diminish or affect in any other manner the common law or statutory rights, duties, or liabilities of employers and employees under any law with respect to injuries, diseases, or death of employees* arising out of, or in the course of, employment. 29 U.S.C. § 653(b)(4) (1994) (emphasis added).

Imposing negligence *per se*, shifting the burden of proof and barring a finding of comparative negligence for an OSHA violation would all "enlarge or diminish or affect in any other manner" the liability of a maritime employer.

155 F. 3d 587, 595, 1999 AMC 324, 334.

2. In *Sentilles v. Inter-Caribbean Corporation*, 361 U.S. 107, 80 S. Ct. 173, 4 L. Ed. 2d 142 (1959), a seaman sued his employer, the shipowner, seeking damages under the Jones Act for injuries sustained in consequence of a seaboard accident. As the vessel encountered a heavy sea, plaintiff was pitched into the air and fell back to the deck, where, upon landing, a wave washed him a considerable distance. Shortly after the accident, plaintiff became ill, was hospitalized and treated for a serious case of tuberculosis. His theory was that the accident aggravated a previously latent tubercular condition.

The case was submitted to a jury, a verdict was returned for plaintiff, and the District Court rendered judgment in his favor. The Court of Appeal reversed on the ground that the evidence did not justify the jury's conclusion that the accident caused aggravation of the pre-existing tubercular condition. The United States Supreme Court granted certiorari and reversed; the Court of Appeal had applied an improper standard in reviewing the medical evidence and in examining the judgment rendered on the jury's verdict.

The medical evidence was not conclusive. A specialist had testified that the aggravation of plaintiff's tubercular condition "might be a consequence of the accident." Another specialist had testified that the trauma and plaintiff's pre-existing diabetic condition were "the most likely causes of the aggravation of the tuberculosis." A third specialist, who had never examined plaintiff, answered when questioned hypothetically that the accident "probably aggravated his condition." The United States Supreme Court held that the jury's power to draw the inference that the aggravation of plaintiff's condition was in fact caused by the accident "was not impaired by the failure of any medical witness to testify that it was in fact the cause." "The members of the jury," the Court declared, "not the medical witnesses, were sworn to make a legal determination of the question of causation. They were entitled to take all the circumstances, including the medical testimony, into consideration.... The focal point of judicial review is the reasonableness of the particular inference or conclusion drawn by the jury.... The proofs here justified with reason the conclusion of the jury that the accident caused the petitioner's serious subsequent illness."

Has the Court dispensed with proof of proximate causation in Jones Act cases? *See Landry v. Oceanic Contractors, Inc.*, 731 F.2d 299, 1986 AMC (5th Cir. 1984), *rehearing denied* 746 F.2d 812 (5th Cir. 1984). For a case in which the court dismissed a claim for lack of causation under the Jones Act standard, *see Martin v. John W. Stone Oil Distributor, Inc.*, 819 F.2d 547, 1988 AMC 1689 (5th Cir. 1987).

———————

CHISHOLM v. SABINE TOWING & TRANSP. CO., INC.

679 F.2d 60 (5th Cir. 1982)

Edwin F. HUNTER, Jr., District Judge:*

Plaintiff, William Chisholm, a member of the crew of the SS San Jacinto, brought this suit against his employer under the Jones Act (46 U.S.C. § 688) and general maritime law, claiming that his injuries resulted from the negligence of defendant and the unseaworthiness of the San Jacinto. Defendant, Sabine Towing and Transportation Company, was the owner and operator of the vessel. The case was tried in the district court by a Magistrate, without a jury. He concluded that the negligence of Sabine and the unseaworthiness of the vessel were each proximate causes of plaintiff's injuries. Judgment was entered and Sabine appeals.

The Magistrate set forth the important facts; we will but summarize. Just prior to the occasion in question, the San Jacinto had been in a shipyard in Tampa, Florida undergoing repairs in her engine room. The scrap iron remaining from the repair work was left unsecured in the engine room. It was customary in instances of this nature for the material to be thrown into the sea after the ship was at sea. Sabine had made a decision to do just that, and on September 4, 1979, four seamen, including the plaintiff, volunteered for overtime work to dispose of the scrap metal. It was not mandatory and additional compensation was paid to the seamen. The work consisted of carrying the individual pieces, each of which weighed between 40 and 50 pounds, up to the vessel's main deck, where they were thrown overboard. Plaintiff alleged that he injured his back while he was lifting a piece of scrap iron. Everyone agrees that this was not dangerous work. The Magistrate expressly found that defendant was not negligent in permitting Chisholm to undertake this job, and that an adequate complement of crewmen was provided to accomplish the assigned task of disposing of the metal. Plaintiff left the vessel about two weeks later, and on December 14, 1979, surgery was performed and resulted in the removal of a herniated disc. In later January of 1980 he returned to the ship in his prior job as an oiler, which job he was retained throughout the trial.

We recite pertinent conclusions of the Court below as they relate to negligence, unseaworthiness and causation:

2. The Defendant, in allowing its vessel to be put to sea with its engine room cluttered with heavy objects of scrap metal and debris, which were in no way secured or removed from the vessel, at the time of the shipyard repair, or before putting to sea, constituted an unseaworthy condition, and the vessel was not reasonably suitable for her intended service.

3. The Defendant knew, or in the exercise of due care, should have known that heavy metal objects, unsecured, left in the working area of employees, could, and would in all probability, cause injury to the employees, and the act of failing to clean the ship before it left the repair docks constituted negligence on the part of the Defendant.

4. The act of the Plaintiff of attempting to remedy a condition which presented a hazard to himself and to others, as a result of the negligence of the Defendant and the unseaworthiness of the vessel, was a cause of his injury, and he is entitled to recover for damages.

5. It is further concluded that inasmuch as Plaintiff was in the course of attempting to remedy the unseaworthy condition, that Defendant had permitted to exist in the engine room of its vessel, that Plaintiff's injuries were proximately caused by said unseaworthy condition and the Defendant is, therefore, liable to Plaintiff for his damages.

* * *

The issue quickly narrows: Was the negligence of Sabine or the unseaworthy condition of the SS San Jacinto a legal cause of Chisholm's injury? Jones Act negligence and unseaworthiness are two separate and distinct claims. This court recognizes two different standards of causation. The "producing cause" standard utilized for Jones Act

---

negligence is the F.E.L.A. Standard. The language selected by Congress to fix liability is simple and direct. Defendant must bear responsibility if his negligence played any part, even the slightest, in producing the injury. *Rogers v. Missouri Pacific R. Co.*, 352 U.S. 500, 506. The standard of causation for unseaworthiness is a more demanding one and requires proof of proximate cause. In either case the plaintiff's burden has been characterized as very light, even "featherweight." *Vallot v. Central Gulf Lines, Inc.*, 641 F.2d 346, 350 (5th Cir. 1981). In *Peymann v. Perini Corporation*, 507 F.2d 1318 (1st Cir. 1974), the court stated (at p. 1324):

> The reason why under the Jones Act the plaintiff is entitled to a charge that he need show only that defendant's negligence contributed to his injury was fully explained in *Rogers*. Basically it is because, as distinguished from the common law, where defendant's negligence must be the 'sole, efficient, producing cause' and plaintiff would be barred if his own negligence was contributing cause, the Jones Act 'expressly imposes liability upon the employer to pay damages for injury or death due "in whole or in part" to its negligence.' *See* 352 U.S. at 505-507. But so does the law of unseaworthiness. *Pope & Talbot, Inc. v. Hawn* (1953), 346 U.S. 406. This does not mean, in either instance, that defendant's fault must not be shown to be a cause—there must, of course be a connection—it merely need not be *the* cause. The distinction was well brought out in *Farnarjian v. American Export Isbrandtsen Lines, Inc.*, (2 Cir. 1973) 474 F.2d 361, at 364.

Nothing that has been said impairs the principle that in Jones Act cases, cause, in fact, is still a necessary ingredient of liability. Here, the conclusion is inescapable that the plaintiff has been unable to shoulder even the featherweight burden. The fact that the debris was not secured had absolutely nothing to do with his injury. The dilapidated condition of a ship is not grounds for liability when there is no suggestion that the dilapidated condition was the cause of plaintiff's injury. Plaintiff, recognizing the tenuousness of its causation argument, suggests the applicability of *Menefee v. Chamberlin*, 176 F.2d 828 (9th Cir. 1949); *Sanford Bros. Boats Inc. v. Vidrine*, 412 F.2d 958 (5th Cir. 1969); and *Stanworth v. American Stern Trawlers, Inc.*, 523 F.2d 46 (9th Cir. 1975). These cases are distinguishable on both the law and the facts. In *Stanworth* the plaintiff slipped in a puddle of diesel oil. The oil was the direct and immediate cause of the slip and fall. In both *Menefee* and *Sanford*, the defendant shipowner had negligently created a dangerous condition which gave rise to an emergency situation, and the plaintiff seaman was injured while responding to that emergency. The danger which invited the response was the cause of the injury in each case. In the present case, plaintiff was not responding to an emergency situation and there was no immediate danger either to him or to the ship. He simply hurt his back carrying the scrap metal to the deck of the ship, a duty which plaintiff readily concedes to be no more than a "normal hazard of his work."

Again, recognizing the tenuousness of his argument, plaintiff seems to rely on the "but for" doctrine, the argument being that if the debris had not been loose, then there would have been no need to throw it overboard. This is just not so. The debris would have been jettisoned in any event. The "but for" argument is not applicable, because the fact that the debris was not secured had nothing to do with its being thrown overboard. Then, too, this Court has rejected, in a Jones Act case, the so-called "but for" argument. *Spinks v. Chevron Oil Company*, 507 F.2d 216, 222 (5th Cir. 1975). There, speaking through Judge Wisdom, we stated:

> The concept of proximate cause often obscures the true analysis of a tort. A court makes a policy judgment on the limits of liability when causation in fact has been established. Prosser, Torts § 42 (4th ed., 1971). This court has applied in maritime law the legal cause analysis, as it is used in common law tort in admiralty....
>
> The American Law Institute's Restatement 2d of Torts adopts the modern concept of legal cause. The elements of legal cause are negligence, a causal connection between the negligence and the injury, the invasion of a legally protected interest, and lack of a countervailing legally protected interest as a defense to liability. Restatement 2d Torts, § 9. *The defendant's negligence must be a substantial factor in bringing about the harm,* with no rule of law relieving the actor of fault. *Id.* § 431. *'Substantial' means more than 'but for' the negligence, the*

harm would not have resulted, (*id.* Com. a.) and more than merely negligible negligence. *Id.* Com. b. The gist of it is that some responsibility for the effect must accompany the cause. *Id.* at 222-23.

The burden of proving the district court's findings "clearly erroneous" is somewhat ameliorated, where as here there are no credibility choices. But with or without that reduced burden, the uncontradicted facts leave us with a definite and firm conviction that a mistake has been committed and that the trial court's findings and conclusions as to causation were patently erroneous.

Reversed.

REAVLEY, Circuit Judge, dissenting:

The trial court findings do not stop at faulting defendant for having unsecured scrap metal in the engine room, where that metal would be a hazard to seamen walking and standing in rough seas. The defendant was found to be negligent and to create an unseaworthy condition by taking the ship to sea with the metal aboard. The metal constituted a hazard in place as well as a hazard in the course of its removal.

The fact that the debris was not secured had nothing to do with its being thrown overboard, but taking the metal to sea for this method of disposal had everything to do with plaintiff seaman's injury in the course of that disposal.

I would affirm.

Notes

1. *Proof of Causation*

Plaintiff need not show that the negligence of the employer is the sole cause of his injuries. *Gajewski v. United States*, 540 F. Supp. 381, 1982 AMC 2830 (S.D.N.Y. 1982). Moreover, plaintiff need not prove proximate cause in the traditional sense. *See Sentilles v. Inter-Caribbean Shipping Corp.*, 361 U.S. 107, 80 S.Ct. 173, 4 L.Ed.2d 142 (1959). For a recent case in which no causation was found, see *Martin v. John W. Stone Oil Distributor, Inc.*, 819 F.2d 547, 1988 AMC 1689 (5th Cir. 1987).

Likewise it has been stated that:

The "producing cause" FELA standard, used for Jones Act negligence, facilitates proof by the employee, incorporating any cause regardless of immediacy. Plaintiff's burden of proving such cause is "featherweight," *Davis v. Hill Engineering, Inc.*, 549 F.2d 314, 331 (5th Cir. 1977), and all that is required is a showing of "slight negligence," *Allen v. Seacoast Products, Inc.*, 623 F.2d 355, 361 (5th Cir. 1980). In keeping with this less demanding standard of proof of causation, the test for sufficiency of evidence in a Jones Act case also requires less evidence to support a finding and directed verdicts and j.n.o.v. motions are granted "only when there is a complete absence of probative facts" to support a verdict. *Lavender v. Kurn*, 327 U.S. 645, 652-53, 66 S. Ct. 740, 743, 90 L. Ed. 2d 916, 922 (1946) (construing standard for FELA cases, applicable to Jones Act cases, *Ferguson v. Moore-McCormick Lines, Inc.*, 352 U.S. 521, 523, 77 S. Ct. 457, 458, 1 L. Ed. 2d 511, 513 (1957)); *Kendrick v. Illinois Central Gulf Railroad Co.*, 669 F.2d 341, 343 n.1 (5th Cir. 1982); *Comeaux v. T.L. James & Co.*, 666 F.2d at 298 n.3; *Allen v. Seacoast Products, Inc.*, 623 F.2d 355, 3359-60 (5th Cir. 1980).

Similarly, we have applied the same standards of proof, causation, and review to the issue of the plaintiff's contributory negligence. *See Campbell v. Seacoast Products, Inc.*, 581 F.2d 98, 99 n.2 (5th Cir. 1978) (applying *Lavender* standard of review to Jones Act case where jury verdict favors plaintiff or defendant); *McBride v. Loffland Brothers Co.*, 422 F.2d 363, (5th Cir. 1970)....

Comeaux v. T.L. James & Co., 702 F.2d 1023, 1024, 1984 AMC 2805 (5th Cir. 1983).

The burden to prove causation in a Jones Act case is "very light" or "featherweight." *Landry v. Two R. Drilling Co.*, 511 F.2d 138, 142 (5th Cir. 1975). Under the Jones Act, a defendant must bear the responsibility for any negligence, however slight, that played a part in producing the plaintiff's injury. *See Landry v. Oceanic Contractors, Inc.*, 731 F.2d 299, 302 (5th Cir. 1984). Although in Jones Act cases a "jury is entitled to make permissible inferences from unexplained events," summary judgment is nevertheless warranted when there is a complete absence of proof of an essential element of the nonmoving party's case. *See Martin v. John W. Stond Oil Distrib., Inc.*, 819 F.2d 547, 549 (5th Cir. 1987). The standard for negligence under general maritime law [not applicable in Jones Act cases] is higher. The plaintiff must demonstrate that there was a duty owed by the defendant to the plaintiff, breach of that duty, injury sustained by plaintiff, and a causal connection between defendant's conduct and the plaintiff's injury. *See Thomas v. Express Boat Co.*, 759 F.2d 444, 448 (5th Cir. 1985). Furthermore, the resultant harm must be reasonably foreseeable. *Daigle v. Point Landing, Inc.*, 616 F.2d 825, 827 (5th Cir. 1980).

In re Cooper/T. Smith, 929 F.2d 1073, 1077, 1991 AMC 2169 (5th Cir. 1991).

2. Recovery for Fright

The Court in *Consolidated Rail Corp. v. Gottshall*, 512 U.S. 532, 114 S. Ct. 2396, 2408, 129 L.Ed.2d 427, 1994 AMC 2113 (1994) held that actions for fright are available under FELA and presumably under the Jones Act. The Court adopted the zone of danger test is the standard of recovery. Actions for fright under FELA are judged according to the common law development of emotional distress. Most states use the "bystander" test and some use the "physical impact" test, but only 14 use the "zone of danger" test adopted by the Supreme Court. *See Jones v. CSX Transp.*, 287 F.3d 1341, 1345-57 (11th Cir. 2002), collecting authorities.

3. Aggravation of Original Injury by Negligent Medical Treatment

A negligent employer is liable not only for the initial injury but for subsequent negligent medical care necessitated by the original injury. *Alholm v. American S.S. Co.*, 144 F.3d 1172, 1998 AMC 2352 (8th Cir. 1998).

B. Conflict of Laws

Introductory Note

When a legal relationship involves foreign contacts, a question arises as to the applicable law. This question is resolved by resorting to *choice of law* rules that may be established by statute, judicial precedents, or by agreement of the parties. The choice of law rules are a part of the law of the forum. Thus, when a foreign seaman is injured aboard a foreign-flag vessel in a United States port, and the action is brought in a federal district court under the grant of admiralty jurisdiction, the court is bound to apply federal law.

The process of choice of law may be simplified by statutes that define their own area of application. For example, the words "any seaman" in the Jones Act were at first taken to require application of the statute to causes of action for personal injuries sustained by a seaman regardless of the nationality of the plaintiff, the flag of the vessel, or the place of the injury. Such an extremely broad application of the Jones Act was impractical and undesirable. The Supreme Court, therefore, sought to establish guidelines for a choice of law process in *Lauritzen v. Larsen*, 345 U.S. 571, 73 S.Ct. 921, 97 L.Ed. 1254, 1953 AMC 1210 (1953), discussed below.

Presumably, questions of choice of law arise *after* the question of jurisdiction is settled. If a court has subject matter jurisdiction of a controversy, and the parties are properly before the court, then it is proper for the court to decide the question of the applicable law. After the choice of law determination, the third step in the analysis is a *forum non conveniens* determination. There are, however, very few examples of cases involving injured seamen in which the court decided that foreign law was applicable but retained jurisdiction. *See Karim v. Finch Shipping Co., Ltd.*, 265 F.3d 258, 2001 AMC 2618 (5th Cir. 2001) (refusing to dismiss on forum non conveniens grounds, applying Bangladeshi law).

In 1982, Congress amended the Jones Act to bar suits for maintenance and cure or personal injury and death by a person not a citizen or resident of the United States who is employed in the production of off-shore mineral or energy resources of nations other than the United States. An exception to this bar can be established by showing that no remedy is available under the laws of the nation asserting jurisdiction. 46 U.S.C.A. § 30105 (formerly 46 U.S.C. § 688b).

HELLENIC LINES LTD. v. RHODITIS

398 U.S. 306, 90 S. Ct. 1731, 26 L. Ed. 2d 252, 1970 AMC 994 (1970)

Mr. Justice DOUGLAS delivered the opinion of the Court.

This is a suit under the Jones Act by a seaman who was injured aboard the ship *Hellenic Hero* in the Port of New Orleans. The District Court, sitting without a jury, rendered judgment for the seaman, 273 F. Supp. 248. The Court of Appeals affirmed. 412 F.2d 919. The case is here on petition for a writ of certiorari which we granted, 396 U.S. 1000, in light of the conflict between the decision below and *Tsakonites v. Transpacific Carriers Corp.*, 368 F.2d 426, in the Second Circuit.

Petitioner Hellenic Lines Ltd. is a Greek corporation that has its largest office in New York and another office in New Orleans. More than 95% of its stock is owned by a United States domiciliary who is a Greek citizen—

Pericles G. Callimanopoulos (whom we call Pericles). He lives in Connecticut and manages the corporation out of New York. He has lived in this country since 1945. The ship *Hellenic Hero* is engaged in regularly scheduled runs between various ports of the United States and the Middle East, Pakistan, and India. The District Court found that its entire income is from cargo either originating or terminating in the United States.

Respondent, the seaman, signed on in Greece, and he is a Greek citizen. His contract of employment provides that Greek law and a Greek collective-bargaining agreement apply between the employer and the seaman and that all claims arising out of the employment contract are to be adjudicated by a Greek court. And it seems to be conceded that respondent could obtain relief through Greek courts, if he desired.

The Jones Act speaks only of "the defendant employer" without any qualifications. In *Lauritizen v. Larsen*, 345 U.S. 571, however, we listed seven factors to be considered in determining whether a particular shipowner should be held to be an "employer" for Jones Act purposes:

(1) the place of the wrongful act; (2) the law of the flag; (3) the allegiance or domicile of the injured seaman; (4) allegiance of the defendant shipowner; (5) the place where the contract of employment was made; (6) the inaccessibility of a foreign forum; and (7) the law of the forum.

Of these seven factors it is urged that four are in favor of the shipowner and against jurisdiction: the ship's flag is Greek; the injured seaman is Greek; the employment contract is Greek; and there is a foreign forum available to the injured seaman.

The *Lauritizen* test, however, is not a mechanical one. 345 U.S. at 582. We indicated that the flag that a ship flies may, at times, alone be sufficient. *Id.*, at 585-586. The significance of one of more factors must be considered in light of the national interest served by the assertion of Jones Act jurisdiction. Moreover, the list of seven factors in *Lauritizen* was not intended as exhaustive. As held in *Pavlou v. Ocean Traders Marine Corp.*, 211 F. Supp. 320, 324, and approved by the Court of Appeals in the present case, 412 F.2d at 923, the shipowner's *base of operations* is another factor of importance in determining whether the Jones Act is applicable; and there well may be others.

In *Lauritizen* the injured seaman had been hired in and was returned to the United States, and the shipowner was served here. Those were the only contacts of that shipping operation with this country.

The present case is quite different.

Pericles became a lawful permanent resident alien in 1952. We extend to such an alien the same constitutional protections of due process that we accord citizens. *Kwong Hai Chew v. Colding*, 344 U.S. 590, 596. The injury occurred here. The forum is a United States court. Pericles' base of operations is New York. The *Hellenic Hero* was not a casual visitor; rather, it and many of its sister ships were earning income from cargo originating or terminating here. We see no reason whatsoever to give the Jones Act a strained construction so that this alien owner, engaged in an extensive business operation in this country, may have an advantage over citizens engaged in the same business by allowing him to escape the obligations and responsibility of a Jones Act "employer." The flag, the nationality of the seaman, the fact that his employment contract was Greek, and that he might be compensated there are in the totality of the circumstances of this case minor weights in the scales compared with the substantial and continuing contacts that this alien owner has with this country. If, as stated in *Bartholomew v. Universe Tankships Inc.*, 263 F.2d 437, the liberal purposes of the Jones Act are to be effectuated, the facade of the operation must be considered as minor, compared with the real nature of the operation and a cold objective look at the actual operational contacts that this ship and this owner have with the United States. By that test the Court of Appeals was clearly right in holding that petitioner Hellenic Lines was an "employer" under the Jones Act.

Affirmed.

Mr. Justice HARLAN, with whom The Chief Justice and Mr. Justice STEWART join, dissenting.

I dissent from today's decision holding that a Greek seaman who signs articles in Greece for employment on a Greek-owned, Greek-flag vessel may recover under the Jones Act for shipboard injuries sustained while the vessel was in American territorial waters. This result is supported neither by precedent, nor realistic policy, and in my opinion is far removed from any intention that can reasonably be ascribed to Congress.

Note: Base of Operations

That a shipowner's base of operations is in the U.S. does not automatically trigger the application of U.S. law. *Warn v. M/V Maridome*, 169 F.3d 625, 629, 1999 AMC 1070 (9th Cir. 1999).

KUKIAS v. CHANDRIS LINES, INC.

839 F.2d 860, 1989 AMC 1277 (1st Cir. 1988)

RE, Chief Judge:

Plaintiff-appellant, Harilaos Kukias (Kukias) appeals from a judgment of the United States District Court for the District of Puerto Rico, which dismissed his claim for failure to state a cause of action under the Jones Act, and under the general maritime law of the United States. Kukias, a Greek seaman, sought to recover damages for personal injuries sustained while employed aboard the cruise ship "M/V The Victoria" (Victoria). Kukias contends that the district court erred in adopting the Magistrate's Report and Recommendation. Specifically, he contends that the Magistrate, after consideration of the various choice-of-law factors, erroneously concluded that Kukias had no remedy under the laws of the United States

The question presented on this appeal is whether Kukias has stated a cause of action for his claim under the Jones Act or the general maritime law of the United States. After a *de novo* review, we hold that the relevant contacts are insufficient to warrant the application of the Jones Act or general maritime law. Accordingly, we affirm the judgment of the district court.

Background

Kukias, a resident and citizen of Greece, was employed aboard the Victoria, a vessel of Panamanian registry, owned by defendant-appellee Phaedon Navegacion, S.A. (Phaedon), a Panamanian corporation, and managed and operated by defendant-appellee Chandris, S.A. (Chandris), a Liberian corporation. The known shareholders of both corporations are Greek domiciliaries and neither corporation maintains any offices or facilities in the United States. An independent entity, Chandris, Inc., incorporated in Delaware, serves as general passenger agent for Chandris, S.A. in the United States. Kukias does not contest the district court's dismissal as to Chandris, Inc.

On April 16, 1984, the Victoria, during its Caribbean cruising season, was on a voyage from San Juan, Puerto Rico to St. Thomas, Virgin Islands. On that date, Kukias was injured when he fell down a stairway. He received treatment aboard the vessel, and was later hospitalized in St. Thomas. Kukias received further medical treatment upon his return to Greece where he apparently continues to reside.

Kukias commenced this action in United States District Court for the District of Puerto Rico, to recover damages for his injuries which he alleged were due to the negligence of the defendants, and their failure to maintain a seaworthy vessel. Jurisdiction was predicated on the Jones Act, 46 U.S.C. § 688 (1982), and general maritime law. Upon defendants' motion to dismiss, Magistrate Arenas, after an analysis of the factors outlined in *Lauritzen v. Larsen*, 345 U.S. 571, 583-91, 73 S. Ct. 921, 928-32, 97 L. Ed. 1254 (1953), and applied and augmented in *Romero v. International Terminal Operating Co.*, 358 U.S. 354, 381-84, 79 S. Ct. 468, 485-86, 3 L. Ed. 2d 368 (1959) and *Hellenic Lines Ltd. v. Rhoditis*, 398 U.S. 306, 308-09, 90 S. Ct. 1731, 1733-34, 26 L. Ed. 2d 252 (1970), determined that United States law was inapplicable. The Magistrate recommended dismissal of the action on the conditions that the defendants submit themselves to the jurisdiction of the Greek courts, and waive defenses of venue and statute of limitations. The defendants agreed to abide by the conditions stated by the Magistrate. Subsequently, Judge Acosta of the district court, entered judgment which adopted the Magistrate's Report and Recommendation, and dismissed the action.

Discussion

At the outset, it is noted that the choice-of-law issue is a question of law, and, therefore, is subject to *de novo* review by this court. *See Sigalas v. Lido Maritime, Inc.*, 776 F.2d 1512, 1516 (11th Cir 1985); *Pereira v. Utah Transp., Inc.*, 764 F.2d 686, 689 (9th Cir. 1985), *cert. dismissed*, 475 U.S. 1040, 106 S. Ct. 1253, 89 L. Ed. 2d 362 (1986).

As is acknowledged by all of the parties, the court's choice-of-law analysis, as to both the Jones Act and general maritime law, should properly be guided by the following factors set forth in both the *Lauritizen* and *Rhoditis* cases:

(1) the place of the wrongful act; (2) the law of the flag; (3) the allegiance or domicile of the injured seaman; (4) the allegiance of the defendant shipowner; (5) the place where the contract of employment was made; (6) the inaccessibility of a foreign forum; and (7) the law of the forum.

Rhoditis, 398 U.S. at 308, 90 S. Ct. at 1733; *Lauritizen*, 345 U.S. at 583-91, 73 S. Ct. at 928-32. In addition, the Court in *Rhoditis* noted that these seven factors were "not intended as exhaustive," and added an eighth factor, the shipowner's base of operations. *Rhoditis*, 398 U.S. at 309, 90 S. Ct. at 1734.

As indicated by Magistrate Arenas, Kukias sustained his injury on the Victoria, somewhere off the coast of Puerto Rico en route to St. Thomas, although the precise location of the vessel, at the time of the incident, is unknown. Even if it is assumed that the accident occurred in United States waters, this first factor is of little significance. As stated by the Supreme Court in the *Romero* case, "[t]he amount and type of recovery which a foreign seaman may receive from his foreign employer while sailing on a foreign ship should not depend on the wholly fortuitous circumstance of the place of injury." *Romero*, 358 U.S. at 384, 79 S. Ct. at 486; *see also Lauritizen*, 345 U.S. at 583, 73 S. Ct. at 928 (test of location of the wrongful act is of limited application to shipboard torts).

The second factor, the law of the flag, has been said to be of "cardinal importance" in determining the choice of law in maritime cases. *See Lauritizen*, 345 U.S. at 584, 73 S. Ct. at 929. At the time of Kukias' accident, the Victoria was registered under the flag of Panama.

Another significant factor is the allegiance or domicile of the injured seaman. There is no doubt that Kukias is a domiciliary and citizen of Greece.

The fourth factor, the allegiance of the shipowner, is often misleading. It is elementary that "only an employer can be liable under the Jones Act." *Karvelis v. Constellation Lines S.A.*, 806 F.2d 49, 52 (2d Cir. 1986), *cert. denied*, — U.S. —, 107 S. Ct. 1891, 95 L. Ed. 2d 498 (1987). In this case, the employer of Kukias was not the owner of the ship, Phaedon, but was Chandris, the company hired to manage and operate the Victoria. Kukias, however, may also be considered the employee of the shipowner, Phaedon, under the borrowed servant doctrine. *See Spinks v. Chevron Oil Co.*, 507 F.2d 216, 224-25 (5th Cir. 1975). Hence, the court must consider the allegiance of Chandris, Kukias' employer, as well as the allegiance of the shipowner, Phaedon. In determining the allegiances of these corporations, the court must "look through the facade of foreign registration and incorporation to find the true ownership of the vessel" and its operator. *See Villar v. Crowley Maritime Corp.*, 782 F.2d 1478, 1481 (9th Cir. 1986).

In this case, it is clear that Phaedon was a Panamanian corporation, and that Chandris was incorporated in Liberia. Looking through the "facade of incorporation," however, the court agrees with the Magistrate's finding that the allegiance of both corporations is with Greece. Even if this were not true, it is beyond dispute that neither corporation is "a foreign shell created by American interests to avoid the requirements of American law." *See Cruz v. Maritime Co. of Philippines*, 549 F. Supp. 285, 288 (S.D.N.Y. 1982), *aff'd*, 702 F.2d 47 (2d Cir. 1983).

Although the fifth factor, the place of contract, is given little weight in maritime law choice-of-law determinations, courts have stated that the "[c]hoice of law expressed in the contract may be much more important." *Villar v. Crowley Maritime Corp.*, 782 F.2d at 1481; *see Lauritizen*, 345 U.S. at 588-89, 73 S. Ct. at 931; *Pereira v. Utah Transp., Inc.*, 764 F.2d at 689. Kukias signed on at Piraeus, Greece, under a contract of employment which specified that "any claim or dispute that may arise from the present agreement or the Ship's Articles will be exclusively subject only to Greek Law and to the Greek Collective Agreement ... and only the Greek Courts will have exclusive jurisdiction...."

The sixth factor, the availability of a foreign forum, to wit, Greece, is assured by the agreement of the defendants to the conditions adopted in the district court's order of dismissal. Hence, there is no doubt that a foreign forum is available.

As for the seventh factor, the law of the forum, even Kukias concedes that the law of the forum "counts for little when the defendants are 'involuntarily made a party.'" *See Sosa v. M/V Lago Izabal*, 736 F.2d 1028, 1031 (5th Cir. 1984); *accord Sigalas*, 776 F.2d at 1518.

The final factor to be considered is the base of operations. From its analysis, the court has concluded that neither the shipowner, Phaedon, nor the manager and operator of the cruiseship, Chandris, has its base of operations in the United States.

From the list of pertinent factors, the only two factors that would support the applicability of United States law are the place of the wrongful act, and the law of the forum. Although the Magistrate concluded that these two factors were insufficient to support a cause of action under the Jones Act or general maritime law, Kukias nevertheless contends that the Magistrate erred in his choice-of-law analysis. Specifically Kukias asserts that the location of his medical treatment, an American hospital in St. Thomas, should have been a factor in the choice-of-law analysis. Kukias also contends that the most significant factor in the choice-of-law analysis should be the "substantial contacts/base of operations" test enunciated in *Hellenic Lines Ltd. v. Rhoditis*, 398 U.S. 306, 90 S. Ct. 1731, 26 L. Ed. 2d 252 (1970). Kukias submits that "the facts overwhelmingly evidence a 'substantial contact' with the United States by Chandris and the Victoria." The court, however, has concluded that none of these contentions are persuasive, and holds that there are insufficient factors to support a cause of action under the Jones Act or the general maritime law of the United States.

It must be noted that, in expanding upon the *Lauritizen* factors, the Court in *Rhoditis* made it clear that "the list of seven factors in *Lauritizen* was not intended as exhaustive." *Rhoditis*, 398 U.S. at 309, 90 S. Ct. at 1734. Kukias, however, has not called to the court's attention any case in which the place of hospitalization was accorded significant weight in deciding the applicability of the Jones Act or general maritime law in a maritime tort action.

Indeed, the courts that have considered the question have decided to the contrary. *See, e.g., Mattes v. National Hellenic Am. Lines, S.A.*, 427 F. Supp. 619, 622 (S.D.N.Y. 1977); *Brillis v. Chandris (U.S.A.) Inc.*, 215 F. Supp. 520, 523 (S.D.N.Y. 1963). In the *Mattes* case, although the Jones Act was held to be applicable because of the shipowner's strong presence in the United States, the court stated that "[t]he fact that plaintiff received initial medical treatment in the United States is simply not sufficiently 'substantial' to justify application of American law." *Mattes*, 427 F. Supp. at 622. Cases from this circuit, although pre-*Rhoditis*, have similarly failed to consider the place of hospitalization as a factor in determining the applicability of the Jones Act or general maritime law in a maritime tort action. *See, e.g., Volkenburg, P.P.A. v. Nederland-Amerik. Stoom v. Maats*, 336 F.2d 480 (1st Cir. 1964); *Zouras v. Menelaus Shipping Co.*, 336 F.2d 209 (1st Cir. 1964). Moreover, even in the absence of persuasive authority, it would seem unwise to allow the choice of law to be influenced by a factor, the place of hospitalization, which is only slightly less fortuitous than that of the place of the wrongful act.

In considering the applicability of the *Lauritizen-Rhoditis* factors, the court must disagree with plaintiff's suggestion that the decision in *Rhoditis* requires that the base of operations must be emphasized over all of the other factors. As correctly noted by defendant's, in *Rhoditis* the Supreme Court stated that "the shipowner's *base of operations* is another factor of importance in determining whether the Jones Act is applicable; and there well may be others." *Rhoditis*, 398 U.S. at 309, 90 S. Ct. at 1734 (emphasis in original); *see DeMateos v. Texaco, Inc.*, 362 F.2d 895, 901 (3d Cir. 1977), *cert. denied*, 435 U.S. 904, 98 S. Ct. 1449, 55 L. Ed. 2d 494 (1978). Surely, this language does not mean that the shipowner's base of operations is the dispositive factor. The post-*Rhoditis* decisions continue to consider the full range of factors relevant to a choice-of-law determination, and, in appropriate cases, have declined to apply the Jones Act despite a finding that the shipowner had substantial domestic contacts. *See, e.g., Pereira v. Utah Transp., Inc.*, 764 F.2d at 689-90; *see also Villar v. Crowley Maritime Corp.*, 782 F.2d 1478, 1482 (9th Cir. 1986) ("even assuming that [defendant's] base of operations is in the United States, under these facts that alone is not a sufficient basis to apply the Jones Act.").

Although it is not dispositive, the base of operations is a significant factor. To determine whether a vessel or its operator has a base of operations in the United States, the court must examine "the substantial and continuing contacts that th[e] alien owner has with this country." *Rhoditis*, 398 U.S. at 310, 90 S. Ct. at 1734.

Kukias contends that "[t]he facts overwhelmingly evidence 'substantial contact' with the United States by Chandris and the Victoria." Kukias stresses that, for a major portion of the year, the Victoria embarks on weekly cruises from Puerto Rico; that substantial revenue from American sources is generated from the operation of the Victoria and is collected by a domestic corporation, Chandris, Inc.; that the vessel is supplied with food and provisions in an American port; and that large sums are spent in advertising the Victoria in the United States. On the basis of these facts, Kukias would have the court decide that the base of operations for Chandris and the Victoria is in the United States, and, therefore he has stated a cause of action under the Jones Act. The court, however, does not agree.

As noted previously, the defendants in this case are foreign corporations controlled by Greek domiciliaries. Defendants maintain no offices in the United States, and management decisions are not made in this country. Furthermore, for portions of the year, the Victoria cruises exclusively in European ports. While the vessel generates revenue from United States sources, and regularly travels to American ports, the management and ownership of the Victoria rest exclusively in the hands of Greeks who do not conduct their activities within the United States.

In resolving the question of the defendants' bases of operations, helpful guidance is found in the case of *Sigalas v. Lido Maritime, Inc.*, 776 F.2d 1512 (11th Cir. 1985). In *Sigalas*, a Greek national died in Senegal while en route from Greece to the United States. The vessel was owned and operated by foreign corporations which had no United States offices but which had a contractual relationship with a ticket agent located in the United States. The vessel cruised the Caribbean, as well as the North Atlantic and Mediterranean. In all seasons over 90% of ticket sales were to American nationals. *Sigalas*, 776 F.2d at 1514.

In affirming the district court's decision that the Jones Act and general maritime law did not apply, the court of appeals in *Sigalas* emphasized that "over 80% of the stock in the relevant corporations is held by Greeks, who exercise complete control over the day-to-day management of the [vessel]." *Id.* at 1518. As for the relevance of ticket sales to Americans, the court stated: "that the bulk of [defendant's] revenue comes from American pocket books ... is not enough to justify application of American law." *Id.*; *see also Rodriguez v. Flota Mercante Grancolombiana, S.A.*, 703 F.2d 1069, 1073 (9th Cir.) ("The fact that [defendant's] vessels have grossed an impressive amount of income in calling on ports o the United States does not prove that [defendant's] base of operations is in the United States."), *cert. denied*, 464 U.S. 820, 104 S. Ct. 84, 78 L. Ed. 2d 94 (1983). A different result clearly is not warranted in this case simply because, at the time of his injury, Kukias was on board a vessel which may have been traveling in United States waters. *See Romero*, 358 U.S. at 383, 79 S. Ct. at 486.

In sum, looking beyond "the facade of the operation," we are convinced that the cumulative significance of the relevant contacts in this case counsels against the applicability of United States law. Hence, we affirm the judgment of dismissal of the district court for failure to state a cause of action under the Jones Act and general maritime law.

Affirmed.

Note: Forum Selection Clauses

The Court of Appeals for the Fifth Circuit has held that a forum selection clause in a foreign seaman's employment contract was enforceable. *Marinechance Shipping, Ltd. v. Sebastian*, 143 F.3d 216, 1998 AMC 2819 (5th Cir. 1998). The same court has held that an arbitration clause in a foreign seaman's employment contract is enforceable, despite the fact that seamen's employment contracts are excluded from the operation of the Federal Arbitration Act by 9 U.S.C. §1. The Fifth Circuit held that that exclusion does not apply to cases where a stay of proceedings is sought pursuant to the part of Title 9 (*i.e.*, 9 U.S.C. §§ 201-208) that implements the Convention on the Recognition and Enforcement of Foreign Arbitral Awards (the New York Convention). *Francisco v. M/T Stolt Achievement*, 293 F.3d 270, 2002 AMC 1529 (5th Cir. 2002).

In *Bodzai v. Arctic Fjord, Inc.*, 990 P.2d 616, 2000 AMC 266 (Ak. 1999), the Supreme Court of Alaska distinguished *Marinechance*, holding claims for maintenance and cure, unseaworthiness and Jones Act did not arise from contract and so could not be affected by a forum selection clause in contract relating to "Any dispute which may arise under the terms of this contract".

Part 3. Actions for Unseaworthiness: Cases and Notes

Introductory Notes

1. The origin of a seaman's right to recover for injuries caused by an unseaworthy ship is far from clear. The earliest codifications of the law of the sea provided only the equivalent of maintenance and cure—medical treatment and wages to a mariner wounded or falling ill in the service of the ship. Markedly similar provisions granting relief of this nature are to be found in the Laws of Oleron, promulgated about 1150 A.D. by Eleanor, Duchess of Guienne; in the Laws of Wisbuy, published in the following century; in the Laws of the Hanse Towns, which appeared in 1597; and in the Marine Ordinances of Louis XIV, published in 1681.

For many years American courts regarded these ancient codes as establishing the limits of a shipowner's liability to a seaman injured in the service of his vessel. During this early period the maritime law was concerned with the concept of unseaworthiness only with reference to two situations quite unrelated to the right of a crew member to recover for personal injuries. The earliest mention of unseaworthiness in American judicial opinions appears in cases in which mariners were suing for their wages. They were required to prove the unseaworthiness of the vessel to excuse their desertion or misconduct which otherwise would result in a forfeiture of their right to wages. The other route through which the concept of unseaworthiness found its way into the maritime law was via the rules covering marine insurance and the carriage of goods by sea.

Not until the late nineteenth century did there develop in American admiralty courts the doctrine that seamen had a right to recover for personal injuries beyond maintenance and cure. During that period it became generally accepted that a shipowner was liable to a mariner injured in the service of a ship as a consequence of the owner's failure to exercise due diligence. The decisions of that era for the most part treated maritime injuries cases on the same footing as cases involving the duty of a shoreside employer to exercise ordinary care to provide his employees with a reasonably safe place to work.

This was the historical background behind Mr. Justice Brown's much quoted second proposition in *The Osceola*, 189 U.S. 158, 175, 23 S.Ct. 483, 47 L.Ed. 760: "That the vessel and her owner are, both by English and American law, liable to an indemnity for injuries received by seamen in consequence of the unseaworthiness of the ship, or a failure to supply and keep in order the proper appliances appurtenant to the ship." In support of this proposition the Court's opinion noted that "[i]t will be observed in these cases that a departure has been made from the Continental codes in allowing an indemnity beyond the expense of maintenance and cure in cases arising from unseaworthiness. This departure originated in England in the Merchants' Shipping Act of 1876 ... and in this country, in a general consensus of opinion among the Circuit and District Courts, that an exception should be made from the general principle before obtaining, in favor of seamen suffering injury through the unseaworthiness of the vessel. We are not disposed to disturb so wholesome a doctrine by any contrary decision of our own." 189 U.S. at 175.

It is arguable that the import of the above-quoted second proposition in *The Osceola* was not to broaden the shipowner's liability, but, rather, to limit liability for negligence to those situations where his negligence resulted in the vessel's unseaworthiness. Support for such a view is to be found not only in the historic context in which *The Osceola* was decided, but in the discussion in the balance of the opinion, in the decision itself (in favor of the shipowner), and in the equation which the Court drew with the law of England, where the Merchant Shipping Act of 1876 imposed upon the owner only the duty to use "all reasonable means" to "insure the seaworthiness of the ship." This limited view of *The Osceola's* pronouncement as to liability for unseaworthiness may be the basis for subsequent decisions of federal courts exonerating shipowners from responsibility for the negligence of their agents because that negligence had not rendered the vessel unseaworthy. Such a reading of the *Osceola* opinion also finds arguable support in several subsequent decisions of the Supreme Court. *Baltimore S.S. Co. v. Phillips*, 274 U.S. 316, 47 S.Ct. 600, 71 L.Ed. 1069; *Plamals v. The Pinar Del Rio*, 277 U.S. 151, 48 S.Ct. 457, 72 L.Ed. 827; *Pacific Co. v. Peterson*, 278 U.S. 130, 49 S.Ct. 75, 73 L.Ed. 220. In any event, with the passage of the Jones Act in 1920, 41 Stat. 1007, 46 U.S.C.A. §§ 30104-5 (formerly 46 U.S.C. § 688), Congress effectively obliterated all distinctions between the kinds of negligence for which the shipowner is liable, as well as limitations imposed by the fellow-servant doctrine, by extending to seamen the remedies made available to railroad workers under the Federal Employers' Liability Act.

The United States Supreme Court began to develop the ancient doctrine of unseaworthiness in *Mahnich v. Southern Steamship Co.*, 321 U.S. 96, 64 S.Ct. 455, 88 L.Ed. 561, 1944 AMC 1 (1944). That case involved the claim of a seaman who was a member of the crew of a vessel. Soon thereafter, the Court extended a warranty of seaworthiness to longshoremen and harbor workers. *Seas Shipping Co. v. Sieracki*, 328 U.S. 85, 66 S.Ct. 872, 90 L.Ed. 1099, 1956 AMC 698 (1946); *Pope & Talbot, Inc. v. Hawn*, 346 U.S. 406, 74 S.Ct. 202, 98 L.Ed. 143, 1954 AMC 1953). During the 1950's and 1960's, most of the cases elaborating on the notion of unseaworthiness involved claims of longshoremen and harbor workers. However, the 1972 amendments to the Longshoremen's and Harbor Workers' Compensation Act (*see infra*) eliminated the unseaworthiness action that longshoremen and harbor workers covered by the Act had against a shipowner. Once again, therefore, the warranty of seaworthiness is largely confined to seamen who are members of the crew of a vessel. Pre-1972 decisions defining the scope of unseaworthiness, even if rendered for claims by longshoremen and harbor workers, continue to be controlling, however, for the determination of claims of seamen.

2. The warranty of seaworthiness applies to the hull of a ship, the ship's cargo-handling machinery, hand tool aboard the ship, ropes and tackle, and, in general, all sorts of equipment either belonging to the ship or brought aboard by stevedores. *See Italia Societa per Azioni di Navigazione v. Oregon Stevedoring Co.*, 376 U.S. 315, 84 S.Ct. 748, 11 L.Ed.2d 732, 1964 AMC 1075 (1964); *Michalic v. Cleveland Tankers, Inc.*, 364 U.S. 325, 81 S.Ct. 6, 5 L.Ed.2d 20, 19760 AMC 2251 (1960); *Crumady v. The J.H. Fisser*, 358 U.S. 423, 79 S.Ct. 445, 3 L.Ed.2d 413, 1959 AMC 580 (1959). Cargo that is improperly packaged or improperly stowed may render a vessel unseaworthy. *See Gutierrez v. Waterman Steamship Corp.*, 373 U.S. 206, 83 S.Ct. 1185, 10 L.Ed.2d 297, 1963 AMC 1649 (1963); *Atlantic & Gulf Stevedores, Inc. v. Ellerman Lines*, 369 U.S. 355, 82 S.Ct. 780, 7 L.Ed.2d 798, 1962 AMC 565 (1962); *Waterman Steamship Corp. v. Dugan & McNamara, Inc.*, 364 U.S. 421, 81 S.Ct. 200, 5 L.Ed.2d 169, 1960 AMC 2260 (1960). Finally, the crew of a vessel is warranted as seaworthy. *See Waldron v. Moore-McCormick Lines*, 386 U.S. 724, 87 S.Ct. 1410, 18 L.Ed.2d 482, 1967 AMC 579 (1967); *Boudoin v. Lykes Brothers Steamship Co.*, 348 U.S. 336, 75 S.Ct. 382, 99 L.Ed. 354, 1955 AMC 488 (1955).

3. A ship may be unseaworthy if it does not have certain types of equipment, such as maps or lifesaving gear. However, the Supreme Court has held that a ship lacking a forced cargo ventilation system is not unseaworthy. *Morales v. City of Galveston*, 370 U.S. 165, 82 S.Ct. 1226, 8 L.Ed.2d 412, 1962 AMC 1450 (1962). The question whether a ship is unseaworthy is ordinarily one of fact. An instruction to the jury that a ship is unseaworthy as a matter of law may be reversible error. *See Dunlap v. G. & C. Towing, Inc.*, 613 F.2d 493, 1980 AMC 1874 (4th Cir. 1980).

4. A seaman employed by the bareboat charterer of a vessel may sue his employer under the Jones Act for negligence and the shipowner *in rem* for unseaworthiness. *See The Barnstable*, 181 U.S. 464, 21 S.Ct. 684, 45 L.Ed. 954 (1901). According to *Baker v. Raymond International*, 656 F.2d 173, 1982 AMC 2752 (5th Cir. 1981), the seaman may also sue the shipowner *in personam* for unseaworthiness (subject to any ceiling established by the Limitation of Liability Act).

A. Application of the Doctrine

MITCHELL v. TRAWLER RACER, INC.

362 U.S. 539, 80 S. Ct. 926, 4 L. Ed. 2d 941, 1960 AMC 1503 (1960)

Mr. Justice STEWART delivered the opinion of the Court

The petitioner was a member of the crew of the Boston fishing trawler *Racer*, owned and operated by the respondent. On April 1, 1957, the vessel returned to her home port from a 10-day voyage to the North Atlantic fishing grounds, loaded with a catch of fish and fish spawn. After working that morning with his fellow crew members in unloading the spawn, the petitioner changed his clothes and came on deck to go ashore. He made his way to the side of the vessel which abutted the dock, and in accord with recognized custom stepped onto the ship's rail in order to reach a ladder attached to the pier. He was injured when his foot slipped off the rail as he grasped the ladder.

To recover for his injuries he filed this action for damages in a complaint containing three counts: the first under the Jones Act, alleging negligence; the second alleging unseaworthiness; and the third for maintenance and cure. At the trial there was evidence to show that the ship's rail where the petitioner had lost his footing was covered for a distance of 10 or 12 feet with slime and fish gurry, apparently remaining there from the earlier unloading operations.

The district judge instructed the jury that in order to allow recovery upon either the negligence or unseaworthiness count, they must find that the slime and gurry had been on the ship's rail for a period of time long enough for the respondent to have learned about it and to have removed it. Counsel for the petitioner requested that the trial judge distinguish between negligence and unseaworthiness in this respect, and specifically requested him to instruct the jury that notice was not a necessary element in proving liability based upon unseaworthiness of the vessel. This request was denied. The jury awarded the petitioner maintenance and cure, but found for the respondent shipowner on both the negligence and unseaworthiness counts.

An appeal was taken upon the sole ground that the district judge had been in error in instructing the jury that constructive notice was necessary to support liability for unseaworthiness. The Court of Appeals affirmed, holding that at least with respect to "an unseaworthy condition which arises only during the progress of the voyage," the shipowner's obligation "is merely to see that reasonable care is used under the circumstances ... incident to the correction of the newly arisen defect." 265 F.2d 426, 432.

* * *

In its present posture this case thus presents the single issue whether with respect to so-called "transitory" unseaworthiness the shipowner's liability is limited by concepts of common-law negligence. There are here no problems, such as have recently engaged the Court's attention, with respect to the petitioner's status as a "seaman." The *Racer* was in active maritime operation, and the petitioner was a member of her crew.

* * *

The first reference in this Court to the shipowner's obligation to furnish a seaworthy ship as explicitly unrelated to the standard of ordinary care in a personal injury case appears in *Carlisle Packing Co. v. Sandanger*, 259 U.S. 255. There it was said "we think the trial court might have told the jury that without regard to negligence the vessel was unseaworthy when she left the dock ... and that if thus unseaworthy and one of the crew received damage as the direct result thereof, he was entitled to recover compensatory damages." 259 U.S. at 259. This characterization of unseaworthiness as unrelated to negligence was probably not necessary to the decision in that case, where the respondent's injuries had clearly in fact been caused by failure to exercise ordinary care (putting gasoline in a can labeled "coal oil" and neglecting to provide the vessel with life preservers). Yet there is no reason to suppose that the Court's language was inadvertent.

During the two decades that followed the *Carlisle* decision there came to be a general acceptance of the view that *The Osceola* had enunciated a concept of absolute liability for unseaworthiness unrelated to principles of negligence law. Personal injury litigation based upon unseaworthiness was substantial. *See*, GILMORE AND BLACK, THE LAW OF ADMIRALTY (1957), p. 316. And the standard texts accepted that theory of liability without question. *See* BENEDICT, THE LAW OF AMERICAN ADMIRALTY (6th ed., 1940), Vol. I, § 83; ROBINSON, ADMIRALTY LAW (1939), p. 303 *et seq.* Perhaps the clearest expression appeared in Judge Augustus Hand's opinion in *The H.A. Scandrett*, 87 F.2d 708:

> In our opinion the libelant had a right of indemnity for injuries arising from an unseaworthy ship even though there was no means of anticipating trouble.
>
> The ship is not freed from liability by mere due diligence to render her seaworthy as may be the case under the Harter Act (46 U.S.C.A. §§ 190-195) where loss results from faults in navigation, but under the maritime law there is an absolute obligation to provide a seaworthy vessel and, in default thereof, liability follows for any injuries caused by breach of the obligation. 87 F.2d. at 711.

In 1944 this Court decided *Mahnich v. Southern S.S. Co.*, 321 U.S. 96. While it is possible to take a narrow view of the precise holding in that case, the fact is that *Mahnich* stands as a landmark in the development of admiralty law. Chief Justice Stone's opinion in that case gave an unqualified stamp of solid authority to the view that *The Osceola* was correctly to be understood as holding that the duty to provide a seaworthy ship depends not at all upon the negligence of the shipowner or his agents. Moreover, the dissent in *Mahnich* accepted this reading of *The Osceola* and claimed no more than that the injury in *Mahnich* was not properly attributable to unseaworthiness. See 321 U.S., at 105-113.

In *Seas Shipping Co. v. Sieracki*, 328 U.S. 85, the Court effectively scotched any doubts that might have lingered after *Mahnich* as to the nature of the shipowner's duty to provide a seaworthy vessel. The character of the duty, said the Court, is "absolute." "It is essentially a species of liability without fault, analogous to other well known instances in our law. Derived from and shaped to meet the hazards which performing the service imposes, the liability is neither limited by conceptions of negligence nor contractual in character ... . It is a form of absolute duty owing to all within the range of its humanitarian policy." 328 U.S., at 94-95. The dissenting opinion agreed as to the nature of the shipowner's duty. "[D]ue diligence of the owner," it said, "does not relieve him from this obligation." 328 U.S., at 104.

* * *

There is no suggestion in any of the decisions that the duty is less onerous with respect to an unseaworthy condition arising after the vessel leaves her home port, or that the duty is any less with respect to an unseaworthy condition which may be only temporary. Of particular relevance here is *Alaska Steamship Co. v. Petterson, supra.* In that case the Court affirmed a judgment holding the shipowner liable for injuries caused by defective equipment temporarily brought on board by an independent contractor over which the owner had no control. That decision is thus specific authority for the proposition that the shipowner's actual or constructive knowledge of the unseaworthy condition is not essential to his liability. That decision also effectively disposes of the suggestion that liability for a temporary unseaworthy condition is different from the liability that attaches when the condition is permanent.

There is ample room for argument, in the light of history, as to how the law of unseaworthiness should have or could have developed. Such theories might be made to fill a volume of logic. But, in view of the decisions in this Court over the last 15 years, we can find no room for argument as to what the law is. What has evolved is a complete divorcement of unseaworthiness liability from concepts of negligence. To hold otherwise now would be to erase more than just a page of history.

What has been said is not to suggest that the owner is obligated to furnish an accident-free ship. The duty is absolute, but it is a duty only to furnish a vessel and appurtenances reasonably fit for their intended use. The standard is not perfection, but reasonable fitness; not a ship that will weather every conceivable storm or withstand every imaginable peril of the sea, but a vessel reasonably suitable for her intended service. *Boudoin v. Lykes Bros. S.S. Co.,* 348 U.S. 336.

The judgment must be reversed, and the case remanded to the District Court for a new trial on the issue of unseaworthiness.

Reversed and remanded.

[Dissenting opinion of Justice FRANKFURTER, with whom Justices HARLAN and WITTAKER join, is omitted.]

MARTINEZ v. SEA-LAND SERVICES, INC.

763 F.2d 26, 1986 AMC 851 (1st Cir. 1985)

BREYER, Circuit Judge

Plaintiff, an ordinary seaman on the SS Boston, sued the ship's owners, claiming (insofar as here relevant) that the ship's "unseaworthiness" caused him to injure his back. The defendant moved for summary judgment. For purposes of deciding that motion, the district court, 589 F. Supp. 844, found

> While plaintiff was carrying two boxes of soft drinks from the main deck to the slop chest of the ship, the boxes slipped because the plastic sleeve on one of the boxes was loose. Plaintiff tried to prevent the boxes from falling and twisted his back.

The court nonetheless granted summary judgment for defendant. It concluded that these facts were insufficient to support a legal conclusion that the ship was "unseaworthy." The court noted that the doctrine of "unseaworthiness"—a warranty of fitness for duty, *see Mitchell v. Trawler Racer, Inc.,* 362 U.S. 539, 80 S. Ct. 926, 4 L. Ed. 2d 941 (1960); *Smith v. American Mail Line, Ltd.,* 525 F.2d 1148 (9th Cir. 1975)—extends to the ship itself, it appurtenances, its crew, its method of cargo storage, and to cargo containers, but not to the cargo itself. *Smith, supra,* 525 F.2d at 1150 (citing cases). The court went on to suggest that the soft drink sleeve was neither a cargo container nor part of the vessel's equipment or appurtenances, and therefore concluded that the warranty of seaworthiness does not apply.

We agree with the plaintiff, who has appealed, that the district court's granting of summary judgment was erroneous. Both parties agree that the soft drinks at issue here were not ordinary "cargo"— that is "goods [or] merchandise ... conveyed in a ship for payment of freight." R. DE KERCHOVE, INTERNATIONAL MARITIME DICTIONARY (2d ed. 1961). Rather, these drinks were part of the ship's stores, destined for the crew's consumption on board and not covered by a bill of lading. And, we believe that the seaworthiness warranty of "fitness for duty" extends to material in which ships' stores are wrapped.

For one thing, the rationale underlying those cases holding that the unseaworthiness doctrine extends to "cargo containers," even if it does not extend to the cargo itself, applies to wrappings of the sort here at issue. That rationale was well stated by the Fourth Circuit as follows:

> Fault is not an essential element of the doctrine of "unseaworthiness" but conceptually and theoretically it may rest upon an irrebuttable presumption of opportunity to prevent harm. Once goods are put aboard, the condition of containers and packaging are within the control of the master of the vessel, and in most instances, although not all, defective packaging is discernible by inspection. If most defects are ascertainable it is a rough sort of justice and not intolerable to assume that all are. Thus it is possible to say that the no-fault concept of unseaworthiness rests in part, at least theoretically, upon the ship's "fault" in failing to discern and correct conditions that may cause injury. Another reason, and perhaps a better one, for imputing responsibility for defective cargo to the ship is that once the ship is at sea the stress and strain of a voyage may break the packages, and it would thereafter be all but impossible to allocate responsibility as between the packager ashore and the ship's officers who subsequently undertake to move the cargo in a dangerous condition.

Pryor v. American President Lines, 520 F.2d 974, 981 (4th Cir. 1975) (footnote omitted). The logic of this argument applies with at least equal strength to boxes of food or drink to be used by the crew during the voyage.

For another thing, this Circuit has specifically said that the unseaworthiness doctrine applies to ships' stores. *Doucette v. Vincent*, 194 F.2d 834, 837-38 (1st Cir. 1952) (maritime law of seaworthiness imposes duty on ship-owner to provide a vessel sufficient in "materials, construction, equipment, stores, officers, men and outfit for the trade or service in which the vessel is employed"). *See also Rodriguez v. The Angelina*, 177 F. Supp. 242, 245 (D.P.R. 1959) (quoting *Doucette*); *In re Gulf & Midlands Barge Line, Inc.*, 509 F.2d 713, 721 (5th Cir. 1975) ("seaworthiness" in marine insurance contract means "that the materials of which the ship is made, its construction, the qualifications of the captain, the number and description of the crew, the tackle, sails, the rigging, stores, equipment, and outfit, generally, are such as to render it in every respect fit for the proposed voyage or service") (quoting Burglass, Marine Insurance and General Average in the United States 20-21 (1973)); *cf.* 46 U.S.C. § 10902 (statutory remedy for unseaworthiness applies to ship's "crew, hull, equipment, tackle, machinery, apparel, furniture, provisions of food or water, or stores"). Though apparently "ships' stores" cases have not arisen often, at least one district court has explicitly held the seaworthiness warranty applicable to their wrapping material, *see Wilson v. Twin Rivers Towing Co.*, 413 F. Supp. 154, 158-59 (W.D. Pa. 1976) (unseaworthiness doctrine applies to improper packaging of meat destined for ships' stores).

Finally, we can find no reasoned distinction between the ship's gear and other material to which the doctrine plainly applies and the stores (or their wrappings) that are to be used on the voyage. *See generally Usner v. Luckenbach Overseas Corp.*, 400 U.S. 494, 499, 91 S. Ct. 514, 517 , 27 L. Ed. 2d 562 (1971) ("But our cases have held that the scope of unseaworthiness is by no means ... limited [to defective conditions of a physical part of the ship itself.] A vessel's condition of unseaworthiness might arise from any number of circumstances.").

For these reasons, the defendant's motion for summary judgment should have been denied. The judgment of the district court is *reversed, and the case is remanded for proceedings consistent with this opinion.*

USNER v. LUCKENBACH OVERSEAS CORP.

400 U.S. 494, 91 S. Ct. 514, 27 L. Ed. 2d 562, 1971 AMC 277 (1971)

Mr. Justice STEWART delivered the opinion of the Court

The petitioner, a longshoreman˙ employed by an independent stevedoring contractor, was injured while engaged with his fellow employees in loading cargo aboard the *S.S. Edgar F. Luckenbach*. He brought this action for damages against the respondents, the owner and the charterer of the ship, in a federal district court, alleging that his injuries had been caused by the ship's unseaworthiness.

In the course of pretrial proceedings the circumstances under which the petitioner had been injured were fully disclosed, and they are not in dispute. On the day in question the ship lay moored to a dock in New Orleans, Louisiana, receiving cargo from a barge positioned alongside. The loading operations were being performed by the petitioner and his fellow longshoremen under the direction of their employer. Some of the men were on the ship, operating the port winch and boom at the No. 2 hatch. The petitioner and others were on the barge, where their job was to "break out" the bundles of cargo by securing them to a sling attached to the fall each time it was lowered from the ship's boom by the winch operator. The loading operations had been proceeding in this manner for some time, until upon one occasion the winch operator did not lower the fall far enough. Finding the sling beyond his reach, the petitioner motioned to the flagman standing on the deck of the ship to direct the winch operator to lower the fall further. The winch operator then lowered the fall, but he lowered it too far and too fast. The sling struck the petitioner, knocking him to the deck of the barge and causing his injuries. Neither before nor after this occurrence was any difficulty experienced with the winch, boom, fall, sling, or any other equipment or appurtenance of the ship or her cargo.

The respondents moved for summary judgment in the District Court, upon the ground that a single negligent act by a fellow longshoreman could not render the ship unseaworthy. The District Court denied the motion, but granted the respondents leave to take an interlocutory appeal under 28 U.S.C. § 1292(b). The United States Court of Appeals for the Fifth Circuit allowed the appeal and, reversing the District Court, directed that the respondents' motion for summary judgment be granted. 413 F.2d 984. It was the appellate court's view that "'[i]nstant unseaworthiness' resulting from 'operational negligence' of the stevedoring contractor is not a basis for recovery by an injured longshoreman." 413 F.2d, at 985-986. We granted certiorari, 397 U.S. 933, because of a conflict among the circuits on the basic issue presented.

The development in admiralty law of the doctrine of unseaworthiness as a predicate for a shipowner's liability for personal injuries or death has been fully chronicled elsewhere, and it would serve no useful purpose to repeat the details of that development here.

* * *

A major burden of the Court's decisions spelling out the nature and scope of the cause of action for unseaworthiness has been insistence upon the point that it is a remedy separate from, independent of, and additional to other claims against the shipowner, whether created by statute or under general maritime law. More specifically, the Court has repeatedly taken pains to point out that liability based upon unseaworthiness is wholly distinct from liability based upon negligence. The reason, of course, is that unseaworthiness is a *condition*, and how that condition came into being—whether by negligence or otherwise—is quite irrelevant to the owner's liability for personal injuries resulting from it.

We had occasion to emphasize this basic distinction again in *Mitchell v. Trawler Racer*, 362 U.S. 539. There the unseaworthy condition causing the plaintiff's injury was a ship's rail made slippery by the presence of fish gurry and slime.

* * *

˙ [At one time the warranty of seaworthiness had been extended to longshoremen engaged on loading and unloading a vessel. Congress eliminated this action in the 1972 amendments to the Longshoremen's and Harbor Worker's Compensation Act. However, decisions in cases involving longshoremen are still relevant to the law of unseaworthiness as applied to seamen. Eds.]

Trawler Racer involved the defective condition of a physical part of the ship itself. But our cases have held that the scope of unseaworthiness is by no means so limited. A vessel's condition of unseaworthiness might arise from any number of circumstances. Her gear might be defective, her appurtenances in disrepair, her crew unfit. The number of men assigned to perform a shipboard task might be insufficient. The method of loading her cargo, or the manner of its stowage, might be improper. For any of these reasons, or others, a vessel might not be reasonably fit for her intended service.

What caused the petitioner's injuries in the present case, however, was not the condition of the ship, her appurtenances, her cargo, or her crew, but the isolated, personal negligent act of the petitioner's fellow longshoreman. To hold that this individual act of negligence rendered the ship unseaworthy would be to subvert the fundamental distinction between unseaworthiness and negligence that we have so painstakingly and repeatedly emphasized in our decisions. In *Trawler Racer, supra,* there existed a condition of unseaworthiness, and we held it was error to require a finding of negligent conduct in order to hold the shipowner liable. The case before us presents the other side of the same coin. For it would be equally erroneous here, where no condition of unseaworthiness existed, to hold the shipowner liable for a third party's single and wholly unforeseeable act of negligence. The judgment of the court of Appeals is affirmed.

It is so ordered.

[Dissenting opinion of Justice DOUGLAS, with whom Justice BLACK and Justice BRENNAN concur, is omitted.]

FEEHAN v. UNITED STATES LINES, INC.

522 F. Supp. 811,1982 A.M.C. 364 (S.D.N.Y. 1980)

STEWART, District Judge:

Plaintiff brought suit for the wrongful death of a merchant seaman against the decedent's employer, United States Lines, Inc., and against the manufacturer and operators of the "straddle carrier" that allegedly struck and killed the decedent. Cross-claims for indemnification or contribution were asserted by the United States and Nacirema Operating Co., Inc. ("Nacirema"), operators of the straddle carrier, as well as by United States Lines, Inc., against Hyster Company, Inc. ("Hyster"), the manufacturer of the machine. Hyster moves to dismiss the complaint and the cross-claims or, alternatively, for summary judgment.

* * *

The circumstances surrounding the accident are as follows. On October 11, 1977, the decedent's ship was docked at a U.S. Navy pier in Norfolk, Virginia. While decedent was walking on the pier, a specialized motor vehicle allegedly manufactured by Hyster that was used to transport, load or unload cargo and was known as a straddle carrier struck and killed the decedent. The straddle carrier was operated by an employee of the United States. An employee of defendant Nacirema allegedly aided in the operation of the straddle carrier by directing vehicular and pedestrian traffic in the vicinity of the straddle carrier.

* * *

Hyster previously moved to dismiss the amended complaint on the basis of the statute of limitations. In response to Hyster's motion, plaintiff sought to change tacks, without amending the complaint, and rely on the Admiralty Extension Act, 46 U.S.C. § 740 (1976), instead of diversity of citizenship over Hyster and Nacirema. By Memorandum Decision dated December 18, 1980, we held that § 740 did not apply as the accident was not "caused by the vessel." Plaintiff now moves for reconsideration of our prior decision. Changing tacks for the second time, plaintiff contends that the Admiralty Extension Act applies as against Hyster because the shipowner, Lines, allegedly breached the implied warranty of seaworthiness owed to the decedent. Plaintiff argues that the breach of the implied warranty of seaworthiness makes the accident one "caused by the vessel" within the meaning of § 740 and permits admiralty jurisdiction over Hyster.

The threshold question is whether injury to a seaman on a dock during loading operations by pier-based equipment states a claim for unseaworthiness against Lines. This case requires us to reconcile *Gutierrez v. Waterman*, 373 U.S. 206, 215 (1963), holding that a longshoreman injured on the dock during unloading operations by defective cargo containers may maintain an unseaworthiness claim against the shipowner, and *Victory Carriers v. Law*, 404 U.S. 202, 213-14 (1971), holding that a longshoreman injured on the dock during loading operations by the stevedore's defective forklift truck may not maintain such an action against the shipowner. The significant factual distinction between *Gutierrez* and *Victory Carriers* is the control or origin of the instrumentality of injury. In *Gutierrez*, the shipowner was under a duty to make the cargo containers safe, while in *Victory Carriers* the stevedore and not the shipowner was required to make the fork lift safe. The *Victory Carriers* court concluded:

> In the present case ... the typical elements of a maritime cause of action are particularly attenuated: respondent Law was not injured by equipment that was part of the ship's usual gear or that was stored on board, the equipment that injured him was in no way attached to the ship, the forklift was not under the control of the ship or its crew, and the accident did not occur aboard ship or on the gangplank.

Victory Carriers, 404 U.S. at 213-14....

* * *

[T]he three claims against Hyster in the amended complaint all relate to defective manufacture and design of the straddle carrier. Thus, *Victory Carriers* apparently forecloses the question whether an unseaworthiness claim ... is properly asserted in this action.

Problem

If a seaman is injured in the course of repairing a defective condition, should he be able to recover on grounds of unseaworthiness? *See, supra.*

B. Damages: Comparative Fault

In *Lewis v. Timco, Inc.*, 716 F.2d 1425, 1427-28, 1984 AMC 191 (5th Cir. 1983), the U.S. Court of Appeals for the Fifth Circuit said:

> Admiralty courts have long engaged in the exercise of comparing plaintiffs' negligence to both fault and non-fault based liability of defendants. For example, comparative fault is applied in the strict liability action for unseaworthiness, *Pope & Talbot, Inc. v. Hawn*, 346 U.S. 406, 408-09, 74 S. Ct. 202, 204, 98 L. Ed. 143 (1953), in personal injury actions under the Jones Act, 46 U.S.C. § 688, in actions brought under the Death on the High Seas Act, 46 U.S.C. § 766, and in longshoremen's suits against vessels under the Longshoremen's and Harbor Worker's Compensation Act, 33 U.S.C. § 901 *et seq. Gay v. Ocean Transport & Trading, Ltd.*, 546 F.2d 1233, 1238 (5th Cir. 1977). "The admiralty rule in personal injury cases is, in effect, one of comparative negligence." G. Gilmore & C. Black, The Law of Admiralty 500 n.70 (2d ed. 1975).

Section II. Longshoremen and Harbor Workers: Cases and Notes

Introductory Note

The notion of "maritime employment" applies to seamen, members of the crew of a vessel, and to a great number of land based workers usually designated as longshoremen and harbor workers. Work is "maritime" when it relates to the shipping industry or when it is done in the hazardous zone over or adjacent to navigable waters. Seamen, *i.e.*, members of the crew of a vessel, have the remedies of maintenance and cure, a Jones Act claim, and a claim for unseaworthiness. Maritime workers other than seamen have remedies under state and federal workers' compensation statutes and, in certain circumstances, actions for negligence. For a proper understanding of the remedies available to such maritime workers against their employers and third persons a historical introduction is necessary.

The movement to provide a system of guaranteed compensation to workers injured in the course of their employment began in the United States in the early twentieth century. Proponents of this legislation concentrated their efforts at the state level, but most legislative bodies proceeded cautiously for fear that workmen's compensation laws might infringe on the due process clause of the federal Constitution. In 1917, the Supreme Court dispelled such apprehensions by upholding the constitutionality of the workmen's compensation laws of New York, Iowa, and Washington. *New York Central Railroad v. White*, 243 U.S. 188, 37 S.Ct. 247, 61 L.Ed. 667 (1917). However, in the companion case of *Southern Pacific Co. v. Jensen*, 244 U.S. 205, 37 S.Ct. 524, 61 L.Ed. 1086, 1996 A.M.C. 2076 (1917), which arose under the New York transit workers' compensation statute, Justice McReynolds declared for the majority that the statute could not constitutionally be applied to a longshoreman who was fatally injured on the gangway of a ship while assisting in unloading operations. He reasoned that the matter was within the admiralty jurisdiction of the United States because the deceased was doing maritime work under a maritime contract and was injured on navigable waters; that the constitutional grant of admiralty jurisdiction contemplates a uniform system of maritime laws; that the power to modify the existing maritime laws is necessarily vested in the Congress; that the inaction of Congress demonstrates an intent to preserve the status quo; and that the saving to suitors clause in the Judiciary Act does not apply to workmen's compensation laws because the remedies under these laws are wholly unknown to the common law. He concluded:

> If New York can subject foreign ships coming into her ports to such obligations as those imposed by her Compensation Statute, other States may do likewise. The necessary consequence would be destruction of the very uniformity in respect to maritime matters which the Constitution was designed to establish; and freedom of navigation between the States and with foreign countries would be seriously hampered and impeded. A far more serious injury would result to commerce than could have been inflicted by the Washington statute authorizing a materialman's lien condemned in *The Roanoke*. The legislature exceeded its authority in attempting to extend the statute under consideration to conditions like those here disclosed. So applied, it conflicts with the Constitution and to that extent is invalid.

Justice Holmes filed a celebrated dissenting opinion:

> The Southern Pacific Company has been held liable under the statutes of New York for an accidental injury happening upon a gangplank between a pier and the company's vessel and causing the death of one of its employees. The company not having insured as permitted, the statute may be taken as if it simply imposed a limited but absolute liability in such a case. The short question is whether the power of the State to regulate the liability in that place and to enforce it in the State's own courts is taken away by the conferring of exclusive jurisdiction of all civil causes of admiralty and maritime jurisdiction upon the courts of the United States.
>
> There is no doubt that saving to suitors of the right of a common-law remedy leaves open the common-law jurisdiction of the state courts, and leaves some power of legislation at least, to the States.
>
> The statute having been upheld in other respects, *New York Central R.R. Co. v. White*, 243 U.S. 188, I should have thought these authorities conclusive. The liability created by the New York act ends in a money judgment, and the mode in which the amount is ascertained, or is to be paid, being one that the State constitutionally might adopt, cannot matter to the question before us if any liability can be imposed that was not known to the maritime law.
>
> The common law is not a brooding omnipresence in the sky but the articulate voice of some sovereign or quasi-sovereign that can be identified; although some decisions with which I have disagreed seem to me to have forgotten the fact. It always is the law of some State, and if the District Courts adopt the common law of torts, as they have shown a tendency to do, they thereby assume that a law not of maritime origin and deriving its authority in that territory only from some particular State of this Union also governs maritime torts in that territory— and if the common law, the statute law has at least equal force, as the discussion in *The Osceola* assumes. On the other hand the refusal of the District Courts to give remedies coextensive with the common law would prove no more than that they regarded their jurisdiction as limited by the ancient lines—not that they doubted that the common law might and would be enforced in the courts of the States as it always has been. This court has recognized that in some cases different principles of liability would be applied as the suit would happen to be brought in a common-law or admiralty court. *Compare The Max Morris*, 137 U.S. 1, *with Belden v. Chase*, 150 U.S. 674, 691. But hitherto it has not been doubted authoritatively, so far as I know, that even when the admiralty had a rule of its own to which it adhered, as in *Workman v. New York City*, 179 U.S. 552, the state law, common or statute, would prevail in the courts of the State. Happily such conflicts are few.

It might be asked why, if the grant of jurisdiction to the courts of the United States imports a power in Congress to legislate, the saving of a common-law remedy, *i.e.*, in the state courts, did not import a like if subordinate power in the States. But leaving that question on one side, such cases as *Steamboat Co. v. Chase*, 16 Wall. 522. *The Hamilton*, 207 U.S. 398, and *Atlantic Transport Co. v. Imbrovek*, 234 U.S. 52, show that it is too late to say that the mere silence of Congress excludes the statute or common law of a State from supplementing the wholly inadequate maritime law of the time of the Constitution, in the regulation of personal rights, and I venture to say that it never has been supposed to do so, or had any such effect.

The *Jensen* decision meant that a longshoreman injured on navigable waters was denied a no-fault remedy against his employer; of course, he could have an action for negligence, but this would be subject to the defenses of assumption of risk and the fellow-servant doctrine. Contributory negligence would not bar recovery, but would result in mitigation of damages. Congress sought to make state no-fault remedies available to longshoremen and harbor workers by a 1917 amendment to the saving suitors clause in the Judiciary Act. The Supreme Court, however, struck down the amendment in *Knickerbocker Ice Co. v. Stewart*, 253 U.S. 149, 40 S.Ct. 438, 64 L.Ed. 834 (1920), on the ground that Congress cannot delegate legislative authority to the states in matters falling within the admiralty jurisdiction of the United States.

Subsequently, in *Western Fuel Co. v. Garcia*, 257 U.S. 233, 42 S.Ct. 89, 66 L.Ed. 210 (1921), the Court held that the California wrongful death statute could be applied to a suit seeking damages for the death of a longshoreman on navigable waters because the subject of the litigation was "maritime but local." Further in *Grant Smith-Portership Co. v. Rhode*, 257 U.S. 469, 42 S.Ct. 157, 66 L.Ed. 321 (1922), the Court held that an action in admiralty for damages brought by a carpenter against his employer on account of injuries sustained on a partially completed ship lying in navigable waters was barred by the Oregon workmen's compensation statute. This statute could be constitutionally applied because the matter was "maritime but local" and the application of state law did not derogate from the uniformity of the maritime workers other than masters and members of the crew of a vessel. In 1922, Congress once again amended the saving to suitors clause to put longshoremen under state workmen's compensation statutes, but exempting the master and the crew of any vessel. The Congressional intent was to preserve the uniformity of maritime law as to seamen and permit the application of state statutes to other maritime workers. The Supreme Court struck down this amendment in *Washington v. Dawson & Co.*, 264 U.S. 219, 44 S.Ct. 302, 68 L.Ed. 646 (1924) as an unconstitutional delegation of power to the states. In the course of its opinion, the Court indicated that the appropriate solution would be the enactment of a workmen's compensation statute by Congress.

In 1926, the legal status of longshoremen and harbor workers was improved by their recognition as "seamen" within the meaning of the Jones Act if they were injured on navigable waters while doing work traditionally done by seamen. *International Stevedoring Co. v. Haverty*, 272 U.S. 50, 47 S.Ct. 19, 71 L.Ed. 157, 1926 A.M.C. 1638 (1926). This decision, however, was soon superseded by the Longshoremen's and Harbor Workers' Compensation Act of 1927, enacted by Congress.

A. Territorial Application of the Longshore and Harbor Workers' Compensation Act (LHWCA): Relationship with State Compensation Acts

Background Note

Section 903(a) of the LHWCA originally provided:

> Compensation shall be payable under this chapter in respect of disability or death of an employee, but only if the disability or death results from an injury occurring upon the navigable waters of the United States (including any dry dock) and if recovery for the disability or death through workmen's compensation proceedings may not validly be provided by State law....

Compensation was thought to be limited to injuries occurring on navigable waters, and the limitation concerning recovery through state workmen's compensation proceedings was thought to be a reference to the "maritime but local" rule that decisions of the Supreme Court had established. If the matter was maritime but local, state statutes could constitutionally apply and there was no need for a federal remedy. As a result of these limitations, if a remedy could be provided by state law for injuries occurring on navigable waters, a claim for compensation under the LHWCA would be dismissed under the act; conversely, if a remedy could not validly be provided by state law, a claim for compensation under state law would be dismissed under that law.

DAVIS v. DEPARTMENT OF LABOR & INDUSTRIES

317 U.S. 249, 63 S. Ct. 225, 87 L. Ed. 246, 1942 AMC 1653 (1942)

Mr. Justice BLACK delivered the opinion of the Court

In this case the Washington Supreme Court held that the State could not, consistently with the Federal Constitution, make an award under its state compensation law to the widow of a workman drowned in a navigable river. The circumstances which caused the court to reach this conclusion were these:

The petitioner's husband, a structural steelworker, was drowned in the Snohomish River while working as an employee of the Manson Construction and Engineering Company, a contributor to the Workmen's Compensation Fund of the State of Washington....

The Washington statute provides compensation for employees and dependents of employees, such as decedent, if its application can be made "within the legislative jurisdiction of the state." A further statement of coverage applies the Act to "all employers or workmen ... engaged in maritime occupations for whom no right or obligation exists under the maritime laws." Rem. Rev. Stat., §§ 7674, 7693a. A line of opinions of this Court, beginning with *Southern Pacific Co. v. Jensen*, 244 U.S. 205, 216, held that under some circumstances states could, but under others could not, consistently with Article III, Par. 2 of the Federal Constitution, apply their compensation laws to maritime employees. State legislation was declared to be invalid only when it "works material prejudice to the characteristic features of the general maritime law or interferes with the proper harmony and uniformity of that law in its international and interstate relations." When a state could, and when it could not, grant protection under a compensation act was left as a perplexing problem, for it was held "difficult, if not impossible," to define this boundary with exactness.

* * *

Harbor workers and longshoremen employed "in whole or in part upon the navigable waters" are clearly protected by this federal act; but employees such as decedent here, occupy that shadowy area within which, at some undefined and undefinable point, state laws can validly provide compensation. This Court has been unable to give any guiding, definite rule to determine the extent of state power in advance of litigation, and has held that the margins of state authority must "be determined in view of surrounding circumstances as cases arise." *Baizley Iron Works v. Span*, 281 U.S. 222, 230. The determination of particular cases, of which there have been a great many, has become extremely difficult. It is fair to say that a number of cases can be cited both in behalf of and in opposition to recovery here.

The very closeness of the cases cited above, and others raising related points of interpretation, has caused much serious confusion. It must be remembered that under the *Jensen* hypothesis, basic conditions are factual: Does the state law "interfere with the proper harmony and uniformity of" maritime law? Yet, employees are asked to determine with certainty before bringing their actions that factual question over which courts regularly divide among themselves and within their own membership. As penalty for error, the injured individual may not only suffer serious financial loss through the delay and expense of litigation, but discover that his claim has been barred by the statute of limitations in the proper forum while he was erroneously pursuing it elsewhere. *See e.g., Ayres v. Parker*, 15 F. Supp. 447. Such a result defeats the purpose of the federal act, which seeks to give "to these hardworking men, engaged in a somewhat hazardous employment, the justice involved in the modern principle of compensation," and the state Acts such as the one before us, which aims at "sure and certain relief for workmen."

* * *

... Since 1917, Congress and the states have sought to restore order out of the confusion which resulted from the *Jensen* decision. That success has not finally been achieved is illustrated by the present case. The Longshoremen's Act, passed with specific reference to the *Jensen* rule, provided a partial solution. The Washington statute represents a state effort to clarify the situation. Both of these laws show clearly that neither was intended to encroach on the field occupied by the other. But the line separating the scope of the two being undefined and undefinable with exact precision, marginal employment may, by reason of particular facts, fall on either side. Overruling the Jensen case would not solve this problem. In our decision in *Parker v. Motor Boat Sales*, 314 U.S. 244, we held that Congress has by the Longshoremen's Act accepted the Jensen line of demarcation between state and federal jurisdiction. Obviously, the determination of the margin becomes no simpler because the standard applied is considered to be embedded in a statute rather than in the Constitution. Nor can we gain assistance in this circumstance from the clause in the federal act which makes that act exclusive. 33 U.S.C. § 905. That section gains meaning only after a litigant has been found to occupy one side or the other of the doubtful jurisdictional line, and is no assistance in discovering on which side he can properly be placed.

There is, in the light of the cases referred to, clearly a twilight zone in which the employees must have their rights determined case by case, and in which particular facts and circumstances are vital elements. That zone includes persons such as the decedent who are, as a matter of actual administration, in fact protected under the state compensation act.

* * *

Not only does the state act in the instant case appear to cover this employee, aside from the constitutional consideration, but no conflicting process of administration is apparent. The federal authorities have taken no action under the Longshoremen's Act, and it does not appear that the employer has either made the special payments required or controverted payment in the manner prescribed in the Act. 33 U.S.C. § 914(b) and (d). Under all the circumstances of this case, we will rely on the presumption of constitutionality in favor of this state enactment; for any contrary decision results in our holding the Washington act unconstitutional as applied to this petitioner. A conclusion of unconstitutionality of a state statute can not be rested on so hazardous a factual foundation here, any more than in the other cases cited.

Notes

1. *Injuries on the Pier*

In *Nacirema Operating Company v. Johnson*, 396 U.S. 212, 90 S. Ct. 347, 24 L. Ed. 2d 1971 (1969), the United States Supreme Court held as a matter of statutory construction that injuries to longshoremen occurring on piers permanently affixed to shore were not compensable under LHWCA. Therefore, state law only applied landward of the *Jensen* line. However, the *Johnson* case was legislatively overruled by the 1972 Amendment to Section 3(a) of LHWCA.

A question has arisen as to the existence of admiralty jurisdiction when longshoremen sustain injuries on the pier on account of the fault of a person other than their land-based employer. LHWCA coverage is broader than the current view of United Stated courts concerning the reach of admiralty jurisdiction under 28 U.S.C. § 1333. *See Parker v. South Louisiana Contractors, Inc.*, 537 F.2d 113, 1976 AMC 2201 (5th Cir. 1976); Note, *infra*.

2. *Injuries on the High Seas*

The LHWCA applies to the high seas since § 39 of the LHWCA calls for compensation districts for injuries sustained on the high seas, and because U.S. navigable waters includes the high seas. *Kollias v. D & G Marine Maintenance*, 29 F.3d 67, 1995 AMC 609 (2d Cir. 1994).

LONGSHORE AND HARBOR WORKERS' COMPENSATION ACT:
AMENDMENTS EXPANDING SITUS

33 U.S.C. § 903(a) (1972 Amendment)

(a) Compensation shall be payable under this chapter in respect of disability or death of an employee, but only if the disability or death results from an injury occurring upon the navigable waters of the United States (including any adjoining pier, wharf, dry dock, terminal, building way, marine railway, or other adjoining area customarily used by an employer in loading, unloading, repairing, or building a vessel).

SUN SHIP, INC. v. PENNSYLVANIA

447 U.S. 715, 100 S. Ct. 2432, 65 L. Ed. 2d 458, 1980 AMC 1930 (1980)

Mr. Justice BRENNAN delivered the opinion of the Court.

The single question presented by these consolidated cases is whether a State may apply its workers' compensation scheme to land-based injuries that fall within the coverage of the Longshoremen's and Harbor Workers' Compensation Act (LHWCA), as amended in 1972. 33 U.S.C. §§ 901-950. We hold that it may.

Appellees are five employees of appellant Sun Ship, Inc., a shipbuilding and ship repair enterprise located on the Delaware River, a navigable water of the United States in Pennsylvania. Each employee was injured after the effective date of the 1972 amendments to the LHWCA while involved in shipbuilding or ship repair activities. Although the LHWCA applied to the injuries sustained, each appellee filed claims for benefits under the Pennsylvania Workmen's Compensation Act with state authorities. Appellant contended that the federal compensation statute was the employee's exclusive remedy. In upholding awards to each respondent, the Pennsylvania Workmen's Compensation Appeal Board ruled that the LHWCA did not preempt state compensation laws. The Commonwealth Court affirmed, and the Supreme Court of Pennsylvania denied petitions for allowance of appeal.

* * *

Before 1972, ... marine-related injuries fell within one of three jurisdictional spheres as they moved landward. At the furthest extreme, *Jensen* commanded that nonlocal maritime injuries fall under the LHWCA. "Maritime but local" injuries "upon the navigable waters of the United States," 33 U.S.C. § 903(a), could be compensated under the LHWCA or under state law. And injuries suffered beyond navigable waters—albeit within the range of federal admiralty jurisdiction—were remediable only under state law.

* * *

The language of the 1972 amendments cannot fairly be understood as pre-empting state workers' remedies from the field of the LHWCA, and thereby resurrecting the jurisdictional monstrosity that existed before the clarifying opinions in *Davis* and *Calbeck*. Appellant focuses our attention upon the deletion from amended § 903(a) of the phrase: "[if] recovery ... through workmen's compensation proceedings may not validly be provided by State law." But, if anything, that change reinforces our previous interpretation of that section as contemplating concurrent jurisdiction. *Calbeck, supra* 370 U.S., at 126. For it was that reference to state law which provided the strongest (although ultimately unsuccessful) argument for reading the pre-1972 § 903(a) as an exclusive jurisdictional provision. *Calbeck, supra,* at 132 (STEWART, J., dissenting). Whether Congress accepted *Calbeck's* view that the state-law clause was *consonant* with concurrent jurisdiction, or the dissenters' construction of the clause as *inconsistent* with concurrent jurisdiction, the deletion of that language in 1972—if it indicates anything—may logically only imply acquiescence in *Calbeck's* conclusion that the LHWCA operates within the same ambit as state workers' remedies.[2] It would be a *tour de force* of statutory misinterpretation to treat the *removal* of phrasing that arguably establishes exclusive jurisdiction as manifesting the intent to command such exclusivity.

Nor does the legislative history suggest a congressional decision to exclude state laws from the terrain newly occupied by the post-1972 Longshoremen's Act. Appellant can draw little support from general expressions of intent to alleviate unjust disparities in recovery conditioned upon the location of marine laborers at the time of an accident; as Part IV, *infra,* demonstrates, concurrency of jurisdiction in no way undercuts that commendable policy. And appellant is not much assisted by fixing upon the sentence in the bill Reports that declares:

---

[2] If Congress joined in *Calbeck's* understanding that the phrase underscored the LHWCA's application where state law compensability had been drawn into question by *Jensen,* then the striking of the language may be explained on the ground of its superfluity once Congress had pushed the federal Act landward beyond the *Jensen* line. If the Court took the dissenters' position that the state law clause imposed jurisdictional exclusivity, then its deletion indicates repeal of any such exclusivity. Finally, Congress may simply have endeavored to reaffirm the correctness of the existing law.

It is apparent that if the Federal benefit structure embodied in Committee bill is enacted, there would be a substantial disparity in benefits payable to a permanently disabled longshoreman, depending on which side of the water's edge the accident occurred, *if State laws are permitted to continue to apply to injuries occurring on land.* S. REP. NO. 1125 92d Cong., 2d Sess., 13 (1972); H.R. REP. NO. 1441, 92d Cong., 2d Sess. 10 (1972), U.S. CODE CONG. & ADMIN. NEWS 1972, pp. 4698, 4707 (emphasis added).

That statement likely means only that state laws should not be permitted to apply *exclusively* to injuries occurring upon land; the "substantial disparity in benefits" that troubled Congress is eliminated once federal law provides a concurrent or supplementary route to compensation. And, in any event, as Professors Gilmore and Black have noted, "the statement does not appear to be entitled to much weight," since the "part of the Committee Report which is devoted to the shoreward extension of [LHWCA] coverage does not so much as mention the pre-1972 case law on 'maritime but local' and the 'twilight zone.' ... "G. GILMORE & C. BLACK, THE LAW OF ADMIRALTY 425 (2d ed. 1975) (hereafter Gilmore & Black). In particular, there is no intimation of intent to overrule *Davis* and *Calbeck*—a significant omission in light of the care which the Reports elsewhere take in identifying the Supreme Court cases to be overturned by the abolition of longshoremen's actions for unseaworthiness. *See* S. REP. NO. 92-1125, *supra*, at 8-12; H.R. REP. NO. 92-1441, *supra*, at 4-8; Gilmore & Black 425.

We therefore find no sign in the 1972 amendments to the LHWCA that Congress wished to alter the accepted understanding that federal jurisdiction would coexist with state compensation laws in that field in which the latter may constitutionally operate under the *Jensen* doctrine.

Appellant vigorously contends, nevertheless, that jurisdictional exclusivity is—in "fact" or in "law"—implied in the LHWCA. Pointing to declarations of congressional policy to eliminate disparities in compensation to marine workers depending on whether they were injured on land or over water, S. REP. NO. 92-1125, *supra*, at 12-13; H.R. REP. NO. 92-1441, *supra*, at 10-11, appellant urges that concurrent remedial jurisdiction on land would defeat the uniformity principle underlying the statute.

As the Reports make clear, the disparities which Congress had in view in amending the LHWCA lay primarily in the paucity of relief under state compensation laws. The thrust of the amendments was to "upgrade the benefits." S. REP. NO. 92-1125, *supra*, at 1; *see Northeast Marine Terminal Co. v. Caputo*, 432 U.S. 249, 261-262 (1977). Concurrent jurisdiction for state and federal compensation laws is in no way inconsistent with this policy of raising awards to a federal minimum. When laborers file claims under the LHWCA, they are compensated under federal standards. And workers who commence their actions under state law will generally be able to make up the difference between state and federal benefit levels by seeking relief under the Longshoremen's Act, if the latter applies.[6]

To be sure, if state remedial schemes are more generous than federal law, concurrent jurisdiction could result in more favorable awards for workers' injuries than under an exclusively federal compensation system. But we find no evidence that Congress was concerned about a disparity between adequate federal benefits and *superior* state benefits....

Finally, we are not persuaded that the bare fact that the federal and state compensation systems are different gives rise to a conflict that, from the employer's standpoint, necessitates exclusivity for each compensation system within a separate sphere. Mandating exclusive jurisdiction will not relieve employers of their distinct obligations under state and federal compensation law. The line that circumscribes the jurisdictional compass of the LHWCA—

---

[6] Most often, state workmen's compensation laws will not be treated as making awards thereunder final or conclusive. *See Calbeck v. Travelers Insurance Co., supra*, at 131-132; *Industrial Comm'n v. McCartin*, 330 U.S. 622 (1947); Gilmore & Black, *supra*, at 431-433; 4 A. LARSON, LAW OF WORKMEN'S COMPENSATION §§ 85.20, 89.53(a) and (b) (1979); Larson, *The Conflict of Laws Problem Between the Longshoremen's Act and State Workmen's Compensation Acts*, 45 S. CAL. L. REV. 699, 729-730 (1972). Admittedly, if a particular state compensation law provision does indisputably declare its awards final, a conflict with the LHWCA may possibly arise where a claimant seeks inferior state benefits in the first instance. But the consequences to the claimant of this error would be less drastic than those of a mistake under the rule appellant contemplates—under which a misstep could result in no benefits. At any rate, although the question is not directly before us, we observe that if federal preclusion ever need be implied to cope with this remote contingency, a less disruptive approach would be to pre-empt the state compensation exclusivity clause, rather than to pre-empt the entire state compensation statute as appellant suggests.

a compound of "status" and "situs"—is no less vague than its counterpart in the pre-"twilight zone" *Jensen* era. Thus, even were the LHWCA exclusive within its field, many employers would be compelled to abide by state-imposed responsibilities lest a claim fall beyond the scope of the LHWCA....

Of one thing we may be certain. The exclusivity rule which appellant urges upon us would thrust employees into the same jurisdictional peril from which they were rescued by *Davis* and *Calbeck v. Travelers Insurance Co. See* Gilmore & Black, *supra*, at 425. The legislative policy animating the LHWCA's landward shift was remedial; the amendments' framers acted out of solicitude for the workers. *See P.C. Pfeiffer Co., supra*, at 74-75; Northeast Marine Terminal Co., 432 U.S., at 268. To adopt appellant's position, then, would blunt the thrust of the 1972 amendments, and frustrate Congress' intent to aid injured maritime laborers. We decline to do so in the name of "uniformity."

Accordingly, we affirm.

Note: Mutual Exclusivity of the LHWCA and the Jones Act

The LHWCA and the Jones Act are mutually exclusive. According to 33 U.S.C. § 903(a)(1), the LHWCA does not apply to "a master or member of the crew of any vessel." *See also id.* § 902(3); *Mcdermott, Inc. v. Boudreaux*, 679 F.2d 452 (5th Cir. 1982). Conversely, the Jones Act does not apply to longshoremen or harborworkers covered by the LHWCA. Thus, a master or member of the crew of a vessel is not entitled to benefits under the LHWCA, and a longshoreman or harborworker may not sue his employer for recovery under the Jones Act (or for maintenance and cure under the general maritime law).

Despite the mutual exclusivity of the LHWCA and the Jones Act, courts have recognized the existence of a "twilight zone," or area of uncertainty in which either statute may apply. *See McDermott, Inc. v. Boudreaux*, 679 F.2d 452, 459 (5th Cir. 1982):

> [W]e, realize that, in a practical sense, a "zone of uncertainty" inevitably connects the two Acts. Confronted by conflicting evidence concerning a worker's duties or undisputed evidence concerning an occupation that exhibits the characteristics of both traditional land and sea duties, a factfinder might be able to draw reasonable inferences to justify coverage under *either* statute.
>
> *Abshire* offers a classic instance of the case that could have gone either way. Plaintiff produced evidence that he was a marine welder and mechanic permanently assigned to a fleet of fishing vessels and spent most of his time performing repairs aboard the employer's boats; defendant produced evidence that plaintiff was a shore-based maintenance employee who never went to sea and whose only contact with vessels under way "was in testing them in connection with repairs and maintenance." *Id.* at 836. The district court properly submitted the issue to a jury, which found that the welder/mechanic was entitled to damages as a Jones Act seaman. Although we affirmed the judgment, we just as easily could have approved a jury's finding that *Abshire* was restricted to compensation under the Longshoremen's Act. Incidentally, the judgment for Abshire under the Jones Act also ordered repayment of two insurers that already had compensated him under the Longshoremen's Act.

Note: State workers' compensation schemes

State workers' compensation acts do not apply to seamen because of the *Jensen* doctrine. *See Knickerbocker Ice Co. v. Stewart*, 253 U.S. 149, 40 S.Ct. 438, 64 L.Ed. 834 (1920); *Bearden v. Leon C. Breaux Towing Co.*, 365 So. 2d 1192 (La. App. 3d Cir. 1978). However, there is authority for the proposition that state compensation schemes may operate concurrently with the Jones Act; that is, there is a "twilight zone" in which either remedy may be available. *See Maryland Cas. Co. v. Toups*, 172 F.2d 542, 1949 AMC 994 (5th Cir. 1949); *Haire v. Devcon Int'l Corp.*, 668 So.2d 775 (Ala. Ct. App. 1995). Conversely, there is a considerable body of authority in state and federal courts to the effect that there is no "twilight zone", and that Jones Act seamen are not entitled to state workers' compensation remedies even if their work is "maritime but local". *Benders v. Board of Governors*, 636 A.2d 1313 (R.I. 1994); *Indiana & Michigan Electric Co. v. Workers' Comp. Comm'r*, 403 S.E.2d 416 (W.Va. 1991); *Bearden v. Leon C. Breaux Towing Co.*, 365 So. 2d 1192 (La. App. 3d Cir. 1978); *Green v. Industrial Com'n*, 717 N.E.2d 457 (Ill. App. 3 Dist. 1999).

SOUTHWEST MARINE, INC. v. GIZONI

502 U.S. 81, 112 S. Ct. 486; 116 L. Ed. 2d 405; 1992 AMC 305 (1991)

Justice WHITE delivered the opinion of the Court.

The question presented is whether a maritime worker whose occupation is one of those enumerated in the Longshore and Harbor Workers' Compensation Act (LHWCA), 44 Stat. 1424, as amended, 33 U.S.C. § 901 *et seq.*, may yet be a "seaman" within the meaning of the Jones Act, 46 U.S.C. App. § 688, and thus be entitled to bring suit under that statute.

I.

Petitioner Southwest Marine, Inc., operates a ship repair facility in San Diego, California. In connection with its ship repair activities, Southwest Marine owns several floating platforms, including a pontoon barge, two float barges, a rail barge, a diver's barge, and a crane barge. These platforms by themselves have no power, means of steering, navigation lights, navigation aids, or living facilities. They are moved about by tugboats, which position the platforms alongside vessels under repair at berths or in drydock at Southwest Marine's shipyard or at the nearby Naval Station. The platforms are used to move equipment, materials, supplies, and vessel components around the shipyard and on to and off of the vessels under repair. Once in place, the platforms support ship repairmen engaged in their work.

Southwest Marine employed respondent Byron Gizoni as a rigging foreman. Gizoni worked on the floating platforms and rode them as they were towed into place. Gizoni occasionally served as a lookout and gave maneuvering signals to the tugboat operator when the platforms were moved. He also received lines passed to the platforms by the ships' crews to secure the platforms to the vessels under repair. Gizoni suffered disabling leg and back injuries in a fall when his foot broke through a thin wooden sheet covering a hole in the deck of a platform being used to transport a rudder from the shipyard to a floating drydock.

Gizoni submitted a claim for, and received, medical and compensation benefits from Southwest Marine pursuant to the LHWCA. He later sued Southwest Marine under the Jones Act in the United States District Court for the Southern District of California, alleging that he was a seaman injured as a result of his employer's negligence. Gizoni also pleaded causes of action for unseaworthiness and for maintenance and cure. App. IV-4, IV-5. In addition to the above facts, Gizoni alleged in his complaint that Southwest Marine's floating platforms were "a group of vessels ... in navigable waters," and that as a rigging foreman, he was "permanently assigned to said group of vessels." *Id.*, at IV-3.

The District Court granted Southwest Marine's motion for summary judgment on two grounds. The District Court determined as a matter of law that Gizoni was not a Jones Act seaman, finding that Southwest Marine's floating platforms were not "vessels in navigation," and that Gizoni was on board to perform work as a ship repairman, not to "aid in navigation." App. to Pet. for Cert. I-1, I-2. More important to our purposes here, the District Court further concluded that Gizoni was a harbor worker precluded from bringing his action by the exclusive remedy provisions of the LHWCA, 33 U.S.C. § 905(a). App. to Pet. for Cert I-2.

The United States Court of Appeals for the Ninth Circuit reversed the determination that Gizoni was not a seaman as a matter of law, 909 F. 2d 385, 387 (1990), holding that questions of fact existed as to seaman status, *e.g.*, whether the floating platforms were vessels in navigation, whether Gizoni's relationship to those platforms was permanent, and whether he aided in their navigation. *Id.*, at 388. The Ninth Circuit also reversed the District Court's determination that the exclusive remedy provisions of the LHWCA precluded Gizoni from pursuing his Jones Act claim. The court concluded that the LHWCA by its terms does not cover "a master or member of a crew of any vessel," 33 U.S.C. § 902(3)(G), that this phrase is the equivalent of "seaman" under the Jones Act, and that the question of his seaman status should have been presented to a jury. 909 F.2d at 389. The Ninth Circuit thus rejected the notion that any employee whose work involved ship repair was necessarily restricted to remedy under the LHWCA, reasoning that coverage under the Jones Act or the LHWCA depended not on the claimant's job title, but on the nature of the claimant's work and the intent of Congress in enacting these statutes. *Ibid.*

We granted certiorari, 498 U.S. — (1991), to resolve the conflict among the Circuits on this issue.[1] We now affirm the judgment of the Ninth Circuit.

II.

The Jones Act and the LHWCA each provide a remedy to the injured maritime worker; however, each specifies different maritime workers to be within its reach. In relevant part, the Jones Act provides that "any seaman who shall suffer personal injury in the course of his employment may, at his election, maintain an action for damages at law, with the right of trial by jury, and in such action all statutes of the United States modifying or extending the common-law right or remedy in cases of personal injury to railway employees shall apply...." 46 U.S.C. App. § 688(a). Under the LHWCA, the exclusiveness of liability provision in part states that the liability of an employer "shall be exclusive and in place of all other liability of such employer to the employee...." 33 U.S.C. § 905(a). However, the term "employee", as defined in the LHWCA does not include "a master or member of a crew of any vessel." 33 U.S.C. § 902(3)(G). The District Court was therefore plainly wrong in holding that, as a matter of law, the LHWCA provided the exclusive remedy for all harbor workers. That cannot be the case if the LHWCA and its exclusionary provision do not apply to a harbor worker who is also a "member of a crew of any vessel," a phrase that is a "refinement" of the term "seaman" in the Jones Act. *McDermott Int'l, Inc. v. Wilander*, 498 U.S. —, — (1991).[3]

The determination of who is a "member of a crew" is "better characterized as a mixed question of law and fact," rather than as a pure question of fact. *Id.*, at —. Even so, "the inquiry into seaman status is of necessity fact-specific; it will depend on the nature of the vessel, and the employee's precise relation to it." *Ibid.* Our decision in *Wilander* jettisoned any lingering notion that a maritime worker need aid in the navigation of a vessel in order to qualify as a "seaman" under the Jones Act. "The key to seaman status is employment-related connection to a vessel in navigation.... It is not necessary that a seaman aid in navigation or contribute to the transportation of the vessel, but a seaman must be doing the ship's work." *Id.*, at —. In arriving at this conclusion, we again recognized that "the Jones Act and the LHWCA are mutually exclusive," *id.*, at — (*citing Swanson v. Marra Brothers, Inc.*, 328 U.S. 1 (1946)), for the very reason that the LHWCA specifically precludes from its provisions any employee who is "a master or member of a crew of any vessel."

Southwest Marine suggests, in line with Fifth Circuit precedent, that this fact-intensive inquiry may always be resolved as a matter of law if the claimant's job fits within one of the enumerated occupations defining the term "employee" covered by the LHWCA. However, this argument ignores the fact that some maritime workers may be Jones Act seamen performing a job specifically enumerated under the LHWCA. Indeed, Congress foresaw this

---

[1] The Ninth Circuit in this case followed a decision by the Sixth Circuit, which held that "[a] plaintiff is not limited to the remedies available under the LHWCA unless he is unable to show that a genuine factual issue exists as to whether he was a seaman at the time of his injury." *Petersen v. Chesapeake & Ohio R. Co.*, 784 F.2d 732, 739 (1986). To the contrary, the Fifth Circuit has previously held that because longshoremen, shipbuilders and ship repairers are engaged in occupations enumerated in the LHWCA, they are unqualifiedly covered by that Act if they meet the Act's situs requirements; coverage of these workmen by the LHWCA renders them ineligible for consideration as seamen or members of the crew of a vessel entitled to claim the benefits of the Jones Act." *Pizzitolo v. Electro-Coal Transfer Corp.*, 812 F.2d 977, 9883 (1987). A later decision by the Fifth Circuit undercut much of the reasoning in *Pizzitolo* by limiting it to cases where "the evidence is insufficient to warrant a finding of seaman's status." *Legros v. Panther Services Group, Inc.*, 863 F.2d 345, 349 (1988). The Fifth Circuit granted rehearing en banc, but the parties later settled and the appeal was dismissed. *Legros v. Panther Services Group, Inc.*, 874 F.2d 953 (1989). With the opinion in *Legros* vacated, *Pizzitolo* remains the law in the Fifth Circuit, although its breadth may be in some question.

[3] Southwest Marine points as well to a separate exclusiveness of liability provision regarding the negligence of a vessel, 33 U.S.C. § 905(b), and places great emphasis on a passage that states:

> If such person was employed to provide shipbuilding, repairing, or breaking services and such person's employer was the owner, owner pro hac vice, agent, operator, or charterer of the vessel, no such action shall be permitted, in whole or in part or directly or indirectly, against the injured person's employer (in any capacity, including as the vessel's owner, owner pro hac vice, agent, operator, or charterer) or against the employees of the employer.

> This exclusivity provision applies, however, only "in the event of injury to a person covered under this chapter [the LHWCA] caused by the negligence of a vessel." 33 U.S.C. § 905(b). As we have already noted, the question whether Gizoni is "a person covered under this chapter" depends upon whether he is a "seaman" under the Jones Act. Like the companion exclusivity provision of § 905(a), § 905(b) does not dictate sole recourse to the LHWCA unless Gizoni is found not to be "a master or member of a crew of any vessel."

possibility, and we have previously quoted a portion of the legislative history to the 1972 amendments to the LHWCA that states: "'The bill would amend the Act to provide coverage of longshoremen, harbor workers, ship repairmen, ship builders, shipbreakers, and other employees engaged in maritime employment (excluding masters and members of the crew of a vessel).'" *Northeast Marine Terminal Co. v. Caputo*, 432 U.S. 249, 266, n.26 (1977) (quoting S. REP. NO. 92—1125, p. 13 (1972)) (emphasis added). As we observed in *Wilander*: "There is no indication in the Jones Act, the LHWCA, or elsewhere, that Congress has excluded from Jones Act remedies those traditional seamen who owe allegiance to a vessel at sea, but who do not aid in navigation." 498 U.S., at —. While in some cases a ship repairman may lack the requisite connection to a vessel in navigation to qualify for seaman status, *see, e.g., Sun Ship, Inc. v. Pennsylvania*, 447 U.S. 715 (1980) (ship repairmen working and injured on land); *P.C. Pfeiffer Co. v. Ford*, 444 U.S. 69, 80, and n.12 (1979), not all ship repairmen lack the requisite connection as a matter of law.[4] This is so because "it is not the employee's particular job that is determinative, but the employee's connection to a vessel." *Wilander, supra*, at —. By its terms the LHWCA preserves the Jones Act remedy for vessel crewmen, even if they are employed by a shipyard. A maritime worker is limited to LHWCA remedies only if no genuine issue of fact exists as to whether the worker was a seaman under the Jones Act.

Southwest Marine submits several arguments in an attempt to foreclose this Jones Act suit. First, Southwest Marine contends that our decision above will conflict with decisions holding that the LHWCA provides the exclusive remedy for certain injured railroad workers otherwise permitted by the Federal Employers' Liability Act, 45 U.S.C. § 51 *et seq.*, to pursue a negligence cause of action. *See, e.g., Chesapeake & Ohio R. Co. v. Schwalb*, 493 U.S. 40 (1989); *Pennsylvania R.R. v. O'Rourke*, 344 U.S. 334 (1953). Such cases, however, can provide no meaningful guidance on the issue here, for the LHWCA contains no exclusion for railroad workers comparable to that for Jones Act seamen.

Next, Southwest Marine advances a "primary jurisdiction" argument suggesting that, where a maritime worker is "arguably covered" by the LHWCA, the district court should stay any Jones Act proceeding pending a final LHWCA "administrative agency" determination that the worker is, in fact, a "master or member of a crew." We find no indication in the LHWCA that Congress intended to preclude or stay traditional Jones Act suits in the district courts. Indeed, the LHWCA anticipates that such suits could be brought. Title 33 U.S.C. § 913(d) tolls the time to file LHWCA claims "where recovery is denied to any person, in a suit brought at law or in admiralty to recover damages in respect of injury or death, on the ground that such person was an employee and the defendant was an employer within the meaning of this chapter and that such employer had secured compensation to such employee under this chapter."

Southwest Marine seeks to support its primary jurisdiction argument by pointing to the relation between the Federal Employees Compensation Act (FECA), 5 U.S.C. § 8101 *et seq.*, and the Federal Tort Claims Act (FTCA), 28 U.S.C. § 2671 *et seq.* But FECA contains an "unambiguous and comprehensive" provision barring any judicial review of the Secretary's determination of FECA coverage. *Lindahl v. OPM*, 470 U.S. 768, 780, and n.13 (1985); *see* 5 U.S.C. § 8128(b). Consequently, the courts have no jurisdiction over FTCA claims where the Secretary of Labor determines that FECA applies. The LHWCA contains no such provision. Likewise, we reject Southwest Marine's argument that agency proceedings under the LHWCA require the jurisdictional limitations we have found the National Labor Relations Act (NLRA), 29 U.S.C. § 151 *et seq.*, to place on state and federal courts in favor of the proceedings conducted by the National Labor Relations Board. *See, e.g., Longshoremen v. Davis*, 476 U.S. 380, 389-390 (1986); *San Diego Building Trades Council v. Garmon*, 359 U.S. 236, 243-245 (1959). The administrative proceedings outlined under the LHWCA in no way approach "the NLRA's 'complex and interrelated federal scheme of law, remedy, and administration'" requiring pre-emption in those cases. *Longshoremen, supra*, at 389 (quoting *Garmon, supra*, at 243)). Neither is it "essential to the administration" of the LHWCA that resolution of the

---

[4] Gizoni stipulates that he was a ship repairman for Southwest Marine and correctly notes that many ship repairmen are excluded from LHWCA coverage, even though ship repairmen are expressly enumerated as a category of "harborworker" included within its coverage. See 33 U.S.C. § 902(3)(F) (individuals employed to repair recreational vessels under 65 feet in length); § 902(3)(H) (persons engaged to repair small vessels under 18 tons net). We find it significant that such clear exclusions of certain ship repairmen fall on either side of the exclusion here at issue for "a master or member of a crew of any vessel." § 902(3)(G).

question of coverage be left "'in the first instance'" to agency proceedings in the Department of Labor. *Longshoremen, supra*, at 390 (quoting *Garmon, supra*, at 244-245)).

Finally, Southwest Marine suggests that an employee's receipt of benefits under the LHWCA should preclude subsequent litigation under the Jones Act. To the contrary, however, we have ruled that where the evidence is sufficient to send the threshold question of seaman status to the jury, it is reversible error to permit an employer to prove that the worker accepted LHWCA benefits while awaiting trial. *Tipton v. Socony Mobil Oil Co.*, 375 U.S. 34, 37 (1963). It is by now "universally accepted" that an employee who receives voluntary payments under the LHWCA without a formal award is not barred from subsequently seeking relief under the Jones Act. G. GILMORE & C. BLACK, LAW OF ADMIRALTY 435 (2d ed. 1975); *see* 4 A. LARSON, WORKMEN'S COMPENSATION LAW § 90.51, p. 16-507 (1989) (collecting cases); *Simms v. Valley Line Co.*, 709 F. 2d 409, 412, and nn. 3 and 5 (CA5 1983). This is so, quite obviously, because the question of coverage has never actually been litigated. Moreover, the LHWCA clearly does not comprehend such a preclusive effect, as it specifically provides that any amounts paid to an employee for the same injury, disability, or death pursuant to the Jones Act shall be credited against any liability imposed by the LHWCA.[5] 33 U.S.C. § 903(e). *See* Gilmore & Black, *supra*, at 435.

III.

Because a ship repairman may spend all of his working hours aboard a vessel in furtherance of its mission—even one used exclusively in ship repair work—that worker may qualify as a Jones Act seaman. By ruling as a matter of law on the basis of job title or occupation alone, the District Court foreclosed Gizoni's ability to make this showing. "If reasonable persons, applying the proper legal standard, could differ as to whether the employee was a 'member of a crew,' it is a question for the jury." *Wilander*, 498 U.S., at ___. The Ninth Circuit concluded that questions of fact existed regarding whether the floating platforms were vessels in navigation, and whether Gizoni had sufficient connection to the platforms to qualify for seaman status.[6] Gizoni alleges facts in support of each of these propositions—facts which Southwest Marine disputes. *Compare* Brief for Respondent 11, with Brief for Petitioner 3. Summary judgment was inappropriate.

The judgment of the Court of Appeals is
Affirmed.

Problems

1. Suppose plaintiff brought suit against his employer claiming recovery under the Jones Act but the court found that he was a longshoreman or harbor worker. If the period of limitations has not run, the plaintiff may claim benefits under the LHWCA (or under a state statute, if applicable).

Suppose, however, that plaintiff brought suit against his employer claiming recovery under the Jones Act and the court found that he was a seaman but not entitled to any recovery because, for example, the employer was free of fault. Can plaintiff now claim benefits under the LHWCA, claiming that he is a longshoreman? Strong argument may be made that such a claim is barred by res judicata or collateral estoppel. However, it has been held that the finding of a seaman's status in the Jones Act suit does not bar a later claim for compensation. *Strachan Shipping Co. v. Shea*, 406 F.2d 521, 1969 AMC 67 (5th Cir. 1969), *cert. denied*, 395 U.S. 920 (1969); *Young v. Shea*, 397 F.2d 185, 1969 AMC 560 (5th Cir. 1968), *cert. denied*, 395 U.S. 920 (1969).

2. Suppose plaintiff claimed benefits under the LHWCA and the administrative law judge found that he was a seaman, *i.e.*, a member of the crew of a vessel. He may now sue his employer under the Jones Act, provided that the period of limitation has not run. It is the same when an administrative law judge finds that plaintiff is a longshoreman or harbor worker but the federal court sets aside the award of benefits on the ground that the plaintiff is a seaman. *See McDermott Inc. v. Boudreaux*, 679 F.2d 452 (5th Cir. 1982).

---

[5] For this same reason, equitable estoppel arguments suggested by amicus Shipbuilders Council of America must fail. Where full compensation credit removes the threat of double recovery, the critical element of detrimental reliance does not appear. *See Heckler v. Community Health Services*, 467 U.S. 51, 59 (1984); *Lyng v. Payne*, 476 U.S. 926, 935 (1986). Argument by amicus would force injured maritime workers to an election of remedies we do not believe Congress to have intended.

[6] The Ninth Circuit also found questions of fact to remain concerning whether Gizoni aided in the navigation of these platforms. After *McDermott Int'l, Inc. v. Wilander*, 498 U.S. —, 111 S. Ct. 807, 112 L. Ed. 2d 866 (1991), however, only "employment-related connection to a vessel in navigation" is required. *Id.*, at —, 111 S. Ct., at 817. To be a seaman, the employee need not aid in navigation.

Suppose, however, that plaintiff recovered compensation under the LHWCA. May he now sue for recovery under the Jones Act? *See Papai v. Harbor Tug and Barge Company*, 67 F.3d 203, 1995 AMC 2888 (9th Cir. 1995), *rvsd. on other grounds*, 520 U.S. 548 (1997); *Biggs v. Norfolk Dredging Co.*, 360 F.2d 360, 1966 AMC 578 (4th Cir. 1966); *Figueroa v. Campbell Industries*, 45 F.3d 311 (9th Cir. 1995); and *C.N.A. Ins. Co. v. Workers' Comp. Appeals Bd.*, 68 Cal. Rptr 2d 115, 1998 AMC 534 (Cal. App. 2d Dist. 1997). In those cases the court held that the plaintiff was not estopped from claiming recovery under the Jones Act, and that there is no need to accord finality to the administrative finding with regard to the status of the plaintiff. *But see Welch v. Elevating Boats, Inc.*, 516 F. Supp. 1245 (E.D. La. 1982), where suit under the Jones Act was dismissed on the grounds that plaintiff was collaterally estopped from claiming seaman's status and, as a matter of law, that he was not a seaman. See also *Sharp v. Johnson Bros. Corp.*, 973 F.2d 423, 426, 1995 AMC 912 (5th Cir. 1992), holding that an administrative determination of LHWCA entitlement precludes Jones Act action if it amounts to a "formal award". In *Reyes v. Delta Dallas Alpha Corp.*, 199 F.3d 626, 2000 AMC 776 (2d Cir. 1999) and *Mooney v. City of New York*, 219 F.3d 123, 2001 AMC 38 (2d Cir. 2000), the Second Circuit held that receipt of *State* workers' compensation benefits by the plaintiff did not constitute a waiver of Jones Act claims, but that waiver would arise if there were a "formal award".

B. Coverage of the Longshore and Harbor Workers' Compensation Act (LHWCA): Status and Situs Requirements

Background Note: Longshore and Harbor Workers' Compensation Act (LHWCA): 1984 Amendments and § 903 Coverage

The 1927 LHWCA was generally applicable to persons engaged in "maritime employment," subject to certain exclusions. The term "employee" applied to longshoremen and harbor workers, but not to "a master or member of the crew of any vessel" (33 U.S.C. §§ 902(3), 903(A)(1)), "an officer or employee of the United States or any agency thereof or of any state or foreign government, or any political subdivision thereof" (33 U.S.C. § 903(a)(2)), or "any person engaged by the master to load or unload or repair any small vessel under eighteen tons net" (33 U.S.C. §§ 903(3), 903(A)(1)). These exclusions have been carried forward without change.

However, the coverage of the act was broadened in 1972 and in 1984. Addition of language to § 903(a) specifies that the term navigable waters of the United States includes "any adjoining pier, wharf, dry dock, terminal, building way, marine railway, or other adjoining area customarily used by an employer in loading, unloading, repairing, or building a vessel." Furthermore, the word "employer" in § 902(4) has been broadened by the addition of the same words.

LHWCA: 1984 Amendment

§ 902. Definitions when used in this chapter.

(2) The term "injury" means accidental injury or death arising out of and in the course of employment, and such occupational disease or infection as arises naturally out of such employment or as naturally or unavoidably results from such accidental injury, and includes an injury caused by the willful act of a third person directed against an employee because of his employment.

(3) The term "employee" means any person engaged in maritime employment, including any longshoreman or other person engaged in longshoring operations, and any harbor-worker including a ship repairman, shipbuilder, and ship-breaker, but such term does not include—

   (A) individuals employed exclusively to perform office clerical, secretarial, security, or data processing work;

   (B) individuals employed by a club, camp, recreational operation, restaurant, museum, or retail outlet;

   (C) individuals employed by a marina and who are not engaged in construction, replacement, or expansion of such marina (except for routine maintenance);

   (D) individuals who (i) are employed by suppliers, transporters, or vendors, (ii) are temporarily doing business on the premises of an employer described in paragraph (4), and (iii) are not engaged in work normally performed by employees of that employer under this chapter;

    (E)   aquaculture workers;

    (F)   individuals employed to build, repair, or dismantle any recreational vessel under sixty-five feet in length;

    (G)   a master or member of a crew of any vessel; or

    (H)   any person engaged by a master to load or unload or repair any small vessel under eighteen tons net;

if individuals described in clauses (A) through (F) are subject to coverage under a State workers' compensation law.

(4)   The term "employer" means an employer any of whose employees are employed in maritime employment, in whole or in part, upon the navigable waters of the United States (including any adjoining pier, wharf, dry dock, terminal, building way, marine railway, or other adjoining area customarily used by an employer in loading, unloading, repairing, or building a vessel).

§ 903. Coverage

(a) Disability or death; injuries occurring upon navigable waters of United States

    Except as otherwise provided in this section, compensation shall be payable under this chapter in respect of disability or death of an employee, but only if the disability or death results from an injury occurring upon the navigable waters of the United States (including any adjoining pier, wharf, dry dock, terminal, building way, marine railway, or other adjoining area customarily used by an employer in loading, unloading, repairing, dismantling, or building a vessel).

(b) Governmental officers and employees

    No compensation shall be payable in respect of the disability or death of an officer or employee of the United States, or any agency thereof, or of any State or foreign government, or any subdivision thereof.

(c) Intoxication; willful intention to kill

    No compensation shall be payable if the injury was occasioned solely by the intoxication of the employee or by the willful intention of the employee to injure or kill himself or another.

(d) Small vessels

(1)   No compensation shall be payable to an employee employed at a facility of an employer if, as certified by the Secretary, the facility is engaged in the business of building, repairing, or dismantling exclusively small vessels (as defined in paragraph (3) of this subsection), unless the injury occurs while upon the navigable waters of the United States or while upon any adjoining pier, wharf, dock, facility over land for launching vessels, or facility over land for hauling, lifting, or drydocking vessels.

(2)   Notwithstanding paragraph (1), compensation shall be payable to an employee—

(A) who is employed at a facility which is used in the business of building, repairing, or dismantling small vessels if such facility receives Federal maritime subsidies; or

(B) if the employee is not subject to coverage under a State workers' compensation law.

(3)   For purposes of this subsection, a small vessel means—

(A) a commercial barge which is under 900 lightship displacement tons; or

(B) a commercial tugboat, towboat, crew boat, supply boat, fishing vessel, or other work vessel which is under 1,600 tons gross.

(e) Credit for benefits paid under other laws

Notwithstanding any other provision of law, any amounts paid to an employee for the same injury, disability, or death for which benefits are claimed under this chapter pursuant to any other workers' compensation law or section 688 of Title 46 (relating to recovery for injury to or death of seamen) shall be credited against any liability imposed by this chapter.

P.C. PFEIFFER CO., INC. v. FORD

444 U.S. 69, 100 S. Ct. 32, 62 L. Ed. 2d 225, 1979 AMC 2319 (1979)

Mr. Justice POWELL delivered the opinion of the Court.

The question in this case is whether two workers were engaged in "maritime employment," as defined by § 2(3) of the Longshoremen's and Harbor Workers' Compensation Act, 44 Stat. 1425, as amended, 86 Stat. 1251, 33 U.C.S. § 902(3), when they sustained injuries for which they sought compensation.

I.

On April 12, 1973, Diverson Ford accidentally struck the middle finger of his left hand with a hammer while working on a public dock in the Port of Beaumont, Tex. On the day of his injury, Ford was employed by the P. C. Pfeiffer Co. to fasten military vehicles onto railroad flatcars. The vehicles had been delivered to the port by ship a number of days before the accident, stored, and then loaded onto flatcars the day before. The flatcars would take the vehicles to their inland designation.

Ford was working out of the warehousemen's local on the day of the accident. Agreements between employers, the warehousemen's union, and the longshoremen's union limit the tasks that warehousemen may perform in the Port of Beaumont. Warehousemen may not move cargo directly from a vessel either to a point of rest in storage or to a railroad car. Nor may they move cargo from a shoreside point of rest directly onto a vessel. These jobs are reserved for longshoremen.

On May 2, 1973, Will Bryant was injured while unloading a bale of cotton from a dray wagon into a pier warehouse. Bryant was working as a cottonheader for the Ayers Steamship Co. in the Port of Galveston, Tex. Cotton arrives at the port from inland shippers and enters storage in cotton compress-warehouses. The cotton then goes by dray wagon to pier warehouses where a driver and two cotton headers unload and store it. Longshoremen later move the cotton from the pier warehouses onto ships.

Contractual agreements between employers, the cotton headers' union, and the longshoremen's union distinguish the work that cotton headers may perform from the tasks assignable to longshoremen. Cotton headers may only load cotton off dray wagons into the pier warehouses or move cotton within a pier warehouse. Cargo moved directly from the ship to shoreside transportation, or directly from shoreside transportation to the ship, is handled solely by longshoremen.

II.

Before 1972, neither Ford nor Bryant could have received compensation under the Longshoremen's and Harbor Workers' Compensation Act because his injury occurred on land. The pre-1972 Act was simply an effort to fill the gap in workmen's compensation coverage created by this Court's decision in *Southern Pacific Co. v. Jensen,* 244 U.S. 205 (1917), which held that state compensation systems could not reach longshoremen injured seaward of the water's edge. A single situs requirement in § 3(a) of the Act governed the scope of its coverage. That requirement limited coverage to workers whose "disability or death [resulted] from an injury occurring upon the navigable waters of the United States (including any dry dock)...." 44 Stat. 1426. In light of Jensen and the limited purpose of the Act, the situs test was understood to draw a sharp line between injuries sustained over water and those suffered on land. Thus, in *Nacirema Operating Co. v. Johnson,* 396 U.S. 212, 218-220 (1969), this Court held that the Act did not extend to injuries occurring on a pier attached to the land. Although the Court recognized that inequities might result from rigid adherence to the Jensen line, the Court concluded that "[the] invitation to move that line landward must be addressed to Congress, not to this Court." 396 U.S., at 224.

Congress responded with the Longshoremen's and Harbor Workers' Compensation Act Amendments of 1972 (1972 Act). The Act now extends coverage to more workers by replacing the single-situs requirement with a two-part situs and status standard. The newly broadened situs test provides compensation for an "employee" whose disability or death "results from an injury occurring upon the navigable waters of the United States (including any adjoining pier, wharf, dry dock, terminal, building way, marine railway, or other adjoining area customarily used by an employer in loading, unloading, repairing, or building a vessel)." § 3(a), 33 U.S.C. § 903(a). The status test defines an employee as "any person engaged in maritime employment, including any longshoreman or other person engaged in longshoring operations, and any harbor worker including a ship repairman, shipbuilder, and shipbreaker...." § 2(3), 33 U.S.C. § 902(3). To be eligible for compensation, a person must be an employee as defined by § 2(3) who sustains injury on the situs defined by § 3(a).

III.

This Court first considered the scope of § 2(3)'s status requirement in *Northeast Marine Terminal Co. v. Caputo*, 432 U.S. 249 (1977). That case concerned the claims of two workers, Blundo and Caputo. Blundo was on a pier checking cargo as it was removed from a container when he suffered a fall. Caputo sustained injury while rolling a loaded dolly into a consignee's truck. We recognized that neither the 1972 Act nor its legislative history states explicitly whether workers like Blundo and Caputo, who handle cargo between sea and land transportation, are employees within the meaning of § 2(3). The Court found, however, that consideration of the legislative history in light of the remedial purposes behind the expansion of coverage reveals a clear intent to cover such workers. 432 U.S., at 267-278.

One of the reasons Congress expanded coverage in 1972 was that containerization permits loading and unloading tasks traditionally conducted aboard ship to be performed on the land. Such tasks are "longshoring operations." *Id.*, at 270-271. Blundo's job of checking and marking goods as they were removed from a container was an integral part of the unloading process even though the container had been removed from a ship and trucked to a different pier before being emptied. Therefore, Blundo was an employee within the meaning of § 2(3). 432 U.S., at 271.

Caputo, working as part of the traditional process of moving goods from ship to land transportation, was unaffected by the advent of containerization. But the Court recognized another congressional purpose relevant to the resolution of Caputo's claim. Congress wanted to ensure that a worker who could have been covered part of the time by the pre-1972 Act would be completely covered by the 1972 Act. By enlarging the covered situs and enacting the status requirement, Congress intended that a worker's eligibility for federal benefits would not depend on whether he was injured while walking down a gangway or while taking his first step onto the land. Congress therefore counted as "longshoremen" persons who spend "at least some of their time in indisputably longshoring operations." *Id.*, at 273. Caputo, who could have been assigned to loading containers and barges as well as trucks, was such a person. *Ibid.* Accordingly, the Court did not have to decide whether Caputo's work was "maritime employment" simply because he "engaged in the final steps of moving cargo from maritime to land transportation: putting it in the consignee's truck." *Id.*, at 272.

In holding that Blundo and Caputo were covered by the Act, Northeast Marine Terminal explicitly rejected the "point of rest" theory. Under that test, maritime employment would include only the portion of the unloading process that takes place before the stevedoring gang places cargo onto the dock. For example, a worker who carried cargo directly from a ship to a warehouse or a truck would be engaged in maritime employment, but one who carried cargo from a warehouse to a truck would not. In loading operations, only workers employed to the seaside of the last point of rest would be covered.

We explained that application of the point-of-rest test would be inconsistent with congressional intent. First, the concept, although well known in the maritime industry, was not mentioned in the Act or its legislative history. Second, the standard excludes from coverage employees like Blundo whose work was shifted landward by the use of containers. Third, the test conflicts with the express purpose of the Act because it allows workers to walk in and out of coverage as their work moves to different sides of a point of rest. *Id.*, at 275-276. In sum, "[a] theory that nowhere appears in the Act, that was never mentioned by Congress during the legislative process, that does not comport with Congress' intent, and that restricts the coverage of a remedial Act designed to extend coverage [was] incapable of defeating our conclusion that Blundo and Caputo [were] 'employees.'" *Id.*, at 278-279.

Most of the litigation in the present case took place before our decision in Northeast Marine Terminal. At the initial administrative level, both Ford's and Bryant's claims for coverage were denied by Administrative Law Judges applying the point-of-rest doctrine. The Benefits Review Board reversed both decisions. The Court of Appeals for the Fifth Circuit affirmed. *Jacksonville Shipyards, Inc. v. Perdue,* 539 F.2d 533 (1976). The court rejected the point-of-rest theory, holding instead that the 1972 Act covers all workers directly involved in the work of loading, unloading, repairing, building, or breaking a vessel. *Id.*, at 539-540. The court found that "Ford's work of fastening the vehicles to the flat cars was ... the last step in transferring this cargo from sea to land transportation," *id.*, at 543, and that Bryant's work "was an integral part of the ongoing process of moving cargo between land transportation and a ship," *id.*, at 544. Accordingly, the Court of Appeals concluded that both men were covered by the 1972 Act.

We granted certiorari, vacated, and remanded for reconsideration in light of *Northeast Marine Terminal.* 433 U.S. 904 (1977). On remand, the Fifth Circuit reaffirmed the reasoning of its earlier opinion. 575 F.2d 79, 80 (1978) (*per curiam*). We again granted certiorari, 439 U.S. 978 (1978), and we now affirm.

IV.

Petitioners urge that Ford and Bryant are not covered by the 1972 Act because they were not engaged in "maritime employment." Petitioners suggest that a person is engaged in maritime employment only if, on the day of his injury, he could have been assigned to perform work upon the navigable waters of the United States. By navigable waters, the petitioners do not mean the broad situs defined in § 3(a), as amended by the 1972 Act; rather they refer to places seaward of the Jensen line. In other words, petitioners argue that the 1972 Act covers only workers who are working or who may be assigned to work over the water itself. They say that this formulation follows congressional intent to cover all workers who, before 1972, could have walked in and out of coverage during any given day.

Petitioners' position is plainly inconsistent with the language and structure of the 1972 Act. The Act, as noted above, contains distinct situs and status requirements. The situs test of § 3(a) allows recovery for an injury suffered on navigable waters or certain adjoining areas landward of the Jensen line. This test defines the broad geographic coverage of the Act. Section 2(3) restricts the scope of coverage by further requiring that the injured worker must have been engaged in "maritime employment." This section defines the Act's occupational requirements. The term "maritime employment" refers to the nature of a worker's activities. Thus, § 2(3) uses the phrase "[longshoremen] or other [persons] engaged in longshoring operations" as one example of workers who engage in maritime employment no matter where they do their job. Since § 3(a) already limits the geographic coverage of the Act, § 2(3) need not provide that longshoremen are covered only if they work in certain places. The use of the term "maritime employment" in § 2(3), therefore, provides no support for the proposition that the statutory definition of an employee imports a geographic limitation narrower than the one defined in § 3(a).

The difficulty with petitioners' position becomes even plainer when their interpretation is applied to a single statutory provision that contains both the status and the situs requirement. Section 2(4), 33 U.S.C. § 902(4), defines an "employer" as one "any of whose employees are employed in maritime employment, in whole or in part, upon the navigable waters of the United States" as broadly defined by § 3(a). If the term "maritime employment" referred only to work that might take employees seaward of the Jensen line, then the broader situs test in the final clause of this section would become virtually superfluous. We decline the invitation to construe "maritime employment" so as to create two differing situs requirements in a single sentence. By understanding the term "maritime employment" to embody an occupational rather than a geographic concept, we give the two phases in § 2(4) distinct and consistent meanings.

The discussion of coverage in the legislative history also shows that Congress intended the term "maritime employment" to refer to status rather than situs. Committees in both Houses of Congress recognized:

> [To] take a typical example, cargo, whether in break bulk or containerized form, is typically unloaded from the ship and immediately transported to a storage or holding area on the pier, wharf, or terminal adjoining navigable waters. The employees who perform this work would be covered under the bill for injuries sustained by them over the navigable waters or on the adjoining land area. The Committee does not intend to cover employees who are not engaged in loading, unloading, repairing, or building a vessel, just because they are injured in an area adjoining navigable waters used for such activity. Thus, employees whose responsibility is only to pick up stored cargo for further trans-shipment would not be covered, nor would purely clerical employees whose jobs do not require them to participate in the loading or unloading of cargo.

This legislative history discusses workers solely in terms of what they are doing and never in terms of where they are working.

In adopting an occupational test that focuses on loading and unloading, Congress anticipated that some persons who work only on land would receive benefits under the 1972 Act. An obvious example of such a worker is Blundo. He was checking and marking cargo from a container that had been removed from a ship and moved over land to another pier before it was opened. Without any indication that he ever would be required to set foot on a ship, this Court held that he was covered by the 1972 Act because this type of work was maritime employment. *Northeast Marine Terminal Co.*, 432 U.S., at 271.

Land-based workers who do not handle containerized cargo also may be engaged in loading, unloading, repairing, or building a vessel. The Senate Subcommittee on Labor heard testimony that 30%-35% of ship repair work is done on land. Furthermore, the usual longshoring crew includes some men whose duties may be carried out solely on the land. A typical loading gang consists of persons who move cargo from a warehouse to the side of a ship, front men who attach the load to the ship's gear for lifting aboard the vessel, and a hold gang which stores cargo inside the ship. Although the workers who carry the cargo to shipside and the front men who attach the cargo to the lifting devices need not board a ship to carry out their duties, they are incontestably longshoremen directly engaged in the loading process. Even the petitioners concede that some land-based workers are covered by the 1972 Act.

V.

The issue in this case thus becomes whether Ford and Bryant are the kind of land-based employees that Congress intended to encompass within the term "maritime employment." Both men engaged in the type of duties that longshoremen perform in transferring goods between ship and land transportation. If the cotton that Bryant was unloading had been brought directly from the compress-warehouse to a ship, his task of moving cotton off a dray wagon would have been performed by a longshoreman. Similarly, longshoremen—not warehousemen like Ford—would fasten military vehicles onto railroad flatcars if those vehicles went directly from a ship to the railroad cars. The only basis for distinguishing Bryant or Ford from longshoremen who otherwise would perform the same work is the point-of-rest theory. That is, longshoremen in the Ports of Beaumont and Galveston would have performed the work done by Bryant and Ford had the cargo moved without interruption between land and sea transportation. Our unanimous opinion in *Northeast Marine Terminal* expressly decided that application of the point-of-rest test to define the scope of maritime employment would be contrary to congressional intent. *Id.*, at 275-279. Thus, there is no principled basis for distinguishing Ford and Bryant from longshoremen who have been injured while performing the same tasks.

We believe that § 2(3)'s explicit use of the terms "longshoreman" and "other person engaged in longshoring operations" to describe persons engaged in maritime employment demonstrates that workers doing tasks traditionally performed by longshoremen are within the purview of the 1972 Act. We do not suggest that the scope of maritime employment depends upon the vagaries of union jurisdiction. 432 U.S., at 268, n.30. Instead, the crucial factor is the nature of the activity to which a worker may be assigned. Persons moving cargo directly from ship to land transportation are engaged in maritime employment. *Id.*, at 267. A worker responsible for some portion of that activity is as much an integral part of the process of loading or unloading a ship as a person who participates in the entire process. We therefore hold that Ford and Bryant were engaged in maritime employment because they were engaged in intermediate steps of moving cargo between ship and land transportation.

Our decision serves the intent of Congress in creating the status requirement. First, it focuses upon the nature, not the location, of employment. Second, it does not extend coverage to all workers in the situs area. There is no doubt for example, that neither the driver of the truck carrying cotton to Galveston nor the locomotive engineer transporting military vehicles from Beaumont was engaged in maritime employment even though he was working on the marine situs. Such a person's "responsibility is only to pick up stored cargo for further trans-shipment." S. Rep. No. 92-1125, p. 13 (1972); H.R. Rep. No. 92-1441, p. 11 (1972); *see Northeast Marine Terminal Co. v. Caputo*, 432 U.S., at 267, 275.

Our decision today also serves the broader congressional purpose of expanding coverage. Congress intended to apply a simple, uniform standard of coverage. Adoption of the petitioners' test would conflict with that goal, because any individual worker's coverage would depend upon the assignment policies of his employer. For example, a land-based worker would be covered if his employer allowed him to alternate assignments with co-workers who work on the water, but he would not be covered if the employer never allowed him to board a ship. Congress did not intend the Act's coverage to shift with the employer's whim. *See id.*, at 276, n.38. In contrast, a definition of maritime employment that reaches any worker who moves cargo between ship and land transportation will enable both workers and employers to predict with reasonable assurance who on the situs is protected by the 1972 Act.

Because the Court of Appeals correctly determined that Ford and Bryant were engaged in maritime employment at the time of their injuries, its judgment is

Affirmed.

Notes: Status and Situs Requirements

1. To recover benefits under the LHWCA, an employee must satisfy both the *status* requirement under § 902(3) and the *situs* requirement under § 903(a). The status test, as discussed in *Pfeiffer*, requires that the employee be engaged in "maritime employment." The situs test requires that the injury take place on the "navigable waters of the United States." The 1972 and 1984 amendments to the act specify that the term "navigable waters" includes "any adjoining pier, wharf, drydock, terminal building way, marine railway, on other adjoining area customarily used by an employer in loading, unloading, repairing, dismantling, or building a vessel."

Courts have struggled to define the parameters of the status and situs requirements. In *Director v. Perini North River Associates*, 459 U.S. 297, 103 S. Ct. 634, 74 L. Ed. 465, 1983 AMC 609 (1983), the Court held that an employee injured on "actual" navigable waters of the United States, as distinguished from the expanded situs under the 1972 amendment to § 903(a), is not bound to show that his employment bears a direct and substantial relation to navigation or commerce to be covered. The standard that situs alone suffices or that the status requirement is satisfied when an employee is injured on "actual" navigable waters of the United States is the same as under the prior law. The Court concluded that Congress in adopting the 1972 Amendments intended to expand coverage and not to exclude anyone who had been covered by prior law. Because the expanded coverage for the first time included workers whose duties may be performed solely on land, it was necessary to apply both a status and situs test to these workers. As to those who work on navigable waters, the Court concluded:

> We hold only that when a worker is injured on the actual navigable waters in the course of his employment on those waters, he satisfies the status requirement in § 2(3), and is covered under the LHWCA, providing, of course, that he is the employee of a statutory "employer," and is not excluded by any other provision of the Act. We consider these employees to be "engaged in maritime employment" not simply because they are injured in a historically maritime locale, but because they are required to perform their duties upon navigable waters. (at p. 323).

Conversely, the status test focuses on the type of occupation rather than the location of employment. The employee must show that the occupation was in some way related to loading, unloading, construction, repair or dismantling of vessels. For example, in *Sanders v. Alabama Dry Dock and Shipbuilding Co.*, 841 F.2d 1085 (11th Cir. 1988), the appeals court held that an industrial relations specialist who oversaw activities in a shipyard *was* engaged in maritime employment because the purpose of his job was to keep the shipyard running smoothly. Yet, the court in *Dorris v. Director, OWCP*, 808 F.2d 1362, 1987 AMC 2730 (9th Cir. 1987) denied that a truck driver who transported cargo to the docks and engaged in a longshore work on an "episodic basis" was involved in maritime employment.

2. The Fifth Circuit has qualified the rule that a worker injured in the course of employment on navigable waters is engaged in maritime employment and meets the status test by excluding those situations where the worker's presence on the water at the time of the injury was either "transient or fortuitous" even though technically in the course of employment. These situations should be distinguished from a worker who spends a "not in substantial amount of time" working on water. For example, the court found that spending 8.3 percent of work time on a vessel was "not in substantial." *Bienvenu v. Texaco, Inc.*, 164 F.3d 901, 1999 AMC 1255(5th Cir. 1999) (en banc).

3. Courts have also refused to extend LHWCA coverage to a worker who satisfies the status, but not the situs requirement of the act. *See, Humphries v. Director, O.W.C.P.*, 834 F.2d 372 (4th Cir. 1987). In *Humphries*, the plaintiff worked as a shift foreman for Cargill, Inc. As part of his employment responsibilities, plaintiff was required to pick up food for employees working overtime. Cargill imposed this responsibility on the shift foreman in order to prevent delays in loading and unloading operations. On the night of the accident, plaintiff drove to a restaurant approximately one and one-half miles from the Cargill terminal to get a meal for an employee working overtime. As he left the restaurant, plaintiff experienced car trouble. Humphries was seriously injured when hit by a passing automobile as he left his car to check under the hood. The Benefits Review Board held that plaintiff's injuries were not covered under the LHWCA because, at the time of his injury, he was not on a maritime situs. The Fourth Circuit first noted that "as a shift foreman supervising and facilitating a loading operation Humphries was clearly 'engaged in maritime employment;'" and therefore met the status requirement. While agreeing with Humphries that the maritime situs requirement should be interpreted broadly, the court held that "[w]ere we to read the situs requirement so broadly as to embrace this claim, however, we would come perilously close to eliminating it entirely."

HERB'S WELDING, INC. v. GRAY

470 U.S. 414, 105 S. Ct. 1421, 84 L. Ed. 2d 406, 1985 AMC 1700 (1985)

Justice WHITE delivered the opinion of the Court

The Longshoremen's and Harbor Workers' Compensation Act (LHWCA or Act), 44 Stat. 1424, as amended, 33 U.S.C. § 901 *et seq.*, provides compensation for the death or disability of any person engaged in "maritime employment," § 902(3), if the disability or death results from an injury incurred upon the navigable waters of the United States or any adjoining pier or other area customarily used by an employer in loading, unloading, repairing, or building a vessel, § 903(a). Thus, a worker claiming under the Act must satisfy both a "status" and a "situs" test. The court below held that respondent Robert Gray, a welder working on a fixed offshore oil-drilling platform in state territorial waters, was entitled to benefits under the Act. We reverse for the reason that Gray was not engaged in maritime employment.

I.

Respondent Gray worked for Herb's Welding, Inc., in the Bay Marchand oil and gas field off the Louisiana coast. Herb's Welding provided welding services to the owners of drilling platforms. The field was located partly in Louisiana territorial waters, *i.e.*, within three miles of the shore, and partly on the Outer Continental Shelf. Gray ate and slept on a platform situated in Louisiana waters. He spent roughly three-quarters of his working time on platforms in state waters and the rest on platforms on the Outer Continental Shelf. He worked exclusively as a welder, building and replacing pipelines and doing general maintenance work on the platforms.

On July 11, 1975, Gray was welding a gas flow line on a fixed platform located in Louisiana waters. He burnt through the bottom of the line and an explosion occurred. Gray ran from the area, and in doing so hurt his knee. He sought benefits under the LHWCA for lost wages, disability, and medical expenses.[3] When petitioner United States

---

[3] Gray did recover under the Louisiana workers' compensation scheme, receiving weekly benefits totalling $3,172.50 over two years as well as $1,696.14 for medical expenses. These payments were credited against his later LHWCA recovery. *See* App. to Pet. for Cert. A-45. State workers'compensation and the LHWCA are not mutually exclusive remedies. *Sun Ship, Inc.v. Pennsylvania*, 447 U.S. 715 (1980).

Fidelity & Guaranty Co., the workers' compensation carrier for Herb's Welding, denied LHWCA benefits, Gray filed a complaint with the Department of Labor. The Administrative Law Judge (ALJ), relying on our decision in *Rodrigue v. Aetna Casualty & Surety Co.*, 395 U.S. 352 (1969), ruled that because Gray's work was totally involved in the exploration for, and development and transmission of, oil and gas from submerged lands, it was not relevant to traditional maritime law and lacked any significant maritime connection. Gray therefore did not satisfy the LHWCA's status requirement.

The Benefits Review Board reversed on other grounds. 12 BRBS 752 (1980). By a vote of 2-1, it concluded that irrespective of the nature of his employment, Gray could recover by virtue of a provision of the Outer Continental Shelf Lands Act, 67 Stat. 462, 43 U.S.C. § 1331 *et seq.* (Lands Act), that grants LHWCA benefits to offshore oil workers injured on the Outer Continental Shelf.[4] Although Gray had been injured in state waters, the Board felt that his injury nonetheless could be said to have occurred, in the words of the statute, "as a result of" operations on the outer shelf. It considered his work "integrally related" to such operations. 12 BRBS, at 757. The dissenting Board member argued that the Lands Act provides LHWCA benefits only for injuries actually occurring in the geographic area of the outershelf. *Id.*, at 761-763.

The Board reaffirmed its position after the case was remanded to the ALJ for entry of judgment and calculation of benefits, and petitioners sought review in the Court of Appeals for the Fifth Circuit. That court affirmed, relying directly on the LHWCA rather than on the Lands Act. 703 F.2d 176 (1983). With regard to the Act's situs requirement, it noted that this Court had compared drilling platforms to wharves in *Rodrigue v. Aetna Casualty & Surety Co., supra.* Given that the 1972 Amendments to the LHWCA extended coverage to accidents occurring on wharves, it would be incongruous if they did not also reach accidents occurring on drilling platforms. Also, since workers injured on movable barges, on fixed platforms on the Outer Continental Shelf, or en route to fixed platforms, are all covered, there would be a "curious hole" in coverage if someone in Gray's position was not. 703 F.2d, at 177-178. As for Gray's status, the Court of Appeals, differing with the ALJ, held that Gray's work bore "a realistically significant relationship to traditional maritime activity involving navigation and commerce on navigable waters," *id.*, at 179-180, because it was an integral part of the offshore drilling process, which, the court had held in *Pippen v. Shell Oil Co.*, 661 F.2d 378 (1981), was itself maritime commerce. We granted certiorari. 465 U.S. 1098 (1984).

II.

A.

When extractive operations first moved offshore, all claims for injuries on fixed platforms proceeded under state workers' compensation schemes. *See Hearings*, at 396, 409, 411. *See also Robertson* 993. With the 1953 passage of the Lands Act, Congress extended LHWCA coverage to oil workers more than three miles offshore. 43 U.S.C. § 1333(b). Because until 1972 the LHWCA itself extended coverage only to accidents occurring on navigable waters, 33 U.S.C. § 903 (1970 ed.), and because stationary rigs were considered to be islands, *Rodrigue v. Aetna Casualty & Surety Co., supra*, oil rig workers inside the 3-mile limit were left to recover under state schemes. *See, e.g., Freeman v. Chevron Oil Co.*, 517 F.2d 201 (CA5 1975); *Gifford v. Aurand Mfg. Co.*, 207 So. 2d 160 (La. App. 1968). Any worker, inside or outside the 3-mile limit, who qualified as a seaman was not covered by the LHWCA, but could sue under the Jones Act, 46 U.S.C. § 688, the Death on the High Seas Act, 46 U.S.C. § 761 *et seq.*, and the general maritime law. Hearings, at 411-414, 450-459, 487; *see* n.1, *supra. See also* Wright, *Jurisdiction in the Tidelands*, 32 TULANE L. REV. 175, 186 (1958).

---

[4] The relevant section provides:

> With respect to disability or death of an employee resulting from any injury occurring as the result of operations conducted on the Outer Continental Shelf for the purpose of exploring for, developing, removing or transporting by pipeline the natural resources, or involving rights to the natural resources, of the subsoil and seabed of the outer Continental Shelf, compensation shall be payable under the provisions of the Longshoremen's and Harbor Workers' Compensation Act. 67 Stat. 463, as amended, 43 U.S.C. § 1333(b).

So matters stood when Congress amended the LHWCA in 1972. What is known about the congressional intent behind that legislation has been amply described in our prior opinions. *See, e.g., Director, OWCP v. Perini North River Associates*, 459 U.S. 297 (1983); *Sun Ship, Inc. v. Pennsylvania*, 447 U.S. 715, 717-722 (1980); *Northeast Marine Terminal Co. v. Caputo*, 432 U.S. 249, 256-265 (1977). The most important of Congress' concerns, for present purposes, was the desire to extend coverage to longshoremen, harbor workers, and others who were injured while on piers, docks, and other areas customarily used to load and unload ships or to repair or build ships, rather than while actually afloat. Whereas prior to 1972 the Act reached only accidents occurring on navigable waters, the amended 33 U.S.C. § 903 expressly extended coverage to "adjoining [areas]." At the same time, the amended definition of an "employee" limited coverage to employees engaged in "maritime employment."

The Act, as amended, does not mention offshore drilling rigs or the workers thereon. The legislative history of the amendments is also silent, although early in the legislative process, a bill was introduced to extend the Act to all offshore oil workers. The bill died in Committee. While hardly dispositive, it is worth noting that the same Committee considered the 1972 Amendments to the LHWCA, and the possible extension of the Lands Act's application of the LHWCA to drilling platforms, apparently without it ever occurring to anyone that the two might have been duplicative. The concurrent but independent reconsideration of both the Lands Act and the LHWCA, the congressional view that the amendments to the latter involved the "[extension] of [coverage] to [shoreside] [areas]," H.R. REP. NO. 92-1441, p. 10 (1972), and the absence of any mention of drilling platforms in the discussion of the LHWCA, combine to suggest that the 1972 Congress at least did not intentionally extend the LHWCA to workers such as Gray.

B.

The rationale of the Court of Appeals was that offshore drilling is maritime commerce and that anyone performing any task that is part and parcel of that activity is in maritime employment for LHWCA purposes. Since it is doubtful that an offshore driller will pay and maintain a worker on an offshore rig whose job is unnecessary to the venture, this approach would extend coverage to virtually everyone on the stationary platform. We think this construction of the Act is untenable.

The Act does not define the term "maritime employment," but our cases and the legislative history of the amendments foreclose the Court of Appeals' reading. *Rodrigue* involved two men killed while working on an offshore drilling rig on the Outer Continental Shelf. Their families brought third-party negligence suits in federal court, claiming recovery under both the Death on the High Seas Act and the state law of Louisiana. The District Court ruled that resort could not be had to state law and that the High Seas Act provided the exclusive remedy. The Court of Appeals for the Fifth Circuit affirmed, holding that the men had been engaged in maritime activity on the high seas and that maritime law was the exclusive source of relief. We reversed. First, the platforms involved were artificial islands and were to be treated as though they were federal enclaves in an upland State. Federal law was to govern accidents occurring on these islands; but, contrary to the Court of Appeals, we held that the Lands Act and borrowed state law, not the maritime law, constituted the controlling federal law. The platforms "were islands, albeit artificial ones, and the accidents had no more connection with the ordinary stuff of admiralty than do accidents on piers." 395 U.S., at 360. Indeed, observing that the Court had previously "held that drilling platforms are not within admiralty jurisdiction," we indicated that drilling platforms were not even suggestive of traditional maritime affairs. *Id.*, at 360-361.

We also went on to examine the legislative history of the Lands Act and noted (1) that Congress was of the view that maritime law would not apply to fixed platforms unless a statute expressly so provided; and (2) that Congress had seriously considered applying maritime law to these platforms but had rejected that approach because it considered maritime law to be inapposite, a view that would be untenable if drilling from a fixed platform is a maritime operation. The history of the Lands Act at the very least forecloses the Court of Appeals' holding that offshore drilling is a maritime activity and that any task essential thereto is maritime employment for LHWCA purposes.

We cannot assume that Congress was unfamiliar with *Rodrigue* and the Lands Act when it referred to "maritime employment" in defining the term "employee" in 1972. It would have been a significant departure from prior understanding to use that phrase to reach stationary drilling rigs generally.

The Fifth Circuit's expansive view of maritime employment is also inconsistent with our prior cases under the 1972 Amendments to the LHWCA. The expansion of the definition of navigable waters to include rather large shoreside areas necessitated an affirmative description of the particular employees working in those areas who would be covered. This was the function of the maritime employment requirement. But Congress did not seek to cover all those who breathe salt air. Its purpose was to cover those workers on the situs who are involved in the essential elements of loading and unloading; it is "clear that persons who are on the situs but not engaged in the overall process of loading or unloading vessels are not covered." *Northeast Marine Terminal Co. v. Caputo*, 432 U.S., at 267. While "maritime employment" is not limited to the occupations specifically mentioned in § 2(3), neither can it be read to eliminate any requirement of a connection with the loading or construction of ships. As we have said, the "maritime employment" requirement is "an occupational test that focuses on loading and unloading." *P.C. Pfeiffer Co. v. Ford*, 444 U.S. 69, 80 (1979). The Amendments were not meant "to cover employees who are not engaged in loading, unloading, repairing, or building a vessel, just because they are injured in an area adjoining navigable waters used for such activity." H.R. REP. NO. 92-1441, p. 11 (1972); S. REP. NO. 92-1125, p. 13 (1972). We have never read "maritime employment" to extend so far beyond those actually involved in moving cargo between ship and land transportation. Both Caputo and *P.C. Pfeiffer Co.* make this clear and lead us to the conclusion that Gray was not engaged in maritime employment for purposes of the LHWCA.[10]

Gray was a welder. His work had nothing to do with the loading or unloading process, nor is there any indication that he was even employed in the maintenance of equipment used in such tasks. Gray's welding work was far removed from traditional LHWCA activities, notwithstanding the fact that he unloaded his own gear upon arriving at a platform by boat. Tr. of Oral Arg. 56. He built and maintained pipelines and the platforms themselves. There is nothing inherently maritime about those tasks. They are also performed on land, and their nature is not significantly altered by the marine environment, particularly since exploration and development of the Continental Shelf are not themselves maritime commerce.

The dissent emphasizes that Gray was generally on or near the water and faced maritime hazards. Post, at 445-449. To the extent this is so, it is relevant to "situs," not "status." To hold that Gray was necessarily engaged in maritime employment because he was on a drilling platform would ignore Congress' admonition that not everyone on a covered situs automatically satisfies the status test. *See* S. REP. NO. 92-1125, p. 13 (1972). The dissent considers "[the] maritime nature of the occupation ... apparent from examining its location in terms of the expanded situs coverage of the 1972 Amendments." Post, at 446. We recognize that the nature of a particular job is defined in part by its location. But to classify Gray's employment as maritime because he was on a covered situs, post, at 448, or in a "maritime environment," post, at 450, would blur together requirements Congress intended to be distinct. We cannot thus read the status requirement out of the statute.

---

[10] This view of "maritime employment" does not preclude benefits for those whose injury would have been covered before 1972 because it occurred "on navigable waters." *Director, OWCP v. Perini North River Associates*, 459 U.S. 297 (1983). No claim is made that Gray was injured "on navigable waters." Indeed, it was agreed by all counsel at oral argument that prior to 1972 Gray would not have been covered, except arguably by operation of the Lands Act. *See* Tr. of Oral Arg. 11, 46, 52-54. *See also* 703 F.2d, at 179.

In light of the dissent's reliance on *Perini*, post, at 442-443, we point out that that decision was carefully limited to coverage of an employee "injured while performing his job upon actual navigable waters." 459 U.S., at 299; *see id.*, at 305, 311-312, 315, 324. The Court's rationale was that, first, any employee injured on navigable waters would have been covered prior to 1972, and, second, Congress did not intend to restrict coverage in adopting its "maritime employment" test. The holding was, "of course," limited to workers covered prior to 1972, *id.*, at 325, n.34, a group to which Gray does not belong. The opinion says nothing about the contours of the status requirement as applied to a worker, like Gray, who was not injured on navigable waters. To hold that enactment of the status requirement did not constrict prior coverage is wholly different from refusing to view that requirement as a meaningful limit on the Act's extended coverage.

III.

Respondents, and the dissenters, object that denying coverage to someone in Gray's position will result in exactly the sort of inconsistent, checkered coverage that Congress sought to eliminate in 1972. In the words of the court below, it creates a "curious hole" in coverage, 703 F.2d, at 178, because Gray would have been covered had he been injured on navigable waters or on the outer shelf.

We do not find the argument compelling. First, this submission goes far beyond Congress' undoubted desire to treat equally all workers engaged in loading or unloading a ship, whether they were injured on the ship or on an adjoining pier or dock. The former were covered prior to 1972; the latter were not. Both are covered under the 1972 Amendments. Second, there will always be a boundary to coverage, and there will always be people who cross it during their employment. *Nacirema Operating Co. v. Johnson*, 396 U.S. 212, 223-224 (1969). If that phenomenon was enough to require coverage, the Act would have to reach much further than anyone argues that it does or should. Third, the inconsistent coverage here results primarily from the explicit geographic limitation to the Lands Act's incorporation of the LHWCA. Gray would indeed have been covered for a significant portion of his work-time, but because of the Lands Act, not because he fell within the terms of the LHWCA. Congress' desire to make LHWCA coverage uniform reveals little about the position of those for whom partial coverage results from a separate statute. This is especially true because that statute draws a clear geographical boundary that will predictably result in workers moving in and out of coverage.

As we have said before in this area, if Congress' coverage decisions are mistaken as a matter of policy, it is for Congress to change them. We should not legislate for them. *See Victory Carriers, Inc. v. Law*, 404 U.S. 202, 216 (1971).

IV.

Because Gray's employment was not "maritime," he does not qualify for benefits under the LHWCA. We need not determine whether he satisfied the Act's situs requirement. We express no opinion on his argument that he is covered by 43 U.S.C. § 1333(b). The judgment is reversed, and the case is remanded to the Court of Appeals for further proceedings consistent with this opinion.

It is so ordered.

Justice MARSHALL, with whom Justice BRENNAN, Justice BLACKMUN, and Justice O'CONNOR join, dissenting.

Today the Court holds that a marine petroleum worker is not covered by the Longshoremen's and Harbor Workers' Compensation Act (LHWCA or Act), 44 Stat. 1424, as amended, 33 U.S.C. § 901 *et seq.*, when pursuing his occupation on a fixed offshore rig within the 3-mile limit of a State's territorial waters. Although such an individual routinely travels over water as an essential part of his job and performs the rest of his job adjacent to and surrounded by water, he is not covered because, in the Court's view, his occupation is not "maritime employment." *See* § 2(3), 33 U.S.C. § 902(3). The Court reaches this conclusion even though a worker of the same occupation, working in the same industry, and performing the same tasks on a rig located in the same place, would be covered if that rig were one that was capable of floating. Neither the Court nor any of the parties have identified any reason why Congress might have desired this distinction. To the contrary, a principal congressional goal behind the 1972 Amendments was to rid the Act of just such arbitrary distinctions derived from traditional admiralty jurisprudence. Because the coverage pattern that the Court adopts is at odds with the Act's 1972 Amendments, and because the accident here meets the Amendments' status and situs tests, I respectfully dissent.

* * *

BLANCQ v. HAPAG-LLOYD A.G.

986 F.Supp. 376, 1998 AMC 1440 (E.D. La. 1997).

V<small>ANCE</small>, District Judge.

Order and Reasons

Before the Court are two motions filed by the defendants: (1) a motion for summary judgment dismissing the claims of plaintiff Ronald Blancq; and (2) a motion to strike plaintiff's demand for a trial by jury. For the reasons set forth below, both motions are DENIED.

I. Background

Captain Ronald Blancq was employed as a Mississippi River pilot and hired by the M/V NEUREMBERG EXPRESS to perform services on or about January 3, 1995. Pet. ¶ III. The M/V NEUREMBERG EXPRESS was owned/operated by defendants Hapag-Lloyd A.G. and Hapag-Lloyd (America), Inc. (collectively referred to hereinafter as "Hapag-Lloyd"). Pet. ¶ IV. Plaintiff alleges that he was injured when he attempted to leave the vessel by way of the ship's Jacob ladder.

* * *

This action was originally filed in the 34th Judicial District Court for the Parish of St. Bernard, State of Louisiana, on January 3, 1996. Defendants timely removed the action from the state court to the Eastern District of Louisiana on January 18, 1996. This Court has diversity jurisdiction over this matter pursuant to 28 U.S.C. § 1332.[1] Hapag-Lloyd now moves this Court for summary judgment and further requests that plaintiff's demand for trial by jury be stricken.

II. Discussion

* * *

A. *Plaintiff's Legal Status*

In maritime law, the standard of care owed by the vessel owner to the plaintiff depends upon the plaintiff's legal status. Hapag-Lloyd argues that plaintiff is covered under the Longshore and Harbor Workers' Compensation Act ("LHWCA"), 33 U.S.C. §§ 901-950, and is owed only a limited duty of care from the vessel owner under § 905(b). Plaintiff asserts that he falls under neither the Jones Act, nor the LHWCA and that the defendants owed him a warranty of seaworthiness under the doctrine articulated in *Seas Shipping Co. v. Sieracki*, 328 U.S. 85, 66 S.Ct. 872, 90 L.Ed. 1099 (1946) (hereinafter the "Sieracki doctrine").

It is generally recognized that "[t]here is some confusion ... over the status of a pilot who suffers personal injury." 2 T<small>HOMAS</small> J. S<small>CHOENBAUM</small>, A<small>DMIRALTY AND</small> M<small>ARITIME</small> L<small>AW</small> § 13-1 at 238 (2d ed.1994). *See generally* Guy C. Stephenson, *A Pilot is a Pilot: Compulsory Pilots—Vessel Owner's Responsibilities for Intervention and Personal Injury*, 70 T<small>UL</small>. L. R<small>EV</small>. 633, 638-46 (1995) (reviewing pilot's coverage under Jones Act, LHWCA, and warranty of seaworthiness); Jack L. Allbritton, *Seaman Status in Wilander's Wake*, 68 T<small>UL</small>. L. R<small>EV</small>. 373, 377-85 (1994) (same); David W. Robertson, *Continuing Issues in the Rights of Injured Maritime Workers in the Wilander-Gizoni Era*, 24 R<small>UTGERS</small> L.J. 443, 451- 59 (1993) (same). Thus, the first question this Court must resolve is the legal status of a river pilot.

Under Louisiana law, river port pilots have the exclusive right to pilot vessels on the Mississippi River between New Orleans and Pilottown, Louisiana, and within certain other geographical limits. La. R.S. 34:996. A river port

---

[1] The Court notes that the "saving to suitors" clause of 28 U.S.C. § 1333 divests the federal courts of exclusive jurisdiction over maritime claims. For purposes of federal question and removal jurisdiction, "[i]t is well established that [general] maritime claims do no 'aris[e]' under the Constitution, treaties or laws of the United States.'" Tennessee Gas Pipeline v. Houston Casualty Ins. Co., 87 F.3d 150, 153 (5th Cir.), *reh'g denied*, 95 F.3d 1151 (5th Cir.1996). Thus, the Fifth Circuit has stated in no uncertain terms that "[a] defendant who desires to remove a maritime action from state court to federal court must establish diversity jurisdiction." *In re Dutile*, 935 F.2d 61, 63 (5th Cir.1991).

pilot must be certified by the Board of River Port Pilot Commissioners for the Port of New Orleans and appointed by the governor. La. R.S. 34:992. River port pilots are intensively regulated under state law—for example, the fees charged to the vessels for the pilotage services is set by statute. La. R.S. 34:997. Although a pilot works on each vessel for only a short period of time, he is exposed to the typical hazards of the sea, and his duties are clearly related to the navigation of the vessel.

1. *Jones Act Coverage*

* * *

Thus, this Court concludes that the holding of *Bach*—that a pilot is not a seaman under the Jones Act because he lacks the requisite connection to a vessel or an identifiable fleet of vessels—is consistent with the Supreme Court's most recent pronouncements. Therefore, Captain Blancq is not entitled to the legal benefits of the Jones Act.[3]

2. *LHWCA Coverage*

The Longshore and Harbor Workers' Compensation Act ("LHWCA"), 33 U.S.C. §§ 901-950, was originally enacted in 1927 to protect longshoremen and other harbor workers doing loading and repair work, who were excluded from state-law workers' compensation coverage and did not fall within federal admiralty jurisdiction. *See generally Northeast Marine Terminal Co. v. Caputo*, 432 U.S. 249, 256-60, 97 S.Ct. 2348, 2353-55, 53 L.Ed.2d 320 (1977). Generally, the Act requires employers to provide compensation to their employees for injury arising out of the course of employment, and, in return, the Act grants the employer immunity from tort liability. 33 U.S.C. §§ 904-905.

Prior to the 1972 Amendments to the LHWCA, all employees injured upon navigable waters in the course of their employment were covered by the LHWCA. Eligibility for coverage depended solely upon a "situs" test. As the Supreme Court explained:

[T]he consistent interpretation given to LHWCA before 1972 by the Director, the deputy commissioners, the courts, and the commentators was that (except for those workers specifically excepted in the statute), any worker injured upon navigable waters in the course of employment was "covered ... without any inquiry into what he was doing (or supposed to be doing) at the time of his injury."

Director v. Perini North River Assocs., 459 U.S. 297, 311, 103 S.Ct. 634, 644, 74 L.Ed.2d 465 (1983) (quoting G. GILMORE & C. BLACK, THE LAW OF ADMIRALTY 429-30 (2d ed.1975)). The statute explicitly excluded from coverage any person who was a "master or member of a crew of any vessel." *Id.* at 306, 103 S.Ct. at 641 (citing 44 Stat. 1424). Significantly, in 1927 the United States Employees' Compensation Commission, the body in charge of implementing the Act, issued an opinion stating that a temporary pilot of a vessel was considered a "master or member of a crew" under the LHWCA and was thus not protected by the Act. Longshoremen's Act, Opinion No. 22 (Nov. 26, 1927), 1928 A.M.C. 263, cited in *Clark v. Solomon Navigation, Ltd.*, 631 F.Supp. 1275, 1281 (S.D.N.Y.1986).

---

[3] The Court notes that another possible basis for denying Captain Blancq the status of a Jones Act seaman is his employment relationship with the defendants. The Jones Act is a statutory remedy available to a seaman only against his employer. The problem in this case is that "[p]ilots are not employees of the vessel. Pilots historically are either self-employed, independent contractors, or, at least, not employed by the vessel owners and operators whose vessels they pilot." *Allbritton, supra*, at 382. *See* Evans v. United Arab Shipping Co. S.A.G., 4 F.3d 207, 215-19 (3d Cir.1993) (holding that a "prerequisite to recovery under the [Jones] Act" is an employment relationship between the plaintiff and defendant and that compulsory pilot failed to establish such a relationship). The Fifth Circuit in *Bach* specifically declined to reach the pilot's employment status. *See Bach*, 920 F.2d at 324 n. 1 ("Because we decided that Bach is not a seaman, we need not consider whether Trident Steamship was his employer for purposes of the Jones Act.").

In 1972, the LHWCA was amended by Congress to expand coverage to "any person engaged in maritime employment, including any longshoreman or other person engaged in longshoring operations, and any harbor-worker including a ship repairman, shipbuilder, and ship-breaker." 33 U.S.C. § 902(3). Further, compensation was available if the injury occurred "upon the navigable waters of the United States (including any adjoining pier, wharf, dry dock, terminal, building way, marine railway, or other adjoining area customarily used by an employer in loading, unloading, repairing, or building a vessel)." *Id.* § 903(a). As interpreted by the Supreme Court, the Amendment's purpose was to expand coverage to those injured in maritime employment on certain areas adjoining previously covered sites but not actually on navigable waters. *See Perini*, 459 U.S. at 316-24, 103 S.Ct. at 646-51; *Caputo*, 432 U.S. at 263-64, 97 S.Ct. at 2357. Thus, the Amendment required certain workers to satisfy both a "situs" test, as well as a "status" test. See *Id.*[4]

In *Perini*, the Supreme Court resolved this apparent tension between the pre-1972 Act and the post-1972 Act and explained that Congress had exhibited no intention to require an employee injured upon the navigable waters in the course of his employment to show that his employment passed the "status" test. *See Perini*, 459 U.S. at 316-24, 103 S.Ct. at 646-51. As the Fifth Circuit recognizes, the current test for coverage under the LHWCA presents a "dual inquiry": "Under *Perini*, an employee may be engaged in maritime employment if he was injured in the course of his employment while on navigable waters. If he was not on navigable waters at the time of his injury, however, he may satisfy the status test only if his work 'is directly connected to the commerce carried on by a ship or vessel under *Gray.*'" *Munguia v. Chevron U.S.A., Inc.*, 999 F.2d 808, 811 (5th Cir.1993) (*quoting Fontenot v. AWI, Inc.*, 923 F.2d 1127, 1130 (5th Cir.1991)). *See also Randall v. Chevron*, 13 F.3d 888, 898 (5th Cir.), *cert. denied*, 513 U.S. 994, 115 S.Ct. 498, 130 L.Ed.2d 408 (1994).[5]

As a result of the LHWCA's expansive breadth, it comes as no surprise that courts are divided over whether river or bar pilots are covered under the LHWCA. Compare *Harwood v. Partredereit AF*, 944 F.2d 1187 (4th Cir.1991) (pilot is covered under LHWCA), *cert. denied*, 503 U.S. 907, 112 S.Ct. 1265, 117 L.Ed.2d 493 (1992), with *Clark v. Solomon Navigation, Ltd.*, 631 F.Supp. 1275 (S.D.N.Y.1986) (pilot is excluded from LHWCA coverage); *see also Ringering v. Compania Maritima De-La Mancha*, 670 F.Supp. 301 (D.Or.1987) (finding that because river pilot was a "seaman," he was not limited to recovery under the LHWCA and was entitled to remedy of seaworthiness), *aff'd*, 848 F.2d 1243 (9th Cir.1988). The split arises in part because some courts conclude that pilots are "master[s] or member[s] of a crew" and are therefore excluded from LHWCA coverage. *See, e.g., Clark*, 631 F.Supp. at 1282. This interpretation of "master or member of a crew" is foreclosed in this Circuit by *Chandris Inc., Wilander*, and *Bach*. The Supreme Court in *Chandris, Inc.* and *Wilander* made clear that the Jones Act and the LHWCA are mutually exclusive compensation regimes, and the term "master or member of a crew" is identical to the term "seaman" for Jones Act purposes— "[i]ndeed, 'it is odd but true that the key requirement for Jones Act coverage now appears in another statute.'" *Chandris*, 515 U.S. at 355-56, 115 S.Ct. at 2183-84 (*quoting Wilander*, 498 U.S. at 347, 111 S.Ct. at 813). Having concluded under *Bach, supra*, that a pilot is not a "seaman" for purposes of the Jones Act, this Court is obligated to find that a pilot is also not a "master or member of a crew of any vessel" and hence not excluded from coverage under the LHWCA on those grounds.

Treating a river pilot who is injured upon navigable waters as falling under the LHWCA is problematic, however, for a number of reasons. First, it is inconsistent with the original purpose of the LHWCA. The Act was passed as a "way to provide workmen's compensation for longshoremen and harborworkers injured on navigable waters" who were excluded from state-law workers' compensation coverage because of the maritime nature of their employment. *Caputo*, 432 U.S. at 257-58, 97 S.Ct. at 2354; see also 1 SCHOENBAUM, *supra*, § 7-1 at 371. As noted supra, when the LHWCA was first passed in 1927, a pilot was excluded because he was thought to be a "member of a crew." Moreover, the persons intended to be covered by the LHWCA are those whose services aboard the vessel are "of the sort performed by longshoremen and harbor workers and thus distinguished from those employees on the

---

[4] Additionally, 33 U.S.C. § 902(3)(A)-(H) provides an expanded list of exceptions to the definition of "employee." Pertinent to this discussion, "a master or member of a crew" remains excluded from coverage. *Id.* § 902(3)(G).

[5] *See also* Herb's Welding, Inc. v. Gray, 470 U.S. 414, 423-24, 105 S.Ct. 1421, 1427-28, 84 L.Ed.2d 406 (1985) (holding that "land-based activity occurring within the § 903 situs will be deemed maritime only if it is an integral or essential part of loading or unloading a vessel").

vessel who are naturally and primarily on board to aid in her navigation." *South Chicago Coal & Dock Co. v. Bassett*, 309 U.S. 251, 260, 60 S.Ct. 544, 549, 84 L.Ed. 732 (1940).

The second problem with extending the LHWCA to river pilots is that the statutory compensation scheme affords them little protection. Because a pilot is typically considered an independent contractor,[6] he is not entitled to LHWCA's primary reward: workers' compensation benefits. The only statutory right that would be available to a pilot if he were covered by the LHWCA is an action in negligence against the vessel owner under 33 U.S.C. § 905(b).

Notably, the Fifth Circuit has expressed doubt over whether the LHWCA covers river pilots. In *Bach*, the appellate court noted that "[t]he LHWCA covers those 'engaged in maritime employment.' The record does not clearly show that Bach was the employee of anyone. It is therefore, unclear whether the LHWCA covered him." 920 F.2d at 326 n. 5. Rather than responding to the question of LHWCA coverage, however, the court reached the merits of both the pilot's negligence claim under 33 U.S.C. § 905(b) and his unseaworthiness claim under the Sieracki doctrine because the court believed the claims were identical. Based on "undisputed summary judgment evidence," the court concluded that both claims failed as a matter of law. *Bach*, 920 F.2d at 327.[7]

In not affirmatively answering whether a river pilot is covered by the LHWCA, the Fifth Circuit avoided the thorny question of a pilot's employment status.[8] As noted *supra*, pilots are generally considered either self-employed, independent contractors, or employees of the pilot's association. See *Evans v. United Arab Shipping Co., S.A.G.*, 4 F.3d 207, 217 (3d Cir.1993) (citing cases). The cases have not held that a pilot is an employee of a vessel he pilots. See *Id.* The Fifth Circuit's comments in *Bach* indicate that coverage under the LHWCA depends in part on the pilot's employee status. If the pilot is not employed by "anyone," his LHWCA-status is called into doubt. Several commentators have recognized the pilots' dilemma and, based upon the pilots' nonemployee status, have concluded that pilots should be entitled to a warranty of seaworthiness under the *Sieracki* doctrine. See *Stephenson, supra*, at 639-46; *Albritton, supra*, at 383-85; see also *Robertson, supra*, at 457 (commenting that providing pilots with protection of seaworthiness is an "unassailable" view and that the proper inquiry to determine a pilot's remedies is his employment status).

River pilots are maritime workers who do not qualify as Jones Act "seamen" and who do not fit comfortably within the LHWCA. Both of these statutory schemes were created in favor of an employee against his employer. In this case, the parties do not dispute that Captain Blancq was self-employed and acted as an independent contractor, with no connection to a particular vessel. Captain Blancq was not employed by the vessel owner. Rather, he is a member and a shareholder of the Crescent River Port Pilots' Association (the "Pilots' Association"). According to its charter, the Pilots' Association is a non-profit corporation, the purpose of which is "[t]o effect the corporate association of licensed and commissioned Louisiana Crescent River Port Pilots, for their mutual benefit and social betterment." Pl.'s Supplemental Mem., Attach., Art. III. Further, another objective of the corporation is "[t]o provide for a pension and welfare plan for retired shareholders of this corporation, and for their families." *Id.* Each pilot-member holds one share in the corporation, which functions to collect pilotage fees and distribute them to the membership "in their just proportion" after deduction of costs and expenses. *Id.*, Art. VII. Additionally, the Pilots'

---

[6] Although not necessarily in the context of determining benefits under the LHWCA, courts generally conclude that pilots function as independent contractors. *See Harwood*, 944 F.2d at 1189; *Bach*, 708 F.Supp. 772, 773-74 (E.D.La.1988), *aff'd on other grounds*, 920 F.2d 322 (5th Cir.), *vacated and remanded*, 500 U.S. 949, 111 S.Ct. 2253, 114 L.Ed.2d 706, *reaff'd on other grounds*, 947 F.2d 1290 (5th Cir.1991), *cert. denied*, 504 U.S. 931, 112 S.Ct. 1996, 118 L.Ed.2d 592 (1992); *see also* Steinhort v. Commissioner of Internal Revenue, 335 F.2d 496, 499 (5th Cir.1964) (noting that pilot's relationship towards the vessel is comparable to an independent contractor); Ehret v. State of Louisiana, 862 F.Supp. 1546, 1550 (E.D.La.1992) (pilots are independent contractors and neither association nor board were "employers" under the Age Discrimination in Employment Act).

[7] The Court also notes that in Meyers v. M/V EUGENIO C, 842 F.2d 815 (5th Cir.1988) (Rubin, J.), *aff'd on reh'g*, 876 F.2d 38 (5th Cir.1989), a bar pilot alleged multiple theories of negligence against the shipowner. The Fifth Circuit did not discuss whether the pilot was covered under either the Jones Act or the LHWCA. Rather, the Court recognized the pilot's claims and affirmed the district court's finding that the vessel was seaworthy. Also, the court reversed the district court's granting of summary judgment, finding that a material question of fact existed concerning whether the crew might have provided an alternative and safer way for the pilot to board the vessel. 842 F.2d at 817-18.

[8] As noted *supra*, the court in *Bach* acknowledged that it was avoiding this discussion when it specifically declined to reach the plaintiff's employment status in regard to his Jones Act claim.

Association makes rules for the assignment of members to pilot jobs. The charter and by-laws do not characterize pilots as employees of the Pilots' Association, but refers to them as shareholders and members. Given plaintiff's unique employment status, and in the absence of Fifth Circuit authority to the contrary, this Court concludes that it is consistent with the purposes behind the LHWCA and general maritime law to exclude a river pilot from coverage under the LHWCA.

3. *Sieracki Liability*

The warranty of seaworthiness is a duty that is generally owed to those employees covered under the Jones Act. See 1 SCHOENBAUM, *supra*, § 6-27, at 345. However, for those workers who "fall into the crack between seamen and longshore workers," the Sieracki doctrine and the warranty of seaworthiness "still rule[ ] the sea." *Id.*, § 6-27, at 347. In *Seas Shipping v. Sieracki*, 328 U.S. 85, 99, 66 S.Ct. 872, 880, 90 L.Ed. 1099 (1946), the Supreme Court extended the remedy of unseaworthiness to longshoremen "doing a seaman's work and incurring a seaman's hazards." The Sieracki doctrine was expanded by the Supreme Court in *Pope & Talbot, Inc. v. Hawn*, 346 U.S. 406, 413, 74 S.Ct. 202, 207, 98 L.Ed. 143 (1953), to include independent contractors who were subject to the same dangers as those crew members directly employed by the vessel. A river pilot who aids in the vessel's navigation is engaged in seaman's work and exposed to typical seaman's dangers.

The 1972 Amendments to the LHWCA eliminated the unseaworthiness remedy from any employee covered under the LHWCA. See 33 U.S.C. § 905(b). Although some courts have concluded that the 1972 Amendments entirely abolished the Sieracki doctrine, *see, e.g., Normile v. Maritime Co. of Philippines*, 643 F.2d 1380 (9th Cir.1981), the Fifth Circuit has made clear that persons excluded from the LHWCA's coverage may qualify as Sieracki seamen for the warranty of seaworthiness. *See Aparicio v. Swan Lake*, 643 F.2d 1109 (5th Cir.1981) (holding that under circumstances in which the maritime worker is not covered by the LHWCA, he may invoke the *Sieracki* unseaworthiness action against the vessel owner); *see also Cormier v. Oceanic Contractors, Inc.*, 696 F.2d 1112, 1113 (5th Cir.1983) (foreign worker outside of LHWCA's coverage entitled to unseaworthiness remedy), *cert. denied*, 464 U.S. 821, 104 S.Ct. 85, 78 L.Ed.2d 94 (1983); *Coats v. Penrod Drilling Corp.*, 785 F.Supp. 614, 622-24 (S.D.Miss.1992) (shore-based worker testing equipment on offshore rig entitled to *Sieracki* claim), *aff'd*, 61 F.3d 1113, 1118 n.2 (en banc) (noting that viability of Sieracki seaman status was not before the court); *Laakso v. Mitsui & Co. USA, Inc.*, Civ.A.No.88-2450, 1989 WL 149186 at *8-*9 (Dec. 6, 1989 E.D.La.) (worker outside of LHWCA's coverage retains his *Sieracki* unseaworthiness action); *Clark*, 631 F.Supp. at 1283 (pilot not covered under LHWCA is clearly due his remedy for unseaworthiness).

Having concluded that Captain Blancq falls outside of both the Jones Act and the LHWCA, he is eligible for the warranty of seaworthiness.[9]

* * *

Accordingly,

IT IS ORDERED that defendant's motion for summary judgment is DENIED.

---

[9] The Court notes that Captain Blancq also has a cause of action for negligence under the general maritime law. The duty of care owed to Captain Blancq by the defendants is one of reasonable care under the particular circumstances. *See* Kermarec v. Compagnie Generale Transatlantique, 358 U.S. 625, 79 S.Ct. 406, 3 L.Ed.2d 550 (1959).

C. Exclusive Liability of the Employer

LONGSHORE AND HARBOR WORKERS' COMPENSATION ACT

§ 905. Exclusiveness of Liability

(a) Employer liability; failure of employer to secure payment of compensation

The liability of an employer prescribed in section 904 of this title shall be exclusive and in place of all other liability of such employer to the employee, his legal representative, husband or wife, parents, dependents, next of kin, and anyone otherwise entitled to recover damages from such employer at law or in admiralty on account of such injury or death, except that if an employer fails to secure payment of compensation as required by this chapter, an injured employee, or his legal representative in case death results from the injury, may elect to claim compensation under the chapter or to maintain an action at law or in admiralty for damages on account of such injury or death. In such action the defendant may not plead as a defense that the injury was caused by the negligence of a fellow servant, or that the employee assumed the risk of his employment, or that the injury was due to the contributory negligence of the employee. For purposes of this subsection, a contractor shall be deemed the employer of a subcontractor's employees only if the subcontractor fails to secure the payment of compensation as required by section 904 of this title.

(b) Negligence of vessel

In the event of injury to a person covered under this chapter caused by the negligence of a vessel, then such person, or anyone otherwise entitled to recover damages by reason thereof, may bring an action against such vessel as a third party in accordance with the provisions of section 933 of this title, and the employer shall not be liable to the vessel for such damages directly or indirectly and any agreements or warranties to the contrary shall be void. If such person was employed by the vessel to provide stevedoring services, no such action shall be permitted if the injury was caused by the negligence of persons engaged in providing stevedoring services to the vessel. If such person was employed to provide shipbuilding, repairing, or breaking services and such person's employer was the owner, owner pro hac vice, agent, operator, or charterer of the vessel, no such action shall be permitted, in whole or in part or directly or indirectly, against the injured person's employer (in any capacity, including as the vessel's owner, owner pro hac vice, agent, operator, or charterer) or against the employees of the employer. The liability of the vessel under this subsection shall not be based upon the warranty of seaworthiness or a breach thereof at the time the injury occurred. The remedy provided in this subsection shall be exclusive of all other remedies against the vessel except remedies available under this chapter.

(c) Outer Continental Shelf

In the event that the negligence of a vessel causes injury to a person entitled to receive benefits under this chapter by virtue of section 1333 of Title 43, then such person, or anyone otherwise entitled to recover damages by reason thereof, may bring an action against such vessel in accordance with the provisions of subsection (b) of this section. Nothing contained in subsection (b) of this section shall preclude the enforcement according to its terms of any reciprocal indemnity provision whereby the employer of a person entitled to receive benefits under this chapter by virtue of section 1333 of Title 43 and the vessel agree to defend and indemnify the other for cost of defense and loss or liability for damages arising out of or resulting from death or bodily injury to their employees.

* * *

§ 933. Compensation for Injuries Where Third Persons Are Liable

(a) Election of remedies

If on account of a disability or death for which compensation is payable under this chapter the person entitled to such compensation determines that some person other than the employer or a person or persons in his employ is liable in damages, he need not elect whether to receive such compensation or to recover damages against such third person.

Note: Relationship Between 33 U.S.C. § 905(b) and 33 U.S.C. § 933

§ 905(b) (*see, supra*) provides a cause of action to a longshoreman injured due to the negligence of a vessel. § 905(b) allows the injured longshoreman or a "third party in accordance with the provisions of section 933 of this title,..." to bring a negligence action against the vessel. § 933(a) provides that where a longshoreman is injured due to the negligence of another he does not need to choose either to receive benefits from his employer under the LHWCA or to sue the negligent third party. Under § 933(b), acceptance of compensation from the employer under the LHWCA operates as an assignment to the employer of all rights of the injured longshoreman, unless the longshoreman commences an action against the third party within six months of the acceptance of compensation. However, if the employer fails to bring the action within ninety days of the assignment, he loses the right to bring any such action and the right reverts to the injured employee. If the employer brings the action, he is entitled to reasonable attorney's fees incurred in bringing the action plus any amounts actually paid to the injured employee and the present value of any amounts that will have to be paid in the future. Any recovery exceeding that amount is to be paid to the party entitled to compensation. (§ 933(e)).

GRANTHAM v. AVONDALE INDUSTRIES, INC.

964 F.2d 471, 1993 AMC 1671 (5th Cir. 1992)

Patrick E. HIGGINBOTHAM, Circuit Judge

The sole issue raised by this appeal is whether the district court was bound by federal or state authority in considering a claim of immunity under federal law in this diversity action. We conclude that although the claim is grounded in state law, whether the state or federal rule of immunity applies is a federal question, and the district court was controlled by the decisions of this court. The district court followed decisions of the Louisiana courts that conflict with this circuit's precedent. We therefore reverse.

I.

In 1989, Fred Grantham was a painter employed by International Marine Industrial Applicators. International Marine contracted with Avondale Industries to sandblast and paint portions of a ship that Avondale was constructing for the United States Navy. While painting the ship, Grantham fell off a platform and was injured. He received benefits from International Marine's insurer pursuant to the Longshore and Harbor Workers' Compensation Act, 33 U.S.C. § 901 *et seq.* Grantham then sued Avondale in federal district court on theories of negligence and strict liability under Louisiana law. The sole basis asserted for federal jurisdiction in the suit was diversity of citizenship.

Avondale moved for summary judgment, arguing that it was entitled to immunity as Grantham's statutory employer under LA. REV. STAT. 23:1032. The district court agreed. It recognized that this Court had held that the immunity provided for statutory employers under state workers' compensation schemes would not preclude a tort suit when a plaintiff elected the federal compensation remedy provided by the LHWCA. It reasoned, however, that because this was a diversity action, it was Erie bound to follow Louisiana law on this issue. The Louisiana courts had explicitly held that an employee cannot sue his statutory employer in tort even if he elects to receive LHWCA benefits rather than state workers' compensation benefits. The district court heeded this authority and found Grantham's claim barred. 774 F. Supp. 408. Grantham appeals.

II.

Workers' compensation programs generally embody a legislative compromise between employers and employees. In return for an expeditious no fault statutory remedy, employees relinquish their common law tort remedies against employers for work related injuries. However, they generally do not give up their rights to sue third parties who caused their injuries through negligence. The question here is whether Avondale is such a third party, and hence subject to a tort suit by Grantham, or whether Avondale is properly characterized as Grantham's employer, since International Marine was Avondale's subcontractor.

It is undisputed that since International Marine paid Grantham disability compensation, Avondale is not Grantham's employer under the LHWCA and therefore is not immune from a tort suit. *See* 33 U.S.C. § 905(a) ("[A] contractor shall be deemed the employer of a subcontractor's employees only if the subcontractor fails to secure the payment of compensation as required by section 904 of this title."); *Martin v. Ingalls Shipbuilding*, 746 F.2d 231, 232 (5th Cir. 1984). It is also undisputed that under the Louisiana compensation statute, Avondale is Grantham's "statutory employer" and is immune from tort liability. *See* La. Rev. Stat. Ann. § 23:1032 (West 1985); *Lewis v. Modular Quarters*, 508 So.2d 975, 980-91 (La. App. 3 Cir. 1987). The more controversial question is whether the federal or state immunity rule applies when the employee has elected to receive benefits under the LHWCA.

The federal and state courts have reached conflicting results on this issue. In *Jenkins v. McDermott, Inc.*, 734 F.2d 229, 233-34 (5th Cir. 1984), this Court reasoned that "the state defense founded upon the state compensation act's coverage scheme, whereby in statutory exchange for his state compensation remedy an injured workman accepts it as the exclusive remedy against his employer and his employer's principal (as "statutory employer"), cannot survive a rejection of the state act's coverage and the election, instead, of the federal remedy." We reasoned that the legislatively intended uniformity of treatment of maritime workers would be thwarted if different remedies were allowed depending on where the injury was sustained.

Jenkins was later vacated in part in light of *Washington Metropolitan Area Transport Authority v. Johnson*, 467 U.S. 925, 104 S. Ct. 2827, 81 L. Ed. 2d 768 (1984), where the Supreme Court held that general contractors are entitled to immunity under the LHWCA if subcontractors pay injured employees disability benefits. *See Jenkins*, 742 F.2d 191 (5th Cir. 1984). But Congress promptly overruled WMATA by amending the Act in September of 1984, see 33 U.S.C. § 905(a), as amended by P.L. 98-426, 98 Stat. 1639 (1984). After this reversal, we again held that the LHWCA's immunity rule controlled in a diversity action in which an employee of a subcontractor sued the contractor on a state law negligence theory. *See Martin*, 746 F.2d at 232. The result was that Mississippi's provision of immunity for statutory employers did not bar claimant's tort suit.

The Louisiana courts have rejected the reasoning of Jenkins and Martin, however. In *Lewis, supra*, a Louisiana court concluded that Congress did not intend to negate the available defenses provided by state law to third party claims brought pursuant to state law. 508 So.2d at 982. It relied on the Fourth Circuit's decision in *Garvin v. Alumax of South Carolina, Inc.*, 787 F.2d 910 (4th Cir. 1986), where the court reasoned that "Congress has not purported to prescribe the immunity rules to be applied by states in actions brought upon state law claims." *Id.* at 917. South Carolina's rule of immunity was not in conflict with the LHWCA and therefore was applied to bar plaintiff's state tort claim. The Louisiana courts have continued to follow this reasoning since *Lewis*. *See Crater v. Mesa Offshore Co.*, 539 So. 2d 88 (La. App. 3rd Cir. 1989); *Griffis v. Gulf Coast Pre-Stress Co.*, 563 So.2d 1254 (La. App. 1st Cir. 1990).

The district court reasoned that it was bound by the Louisiana courts' resolution of this issue because it sat as a diversity court. *See Erie Railroad v. Tompkins*, 304 U.S. 64, 58 S. Ct. 817, 82 L. Ed. 1188 (1938); *Mozeke v. International Paper Co.*, 856 F.2d 722, 724 (5th Cir. 1988). It noted that Jenkins and Martin were decided before *Lewis* and its progeny, and that "federal courts sitting in diversity in this Circuit are obliged to apply the latest and most authoritative expression of state law applicable to the facts of a case." *Lamarque v. Massachusetts Indemnity & Life Insurance Co.*, 794 F.2d 194, 196 (5th Cir. 1986).

We agree with the district court's reasoning for issues of state law. The Erie doctrine does not apply, however, in matters governed by the federal Constitution or by acts of Congress. 304 U.S. at 78, 58 S. Ct. at 822. It is beyond cavil that we are not bound by a state court's interpretation of federal law regardless of whether our jurisdiction is based on diversity of citizenship or a federal question. *See Pauk v. Board of Trustees of City University of New York*, 654 F.2d 856, 866 n.6 (2nd Cir. 1981) (a state court decision cannot preclude a federal court's more authoritative decision on matters of federal law); *cf. In re Asbestos Litigation*, 829 F.2d 1233, 1237 (3rd Cir. 1987) ("The federal district court ... takes as its authority on federal constitutional issues decisions of the United States courts of appeals and the United States Supreme Court, rather than those of the state supreme court.").

The issue of whether the state or federal immunity rule applies here is a question of federal law. As the Supreme Court has observed, "[w]hen state law creates a cause of action, the state is free to define the defenses to the claim, including the defense of immunity, unless the state rule is in conflict with federal law." *Ferri v. Ackerman*, 444 U.S. 193, 100 S. Ct. 402, 62 L. Ed. 2d 355 (1979). When the Court considered in Ferri whether federal law was in fact in conflict with the state immunity rule, that is whether the Criminal Justice Act required the state to accept respondent's immunity defense, it did so as a matter of federal law. The issue may properly be characterized as whether federal law preempts state law, which is of course a federal law matter. *See Silkwood v. Kerr-McGee Corp.*, 464 U.S. 238, 104 S. Ct. 615, 78 L. Ed. 2d 443 (1984); *Atkinson v. Gates, McDonald & Co.*, 838 F.2d 808 (5th Cir. 1988). Indeed, the state court decisions on which the district court relies indicated that their rulings were governed by federal law—the effect of the LHWCA on the availability of the state law immunity for statutory employers. *See Lewis*, 508 So.2d at 981-82 (relying on the Fourth Circuit's interpretation of the LHWCA in *Garvin*).

Of course, the fact that a federal issue is involved in the case does not mean that the case "arises under" federal law for the purposes of asserting federal question jurisdiction. *See Franchise Tax Bd. v. Construction Laborers Vacation Trust*, 463 U.S. 1, 103 S. Ct. 2841, 77 L. Ed. 2d 420 (1983). We have in fact explained that s 905(a) of the LHWCA does not give rise to federal question jurisdiction. *Griffis v. Gulf Coast Pre-Stress Co.*, 850 F.2d 1090, 1092 (5th Cir. 1988). The issue of whether the state immunity rule is preempted by the LHWCA is nevertheless an issue of federal law.

The district court erred in following the decisions of the Louisiana courts rather than that of this circuit on an issue of federal law. We recognize that our decisions in Jenkins and Martin did not address the Supreme Court's holding in *Sun Ship Inc. v. Pennsylvania*, 447 U.S. 715, 100 S. Ct. 2432, 65 L. Ed. 2d 458 (1980), where the court held that the LHWCA supplements rather than supplants state workers' compensation schemes. We do not purport to address Sun Ship here; nor do we consider whether our decision in Martin or those of the Fourth Circuit and the courts of Louisiana reach the better result. There is a powerful argument that we have taken a wrong turn. A conflict between the Fourth and Fifth Circuits over a significant maritime issue should not be left unresolved by our court en banc. This panel can only say that it is bound by the prior decisions of this court as was the district court.

Reversed.

Note

In *Garvin v. Alumax of South Carolina*, 787 F.2d 910, 1987 AMC 402 (4th Cir.), *cert. denied*, 479 U.S. 915 (1986), the court stated:

* * *

As initially enacted, when the application of the LHWCA stopped at the water's edge, the third party claim would usually be one in admiralty. When application of the federal statute was moved inland to supplement state workmen's compensation statutes without displacing them, a third party claim under state law by a recipient of benefits under the LHWCA was not converted into a maritime claim. Its scope, including available defenses, is governed by state law. Thus in *Holland v. Sea-Land Service*, 655 F.2d 556 (4th Cir. 1981), *cert. denied* 455 U.S. 919 (1982), we held that the defendant, in an action brought by a recipient of benefits under the LHWCA for damages on account of injury for which he was receiving compensation, could defend on the basis of the state's contributory negligence rule.

A similar result was reached in *Millspaugh v. Port of Portland*, 25 Ore. App. 389, 671 P.2d 743 (1983), in which it was held that Oregon's rule of municipal immunity is applicable to such a claim.

The Supreme Court itself left no doubt about the matter in *Victory Carriers, Inc. v. Law*, 404 U.S. 202 (1971). The third party action, when founded on state law, is a creature of state law and is to be governed entirely by it. Indeed, in *Ferri v. Ackerman*, 444 U.S. 1983 (1979), the Supreme Court stated with respect to such a third party claim by an LHWCA compensation recipient:

When state law creates a cause of action, the state is free to define the defenses to the claim, including the defense of immunity, unless the state rule is in conflict with federal law.

The South Carolina rule of immunity of a contractor in the position of Alumax is different from that under the LHWCA, but not in conflict with it, for Congress has not purported to prescribe the immunity rules to be applied by states in actions brought upon state law claims. The federal immunity rule is to be applied when the third party claim is a federal claim; when the third party claim is a state law claim, the immunity rules of that state are to be applied. The federal and state statutes are readily harmonized, and each may function in its own sphere without interference with the other.

* * *

In *Brown v. Avondale Industries, Inc.*, 617 So. 2d 482 (La. 1993), the Supreme Court of Louisiana held that a Louisiana statute providing immunity was not available where the plaintiff was proceeding under LHWCA because the issue was governed by federal law, not state law. By doing so, the court implicitly followed *Grantham* and disagreed with *Garvin*.

D. Suits Against Shipowners

Introductory Notes

1. A shipowner who negligently inflicts injuries on a maritime worker commits a maritime tort. *See Pope & Talbot v. Hawn*, 346 U.S. 406, 74 S. Ct. 202, 1954 AMC 1 (1953); *see also.International Stevedoring Co. v. Haverty*, 272 U.S. 40, 1926 AMC 1638 (1926).The matter is within the admiralty jurisdiction and subject to federal maritime law. In such a case, contributory negligence is not a bar to the action by the injured worker but results in mitigation of damages. *Pope v. Talbot v. Hawn, supra.*

2. In *Seas Shipping Co. v. Sieracki*, 328 U.S. 85, 66 S.Ct. 872, 90 L.Ed. 1099,1946 AMC 689 (1946), the Supreme Court held that the warranty of seaworthiness extends to longshoremen and other harbor workers. Thus, an injured longshoreman could proceed directly against a shipowner to recover for injuries sustained as a result of the unseaworthiness of the vessel. In turn, the shipowner could proceed against the employer of the longshoreman for indemnity under the *Ryan* doctrine.

The 1972 amendments to the LHWCA purport to eliminate the action for unseaworthiness that was available to a longshoreman or harbor worker under the *Sieracki* doctrine. However doubts continue to be voiced as to the viability of *Sieracki* with respect to longshoremen and harbor workers *not* covered by the LHWCA. For this reason the following subsection addresses actions brought against a shipowner under the theory of unseaworthiness as well as negligence.

3. In *Gutierrez v. Waterman Steamship Corporation*, 373 U.S. 206, 83 S.Ct. 1185, 10 L.Ed.2d 297, 1963 AMC 1649 (1963), the United States Supreme Court allowed recovery for personal injuries sustained by a longshoreman on a pier on grounds of the unseaworthiness of the vessel. Beans had spilled on the pier from defective sacks, found to be an instrumentality of the vessel, and plaintiff slipped and fell when he stepped on loose beans. In *Victory Carriers v. Law*, 404 U.S. 202, 92 S.Ct. 418, 30 L.Ed.2d 383, 1972 AMC 1 (1971), a longshoreman was likewise injured on the pier while driving a forklift loaded with cargo. The forklift belonged to his land-based employer; it was not an instrumentality of the ship. In an action brought by the longshoreman against the shipowner on grounds of unseaworthiness of the vessel, the Court held that because the injury occurred on the pier, admiralty jurisdiction was lacking. Accordingly, the matter was governed by state law.

After the 1972 Amendments to LHWCA, a longshoreman's action under the statute cannot be grounded on unseaworthiness. However, question remains as to the existence of admiralty jurisdiction in an action by a longshoreman grounded on negligence for injuries sustained on the pier. According to § 903(a) of LHWCA, for purposes of compensation, a pier is considered to be "navigable waters" of the United States. However, LHWCA coverage is broader than the current view concerning the limits of admiralty tort jurisdiction under 28 U.S.C. § 1333. In this respect, the *Law* case still controls. *See Parker v. South Louisiana Contractors, Inc.*, 537 F.2d 113, 1976 AMC 2201 (5th Cir. 1976); *Holland v. Sea-Land Service, Inc.*, 655 F.2d 556, 1981 AMC 2474 (4th Cir. 1981). *Gutierrez* may still be pertinent when injuries on the pier are negligently caused by operations involving an instrumentality of the ship.

1. Negligence: Duty and Standard of Care

SCINDIA STEAM NAVIGATION CO., LTD. v. DE LOS SANTOS

451 U.S. 156, 101 S.Ct. 1614, 68 L.Ed.2d 1, 1981 A.M.C. 601 (1981)

Justice WHITE delivered the opinion of the Court.

Respondent Santos, a longshoreman and an employee of respondent Seattle Stevedore Co., was injured while he was helping load the M/S *Jalaratna*, a vessel owned by petitioner Scindia Steam Navigation Co., Ltd. He later brought an action against Scindia pursuant to § 5(b) of the Longshoremen's and Harbor Workers' Compensation Act (Act), as amended in 1972, which, as set forth in 33 U.S.C. § 905(b), ...

* * *

The District Court granted petitioner's motion for summary judgment; the Court of Appeals, disagreeing with the District Court on both the facts and the law, reversed and remanded for further proceedings. 598 F.2d 480 (CA9 1979). We granted certiorari, 446 U.S. 934, 100 S.Ct. 2150, 64 L.Ed.2d 786, because the Courts of Appeals are in considerable disagreement as to the meaning and application of § 905(b).

I

For present purposes, we take the facts from the opinion of the Court of Appeals, which properly viewed the case in the light most favorable to Santos, against whom summary judgment had been granted.

On December 10, 1972, Seattle Stevedore Co., pursuant to its undertaking with Scindia, was engaged in loading a cargo of wheat into a hold of the M/S *Jalaratna*. A winch, part of the ship's gear, was being used to lower wooden pallets, each containing seventy 50-pound sacks of wheat, into the hold. Because of the location of the winch controls, the longshoreman operator relied on the hatch tender, another longshoreman, to signal him when to start and stop the winch while lowering a pallet of sacks into the hold. Santos and three other longshoremen were in the hold. Their task was to remove sacks of wheat from the pallet and properly stow them.

On the day of the accident, as it had for the two previous days, the braking mechanism of the winch was malfunctioning in that it would not quickly stop the descent of a loaded pallet, which would continue to drop for several feet before coming to a stop. At the time important here, while a pallet was being lowered, the hatch tender signaled the winch operator to stop the descent of the load. The brake was applied, but the pallet did not stop before striking a pallet jack[5] with some force and spilling about half the sacks of wheat from the pallet. The hatch tender signaled the operator to raise the pallet about 15 feet and, believing that the remaining sacks on the pallet were secure enough not to fall, permitted Santos and the other men to clear away the spilled sacks then lying below in the hold. Some minutes later, however, more sacks fell from the pallet, striking and injuring Santos. There was dispute as to whether the additional sacks fell because the suspended pallet was swinging back and forth or because while the pallet was suspended the braking mechanism slipped on three or four occasions, each time requiring the operator to raise it again, thus working loose the additional sacks that fell on Santos.

Relying on the legislative history of the 1972 Amendments to the Act, the District Court held that the negligence standards governing the longshoreman's action against a shipowner under § 905(b) are best expressed in Restatement (Second) of Torts §§ 343 and 343A (1965), which purport to state the prevailing or preferred rules governing the liability of a possessor of land to an invitee.[6] Under these land-based negligence standards, the District Court thought

---

[5] A pallet jack is a small, wheeled, cartlike vehicle with prongs on the front like a forklift with which the longshoremen in the hold would cart the pallet load to the wings of the hold where they would then remove the sacks and stow them by hand. Record 77.

[6] Restatement (Second) of Torts § 343 provides:

"§ 343. Dangerous Conditions Known to or Discoverable by Possessor
"A possessor of land is subject to liability for physical harm caused to his invitees by a condition on the land if, but only if, he

"a shipowner is not liable for dangerous conditions created by the stevedore's negligence while the stevedore [is] in exclusive control over the manner and area of the work ..., nor is the shipowner under a duty to warn the stevedore or his employees of dangers or open and obvious defects which are known to the stevedore or his employees or which are so obvious and apparent that they may reasonably be expected to discover them." 1976 A.M.C. 2583, 2585.

Based on the admissions of the parties and the depositions available to the court, the District Court concluded (1) that there was no dispute that the premises were in the exclusive control of Seattle during the loading operation and that (2) even if Scindia knew or should have known of the defective winch,[7] the condition of the winch "was open and obvious to the plaintiff" and "the fact that plaintiff undertook his actions free from any direction by the defendant while recognizing that the circumstances were so dangerous, is such that the defendant cannot be held liable as a matter of law." *Id.*, at 2586-2587. In addition, the District Court found that "the alleged defective condition of the winch had only a remote cause-in-fact relationship to plaintiff's accident and could not have been the proximate cause thereof as a matter of law." *Id.*, at 2587. Hence, summary judgment was granted.

Reversing, the Court of Appeals disagreed with the District Court and with other Courts of Appeals with respect to the applicable law. Sections 343 and 343A of the Restatement were improper measures of the shipowner's liability for negligence under § 905(b)[9] because those sections in effect incorporated notions of contributory negligence and assumption of risk that were inapplicable under the maritime law. Instead, the Court of Appeals declared the controlling standard under § 905(b) to be the following:

"A vessel is subject to liability for injuries to longshoremen working on or near the vessel caused by conditions on the vessel if, but only if, the shipowner

"(a) knows of, or by the exercise of reasonable care would discover, the condition, and should realize that it involves an unreasonable risk of harm to such longshoremen, and

"(b) the shipowner fails to exercise reasonable care under the circumstances to protect the longshoremen against the danger." 598 F.2d, at 485.

"(a) knows or by the exercise of reasonable care would discover the condition, and should realize that it involves an unreasonable risk of harm to such invitees, and

"(b) should expect that they will not discover or realize the danger, or will fail to protect themselves against it, and

"(c) fails to exercise reasonable care to protect them against the danger."

Restatement (Second) of Torts § 343A provides:

"§ 343A. Known or Obvious Dangers

"(1) A possessor of land is not liable to his invitees for physical harm caused to them by any activity or condition on the land whose danger is known or obvious to them, unless the possessor should anticipate the harm despite such knowledge or obviousness.

"(2) In determining whether the possessor should anticipate harm from a known or obvious danger, the fact that the invitee is entitled to make use of public land, or of the facilities of a public utility, is a factor of importance indicating that the harm should be anticipated."

[7] The District Court stated, 1976 A.M.C., at 2586, that "[p]laintiff does not controvert defendant's claim that no one from the ship's crew was ever informed of the winch's condition prior to the accident" and further stated that if the winch was defective, it was a "condition [about] which the Court finds the shipowner did not know nor should it reasonably have been expected to know, given the exclusive control of the gear by the stevedores during the relevant time period." *Ibid.* Scindia contended in any event that the winch was not defective but concedes that for present purposes the case should be judged on the assumption that it was.

[9] The Court of Appeals acknowledged that the Courts of Appeals for the Second, Fourth, and Fifth Circuits had relied on these sections in § 905(b) suits. See, *e. g., Canizzo v. Farrell Lines, Inc.*, 579 F.2d 682 (CA2 1978); *Gay v. Ocean Transport & Trading, Ltd.*, 546 F.2d 1233 (CA5 1977); *Anuszewski v. Dynamic Mariners Corp., Panama*, 540 F.2d 757 (CA4 1976); *Napoli v. Hellenic Lines, Ltd.*, 536 F.2d 505 (CA2 1976). The Court of Appeals for the Second Circuit has recently reaffirmed its position. *Evans v. S.S. "Campeche,"* 639 F.2d 848 (1981). On the other hand, the First and Third Circuits, like the Ninth Circuit, have held that these sections should not apply in § 905(b) suits since they might bar a longshoreman from recovery because he was contributorily negligent or because he voluntarily encountered a known or obvious risk. See *Sarauw v. Oceanic Navigation Corp.*, 622 F.2d 1168 (CA3 1980); *Johnson v. A/S Ivarans Rederi*, 613 F.2d 334 (CA1 1980); *Griffith v. Wheeling Pittsburgh Steel Corp.*, 610 F.2d 116 (CA3 1979); *Lawson v. United States*, 605 F.2d 448 (CA9 1979); *Bachtel v. Mammoth Bulk Carriers, Ltd.*, 605 F.2d 438 (CA9 1979); 598 F.2d 480 (CA9 1979) (case below).

Under this standard, Scindia's duty to inspect did not end even if the vessel was turned over to the stevedore in safe condition. If conditions dangerous to the longshoremen subsequently developed, in light of the vessel's practical opportunities to discover the dangers and remedy them, failure to do so could be negligence on its part.

Under the Court of Appeals' view of the law there were several material facts in dispute that were for a jury to resolve: whether the shipowner knew or should have known of the defective winch; whether Seattle was in exclusive control of the loading in the sense that only Seattle could have repaired the winch; whether the defective operation of the winch had caused the initial spillage of the sacks, thus necessitating a cleanup, or had later been the proximate cause of the additional sacks falling from the pallet and injuring Santos. Accordingly, the Court of Appeals set aside the judgment of the District Court and remanded for further proceedings.

II

Initially, we must briefly revisit the 1972 Amendments to the Act. Prior to 1972, a longshoreman injured while loading or unloading a ship could receive compensation payments and also have judgment against the ship-owner if the injury was caused by the ship's unseaworthiness or negligence. *Seas Shipping Co. v. Sieracki*, 328 U.S. 85, 66 S.Ct. 872, 90 L.Ed. 1099 (1946). Proof of unseaworthiness required no proof of fault on the part of the shipowner other than an unsafe, injury-causing condition on the vessel. This was true even though the condition was caused, created, or brought into play by the stevedore or its employees. In the latter event, the shipowner could recover over against a stevedore for breach of express or implied warranty to handle the cargo in a reasonably safe manner. *Ryan Stevedoring Co. v. Pan-Atlantic S.S. Corp.*, 350 U.S. 124, 76 S.Ct. 232, 100 L.Ed. 133 (1956).

The 1972 Amendments, particularly by adding § 905(b), radically changed this scheme of things. The compensation payments due the longshoreman from the stevedore for injuries incurred in the course of his employment were substantially increased; the longshoreman's right to recover for unseaworthiness was abolished; his right to recover from the shipowner for negligence was preserved in § 905(b), which provided a statutory negligence action against the ship; and the stevedore's obligation to indemnify the shipowner if the latter was held liable to the longshoreman was abolished.

Section 905(b) did not specify the acts or omissions of the vessel that would constitute negligence. In light of the differences among the lower federal courts as to the construction and application of § 905(b), neither can it be said that the legislative history, which has been analyzed and reanalyzed in the course of these cases, furnishes sure guidance for construing § 905(b).[13] Much was left to be resolved through the "application of accepted principles of tort law and the ordinary process of litigation." Rep., p. 11.

---

[13] Section 905(b) itself negates the vessel's liability for unseaworthiness, and the Committee Reports state that the purpose of eliminating this remedy was to place the injured longshoreman "in the same position he would be if he were injured in non-maritime employment ashore ... and not to endow him with any special maritime theory of liability or cause of action under whatever judicial nomenclature it may be called, such as 'unseaworthiness', 'non-delegable duty', or the like." S.Rep.No.92-1125, p. 10 (1972) (hereafter Rep.). (H.R.Rep.No.92- 1441 (1972), U.S.Code Cong. & Admin.News 1972, 4698, is in all relevant respects identical to the Senate Report.) The vessel was not to be liable on the theory of unseaworthiness for the acts or omissions of stevedores, or of the employees of stevedores, for the manner in which the stevedore performed its work, or for its defective gear or equipment. Rep., p. 10. Its liability was to be "based on its own negligence" and could be proved only if it was shown "to have acted or have failed to act in a negligent manner such as would render a land-based third party in non-maritime pursuits liable under similar circumstances." *Id.*, at 11.

At the same time, the Committees observed that the statutory cause of action for negligence would "meet the objective of encouraging safety because the vessel would still be required to exercise the same care as a land-based person in providing a safe place to work." *Id.*, at 10. Nothing was intended "to derogate from the vessel's responsibility to take appropriate corrective action where it knows or should have known about a dangerous condition" as long as the vessel was not "chargeable with the negligence of the stevedore or employees of the stevedore." *Id.*, at 10, 11.

The Committees also anticipated that in § 905(b) cases, as in other admiralty cases, the rule of comparative negligence would apply and the defense of assumption of risk would be barred. Furthermore, the Reports emphasized that the amendments were not intended to relieve any person from his duties and obligations under the Occupational Safety and Health Act of 1970.

Otherwise, the definition of the vessel's negligence and its resulting liability were left to be "resolved through the application of accepted principles of tort law and the ordinary process of litigation--just as they are in cases involving alleged negligence by land-based third parties." Rep., p. 11. It was anticipated, however, that questions arising in § 905(b) cases "shall be determined as a matter of Federal law." Rep., p. 12.

III

We held in *Marine Terminals v. Burnside Shipping Co.*, 394 U.S. 404, 415, 89 S.Ct. 1144, 1150, 22 L.Ed.2d 371 (1969), that the vessel owes to the stevedore and his longshoremen employees the duty of exercising due care "under the circumstances." This duty extends at least to exercising ordinary care under the circumstances to have the ship and its equipment in such condition that an expert and experienced stevedore will be able by the exercise of reasonable care to carry on its cargo operations with reasonable safety to persons and property, and to warning the stevedore of any hazards on the ship or with respect to its equipment that are known to the vessel or should be known to it in the exercise of reasonable care, that would likely be encountered by the stevedore in the course of his cargo operations and that are not known by the stevedore and would not be obvious to or anticipated by him if reasonably competent in the performance of his work. *Id.*, at 416, n. 18, 89 S.Ct., at 1151. The shipowner thus has a duty with respect to the condition of the ship's gear, equipment, tools, and work space to be used in the stevedoring operations; and if he fails at least to warn the stevedore of hidden danger which would have been known to him in the exercise of reasonable care, he has breached his duty and is liable if his negligence causes injury to a longshoreman. … It is also accepted that the vessel may be liable if it actively involves itself in the cargo operations and negligently injures a longshoreman or if it fails to exercise due care to avoid exposing longshoremen to harm from hazards they may encounter in areas, or from equipment, under the active control of the vessel during the stevedoring operation.

The parties, however, like the District Court and the Court of Appeals, are in sharp disagreement as to the vessel's duty under § 905(b) once the stevedore's cargo operations have begun. Scindia contends that the shipowner has no duty to supervise or inspect the stevedore's cargo operations or to take reasonable care to discover dangerous conditions that develop or come to light during the loading or unloading. Scindia also submits that even if the vessel learns of the hazard, it has no duty to correct it and is entitled as a matter of law to rely on the stevedore to protect his employees from injury. This is true, Scindia argues, even though the hazard is an obviously defective ship's winch being used by the stevedore and his longshoremen employees,[14] and even if the winch was defective when the stevedore came aboard and the vessel is charged with knowledge of the condition. Respondents, on the other hand, defend the view of the Court of Appeals that the vessel is subject to a continuing duty to use reasonable care to discover dangerous conditions exposing longshoremen to unreasonable risk of harm and to exercise reasonable care under the circumstances to protect them. We are unable to agree wholly with either of these submissions.

Considering first the position of the Court of Appeals, we cannot agree that the vessel's duty to the longshoreman requires the shipowner to inspect or supervise the stevedoring operation. Congress intended to make the vessel answerable for its own negligence and to terminate its automatic, faultless responsibility for conditions caused by the negligence or other defaults of the stevedore. Cases holding the vessel liable on the ground that it owed nondelegable duties to protect the longshoremen from injury were rejected.[15] It would be inconsistent with the Act to hold, nevertheless, that the shipowner has a continuing duty to take reasonable steps to discover and correct dangerous conditions that develop during the loading or unloading process. Such an approach would repeatedly result in holding the shipowner solely liable

---

[14] Because the legislative history suggests that the shipowner's liability is to be judged by land-based standards, see n. 13, *supra*, it is urged that the District Court properly turned to and applied §§ 343 and 343A of the Restatement (Second) of Torts. But the legislative history does not refer to the Restatement and also states that land-based principles of assumption of risk and contributory negligence are not to be applied in § 905(b) cases. This strongly suggests, as *Kermarec v. Compagnie Generale Transatlantique*, 358 U.S. 625, 79 S.Ct. 406, 3 L.Ed.2d 550 (1959), indicated, that maritime negligence actions are not necessarily to be governed by principles applicable in nonmaritime contexts. Furthermore, since the lower courts are in disagreement not only as to the applicability of §§ 343 and 343A but also as to their import and meaning when applied in the maritime context, those sections, while not irrelevant, do not furnish sure guidance in cases such as this.

[15] "Thus a vessel shall not be liable in damages for acts or omissions of stevedores or employees of stevedores subject to this Act. *Crumedy vs. The J. H. Fisser*, 358 U.S. 423 [79 S.Ct. 445, 3 L.Ed. 413]; *Albanese vs. Matts [Maats]*, 382 U.S. 283 [86 S.Ct. 429, 15 L.Ed.2d 327], *Skibinski vs. Waterman SS Corp.*, [360] F.2d 539; for the manner or method in which stevedores or employees of stevedores subject to this Act perform their work, *A. N. G. [A. & G.] Stevedores vs. Ellerman Lines*, 369 U.S. 355 [82 S.Ct. 780, 7 L.Ed.2d 798], *Blassingill vs. Waterman SS Corp.*, 336 F.2d 367; for gear or equipment of stevedores or employees of stevedores subject to this Act whether used aboard ship, or ashore, *Alaska SS Co. vs. Peterson*, 347 U.S. 396 [74 S.Ct. 601, 98 L.Ed. 798], *Italia Societa vs. Oregon Stevedoring Co.*, 376 U.S. 315 [84 S.Ct. 748, 11 L.Ed.2d 732], or for other categories of unseaworthiness which have been judicially established. This listing of cases is not intended to reflect a judgment as to whether recovery on a particular actual setting could be predicated on the vessel's negligence." Rep., p. 10.

for conditions that are attributable to the stevedore, rather than the ship. True, the liability would be cast in terms of negligence rather than unseaworthiness, but the result would be much the same. "[C]reation of a shipowner's duty to oversee the stevedore's activity and insure the safety of longshoremen would ... saddle the shipowner with precisely the sort of nondelegable duty that Congress sought to eliminate by amending section 905(b)." *Hurst v. Triad Shipping Co.*, 554 F.2d 1237, 1249-1250, n. 35 (CA3 1977); *Evans v. S.S. "Campeche,"* 639 F.2d 848, 856 (CA2 1981).[16]

As a general matter, the shipowner may rely on the stevedore to avoid exposing the longshoremen to unreasonable hazards. Section 41 of the Act, 33 U.S.C. § 941, requires the stevedore, the longshoremen's employer, to provide a "reasonably safe" place to work and to take such safeguards with respect to equipment and working conditions as the Secretary of Labor may determine to be necessary to avoid injury to longshoremen. The ship is not the common employer of the longshoremen and owes no such statutory duty to them. Furthermore, as our cases indicate, the stevedore normally warrants to discharge his duties in a workman-like manner; and although the 1972 Amendments relieved the stevedore of his duty to indemnify the shipowner for damages paid to longshoremen for injuries caused by the stevedore's breach of warranty, they did not otherwise disturb the contractual undertaking of the stevedore nor the rightful expectation of the vessel that the stevedore would perform his task properly without supervision by the ship.

The approach of the indemnity cases in this Court, beginning with *Ryan Stevedoring Co. v. Pan-Atlantic S.S. Corp.*, 350 U.S. 124, 76 S.Ct. 232, 100 L.Ed. 133 (1956), was that the stevedore was in the best position to avoid accidents during cargo operations and that the shipowner could rely on the stevedore's warranty to perform competently. In *Italia Societa v. Oregon Stevedoring Co.*, 376 U.S. 315, 84 S.Ct. 748, 11 L.Ed.2d 732 (1964), for example, the vessel was found liable for injuries to a longshoreman caused by an unseaworthy condition arising when the stevedore, without negligence, supplied defective equipment used in handling the cargo. We held the vessel entitled to recover over against the stevedore, saying:

"Oregon, a specialist in stevedoring, was hired to load and unload the petitioner's vessels and to supply the ordinary equipment necessary for these operations. The defective rope which created the condition of unseaworthiness on the vessel and rendered the shipowner liable to the stevedore's employee was supplied by Oregon, and the stevedoring operations in the course of which the longshoreman was injured were in the hands of the employees of Oregon. Not only did the agreement between the shipowner place control of the operations on the stevedore company, but Oregon was also charged under the contract with the supervision of these operations. Although none of these factors affect the shipowner's primary liability to the injured employee of Oregon, since its duty to supply a seaworthy vessel is strict and nondelegable, and extends to those who perform the unloading and loading portion of the ship's work, *Seas Shipping Co. v. Sieracki*, 328 U.S. 85 [66 S.Ct. 872, 90 L.Ed. 1099], cf. *Pope & Talbot v. Hawn*, 346 U.S. 406 [74 S.Ct. 202, 98 L.Ed. 143], they demonstrate that Oregon was in a far better position than the shipowner to avoid the accident. The shipowner defers to the qualification of the stevedoring contractor in the selection and use of equipment and relies on the competency of the stevedore company." *Id.*, at 322-323, 84 S.Ct., at 752-753.

---

[16] Much is made of the Committees' statement that nothing in the bill "is intended to derogate from the vessel's responsibility to take appropriate corrective action where it knows or should have known about a dangerous condition." *Ibid.* But the statement did not explain what the vessel's "responsibility" is and what "appropriate" action might be, or when it "should have known" of the condition. The Committees did offer an example:

"So, for example, where a longshoreman slips on an oil spill on a vessel's deck and is injured, the proposed amendments to Section 5 would still permit an action against the vessel for negligence. To recover, he must establish that: 1) the vessel put the foreign substance on the deck, or knew that it was there, and willfully or negligently failed to remove it; or 2) the foreign substance had been on the deck for such a period of time that it should have been discovered and removed by the vessel in the exercise of reasonable care by the vessel under the circumstances." *Id.*, at 10-11.

However, when the failure to remove the oil spill would be "willful" or "negligent" or what the exercise of reasonable care under the circumstances would require was not explicated except to say that the "vessel will not be chargeable with the negligence of the stevedore or employees of the stevedore." *Id.*, at 11.

The 1972 Amendments foreclosed indemnity of the shipowner by the stevedore in § 905(b) cases; but they also rejected the notion of a nondelegable duty on the shipowner to provide a safe place to work and did not undermine the justifiable expectations of the vessel that the stevedore would perform with reasonable competence and see to the safety of the cargo operations.

We are of the view that absent contract provision, positive law, or custom to the contrary--none of which has been cited to us in this case--the shipowner has no general duty by way of supervision or inspection to exercise reasonable care to discover dangerous conditions that develop within the confines of the cargo operations that are assigned to the stevedore. The necessary consequence is that the shipowner is not liable to the longshoremen for injuries caused by dangers unknown to the owner and about which he had no duty to inform himself. This conclusion is plainly consistent with the congressional intent to foreclose the faultless liability of the shipowner based on a theory of unseaworthiness or nondelegable duty. The shipowner, within limits, *is* entitled to rely on the stevedore, and owes no duty to the longshoremen to inspect or supervise the cargo operations. To the extent that the judgment of the Court of Appeals rested on a contrary view, we disagree.

IV

We arrive at the more difficult and recurring issue involved in this case: What are the shipowner's duties when he learns that an apparently dangerous condition exists or has developed in the cargo operation, which is known to the stevedore and which may cause injury to the longshoreman? Must the owner take some action? Scindia and the District Court would have it that the vessel is entitled to rely on the expertise and responsibility of the stevedore and is not liable for injuries caused by dangers known by or obvious to the stevedore, who, if he fails to take proper precautions, is necessarily the sole and proximate cause of the injury. There is arguable support for this position in our cases.

* * *

In *Crumady*, the Court declared that "those acting for the vessel owner" had adjusted the winch "in a way that made it unsafe and dangerous for the work at hand." *Id.*, at 427, 79 S.Ct., at 447. It thus appeared that the vessel had at least been negligent, yet it was entitled to shift its entire liability to the stevedore because it was entitled to rely on the stevedore's undertaking to perform in a workmanlike manner. Arguably, Scindia should likewise be justified in expecting Seattle to perform its undertaking and should therefore have no duty or responsibility with respect to the ship's winch, which, if defective, was obviously so and which the stevedore continued to use.

The court below rejected this position, holding that if the vessel should realize that the condition presents an unreasonable risk of harm, it is liable if it "fails to exercise reasonable care under the circumstances" to protect the longshoremen. The court did not suggest how to recognize an "unreasonable risk" of harm from an obvious danger or suggest what reasonable care under the circumstances might be.

The Court of Appeals for the Second Circuit, while disagreeing with the duty-to-inspect thesis of the Court of Appeals in the present case, has also rejected this position, ruling that although the shipowner is normally entitled to rely on the stevedore to guard against hazards to its employees, "there may be circumstances in which it would not be reasonable for the shipowner to assume that the stevedore will correct the problem." *Evans v. S.S. "Campeche,"* 639 F.2d, at 856. As that court sees it, mere knowledge of the danger would not be sufficient in itself to fasten such a duty on the shipowner, but if the shipowner should anticipate that the stevedore will not or cannot correct the danger and that the longshoremen cannot avoid it, then the shipowner's duty is triggered to take steps, reasonable in the circumstances, to eliminate or neutralize the hazard. We are presently unprepared to agree that the shipowner has precisely the duty described by the Court of Appeals for the Second Circuit, but for the reasons that follow we agree that there are circumstances in which the shipowner has a duty to act where the danger to longshoremen arises from the malfunctioning of the ship's gear being used in the cargo operations.

On the facts posited here, for two days prior to the accident, it had been apparent to those working with the winch that this equipment was malfunctioning. Even so, whether it could be safely used or whether it posed an unreasonable risk of harm to Santos or other longshoremen was a matter of judgment committed to the stevedore in the first instance. The malfunctioning being obvious and Seattle having continued to use it, Scindia submits that if it was aware of the condition or was charged with knowledge of it, it was nevertheless entitled to assume that Seattle, the specialist in loading and unloading, considered the equipment reasonably safe and was entitled to rely on that judgment.

Yet it is quite possible, it seems to us, that Seattle's judgment in this respect was so obviously improvident that Scindia, if it knew of the defect and that Seattle was continuing to use it, should have realized the winch presented an unreasonable risk of harm to the longshoremen, [FN22] and that in such circumstances it had a duty to intervene and repair the ship's winch. The same would be true if the defect existed from the outset and Scindia must be deemed to have been aware of is condition.

As we have indicated, the legal duties placed on the stevedore and the vessel's justifiable expectations that those duties will be performed are relevant in determining whether the shipowner has breached its duty. The trial court, and where appropriate the jury, should thus be made aware of the scope of the stevedore's duty under the positive

law. But an equally necessary inquiry is whether the pertinent statutes, regulations, or custom place or assume a continuing duty on the vessel to repair defective ship's gear being used by the stevedore in the cargo operation.

... Even in the absence of other statutory or regulatory law placing on the shipowner the obligation to repair a defective winch, a possible inference from the provisions already described is that when a defective winch is discovered, it should not be repaired by the stevedore but should be reported to and repaired by the shipowner. If this is the case, the situation comes down to this: If Scindia was aware that the winch was malfunctioning to some degree, and if there was a jury issue as to whether it was so unsafe that the stevedore should have ceased using it, could the jury also have found that the winch was so clearly unsafe that Scindia should have intervened and stopped the loading operation until the winch was serviceable?

... Based on our own examination of the record, we agree with the Court of Appeals in this respect and with its conclusion that the District Court erred in granting summary judgment. The case should be returned to the District Court and, if necessary, tried to a jury under appropriate instructions.

Accordingly, we affirm the judgment of the Court of Appeals and remand the case to that court for further proceedings consistent with this opinion.

So ordered.

* * *

Justice POWELL, with whom Justice REHNQUIST joins, concurring.

* * *

The difficulty with a more general reasonableness standard like that adopted by the court below is that it fails to deal with the problems of allocating responsibility between the stevedore and the shipowner. It may be that it is "reasonable" for a shipowner to rely on the stevedore to discover and avoid most obvious hazards. But when, in a suit by longshoreman, a jury is presented with the single question whether it was "reasonable" for the shipowner to fail to take action concerning a particular obvious hazard, the jury will be quite likely to find liability. If such an outcome were to become the norm, negligent stevedores would be receiving windfall recoveries in the form of reimbursement for the statutory benefit payments made to the injured longshoremen.[2] This would decrease significantly the incentives toward safety of the party in the best position to prevent injuries, and undercut the primary responsibility of that party for ensuring safety.

---

[2] Under 33 U.S.C. § 905(b), the shipowner is liable in damages to the longshoreman if it was negligent, and it may not seek to recover any part of this liability from the stevedore. The longshoreman's recovery is not reduced to reflect the negligence of the stevedore. *Edmonds v. Compagnie Generale Transatlantique*, 443 U.S. 256, 99 S.Ct. 2753, 61 L.Ed.2d 521 (1979). Under 33 U.S.C. § 933, the stevedore--even if concurrently negligent-receives reimbursement for its statutory benefit payments to the longshoreman, up to the full amount of those payments. See also *Bloomer v. Liberty Mutual Ins. Co.*, 445 U.S. 74, 100 S.Ct. 925, 63 L.Ed. 215 (1980) (stevedore's lien is not reduced by its proportional share of the costs of

Notes on the Scindia Rules

1. The Supreme Court again examined the relative duties of the shipowner and the stevedore with regard to the safety of longshoremen in *Howlett v. Birkdale Shipping Co., S.A.*, 512 U.S. 92, 114 S.Ct. 2057, 129 L.Ed. 2d 78, 1194 A.M.C. 1817 (1994). In *Scindia*, the Court articulated three duties that the law imposes on shipowners, succinctly summarized in *Howlett* as:

> The starting point in this regard must be our decision in *Scindia Steam,* which outlined the three general duties shipowners owe to longshoremen. The first, which courts have come to call the "turnover duty," relates to the condition of the ship upon the commencement of stevedoring operations. The second duty, applicable once stevedoring operations have begun, provides that a shipowner must exercise reasonable care to prevent injuries to longshoremen in areas that remain under the "active control of the vessel." The third duty, called the "duty to intervene," concerns the vessel's obligations with regard to cargo operations in areas under the principal control of the independent stevedore.

In *Howlett*, a longshoreman engaged in unloading cargo was injured allegedly because the foreign stevedore improperly loaded the cargo. Howlett asserted that the shipowner was negligent in not supervising the work of the loading stevedore and for not inspecting the stow after the loading had been completed. The Supreme Court rejected these contentions and concluded:

> In sum, the vessel's turnover duty to warn of latent defects in the cargo stow and cargo area is a narrow one. The duty attaches only to latent hazards, defined as hazards that are not known to the stevedore and that would be neither obvious to nor anticipated by a skilled stevedore in the competent performance of its work. Furthermore, the duty encompasses only those hazards that "are known to the vessel or should be known to it in the exercise of reasonable care." Contrary to Howlett's submission, however, the exercise of reasonable care does not require the shipowner to supervise the ongoing operations of the loading stevedore (or other stevedores who handle the cargo before its arrival in port) or to inspect the completed stow.

2. Open and Obvious hazards.

The court in *Kirsh v. Plovida*, 971 F. 2d 1036 (3d Cir. 1992) engaged in an extensive discussion of the "turnover duty" as it related to open and obvious conditions. In some circumstances such as where longshoremen cannot avoid the hazard, the open and obvious rule may not be a bar to recovery. The approach to the open and obvious situation is important because if a shipowner has no duty with respect to such conditions then the issue of comparative negligence does not come into play. Approaching the issue in terms of "duty" is much like the common law approach to contributory negligence and assumption of risk. The case also reveals a possible link between the turnover duty and the duty to intervene. For example, in a situation where a shipowner is aware of a hazardous condition and relies on the stevedore to "work around" it, what if any is the shipowner's duty when it learns that the stevedore has not does so?

It has also been suggested that the open and obvious rule should not apply where a longshoreman's only alternative is to continue to work despite knowledge of the hazard or "to leave his job or face trouble for delaying the work. *Stass v. American Commercial Lines, Inc.,* 720 F.2d 879 (5th Cir. 1983).

3. The "operational control" duty.

A shipowner's duty when it has retained operational control of an area or has involved itself in the cargo loading or unloading process is examined extensively in *Davis v. Portline Transportes Maritime Internacional*, 16 F.3d 532 (3d Cir. 1994).

4. Scindia and other maritime employees.

The *Scindia* rationale and duties have been applied in cases involving maritime worker other than longshoremen such as ship repairmen. *Mayer v. Lykes Bros. S.S. Co., Inc.*, 585 F. Supp. 1222 (E.D. La. 1984).

---

litigating the negligence suit). As a result of this automatic reimbursement, there is a danger that "concurrently negligent stevedores will be insulated from the obligation to pay statutory workmen's compensation benefits, and thus will have inadequate incentives to provide a safe working environment for their employees." *Edmonds, supra*, 443 U.S., at 274, 99 S.Ct., at 2764 (BLACKMUN, J., dissenting). In cases involving obvious and avoidable hazards, this danger will be realized unless the shipowner's liability is limited to the unusual case in which it should be anticipated that the stevedore will fail to act reasonably. Any more stringent, or less defined, rule of shipowner liability will skew the statutory scheme in a way Congress could not have intended. Cf. *Canizzo v. Farrell Lines, Inc.*, 579 F.2d 682, 687-688 (CA2 1978) (Friendly, J., dissenting).

Notes

1. *Vessel for Purposes of Section 905 Actions*

Section 902(21) of LHWCA provides generally:

Unless the context requires otherwise, the term "vessel" means any vessel upon which or in connection with which any person entitled to benefits under this chapter suffers injury or death arising out of or in the course of his employment, and said vessel's owner, owner pro hac vice, agent, operator, charter or bareboat charterer, master, officer, or crew member.

For the definition of the word "vessel" for purposes of Section 905 of LHWCA, *see Stewart v. Dutra Construction Co.* 543 U.S. 481, 125 S. Ct. 1118.

2. *The Character of the Section 905(b) Action*

The question has arisen whether an action under 33 U.S.C. § 905(b) is a tort action under principles of land law or under principles of maritime law. Numerous appeals courts initially held that § 905(b) was intended to establish liability under "land-based principles of negligence." *Griffith v. Wheeling Pittsburgh Steel Corp.*, 610 F.2d 116 (3d Cir. 1979), *vacated*, 451 U.S. 965, *reinstated*, 657 F.2d 25, 1981 AMC 2974 (3d Cir. 1981); *Gay v. Ocean Transport and Trading, Ltd.*, 546 F.2d 1233, 1977 AMC 996 (5th Cir. 1977).

Courts have recently emphasized that the § 905(b) action is for maritime tort only. *See Richendollar, supra; see also May v. Transworld Drilling Co.*, 786 F.2d 1261, 1987 AMC 971 (5th Cir. 1986) ("injury on navigable waters is a *sina qua non* of the maritime tort"). Thus, a plaintiff in a § 905(b) action must show that the case falls within admiralty jurisdiction: the tort must involve a vessel on navigable waters (or in accordance with the Admiralty Extension Act) and have a significant relationship with traditional maritime activity. For its basis in jurisdiction, the plaintiff's action arises under the general maritime law and not the LHWCA. *Stevenson v. Point Marine, Inc.*, 697 F. Supp. 285 (E.D. La. 1988); *see also Comment, Jurisdiction in Section 905(b) Actions—Wrong Test Doomed to Wrong Results*, 13 Tul. Mar. L.J. 121 (1988).

3. *The Land-Based Employer as Shipowner*

Certain land-based employers, such as stevedores and ship repairers, own or operate vessels in the course of their business. In such cases, the question arises whether the liability of the land-based employer is limited to the payment of benefits under the LHWCA or whether the injured employee may sue his employer in his capacity as shipowner for damages under the general maritime law. The problem is the same when a shipowner chooses to undertake certain operations, such as stevedoring or ship repairing, instead of engaging the services of an independent contractor. *See Smith v. M/V Captain Fred*, 546 F.2d 119, 1977 AMC 353 (5th Cir. 1977); *Fanetti v. Hellenic Lines, Ltd.*, 678 F.2d 424, 1982 AMC 1521 (2d Cir. 1982).

In *Reed v. Yaka*, 373 U.S. 410, 83 S.Ct. 1349, 10 L.Ed.2d 448, 1963 A.M.C. 1373 (1963), a longshoreman filed a libel *in rem* against the steamship *Yaka* to recover for injuries he sustained due to the unseaworthiness of the vessel in the process of loading operations. The shipowner impleaded plaintiff's land-based employer, who was the bareboat charterer of the *Yaka*, alleging that the employer's negligence was the sole cause of the injury. The Supreme Court declared that a bareboat charterer as owner *pro hac vice* incurs the liabilities of a shipowner. And, since the unseaworthiness of the *Yaka* was not in dispute, the court held that the plaintiff was not barred by the Longshoremen's Act from relying on his employer's liability as shipowner for the *Yaka's* unseaworthiness in order to support his label *in rem* against the vessel.

The 1972 Amendments to the LHWCA eliminated the unseaworthiness action that an employee covered by the Act had against a shipowner. 33 U.S.C. § 905(b). However, the question arose whether a land-based employee of an independent contractor could still have a negligence action against his employer under § 905(b) if the employer was also shipowner or owner *pro hac vice*, *see Bossard v. Port Allen Marine Service, Inc.*, 624 F.2d 671, 1984 AMC 303 (5th Cir. 1980). The court held that a ship repairer, though having control of the vessel, is not an owner *pro hac vice*; only a bareboat charterer has this status. Hence, an injured employee does not have a § 905(b) action against the ship repairer-employer. *See also Ducote v. International Operating Co.*, 678 F.2d 543, 1985 AMC 2405 (5th Cir. 1981) (a terminal operator was found, as a matter of law, not to be an owner *pro hac vice*). Did Congress mean to overrule the *Yaka* case legislatively in all respects?

The Supreme Court resolved this question in *Jones & Laughlin Steel Corp. v. Pfeifer*, 462 U.S. 523, 103 S. Ct. 2541, 2546-57, 76 L. Ed. 2d 768, 1983 AMC 1881 (1983), stating as follows:

Most longshoremen who load and unload ships are employed by independent stevedores, who have contracted with the vessel owners to provide such services. In this case, however, the respondent longshoreman was employed directly by the petitioner vessel owner. Under § 4 of the Act, a longshoreman who is injured in the course of his employment is entitled to a specified amount of compensation from his employer, whether or not the injury was caused by the employer's negligence. Section 5(a) of the Act appears to make that liability exclusive. It reads, "The liability of an employer prescribed in § 4 of this act shall be exclusive and in place of all other liability of such an employer to the employee...." 44 Stat. 1526, 33 U.S.C. § 905(a). Since the petitioner was the respondent's employer and paid him benefits pursuant to § 4 of the Act, it contends that § 5(a) absolves it of all other responsibility for damages.

Although petitioner's contention is, indeed, supported by the language of § 5(a), it is undermined by the plain language of § 5(b). The first sentence of § 5(b) authorizes a longshoreman whose injury is caused by the negligence of a vessel to bring a separate action against such a vessel as a third party. Thus, in the typical tripartite situation, the longshoreman is not only guaranteed the statutory compensation from his employer; he may also recover tort damages if he can prove negligence by the vessel. The second sentence of § 5(b) makes it clear that such a separate action is authorized against the vessel even when there is no independent stevedore and the longshoreman is employed directly by the vessel owner. That sentence provides, "If such person was employed by the vessel to provide stevedoring services, no such action shall be permitted if the injury was caused by the negligence of persons engaged in providing stevedoring services to the vessel." If § 5(a) had been intended to bar all negligence suits against owner-employes, there would have been no need to put an additional sentence in § 5(b) barring suits against owner-employers for injuries caused by fellow servants.

The history of the Act further refutes petitioner's contention that § 5(a) of the Act bars respondent's suit under § 5(b). Prior to 1972, this Court had construed the Act to authorize a longshoreman employed directly by the vessel to obtain a recovery from his employer in excess of the statutory schedule even though § 5 of the Act contained the same exclusive liability language as today. *Reed v. The Yaka*, 373 U.S. 410 (1963); *Jacksonville v. Lykes Brothers Steamship Co.*, 386 U.S. 731 (1967). Although the 1972 Amendments changed the character of the longshoreman's action against the vessel by substituting negligence for unseaworthiness as the basis for liability, Congress clearly intended to preserve the rights of longshoremen employed by the vessel to maintain such an action.

Employees not covered by the LHWCA may still have an action for unseaworthiness against then land-based employer who also happens to be a shipowner.

4. *Vessel Negligence*

The question of whether a longshoreman's injuries are attributed to the negligence of his employer in his capacity as shipowner or in his capacity as land-based employer is not always easy to determine. In *White v. Cooper/T. Smith Corporation*, 690 F. Supp. 534 (E.D. La. 1988), a longshoreman injured in two separate accidents brought suit against his employer in his capacity as shipowner, and his wife joined in the suit seeking recovery for loss of consortium. The court ruled as a matter of law that under the facts alleged in the complaint with respect to the first accident, there was no vessel negligence. In the first incident plaintiff slipped while working on a mooring buoy after he had left his employer's vessel. As to the second accident, however, the court found that the petition stated sufficient facts to engage the liability of the employer under § 905(b), that is, in his capacity as shipowner. In this incident, plaintiff was injured on his employer's vessel while turning its steering wheel. The court found that the first incident lacked "vessel negligence" but there was a material fact in issue with respect to "vessel negligence" as to the second incident. The court also held that when an action under § 905(b) is available to a longshoreman, his spouse may institute action for loss of consortium.

5. *Unseaworthiness*

A longshoreman, assigned by his land-based employer to work on board a vessel belonging to the employer may qualify as a member of the crew of that vessel under the *Robison* test or may retain the status of a longshoreman. In the latter situation, he may recover from his employer damages for personal injuries in accordance with § 905(b) of the LHWCA. *See Jones & Laughlin Steel Corporation v. Pfeiffer*, 462 U.S. 523, 103 S. Ct. 2541, 76 L. Ed. 2d 768, 1983 AMC 1881 (1983), *supra*. A longshoreman, assigned by his land-based employer to work on board a vessel belonging to another person, may also be a seaman, a member of the crew of that vessel, if he meets the *Robison* test. In such a case, the longshoreman, in his capacity as a *borrowed servant*, may bring a Jones Act action or an action for unseaworthiness under the general maritime law against the shipowner. *See Wheatly v. Gladden*, 660 F.2d 1024, 1982 AMC 618 (4th Cir. 1981); Note, *supra*. A question remains, however, as to whether a longshoreman who is not covered by the LHWCA may bring an action grounded on *unseaworthiness* against a non-employer shipowner. In *Aparicio v. Swan Lake*, 643 F.2d 1109, 1981 AMC 1887 (5th Cir. 1981), the court held that a longshoreman who is *not* covered by LHWCA may bring an action against a shipowner for the recovery of damages caused by the unseaworthiness of the vessel. *But see Normile v. Maritime Company*, 643 F.2d 1380, 1981 AMC 2470 (9th Cir. 1981). In this case, the court held that the 1972 Amendments to the LHWCA suppressed the unseaworthiness action as to *all* longshoremen whether or not covered by the act. There is a general agreement that the unseaworthiness action is no longer available to a longshoreman who is covered by the LHWCA. *See Burks v. American River Transportation Company*, 679 F.2d 69, 1983 AMC 2208 (5th Cir. 1982). In this case, a longshoreman was injured on a vessel belonging to a person other than his employer while performing stevedoring work and sued the shipowner on grounds of unseaworthiness. Plaintiff claimed that he was a seaman, permanently assigned by his employer to do the work of a seaman on a vessel belonging to his employer but a longshoreman as to the vessel on which he was injured. The court held that whether or not plaintiff was a seaman as to his employer, he was a longshoreman covered by the LHWCA as to the defendant shipowner; therefore, after the 1972 Amendments to the LHWCA, plaintiff was not entitled to sue the shipowner for unseaworthiness.

May a seaman, member of the crew of a vessel, assigned to perform stevedoring duties on a vessel belonging to a person other than his employer claim from the non-employer shipowner benefits under the LHWCA? *See Smith v. Harbor Towing & Fleeting, Inc.*, 910 F.2d 312, 1991 AMC 986 (5th Cir. 1990). In this case, a seaman was injured on a vessel belonging to a person other than his employer while assisting in loading and unloading operations. He sued his employer under the Jones Act and under the general maritime law for unseaworthiness. He also sued the owner of the vessel on which he was injured for negligence and unseaworthiness under the general maritime law. Cognizant of the rule that the remedy of unseaworthiness is reserved for members of the crew of a vessel, plaintiff argued that, as to the vessel on which he was injured, he was a longshoreman not covered by LHWCA and, therefore, entitled to a remedy for unseaworthiness. The court granted a motion for partial summary judgment in favor of the non-employer shipowner, on the authority of *Bridges v. Penrod Drilling Co.*, 740 F.2d 361, 1986 AMC 1777 (5th Cir. 1984). The court concluded:

> In summary, we hold that a Jones Act seaman, who possesses the full range of traditional seamen's rights and remedies, cannot maintain a *Sieracki* seaworthiness action against a vessel on which he is not a crew member. In reaching this conclusion, we are not unmindful of the fact that longshoremen performing a seaman's task on a nonemployer's vessel are entitled to an unseaworthiness remedy while seamen performing the same task are not. Although this court may wish to reexamine this issue en banc, until then the holding in *Bridges* controls this case. Thus, we hold that Smith may not assert a *Sieracki* unseaworthiness claim against Chotin, and the judgment of the district court is hereby affirmed.

6. Products Liability and Unseaworthiness

The law of products liability, including strict liability, is a part of the general maritime law. *See East River Steamship Corporation v. Transamerica Delaval, Inc.*, 476 U.S. 858, 106 S. Ct. 2295, 90 L. Ed. 2d 865, 1986 AMC 2027 (1986). Unseaworthiness gives rise to a liability without negligence that is often called "absolute" or "strict liability." The 1972 Amendments to LHWCA suppressed the action for unseaworthiness that was available to longshoremen against shipowners under the general maritime law, and question has arisen as to whether *all* actions brought by longshoremen on grounds of strict liability were suppressed. In *Streach v. Associated Container Transportation, Ltd.*, 388 F. Supp. 953 (C.D. Cal. 1975), the court held that a strict products liability suit by a longshoreman is not the same as a proscribed action grounded on unseaworthiness and that such an action is not barred by the 1972 Amendments to LHWCA. Of course, a shipowner would then be liable in his capacity as manufacturer, designer, or distributor of a defective product.

Occasionally, injured longshoremen allege that their injuries on board the vessel were caused by a *negligently designed product* rather than the unseaworthiness of the vessel in order to prevent a summary dismissal of the action by application of LHWCA. Courts, however, can see through the pleadings. *See Bilderbeck v. World Wide Shipping Agency*, 776 F.2d 817 (9th Cir. 1985). The court affirmed a judgment discussing the action, stating:

> In the absence of specific allegations of negligence, the trial court acted within its discretion in disregarding the generalizations as simply another attempt to get seaworthiness into the case in the face of clear Congressional intent to remove it. There was no reversible error.
>
> We leave for later cases the question left open in *Scindia*, whether the functional equivalent of unseaworthiness can be brought back into these cases by pleading and proving that the vessel carried a negligently created defect that made the vessel hazardous to longshoremen and that the shipowner knew or reasonably should have known of the hazard, and nonetheless failed to warn the stevedore company so that it could take steps to protect its workmen. That was not this case.

E. Contribution and Indemnity

Background Note

Section 5 (33 U.S.C. § 905) of the LHWCA originally provided:

> *The liability of an employer prescribed in section 4* [for compensation] *shall be exclusive and in place of all other liability of such employer to the employee,* his legal representative, husband or wife, parents, dependents, next of kin, *and any one otherwise entitled to recover damages from such employer at law or in admiralty on account of such injury or death.* [Emphasis added.]

Nevertheless, the Supreme Court imposed *tort* liability on the land-based employer of a longshoreman or harbor worker in two situations: (a) when a longshoreman or harbor worker injured aboard a ship recovered damages from the shipowner, and the shipowner brought a suit for indemnity or contribution against the land-based employer; and (b) when the land-based employer also qualified as an owner *pro hac vice* of a vessel.

Frequently a longshoreman or harbor worker is injured in circumstances implicating the liability of a person other than his land-based employer. For example, the injuries sustained by a longshoreman may have been caused, in whole or in part, by the negligence of a shipowner. If the shipowner is solely liable under principles of tort law, the injured longshoreman or harbor worker may receive compensation under the LHWCA from his employer and sue the shipowner for damages. The employer of the injured worker may also sue the third-party tortfeasor to recover the payments made to the employee under LHWCA. This suit for indemnity may be based on a statutory assignment under 33 U.S.C. § 933 or on the general maritime law. For a discussion of actions for indemnity, as distinguished from actions for contribution, *see Federal Marine Terminals, Inc. v. Burnside Shipping Co.*, 394 U.S. 404, 1969 AMC 745 (1969). There, an employer brought an action against a shipowner claiming indemnity for payments made to an injured employee under the LHWCA on the ground that the injury had been caused by the negligence of the shipowner. The court held that the employer was not limited to the right of subrogation under the LHWCA but could maintain a direct action against the vessel for indemnity.

If the longshoreman or harbor worker is injured through the concurrent fault of his employer and a third party, questions arise as to the liability of each party toward the injured worker and toward each other. Matters become more complex when the liability of one party is based on negligence or products liability, whereas the liability of the other party is limited to benefits under the LHWCA.

In *Halcyon Lines v. Haenn Ship Ceiling & Refitting Corp.*, 342 U.S. 282, 72 S.Ct. 277, 96 L.Ed. 318, 1952 AMC 1 (1952), a ship repairman employed by Haenn was injured aboard a vessel belonging to Halcyon, and brought suit against Halcyon for negligence and unseaworthiness. Halcyon impleaded Haenn, and the jury found that plaintiff's injuries were attributable seventy-five percent to the fault of Haenn and twenty-five percent to the fault of Halcyon. Before the Supreme Court, Halcyon claimed contribution in proportion to the fault of each defendant. Haenn, however, maintained that there is no contribution among joint tortfeasors under the general maritime law in cases other than collisions, and the Court agreed. As a result, an injured longshoreman was able to recover his entire loss from the shipowner in an action based on negligence and unseaworthiness, and the shipowner had no recourse against the employer of the longshoreman, even if the injury had been proximately caused by the fault of the employer. The liability of the employer was limited to that established by the LHWCA. In *Cooper Stevedoring Co. v. Fritz Kopke, Inc.*, 417 U.S. 106, 94 S.Ct. 2174, 40 L.Ed.2d 694, 1974 AMC 537 (1974), a case governed by the law as it existed prior to the 1972 amendments to the LHWCA, the Supreme Court restricted the *Halcyon* case to its own facts. The Court held that the general maritime law provided a rule for contribution among joint tortfeasors in cases other than collisions and in which the employer could not claim exclusive liability under the LHWCA. Thus, in a suit by an injured longshoreman against a shipowner and a third-party stevedore (other than plaintiff's employer), the Court allowed contribution between joint tortfeasors. For an action for contribution against the United States for injuries compensable under the Federal Employees Compensation Act, *see Galimi v. Jetco, Inc.*, 514 F.2d 949, 1975 AMC 681 (2d Cir. 1975).

Subsequently, however, the Supreme Court held that a right to contribution or indemnity, though nonexistent under tort theory, may be based on the breach of an express or implied warranty of workmanlike service when the unseaworthiness of the vessel was produced by the fault of the contracting stevedoring company. *Ryan Stevedoring Co. v. Pan-Atlantic Steamship Co.*, 350 U.S. 124, 76 S.Ct. 232, 100 L.Ed. 133 (1956) [implied warranty]. Further, in *Italia Societa per Azioni di Navigazione v. Oregon Stevedoring Co.*, 376 U.S. 315, 84 S.Ct. 748, 11 L.Ed.2d 732, 1964 AMC 1075 (1964), the Supreme Court found breach of warranty where equipment furnished by the stevedore failed because of a latent defect. In the framework of the tripartite relationship among a longshoreman, his employer, and the shipowner, these decisions meant that the liability of the employer was no longer exclusively governed by the LHWCA. Instead, liability for the payment of damages rested entirely on the employer, even if the injuries had been caused to a large extent by the fault of the shipowner.

Then the 1972 amendments to the LHWCA were enacted. According to the provisions of 33 U.S.C. § 905(b) a shipowner may not recover damages he has paid to a longshoreman from the longshoreman's employer under any theory of warranty, express or implied, in tort or in contract. It should be noted, however, that the 1972 amendments to the LHWCA do not affect the applicability of the warranty of workmanlike service to persons other than employers of longshoremen and harbor workers. *See Stevens v. East-West Towing Co.*, 649 F.2d 1104, 1982 AMC 2820 (5th Cir. 1981) [charter party]; *Leckelt v. Superior Oil Co.*, 608 F.2d 592 (5th Cir. 1979) [vessel manufacture]; *Fairmont Shipping Corp. v. Clevron International Oil Co.*, 511 F.2d 1252, 1975 AMC 261 (5th Cir. 1979) [towage]. Thus, pre-1972 decisions extending the *Ryan* doctrine to a variety of maritime contracts continue to be valid. *See, e.g., Parfact v. Jahncke Service, Inc.*, 484 F.2d 296, 1974 AMC 1892 (5th Cir. 1973) [diesel dredge repair contract]; *Whisenant v. Brewster-Bartle Offshore Co.*, 446 F.2d 394, 1970 AMC 1713 (4th Cir. 1969) [towage]; *Lusich v. Bloomfield Steamship Co.*, 355 F.2d 770, 1966 AMC 191 (5th Cir. 1966) [ship repair]; *United States v. Tug Manzanillo*, 310 F.2d 220, 1963 AMC 365 (9th Cir. 1062) [towage]; *McWilliams Blue Line, Inc. v. Esso Standard Oil Co.*, 245 F.2d 84, 1957 AMC 1213 (2d Cir. 1957) [towage]. *But see General Construction Co. v. Umpqua River Navigation Co.*, 458 F.2d 1186, 1972 AMC 1615 (9th Cir. 1972) [dredging contract].

EDMONDS v. COMPAGNIE GENERALE TRANSATLANTIQUE

443 U.S. 256, 99 S. Ct. 2753, 61 L. Ed. 2d 521, 1979 AMC 1167 (1979)

Mr. Justice WHITE delivered the opinion of the Court.

On March 3, 1974, the S.S. *Atlantic Cognac*, a containership owned by respondent, arrived at the Portsmouth Marine Terminal, Va. Petitioner, a longshoreman, was then employed by the Nacirema Operating Co., a stevedoring concern that the shipowner had engaged to unload cargo from the vessel. The longshoreman was injured in the course of that work, and he received benefits for that injury from his employer under the Longshoremen's and Harbor Workers' Compensation Act. 44 Stat. 1424, as amended, 33 U.S.C. § 901 *et seq*. In addition, the longshoreman brought this negligence action against the shipowner in Federal District Court.

A jury determined that the longshoreman had suffered total damages of $100,000, that he was responsible for 10% of the total negligence resulting in his injury, that the stevedore's fault, through a co-employee's negligence, contributed 70%, and that the shipowner was accountable for 20%. Following an established principle of maritime law, the District Court reduced the award to the longshoreman by the 10% attributed to his own negligence. But also in accordance with maritime law, and the common law as well, the court refused further to reduce the award against the shipowner in proportion to the fault of the employer.

The United States Court of Appeals for the Fourth Circuit, with two judges dissenting, reversed en banc, holding that the 1972 Amendments to the Act, 86 Stat. 1251, had altered the traditional admiralty rule by making the shipowner liable only for that share of the total damages equivalent to the ratio of its fault to the total fault. 577 F.2d 1153, 1155-1156 (1978). Other Courts of Appeals have reached the contrary conclusion. We granted certiorari to resolve this conflict

I.

Admiralty law is judge-made law to a great extent, and a longshoreman's maritime tort action against a shipowner was recognized long before the 1972 Amendments, *see Pope & Talbot, Inc. v. Hawn*, 346 U.S. 406, 413-414 (1953), as it has been since. As that law had evolved by 1972, a longshoreman's award in a suit against a negligent shipowner would be reduced by that portion of the damages assignable to the longshoreman's own negligence; but, as a matter of maritime tort law, the shipowner would be responsible to the longshoreman in full for the remainder, even if the stevedore's negligence contributed to the injuries. This latter rule is in accord with the common law, which allows an injured party to sue a tortfeasor for the full amount of damages for an indivisible injury that the tortfeasor's negligence was a substantial factor in causing, even if the concurrent negligence of others contributed to the incident.

The problem we face today, as was true of similar problems the Court has dealt with in the past, is complicated by the overlap of loss-allocating mechanisms that are guided by somewhat inconsistent principles. The liability of the ship to the longshoreman is determined by a combination of judge-made and statutory law and, in the present context, depends on a showing of negligence or some other culpability. The longshoreman-victim, however, and his stevedore-employer—also a tortfeasor in this case—are participants in a workers' compensation scheme that affords benefits to the longshoreman regardless of the employer's fault and provides that the stevedore's only liability for the longshoreman's injury is to the longshoreman in the amount specified in the statute. 33 U.S.C. § 905. We have more than once attempted to reconcile these systems.

We first held that the shipowner could not circumvent the exclusive-remedy provision by obtaining contribution from the concurrent tortfeasor employer. *Halcyon Lines v. Haenn Ship Ceiling & Refitting Corp.*, 342 U.S. 282 (1952); *Pope & Talbot, Inc. v. Hawn, supra; see Cooper Stevedoring Co. v. Fritz Kopke, Inc.*, 417 U.S. 106, 111-113 (1974). As a matter of maritime law, we also held that a longshoreman working on a vessel was entitled to the warranty of seaworthiness, *Seas Shipping Co. v. Sieracki*, 328 U.S. 85, 94 (1946), which amounted to liability without fault for most onboard injuries. However, we went on to hold, as a matter of contract law, that the shipowner could obtain from the stevedore an express or implied warranty of workman like service that might result in indemnification of the shipowner for its liability to the longshoreman. *Ryan Stevedoring Co. v. Pan-Atlantic S.S. Corp.*, 350 U.S. 124 (1956).

Against this background, Congress acted in 1972, among other things, to eliminate the shipowner's liability to the longshoreman for unseaworthiness and the stevedore's liability to the shipowner for unworkmanlike service resulting in injury to the longshoreman—in other words, to overrule *Sieracki* and *Ryan. See Northeast Marine Terminal Co. v. Caputo*, 432 U.S. 249, 260-261, and n.18 (1977); *Cooper Stevedoring Co. v. Fritz Kopke, Inc., supra*, at 113 n.6. Though admitting that nothing in either the statute or its history expressly indicates that Congress intended to modify as well the existing rules governing the longshoreman's maritime negligence suit against the shipowner by diminishing damages recoverable from the latter on the basis of the proportionate fault of the nonparty stevedore, 577 F.2d, at 1155, and n.2, the en banc Court of Appeals found that such a result was necessary to reconcile two sentences added in 1972 as part of 33 U.S.C. § 905(b). The two sentences state:

> In the event of injury to a person covered under this chapter caused by the negligence of a vessel, then such person, or anyone otherwise entitled to recover damages by reason thereof, may bring an action against such vessel as a third party in accordance with the provisions of section 933 of this title, and the employer shall not be

liable to the vessel for such damages directly or indirectly and any agreements or warranties to the contrary shall be void. If such person was employed by the vessel to provide stevedoring services, no such action shall be permitted if the injury was caused by the negligence of persons engaged in providing stevedoring services to the vessel. 33 U.S.C. § 905(b).

The Court of Appeals described the perceived conflict in this fashion:

> The first sentence says that if the injury is caused by the negligence of a vessel the longshoreman may recover, but the second sentence says he may not recover anything of the ship if his injury was caused by the negligence of a person providing stevedoring services. The sentences are irreconcilable if read to mean that any negligence on the part of the ship will warrant recovery while any negligence on the part of the stevedore will defeat it. They may be harmonized only if read in apportioned terms. 577 F.2d, at 1155.

For a number of reasons, we are unpersuaded that Congress intended to upset a "long-established and familiar [principle]" of maritime law by imposing a proportionate-fault rule.

A.

In the first place, the conflict seen by the Court of Appeals is largely one of its own creation. Both sides admit that each sentence may be read so as not to conflict with the other. The first sentence addresses the recurring situations, reflected by the facts in this case, where the party injured by the negligence of the vessel is a longshoreman employed by a stevedoring concern. In these circumstances, the longshoreman may sue the vessel as a third party, but his employer, the stevedore, is not to be liable directly or indirectly for any damages that may be recovered. This first sentence overrules *Ryan* and prevents the vessel from recouping from the stevedore any of the damages that the longshoreman may recover from the vessel. But the sentence neither expressly nor implicitly purports to overrule or modify the traditional rule that the longshoreman may recover the total amount of his damages from the vessel if the latter's negligence is a contributing cause of his injury, even if the stevedore, whose limited liability is fixed by statute, is partly to blame.

The second sentence of the paragraph is expressly addressed to the different and less familiar arrangement where the injured longshoreman loading or unloading the ship is employed by the vessel itself, not by a separate stevedoring company—in short, to the situation where the ship is its own stevedore. In this situation, the second sentence places some limitations on suits against the vessel for injuries caused during its stevedoring operations. Whatever these limitations may be, there is no conflict between the two sentences, and one arises only if the second sentence is read, as the Court of Appeals read it, as applying to all injured longshoremen, whether employed by the ship or by an independent stevedore. Nothing in the legislative history advises this construction of the sentence, and we see no reason to depart from the language of the statute in this respect.

Respondent insists that, even though the two sentences may deal with different business arrangements, problems still arise. If under the first sentence a third-party suit against the vessel is authorized when *any* part of the negligence causing the injury is that of the vessel, it is argued that suit against the vessel under the second sentence should be barred when *any* part of the negligence causing the injury is that of a co-worker also providing stevedoring services to the vessel. Under this interpretation, the employee of the independent stevedore could recover from the ship where the stevedore was responsible for 99% of the negligence, though a ship's employee performing stevedoring services could not hold the vessel liable if his co-worker's negligence was the slightest cause of the injury. This is said to be preposterous and contrary to the legislative intent to treat the vessel that provides its own stevedoring services just like other shipowners when and if it negligently causes injury in its capacity as a shipowner and just like other stevedores when it negligently injures in the course of providing its own loading or unloading services.

Aside from the fact that the problem suggested would arise only in the application of the second sentence, which is not involved in this case, the argument that the words "caused by the negligence of" in the two sentences must be given the same meaning and that they cannot have the meaning ascribed to them by petitioner's construction of the first sentence, logically leads to the conclusion that the injured longshoreman should *never* be able to bring suit against the vessel unless it is the sole cause of the injury. This is a doubly absurd conclusion. It is supported by no one, and to avoid it, it is necessary only to construe the second sentence to permit a third-party suit against the vessel providing its own loading and unloading services when negligence in its nonstevedoring capacity contributes to the injury. The second sentence means no more than that all longshoremen are to be treated the same whether their employer is an independent stevedore or a shipowner-stevedore and that all stevedores are to be treated the same whether they are independent or an arm of the shipowner itself.

This leaves the question of the measure of recovery against a shipowner, whether or not it is doing its own stevedoring, when as shipowner it is only partially responsible for the negligence, but we are quite unable to distill from the face of the obviously awkward wording of the two sentences any indication that Congress intended to modify the pre-existing rule that a longshoreman who is injured by the concurrent negligence of the stevedore and the ship may recover for the entire amount of his injuries from the ship.

B.

The legislative history strongly counsels against the Court of Appeals' interpretation of the statute, which modifies the longshoreman's pre-existing rights against the negligent vessel. The reports and debates leading up to the 1972 Amendments contain not a word of this concept. This silence is most eloquent, for such reticence while contemplating an important and controversial change in existing law is unlikely. Moreover, the general statements appearing in the legislative history concerning § 905(b) are inconsistent with what respondent argues was in the back of the legislators' minds about this specific issue. The Committees repeatedly refer to the refusal to limit the shipowner's liability for negligence, which they felt left the vessel in the same position as a land-based third party whose negligence injures an employee. Because an employee generally may recover in full from a third-party concurrent tortfeasor, these statements are hardly indicative of an intent to modify the law in the respect found by the Court of Appeals. At the very least, one would expect some hint of a purpose to work such a change, but there was none.

The shipowner denies that the legislative history is so one-sided, relying upon statements that vessels "will not be chargeable with the negligence of the stevedore or [the] employees of the stevedore." S. REP. 11; *see* 577 F.2d, at 1156 n.2. But in context these declarations deal only with removal of the shipowner's liability under the warranty of seaworthiness for acts of the stevedore—even nonnegligent ones.

C.

Finally, we note that the proportionate-fault rule adopted by the Court of Appeals itself produces consequences that we doubt Congress intended. It may remove some inequities, but it creates others and appears to shift some burdens to the longshoreman.

As we have said, § 905 permits the injured longshoreman to sue the vessel and exempts the employer from any liability to the vessel for any damages that may be recovered. Congress clearly contemplated that the employee be free to sue the third-party vessel, to prove negligence and causation on the vessel's part, and to have the total damages set by the court or jury without regard to the benefits he has received or to which he may be entitled under the Act. Furthermore, under the traditional rule, the employee may recover from the ship the entire amount of the damages so determined. If he recovers less than the statutory benefits, his employer is still liable for the statutory amount.

Under this arrangement, it is true that the ship will be liable for all of the damages found by the judge or jury; yet its negligence may have been only a minor cause of the injury. The stevedore-employer may have been predominantly responsible; yet its liability is limited by the Act, and if it has lien rights on the longshoreman's recovery it may be out-of-pocket even less.

Under the Court of Appeals' proportionate-fault rule, however, there will be many circumstances where the longshoreman will not be able to recover in any way the full amount of the damages determined in his suit against the vessel. If, for example, his damages are at least twice the benefits paid or payable under the Act and the ship is less than 50% at fault, the total of his statutory benefits plus the reduced recovery from the ship will not equal his total damages. More generally, it would appear that if the stevedore's proportionate fault is more than the proportion of compensation to actual damages, the longshoreman will always fall short of recovering the amount that the factfinder has determined is necessary to remedy his total injury, even though the diminution is due not to his fault, but to that of his employer.

But the impact of the proportionate-fault rule on the longshoreman does not stop there. Under § 933(b), an administrative order for benefits operates as an assignment to the stevedore-employer of the longshoreman's rights against the third party unless the longshoreman sues within six months. And a corresponding judicially created lien in the employer's favor operates where the longshoreman himself sues. In the past, this lien has been for the benefits paid up to the amount of the recovery. And under § 933(c), which Congress left intact in 1972, where the stevedore-employer sues the vessel as statutory assignee it may retain from any recovery an amount equal in general to the expenses of the suit, the costs of medical services and supplies it provided the employee, all compensation benefits paid, the present value of benefits to be paid, plus one-fifth of whatever might remain. Under the Court of Appeals' proportionate-fault system, the longshoreman would get very little, if any, of the diminished recovery obtained by his employer. Indeed, unless the vessel's proportionate fault exceeded the ratio of compensation benefits to total damages, the longshoreman would receive nothing from the third-party action, and the negligent stevedore might recoup all the compensation benefits it had paid.

Some inequity appears inevitable in the present statutory scheme, but we find nothing to indicate and should not presume that Congress intended to place the burden of the inequity on the longshoreman whom the Act seeks to protect. Further, the 1972 Amendments make quite clear that "the employer shall not be liable to the vessel for such damages *directly or indirectly*," 33 U.S.C. § 905(b) (emphasis supplied), and that with the disappearance of the ship's contribution and indemnity right against the stevedore the latter should no longer have to appear routinely in suits between longshoreman and shipowner. Consequently, as we have done before, we must reject a "theory that nowhere appears in the Act, that was never mentioned by Congress during the legislative process, that does not comport with Congress' intent, and that restricts ... a remedial Act...." *Northeast Marine Terminal Co. v. Caputo*, 432 U.S., at 278-279.

II.

Of course, our conclusion that Congress did not intend to change the judicially created rule that the shipowner can be made to pay all the damages not due to the plaintiff's own negligence does not decide whether we are free to and should change that role so as to make the vessel liable only for the damages in proportion to its own negligence. Indeed, some amici in support of respondent share the view that Congress did not change the rule but argue that this Court should do so. We disagree.

Though we recently acknowledged the sound arguments supporting division of damages between parties before the court on the basis of their comparative fault, *see United States v. Reliable Transfer Co.*, 421 U.S. 397 (1975), we are mindful that here we deal with an interface of statutory and judge-made law. In 1972 Congress aligned the rights and liabilities of stevedores, shipowners, and longshoremen in light of the rules of maritime law that it chose not to change. "One of the most controversial and difficult issues which [Congress was] required to resolve ... [concerned] the liability of vessels, as third parties, to pay damages to longshoremen who are injured while engaged in stevedoring operations." S. REP. 8. By now changing what we have already established that Congress understood to be the law, and did not itself wish to modify, we might knock out of kilter this delicate balance. As our cases advise, we should stay our hand in these circumstances. *Cooper Stevedoring Co. v. Fritz Kopke, Inc.*, 417 U.S., at 112; *Halcyon Lines v. Haenn Ship Ceiling & Refitting Corp.*, 342 U.S., at 285-286. Once Congress has relied upon conditions that the courts have created, we are not as free as we would otherwise be to change them. A change in the conditions would effectively alter the statute by causing it to reach different results than Congress envisioned. Indeed, Congress might have intended to adopt the existing maritime rule even for third-party actions under the Act that are not within the admiralty jurisdiction, though we need not and do not reach that issue today.

Accordingly, we reverse the judgment below and remand for proceedings consistent with this opinion.

Mr. Justice POWELL took no part in the consideration or decision of this case.

Mr. Justice BLACKMUN, with whom Mr. Justice MARSHALL and Mr. Justice STEVENS join, dissenting.

The jury in this case found that the shipowner, the stevedore, and the longshoreman were each partially responsible for the latter's (petitioner Stanley Edmonds) injury. A member of the ship's crew instructed Edmonds to remove a jack from the rear wheel of a large cargo container. As Edmonds went behind the container to remove the jack, another longshoreman backed a truck into the container, causing it to roll backwards and pin Edmonds against the bulkhead. The jury concluded that the shipowner, as the employer of the crewman, was 20% responsible for the accident; the stevedore, as the employer of the longshoreman driving the truck, was 70% responsible; and Edmonds himself was 10% responsible.

The Court holds that the shipowner, who was 20% negligent, must pay 90% of Edmonds' damages. Edmonds, because of his comparative negligence, must absorb 10% of the damages himself. But the stevedore, who, the jury determined, was 70% at fault, will recoup its statutory compensation payments out of the damages payable to Edmonds, and thus will go scot-free.

The Court does not, and indeed could not, defend this result on grounds of reason or fairness. Today's ruling means that concurrently negligent stevedores will be insulated from the obligation to pay statutory workmen's compensation benefits, and thus will have inadequate incentives to provide a safe working environment for their employees. It also means that shipowners in effect will be held vicariously liable for the negligence of stevedores, and will have to pay damages far out of proportion to their degree of fault. Nor does the Court suggest that its holding is compelled by the language or legislative history of § 5(b) of the Longshoremen's and Harbor Workers' Compensation Act (LHWCA), 33 U.S.C. § 905(b). The Court appears to advance two justifications for its decision: first, that principles of comparative negligence did not apply under the traditional law of admiralty, and Congress intended to preclude judicial modification of that law when it passed the 1972 Amendments to the LHWCA; and second, that a rule of comparative negligence would be unfair to injured longshoremen. Since I find both purported justifications wholly inadequate to support the Court's decision, I respectfully dissent.

Note: Contribution and Indemnity When LHWCA Does Not Apply

Is a land-based employer immune to suits for contribution or indemnity in situations in which the LHWCA does *not* apply? In *White v. Johns-Manville Corp.*, 662 F.2d 243, 1982 AMC 1770 (4th Cir. 1981), harbor workers brought suit against a manufacturer for injuries caused by asbestos, and the manufacturer impleaded the land-based employer, seeking indemnity. The court held that contractual indemnity is governed by state law, but noncontractual (tort) indemnity is within admiralty jurisdiction. The court held that no indemnity was due under any theory advanced by the manufacturers but reserved decision as to the exclusivity of the liability of the employer under § 905(b).

McDERMOTT, INC. v. AMCLYDE

511 U.S. 202, 114 S. Ct. 1461, 128 L. Ed. 2d 148, 1994 AMC 1521 (1994)

Justice STEVENS delivered the opinion of the Court.

A construction accident in the Gulf of Mexico gave rise to this admiralty case. In advance of trial, petitioner, the plaintiff, settled with three of the defendants for $1 million. Respondents, however, did not settle, and the case went to trial. A jury assessed petitioner's loss at $2.1 million and allocated 32% of the damages to respondent AmClyde and 38% to respondent River Don. The question presented is whether the liability of the nonsettling defendants should be calculated with reference to the jury's allocation of proportionate responsibility, or by giving the nonsettling defendants a credit for the dollar amount of the settlement. We hold that the proportionate approach is the correct one.

I

Petitioner McDermott, Inc., purchased a specially designed, 5,000-ton crane from AmClyde. When petitioner first used the crane in an attempt to move an oil and gas production platform—the "Snapper deck"—from a barge to a structural steel base affixed to the floor of the Gulf of Mexico, a prong of the crane's main hook broke, causing massive damage to the deck and to the crane itself. The malfunction may have been caused by petitioner's negligent operation of the crane, by AmClyde's faulty design or construction, by a defect in the hook supplied by River Don Castings, Ltd. (River Don), or by one or more of the three companies (the "sling defendants") that supplied the supporting steel slings.

Invoking the federal court's admiralty jurisdiction under 28 U.S.C. § 133(1), petitioner brought suit against AmClyde and River Don and the three sling defendants. The complaint sought a recovery for both deck damages and crane damages. On the eve of trial, petitioner entered into a settlement with the sling defendants. In exchange for $1 million, petitioner agreed to dismiss with prejudice its claims against the sling defendants, to release them from all liability for either deck or crane damages, and to indemnify them against any contribution action. The trial judge later ruled that petitioner's claim for crane damages was barred by *East River Steamship Corp. v. Transamerica Delaval Inc.*, 476 U.S. 858, 106 S. Ct. 2295, 90 L. Ed. 2d 865 (1986).

In its opening statement at trial, petitioner McDermott "accepted responsibility for any part the slings played in causing the damage." The jury found that the total damages to the deck amounted to $2.1 million and, in answer to special interrogatories, allocated responsibility among the respective parties: 32% to AmClyde, 38% to River Don, and 30% jointly to McDermott and the sling defendants.[5] The Court denied a motion by respondents to reduce the judgment pro tanto by the $1 million settlement, and entered judgment against AmClyde for $672,000 (32% of $2.1 million) and against River Don for $798,000 (38% of $2.1 million). Even though the sum of those judgments plus the settlement proceeds exceeded the total damages found by the jury, the District Court concluded that petitioner had not received a double recovery because the settlement had covered both crane damages and deck damages.[6]

The Court of Appeals held that a contractual provision precluded any recovery against AmClyde and that the trial judge had improperly denied a pro tanto settlement credit. It reversed the judgment against AmClyde entirely and reduced the judgment against River Don to $470,000. It arrived at that figure by making two calculations. First, it determined that petitioner's "full damage award is $1.47 million ($2.1 million jury verdict less 30% attributed to McDermott/sling defendants)." 979 F.2d, at 1081. Next, it deducted the "$1 million received in settlement to reach $470,000." *Ibid.* It treated this figure as the maximum that could be recovered from the non-settling defendants. Because it was less than River Don's liability as found by the jury (38% of $2.1 million or $798,000), it directed the entry of judgment against River Don in that amount. *Ibid.*

* * *

II

Although Congress has enacted significant legislation in the field of admiralty law, none of those statutes provides us with any "policy guidance" or imposes any limit on our authority to fashion the rule that will best answer the question presented by this case. *See Miles v. Apex Marine Corp.*, 498 U.S. 19, 27, 111 S. Ct. 317, 322, 112 L. Ed. 2d 275 (1990). We are, nevertheless, in familiar waters because "the Judiciary has traditionally taken the lead in formulating flexible and fair remedies in the law maritime." *United States v. Reliable Transfer Co.*, 421 U.S. 397, 409, 95 S. Ct. 1708, 1714, 44 L. Ed. 2d 251 (1975).

---

[5] The special interrogatory treated McDermott and the sling defendants as a single entity and called for a percentage figure that covered them both. This combined treatment reflected McDermott's acceptance of responsibility for the damages caused by the sling defendants.

[6] The trial judge also noted that "[t]o hold as the defendants request would result in the settling defendants, who were at the most thirty percent (30%) responsible for the accident (no separate contributory negligence, if any, finding was made as to McDermott), paying One Million Dollars ($1,000,000.00) while the defendants who insisted on a trial and were found to be seventy percent (70%) liable would pay Four Hundred and Seventy Thousand Dollars ($470,000.00) between them. That is unjust...." App. to Pet. for Cert. A-52—A-53.

In the Reliable Transfer case we decided to abandon a rule that had been followed for over a century in assessing damages when both parties to a collision are at fault. We replaced the divided damages rule, which required an equal division of property damage whatever the relative degree of fault may have been, with a rule requiring that damages be assessed on the basis of proportionate fault when such an allocation can reasonably be made. Although the old rule avoided the difficulty of determining comparative degrees of negligence, we concluded that it was "unnecessarily crude and inequitable" and that "[p]otential problems of proof in some cases hardly require adherence to an archaic and unfair rule in all cases." *Id.*, at 407, 95 S. Ct., at 1714. Thus the interest in certainty and simplicity served by the old rule was outweighed by the interest in fairness promoted by the proportionate fault rule.

Our decision in Reliable Transfer was supported by a consensus among the world's maritime nations and the views of respected scholars and judges. *See id.*, at 403-405, 95 S. Ct., at 1711-1713. No comparable consensus has developed with respect to the issue in the case before us today. It is generally agreed that when a plaintiff settles with one of several joint tortfeasors, the nonsettling defendants are entitled to a credit for that settlement. There is, however, a divergence among respected scholars and judges about how that credit should be determined. Indeed, the American Law Institute has identified three principal alternatives and, after noting that "[e]ach has its drawbacks and no one is satisfactory," decided not to take a position on the issue. RESTATEMENT (SECOND) OF TORTS s 886A, pp. 343-344 (1977). The ALI describes the three alternatives as follows: "(1) The money paid extinguishes any claim that the injured party has against the party released and the amount of his remaining claim against the other tortfeasor is reached by crediting the amount received; but the transaction does not affect a claim for contribution by another tortfeasor who has paid more than his equitable share of the obligation." *Id.*, at 343. "(2) The money paid extinguishes both any claims on the part of the injured party and any claim for contribution by another tortfeasor who has paid more than his equitable share of the obligation and seeks contribution." *Ibid.* (As in Alternative (1), the amount of the injured party's claim against the other tortfeasors is calculated by subtracting the amount of the settlement from the plaintiff's damages.) "(3) The money paid extinguishes any claim that the injured party has against the released tortfeasor and also diminishes the claim that the injured party has against the other tortfeasors by the amount of the equitable share of the obligation of the released tortfeasor." *Id.*, at 344.

The first two alternatives involve the kind of "pro tanto" credit that respondents urge us to adopt. The difference between the two versions of the pro tanto approach is the recognition of a right of contribution against a settling defendant in the first but not the second. The third alternative, supported by petitioner, involves a credit for the settling defendants' "proportionate share" of responsibility for the total obligation. Under this approach, no suits for contribution from the settling defendants are permitted, nor are they necessary, because the nonsettling defendants pay no more than their share of the judgment.

The proportionate share approach would make River Don responsible for precisely its share of the damages, $798,000 (38% of $2.1 million).[10] A simple application of the pro tanto approach would allocate River Don $1.1 million in damages ($2.1 million total damages minus the $1 million settlement).[11] The Court of Appeals, however,

---

[10] It might be thought that, since AmClyde is immune from damages, River Don's liability should be $1.47 million (McDermott's $2.1 million loss minus 30% of $2.1 million, the share of liability attributed to the settling defendants and McDermott). This calculation would make River Don responsible not only for its own 38% share, but also for the 32% of the damages allocated by the jury to AmClyde. This result could be seen as mandated by principles of joint and several liability and by *Edmonds v. Compagnie Generale Transatlantique*, 443 U.S. 256, 99 S. Ct. 2753, 61 L. Ed. 2d 521 (1979). *See infra*, at 1471-1472. Nevertheless, McDermott has not requested that River Don pay any more than its 38% share of the damages. AmClyde is immune from damages because its contract with McDermott provided that free replacement of defective parts "shall constitute fulfillment of all liabilities ... whether based upon Contract, tort, strict liability or otherwise." 979 F.2d, at 1075 (emphasis omitted). The best way of viewing this contractual provision is as a quasi-settlement in advance of any tort claims. Viewed as such, the proportionate credit in this case properly takes into account both the 30% of liability apportioned to the settling defendants (and McDermott) and the 32% allocated to AmClyde. This leaves River Don with $798,000 or 38% of the damages.

[11] For simplicity, we ignore AmClyde, which was found to be immune from damages by the Court of Appeals. *Id.*, at 1075-1076. No party appeals that holding. Although AmClyde spent a considerable amount replacing the defective hook, River Don does not argue that that amount should be included in the calculation of its liability.

made a different calculation. Because McDermott "accepted responsibility for any part the sling played in causing the damage," 979 F.2d, at 1070, the Court of Appeals treated the 30% of liability apportioned to "McDermott/sling defendants" as if that 30% had been caused solely by McDermott's own negligence. *Id.*, at 1081. The Court of Appeals, therefore, gave River Don a double credit, first reducing the total loss by the McDermott/sling defendants' proportionate share and then applying the full pro tanto reduction to that amount. This double credit resulted in an award of only $470,000 ($2.1 million minus 30% of $2.1 million minus $1 million).

III

In choosing among the ALI's three alternatives, three considerations are paramount: consistency with the proportionate fault approach of *Reliable Transfer*, 421 U.S. 397, 95 S. Ct. 1708, 44 L. Ed. 2d 251 (1975), promotion of settlement, and judicial economy. ALI Option 1, pro tanto setoff with right of contribution against the settling defendant, is clearly inferior to the other two, because it discourages settlement and leads to unnecessary ancillary litigation. It discourages settlement, because settlement can only disadvantage the settling defendant. If a defendant makes a favorable settlement, in which it pays less than the amount a court later determines is its share of liability, the other defendant (or defendants) can sue the settling defendant for contribution. The settling defendant thereby loses the benefit of its favorable settlement. In addition, the claim for contribution burdens the courts with additional litigation. The plaintiff can mitigate the adverse effect on settlement by promising to indemnify the settling defendant against contribution, as McDermott did here. This indemnity, while removing the disincentive to settlement, adds yet another potential burden on the courts, an indemnity action between the settling defendant and plaintiff.

The choice between ALI Options 2 and 3, between the pro tanto rule without contribution against the settling tortfeasor and the proportionate share approach, is less clear. The proportionate share rule is more consistent with *Reliable Transfer*, because a litigating defendant ordinarily pays only its proportionate share of the judgment.

Under the pro tanto approach, however, a litigating defendant's liability will frequently differ from its equitable share, because a settlement with one defendant for less than its equitable share requires the nonsettling defendant to pay more than its share.[14] Such deviations from the equitable apportionment of damages will be common, because settlements seldom reflect an entirely accurate prediction of the outcome of a trial. Moreover, the settlement figure is likely to be significantly less than the settling defendant's equitable share of the loss, because settlement reflects the uncertainty of trial and provides the plaintiff with a "war chest" with which to finance the litigation against the remaining defendants. Courts and legislatures have recognized this potential for unfairness and have required "good-faith hearings" as a remedy. When such hearings are required, the settling defendant is protected against contribution actions only if it shows that the settlement is a fair forecast of its equitable share of the judgment. Nevertheless, good-faith hearings cannot fully remove the potential for inequitable allocation of liability. First, to serve their protective function effectively, such hearings would have to be minitrials on the merits, but in practice they are often quite cursory. More fundamentally, even if the judge at a good-faith hearing were able to make a perfect forecast of the allocation of liability at trial, there might still be substantial unfairness when the plaintiff's success at trial is uncertain.[19] In sum, the pro tanto approach, even when supplemented with good-faith hearings, is likely to lead to inequitable apportionments of liability, contrary to Reliable Transfer.

---

[14] Suppose, for example, that a plaintiff sues two defendants, each equally responsible, and settles with one for $250,000. At trial, the non-settling defendant is found liable, and plaintiff's damages are assessed at $1 million. Under the pro tanto rule, the nonsettling defendant would be liable for 75% of the damages ($750,000, which is $1 million minus $250,000). The litigating defendant is thus responsible for far more than its proportionate share of the damages. It is also possible for the pro tanto rule to result in the nonsettlor paying less than its apportioned share, if, as in this case, the settlement is greater than the amount later determined by the court to be the settlors' equitable share. For a more complex example illustrating the potential for unfairness under the pro tanto rule when the parties are not equally at fault, *see Kornhauser & Revesz* 68 N.Y.U. L. Rev., at 455-456 (pro tanto rule can lead to defendant responsible for 75% of damages paying only 37.5% of loss, while 25% responsible defendant pays 31.25%).

[19] Suppose again, as in footnote 14, that plaintiff sues two equally culpable defendants for $1 million and settles with one for $250,000. At the good-faith hearing, the settling defendant persuasively demonstrates that the settlement is in good faith, because it shows that its share of liability is 50% and that plaintiff has only a 50% chance of prevailing at trial. The settlement thus reflects exactly the settling defendant's expected liability. If plaintiff

The effect of the two rules on settlements is more ambiguous....

* * *

The effect of the two rules on judicial economy is also ambiguous....

* * *

In sum, although the arguments for the two approaches are closely matched, we are persuaded that the proportionate share approach is superior, especially in its consistency with *Reliable Transfer*.

IV

* * *

Respondents also argue that the proportionate share rule is inconsistent with *Edmonds v. Compagnie Generale Transatlantique*, 443 U.S. 256, 99 S. Ct. 2753, 61 L. Ed. 2d 521 (1979). In that case, we refused to reduce the judgment against a shipowner by the proportionate fault attributed to a stevedore whose liability was limited by the Longshoremen's and Harbor Workers' Compensation Act. Instead, the Court allowed the plaintiff to collect from the shipowner the entirety of his damages, after adjusting for the plaintiff's own negligence. There is no inconsistency between that result and the rule announced in this opinion. *Edmonds* was primarily a statutory construction case and related to special interpretive questions posed by the 1972 amendments to the Longshoremen's and Harbor Workers' Compensation Act. Both parties acknowledge that this case must be resolved by judge-made rules of law. Moreover, *Edmonds* did not address the issue in this case, the effect of a settlement on nonsettling defendants. Indeed, there was no settlement in that case. Instead, one can read that opinion as merely reaffirming the well-established principle of joint and several liability. As the Court pointed out, that principle was in no way abrogated by Reliable Transfer's proportionate fault approach. *Edmonds*, 443 U.S., at 271-272, n.30, 99 S. Ct., at 2762-2763, n.30. In addition, as the Commissioners on Uniform State Laws have noted, there is no tension between joint and several liability and a proportionate share approach to settlements. Joint and several liability applies when there has been a judgment against multiple defendants. It can result in one defendant's paying more than its apportioned share of liability when the plaintiff's recovery from other defendants is limited by factors beyond the plaintiff's control, such as a defendant's insolvency. When the limitations on the plaintiff's recovery arise from outside forces, joint and several liability makes the other defendants, rather than an innocent plaintiff, responsible for the shortfall. *Ibid.* Unlike the rule in *Edmonds*, the proportionate share rule announced in this opinion applies when there has been a settlement. In such cases, the plaintiff's recovery against the settling defendant has been limited not by outside forces, but by its own agreement to settle. There is no reason to allocate any shortfall to the other defendants, who were not parties to the settlement. Just as the other defendants are not entitled to a reduction in liability when the plaintiff negotiates a generous settlement, *see supra*, at 1470-1471, so they are not required to shoulder disproportionate liability when the plaintiff negotiates a meager one.

V

The judgment of the Court of Appeals is reversed, and the case is remanded for further proceedings consistent with this opinion.

It is so ordered.

---

prevails at trial, the nonsettling defendant will again be liable for 75% of the judgment even though its equitable share is only 50%. The only way to avoid this inequity is for the judge at the good-faith hearing to disallow any settlement for less than $500,000, that is any settlement which takes into account the uncertainty of recovery at trial. Such a policy, however, carries a grave cost. It would make settlement extraordinarily difficult if not impossible in most cases. As a result, every jurisdiction which conducts a good-faith inquiry into the amount of the settlement takes into account the uncertainty of recovery at trial. *Miller*, 887 F.2d, at 907-908; *Tech-Bilt*, 38 Cal. 3d, at 499, 213 Cal. Rptr., at 265, 698 P.2d, at 166; *TBG Inc.*, 811 F. Supp., at 600.

Note

A panel of the Court of Appeals for the Fifth Circuit in *Coats v. Penrod Drilling Corporation*, 61 F.3d 1113, 1996 AMC 1 (5th Cir. 1995) reiterating that joint and several liability is the rule in maritime personal injury cases, rejected one defendant's proposed modification of the rule. Under the proposal a contributorily negligent plaintiff would bear his proportionate share of the risk that part of the judgment in his favor may be uncollectible from one or more of the defendants.

F. Stevedore's Lien and Assignment of the Employee's Action

LONGSHORE AND HARBOR WORKERS' COMPENSATION ACT

§ 933. Compensation for Injuries Where Third Persons Are Liable

(a) Election of remedies

If on account of a disability or death for which compensation is payable under this chapter the person entitled to such compensation determines that some person other than the employer or a person or persons in his employ is liable in damages, he need not elect whether to receive such compensation or to recover damages against such third person.

(b) Acceptance of compensation operating as assignment

Acceptance of compensation under an award in a compensation order filed by the deputy commissioner, an administrative law judge, or the Board shall operate as an assignment to the employer of all rights of the person entitled to compensation to recover damages against such third person unless such person shall commence an action against such third person within six months after such acceptance. If the employer fails to commence an action against such third person within ninety days after the cause of action is assigned under this section, the right to bring such action shall revert to the person entitled to compensation. For the purpose of this subsection, the term "award" with respect to a compensation order means a formal order issued by the deputy commissioner, an administrative law judge, or Board.

(c) Payment into section 944 fund operating as assignment

The payment of such compensation into the fund established in section 944 of this title shall operate as an assignment to the employer of all right of the legal representative of the deceased (hereinafter referred to as "representative") to recover damages against such third person.

(d) Institution of proceedings or compromise by assignee

Such employer on account of such assignment may either institute proceedings for the recovery of such damages or may compromise with such third person either without or after instituting such proceeding.

(e) Recoveries by assignee

Any amount recovered by such employer on account of such assignment, whether or not as the result of a compromise, shall be distributed as follows:

    (1) The employer shall retain an amount equal to—

(A) the expenses incurred by him in respect to such proceedings or compromise (including a reasonable attorney's fee as determined by the deputy commissioner or Board);

(B) the cost of all benefits actually furnished by him to the employee under section 907 of this title;

(C) all amounts paid as compensation;

(D) the present value of all amounts thereafter payable as compensation, such present value to be computed in accordance with a schedule prepared by the Secretary, and the present value of the cost of all benefits thereafter to be furnished under section 907 of this title, to be estimated by the deputy commissioner, and the amounts so computed and estimated to be retained by the employer as a trust fund to pay such compensation and the cost of such benefits as they become due, and to pay any sum finally remaining in excess thereof to the person entitled to compensation or to the representative; and

(2) The employer shall pay any excess to the person entitled to compensation or to the representative.

(f) Institution of proceedings by person entitled to compensation

If the person entitled to compensation institutes proceedings within the period prescribed in subsection (b) of this section the employer shall be required to pay as compensation under this chapter a sum equal to the excess of the amount which the Secretary determines is payable on account of such injury or death over the net amount recovered against such third person. Such net amount shall be equal to the actual amount recovered less the expenses reasonably incurred by such person in respect to such proceedings (including reasonable attorneys' fees).

(g) Compromise obtained by person entitled to compensation

(1) If the person entitled to compensation (or the person's representative) enters into a settlement with a third person referred to in subsection (a) of this section for an amount less than the compensation to which the person (or the person's representative) would be entitled under this chapter, the employer shall be liable for compensation as determined under subsection (f) of this section only if written approval of the settlement is obtained from the employer and the employer's carrier, before the settlement is executed, and by the person entitled to compensation (or the person's representative). The approval shall be made on a form provided by the Secretary and shall be filed in the office of the deputy commissioner within thirty days after the settlement is entered into.

(2) If no written approval of the settlement is obtained and filed as required by paragraph (1), or if the employee fails to notify the employer of any settlement obtained from or judgment rendered against a third person, all rights to compensation and medical benefits under this chapter shall be terminated, regardless of whether the employer or the employer's insurer has made payments or acknowledged entitlement to benefits under this chapter.

(3) Any payments by the special fund established under section 944 of this title shall be a lien upon the proceeds of any settlement obtained from or judgment rendered against a third person referred to under subsection (a) of this section. Notwithstanding any other provision of law, such lien shall be enforceable against such proceeds, regardless of whether the Secretary on behalf of the special fund has agreed to or has received actual notice of the settlement or judgment.

(4) Any payments by a trust fund described in section 917 of this title shall be a lien upon the proceeds of any settlement obtained from or judgment recorded against a third person referred to under subsection (a) of this section. Such lien shall have priority over a lien under paragraph (3) of this subsection.

(h) Subrogation

Where the employer is insured and the insurance carrier has assumed the payment of the compensation, the insurance carrier shall be subrogated to all the rights of the employer under this section.

(i) Right to compensation as exclusive remedy

The right to compensation or benefits under this chapter shall be the exclusive remedy to an employee when he is injured, or to his eligible survivors or legal representatives if he is killed, by the negligence or wrong of any other person or persons in the same employ: *Provided.* That this provision shall not affect the liability of a person other than an officer or employee of the employer.

Notes

1. In *Bloomer v. Liberty Mutual Ins. Co.*, 445 U.S. 74, 100 S.Ct. 925, 63 L.Ed.2d 215, 1980 AMC 338 (1980), the issue was "whether the stevedore's lien must be reduced by a proportionate share of the longshoremen's expenses in obtaining a recovery from the shipowner, or whether the stevedore is instead entitled to be reimbursed for the full amount of the compensation on the vessel, *S.S. Pacific Breeze*. He received $17,152.83 in compensation from Liberty Mutual, his employer's insurance carrier. Plaintiff thereafter brought a diversity action against the vessel owner under 33 U.S.C. § 905(b), in which plaintiff and the vessel owner settled for $60,000. Liberty Mutual sought to recover the full amount it had paid to *Bloomer* in compensation, while *Bloomer* argued that the stevedore's lien should be reduced by an amount representing a proportionate share of the expenses of the suit against the shipowner. The court denied plaintiff's request, holding that under the legislative history and clear provisions of 33 U.S.C. § 933, Congress intended "that the longshoreman's attorney's fees would be paid by the longshoreman alone."

The *Bloomer* rule was applied by the United States Fifth Circuit Court of Appeals in *Bartholomew v. CNG Producing Co.*, 862 F.2d 555, 1989 AMC 741 (5th Cir. 1989). The plaintiff in that case argued (1) that an amendment of 33 U.S.C. § 933(f) in 1984 overruled the *Bloomer* holding, and (2) that it was not equitable to allow a stevedore's insurance company to gain from a longshoreman's suit against a negligent third party without having to pay its proportionate share of the costs. The court held that that 1984 amendment to 33 U.S.C. § 933(f), rather of overruling the *Bloomer* holding, actually reinforced it. While sympathizing with the plaintiff's equity argument, the court stated that "Congress' intent that the compensation carrier's lien remain inviolate, ... seems ... to be clear." The court therefore felt that only Congress had the power to change its decision, and accordingly awarded to the insurance company the full amount it paid in compensation to the plaintiff.

2. In *Pallas Shipping Agency, Ltd. v. Duris*, 461 U.S. 529, 103 S.Ct. 1991, 76 L.Ed.2d 120, 1983 AMC 1724 (1983), the Supreme Court held that in the absence of a formal award, an employee's acceptance of compensation payments cannot lead to an assignment of his right of action against third parties.

> Petitioner contends that the requirement of a formal compensation order prior to the assignment of an injured longshoreman's claims will frustrate the Act's aims of ensuring prompt payment to injured workers and of relieving burden of litigating compensation claims. It is said that employers who desire to seek indemnification from the negligent third party will be encouraged to contest their liability in order to obtain a compensation order instead of making voluntary payments. We do not find this contention persuasive. Employers are not required to contest their liability in order to obtain a formal compensation award. Department of Labor regulations permit an employer who makes voluntary payments to obtain a compensation order upon request if there is not disagreement among the parties. 20 CFR 702.315(a) (1982). Moreover, even without a statutory assignment of the longshoreman's claims, an employer can seek indemnification from negligent third parties for payments it has made to the longshoreman. *See Federal Marine Terminals v. Burnside Shipping Co.*, 394 U.S. 404 (1969); *Crescent Wharf & Warehouse Co. v. Barracuda Tanker Corp.*, 696 F.2d 703 (CA9 1983). For these reasons, the employer who seeks to bring an action against a shipowner, charterer, or other third person has little to gain from contesting his liability to the longshoreman under the LHWCA.

> We therefore conclude that respondent's acceptance of voluntary compensation payments did not constitute "[a]cceptance of such compensation under an award in a compensation order" so as to give rise to the assignment of respondent's claims against third persons.

Section III. Remedies for Wrongful Death

Part 1. Death on the High Seas: Cases and Notes

A. Introduction

In *The Harrisburg*, 119 U.S. 199, 7 S.Ct. 140, 30 L.Ed. 358 (1886), the Supreme Court held that the general maritime law does not afford a cause of action for wrongful death. However, in *The Hamilton*, 207 U.S. 398, 28 S.Ct. 133, 52 L.Ed. 264 (1907), the Court declared that the lacuna in maritime law created by the lack of a cause of action for wrongful death could be filled by the application of a state wrongful death statute. Thus, dependents of persons wrongfully killed on state territorial waters or, perhaps, on the high seas had remedies under state laws.

In 1920, Congress enacted the Death on the High Seas Act (DOHSA), now 46 U.S.C.A. §§ 30301-30308 (formerly 46 U.S.C. §§ 761-768), which established a cause of action for death "caused by wrongful act, neglect, or default occurring on the high seas beyond a marine league from the shore of any State, dependency, or territory." 46 U.S.C.A. § 30302 (formerly 46 U.S.C. § 761). In the same year, Congress also enacted the Jones Act, which incorporated the wrongful death provision of the Federal Employers' Liability Act (FELA), now 45 U.S.C. §§ 51-60. The two statutes are not entirely consistent as to the nature of the wrongful death recovery and as to the classes of persons entitled to recovery.

Subsequently jurisprudence established that DOHSA furnished the exclusive remedy for the wrongful death of a person other than a seaman on the high seas, and state statutes furnished remedies for wrongful death on territorial waters. The Jones Act provided the exclusive remedy for the death of a seaman in territorial waters, and both DOHSA (unseaworthiness) and the Jones Act (negligence) offered remedies for the death of a seaman on the high seas.

In 1946, in *Seas Shipping Co. v. Sieracki*, 328 U.S. 85, 66 S.Ct. 872, 90 L.Ed. 1099, 1956 AMC 698 (1946), the warranty of seaworthiness, which theretoforce was applicable to seamen only, was extended to longshoremen and other harbor workers. It was not clear, however, whether state wrongful death statutes gave recovery for wrongful death caused by the unseaworthiness of a vessel, and the extent to which state law applied to matters within the admiralty jurisdiction of the United States. The Supreme Court, in initial attempts to resolve practical questions concerning the extent to which state law imposed substantive limitations on recovery, instead engaged in meta-physical discussion concerning the distinction between "right" and "remedy." *See The Tungus v. Skovgaard*, 358 U.S. 588, 79 S.Ct. 503, 3 L.Ed.2d 524, 1959 A.M.C. 813; *Hess v. United States*, 361 U.S. 314, 80 S.Ct. 341, 4 L.Ed.2d 305, 1960 A.M.C. 527 (1960); *Goett v. Union Carbide Corp.*, 361 U.S. 340, 1960 A.M.C. (1960). Faced with confusion and uncertainty, the Supreme Court overruled *The Harrisburg* in *Moragne v. States Marine Lines, Inc.* 398 U.S. 375, 90 S.Ct. 1772, 26 L.Ed.2d 339, 1970 A.M.C. 967 (1970). These matters are explored in the following materials.

Wrongful-death statutes are to be distinguished from survival statutes. The latter have been separately enacted to abrogate the common-law rule that an action for tort abated at the death of either the injured person or the tortfeasor. Survival statutes permit the deceased's estate to prosecute any claims for personal injury the deceased would have had, but for his death. They do not permit recovery from harms suffered by the deceased' family as a result of his death. *See Michigan C.R. Co. v. Vreeland*, 227 U.S. 59, 33 S.Ct. 192, 57 L.Ed. 417 (1913).

B. The Death on the High Seas Act

[handwritten: only permission damages under DOSHA]

46 U.S.C.A. §§ 30301-30308

§ 30301. Short title

This chapter may be cited as the "Death on the High Seas Act".

[handwritten: Allows for (unseaworthiness) (which is not allowed under Jones).]

§ 30302. Cause of action

When the death of an individual is caused by a wrongful act, neglect, or default occurring on the high seas beyond 3 nautical miles from the shore of the United States, the personal representative of the decedent may bring a civil action in admiralty against the person or vessel responsible. The action shall be for the exclusive benefit of the decedent's spouse, parent, child, or dependent relative.

§ 30303. Amount and apportionment of recovery

The recovery in an action under this chapter shall be a fair compensation for the pecuniary loss sustained by the individuals for whose benefit the action is brought. The court shall apportion the recovery among those individuals in proportion to the loss each has sustained.

§ 30304. Contributory negligence

In an action under this chapter, contributory negligence of the decedent is not a bar to recovery. The court shall consider the degree of negligence of the decedent and reduce the recovery accordingly.

§ 30305. Death of plaintiff in pending action

If a civil action in admiralty is pending in a court of the United States to recover for personal injury caused by wrongful act, neglect, or default described in section 30302 of this title, and the individual dies during the action as a result of the wrongful act, neglect, or default, the personal representative of the decedent may be substituted as the plaintiff and the action may proceed under this chapter for the recovery authorized by this chapter.

§ 30306. Foreign cause of action

When a cause of action exists under the law of a foreign country for death by wrongful act, neglect, or default on the high seas, a civil action in admiralty may be brought in a court of the United States based on the foreign cause of action, without abatement of the amount for which recovery is authorized.

§ 30307. Commercial aviation accidents

(a) Definition—In this section, the term "nonpecuniary damages" means damages for loss of care, comfort, and companionship.

(b) Beyond 12 Nautical Miles—In an action under this chapter, if the death resulted from a commercial aviation accident occurring on the high seas beyond 12 nautical miles from the shore of the United States, additional compensation is recoverable for nonpecuniary damages, but punitive damages are not recoverable.

(c) Within 12 Nautical Miles—This chapter does not apply if the death resulted from a commercial aviation accident occurring on the high seas 12 nautical miles or less from the shore of the United States.

§ 30308. Nonapplication

(a) State Law—This chapter does not affect the law of a State regulating the right to recover for death.

(b) Internal Waters—This chapter does not apply to the Great Lakes or waters within the territorial limits of a State.

46 U.S.C. App. §§ 761-768
(Superseded Version)

§ 761. Right of action; where and by whom brought

(a) subject to subsection (b), whenever the death of a person shall be caused by wrongful act, neglect, or default occurring on the high seas beyond a marine league from the shore of any State, or the District of Columbia, or the Territories or dependencies of the United States, the personal representative of the decedent may maintain a suit for damages in the district courts of the United States, in admiralty, for the exclusive benefit of the decedent's wife, husband, parent, child, or dependent relative against the vessel, person, or corporation which would have been liable if death had not ensued.

(b) In the case of a commercial aviation accident, whenever the death of a person shall be caused by wrongful act, neglect, or default occurring on the high seas 12 nautical miles or closer to the shore of any State, or the District of Columbia, or the Territories or dependencies of the United States, this Act shall not apply and the rules applicable under Federal, State, and other appropriate law shall apply.

§ 762. Amount and apportionment of recovery

(a) The recovery in such suit shall be a fair and just compensation for the pecuniary loss sustained by the persons for whose benefit the suit is brought and shall be apportioned among them by the court in proportion to the loss they may severally have suffered by reason of the death of the person by whose representative the suit is brought.

(b) (1) If the death resulted from a commercial aviation accident occurring on the high seas beyond 12 nautical miles from the shore of any State, or the District of Columbia, or the Territories or dependencies of the United States, additional compensation for nonpecuniary damages for wrongful death of a decedent is recoverable. Punitive damages are not recoverable.

(2) In this subsection, the term "nonpecuniary damages" means damages for loss of care, comfort, and companionship.

§ 763a. Limitations

[This section was not enacted as part of the Death on the High Seas Act and is obviously broader in application. Eds.]

Unless otherwise specified by law, a suit for recovery of damages for personal injury or death, or both, arising out of a maritime tort, shall not be maintained unless commenced within three years from the date the cause of action accrued.

§ 764. Rights of action given by laws of foreign countries

Whenever a right of action is granted by the law of any foreign State on account of death by wrongful act, neglect, or default occurring upon the high seas, such right may be maintained in an appropriate action in admiralty in the courts of the United States without abatement in respect to the amount for which recovery is authorized, any statute of the United States to the contrary notwithstanding.

§ 765. Death of plaintiff pending action

If a person die as the result of such wrongful act, neglect, or default as is mentioned in section 761 of this title during the pendency in a court of admiralty of the United States of a suit to recover damages for personal injuries in respect of such act, neglect, or default, the personal representative of the decedent may be substituted as a party and the suit may proceed as a suit under this chapter for recovery of the compensation provided in section 762 of this title.

§ 766. Contributory negligence

In suits under this chapter the fact that the decedent has been guilty of contributory negligence shall not bar recovery, but the court shall take into consideration the degree of negligence attributable to the decedent and reduce the recovery accordingly.

§ 767. Exceptions from operation of chapter

The provisions of any State statute giving or regulating rights of action or remedies for death shall not be affected by this chapter. Nor shall this chapter apply to the Great Lakes or to any waters within the territorial limits of any State, or to any navigable waters in the Panama Canal Zone.

Note: Coverage of DOHSA

DOHSA permits recovery for wrongful death caused by negligence or unseaworthiness. *Bodden v. American Offshore, Inc.*, 681 F.2d 319, 1982 A.M.C. 2409 (5th Cir. 1982). Plaintiffs under DOHSA may recover only their pecuniary loss, including loss of services and loss of support. *Mobile Oil Corp. v. Higginbotham*, 436 U.S. 618, 1978 A.M.C. 1059 (1978); *Smith v. Ithaca Corp.*, 612 F.2d 215, 1981 A.M.C. 1029 (5th Cir. 1980). Punitive damages are not recoverable under DOHSA. *Bergen v. F/V St. Patrick*, 816 F.2d 1345, 1987 A.M.C. 2024 (9th Cir. 1987); *Jennings v. The Boeing Co.*, 660 F. Supp. 796 (E.D. Pa. 1987).

DOHSA applies in foreign territorial waters as well as the high seas. *See Howard v. Crystal Cruise Line*, 41 F.3d 527 (9th Cir.), 1995 A.M.C. 305 (1994); *Public Administrator v. Angela Compania Naviera*, 592 F.2d 58, 1979 AMC 106 (2d Cir. 1979). Moreover, DOHSA applies to maritime torts only. Thus, if a tort is not within the purview of admiralty jurisdiction, DOHSA does not apply. *See Brons v. Beech Aircraft Corp.*, 627 F. Supp 230 (S.D. Fla. 1985). But compare *Kunreuther v. Outboard Marine Corp.*, 757 F. Supp. 633, 1991 AMC 1812 (E.D. Pa. 1991).

C. State Remedies

OFFSHORE LOGISTICS, INC. v. TALLENTIRE

477 U.S. 207, 106 S. Ct. 2485, 91 L. Ed. 2d 174, 1986 AMC 2113 (1986)

Justice O'CONNOR delivered the opinion of the Court

Respondents' husbands were killed when petitioner Air Logistic's helicopter, in which the decedents were traveling crashed in the high seas. The issues presented is whether the Death on the High Seas Act (DOHSA), 41 Stat. 537, 46 U.S.C. § 761 *et seq.*, provides the exclusive remedy by which respondents may recover against petitioner for the wrongful death of their husbands, or whether they may also recover the measure of damages provided by the Louisiana wrongful death statute, La. Civ. Code Ann., Art 2315 (West Supp. 1986), applying either of its own force or as surrogate federal law under the Outer Continental Shelf Lands Act (OCSLA), 67 Stat. 462, as amended, 43 U.S.C. § 1331 *et seq.*

I.

The husbands of respondents Corrine Taylor and Beth Tallentire worked on drilling platforms in the Gulf of Mexico, off the coast of Louisiana. On August 6, 1980, respondents' husbands were killed while being transported in a helicopter owned and operated by petitioner Air Logistics (hereafter petitioner), a Division of Offshore Logistics, Inc., from a drilling platform to Houma, Louisiana. The crash occurred approximately 35 miles off the coast of Louisiana, well over the 3-mile limit that separates Louisiana's territorial waters from the high seas for purposes of DOHSA.

Respondents each filed wrongful death suits in United States District Court, raising claims under DOHSA, OCSLA, and the law of Louisiana. These actions were later consolidated in the Eastern District of Louisiana. Upon petitioner's pretrial motion for partial summary judgment, the District Court ruled that DOHSA provides the exclusive remedy for death on the high seas, and it therefore dismissed respondents' claims based upon the Louisiana wrongful death statute.

Petitioner admitted liability and the trial was limited to the question of damages. Because DOHSA limits recovery to "fair and just compensation for ... pecuniary loss," the District Court's awards to respondents did not include damages for nonpecuniary losses. 46 U.S.C. § 762.

Respondents appealed the District Court's dismissal of their OCSLA and state law wrongful death claims, contending that they were entitled to nonpecuniary damages under the Louisiana wrongful death statute. *See* LA. CIV. CODE ANN., Art. 2315(B) (West Supp. 1986) (permitting recovery for both pecuniary and nonpecuniary damages, "[including] loss of consortium, service, and society"). They argued that the Louisiana statute applied to this helicopter crash on the high seas, either of its own force by virtue of the saving provision in § 7 of DOHSA, 46 U.S.C. § 767, or as adopted federal law through OCSLA. *See* 43 U.S.C. § 1333(a)(2)(A). The Court of Appeals for the Fifth Circuit reversed the District Court's denial of benefits recoverable under Louisiana law, with one judge specially concurring and another judge dissenting. *See* 754 F.2d 1274 (1985).

* * *

Because the Fifth Circuit's decision creates the potential for disunity in the administration of wrongful death remedies for causes of action arising from accidents on the high seas and is in conflict with the prevailing view in other courts that DOHSA pre-empts state law wrongful death statutes in the area of its operation, we granted certiorari. 474 U.S. 816 (1985). We now hold that neither OCSLA nor DOHSA requires or permits the application of Louisiana law in this case, and accordingly reverse the judgment of the Court of Appeals for the Fifth Circuit.

II.

* * *

In 1920, Congress enacted DOHSA, in which it finally repudiated the rule of *The Harrisburg* for maritime deaths occurring beyond state territorial waters by providing for a federal maritime remedy for wrongful deaths more than three miles from shore.[1] DOHSA limits the class of beneficiaries to the decedent's "wife, husband, parent, child, or dependent relative," 46 U.S.C. § 761, establishes a 3-year statute of limitations period, § 763a, allows a suit filed by the victim to continue as a wrongful death action if the victim dies of his injuries while suit is pending, § 765, provides that contributory negligence will not bar recovery, § 766, and declares that "recovery ... shall be a fair and just compensation for the pecuniary loss sustained by the persons for whose benefit the suit is brought...." § 762.

* * *

III.

As explained above, DOHSA is intended to provide a maritime remedy for deaths stemming from wrongful acts or omissions "occurring on the high seas." 46 U.S.C. § 761. OCSLA, by contrast, provides an essentially nonmaritime remedy and controls only on "the subsoil and seabed of the outer Continental Shelf, and artificial islands and fixed structures" erected thereon. 43 U.S.C. § 1333(a)(2)(A). By its terms, OCSLA must be "construed in such a manner that the character of the waters above the outer Continental Shelf as high seas ... shall not be affected." § 1332(2). Within the area covered by OCSLA, federal law controls but the law of the adjacent State is adopted as surrogate federal law to the extent that it is not inconsistent with applicable federal laws or regulations. § 1333(a)(2)(A).

The intent behind OCSLA was to treat the artificial structures covered by the Act as upland islands or as federal enclaves within a landlocked State, and not as vessels, for purposes of defining the applicable law because maritime

---

[1] DOHSA does not include a survival provision authorizing recovery for pain and suffering before death. We do not address the issue whether the DOHSA recovery for the beneficiaries' pecuniary loss may be "supplemented" by a recovery of the decedent's pain and suffering before death under the survival provision of some conceivably applicable state statute that is intended to apply on the high seas. *See generally Barbe v. Drummond*, 507 F.2d 794, 797-798 (CA 1 1974); *Dugas v. National Aircraft Corp.*, 438 F.2d 1386 (CA 3 1971).

law was deemed inapposite to these fixed structures. *See Rodrigue v. Aetna Casualty & Surety Co.*, 395 U.S. 352, 361-366 (1969). This Court endorsed the congressional assumption that admiralty law generally would not apply to the lands and structures covered by OCSLA in *Rodrigue*, noting that accidents on the artificial islands covered by OCSLA "had no more connection with the ordinary stuff of admiralty than do accidents on piers." *Id.*, at 360. *See also Herb's Welding, Inc. v. Gray*, 470 U.S. 414, 422 (1985). Thus, in *Rodrigue*, the Court held that an admiralty action under DOHSA does not apply to accidents "actually occurring" on these artificial islands, and that DOHSA therefore does not preclude the application of state law as adopted federal law through OCSLA to wrongful death actions arising from accidents on offshore platforms. *Rodrigue v. Aetna Casualty Co., supra*, at 366, 89 S. Ct., at 1842.

Respondents argue that because the decedents were platform workers being transported from work to the mainland, OCSLA, not DOHSA, governs their cause of action.

* * *

We do not interpret § 4 of OCSLA, 43 U.S.C. § 1333, to require or permit us to extend the coverage of the statute to the platform workers in this case who were killed miles away from the platform and on the high seas simply because they were platform workers. Congress determined that the general scope of OCSLA's coverage, like the operation of DOHSA's remedies, would be determined principally by locale, not by the status of the individual injured or killed.

* * *

In the circumstances presented, then, the conclusion is inescapable that the remedies afforded by DOHSA, not OCSLA, govern this action. Thus, respondents may secure the nonpecuniary damages made available by Louisiana's wrongful death statute only if it is found that DOHSA preserves, or does not pre-empt, state remedies on the high seas.

* * *

Respondents argue that the first sentence of § 7 of DOHSA was intended to ensure the applicability of state wrongful death statutes to deaths on the high seas. We conclude that provision will not bear respondents' reading when evaluated in light of the language of the Act as a whole, the legislative history of § 7, the congressional purposes underlying the Act, and the importance of uniformity of admiralty law. *See Mastro Plastics Corp. v. NLRB*, 350 U.S. 270, 285 (1956) ("'In expounding a statute, we must not be guided by a single sentence or member of a sentence, but look to the provisions of the whole law, and to its object and policy'") (quoting *United States v. Heirs of Boisdoré*, 8 How. 113, 122 (1849)). These references persuade us that the first sentence of § 7 was intended only to serve as a jurisdictional saving clause, ensuring that state courts enjoyed the right to entertain causes of action and provide wrongful death remedies both for accidents arising on territorial waters and, under DOHSA, for accidents occurring more than one marine league from shore.

The first sentence of § 7 of DOHSA, as originally drafted, provided that "the provisions of any State statute giving or regulating rights of action or remedies for death shall not be affected by this act as to causes of action accruing within the territorial limits of any State." *See* 59 CONG. REC. 4482 (1920). During the House debate, Representative Mann proposed an amendment deleting the words "as to causes of action accruing within the territorial limits of any state." Although at first blush the language of the amended § 7 seems to support respondents' position, a closer comparison of the language of § 7, both before and after its amendment, with the language of § 4 of the Act belies respondents' facial argument.

* * *

In sum, the language of § 7 and its legislative history, as well as the congressional purposes underlying DOHSA, mandate that § 7 be read not as an endorsement of the application of state wrongful death statutes to the high seas, but rather as a jurisdictional saving clause. Viewed in this light, § 7 serves not to destroy the uniformity of wrongful death remedies on the high seas but to facilitate the effective and just administration of those remedies. The recognition of concurrent state jurisdiction to hear DOHSA actions makes available to DOHSA beneficiaries a convenient forum for the decision of their wrongful death claims. *See* Note, *Admiralty: Death on the High Seas by Wrongful Act*, 47 CORNELL. L.Q. 632, 638 (1962) (hereinafter Note). Because the resolution of DOHSA claims does not normally require the expertise that admiralty courts bring to bear, DOHSA actions are clearly within the competence of state courts to adjudicate. *See* ALI Study, at 237; Note, at 637. Also, the availability of concurrent jurisdiction prevents disunity in the provision of forums to survivors of those killed on the high seas; it ensures that if a seaman and a passenger are killed at sea in the same accident, the beneficiaries of both are able to choose the forum in which they prefer to proceed. *See Engel v. Davenport*, 271 U.S. 33 (1926) (state and federal courts have concurrent jurisdiction over Jones Act claims). *See also* ALI Study § 1316(b), at 237; Note, at 638. *Cf. also Gulf Offshore Co. v. Mobil Oil Corp.*, 453 U.S. 473 (1981) (recognizing state courts' concurrent jurisdiction over OCSLA claims).

Once it is determined that § 7 acts as a jurisdictional saving clause, and not as a guarantee of the applicability of state substantive law to wrongful deaths on the high seas, the conclusion that the state statutes are pre-empted by DOHSA where it applies is inevitable. As we held in *Higginbotham*, Congress has "struck the balance for us" in determining that survivors should be restricted to the recovery of their nonpecuniary losses, and when DOHSA "does speak directly to a question, the courts are not free to 'supplement' Congress' answer so thoroughly that the Act becomes meaningless." 436 U.S., at 625, 98 S. Ct. at 2015.

Admittedly, in the circumstances of this case, the recognition of a state damages remedy for loss of society would bring respondents' DOHSA recovery into line with the damages available to a beneficiary of a federal *Moragne* maritime cause of action arising from a death on territorial waters. *See Sea-Land Services, Inc. v. Gaudet*, 414 U.S. 573 (1974) (holding that awards under the general federal maritime cause of action for wrongful death could include compensation for loss of society). However, the questionable practical significance of this difference in recovery, *see Mobil Oil Corp. v. Higginbotham, supra*, at 624, and n.20, is far overshadowed by the potential for serious conflicts between DOHSA and state substantive law in such areas as limitations periods, classes of beneficiaries, and the definition of potential defenses. We defer to Congress' purpose in making a uniform provision for recovery for wrongful deaths on the high seas, an area where the federal interests are primary.

The judgment of the Court of Appeals for the Fifth Circuit is reversed, and the case is remanded for further proceedings consistent with this opinion.

It is so ordered.

Justice POWELL, with whom Justice BRENNAN, Justice MARSHALL, and Justice STEVENS join, concurring in Part III and dissenting.

The Court today holds that § 7 of the Death on the High Seas Act (DOHSA), 41 Stat. 538, 46 U.S.C. § 767, forecloses application of state remedies for wrongful deaths on the high seas. Thus, the Court confines state courts to the adjudication of causes of action brought under DOHSA. Because I believe that the Court's reading of § 7 is at odds with the language of the statute and its legislative history, I dissent.

* * *

II.

The starting point in statutory construction is, of course, the language of the statute itself. *Blue Chip Stamps v. Manor Drug Stores*, 421 U.S. 723, 756 (1975) (POWELL, J., concurring). *See Consumer Product Safety Comm'n v. GTE Sylvania, Inc.*, 447 U.S. 102 (1980). The language of § 7, given scant attention by the Court, reads as codified:

§ 767. Exceptions from operation of chapter
The provisions of any State statute *giving or regulating rights of action or remedies for death* shall not be affected by this chapter. Nor shall this chapter apply to the Great Lakes or to any waters within the territorial limits of any State, or to any navigable waters in the Panama Canal Zone. 46 U.S.C. § 767 (emphasis added).

The terms of the provision are clear. The provision preserves state rights of action and state remedies for wrongful death without any territorial qualification. It encompasses not only jurisdiction, but also "rights of action" and "remedies." The geographic reach of these traditional rights of action is therefore undiminished by DOHSA. The congressional debate and other legislative history cast no doubt on the plain meaning of § 7.

* * *

It is not easy to understand how § 7 was transformed from a provision that preserved both state jurisdiction and state rights of action in territorial waters, into a mere "jurisdictional saving clause" with no power to preserve state rights of action on the high seas. The Mann Amendment did nothing more than remove a territorial restriction; all other clauses of § 7 remained intact. As Representative Mann stated: "If the amendment which I have suggested should be agreed to, the bill *would not interfere in any way with rights now granted by any State statute*, whether the cause of action accrued within the territorial limits of the State or not." 59 Cong. Rec. 4484 (1920) (emphasis added). Moreover, as already noted, construing § 7 as preserving only state jurisdiction on the high seas is at odds with the terms of the provision itself. The language plainly refers to "[the] provisions of any State statute giving or regulating rights of action or remedies for death."

* * *

IV.

The Court argues that preserving state rights of action for death on the high seas, in accordance with the plain language of § 7, would undermine a uniform federal remedy and conflict with the *exclusive*, federal character of most aspects of admiralty law. I agree that such a result undercuts a federal uniformity that seems desirable here, but it is not the role of this Court to reconsider the wisdom of a policy choice that Congress has already made. Congress enacted the Mann Amendment to remove the territorial restriction from § 7's preservation of state-law rights of action for wrongful death. The Court now holds that those rights of action may not be enforced on the high seas, and thereby imposes an exclusive federal remedy that Congress declined to enact. We should respect the outcome of the legislative process and preserve State rights of action for wrongful death on the high seas until Congress legislates otherwise. Accordingly, I dissent.

Note: Jury Trial

Is there a possibility for a jury trial in a suit under DOHSA? In *Friedman v. Mitsubishi Aircraft International, Inc.*, 678 F. Supp. 1064 (S.D.N.Y. 1988), an aircraft crashed on the high seas and plaintiff moved for a trial by jury. The motion was grounded on the theory that DOHSA was inapplicable in the absence of a traditional maritime activity and, in the alternative, if DOHSA was applicable, on the assertion that Section 7 of DOHSA preserves the right to a jury trial, especially when diversity jurisdiction exists. The court denied the motion. In the opinion of the court, DOHSA provides the exclusive remedy for all deaths on the high seas, regardless of any traditional maritime activity, and substantive state wrongful death remedies are preempted outside the territorial waters of a state. "It follows, therefore," the court concluded that "since DOHSA provides a remedy in admiralty, admiralty principles are applicable and a DOHSA plaintiff has no right to a jury trial of wrongful death claims."

Is the right to a jury trial a "substantive" remedy or a part of procedural law? If Section 7 of DOHSA is a jurisdictional saving clause that preserves the jurisdiction of a state court to hear DOHSA claims, what prevents the state court from granting a motion for a jury trial? *See Favaloro v. S.S. Golden Gate*, 687 F. Supp. 475, 1988 AMC 818 (N.D. Cal. 1987); *In re Korean Airlines Disaster of September 1, 1983*, 704 F. Supp. 1135 (Dist. Colum. 1988), *aff'd* in part, 932 F.2d 1475 (D. Col. Cir. 1991).

Part 2. Wrongful Death Actions Under General Maritime Law—(Within State Territorial Waters): Cases and Notes

A. Creation of a Cause of Action

MORAGNE v. STATES MARINE LINES, INC.

398 U.S. 375, 90 S. Ct. 1772, 26 L. Ed. 2d 339, 1970 AMC 967 (1970)

Mr. Justice HARLAN delivered the opinion of the Court.

We brought this case here to consider whether *The Harrisburg*, 119 U.S. 199, in which this Court held in 1886 that maritime law does not afford a cause of action for wrongful death, should any longer be regarded as acceptable law.

The complaint sets forth that Edward Moragne, a longshoreman, was killed while working aboard the vessel *Palmetto State* in navigable waters within the State of Florida. Petitioner, as his widow and representative of his estate, brought this suit in a state court against respondent States Marine Lines, Inc., the owner of the vessel, to recover damages for wrongful death and for the pain and suffering experienced by the decedent prior to his death. The claims were predicated upon both negligence and the unseaworthiness of the vessel.

* * *

I.

The Court's opinion in *The Harrisburg* acknowledged that the result reached had little justification except in primitive English legal history—a history far removed from the American law of remedies for maritime deaths.

II.

We need not, however, pronounce a verdict on whether *The Harrisburg*, when decided, was a correct extrapolation of the principles of decisional law then in existence. A development of major significance has intervened, making clear that the rule against recovery for wrongful death is sharply out of keeping with the policies of modern American maritime law. This development is the wholesale abandonment of the rule in most of the areas where it once held sway, quite evidently prompted by the same sense of the rule's injustice that generated so much criticism of its original promulgation.

* * *

In the United States, every State today has enacted a wrongful-death statute. *See Smith, supra,* 44 N.C. L. REV. 402. The Congress has created actions for wrongful deaths of railroad employees, Federal Employers' Liability Act, 45 U.S.C. §§ 51-59; of merchant seamen, Jones Act, 46 U.S.C. § 688; and of persons on the high seas, Death on the High Seas Act, 46 U.S.C. §§ 761, 762. Congress has also, in the Federal Tort Claims Act, 28 U.S.C. § 1346(b), made the United States subject to liability in certain circumstances for negligently caused wrongful death to the same extent as a private person. *See, e.g., Richards v. United States,* 369 U.S. 1 (1962).

These numerous and broadly applicable statutes, taken as a whole, make it clear that there is no present public policy against allowing recovery for wrongful death. The statutes evidence a wide rejection by the legislatures of whatever justifications may once have existed for a general refusal to allow such recovery.

This legislative establishment of policy carries significance beyond the particular scope of each of the statutes involved. The policy thus established has become itself a part of our law, to be given its appropriate weight not only in matters of statutory construction but also in those of decisional law.

* * *

III.

Our undertaking, therefore, is to determine whether Congress has given such a direction in its legislation granting remedies for wrongful deaths in portions of the maritime domain. We find that Congress has given no affirmative indication of an intent to preclude the judicial allowance of a remedy for wrongful death to persons in the situation of this petitioner.

From the date of *The Harrisburg* until 1920, there was no remedy for death on the high seas caused by breach of one of the duties imposed by federal maritime law. For deaths with state territorial waters, the federal law accommodated the humane policies of state wrongful-death statutes by allowing recovery whenever an applicable state statute favored such recovery. Congress acted in 1920 to furnish the remedy denied by the courts for deaths beyond the jurisdiction of any State, by passing two landmark statutes. The first of these was the Death on the High Seas Act, 41 Stat. 537, 46 U.S.C. § 761 *et seq.*

... The second statute was the Jones Act, 41 Stat. 1007, 46 U.S.C. § 688, which, by extending to seamen the protections of the Federal Employers' Liability Act, provided a right of recovery against their employers for negligence resulting in injury or death. This right follows from the seamen's employment status and is not limited to injury or death occurring on the high seas.

The United States, participating as *amicus curiae*, contended at oral argument that these statutes, if construed to forbid recognition of a general maritime remedy for wrongful death within territorial waters, would perpetuate three anomalies of present law. The first of these is simply the discrepancy produced whenever the rule of *The Harrisburg* holds sway: within territorial waters, identical conduct violating federal law (here the furnishing of an unseaworthy vessel) produces liability if the victim is merely injured, but frequently not if he is killed. As we have concluded, such a distinction is not compatible with the general policies of federal maritime law.

The second incongruity is that identical breaches of the duty to provide a seaworthy ship, resulting in death, produce liability outside the three-mile limit—since a claim under the Death on the High Seas Act may be founded on unseaworthiness, *see Kernan v. American Dredging Co.*, 355 U.S. 426, 430 n.4 (1958)—but not within the territorial waters of a State whose local statute excludes unseaworthiness claims. The United States argues that since the substantive duty is federal, and federal maritime jurisdiction covers navigable waters within and without the three-mile limit, no rational policy supports this distinction in the availability of a remedy.

The third, and assertedly the "strangest" anomaly is that a true seaman—that is, a member of a ship's company, covered by the Jones Act—is provided no remedy for death caused by unseaworthiness within territorial waters, while a longshoreman, to whom the duty of seaworthiness was extended only because he performs work traditionally done by seamen, does have such a remedy when allowed by a state statute.

There is much force to the United States' argument that these distinctions are so lacking in any apparent justification that we should not, in the absence of compelling evidence, presume that Congress affirmatively intended to freeze them into maritime law. There should be no presumption that Congress has removed this Court's traditional responsibility to vindicate the policies of maritime law by ceding that function exclusively to the States.

* * *

Read in light of the state of maritime law in 1920, we believe this legislative history indicates that Congress intended to ensure the continued availability of a remedy, historically provided by the States, for deaths in territorial waters; its failure to extend the Act to cover such deaths primarily reflected the lack of necessity for coverage by a federal statute, rather than an affirmative desire to insulate such deaths from the benefits of any federal remedy that might be available independently of the Act. The void that existed in maritime law up until 1920 was the absence of any remedy for wrongful death on the high seas. Congress, in acting to fill that void, legislated only to the three-mile limit because that was the extent of the problem. The express provision that state remedies in territorial waters were not disturbed by the Act ensured that Congress' solution of one problem would not create another by inviting the courts to find that the Act pre-empted the entire field, destroying the state remedies that had previously existed.

The beneficiaries of persons meeting death on territorial waters did not suffer at that time from being excluded from the coverage of the Act. To the contrary, the state remedies that were left undisturbed not only were familiar but also may actually have been more generous than the remedy provided by the new Act....

* * *

We conclude that the Death on the High Seas Act was not intended to preclude that availability of a remedy for wrongful death under general maritime law in situations not covered by the Act. Because the refusal of maritime law to provide such a remedy appears to be jurisprudentially unsound and to have produced serious confusion and hardship, that refusal should cease unless there are substantial countervailing factors that dictate adherence to *The Harrisburg* simply as a matter of *stare decisis*. We now turn to a consideration of those factors.

V.

* * *

The one aspect of a claim for wrongful death that has no precise counterpart in the established law governing nonfatal injuries is the determination of the beneficiaries who are entitled to recover. General maritime law, which denied any recovery for wrongful death, found no need to specify which dependents should receive such recovery. On this question, petitioner and the United States argue that we may look for guidance to the expressions of Congress, which has spoken on this subject in the Death on the High Seas Act, the Jones Act, and the Longshoremen's and Harbor Workers' Compensation Act. Though very similar, each of these provisions differs slightly in the naming of dependent relatives who may recover and in the priority given in their claims.

The United States contends that, of the three, the provision that should be borrowed for wrongful-death actions under general maritime law is that of the Death on the High Seas Act. It is the congressional enactment that deals specifically and exclusively with actions for wrongful death, and that simply provides a remedy—for deaths on the high seas—for breaches of the duties imposed by general maritime law. In contrast, the beneficiary provisions of the Jones Act are applicable only to a specific class of actions—claims by seamen against their employers—based on violations of the special standard of negligence that has been imposed under the Federal Employers' Liability Act. That standard appears to be unlike any imposed by general maritime law. Further, although the Longshoremen's and Harbor Workers' Compensation Act is applicable to longshoremen such as petitioner's late husband, its principles of recovery are wholly foreign to those of general maritime law—like most workmen's compensation laws, it deals only with the responsibilities of employers for death or injury to their employees, and provides standardized amounts of compensation regardless of fault on the part of the employer.

The only one of these statutes that applies not just to a class of workers but to any "person," and that bases liability on conduct violative of general maritime law, is the Death on the High Seas Act. The borrowing of its schedule of beneficiaries, argues the United States, will not only effectuate the expressed congressional preferences in this area but will also promote uniformity by ensuring that the beneficiaries will be the same for identical torts, rather than varying with the employment status of the decedent. There is no occasion, according to this argument, to borrow from the law of the relevant coastal State, since the underlying duties to be effectuated are entirely federal and Congress has expressed its preference of beneficiaries for violations of maritime law.

We do not determine this issue now, for we think its final resolution should await further sifting through the lower courts in future litigation. For present purposes we conclude only that its existence affords no sufficient reason for not coming to grips with *The Harrisburg*. If still other subsidiary issues should require resolution, such as particular questions of the measure of damages, the courts will not be without persuasive analogy for guidance. Both the Death on the High Seas Act and the numerous state wrongful-death acts have been implemented with success for decades. The experience thus built up counsels that a suit for wrongful death raises no problems unlike those that have long been grist for the judicial mill.

* * *

We accordingly overrule *The Harrisburg*, and hold that an action does lie under general maritime law for death caused by violation of maritime duties. The judgment of the Court of Appeals is reversed, and the case is remanded to that court for further proceedings consistent with this opinion.

It is so ordered.

Notes

1. *The Moragne Action*

The *Moragne* decision itself was concerned with death caused by unseaworthiness. However, the *Moragne* action also provides a remedy for wrongful death caused to a maritime worker by negligence within territorial waters. *Garris v. Norfolk Shipbuilding & Drydock Corp.*, 532 U.S. 811, 121 S. Ct. 1927, 2001 AMC 1817 (2001).

The *Moragne* action survives the death of the decedent. *McKeithen v. M/V Frosta*, 435 F. Supp. 584, 1978 AMC 51 (E.D. La. 1977). The claim gives rise to a maritime lien, and the suit may be brought *in rem* and *in personam. Palmer v. Ribax, Inc.*, 407 F. Supp. 974, 1976 AMC 1056 (M.D. Fla. 1976). Suit may be brought by a stepchild. *Spiller v. Lowe & Associates*, 466 F.2d 903 1972 AMC 2510 (8th Cir. 1972). It may also be brought by the parents of a seaman, even if the deceased is survived by closer relatives, such as children, legitimate or illegitimate, when the parents cannot recover under the Jones Act. *Hamilton v. Canal Barge Co.*, 395 F. Supp. 978 (E.D. La. 1975); *Palmer v. Ribax, Inc., supra.* A fiancée has no standing to sue under *Moragne. Hamilton v. Canal Barge Co., supra.* Questions of filiation in a *Moragne* suit are determined under state law, as incorporated into the maritime law. *In re Industrial Transportation Corp.*, 344 F. Supp. 1371, 1972 AMC 2380 (E.D.N.Y. 1972).

When a seaman is fatally injured in territorial waters, the *Moragne* action applies along with the Jones Act. Application of the *Moragne* action is particularly desirable when death results from unseaworthiness rather than negligence. *Ivy v. Security Barge Lines, Inc.*, 606 F.2d 524, 1980 AMC 356 (5th Cir. 1979). In any case, however, the Jones Act precludes recovery under the general maritime law for the non-pecuniary loss sustained by the seaman's survivors. *See Miles v. Apex Marine Corp.*, 498 U.S. 19, 111 S. Ct. 317, 112 L. Ed. 2d 275, 1991 AMC 1 (1990).

When a person dies in state territorial waters, the issue arises as to whether state law or rules of general maritime law govern the remedies for such action. In such circumstance, DOHSA only provides for deaths which occur on the high seas, and the Jones Act only provides for the wrongful deaths of seamen caused by employer negligence. After the enactment of DOHSA, the Supreme Court in *Moragne v. States Marine Lines*, 398 U.S. 375, 90 S. Ct. 1772, 26 L. Ed. 2d 339 (1970) provided a general maritime law cause of action for a longshoreman (Sieracki seaman) killed in the territorial waters of the United States.

In *Miles v. Apex Marine Corp., supra*, the Supreme Court "extended" the *Moragne* general maritime wrongful death action to seamen killed in territorial waters.

Subsequently, in *Norfolk Shipbuilding & Drydock Corp. v. Garris*, 532 U.S. 811, 121 S.Ct. 1927, 150 L. Ed. 2d 34, 2001 AMC 1817 (2001), the Supreme Court held that a general maritime law action for deaths that occur in state waters may be maintained for the negligent breach of a maritime duty of care. In other words, the Court extended *Moragne* which was an unseaworthiness case to apply to negligence actions as well.

Prior to *Moragne*, the Supreme Court had held that state wrongful death statutes could be invoked for deaths that occur in state waters under the "maritime but local" doctrine. *Western Fuels v. Garcia*, 257 U.S. 233 (1921). In fact, such actions could be brought in federal court under admiralty jurisdiction. These state wrongful death statutes were available to all classes of persons, including maritime workers, except that the Jones Act provided the exclusive remedy for seamen. *Lindgren v. United States*, 281 U.S. 38, 50 S.Ct. 207, 74 L.Ed. 686 (1930).

The question after *Moragne* was whether or not the general maritime law action created by *Moragne* displaced state law. *See Yamaha Motor Corp., U.S.A. v. Calhoun, infra.*

2. *DOHSA and the Moragne Action*

In *Mobil Oil Corp. v. Higginbotham*, 436 U.S. 618, 98 S. Ct. 2010, 56 L. Ed. 2d 581, (1978) the Supreme Court was faced with the question as to whether to extend *Moragne* and *Gaudet* line of authorities to a death on the high seas. The Court held that the congressionally provided remedy contained in the Death on the High Seas Act was the exclusive remedy and is not supplemented by the general maritime law.

YAMAHA MOTOR CORP., U.S.A. v. CALHOUN

516 U.S. 199, 116 S. Ct. 619, 133 L. Ed. 2d 578, 1996 AMC 305 (1996)

Justice GINSBURG delivered the opinion of the Court.

Twelve-year-old Natalie Calhoun was killed in a jet ski accident on July 6, 1989. At the time of her death, she was vacationing with family friends at a beach-front resort in Puerto Rico. Alleging that the jet ski was defectively designed or made, Natalie's parents sought to recover from the manufacturer pursuant to state survival and wrongful death statutes. The manufacturer contended that state remedies could not be applied because Natalie died on navigable waters; federal, judge-declared maritime law, the manufacturer urged, controlled to the exclusion of state law.

Traditionally, state remedies have been applied in accident cases of this order—maritime wrongful death cases in which no federal statute specifies the appropriate relief and the decedent was not a seaman, longshore worker, or person otherwise engaged in a maritime trade. We hold, in accord with the United States Court of Appeals for the Third Circuit, that state remedies remain applicable in such cases and have not been displaced by the federal maritime wrongful death action recognized in *Moragne v. States Marine Lines, Inc.*, 398 U.S. 375, 90 S. Ct. 1772, 26 L. Ed. 2d 339 (1970).

I

Natalie Calhoun, the twelve-year-old daughter of respondents Lucien and Robin Calhoun, died in a tragic accident on July 6, 1989. On vacation with family friends at a resort hotel in Puerto Rico, Natalie had rented a "WaveJammer" jet ski manufactured by Yamaha Motor Company, Ltd., and distributed by Yamaha Motor Corporation, U.S.A. (collectively, "Yamaha"), the petitioners in this case. While riding the WaveJammer, Natalie slammed into a vessel anchored in the waters off the hotel frontage, and was killed.

The Calhouns, individually and in their capacities as administrators of their daughter's estate, sued Yamaha in the United States District Court for the Eastern District of Pennsylvania. Invoking Pennsylvania's wrongful death and survival statutes, 42 Pa. Cons.Stat. §§ 8301-8302 (1982 and Supp. 1995), the Calhouns asserted several bases for recovery (including negligence, strict liability, and breach of implied warranties), and sought damages for lost future earnings, loss of society, loss of support and services, and funeral expenses, as well as punitive damages. They grounded federal jurisdiction on both diversity of citizenship, 28 U.S.C. § 1332,[1] and admiralty, 28 U.S.C. § 1333.

Yamaha moved for partial summary judgment, arguing that the federal maritime wrongful death action this Court recognized in *Moragne v. States Marine Lines, Inc.*, 398 U.S. 375, 90 S. Ct. 1772, 26 L. Ed. 2d 339 (1970), provided the exclusive basis for recovery, displacing all remedies afforded by state law. Under *Moragne*, Yamaha contended, the Calhouns could recover as damages only Natalie's funeral expenses. The District Court agreed with Yamaha that *Moragne's* maritime death action displaced state remedies; the court held, however, that loss of society and loss of support and services were compensable under *Moragne*.

* * *

Although the Court of Appeals granted the interlocutory review petition, the panel to which the appeal was assigned did not reach the questions presented in the certified order, for it determined that an anterior issue was pivotal. The District Court, as just recounted, had concluded that any damages the Calhouns might recover from Yamaha would be governed exclusively by federal maritime law. But the Third Circuit panel questioned that conclusion and inquired whether state wrongful death and survival statutes supplied the remedial prescriptions for the Calhouns' complaint. The appellate panel asked whether the state remedies endured or were "displaced by a federal maritime rule of decision." 40 F.3d 622, 624 (1994). Ultimately, the Court of Appeals ruled that state law remedies apply in this case. *Id.*, at 644.

---

[1] The Calhouns are citizens of Pennsylvania. Yamaha Motor Corporation, U.S.A. is incorporated and has its principal place of business in California; Yamaha Motor Company, Ltd. is incorporated and has its principal place of business in Japan.

II

* * *

We therefore proceed to the issue on which certiorari was granted: Does the federal maritime claim for wrongful death recognized in *Moragne* supply the exclusive remedy in cases involving the deaths of nonseafarer[2] in territorial waters?

III

Because this case involves a watercraft collision on navigable waters, it falls within admiralty's domain. *See Sisson v. Ruby*, 497 U.S. 358, 361-367, 110 S. Ct. 2892, 2895-2898, 111 L. Ed. 2d 292 (1990); *Foremost Ins. Co. v. Richardson*, 457 U.S. 668, 677, 102 S. Ct. 2654, 2659, 73 L. Ed. 2d 300 (1982). "With admiralty jurisdiction," we have often said, "comes the application of substantive admiralty law." *East River S.S. Corp. v. Transamerica Delaval Inc.*, 476 U.S. 858, 864, 106 S. Ct. 2295, 2298-2299, 90 L. Ed. 2d 865 (1986). The exercise of admiralty jurisdiction, however, "does not result in automatic displacement of state law." *Jerome B. Grubart, Inc. v. Great Lakes Dredge & Dock Co.*, 513 U.S. —, —, 115 S. Ct. 1043, 1046, 130 L. Ed. 2d 1024 (1995). Indeed, prior to *Moragne*, federal admiralty courts routinely applied state wrongful death and survival statutes in maritime accident cases.[3] The question before us is whether *Moragne* should be read to stop that practice.

Our review of maritime wrongful death law begins with *The Harrisburg*, 119 U.S. 199, 7 S. Ct. 140, 30 L. Ed. 358 (1886), where we held that the general maritime law (a species of judge-made federal common law) did not afford a cause of action for wrongful death. The *Harrisburg* Court said that wrongful death actions are statutory and may not be created by judicial decree. The Court did not question the soundness of this view, or examine the historical justifications that account for it. Instead, the Court merely noted that common law in the United States, like the common law of England, did not allow recovery "for an injury which results in death," *id.*, at 204, 7 S. Ct., at 142 (internal quotation marks omitted), and that no country had "adopted a different rule on this subject for the sea from that which it maintains on the land," *id.*, at 213, 7 S. Ct., at 146. The Court did not consider itself free to chart a different course by crafting a judge-made wrongful death action under our maritime law.

Federal admiralty courts tempered the harshness of *The Harrisburg's* rule by allowing recovery under state wrongful death statutes. *See, e.g., The Hamilton*, 207 U.S. 398, 28 S. Ct. 133, 52 L. Ed. 264 (1907); *The City of Norwalk*, 55 F. 98 (S.D.N.Y. 1893).[4] We reaffirmed this practice in *Western Fuel Co. v. Garcia*, 257 U.S. 233, 42 S. Ct. 89, 66 L. Ed. 210 (1921), by holding that California's wrongful death statute governed a suit brought by the widow of a maritime worker killed in that State's territorial waters. Though we had generally refused to give effect to state laws regarded as inconsonant with the substance of federal maritime law, we concluded that extending state wrongful death statutes to fatal accidents in territorial waters was compatible with substantive maritime policies: "The subject is maritime and local in character and the specified modification of or supplement to the rule applied in admiralty courts ... will not work material prejudice to the characteristic features of the general maritime law, nor interfere with the proper harmony and uniformity of that law in its international and interstate relations." *Id.*, at 242, 42 S. Ct., at 90.[5] On similar reasoning, we also held that state survival statutes may be applied in cases arising out of accidents in territorial waters. *See Just v. Chambers*, 312 U.S. 383, 391-392, 61 S. Ct. 687, 692-693, 85 L. Ed. 903 (1941).

---

[2] By "nonseafarers," we mean persons who are neither seamen covered by the Jones Act, 46 U.S.C. App. § 688 (1988 ed.), nor longshore workers covered by the Longshore and Harbor Workers' Compensation Act, 33 U.S.C. § 901 *et seq.*

[3] Throughout this opinion, for economy, we use the term wrongful death remedies or statutes to include survival statutes.

[4] Congress also mitigated the impact of *The Harrisburg* by enacting two statutes affording recovery for wrongful death. In 1920, Congress passed the Death on the High Seas Act (DOHSA), 46 U.S.C. App. § 761 *et seq.* (1988 ed.), which provides a federal claim for wrongful death occurring more than three nautical miles from the shore of any State or Territory. In that same year, Congress also passed the Jones Act, 46 U.S.C. App. § 688 (1988 ed.), which provides a wrongful death claim to the survivors of seamen killed in the course of their employment, whether on the high seas or in territorial waters.

[5] Indeed, years before *The Harrisburg*, this Court rendered a pathmarking decision, *Steamboat Co. v. Chase*, 83 U.S. 522, 21 L. Ed. 369, 16 Wall. 522 (1873). In *Steamboat*, the Court upheld, under the "saving-to-suitors" proviso of the Judiciary Act of 1789 (surviving currently in 28 U.S.C. § 1333(1)), a state court's application of the State's wrongful death statute to a fatality caused by a collision in territorial waters between defendants' steamboat and a sailboat in which plaintiff's decedent was passing.

State wrongful death statutes proved an adequate supplement to federal maritime law, until a series of this Court's decisions transformed the maritime doctrine of unseaworthiness into a strict liability rule. Prior to 1944, unseaworthiness "was an obscure and relatively little used" liability standard, largely because "a shipowner's duty at that time was only to use due diligence to provide a seaworthy ship." *Miles v. Apex Marine Corp.*, 498 U.S. 19, 25, 111 S. Ct. 317, 322, 112 L. Ed. 2d 275 (1990) (internal quotation marks omitted). *See also Moragne*, 398 U.S., at 398-399, 90 S. Ct., at 1786-1787. *Mahnich v. Southern S.S. Co.*, 321 U.S. 96, 64 S. Ct. 455, 88 L. Ed. 561 (1944), however, notably expanded a shipowner's liability to injured seamen by imposing a nondelegable duty "to furnish a vessel and appurtenances reasonably fit for their intended use." *Mitchell v. Trawler Racer, Inc.*, 362 U.S. 539, 550, 80 S. Ct. 926, 933, 4 L. Ed. 2d 941 (1960). The duty imposed was absolute; failure to supply a safe ship resulted in liability "irrespective of fault and irrespective of the intervening negligence of crew members." *Miles*, 498 U.S., at 25, 111 S. Ct., at 322. The unseaworthiness doctrine thus became a "species of liability without fault," *Seas Shipping Co. v. Sieracki*, 328 U.S. 85, 94, 66 S. Ct. 872, 877, 90 L. Ed. 1099 (1946), and soon eclipsed ordinary negligence as the primary basis of recovery when a seafarer was injured or killed. *Miles*, 498 U.S., at 25-26, 111 S. Ct., at 321-322.[6]

The disparity between the unseaworthiness doctrine's strict liability standard and negligence-based state wrongful death statutes figured prominently in our landmark *Moragne* decision. Petsonella Moragne, the widow of a longshore worker killed in Florida's territorial waters, brought suit under Florida's wrongful death and survival statutes, alleging both negligence and unseaworthiness. The district court dismissed the claim for wrongful death based on unseaworthiness, citing this Court's decision in *The Tungus v. Skovgaard*, 358 U.S. 588, 79 S. Ct. 503, 3 L. Ed. 2d 524 (1959). There, a sharply-divided Court held that "when admiralty adopts a State's right of action for wrongful death, it must enforce the right as an integrated whole, with whatever conditions and limitations the creating State has attached." *Id.*, at 592, 79 S. Ct., at 506. Thus, in wrongful death actions involving fatalities in territorial waters, state statutes provided the standard of liability as well as the remedial regime. Because the Florida Supreme Court had previously held that Florida's wrongful death statute did not encompass unseaworthiness as a basis of liability, the Court of Appeals affirmed the dismissal of *Moragne*'s unseaworthiness claim. *See Moragne*, 398 U.S., at 377, 90 S. Ct., at 1775-1776.

The Court acknowledged in *Moragne* that *The Tungus* had led to considerable uncertainty over the role state law should play in remedying deaths in territorial waters, but concluded that "the primary source of the confusion is not to be found in *The Tungus*, but in *The Harrisburg*." 398 U.S., at 378, 90 S. Ct., at 1776. Upon reexamining the soundness of *The Harrisburg*, we decided that its holding, "somewhat dubious even when rendered, is such an unjustifiable anomaly in the present maritime law that it should no longer be followed." 398 U.S., at 378, 90 S. Ct., at 1776. Accordingly, the Court overruled *The Harrisburg* and held that an action "lie[s] under general maritime law for death caused by violation of maritime duties." 398 U.S., at 409, 90 S. Ct., at 1792.

IV

Yamaha argues that *Moragne*—despite its focus on "maritime duties" owed to maritime workers—covers the waters, creating a uniform federal maritime remedy for all deaths occurring in state territorial waters, and ousting all previously available state remedies. In Yamaha's view, state remedies can no longer supplement general maritime law (as they routinely did before *Moragne*), because *Moragne* launched a solitary federal scheme.[7] Yamaha's reading of *Moragne* is not without force; in several contexts, we have recognized that

---

[6] The Court extended the duty to provide a seaworthy ship, once owed only to seamen, to longshore workers in *Seas Shipping Co. v. Sieracki*, 328 U.S. 85, 66 S. Ct. 872, 90 L. Ed. 1099 (1946). Congress effectively overruled this extension in its 1972 amendments to the Longshore and Harbor Workers' Compensation Act, 33 U.S.C. § 901 *et seq. See* 33 U.S.C. § 905(b). We have thus far declined to extend the duty further. *See Kermarec v. Compagnie Generale Transatlantique*, 358 U.S. 625, 629, 79 S. Ct. 406, 409, 3 L. Ed. 2d 550 (1959) (unseaworthiness doctrine inapplicable to invitee aboard vessel).

[7] If *Moragne*'s wrongful death action did not extend to nonseafarers like Natalie, one could hardly argue that Moragne displaced the state law remedies the Calhouns seek. Lower courts have held that *Moragne*'s wrongful death action extends to nonseafarers. *See, e.g., Sutton v. Earles*, 26 F.3d

vindication of maritime policies demanded uniform adherence to a federal rule of decision, with no leeway for variation or supplementation by state law. *See, e.g., Kossick v. United Fruit Co.*, 365 U.S. 731, 742, 81 S. Ct. 886, 894, 6 L. Ed. 2d 56 (1961) (federal maritime rule validating oral contracts precluded application of state Statute of Frauds); *Pope & Talbot, Inc. v. Hawn*, 346 U.S. 406, 409, 74 S. Ct. 202, 204-205, 98 L. Ed. 143 (1953) (admiralty's comparative negligence rule barred application of state contributory negligence rule); *Garrett v. Moore-McCormack Co.*, 317 U.S. 239, 248-249, 63 S. Ct. 246, 252-253, 87 L. Ed. 239 (1942) (federal maritime rule allocating burden of proof displaced conflicting state rule).[8] In addition, Yamaha correctly points out that uniformity concerns informed our decision in *Moragne*.

The uniformity concerns that prompted us to overrule *The Harrisburg*, however, were of a different order than those invoked by Yamaha. *Moragne* did not reexamine the soundness of *The Harrisburg* out of concern that state damage awards in maritime wrongful death cases were excessive, or that variations in the remedies afforded by the States threatened to interfere with the harmonious operation of maritime law. Variations of this sort had long been deemed compatible with federal maritime interests. *See Western Fuel*, 257 U.S., at 242, 42 S. Ct., at 90-91. The uniformity concern that drove our decision in *Moragne* related, instead, to the availability of unseaworthiness as a basis of liability.

By 1970, when *Moragne* was decided, claims premised on unseaworthiness had become "the principal vehicle for recovery" by seamen and other maritime workers injured or killed in the course of their employment. *Moragne*,

398 U.S., at 399, 90 S. Ct., at 1786-1787. But with *The Harrisburg* in place, troubling anomalies had developed that many times precluded the survivors of maritime workers from recovering for deaths caused by an unseaworthy vessel. The *Moragne* Court identified three anomalies and concluded they could no longer be tolerated.

First, the Court noted that "within territorial waters, identical conduct violating federal law (here the furnishing of an unseaworthy vessel) produces liability if the victim is merely injured, but frequently not if he is killed." *Id.*, at 395, 90 S. Ct., at 1785. This occurred because in nonfatal injury cases, state substantive liability standards were superseded by federal maritime law, *see Kermarec v. Compagnie Generale Transatlantique*, 358 U.S. 625, 628, 79 S. Ct. 406, 408-409, 3 L. Ed. 2d 550 (1959); *Pope & Talbot*, 346 U.S., at 409, 74 S. Ct., at 204-205, which provided for maritime worker recovery based on unseaworthiness. But if the same worker met death in the territorial waters of a State whose wrongful death statute did not encompass unseaworthiness (as was the case in *Moragne* itself), the survivors could not proceed under that generous standard of liability. *See The Tungus*, 358 U.S., at 592-593, 79 S. Ct., at 506-507.

Second, we explained in *Moragne* that "identical breaches of the duty to provide a seaworthy ship, resulting in death, produce liability outside the three-mile limit ... but not within the territorial waters of a State whose local statute excludes unseaworthiness claims." *Moragne*, 398 U.S., at 395, 90 S. Ct., at 1785. This occurred because survivors of a maritime worker killed on the high seas could sue for wrongful death under the Death on the High Seas Act (DOHSA), 46 U.S.C. App. § 761 *et seq.* (1988 ed.), which encompasses unseaworthiness as a basis of liability. *Moragne*, 398 U.S., at 395, 90 S. Ct., at 1784-1785 (*citing Kernan v. American Dredging Co.*, 355 U.S. 426, 430, n.4, 78 S. Ct. 394, 397 n.4, 2 L. Ed. 2d 382 (1958)).

---

903 (C.A. 9 1994) (recreational boater); *Wahlstrom v. Kawasaki Heavy Industries, Ltd.*, 4 F.3d 1084 (C.A. 2 1993) (jet skier), *cert. denied*, 510 U.S. —, 114 S. Ct. 1060, 127 L. Ed. 2d 380 (1994). We assume, for purposes of this decision, the correctness of that position. Similarly, as in prior encounters, we assume without deciding that *Moragne* also provides a survival action. *See Miles v. Apex Marine Corp.*, 498 U.S. 19, 34, 111 S. Ct. 317, 326-327, 112 L. Ed. 2d 275 (1990). The question we confront is not what *Moragne* added to the remedial arsenal in maritime cases, but what, if anything, it removed from admiralty's stock.

[8] The federal cast of admiralty law, we have observed, means that "state law must yield to the needs of a uniform federal maritime law when this Court finds inroads on a harmonious system[,] [b]ut this limitation still leaves the States a wide scope." *Romero v. International Terminal Operating Co.*, 358 U.S. 354, 373, 79 S. Ct. 468, 480, 3 L. Ed. 2d 368 (1959). Our precedent does not precisely delineate that scope. As we recently acknowledged, "[i]t would be idle to pretend that the line separating permissible from impermissible state regulation is readily discernible in our admiralty jurisprudence." *American Dredging Co. v. Miller*, 510 U.S. —, —, 114 S. Ct. 981, 987, 127 L. Ed. 2d 285 (1994). We attempt no grand synthesis or reconciliation of our precedent today, but confine our inquiry to the modest question whether it was *Moragne's* design to terminate recourse to state remedies when nonseafarers meet death in territorial waters.

Finally, we pointed out that "a true seaman [a member of a ship's company] ... is provided no remedy for death caused by unseaworthiness within territorial waters, while a longshoreman, to whom the duty of seaworthiness was extended only because he performs work traditionally done by seamen, does have such a remedy when allowed by a state statute." 398 U.S., at 395-396, 90 S. Ct., at 1785. This anomaly stemmed from the Court's rulings in *Lindgren v. United States*, 281 U.S. 38, 50 S. Ct. 207, 74 L. Ed. 686 (1930), and *Gillespie v. United States Steel Corp.*, 379 U.S. 148, 85 S. Ct. 308, 13 L. Ed. 2d 199 (1964), that the Jones Act, 46 U.S.C. App. § 688 (1988 ed.), which provides only a negligence-based claim for the wrongful death of seamen, precludes any state remedy, even one accommodating unseaworthiness. As a result, at the time *Moragne* was decided, the survivors of a longshore worker killed in the territorial waters of a State whose wrongful death statute incorporated unseaworthiness could sue under that theory, but the survivors of a similarly-situated seaman could not.[9]

The anomalies described in *Moragne* relate to ships and the workers who serve them, and to a distinctly maritime substantive concept—the unseaworthiness doctrine. The Court surely meant to "assure uniform vindication of federal policies," 398 U.S., at 401, 90 S. Ct., at 1788, with respect to the matters it examined. The law as it developed under *The Harrisburg* had forced on the States more than they could bear—the task of "provid[ing] the sole remedy" in cases that did not involve "traditional common-law concepts," but "concepts peculiar to maritime law." 398 U.S., at 401, n.15, 90 S. Ct., at 1788, n.15 (internal quotation marks omitted). Discarding *The Harrisburg* and declaring a wrongful death right of action under general maritime law, the Court concluded, would "remov[e] the tensions and discrepancies" occasioned by the need "to accommodate state remedial statutes to exclusively maritime substantive concepts." 398 U.S., at 401, 90 S. Ct., at 1788.[10]

Moragne, in sum, centered on the extension of relief, not on the contraction of remedies. The decision recalled that " 'it better becomes the humane and liberal character of proceedings in admiralty to give than to withhold the remedy, when not required to withhold it by established and inflexible rules.' " *Id.*, at 387, 90 S. Ct., at 1781 (quoting *The Sea Gull*, 21 F.Cas. 909, 910 (C.C. Md. 1865) (CHASE, C.J.)). The Court tied Petsonella Moragne's plea based on the unseaworthiness of the vessel to a federal right-of-action anchor,[11] but notably left in place the negligence claim she had stated under Florida's law. *See* 398 U.S., at 376-377, 90 S. Ct. at 1775-1776.[12]

Our understanding of *Moragne* accords with that of the Third Circuit, which Judge Becker set out as follows:

Moragne ... showed no hostility to concurrent application of state wrongful death statutes. Indeed, to read into *Moragne* the idea that it was placing a ceiling on recovery for wrongful death, rather than a floor, is somewhat ahistorical. The *Moragne* cause of action was in many respects a gap-filling measure to ensure that seamen (and their survivors) would all be treated alike. The 'humane and liberal' purpose underlying the general maritime remedy of *Moragne* was driven by the idea that survivors of seamen killed in state territorial waters should not have been barred from recovery simply because the tort system of the particular state in which a seaman died did not

---

[9] As noted earlier, unseaworthiness recovery by longshore workers was terminated by Congress in its 1972 amendments to the Longshore and Harbor Workers' Compensation Act, 33 U.S.C. § 901 *et seq*. *See* 33 U.S.C. § 905(b).

[10] The Court might have simply overruled *The Tungus, see supra* pp. 624-625, thus permitting plaintiffs to rely on federal liability standards to obtain state wrongful death remedies. The petitioner in *Moragne*, widow of a longshore worker, had urged that course when she sought certiorari. *See Moragne v. States Marine Lines, Inc.*, 398 U.S. 375, 378, n.1, 90 S. Ct. 1772, 1776, n.1, 26 L. Ed. 2d 339 (1970). But training *Moragne* solely on *The Tungus* would have left untouched the survivors of seamen, who remain blocked by the Jones Act from pursuing state wrongful death claims—whether under a theory of negligence or unseaworthiness. *See Gillespie v. United States Steel Corp.*, 379 U.S. 148, 154-155, 85 S. Ct. 308, 312-313, 13 L. Ed. 2d 199 (1964). Thus, nothing short of a federal maritime right of action for wrongful death could have achieved uniform access by seafarers to the unseaworthiness doctrine, the Court's driving concern in *Moragne*. *See* 398 U.S., at 396, n.12, 90 S. Ct., at 1785, n.12.

[11] While unseaworthiness was the doctrine immediately at stake in *Moragne*, the right of action, as stated in the Court's opinion, is "for death caused by violation of maritime duties." *Moragne*, 398 U.S., at 409, 90 S. Ct., at 1792. *See East River S.S. Corp. v. Transamerica Delaval Inc.*, 476 U.S. 858, 865, 106 S. Ct. 2295, 2299, 90 L. Ed. 2d 865 (1986) (maritime law incorporates strict product liability); *Kermarec*, 358 U.S., at 630, 79 S. Ct., at 409-410 (negligence). *See also* G. GILMORE & C. BLACK, THE LAW OF ADMIRALTY 368 (2d ed.1975).

[12] *Moragne* was entertained by the Court of Appeals pursuant to a 28 U.S.C. § 1292(b) certification directed to the District Court's order dismissing the unseaworthiness claim. *See* 398 U.S., at 376, 90 S. Ct., at 1775.

incorporate special maritime doctrines. It is difficult to see how this purpose can be taken as an intent to preclude the operation of state laws that do supply a remedy. 40 F.3d, at 641-642 (citation omitted).

We have reasoned similarly in *Sun Ship, Inc. v. Pennsylvania*, 447 U.S. 715, 100 S. Ct. 2432, 65 L. Ed. 2d 458 (1980), where we held that a State may apply its workers' compensation scheme to land-based injuries that fall within the compass of the Longshore and Harbor Workers' Compensation Act, 33 U.S.C. § 901 *et seq. See Sun Ship*, 447 U.S., at 724, 100 S. Ct., at 2438-2439 (a State's remedial scheme might be "more generous than federal law" but nevertheless could apply because Congress indicated no concern "about a disparity between adequate federal benefits and superior state benefits") (emphasis in original).[13]

When Congress has prescribed a comprehensive tort recovery regime to be uniformly applied, there is, we have generally recognized, no cause for enlargement of the damages statutorily provided. *See Miles*, 498 U.S., at 30-36, 111 S. Ct., at 324-328 (Jones Act, rather than general maritime law, determines damages recoverable in action for wrongful death of seamen); *Offshore Logistics, Inc. v. Tallentire*, 477 U.S. 207, 232, 106 S. Ct. 2485, 2499, 91 L. Ed. 2d 174 (1986) (DOHSA, which limits damages to pecuniary losses, may not be supplemented by nonpecuniary damages under a state wrongful death statute); *Mobil Oil Corp. v. Higginbotham*, 436 U.S. 618, 624-625, 98 S. Ct. 2010, 2014-2015, 56 L. Ed. 2d 581 (1978) (DOHSA precludes damages for loss of society under general maritime law). But Congress has not prescribed remedies for the wrongful deaths of nonseafarers in territorial waters. *See Miles*, 498 U.S., at 31, 111 S. Ct., at 325. There is, however, a relevant congressional disposition. Section 7 of DOHSA states: "The provisions of any State statute giving or regulating rights of action or remedies for death shall not be affected by this chapter." 46 U.S.C. App. § 767. This statement, by its terms, simply stops DOHSA from displacing state law in territorial waters. *See Miles*, 498 U.S., at 25, 111 S. Ct., at 321-322; *Tallentire*, 477 U.S., at 224-225, 106 S. Ct., at 2495-2496; *Moragne*, 398 U.S., at 397-398, 90 S. Ct., at 1785-1786. Taking into account what Congress sought to achieve, we preserve the application of state statutes to deaths within territorial waters.

* * *

For the reasons stated, we hold that the damages available for the jet ski death of Natalie Calhoun are properly governed by state law.[14] The judgment of the Court of Appeals for the Third Circuit is accordingly
Affirmed.

Note

1. The Supreme Court in *Calhoun* left open the question of *which* state law would govern the remedies available. On remand, the District Court held, and on appeal, the Third Circuit confirmed, that Pennsylvania law governed the determination of compensatory damages, Puerto Rico law governed determination of punitive damages, and federal maritime law governed determination of liability. *Calhoun v. Yamaha Motor Corp., U.S.A.*, 216 F.3d 338, 2000 AMC 1865 (3d Cir. 2000). This determination proved fatal to the bulk of the parents' claim, because Puerto Rico law

---

[13] Federal maritime law has long accommodated the States' interest in regulating maritime affairs within their territorial waters. *See, e.g., Just v. Chambers*, 312 U.S. 383, 390, 61 S. Ct. 687, 692, 85 L. Ed. 903 (1941) ("maritime law [is] not a complete and perfect system"; "a considerable body of municipal law ... underlies ... its administration"). States have thus traditionally contributed to the provision of environmental and safety standards for maritime activities. *See, e.g., Askew v. American Waterways Operators, Inc.*, 411 U.S. 325, 93 S. Ct. 1590, 36 L. Ed. 2d 280 (1973) (oil pollution); *Huron Portland Cement Co. v. Detroit*, 362 U.S. 440, 80 S. Ct. 813, 4 L. Ed. 2d 852 (1960) (air pollution); *Kelly v. Washington ex rel. Foss Co.*, 302 U.S. 1, 58 S. Ct. 87, 82 L. Ed. 3 (1937) (safety inspection); *Cooley v. Board of Wardens of Port of Philadelphia ex rel. Soc. for Relief of Distressed Pilots*, 53 U.S. 299, 13 L. Ed. 996, 12 How. 299 (1852) (pilotage regulation). Permissible state regulation, we have recognized, must be consistent with federal maritime principles and policies. *See Romero*, 358 U.S., at 373-374, 79 S. Ct., at 480-481.

[14] The Third Circuit left for initial consideration by the District Court the question whether Pennsylvania's wrongful death remedies or Puerto Rico's apply. 40 F.3d 622, 644 (1994). The Court of Appeals also left open, as do we, the source—federal or state—of the standards governing liability, as distinguished from the rules on remedies. We thus reserve for another day reconciliation of the maritime personal injury decisions that rejected state substantive liability standards, and the maritime wrongful death cases in which state law has held sway. *Compare Kermarec*, 358 U.S., at 628, 79 S. Ct., at 408-409 (personal injury); *Pope & Talbot, Inc. v. Hawn*, 346 U.S. 406, 409, 74 S. Ct. 202, 204-205, 98 L. Ed. 143 (1953) (same), with *Hess v. United States*, 361 U.S. 314, 319, 80 S. Ct. 341, 345-346, 4 L. Ed. 2d 305 (1960) (wrongful death); *The Tungus v. Skovgaard*, 358 U.S. 588, 592-594, 79 S. Ct. 503, 506-508, 3 L. Ed. 2d 524 (1959) (same).

does not permit the award of punitive damages. The Calhouns applied to the Supreme Court again for certiorari, but this time they were unsuccessful (*Calhoun v.. Yamaha Motor Corp., U.S.A.*, 531 U.S. 1037, 121 S. Ct. 627 (2000)) despite an application for rehearing of the cert. application (*Calhoun v.. Yamaha Motor Corp., U.S.A.*, 531 U.S. 1105, 121 S. Ct. 797 (2001)). When the suit finally went to trial, the jury entered a verdict for the defendant, holding that the jet ski was not a defective product. The Calhouns appealed unsuccessfully. *Calhoun v.. Yamaha Motor Corp., U.S.A.*, 350 F.3d 316 (3d Cir. 2003). Thus, the 14-year saga of their lawsuit ended with them receiving no damages for Natalie Calhoun's death.

2. Following *Calhoun*, the Court of Appeals for the Eleventh Circuit approved application of Florida law, which allows recovery of non-pecuniary damages, in a wrongful death action where a non-seaman was killed in state waters. *American Dredging Co. v.. Lambert*, 81 F.3d 127, 1996 AMC 2929 (11th Cir. 1996). However, state law provides only the remedy; uniformity demands that federal general maritime law determines the standard of liability. *In re Amtrak "Sunset, Ltd.." Train Crash*, 121 F.3d 1421, 1997 AMC 2962 (11th Cir. 1997); *Calhoun v.. Yamaha Motor Corp., U.S.A.*, 216 F3d 338, 2000 AMC 1865 (3d Cir. 2000). Thus, in *In re Amtrak*, the Eleventh Circuit held that although punitive damages where available under Alabama state law to non-seafarers killed in state waters, the standard of liability for recovery of those punitive damages was determined by federal law ("intentional or wanton and reckless conduct" necessary), rather than Alabama state law (by which simple negligence sufficed).

B. Survival Actions

DOOLEY v. KOREAN AIR LINES CO., LTD.
524 U.S. 116, 118 S. Ct. 1890, 141 L. Ed. 2d 102, 1998 AMC 1940 (1998)

Justice THOMAS delivered the opinion of the Court.

In a case of death on the high seas, the Death on the High Seas Act, 46 U.S.C.App. § 761 *et seq.*, allows certain relatives of the decedent to sue for their pecuniary losses, but does not authorize recovery for the decedent's pre-death pain and suffering. This case presents the question whether those relatives may nevertheless recover such damages through a survival action under general maritime law. We hold that they may not.

I

On September 1, 1983, Korean Air Lines Flight KE007, en route from Anchorage, Alaska, to Seoul, South Korea, strayed into the airspace of the former Soviet Union and was shot down over the Sea of Japan. All 269 people on board were killed.

Petitioners, the personal representatives of three of the passengers, brought lawsuits against respondent Korean Air Lines Co., Ltd. (KAL), in the United States District Court for the District of Columbia. These cases were consolidated in that court, along with the other federal actions arising out of the crash. After trial, a jury found that KAL had committed "willful misconduct," thus removing the Warsaw Convention's $75,000 cap on damages, and in a subsequent verdict awarded $50 million in punitive damages. The Court of Appeals for the District of Columbia Circuit upheld the finding of willful misconduct, but vacated the punitive damages award on the ground that the Warsaw Convention does not permit the recovery of punitive damages. *In re Korean Air Lines Disaster of Sept. 1, 1983*, 932 F.2d 1475, *cert. denied*, 502 U.S. 994, 112 S. Ct. 616, 116 L.Ed.2d 638 (1991).

The Judicial Panel on Multidistrict Litigation thereafter remanded, for damages trials, all of the individual cases to the District Courts in which they had been filed. In petitioners' cases, KAL moved for a pretrial determination that the Death on the High Seas Act (DOHSA), 46 U.S.C.App. § 761 *et seq.*, provides the exclusive source of recoverable damages. DOHSA provides in relevant part:

> "Whenever the death of a person shall be caused by wrongful act, neglect, or default occurring on the high seas beyond a marine league from the shore of any State, or the District of Columbia, or the Territories or dependencies of the United States, the personal representative of the decedent may maintain a suit for damages in the district courts of the United States, in admiralty, for the exclusive benefit of the decedent's wife, husband, parent, child or dependent relative ..." § 761.

> "The recovery in such suit shall be a fair and just compensation for the pecuniary

loss sustained by the persons for whose benefit the suit is brought ..." § 762.

KAL argued that, in a case of death on the high seas, DOHSA provides the exclusive cause of action and does not permit damages for loss of society, survivors' grief, and decedents' pre-death pain and suffering. The District Court for the District of Columbia disagreed, holding that because petitioners' claims were brought pursuant to the Warsaw Convention, DOHSA could not limit the recoverable damages. The Court determined that Article 17 of the Warsaw Convention "allows for the recovery of all 'damages sustained,'" meaning any "actual harm" that any party "experienced" as a result of the crash. App. 59.

While petitioners' cases were awaiting damages trials, we reached a different conclusion in *Zicherman v. Korean Air Lines Co.*, 516 U.S. 217, 116 S.Ct. 629, 133 L.Ed.2d 596 (1996), another case arising out of the downing of Flight KE007.

[Remainder of this page is intentionally blank.]

In *Zicherman*, we held that the Warsaw Convention "permit[s] compensation only for legally cognizable harm, but leave[s] the specification of what harm is legally cognizable to the domestic law applicable under the forum's choice-of-law rules," and that where "an airplane crash occurs on the high seas, DOHSA supplies the substantive United States law." *Id.*, at 231, 116 S.Ct., at 637. Accordingly, the petitioners could not recover damages for loss of society: "[W]here DOHSA applies, neither state law, *see Offshore Logistics, Inc. v. Tallentire*, 477 U.S. 207, 232-233, 106 S.Ct. 2485, 2499-2500, 91 L.Ed.2d 174 (1986), nor general maritime law, *see Mobil Oil Corp. v. Higgginbotham*, 436 U.S. 618, 625-626, 98 S.Ct. 2010, 2015, 56 L.Ed.2d 581 (1978), can provide a basis for recovery of loss-of-society damages." *Id.*, at 230, 106 S.Ct., at 2498. We did not decide, however, whether the petitioners in *Zicherman* could recover for their decedents' pre-death pain and suffering, as KAL had not raised this issue in its petition for certiorari. *See id.*, at 230, n.4, 116 S.Ct., at 636, n.4.

After the *Zicherman* decision, KAL again moved to dismiss all of petitioners' claims for nonpecuniary damages. The District Court granted this motion, holding that United States law (not South Korean law) governed these cases; that DOHSA provides the applicable United States law; and that DOHSA does not permit the recovery of nonpecuniary damages—including petitioners' claims for their decedents' pre-death pain and suffering. *In Re Korean Air Lines Disaster of Sept. 1, 1983*, 935 F.Supp. 10, 12-15 (1996).

On appeal, petitioners argued that although DOHSA does not itself permit recovery for a decedent's pre-death pain and suffering, general maritime law provides a survival action that allows a decedent's estate to recover for injuries (including pre-death pain and suffering) suffered by the decedent. The Court of Appeals rejected this argument and affirmed. *In Re Korean Air Lines Disaster of Sept. 1, 1983*, 117 F.3d 1477 (C.A.D.C.1997). Assuming arguendo that there is a survival cause of action under general maritime law, the court held that such an action is unavailable when the death is on the high seas:

> For deaths on the high seas, Congress decided who may sue and for what. Judge-made general maritime law may not override such congressional judgments, however ancient those judgments may happen to be. Congress made the law and it is up to Congress to change it. *Id.*, at 1481.

We granted certiorari, 522 U.S. ___, 118 S.Ct. 679, 139 L.Ed.2d 628 (1998), to resolve a Circuit split concerning the availability of a general maritime survival action in cases of death on the high seas. *Compare, e.g., In Re Korean Air Lines Disaster*, 117 F.3d, at 1481, *with Gray v. Lockheed Aeronautical Systems Co.*, 125 F.3d 1371, 1385 (C.A.11 1997).

II

Before Congress enacted DOHSA in 1920, the general law of admiralty permitted a person injured by tortious conduct to sue for damages, but did not permit an action to be brought when the person was killed by that conduct. *See generally* R. HUGHES, HANDBOOK OF ADMIRALTY LAW 222-223 (2d ed.1920). This rule stemmed from the theory that a right of action was personal to the victim and thus expired when the victim died. Accordingly, in the absence of an act of Congress or state statute providing a right of action, a suit in admiralty could not be maintained in the courts of the United States to recover damages for a person's death. *See The Harrisburg*, 119 U.S. 199, 213, 7 S.Ct. 140, 146-147, 30 L.Ed. 358 (1886); *The Alaska*, 130 U.S. 201, 209, 9 S.Ct. 461, 463, 32 L.Ed. 923 (1889).[1]

Congress passed such a statute, and thus authorized recovery for deaths on the high seas, with its enactment of DOHSA. DOHSA provides a cause of action for "the death of a person ... caused by wrongful act, neglect, or default occurring on the high seas," § 761; this action must be brought by the decedent's personal representative "for the exclusive benefit of the decedent's wife, husband, parent, child, or dependent relative," *ibid.* The Act limits recovery in such a suit to "a fair and just compensation for the pecuniary loss sustained by the persons for whose benefit the suit is sought." § 762. DOHSA also includes a limited survival provision: In situations in which a person injured on the high seas sues for his injuries and then dies prior to completion of the suit, "the personal representative of the decedent may be substituted as a party and the suit may proceed as a suit under this chapter for the recovery of the compensation provided in section 762." § 765. Other sections establish a limitations period, § 763a, govern actions under foreign law, § 764, bar contributory negligence as a complete defense, § 766, exempt the Great Lakes, navigable waters in the Panama Canal Zone, and state territorial waters from the Act's coverage, § 767, and preserve certain state law remedies and state court jurisdiction, *ibid.* DOHSA does not authorize recovery for the decedent's own losses, nor does it allow damages for non-pecuniary losses.In *Mobil Oil Corp. v. Higginbotham*, 436 U.S. 618, 98 S.Ct. 2010, 56 L.Ed.2d 581 (1978), we considered whether, in a case of death on the high seas, a decedent's survivors could recover damages under general maritime law for their loss of society. We held that they could not, and thus limited to territorial waters those cases in which we had permitted loss of society damages under general maritime law. *Id.*, at 622-624, 98 S.Ct., at 2013-2014; see n. 1, *supra*. For deaths on the high seas, DOHSA "announces Congress' considered judgment on such issues as the beneficiaries, the limitations period, contributory negligence, survival, and damages." 436 U.S., at 625, 98 S.Ct., at 2015. We thus noted that while we could "fil[l] a gap left by Congress' silence," we were not free to "rewrit[e] rules that Congress has affirmatively and specifically enacted." *Ibid.* Because "Congress ha[d] struck the balance for us" in DOHSA by limiting the available recovery to pecuniary losses suffered by surviving relatives, *id.*, at 623, 98 S.Ct., at 2014, we had "no authority to substitute our views for those expressed by Congress." *Id.*, at 626, 98 S.Ct., at 2015. Higginbotham, however, involved only the scope of the remedies available in a wrongful death action, and thus did not address the availability of other causes of action.

Conceding that DOHSA does not authorize recovery for a decedent's pre- death pain and suffering, petitioners seek to recover such damages through a general maritime survival action. Petitioners argue that general maritime law recognizes a survival action, which permits a decedent's estate to recover damages that the decedent would have been able to recover but for his death, including pre-death pain and suffering. And, they contend, because DOHSA is a wrongful death statute—giving surviving relatives a cause of action for losses they suffered as a result of the decedent's death—it has no bearing on the availability of a survival action.

We disagree. DOHSA expresses Congress' judgment that there should be no such cause of action in cases of death on the high seas. By authorizing only certain surviving relatives to recover damages, and by limiting damages to the pecuniary losses sustained by those relatives, Congress provided the exclusive recovery for deaths that occur on the high seas. Petitioners concede that their proposed survival action would necessarily expand the class of beneficia-

---

[1] We later rejected this rule in *Moragne v. States Marine Lines, Inc.*, 398 U.S. 375, 408-409, 90 S.Ct. 1772, 1791-1792, 26 L.Ed.2d 339 (1970), by overruling *The Harrisburg*, 119 U.S. 199, 7 S.Ct. 140, 30 L.Ed. 358 (1886), and holding that a federal remedy for wrongful death exists under general maritime law. In *Sea-Land Services, Inc. v. Gaudet*, 414 U.S. 573, 574, 94 S.Ct. 806, 809-810, 39 L.Ed.2d 9 (1974), we further held that such wrongful death awards could include compensation for loss of support and services and for loss of society.

ries in cases of death on the high seas by permitting decedents' estates (and their various beneficiaries) to recover compensation. They further concede that their cause of action would expand the recoverable damages for deaths on the high seas by permitting the recovery of non-pecuniary losses, such as pre-death pain and suffering. Because Congress has already decided these issues, it has precluded the judiciary from enlarging either the class of beneficiaries or the recoverable damages. As we noted in *Higginbotham*, "Congress did not limit DOHSA beneficiaries to recovery of their pecuniary losses in order to encourage the creation of nonpecuniary supplements." 436 U.S., at 625, 98 S.Ct., at 2015.

The comprehensive scope of DOHSA is confirmed by its survival provision, see supra, at 1894, which limits the recovery in such cases to the pecuniary losses suffered by surviving relatives. The Act thus expresses Congress' "considered judgment," *Mobil Oil Corp. v. Higginbotham, supra*, at 625, 98 S.Ct., at 2015, on the availability and contours of a survival action in cases of death on the high seas. For this reason, it cannot be contended that DOHSA has no bearing on survival actions; rather, Congress has simply chosen to adopt a more limited survival provision. Indeed, Congress did so in the same year that it incorporated into the Jones Act, which permits seamen injured in the course of their employment to recover damages for their injuries, a survival action similar to the one petitioners seek here. *See* Act of June 5, 1920, § 33, 41 Stat. 1007 (incorporating survival action of the Federal Employers' Liability Act, 45 U.S.C. § 59). Even in the exercise of our admiralty jurisdiction, we will not upset the balance struck by Congress by authorizing a cause of action with which Congress was certainly familiar but nonetheless declined to adopt.

In sum, Congress has spoken on the availability of a survival action, the losses to be recovered, and the beneficiaries, in cases of death on the high seas. Because Congress has chosen not to authorize a survival action for a decedent's pre-death pain and suffering, there can be no general maritime survival action for such damages.[2] The judgment of the Court of Appeals is

Affirmed.

Note

Although *Dooley* did not expressly reject the possibility that DOHSA could be supplemented by a *State* survival action (as opposed to a general maritime law one) that was implicit. See *Jacobs v. Northern King Shipping Co., Ltd.*, 180 F.3d 713, 1999 AMC 2341 (5th Cir. 1999). *Offshore Logistics v. Tallentire, supra*, had previously held that DOHSA pre-empted recovery of non-pecuniary losses under State *wrongful death* states. *Tallentire* left open the possibility of a state *survival* action supplementing DOHSA, but that possibility has been foreclosed by *Jacobs*.

C. Restrictions on Damages

MILES v. APEX MARINE CORP.

498 U.S. 19, 111 S. Ct. 317, 112 L. Ed. 2d 275, 1991 AMC 1 (1990)

Justice O'CONNOR delivered the opinion of the Court.

We decide whether the parent of a seaman who died from injuries incurred aboard respondents' vessel may recover under general maritime law for loss of society, and whether a claim for the seaman's lost future earnings survives his death.

I.

Ludwick Torregano was a seaman aboard the vessel *M/V Archon*. On the evening of July 18, 1984, Clifford Melrose, a fellow crew member, stabbed Torregano repeatedly, killing him. At the time, the ship was docked in the harbor of Vancouver, Washington.

---

[2] Accordingly, we need not decide whether general maritime law ever provides a survival action.

Mercedel Miles, Torregano's mother and administratrix of his estate, sued Apex Marine Corporation and Westchester Marine Shipping Company, the vessel's operators, Archon Marine Company, the charterer, and Aeron Marine Company, the *Archon's* owner (collectively Apex), in United States District Court for the Eastern District of Louisiana. Miles alleged negligence under the Jones Act, 46 U.S.C. App. § 688, for failure to prevent the assault on her son, and breach of the warranty of seaworthiness under general maritime law for hiring a crew member unfit to serve. She sought compensation for loss of support and services and loss of society resulting from the death of her son, punitive damages, and compensation to the estate for Torregano's pain and suffering prior to his death and for his lost future income.

At trial, the District Court granted Apex's motion to strike the claim for punitive damages, ruled that the estate could not recover Torregano's lost future income, and denied Miles' motion for a directed verdict as to negligence and unseaworthiness. The court instructed the jury that Miles could not recover damages for loss of society if they found that she was not financially dependent on her son.

The jury found that Apex was negligent and that Torregano was 7% contributorily negligent in causing his death, but that the ship was seaworthy. After discounting for Torregano's contributory negligence, the jury awarded Miles $7,254 for the loss of support and services of her son and awarded the estate $130,200 for Torregano's pain and suffering. The jury also found that Miles was not financially dependent on her son and therefore not entitled to damages for loss of society. The District Court denied both parties' motions for judgment notwithstanding the verdict and entered judgment accordingly.

The United States Court of Appeals for the Fifth Circuit affirmed in part, reversed in part, and remanded. 882 F.2d 976 (1989). The court affirmed the judgment of negligence on the part of Apex, but held that there was insufficient evidence to support the contributory negligence finding. *Id.*, at 983-985. Miles was therefore entitled to the full measure of $7,800 for loss of support and services, and the estate entitled to $140,000 for Torregano's pain and suffering. The court also found that Melrose's extraordinarily violent disposition demonstrated that he was unfit, and therefore that the Archon was unseaworthy as a matter of law. *Id.*, at 983. Because this ruling revived Miles' general maritime claim, the court considered two questions concerning the scope of damages under general maritime law. The court reaffirmed its prior decision in *Sistrunk v. Circle Bar Drilling Co.*, 770 F.2d 455 (CA5 1985), holding that a nondependent parent may not recover for loss of society in a general maritime wrongful death action. 882 F.2d, at 989. It also held that general maritime law does not permit a survival action for decedent's lost future earnings. *Id.*, at 987.

We granted Miles' petition for certiorari on these two issues, 494 U.S. —, 110 S. Ct. 1295, 108 L. Ed. 2d 472 (1990), and now affirm the judgment of the Court of Appeals.

II.

We rely primarily on *Moragne v. States Marine Lines, Inc.*, 398 U.S. 375 , 90 S. Ct. 1772, 26 L. Ed. 2d 339 (1970).

* * *

III.

* * *

The Jones Act provides an action in negligence for the death or injury of a seaman. It thereby overruled *The Osceola*, 189 U.S. 158, 23 S. Ct. 483, 47 L. Ed. 760 (1903), which established that seamen could recover under general maritime law for injuries resulting from unseaworthiness, but not negligence. The Jones Act evinces no general hostility to recovery under maritime law. It does not disturb seamen's general maritime claims for injuries resulting from unseaworthiness, *Pacific Steamship Co. v. Peterson*, 278 U.S. 130, 139, 49 S. Ct. 75, 78, 73 L. Ed. 220 (1928), and it does not preclude the recovery for wrongful death due to unseaworthiness created by its companion statute DOHSA. *Kernan v. American Dredging Co.*, 355 U.S. 426, 430, n.4, 78 S. Ct. 394, 397, n.4, 2 L. Ed. 2d 382 (1958). Rather, the Jones Act establishes a uniform system of seamen's tort law parallel to that available to employees of interstate railway carriers under FELA. As the Court concluded in *Moragne*, the extension of the DOHSA wrongful death action to territorial waters furthers rather than hinders uniformity in the exercise of admiralty jurisdiction. *Moragne, supra*, 398 U.S., at 396, n.12, 90 S. Ct., at 1785, n.12.

There is also little question that *Moragne* intended to create a general maritime wrongful death action applicable beyond the situation of longshoremen. For one thing, *Moragne* explicitly overruled *The Harrisburg. Moragne, supra*, 398 U.S., at 409, 90 S. Ct., at 1792. *The Harrisburg* involved a true seaman. *The Harrisburg*, 119 U.S., at 200, 7 S. Ct., at 141. In addition, all three of the "anomalies" to which the *Moragne* cause of action was directed involved seamen. The "strangest" anomaly—that recovery was available for the wrongful death in territorial waters of a longshoreman, but not a true seaman—could only be remedied if the *Moragne* wrongful death action extended to seamen. It would be strange indeed were we to read *Moragne* as not addressing a problem that in large part motivated its result. If there has been any doubt about the matter, we today make explicit that there is a general maritime cause of action for the wrongful death of a seaman, adopting the reasoning of the unanimous and carefully crafted opinion in *Moragne*.

IV.

Moragne did not set forth the scope of the damages recoverable under the maritime wrongful death action. The Court first considered that question in *Sea-Land Services, Inc. v. Gaudet*, 414 U.S. 573, 94 S. Ct. 806, 39 L. Ed. 2d 9 (1974). Respondent brought a general maritime action to recover for the wrongful death of her husband, a longshoreman. The Court held that a dependent plaintiff in a maritime wrongful death action could recover for the pecuniary losses of support, services, and funeral expenses, as well as for the nonpecuniary loss of society suffered as the result of the death. *Id.*, at 591, 94 S. Ct., at 818. *Gaudet* involved the death of a longshoreman in territorial waters.[1] Consequently, the Court had no need to consider the preclusive effect of DOHSA for deaths on the high seas, or the Jones Act for deaths of true seamen.

We considered DOHSA in *Mobil Oil Corp. v. Higginbotham*, 436 U.S. 618, 98 S. Ct. 2010, 56 L. Ed. 2d 581 (1978). That case involved death on the high seas and, like *Gaudet*, presented the question of loss of society damages in a maritime wrongful death action. The Court began by recognizing that *Gaudet*, although broadly written, applied only in territorial waters and therefore did not decide the precise question presented. *Id.*, at 622-623, 98 S. Ct., at 2013-2014. Congress made the decision for us. DOHSA, by its terms, limits recoverable damages in wrongful death suits to "*pecuniary* loss sustained by the persons for whose benefit the suit is brought." 46 U.S.C. App. § 762 (emphasis added). This explicit limitation forecloses recovery for non-pecuniary loss, such as loss of society, in a general maritime action.

Respondents argued that admiralty courts have traditionally undertaken to supplement maritime statutes. The Court's answer in *Higginbotham* is fully consistent with those principles we have here derived from *Moragne*: Congress has spoken directly to the question of recoverable damages on the high seas, and "when it does speak directly to a question, the courts are not free to 'supplement' Congress' answer so thoroughly that the Act becomes meaningless." *Higginbotham, supra*, at 625, 98 S. Ct., at 2015. *Moragne* involved gap-filling in an area left open by statute; supplementation was entirely appropriate. But in an "area covered by the statute, it would be no more appropriate to prescribe a different measure of damages than to prescribe a different statute of limitations, or a different class of beneficiaries." *Higginbotham, supra*, at 625, 98 S. Ct., at 2015.

The logic of *Higginbotham* controls our decision here. The holding of Gaudet applies only in territorial waters, and it applies only to longshoremen. *Gaudet* did not consider the preclusive effect of the Jones Act for deaths of true seamen. We do so now.

Unlike DOHSA, the Jones Act does not explicitly limit damages to any particular form. Enacted in 1920, the Jones Act makes applicable to seamen the substantive recovery provisions of the older FELA. *See* 46 U.S.C. App. § 688. FELA recites only that employers shall be liable in "damages" for the injury or death of one protected under the

---

[1] As with *Moragne*, the 1972 amendments to LHWCA have rendered *Gaudet* inapplicable on its facts. *See supra*, at 323; 33 U.S.C. § 905(b). Suit in *Gaudet* was filed before 1972. *Gaudet v. Sea-Land Services, Inc.*, 463 F.2d 1331, 1332 (CA 5 1972).

Act. 45 U.S.C. § 51. In *Michigan Central R. Co. v. Vreeland*, 227 U.S. 59, 33 S. Ct. 192, 57 L. Ed. 417 (1913), however, the Court explained that the language of the FELA wrongful death provision is essentially identical to that of Lord Campbell's Act, 9 & 10 Vict. ch. 93 (1846), the first wrongful death statute. Lord Campbell's Act also did not limit explicitly the "damages" to be recovered, but that Act and the many state statutes that followed it consistently had been interpreted as providing recovery only for pecuniary loss. *Vreeland, supra*, at 69-71. The Court so construed FELA. *Ibid.*

When Congress passed the Jones Act, the *Vreeland* gloss on FELA, and the hoary tradition behind it, were well established. Incorporating FELA unaltered into the Jones Act, Congress must have intended to incorporate the pecuniary limitation on damages as well. We assume that Congress is aware of existing law when it passes legislation. *See Cannon v. University of Chicago*, 441 U.S. 677, 696-697, 99 S. Ct. 1946, 1957, 60 L. Ed. 2d 560 (1979). There is no recovery for loss of society in a Jones Act wrongful death action.

The Jones Act also precludes recovery for loss of society in this case. The Jones Act applies when a seaman has been killed as a result of negligence and it limits recovery to pecuniary loss. The general maritime claim here alleged that Torregano had been killed as a result of the unseaworthiness of the vessel. It would be inconsistent with our place in the constitutional scheme were we to sanction more expansive remedies in a judicially-created cause of action in which liability is without fault than Congress has allowed in cases of death resulting from negligence. We must conclude that there is no recovery for loss of society in a general maritime action for the wrongful death of a Jones Act seaman.

Our decision also remedies an anomaly we created in *Higginbotham*. Respondents in that case warned that the elimination of loss of society damages for wrongful deaths on the high seas would create an unwarranted inconsistency between deaths in territorial waters, where loss of society was available under *Gaudet*, and deaths on the high seas. We recognized the value of uniformity, but concluded that a concern for consistency could not override the statute. *Higginbotham*, 436 U.S., at 624, 98 S. Ct., at 2014. Today we restore a uniform rule applicable to all actions for the wrongful death of a seaman, whether under DOHSA, the Jones Act, or general maritime law.

V.

We next must decide whether, in a general maritime action surviving the death of a seaman, the estate can recover decedent's lost future earnings. Under traditional maritime law, as under common law, there is no right of survival; a seaman's personal cause of action does not survive the seaman's death. *Cortes v. Baltimore Insular Line, Inc.*, 287 U.S. 367, 371, 53 S. Ct. 173, 174, 77 L. Ed. 368 (1932); *Romero v. International Terminal Operating Co.*, 358 U.S. 354, 373, 79 S. Ct. 468, 480, 3 L. Ed. 2d 368 (1959); *Gillespie*, 379 U.S., at 157, 85 S. Ct., at 313-314.

Congress and the States have changed the rule in many instances. The Jones Act, through its incorporation of FELA, provides that a seaman's right of action for injuries due to negligence survives to the seaman's personal representative. *See* 45 U.S.C. § 59; *Gillespie, supra*, at 157, 85 S. Ct., at 313. Most States have survival statutes applicable to tort actions generally, *see* 1 S. Speiser, Recovery for Wrongful Death 2d § 3.2, (1975 and Supp. 1989), 2 *id.*, §§ 14.1, 14.3, App. A., and admiralty courts have applied these state statutes in many instances to preserve suits for injury at sea. *See, e.g., Just v. Chambers* 312 U.S. 383, 391, 61 S. Ct. 687, 693, 85 L. Ed. 903 (1941). *See also Kernan v. American Dredging Co.*, 355 U.S. 426, 430, n.4, 78 S. Ct. 394, 397, n.4, 2 L. Ed. 2d 382 (1958); *Kossick v. United Fruit Co.*, 365 U.S. 731, 739, 81 S. Ct. 886, 892, 6 L. Ed. 2d 56 (1961); *Gillespie, supra*, 379 U.S., at 157, 85 S. Ct., at 313-314; Comment, *Application of State Survival Statutes in Maritime Causes*, 60 Colum. L. Rev. 534, 535, n.11 (1960); Nagy, *The General Maritime Law Survival Action: What are the Elements of Recoverable Damages?*, 9 U. Haw. L. Rev. 5, 27 (1987). Where these state statutes do not apply,[2] however, or where there is no state survival statute, there is no survival of unseaworthiness claims absent a change in the traditional maritime rule.

---

[2] In *Offshore Logistics, Inc. v. Tallentire*, 477 U.S. 207, 215, n.1, 106 S. Ct. 2485, 2490, n.1, 91 L. Ed. 2d 174 (1986), we declined to approve or disapprove the practice of some courts of applying state survival statutes to cases involving death on the high seas.

Several Courts of Appeals have relied on *Moragne* to hold that there is a general maritime right of survival. *See Spiller v. Thomas M. Lowe, Jr., & Assocs., Inc.*, 466 F.2d 903, 909 (CA8 1972); *Barbe v. Drummond*, 507 F.2d 794, 799-800 (CA1 1974); *Law v. Sea Drilling Corp.*, 523 F.2d 793, 795 (CA5 1975); *Evich v. Connelly*, 759 F.2d 1432, 1434 (CA9 1985). As we have noted, *Moragne* found that congressional and state abrogation of the maritime rule against wrongful death actions demonstrated a strong policy judgment, to which the court deferred. *Moragne*, 398 U.S., at 388-393, 90 S. Ct., at 1781-1784. Following this reasoning, the lower courts have looked to the Jones Act and the many state survival statutes and concluded that these enactments dictate a change in the general maritime rule against survival. *See, e.g., Spiller, supra*, at 909; *Barbe, supra*, at 799-800, and n.6.

Miles argues that we should follow the Courts of Appeals and recognize a general maritime survival right. Apex urges us to reaffirm the traditional maritime rule and overrule these decisions. We decline to address the issue, because its resolution is unnecessary to our decision on the narrow question presented: whether the income decedent would have earned but for his death is recoverable. We hold that it is not.

Recovery of lost future income in a survival suit will, in many instances, be duplicative of recovery by dependents for loss of support in a wrongful death action; the support dependents lose as a result of a seaman's death would have come from the seaman's future earnings.

* * *

The Jones Act/FELA survival provision limits recovery to losses suffered during the decedent's lifetime. *See* 45 U.S.C. § 59. This was the established rule under FELA when Congress passed the Jones Act, incorporating FELA. *see St. Louis, I.M. & S.R. Co., supra*, 237 U.S., at 658, 35 S. Ct., at 706, and it is the rule under the Jones Act. *See Van Beeck, supra*, at 347 Congress has limited the survival right for seamen's injuries resulting from negligence. As with loss of society in wrongful death actions, this forecloses more expansive remedies in a general maritime action founded on strict liability. We will not create, under our admiralty powers, a remedy disfavored by a clear majority of the States and that goes well beyond the limits of Congress' ordered system of recovery for seamen's injury and death. Because Torregano's estate cannot recover for his lost future income under the Jones Act, it cannot do so under general maritime law.

VI.

Cognizant of the constitutional relationship between the courts and Congress, we today act in accordance with the uniform plan of maritime tort law Congress created in DOHSA and the Jones Act. We hold that there is a general maritime cause of action for the wrongful death of a seaman, but that damages recoverable in such an action do not include loss of society. We also hold that a general maritime survival action cannot include recovery for decedent's lost future earnings. Accordingly, the judgment of the Court of Appeals is

Affirmed.

Note

Courts are divided about whether *Miles* controls the decision in *Gaudet* where loss of consortium was available under general maritime law to beneficiaries of maritime workers, non-seamen, and seamen in actions against non-employers. Although some courts allow loss of consortium to relatives of maritime workers and non-maritime plaintiffs, other courts refuse to allow relatives of non-seamen to collect greater recovery than relatives of true seamen because seamen were traditionally the wards of the courts. The latter courts have focused on an interest in uniformity.

There is also a split of authority as to whether punitive damages may be recovered in a seaman's unseaworthiness action brought under the general maritime law.

The conflicting cases are discussed at length in Force, *The Curse of Miles v. Apex Marine Corp.: The Mischief of Seeking "Uniformity" and "Legislative Intent" in Maritime Personal Injury Cases*, 55 LA. L. REV. 745 (1995).

Notes

1. *Punitive Damages*

May punitive damages be recovered in a seaman's action brought under the general maritime law or the Jones Act? *Complaint of Merry Shipping, Inc.*, 650 F.2d 622, 1981 AMC 2839 (5th Cir. 1981) which allowed such recovery was overruled in dictum on the authority of *Miles* in *Guevara v. Maritime Overseas Corporation*, 59 F.3d 1496, 1995 AMC 2409 (5th Cir. 1995), *cert. denied*, 116 S. Ct. 706 (1996).

2. *Loss of Consortium in Injury Cases*

In *American Export Lines, Inc. v. Alvez*, 446 U.S. 274, 100 S.Ct. 1673, 64 L.Ed.2d 284 (1980), the Supreme Court held that the wife of a harbor worker who was injured non-fatally aboard a vessel in state territorial waters could recover for loss of society. Has this decision been overruled impliedly by *Miles v. Apex Marine Corp., supra*?

Although *American Export Lines* has never been expressly overruled, it is wise to ask if it is good law. The holding that the wife of an injured longshoreman may recover non-pecuniary damages was based on an extension of the rule in *Sea-Land Services, Inc. v. Gaudet*, 414 U.S. 573, 94 S.Ct. 806, 39 L.Ed.2d 9, 1973 AMC 2572 (1974). Yet, *Gaudet* has since been severely limited in two subsequent Supreme Court cases. *See Miles v. Apex Marine Corp.*, 498 U.S. 19, 1991 A.M.C. 1 (1990); *Mobil Oil Co. v. Higginbotham*, 436 U.S. 618 (1978). Many have argued that *Gaudet's* continued presence creates a wrinkle in the uniformity of maritime law that should soon be resolved. *See* C. Taylor Simpson, *Sailing the Statutory Seas Toward Uniformity in Maritime Tort Law:* Miles v. Apex Marine Corp. 15 Tul. Mar. L.J. 449 (1991).

The decision in *American Export Lines* conflicts with all other remedies available under the maritime law. Non-pecuniary damages are not available under the Jones Act nor under the LHWCA when a seaman or worker is injured. To provide such damages under the general maritime law, when a longshoreman sues a vessel owner under 905(b), would give claimants a remedy that is not available to any seaman nor to any longshoreman injured while not aboard a ship. There seems to be no policy reason for making the availability of non-pecuniary damages dependent solely on the basis of where the longshoreman was injured. Thus, an argument for uniformity in the remedies available to injured workers seems to be warranted.

Nevertheless, in *Moore v. M/V Angela*, 353 F.3d 376, 2004 AMC 59 (5th Cir. 2003), the court held that an award of damages for loss of consortium to the widow of a longshoreman was permissible in a §905(b) action. The court said:

Despite the illogical discrepancies between the law governing injuries to longshoremen in territorial waters and persons governed by the Death on the High Seas Act or the Jones Act, we must apply the law as it is.

Moore v. M/V Angela, 353 F.3d 376, 383 (5th Cir. 2003).

In *In re Amtrak "Sunset, Ltd" Train Crash*, 121 F.3d 1421, 1997 AMC 2962 (11th Cir. 1997), the Eleventh Circuit held that punitive damages and damages for loss of society or consortium are not available in personal injury actions under maritime law; they are unaffected by *Yamaha v. Calhoun, supra*, which dealt only with death cases.

3. *Discounting: Inflation and Interest*

When calculating damages, the court or jury should take into account both the anticipated rate of inflation and the fact that the lump sum award can be invested to earn interest. In *Jones & Laughlin Steel Corp. v. Pfeifer*, 462 U.S. 523, 538-47, 103 S. Ct. 2541, 2551-55, 76 L. Ed. 768 (1983), the Supreme Court rejected the "total offset method", which regards any investment gains as being effectively canceled out by the effect of inflation. As a result, the award should be discounted to some extent, to reflect the present value of the future loss (i.e., the sum which, if given now, would produce the required figure over the period of years remaining in the plaintiff's life). The Court reviewed several different approaches taken by lower courts to the process of discounting, but refused to adopt any one of them "and establish it for all time as the exclusive method in all federal trials for calculating an award for lost earnings in an inflationary economy". *Id.* at 546, 2555.

Section IV. Remedies of Non-Maritime Persons

1. *Duty and Standard of Care Generally*

A variety of individuals other than seamen and other maritime employees may be lawfully present on a vessel. Every day, passengers board cruise ships, merchant ships are inspected by various government officials, and seamen receive visitors aboard the vessel. These persons are entitled to be protected by a certain standard of care notwithstanding their non-maritime status.

As a general rule, the shipowner owes a duty of exercising reasonable care toward the persons lawfully present aboard the vessel, *see Leathers v. Blessing*, 105 U.S. 626, 26 L.Ed. 1192 (1881); *The Max Morris*, 137 U.S. 1, 11 S.Ct. 29, 34 L.Ed. 586 (1890); *The Admiral Peoples*, 295 U.S. 649, 55 S.Ct. 885, 79 L.Ed. 1633 (1935). In *Kermarec v. Companie Generale Transatlantique*, the Supreme Court also refused to elaborate a standard of care which depends upon whether the injured person is a licensee or invitee on the vessel. The Court held that "the owner of a ship in navigable waters owes to all who are on board for purposes not inimical to his legitimate interests the duty of exercising reasonable care under the circumstances of each case." *Kermarec v. Compagnie Generale Transatlantique*, 358 U.S. 625, 79 S.Ct. 406, 3 L.Ed.2d 550 (1959). Nevertheless, such standard of care is only applicable where the injured person was lawfully present aboard the vessel. Stowaways and all individuals who have no legal right to remain aboard the vessel are entitled only to a lessened standard of care limited to humane treatment, *see The Laura Madsen*, 112 F. 72 (W.D. Wash. 1901). In such situations the shipowner is only liable for his willful or wanton misconduct towards stowaways, *see Taylor v. Alaska Rivers Navigations Co.*, 391 P.2d 15 (Ala. 1964).

The issue of liability is to be determined upon principles not foreign to the common law of torts notwithstanding its maritime flavor. A shipowner is liable when he, or an employee (under the doctrine of respondeat superior) negligently caused an injury to a person lawfully present aboard the vessel, namely, when he has breached his duty to exercise reasonable care, *see Monteleone v. Bahama Cruise Line, Inc.*, 838 F.2d 63, 64, 1988 AMC 1146 (2d Cir. 1988).

In determining the standard of care to which a shipowner is held accountable, "the extent to which the circumstances surrounding maritime travel are different from those encountered in daily life and involve more danger to the passenger, will determine how high a degree of care is reasonable in each case." *See Rainey v. Paquet Cruises, Inc.*, 709 F.2d 169, 172, 1983 AMC 2100 (2d Cir. 1983). Early case law considered the shipowner accountable to a heightened standard of care. This position was based upon the premise that "... when carriers undertake to convey persons by the powerful and dangerous agency of steam, public policy and safety require that they be held to the greatest possible care and diligence,—that the personal safety of passengers should not be left to the sport of chance, or the negligence of careless agents," *see Pennsylvania Co. v. Roy*, 102 U.S. 451, 453, 26 L.Ed. 141 (1880); *see also Ludena v. the Santa Luisa*, 112 F. Supp. 401 (D.C.N.Y. 1953) (duty of care characterized as "... the greatest possible care...."); *Moore-McCormack Lines, Inc. v. Russack*, 266 F.2d 573 (9th Cir. 1959). The Supreme Court, however, in *Kermarec*, concluded that a shipowner is accountable to no more than a duty to exercise reasonable care, as a reasonable shipowner. A court's inquiry should focus on the amount of control the shipowner and the crew of the vessel possessed or should have possessed over a given situation. For example, in *Monteleone v. Bahama Cruise Lines, Inc.*, the court refused to hold a shipowner liable when a passenger tripped on a protruding screw and sustained injuries when she fell down a flight of stairs on a cruise ship. Taking into consideration the fact that the shipowner had demonstrated that the stairs were regularly inspected to guard against such defects, the court held that the "(shipowner's) liability properly turns on whether it had notice of the screw's protrusion [and that] merely allowing the screw to protrude did not constitute a breach of duty." *Id.* at 65.

The standard of care which is owed to passengers and other non-seafarers was discussed by the Ninth Circuit which stated:

We conclude that the district court applied the proper standard of care. The district court correctly noted that a shipowner owes a duty of reasonable care to those aboard the ship who are not crew members. *See Kermarec v. Compagnie Generale Transatlantique*, 358 U.S. 625, 630, 79 S.Ct. 406, 409-10, 3 L.Ed.2d 550 (1959). In *Kermarec*, the Supreme Court held that "the owner of a ship in navigable waters owes to all who are on board for purposes not inimical to his legitimate interests the duty of exercising reasonable care under the circumstances of each case." *Id.* at 632, 79 S.Ct. at 410; accord *Morton v. De Oliveira*, 984 F.2d 289, 291 (9th Cir.), *cert. denied*, 510 U.S. 907, 114 S.Ct. 289, 126 L.Ed.2d 238 (1993).

The degree of care required is always that which is reasonable, but the application of reasonable will of course change with the circumstances of each particular case. The Second Circuit has described the standard accurately:

> What is required ... is merely the conduct of the reasonable man of ordinary prudence under the circumstances, and the greater danger, or the greater responsibility, is merely one of the circumstances, demanding only an increased amount of care. In some instances, reasonable care under the circumstances may be a very high degree of care; in other instances, it may be something less.

Rainey v. Paquet Cruises, Inc., 709 F.2d 169, 170-71 (2d Cir.1983) (internal quotations and citations omitted). The district court correctly determined that the standard of care is one of reasonableness, but in a situation such as this, where the risk is great because of high seas, an increased amount of care and precaution is reasonable.

Furthermore, the district court's finding that Catalina Cruises breached this standard of reasonable care is not clearly erroneous. The crew of the COUNTESS had significant information regarding the weather they would encounter when crossing. The conditions had steadily deteriorated throughout the morning hours and had not shown any signs of improving. Captain Martin and Dennis were aware that the crossing would be rough and that they could be facing rather severe wind gusts. Knowing all this, Captain Martin ventured into this weather with over 300 passengers on board, many of them young campers.

During the voyage, the MONARCH radioed the COUNTESS and informed Dennis that the MONARCH'S crossing had been miserable. Dennis failed to inform Captain Martin of the conditions the MONARCH reported. The COUNTESS continued to encounter rough seas, until a large wave caused one of the vessel's windows to shatter. After the window shattered, and water literally washed many passengers from their seats, Captain Martin slowed the vessel and changed course so the ride would be more comfortable. Many on board noticed an extreme change in the smoothness of the ride.

A person exercising reasonable care under the circumstances would have slowed the vessel sooner, sought refuge at Long Point once he realized the severity of the conditions, or decided not to risk venturing out into the hazardous conditions at all. Accordingly, we hold that the district court did not commit clear error in determining that Catalina Cruises did not act with reasonable care under the circumstances of this case.

In re: Catalina Cruises, Inc., 137 F.3d 1422, 1998 AMC 1282 (9th Cir. 1998).

The shipowner, however, may be absolutely liable for the intentional torts of the members of its crew, *see Morton v. De Oliveira*, 984 F.2d 289, 1993 AMC 843 (9th Cir. 1993). In *Morton*, a passenger was allegedly raped by a crew member. The court held that the passenger could recover against a shipowner without showing any negligence on the part of the the shipowner. Other circuits disagree, however. *Morton v. De Oliveira*, 984 F.2d 289, 292 (2d Cir. 1993); *York v. Commodore Cruise Line, Ltd*, 863 F. Supp. 159, 162, 1995 AMC 339, 342-43 (S.D.N.Y. 1994); *Doe v. Celebrity Cruises*, 145 F. Supp. 2d 1337, 1342ff., 2001 AMC 2672, 2675ff. (S.D. Fla. 2001).

The shipowner's liability to non-maritime persons has also been held to not be limited to the confines of the ship, *see Gillmor v. Caribbean Cruise Line. Ltd.*, 789 F. Supp. 488, 1994 AMC 1329 (D.P.R. 1992) (Vessel owner liable if the crew knew or should have known about the high probability of criminal activity in the area adjacent to the vessel's moorage and failed to warn the passengers of the danger).

The principles of comparative negligence may also be used by a shipowner to reduce the amount of damages. *See Carey v. Bahama Cruise Lines*, 864 F.2d 201, 1989 AMC 852 (1st Cir. 1988).

---

2. Wrongful Death Actions

a. Deaths on the High Seas

When a tort on the high seas causes the death of a passenger, the court applies the Death On the High Seas Act, 46 U.S.C.A. §§ 30301-30308 (DOHSA, formerly 46 U.S.C. §§ 761-768). State law is displaced in such action since DOHSA has been held to provide the exclusive federal remedy, *see Offshore Logistics v. Tallentire*, 477 U.S. 207, 106 S.Ct. 2485, 91 L.Ed.2d 174, 1986 AMC 2113 (1986) (Dependents of offshore workers killed in a helicopter crash on the high seas held to be limited to DOHSA remedies. Such remedies may not be supplemented by any state law). Courts have also determined that wrongful deaths which occur in foreign territorial waters are considered as within the ambit of DOHSA, *see Howard v. Crystal Cruises, Inc.*, 41 F.3d 527, 1995 AMC 305 (9th Cir. 1994) (Dependents of a passenger who had been injured in foreign territorial waters and from which he subsequently died held to be limited to DOHSA's pecuniary damages although the accident causing the death of the passenger occurred in foreign territorial waters. The court considered that the primary purpose of DOHSA was to create a remedy for deaths occurring outside the reach of the state courts of the United States).

---

b. Deaths in Territorial Waters

See *Yamaha Motor Corp., U.S.A. v. Calhoun*, and accompanying Note, *supra*.

---

3. Choice of Law: Choice of Forum Clauses

Many nations have accepted the Athens Convention Relating to the Carriage of Passengers and Their Luggage By Sea (1974), which deals with the recovery of damages by passengers for personal injury and death as well as loss of baggage. Under the Convention, the carrier is liable for losses caused by the fault or neglect of the shipowner or his employees. Fault or neglect is presumed (although subject to rebuttal evidence) in the case of death, injury or loss of baggage due to shipwreck, collision, standing, explosion, fire, or a defect in the ship. No contractual alteration of these rules is permitted. Under the Convention liability is limited to 70,000 gold francs per passenger for death or injury; 50,000 gold francs for loss or damage to a vehicle; 12,5000 gold francs for loss of cabin baggage; and 18,000 gold francs for any other loss.

The United States has not ratified the Athens Convention. Liability for death, personal injury or loss of baggage is based upon common-law negligence, but a generally high standard of care is applied. *See Allen v. Matson Navigation Co.*, 255 F.2d 273, 1958 AMC 1343 (9th Cir. 1958). Contract clauses that relieve a carrier from liability for negligence or limit damages are void by statute. 46 U.S.C.A. § 30509 (formerly 46 U.S.C. § 183(c)). Contract provisions placing limits on liability for loss of passenger baggage are valid if reasonable under the circumstances. *See The Leviathan*, 4 F. Supp. 918, 1933 AMC 1394 (E.D.N.Y. 1933); *Miller v. International Freighting Corp.*, 97 F. Supp. 60, 1951 AMC 944 (S.D.N.Y. 1951).

Is a provision on the contract of passage specifying a time limit for suit valid? *Compare DeNicola v. Cunard Line, Inc.*, 642 F.2d 5, 1981 AMC 1388 (1st Cir. 1981) with *Raskin v. Compania de Vapores Realma*, 521 F. Supp. 337, 1983 AMC 814 (S.D.N.Y. 1981).

Is a forum selection clause contained in a form passage contract valid? In *Carnival Cruise Lines, Inc. v. Shute*, 499 U.S. 585, 111 S. Ct. 1522, 113 L. Ed. 2d 622, 1991 AMC 1697 (1991), a Washington state couple, the Shutes, purchased passage on a ship owned by Carnival Cruise Lines which sent the Shutes tickets that contained a clause designating courts in Florida as the agreed-upon forum for the resolution of any disputes. The Shutes boarded the ship in Los Angeles and, while in international waters off the Mexican coast, Mrs. Shute suffered injuries when she slipped and fell. The Shutes filed suite in a Washington Federal District Court, which granted summary judgment for the cruise line. The

Court of Appeals reversed, holding, *inter alia*, that the forum selection clause should not be enforced because it was not freely bargained for and because its enforcement would deprive the Shutes of their day in court since the couple was physically and financially incapable of pursuing litigation in Florida.

The Supreme Court, reversing the judgment of the Court of Appeals, emphasized that forum-selection clauses contained in form passage contracts are subject to judicial scrutiny for fundamental fairness. In the instant case the Court held that the forum selection clause at issue was reasonable and enforceable. Florida was not a "remote alien forum" nor, given the fact that the accident occurred off the Mexican coast, was Washington inherently more suited to resolution of the dispute than Florida. Further, the Court found no indication that the cruise line designated Florida as the forum in order to discourage cruise passengers from pursuing legitimate claims, no evidence that the Company obtained passengers' assent to the clause by fraud or overreaching, and the passengers conceded that they were given notice of the provision. Finally, the Court ruled that the forum selection clause did not violate 46 U.S.C.A. § 30509 (formerly 46 U.S.C. § 183(c)) which prohibits a vessel owner from inserting in any contract a provision depriving a claimant of trial by a court of competent jurisdiction for loss of life or personal injury resulting from negligence. The Court characterized the forum selection clause as merely stating that actions arising out of passage contracts were to be brought, if at all, in a court located in Florida which would be a court of competent jurisdiction within the meaning of the statute.

The result in *Carnival Cruise Lines, Inc.* was legislatively overruled with an amendment to 46 U.S.C.A. § 30509 (formerly 46 U.S.C. § 183(c)) which precludes a carrier from limiting a passenger's choice of an otherwise valid forum by a forum selection clause. This amendment was itself overruled, presumably reinstating the effect of *Carnival Cruise Lines, Inc.*

Section V. Products Liability

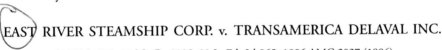

EAST RIVER STEAMSHIP CORP. v. TRANSAMERICA DELAVAL INC.

476 U.S. 858, 106 S. Ct. 2295, 90 L. Ed. 2d 865, 1986 AMC 2027 (1986)

Justice BLACKMUN delivered the opinion of the Court.

In this admiralty case, we must decide whether a cause of action in tort is stated when a defective product purchased in a commercial transaction malfunctions, injuring only the product itself and causing purely economic loss. The case requires us to consider preliminarily whether admiralty law, which already recognizes a general theory of liability for negligence, also incorporates principles of products liability, including strict liability. Then, charting a course between products liability and contract law, we must determine whether injury to a product itself is the kind of harm that should be protected by products liability or left entirely to the law of contracts.In 1969, Seatrain Shipbuilding Corp. (Shipbuilding), a wholly owned subsidiary of Seatrain Lines, Inc. (Seatrain), announced it would build the four oil-transporting supertankers in issue—the T.T. Stuyvesant, T.T. Williamsburgh, T.T. Brooklyn, and T.T. Bay Ridge. Each tanker was constructed pursuant to a contract in which a separate wholly owned subsidiary of Seatrain engaged Shipbuilding. Shipbuilding in turn contracted with respondent, now known as Transamerica Delaval Inc. (Delaval), to design, manufacture, and supervise the installation of turbines (costing $1.4 million each, *see* App. 163) that would be the main propulsion units for the 225,000-ton, $125 million, *ibid.*, supertankers. When each ship was completed, its title was transferred from the contracting subsidiary to a trust company (as trustee for an owner), which in turn chartered the ship to one of the petitioners, also subsidiaries of Seatrain. Queensway Tankers, Inc., chartered the Stuyvesant; Kingsway Tankers, Inc., chartered the Williamsburgh; East River Steamship Corp. chartered the Brooklyn; and Richmond Tankers, Inc., chartered the Bay Ridge. Each petitioner operated under a bareboat charter, by which it took full control of the ship for 20 or 22 years as though it owned it, with the obligation afterwards to returnthe ship to the real owner. *See* G. GILMORE & C. BLACK, ADMIRALTY

§§ 4-1, 4-22 (2d ed. 1975). Each charterer assumed responsibility for the cost of any repairs to the ships. Tr. of Oral Arg. 11, 16-17, 35.

The Stuyvesant sailed on its maiden voyage in late July 1977. On December 11 of that year, as the ship was about to enter the Port of Valdez, Alaska, steam began to escape from the casing of the high-pressure turbine. That problem was temporarily resolved by repairs, but before long, while the ship was encountering a severe storm in the Gulf of Alaska, the high-pressure turbine malfunctioned. The ship, though lacking its normal power, was able to continue on its journey to Panama and then San Francisco. In January 1978, an examination of the high-pressure turbine revealed that the first-stage steam reversing ring virtually had disintegrated and had caused additional damage to other parts of the turbine. The damaged part was replaced with a part from the Bay Ridge, which was then under construction. In April 1978, the ship again was repaired, this time with a part from the Brooklyn. Finally, in August, the ship was permanently and satisfactorily repaired with a ring newly designed and manufactured by Delaval.

The Brooklyn and the Williamsburgh were put into service in late 1973 and late 1974, respectively. In 1978, as a result of the Stuyvesant's problems, they were inspected while in port. Those inspections revealed similar turbine damage. Temporary repairs were made, and newly designed parts were installed as permanent repairs that summer.

When the Bay Ridge was completed in early 1979, it contained the newly designed parts and thus never experienced the high-pressure turbine problems that plagued the other three ships. Nonetheless, the complaint appears   to   claim

damages as a result of deterioration of the Bay Ridge's ring that was installed in the Stuyvesant while the Bay Ridge was under construction. In addition, the Bay Ridge experienced a unique problem. In 1980, when the ship was on its maiden voyage, the engine began to vibrate with a frequency that increased even after speed was reduced. It turned out that the astern guardian valve, located between the high-pressure and low-pressure turbines, had been installed backwards. Because of that error, steam entered the low-pressure turbine and damaged it. After repairs, the Bay Ridge resumed its travels.

II.

The charterers' second amended complaint, filed in the United States District Court for the District of New Jersey, invokes admiralty jurisdiction. It contains five counts alleging tortious conduct on the part of respondent Delaval and seeks an aggregate of more than $8 million in damages for the cost of repairing the ships and for income lost while the ships were out of service. The first four counts, read liberally, allege that Delaval is strictly liable for the design defects in the high-pressure turbines of the Stuyvesant, the Williamsburgh, the Brooklyn, and the Bay Ridge, respectively. The fifth count alleges that Delaval, as part of the manufacturing process, negligently supervised the installation of the eastern guardian valve on the Bay Ridge. The initial complaint also had listed Seatrain and Shipbuilding as plaintiffs and had alleged breach of contract and warranty as well as tort claims. But after Delaval interposed a statute of limitationsdefense, the complaint was amended and the charterers alone brought the suit in tort. The nonrenewed claims were dismissed with prejudice by the District Court. Delaval then moved for summary judgment, contending that the charterers' actions were not cognizable in tort.

The District Court granted summary judgment for Delaval, and the Court of Appeals for the Third Circuit, sitting *en banc*, affirmed. *East River S.S. Corp. v. Delaval Turbine, Inc.*, 752 F.2d 903 (1985). The Court of Appeals held that damage solely to a defective product is actionable in tort if the defect creates an unreasonable risk of harm to persons or property other than the product itself, and harm materializes. Disappointments over the product's quality, on the other hand, are protected by warranty law. *Id.*, at 908, 909-910. The charterers were dissatisfied with product quality: the defects involved gradual and unnoticed deterioration of the turbines' component parts, and the only risk created was that the turbines would operate at a lower capacity. *Id.*, at 909. *See Pennsylvania Glass*

Sand Corp. v. Caterpillar Tractor Co., 652 F.2d 1165, 1169-1170 (CA3 1981). Therefore, neither the negligence claim nor the strict-liability claim were cognizable.

Judge Garth concurred on "grounds somewhat different," 752 F.2d, at 910, and Judge Becker, joined by Judge Higginbotham, concurred in part and dissented in part. *Id.*, at 913. Although Judge Garth agreed with the majority's analysis on the merits, he found no strict-liability claim presented because the charterers had failed to allege unreasonable danger or demonstrable injury.

Judge Becker largely agreed with the majority's approach, but would permit recovery for a "near miss," where the risk existed but no calamity occurred. He felt that the first count, concerning the Stuyvesant, stated a cause of action in tort. The exposure of the ship to a severe storm when the ship was unable to operate at full power due to the defective part created an unreasonable risk of harm.

We granted certiorari to resolve a conflict among the Courts of Appeals sitting in admiralty. 474 U.S. 814, 106 S. Ct. 56, 88 L. Ed. 2d 45 (1985).

III.

* * *

B.

The torts alleged in the first, second, third, and fifth counts clearly fall within the admiralty jurisdiction. The claims satisfy the traditional "locality" requirement—that the wrong must have occurred on the high seas or navigable waters. *See, e.g., The Plymouth*, 3 Wall. 20, 35-36 (1866). The first and fifth counts allege that the injury to the Stuyvesant's high-pressure turbine and the Bay Ridge's low-pressure turbine occurred while the ships were sailing on the high seas. The damage to the Williamsburgh and the Brooklyn, alleged in the second and third counts, occurred at sea, and was discovered in port, also a maritime locale. *See Southern S.S. Co. v. NLRB*, 316 U.S. 31, 41, 93 S. Ct. 493, 504, 34 L. Ed. 2d 1246 (1942).

When torts have occurred on navigable waters within the United States, the Court has imposed an additional requirement of a "maritime nexus"— that the wrong must bear "a significant relationship to traditional maritime activity." *See Executive Jet Aviation, Inc. v. Cleveland*, 409 U.S. 249, 268, 93 S. Ct. 493, 504, 34 L. Ed. 2d 454 (1972); *Foremost Ins. Co. v. Richardson*, 457 U.S. 668, 102 S. Ct. 2654, 73 L. Ed. 2d 300 (1982). We need not reach the question whether a maritime nexus also must be established when a tort occurs on the high seas. Were there such a requirement, it clearly was met here, for these ships were engaged in maritime commerce, a primary concern of admiralty law.

C.

With admiralty jurisdiction comes the application of substantive admiralty law. *See Executive Jet Aviation*, 409 U.S., at 255. Absent a relevant statute, the general maritime law, as developed by the judiciary, applies. *United States v. Reliable Transfer Co.*, 421 U.S. 397, 409, 95 S. Ct. 1708, 1714, 44 L. Ed. 2d 251 (1975); *Knickerbocker Ice Co. v. Stewart*, 253 U.S. 149, 160-161, 40 S. Ct. 438, 440, 64 L. Ed. 834 (1920). Drawn from state and federal sources, the general maritime law is an amalgam of traditional common-law rules, modifications of those rules, and newly created rules. *See Kermarec v. Compagnie Generale Transatlantique*, 358 U.S. 625, 630, 79 S. Ct. 406, 409, 3 L. Ed. 2d 550 (1959); *Romero v. International Terminal Operating Co.*, 358 U.S. 354, 373-375, 79 S. Ct. 468, 480-81, 3 L. Ed. 2d 368 (1959). This Court has developed a body of maritime tort principles, *see, e.g., Kermarec, supra*, 358 U.S. at 632, 79 S. Ct., at 410; *see generally* Currie, *Federalism and the Admiralty: "The Devil's Own Mess,"* 1960 S. Ct. Rev. 158, 164, and is now asked to incorporate products-liability concepts, long a part of the common law of torts, into the general maritime law. *See Igneri v. Cie. de Transports Oceaniques*, 323 F.2d 257, 260 (CA2 1963), *cert. denied*, 376 U.S. 949, 84 S. Ct. 965, 11 L. Ed. 2d 969 (1964).

The Courts of Appeals sitting in admiralty overwhelmingly have adopted concepts of products liability, based both on negligence, *Sieracki v. Seas Shipping Co.*, 149 F.2d 98, 99-100 (CA3 1945), *aff'd* on other grounds, 328 U.S. 85, 66 S. Ct. 872, 90 L. Ed. 1099 (1946), and on strict liability, *Pan-Alaska Fisheries, Inc. v. Marine Constr. &*

Design Co., 565 F.2d 1129, 1135 (CA9 1977) (adopting RESTATEMENT (SECOND) OF TORTS § 402A (1965)). Indeed, the Court of Appeals for the Third Circuit previously had stated that the question whether principles of strict products liability are part of maritime law "is no longer seriously contested." *Ocean Barge Transport Co. v. Hess Oil Virgin Islands Corp.*, 726 F.2d 121, 123 (1984) (*citing* cases).

We join the Courts of Appeals in recognizing products liability, including strict liability, as part of the general maritime law. This Court's precedents relating to injuries of maritime workers long have pointed in that direction. *See Seas Shipping Co. v. Sieracki*, 328 U.S. 85, 94, 66 S. Ct. 872, 877, 90 L. Ed. 1099 (1946) (strict liability for unseaworthiness); *Italia Societa per Azioni di Navigazione v. Oregon Stevedoring Co.*, 376 U.S. 315, 322, 84 S. Ct. 748, 752, 11 L. Ed. 2d 732 (1964) (strict liability for breach of implied warrant of workmanlike service). The Court's rationale in those cases—that strict liability should be imposed on the party best able to protect persons from hazardous equipment—is equally applicable when the claims are based on products liability. *Compare Sieracki*, 328 U.S., at 93-94, 66 S. Ct., at 876-877, with *Escola v. Coca Cola Bottling Co. of Fresno*, 24 Cal. 2d 453, 462, 150 P.2d 436, 441 (1944) (concurring opinion). And to the extent that products actions are based on negligence, they are grounded in principles already incorporated into the general maritime law. *See Kermarec v. Compagnie Generale Transatlantique*, 358 U.S., at 632, 79 S. Ct., at 410. Our incorporation of products liability into maritime law, however, is only the threshold determination to the main issue in this case.

IV.

Products liability grew out of a public policy judgment that people need more protection from dangerous products than is afforded by the law of warranty. *See Seely v. White Motor Co.*, 63 Cal. 2d 9, 15, 403 P.2d 145, 149 (1965). It is clear, however, that if this development were allowed to progress too far, contract law would drown in a sea of tort. *See* G. GILMORE, THE DEATH OF CONTRACT 87-94 (1974). We must determine whether a commercial product injuring itself is the kind of harm against which public policy requires manufacturers to protect, independent of any contractual obligation.

* * *

B.

The intriguing question whether injury to a product itself may be brought in tort has spawned a variety of answers. At one end of the spectrum, the case that created the majority land-based approach, *Seely v. Shite Motor Co.*, 63 Cal. 2d 9, 403 P.2d 145 (1965) (defective truck), held that preserving a proper role for the law of warranty precludes imposing tort liability if a defective product causes purely monetary harm. *See also Jones & Laughlin Steel Corp. v. Johns-Manville Sales Corp.*, 626 F.2d 280, 287, and n.13 (CA3 1980) (*citing* cases).

At the other end of the spectrum is the minority land-based approach, whose progenitor, *Santor v. A & M Karagheusian, Inc.*, 44 N.J. 52, 66-67, 207 A.2d 305, 312-313 (1965) (marred carpeting), held that a manufacturer's duty to make nondefective products encompassed injury to the product itself, whether or not the defect created an unreasonable risk of harm. *See also LaCrosse v. Schubert, Schroeder & Associates, Inc.*, 72 Wis. 2d 38, 44-45, 240 N.W.2d 124, 127-128 (1976). The courts adopting this approach, including the majority of the Courts of Appeals sitting in admiralty that have considered the issue, *e.g., Emerson G. M. Diesel, Inc. v. Alaskan Enterprise*, 732 F.2d 1468 (CA9 1984), find that the safety and insurance rationales behind strict liability apply equally where the losses are purely economic. These courts reject the *Seely* approach because they find it arbitrary that economic losses are recoverable if a plaintiff suffers bodily injury or property damage, but not if a product injures itself. They also find no inherent difference between economic loss and personal injury or property damage, because all are proximately caused by the defendant's conduct. Further, they believe recovery for economic loss would not lead to unlimited liability because they think a manufacturer can predict and insure against product failure. *See Emerson G. M. Diesel, Inc. v. Alaskan Enterprise*, 732 F.2d, at 1474. Between the two poles fall a number of cases that would permit a product-liability action under certain circumstances when a product injures only itself. These cases attempt to differentiate between "the disappointed users ... and the endangered ones," *Russell v. Ford Motor Co.*, 281 Ore. 587, 595, 575 P.2d 1383, 1387

(1987), and permit only the latter to sue in tort. The determination has been said to turn on the nature of the defect, the type of risk, and the manner in which the injury arose. *See Pennsylvania Glass Sand Corp. v. Caterpillar Tractor Co.*, 652 F.2d, at 1173 (relied on by the Court of Appeals in this case). The Alaska Supreme Court allows a tort action if the defective product creates a situation potentially dangerous to persons or other property, and loss occurs and a proximate result of that danger and under dangerous circumstances. *Northern Power & Engineering Corp. v. Caterpillar Tractor Co.*, 623 P.2d 324, 329 (1981).

We find the intermediate and minority land-based positions unsatisfactory. The intermediate positions, which essentially turn on the degree of risk, are too indeterminate to enable manufacturers easily to structure their business behavior, Nor do we find persuasive a distinction that rests on the manner in which the product is injured. We realize that the damage may be qualitative, occurring through gradual deterioration or internal breakage. Or it may be calamitous. *Compare Morrow v. New Moon Homes, Inc.*, 548 P.2d 279 (Alaska 1976), with *Cloud v. Kit Mfg. Co.*, 563 P.2d 248, 251 (Alaska 1977). But either way, since by definition no person or other property is damaged, the resulting loss is purely economic. Even when the harm to the product itself occurs through an abrupt, accident-like event, the resulting loss due to repair costs, decreased value, and lost profits is essentially the failure of the purchaser to receive the benefit of its bargain—traditionally the core concern of contract law. *See* E. FARNSWORTH, CONTRACTS § 12.8, pp. 839-840 (1982).

We also decline to adopt the minority land-based view espoused by *Santor* and *Emerson*. Such cases raise legitimate questions about the theories behind restricting products liability, but we believe that the countervailing arguments are more powerful. The minority view fails to account for the need to keep products liability and contract law in separate spheres and to maintain a realistic limitation on damages.

C.

Exercising traditional discretion in admiralty, *see Pope & Talbot, Inc. v. Hawn*, 346 U.S. 406, 409 (1953), we adopt an approach similar to *Seely* and hold that a manufacturer in a commercial relationship has no duty under either a negligence or strict products-liability theory to prevent a product from injuring itself.

* * *

Notes

1. *"Other Property"*

In *Saratoga Fishing Co. v. J.M. Martinac and Co.*, 520 U.S. 875, 117 S.Ct. 1783, 138 L.Ed.2d 76, 1997 AMC 2113 (1997), the Supreme Court held the rule that precludes a purchaser from recovering damages in a products liability action when the only injury is to the product itself does not preclude recovery where there is injury to "other property". "Other property" includes equipment added to a product after the manufacturer or distributor selling in the initial distribution change has sold the product to an initial user.

* * *

2. *Products Liability and Personal Injuries*

Cases after *East River* have allowed recovery for personal injury under admiralty products liability law. *See, e.g., Robinson v. United States*, 730 F. Supp. 551, 1990 AMC 1493 (S.D.N.Y. 1990) (action for personal injury products liability claim maintained); *Frantz v. Brunswick Corp.*, 866 F. Supp. 527, 1994 AMC 1954 (S.D. Ala. 1994) (general maritime law applied to products liability action against seller where boat owner was injured in crash). A great number of claims have resulted from asbestos-related injuries or health damage claims. Asbestosis litigation in maritime law usually involves one of three types. Many of these cases have been disposed of on jurisdictional grounds. *See, e.g., Johns-Manville Corp.*, 764 F.2d 224, 1985 AMC 2317 (4th Cir. 1985).

* * *

CHAPTER 4 — COLLISION AND OTHER ACCIDENTS

A. Liability

1. Inevitable Accident

THE JUMNA

149 F. 171 (2d Cir. 1906)

On appeal and cross-appeal from a decree of the District Court for the Southern District of New York dismissing the libel and cross-libels and deciding that the collision between barge No. 19, in tow of the tug Gypsum King, and the steamship Jumna, and the subsequent collision of said barge and the schooner Gypsum Emperor with the New Haven Railroad's pier No. 38, East River, was the result of inevitable accident.

The opinion of Judge Holt in the District Court is reported in 140 F. 743....

COXE, Circuit Judge

It is conceded on all hands that, except in a few unimportant details, the facts are fully and accurately stated in the opinion of the district judge. He has carefully considered the conflicting theories of fault and has reached the conclusion that negligence has not been established as to any of the vessels participating in the collision. To arrive at this result it was necessary for him to determine several disputed questions of fact regarding which it is sufficient to say that in many instances he was unquestionably right and in no instance is the finding so clearly against the preponderance of proof as to warrant us in setting it aside.

For instance, was the Jumna's hawser sufficient and in proper condition? Was the tow of the Gypsum King properly made up? Did the McCaldin Brothers make proper effort to reach the port side of the Jumna? Did the Dalzell put a sudden strain on the hawser?

In each of these instances the district judge found against the asserted negligence and we think the weight of testimony sustains these findings. Like him we are unable to localize the blame for the collision. We had some doubt as to whether the tugs in charge of the Jumna, and particularly the McCaldin Brothers, can be exculpated but, after an examination of the testimony, we incline to the opinion that they did everything which could be reasonably expected of them and that the McCaldin Brothers started to make fast to the port quarter of the Jumna as soon as the latter cleared the pier and it was possible to get around her stern.

The judge of the District Court has found that the collision was the result of an inevitable accident. Such an accident usually happens when it is not possible to prevent it by the exercise of due care, caution and nautical skill. It is generally, though not invariably, attributed to an act of God, as where a tremendous tempest arises, such as devastated Galveston a few years ago, or more recently destroyed the shipping in the harbor of Havana. So, where a dense fog or falling snow obstructs the vision, where a gale and high seas unite to make navigation difficult, or where a severe storm is prevailing upon a dark night, a collision happening in such circumstances, the colliding vessels exercising the care, skill and caution required by prudent navigation, would be attributed to inevitable accident. Such accidents usually occur when safe navigation is rendered impossible from causes which no human foresight can prevent; when the forces of nature burst forth in unforeseen and uncontrollable fury so that man is helpless, and the stoutest ship and the most experienced mariner are at the mercy of the winds and waves.

In admiralty law, however, the phrase has a more comprehensive meaning. It is not necessary that the accident should be the result of a vis major. If no negligence can be imputed to either vessel there is a presumption that they are navigating in a lawful manner and where no fault can be shown the accident may be said to be inevitable.

* * *

The test is, could the collision have been prevented by the exercise of ordinary care, caution and maritime skill? In the case at bar we are unable upon the testimony before us to specify any particular fault, to put our finger upon any act or omission and assert that to it the accident was attributable. Fault may exist, but we are unable to discover it; it is inscrutable. Where the evidence is so conflicting that it is impossible to determine to what direct and specific acts the collision is attributable, it is a case of damage arising from a cause that is inscrutable. *The Fern and The Swann*, Newb. 158, Fed. Cas. No. 8,588. Whether the case at bar be thus classified, or whether it be held to come within the admiralty definition of inevitable accident is not material; in either event the loss must be borne by the party on whom it falls....

Note

Fault in a collision case may arise because of (1) negligence on the part of the navigators, lack of proper care or skill; (2) violation of the rules of the road, the applicable rules of navigation laid down by or under the authority of statute: or (3) failure to comply with local navigational customs or usage.

THE LOUISIANA

70 U.S. (3 Wall.) 164, 18 L. Ed. 85 (1865)

[The steamship LOUISIANA broke free from its moorings in a strong gale and drifted until it collided with the steamship FLUSHING, which was hard aground on a sandbar. The owners of the FLUSHING sued the LOUISI-ANA *in rem*. The District Court held that the LOUISIANA was not at fault. The Circuit Court for Maryland reversed, holding the LOUISIANA to be entirely at fault. Eds.]

* * *

Mr. Justice GRIER delivered the opinion of the court.

The steamer Flushing being aground on Hampton Bar, out of the channel or course of vessels navigating the bay or harbor, and incapable of motion, cannot be justly charged with any participation in causing the collision.

The collision being caused by the Louisiana drifting from her moorings, she must be liable for the damages consequent thereon, unless she can show affirmatively that the drifting was the result of inevitable accident, or a *vis major*, which human skill and precaution, and a proper display of nautical skill could not have prevented.

Now the facts show that the Louisiana has entirely failed to establish her defence.

1. The drifting of this vessel was not caused by any sudden hurricane which nautical experience could not anticipate. None of the other numerous vessels, at that time in the harbor, were driven from their moorings. The wind which arose was only of such a character that its effects might have been anticipated, and, by proper precaution, prevented;—"a half gale," "a stiff breeze," "a little more than ordinary."

The fact that the steamer was ordered by the government officers to take in coal at the old wharf, which had a narrow front when compared with the great length of the vessel, could not relieve the officers of the boat from the duty of securing her in such a manner as to prevent her drifting when the change of the tide and winds changed the direction of the forces acting upon the vessel. And the fact that under these circumstances she *did* drift, is conclusive evidence that she was not sufficiently and properly secured.

It requires no assumption or affectation of any very great nautical skill in this court to point out the defects of the management of this vessel by the mate, who was left in charge of her. If the tide and wind could have been reasonably expected to remain as it was when, according to the mate's idea, the vessel was lying so "*very nice to the wharf,*" we should probably not have heard of this case.

So long as things were in the condition in which they were when the vessel was first moored, she was sufficiently secured to meet any stress or force likely to be opposed to her in that direction. But when the tide changed so as to strike the stern with a momentum increased by a high wind, and multiplied by the leverage resulting from the length of the vessel exposed below the wharf, the "necessity" for a change of position ought to have suggested itself to a person of nautical skill, as a proper precaution against a danger which might justly have been anticipated. The fact that the captain and mate "did not anticipate the breaking away of the vessel, and thought the lines sufficient to hold her," may prove their want of judgment, but not that "the accident was unavoidable;" and this more especially, as other person of nautical skill—disinterested witnesses in this case—found no difficulty in securing their vessels at the same place, and under similar circumstances.

2. It is not necessary to a decision of the cause to show that this collision might have been averted by a proper use of the anchors of the Louisiana, after she had broken away from her mooring at the wharf, or by a proper use of her steam power, further than to say, that the testimony in the case would well justify that conclusion.

We are of opinion, therefore, that the appellant has failed to show that the collision is the result of inevitable accident, and that the decree of the Circuit Court should be

AFFIRMED WITH COSTS.

---

2. Error In Extremis

PUERTO RICO PORTS AUTH. v. M/V MANHATTAN PRINCE

897 F.2d 1, 1990 AMC 1475 (1st Cir. 1990)

BOWNES, Circuit Judge

Shortly after 8 p.m. (2012 hours) on August 15, 1985, the tanker Manhattan Prince, while in the process of docking, collided with a pier. The allision occurred in the Army Terminal Turning Basin, Puerto Nuevo Channel, San Juan Harbor, Puerto Rico. An *in rem* action against the vessel was brought by the Puerto Rico Ports Authority (PRPA) and the Puerto Rico Electric Authority for damages caused to facilities on the pier owned by both authorities. Shortly thereafter, Sujeen Trading PTE., LTD., (Sujeen), the owner of the tanker, brought an action for damage to the tanker's bow incurred in the allision and damages due to loss of hire against Crowley Towing and Transportation Company (Crowley) and against Captain Oscar Camacho, the compulsory pilot. Crowley was the owner of two tugboats, the Borinquen and El Morro, which had been hired by the tanker to help her dock. The claim against Crowley by the tanker was based on the alleged negligence of the tug Borinquen; the tug El Morro is not involved in the case. In both cases, the defendants filed cross claims and counterclaims against each other.

The cases were consolidated for trial and a bench trial was held in August, 1987. The district court found the vessel and the pilot "jointly, severally and equally liable" for damages to the pier facilities, which amounted to $53,000. It found Crowley and the Electric Authority not liable to Sujeen for damages to the tanker. It found the pilot, Camacho, liable to Sujeen for half of the vessel's damages. These amounted to $194,723.40 for repairs to the bow of the tanker and $142,951.49 for loss of hire. The court further found that the PRPA was not liable for the negligence of the pilot. The court addressed the vicarious liability of the PRPA in an opinion published at 669 F. Supp. 34 (D.P.R. 1987).

Sujeen has appealed the holding that the ship was at fault for the allision and the ruling that the PRPA was not vicariously liable for the negligence of the pilot. The pilot has not appealed, and there has been no appeal on the computation of damages. There are, therefore, two basic issues to be reviewed: whether the tanker was 50% at fault for the allision, and whether the PRPA is responsible for the negligence of the pilot. We start with the negligence issue.

I.

* * *

B. The Facts

Most of the facts are undisputed; it is the conclusions drawn from them by the district court that has drawn Sujeen's fire. The tanker, Manhattan Prince, was carrying 34,800 metric tons of fuel oil to San Juan. The vessel is 805 feet long, has a 124 foot beam, and at the time of the allision had a draft of approximately 32 feet, since she was fully loaded. The vessel was powered by a diesel engine with one right-hand screw.

The Manhattan Prince was manned by Polish officers and crew. Neither the captain nor the two mates had been to San Juan Harbor prior to August 15, 1985, the date of the allision. None of the ship's officers spoke or understood Spanish. The compulsory pilot, Oscar Comacho, did not speak or understand Polish. He boarded the ship about 2½ miles from the entrance to San Juan Harbor at 7:12 p.m. (1912 hours). The pilot had never before docked a ship of the size of the Manhattan Prince. He did not know when he first went on board where the ship was to dock. He obtained this information by radio from Port Control.

At the time the pilot boarded the ship, darkness had fallen. After a discussion with the captain about the maneuverability and other characteristics of the vessel and the layout of San Juan Harbor, the pilot stationed himself in the port wing of the bridge. The captain moved back and forth across the bridge as conditions dictated. The pilot guided the ship by giving course and speed orders to the captain in English who relayed them in Polish to the crew member responsible for carrying them out. At times the pilot gave orders directly to a crew member. The second mate of the Manhattan Prince was on the bow. His responsibility was to act as a lookout and count down the distances as the ship approached the dock.

The course the ship followed was through the mouth of San Juan Harbor, down the Bar Channel to Anegado Channel, then a turn to port and down Anegado Channel to Army Terminal Channel. The ship then turned to starboard and followed Army Terminal Channel to the Army Terminal Turning Basin where it docked.

The tugs owned by Crowley, the Borinquen and El Morro, tied onto the tanker in Anegado Channel before she turned into Army Terminal Channel. The Borinquen was secured to the starboard bow with two lines; the El Morro was made fast to the starboard quarter. The tugs were manned by Puerto Ricans so the only one who could talk to the tug captains was the pilot which he did via a VHF radio in Spanish and "Spanglish," a combination of Spanish and English. From his position on the port wing of the bridge, the pilot was unable to see the Borinquen. The second mate who was stationed on the bow could see the tug but could not talk to its crew because of the language barrier and because his VHF radio, which enabled him to talk with the tanker captain, was on a different frequency from the radios of the pilot and the tug captains. This meant that the pilot could not hear the communications between the bow and the captain of the tanker, the tug captains could not hear the communications between the tanker's captain and the bow, and the bow could not hear the communications between the tug captains and the pilot.

In addition to the communications problems, the ship was attempting to dock at night in a constricted area. It was commanded by a master who had never even seen San Juan Harbor prior to this, much less transited it by ship, and it was piloted by one who had never before guided a vessel of this size. This was a prescription for an accident.

The tanker and tugs proceeded down Army Terminal Channel to the turning basin. The basin is at the south end of the channel, which runs almost directly from north to south. At its widest point, the basin measures about 200 yards. The distance from the basin entrance to the pier at which the ship was to dock was approximately 400 yards.

Two piers jutted out into the water at the southern terminus of the basin. The Army Terminal pier, which was where the tanker was to dock, lay to the west of Catano pier. Both piers are about 150 yards long. The Catano pier is considerably narrower than the Terminal pier. The piers are about 100 yards apart. The depth of the basin is between twenty-eight and thirty-nine feet. On the west side of the Terminal pier, where the ship was to be docked, the water depth is thirty-six to thirty-seven feet.

There are two buoys on the east side of the basin, numbered 7 and 9, marking the beginning of shallow water (3 to 5 feet). It must be kept in mind that the ship was a little more than 268 yards long, its beam was 41.3 yards and it had a draft of about 32 feet. There was not much room for maneuvering.

When the tanker entered the turning basin, it was moving forward. The estimates of its speed vary from less than 1 knot to 4 knots. The first task for the ship and tugs was to keep the stern from going aground in the shallow waters marked by buoys 7 and 9. This was accomplished. The ship, which continued to move forward, had to be positioned so that it would dock with its port side next to the Terminal pier. This meant that it had to be moved to the starboard (west) of the Catano pier and then just past the Terminal pier so its port side could be nudged against the pier. The ship continued its forward and sidewards motion past the Catano pier. At some point, the pilot asked the captain of the tug Borinquen how far the ship was from the pier. When it was about fifty feet from the Terminal pier, the tug Borinquen cast off its lines and backed off. There is a dispute as to how far and in what direction the tug moved. The ship continued forward and struck the front of the Terminal pier at a 90° angle—head on. The Borinquen picked up the lines and the ship, which was now dead in the water, was brought alongside the Terminal pier and docked.

C. The Findings and Conclusions of the District Court

The district court found that the allision occurred because the vessel was travelling too fast down Army Terminal Channel and was not slowed down sufficiently for a safe docking. The court did not credit the testimony of the pilot that he had ordered slow astern at buoy number 6 in the channel, which is about 900 yards from the dock. The court's conclusion as to the pilot's negligence was as follows:

> The pilot's negligence and failure to exercise due care in docking the vessel was a proximate cause of the allision which caused damages to the "*Manhattan Prince*" and the dock facilities. The pilot was negligent in attempting to dock the vessel at an excessive speed. Due to the large size of the vessel, the restricted space in the turning basin, and the pilots, [sic] lack of previous experience in docking a vessel the size of the "*Manhattan Prince*," the proper method would have been to stop the tanker dead in the water before attempting the final maneuvers to the dock. A prudent pilot would have proceeded with extreme caution given the situation.

The court's assessment of liability on the part of the ship was stated thus:

> The Court has found that distances were not relayed to the pilot by the master even though the bow watch was relaying the distances of the master upon approaching the dock. The pilot was forced to request a distance report from the captain of the "*Borinquen*" at a time when the vessel was too close to impact to matter. Whether this lack of communication resulted from the mish-mash of languages being spoken over the various radios, from the inconsistency occurring in the pilot sometimes giving commands through the master and sometimes directly, as evidenced by the statement of the chief officer who was stationed on the lee helm on the bridge, or from sheer negligence on the part of the master, this crucial information did not reach the pilot's ears. Responsibility for this omission must be attributed to the "*Manhattan Prince*." Thus, the ship's failure to report distances to the pilot, under these circumstances, was also a proximate cause of the allision. Had the pilot been better apprised of the ship's proximity to the dock and of the rate of the rapidly decreasing distances he could have better judged the ship's speed and distance and taken appropriate maneuvers to avoid allision.

In concluding that the tug Borinquen's actions were not a proximate cause of the allision, the court found that the tug was "*in extremis.*" It stated:

The extremely close passage by the Catano Oil Dock, her [the tug's] position near the bow of the tanker, and the tanker's massive size and continued forward way and 90° angle to the dock at a position only 30-50 feet from the dock, all conspired to put the *"Borinquen"* in extremis. The captain of the *"Borinquen"* was reasonable in letting go the lines. Whether the allision could have been avoided or mitigated if the *"Borinquen"* had held steady is mere speculation. The captain of the *"Borinquen"* cannot be held negligent for not choosing to risk his tug or the lives of his crew by holding fast to the ship while it allided with the dock.

D. The Issues

Sujeen mounts a four-pronged attack on the negligence findings of the district court: (1) the district court misapplied the *in extremis* doctrine and therefore the tug Borinquen should have been found negligent for casting off its lines when it did (2) the Manhattan Prince was not negligent (3) the admission in evidence of the Coast Guard's report of the accident was error and (4) the tug *Borinquen* breached its implied warranty of performance in a workmanlike manner and is therefore liable for the damages suffered by the tanker. We reject all four claims and affirm the district court's negligence findings.

We note at the outset that although appellant pays lip service to the clearly erroneous standard, its brief is written as if we were reviewing the facts *de novo*; its oral argument also proceeded on the same tack.

(1) The In Extremis Finding

The doctrine of *in extremis* has long been a part of admiralty law. In *The Blue Jacket*, 144 U.S. 371, 392, 12 S. Ct. 711, 719, 36 L. Ed. 469 (1892), the rule was stated as follows:

As was held in *The Bywell Castle*, 4 Prob. Div. 219, "where one ship has, by wrong manoeuvres, placed another ship in a position of extreme danger, that other ship will not be held to blame if she has done something wrong, and has not been manoeuvred with perfect skill and presence of mind."

The doctrine was invoked again by the Court in *The Oregon*, 158 U.S. 186, 204, 15 S. Ct. 804, 812, 39 L. Ed. 943, (1895), where it stated, "the judgment of a competent sailor *in extremis* cannot be impugned." In *Bucolo, Inc. v. S/V Jaguar*, 428 F.2d 394, 396 (1st Cir. 1970), we stated: "This doctrine is applicable only when the party asserting it was free from fault until the emergency arose." One of the most recent applications of the doctrine was in a case remarkably similar to this one, *Chevron U.S.A., Inc. v. Vessel J. Louis*, 702 F. Supp. 887 (M.D. Fla. 1988). The court there found that the allision occurred because of "the negligence of the pilot and vessel master in navigating the vessel at an excessive rate of speed so that she ran aground...." *Id.* at 891. As here, there was a tug tied to the vessel, and it loosened its line to the vessel to avoid being crushed against the dock. The court found the tug to be without fault, stating:

The tug was placed, by the pilot and master of the vessel, in a position of sudden peril and emergency, which situation did not arise as a result of the tug's own previous fault. Therefore, even if the Court were to decide that the Tampa was somehow negligent in failing to keep the towline from slipping as it backed full astern, as the pilot ordered, such alleged negligence must be excused under the *in extremis* doctrine. *Id.* at 891.

There was no misapplication of the *in extremis* doctrine here. The captain of the tug Borinquen testified in effect as follows: He had no problem communicating with the pilot. After the ship cleared the Catano dock, the pilot told him to stop pushing. At that time, the tug was between the head of the Catano dock and the bulkhead of the terminal pier. He told the pilot that he was about 50 feet from the pier, that there would be a collision, and he was going to release the lines because the tug was in danger. It was his judgment that if the tug had not backed away from the tanker, it would have been sandwiched between the tanker and the Catano pier.

Robert Leith, shipping agent for the Manhattan Prince, was on the pier waiting for it to dock. He testified that the ship approached the pier at a steady speed of between four and seven knots. He had seen vessels dock at this pier for thirty years and they approached at much less speed and much less under the control of tugs. Leith testified that the bow tug (*Borinquen*) "got out of there" when its captain saw that there was going to be a collision with the dock. It was Leith's testimony that the tug dropped its lines and backed away from the tanker, when the vessel was 50 to 60 feet from the pier.

It was the opinion of expert witness John Deck III that even if the tug *Borinquen* had not dropped the lines, the tanker would still have hit the pier.

Captain Stillwaggeon, an expert witness with extensive experience as a pilot, testified that if the tug had not dropped its lines it would have been endangered. He further testified that the tug did not desert the ship, but simply moved to a safe position and that the tug could not have prevented the collision.

From this evidence the court could have found that the tug did not do anything to create the emergency, that the safety of the tug and its crew was put in peril as the ship continued forward towards the piers and that casting off the lines was a reasonable response to the danger thrust upon the tug by the tanker.

The testimony is more than sufficient to sustain the district court's finding that the tug Borinquen was *in extremis* when it cast off the lines and therefore did not act negligently.

(2) The Negligence of the Manhattan Prince

The district court invoked a presumption of negligence against "all parties participating in the management of the vessel" because the vessel was moving and collided with a stationary object. It specifically found that the presumption applied to the tug *Borinquen* and the pilot as well as the vessel. It found that only the *Borinquen* overcame the presumption because it went forward and proved that when it cast off the lines, it was *in extremis*. The court found that neither the ship nor the pilot overcame the presumption.

This presumption of negligence goes back at least to *The Louisiana*, 70 U.S. 164, 18 L. Ed. 85 (1865). In that case the Court held:

> The streamer Flushing being aground on Hampton Bar, out of the channel or course of vessels navigating the bay or harbor, and incapable of motion, cannot be justly charged with any participation in causing the collision.
>
> The collision being caused by the Louisiana drifting from her moorings, she must be liable for the damages consequent thereon, unless she can show affirmatively that the drifting was the result of inevitable accident, or a *vis major*, which human skill and precaution, and a proper display of nautical skill could not have prevented.

Id. at 173. *See Weyerhaeuser Co. v. Atropos Island*, 777 F.2d 1344, 1347 (9th Cir. 1985). Although the circumstances here did not involve a vessel that had broken loose from her moorings as in *The Louisiana* and *Atropos Island*, it was not error to invoke the presumption against the Manhattan Prince. When a fully manned vessel accompanied by two tugs strikes a pier head-on, it ought to be presumed, unless the vessel proves otherwise, that the vessel was negligent. Under the facts here, however, considering especially the communication obstacles between the pilot, the ship's officers and the tug and the evidence of the speed of the ship in the turning basin, no presumption of negligence was needed; with or without such presumption the pilot and the ship were clearly negligent.

There is no reason to regurgitate the evidence establishing the tanker's negligence. We have read the entire record, including all depositions bearing on the issue and have examined carefully all pertinent exhibits. We hold that the district court's finding that the Manhattan Prince was 50% at fault was not clearly erroneous.

* * *

Affirmed. Costs awarded to appellees.

Note: Vicarious Liability for Acts of Compulsory/Noncompulsory Pilots

The court's finding in *Puerto Rico Ports Auth. v. M/V Manhattan Prince, supra*, that the PRPA was not vicariously liable for the negligence must be understood in the context of the rule in *The China*, 74 U.S. (7 Wall.) 53, 19 L. Ed. 67 (1868). The rule in *The China* is that a shipowner is not vicariously liable *in personam* for the negligence of a compulsory pilot, but the ship is vicariously liable *in rem*. The rule in *The China* is still in force. *See Afran Transport Co. v. Steamship Transcolorado*, 468 F.2d 772, 1974 AMC 2034 (5th Cir. 1972); *State of California v. Italian Motorship Ilice*, 534 F.2d 836, 1976 AMC 2290 (9th Cir. 1976); *Hogge v. Steamship Yorkman*, 434 F. Supp. 715, 1977 AMC 805 (D. Md. 1977); *Logue Stevedoring Corp. v. The Dalzellance*, 198 F.2d 369, 1952 AMC 1297 (2d Cir. 1952); *Homer Ramsdell Transportation Co. v. La. Compagnie Generale Transatlantique*, 182 U.S. 406, 21 S. Ct. 831, 45 L. Ed. 1155 (1901). Thus, the *M/V Manhattan Prince* would have been vicariously liable for the negligence of the compulsory pilot Camacho. The end result would have been that Sujeen's right to contribution from Camacho would effectively have been worthless.

The PRPA was not vicariously liable for the negligence of the compulsory pilot because it enjoyed Eleventh Amendment sovereign immunity from suit as a state agency. *Puerto Rico Ports Auth. v. M/V Manhattan Prince*, 897 F.2d 1, 1990 AMC 1475 (1st Cir. 1990), in passages not reproduced *supra*. Municipal authorities and port commissions that provide pilotage services may not share the same constitutional immunity. *See Principe Compania Naviera, S.A. v. Board of Commissioners of Port of New Orleans*, 333 F. Supp. 353, 1971 AMC 2639 (E.D. La. 1971). However, pilotage associations are not vicariously liable for the negligence of their member pilots. *Guy v. Donald*, 203 U.S. 399, 27 S. Ct. 63, 51 L. Ed. 245 (1906).

When the pilot is voluntarily taken aboard ship and his or her fault is the cause of injury or damage, the ship operator is liable both *in rem* and *in personam* under the generally recognized rules of *respondeat superior*. The rule in *The China* applies only to compulsory pilots. When is a pilot "compulsory" for these purposes? What if the services of a pilot are required by the private owner of a port facility? *See Texaco Trinidad, Inc. v. Afran Transport Co.*, 538 F. Supp. 1038, 1983 AMC 1582 (E.D. Pa. 1982) (pilot compulsory when required by berth or terminal owner even though pilotage not required by law or regulation).

If an onshore terminal employs a mooring master to assist in the docking of vessels, can the risk of liability from negligent mooring of the vessel be shifted from the terminal to the vessel through a pilotage clause in the agreement between the terminal and the ship that makes the mooring master the servant of the ship? *See Kane v. Hawaiian Independent Refinery, Inc.*, 690 F.2d 722, 1984 AMC 1323 (9th Cir. 1982) (the validity of pilotage clause upheld). For pilotage clauses in towing contracts, see Chapter 5, on Towage, Pilotage and Salvage.

In *Guangco v. Edward Shipping & Mercantile, S.A.*, 705 F.2d 360 (9th Cir. 1983), a crew member aboard the *M/V Pacific Queen* was injured while the ship was being docked in Apra Harbor, Guam, by a compulsory pilot. In the resulting litigation, the pilot company denied liability, relying on a clause in the pilotage agreement that the shipowner ["Edward"] would indemnify the pilot company for any injury resulting from the pilot's negligence. The court upheld the pilotage clause, stating as follows:

For the first argument, Edward relies upon Guam Civil Code § 2384, which provides:

The owner or master of a ship is not responsible for the negligence of a pilot whom he bound by law to employ; but if he is allowed an option between pilots, some of whom are competent, or is required only to pay compensation to a pilot, whether he employs him or not, he is also responsible to third persons.

It codifies the common law rule that a shipowner will not be held liable when the selection of a pilot is not a voluntary act. *Homer Ramsdell Transportation Co. v. La Compagnie Generale Transatlantique*, 182 U.S. 406 (1901). The rule grew out of the traditional pilotage system in which a shipmaster was required to accept the first pilot to offer his services to the vessel as it entered the harbor.

In Apra Harbor, however, a shipmaster has a choice among pilots. There are two companies providing local pilotage service. And under the plain language of Guam Civil Code § 2384, as long as the shipmaster can reject a pilot, he will be held responsible if he accepts the services of that pilot. This responsibility is reinforced by an administrative regulation, which imposes on a shipmaster the duty to relieve any incompetent or negligent pilot on board his ship. 9 GUAM ADMIN. R. § 8004.8. If the pilot aboard the Pacific Queen was negligent, Edward's shipmaster had a duty to replace that pilot.

... The exculpatory clause is reasonable. When the pilot boards the ship and takes over direction of its movement, he becomes independent of his employer, the pilotage company. He must serve the interest of the shipowner, and not of the pilotage company. Consequently the shipowner, who has a right to the best efforts of the pilot, bears the responsibility for the acts of the pilot.

... Because of the particular nature of the pilot's duties, it is fair and reasonable to indemnify the company which employs the pilot for that period when the pilot is on board another vessel, directing the movements of that vessel. The contract which Edward signed with Cabras is enforceable, even if Edward did not and could not bargain over the exculpatory clause. The clause is fair and reasonable in the light of the customary business practices of pilotage companies in Guam and elsewhere throughout the United States.

3. *Allocation of Fault—The Modern Rule*

UNITED STATES v. RELIABLE TRANSFER CO., INC.

421 U.S. 397, 95 S. Ct. 1708, 44 L. Ed. 2d 251, 1975 AMC 541 (1975)

Mr. Justice STEWART delivered the opinion of the Court.

More than a century ago, in *The Schooner Catharine v. Dickinson*, 17 How. 170, this Court established in our admiralty law the rule of divided damages. That rule, most commonly applied in cases of collision between two vessels, requires the equal division of property damage whenever both parties are found to be guilty of contributing fault, whatever the relative degree of their fault may have been. The courts of every major maritime nation except ours have long since abandoned that rule, and now assess damages in such cases on the basis of proportionate fault when such an allocation can reasonably be made. In the present case we are called upon to decide whether this country's admiralty rule of divided damages should be replaced by a rule requiring, when possible, the allocation of liability for damages in proportion to the relative fault of each party.

On a clear but windy December night in 1968, the Mary A. Whalen, a coastal tanker owned by the respondent Reliable Transfer Co., embarked from Constable Hook, N.J., for Island Park, N.Y., with a load of fuel oil. The voyage ended, instead, with the vessel stranded on a sand bar off Rockaway Point outside New York Harbor.

The Whalen's course led across the mouth of Rockaway Inlet, a narrow body of water that lies between a breakwater to the southeast and the shoreline of Coney Island to the northwest. The breakwater is ordinarily marked at its southernmost point by a flashing light maintained by the Coast Guard. As, however, the Whalen's captain and a deckhand observed while the vessel was proceeding southwardly across the inlet, the light was not operating that night. As the Whalen approached Rockaway Point about half an hour later, her captain attempted to pass a tug with a barge in tow ahead, but, after determining that he could not overtake them, decided to make a 180 degree turn to pass astern of the barge. At this time the tide was at flood, and the waves, whipped by northwest winds of gale force, were eight to ten feet high. After making the 180 degree turn and passing astern of the barge, the captain headed the Whalen eastwardly, believing that the vessel was then south of the breakwater and that he was heading her for the open sea. He was wrong. About a minute later the light structure on the southern point of the breakwater came into view. Tuning to avoid rocks visible ahead, the Whalen ran aground in the sand.

The respondent brought this action against the United States in Federal District Court, under the Suits in Admiralty Act, 41 Stat. 525, 46 U.S.C. § 741 *et seq.*, and the Federal Tort Claims Act, 28 U.S.C. § 1346 *et seq.*, seeking to recover for damages to the Whalen caused by the stranding. The District Court found that the vessel's grounding was caused 25% by the failure of the Coast Guard to maintain the breakwater light and 75% by the fault of the Whalen. In so finding on the issue of comparative fault, the court stated:

> The fault of the vessel was more egregious than the fault of the Coast Guard. Attempting to negotiate a turn to the east, in the narrow space between the bell buoy No. 4 and the shoals off Rockaway Point, the Captain set his course without knowing where he was. Obviously, he would not have found the breakwater light looming directly ahead of him within a minute after his change of course, if he had not been north of the point where he believed he was.
>
> Equipped with look-out, chart, searchlight, radio-telephone, and radar, he made use of nothing except his own guesswork judgment. After ... turning in a loop toward the north so as to pass astern of the tow, he should have made sure of his position before setting his new 73 degree course. The fact that a northwest gale blowing at 45 knots with eight to ten foot seas made it difficult to see, emphasizes the need for caution rather than excusing a turn into the unknown....

The court held, however, that the settled admiralty rule of divided damages required each party to bear one-half of the damages to the vessel.[1]

The Court of Appeals for the Second Circuit affirmed this judgment. 497 F.2d 1036....

We granted certiorari, 419 U.S. 1018, to consider the continued validity of the divided damages rule.

The precise origins of the divided damages rule are shrouded in the mists of history. In any event it was not until early in the 19th century that the divided damages rule as we know it emerged clearly in British admiralty law. In 1815, in *The Woodrop-Sims*, 2 Dods. 83, 165 Eng. Rep. 1422, Sir William Scott, later Lord Stowell, considered the various circumstances under which maritime collisions could occur and stated that division of damages was appropriate in those cases "where both parties are to blame." *Id.*, at 85, 165 Eng. Rep., at 1423. In such cases the total damages were to be "apportioned between" the parties "as having been occasioned by the fault of both of them." *Ibid.* Nine years later the divided damages rule became settled in English admiralty law when the House of Lords in a maritime collision case where both ships were at fault reversed a decision of a Scottish court that had apportioned damages by degree of blame, and, relying on *The Woodrop-Sims*, ordered that the damages be divided equally. *Hay v. Le Neve*, 2 Shaw H.L. 395.

It was against this background that in 1855 this Court adopted the rule of equal division of damages in *The Schooner Catharine v. Dickinson*, 17 How. 170. The rule was adopted because it was then the prevailing rule in England, because it had become the majority rule in the lower federal courts, and because it seemed the "most just and equitable, and ... best [tended] to induce care and vigilance on both sides, in the navigation." *Id.*, at 177-178. There can be no question that subsequent history and experience have conspicuously eroded the rule's foundations.

It was true at the time of *The Catharine* that the divided damages rule was well entrenched in English law. The rule was an ancient form of rough justice, a means of apportioning damages where it was difficult to measure which party was more at fault. *See* 4 R. Marsden, British Shipping Laws, *Collisions at Sea* §§ 119-147 (11th ed. 1961); Staring, *Contribution and Division of Damages in Admiralty and Maritime Cases*, 45 Calif. L. Rev. 304, 305-310 (1957). But England has long since abandoned the rule and now follows the Brussels Collision Liability Convention of 1910 that provides for the apportionment of damages on the basis of "degree" of fault whenever it is possible to do so. Indeed, the United States is now virtually alone among the world's major maritime nations in not adhering to the Convention with its rule of proportional fault—a fact that encourages transoceanic forum shopping. *See* G. Gilmore & C. Black, The Law of Admiralty 529 (2d ed. 1975) (hereinafter Gilmore & Black).

While the lower federal courts originally adhered to the divided damages rule, they have more recently followed it only grudgingly, terming it "unfair," "illogical," "arbitrary," "archaic and frequently un-just." Judge Learned Hand was a particularly stern critic of the rule. Dissenting in *National Bulk Carriers v. United States*, 183 F. 2d 405, 410 (CA2), he wrote: "An equal division [of damages] in this case would be plainly unjust; they ought to be divided in some such proportion as five to one. And so they could be but for our obstinate cleaving to the ancient rule which has been abrogated by nearly all civilized nations." And Judge Hand had all but invited this Court to overturn the rule when, in an earlier opinion for the Court of Appeals for the Second Circuit, he stated that "we have no power to divest ourselves of this vestigial relic; we can only go so far as to close our eyes to doubtful delinquencies." *Oriental*

---

[1] The operation of the rule was described in *The Sapphire*, 18 Wall. 51, 56. 21 L.Ed. 814: "It is undoubtedly the rule in admiralty that where both vessels are in fault the sums representing the damage sustained by each must be added together and the aggregate divided between the two. This is in effect deducting the lesser from the greater and dividing the remainder.... If one in fault has sustained no injury, it is liable for half the damages sustained by the other, though that other was also in fault."

Similarly, in *The North Star*, 106 U.S. 17, 22, the rule was thus stated:

[A]ccording to the general maritime law, in cases of collision occurring by the fault of both parties, the entire damage to both ships is added together in one common mass and equally divided between them, and thereupon arises a liability of one party to pay to the other such sum as is necessary to equalize the burden.

* * *

It has long been settled that the divided damages rule applies not only in cases of collision between two vessels, but also in cases like this one where a vessel party at fault is damaged in collision or grounding because of the mutual contributing fault of a nonvessel party....

Trading & Transport Co. v. Gulf Oil Corp., 173 F. 2d 108, 111. Some courts, even bolder, have simply ignored the rule. *See* J. Griffin, The American Law of Collision 564 (1949); *Staring, supra*, at 341-342. *Cf. The Margaret*, 30 F. 2d 923 (CA3).

It is no longer apparent, if it ever was, that this Solomonic division of damages serves to achieve even rough justice. An equal division of damages is a reasonably satisfactory result only where each vessel's fault is approximately equal and each vessel thus assumes a share of the collision damages in proportion to its share of the blame, or where proportionate degrees of fault cannot be measured and determined on a rational basis. The rule produces palpably unfair results in every other case. For example, where one ship's fault in causing a collision is relatively slight and her damages small, and where the second ship is grossly negligent and suffers extensive damage, the first ship must still make a substantial payment to the second. "This result hardly commends itself to the sense of justice any more appealingly than does the common law doctrine of contributory negligence...." Gilmore & Black 528.

And the potential unfairness of the division is magnified by the application of the rule of *The Pennsylvania*, 19 Wall. 125, whereby a ship's relatively minor statutory violation will require her to bear half the collision damage unless she can satisfy the heavy burden of showing "not merely that her fault might not have been one of the causes, or that it probably was not, but that *it could not have been.*" *Id.*, at 136 (emphasis added).

The Court has long implicitly recognized the patent harshness of an equal division of damages in the face of disparate blame by applying the "major-minor" fault doctrine to find a grossly negligent party solely at fault. But this escape valve, in addition to being inherently unreliable, simply replaces one unfairness with another. That a vessel is primarily negligent does not justify its shouldering all responsibility, nor excuse the slightly negligent vessel from bearing any liability at all....

The divided damages rule has been said to be justified by the difficulty of determining comparative degrees of negligence when both parties are concededly guilty of contributing fault. *The Max Morris*, 137 U.S. 1. Although there is some force in this argument, it cannot justify an equal division of damages in every case of collision based on mutual fault. When it is impossible fairly to allocate degrees of fault, the division of damages equally between wrongdoing parties is an equitable solution. But the rule is unnecessarily crude and inequitable in a case like this one where an allocation of disparate proportional fault has been made. Potential problems of proof in some cases hardly require adherence to an archaic and unfair rule in all cases. Every other major maritime nation has evidently been able to apply a rule of comparative negligence without serious problems, *see* Mole & Wilson, *A Study of Comparative Negligence*, 17 Corn. L.Q. 333, 346 (1932); *In re Adams' Petition*, 125 F. Supp. 110, 114 (SDNY), *affd.* 237 F.2d 884 (CA2), and in our own admiralty law a rule of comparative negligence has long been applied with no untoward difficulties in personal injury actions. *See, e.g., Pope & Talbot, Inc. v. Hawn*, 346 U.S. 406, 409. *See also* Merchant Marine (Jones) Act, 38 Stat. 1185, *as amended*, 41 Stat. 1007, 46 U.S.C. § 688; Death on the High Seas Act, 41 Stat. 537, 46 U.S.C. § 766.

The argument has also been made that the divided damages rule promotes out-of-court settlements, because when it becomes apparent that both vessels are at fault, both parties can readily agree to divide the damages—thus avoiding the expense and delay of prolonged litigation and the concomitant burden on the courts. It would be far more difficult, it is argued, for the parties to agree on who was more at fault and to apportion damages accordingly. But the argument is hardly persuasive. For if the fault of the two parties is markedly disproportionate, it is in the interest of the slightly negligent party to litigate the controversy in the hope that the major-minor fault rule may eventually persuade a court to absolve it of all liability. And if, on the other hand, it appears after a realistic assessment of the situation that the fault of both parties is roughly equal, then there is no reason why a rule that apportions damages would be any less likely to induce a settlement than a rule that always divides damages equally. Experience with comparative negligence in the personal injury area teaches that a rule of fairness in court will produce fair out-of-court settlements. But even if this argument were more persuasive than it is, it could hardly be accepted. For, at bottom, it asks us to continue the operation of an archaic rule because its facile application out of court yields quick, though inequitable, settlements, and relieves the courts of some litigation. Congestion in the courts cannot justify a legal rule that produces unjust results in litigation simply to encourage speedy out-of-court accommodations.

Finally, the respondent suggests that the creation of a new rule of damages in maritime collision cases is a task for Congress and not for this Court. But the Judiciary has traditionally taken the lead in formulating flexible and fair remedies in the law maritime, and "Congress has largely left to this Court the responsibility for fashioning the controlling rules of admiralty law." *Fitzgerald v. United States Lines Co.*, 374 U.S. 16, 20. *See also Moragne v. States Marine Lines*, 398 U.S. 375, 405 n.17; *Kermarec v. Compagnie Generale Transatlantique*, 358 U.S. 625, 630-632. No statutory or judicial precept precludes a change in the rule of divided damages, and indeed a proportional fault rule would simply bring recovery for property damage in maritime collision cases into line with the rule of admiralty law long since established by Congress for personal injury cases. *See* the Jones Act, 46 U.S.C. § 688.

* * *

The rule of divided damages in admiralty has continued to prevail in this country by sheer inertia rather than by reason of any intrinsic merit. The reasons that originally led to the Court's adoption of the rule have long since disappeared. The rule has been repeatedly criticized by experienced federal judges who have correctly pointed out that the result it works has too often been precisely the opposite of what the Court sought to achieve in *The Schooner Catharine*—the "just and equitable" allocation of damages. And worldwide experience has taught that that goal can be more nearly realized by a standard that allocates liability for damages according to comparative fault whenever possible.

We hold that when two or more parties have contributed by their fault to cause property damage in a maritime collision or stranding, liability for such damage is to be allocated among the parties proportionately to the comparative degree of their fault, and that liability for such damages is to be allocated equally only when the parties are equally at fault or when it is not possible fairly to measure the comparative degree of their fault.

Accordingly, the judgment before us is vacated and the case is remanded for further proceedings consistent with this opinion.

---

4. Proximate Cause

EXXON CO., U.S.A. v. SOFEC, INC.

517 U.S. 830, 116 S. Ct. 1813, 135 L. Ed. 2d 113, 1996 AMC 1817 (1996)

Justice THOMAS delivered the opinion of the Court.

In *United States v. Reliable Transfer Co.*, 421 U.S. 397, 95 S.Ct. 1708, 44 L.Ed.2d 251 (1975), we abandoned the "divided damages" rule previously applied to claims in admiralty for property damages, and adopted the comparative fault principle for allocating damages among parties responsible for an injury. In this case we affirm that the requirement of legal or "proximate" causation, and the related "superseding cause" doctrine, apply in admiralty notwithstanding our adoption of the comparative fault principle.

I

This case arises from the stranding of a tanker, the Exxon Houston, several hours after it broke away from a Single Point Mooring System (SPM) owned and operated by the HIRI respondents and manufactured by respondent Sofec, Inc.[1] The Houston was engaged in delivering oil into HIRI's pipeline through two floating hoses, pursuant to a contract between Exxon and respondent PRII, when a heavy storm broke the chafe chain linking the vessel to the SPM. As the vessel drifted, the oil hoses broke away from the SPM. The parting of the second hose at

---

[1] The Houston was owned and operated by petitioner Exxon Shipping Company, whose vessels carried crude oil for petitioner Exxon Company, U.S.A. We will refer to both of these companies as Exxon. The HIRI respondents are several affiliated corporations: Pacific Resources, Inc.; Hawaiian Independent Refinery, Inc.; PRI Marine, Inc.; and PRI International, Inc. (PRII).

approximately 1728 nautical time was designated below as the "breakout." The hoses were bolted to the ship, and a portion of the second hose remained attached to the ship. So long as the hose was attached to and trailing from the ship, it threatened to foul the ship's propeller, and consequently the ship's ability to maneuver was restricted.

During the 2 hours and 41 minutes following the breakout, the captain of the Houston, Captain Coyne, took the ship through a series of maneuvers described in some detail in the District Court's findings of fact. The District Court found that by 1803, a small assist vessel, the Nene, was able to get control of the end of the hose so that it was no longer a threat to the Houston. See 54 F.3d 570, 572 (C.A.9 1995). Between 1803 and 1830, Captain Coyne maneuvered the Houston out to sea and away from shallow water. The District Court, and on appeal, a panel of the Court of Appeals for the Ninth Circuit, found that by 1830, the Houston had successfully avoided the peril resulting from the breakout. App. to Pet. for Cert. 65; 54 F.3d, at 578-579. The ship had "reached a safe position," App. to Pet. for Cert. 64, and was "heading out to sea and in no further danger of stranding," *id.*, at 65; 54 F.3d, at 578.

Many of Captain Coyne's actions after 1830 were negligent, according to the courts below. Most significant was his failure to have someone plot the ship's position between 1830 and 2004, a period during which the crews of the Houston and the Nene were working to disconnect the hose from the Houston. Without knowing his position, Captain Coyne was unable to make effective use of a navigational chart to check for hazards. The courts found that this failure to plot fixes of the ship's position was grossly and extraordinarily negligent. App. to Pet. for Cert. 61; 54 F.3d, at 578. The District Court found that "Captain Coyne's decisions were made calmly, deliberately and without the pressure of an imminent peril." App. to Pet. for Cert. 60. His failure to plot fixes after 1830 "was entirely independent of the fact of breakout; he voluntarily decided not to plot fixes in a situation where he was able to plot fixes." *Id.*, at 64.

At 1956, Captain Coyne initiated a final turn toward the shore. Because he had not plotted the ship's position, Captain Coyne was unaware of its position until he ordered another crew member to plot the fix at 2004. Upon seeing the fix on the chart, the captain apparently realized that the ship was headed for a reef. Captain Coyne's ensuing efforts to avoid the reef came too late, and moments later the ship ran aground, resulting in its constructive total loss. The District Court found that Captain Coyne's decision to make this final turn "was not foreseeable." *Id.*, at 65.

Exxon filed a complaint in admiralty against the HIRI respondents and respondent Sofec for, *inter alia*, the loss of its ship and cargo. The complaint contained claims for breach of warranty, strict products liability, and negligence. HIRI filed a complaint against several third-party respondents, who had manufactured and supplied the chafe chain that held the tanker to the SPM.

Before trial, respondents suggested that Captain Coyne's conduct was the superseding and sole proximate cause of the loss of the ship, and they moved to bifurcate the trial. Respondents and the third-party respondents disputed among themselves the cause of the breakout, and they apparently sought bifurcation of the trial to avoid lengthy proceedings to resolve those factual disputes prior to a determination whether Captain Coyne's conduct was the superseding cause of Exxon's injury. The District Court granted the motion, limiting the first phase of the trial to the issue of proximate causation with respect to actions taken after the breakout, and leaving the issue of causation of the breakout itself for the second phase.

Following a 3-week bench trial in admiralty, the District Court found that Captain Coyne's (and by imputation, Exxon's) extraordinary negligence was the superseding and sole proximate cause of the Houston's grounding. *Id.*, at 63. The court entered final judgment against Exxon with respect to the loss of the Houston, and Exxon appealed.

The Ninth Circuit held that the District Court's findings "that Captain Coyne had ample time, as well as opportunity and available manpower, to take precautions which would have eliminated the risk of grounding, and that his failure to do so amounted to extraordinary negligence, superseding any negligence of the defendants with regard to the breakout or provision of safe berth after the breakout," were "well supported by the record," and not clearly erroneous. 54 F.3d, at 579. The court rejected Exxon's contention that the captain's actions were foreseeable reactions to the breakout; rather, it noted, Captain Coyne himself had explained that he did not plot fixes "because he felt it was unnecessary to do so." *Id.*, at 578.

Relying upon Circuit precedent, the court rejected Exxon's legal argument that the doctrines of proximate causation and superseding cause were no longer applicable in admiralty in light of this Court's decision in *Reliable Transfer*. "[A]n intervening force supersedes prior negligence" and thus breaks the chain of proximate causation required to impose liability on the original actor, the court held, "where the subsequent actor's negligence was 'extraordinary' (defined as 'neither normal nor reasonably foreseeable')." *Id.*, at 574. The court also rejected Exxon's argument that the District Court erred in rendering judgment against Exxon on its breach of warranty claims. "Where, as here, the district court finds the injured party to be the superseding or *sole* proximate cause of the damage complained of, it cannot recover from a party whose actions or omissions are deemed to be causes in fact, but not legal causes of the damage." *Id.*, at 576. Finally, the court held that under the circumstances of the case, the District Court's bifurcation of the trial was not an abuse of discretion. We granted certiorari. 516 U.S. —, 116 S.Ct. 493, 133 L.Ed.2d 419 (1995).

II

Exxon makes four arguments for the reversal of the judgment below: (1) that the superseding cause doctrine does not or should not apply in admiralty; (2) that respondents' breaches of warranty were causes in fact of the loss of the Houston and hence respondents should be liable for that loss; (3) that the lower courts' finding that Captain Coyne's extraordinary negligence was the sole proximate cause of the loss of the Houston was in error; and (4) that the District Court abused its discretion and deprived Exxon of due process in bifurcating the issue of proximate causation from the other issues.

A

Exxon's primary argument is that the proximate causation requirement, and the related superseding cause doctrine, are not or should not be applicable in admiralty. In particular, Exxon asserts that the lower courts' refusal to allocate any share of damages to parties whose fault was a cause in fact of Exxon's injury conflicts with our decision in *Reliable Transfer*.

We disagree. In *Reliable Transfer*, we discarded a longstanding rule that property damages in admiralty cases are to be divided equally between those liable for injury, "whatever the relative degree of their fault may have been," 421 U.S., at 397, 95 S.Ct., at 1709, and adopted the comparative fault principle in its stead.[2] The proximate causation requirement was not before us in *Reliable Transfer*, and we did not suggest that the requirement was inapplicable in admiralty. (Nor, for that matter, did we consider whether the injury had been proximately caused by the defendant in that case.)

There is nothing internally inconsistent in a system that apportions damages based upon comparative fault only among tortfeasors whose actions were proximate causes of an injury. Nor is there any repugnancy between the superseding cause doctrine, which is one facet of the proximate causation requirement, and a comparative fault method of allocating damages. As Professor Schoenbaum has said:

> The doctrine of superseding cause is ... applied where the defendant's negligence in fact substantially contributed to the plaintiff's injury, but the injury was actually brought about by a later cause of independent origin that was not foreseeable. It is properly applied in admiralty cases. [T]he superseding cause doctrine can be reconciled with comparative negligence. Superseding cause operates to cut off the liability of an admittedly negli-

---

[2] Some commentators have suggested that there may be a distinction between a system allocating damages on the basis of comparative culpability, and a system allocating damages on the basis of both comparative culpability and the degree to which fault proximately or foreseeably contributed to an injury. W. Keeton, Prosser and Keeton on the Law of Torts 474 (5th ed.1984); 1 T. Schoenbaum, Admiralty and Maritime Law § 5-4, p. 167 (2d ed.1994); Owen & Whitman, Fifteen Years Under *Reliable Transfer*: 1975-1990, Developments in American Maritime Law in Light of the Rule of Comparative Fault, J. Mar. L. & Com. 445, 476-483 (1991). We continue to use the term "comparative fault" employed in *Reliable Transfer*, but we do not mean thereby to take a position on which of these systems is the appropriate one, assuming that there is in fact a distinction between them.

gent defendant, and there is properly no apportionment of comparative fault where there is an absence of proximate causation." 1 T. Schoenbaum, Admiralty and Maritime Law § 5-3, pp. 165-166 (2d ed.1994).

Indeed, the HIRI respondents assert that of the 46 States that have adopted a comparative fault system, at least 44 continue to recognize and apply the superseding cause doctrine. Brief for HIRI Respondents 28, and n. 31; *id.*, at App. A (listing state court decisions). Exxon does not take issue with this assertion and concedes that it is not aware of any state decision that holds otherwise. Tr. of Oral Arg. 10.

Exxon also argues that we should in any event eschew in the admiralty context the "confusing maze of common-law proximate cause concepts"; a system in which damages are allocated based upon the degree of comparative fault of any party whose act was a cause in fact of injury is "fairer and simpler," it says. Reply Brief for Petitioners 2. It is true that commentators have often lamented the degree of disagreement regarding the principles of proximate causation and confusion in the doctrine's application, see, *e.g.*, W. Keeton, Prosser and Keeton on the Law of Torts 263 (5th ed.1984), but it is also true that proximate causation principles are generally thought to be a necessary limitation on liability, see, *e.g.*, *id.*, at 264, 293, 294, 312. Indeed, the system Exxon apparently proposes either would let proximate causation principles, with all of their complexity, creep back in as one factor in the "comparative fault" analysis itself, see n. 2, *supra*, or would produce extreme results. "In a philosophical sense, the consequences of an act go forward to eternity, and the causes of an event go back to the dawn of human events, and beyond." Keeton, *supra*, at 264. Nevertheless,

> the careless actor will [not] always be held for all damages for which the forces that he risked were a cause in fact. Somewhere a point will be reached when courts will agree that the link has become too tenuous—that what is claimed to be consequence is only fortuity. Thus, if the [negligent] destruction of the Michigan Avenue Bridge had delayed the arrival of a doctor, with consequent loss of a patient's life, few judges would impose liability.

Petition of Kinsman Transit Co., 338 F.2d 708, 725 (C.A.2 1964), quoted in 1 Schoenbaum, *supra*, § 5-3, at 164.

In ruling upon whether a defendant's blameworthy act was sufficiently related to the resulting harm to warrant imposing liability for that harm on the defendant, courts sitting in admiralty may draw guidance from, *inter alia*, the extensive body of state law applying proximate causation requirements and from treatises and other scholarly sources. See Keeton, *supra*, at 279 ("'The best use that can be made of the authorities on proximate cause is merely to furnish illustrations of situations which judicious men upon careful consideration have adjudged to be on one side of the line or the other'") (quoting 1 T. Street, Foundations of Legal Liability 110 (1906)).

B

Exxon's argument that the District Court erred in rendering judgment against Exxon on its breach of warranty claims fares no better. Exxon implicitly argues that because the respondents breached various contractual warranties, they were "best situated" to prevent the loss of the Houston; and Exxon invokes a passage from *Italia Societa per Azioni di Navigazione v. Oregon Stevedoring Co.*, 376 U.S. 315, 84 S.Ct. 748, 11 L.Ed.2d 732 (1964). In *Italia Societa*, we held that a stevedore breaches its implied warranty of workmanlike service to a shipowner when the stevedore nonnegligently supplies defective equipment that injures one of its employees during stevedoring operations. That case does not purport to deal with the proximate causation limitation for damages on a warranty claim and is not relevant to the question presented here.

We agree with the Ninth Circuit that where the injured party is the sole proximate cause of the damage complained of, that party cannot recover in contract from a party whose breach of warranty is found to be a mere cause in fact of the damage. Although the principles of legal causation sometimes receive labels in contract analysis different from the "proximate causation" label most frequently employed in tort analysis, these principles nevertheless exist to restrict liability in contract as well. Indeed, the requirement of foreseeability may be more stringent in the context of contract liability than it is in the context of tort liability. See *East River S.S. Corp. v. Transamerica Delaval Inc.*, 476 U.S. 858, 874-875, 106 S.Ct. 2295, 2303-2304, 90 L.Ed.2d 865 (1986); Restatement (Second) of Contracts § 351 and Comment *a*, pp. 135-136 (1979); 11 W. Jaeger, Williston on Contracts § 1344, pp. 227-228 (3d ed.1968); 5 A. Corbin, Corbin on Contracts § 1008, pp. 75-76 (1964); *id.*, § 1019, at 113-116; cf. 3 E. Farnsworth, Farnsworth on Contracts § 12.14, pp. 241-243 (1990) (*Hadley v. Baxendale*, 9 Ex. 341, 156 Eng. Rep. 145 (1854), "impose[s] a more severe limitation on the recovery of damages for breach of contract than that applicable to actions in tort or for breach of warranty, in which substantial or proximate cause is the test"). The finding that Captain Coyne's extraordinary negligence was the sole proximate cause of Exxon's injury suffices to cut off respondents' liability for that injury on a contractual breach of warranty theory as well.

C

The legal question that we took this case to address is whether a plaintiff in admiralty that is the superseding and thus the sole proximate cause of its own injury can recover part of its damages from tortfeasors or contracting partners whose blameworthy actions or breaches were causes in fact of the plaintiff's injury. As we have held above, the answer is that it may not. Apparently anticipating that this legal issue would not likely be resolved in its favor, Exxon devotes a large portion of its briefs to arguing that the findings by the lower courts that Captain Coyne's extraordinary negligence was the sole proximate cause of Exxon's injury were in error. The issues of proximate causation and superseding cause involve application of law to fact, which is left to the factfinder, subject to limited review. See, *e.g.*, *Milwaukee & St. Paul R. Co. v. Kellogg*, 94 U.S. 469, 473-476, 24 L.Ed. 256 (1876); Keeton, Prosser and Keeton on Torts, at 320-321; 5 Corbin, *supra*, § 998, at 22-23. "A court of law, such as this Court is, rather than a court for correction of errors in fact finding, cannot undertake to review concurrent findings of fact by two courts below in the absence of a very obvious and exceptional showing of error." *Graver Tank & Mfg. Co. v. Linde Air Products Co.*, 336 U.S. 271, 275, 69 S.Ct. 535, 538, 93 L.Ed. 672 (1949); see also *Goodman v. Lukens Steel Co.*, 482 U.S. 656, 665, 107 S.Ct. 2617, 2623, 96 L.Ed.2d 572 (1987); *Reliable Transfer*, 421 U.S., at 401, n. 2, 95 S.Ct., at 1711, n. 2. Although Exxon identifies some tension in the various findings made by the courts below,[3] we nevertheless conclude that Exxon has not made an "obvious and exceptional showing of error" that would justify our reversal of the courts' ultimate conclusion, reached after a 3-week trial and review of a lengthy and complex record. Without necessarily ratifying the application of proximate causation principles by the courts below to the particular facts here, we decline to reconsider their conclusion.

D

Finally, Exxon argues that the District Court erred in bifurcating the trial. This issue is not within the questions upon which we granted certiorari. See Pet. for Cert. i. To the extent that Exxon argues that the issue involved here—whether one cause of injury is a superseding cause—can never be bifurcated from other issues, we reject that contention. Again, Exxon relies upon *Reliable Transfer* in asserting that the fault of all parties must be considered together in order that they may be compared. As explained above, that argument is wrong: A party whose fault did not proximately cause the injury is not liable at all. To the extent that Exxon argues that the District Court abused its discretion in dividing the trial in the particular way that it did here, we decline to address that argument.

The judgment is affirmed.

It is so ordered.

---

[3] Exxon argues that the courts' findings—that by 1803, the Nene had gained control of the end of the hose so that it was no longer a threat to the Houston, and that by 1830, the Houston had successfully avoided the peril resulting from alleged breaches of duty on respondents' part, had "reached a safe position," and was "heading out to sea and in no further danger of stranding"—are inconsistent with the apparently uncontested finding that the hose, which was suspended from the ship's crane during efforts to disconnect the hose from the ship, caused the crane to topple at 1944, injuring a crewman. We note in this regard that the District Court expressly found that the captain's failure to plot fixes after 1830 "was entirely independent of the fact of breakout" and that "he voluntarily decided not to plot fixes in a situation where he was able to plot fixes"; the Court of Appeals also relied upon the fact that Captain Coyne himself had explained that he did not plot fixes "because he felt it was unnecessary to do so."

5. Violation of Safety Standards: The Pennsylvania Rule

Introductory Note

In *The Pennsylvania*, 86 U.S. (19 Wall) 125, 22 L. Ed. 148 (1873), a collision between the sailing bark MARY TROOP and the steamship PENNSYLVANIA occurred in very dense fog. The MARY TROOP was moving slowly, ringing a bell as a fog signal, although the collision regulations stipulated use of a foghorn. The PENNSYLVANIA was proceeding at a speed of seven knots, although the collision regulations required ships "to go at a moderate speed" in fog. The Supreme Court held that the PENNSYLVANIA was at fault by going too fast and the MARY TROOP by ringing a bell rather than sounding a foghorn. The Court said (*id.* at 136):

Concluding then, as we must, that the bark was in fault, it still remains to inquire whether the fault contributed to the collision, whether in any degree it was the cause of the vessels coming into a dangerous position. It must be conceded that if it clearly appears the fault could have had nothing to do with the disaster, it may be dismissed from consideration. The liability for damages is upon the ship or ships whose fault caused the injury. But when, as in this case, a ship at the time of a collision is in actual violation of a statutory rule intended to prevent collisions, it is no more than a reasonable presumption that the fault, if not the sole cause, was at least a contributory cause of the disaster. In such a case the burden rests upon the ship of showing not merely that her fault might not have been one of the causes, or that it probably was not, but that it could not have been. Such a rule is necessary to enforce obedience to the mandate of the statute.

CANDIES TOWING CO., INC. v. M/V B & C ESERMAN

673 F.2d 91, 1983 AMC 2033 (5th Cir. 1982)

John R. BROWN, Circuit Judge

In this sugary sweet tale of oceangoing disaster, Candies Towing, owner of a sunken barge, and ProRico, owner of its cargo, sue the tug *M/V B&C Eserman*, and its owners, for the loss of barge and cargo. Trial before the District Court resulted in a judgment for the vessel. Ensnared in the rigging of the clearly erroneous rule, we affirm the factual findings and decree but modify in one important respect.

A. Cargo of Molasses for Neptune's Graveyard

Following in the wake of the District Court, which set forth all the important facts, we will but summarize. Candies Towing, a Louisiana corporation, owned a steel hull, oceangoing barge, OC-250. It measured 250 feet in length, 72 feet of beam, and a depth of 15 feet. Built in 1970 as a deck barge, OC-250 later was converted by its owners for use as a liquid bulk carrier. It carried an A-1 certification of the American Bureau of Shipping and satisfied Coast Guard standards for a seagoing barge. The Coast Guard, in fact, inspected the barge and gave its approval on March 24, 1977, less than nine months before it sank.

The tug *B&C Eserman* is an 80-foot, 1250 horsepower twin screw diesel tug that carries a crew of four. It routinely operated with OC-250 to carry cargoes of liquid molasses between Mobile, Alabama and West Palm Beach, Florida.

From October 15-25, 1977, the barge underwent substantial maintenance and repair work at Hunt's Shipyard in Harvey, Louisiana. Although OC-250 had not suffered any accident or casualty, Hunt's employees repaired deck cracks, separations of welds in the internal frame work, two splits in the bottom, damage to the longitudinal bulkhead, and repaired or replaced internal frames and supports. All this work concentrated on the forward section of the barge in way of the first two compartments. Following completion of the repairs and an inspection, OC-250 returned to service.

On November 27, 1977, *B&C Eserman*, while en route to Wilmington, North Carolina from West Palm Beach, grounded its laden tow, OC-250, on Frying Pan Shoal Reef. Although some question exists, it appears that the barge grounded stern-first on a hard sand reef, at a speed of 1 to 1½ miles per hour, in calm seas. At the time, OC-250 carried a cargo of molasses to a draft of 10½ feet forward and 11½ aft.

Captain Jones, at the conn, lacked a fathometer, channel charts, tide tables, light lists, or other such aids to navigation. It was his first trip to Wilmington. He had no offshore license and was not a qualified navigator. His prior experience on seagoing tugs was as a wheelman or mate, not as a captain. Nor did he have the requisite number of licensed watchstanders on board.

Approximately ten hours later, high tide freed OC-250 from its strand, and the tow proceeded into Wilmington. There Captain Leo Spooner, Candies' representative, met the vessel as usual. Spooner, already aware from radio communications that OC-250 had gone aground, checked it out. He inspected each of the tanks after unloading and found no water in any of them. Personnel from ProRico and American Molasses also inspected the barge. No one found any damage or cause for concern. Following these inspections, Captain Spooner cleared OC-250 as fit to resume travel. The tow thus returned to West Palm Beach for the next voyage.

Spooner and ProRico's representative again inspected OC-250 in West Palm Beach. After seeing its trim, freeboard and draft, Spooner found it fit. Despite deteriorating weather conditions, it set out for Mobile on December 4. After passing Dry Tortugas, the last point of land along the Florida Keys, Captain Jones noticed that the barge had sheered to the left. He had the tug circle the barge but found nothing wrong.

The weather indeed worsened. One winter storm, called a norther, hit on December 7, with seas of up to 15 feet. A second struck on December 9, with seas up to 20 feet and winds around 100 miles per hour. At dawn on December 10, Captain Jones noticed that the freeboard at the bow of the barge had increased, indicating that the stern was going down. Down, indeed, it went, in some 1300 feet of water, a total loss of both the barge and its cargo of 4248 short tons of bulk molasses.

Bittersweet Results in the District Court

The District Court made extensive findings of fact. It held that the tug did not breach a duty to Candies, Captain Jones acted reasonably in sailing for Mobile despite the bad weather, and Candies failed to show that any of the clear statutory violations with regard to crew qualifications and watchstanding at sea "were in any way connected to" the sinking of the barge. The Court specifically found that the rule of *The Pennsylvania*, 86 U.S. (19 Wall) 125, 22 L. Ed. 148 (1873) did not apply since no collision had occurred, citing *Garner v. Cities Service Tankers Corp.*, 456 F.2d 476, 1972 A.M.C. 1980 (5th Cir. 1972). It therefore granted a decree in favor of the tug *B&C Eserman*.

M/V Scope of Review

The findings of the District Judge, confronted with a mystery for which no apparent cause exists, float well above that Plimsoll Line. We affirm the findings and judgment of the District Court.

Accepting the factual findings does not yet put an end to this watery donnybrook, for we cannot anchor until we have addressed the District Court's treatment of the rule of *The Pennsylvania, supra.*

In simplest terms, that rule states that where a vessel is guilty of a statutory violation, the defaulting ship must show "not merely that her fault might not have been one of the causes, or that it probably was not, but that it could not have been." 86 U.S. (19 Wall) at 136, 22 L. Ed. at 151. *See also Allied Chemical, supra*, at 1052; G. GILMORE & C. BLACK, THE LAW OF ADMIRALTY (2d ed. 1975) § 10-25, at 898. It thus constitutes an evidentiary rule reversing the burden of proof. It does not render immaterial negligence, fault or damages but does impose a substantial burden upon the party at fault in proving its innocence.

The District Court simply erred as a matter of law in concluding that the rule of *The Pennsylvania* applies only in collision cases. The case on which the District Judge relied, *Garner, supra*, neither establishes nor supports any such holding. A hot water tank on the SS Bradford Island exploded, killing one employee and injuring two others. The vessel owners sought to apply the rule of *The Pennsylvania* to force the shipyard, which had connected its 125 pounds per square inch (PSI) saturated steam system to the vessel's 70 PSI system, to prove that its action could not have contributed to the cause of the accident. This court, per the late Judge Gewin, refused. We began by pointing out:

Within the Fifth Circuit, the rule of *The Pennsylvania* has not been viewed as a rule of liability. The rule creates a shift in the burden of proof as to causation.... Although Cities Services cites authority in other circuits where the rule has been applied in cases not involving collisions between ships, we have found no instance where this court has done so.

456 F.2d at 480, 1972 A.M.C. at 1985 (citations omitted).

The inability to find such precedent, of course, by no means stamps such a possibility as incorrect. Indeed, our specific holding belied the District Court's broad generalization. We did not hold, nor have we ever held, that the rule of *The Pennsylvania* applies only to collision cases. Rather, we merely declined "to extend the rule of *The Pennsylvania* from its tort origins to the setting of contractual indemnity or breach of WWLP." *Id*. Thus, although the rule of *The Pennsylvania* rightfully has little application in a contractual indemnity action, an action far removed from its original port of call, Garner does not state and we do not interpret it to mean that in other tort actions, such as here, the rule does not apply.

The Appropriate Vantage Point

This Court recently spoke on the subject and clarified the ramifications of Garner. In *Reyes v. Vantage Steamship Co.*, 558 F.2d 238 (5th Cir. 1977), on rehearing, 609 F.2d 140 (5th Cir. 1980), we applied the rule of *The Pennsylvania* where a vessel lacked a required line-throwing device and its crew, in violation of the maritime rescue doctrine, made no effort to save a drowning sailor. The sailor, legally drunk at the time, decided to take a swim in the ocean and dived some 35 feet off the side of the vessel. He was spotted immediately by other crew members, who knew from the outset that he was in danger. Yet no one made any effort to rescue Reyes. These facts and the absence of the statutorily required line throwing device established negligence as a matter of law. Citing *In re Seaboard Shipping Corp.*, 499 F.2d 132, 136, 1971 A.M.C. 2145, 2152 (2d Cir. 1971), *cert. denied*, 406 U.S. 949, 92 S. Ct. 2038-39, 32 L. Ed. 2d 337 (1972), we explicitly held that the rule of *The Pennsylvania* extended to this man overboard situation:

Nothing that has been said impairs the principle that ... in Jones Act cases ... cause in fact is still necessary.... Combining this slight standard of causation with the presumption of causation to which the plaintiff is here entitled means that on remand the ship owner must show that the ship's inaction and regulatory violations *could not have been* even a contributing cause of Reyes' death.

609 F.2d at 146, (emphasis added).

In *Seaboard Shipping, supra*, two crew members of a barge died during a wild storm on Lake Michigan. The Second Circuit found that the barge was unseaworthy in three respects: its radio was out of order, its lifeboat was damaged, and its inflatable liferaft was improperly stowed. Seaboard, the barge owner, argued that in all probability none of those defects caused the deaths. Yet the Court refused to exonerate Seaboard, declaring,

We need go no further here than to say, however, that given the statutory violations alone (the liferaft stowage and the overloading), Seaboard is not entitled to exoneration. *The Pennsylvania* ... makes it clear that the burden is on a ship in violation of a safety statute—in this case the barge—to show "not merely that her fault might not have been one of the causes, or that it probably was not, but that it could not have been." Seaboard is wrong in its contention that admiralty applies their rule only in collision cases. *Kernan v. American Dredging Co.*, 355 U.S. 426 (1958) (fire on a tug caused by open-flame kerosene lamp carried on scow in statutory violation); *The Denali*, 112 F.2d 952 (9th Cir. 1940) (stranding case).

449 F.2d at 136, 1971 A.M.C. at 2152. These cases, we believe, establish beyond doubt that the rule of *The Pennsylvania* does apply in non-collision cases.

Nor does *U.S. v. Reliable Transfer Co.*, 421 U.S. 397, 95 S. Ct. 1708, 44 L. Ed. 2d 251, 1975 A.M.C. 541 (1975), in any way alter our conclusion. *Reliable Transfer*, a tidal wave case in the admiralty, overruled only the time honored policy practice of dividing damages in a case of mutual or joint fault on a 50/50 basis. It does not bring into question the rule shifting the burden of proof.

* * *

No Candy

Given our conclusion that the District Court erred in its discussion of *The Pennsylvania* rule, we necessarily must address its findings to determine whether we must remand. We conclude that we need not do so.

Two separate incidents took place: the grounding and the sinking. As to the first, we have fault but no damage; in the second, damage but no fault. While *The Pennsylvania* does impose a strenuous burden upon one guilty of statutory default, and we hesitate not a moment in declaring *B&C Eserman* negligent as to the grounding of the barge, it does not delete the requirement of causation with respect to the loss of the barge many days later under severe conditions of wave and weather. The District Court concluded, and we cannot disagree, that whatever *B&C Eserman's* statutory violations, whatever its negligence insofar as the grounding is concerned, neither had anything to do with the sinking. "Plaintiffs failed to show that any of the factors above, either individually or collectively, were in any way connected to the sinking of the barge." (emphasis supplied) *B&C Eserman* introduced testimony that the barge suffered from a weak internal framework. Such a weakness could cause the barge to "work", causing metal fatigue and, ultimately, breaking the internal structure. The extensive repair work done on OC-250, according to expert testimony, established such a weakness. The District Judge apparently credited this testimony and believed it furnished a more logical explanation for the sinking then the grounding two weeks previously. Thus, even if the District Court had correctly interpreted the rule of *The Pennsylvania*, it still would have granted judgment for the tug since neither the negligent grounding some two weeks before nor the statutory violations on the trip to Mobile could have caused the sinking.

The Court of Appeals, no less than Coke, does not require the performance of a useless act. We there-fore modify the opinion of the District Court as regards the rule of *The Pennsylvania* and, as modified, affirm.

Affirmed as modified.

OTTO CANDIES, INC. v. M/V MADELINE D

721 F.2d 1034, 1987 AMC 911 (5th Cir. 1983)

TATE, Circuit Judge

In this maritime case of negligent towage, the plaintiff owner ("Candies") sues the *Madeline D*, a towing vessel, and its owner to recover damages arising out of the capsizing and sinking of its tug the *Ferdie Candies*. Candies appeals from adverse judgment, contending, inter alia, that the district court, after finding that both vessels were operated in violation of a rule designed to assure navigational safety, erroneously refused to apply the "*Pennsylvania*" rule (creating a heavy presumption of fault for a maritime accident occurring when a vessel is being operated in violation of the rules of navigation). Finding merit to this contention, we reverse and remand to the district court.

The relevant facts as to the accident itself may be briefly stated:

The defendant *Madeline D* and the plaintiff's *Ferdie Candies* were part of a flotilla towing a barge. *Madeline D* was in the lead, in charge of steering and navigation of the flotilla. The *Ferdie Candies* was attached by a fifteen-foot towing hawser astern of the *Madeline D*, and participated solely for the purpose of providing additional power. The towed barge was some forty feet behind the *Ferdie Candies*. The parties' witnesses differed as to the cause of the accident, which occurred when the towed barge struck the *Ferdie Candies* and caused it to capsize: the plaintiff Candies presented testimony that the mishap occurred when the *Madeline D* veered sharply to the right and pulled the *Ferdie Candies* out of alignment with the two, causing the barge to strike it; the defendant *Madeline D's* witnesses denied the sharp turn and testified that the cause of the accident was the *Ferdie Candies's* helmsman playing with the steering system and thus putting that vessel out of line with the rest of the flotilla and causing it to be struck by the towed barge.

The district court, after making findings of fact that merely summarized the testimony of the opposing witnesses,[1] concluded that "[t]here was little or no proof of the actual cause of the casualty" and that proof of the casualty alone was "insufficient to shift the responsibility for the accident to the *Madeline D*", since "[t]o do so would be to allow plaintiff to prove its case by speculation and hypothesis." In therefore dismissing the plaintiff's suit, Candies, the owner of the tug, was thus required to bear the entire loss of the mishap.

The Pennsylvania Rule Issue

The district court also found that both vessels were at the time of the mishap being operated in violation of a statutory regulation designed "to assure safe navigation," which provides that an uninspected towing vessel shall be under "the actual direction and control" of a person licensed to operate that type of vessel in the particular geographic area. 46 U.S.C. § 405(b)(2).[2] At the time of the accident, an unlicensed deckhand was at the steering controls of both vessels, while the captain of the *Madeline D* was not licensed.[3]

Accepting this conclusion of the district court,[4] we find that the district court erred as a matter of law in concluding that, because of the mutual statutory fault of both vessels, the plaintiff was "estopped from transferring its heavy burden of proof to defendant by invoking the rule of *The Pennsylvania*." This rule provides that when a ship violates a statutory rule of navigation intended to prevent collisions, "the burden rests on the ship of showing not merely that her fault might not have been one of the causes, or that it probably was not, but that it could not have been." *The Pennsylvania*, 86 U.S. (19 Wall.) 125, 136, 22 L. Ed. 148 (1873). *See also* GILMORE & BLACK, THE LAW OF ADMIRALTY § 10-25 at 898 (2d ed. 1975).

The rule shifts the burden of proof as to causation to the statutory offender, but it does not ipso facto impose liability. *Florida East Coast Railway Company v. Revilo Corporation*, 637 F.2d 1060, 1065-66 (5th Cir. 1981); *Green v. Crow*, 243 F.2d 401, 403 (5th Cir. 1957). Where both parties to a collision are guilty of statutory fault, the heavy presumption that the fault of each contributed to the accident may be rebutted by proof that, in fact, the fault of either of the parties was the sole cause of the accident or, instead, not a substantial contributing cause thereof. *Id.*

---

[1] Candies also argues, with some force, that remand would be required because these "findings of fact" were not specific enough on the subsidiary facts relating to the critical issues of fault and credibility to afford a sufficiently definite predicate for appellate review. *See, e.g., Hydrospace-Challenger, Inc. v. Tracor/Mas, Inc.*, 520 F.2d 1030, 1033-34 (5th Cir. 1975); *see also Golf City, Inc. v. Wilson Sporting Goods Co., Inc.*, 555 F.2d 426, 432-36 (5th Cir. 1977). Because remand is required for the district court's error of law in failing to apply to Pennsylvania rule, we do not reach these forceful contentions, although by citing them we wish to alert the district court to them on the remand.

[2] 46 U.S.C. § 405(b)(2) provides:

> An uninspected towing vessel in order to assure safe navigation shall, while underway, be under the actual direction and control of a person licensed by the Secretary to operate in the particular geographic area and by type of vessel under regulations prescribed by him. A person so licensed may not work a vessel while underway or perform other duties in excess of a total of twelve hours in any consecutive twenty-four hour period except in case of emergency. (Emphasis added).

[3] The district court also noted that the *Ferdie Candies'* master, in violation of this statute, had been standing watch for sixteen hours straight (in excess of the statutory maximum of twelve, *see* 46 U.S.C. § 405(b)(2), quoted in note 2), before going down to sleep and leaving the craft under the actual direction and control of an inexperienced and unlicensed deckhand.

[4] Both parties contend that the other vessel, but not their own, was not within the regulation provided by 46 U.S.C. § 405(b)(2). The plaintiff Candies contends, without citation of authority, that the *Ferdie Candies* should not be considered a "towing vessel" within the meaning of the statute, because it merely provided an additional engine and was more in the nature of a "tow". The *Madeline D* parties contend, based on inferences that they assert may be made from the record, that their vessel was exempt from the statutory requirements by virtue of 46 U.S.C. § 405(b)(3) which provides that the statutory regulation does not apply to towing vessels of less than two hundred tons engaged in a service to the offshore oil and mineral exploitation industry, where the vessel's point of departure or ultimate destination is an offshore mineral exploitation site. Again, because of the conclusory nature of the district court's findings (*see* note 1), we are unable to review the merits of the latter contention and accept, for present purposes (but without prejudice to renewal of the contention on the remand), the district court's presumptively valid, FED. R. CIV. P. 52(a), implicit conclusion that the facts in the record do not support such exemption.

Here, the district court was unable to determine the cause of the *Ferdie Candies'* collision and, for whatever reason, made no credibility determination as between the opposing contentions as to whether steering negligence by an unlicenced deckhand on the part of either one vessel or the other factually caused the accident. In that posture of the case, the invoked *Pennsylvania* rule required the district court to find that the statutory fault of both vessels contributed to the accident, unless it found that the fault of either (or of both, for that matter) could not have been a cause of the collision. The district court was in error of law in holding that one party or the other, because of mutual fault, was estopped from invoking the *Pennsylvania* rule, which is a rule of presumed causation not of clean hands-dirty hands moral blameworthiness.

In the absence of the requisite findings by the district court that would permit effective appellate review (*see* note 1, *supra*), it is necessary for us to vacate the take-nothing judgment entered against the plaintiff Candies and to remand this case to the district court for it to make such additional findings of fact as are necessary to decide the Pennsylvania-rule causation issues presented. If both parties are guilty of statutory fault (*but see* note 4 *supra*), these determinations should include: (a) whether either party had proved that its own fault could not have contributed to the collision; (b) the proportionate degree of fault of both, *Florida East Coast Railway Company, supra*, 637 F.2d at 1067, if neither vessel is exonerated from collision causing statutory fault; and (c) if comparable fault cannot be fairly measured, a determination to that effect, with the consequence that the damages are to be allocated equally between the opposing parties, *see United States v. Reliable Transfer Co., Inc.*, 421 U.S. 397, 421, 95 S. Ct. 1708, 1716, 44 L. Ed. 2d 251 (1975).

Conclusion

Accordingly, we VACATE the judgment of the district court, and we REMAND this case for further proceedings not inconsistent with this opinion. The defendants-appellees to pay the costs of this appeal.

––––––––––

Notes

1. The 1910 Brussels Collision Convention

As stated in *Reliable Transfer*, the basic international law concerning collision is embodied in the 1910 Brussels Collision Convention. The basis for liability is fault, and the proportional fault rule applies (Arts. 3-4). The United States is one of the few nations of the world that has not adhered to this convention. Despite the adoption of the proportional fault rule in *Reliable Transfer*, important differences still exist between U.S. and the international law relating to collisions, as will be made clear below.

2. The Rules of the Road

The Basic Collision Regulations or International Rules were developed by the Intergovernmental Maritime Commission (IMCO) and agreed upon in the 1972 Convention on the International Regulations for Preventing Collisions at Sea, done at London in 1972. In 1977, these rules were adopted by statute in the United States. 33 U.S.C. §§ 1601-1608. In the internal waters of the United States the Inland Navigational Rules, 33 U.S.C. §§ 2001-2073, apply.

Consider the following selected provisions of the International Rules:

Rule 2. Responsibility
  a) Nothing in these Rules shall exonerate any vessel, or the owner, master or crew thereof, from the consequences of any neglect to comply with these Rules or of the neglect of any precaution which may be required by the ordinary practice of seamen, or by the special circumstances of the case.
  b) In construing and complying with these Rules due regard shall be had to all dangers of navigation and collision and to any special circumstances, including the limitations of the vessels involved, which may make a departure from these Rules necessary to avoid immediate danger.
Rule 9. Narrow Channels
  a) A vessel proceeding along the course of a narrow channel or fairways shall keep as near to the outer limit of the channel or fairway which lies on her starboard side as is safe and practicable....
Rule 13. Overtaking

a) Notwithstanding anything contained in the Rules of this Section any vessel overtaking any other shall keep out of the way of the vessel being overtaken....

Rule 14. Head-on situation

a) When two power-driven vessels are meeting on reciprocal or nearly reciprocal courses so as to involve risk of collision each shall alter her course to starboard so that each shall pass on the port side of the other....

Rule 15. Crossing situation

When two power-driven vessels are crossing so as to involve risk of collision, the vessel which has the other on her own starboard side shall keep out of the way and shall, if the circumstances of the case admit, avoid crossing ahead of the other vessel.

Rule 16. Action by give-way vessel

Every vessel which is directed to keep out of the way of another vessel shall, so far as possible, take early and substantial action to keep well clear.

Rule 17. Action by stand-on vessel

(a)(i) Where one of two vessels is to keep out of the way the other shall keep her course and speed.

(ii) The latter vessel may however take action to avoid collision by her manoeuvre alone, as soon as it becomes apparent to her that the vessel required to keep out of the way is not taking appropriate action in compliance with these Rules.

b) When, from any cause, the vessel required to keep her course and speed finds herself so close that collision cannot be avoided by the action of the give-way vessel alone, she shall take such action as will best aid to avoid collision.

c) A power-driven vessel which takes action in a crossing situation in accordance with sub-paragraph (a)(ii) of this Rule to avoid collision with another power-driven vessel shall, if the circumstances of the case admit, not alter course to port for a vessel on her own port side.

d) This Rule does not relieve the give-way vessel of her obligation to keep out of the way.

Rule 19. Conduct of vessels in restricted visibility

a) This Rule applies to vessels not in sight of one another when navigating in or near an area of restricted visibility.

b) Every vessel shall proceed at a safe speed adapted to the prevailing circumstances and conditions of restricted visibility. A power-driven vessel shall have her engines ready for immediate manoeuvre.

For an application of these rules, *see Cap'n Mark v. Sea Fever Corp.*, 692 F.2d 163, 1983 AMC 2651 (1st Cir. 1982); *Ching Sheng Fishery Co., Ltd. v. United States*, 124 F.3d 152, 1998 AMC 370 (2d Cir. 1997). *See also Partenreederei M.S. Bernd Leonhardt v. U.S.*, 393 F.2d 756, 1968 AMC 910 (4th Cir. 1968).

3. *Place of Suit and Choice of Law*

Where should suit be brought in the case of a collision on the high seas? Should some connection to the forum state be required before a court in that state can exercise jurisdiction? Such a requirement was a feature of the 1952 Brussels Convention on Civil Jurisdiction in Matters of Collision (Art. 1 (1)(b)), but this convention has not been adopted by most important maritime states. United States courts can be expected to apply principles of *forum non conveniens* in such cases. If an American court takes jurisdiction of a collision case involving vessels registered in countries that have accepted the 1910 Collision Convention, will the court apply the law of the Convention? *See The Mandu*, 102 F.2d 459 (2d Cir. 1939).

What law will the court apply in the case of a collision on the high seas? In *Alemeon Naviera, S.A. v. M/V "Marina L."*, 633 F.2d 789, 792-93, 1982 AMC 153 (9th Cir. 1980), the court stated as follows:

To decide Elmarina's claim, we must first decide what law controls. In collisions occurring on the high seas, general maritime law usually applies. *The Scotland*, 105 U.S. 24, 29 (1881); *Fitzgerald v. Texaco, Inc.*, 521 F.2d 448, 452 (2d Cir. 1975), *cert. denied*, 423 U.S. 1052 (1976). Where, however, both ships are of the same registry, the law of the common flag applies. *The Scotland*, 105 U.S. at 29-30; *The Gelgenland*, 114 U.S. 355, 370 (1885); *Pacific Vegetable Oil Corp. v. S/S Shalom*, 257 F. Supp. 944, 946 (S.D.N.Y. 1966). *Compare Arbitration of Paeuz-Pamare*, 1949 A.M.C. 508, 512 (N.Y. 1948) (collision in Gulf of Venezuela between ships of Venezuela registry; Venezuelan law applies) with *Arbitration of Catatumbo-Quiriquire*, 1949 A.M.C. 513, 520 (N.Y. 1948) (collision eight months later in same area between ships of Venezuelan and British registry; *lex fori*, or New York law, applies). Here, since both ships are of Greek registry, the parties have agreed that Greek law controls. This does not mean, however, that our task becomes one of determining and applying foreign law; Greece, in common with most nations involved in commercial shipping, is a party to the 1960 Safety of Life at Sea Convention [1960 SOLAS]. 6B A. KNAUTH & C. KNAUTH, BENEDICT ON ADMIRALTY 1064 (7th rev. ed. 1969). The United States is also a member of that convention. *Id.* The provisions and annexes promulgated under the 1960 SOLAS were therefore not only the law of Greece, but also were the positive law of the United States, Act of September 24, 1963, Pub. L. 88-131, 77 Stat. 195; Executive Order No. 239, 30 Fed. Reg. 9671 (1965) (implementing regulations and annexes). The guidelines of the 1960 SOLAS represent a uniform set of internationally recognized navigational rules and thus they have the status of general maritime law. Indeed, Professors Gilmore and Black have noted that "the more competent [ship officers] have most of the [rules] substantially committed to memory." G. GILMORE & C. BLACK, THE LAW OF ADMIRALTY 489 (2d ed. 1975).

The parties have also conceded that certain provisions of the 1960 SOLAS control this case. As noted above, however, the provisions of the 1960 SOLAS constitute not only Greek and general maritime law, but American law as well. Thus, we are not presented with the thorny, question of whether American precedent is applicable in interpreting another country's general maritime law of personal injury, *see id.* at 482-84; rather, we are presented with the interpretation of uniform international collision regulations which are not only the law of Greece and the United States, but also are the law of most seafaring nations. In order to achieve the uniformity of application and certainty of decision that the 1960 SOLAS was designed to promote, we consider all apposite precent; this includes American law as well as the law of other signatories to the 1960 SOLAS. *See e.g., McDonald v. M/V Betty K II*, 1958 A.M.C. 523, 525 (S.D. Fla. 1958).

In *Ching Sheng Fishery Co. Ltd v. U.S.*, 124 F.3d 152, 1998 AMC 370 (2d Cir. 1997), the court applied the U.S. enactment of the international Collision Regulations and the *Pennsylvania* rule to a collision in the Malacca Strait (which lies between Malaysia and Indonesia) between a Taiwanese-flagged fishing vessel and a ship operated by the U.S. Navy's Military Sealift Command.

In *Otal Investments, Ltd. v. M/V Clary* ___ F. 3d ___, 2007 AMC ___ (2d Cir. 2007), the Second Circuit applied the 1910 Collision Convention to a collision in international waters between vessels flying flags of signatory states. The court also held that the *Pennsylvania* rule is substantive, not procedural, and therefore should not be applied to a collision governed by the Convention, which abolishes all presumptions of causative fault.

4. *The Pennsylvania Rule*

Was the court in *Candies Towing Co., Inc. v. M/V B & C Eserman*, 673 F.2d 91, 1983 AMC 2033 (5th Cir. 1982) correct in concluding that *The Pennsylvania* rule survives *Reliable Transfer*? *See also, Getty Oil Co., Inc. v. SS Ponce de Leon*, 555 F.2d 328, 1977 AMC 711 (2d Cir. 1977). What is the purpose of the *Pennsylvania* rule? *See First Nat'l Bank of Chicago v. Material Service Co.*, 544 F.2d 911, 1978 AMC 193 (7th Cir. 1976). Article 6 of the 1910 Collision Convention states that "[a]ll legal presumptions of fault in regard to liability are abolished." Should *The Pennsylvania* rule be overruled? *See* William Tetley, *The Pennsylvania Rule—An Anachronism?*, 13 J. Mar. L. & Com. 127 (1982).

5. *The "Major-Minor" Fault Rule*

Did the "major-minor" fault rule survive *Reliable Transfer*? Is the rule of "last clear chance" applied in collision cases? *See Getty Oil, supra.*

6. *Radar*

Is failure to use radar a basis for fault? *See Allied Chemical Corp. v. Hess Tankship Co.*, 661 F.2d 1044, 1053, 1982 AMC 1271 (5th Cir. 1981) and *Afran Transport Co., v. The Bergechief*, 274 F.2d 469 (2d Cir. 1960). Rule 7 of the International Rules requires that "proper use" be made of "radar equipment if fitted and operational." Should failure to equip a vessel with radar be a basis of fault? For a proposal to require radar equipment, *see* Robert G. Martinez, *Marine Radar, A Proposal for Mandatory Usage*, 11 J. Mar. L & Com. 109 (1979).

7. *Error "In Extremis"*

Under the error *in extremis* rule negligence committed by navigators of a vessel that is in imminent peril of collision is excused. *See The Stifinder*, 275 F. 271 (2d Cir. 1921), overruled on other grounds in *American Tobacco Co. v. The Katingo Hadjipatera*, 211 F.2d 666, 1954 AMC 874 (2d Cir.), *cert. denied*, 348 U.S. 828, 75 S. Ct. 48, 99 L. Ed. 653 (1954). Did this rule survive *Reliable Transfer*?

8. *Ship-To-Shore Collisions (Allisions)*

Does the proportional fault rule apply in ship-to-shore collision cases? *See Feeder Line Towing Service, Inc. v. Toledo, Peoria & Western Railroad*, 539 F.2d 1107 (7th Cir. 1976).

9. *Underwater Pipelines*

Another type of marine casualty is an allision between a vessel and an underwater pipeline. Does *The Pennsylvania* rule apply in this kind of case? *See Orange Beach Water, Sewer, & Fire Protection Authority v. M/V Alva*, 680 F.2d 1374 (11th Cir. 1982).

10. *The Wreck Act*

This statute, 33 U.S.C. §§ 409, 411, requires the owner of a vessel sunk "accidentally or otherwise" to visibly mark it and to remove it. The United States Supreme Court has held that this statute is not exclusive, and that under principles of tort liability a negligent non-owner may be liable for the costs of removal or may be required by the United States through injunctive relief to remove the vessel. *Wyandotte Transportation Co. v. United States*, 389 U.S. 191, 88 S. Ct. 379, 19 L. Ed. 2d 407 (1967).

Can the owner or negligent non-owner be liable from a post-sinking collision with an unmarked wreck? *See Nunley v. M/V Dauntless Colocotronis*, 696 F.2d 1141 (5th Cir. 1983) and *Ison v. Roof*, 698 F.2d 294 (6th Cir.), *cert. denied sub nom. Great Southwest Fire Ins. Co. v. Iron*, 461 U.S. 957, 103 S. Ct. 2429, 77 L. Ed. 2d 1316 (1983).

11. *Presumptions*

In addition to the Pennsylvania Rule, other presumptions are recognized under U.S. collision law. One of the most common is that where a moving vessel hits a stationary object, the moving vessel is presumed to be at fault. *The Oregon*, 158 U.S. 186, 15 S. Ct. 804, 39 L. Ed. 943 (1895); *The Louisiana*, 70 U.S. (3 Wall.) 164, 18 L. Ed. 85 (1865). This presumption, like others, is a rebuttable presumption. Thus, in a case where a vessel struck a bridge, evidence that the Coast Guard had determined pursuant to an investigation that the bridge was an obstruction to navigation may be sufficient to overcome the presumption. *I&M Rail Link, LLC v. Northstar Navigation, Inc.*, 198 F.3d 1012, 2000 AMC 736 (7th Cir.), *cert. denied*, 531 U.S. 917, 121 S. Ct. 276, 148 L. Ed. 2d 201 (2000).

B. Damages

Note: *Total and Partial Losses*

When the vessel involved in a collision or accident is a total loss, the damages include (1) the market value of the vessel at the time of the loss (plus pending freight) and (2) pollution cleanup, salvage, wreck removal, and other incidental costs proximately resulting from the casualty. For problems of valuation of the vessel, *see Oliver J. Olson & Co. v. American Steamship Marine Leopard*, 356 F.2d 728, 1966 AMC 1064 (9th Cir. 1966). Loss of earnings and detention are not recoverable. *See The Umbria*, 166 U.S. 404, 17 S. Ct. 610, 41 L. Ed. 1053 (1897).

In a case of damage other than total loss, damages include (1) the cost of repairs (or diminution of value if no repairs are made), (2) detention, *i.e.* loss of earnings for the period the vessel is out of service, and (3) incidental costs such as wharfage, pilotage, and salvage costs. *See Skou v. United States*, 478 F.2d 343, 1973 AMC 1482 (5th Cir. 1973). In a repair—loss of use case, suppose the vessel owner uses the occasion to advance the regularly scheduled drydocking of the vessel? *See Bouchard Transp. Co., Inc. v. The Tug Ocean Prince*, 691 F.2d 609, 1982 AMC 2944 (2d Cir. 1982).

More difficult issues of damage recovery are raised in the following cases.

---

1. *Economic Loss*

MOORE-McCORMACK LINES v. THE ESSO CAMDEN

244 F.2d 198, 1957 AMC 971 (2d Cir.), *cert. denied*, 355 U.S. 822, 78 S. Ct. 29, 2 L. Ed. 2d 37 (1957)

LUMBARD, Circuit Judge

Cross appeals are taken by two ships from damages awarded resulting from a collision in 1946 for which both ships were held to be at fault. The questions raised concern the measure of reimbursement to both ships for losses from their respective detentions and for the outlay by libellant of general average disbursements.

On November 2, 1946, *The S.S. William S. Halsted* collided with the tank steamship *Esso Camden* in Chesapeake Bay. *The Halsted*, owned by Moore-McCormack Lines, Inc., had just commenced a voyage to ports on the Baltic Sea. *The Camden*, owned by Standard Oil Company (N.J.) (hereinafter "owner"), and under charter to its subsidiary, Standard Oil Company of New Jersey (hereinafter "charterer"), was enroute to Baltimore from Baytown, Texas. As a result of the collision, *The Halsted* was laid up for 17 days, after which she resumed her scheduled run to the Baltic. Upon her return, the season for Baltic trade being over, *The Halsted* turned to a South American cruise. *The Camden*, previously scheduled for a two-day lay-off for repairs, was detained 15.986 days because of the collision.

The commissioner awarded *The Halsted* $20,342.28 detention damages for the 17 day delay, based on the average per diem profit of her collision and pre-collision voyages and $6,194.83, representing 2% commission and 6% interest on general average disbursements and 2½% settling agent's commission for collecting and settling the general average.

The Camden was awarded $22,181.29 detention damages. At the time of the collision, *The Camden* was carrying oil under a charter party between owner and charterer. The charter party having been prematurely terminated as a result of the collision, the commissioner looked to the potential earnings thereunder as a basis for ascertaining loss. Because of the accident the owner of *The Camden* was required to refund $38,395, representing a portion of the gross rate of hire which had been paid in advance by the charterer. This refund included profits and certain voyage maintenance expenses which it was agreed by stipulation would have been incurred by the owner. The commissioner therefore deducted $16,231.71, the stipulated voyage maintenance expenses, from the $38,395 refunded to the charterer in arriving at the $22,181.29 damages occasioned to the owner by the loss of use of *The Camden*. Nothing was allowed to *The Camden* for its maintenance expenses while laid up for repairs.

The commissioner's report was first affirmed in its entirety by the district court and later modified as to two minor items.[1]

The principal issue regarding the award to *The Halsted* concerns detention damages. In estimating the loss from the 17 day delay, the commissioner used an average of the per diem profits for *The Halsted's* collision and pre-collision voyages to the Baltic, $1,227.06 and $1,156.36 respectively, and ignored the post-collision voyages to South America which netted *The Halsted* only $413.25 daily profits. *The Camden* urges that the earnings of the post-collision voyage are the correct measure of the damages, or, at most, an average of the daily net earnings of the collision voyage and the post-collision voyage. Either of these measures would reduce the damages allowed by the commissioner.

It is well established that demurrage is recoverable only when profits have actually been, or may reasonably be supposed to have been lost, and such profits can be proven with reasonable certainty. *The Conqueror*, 1897, 166 U.S. 110, 125, 17 S. Ct. 510, 41 L. Ed. 937. Although *The Halsted* was able to complete successfully the interrupted voyage, she was active in a ready market at the time of the collision and for her loss of potential earnings she is entitled to reparation. *The Mayflower*, D.C.E.D. Mich. 1872, 16 Fed. Cas. page 1243, No. 9,345.

The only facts before us bearing on loss of profits from the detention are the stipulated earnings of *The Halsted* for three voyages: (1) the pre-collision Baltic voyage of 59 days showing a profit of $68,224.47, (2) the collision voyage to the Baltic for 78 days with $95,710.40 profit, and (3) the post-collision voyage to South American ports lasting 104 days and earning $42,978.06.

On consideration of all the circumstances, it seems to us that a fairer measure of lost profits is the average daily earnings over the entire period of the three voyages in evidence. The measure of a ship's demurrage is the amount the vessel would have earned in the business in which she has been customarily employed. *Williamson v. Barrett*, 1851, 13 How. 101, 54 U.S. 101, 110, 14 L. Ed. 68. The three voyages (not including the detention period) here cover a total of 241 days. This period is sufficient in point of time and activity to evaluate the Halsted's probable loss of profits from detention. For that matter, *The Halsted's* earnings over a longer period of time, or, perhaps earnings of similar ships in the same market at or about the period of detention, would also be relevant on the question of what was a fair measure of *The Halsted's* lost profits.[2] But no such proof was offered here. Under the circumstances of this case the average daily earnings during the 241 days is sufficient evidence of lost profits during detention.

Clearly *The Halsted* suffered no losses on the interrupted voyage, and it could make no difference to her regular course of business whether the collision occurred towards the beginning or the end of the successfully completed run. There is no proof offered that another Baltic voyage would have been undertaken but for the delay. The itineraries of *The Halsted's* three voyages apparently represent her normal course of business. On the record we must

---

[1] On reargument the district court amended its decision to correct two errors: (1) adjusting the commissioner's finding of $16,213.71 unincurred voyage maintenance expenses for the *Camden* to $16,313.71, to account for an error of $100 in computation; and (2) adding $1,508.19 to these unincurred expenses, constituting anticipated port charges which the commissioner, by oversight, failed to include. Thus corrected these expenses totalled $17,821.90. When deducted from the $38,395 refunded, instead of the original award of $22,181.29, the *Camden's* detention damages were held to be $20,573.10.

The final award was as follows:

Damages to the *Halsted* (by stipulation) $41,017.31; detention damages $20,342.28 (loss of 17 days profit) plus $687.24 (detention maintenance expenses); general average disbursements $6,194.83; total $68,241.66; recovery of one half, or $34,120.83.

Damages to the *Camden* (by stipulation) $43,402.38; detention damages $20,573.10; cargo damages (by stipulation) $1,392.75; total $65,368.23; recovery of one half, or $33,691.92.

The *Halsted's* recovery exceeded the *Camden's*, and accordingly libellant was awarded the $428.91 difference.

[2] *The Conqueror, supra*, 166 U.S. at page 127, 17 S. Ct. at page 516. See *The Europe*, 9 Cir., 1911, 190 F. 475, 482, using an average of per diem profits for the preceding five years; *Simpson v. State of California*, 9 Cir., 1893, 54 F. 404, 407, using the average daily earnings for a period of six months before and six months after the collision.

conclude that the evidence of earnings during the 241 days, covering three voyages, fairly represents what her average daily earnings would have been had she not been detained by the collision.[3] We therefore modify the commissioner's award and the district court's affirmance of it and direct that *The Halsted's* detention damages be computed at the average of the daily earnings, or $858.56 per day for 17 days, amounting to $14,595.52.

The other disputed item concerns the commissioner's award to the libellant of $6,194.83 for general average disbursements made by the Halsted as a result of the collision, consisting of 6% interest, 2% commission, and 2½% settling agent's commission.

General average disbursements made by the owner of a ship are funds advanced to meet the extraordinary expenses necessary to keep the ship going after a collision for the benefit of both hull and cargo owners. These funds, in effect, constitute a loan and the owner is therefore allowed interest on money advanced for the common purpose. Rule XXII, York-Antwerp Rules of 1924; *see* Lowndes and Rudolf, General Average, pp. 16, 27 (7th ed. 1948).

The Camden, in opposing interest on the general average disbursements, argues that because these disbursements included an amount for repairs to *The Halsted*, she has been allowed to recover interest on her own collision damages. This is alleged to be contrary to our decision in *The Wright*, 2 Cir., 1940, 109 F.2d 699 and in *Canadian Aviation, Ltd. v. United States*, 2 Cir., 1951, 187 F.2d 100, 101, which held that no interest is to be allowed on damages where there is a "both to blame" collision. In The Wright and Canadian Aviation cases, however, the interest which was disallowed was on the final award for damages before decree; no question of use of money for general average disbursements was involved. The award allowed by the Commissioner cannot be considered interest on damages. It is payment for the use of money which was necessary to keep the ship under way and the fact that repairs to the ship were included is immaterial. We therefore affirm the district court's holding on this issue.

As to the 2% commission awarded to *The Halsted* on her general average disbursements, Rule XXI of the York-Antwerp Rules of 1924 expressly provides for such commission; this ruling of the district court was clearly correct.

The 2½% settling agent's commission which *The Halsted* advanced is also a well established item of recovery. *See Gulf Refining Co. v. Universal Ins. Co.*, 2 Cir., 1929, 32 F.2d 555, *certiorari denied*, 280 U.S. 584, 50 S. Ct. 35, 74 L. Ed. 634. As the general average disbursements were advanced for the benefit of all interests in and aboard the ship, it became necessary thereafter to have a general average adjustment to apportion the loss between hull and cargo and to determine which items were properly included in general average. For this the settling agent was properly employed and the ruling of the district court was correct.

The Camden's Damages

At the time of the collision, the Camden was sailing under a charter party entered into between Standard Oil Company (N.J.) (the owner) and Standard Oil Company of New Jersey, its subsidiary (the charterer). The commissioner used the charter party rate as a basis for measuring the owner's loss from the 15.986 days detention required to make repairs. *The Halsted* claims that because the charter party was entered into between parent and subsidiary the charter party rate was not a proper yardstick to be used to measure *The Camden's* detention damages and the owner should be made to prove the cost of hiring substitute vessels. We do not agree. The charter party rate constituted appropriate evidence from which to measure damages. *See The Conqueror, supra*, 166 U.S. at page 133, 17 S. Ct. at page 519. There is no evidence that the parent overreached the subsidiary in setting the rate of hire in the charter party, which was manifestly fair, being in accord with or lower than the current market. Accordingly, we affirm the district court's consideration of the charter party rate as proper and persuasive evidence for measuring *The Camden's* detention damages.

We turn now to *The Camden's* objections to the commissioner's findings regarding her damages during detention of 17.986 days for repairs. As *The Camden* had already been scheduled for a two day layoff to have some of her

---

[3] Where the voyages do not fairly represent normal average earnings they should not be considered. Thus in *The Gylfe v. The Trujillo*, 2 Cir., 1954, 209 F.2d 386, 389, consideration of the precollision voyage was ruled out because the market had gone into a sudden decline. In *Quevvilly-Sampson*, D.C.S.D.N.Y., 1938, A.M.C. 347, 357, the post-collision voyage was ruled out because World War I had caused an artificial and rapid inflation in market prices. *But see The Bulgaria*, D.C.N.D.N.Y. 1897, 83 F. 312, using the average earnings of the precollision, collision and post-collision voyages.

bulkheads tightened,[4] *The Halsted* is responsible for only 15.986 days detention. Under the charter party the charter hire had been paid in advance and after the collision the owner was required to and did return $43,196.33 for the full layoff period of *The Camden*, or $38,395 for 15.986 days.

The owner's recovery is limited to profits lost as a result of the collision. As the owner was required to pay certain voyage maintenance expenses, this is some amount less than the charter hire of $38,395. It was agreed by stipulation between the parties that *The Camden's* owner "... would have incurred port charges for a single round trip voyage of $1,508.19, and in addition would have incurred per diem operating costs of $1,020.50, made up of wages of $444.19, provisions, $70.00; fuel $436.15, and stores, $70.16". *The Camden's* expenses for 15.986 days thus would have totalled $17,821.90. Deducting these expenses from the $38,395 gross charter hire to arrive at the profits which *The Camden* would have earned over the detention period, the detention loss awarded to *The Camden* came to $20,573.10.

The owner of *The Camden* does not question the reasoning behind the award of detention damages. It does object, however, to the use of the stipulation to determine the voyage expenses. The owner of *The Camden* urges that according to the terms of the charter party, port charges and fuel costs were for the account of the charterer, and, as a result, would never have been among the voyage expenses of the owner. It therefore claims that as it would not have had to pay them, the deductions for these expenses was incorrect.

We do not dispute the owner's reading of the charter party. The stipulation, however, is the later instrument entered into between the parties to this action for the purpose of determining liability and, as between the two, the stipulation must control. *The Camden* contends that these figures were included in the stipulation for the sole purpose of placing all the material data before the commissioner. We cannot agree with this reading. Clearly, the stipulation was entered into to indicate the costs of the parties relevant to the damages claimed and the parties are bound by the language they have used. The stipulation expressly includes the disputed costs among the expenses which the owner "would have incurred." Under the circumstances, we can find no reason to give these words any other than their plain meaning. We therefore affirm the deduction of $17,821.90 from the $38,395 refund in order to arrive at the profits which the owner lost.

The owner also claims damages for $7,527.17 which it actually expended for maintenance of *The Camden* during the detention period.[5] The commissioner ruled against the owner, apparently on the theory that the maintenance had already been recovered once as voyage maintenance expenses as it had been considered in computing lost profits during detention. His report states:

Since that detention recovery represents gross charter hire on a time charter, no reason exists why the shipowner should recover, in addition to the charter hire, the expense of the ship while undergoing repairs. Those expenses would have been incurred in any event, and the only compensation to the shipowner would be the gross charter hire, in any event.

The commissioner's ruling was followed by the district court on the ground that to allow the expenses "would involve duplication." On reargument the district court adhered to its original decision. We believe the commissioner was clearly wrong.

The money actually expended in maintaining the Camden during detention was an expense incurred by reason of the collision and the owner was entitled to recover therefor. The fact that voyage maintenance costs were considered in computing lost profits does not mean that the owner has been given the benefit of this item. Quite the contrary: all the commissioner did was to reduce the gross hire fee by such amount as the owner would have been required to spend in order to earn the fee; but the money was never spent. What was disbursed was $7,527.17. This

---

[4] While nothing appears in the record on the subject, both parties seem to assume that the bulkhead work was done during the detention and that this work took two days, and we so treat it.

[5] The detention expenses actually came to $9,037.27 and included fuel, wages and provisions costs. In accordance with its argument on the stipulation-charter party issue, *supra*, the owner does not ask for fuel charges, thus reducing its maintenance claim to the stated $7,527.17, (Claimant's brief, p. 15.)

fact was stipulated to by both parties and constitutes actual damages resulting from the collision. We therefore reverse the holding on this issue and direct that $7,527.17 detention maintenance expenses be awarded to *The Camden*.

In summary, we affirm the commissioner's report and the holding of the district court as to: (1) the award to *The Halsted* of interest and commission on general average disbursement and the settling agent's commission; (2) the use of the charter party rate as a proper measure of *The Camden's* detention damages; and (3) the use of the stipulation as to the deductions necessary to determine *The Camden's* lost profits.

We reverse and direct that judgment be entered in accordance with our conclusions: (1) an average of the daily earnings over the entire period of the three voyages be used to measure *The Halsted's* damages from detention, reducing them from $20,342.28 to $14,595.52; and (2) the damages awarded to *The Camden* include the $7,527.17 maintenance expenses during her detention for repairs.

The Halsted's damages are therefore reduced by $5,746.76 to a total of $62,494.90. *The Camden's* damages are therefore increased by $7,527.17 to $72,895.40. Since both parties were at fault, each is entitled to recover one half of his damages from the other: *The Halsted* $31,247.45; *The Camden* $36,447.70. We direct that judgment be entered in favor of the claimant, Standard Oil Company (N.J.) for the difference, $5,200.22.

––––––––––––

VENORE TRANSPORTATION. CO. v. M/V STRUMA

583 F.2d 708, 1978 AMC 2146 (4th Cir. 1978)

HAYNSWORTH, Chief Judge

Venore Transportation Company, time charterer of the 55,000 ton *S.S. Oswego Liberty*, sought damages from the 60,000 ton *M/V Struma* and her owner, Bulk Transport Corporation, for loss of use of the *Oswego Liberty* after the two vessels had been in a collision. The district court entered summary judgment for the defendants, reasoning that the claim was foreclosed by the Supreme Court's decision in *Robins Dry Dock and Repair Co. v. Flint*, 275 U.S. 279. Because there was no suspension in the payment of charter hire while the *Oswego Liberty* was being repaired, we conclude that *Robins* is inapplicable and that recovery of charter hire should be allowed.

In January 1972 the Oswego Shipping Corporation let the *Oswego Liberty* to Venore Transportation Company for a term of thirteen and a half years. The time charter party fixed the charter hire at monthly rates of more than $90,000.

* * *

On November 27, 1974 the *Oswego Liberty* and the *Struma* were in a collision, and the *Oswego Liberty* was withdrawn from service and laid up for repairs until January 17, 1975. During the time she was under repair, escalated charter hire of $225,380.64 accrued, which Venore has paid to the owner.

For the purpose of these proceedings, the *Struma* has conceded her fault, and the owner's claim against her has been settled. The owner's claim, however, consisted entirely of the expenses to which it was put to repair the physical damage sustained by the *Oswego Liberty*. It claimed nothing for its loss of use of the vessel. Indeed, it could not have made such a claim, for it had received the full charter hire for the period during which the vessel was under repair.

Robins Dry Dock was not a case arising out of a collision. The charter party there required that the vessel be dry docked periodically. While in dry dock, her propeller was negligently damaged and had to be replaced. That enlarged the time during which the vessel was out of service, and it was for the loss of use of the vessel during that period that the time charterer claimed. The Supreme Court reasoned that the dry dock's duty arose out of its contract with the owner, and that it had no such contractual duty to the time charterer. Since there had been no demise of the vessel, it was technically in the possession of the owner, and the time charterer had no property interest in it. Thus there was applicable the principle that one who unintentionally but negligently damages the property of another is not liable to others who may suffer economic loss because the owner is unable to perform contractual commitments to those others.

It is essentially a principle of disallowance of damages because of remoteness, and because of the concern that the number and the amount of potential claims in a given instance may be staggering. The time charterer in *Robins Dry Dock* had not paid charter hire for the period during which the vessel was out of service. The claim was essentially one for loss of anticipated profits.

The principle has found expression in a variety of cases since *Robins Dry Dock*.

* * *

The principle of *Robins Dry Dock* is perfectly defensible, if pragmatic considerations require the foreclosure of remote damage claims. The tort feasor, having paid the owner for its loss of use of the vessel, should not be required to pay additionally for the time charterer's loss of anticipated profits. A pragmatic approach would require that the offending vessel pay for loss of use of the damaged vessel once, but no more. Unless the offending vessel is required to pay for the loss of use of the *Oswego Liberty* in this case, however, it would never be required to pay at all. The owner lost no charter hire. It could not claim a loss it had not suffered, and it did not do so. But payment for loss of use of the damaged vessel is a conventional item of recovery, and the fact that the charter party has transferred the risk of loss of use from the owner to the time charterer should not extinguish the right to a recovery of a traditional item of damages. There is nothing remote about these damages; the only objection is that they were suffered by the time charterer rather than by the owner.

* * *

We do not intend, however, to suggest that the time charterer is entitled to lost profits. That kind of claim is foreclosed by *Robins Dry Dock*. The traditional item of recoverable damage is the owner's claim for loss of use. When the vessel is under a time charter, the starting point for the measurement of those damages is lost charter hire. Our only holding is that when there has been no suspension in the payment of charter hire during the period when the vessel is out of service, the time charterer who has paid the charter hire is entitled to recover what the owner would have been entitled to recover had those payments been suspended.

In *Robins Dry Dock*, Mr. Justice Holmes wrote broadly, as he customarily did, but there is no inconsistency in our holding and that of the Supreme Court in *Robins Dry Dock*. Nor do we enlarge in any way the types of damages which have been traditionally recoverable, nor the offending vessel's obligation of recompense. Under our holding, the STRUMA and her owner will pay no more than they would have if the charter had provided for a suspension of charter hire while the vessel was laid up.

Thus we conclude that either the owner or the time charterer, but not both, may claim damages for loss of use depending upon the charter's placement of the risk of loss of use.

Reversed and remanded.

WINTER, Circuit Judge, dissenting.

... Recovery in *Robins Dry Dock* was denied, not on the ground that the damages were too remote, but on the ground that a time charterer has no standing or property interest to recover from an unintentional wrongdoer.... *Robins Dry Dock* thus establishes a rule of liability, not of damages, as the majority would read it.

The majority also justifies the result it reaches on the pragmatic ground that the tortfeasor, the offending vessel, should pay for loss of use of the damaged vessel once, but no more, and that where the owner suffers no loss of use because the time charterer, by the terms of the time charter, has not been excused from paying hire, the time charterer should be permitted to recover its direct loss, *i.e.* the hire it must pay, but not its loss of profits. This very argument was rejected in *Robins Dry Dock*....

* * *

STATE OF LOUISIANA, EX REL. GUSTE v. M/V TESTBANK

752 F.2d 1019, 1985 AMC 1521 (5th Cir. 1985) (en banc)

Patrick E. HIGGINBOTHAM, Circuit Judge

We are asked to abandon physical damage to a proprietary interest as a prerequisite to recovery for economic loss in cases of unintentional maritime tort. We decline the invitation.

I.

In the early evening of July 22, 1980, the *M/V Sea Daniel*, an inbound bulk carrier, and the *M/V Testbank*, an outbound container ship, collided at approximately mile forty-one of the Mississippi River Gulf outlet. At impact, a white haze enveloped the ships until carried away by prevailing winds, and containers aboard *Testbank* were damaged and lost overboard. The white haze proved to be hydrobromic acid and the contents of the containers which went overboard proved to be approximately twelve tons of pentachlorophenol, PCP, assertedly the largest such spill in United States history. The United States Coast Guard closed the outlet to navigation until August 10, 1980 and all fishing, shrimping, and related activity was temporarily suspended in the outlet and four hundred square miles of surrounding marsh and waterways.

Forty-one lawsuits were filed and consolidated before the same judge in the Eastern District of Louisiana. These suits presented claims of shipping interests, marina and boat rental operators, wholesale and retail seafood enterprises not actually engaged in fishing, seafood restaurants, tackle and bait shops, and recreational fishermen. They proffered an assortment of liability theories, including maritime tort, private actions pursuant to various sections of the River & Harbors Appropriation Act of 1899 and rights of action under Louisiana law. Jurisdiction rested on the proposition that the collision and contamination were maritime torts and within the court's maritime jurisdiction. *See* 28 U.S.C. § 1333.

Defendants moved for summary judgment as to all claims for economic loss unaccompanied by physical damage to property. The district court granted the requested summary judgment as to all such claims except those asserted by commercial oystermen, shrimpers, crabbers and fishermen who had been making a commercial use of embargoed waters. The district court found these commercial fishing interests deserving of a special protection akin to that enjoyed by seamen. *See State of Louisiana ex rel. Guste v. M/V Testbank*, 524 F. Supp. 1170, 1173-74 (E.D. La. 1981).

On appeal a panel of this court affirmed, concluding that claims for economic loss unaccompanied by physical damage to a proprietary interest were not recoverable in maritime tort. 728 F.2d 748 (5th Cir. 1984). The panel, as did the district court, pointed to the doctrine of *Robins Dry Dock & Repair Co. v. Flint*, 275 U.S. 303, 48 S. Ct. 134, 72 L. Ed. 290 (1927), and its development in this circuit. Judge Wisdom specially concurred, agreeing that the denial of these claims was required by precedent, but urging reexamination en banc. We then took the case en banc for that purpose. After extensive additional briefs and oral argument, we are unpersuaded that we ought to drop physical damage to a proprietary interest as a prerequisite to recovery for economic loss. To the contrary, our reexamination of the history and central purpose of this pragmatic restriction on the doctrine of foreseeability heightens our commitment to it. Ultimately we conclude that without this limitation foreseeability loses much of its ability to function as a rule of law.

II.

Plaintiffs first argue that the "rule" of *Robins Dry Dock* is that "a tort to the property of one which results in the negligent interference with contractual relationships of another does not state a claim," and that so defined, *Robins Dry Dock* is here inapplicable. Next and relatedly, plaintiffs urge that physical damage is not a prerequisite to recovery of economic loss where the damages suffered were foreseeable. Third, plaintiffs argue that their claims are cognizable in maritime tort because the pollution from the collision constituted a public nuisance and violated the Rivers and Harbors Appropriation Act of 1899, as well as Louisiana law.

Defendants urge the opposite: that *Robins Dry Dock* controls these cases; that the physical damage limitation on foreseeability ought to be retained; and that plaintiffs stated no claim for "federal pollution," either as a nuisance or under the Rivers and Harbors Act. Finally, defendants reply that state law is not applicable to this maritime collision case and in any event provides plaintiffs no claim.

III.

The meaning of *Robins Dry Dock v. Flint*, 275 U.S. 303, 48 S. Ct. 134, 72 L. Ed. 290 (1927) (HOLMES, J.) is the flag all litigants here seek to capture. We turn first to that case and to its historical setting.

Robins broke no new ground but instead applied a principle, then settled both in the United States and England, which refused recovery for negligent interference with "contractual rights." Stated more broadly, the prevailing rule denied a plaintiff recovery for economic loss if that loss resulted from physical damage to property in which he had no proprietary interest. *See, e.g., Byrd v. English*, 117 Ga. 191, 43 S.E. 419 (1903); *Cattle v. Stockton Waterworks Co.,* 10 Q.B. 453, 457 (C.A. 1875).

* * *

In *Robins*, the time charterer of a steamship sued for profits lost when the defendant dry dock negligently damaged the vessel's propeller. The propeller had to be replaced, thus extending by two weeks the time the vessel was laid up in dry dock, and it was for the loss of use of the vessel for that period that the charterer sued. The Supreme Court denied recovery to the charterer, noting:

> ...no authority need to be cited to show that, as a general rule, at least, a tort to the person or property of one man does not make the tort-feasor liable to another merely because the injured person was under a contract with that other unknown to the doer of the wrong. (citation omitted). The law does not spread its protection so far.

275 U.S. at 309, 48 S. Ct. at 135....

* * *

Plaintiffs would confine *Robins* to losses suffered for inability to perform contracts between a plaintiff and others, categorizing the tort as a species of interference with contract. When seen in the historical context described above, however, it is apparent that *Robins Dry Dock* represents more than a limit on recovery for interference with contractual rights. Apart from what it represented and certainly apart from what it became, its literal holding was not so restricted. If a time charterer's relationship to its negligently injured vessel is too remote, other claimants without even the connection of a contract are even more remote.

It is true that in *Robins* the lower courts had sustained recovery on contract principles, but the Supreme Court pushed the steamship company's contract arguments aside and directly addressed its effort to recover in tort.... The language and the cases the *Robins* Court pointed to as "good statement[s]" of the principle make plain that the charterer failed to recover its delay claims from the dry dock because the Court believed them to be too remote. Notably, although the dry dock company did not know of the charter party when it damaged the propeller, delay losses by users of the vessel were certainly foreseeable. Thus *Robins* was a pragmatic limitation imposed by the Court upon the tort doctrine of foreseeability.

* * *

In sum, the decisions of courts in other circuits convince us that *Robins Dry Dock* is both a widely used and necessary limitation on recovery for economic losses. The holdings in *Kinsman* and *Union Oil* are not to the contrary. The courts in both those cases made plain that restrictions on the concept of foreseeability ought to be imposed where recovery is sought for pure economic losses.

Jurisprudence developed in the Gulf states informs our maritime decisions. It supports the *Robins* rule. Courts applying the tort law of Texas, Georgia, Florida, Alabama, Mississippi and Louisiana have consistently denied recovery for economic losses negligently inflicted where there was no physical damage to a proprietary interest.

* * *

IV.

Plaintiffs urge that the requirement of physical injury to a proprietary interest is arbitrary, unfair, and illogical, as it denies recovery for foreseeable injury caused by negligent acts. At its bottom the argument is that questions of remoteness ought to be left to the trier of fact. Ultimately the question becomes who ought to decide—judge or jury—and whether there will be a rule beyond the jacket of a given case. The plaintiffs contend that the "problem" need not be separately addressed, but instead should be handled by "traditional" principles of tort law. Putting the problem of which doctrine is the traditional one aside, their rhetorical questions are flawed in several respects.

Those who would delete the requirement of physical damage have no rule or principle to substitute. Their approach failed to recognize limits upon the adjudicating ability of courts. We do not mean just the ability to supply a judgment; prerequisite to this adjudicatory function are preexisting rules, whether the creature of courts or legislatures. Courts can decide cases without preexisting normative guidance but the result becomes less judicial and more the product of a managerial, legislative or negotiated function.

Review of the foreseeable consequences of the collision of the *Sea Daniel* and *Testbank* demonstrates the wave upon wave of successive economic consequences and the managerial role plaintiffs would have us assume. The vessel delayed in St. Louis may be unable to fulfill its obligation to haul from Memphis, to the injury of the shipper, to the injury of the buyers, to the injury of their customers. Plaintiffs concede, as do all who attack the requirement of physical damage, that a line would need to be drawn—somewhere on the other side, each plaintiff would say in turn, of its recovery. Plaintiffs advocate not only that the lines be drawn elsewhere but also that they be drawn on an ad hoc and discrete basis. The result would be that no determinable measure of the limit of foreseeability would precede the decision on liability. We are told that when the claim is too remote, or too tenuous, recovery will be denied. Presumably then, as among all plaintiffs suffering foreseeable economic loss, recovery will turn on a judge or jury's decision. There will be no rationale for the differing results save the "judgment" of the trier of fact. Concededly, it can "decide" all the claims presented, and with comparative if not absolute ease. The point is not that such a process cannot be administered but rather that its judgments would be much less the products of a determinable rule of law. In this important sense, the resulting decisions would be judicial products only in their draw upon judicial resources.

The bright line rule of damage to a proprietary interest, as most, has the virtue of predictability with the vice of creating results in cases at its edge that are said to be "unjust" or "unfair." Plaintiffs point to seemingly perverse results, where claims the rule allows and those it disallows are juxtaposed—such as vessels striking a dock, causing minor but recoverable damage, then lurching athwart a channel causing great but unrecoverable economic loss. The answer is that when lines are drawn sufficiently sharp in their definitional edges to be reasonable and predictable, such differing results are the inevitable result—indeed, decisions are the desired product. But there is more. The line drawing sought by plaintiffs is no less arbitrary because the line drawing appears only in the outcome—as one claimant is found too remote and another is allowed to recover. The true difference is that plaintiff's approach would mask the results. The present rule would be more candid, and in addition, by making results more predictable, serves a normative function. It operates as a rule of law and allows a court to adjudicate rather than manage.

V.

That the rule is identifiable and will predict outcomes in advance of the ultimate decision about recovery enables it to play additional roles. Here we agree with plaintiffs that economic analysis, even at the rudimentary level of jurists, is helpful both in the identification of such roles and the essaying of how the roles play. Thus it is suggested that placing all the consequence of its error on the maritime industry will enhance its incentive for safety. While correct, as far as such analysis goes, such in terrorem benefits have an optimal level. Presumably, when the cost of an unsafe condition exceeds its utility there is an incentive to change. As the costs of an accident become increasing multiples of its utility, however, there is a point at which greater accident costs lose meaning, and the incentive curve flattens. When the accidents costs are added in large but unknowable amounts the value of the exercise is diminished.

With a disaster inflicting large and reverberating injuries through the economy, as here, we believe the more important economic inquiry is that of relative cost of administration, and in maritime matters administration quickly involves insurance. Those economic losses not recoverable under the present rule for lack of physical damage to a proprietary interest are the subject of first party or loss insurance. The rule change would work a shift to the more costly liability system of third party insurance. For the same reasons that courts have imposed limits on the concept of foreseeability, liability insurance might not be readily obtainable for the types of losses asserted here. As Professor James has noted, "[s]erious practical problems face insurers in handling insurance against potentially wide, open-ended liability. From an insurer's point of view it is not practical to cover, without limit, a liability that may reach catastrophic proportions, or to fix a reasonable premium on a risk that does not lend itself to actuarial measurement." James, *supra*, at 53. By contrast, first party insurance is feasible for many of the economic losses claimed here. Each businessman who might be affected by a disruption of river traffic or by a halt in fishing activities can protect against that even-tuality at a relatively low cost since his own potential losses are finite and readily discernible. Thus, to the extent that economic analysis informs our decision here, we think that it favors retention of the present rule.

VI.

Plaintiffs argue alternatively that their claims of economic losses are cognizable in maritime tort because the pollution from the collision constituted a public nuisance, and violated the Rivers and Harbors Appropriation Act of 1899 and Louisiana law. We look to each in turn.

* * *

Were we to allow plaintiffs recovery for their losses under a public nuisance theory we would permit recovery for injury to the type of interest that, as we have already explained, we have consistently declined to protect. Nuisance, as Dean Prosser has explained, is not a separate tort subject to rules of its own but instead is a type of damage. W. PROSSER, LAW OF TORTS § 87 (4th ed. 1971). Our decisions under *Robins* have emphasized the nature of the interest harmed rather than the theory of recovery. As we noted in *Dick Meyers Towing*, "rephrasing the claim as a public nuisance claim does not change its essential character." *Dick Meyers*, 577 F.2d at 1025 n.4. Thus we conclude that plaintiffs may not recover for pure economic losses under a public nuisance theory in maritime tort.

Plaintiffs' arguments that the Rivers and Harbors Appropriation Act affords them an avenue of relief are foreclosed by Supreme Court decision. Plaintiffs suggest that both Section 10 of the Act, which prohibits the obstruction of navigable waters, and Section 13 of the Act, which prohibits the deposit of refuse into navigable waters, have been violated, and that such violations provide a basis for civil liability. In *California v. Sierra Club*, 451 U.S. 287, 101 S. Ct. 1775, 68 L. Ed. 2d 101 (1981), the Court held that the Rivers and Harbors Appropriation Act did not authorize private actions to be brought for violation of its provisions. Accordingly, plaintiffs' claims under the Rivers and Harbors Act may not be maintained.

Plaintiffs also urge that their economic losses are recoverable as state law claims in negligence, nuisance or under the Louisiana Environmental Affairs Act of 1980. Because established principles of general maritime law govern the issue of recovery in this case, we reject these state law theories.

* * *

VII.

In conclusion, having reexamined the history and central purpose of the doctrine of *Robins Dry Dock* as developed in this circuit, we remain committed to its teaching. Denying recovery for pure economic losses is a pragmatic limitation on the doctrine of foreseeability, a limitation we find to be both workable and useful. Nor do we find persuasive plaintiffs' arguments that their economic losses are recoverable under a public nuisance theory, as damages for violation of federal statutes, or under state law.

Accordingly, the decision of the district court granting summary judgment to defendants on all claims for economic losses unaccompanied by physical damage to property is AFFIRMED.

GEE, Circuit Judge, with whom CLARK, Chief Judge, joins, concurring.

Both the majority opinion and the dissent do our Court proud, joining a few others on that relatively short list of truly distinguished and thoughtful legal writings of which it or any court can boast. Neither opinion, however, confronts explicitly what is for me the overarching issue in the appeal. That issue, a legal one only in the broadest sense and only implicitly presented, is perhaps best addressed in a brief collateral writing such as this will be.

The issue to which I refer is, who should deal with questions of such magnitude as the rule for which the dissent contends would, again and again, draw before the courts? An oil spill damages hundreds, perhaps thousands, of miles of coastal area. A cloud of noxious industrial gas leaks out, kills thousands, and injures thousands more. A commonly-used building material is discovered, years after the fact, to posses unforeseen lethal qualities affecting thousands who have worked with it. The long-term effects of inhaling coal dust are found to be disabling to a significant proportion of veteran miners. None of these illustrations is fanciful; each has arisen in recent times and presented itself for resolution to our body politic. Congress has dealt effectively with Black Lung; it has signally failed to deal with the ravages of asbestosis—a scourge, I suspect, far more general and widespread—and a swelling wave of individual asbestosis claims, to be resolved on a case by case basis, pushes slowly through our court system, threatening to inundate it and to consume in punitive damage awards to early claimants the relatively meager assets available to compensate the general class affected, many of whom have not yet suffered the onset of symptoms. It is my thesis that the dispute-resolution systems of courts are poorly equipped to manage disasters of such magnitude and that we should be wary of adopting rules of decision which, as would that contended for by the dissent, encourage the drawing of their broader aspects before us.

* * *

Jerre S. WILLIAMS, Circuit Judge, concurring specially.

My concern is that I have considerable doubt that commercial fishermen can establish a proprietary interest in the right to fish in their fishing waters. Certainly the common legal synonym for "proprietary interest" is "ownership", as legal lexicons attest. Yet the bright line rule of the Court's opinion places emphasis upon a requisite proprietary interest.

It would be preferable, in my view, to have the rule include a clear recognition that the rights of commercial fishermen were more accurately defined by the Court in *Union Oil Co. v. Oppen*, 501 F.2d 558 (9th Cir. 1974), one of the cases discussed by Judge Higginbotham. The Court agreed that ordinarily there is no recovery for economic losses unaccompanied by physical damage. It found, however, that commercial fishermen were foreseeable plaintiffs whose interests the oil company had a duty to protect when conducting its operations which resulted in the spillage. The rule that should prevail was effectively stated by Judge Sneed in that case in the quotation set out in Judge Higginbotham's opinion.

* * *

The commercial fishermen properly recover because their livelihood comes from a "resource" of the water which was polluted. Yet, physical property owned by them was not damaged and it is doubtful that a proprietary interest could have been shown.

GARWOOD, Circuit Judge, delivered a concurring opinion.

WISDOM, Circuit Judge, with whom Alvin B. RUBIN, POLITZ, TATE, and JOHNSON, Circuit Judges, join dissenting.

Robins is the Tar Baby of tort law in this circuit. And the brier-patch is far away. This Court's application of *Robins* is out of step with contemporary tort doctrine, works substantial injustice on innocent victims, and is unsupported by the considerations that justified the Supreme Court's 1927 decision.

Robins was a tort case grounded on a contract. Whatever the justification for the original holding, this Court's requirement of physical injury as a condition to recovery is an unwarranted step backwards in torts jurisprudence.

The resulting bar for claims of economic loss unaccompanied by any physical damage conflicts with conventional tort principles of foreseeability and proximate cause. I would analyze the plaintiffs' claims under these principles, using the "particular damage" requirement of public nuisance law as an additional means of limiting claims. Although this approach requires a case-by-case analysis, it comports with the fundamental idea of fairness that innocent plaintiffs should receive compensation and negligent defendants should bear the cost of their tortious acts. Such a result is worth the additional costs of adjudicating these claims, and this rule of liability appears to be more economically efficient. Finally, this result would relieve courts of the necessity of manufacturing exceptions totally inconsistent with the expanded *Robins* rule of requiring physical injury as a prerequisite to recovery.

* * *

I. Alternate Statement of the Case

The commercial fishing industry in the area sustained serious losses, primarily from the depressed market in that industry in southern Louisiana. Other businesses suffered losses. Numerous parties filed suit against the vessels and their owners, seeking compensation for their expenses and their lost profits caused by the collision, pollution, and bans to navigation and fishing. The claimants may be classified as follows:

(1) commercial fishermen, crabbers, oystermen, and shrimpers who routinely operated in and around the closed area;
(2) fishermen, crabbers, oystermen, and shrimpers who engaged in these practices only for recreation;
(3) operators of marinas and boat rentals, and marine suppliers;
(4) tackle and bait shops;
(5) wholesale and retail seafood enterprises not actually engaged in fishing, shrimping, crabbing, or oystering in the closed area;
(6) seafood restaurants;
(7) cargo terminal operators;
(8) an operator of railroad freight cars seeking demurrage;
(9) vessel operators seeking expenses (demurrage, crew costs, tug hire) and losses of revenues caused by the closure of the outlet.

In its decision and judgment entered in *State of Louisiana ex rel. Guste v. M/V Testbank*, E.D. La.1981, 524 F. Supp. 1170, *aff'd*, 728 F.2d 748 (per curiam), the district court dismissed the claims of shipping interests, marine and boat rental operators, wholesale and retail seafood enterprises not actually engaged in fishing, seafood restaurants, tackle and bait shops, and recreational fishermen. On February 22, 1982, a panel of this Court heard oral argument, and that panel affirmed the decision of the district court, holding that it was bound by *Robins* and by *Akron Corp. v. M/T Cantigny*, 5 Cir.1983, 706 F.2d 151 (per curiam). *See State of Louisiana ex rel. Guste v. M/V Testbank*, 5 Cir.1984, 728 F.2d 748 (per curiam). Now a majority of our Court en banc has affirmed that determination.

* * *

III. An Alternate Rule of Recovery

Rather than limiting recovery under an automatic application of a physical damage requirement, I would analyze the plaintiffs' claims under the conventional tort principles of negligence, foreseeability, and proximate causation. I would confine *Robins* to the "factual contours" of that case: A plaintiff's claim may be barred only if the claim is derived solely through contract with an injured party. The majority's primary criticism of this approach to a determination of liability is that it is potentially open ended. Yet, there are well-established tort principles to limit liability for a widely-suffered harm. Under the contemporary law of public nuisance, courts compensate "particularly" damaged plaintiffs for harms suffered from a wide- ranging tort, but deny recovery to more generally damaged parties. Those parties who are foreseeably and proximately injured by an oil spill or closure of a navigable river, for example, and who can also prove damages that are beyond the general economic dislocation that attends such disasters should recover whether or not they had contractual dealings with others who were also damaged by the tortious act. The limitation imposed by "particular" damages, together with refined notions of proximate cause and forseeability, provides a workable scheme of liability that is in step with the rest of tort law, compensates innocent plaintiffs, and imposes the costs of harm on those who caused it.

A. Public Nuisance Law and Particular Damages

To assert a cause of action under public nuisance law, a plaintiff must assert "particular damages". As Dean Prosser, Reporter for the Second Restatement of Torts, has written, although courts once required physical injury for a recovery under nuisance, this limitation was quickly abandoned:

> The origin of this notion is obscure, although there is an obvious derivation from the old distinction between the actions of trespass and case. It has been expressly repudiated often enough; and the whole tenor of the cases in which particular damage has been found makes it quite clear that it is not now the law, if indeed it ever was.

Prosser, *Private Action for Public Nuisance*, 52 VA. L. REV. 997, 1007-08 (1966).

Instead, to state a cause of action under public nuisance, a plaintiff must prove "particular" damages from the alleged wrong. These damages must be different in kind and degree from those suffered by the general public. If other individuals suffer the same kind of damage, although in lesser degree, a private plaintiff might still recover. *Id.* at 1009. "It is only when the class becomes so large and general as to include all members of the public who come in contact with the nuisance, that the private action will fail." *Id.*

Generally, pecuniary loss to the plaintiff results in particular damage that sets him apart from the general public. When the plaintiff is prevented from performing a specific contract, or is put to additional expense in performing it, he can maintain his action because the contract is an individual matter that is not common to the public. *Id.* Also, those who have established businesses which make common use of the public right that the nuisance infringes have been allowed recovery. When a river is blocked, for example, a steamboat line operating on it and a company that rafts logs or collects tolls for passage have been permitted to maintain the action. There are also cases in which commercial fisheries making a localized use of public waters have been allowed to recover under nuisance law. And although plaintiffs who are delayed by a public nuisance cannot recover money for the delay itself (*e.g.*, the profitable opportunities that the plaintiff had to forego), they can recover for actual additional expenses, such as extra fuel, additional crew expenses, and greater demurrage charges.

The Supreme Court of Louisiana has recognized that a business may sustain the requisite "particular kind of business damages as a consequence of the obstruction of a navigable channel". *Pharr v. Morgan's L. & T.R. & S.S. Co.*, La. 1905, 115 La. 138, 38 So. 943. In that case, the defendant had negligently damaged a railroad bridge spanning the Atchafalaya River. The barges could pass under the repair framework, but the steamboat could not. The plaintiff was forced to employ an extra steamboat to transport the sugar cane from the sugar fields below the bridge to the refinery above the bridge. *Id.*, 38 So. at 944. The Court held:

> The negligent breaking of the bridge was the primary, paramount cause, which lead to the obstruction of navigation as well as the work of reparation; and if, as argued, such work was the immediate cause of the injury, it was simply an intervening cause set in motion by the party originally in fault. It may be said that the remedy was worse than the disease. "We therefore are of opinion that defendants are responsible in damages caused by the obstruction of navigation.

Id. at 945. The Louisiana Supreme Court awarded damages for the extra transportation costs incurred, but refused to award delay damages because of the uncertainty of the evidence; the plaintiff would have been entitled to such damages had he been able to prove them.

The closest federal case in point is probably *Burgess v. M/V Tamano*, D. Me.1973, 370 F. Supp. 247, *aff'd*, 1 Cir. 1977, 559 F.2d 1200. There, the court denied the plaintiff's motion to dismiss the claims of fishermen and clam diggers seeking damages as a result of an oil spill in a Maine bay. The court decided the motion for dismissal on the basis of public nuisance, holding that the commercial fishermen and clam diggers had suffered "particular damage different in kind, rather than degree, from that asserted by the general public". The court denied recovery to businessmen in Old Orchard Beach because their damage was "derivative from that of the public at large, is common to all businesses and residents of the Old Orchard Beach area". *Id.* at 251.

The line of demarcation provided by the *Burgess* court under an analysis of public nuisance and the line suggested in this dissent are similar. Those who incur a direct pecuniary loss (and thus fall within the field of "particular damages") will frequently also have been injured both proximately and foreseeably by the spill. Ships bottled up in the Mississippi River that had to pay additional crew expenses and docking and demurrage charges, for example, would recover these expenses. Similarly, fishermen would be entitled to compensation for the loss of their livelihood.

IV. Advantages of the Alternate Rule of Recovery

The advantages of this alternate rule of recovery are that it compensates damaged plaintiffs, imposes the cost of damages upon those who have caused the harm, is consistent with economic principles of modern tort law, and frees courts from the necessity of creating a piecemeal quilt of exceptions to avoid the harsh effects of the *Robins* rule.

* * *

Alvin B. RUBIN, Circuit Judge, with whom WISDOM, POLITZ and TATE, Circuit Judges, join, dissenting.

While voting to deny damages to all of the plaintiffs who joined in this appeal on the basis of the *Robins* rule, several of our colleagues who joined to make up the majority have indicated some concern about applying the rule so as to deny damages to every claimant who has not suffered a physical injury to a proprietary interest. Thus, the majority opinion refrains from agreeing or disagreeing with the Ninth Circuit decision in Union Oil, permitting recovery, in the absence of physical injury to a proprietary interest, by "commercial fishermen, plaintiffs whose economic losses were characterized as 'of a particular and special nature,' " and would leave that question "for later." It may be assumed, therefore, that some who joined in the opinion may not be disposed to deny damages to fishermen. Judge Williams would go further and expressly recognize the right of commercial fishermen as "foreseeable plaintiffs whose interests the oil company had a duty to protect when conducting its operations which resulted in the spillage." Judge Garwood does not think that *Robins* requires proof of physical injury in every case. These views evidence that in fact a majority of the court is unwilling to impose an unqualified requirement of physical injury to a proprietary interest.

Judge Gee's view, in which Chief Judge Clark joins, is that, while we should not go beyond the physical-injury requirement, the question of scope of liability for damages should never be resolved by legislature action. If, however, the limited-recovery rule is fair, it does not require Congressional consideration.

I agree with Judge Gee and Chief Judge Clark that the subject calls for legislative consideration and that the necessary application of principle accompanied by suitable line drawing can be better accomplished by statute. However, I would not await such action, for, in default of it, every time we reject a claim we act as decisively and finally as if we had allowed it—as definitively as if we were adhering to a statutory command not to allow damages when no such command has been given. The constitutional grant of jurisdiction to federal courts over cases and controversies not only empowers but requires us to review the constitutionality of legislation, as the Court held in *Marbury v. Madison* a century and a half ago. It equally empowers and requires us to decide other cases within our jurisdiction whether or not Congress has provided a rule of decision and even when we think Congress should have acted and has not done so.

* * *

Note: Lessees and "Proprietary Interest"

An interesting application of the *Robins Drydock* doctrine was presented when the M/V Bright Field allided with the Riverwalk Shopping Center causing extensive physical damage to the structure of the center and to many shops. Lessees of various shops brought suit to recover not only for physical damages to their stock and equipment but for loss of business during the period the stores were closed for repairs. Does their status as "lessees" satisfy the *Robins Drydock* "proprietary interest" test? *Complaint of Clearsky Shipping Corp.*, 1998 WL 770498, 1999 AMC 531 (E.D. La. 1998).

---

2. Total Loss

A & S TRANSPORTATION CO. v. THE TUG FAJARDO

688 F.2d 1, 1983 AMC 10 (1st Cir. 1982)

Levin H. CAMPBELL, Circuit Judge

Plaintiff PCI International, Inc. (PCI) seeks damages from Puerto Rico Lighterage Company and its underwriters for loss of use of a waste disposal barge of which it was the bareboat charterer. The barge was stranded, and became a total loss, while being towed by a tug (the "Fajardo") owned by Lighterage pursuant to a written agreement of towage with PCI. PCI asserts that the stranding was due to the carelessness of the tug, and that because of loss of use of the barge, and the difficulty of securing a suitable replacement, it was put to great expense in order to meet commitments to customers who had contracted for PCI to dispose of their chemical wastes at sea.

After the stranding, the underwriters of the barge determined that it was a constructive total loss, and reimbursed the owner, A & S Transportation Co., from whom PCI had chartered it, the full insured value of the hull (with certain adjustments) plus an additional sum under the sue and labor provisions of the policy. The owner, in return, assigned all its rights respecting the barge to the underwriters. The underwriters also reimbursed PCI, under the sue and labor provisions of the policy, PCI having been named in the policy as an additional insured, for certain amounts PCI had expended to preserve the wreck.

Thereafter PCI joined the owner and the barge's underwriters in this damages action against the tug, Lighterage, and their underwriters. Before trial, however, the barge's underwriters effected a settlement with defendants. As part of the settlement, they released defendants and assigned to them all rights of action, including all the rights which had been assigned to them by A & S.

After a trial, the district court sitting in admiralty rejected the owner's claims for damages in excess of the amount already received from its underwriters. The court held that the owner had effectively divested itself of any claims in the matter by its previous settlement and assignment to its own underwriters, who had thereafter settled with defendants. The owner has not appealed from this judgment.

The court also rejected appellant PCI's claims for consequential damages based on the uniqueness of the barge and alleged expenses incurred in procuring a substitute. Although PCI had not been a party to the settlement between the owner and the barge's underwriters, the court held that PCI, as a bareboat charterer, stood in the shoes of the owner. The court relied upon,

> The well-settled rule where a ship is a total loss ... the aggrieved party may not recover compensation for contemplated profits or the loss of use of the ship. Damages are limited to the value of the ship, plus interest and the net freight pending at the time of the collision. *The Umbria*, 166 U.S. 404 (1897); *Barger v. Hanson*, [426] F.2d 640, 641 (9th Cir. 1970).

The court acknowledged PCI's claims that the tug had been negligent as to it; that the tug's owner had committed a breach of duties owed to PCI individually under the towing contract; and, finally, that it had violated its implied warranty of workmanlike service owed to PCI under the towing contract. However, the court ruled that as bareboat charterer PCI was limited to the same damages an owner could have claimed in like circumstances, and that these would not have gone beyond the value of the totally lost vessel and of certain other items not material to PCI's claim. The court contrasted the situation with that which would have prevailed if the barge had been a partial, not a total, loss. In such case, the court said, the owner would have been entitled to lost earnings or to the cost of providing a substitute ship, citing *The Emma Kate Ross v. Myers Excursion Nav. Corp.*, 50 F. 845 (3d Cir. 1892).

We sustain the judgment of the district court. Where a vessel is totally lost, the measure of damages is its value at the time of loss, plus interest and the net freight pending at the time of the collision. *The Umbria*, 166 U.S. 404, 421-22 (1897). Loss of use is not allowable. *Alkmeon Naviera, S.A. v. M/V Marina L*, 633 F.2d 789, 797 (9th Cir. 1980); *Ozanic v. United States*, 165 F.2d 738, 743 (2d Cir. 1948); *The Hamilton*, 95 F. 844 (E.D.N.Y. 1899). While termed a "collision" rule, courts have applied it where barges under tow have been damaged or lost because of the inattention of the tug, and we see no reason not to apply it where the barge was stranded by the tug as here. *The June Ames*, 66 F.2d 415, 416 (2d Cir. 1933) (tow damaged by hitting abutment of a bridge through negligence of tug; rule in issue followed); *Mobile Towing & Wrecking Co. v. Dredge*, 299 F. Supp. 358, 367 (N.D. Fla. 1969) (tow sank as a result of tug's negligence; consequential damages denied). As the district court here recognized, damages for loss of use would have been recoverable had the loss been partial.

* * *

We think the rule in question is too well-established to be altered now, at least at our level. While arguments may be made, pro and con, for its soundness as an original proposition, it was announced by the Supreme Court and has been followed by admiralty judges of the stature of Learned and Augustus Hand. *The June Ames, supra*. There is much to be said in the world of shipping and commerce for predictability, simplicity and stability of rules, so that shipowners and insurers may plan their financial exposure. PCI could have insured itself against the consequences of loss of use of this special barge had it thought to do so. G. Gilmore & C. Black, The Law of Admiralty § 4-22 (2d ed. 1975); Arnould, Marine Insurance § 300 (15th ed. 1961).

PCI argues that, as a bareboat charterer, not an owner, it should not be bound by a rule developed for owners—otherwise it will receive no recompense for the tug's mistake. Bareboat charterers, however, are ordinarily treated as if they are owners, *Reed v. Yaka*, 373 U.S. 410, 412 (1963); *Williams v. McAllister Bros., Inc.*, 534 F.2d 19 (2d Cir. 1976); they acquire the character and become subject to the legal duties and responsibilities of ownership. *See Reed v. United States*, 78 U.S. (11 Wall.) 591, 600-07 (1871); *Leary v. United States*, 81 U.S. (14 Wall.) 607, 610 (1872). We recognize that the Supreme Court cases dealt only with situations in which the bareboat charterer as a defendant was held to stand in the shoes of the owner, but we think that it must wear the same shoes here. It would be illogical to restrict owners in the recovery of special damages of this nature but to allow bareboat charterers to recover them. Owners, it is true, will in any event receive the value of their investment with interest, but these amounts will not necessarily make up for additional damages from the loss of a profitable charter or the inability to perform pending contracts with third parties. If owners are denied special damages of this type, it is difficult to see why a bareboat charterer should recover them. The liability of those responsible for the loss should not depend on whether the injured party is an owner or a bareboat charterer. As a practical matter, the question may often come down to whether the bareboat charterer or the putative tortfeasor should procure insurance against consequential damages. A good reason for placing this requirement on the charterer—at least where, as here, the uniqueness of the vessel or other special circumstances are claimed to create exceptionally high consequential damages—is that he is better able to predict the extent of consequential damages in the event the chartered vessel is lost. *Cf.* R. Posner, Economic Analysis of Law §§ 4.11, 6.8 (2d ed. 1977) (party best able to foresee consequences should take precaution against anticipated losses). When a bareboat charterer raised a claim similar to the present one in 1969, the district court dismissed it as "novel and imaginative" but "without basis in law." *Mobile Towing & Wrecking Co. v. Dredge*, 299 F. Supp. 358, 367 (N.D. Fla. 1969). We agree that the claim for lost profits and other consequential damages lacks a basis in law.

Affirmed.

3. Cargo Losses

AMOCO TRANSPORT CO. v. S/S MASON LYKES

768 F.2d 659, 1986 AMC 563 (5th Cir. 1985)

[*Mason Lykes* collided with *Amoco Cremona* in dense fog; *Mason Lykes* was 90% at fault and *Amoco Cremona* 10%. Can the owners of cargo carried on *Mason Lykes* recover damages from *Amoco Cremona*? How much? Eds.]

* * *

Citing *Robins Dry Dock & Repair Co. v. Flint*, 275 U.S. 303, 48 S. Ct. 134, 72 L. Ed. 2d 290 (1927), the district court held that the cargo interests could not recover freight damages from the owners of the *Amoco Cremona* because freight losses are purely economic losses and a victim who does not suffer physical damage to property is precluded from recovering economic losses. We disagree with the district court's finding that *Robins Dry Dock* mandates the disposition of this case. We also disagree with the court's distinguishing of *Aktieselskabet Cuzco v. The Sucaresco ("The Toluma")*, 294 U.S. 394, 55 S. Ct. 467, 79 L. Ed. 2d 942 (1935). We conclude that the facts at bar are more nearly akin to the facts in *The Toluma* than to the facts in *Robins Dry Dock* and it progeny.

In *Robins Dry Dock* a vessel was negligently damaged by employees of a dry dock while undergoing ordinary maintenance. The damage to the vessel delayed its return to service. The vessel was subject to a charter. Although the charter suspended the charter hire while the vessel was in dry dock, the time charterer sued the dry dock for damages resulting from loss of use of the vessel during the damage-induced extension. Justice Holmes, writing for a unanimous court, denied recover, stating that "a tort to the person or property of one man does not make the tort-feasor liable to another merely because the injured person was under a contract with that other, unknown to the doer of the wrong." 275 U.S. at 309, 48 S. Ct. at 135. This circuit and others have interpreted *Robins Dry Dock* to mean that there can be no recovery for economic losses caused by an unintentional maritime tort absent physical damage to property in which the victim has a proprietary interest. Our most recent expression is *State of Louisiana ex rel. Guste v. M/V Testbank*, 752 F.2d 1019 (5th Cir. 1985) (*en banc*).

In the *Toluma* a collision occurred between the *Toluma* and the *Sucaresco* as a result of the fault of both vessels. Both vessels were damaged, but the *Sucaresco* was able to continue her voyage. While the *Toluma* was too badly damaged to proceed without repairs, her cargo was not physically damaged and she put into port. Part of her cargo was unloaded and stored to permit necessary repairs. After the repairs, the *Toluma* continued her voyage. A clause in the bill of lading gave the owners of the *Toluma* the right to collect the cost of unloading, reloading, and storage from the cargo interests despite the fact that the costs were incurred as a result of the owner's partial fault in the collision. The innocent cargo interests in turn sought to recover the money paid to the owners of the *Toluma* from the owners of the other negligent non-carrying vessel. In allowing the cargo interests to recover, the Supreme Court stressed the common adventure nature of the relationship between the vessel owner and the cargo interests. The Court also noted that the expenses in question were expenses arising directly from the collision, expenses for which the negligent non-carrying vessel would have been liable even in the absence of a general average right by the vessel owners against the cargo interests:

> That the extraordinary expenses, thus shared, were due to the collision cannot be gainsaid. It is because they were thus directly caused, that these expenses form part of the damages to be divided between the two vessels. On this basis they were included in the decree for division made by the District Court and the propriety of the inclusion of these amounts in the total damages to be divided between the vessels is not questioned. But the right to that inclusion springs directly from the tort and in that relation no question is raised as to proximate cause or foreseeable consequences.

The nature of these expenditures and the fact that they are traceable directly to the collision are not changed by the sharing in general average. That merely affects the distribution of the loss, not its cause. The claim of the cargo owners for their general average contributions is not in any sense a derivative claim. It accrues to the cargo owners in their own right. It accrues because of cargo's own participation in the common adventure and the action taken on behalf of cargo and by its representative to avert a peril with which that adventure was threatened. Being cargo's own share of the expense incurred in the common interest, the amount which is paid properly belongs in the category of damage which the cargo owners have suffered by reason of the collision. *The Energia* (D.C. [1894]) 61 F. 222 (C.C.A.2d [1895]) 66 F. 604, 608.

* * *

As we have said, the "Jason clause" merely distributed a loss for which *Sucaresco* was responsible and in that view the cargo owners are entitled to recover that part of the loss which they have sustained.

294 U.S. at 403-05, 55 S. Ct. at 470-71. Chief Justice Hughes, writing for a unanimous court, distinguished *Robins Dry Dock*, observing:

This is not a case of an attempt, by reason of "a tort to the person or property of one man," to make the tortfeasor liable to another "merely because the injured person was under a contract with that other, unknown to the doer of the wrong." *See Robins Dry Dock & Repair Co. v. Flint*, 275 U.S. 303, 309, 72 L. Ed. 2d 290, 292, 48 S. Ct. 134 [135]; *Elliott Steam Tug Co. v. The Shipping Controller* [1922] 1 K.B. 127, 139, 142-C.A.; *The Federal No. 2* (C.C.A.2d) 21 F.(2d) 313. Here, cargo as well as ship was placed in jeopardy. That jeopardy was due in part to the negligence of the vessel against which the claim is made. The fact that the vessel and the cargo under the "Jason clause" bear their proportionate shares of the expenses gives *Sucaresco* no ground for a contention that the expenses themselves, or the share that cargo bears, were not occasioned directly by the tort. In the light of the nature of the general average contributions, and of the event which made them necessary, the fact that they were made under the stipulation in the "Jason clause" is no more a defense to *Sucarseco* than is the fact that the cargo was placed on board under a contract to carry it.

294 U.S. at 404-05, 55 S. Ct. at 471.

The common adventure concept is a venerable one and is firmly established. Reflecting on vintage cases, the authors of Benedict on Admiralty observe, almost in passing, that "upon stowage of the cargo ... hull and cargo [are] bound together in a venture." 2A Benedict on Admiralty, § 35, at 4-17 (6th Ed. 1985).

The bills of lading in this case indicate that the voyage of the *Mason Lykes* was a common adventure between the vessel and cargo owners similar to the participants in the voyage of the *Toluma*. The instant bills of lading contain a "Jason clause" similar to the clause under which the owners of the *Toluma* passed along the expenses of unloading, loading, and storage to the cargo interests. The purpose of the Jason clause is to spread the risks among all participants in the venture. *The Toluma*. The freight earned clause under which the cargo interests in this case were obligated to pay Lykes also supports the common adventure nature of the voyage for freight earned clauses were also developed to spread the risks between common adventures in ocean transportation. As the district court observed in *9655 Long Tons, No. 2 Yellow Milo*: "The prepaid freight clause involved here was developed to require the cargo owner to share with the vessel owner to some extent the inherent risks of ocean transportation...." 238 F. Supp. at 574. Thus the terms of the bills of lading support the proposition that the owners of the *Mason Lykes* and the owners of her cargo were engaged in a common venture. That common venture sustained physical injury when the *Amoco Cremona* collided with the *Mason Lykes*. It cannot be gainsaid that the damages in this case, lost freight, are similar to the costs of unloading, reloading, and storage in *The Toluma*; they, too, are damages arising directly from the collision for which the negligent non-carrying vessel would have been liable even in the absence of a freight earned clause. *The Baltimore*, 75 U.S. (8 Wall.) 377, 19 L. Ed. 2d 463 (1869).

Robins Dry Dock is inapposite for another reason. In the absence of a freight earned clause, Lykes would not have had the right to retain the freight. *Alcoa Steamship Co. v. United States.* When a collision causes a vessel to lose freight by preventing delivery of the cargo to its final destination, the cargo-carrying vessel can recover the lost freight from the negligent non-carrying vessel. *The Baltimore.* Thus the loss of the original freight for the voyage would be an economic loss of the owner of the damaged vessel. *Robins Dry Dock* does not prevent recovery for such economic losses by the owner of the physically damaged vessel. *See Vicksburg Towing Co. v. Mississippi Marine Transport Co.,* 609 F.2d 176 (5th Cir. 1980); *State of Louisiana ex rel Guste v. M/V Testbank; Venore Transportation Co. v. M/V Struma,* 583 F.2d 708 (4th Cir. 1978). Nor does *Robins Dry Dock* prevent recovery for such losses by a person to whom they have been contractually shifted. *Standard Navigazione v. K. Z. Michalos,* 1981 A.M.C. 748 (S.D. Tex. 1981); *Venore Transportation Co. v. M/V Struma.* Nothing in the *Robins Dry Dock* or the *Testbank* holding or rationale prohibits recovery in tort by the person to whom the economic losses suffered by the owner of physically damaged property have been shifted. The effect of a freight earned clause is similar to the effect of a clause providing that charter hire continues to run while a vessel is disabled; it contractually shifts the risk of economic loss, which would normally fall upon the property owner, to a third part. That third party is entitled to recover those losses. The risk of double recovery from the tortfeasor is not extant. *Struma.*

The spectre of runaway recovery lies at the heart of the *Robins Dry Dock* rubric. As Professors Prosser and Keeton noted in their most recent work:.

> The policy against recovery based on negligence is rooted at least in part on what Professor James has called the "pragmatic objection," that while physical harm generally has limited effects, a chain reaction occurs when economic harm is done and may produce an unending sequence of financial effects best dealt with by insurance, or by contract, or by other business planning devices.

Prosser & Keeton on The Law of Torts (5th Ed. 1984), § 129, p. 1001, *citing* James, *Tort Liability for Economic Loss,* 1972, 25 Vand. L. Rev. 43, 45.

The claim against Amoco by the cargo owners is in the nature of an equitable subrogation of Lykes' rights. So viewed, there would be no double recovery, much less runaway recovery. As the professors again observed, "subrogation recoveries involve only one loss ... there is no potential in such cases for a chain of recoveries...." *Id.* at 999.

The instant case is not within the parameters of the evil to be remedied. There is no danger of an unlimited round of recoveries. The cargo owners make no attempt to recover for remote contractual losses or real or speculative lost profits. Rather, they seek only to recover, with and through the vessel, those actual, out-of-pocket expenses they incurred which were directly occasioned by the collision. But for the freight earned clause, Amoco would have been liable exclusively to Lykes. As a consequence of the freight earned clause, the claim is transferred to the cargo owners and may be asserted by them under the umbrella of this equitable principle. *See Compania Anonima Venezolana de Nav. v. A.J. Perez Export Co.,* 303 F.2d 692 (5th Cir. 1962), and other authorities cited therein.

Collection of Damages

The cargo interests are entitled to recover their damages from either Lykes or Amoco, for they have a valid cause of action against both. Because Lykes' decision to abandon the voyage was unreasonable, the cargo interests are entitled to recover the full amount of retained freight on the voyage of the *Mason Lykes* from Lykes. *T.J. Stevenson & Co. v. 81,193 Bags of Flour.* The cargo interests are also entitled to recover the entire amount of the forfeited freight. *The Toluma.* However, they may recover only once. If the cargo interests collect full damages from Amoco, Amoco in turn may include these costs in the apportionment of the damages between the vessels. *See The Toluma* and *United States v. Reliable Transfer Co.,* 421 U.S. 397, 95 S. Ct. 1708, 44 L. Ed. 2d 251 (1975). If the cargo interests collect full damages from Lykes, Lykes may include the lost freight in the apportionment of the damages between the vessels. *The Baltimore; United States v. Reliable Transfer Co.*

Accordingly, we *Reverse* and *Remand* to the district court for the determination of the amount of freight actually paid by the cargo interests for the aborted voyage of the *Mason Lykes* and to enter judgment for the appellants in that amount, together with any interests deemed appropriate, and costs.

UNITED STATES v. ATLANTIC MUTUAL INSURANCE CO.

343 U.S. 236, 72 S. Ct. 666, 96 L. Ed. 907, 1952 AMC 659 (1952)

Mr. Justice BLACK delivered the opinion of the Court.

Respondents are cargo owners who shipped goods on the steamship *Nathaniel Bacon* owned by petitioner, the United States, and operated as a common carrier of goods for hire. It collided with the *Esso Belgium* and respondents' cargo was damaged. The ships were also damaged. This litigation was brought in the District Court to determine liability for the damages suffered by the cargo owners and for the physical damage caused the ships. It was agreed in the District Court that:

(a) The collision was due to negligent navigation by employees of both ships. The cargo owners were in no way at fault.

(b) *The Belgium*, as one of two joint tortfeasors, must pay "100%" of damages suffered by the Bacon's cargo owners.

(c) Because of § 3 of the Harter Act and § 4(2) of the Carriage of Goods by Sea Act, the cargo owners are barred from directly suing the Bacon for cargo damages.

(d) Since the two ships were mutually at fault, the aggregate of all damages to both should be shared by both.

(e) In computing the aggregate damages caused both ships, account should be taken of the cargo damages recovered from the *Belgium* by the cargo owners.

(f) The bill of lading issued by the Bacon to the cargo owners contained a "Both-to-Blame" clause.[5] This clause, if valid, requires the cargo owners to indemnify the carrier Bacon for any amounts the Bacon loses because damages recovered by the cargo owners from the *Belgium* are included in the aggregate damages divided between the two ships.

The only question presented to us is whether the "Both-to-Blame" clause is valid. Respondent cargo owners contend that it is void and unenforceable as a violation of the long-standing rule of law which forbids common carriers from stipulating against the consequences of their own or their employees' negligence. Petitioner, the United States, contends that § 3 of the Harter Act, as substantially reenacted in § 4(2) of the Carriage of Goods by Sea Act, provides special statutory authorization permitting ocean carriers to deviate from the general rule and to stipulate against their negligence as they did here. The District Court held the clause valid. 90 F. Supp. 836. The Court of Appeals reversed. 191 F.2d 370. Deeming the question decided of sufficient importance to justify our review, this Court granted certiorari.

There is a general rule of law that common carriers cannot stipulate for immunity from their own or their agents' negligence. While this general rule was fashioned by the courts, it has been continuously accepted as a guide to common-carrier relationships for more than a century and has acquired the force and precision of a legislative enactment. Considering the relationship of the rule to the Harter Act, this Court said in 1901

---

[5] The clause reads as follows:

If the ship comes into collision with another ship as a result of the negligence of the other ship and any act, neglect or default of the Master, mariner, pilot or the servants of the Carrier in the navigation or in the management of the ship, the owners of the goods carried hereunder will indemnify the Carrier against all loss or liability to the other or non-carrying ship or her owners in so far as such loss or liability represents loss of, or damage to, or any claim whatsoever of the owners of said goods, paid or payable by the other or non-carrying ship or her owners to the owners of said goods and set-off, recouped or recovered by the other or non-carrying ship or her owners as part of their claim against the carrying ship or Carrier.

that "in view of the well-settled nature of the general rule at the time the statute was adopted, it must result that legislative approval was by clear implication given to the general rule as then existing in all cases where it was not changed." *The Kensington*, 183 U.S. 263, 268-269. Our question therefore is whether the language of the Harter Act, substantially reenacted in the Carriage of Goods by Sea Act, has carved out a special statutory exception to the general rule so as to permit a carrier to deprive its cargo owners of a part of the fruits of any judgment they obtain in a direct action against a noncarrying vessel that contributes to a collision.

Prior to the passage of the Harter Act in 1893, cargo damages incurred in a both-to-blame collision could be recovered in full from either ship. *The Atlas*, 93 U.S. 302. The Harter Act, under some circumstances, took away the right of the cargo owner to sue his own carrier for cargo damages caused by the negligent navigation of the carrier's servants or agents. It did not deprive the cargo owner of his tort action against the noncarrying ship. *The Chattahoochee*, 173 U.S. 540, 549-550. Nor did the Harter Act go so far as to insulate the carrier from responsibility to another vessel for physical damages caused to the ship by negligent navigation of the carrier's servants or agents. In *The Delaware*, 161 U.S. 459, 471, 474, this Court declined to give the Harter Act such a broad interpretation even though the language itself, if "broadly construed" and considered alone, would have justified such an interpretation. In addition, the Harter Act does not exonerate the carrier from its obligation to share with the noncarrier one-half the damages paid by the noncarrier to the cargo owners....

Apparently it was not until about forty years after the passage of the Harter Act that shipowners first attempted by stipulation to deprive cargo owners of a part of their recovery against noncarrying ships.... The present effort of shipowners appears to date from 1937 when the North Atlantic Freight Conference adopted the "Both-to-Blame" clause. So far as appears, this is the first test of the legality of the clause that has appeared in the courts. When Congress passed the Carriage of Goods by Sea Act in 1936, it indicated no purpose to bring about a change in the long-existing relationships and obligations between carriers and shippers which would be relevant to the validity of the "Both-to-Blame" clause.

Petitioner argues that the clause does nothing more than remove an "anomaly" which arises from this Court's construction of the Harter Act. It is said to be "anomalous" to hold a carrier not liable at all if it alone is guilty of negligent navigation but at the same time to hold it indirectly liable for one-half the cargo damages if another ship is jointly negligent with it. Assuming for the moment that all rules of law must be symmetrical, we think it would be "anomalous" to hold that a cargo owner, who has an unquestioned right under the law to recover full damages from a noncarrying vessel, can be compelled to give up a portion of that recovery to his carrier because of a stipulation exacted in a bill of lading. Moreover, there is no indication that either the Harter Act or the Carriage of Goods by Sea Act was designed to alter the long-established rule that the full burden of the losses sustained by both ships in a both-to-blame collision is to be shared equally.

ALLIED CHEMICAL CORP. v. HESS TANKSHIP CO. OF DEL.

661 F.2d 1044, 1982 AMC 1271 (5th Cir. 1981)

John R. BROWN, Circuit Judge:

It was a dark and stormy night. A patchy, low-lying fog covered the murky waters of the river and obscured the banks. Ships, passing in the night, were but phantoms, vague outlines disappearing into the mist. Ships' whistles, echoing across the dark expanse, seemed like mournful cries from another world. Then suddenly, looming out of the darkness, another ship appeared. The distance was too small; time too short; before anyone could do more than cry out, the unthinkable occurred. The ships collided. The tug, helpless, drifted downriver. Floundering like some giant behemoth wounded in battle, the tanker came to ground and impaled itself on some voracious underwater obstruction. And still the whistles, echoing, seemed like cries from another world.

This apparent screenplay for a Grade B film, in fact, came to Southwest Pass of the Mississippi River, about 3 miles below Head of Passes, in Louisiana, on February 1, 1973. The cast of characters included the *S.S. Hess Refiner* *(Refiner)*, a jumboized T-2 tanker approximately 605 feet in length and 75 feet in beam and drawing, that fateful night, 32 feet, 1 inch forward and 34 feet, 7 inches aft; the *Socrates*, a 125-foot seagoing tug drawing 14 feet, equipped with twin pilot-house-controlled engines boasting 3200 h.p.; and its tow, the barge *Allied Chemical No. 44 (AC-44)*, which measured some 340 feet in length, 68 feet in beam, drawing approximately 17 feet forward and 18 feet aft. *Refiner* is owned by Hess Tankship Company and was bareboat chartered to Amerada Hess Corporation (collectively Hess). SOCRATES is owned by Allied Towing Corporation (Allied Towing). AC-44 belongs to Allied Chemical Corporation (Allied Chemical), which, despite the apparent filial connection, bears no relation to Allied Towing.

* * *

The District Court found the parties equally to blame and allocated fault accordingly in conformity with *Reliable Transfer*.... The equal 50/50 allocation of fault finds ample support in the facts and the record, and we affirm.

Allied Towing labels as error the District Court's holding that Allied Chemical may recover its full damages from Hess. The reason for this counter-intuitive strategy is that, under long-standing admiralty practice, this loss goes into Hess' damage claim which, on striking the balance, means that Hess will be entitled to recover 50% of such amount against Allied Towing. *The Chattahoochee*, 173 U.S. 540, 19 S. Ct. 491, 43 L. Ed. 801 (1899); *The New York*, 175 U.S. 187 (1899); *Griffin on Collision* §§ 245, 246.

Allied Towing informs us that *Alamo Chemical Transportation Co. v. M/V Overseas Valdes*, 469 F. Supp. 203 (E.D. La. 1979), interpreting the *Reliable Transfer* mandate, supplants that traditional rule. We disagree....

In arriving at that decision, the *Overseas Valdes* Court explicitly rejected prior contrary holdings. In *Complaint of Flota Mercante Grancolombiana, S.A.*, 440 F. Supp. 704, 725 (S.D.N.Y. 1977), the Court, taking due notice of *Reliable Transfer*, stated:

This Court believes that the better rule would be to allow ... a full recovery against the non-carrying vessel, allow the latter to add the payments it makes to cargo to its own damages, and then to permit it to recover this total from the carrying vessel in proportion to the fault of the carrying vessel. This resolution would be more in accord with the principles enunciated in *Reliable Transfer* [which] was intended to change the rule of damages so that the burden would fall more equitably on those parties whose fault contributed to the collision.

We believe that Flota Mercante more nearly charts a Reliable course. The Supreme Court acted to abolish the doctrine of mutual fault-equal contribution, an anachronism which every other maritime nation had already rejected. The decision only alters the proportions in which damages are fixed—it does not abolish the procedure by which an innocent cargo owner traditionally could recover his damages in full from the tortious non-carrying vessel no matter what the degree of fault between the tortious actors.[24]

The Supreme Court provides support for our view in *Edmonds v. Compagnie Generale Transatlantique*, 443 U.S. 256, (1979).... Citing *Reliable Transfer*, the Court observed "*Reliable Transfer* merely changed the apportionment from equal division to division on the basis of relative fault. But we did not upset the rule that the plaintiff may recover from one of the colliding vessels the damage concurrently caused by the negligence of both." 443 U.S. at 272 (n. 30).

Overseas Valdes, decided before Edmonds, involved a Both-to-Blame clause that recovery under the traditional rule would sidestep. The Court, by confining Firestone to its percentage recovery against Maritime, did an end-run around the problem. In so doing, it created a greater problem.

---

[24] *See also Gulfcoast Transit v. ANCO PRINCESS*, 1978 A.M.C. 2471 (E.D. La. 1977), *citing Oriental Hero-Caster*, 1976 A.M.C. 1287, 1306 (S.D.N.Y. 1976) ("*The Reliable Transfer* decision has no application to an action between innocent cargo and one of the vessels in a collision."); *Florida East Coast Railway, supra; Samuels v. Empresa Lineas Maritimas Argentinas*, 573 F.2d 884, 887-888 (5th Cir. 1978), *cert. denied*, 443 U.S. 915, 99 S. Ct. 3106, 61 L. Ed. 2d 878 (1979).

The Court's decision in *Overseas Valdes* leaves the innocent cargo, "the one party both aggrieved and free to do something about it," *O/Y Finlayson-Forssa v. Pan Atlantic Steamship Co.*, 259 F.2d 11, 13 (5th Cir. 1958), *cert. denied*, 361 U.S. 882, (1959), in the lurch. Where a cargo suffers damages from a collision where both vessels were negligent, it is the only innocent party. *Reliable Transfer* certainly did not intend to shift the risk of loss away from the negligent parties. Yet *Overseas Valdes* does precisely that.

We reject Allied Towing's argument and the decision in *Overseas Valdes* to the extent it is inconsistent with out holding.[25] We therefore affirm the District Court's grant of full recovery against Hess, which automatically goes into its damages for ultimate division.

Notes

1. Third-Party Damages in Marine Casualty Cases

The rule in *Robins Dry Dock* holds that "a tort to the person or property of one man does not make the tortfeasor liable to another merely because the injured person was under contract with that other, unknown to the doer of the wrong." 275 U.S. 303, 309, 48 S. Ct. 134, 72 L. Ed. 290 (1927). This rule has been questioned, but it is still valid. In *The Sucarseco*, 294 U.S. 394, 55 S. Ct. 467, 79 L. Ed. 942 (1935), the Court required a negligent noncarrying vessel to pay for a share of a general average that cargo had to bear under the bill of lading's Jason clause. How is this reconcilable with *Robins*?

If, as a result of a collision, the subcharterer of a vessel puts the vessel off-hire pursuant to a contract right, can the charterer recover the lost profits?

2. Damages Recoverable by Owners of Cargo

Under Article 4 of the Collision Convention of 1910, cargo can only recover from the noncarrying vessel to the extent of that vessel's degree of fault. Compare this to the American rule in the foregoing cases. Is there a good argument that *Reliable Transfer* should be interpreted to overrule the American rule?

3. Damages Recoverable by Personal Injury and Death Claimants

Personal injury and death claimants recover the full amount of their damages except where limitation of liability applies. In a both-to-blame collision each vessel is jointly and severally liable, and the amounts paid are included as collision damages. The matter of personal injury and death is covered extensively in Chapter 3, *supra*.

4. Prejudgment Interest

This item is often an important aspect of a damage award in marine casualty cases. The law concerning when prejudgment interest will be given was set out by the court in *Alkmeon Naviera, S.A. v. M/V "Marina L,"* 633 F.2d 789, 793-94, 1982 AMC 153 (9th Cir. 1980):

> While the award of prejudgment interest is in the discretion of the trial judge, this discretion must be "exercised with a view to the right to interest unless the circumstances are exceptional." [*The President Madison*, 91 F.2d 845,] 847. The rationale for restricting discretion to exceptional cases is that, in admiralty collisions, prejudgment interest is an element of compensation and not a penalty. *Federal Barge Lines, Inc. v. Republic Marine, Inc.*, 616 F.2d 372, 373 (8th Cir. 1980); *Rosa v. Insurance Co. of Pa.*, 421 F.2d 390, 393 (9th Cir. 1970). As such, it is usually denied only when a party "deprive[s] himself of interest." *The President Madison*, 91 F.2d at 847. Unwarranted delay by counsel is the most common ground for denial, *American Zinc Co. v. Foster*, 441 F.2d 1100, 1101 (5th Cir.), *cert. denied*, 404 U.S. 855 (1971); *The President Madison*, 91 F.2d at 847, but other cases arise. This circuit, for example, has denied prejudgment interest where there was less than actual loss and no proof of of deprivation of use, *Firemen's Fund Ins. Co., v. Standard Oil Co. of Cal.*, 339 F.2d 148, 159 (9th Cir. 1964); where the parties have excluded prejudgment interest in their stipulation of damages, *Grace Line, Inc. v. Todd Shipyards Corp.*, 500 F.2d 361, 366 (9th Cir. 1974); or where the parties assert claims or defenses in bad faith, *Darling v. Scheimer*, 444 F.2d 514, 515 (9th Cir. 1971). Other circuits have considered uncertainty regarding claims or damages as "peculiar circumstances." *Sinclair Refining Co. v. S/S Green Island*, 426 F.2d 260, 262 (5th Cir. 1970). *Contra: Ore Carriers of Liberia, Inc. v. Navigen Co.*, 305 F. Supp. 895, 897 (S.D.N.Y. 1969), *affd*, 435 F.2d 549, 551 (2d Cir. 1970).

---

[25] In proceedings fixing damages and striking the balance, Allied Towing, of course, may urge all contractual exemptions and limitations from liability to cargo.

In *City of Milwaukee v. Cement Div., Nat. Gypsum Co.*, 515 U.S. 189, 115 S. Ct. 2091, 132 L. Ed. 2d 148, 1995 AMC 1882 (1995), the Court confirmed that the general rule is that prejudgment interest should be awarded in maritime collision cases, subject to a limited exception for "peculiar" or "exceptional" circumstances.

Problem

Suppose two vessels, the Ajax and Bjax, are involved in a collision and it is determined that the Ajax is 20% at fault while the Bjax is 80% at fault. The following damages are proved:

Vessel Ajax

1. Cost of repairs and incidentals	$ 600,000
2. Lost profits based on the charter rate	50,000
3. Damage paid to injured seaman	50,000
Total	$ 700,000

Vessel Bjax

1. Market value of vessel (total loss)	$ 950,000
2. Wreck removal	50,000
Total	$ 1,000,000

How would damages be allocated if it were determined that cargo aboard the Bjax was also a total loss valued at $300,000?

CHAPTER 5 — TOWAGE, PILOTAGE, AND SALVAGE

Section 1. Towage

A. Towage and Affreightment Contracts Distinguished

AGRICO CHEMICAL CO. v. M/V BEN W. MARTIN
664 F.2d 85, 1985 AMC 563 (5th Cir. 1981)

Alvin B. RUBIN, Circuit Judge

A barge loaded with liquid nitrogen fertilizer capsized. The parties involved in supplying and moving the barge concede their liability to the owner of the cargo but each contends that the other was liable for the loss. Based on what we consider to be a misconstruction of the contractual relationship between the parties, the district court found only one party at fault. We find both negligent, apportion the liability equally between them, and remand for further proceedings.

Agrico Chemical Company manufactures and sells various chemical products, including 32% liquid nitrogen fertilizer (urea ammonium nitrate or UAN), which it manufactures at a plant near Tulsa, Oklahoma. Agrico contracted with Brent Towing Company to provide the marine services and equipment necessary to transport Agrico's products on a continuing basis. During October 1977, Agrico advised Brent that, pursuant to the contract, it had more than 5000 tons of UAN to be moved from its Oklahoma plant to Westwego, Louisiana. Brent assigned two of its barges to the task and engaged Logicon's tow boat, the M/V GREENVILLE, to tow the barges on a mills-per-ton-mile basis, the usual way in which it engaged a tow. Brent concedes that its contract with Agrico was not a charter but a contract of affreightment. Logicon provided the tug and crew, arranged and paid for insurance, paid the expenses of the trip and was compensated in the same manner in which a taxi would be paid.

Agrico then informed Brent that it wished to move an additional 3,000 tons of UAN. Brent had no other barge available, so Malcolm Gunter, Brent's traffic manager, communicated with Herman Pardue, Logicon's port captain, seeking sufficient space on a Logicon barge to move the additional cargo.

Pardue informed Gunter that the Logicon 2702, a 27,000 barrel, single-skinned barge, was available and could be added to the GREENVILLE's tow. This barge, however, had previously been loaded with diesel fuel, and was scheduled for another fuel charter in fifteen days. Therefore, Pardue requested that Brent clean the barge's tanks after it had been used to transport UAN, so that it would be fit again to haul diesel fuel. Payment was to be made on a mills-per-ton-mile basis without regard to the number of days the trip took. Logicon was to provide insurance on the barge. No on-charter survey of the Logicon barge was intended, and none was made.

Brent's tankermen were to load the two Brent barges. There is conflict in the testimony concerning whose tankermen were to load the Logicon barge; the district court found, however, that this was to be Brent's responsibility. Brent was to receive daily position reports on the barge but furnished no crew and did not direct its movement.

The interior of the Logicon barge consisted of ten cargo tanks, five on each side of a centerline bulkhead. The centerline bulkhead was liquid-tight only at the number one (forward-most) port and starboard tanks; that part of the bulkhead separating cargo compartments two through five contained "baffles" or openings that permitted liquid to flow between the port and starboard tanks. Diesel fuel is lighter than water, and the barge can be loaded almost to its top with diesel fuel without causing the barge to be overloaded. UAN, however, is so much heavier than water that the vessel is down to its draft line when loaded with a much smaller volume of UAN than of diesel fuel. Thus, there is more empty space in the cargo tanks, leaving more room for the liquid to shift when the barge is loaded with UAN rather than with diesel fuel. When the heavier fluid, UAN, shifts from one side of the barge to another, the stability of the barge is threatened.

Most barges used to transport liquids have a liquid-tight centerline bulkhead. Barge 2702 was, therefore, unusual, although the conventional exterior of the barge gave no visible suggestion of its internal structure. Gunter testified that he told Pardue that the cargo to be transported was UAN and that Pardue said nothing about the construction of the barge. This testimony was not contradicted, and the district court made no finding of fact with regard to these matters.

One of Logicon's employees, a tankerman named Homer Bland, testified that, while the barge was en route to Oklahoma, he overheard a radio conversation between Pardue and the GREENVILLE's master, Captain Cecil Jacobs, in which the intended cargo of UAN was mentioned. Thereupon, Bland, who had thought the intended cargo was oil, said to Captain Jacobs, "I wouldn't think it was a good barge to load with fertilizer. The way it is made, it is made odd, and it just takes a pretty good tankerman to understand it before you would undertake a job like that." Bland testified that the barge "will roll on you" because "the compartments are together as one complete compartment, instead of having port and starboard compartments." Thus, when the cargo shifts, as he later testified, all of it "goes to one side and causes it to roll."

Bland testified that he was directed to explain the barge's construction and the proper loading procedure to Brent's employees. When the barge arrived at Agrico's plant, two Brent tankermen, experienced in handling UAN, began loading. Bland testified that he suggested to the tankermen the order the tanks should be filled. After four hours of loading, the 2702 began to list. One of Brent's tankermen then sought out Bland, who informed the Brent tankerman of the nature of the bulkheads, which permitted the cargo to shift from one side to the other. The district judge found that "[w]ith this knowledge [Brent's employees] continued with the loading, and with the advice and counsel, and at times the assistance, of Mr. Bland the matter was completed."

Loading the barge required twelve hours to complete. The Brent tankermen then left. The barge was afloat and appeared to be stable and level. "[A] little after" the Brent tankermen left, and before the tow commenced, however, the barge began to roll. Captain Jacobs telephoned Pardue for instructions, then directed Bland to get the barge leveled off so the tow could begin. Bland put pumps on the barge and transferred some of the cargo from the first compartment to the other compartments, thus, of course, altering the distribution of the cargo. The barge was left tied up overnight, and the tow commenced the next morning.

The GREENVILLE towed the three barges, including the two Brent barges and the Logicon barge, to Greenville, Mississippi. There the barges were tied up, and the GREENVILLE went into dry dock for a wheel change. Coast Guard Chief Warrant Officer Frank Self testified that, while the barge was in Greenville, he had a conversation with Pardue, Logicon's port captain, and commented that the Logicon barge was listing to port. Pardue stated that he does not recall the subject matter of his conversation with the Coast Guard warrant officer. Self testified that Pardue mentioned that the barge had a cargo of liquid nitrogen fertilizer. Self also testified that he said to Pardue that he did not "really understand how you made it this far, because I am very familiar with that barge, and only the number one cargo tank has a solid centerline bulk-head in it, and with the free flow of fertilizer, it just will not stay upright, it is going to flow to one side or the other." To this, he said Pardue responded, "Well, I am going to Baton Rouge.... I am going down there and ... I will tie it off. I will pump the cargo out and I will return it back and make all those compartments watertight, the centerline bulkheads watertight." Self said that Captain Jacobs had informed him that, during the downriver trip, "when he was making turns in the river that the barge [Logicon 2702] would lean quite extensively, to port or starboard, which ever way he was turning."

On the morning of November 12, the crew of the M/V GREENVILLE was attempting to make up the tow so that it could continue the downriver voyage. The GREENVILLE was brought outside Logicon 2702 and was being used to slide the barge forward when the barge began to roll and then suddenly capsized.

Agrico sued only Logicon and its vessels. Logicon filed a third-party complaint against Brent seeking indemnity or contribution, and also seeking the damages suffered by its barge. After an evidentiary hearing on liability issues only, the district judge held that the arrangement between Brent and Logicon constituted a charter, and that Brent was functioning as a stevedore in loading the 2702. The court noted that as a stevedore Brent owed a duty of workmanlike performance to Logicon and that Brent's tankerman had committed a breach of this duty in continuing to load the barge after they knew of the openings in the centerline bulkhead. "[I]t was Brent's duty at that time ... to discontinue the loading of the barge and thereby avoid an unseaworthy condition in connection therewith."

The judge also found that Logicon was not skilled or knowledgeable in connection with the movement of this kind of product and made no representation that the barge would be seaworthy for its movement. He added, however, that the

> master of the tug and its tankerman [presumably Bland] were familiar with this situation, that this was an unseaworthy vessel at the time they took it in tow. The fact that it might have been level and was not listing ... would not in my opinion relieve them of the duty and responsibility of knowing that, in the voyage the tug would undertake the product would move from place to place and render the barge unseaworthy during its passage.

The judge concluded, nonetheless, that Logicon's acts did not cause the loss, for the cargo was not lost "in the movement between the place where the movement started and Greenville." The "sole and only reason the cargo was lost was the shifting of the cargo within the barge so as to make it capsize. The towage of the vessel did not have any causal connection with the capsizing of the barge."

Holding that sole liability rested on Brent, the district judge entered judgment for Agrico against Logicon for the full amount of its damages, to be determined later, and awarded Logicon indemnity from its damages against Brent. The key issue, about which the other determinations revolve, is the nature of the contract between Brent and Logicon, for that determines the rights and duties of each. Accordingly, we first examine that question.

I.

Barges are vessels, but of a peculiar kind. A. Parks, Law of Tug, Tow and Pilotage 4 (1971). Lacking power and usually crew, barges depend upon another vessel, a tug, for movement. A contract for a tug to move a barge is one of towage. The tug is neither a bailee nor an insurer of the tow. *See South-western Sugar and Molasses Co. v. River Terminals Corp.*, 360 U.S. 411, 418 n.6, 79 S. Ct. 1210, 1215 n.6, 3 L. Ed. 2d 1334, 1341 n.6 (1959); *Nat G. Harrison Overseas Corp. v. American Tug Titan*, 516 F.2d 89, 94 (5th Cir. 1974), *as modified*, 520 F.2d 1104 (5th Cir. 1975); *Humble Oil & Refining Co. v. Tug Crochet*, 422 F.2d 602, 606 (5th Cir. 1970); *First Mississippi Corp. v. Fielder Towing Co.*, 469 F. Supp. 1080, 1084 (N.D. Miss. 1979). The tug is, however, obliged to use "'such reasonable care and maritime skill as prudent navigators employ for the performance of similar service.'" *First Mississippi Corp. v. Fielder Towing Co.*, 469 F. Supp. at 1084, quoting from, *Stevens v. The White City*, 285 U.S. 195, 202, 52 S. Ct. 347, 350, 76 L. Ed. 699, 703 (1932).

A towage contract, imposing the duties we have described, arises when one vessel is employed to expedite the movement of another. A. Parks, *supra*, at 22. If, however, the tug is engaged to do more than merely tow another's vessel, the contract is considered one for the movement of the tow and its contents, a contract of affreightment, subject to the more exacting duties applicable to those who undertake as carriers to transport cargo. *See Southwestern Sugar and Molasses Co. v. River Terminals Corp.*, 360 U.S. 411, 417 n.6, 79 S. Ct, 1210, 1215 n.6, 3 L. Ed. 2d 1334, 1341 n.6 (1959) (a common carrier is liable "without proof of negligence, for all damage to the goods transported by it," but liability in the normal tug-tow relationship has not been held to extend this far). Thus, "when a tug and barge are owned by the same person (or when either the tug or barge is bareboat-chartered to the same person) and are utilized, by contract to tow cargo from one point to another, the contract is one of affreightment and not towage." A. Parks, *supra* at 22. *Sacramento*

Navigation Co. v. Salz, 273 U.S. 326, 328, 47 S. Ct. 368, 369, 71 L. Ed. 663, 664 (1927); *Continental Grain Co. v. American Commercial Barge Line Co.*, 332 F.2d 26, 27 (7th Cir. 1964).

The owner of a barge may, like the owners of other vessels, agree by contract to allow another to use it. This contract, usually called a charter party or charter, may assume a variety of forms. If full possession and control of the vessel is turned over to the charterer, the contract is a demise or bareboat charter. The primary obligation of the owner under such a charter is to furnish a vessel in seaworthy state when it is delivered to the charterer. G. GILMORE & C. BLACK, THE LAW OF ADMIRALTY 241 (2d ed. 1975). The charterer is regarded as the owner of the vessel for the period of the charter and is responsible for the vessel's operation. *Id.* at 242.

A "bareboat" or demise charter requires "complete transfer of possession, command, and navigation of the vessel from the owner to the charterer." *Gaspard v. Diamond M. Drilling Co.*, 593 F.2d 605, 606 (5th Cir. 1979). A demise is "tantamount to, though just short of, an outright transfer of ownership." *Guzman v. Pichirilo*, 369 U.S. 698, 700, 82 S. Ct. 1095, 1096, 8 L. Ed. 2d 205, 208 (1962). It need not, however, be in writing.

A vessel may, of course, be chartered in some other fashion, for example for a single voyage ("voyage charter"), or for a fixed period of time ("time charter"). Typically in the case of conventional vessels, the owner remains in control during such charters, and provides the master and crew. Because barges lack power and usually have no crew, contracts for the mere use of a barge are usually bareboat, A. Parks, *supra*, at 394, although this is not inevitable. The owner may not only charter the barge but may also provide a tow and remain in control of the barge.

Whatever the nature of the vessel, the rules concerning responsibility for its operation are the same. If the owner retains control, he remains liable for all damages arising out of its operation whether the charter be only for a single voyage ("voyage charter") or for a fixed time ("time charter"). If the charter is a demise, the charterer is responsible. The charter may describe the duties of the parties and provide for the shifting of risks between them, but, in general, control entails responsibility for fault.

Thus, if the Logicon-Brent agreement for use of the Logicon barge was a bareboat charter and the agreement to tow that barge was a contract of towage, Logicon would be liable only if it were negligent in towage or if it failed to provide a seaworthy vessel. If, however, their arrangement was a contract of affreightment for the benefit of Agrico, primary liability to Agrico for damage to its cargo rests on Logicon. A. Parks, *supra*, at 24.

The agreement between Agrico and Brent was certainly a contract of affreightment, as it was declared to be by the district court. The contract between Brent and Logicon to tow Brent's two barges from Oklahoma to Louisiana was equally clearly a towage contract. As to Agrico, the cargo owner, Brent was responsible for the delivery of the cargo. Brent in turn could look to Logicon only for reasonable diligence in towage. The agreement by Logicon to supply and to tow the third barge is more difficult to characterize. We look to its terms to determine whether the arrangement should be considered two separate contracts, one a barge charter, the other a towage contract, or whether the terms for the use of the barge made that agreement an affreightment contract.

> The district court found that
> The nature of the contract was one of charter rather than a contract of affreightment. That is, for the period of time necessarily involved in the shipment, that the barge was made available to Brent for that purpose.... [T]he barge was then placed in the tow of the vessel which was to transport the other two barges to the plaintiff's plant in Oklahoma in order to receive the cargo that was to be transported by Brent under its contract of affreightment with [Agrico].

The district court made only one other factual finding of any possible relevance to the issue: that Brent's tankermen were in control of the loading process and that Brent was, therefore, a stevedore.

The terms of the oral agreement between Gunter, representing Brent, and Pardue, representing Logicon, all point away from bareboat charter. The bareboat charter is not a device for the conduct of the business of shipping but is instead an instrument designed to vest in one person most of the incidents of ownership in a capital asset of that business, a vessel, while another retains its general ownership and the right of reversion. G. Gilmore & C. Black, *supra* at 239. The bareboat charterer typically is required to carry insurance on the vessel as well as protection and indemnity insurance and crew insurance. *See* A. Parks, *supra*, at 406 (The Standard Form of Bareboat Charter, P4). Though not essential, a survey of the vessel on delivery and redelivery is customary to determine the condition of the vessel at the beginning of the charter and its condition at the end, so as to fix responsibility for and limit disputes about damage during the charter. Because the charter is for the use of the boat bare, the compensation is for the furnishing only of that asset. The term for a bareboat charter would not be for a single, short voyage. Indeed, the usual single voyage charter or charter for a limited period of time provides for control by the owner. A. Parks, *supra* at 394.

Payment for the Logicon was to be made on the basis of mills-per-ton-mile, a measure that included compensation both for furnishing towing and for use of the barge. Such a measure is inherently inconsistent with the concept of the charter bare of a dumb barge. There was testimony that such payment is typical of affreightment contracts. Both the master who had control of the barge and the crew were Logicon's employees. Logicon was responsible for insurance. No survey was made or contemplated either on delivery or redelivery.

Thus Logicon had "possession, command and navigation" of the barge under an agreement to transport it from one port to another. *See Guzman v. Pichirilo*, 369 U.S. 698, 699, 82 S. Ct. 1095, 1096, 8 L. Ed. 2d 205, 208 (1963); *Reed v. United States*, 78 U.S. (11 Wall) 591, 600-01, 20 L. Ed. 220, 222-23 (1871); *Anderson v. United States*, 450 F.2d 567, 572 & n.15 (5th Cir. 1971), *cert. denied*, 406 U.S. 906, 92 S. Ct. 1608, 31 L. Ed. 2d 816 (1972); *Stockton Sand & Crushed Rock Co. v. Bundensen*, 148 F.2d 159 (9th Cir. 1945). *But see The Independent*, 122 F.2d 141 (5th Cir. 1941) (holding no contract of affreightment when a barge was chartered for $500 a month and the charterer then contracted with the owner to tow the barge on a short trip for $50). We conclude that the contract between Brent and Logicon was a contract of affreightment whereby Brent subcontracted with Logicon to perform part of its duties under its own affreightment contract with Agrico.[2]

II.

The district court also concluded that Brent was the stevedore for loading the Logicon 2702 and, as such, owed a duty of workmanlike performance to the vessel's owner, as recognized in *Ryan Stevedoring Co. v. Pan-Atlantic S.S. Corp.*, 350 U.S. 124, 133-34, 76 S. Ct. 232, 237, 100 L. Ed. 133, 141 (1956). The duty of workmanlike performance arises out of the stevedoring contract, but it does not automatically imply that the stevedore owes the owner indemnity against all liability under all circumstances. Ryan arose out of a suit by a longshoreman, injured by cargo improperly stowed by the stevedore, against the vessel owner for liability based on unseaworthiness of the vessel, a liability without fault, *Seas Shipping Co. v. Sieracki*, 328 U.S. 85, 66 S. Ct. 872, 90 L. Ed. 1099 (1946). The shipowner was allowed indemnity because the stevedore had impliedly warranted performance of its contract to load the vessel in a workmanlike manner. In this situation, the shipowner's failure to discover and correct the stevedore's breach did not reduce or diminish the indemnity.

The *Ryan* doctrine thus includes two facets: an implied undertaking by a stevedore to render workmanlike performance and the stevedore's duty to indemnify the owner for liability arising out of its breach of the duty. The doctrine was developed in response to the *Sieracki* rule imposing on the shipowner a nondelegable duty, regardless of fault, to provide a seaworthy vessel to seamen and those who do seamen's work. We have recognized "that the *Ryan* doctrine is designed to serve special problems in maritime law arising from the absolute and nondelegable duty of seaworthiness which general maritime law imposes upon all vessel owners." *Hobart v. Sohio Petroleum Co.*, 445 F.2d 435, 438 (5th Cir.), *cert. denied*, 404 U.S. 942, 92 S. Ct. 288, 30 L. Ed. 2d 256 (1971). "[T]he predicate of the doctrine is the shipowner's absolute nondelegable liability under the seaworthiness guaranty." *Id.* at 439. Therefore,

---

[2] In view of this conclusion, we need not consider whether the Logicon 2702 was unseaworthy, or what Logicon's duty would have been as tower of a barge bareboat chartered to another.

in *Hobart*, we refused to extend *Ryan's* indemnity to protect a party who "owes no more than an ordinary duty to act as would a reasonably prudent person." 445 F.2d at 440 (in that case, the shipper, rather than the shipowner).[3] "[P]roof of a breach of the warranty of workmanlike performance does not ipso facto establish a right to indemnity by the vessel." *F.J. Walker Ltd. v. Motor Vessel "LEMONCORE"*, 561 F.2d 1138, 1148 (5th Cir. 1977). "Obviously, if such breach is not an operative factor in the damages that occur; or if conduct on the part of the shipowner causes the injury ... indemnity should be denied." *Id.* Therefore, in *Gator Marine Service Towing, Inc. v. J. Ray McDermott & Co.*, 651 F.2d 1096 (5th Cir. 1981), we refused to extend *Ryan*, pointing out that, "[t]here is little logical appeal in this proposed extension of a doctrine so withered. Disputes between vessels and stevedores over damaged cargo are best accommodated by a straightforward application of the usual maritime comparative fault system." *Id.* at 1100. "Proportional damages based on degrees of fault is now the general rule for damages in maritime property damage cases." *Gorman, supra* note 3, at 55.

We have recently applied these rules to apportion fault, rather than impose full indemnity, as between the parties whose fault occasioned a cargo loss. In *Gator Marine Service Towing, Inc. v. J. Ray McDermott & Co.*, 651 F.2d 1096 (5th Cir. 1981), we found the cargo-loader (which happened to be the owner of the cargo) and the transporting vessel concurrently negligent in causing a vessel to capsize. The loader was negligent in loading a fifteen-ton spool of wire on the deck without securing it against sideward movement. The vessel crew was concurrently negligent in failing to conduct periodic inspections of the cargo during the voyage. The intervening vessel negligence was "precisely the sort of conduct the Supreme Court anticipated in leaving open the possibility that an indemnity claim under the *Ryan* doctrine might be defeated or reduced." *Id.* at 1100. Damages were devided in proportion to fault, in reliance on *United States v. Reliable Transfer Co.*, 421 U.S. 397, 407, 95 S. Ct. 1708, 1713-1714, 44 L. Ed. 2d 251, 259-60 (1975).

Application of these principles to the present case leads to a readily predictable result. Brent was negligent in loading the cargo. As a stevedore, Brent violated its duty of workmanlike performance. Logicon, however, was negligent in considering that mere redistribution of the UAN would correct the barge's condition, in taking the barge in tow while it was unstable, in unhitching it at Greenville, and, perhaps, in even supplying the barge without warning of its hidden quality that made it unsuitable for this cargo.

We deem it unnecessary to remand for fault-apportionment. The fault appears to have been equal and damages to the cargo and the barge should be divided between Logicon and Brent.

The judgment of the district court is REVERSED and the case is REMANDED for further proceedings consistent with this opinion.

Note: Warranty of Workmanlike Performance

1. Breach of the warranty of workmanlike service by tow permits barge owner to recover amounts paid to its seaman for maintenance and cure. *Rogers v. New Jersey Barging Corp.*, 567 F. Supp. 822 (S.D.N.Y. 1983).

2. In a case decided before *Reliable Transfer*, one court had described the warranty of workmanlike performance as follows:

The doctrine of an implied warranty of workmanlike performance in maritime service contracts is most frequently applied in the context of agreements between shipowner and stevedoring companies. *See Ryan Stevedoring Co. v. Pan-Atlantic S.S. Corp.*, 350 U.S. 124, 76 S. Ct. 232, 100 L. Ed. 133 (1956). The reasoning of these cases is that shipowners are entitled to the benefits of the warranty because a stevedoring company's expertise and its control and supervision of the stevedoring operations make it the party best situated to prevent

---

[3] "The Fifth Circuit has resisted the expansion of *Ryan* indemnity beyond the facts of *Ryan*." Gorman, *Ryan Indemnity in Maritime Property Damage Cases: What of Proportionate Fault?* 8 BALT. L. REV. 42, 48 & n.39 (1978). Even if the undiluted *Ryan* doctrine applies, indemnity is due only "absent conduct on [the owner's] part sufficient to preclude recovery." *Weyerhaeuser S.S. Co. v. Nacirema Operating Co.*, 355 U.S. 563, 567, 78 S. Ct. 438, 441, 2 L. Ed. 2d 491, 494 (1958). In the classical *Ryan* situation this means only conduct on the part of the shipowner which prevents the stevedore's workmanlike performance, *Waterman S.S. Corp. v. David*, 353 F.2d 660, 665 (5th Cir. 1965), *cert denied*, 384 U.S. 972, 86 S. Ct. 1863, 16 L. Ed. 2d 683 (1966); *Brock v. Coral Drilling, Inc.*, 477 F.2d 211, 217 (5th Cir. 1973).

In 1972, amendments to the Longshoremen's and Harbor Workers' Compensation Act abrogated the *Ryan* doctrine as it applies to personal injury and death actions by employees. 33 U.S.C. § 905(b) (a stevedore will not be allowed to bring an action against the vessel if the injury was caused by the negligence of the stevedore).

accidents. *See Italia Societa per Azioni de Navigazione v. Oregon Stevedoring Co.*, 376 U.S. 315, 323-324, 84 S. Ct. 748, 11 L. Ed. 2d 732 (1964). A similar warranty has been implied in other service contracts involving comparable relationships.

A contract of towage, like the various agreements in the cited cases, gives rise to an implied warranty of workmanlike service. *Dunbar v. Henry DuBois' Sons Co.*, 275 F.2d 304, 307 (2d Cir. 1960); *James McWilliams Blue Line, Inc. v. Esso Standard Oil Co.*, 245 F.2d 84 (2d Cir. 1957); *Singer v. Dorr Towing Co.*, 272 F. Supp. 931, 934 (E.D. La. 1967). The shipowner turns his vessel over to the control of the tug owner and relies on the latter's expertise in conducting safe towing operations. The tug does not of course become an insurer against accidents; the extent of the warranty depends on "the circumstances of [the] case relating to control, supervision, and expertise." *H & H Ship Service Co. v. Weyerhaeuser Line*, 382 F.2d 711, 713 (9th Cir. 1967).

Tebbs v. Baker-Whiteley Towing Company, 407 F.2d 1055, 1058-59 (4th Cir. 1969).

B. Duties of Tug and Tow

CONSOLIDATED GRAIN & BARGE CO. v. MARCONA CONVEYOR CORP.

716 F.2d 1077, 1985 AMC 117 (5th Cir. 1983)

PER CURIAM

At about 6:40 a.m. on March 25, 1977, Barge BUNGE-28, loaded with aragonite, a fine sand, buckled in the middle and sank, carrying its cargo to the bottom of the Mississippi River. In the proceedings below, the legal owners of Barge BUNGE-28, Consolidated Grain and Barge Company (Consolidated),[1] sued for the loss of the barge, alleging that Barge BUNGE-28 sank because its cargo was improperly concentrated in the center of the hopper compartment; the owners of the conveyor ship, Marcona Conveyor Corporation and Marcona Ocean Carriers, Ltd. (hereinafter jointly referred to as Marcona), and the stevedore in charge of the loading, Hollywood Marine, Inc. (Hollywood), countered that Barge BUNGE-28 sank because it was unseaworthy. At the conclusion of a four-day bench trial, the district court ruled that Consolidated had failed to rebut the presumption of unseaworthiness which arises when a barge in tow sinks in normal use for no apparent reason and had failed to establish that negligent loading caused the sinking of Barge BUNGE-28. Accordingly, the district court rendered judgment for the defendants. Consolidated appeals, arguing that the trial judge misapplied the presumption of unseaworthiness, that his findings as to the proximate cause of Barge BUNGE-28's sinking and as to defendant's negligence are clearly erroneous, and that he abused his discretion in not allowing Consolidated to put into evidence the complete loading records of Barge BUNGE-28 and evidence as to the loading of all 38 of the barges loaded contemporaneously with Barge BUNGE-28. For the reasons set out below, we find Consolidated's arguments to be without merit and accordingly affirm the judgment of the trial court.

I.

On March 22-23, 1977, the M/V MARCONA CONVEYOR, a 32,607 gross ton self-discharging bulk carrier owned and operated by Marcona,[2] was anchored in the Mississippi River near Davant, Louisiana, laden with a cargo of aragonite.[3] The cargo owner, Marcona Sales, Inc. (Marcona Sales), had contracted with Consolidated to transport a portion of the ship's cargo of aragonite from the side of the vessel to various points of destination upriver. In order to comply with this contract, Consolidated assembled a fleet of 26 barges, one of which was Barge BUNGE-28, together with several tugs owned and/or operated by T. Smith & Son, Inc. (T. Smith) which would tow the barges from various fleeting facilities in the New Orleans area to the "staging" or loading point, and tow the barges back up to various fleeting facilities in the New Orleans area once they had been loaded.

Marcona Sales also contracted with T. Smith to shift 38 barges (including the 26 barges provided by Consolidated) alongside the M/V MARCONA CONVEYOR as they were being loaded "mid-stream" in the Mississippi

---

[1] As the bareboat charterer, Consolidated was the owner pro hac vice of Barge BUNGE-28. GILMORE & BLACK, ADMIRALTY, § 4-23 (1975 edition).

[2] The vessel was owned by Marcona Conveyor Corporation, under bareboat charter to Marcona Ocean Carriers, Ltd., and was transporting a cargo of aragonite for Marcona Sales, Inc.

[3] Argonite is a fine grain sand mined from the ocean floor offshore of the Bahamas and used in the construction industry.

River. The loading operation was under the supervision of Hollywood, an expert loading stevedore under contract to Marcona Sales to unload the cargo of aragonite into the barges.

During the morning of March 23, each of the 38 barges, including Barge BUNGE-28, was brought alongside the M/V MARCONA CONVEYOR and loaded under the supervision of Hollywood personnel. According to the barge capacity tables furnished by Bunge Corporation, the owner of Barge BUNGE-28, the cargo of aragonite aboard Barge BUNGE-28 was well within the cubic capacity and weight capacity listed for that particular barge.

No witness who testified at trial could recall the exact cargo distribution of the aragonite loaded aboard the Barge BUNGE-28; however, no witness could recall anything unusual about the way in which the barge was loaded.[4]

On the morning of March 24, Barge BUNGE-28 was taken in tow by the M/V LADY HAZEL, a vessel under contract to T. Smith, and was towed upriver approximately 65 miles to Triangle Fleeting Corporation's (Triangle) fleeting area in New Orleans, Louisiana. That evening, Barge BUNGE-28 was placed into a tow at the Triangle fleeting area for subsequent towage to its final destination upriver. When Barge BUNGE-28 was placed into its northbound tow, the barge appeared to be in good shape, it was on an even keel with adequate freeboard, and was even with the other barges in the tow.

At approximately 6:00 a.m. on March 25, 1977, the tow was made up to the M/V MABA KELCE tug owned by Mid-America Transportation Company (Mid-America). The M/V MABA KELCE was faced up to the Barge BUNGE-28 and the barge to its immediate starboard side. The captain of the M/V MABA KELCE backed the stern of the tow away from the fleet and was about to push ahead on the tow when, at approximately 6:40 a.m., the Barge BUNGE-28 buckled in the center without warning and sank.

Consolidated subsequently sued Marcona and others for loss of the barge.[5] At trial, Consolidated attempted to prove that Barge BUNGE-28 was improperly loaded by introducing survey reports of 25 of the 38 barges loaded alongside the M/V MARCONA CONVEYOR with Barge BUNGE-28.[6] The trial court received ten representative survey reports into evidence. These surveys showed that on some of the other barges there was as much as 21 feet of bare metal at either end of the hopper compartment. The parties' experts disagreed as to whether this would be an acceptable cargo distribution.[7]

Defendants Marcona and Hollywood contended that Barge BUNGE-28 sank because it was unseaworthy—*i.e.* unfit for normal use.[8] They pointed specifically to the fact that the barge, at 15 years of age, was approaching the end of its useful life, that its transversal frame construction made the barge more susceptible to bucking with age, and that the barge had an extensive history of repairs, including an improperly fused double V butt on its starboard midship side.

At the close of the evidence, the trial court concluded that "[t]here has been no evidence ... to establish what was the proximate cause of the sinking of the barge."[9] The court concluded that "when there is a sinking of the barge as this barge did with no apparent reason in normal use, there is a presumption that it is unseaworthy and the obligation is on the plaintiff to overcome that presumption." The trial court found that Consolidated had failed to

---

[4] Representatives of Hollywood testified that Barge BUNGE-28 was loaded in accordance with standard loading procedure. A surveyor employed by Marcona, who conducted a loaded draft survey of the barges at the staging area shortly after loading, noted nothing unusual about the cargo distribution on Barge BUNGE-28.

[5] Consolidated originally filed suit against Marcona Conveyor Corporation, Marcona Carriers, Ltd., Hollowood, T. Smith, Mid-America, Triangle, and various unidentified insurance companies, *in personam*, and the M/V MARCONA CONVEYOR and M/V MABA KELCE, *in rem*, seeking damages for the sinking of Barge BUNGE-28. Shortly thereafter, Marcona Sales, Inc. filed a complaint against Consolidated, Hollywood and Mid-America, *in personam*, and the Barge BUNGE-28 and M/V MABA KELCE, *in rem*, seeking recovery for damages and the loss of the cargo of aragonite which was aboard the BUNGE-28 when it sank. The two cases were consolidated. Prior to trial, Consolidated paid Marcona Sales, Inc. $7,385.00 for the cargo of aragonite lost aboard the Barge BUNGE-28, thus rendering moot the claim of Marcona Sales, Inc. for the loss of cargo. Various counterclaims, third-party claims and cross-claims were subsequently filed.

* * *

[6] These surveys were conducted approximately eight days after the barges had been loaded and after they had been towed a considerable distance upriver.

[7] Both parties' witnesses agreed that the ideal distribution of such a cargo would be to have the aragonite spread evenly throughout the entire length of the hopper compartment, but that such a distribution is rarely achieved in practice.

[8] "Seaworthiness, as that term has been defined and redefined, is reasonable fitness to perform or do the work at hand." *Lamar Towing Inc. v. Fireman's Fund Insurance Company*, 352 F. Supp. 652, 661 (E.D. La.), *aff'd* 471 F.2d 609 (5th Cir. 1972), *cert. denied*, 414 U.S. 976, 94 S. Ct. 292, 38 L. Ed. 2d 219 (1973), quoting *Walker v. Harris*, 335 F.2d 185, 191 (5th Cir.), *cert. denied*, 379 U.S. 930, 85 S. Ct. 326, 13 L. Ed. 2d 342 (1964).

[9] The court refused to infer the distribution of the cargo on the Barge BUNGE-28 from the reports submitted by Consolidated regarding the distribution of cargo on the other barges.

overcome that presumption of unseaworthiness and also found that Consolidated had failed to establish that any alleged negligence in loading the barge was the proximate cause of its sinking.

II.

On this appeal, Consolidated raises several challenges to the judgment below. First, Consolidated challenges the district court's interpretation and application of the presumption of unseaworthiness. Next, Consolidated challenges the district court's findings of fact: that Consolidated failed to overcome this presumption, and that Consolidated failed to prove that the proximate cause of the sinking was any alleged negligence in the loading of the barge. Last, Consolidated challenges the district court's exclusion of certain evidence. Our review of Consolidated's arguments reveals that each is without merit.

The Presumption of Unseaworthiness.

Under general maritime law, in a towage situation such as that involved in this case the owner of the barge is responsible for the seaworthiness of his vessel, while those responsible for the handling (*e.g.* towing, loading, etc.) of the barge are obligated to perform these tasks using such care as a prudent person would under similar situations. *Derby Company v. A.L. Mechling Barge Lines, Inc.*, 258 F. Supp. 206, 211 (E.D. La. 1966), *aff'd*, 399 F.2d 304 (5th Cir. 1968) (and cases cited therein); *Massman Construction v. Sioux City & N.O. Barge Lines*, 462 F. Supp. 1362, 1369 (W.D. Mo. 1979). *See Winn v. C.I.R.*, 595 F.2d 1060 (5th Cir. 1979) (barge owner has non-delegable duty to furnish seaworthy vessel in contract of towage). Where, as here, a barge in tow sinks in calm water for no immediately ascertainable cause, the law translates these duties into burdens of proof: in the absence of proof that the barge was improperly handled, the vessel's sinking is presumed to be a direct result of her unseaworthiness. *Derby*, 258 F. Supp. at 211. Here, the district judge found there was no evidence that the Barge BUNGE-28 was improperly loaded or otherwise improperly handled. Accordingly, he applied this presumption of unseaworthiness against Consolidated, the legal owners of the barge. This application of the presumption was correct. The cases applying this presumption of unseaworthiness to allocate burdens of proof in litigation between owners and handlers of a barge[10] make clear that the burden is on the owner of the tow to establish any alleged negligence on the part of the handler; if he cannot do so, the tow "simply cannot recover." *Massman*, 462 F. Supp. 1362 at 1369.

Consolidated relies heavily on a 1940 case from the Second Circuit: *Commercial Molasses Corporation v. New York Tank Barge Corporation*, 114 F.2d 248 (2d Cir.), *aff'd*, 314 U.S. 104, 62 S. Ct. 156, 86 L. Ed. 89 (1940). This reliance is misplaced. The principles enunciated in *Commercial Molasses* derive from the relationship of bailor-bailee which existed in that case.[11] Such a relationship does not exist here[12] and those principles are, therefore, not appli-

---

[10] A related but not identical presumption operates in marine insurance litigation; there it is used to allocate burdens of proof where the issue is whether the sinking was attributable to an insured risk (*e.g.* a peril of the sea) or to a risk against which the vessel was not insured (*e.g.* unseaworthiness). *See, e.g., Darien Bank v. Travelers Indemnity Company*, 654 F.2d 1015 (5th Cir. 1981); *Reisman v. New Hampshire Fire Insurance Co.*, 312 F.2d 17 (5th Cir. 1963).

[11] In *Commercial Molasses*, the owner of a cargo of molasses sued a private carrier for loss of the cargo when a molasses-freighted barge chartered by the private carrier sank without apparent explanation. The private carrier filed for limitation of liability. The trial judge found that "upon all the evidence, the cause of the accident ha[d] been left in doubt," *Commercial Molasses*, 314 U.S. at 107, 62 S. Ct. at 159, and applied the presumption of unseaworthiness to tip the scales against the barge owner. However, the trial judge read an insurance clause in the contract of affreightment to require the cargo owner to effect cargo insurance, which it failed to do; on this basis he dismissed petitioner's claim. *Id.* The Second Circuit (L. HAND., J.) affirmed, but on a different basis. That court held that the burden was on the cargo owner to prove that the carrier had furnished an unseaworthy barge. *See* 114 F.2d 248. By a five-to-four majority, the Supreme Court affirmed the Court of Appeals but narrowly restricted the position advanced by the Second Circuit to the facts of the particular case. The Court emphasized that *Commercial Molasses* was a suit between the cargo owner and a private carrier pursuant to a contract which "gave to (the private carrier) the status of a bailee for hire of the molasses." 314 U.S. at 108, 62 S. Ct. at 159. The Court reiterated that this case did not involve a contract of towage, but rather one of affreightment. Thus, the result in no way altered the applicable assumptions of liability and the corresponding burdens of proof in cases involving towage situations, *id.* at 109, 62 S. Ct. at 160. *See Dow Chemical Co. v. M/V CHARLES DITMAR, JR.*, 545 F.2d 1091, 1096 (7th Cir. 1976) (*Commercial Molasses* confined to contracts of affreightment).

[12] The instant litigation is not a suit between cargo interests and a bailee of the goods as *Commercial Molasses* was, but a suit between the legal owner of the barge and those who handled the barge at various points in its journey. This suit does not involve a contract of affreightment, and the claim here is not for loss of the cargo but for loss of the vessel.

cable. The burden of persuasion as to the seaworthiness of Barge BUNGE-28 remains with Consolidated as the legal owner of the barge.[13]

The District Court's Findings of Fact

In admiralty cases, questions of proximate cause are treated as factual issues for purposes of appellate review, *Kratzen v. Capital Marine Supply, Inc.*, 645 F.2d 477 (5th Cir. 1981), as are questions of negligence, *Noritake Co., Inc. v. M/V Hellenic Enterprises Champion*, 627 F.2d 724, 728 (5th Cir. 1980). Accordingly, findings as to both issues are reviewed under the "clearly erroneous" standard on appeal. *McAllister v. United States*, 348 U.S. 19, 75 S. Ct. 6, 99 L. Ed. 20 (1954); *Noritake*, 627 F.2d at 727. A finding is clearly erroneous "when, although there is evidence to support it, the reviewing court on the entire evidence is left with a definite and firm conviction that a mistake has been committed." *Verrett v. McDonough Marine Service*, 705 F.2d 1437, 1441 (5th Cir. 1983), quoting *United States v. United States Gypsum Co.*, 333 U.S. 364, 395, 68 S. Ct. 525, 542, 92 L. Ed. 746 (1948).

We hold that it was not clearly erroneous for the trial court to find that no evidence had been presented which established the actual proximate cause of the sinking of Barge BUNGE-28, that Consolidated had failed to overcome the applicable presumption of unseaworthiness, and that Consolidated had failed to prove that the manner in which Barge BUNGE-28 was loaded was the proximate cause of the barge's sinking. There is ample support in the record for these findings. Having reviewed the entire record, we find we do not have the "definite and firm conviction that a mistake has been committed." The trial court's findings against Consolidated are affirmed.

* * *

RYAN WALSH STEVEDORING CO. v. JAMES MARINE SERVICE

557 F. Supp 457 (E.D. La. 1983), aff'd., 729 F.2d 1457, 1984 AMC 3000 (5th Cir. 1984).

Findings of Fact and Conclusions of Law

MENTZ, District Judge

This litigation arises out of an accident that occurred when the D/B FRANK L, while in tow of the M/V HIAWATHA, collided with the Huey P. Long Bridge. As a result of the collision, both the bridge and the barge sustained damage. So, too, did the crane located on the D/B FRANK L. Indeed, as a result of the collision, the crane was lifted from its turntable and fell into the river. The owners and underwriters of the M/V HIAWATHA settled the claims of the bridge owners and filed a cross-claim against the D/B FRANK L, her owner and insurer for those damages. Southern Pacific Transportation Company, the owner and operator of a railroad, claims damages for loss of revenue during the time the bridge was being repaired because its trains were delayed in crossing the bridge. Jefferson Disposal Company, Inc., claims damages because during that time its garbage trucks could not use the bridge. This opinion addresses questions of liability only. It does not cover the limitation of liability prayed for by James Marine Service in Civil Action No. 80-3760. A non-jury trial was held on September 2 and 3, 1982.

Ryan Walsh Stevedoring Company, Inc. ("Ryan Walsh"), is an Alabama corporation engaged in stevedoring operations in the Port of New Orleans area and, in connection therewith, owned and operated the D/B FRANK L at all times pertinent to this litigation ("the barge"). James Marine Service, Inc. ("James Marine"), is a Louisiana corporation that owned and oeprated the M/V HIAWATHA (the "tug") at all times pertinent to this litigation.

On April 2, 1980, the boom of D/B FRANK L struck the highest span of the Huey P. Long Bridge. This bridge, which crosses the Mississippi River at Mile 106, just above the Port of New Orleans, is a fixed structure with roadways for automobile traffic on either side and railroad tracks in its mid-section. Maximum vertical clearance of the bridge is 153 feet at the low-water reference plane and 133 feet based upon 1950 high water.

---

[13] The Fourth Circuit case of *Hampton Roads Carriers v. Allied Chemical Corp.*, 329 F.2d 387 (4th Cir.), *cert. denied*, 379 U.S. 839, 85 S. Ct. 78, 13 L. Ed. 2d 46 (1964), on which Consolidated also relies, also involves a claim for loss of cargo and does not help Consolidated's claim for loss of the barge.

At the time of the collision, the D/B FRANK L was in tow of the M/V HIAWATHA. Captain Burgo and one deckhand manned the tug; the usual navigational equipment was aboard the tug. The barge was approximately 106 feet in length with an American Hoist revolving crane mounted near its stern. The boom of the crane was set in a partially elevated position in line with the center line of the barge. The crown of the boom plumbed even with the bow of the barge. The barge itself was unmanned. This practice was customary for Ryan Walsh in towing barges from one place to another.

At about 1:30 p.m. on April 2, 1980, the Ryan Walsh barge superintendent telephoned Joe Domino, Inc. ("Domino") a tug broker, and requested that Domino assign a tug to move the two derrick barges to the Celeste Street Wharf. Domino's dispatcher agreed to make the necessary arrangements for a tug but subsequently called back and said it would be necessary, owing to high river conditions,[2] to move the two barges individually using two tugs. The barge superintendent agreed. At no time, however, did the dispatcher and the barge superintendent discuss the height of the boom on either barge. There is conflict in the testimony over whether the Ryan Walsh superintendent told Domino's dispatcher that "the barge was ready to go."[3] At trial, the Court asked the dispatcher if that expression had any meaning to him, insofar as navigation was concerned. The dispatcher explained that the expression merely meant "Come get the barge now." On the basis of this testimony the Court finds that the dispatcher did not interpret the expression to mean the crane was in a position to clear the bridge safely.[4]

When the HIAWATHA arrived to pick up the barge, it was unable to make up to the barge because of the placement of various winch wires that helped to secure the barge at its mooring. Captain Burgo communicated this difficulty to the Domino dispatcher, who suggested that Burgo obtain assistance from Ryan Walsh personnel on another crane barge in the area. Captain Burgo then contacted the crew of a nearby Ryan Walsh crane barge. The foreman of that vessel sent over a Ryan Walsh deckhand, who released the winch wires and told Captain Burgo that the FRANK L was "ready to go."

At approximately 7:00 in the evening of April 2, 1980, Captain Burgo turned the FRANK L around in the river and headed south toward the New Orleans harbor. The weather was clear and there was almost no wind. With the barge in front and the boom extending over the wheelhouse, the tug proceeded downriver at approximately 10 knots without a lookout. As he approached the bridge, Captain Burgo failed to shine his spotlight on either the boom or the bridge. Suddenly, Captain Burgo felt a jerk on the vessel. Immediately thereafter, the crane cab and boom slid off the starboard side of the barge into the river.

Experts estimated that the boom of the crane failed to clear the bridge by five to six feet. Burgo admitted he did not know the vertical clearance of the bridge and did not look in his Book of Maps to ascertain it; nor did he know or try to ascertain the river stage to determine clearance. This is especially important since the river was high enough to prompt the tug broker to recommend one tug per barge rather than one tug for both barges, as Ryan Walsh had originally requested.

* * *

At issue is whether the tug or the tow was responsible for ascertaining that the boom of the crane on D/B FRANK L could safely pass under the Huey P. Long Bridge. James Marine correctly asserts both that Ryan Walsh, as a party to a contract of towage, warranted that the D/B FRANK L was sufficiently seaworthy "to withstand the ordinary perils to be encountered on the voyage." *South, Inc. v. Moran Towing and Transportation Co., Inc.*, 360 F.2d 1002, 1005 (2d Cir. 1966), and that in determining whether the barge was sufficiently seaworthy to withstand the ordinary perils to be encountered on its voyage, the Court must consider whether the barge was "reasonably fit for its intended purpose." *S.C. Loveland v. East West Towing, Inc.*, 415 F. Supp. 596, 605 (S.D. Fla. 1976), *aff'd*, 608 F.2d 160 (5th Cir. 1979). Additionally, James Marine plausibly argues that, to be reasonably fit for its intended purpose, a floating crane barge must have the ability to function at different sites and the capacity to travel safely

---

[2] Marine surveyor, Jules Schubert, stated that the river stage was fourteen feet and if the river had been 7 feet lower, the boom would have cleared.

[3] James Marine argues that this expression assured the tug of the barge's readiness for its intended voyage, *i.e.*, that it was seaworthy. Ryan Walsh counters that McKee simply asked the Domino dispatcher to get a tug to move two derrick barges from Ama to the Port of New Orleans.

[4] It should be noted that Captain Burgo met the tug at the Ama Anchorage and relieved the earlier skipper; there is no suggestion in the testimony that Burgo was told at this time that the tow was "ready to go."

from one site to another. Given this, James Marine argues, the FRANK L was not seaworthy and fit for its purpose on April 2, 1980, because its boom height exceeded the vertical clearance of the Huey P. Long Bridge.

James Marine also correctly asserts that a tug is not responsible for accidents which occur as a result of the unseaworthiness of its tow. However, even assuming that the barge was unseaworthy because of the positioning of its boom,[5] James Marine's argument fails, for the Court finds that the instant case falls within an exception to that rule, *i.e.*, the tug is responsible if the alleged unseaworthiness is so apparent that it would be negligent for the tug to attempt to proceed. *Dameron White Co. v. Angola Transfer Co.*, 19 F.2d 12, 14 (5th Cir. 1927); *Otto Candies, Inc. v. Great American Insurance Co.*, 221 F. Supp. 1014, 1018 (E.D. La. 1963), *aff'd* 332 F.2d 372 (5th Cir. 1964). Even a casual inspection of the D/B FRANK L with its boom in an upright position should have prompted a reasonably prudent tug captain at least to inquire about the height of the boom relative to the bridge clearance. "The duty of the towing vessel is 'to exercise such reasonable care and maritime skill as prudent navigators employ for the performance of similar service.'" *Houma Well Service, Inc. v. Tug CAPT. O'BRIEN*, 312 F. Supp. 257, 260 (E.D. La. 1970), quoting *Stevens v. The WHITE CITY*, 285 U.S. 195, 202, 52 S. Ct. 347, 350, 76 L. Ed. 699 (1932). Based on his earlier trips under the bridge with this derrick barge, Captain Burgo, as a prudent navigator, should have been aware of the obvious danger of a collision, especially in view of the high water stage of the river on April 2, 1980.

James Marine also argues that it was entitled to rely on the barge superintendent's "assurances" that the D/B FRANK L "was ready" for the contemplated voyage. Again, even assuming that the expression "ready to go" was used, the Court finds that this was not meant to certify that the barge was capable of clearing the bridge; it merely meant that the barge superintendent wanted the tug to move the derrick barge to its next assignment. *City of New York v. McAllister Brothers, Inc.*, 299 F.2d 227 (2d Cir. 1962), wherein a navy tug captain told the towing tug captain that a derrick was "ready to tow", supports this interpretation:

We do not consider that either the initial order from the Navy ensign or the response of the Navy tug captain warranted the fitness of the Y.D. 209 to pass under the bridge; we construe both as saying merely that she had no more work to do at Gravesend Bay. *Id.* at 228.

Ryan Walsh argues that the collision was the result of negligent navigation and that the tug alone was responsible for the safe navigation of her unmanned tow. The barge owners contend that a tug which tows her tow into collision, especially with a stationary object, is presumptively at fault. *See, e.g., Bunge Corp. v. M/V FURNESS BRIDGE*, 558 F.2d 790, 794-95 (5th Cir. 1977); *Alter Co. v. M/V MISS SUE and M/V JOHN ROD*, 536 F. Supp. 313, 316 (E.D. La. 1982) ("Dominant Mind" Doctrine).

The master of a tug towing an unmanned barge must know all conditions essential to the safe accomplishment of the undertaking or voyage. This knowledge includes the depth of the water, the ordinary obstructions, the state of the tides and water levels in the channel, and the clearance of bridges to be negotiated. *Linde-Griffith Const. Co. v. Tug Authentic*, 1952 AMC 932, 935 (S.D.N.Y.), *rev'd on other grounds* 1954 AMC 582 (2d Cir.); *see also, Humble Oil & Refining Co. v. Tug CRO-CHET*, 288 F. Supp. 147, 150 (E.D. La. 1968), *aff'd* 422 F.2d 602 (5th Cir. 1972). A tug must make a reasonable inspection of her tow before undertaking a voyage. The tug master, moreover, must obtain knowledge from personal cognizance, or avail himself of the means of knowledge, of conditions likely to produce or contribute to a loss, unless appropriate means are adapted to prevent it. *Tebbs v. Baker-Whiteley Towing Co.*, 271 F. Supp. 529, 538 (D. Md. 1967); *Avera v. Florida Towing Corporation*, 322 F.2d 155, 166 (5th Cir. 1963); *Great Atlantic & Pacific Tea Co. v. Brasileiro*, 159 F.2d 661, 664 (2d Cir. 1947). "[C]aptains [are] held to a standard of prudent navigation, including the knowledge they should have had." *Houma Well Service v. Capt. O'Brien*, 312 F. Supp. 257, 262 (E.D. La. 1970).

The HIAWATHA has not offered sufficient proof to overcome the presumption that a tug which tows her tow into collision, especially with a stationary object, is presumptively at fault. Captain Burgo did not look at the Corps of Engineers Book of Maps aboard the tug to ascertain the vertical clearance of the Huey P. Long Bridge. Nor did he ascertain the level of the water in the river, although that information was readily available from the U.S. Corps of Engineers in New Orleans and was essential to determine the vertical clearance of the bridge. Nor did he attempt to

---

[5] The Court is not determining whether or not this rendered the barge unseaworthy.

ascertain the height of the boom of the D/B FRANK L. Indeed, Captain Burgo undertook the towage of the D/B FRANK L on the voyage in question on the basis of unsubstantial and erroneous assumptions, using only his past experience as a guide. The fact that he had successfully navigated the same barge under the same bridge on at least two earlier occasions did not relieve him of his responsibility to check the bridge clearance and boom height before embarking on this voyage. "'What usually is done may be evidence of what ought to be done, but what ought to be done is fixed by a standard of reasonable prudence, whether it is usually complied with or not.'" *City of New York v. McAllister Brothers, Inc.*, supra 7, at 228-29 (quoting Mr. Justice Holmes in *Texas & Pacific Ry. Co. v. Behymer*, 189 U.S. 468, 470, 23 S. Ct. 622, 623, 47 L. Ed. 905 (1903)).

Under traditional principles of maritime law, once the master of the M/V HIAWATHA took over the D/B FRANK L without knowing the height of the boom or the vertical clearance of the bridge, all responsibility for the safe conduct of the voyage shifted to him. He could have made the decision either to get the requisite information or, failing, that not to proceed with the tow. *Houma Well Service v. Capt. O'Brien*, supra, at 262; *The City of New York v. McAllister Brothers, Inc.*, supra; *N.Y. Thruway Authority v. Merritt-Chapman*, 1969 AMC 375, 380 (S.D.N.Y.); *Linde-Griffith Const. Co. v. Tug Authentic*, 1952 AMC 932, 934 (S.D.N.Y.).

In light of the foregoing, the Court holds that James Marine, as owner of the tug, is solely liable for damages, including the loss of the crane, resulting from the collision of the boom of D/B FRANK L with the Huey P. Long Bridge on April 2, 1980.

Note

At the same time, the tug cannot complain about a condition of unseaworthiness or other weakness that caused the loss if it knew of the condition and failed to use reasonable care under the circumstances. *Tidewater Marine Activities, Inc. v. American Towing Co.*, 437 F.2d 124, 130 (5th Cir. 1970); *Horton & Horton, Inc. v. T/S J.E. Dyer*, 428 F.2d 1131, 1134 (5th Cir. 1970); *Bisso v. Waterways Transportation Co.*, 235 F.2d 741, 745 (5th Cir. 1956). If the alleged unseaworthiness is so apparent that it would be negligent for the tow to attempt to proceed, it cannot disclaim responsibility for the loss. *Damaron-White Co. v. Angola Transfer Co.*, 19 F.2d 12, 14 (5th Cir. 1927); *Otto Candies, Inc. v. Great American Insurance Co.*, 221 F. Supp. 1014, 1018 (E.D. La 1963) *aff'd* 332 F.2d 372 (5th Cir. 1964). As the district court recognized, King Fisher had the burden of proving Newpark negligent. *See Consolidated Grain & Barge Co.v. Marcona Conveyor Corp.*, 716 F.2d 89, 94 (5th Cir. 1975). In admiralty, findings of proximate cause and negligence are reviewed under the clearly erroneous standard. *Consolidated Grain & Barge Company v. Marcona Conveyor Corp.*, 716 F.2d at 1082.

King Fisher Marine Service, Inc. v. NP Sunbonnet, 724 F.2d 1181, 1984 AMC 1769 (5th Cir. 1984).

Note: Duty to Save Tow

A separate basis for the tug's liability exists, however, in the principles articulated by Judge Hand in *Chemical Transporter, Inc. v. M. Turecamo, Inc.*, 290 F.2d 496, 497 (2d. Cir. 1961). There, although the barge being towed got into trouble because of inadequate maintenance by its owner, the tug that had it under tow had a duty to prevent the barge from sinking, if it could. Here, also, the tug failed to exercise due care after the hawser parted. The evidence as to the efforts undertaken to pump out the barge is inconsistent, and on balance shows that no serious effort was made to use the emergency pump which the tug had aboard. The tug's personnel had a considerable period of time available to them before water was so deep on the deck as to preclude pumping. *See* Depo. Rittenhouse 14; Depo O'Neil 18-20. Captain Pulley claimed that Mate Quinn attempted to use the pump, but could not do so because the bow was already underwater when the tug pulled aside at around 0245 hours. Nothing in either Pulley's or Quinn's written reports of the incident indicates, however, that an effort was made to pump. *See* Ex. C-3 & C-4. In fact, Quinn's report says "the bow was partially submerged" which is consistent with the testimony of crewmembers O'Neil and Tittenhouse, the latter of whom said that, although the decks were not awash, no effort was made to pump because there was "[n]o place to put the pump to hook it up." Depo. Rittenhouse 14, 16. What seems to have happened is that the crew after checking for leaks and finding nothing obvious, merely went to work rigging the hawser, and then attempted to tow the barge back to Newport News. They should have been able to set up the pump within the time available and their failure to do so seems more likely than not to have contributed to the vessel's sinking slowly when the hawser parted, so a successful pumping operation might have kept the barge from sinking long enough to enable the tug company to get more pumps on the scene.

Champion Intern. Corp. v. S.S. Lash Pacifico, 569 F. Supp. 1557, 1560-61, 1984 AMC 444 (D.C. S.D. 1983).

C. Exculpatory Clauses

DILLINGHAM TUG & BARGE CORP. v. COLLIER CARBON & CHEMICAL CORP.

707 F.2d 1086, 1984 AMC 1990 (9th Cir. 1983)

* * *

Factual and Procedural Background

This case arises out of the sinking of the barge Columbia, which was owned by the Collier Carbon & Chemical Corporation, a division of the Union Oil Company (Union). The tower of the barge, the Dillingham Tug & Barge Corporation (Dillingham), initiated this action by suing Union for its towing fees. Union counterclaimed against Dillingham, alleging that its negligence caused the loss of the *Columbia*, and also filed a third party complaint against the Salvage Association (Salvage), Nickum & Spaulding (N&S), and Todd Shipyards alleging that their negligence contributed to the loss of the barge. Todd Shipyards settled before trial and is no longer a party in this action.

Union purchased the barge *Columbia* in the spring of 1976. Union wished to have the *Columbia* ocean towed from Galveston, Texas, to Portland, Oregon. The *Columbia* had been built as an inland barge, and Union intended to use it as an inland barge, but it was necessary to modify it somewhat so that it could survive the ocean tow. Union retained N&S to perform the naval architectural and marine engineering services necessary to allow the barge to make the ocean tow. N&S originally proposed that a hopper cover be built for the barge, to prevent it filling with water. However, this would have been very expensive, and so Union asked N&S if the barge could survive an ocean voyage without the hopper cover. N&S advised Union that it could, if the tie-down devices on the barge were strengthened.

Union's underwriters required the barge to be surveyed by a designated surveyor or salvage association. Union hired Salvage to perform the necessary survey. Salvage determined that the barge was seaworthy for the proposed tow, and issued the survey certificate required by Union's underwriters. As part of their survey, Salvage reviewed the calculations performed by N&S. Salvage also made recommendations for the tow, *inter alia* that the maximum speed should be restricted to eight knots through the water, that the crew should check the barge periodically to insure that it was not taking on water, and that if it was, the water should be pumped out.

Union hired Dillingham to perform the tow. The towing contract required Dillingham to give "due regard" to Salvage's recommendation. The towing contract also required Union to maintain Hull and Machinery insurance on the barge to its full value naming Dillingham as an additional assured with loss payable to Union. The contract further required a waiver of subrogation against Dillingham, and stated that Union would look only to the insurance for recovery for any loss or damage to the barge. The Columbia was placed on Union's fleet Hull and Machinery policy, with the required waiver of subrogation against Dillingham, but also with a $1,000,000 deductible. The parties dispute whether Dillingham was informed of this deductible before or after the commencement of the tow, and the trial judge made no finding of fact on this issue.

The tow commenced on January 29, 1977. By the time the barge reached the Panama Canal, several feet of water had accumulated in the barge's hopper, but the towing crew did not pump it out. After leaving the Canal, the tow consistently exceeded the recommended speed of eight knots. On February 25, the tow encountered heavy seas, speed was reduced at this time, but the barge continued to take on water. After some time, and several speed reductions, the captain of the tug decided to head for Bahia Ballenas to pump out the barge. Bahia Bellenas was over one hundred miles away at this point, and the tug had to head into the northwesterly seas to reach it, while the port of Bahia Santa Maria was only about twenty miles away, and was due east of the tug and tow. Eventually, the captain changed course for Bahia Santa Maria, but it was too late, the straps on the barge gave way, the cargo tanks broke off the barge, and the barge was lost.

The trial court found that Dillingham, Salvage and N&S were liable for the loss of the Columbia, and apportioned their fault for the loss at 60%, 20% and 20% respectively. The Court further found that Union's recovery should be reduced by $1,000,000 for its failure to fully insure the barge, and that each defendant would be liable for its proportionate fault only.

Discussion

I. Effect of the Insurance Provision in the Towage Contract Between Dillingham and Union

The towing contract entered into between Dillingham and Union contained a clause providing that Union would insure the *Columbia* to its full value with Hull and Machinery insurance. The insurance policy was to name Dillingham as an additional assured, with a waiver of right of subrogation against Dillingham. The provision also required Union to look solely to its insurance for the recovery of any loss or damage to the barge.

Union argues that this provision is invalid under *Bisso v. Inland Waterways Corp.*, 349 U.S. 85 (1955). In *Bisso* the Supreme Court held that exculpatory provisions in towing contracts were invalid. Union argues that the insurance provision in this contract is merely an indirect exculpatory clause, since it effectively seeks to shield Dillingham from any liability for the loss of the barge.

The Supreme Court's holding in *Bisso* was based on two public policy factors. The Court wished to discourage negligence by making wrongdoers pay for damage they cause, and the Court also wished to protect those in need of goods and services from being overreached by others who have the power to drive hard bargains.[1] *Bisso* dealt with pure exculpatory clause. That is not the case herein, though, and the public policy factors key to the holding in *Bisso* do not carry the same weight in the case of an insurance provision like the one at hand. In fact, there are public policy considerations in favor of such provision.

The Fifth Circuit has previously considered this issue in several cases.[2] In *Fluor Western, Inc. v. G&H Offshore Towing Co.*, 447 F.2d 35 (5th Cir. 1971), *cert. denied*, 405 U.S. 922 (1972), a cargo owner had been required to get insurance under a provision similar to the one in question. The court held that the provision was valid, finding several distinctions between it and the exculpatory provision in *Bisso*. First, the court stated that there was no absolute exculpation under the provision; if the cargo owner couldn't collect from the insurer he could sue the tower. Union argues that this distinguishes the present cases, because the provision appears to eliminate any suit against the tower, whether the insurer pays or not. However, this is not at issue in this case; Union was paid by its insurers for the full value of the barge, minus the $1,000,000 deductible. Whether the provision could shield Dillingham from liability in the absence of such a payment need not be determined.

The *Fluor Western* court went on to note that the contract containing the insurance provision did not bind the underwriters; they bound themselves in a separate agreement, and it was they who would have to bear the loss. The court did not see how any overreaching in the towing industry could have affected the underwriters. The only possible adhesiveness in the contract with regard to the cargo owner was the requirement that he pay the premiums for the insurance, but the court found that public policy was not concerned with which party paid for the insurance.

Fluor Western was followed in *Twenty Grand Offshore, Inc. v. West India Carriers, Inc.*, 492 F.2d 679 (5th Cir.), *cert. denied*, 419 U.S. 836 (1974). The court again noted that the provision in question did not shield the tower from all liability; he could still be liable for loss of use of the barge, or injuries to third persons. Similarly, in the case at hand, the Hull and Machinery insurance obtained would not have paid for loss of use, or injuries to third persons, so it did not shield Dillingham from all liability. Union notes that in Twenty Grand there were mutual insurance provisions; since both parties had to insure one another. Union claims that fact distinguishes the present case.

---

[1] *Bisso, supra* at 91.

[2] The only other circuit which has considered this question found an insurance provision to be unenforceable, saying it had not been bargained for, without giving further explanation. *PPG Industries v. Ashland Oil Co.*, 592 F.2d 138 (3rd Cir. 1978), *cert. denied*, 444 U.S. 830 (1979).

However, in BASF *Wyandotte Corp. v. Tug Leander, Jr.*, 590 F.2d 96 (5th Cir. 1979), the court explicitly held that such mutuality was not required for the enforcement of such a provision.

We believe that the reasoning of the Fifth Circuit is sound, and that it is not against public policy to enforce an insurance provision in a towage contract. Furthermore, it is economically efficient to allow the enforcement of such provision. The parties to a towage contract with such a provision are effectively insuring themselves under one policy against any loss due to the fault of either one of them, instead of each obtaining separate policies for this purpose. A single policy can be obtained cheaper than two individual policies. In the event of a loss, the same insurance company pays for the loss, despite who is at fault.

Union argues that even if such provisions are not invalid per se, this one should be held invalid because Union produced uncontradicted evidence of overreaching in the towing industry regarding such provision. The trial judge found that there was no monopoly in the towing industry, and that there had been no overreaching by Dillingham. The evidence to which Union refers was testimony by an employee of Dillingham that he couldn't recall ever negotiating a contract without such a provision (RT 270-271), and that other major towing companies also used such provisions (RT 272-273). Union also relies on the testimony by a Union employee that Dillingham refused to delete the provision from the contract (RT 532-3, 1537-8). This evidence does not justify a finding that the trial court was clearly erroneous. We uphold the trials court's finding that Union failed to meet their burden of establishing the existence of overreaching.

Having decided that the insurance provision in the towage contract should be enforced, we must determine what effect it has in this case. While finding that the insurance provision was enforceable, the trial judge still allowed Union to collect from Dillingham for its negligence in losing the Columbia. We find this to be error.

Normally, the right to sue a party responsible for a loss passes to an insurer once the insurer has paid for the loss. The trial court found that in this case, since a right of subrogation against Dillingham had been waived, and the insurer could therefore not sue Dillingham, the right to sue Dillingham remained with Union. The trial judge went on to rule that, under the collateral source rule, Union's recovery against Dillingham would not be reduced by the amount it had received from its insurer.

We disagree with the trial court's ruling for two reasons. First, the insurance provision in question explicitly provided that Union would look "solely to its Hull and Machinery insurance for the recovery of any loss or damage to the Barge." To allow Union to collect from Dillingham for its negligence violates this provision, which we have found to be enforceable. Second, the collateral source rule only applies to money received from "wholly independent" sources. Union was required to purchase the insurance for Dillingham's benefit. Presumably, Dillingham gave up something in return. Therefore, the insurance payment was not a source wholly independent of Dillingham. In conclusion, to the extent that Union has been paid for its loss by its insurer, Union cannot now collect from Dillingham.

Since the policy under which Union insured the Columbia had a $1,000,000 deductible, Union's insurance did not pay for the full value of the barge. The trial court found that Union breached its agreement to insure the barge for its full value by insuring it with a $1,000,000 deductible, and concluded that Union therefore became a self insurer for this $1,00,000. We agree. Union argues that Dillingham either agreed to the deductible, or waived any objection to it. The contract provided that "[Union] shall maintain ... insurance on the barge to its full value in form and amount satisfactory to [Dillingham]". Union argues that "full value" merely meant last dollar coverage and did not rule out a deductible. While some deductible might have reasonably been anticipated under the contract, we do not believe that insuring the barge for half its value was insuring it to "full value".

Union also argues that Dillingham waived any objection to the deductible because it was informed of the deductible prior to the commencement of the tow, and did not object until after the sinking. There was a dispute in the testimony as to when Dillingham was informed of the deductible, and the trial judge did not make a finding as to whether Dillingham was informed before or after the commencement of the tow. The trial judge concluded that whether they had been informed just prior to the tow or after it had begun they did not waive their objection to the deductible. There does not appear to be any basis for concluding that the trial judge was clearly erroneous in making this finding.

II. Towing Fees and Panama Canal Fees.

The towage contract provided that towage fees "shall be deemed earned by Dillingham upon commencement of the voyage even though at any stage of the venture thereafter the barge or tug be lost...." The trial court found that the contract contained an implied warranty to perform the services required in a workmanlike manner, following *Fairmont Shipping Corp. v. Chevron International Oil Co.*, 511 F.2d 1252, 1259-60 (2nd Cir.), *cert denied*, 423 U.S. 838 (1975). The court further found that Dillingham had breached this implied warranty, and was therefore not entitled to its towing fees. However, the trial court did find that Dillingham was entitled to be reimbursed for the Panama Canal fees it had paid for the tow. Both Dillingham and Union agree that there is no reason why the Panama canal fees should have been treated any differently that the towage fees, and there does not in fact seem to be any basis for making such a distinction. Since there is ample evidence to support the trial court's finding that Dillingham breached the implied warranty to perform the tow in a workmanlike manner,[3] the trial court was correct in refusing to allow Dillingham to collect its towing fees, but it erred in allowing Dillingham to collect the Panama Canal Fees.

* * *

Notes

1. "... On December 21, 1979, the Court denied plaintiff's Motion to Dismiss and/or Strike defendant's Counterclaim, holding that the exculpatory clauses in the contract in this case, purporting to limit plaintiff's liability for cargo damage and delay, must be evaluated in light of "the individual contract, the factors which went into its making, the relative economic positions of the parties, and the general nature of the industry." *Hercules Powder Co. v. Commercial Transport Corp.*, 270 F. Supp. 676, 681 (N.D. Ill. 1967).

* * *

"In its order of December 21, 1979, the Court refused to hold as a matter of law that *Bisso* applies only to towage contracts and has no bearing on private contracts of affreightment. The more circumspect route taken by the Court in *Hercules Powder, supra*, seemed the best way to develop a disputed set of facts. The Court's findings today make clear that defendants have failed to show under any of the *Hercules Powder* criteria the individual contract, the factors which went into its making, the relative economic positions of the parties, and the general nature of the industry—why *Bisso* should work to defeat the arrangement made by these parties.

"... The arrangement is a contract for private carriage. Styled as such in the written agreement, the contract provides that plaintiffs were to make the entire barge available for carriage of defendants' cargo alone. They had authority to carry cargo for no others. *See Alamo Chemical Transportation Co. v. M/V Overseas Valdez*, 469 F. Supp. 203, 209 (E.D. La. 1979).

"... The arrangement is also one of affreightment. Plaintiff agreed to transport defendants' equipment to Haiti by means of a tug and barge belonging to plaintiff. Plaintiff did not undertake merely to provide towage for a barge belonging to defendant. The tug and barge constituted a single conveyance. Unlike the arrangement in *Bisso*, there was no divided interest between the tug and barge owner. *Compare* 349 U.S. at 95, 75 S. Ct. at 635. ("[T]he owners of the barge being towed never had any relationship of any kind or character with those who controlled or operated the towboat.") *See Pure Oil Co. v. M/V Caribbean*, 235 F. Supp. 299, 304 (W.D. La. 1964), *aff'd*, 370 F.2d 121 (5th Cir. 1966).

"... In private contracts of affreightment, barring the presence of factors suggesting an unconscionable bargain (as in *Hercules Powder, supra*), the relationship is one of bailment and the rights and obligations of one party to the other are to be determined according to the terms of the agreement. *See Commercial Molasses Corp. v. New York Tank Barge Co.*, 314 U.S. 104, 110, 62 S. Ct. 156, 160, 86 L. Ed. 89, (1941). There has been no suggestion by either party that the contract here was intended to incorporate the provisions of the Harter Act, 46 U.S.C. § 190 *et seq.*, or of the Carriage of Goods by Sea Act, 46 U.S.C. § 1300 *et seq.*, limiting a carrier's ability to contract against the consequences of its own negligence. As the court said in *Kerr-McGee Corp. v. Law*, 479 F.2d 61 (3rd Cir. 1973), when considering an exculpatory clause whereby the shipper waived all claims for loss, damage and/or expense against the carrier no matter what the nature or cause,

"Nor does the clause contravene public policy. Although section 1 of the Harter Act, 46 U.S.C. § 190, forbids stipulations against negligence by carriers, the Act applies only to contracts of common carriage unless it is specifically incorporated into the agreement for private affreightment. (citations omitted). The district court found, and the parties do not suggest otherwise, that the cargo was shipped under a contract of private carriage. Section 1 of the Harter Act was not incorporated into the transportation agreement. Allied and Kerr-McGee, therefore, were free to make whatever contractual allocation of risk they desired. (citations omitted). Kerr-McGee's reliance on *Bisso v. Inland*

---

[3] It is undisputed that Dillingham towed the barge in excess of the recommended speed, and failed to pump water out of the barge's hopper when it had an opportunity to do so. In addition, when it became obvious that the barge was in trouble, the tug headed directly into the pounding seas toward a port over 100 miles away, when another port was available at a distance of only twenty miles.

Waterways Corp., 349 U.S. 85, 75 S. Ct. 629, 99 L. Ed. 911 (1955), does not require a contrary result. Mr. Justice Black was careful to point out that the decision was based on the particular nature of the tug-tow relationship, and specifically stated that the considerations which invalidated exculpatory clauses in towage contracts did not necessarily command a similar result in other maritime contracts. 349 U.S. at 91, 93, 75 S. Ct. 629. Both before and after *Bisso*, it has been held that exculpatory clauses in private contracts of affreightment are not contrary to public policy. [citations omitted]. 479 F.2d at 64.'"

Caribe Tugboat Corp. v. J.D. Barter Const. Co., Inc., 509 F. Supp. 312, 318, 321-22 (M.D. Fla. 1981).

2. In *The Bremen v. Zapata Off-Shore Co.*, 407 U.S. 1, 15-16 (1972). the Supreme Court has said that "*Bisso* rested on considerations with respect to the towage business strictly in American waters, and those considerations are not controlling in an international commercial agreement", in this case a contract to tow a drilling rig from Louisiana to Italy.

Note: Liability to Third Parties

1. In *Boston Metals Co. v. Winding Gulf*, 349 U.S. 122, 123 (1955). The court stated regardless of the rights of the parties to a towing contract *inter se*, a provision which purports to attribute the tug master's negligence to the vessel being towed does not create rights in "third parties injured as a consequence of the negligence of the tug". The fact that the tow may have agreed to indemnify the tug against third party claims did not give such third parties an action against the tow.

2. "This is a maritime property damage case under Rule 9(h). On October 28, 1986, defendants' vessel the M/V ROBERT N. STOUT picked up thirteen loosely-rigged barges in the Chain of Rocks Canal near St. Louis, Missouri. Without first having his crew completely tighten the rigging, the captain proceeded down the canal and into the Mississippi River, where eleven of these barges soon broke away in an unexpected current. One or more of these barges struck and severely damaged two of plaintiffs' marine structures in the river, namely, a mooring cell at the ICG/Peabody facility and a mooring dolphin at the Pillsbury Sauget facility. Plaintiffs seek to recover the replacement costs for these two structures, as well as certain incidental expenses relating to the damage.

* * *

"When an unmanned barge strikes a stationary object such as a dolphin or cell, the custodian of the barge has the burden to prove that his negligence was not a proximate cause of the allision.[42] Where the barge is in the custody of a towboat, the barge's custodian is held to include both the operator[43] (including the towboat captain's employer)[44] and the owner[45] of the towboat; in other words, this rule "operates against all parties who participated in the management of" the towboat.[46] This burden-shifting, which is more than simply a rebuttable presumption governed by F. R. Ev. 301,[47] applies whether or not the barge breaks loose from its custodian,[48] and whether or not the barge was owned by its custodian.[49]

---

[42] *Koch-Ellis*, 218 F.2d at 772 & n.3; *see James*, 686 F.2d at 1131-33 (upholding liability against owner/operator of fleeting facility an errant barge from which struck moored barge downriver, where plaintiff presented no evidence of cause of breakaway); *cf. Bunge Corp v. M/V Furness Bridge*, 558 F.2d 790, 794 (5th Cir.) (same rule for claim where manned ship struck mooring dolphin), *cert. denied mem.*, 564 F.2d 97 (5th Cir. 1977), *cert. denied sub nom. Furness Withy & Co. v. Bunge Corp.*, 435 U.S. 924, 98 S. Ct. 1488, 55 L. Ed. 2d 518 (1978).

[43] *See Woods v. United States*, 681 F.2d 988, 990 (5th Cir. 1982) (compulsory pilot was presumed negligent); *cf. Compania de Navigacion Porto Ronco v. S/S American Oriole*, 474 F. Supp. 22, 27 (E.D. La. 1976) (holding liable Wharfinger with sole custody of another's unmanned vessel that broke away and struck moored vessel and dock), *aff'd* on basis of opinion below, 585 F.2d 1326 (5th Cir. 1978).

[44] *See Delta Transload, Inc. v. M/V Navios Commander*, 818 F.2d 445, 451-52 (5th Cir. 1987) (applying the doctrine of respondeat superior).

[45] *See City of New Orleans v. American Commercial Lines, Inc.*, 662 F.2d 1121, 1123 (5th Cir. Dec. 1981) (holding towboat owner liable where barge in tow damaged fender on dolphin; no mention of who operated towboat or who owned barge); *Koch-Ellis*, 218 F.2d at 772 & n.3 (no mention of who operated towboat).
While towboat owners often seek limitation of liability for lack of privity and knowledge of any navigational negligence by a towboat captain, defendants have raised no such defense. Nor would they have been entitled to such, for they did not file a complaint of limitation "not later than six months after receipt of a claim in writing" (*viz.*, April 29, 1987, which was six months after O'Brien sent Dykes the telex). *See Exxon Shipping Co. v. Cailleteau*, 869 F.2d 843, 846 (5th Cir. 1989); 46 U.S.C. § 185; F. R. Civ. P. Supp. R. F(1).

[46] *See Delta Transload*, 818 F.2d at 449 & n.8.

[47] *Id.*; *James*, 686 F.2d at 1132-33. Dictum to the contrary in *S.C. Loveland Inc. v. East West Towing, Inc.*, 608 F.2d 160, 165 n.3 (5th Cir. 1979) (*citing Pennsylvania Railroad Co. v. S/S Marie Leonhardt*, 320 F.2d 262, 264 (3d Cir. 1963)), *reh'g denied mem.*, 611 F.2d 882 (5th Cir.), *cert. denied sub nom. St. Paul Mercury Insurance Co. v. East West Towing, Inc.*, 446 U.S. 918, 100 S. Ct. 1852, 64 L. Ed. 2d 272 (1980), had already been rejected in *Bunge Corp.*, 558 F.2d at 795 n.3.

[48] *Compare Brown & Root Marine Operators, Inc. v. Zapata Off-Shore Co.*, 377 F.2d 724, 726 (5th Cir. 1967) (tug towing integrated barge) and *The Victor*, 153 F.2d 200, 203 (5th Cir. 1946) (tug towing loosely rigged barges) *with James*, 686 F.2d 1129 (barges broke away from fleeting facility) and *Koch-Ellis*, 218 F.2d 771 (barges broke away from tree).

[49] *See Compania de Navigacion*, 474 F. Supp. at 27 (Wharfinger had sole custody, but not ownership, of unmanned vessel); *cf. City of New Orleans*, 662 F.2d 1121 (no mention of who owned the barges); *The Victor*, 153 F.2d 200 (same).

"A person may meet this heavy[50] burden by proving by a preponderance of the evidence that the allision was an "unavoidable," or "inevitable," accident such as a *vis major* (greater force, or Act of God);[51] to establish this defense, the person against whom the burden-shifting is applied "'must exhaust every reasonable possibility which the circumstances admit and show that in each [he] did all that reasonable care required.'"

"In this case, the Court finds not only that defendants have not established any inevitable-accident or other defense to meet this burden-shifting rule, but also that plaintiffs have overwhelmingly established by affirmative evidence that the negligence of both Captain Wolfe and defendants' management was a proximate cause of the breakup.

Pillsbury Co. v. Midland Enterprises, Inc., 715 F. Supp. 738, 758-59, 1989 AMC 2113, *cert denied* 111 S. Ct. 515, 112 L. Ed 2d 527 (E.D. La. 1989).

Section 2. Pilotage

A. Duty of Pilot

ATLEE v. PACKET CO.
88 U.S. 389, 22 L. Ed. 619 (1875)

* * *

The character of the skill and knowledge required of a pilot in charge of a vessel on the rivers of the country is very different from that which enables a navigator to carry his vessel safely on the ocean. In this latter case a knowledge of the rules of navigation, with charts which disclose the places of hidden rocks, dangerous shores, or other dangers of the way, are the main elements of his knowledge and skill, guided as he is in his course by the compass, by the reckoning, and the observations of the heavenly bodies, obtained by the use of proper instruments. It is by these he determines his locality and is made aware of the dangers of such locality if any exist. But the pilot of a river steamer, like the harbor pilot, is selected for his personal knowledge of the topography through which he steers his vessel. In the long course of a thousand miles in one of these rivers, he must be familiar with the appearance of the shore on each side of the river as he goes along. Its banks, towns, its landings, its houses and trees, and its openings between trees, are all landmarks by which he steers his vessel. The compass is of little use to him. He must know where the navigable channel is, in its relation to all these external objects, especially in the night. He must also be familiar with all dangers that are permanently located in the course of the river, as sand-bars, snags, sunken rocks or trees, or abandoned vessels or barges. All this he must know and remember and avoid. To do this he must be constantly informed of changes in the current of the river, of sand-bars newly made, of logs or snags, or other objects newly presented, against which his vessel might be injured. In the active life and changes made by the hand of man or the action of the elements in the path of his vessel, a year's absence from the scene impairs his capacity, his skilled knowledge, very seriously in the course of a long voyage. He should make a few of the first "trips," as they are called, after his return, in company with other pilots more recently familiar with the river.

It may be said that this is exacting a very high order of ability in a pilot. But when we consider the value of the lives and property committed to their control, for in this they are absolute masters, the high compensation they receive, and the care which Congress hastaken to secure by rigid and frequent examinations and renewal of licenses, this very class of skill, we do not think we fix the standard too high.

* * *

---

[50] *See Brown & Root*, 377 F.2d at 726 (finding that defendant did not meet the defense); *Petition of United States*, 425 F.2d 991, 995 (5th Cir. 1970) (upholding defense, where barge owners had taken reasonable precautionary measures before the impending hurricane whose winds caused the barges to break loose).

[51] *American Petrofina*, 837 F.2d at 1326 ("unavoidable"), *Nunley v. M/V Dauntless Colocotronis*, 863 F.2d 1190, 1197 (5th Cir.) ("inevitable"), *reh'g denied mem.*, 869 F.2d 1487 (5th Cir. 1989).

Note: Knowledge of Local Conditions

Thus absent a finding of actual knowledge, the pilot may be charged with knowledge of a local condition as a matter of law. *General Const. Co. v. Isthmian Lines, Inc.*, 259 F. Supp. 336, 339 (D. Or. 1966). In the instant case, the compulsory pilot was charged with constructive, if not actual, knowledge of the mooring dolphins and the risk they presented.

Bunge Corp. v. M/V Furness Bridge, 558 F.2d 790, 798 n.6 (5th Cir. 1977).

B. Liability of Pilots, Pilot Associations and Governmental Regulatory Agencies

Notes

1. *Liability of Pilots*

A pilot may be held liable to third parties for damage caused by his ngeligence (*Gulf Towing Co., Inc. v. Steam Tanker, Amoco, N.Y.*, 648 F.2d 242 (5th Cir. 1981) (held liable for sinking of assisting tug), and, in the absence of a valid contractual provision to the contrary, may be liable for damage to the vessel he was piloting. (*Bethlehem Steel Corp. v. Yates*, 438 F.2d 798 (5th Cir. 1971). But see discussion of exculpatory clauses, *infra*.

2. *Liability of Others*

a. *Pilots' Associations*

Pilots' Associations generally have been found not to be liable for the negligent acts of individual pilots. Thus, in *General v. Pilots' Association for Bay & River Delaware*, 254 F. Supp. 447 (D. Del. 1966), the court found:

> The Pilots' Association has also adopted by-laws in amplification of the constitution. The by-laws provide, inter alia, (1) that all the pilots will render services in rotation (No. 17); (2) that bills or statements for pilotage fees will be made out in the name of the pilot, with the Association named as agent (No. 15); (3) that the net earnings of the members of the Association will be divided among all members in accordance with agreed ratios (Nos. 40, 41); and (4) that members of the Association cannot contract for or on behalf of the Association (No. 32).
>
> It should be noted, conversely, that there is no provision in either constitution or by-laws for expelling a member, taking an action with respect to suspension or revocation of a member's license or controlling in any fashion the rendition of pilotage services. The only qualifications for membership in the Association are the possession of a state license and purchase of a certificate of membership.
>
> The existing legislation of Delaware concerning pilots and pilotage is found in Title 23, Del.C., Secs. 101-137. Substantially parallel legislation is found in the Pennsylvania statutes, 55 P.S. Secs. 1-194. Both states provide for the creation of a Commission or Board invested with power to grant deserving applicants a license, subject to a restriction in the number licensed at any time, to perform the duties and services of a pilot on the Delaware River (Del. Secs. 101, 102, 111, 113; Pa. 1, 31, 41, 42). Applicants examined by the Board and found deserving must first serve a minimum of four years apprenticeship, followed by one year as a third-class pilot, and one year as a second-class pilot before receiving the license of a first-class pilot (Del. Sec. 113; Pa. 44).
>
> The laws provide, *inter alia*, (1) for suspension or forfeiture of pilot licenses in the event of neglect of duties or misconduct (Del. Secs. 116, 118; Pa. 71, 73); (2) for pilotage rates (Del. Secs. 131; Pa. 131); (3) for compulsory pilotage (Del. Sec. 121; Pa. 171-173); and (4) for Board determination of disputes (Del. Secs. 102, 118; Pa. 72, 194).
>
> It should be noted that both Delaware and Pennsylvania grant licenses to perform the duties of a pilot on the Delaware River only to individual persons who meet the rigid standards set by the respective Boards; that, after a person receives a pilot's license, he is bound to perform faithfully his duties in accordance with the law. It is also noteworthy that legislation requires each pilot to post his individual bond to assure proper performance of his personal duties (Del.Sec. 113; Pa. 44).
>
> The recited facts justify the conclusion that the Pilots' Association is the personal agent for each pilot member. It acts as a clearing house for the transmittal of requests for pilotage; it assists each member in the collection of the statutory pilotage fees by rendering bills in the name of the pilot for whose service a fee is owing; it enables members to share the cost of common expenses, including station boat, launches, transportation, office and sleeping accommodations, and it distributes designated benefits in the event of incapacity, retirement or death. In all of the above ways, the Association as an entity is extremely active; the Association, however, is powerless to control members in the performance of their profession as pilots. In this area, as the law dictates, the individual pilot is answerable only to himself. For dereliction of duty, it is the licensing State, by its Board of Commissioners, and not the Pilots' Association, which has disciplinary power to act with respect to a pilot's license. In an unbroken line of authorities, extending well over half a century,[2] these features have been considered sufficient to warrant a finding that a pilots' association and its other members are not responsible for any faults by a member rendering pilotage service.

---

[2] A much criticized decision is *The Joseph Vaccaro*, 180 F. 272 (E.D. La., 1910). *Compare The Griffdu*, 25 F.2d 312 (S.D. Texas, 1928).

The court applied the test used by the Supreme Court in *Guy v. Donald*, 203 U.S. 399, 406:

... When a man is carrying on business in his private interest and intrusts a part of the work to another, the world has agreed to make him answer for that other as if he had done the work himself. But there is always a limitation. It is true that he is not excused by care in selection or orders sufficient to secure right conduct, if obeyed. But when he could not select, could not control, and could not discharge, the guilty, he does not answer for his torts. (Emphasis supplied.)

It held:

There being no power of direction or control by the Association over its members while rendering their services as pilots, the Association is not liable and its motion for summary judgment must be granted.

Liability was rejected in *McKeithen v. S.S. Frosta*, 441 F. Supp. 1213 (E.D. La. 1977) where the court found that the pilots association did not "guarantee the professional conduct of its members to the general public." (at 1217). The court rejected claims that the association itself was negligent in not properly securing prospective members, educating its members, or in selecting and assigning the pilot in this case.

Another court has interpreted the decisions on this issue as "judicially creating a doctrine of immunity for pilot associations *and individual pilots,...*". (emphasis added) *In Re China Union Lines, Ltd.*, 342 F. Supp. 426 (E.D. La. 1971). The court, here, not only found for the association but for the estate of the deceased pilot who had piloted the vessel.

b. *State and Local Agencies*

Whether or not a state or local pilot board or commission may be liable for the negligent acts of pilots depends on the relationship between the board or commission and the pilot, *i.e.*, the powers and duties of the governmental body.

In *State of Wash v. M/V Dilkara*, 470 F. Supp. 437 (W.D. Wash. 1979), the court stated:

The Washington Pilotage Act, R.C.W. § 88.16 *et seq.*, vests in the State Board of Pilotage commissioners broad and exclusive powers to regulate and control the professional behavior of Washington pilots. The Board's powers include the issuance and revocation or suspension of pilots' licenses, the promulgation of rules promoting efficient and competent pilotage services, and the enforcement of penalties for violations of Board rules or the Pilotage Act itself. R.C.W. §§ 88.16.030, 090, 100. The licensing and regulation of the pilots, however, does not create an employer/employee or principal/agent relationship between the State and the pilots.

Washington's compulsory pilot laws, R.C.W. §§ 88.16.070, 180, do not change the relationship between the State and the pilot. The pilots remain licensed independent contractors, hired by the vessels. *See Port of Seattle v. M/V Maria Rubicon*, 404 F. Supp. 302 (W.D. Wash. 1975).

A governmental agency may be vicariously liable for the actions of a compulsory pilot if the agency, in addition to regulating the pilot's profession, is the pilot's employer. *City of Long Beach v. American President Lines*, F.2d 853 (9th Cir. 1955); *National Development Co. v. City of Long Beach*, 187 F. Supp. 109 (S.D. Calif. 1960), *aff'd* 289 F.2d 586 (9th Cir. 1961), *cert denied* 368 U.S. 901, 82 S. Ct. 177, 7 L. Ed. 2d 95 (1961). More than mere licensing and regulation of the pilots is required for liability. The government agency must benefit from the contract between the pilot and the vessel, or have direct control over the pilot's actions. *City of Long Beach v. American President Lines, supra*. In the present case the State only requires vessels operating under its jurisdiction to have a state licensed pilot on board. The State does not benefit from the contract between the vessel and the pilot, or control the pilot's actions. DILKARA relies heavily on *City of Long Beach v. American President Lines, id*. Apparently counsel overlooked the following passages: "[m]uch different would it be if Long Beach provided by ordinance only that a pilot licensed by Long Beach would be permitted to perform pilotage." *Id*. at 858.

Further light was shed on this subject in *Kitanihon-oi S.S. Co. v. General Const. Co.*, 678 F.2d 109 (9th Cir. 1982):

Our discussion must commence with *City of Long Beach v. American President Lines*, 223 F.2d 853 (9th Cir. 1955). There we held that a city which requires the use of pilots furnished by it through an independent contractor on ships in its harbor is liable for the negligent performance of those pilots under an implied covenant to perform personal service with the necessary skill and without neglect.

In *City of Long Beach* there was no written contract between the shipowner and the city other than the tariff. The shipowner paid the city pilotage fees of which the city retained 40% and paid over the remaining 60% to the independent contractor, Jacobsen. We found that the city acted in a proprietary capacity in maintaining and operating its harbor "because it thinks it is good business for it, representing its citizens, to do so." *Id*. at 856. The pilot boarded and navigated the vessel pursuant to the city's tariff requirement of compulsory pilotage, as a member of the city's "staff of pilots."[1] *Id*. at 857. Under these circumstances the shipowner had a contract of pilotage with the city, which was liable in tort and contract to the shipowner for negligence of the pilot.

---

[1] The pilots were not city employees; they worked for an independent contractor under contract to the City.

The present case differs from *City of Long Beach* in one significant way. Here, Shipowner paid the pilot directly, and the Port itself paid no fees to the pilot. The Port commissions a limited number of pilots in order to protect the earning capacity of those commissioned, who in February 1977 numbered eight. The standard pilot's fee schedule is arrived at by negotiations between the Bay Area pilots and the maritime steamship associations conducted at meetings which the Port attends. Shipowners must use a commissioned ship's pilot to comply with the compulsory pilotage clause of the Port's tariff.[2] The Port's primary relationship with the pilot is as the source of his commission, which the pilot holds at the pleasure of the Port through its Pilot Advisory Board. While the Port's power to decommission a pilot temporarily or permanently at its sole discretion gives teeth to its rules and regulations governing commissioned pilots and use of the Channel,[3] the Port does not hire the pilot either directly or indirectly. *Cf. Washington v. M/V Dilkara*, 470 F. Supp. 437 (W.D. Wash. 1979) (state that regulates, controls, and requires the use of licensed pilot not liable for pilot's negligence).

Shipowner argues that the economic substance of the arrangements in *City of Long Beach* and here is the same. In both cases, Shipowner insists, pilots provide pilotage services to the shipowners and fees paid by the shipowners compensate the pilot. That the City in *City of Long Beach* acted as a middle-man collecting tariffs from shipowners and paying a portion of those tariffs to an independent subcontractor who employs the pilots should make no difference. In either case, the shipowners' money ends up in the pilots' pockets.

That the presence of an employment contract between the shipowner and the pilot distinguishes the cases provides small comfort to Shipowner. In *City of Long Beach* we considered the presence of such an employment contract decisive. In finding liability we characterized the City's conduct thus: "Long Beach said, 'Stay out unless you let us furnish you our pilot at a price we fix, which you shall pay us, and which you shall not pay the pilot.'" *Id.* at 858. While here the Port arguably "furnished" a pilot (although Shipowner had a choice from eight pilots then commissioned), the Port did not fix the price, Shipowner did not pay the pilotage fee to the Port, and Shipowner *did* pay the fee to the pilot. Thus, most of the factors considered crucial to implied warranty liability in *City of Long Beach* are lacking here.

There is appeal to Shipowner's contention that the required use of only pilots commissioned by the Port in fairness should entitle it to look to the Port for compensation for negligent performance by those pilots. At first glance, it seems unjust to permit the Port to shoulder Shipowner's preferred pilot from the helm while disclaiming all responsibility when its commissioned pilot runs the ship aground. More careful scrutiny, however, reveals this perception to be much less compelling.

The Port in requesting that the Shipowner's pilot be one commissioned by it serves an interest unrelated to the welfare of particular pilots. It no less than the shipowners has every incentive to avoid collisions and groundings in the Channel, the "lifeline" for the Port's existence. Excerpt of Record 187. The Port included compulsory pilotage in the tariff to prevent blockage of the Channel, which would reduce the Port's business. *Id.* The monopoly the Port grants its commissioned pilots to protect their livelihood also increases the pilots' specialized local knowledge by virtue of more frequent piloting of the Channel. Thus, the Port's interest in safety—which is identical to the shipowners'—may well be best served by compulsory pilotage.

Given the lack of any contract between the Port and Shipowner for pilotage services such as existed in *City of Long Beach*, and the sound justification for the Port's pilotage arrangements, we affirm the district court's holding that Shipowner has no cause of action against the Port for the negligence of its commissioned pilot.

This result gains strength when access to insurance is considered. Assuming that accidents will occur even when competent pilots are employed, the cost of those accidents should no doubt fall on those best able to insure against them.[4] A shipowner knows or can easily ascertain the value of his ship and its cargo, and the cost to him of damage or delay. He is in a better position to match his insurance coverage precisely to the risk than is the Port. Moreover, the protection and indemnity insurance carried by all sea-going vessels already covers accidents under pilotage like that of the Oji Maru. A. PARKS, LAW OF TUG, TOW & PILOTAGE, 1035 (2d ed. 1982). Imposing liability on the Port here would require it to carry insurance whose cost it would have to recoup in higher tariffs. No deterrent effect can be expected from imposing such liability inasmuch as the Port already has ample incentive to avoid accidents. The net effect on imposing liability on the Port would be

---

[2] The Port's tariff applies to all sea-going ships using the Port of Sacramento. In February 1977 its pilotage clause read as follows:

(a) Except as provided in paragraph (b) below, the privilege of using any wharf or terminal facility of the Port of Sacramento will be denied to any seagoing vessels entering or leaving the Port of Sacramento without the services of a pilot commissioned by the Port of Sacramento. It is understood that such pilot shall act only in the capacity of advisor to the master of the vessel.

(b) Vessels enrolled by the United States of America and exempt from federal laws are not subject to requirements provided in paragraph (a) above. Excerpt of Record 40. "Enrollment" is limited to United States flag vessels that do not call at foreign ports. 46 U.S.C. §§ 252, 278 (1976).

[3] Among other requirements, pilots must obtain clearance to leave the Port from the Port's Operations Manager; make vessel position reports at five specified locations; and notify the Port of any collisions and groundings en route. Excerpt of Record 30. The Port also has the power to close the Channel by ordering the commissioned pilots not to take any ships up or down it, as the Port Director did after the grounding of the Oji Maru. Excerpt of Record 196-98.

[4] Because shipowners must hire a commissioned pilot, they are not in a position to demand that pilots insure. And pilots have no incentive to insure—although the clause in their form contract exculpating them from liability for all acts as pilot is void as against public policy, ER 261; *United States v. SS President Van Buren*, 490 F.2d 504, 509 (9th Cir. 1974) (by implication), they are usually judgment-proof in any event.

an increase in fees to shipowners without any corresponding increase in insurance coverage.[5] This would achieve very little. The loss should remain where it fell, on the Shipowner. He must look to his insurance carrier.

The dissenting opinion stated:

I am not persuaded that this is a case of first impression. This case cannot be distinguished in a principled way from *City of Long Beach v. American President Lines*, 223 F.2d 853 (9th Cir. 1955), and we should apply its holding here.

The mere fact that this small cadre of compulsory pilots is not directly employed or paid by the Port is not dispositive. As urged by Shipowner, the economic reality and substance is the same here as in *City of Long Beach*. The realistic situation is that the Port has plenary power to reject any pilot not commissioned by it. Through its tariff and the negotiations with Bay Area pilots and maritime associations, the crucial fact, like *City of Long Beach*, is that the Port has arrogated unto itself total control of pilotage for its own benefit and for the benefit of a few select pilots.

Finally, the existence of insurance or not has nothing to do with the determination of the liability issue in this case.

There is an implied covenant to perform the personal pilot service with the necessary skill and without neglect. I respectfully dissent and would reverse the district court's contrary ruling.

C. Exculpatory Pilotage Clauses

THE CHINA

74 U.S. 53, 19 L.Ed 67 (1869)

ERROR to the Circuit Court for the Southern District of New York.

The pilot act of New York, having provided for the education and licensing of a body of pilots, enacts that all masters of foreign vessels, bound to or from the port of New York, "*shall* take a licensed pilot, or, in case of refusal to take such pilot, *shall* pay pilotage as if one had been employed." It enacts, further, that any person not licensed as a pilot, who shall attempt to pilot a vessel bound as aforesaid, "shall be deemed *guilty of a misdemeanor*, and be punished by a fine not exceeding $100; OR, *imprisonment not exceeding sixty days*. And all persons employing a person to act as pilot, not holding a license, shall forfeit and pay to the board of commissioners of pilots the sum of $100." The pilot first offering his services to a vessel inward bound is entitled to pilot her in, and when she goes out has the right, by port rules, to pilot her out.

This pilot act of New York, it may be observed—differing from certain acts of Great Britain, known as the "*General Pilot Acts*," though agreeing with others, sometimes called local pilot acts, to wit, the Liverpool pilot act and the Newcastle pilot act, and also in its main features with a Pennsylvania pilot act (though this inflicts no penalty of imprisonment, and provides only for a money fine of half pilotage, in case of refusal)—does not contain any provision to the effect that the owner or master of any ship shall not be liable for any loss or damage occasioned by the neglect, incompetency, or default of any licensed pilot.

With the pilot act of New York, above set forth, in force, the steamer China, a foreign vessel bound from the port of New York, and being then in pilot waters, and in charge of a licensed pilot of that port, ran into the Kentucky, a vessel of the United States, and sunk her. The collision was occasioned by gross fault of the licensed pilot then in charge of the China. The owners of the Kentucky accordingly libelled the offending vessel in the District Court of New York. Her owners set up for defence, that at the time of the collision she was in charge of a pilot duly licensed by the State of New York; that the said pilot was taken in conformity with the laws of that State; that he directed all the maneuvers of the steamer which preceded the collision, and that the same was not in consequence of any negligence of her officers or crew.

---

[5] We note that the extra cost of redundant insurance coverage resulting from the imposition of liability for pilots' negligent performance has received the attention of the Oregon State Legislature, which has authorized pilots to limit the imposition of such liability by contract. Under the statute, pilots so contracting must offer "trip" insurance coverage to vessels that specially request it. The pilots are authorized to raise the tariff to such vessels in an amount equal to the "trip" insurance premium. OR. REV. STAT. § 776.520 (1979). *See* A. PARKS, LAW OF TUG, TOW & PILOTAGE 1034-36 (2d ed. 1982) (approving statute).

The case thus presented the question whether a vessel, in charge of a licensed pilot, whom the statutes of the State governing the port whence she sailed, enacted positively that the vessel should take aboard under penalties named, was liable *in rem* for a tort committed by her, the result wholly of this pilot's negligence.

The District Court held that she was, and the Circuit Court having affirmed the decree, the question was now here on appeal.

* * *

Mr. Justice SWAYNE delivered the opinion of the court

This is a case arising out of a collision between the steamship China, a British vessel, then leaving the port of New York for Liverpool, and the brig Kentucky, then on a voyage from Cardenas to New York. The facts are few and undisputed. The collision occurred on the 15th of July, 1863, a short distance outside of Sandy Hook. The brig was sunk. The steamship was wholly in fault. It was not alleged, in the argument here for the appellants, that there was either fault or error on the part of the brig. The case turns upon the effect to be given to the statute of New York, of the 3d of April, 1857. At the time of the collision the steam-ship was within the pilot waters of the port of New York, and was in charge of a pilot, licensed under this act, and taken by the master pursuant to its provisions. The pilot's orders were obeyed, and the catastrophe was entirely the result of his gross and culpable mismanagement. No question was made in the argument, upon the subject; the evidence is too clear to admit of any. These are all the facts material to be considered.

The questions with which we have to deal, are questions of law. No others arise in the case.

It is insisted by the appellants that the statute referred to compelled the master of the steamship to take the pilot, and that they are therefore not liable for the results of his misconduct.

British adjudications are relied upon in support of both these propositions. In order to appreciate these authorities, the British pilot acts must be understood. They are the 52 George III, ch. 30; the 6 George IV, ch. 125; the Shipping Act of the 17 and 18 Victoria, ch. 104; the Liverpool Pilot Act of 37 George III, ch. 789, and the Newcastle Pilot Act of the 41 George III, ch. 86. The three first mentioned contain equivalent provisions. The same remark applies to the two latter. The former all contain a clause to the effect that the "owner or master of any ship shall not be answerable for any loss or damage occasioned by the neglect, default, incompetency, or incapacity of any licensed pilot." The latter contain a system of local pilot regulations, but have no such provision. They require that a pilot shall be taken, and if not taken, that pilotage shall, nevertheless, be paid. In these respects, and in most others, they are substantially the same with the statute of New York.

* * *

1. Was the steamship *compelled* to take the pilot?

* * *

Giving to the statute either construction, it seems to us clear, in the light of both reason and authority, that the pilot was taken by the steamship upon compulsion.

2. This brings us to the examination of the second proposition. Does the fact that the law compelled the master to take the pilot, exonerate the vessel from liability?

The immunity of the wrongdoing vessel when the pilot is in charge, and alone in fault, is now well settled in English jurisprudence, both in the Admiralty Court and in the courts of common law. The rule must necessarily be the same in both. In such cases the liability of the ship and of the owner are convertible terms. The ship is not liable if the owners are not; and no responsibility can attach to the owners, if the ship is not liable to be proceeded against.[a]

Some of the leading English cases will be adverted to, according to the order of time in which they were determined.

---

[a] *The Druid*, 1 W. Robinson, 899.

[The Court then considered a series of English cases before continuing:]

These judgments have stood unquestioned down to the present time. There have been numerous adjudications settling the construction of the statutory provision that the vessel shall be exonerated where the pilot is in fault.

The following propositions may be deduced from them:

- The statute giving the immunity where a licensed pilot is employed, abridges the natural right of the injured party to compensation, and is therefore to be construed strictly.
- The exemption applies only where the pilot is actually in charge of the vessel, and solely in fault.
- If there be anything which concurred with the fault of the pilot, in producing the accident, the exemption does not apply, and the vessel, master, and owners are liable.
- The colliding vessel is in all cases *prima facie* responsible.
- The burden of proof rests upon the party claiming the benefit of the exemption. He must show affirmatively that the pilot was in fault, and that there was no fault on the part of the officers or crew, "which might have been in any degree conducive to the damage."[k]

* * *

The question is now, for the first time, presented in this court.

The New York statute creates a system of pilotage regulations. It does not attempt, in terms, to give immunity to a wrongdoing vessel. Such a provision in a State law would present an important question, which, in this case, it is not necessary to consider.

The argument for the appellants proceeds upon the general legal principle that one shall not be liable for the tort of another imposed upon him by the law, and who is, therefore, not his servant or agent.

The reasoning by which the application of this principle to the case before us is attempted to be maintained, is specious rather than solid. It is necessary that both outward and inward bound vessels, of the classes designated in the statute, should have pilots possessing full knowledge of the pilot grounds over which they are to be conducted. The statute seeks to supply this want, and to prevent, as far as possible, the evils likely to follow from ignorance or mistake as to the qualifications of those to be employed, by providing a body of trained and skilful seamen, at all times ready for the service, holding out to them sufficient inducements to prepare themselves for the discharge of their duties, and to pursue a business attended with so much of peril and hardship. The services of the pilot are as much for the benefit of the vessel and cargo as those of the captain and crew. His compensation comes from the same source as theirs. Like them he serves the owner and is paid by the owner. If there be any default on his part, the owner has the same remedies against him as against other delinquents on board. The difference between his relations and those of the master is one rather of form than substance. It is the duty of the master to interfere in cases of the pilot's intoxication or manifest incapacity, in cases of danger which he does not foresee, and in all cases of great necessity.[**] The master has the same power to displace the pilot that he has to remove any subordinate officer of the vessel. He may exercise it or not, according to his discretion.

The maritime law as to the position and powers of the master, and the responsibility of the vessel, is not derived from the civil law of master and servant, nor from the common law. It had its source in the commercial usages and jurisprudence of the middle ages. Originally, the primary liability was upon the vessel, and that of the owner was not personal, but merely incidental to his ownership, from which he was discharged either by the loss of the vessel or by abandoning it to the creditors. But while the law limited the creditor to this part of the owner's property, it gave him a lien or privilege against it in preference to other creditors.[***]

---

[k] *The Gen. De Caen*, 1 Swabey, 10; *The Diana*, 1 W. Robinson, 135; *The Protector, Ib.* 60; *The Christiana*, 7 Moore, P. C. 171; *The Minna*, Law Rep. Ad. & Ecc. pt. 2, Nov. 1868, p. 97; *The Iona*, Law Reports, 1 Privy Council, 432.
[**] *The Argo*, 1 Swabey, 464; *The Christiana*, 7 Moore P.C. 192.
[***] *The Phoebe*, Ware, 273; *The Creole*, 2 Wallace, Jr., 519.

The maxim of the civil law—*sic utere tuo ut non laedas alienum*—may, however, be fitly applied in such cases as the one before us. The remedy of the damaged vessel, if confined to the culpable pilot, would frequently be a mere delusion. He would often be unable to respond by payment—especially if the amount recovered were large. Thus, where the injury was the greatest, there would be the greatest danger of a failure of justice. According to the admiralty law, the collision impresses upon the wrongdoing vessel a maritime lien. This the vessel carries with it into whosesoever hands it may come. It is inchoate at the moment of the wrong, and must be perfected by subsequent proceedings. Unlike a common-law lien, possession is not necessary to its validity. It is rather in the nature of the hypothecation of the civil law. It is not indelible, but may be lost by laches or other circumstances.[*]

The proposition of the appellants would blot out this important feature of the maritime code, and greatly impair the efficacy of the system. The appellees are seeking the fruit of their lien.

All port regulations are compulsory. The provisions of the statute of New York are a part of the series within that category. A damaging vessel is no more excused because she was compelled to obey one than another. The only question in all such cases is, was she in fault? The appellants were bound to know the law. They cannot plead ignorance. The law of the place makes them liable. This ship was brought voluntarily within the sphere of its operation, and they cannot complain because it throws the loss upon them rather than upon the owners of the innocent vessel. We think the rule which works this result is a wise and salutary one, and we feel no disposition to disturb it.

The steamship is a foreign vessel. We have, therefore, considered the learned and able argument of the counsel for the appellants with more care than we should otherwise have deemed necessary. Maritime jurisprudence is a part of the law of nations. We have been impressed with the importance of its right administration in this case.

[Mr. Justice CLIFFORD (with whom concurred Mr. Justice FIELD) delivered a separate concurrence. Eds.]

DECREE AFFIRMED.

Note

The owner of a vessel under the control of a compulsory pilot escapes liability *in personam* for collision damage only if the pilot was solely at fault. If the pilot was not negligent the rule exempting the owner is not applicable. *Mount Washington Tanker Co. v. Wahyuen Shipping, Inc.*, 833 F.2d 1541 (11th Cir. 1987), 1988 A.M.C. 1601.

UNITED STATES v. S.S. PRESIDENT VAN BUREN

490 F.2d 504 (9th Cir. 1973)

Alfred T. GOODWIN, Circuit Judge

American President Lines, Ltd., challenges in this ship-collision case district court orders which dismissed its cross-claim against a pilot and its third-party complaint against the City of Long Beach. The court ruled that the tariff of the Port of Long Beach provided for noncompulsory pilotage services and that the exculpatory provisions of this tariff were valid. We agree with these conclusions, and affirm.

On the morning of July 5, 1968, while the government-owned USS Capacon was moored in its berth in Long Beach inner harbor, American President Lines requested the port to furnish pilotage services to the SS President Van Buren for a movement into the inner harbor. Municipal Pilot Carl Aultman boarded the President Van Buren and assumed his duties. The President Van Buren, while proceeding under pilotage, collided with the Capacon, damaging both vessels.

The United States subsequently filed its complaint against the President Van Buren, *in rem*, and against American President Lines and Carl Aultman, in personam, to recover the damages sustained by the Capacon. No service was accomplished in the in-rem proceeding, and that action has been dormant pending resolution of this one.

---

[*] *The Bold Buccleugh*, 7 Moore P.C. 284; *Edwards v. The Steamer R.F. Stockton*, Crabbe, 580; *The American*, 16 Law Reports, 264; *The Lion*, Law Rep., November, 1868, Ad. and Ecc. 107.

American President Lines (APL) denied liability and counterclaimed against the United States for property damage sustained by the President Van Buren. APL also filed a cross-claim against Aultman, and a third-party complaint against the Port of Long Beach and Jacobsen Pilot Services, Inc., the pilotage contractor which, pursuant to its contract with the port, had placed Aultman aboard the President Van Buren.

The district court, sitting in admiralty, without a jury, awarded the United States its full damages against APL. The court dismissed the government's complaint against Aultman, APL's counterclaim against the government, APL's cross-claim against Aultman, and APL's third-party complaint against Long Beach and Jacobsen. These rulings raise two issues.

The first question is whether Aultman was a noncompulsory pilot. If so, he was in much the same position as one of the ship's officers. Under the ordinary rules of *respondeat superior*, the shipowner would be responsible for Aultman's actions. If, on the other hand, the district court had concluded that pilotage was compulsory, the *respondeat superior* nexus would have been broken, and APL would not be personally liable for the results of the pilot's negligence. *See Homer Ramsdell Transportation Co. v. La Compagnie Generale Transatlantique*, 182 U.S. 406 (1901); G. Gilmore & C. Black, The Law of Admiralty, 429-30 (1957).

The tariff of the Port of Long Beach, under which Aultman boarded the President Van Buren, on its face provides for optional pilotage services to vessels entering, leaving, or shifting within the port.[1] However, if a vessel subject to the payment of pilotage elects not to take aboard a municipal pilot, an assessment of three quarters of the applicable charge is payable to the port.[2] APL argues that this financial inducement makes compulsory the use of the port's pilots.

In *The China*, 74 U.S. (7 Wall.) 53 (1869), the Supreme Court held that under a New York statute which made the master liable for the payment of full pilotage even if he chose to proceed without one, vessels were compelled to take a pilot. The Court further held, however, that, even though the shipowner was not liable in personam, the vessel itself still was liable *in rem*.

Three years later, in *The Merrimac*, 81 U.S. (14 Wall.) 199 (1872), the Court said:

> ... State pilot laws which compel the owners of vessels to pay half-pilotage in cases where the pilot offers his services and they are refused, where the law is not enforced by any penalty, are not regarded as compulsory, and therefore, the fact that the vessel was in charge of a pilot under such a law at the time of the collision is no defence to a libel for damages, if it appears that the collision was occasioned by negligence or unskilful navigation.... 81 U.S. at 203.

This holding was cited in dicta in the Supreme Court's most recent opinion on the subject of compulsory pilotage. *Homer Ramsdell Transportation Co. v. La Compagnie Generale Transatlantique*, 182 U.S. at 415.

The trial court correctly relied upon the portion of *The Merrimac* quoted above, even though this court had held that an earlier version of the tariff of the Port of Long Beach provided for compulsory pilotage. *National Development Co. v. City of Long Beach*, 187 F. Supp. 109, 113 (S.D. Cal. 1960), *aff'd*, 289 F.2d 586 (9th Cir.), *cert. denied*, 368 U.S. 901 (1961); *City of Long Beach v. American President Lines, Ltd.*, 223 F.2d 853, 856 (9th Cir. 1955). Neither of our cases would support a holding today that the pilotage is compulsory. The *Long Beach* tariff

---

[1] Port of Long Beach, Tariff No. 3, Item No. 205 (1967):

(a) The City of Long Beach maintains a force of municipal pilots, pursuant to a contract with an independent pilotage contractor, to perform the service of piloting vessels within, into and out of the Port of Long Beach. Any vessel entering, leaving or shifting within the Port of Long Beach may, but is not required to, request the services of and be piloted by a municipal pilot. Such pilotage services are understood to be voluntarily requested and voluntarily rendered.

[2] Port of Long Beach, Tariff No. 3, Item No. 215(a), Exception 1 (1967):

Three-fourths (3/4) the applicable charge, including minimum or maximum charge, shall be assessed when vessel subject to the payment of pilotage is not piloted by a municipal pilot.

has been significantly amended. The earlier version provided that "all vessels entering and leaving, and shifting within, the Port of Long Beach ... must be piloted by a municipal pilot...."[3] (Emphasis added.) Its current version, by contrast, purports to provide that pilotage is completely voluntary. *See* note 1, *supra.*

The three-quarter charge on vessels that elect not to take on a municipal pilot, the port explains, is assessed in order to generate needed revenues to help defray the many costs of operating a major port. We have no basis for holding this explanation to be unreasonable. *Cf. Cooley v. Board of Wardens of Port of Philadelphia*, 53 U.S. (12 How.) 299, 311-14 (1851).

Accordingly, we hold that Aultman was a noncompulsory pilot for the purposes of fixing the respondeat liability of the owner of the vessel under pilotage. The court correctly held APL responsible for the damages sustained by the Capacon.

Having agreed with the trial court that pilotage was noncompulsory, we come to the second issue: are the sweeping immunity provisions of the tariff of the Port of Long Beach valid?

Normally, a pilot is personally liable for his own negligence, and his employers are responsible for his actions under the rules of respondeat superior. *See* G. Gilmore & C. Black, *supra* at 430-32 A. Parks, Law of Tug, Tow and Pilotage 484 (1971).

In this case, the tariff of the Port of Long Beach provided that pilotage services are furnished on the understanding that the pilot is acting as the servant of the vessel, and that the vessel and its owners agree not to assert any liability against the pilot, Long Beach, the Board of Harbor Commissioners, and the pilotage contractor, and to hold those parties harmless with respect to any liability arising out of the negligence of the pilot except such personal liability as may arise by reason of the willful misconduct or gross negligence of the pilot.[4] APL argues that these exculpatory provisions are void, as against public policy, and unconstitutional.

Sun Oil Co. v. Dalzell Towing Co., 287 U.S. 291 (1932), enforced a contractual clause very similar to the one at issue here. The clause in *Sun Oil* provided that a tug captain who piloted a vessel propelled by its own power should be considered the servant of that vessel and that the tug owners should not be liable for his negligent pilotage. 287 U.S. at 292-93.

Bisso v. Inland Waterways Corp., 349 U.S. 85 (1955), distinguished *Sun Oil*, and held invalid an exculpatory contract designed to relieve a tugboat owner from liability for negligent towage of a dead ship:

---

[3] Port of Long Beach, Tariff No. 3, Item No. 205 (amended 1967):

(a) The City of Long Beach, acting through its Board of Harbor Commissioners, the governing body of the Port of Long Beach, maintains a force of pilots duly licensed to perform the service of piloting vessels in the Port of Long Beach, and all vessels entering and leaving, and shifting within, the Port of Long Beach, not exempt from the payment of pilotage, must be piloted by a municipal pilot, except that any such vessel may be piloted by the bona fide master thereof, if such master holds a federal pilot's license for the Port of Long Beach and excepting, further, that, if necessary, any such vessel may be piloted by the bona fide master thereof into the Port of Long Beach to anchor in the outer harbor to await the services of a municipal pilot.

[4] Port of Long Beach, Tariff No. 3, Item No. 205 (1967):

(e) It is understood and agreed, and is the essence of the contract under which pilotage services are proffered and rendered, and are requested and accepted by the vessel, that the services of the pilot are requested and accepted on the express understanding that such pilotage services are given, done or performed solely in the pilot's capacity as the servant of the vessel and of her owners, master, operators, charterers or agents, and not otherwise, and the owners, master, operators, charterers and agents of the vessel expressly covenant and agree to comply with the provisions of paragraphs (c) and (d) of this Item 205 and not to assert any personal liability against the pilot or the City of Long Beach, the Board of Harbor Commissioners, or any of their officers, employees or pilotage contractor, to respond in damage (including any rights over) arising out of or connected with, directly or indirectly, any damage, loss or expense sustained by the vessel, her owners, master, operators, charterers, agents or crew, and by any third parties, even though resulting from acts, omissions or negligence of the pilot; and provided, further, that to the extent only to which liability is legally imposed against the vessel, taking into consideration any limitation thereof to which the vessel or its owners, master, operators, charterers or agents are entitled by reason of any contract or bill of lading, or of any statute or rule of law in force, such vessel and her owners, master, operators, charterers and agents further covenant and agree to indemnify and hold harmless said pilot, the City of Long Beach, the Board of Harbor Commissioners, and each of their officers, employees and pilotage contractor, in respect to any liability arising out of claims, suits or actions against the municipal pilot, the City of Long Beach, the Board of Harbor Commissioners, or any of their officers, employees or pilotage contractor, or by third parties, resulting from acts, omissions or negligence of said pilot, excepting, however, such personal liability and rights over as may arise by reason of the willful misconduct or gross negligence of the pilot....

... It is one thing to permit a company to exempt itself from liability for the negligence of a licensed pilot navigating another company's vessel on that vessel's own power. That was the *Sun Oil* case. It is quite a different thing, however, to permit a towing company to exempt itself by contract from all liability for its own employees' negligent towage of a vessel.... 349 U.S. at 94.

APL argues, however, that the controlling distinction between *Sun Oil* and *Bisso* is not the difference between a live ship and a dead tow, but rather the degree of disparity in the relative bargaining positions of the parties. APL points particularly to the statement in *Sun Oil* that:

... Respondent had no exclusive privilege or monopoly in respect to the services that petitioner desired to have performed for its tanker. And petitioner was under no compulsion to accept the terms of respondent's pilotage clause. There is nothing to suggest that the parties were not on equal footing or that they did not deal at arm's length.... 287 U.S. at 294.

APL concludes that, unlike the contract involved in *Sun Oil*, but like that in *Bisso*, the port's tariff here is adhesive in light of the relative bargaining positions of the parties and should be held invalid.

However, the exculpatory provisions of the Long Beach tariff are integrated within a pilotage scheme which we have held to be non-compulsory. APL was not forced to use a municipal pilot, and in this sense it was not compelled to accept the exculpatory provisions of the port's tariff.

Moreover, Long Beach had anticipated APL's argument by making available to owners of piloted vessels "trip insurance" at a nominal charge of $4.50 per trip in addition to the pilotage fee. A steamship company can purchase in advance insurance covering all movements of its ships within the harbors of Long Beach and Los Angeles while piloted by municipal pilots, or a shipowner can purchase insurance solely for a specific ship movement. If not arranged earlier, the ship's master or agent can request single-trip insurance from the pilot himself at the time he boards the vessel. The insurance offered covers the legal liability for negligent acts or omissions of pilots furnished by Long Beach. In effect, then, Long Beach has offered two types of pilotage—one for an uninsured passage at a fixed rate, and the other for an insured passage at a slightly higher rate. APL had a free choice between uninsured and insured pilotage, and it chose the former.[5] To quote from *Sun Oil*: "It would be unconscionable for petitioner upon occurrence of a mishap to repudiate the agreement upon which it obtained the service." 287 U.S. at 295.

Because of the voluntary nature of the pilotage, and the availability of trip insurance at a nominal cost, the provisions of the tariff of the Port of Long Beach exculpating the pilot and his employers from liability are valid and enforceable.

The judgment is affirmed.

UNITED STATES v. NIELSON

349 U.S. 129, 75 S. Ct. 654, 99 L. Ed. 939, 1955 AMC 935 (1955)

Mr. Justice BLACK delivered the opinion of the Court

The respondent, Dauntless Towing Line, contracted to use two of its tugs in assisting the United States, petitioner here, move its steamship *Christopher Gale* from Hoboken to a Brooklyn pier. The *Gale* was to move under its own propelling power under guidance of one of respondent's tugboat captains or some other licensed pilot. The

---

[5] For an interesting discussion of the economics of pilotage insurance, and statutory efforts to institutionalize exculpatory tariffs, *see* A. Parks *supra* at 484-489.

contract further provided that a tugboat captain or pilot going on board would become the "servant of the owners of the vessel assisted in respect to the giving of orders to any of the tugs furnished to or engaged in the assisting service and in respect to the handling of such vessel, and neither those furnishing the tugs and/or pilot nor the tugs, their owners, agents, or charterers shall be liable for any damage resulting therefrom." One of the respondent's tug captains went aboard the government vessel to pilot it in connection with the moving operation. The two tugs of respondent were at the time fastened to the *Gale* by lines to help guide its movements. One of the tugs was crushed between the *Gale* and a pier while attempting to carry out a maneuver under orders of the tug captain piloting the *Gale.*

The respondent brought this suit in admiralty to recover damages from the United States alleging that damages to the tug were caused by negligent pilotage orders of the tug captain while temporarily acting as "servant" of the *Gale.* After hearings the District Court found that the damages were caused by the pilot's negligence "in persisting in his attempt to enter the slip after he knew or should have known that he could not overcome the force of the wind and tide and keep the CHRISTOPHER GALE from sagging down on Pier 1." On this finding the District Court entered a decree requiring the United States to pay respondent for damages brought about by this negligence. This decree was entered over the Government's contention that the contract was invalid if construed as exempting respondent from liability for its own servant's negligence. 112 F. Supp. 730. Agreeing with the District Court's reasoning and decree, the Court of Appeals affirmed. 209 F.2d 958. We granted certiorari to consider the meaning and validity of the pilotage clause, 348 U.S. 811, and at the same time granted certiorari in two other cases, today decided, which involve validity of contracts exempting towers from liability for negligent towage. *Bisso v. Inland Waterways Corp.,* ante, p. 85; *Boston Metals Co. v. The Winding Gulf,* ante, p. 122.

Sun Oil Co. v. Dalzell Towing Co., 287 U.S. 291, involved the meaning and validity of a pilotage contract substantially the same as the one here. One of Dalzell's tug captains negligently piloted Sun Oil's vessel causing the boat to ground and suffer damages. Sun Oil sued Dalzell. The contract exempting Dalzell from liability for pilotage was pleaded as a defense. This Court held that the tug company could validly contract against being "liable for any damage" caused by the negligence of one of its captains in piloting Sun Oil's vessel and construed the contract there as having that effect. The question in this case, however, is whether the agreement of the ship being piloted to release the tug company from being "liable for any damage resulting" from negligent pilotage not only relieves the tug company from liability for damage, but allows it affirmatively to collect damages for injury to its own tug due to negligent pilotage by one of its tug captains.

An agreement that one shall not be liable for negligence of a third person cannot easily be read as an agreement that one is entitled to collect damages for negligence of that third person. And there is no reason to stretch contractual language to force payment of damages under circumstances like these. A person supplying his own employees for use by another in a common undertaking cannot usually collect damages because of negligent work by the employee supplied. Clear contractual language might justify imposition of such liability. But the contractual language here does not meet such a test and we do not construe it as authorizing respondent to recover damages from petitioner.

Reversed.

Notes

1. A provision in contract of pilotage to the effect "that neither the owners nor the operators of a vessel making use of or having available her own propelling power will assert any personal liability to respond in damages, including any rights over, against the pilot for any damage sustained or caused by the vessel, even though resulting from the pilot's negligence", ... was held to be valid in *Reederei Franz Hagen v. Diesel Tug Resolute,* 400 F. Supp. 680 (D. Md. 1975) and relieved the pilot of liability. The court found this exculpatory clause not to be contrary to public policy because pilots are not paid enough to carry insurance to protect themselves and shipowners are no notice from the contract to procure their own insurance.

2. The relationship between exculpatory clauses and compulsory pilotage was discussed in *Kane v. Hawaiian Independent Refinery, Inc.,* 690 F.2d 722, 724 (9th Cir. 1982), 1984 A.M.C. 1323.

While compulsory pilotage may invalidate a pilotage clause in particular circumstances, *see City of Long Beach*, 223 F.2d at 856-57, the degree of compulsion here does not justify such a remedy. The use of HIRI's mooring masters was not required by law, but was merely a condition to doing business with HIRI. The clause was not motivated by HIRI's monopolistic bargaining position, but rather by HIRI's understandable and reasonable reluctance to risk responsibility for damage to a costly vessel moving under its own power. *See Transpacific Carriers Corp. v. The Tug Ellen F. McAllister*, 336 F.2d 371, 373-76 (2d Cir. 1964); *Federal Steam Navigation Co*, 305 F. Supp. at 1297.

3. *Compare Texaco Trinidad, Inc. v. Afran Transport Co.*, 538 F. Supp. 1038, 1043-44 (E.D. Pa. 1982), *aff'd* 707 F.2d 1395 (3rd Cir. 1983). In this case *Texaco Trinidad* required the vessel to take its pilot, and then sued when the pilot's negligence damaged its property.

Usually a ship owner is liable for negligence or negligent acts committed by a voluntary pilot. *See Homer Ramsdell Transportation Co. v. La Compagnie Generale Transatlantique*, 182 U.S. 406 (1901). That authority stands for the proposition that the pilot, that is, a voluntary pilot, is regarded as the servant of the ship owner. However, that case also teaches us that a ship owner is not liable in personam for the negligence or fault of a compulsory pilot.

It appears to be true that under existing case law a pilot has been held to be a compulsory pilot only where the requirement is imposed by law. Authority for that is the *Homer* case as well as *People of State of California v. Italian Motorship Ilice*, 534 F.2d 836 (9th Cir. 1976) and *Hogge v. SS YORKMAR*, 434 F. Supp. 715 (D. Md. 1977). No case has been cited by either party, though, nor has the Court found a case, that discussed whether or not a pilot could be held to be compulsory when the requirement is imposed by a source other than a governmental entity. This then becomes a critical issue for the Court to decide—whether or not under these circumstances the compulsory pilot rationale should nevertheless extend to a circumstance where the pilot is on board, whether or not there is any application of a rule or regulation or statute.

In determining whether the compulsory pilotage exception to the ship owner's liability in personam applies in this case, we have to examine the reason behind the rule. In *Homer*, the Supreme Court explained that the ship owner is not liable for the fault of a compulsory pilot because when the employment of the pilot is under compulsion of law, a true relation of master and servant does not exist and the doctrine of respondeat superior is not applicable. *See also* J. GRIFFIN, AMERICAN LAW OF COLLISION, 193, at 443-444 (1949). In those jurisdictions where there is a lawful requirement for a pilot to manage the mooring responsibility, *Homer* tells us that:

[t]he object of a legislature, in establishing [such] pilots, has been to secure, as far as possible, protection to life and property, by supplying a class of men better qualified than ordinary mariners to take charge of ships in places where, from local causes, navigation is attendant with more than common difficulty. To effect this object, it has in general been made the duty of a master in every ship, or arriving at any of the places in question, to take a pilot on board, and to give up to him the navigation of the vessel. The master, however well qualified to conduct the ship himself, is bound under a penalty in a great measure to divest himself of its control and to give up the charge to the pilot. As a necessary consequence, the master and owners are exempted from responsibility for acts resulting from the mismanagement of the pilot.

Homer Ramsdell Transportation Co. v. La Compagnie General Transatlantique, supra, at 412, quoting *Lucey v. Ingram*, 6 M & W. *Homer* also points out that if it is compulsive upon the master to take a pilot, and if he is bound to do so under a penalty, then and in such case neither he nor the owner will be liable for injuries occasioned by the negligence of a pilot. *Id.* at 416. In such a case, the pilot cannot be deemed properly the servant of the master or the owner but is forced upon them.

While we do not have a statute or a law requiring a pilot in this instance, nevertheless the principle would appear to be the same. While there is no criminal or monetary penalty embodied in the statute, there is a penalty of not being able to deliver the ship or deliver the cargo to its intended destination. That is to say, if the pilot is not accepted by the master, the only reasonable conclusion that can be drawn on the record of this case is that the ship is not permitted to moor and unload or indeed engage in anything other than presumably anchorage or departure from the area governed by the party imposing the requirement.

In this case, the evidence is clear that Texaco Trinidad required ships mooring at the SPM buoy to take a pilot—and for good reason. These buoys, it is quite plain, represent the investment of a considerable amount of resources in their placement, management, and use, as well as a need to accommodate the deep-draft vessels that allow this particular refinery to function. Common sense would suggest that Texaco has an interest not only in the property, but also in the operation of its refinery and the safety of personnel engaged in the delicate and important and often difficult task of fulfilling a mooring operation in such waters.

The record is plain as well that these pilots were considered to be local experts in regard to local conditions. It is this very type of requirement that *Homer* speaks of. It cannot be said, therefore, that Afran had any choice but to accept the pilot provided by Texaco. Afran was entitled to have a pilot that was prudently equipped and prudently advised, and who functioned in a way that would assure that his local expertise would prevent injury to property or persons associated with the mooring procedure.

The Court does not believe that the fact that Texaco Trinidad is not a governmental entity is dispositive. Indeed many of Texaco Trinidad's interests are the same as those that governmental entities have when compulsory pilotage is considered. The principal interest, of course, is in preventing damage to its own property. That is a direct proprietary interest in having competent pilotage. Secondly, there is the interest in having successful and expeditious operations in mooring so that Texaco Trinidad will gain maximum use from the facilities that are installed, in this instance, the SPM buoy. There is also an interest in preventing injury to persons involved, irrespective of whom those persons are employed by. The interest in preventing injury or death to persons involved in these procedures can be said to be an interest that would support the need by Texaco to have a local expert become the pilot and take over the navigation of a vessel, especially vessels of this size.

4. In *United States v. SS President Van Buren, supra,* the exculpatory pilotage clause was contained in the tariff of the Port of Long Beach. Often such clauses are accepted by a vessel at the time the pilot boards her. For example, in *American Oil Company v. M/T Lacon,* 398 F. Supp. 1181 (S.D. Ga. 1973), *aff'd* 518 F.2d 1405 (5th Cir. 1974), the court found that a valid pilotage clause had attached when the pilot on reaching the bridge "handed the Master a copy of Atlantic Towing Company's Schedule of Rates, Terms and Conditions for Tug Services. The Master signed another document submitted to him under which he acknowledged the services of the tugs...." The Rate Sheet contained a provision immunizing the towing company from acts of the pilot and provided that when he went aboard the vessel assisted by a tug he became the servant of the shipowner.

There must, however, be a contractual basis for the pilotage clause either expressly or by implication. *See Tankers and Tramps Corp. v. Tug Jane McAllister, etc.,* 358 F.2d (2d Cir. 1966), where the court stated:

> A contract arose from the telephone conversation calling for the furnishing of the services. This is so even though there was no price specified, for a reasonable price was implied and the services were furnished. WILLISTON ON CONTRACTS, 3rd Ed. Vol. 1, Sec. 41. Since the contract was complete at the time of the telephone conversation, the pilotage clause can defeat libelant's claim only if it was part of that contract, or if it was later agreed to in some subsequent addition to or substitution for the original contract. If prior dealings between the parties involving the clause were proved, an inference that it was a term of this contract might be justified. *Sun Oil Co. v. Dalzell Towing Co.,* 55 F.2d 63, 64 (2 Cir.), *aff'd* 287 U.S. 291, 53 S. Ct. 135, 77 L. Ed. 311 (1932). The proof of such prior dealings as would justify such an inference is, however, lacking here. To be sure, there are circumstances which indicate that such a restrictive clause has been in use at times in the trade. The title of the clause, reference to it in a number of other cases, McAllister's printing of it on schedules, tug assistance slips and bills, all show that it has been utilized in such contracts, perhaps with some frequency in the trade in this harbor.[2] There was, however, no testimony that there was in fact use with such frequency as to justify a finding that such a transfer of liability was a custom in the trade, or in what percentage of New York Harbor towage contracts such a provision was included, or what knowledge Tankers had of any such custom.

5. How far-reaching is the exculpatory clause? May it be used by a towing company to indemnify itself from the vessel for damages it has paid to a third party? May it be used by a towing company to recover damages to its tug?

6. For a case involving negligence of both the pilot and the crew, see *Petition of Marine Mercante Nicaraguense, S.A.,* 364 F.2d 118, 1966 AMC 2392 (2d. Cir. 1966).

Section 3. Salvage

A. Introduction

B.V. BUREAU WIJSMULLER v. UNITED STATES

702 F.2d 333 (2d Cir. 1983)

* * *

Discussion

I.

Unknown to the common law, the law of salvage occupies a unique position in the the Anglo-American legal system. In *Mason v. The Ship Blaireau,* 6 U.S. (2 Cranch) 143 (1804), Chief Justice Marshall commented that when property on land exposed to grave peril is saved by a volunteer, no remuneration is given. "Let precisely the same service, at precisely the same hazard, [b]e rendered at sea, and a very ample reward will be bestowed in the courts of justice." *Id.* at 158. *See Wright v. The Felix,* 62 F. 620, 621 (E.D. Pa. 1894).

---

[2] *Compare The West Eldara,* 101 F.2d 45 (2 Cir.), *cert. den. sub nom. McAllister Towing & Tr. Co. v. American Diamond Lines, Inc.,* 308 U.S. 607, 60 S. Ct. 144, 84 L. Ed. 507 (1939), *modified on rehearing* 104 F.2d 670, 671 (2 Cir. 1939), in which the charterer was shown to be in possession of the towage schedule containing the pilotage clause, but the master was not shown to have knowledge of a custom to include the clause in docking agreements so as to bind the owner.

The history of salvage law dates back to the earliest civilizations. Although Phoenicia, Carthage and Athens were distinguished for their navigation and commerce, none of them founded an authoritative digest of maritime law. Rhodes, the cradle of nautical jurisprudence, was sovereign of the seas about 900 years before the Christian era and it was the Rhodians who formulated the first maritime code. The Romans who conquered Rhodes preserved these laws. Emperor Augustus first sanctioned the use of Rhodian laws to decide maritime cases in Rome. The Romans added the notion of rewarding a volunteer who preserved or improved the property of another, even though such act was without the owner's knowledge or consent. This concept was carried under the title "Rhodian Code" into the marine law of various European countries. Anglo-American jurisprudence adopted this equitable doctrine from the Romans, providing for a reward to the salvor volunteer for his efforts based on the circumstances of the case, and proportionate to the dangers involved. *The Felix*, 62 F. at 621-622; *The "Calypso"*, 166 Eng. Rep. 221, 224 (1828); *See* 3A M. Norris, Benedict on Admiralty §§ 5-11 (6th ed. 1980) (Bendict); 3 Kent's Commentaries 1-5 (12th ed. 1873).

The law of salvage originated to preserve property and promote commerce.[1] *See Seven Coal Barges*, 21 F. Cas. 1096, 1097 (C.C.D. Ind. (1870) (No. 12,677) ("The very object of the law of salvage is to promote commerce and trade, and the general interests of the country, by preventing the destruction of property...."); Palaez, *Salvage—A New Look at an Old Concept*, 7 J. Mar. L. & Com. 505 (1976). These remain its most compelling goals. In order to accomplish these purposes courts of admiralty do not view salvage awards therefore "merely as pay, on the principal of a *quantum meruit*, or as a remuneration *pro opere et labore*, but as a reward given for perilous services, voluntarily rendered, and as an inducement to seamen and others to embark in such undertaking to save life and property." *The Blackwall*, 77 U.S. (10 Wall.) 1, 14 (1870); *see* Benedict, *supra*, § 235. For these reasons courts sitting in admiralty are liberal in fixing awards. *The Felix*, 62 F. at 622.

Note: Cargo Liability for Salvage

"The saving of cargo, fuel, or other property on the salved vessel is a salvage service that merits compensation in the same way as does saving of the vessel itself, and anyone with a direct pecuniary interest in the property may be held liable for the award." *Allseas Maritime, S.A. v. M/V Mimosa*, 812 F.2d 243, 248 (5th Cir. 1987).

Generally, if a ship is imperiled that same situation will also place the cargo in peril. Although one can think of situations where a vessel may be in peril but its cargo is not and converse situations where some or all of cargo is imperiled but the vessel is not, "[i]f one part of the property making the common adventure is in peril then the whole adventure is treated as being in peril and pays the salvage remuneration rateably to salved shares: this principle is confirmed in Article 13.2 (first sentence) of the London Salvage Convention 1989. The different interests are all treated as having a unity of interest. The position is the same in American law." G. Brice, Maritime Law of Salvage 53 (2d ed. 1993).

---

[1] While the wish to protect human life may have played a role in the historical development of salvage law, it was not the prime motivating factor. The Brussels Convention of 1910, which conformed international law to that generally applicable in the United States. G. Gilmore & C. Black, Jr., The Law of Admiralty § 8-1, at 534 (2d ed. 1975), expressly provided that no remuneration was due from people whose lives were saved. Two years later the United States enacted the Salvage Act which rewarded salvors who saved human life.

B. Elements of Salvage Claim

1. *Generally*

THE SABINE

101 U.S. 384, 25 L. Ed. 982 (1880)

Mr. Justice CLIFFORD

Salvage is the compensation allowed to persons by whose voluntary assistance is a ship at sea or her cargo or both have been saved in whole or in part from impending sea peril, or in recovering such property from actual peril or loss, as in cases of shipwreck, derelict, or recapture.

Three elements are necessary to a valid salvage claim: 1. A marine peril. 2. Service voluntarily rendered when not required as an existing duty or from a special contract. 3. Success in whole or in part, or that the service rendered contributed to such success.

Proof of success, to some extent, is as essential as proof of service, for if the property is not saved, or if it perishes, or, in case of capture, if it is not retaken, no compensation will be allowed. Compensation as salvage is not viewed by the admiralty courts merely as pay on the principle of *quantum meruit* or as a remuneration pro opere et labore, but as a reward given for perilous services voluntarily rendered, and as an inducement to mariners to embark in such dangerous enterprises to save life and property.

Sufficient appears to show that important assistance was rendered by the steamer "Mayflower" and her crew to the steamer "Sabine," in the nature of salvage service, as alleged in the libel. Both steamers were at the time in the Ouachita River, and each was bound on a trip to the port of New Orleans. When the "Mayflower" approached the landing described in the libel, those in charge of her deck discovered that the steamer "Sabine" was in distress, and it appears that those in command of the latter steamer hailed the "Mayflower" and requested assistance. It also appears from the pleadings that the injured steamer had a cargo of six hundred and nineteen bales of cotton, consigned to various merchants at the port of destination, together with a number of passengers; that she and her cargo were in peril, owing to the fact that in attempting to back out from the landing she struck a snag or other obstruction beneath the surface of the river and became fast. Many of her flooring timbers and bottom planks were broken, and it is alleged that she had in her hold sixteen to eighteen inches of water, which was rapidly gaining on her pumps.

Success attended the efforts of the salvors, both as to the steamer and her cargo, and they delivered all the cotton to the consignees.

* * *

MERRITT & CHAPMAN CO. v. UNITED STATES

274 U.S. 611, 47 S. Ct. 663, 71 L. Ed. 1232, 1927 AMC 953 (1927)

Mr. Justice BUTLER delivered the opinion of the Court

Plaintiff in error sued under the Tucker Act, § 359, 24 Stat. 505, upon a claim for salvage on account of service alleged to have been rendered the Steamship Leviathan owned by the defendant in error. *United States v. Cornell Steamboat Co.*, 202 U.S. 184, 189. On defendant's motion the court, May 7, 1925, dismissed the petition on the ground that it fails to state a cause of action. The case is here on writ of error to that court. *J. Homer Fritch, Inc. v. United States*, 248 U.S. 458.

The petition alleges the following. August 24-25, 1921, at Hoboken, there was a fierce and extensive fire on Pier 5. The Leviathan lay bow in at the south side of Pier 4. She could not be towed out. She had only a skeleton crew, and it would have required a large number to man her and many hours of preparation to get up sufficient steam and move her by means of her own engines. The fire started at half after six in the evening and was not extinguished until seven in the morning. A part of the time it covered the whole length of Pier 5, the bulkhead and adjacent houses. The wind was from the south and tended to carry the fire across the slip and onto the Leviathan. Her port side was considerably scorched, and several times fire broke out on her super-structure. Ammunition was stored in a building near the bulkhead, and the possibility of an explosion added to the danger. Plaintiff's steamers Commissioner and Chapman Brothers were powerful boats, specially built, equipped and manned for salvage and fire fighting service. The former from seven until half after nine in the evening the latter from about seven in the evening until seven in the morning continuously fought the fire. They played heavy streams of water on the burning pier where the fire threatened the Leviathan. And, by way of conclusion, it is stated that "The service was a direct aid and benefit to the steamer Leviathan in preventing the spread of flames from Pier 5 to that vessel, and had it not been for the said service great damage to, if not total loss of, the said steamship would have resulted." Limiting the general statement by the specific, in accordance with the context, (*United States v. Union Pacific R. Co.*, 169 Fed. 65, 67, and cases cited) the substance of the allegation is that plaintiff in error, by preventing the spread of the fire from the pier to the Leviathan, rendered her direct aid and benefit.

There is no claim that the Leviathan, or any one in her behalf, requested or accepted assistance from plaintiff in error, or that its fireboats played any water on that vessel or did anything to extinguish fire thereon or to give her any assistance other than that involved in fighting the fire on and about Pier 5. The distance between the Leviathan and that fire is not stated, and there is nothing to indicate that she did not have adequate protection from other sources. Indeed, the circumstances disclosed by the petition rather than to show that she did not need any assistance from plaintiff in error.

While salvage cannot be exacted for assistance forced upon a ship (*The Bolivar v. The Chalmette*, 1 Woods C.C. 397), her request for or express acceptance of the service is not always essential to the validity of the claim. It is enough if under the circumstances any prudent man would have accepted. *The Annapolis*, (In the Privy Council), *Lushington* 355, 375. Plaintiff in error claims as a volunteer salvor going at his own risk to the assistance of the ship on the chance of reward in case of success, and not as one employed rendering service for pay according to his effort or the terms of his contract. *The Sabine*, 101 U.S. 384, 390. It did not communicate with or enter into the service of the Leviathan. Its fireboats did not put water upon her. The fires that started on her were put out by other means. All effort of plaintiff in error was put forth directly for the purpose of extinguishing fire at and about Pier 5 and to save property not at all related to the Leviathan. The elimination of that fire contributed mediately to her safety. But, whatever the aid or benefit resulting to her, it was incidental and indirect for which, in the absence of request for or acceptance of the service, a claim for salvage cannot be sustained. *The Annapolis, supra*; *The City of Atlanta*, 56 Fed. 252, 254; *The San Cristobal*, 215 Fed. 615; 230 Fed. 599.

Judgment affirmed.

---

2. Marine Peril

MARKAKIS V. S/S VOLENDAM

486 F. Supp. 1103, 1980 AMC 915 (S.D.N.Y. 1980)

Opinion

Findings of Fact and Conclusions of Law

Edward WEINFELD, District Judge

Plaintiff, master of the vessel S.S. Monarch Sun (the "Sun") commenced this suit on behalf of himself and the crew members of the Sun, to recover a salvage award for services allegedly rendered to the S.S. Monarch Star (the "Star") between January 10, 1977 and January 11, 1977.[1] At the time of the alleged salvage service, the Sun and the Star were both Panamanian flag passenger cruise vessels, each weighing about 15,000 gross tons. Both were engaged in passenger cruise voyages from Miami, Florida, to various points in the Caribbean Sea, and return. Both vessels were owned by Monarch Cruise Lines, N.V., and operated by the same agent, Technical Marine Planning ("TMP") of Miami, Florida.

The basic material facts are not seriously disputed. On January 10, 1977, the Star, which was carrying 368 passengers and a crew of an almost equal number, sustained an engine failure while sailing off the northern coast of Cuba. Her deck log indicates that at 14:35 hours on that day, she was "rendered powerless due to engine difficulties and blackout." The main engine was "completely stopped," although the emergency generator, which supplied power for lights and for the radio, was still in operation. Almost eight hours later, at 23:30, while the ship was still "lying stopped in [the] [Old] [Bahama] [Channel]," north of Cuba, its captain reported that the emergency generator had also failed. Thus, the ship was left without power or lights, and with only batteries to operate its radio. According to the ship's radio log, the emergency generator remained inoperative until January 11 at 9:21 hours.[2] Throughout this time, the Star was having difficulty communicating with the head office in Miami.

During the aforementioned period, the Sun was enroute from Florida to Puerto Rico. At 21:15 hours on January 10, or almost seven hours after the Star's initial engine failure, TMP, the agent for the owners of both vessels, radio-telephoned the master of the Sun, the plaintiff Markakis, that the Star was disabled and instructed him to change course, head toward, and render assistance to the Star. The Sun thereupon altered course and headed toward the northern coast of Cuba, where the Star lay disabled off the Cuban coast at various distances estimated from between twelve to fifteen miles. The ships rendezvoused on January 11 at 11:00 a.m. The two captains agreed on procedures for transferring the passengers, some of the crew, baggage, and provisions of the crippled ship to the Sun. The transfer operation, carried out on tenders sent from the Sun and manned by the Sun's crew, began at noon on January 11, and was completed five hours later. One crewman was slightly injured in the operation when he fell off one of the tenders. After it was completed, Captain Avdelas and other members of his crew remained on board the [S]tar. Thereafter, at Captain Avdelas' request, TMP ordered Markakis to tow the Star farther away from the coast of Cuba and into the Old Bahama Channel, a deep and well-traveled shipping route. Avdelas himself acknowledged that the purpose of the tow was to bring the ship "to a safer place" until a tugboat sent from Miami by the Star's owners arrived and finished the job.

Towing by the Star commenced at 18:05 and lasted about four hours. The Sun, with passengers from both vessels aboard, towed the Star a distance of approximately 13 miles in a generally northeasterly direction and away from the coast of Cuba. At 22:00 the tow lines were released at the request of Captain Avdelas. The Sun resumed its journey, embarking at destinations on its own route as well as those that would have been on the Star's itinerary. The Star was left in the Old Bahama Channel to await its appointed rendezvous with the tug Curb, which arrived on January 12 at about 13:00 and which eventually towed the Star 324 miles back to Miami.

---

[1] The Sun is now known as the S.S. Volendam. The other defendant, the S.S. Veendam, was formerly known as the Monarch Star. At trial plaintiff abandoned any claim against his own vessel, the Volendam.

[2] Captain Avdelas, the master of the Star, testified that the emergency generator resumed functioning at 3:00 a.m. on January 11. However, the contemporaneously recorded entries of the ship's radio-telephone logbook indicate that it was still not working at 06:01, and that it was "restored to service" at 09:21. We credit these entries as more accurate than the Captain's memory.

From the time that its engines first failed until the time of its rendezvous with the Curb, the Star remained close to the coast of Cuba and in constant motion. When its engines first stopped, the Star was located 12 miles off the coast. The Captain reported that he could see lights from the land and two Cuban gunboats were visible on the horizon. Immediately thereafter, the ship began to drift with the currents; first it was carried slightly south toward Cuba,[3] and thereafter, on a steady line to the northwest along the Channel, running roughly parallel to the coast, although gradually moving away from it. During part of this time, the ship was in total blackness. The seas were calm. Although the prevailing winds at this time of the year were from the northeast and, if active, would have tended to push a drifting vessel toward the coast of Cuba, during this portion of the drift there was no wind. The vessel was directed solely by the force of the currents, which ran parallel to the coast of Cuba. By the time of its rendezvous with the Sun, the Star had drifted 34.4 miles northwest from the point of its breakdown; when the Sun began to tow the Star it was then 23.3 miles off the coast of Cuba. It was towed 13.8 miles directly east, which brought it six more miles away from the coast. After the Sun had released its tow ropes, the wind picked up from the east, carrying the Star across the water currents and directly toward the Cuban coast. By the time of the arrival of the Curb, on January 12 at 13:00 hours, the Star had drifted 23 miles back toward Cuba and was only 17 miles from its coast. Although Captain Avdelas vehemently contended that the ship was in no danger, in that the water current flowing parallel to the coast was stronger than the wind blowing toward it, he did admit that a "very stormy" east wind could have carried the ship all the way to the coast. At the point toward which the Star was drifting, the shore is rocky and lined with reefs; there is no shallow water in which to anchor. The captain also admitted that when he asked the Sun to tow him away from the coast he was "apprehensive about an easterly wind." Indeed, by the time the tug Curb had arrived, the Star reported the weather as "Fresh breeze, rough sea." Captain Avdelas' fears were allayed, however, by the knowledge that the Sun would tow him to the middle of the Old Bahama Channel, that at least one other ship, the Stella Solaris, was available and ready to assist; that the Coast Guard cutter Dauntless was patrolling the vicinity; and that the tug Curb had been dispatched to complete the rescue.

In order to prevail upon a claim for a salvage award, the plaintiff must prove three essential elements: "1. A marine peril. 2. Service voluntarily rendered when not required as an existing duty or from a special contract. 3. Success in whole or in part, or that the service rendered contributed to such success."[4] There is no dispute that the third element has been satisfied. The combined efforts of the Sun and the tugboat Curb eventually did bring success; the passengers, their baggage, and the ship's provisions were all successfully transferred to the Sun to complete the balance of the voyage. The Star safely reached Miami, where it was repaired.

However, the defendant disputes both of the other elements. It claims that the Star's predicament was not sufficiently perilous to warrant a salvage award, and that the actions of the plaintiff and the crew of the Sun in coming to the Star's assistance were involuntary, because they were taken at the direction and under the orders of the ship's owners. We find neither of these arguments persuasive and hold that plaintiff has sustained the claim for a salvage award.

A. Marine Peril

In determining whether there exists a marine peril sufficient to justify a salvage award, the Court must decide "not whether the peril is imminent, but rather whether it is 'reasonably to be apprehended.'"[5] In order to prevail, the plaintiff need only establish that "'at the time the assistance [was] rendered, the ship [had] encountered any damage or misfortune which might expose her to destruction if the service were not rendered.'"[6]

---

[3] *See* Plaintiff's Exh. 2.

[4] *The Sabine*, 101 U.S. 384 ... (1879). *See The Blackwell*, 77 U.S. (10 Wall.) 1, 12, ... (1869); *M'Connochie v. Kerr*, 9 F. 50, 53 (S.D.N.Y. 1881); *In re Petition of Sun Oil Co.*, 342 F. Supp. 976, 981-82 (S.D.N.Y. 1972) (citing cases), *aff'd*, 474 F.2d 1048 (2d Cir. 1973).

[5] *Fort Myers Shell & Dredging Co. v. Barge NBC 512*, 404 F.2d 137, 139 (5th Cir. 1968) (citation omitted). *See also The Leonie O. Louise*, 4 F.2d 699, 700 (5th Cir. 1925); *The Neshaminy*, 228 F. 285, 288 (3d Cir. 1915) ("Assistance to a vessel in a situation of actual apprehension, though not of actual danger, is salvage service."); *M'Connochie v. Kerr*, 9 F. 50, 53 (S.D.N.Y. 1881).

[6] *Conolly v. S.S. Karina II*, 302 F. Supp. 675, 679 (E.D.N.Y. 1969) (quoting NORRIS, THE LAW OF SALVAGE § 188) (emphasis supplied). *See The Mercer*, 297 F. 981, 984 (2d Cir. 1924); *The Saragossa*, 21 Fed. Cas. 425, at 426 (No. 12,334) (S.D.N.Y. 1867).

A variety of services, many of which seem more mundane than daring, qualify for salvage awards. As one commentator has stated:

> The prototypical act [of salvage] is rescuing a ship in peril at sea and towing her to a place of safety.... In deciding [whether to make an award] ... courts look to the situation that existed at the time the ship was taken in tow: If she was not under command, unable to navigate or to reach port unaided, the service will be considered salvage even though the ship was not in imminent danger of destruction and even though the towage itself was calm and uneventful.... The act of salvage need not be so dramatic and need not even consist in rendering physical assistance: standing by or escorting a distressed ship in a position to give aid if it becomes necessary, giving information on the channel to follow ... to avoid running aground, carrying a message as a result of which necessary aid and equipment are forthcoming have all qualified. So long as the ship is in peril, any voluntary act which contributes to her ultimate safety may rank as an act of salvage.[7]

The most frequent instances of salvage awards involve situations in which the salvor renders assistance to a vessel lodged in a sandbar or run aground on a reef. In such situations, the courts often justify the award by citing the possibility that storms could arise and further injure the stranded vessel, which is incapable of dislodging itself under its own power.[8] Nevertheless, salvage awards have been granted even where the vessel could safely have remained grounded for an indefinite period of time.[9] Indeed, whenever a vessel is stranded, "she and her cargo are practically always in a substantial peril. Such a vessel is helpless because she cannot pursue her intended voyage or deal effectively with any emergency which may arise."[10]

Just as a stranded ship is imperiled, so too, one adrift without power may be equally endangered. Salvage awards have long been accorded to those who tow disabled and imperiled vessels from the open sea into port. In *Steamer Avalon Co. v. Hubbard S.S. Co. (The General Hubbard)*,[11] for example, the Ninth Circuit approved an award for the rescue of a ship whose crankshaft had broken while sailing fourteen miles out at sea. That the vessel was disabled and incapable of guiding its own course were sufficient reasons to justify a substantial award, which the Court made, even though it concluded that the service of the salving crew was not perilous, and that there was little if any danger of the salved vessel drifting to shore.[12] Other courts have reached the same result in similar situations.[13]

The facts of the instant case clearly support the conclusion that on January 10 and 11, 1977, the Star was exposed to peril "'reasonably to be apprehended.'"[14] Not only was the ship unable to "pursue her intended voyage or deal effectively with any emergency"[15] that might have arisen, she was left to drift, at times in total darkness and without adequate power to communicate by radio. Although the weather was calm from the time of the engine failure until the completion of the Star's towing operation, the accident occurred in an area known for sudden, intense storms.[16] In fact, after the Sun had cast off its tow lines, the east wind, which

---

[7] GILMORE & BLACK, THE LAW OF ADMIRALTY, § 8-2, at 536-37 (2d ed. 1975).

[8] *See, e.g., Sobonis v. Steam Tanker National Defender*, 298 F. Supp. 631, 636 (S.D.N.Y. 1969); *The Leonie O. Louise*, 4 F.2d 699, 700 (5th Cir. 1925); *The St. Paul*, 86 F. 340, 343 (2d Cir. 1898); *The Sahara*, 246 F. 141, 142 (D. Md. 1917).

[9] *The St. Paul*, 86 F. 340, 343 (2d Cir. 1898). *Cf. The Naiwa*, 3 F.2d 381, 382-83 (4th Cir. 1924) (large award granted to salvors of McAllister would not be entitled to indemnification for negligent acts of Skogen before boarding the El Salvador or for improper stranded vessel even though the "most favorable weather conditions" had prevailed during the month in which salved vessel lay stranded).

[10] *Navigazione Generale Italiana v. Spencer Kellogg & Sons, Inc.*, 92 F.2d 41, 44 (2d Cir.), *cert. denied*, 302 U.S. 751 (1937) (A. HAND, J.). *See Sobonis v. Steam Tanker National Defender*, 298 F. Supp. 631, 636 (S.D.N.Y. 1969). *Cf. The St. Paul*, 86 F. 340, 343 (2d Cir. 1898).

[11] 255 F. 854 (9th Cir. 1919).

[12] The Court said that at the time of the rescue "there was little wind or sea, and there was reasonable expectation of a continuation of favorable conditions, and the steamship lay in an ocean path not infrequently traveled by vessels." 255 F. at 856 (9th Cir. 1919). In short, the General Hubbard's predicament was almost precisely equivalent to that of the Star.

[13] *See e.g., The Roanoke*, 214 F. 63 (9th Cir. 1914)., *The Mercer*, 297 F. 981, 984 (2d Cir. 1924); *The Henry Maurer*, 215 F. 238 (D. Mass. 1914); *Squires v. The Ionian Leader*, 100 F. Supp. 829 (D.N.J. 1951). *The Angie & Florence*, 77 F. Supp. 404 (D. Mass 1948).

[14] *See note 5 supra.*

[15] *Navigazione Generale Italiana v. Spencer Kellogg & Sons, Inc.*, 92 F.2d 41, 44 (2d Cir.), *cert. denied*, 302 U.S. 751 (1937) (A. HAND, J.).

[16] *See Fort Myers Shell & Dredging Co. v. Barge NBC 512*, 404 F.2d 137, 139 (5th Cir. 1968).

made Captain Avdelas "apprehensive," increased, and the sea became "choppy." Between the time of the Sun's departure and the Curb's arrival, the Star drifted 23 miles back toward the coast of Cuba. Had that drift occurred before the Sun had towed her, the Star might well have been dashed against the reefs lining the northern coast of Cuba.

In addition, it is noted that at the time of the breakdown, the Star was about 12 miles off the shore of Cuba, or at the edge of the territorial waters claimed by that country; and that it was in sight of at least two Cuban warships. Had it drifted closer to the shore, it faced a real possibility of interception or even reprisal.[17] None of these dangers was as remote as the claimant has suggested. Indeed, Captain Avdelas' assertion that the Star was never in peril is belied by his own radio requests for aid,[18] by his request to be towed "to a safer place" to await the arrival of the Curb, and by the unsolicited offers of assistance from other vessels in the area, including a Coast Guard cutter. Though the danger to the Star was less than compelling and the rescue operation short of heroic, the ship was sufficiently imperiled to justify a salvage award.

* * *

The fact that the Sun was not called upon to tow the Star back to Miami and that this service was performed by the Curb does not invalidate plaintiff's right to relief. The quality and degree of contributory service need only be slight to justify a salvage award; the extent of the service may effect the amount of the award, but not its validity.[29]

The Court holds the owners of the Star liable to the captain and crew of the Sun for salvage services performed. The matter will be referred, pursuant to the parties' stipulation, to a special master for a computation of the award.

The foregoing shall constitute the Court's Findings of Fact and Conclusions of Law.

---

3. Voluntariness: Who Can Qualify as a Salvor?

MARKAKIS v. S/S VOLENDAM

486 F. Supp. 1103, 1980 AMC 915 (S.D.N.Y. 1980)

[The facts are stated *supra*.]

* * *

B. Voluntary Act

The claimant also contends that the Sun's crew acted under compulsion, rather than voluntarily, in that they were ordered by the owners to change course, rendezvous with the Star, and render assistance. Initially, the claimant argues that the vessels' joint ownership by Monarch Lines precludes a salvage award. In essence, the claimant seeks to analogize this situation to those cases in which courts have refused to permit awards to crews that perform salvage services to their own vessels. The principles of those cases, however, are not apt here. At least since 1912, when

---

[17] On December 28, 1977 the United States Coast Guard issued an "Advisory Notice" to inform the United States Maritime Community that the Cuban government was enforcing its claim to a 12-mile territorial sea by stopping, and at times detaining, vessels approaching within 30 miles of the north coast of Cuba. *See* Local Notice to Mariners No. 52-77 (Dec. 28, 1977) [Pltf's Exh. 9]. It is admitted that the Star was a Panamanian flagship and not an American vessel, and its engine failure occurred eleven months before the publication of this advisory bulletin. Nevertheless, we take notice of the fact that the policies of the Cuban government, its claim to an expansive territorial sea, and the proximity of two Cuban warships may have posed more than a theoretical prospect of the detention of the vessel with its many Americans on board.

[18] A master's requests for assistance are strong evidence that a marine peril is genuine and that the salvor's efforts, if voluntary and successful, are worthy of reward. *See The Pendragon Castle*, 5 F.2d 56 (2d Cir. 1924); *The St. Paul*, 86 F. 340, 342 (2d Cir. 1898). *Cf. The Roanoke*, 214 F. 63, 65 (9th Cir. 1914).

[29] *See, e.g, W.E. Rippon & Son v. United States*, 348 F.2d 627, 629 (2d Cir. 1965) (minimal contributory service is compensable); *Nadle v. M/V Tequila*, 377 F. Supp. 414, 417 (S.D.N.Y. 1974); *Conolly v. S.S. Karina II*, 302 F. Supp. 675, 680 (E.D.N.Y. 1969).

Congress codified the trend of the common law, the fact of common ownership of the salvor and salved vessels has played no part in the grant of salvage awards.[20]

The claimant also contends that the Sun's crew were, in effect, under a duty to obey the orders of their owner, and that they had no choice in the matter. Although there are instances in which a would-be salvor's pre-existing duty to act defeats his claim, those cases are rare.[21] Where an individual performs a salvage service outside the normal scope of his employment, the rule is that "nothing short of a contract [between the owners of the salved vessel and the salvors] to pay a given sum for the services to be rendered, or a binding agreement to pay at all events, whether successful or unsuccessful, in the enterprise, will operate as a bar to a meritorious claim for salvage."[22] Indeed, even if the master, the owner or the charterer of the salvor vessel is found expressly to have waived his rights, the crew is not bound by the waiver.[23]

Thus, in *Kimes v. United States*[24] the Court allowed an award to one United States government vessel that saved the cargo of another during the Second World War. Even though the employees of the salvor ship were under a "moral obligation to render [their] services for the effective prosecution of an all-out war effort," the Court held that because they were under no "legal duty to perform this salvage work,"[25] they were entitled to an award. Moreover, it noted that salvaging vessels was not an ordinary task performed within the scope of the crew's employment; it involved an extra increment, however slight, of physical danger. Granting the award was in the interest of public policy. Likewise, in *Sobonis v. Steam Tanker National Defender*[26] the Court allowed an award to a crew hired at fixed salaries by the same company that owned the salvaged vessel; the Court reasoned that public policy supports salvage awards unless the contract of hire expressly waives salvage rights.

In the instant case there is not even a suggestion that the articles of employment of the Sun's crew contemplate salvage service. When the Sun responded to the Star's call for help, the crew were called upon to perform tasks beyond the ordinary scope of their employment, in an unusual situation, and with an added degree, however slight, of peril. Their decision to follow an order that their employer could not otherwise lawfully have required them to obey is a voluntary act for the purposes of a salvage award.[27] If their claim could be defeated merely because their employer had ordered them to perform salvage service, Congress' purpose of fostering salvage service by eliminating

---

[20] 46 U.S.C. § 727 [effective August 1, 1912] provides:

> The right to remuneration for assistance or salvage service shall not be affected by common ownership of the vessels rendering and receiving such assistanc or salvage services.

See Kimes v. United States, 207 F.2d 60, 62-63 (2d Cir. 1953) (citing cases); *Spivak v. United States*, 203 F.2d 881, 82-83 (3d Cir. 1953). Even before the Act's effective date, the common ownership of the salvor and salved vessels did not preclude a salvage award. *See, e.g.*, NORRIS, THE LAW OF SEAMEN § 238 (3d ed.) (citing cases).

[21] Firemen who aid in extinguishing blazes upon ships are precluded from obtaining salvage awards, *see Firemen's Charitable Ass'n v. Ross*, 60 F. 456, 458-59 (5th Cir. 1893), as are pilots acting within the scope of their employment duties, *see The Cachemire*, 38 F. 518, 522 (D.S.C. 1889) (citing cases). The "pre-existing duty" exception has been considerably narrowed in modern cases; for example, Coast Guard personnel performing rescue tasks in the line of duty are deemed voluntary actors whose services may generate salvage awards, *see, e.g., In re American Oil Co.*, 417 F.2d 164, 168 (5th Cir. 1969); *Frank v. United States*, 250 F.2d 178, 180 (3d Cir. 1957), *cert. denied*, 356 U.S. 962 (1958). The same is true for members of the armed forces. *See, e.g., W.E. Rippon & Son v. United States*, 348 F.2d 627, 628 (2d Cir. 1965); *Tampa Tugs and Towing, Inc. v. M/V Sandanger*, 242 F. Supp. 576, 581 (S.D. Cal. 1965).

[22] *The Camanche*, 75 U.S. (8 Wall.) 448, 477 (1869). *See Smith v. Union Oil Co. of Calif.*, 274 F. Supp. 248, 251 (W.D. Wash. 1966); *Sobonis v. Steam Tanker National Defender*, 298 F. Supp. 631, 637 (S.D.N.Y. 1969).

[23] *Sobonis v. Steam Tanker National Defender*, 298 F. Supp. 631, 637-38 (S.D.N.Y. 1969) (citing cases); *Squires v. The Ionian Leader*, 100 F. Supp. 829, 835 (D.N.J. 1951) (citing cases).

[24] 207 F.2d 60 (2d Cir. 1953).

[25] *Id.* at 63. The decision of the Third Circuit in *Spivak v. United States*, 203 F.2d 881 (3d Cir. 1953), cited by the defendant, is not to the contrary. The plaintiff in *Spivak* was a single civilian seaman, employed at a fixed salary as a kind of general factotum by the War Department in Korea shortly before war broke out in that country. The Court denied his claim for a salvage award only after it reached the factual conclusion that the services he had performed in rescuing the cargo of a distressed ship were within the scope and ordinary course of his employment. *Spivak's* presidential value has been limited to its own factual circumstances. *See Kimes v. United States*, 207 F.2d 60, 63 (2d Cir. 1953).

[26] 298 F. Supp. 631 (S.D.N.Y. 1969).

[27] *See, id* at 637 (*quoting The Sarpen*, [1916] pp. 306, 315, per PICKFORD L.J.):

> The test of voluntariness is only applicable as between the salvor and salved, and if the services be voluntary in relation to the salved, *i.e.*, not rendered by reason of any obligation towards him, it is quite immaterial that the salvor has been ordered by someone who has control of his movements to render them.

common ownership as an impediment to an award would likewise be defeated: the owner of a vessel in distress could always order other, commonly-owned vessels to the rescue, without the requirement of a salvage contract and without being required to pay any salvage award. Plainly such a result is contrary to the Congressional purpose. We hold that Captain Markakis and the crew of the Sun performed voluntary salvage service on January 10 and 11, 1977, when they rescued baggage and provisions of the Star and towed the vessel to safety.

Note

1. In *Clifford v. M/V Islander*, 751 F.2d 1, 1985 AMC 1855 (1st Cir. 1984), it was held that although the parties had not made a salvage contract, they had made an oral maritime contract for the provision of services, which was sufficient to render those services non-voluntary for the purposes of salvage reward.

However, there are views to the contrary. In *Smith v. Union Oil Company of California*, 274 F. Supp. 248, 251-252 (N.D. Calif. 1966) defendant attempted to resist a claim of "pure" salvage by asserting that the parties had arranged for contract salvage. The court rejected this contention:

> As to respondents' defense that libelants entered into a contract for the salvage services which they rendered, the law imposes a heavier burden of proof upon respondents than would apply in a non-salvage case. *See* NORRIS, SALVAGE § 160, wherein it is stated, "The salvage contract need not be in writing but the terms must be clear, definite and explicit as to the amount and that there is a mutual understanding that the services involved are in the nature of salvage." *See also* the discussion of this issue in *Kimes, supra*, and in *Lago Oil & Transport Co. Ltd. v. United States*, 218 F.2d 631 (2d Cir. 1955). Both courts placed considerable reliance on *The Camanche*, 75 U.S. 448, 477 (8 Wall.), 19 L. Ed. 397, 405 (1869), wherein the rule was set forth that "nothing short of a contract to pay a given sum for the services to be rendered, or a binding engagement to pay at all events, whether successful or unsuccessful in the enterprise, will operate to bar a meritorious claim for salvage."
>
> The alleged oral contract in this case is evidenced by the unsigned memorandum. Exhibit A133. Applying the above cited principles to the terms of the contract the court finds that respondents have sustained their burden only in so far as the contract is applied to work "in discharging the cargo ... and readying the ship for towing to Seattle." The court further finds that the work performed to and including October 23 was predominantly concerned with firefighting and controlling the flow of sea water into the engine room. The fires and the flooding were both brought under control on that date. The work performed on October 24 and thereafter was predominantly concerned with cleanup, discharge of cargo and readying the vessel for the tow to Seattle. As to the first period, respondents have not sustained their burden of proving that a salvage contract was made or ratified by libelants or their agents. The alleged contract was negotiated by Mr. Snow and Mr. Ellis. The evidence is undisputed that neither one of them considered in such negotiations the hazards to the SANTA MARIA and its cargo or the value thereof or the risks to which libelants exposed themselves. One of the fundamental purposes of the law of salvage is to encourage action such as was voluntarily undertaken by libelants. Such encouragement in this instance was in respondents' own interest as well as that of the public. As stated by First Mate Joe Itson, libelants were the only ones available to do the job. Payment of $5.72 per hour can hardly be said to be in furtherance of the policy of encouraging salvage.

The court also said that the fact that the person who renders services is under contract, even an employment contract, does not necessarily preclude a claim for pure salvage.

> While the court finds no evidence of an agreement to pay wages in all events, the court does find that libelants considered themselves employees of the company in that they believed they would be paid wages in an unspecified amount irrespective of success. The court, however, does not agree with respondents that this bars a salvage award. The law is clear that an employee who receives wages for work of a salvage nature may nevertheless be a volunteer who is entitled to a salvage award in addition thereto. The issues of this case are much the same as those raised in *Kimes v. United States*, 207 F. 2d 60 (2d Cir. 1953). The court there found the crew of the salving vessel entitled to a salvage award even though the crew had already received a base wage, overtime, supplementary overtime, a 166-2/3% war bonus and an area bonus of $5 per day. Because the crew was exposed to greater risks than were part of their normal duties the court allowed a salvage award. The court held that libelants undertook the work voluntarily in that they were under no legal duty to do so. In the case at bar the court finds no legal duty on the part of any libelants to render aid to the SANTA MARIA and that the voluntariness of libelants' services is not negated by their expectation of wages regardless of the success of the salvage operation.

2. In *Fort Myers Shell and Dredging Co. v. Barge NBC 512*, 404 F.2d 137 (5th Cir. 1968) the court held:

> The District Court's determination that Fort Myers was contractually obligated to unbeach the barges lacks adequate support in the record. By agreeing to a modification and continuation of the prior towing contract whereby it would be obligated to refloat the barges on

the beach rather than pick them up at the sea buoy, Fort Myers would have undertaken a time-consuming and extensive unbeaching operation for the same fee that had been set for a relatively simple towing job. We are unable to find sufficient evidence to indicate that such an agreement was made. The fact that a shipowner requests a salvage service and that the salvors in response furnish it, standing alone, does not create an implied contract so as to defeat a salvage claim. *See Atlantic Towing Co. v. The Caliche*, 47 F. Supp. 610, 614 (S.D. Ga. 1942).

Does it make any difference that the barges had been beached before the towing operation commenced? Fort Myers had agreed to tow, but before its tug could take control and while the barges were in control of another tug, the latter tug and barges were beached by bad weather. Fort Myers was then asked to see what it could do. Would it have made any difference if the barges had become beached while in control of Fort Myers? *See* "Note: Duty to save tow" in the section on Towage, *supra*.

3. The fact that services are rendered by a "professional" salvor does not preclude eligibility for a salvage award. *See B. V. Bureau Wijsmuller v. United States*, 702 F.2d 333, 338-339 (2d Cir. 1983) where the court at 338-39 stated:

The second element is voluntary service. Voluntary service, the *sine qua non* of marine salvage, is rendered in the absence of a legal duty or obligation. *See The Clarita and The Clara*, 90 U.S. (23 Wall.) 1, 16-17, 23 L. Ed. 146, 150 (1875); *Elrod*, 62 F. Supp. at 936. Whatever motive impels the true volunteer, be it monetary gain, humanitarian purposes or merely error, it will not detract from the status accorded him by law. Benedict, *supra*, § 68 at 6-2. Thus professional salvors—who perform their services for monetary gain—may claim salvage awards. *The Camanche*, 75 U.S. (8 Wall.) 448, 19 L. Ed. 397 (1869).

Note: Lack of Request by Owners

May a claim for salvage be made by one who renders services to a vessel without having been requested by the owner, master or other agent to do so? *Lambros Seaplane Base v. Batory*, 215 F.2d 228 (2d Cir. 1954) involved a salvage claim which arose when plaintiffs brought aboard its vessel a seaplane which had landed in the water. The pilot who asked to be "rescued" stated that he had run out of gas. The pilot was not the owner of the plane but had merely rented it from the defendant. Plaintiff's vessel was a transatlantic liner with 500 passengers aboard and was proceeding to Europe, with Southampton, England being its first port of call. The plane had landed in the water about twelve miles south of Fire Island and some fifty miles from New York. After taking the plane aboard, the vessel continued on to Southampton. Plaintiff notified defendant that it could have its plane back if it paid the expense of transporting it to the United States. When defendant failed to respond, plaintiff commenced an action to recover a salvage award.

The court first determined that a sea plane because it was designed to take off and land on water was the kind of "maritime" property to which an action in salvage would extend. It then addressed defendant's contentions that plaintiff should be denied an award because it did not request plaintiff's services, that it was unnecessary to bring the plane aboard the ship, and that it did not request nor was it necessary to carry the plane to England in order to save it.

The court stated:

It follows, we think, that Batory had a right, unrequested, to furnish salvage service to the derelict. True, there was no obligation to furnish such service. And a more limited salvage service might have been furnished by leaving the plane where it was with suitable lights and advising those concerned by wireless of her location. However, Batory was not legally required to forego more extensive service in favor of other salvors (including the owner) who might possibly, or even probably, arrive in time to save the plane,—not even in favor of salvage service by the Coast Guard without cost to the owner. *Cf.* ROBINSON ON ADMIRALTY, page 761. We are pointed to no case holding that a fragile vessel left derelict at sea and exposed to the hazard of a summer thunderstorm is not in peril enough to justify unrequested salvage service. Indeed, such a holding, we think, would be a most unwise innovation in the maritime law. We hold, rather, that Batory was entitled to take possession of the derelict and bring it to a place of safety.

Was right to salvage forfeited by carrying the plane to England instead of leaving it in safety at a nearer American port? In *Western Transportation Co. v. The Great Western*, D.C. N.D.N.Y 1862, 20 Fed. Cas. page 788, No. 17,443, the governing rule was stated as follows:

There is, however, no inflexible rule that salvors must take the property saved to the nearest convenient port, or retain the property for adjudication at the first port at which it arrives in safety. *Post v. Jones*, 19 How. 150 [15 L. Ed. 618]. In all their proceedings, they should act in good faith, and with reasonable skill and judgment; and, while they are entitled to protect their own interests by proper means, they must not forget or disregard the interests of the owners of the property saved.

See also Hartshorn v. Twenty-Five Cases of Silk, D.C.S.D.N.Y., 1841, 11 Fed. Cas. page 713, No. 6,168a. *Cf. The Sapinero*, 2 Cir., 5 F.2d 56. We think this principle as sound today as in 1862 when *The Great Western* was decided, although of course the intervening development of techniques in aid of marine shipping, such principally as wireless communication, may occasionally require a modified application of the principle.

In applying this principle it is proper and necessary to remember that amongst the factors which affect a salvage claim are the values not only of the vessel or property saved but also of the salvor vessel including the obligations under which the salvor vessel operates.[4] Time lost by a transatlantic liner, under obligation to transport some 500 passengers without avoidable delay, would obviously constitute a factor of large dimensions. And with Southampton, England her next port of destination, obviously at least several hours would have been lost if Batory had put in at some unscheduled port in which to deposit the plane in safety or even if she had stood by for the indefinite period of time required for the arrival of other salvors, whom she might have notified by wireless. In this connection it must also be remembered that having once taken possession of the plane she could not, without hazard of a damage suit, abandon the plane, at least unless forced to do so by the perils of the sea, short of the time when she should place it in a place of safety in which it would be available to the owner, subject to a libel *in rem* for salvage if desired. *Serviss v. Gerguson*, 2 Cir., 84 F. 202. There was no evidence that there was a port nearer than New York suitable for entry by a liner of Batory's dimensions. And even if it would have been feasible for her to have entered some nearer port, the Master might reasonably have expected that considerable time would be lost in finding a safe place for the deposit of the plane pending its repossession by its owner. In practical effect, the Master, under constraint to make judicious use of the vast property interests entrusted to him, was confronted with need to make an immediate choice between two alternatives, *viz.*, the removal of the plane to a place of safety at his next port of call or its abandonment coupled with notice by wireless of its location.

In the case of *The Annapolis*, decided by the Court of Privy Council in 1862, Lushington's Admiralty Reports, Vol. 1, page 355, it was said (page 375) "that it would be dangerous to hold that if salvage service be actually furnished to a ship, she cannot be called upon to pay anything unless it can be shown that she either requested or expressly accepted service. In many cases the urgency of the case would be too great to admit of previous discussion, and if a salvor were required to prove such an agreement before he could recover, it is feared that there would be much slackness in cases which most require energy and activity." The court agreed "that it is sufficient if the circumstances of the cases are such that, if an offer of service had been made, any prudent man would have accepted it." This was said as to the right of one claiming salvage on account of assistance to a ship lying at anchor in a harbor, fully manned. Here we are concerned with a derelict seaplane adrift twelve miles from shore with night approaching. We think the Master of the Batory might reasonably have believed that a prudent owner would have preferred to have its plane safe in Southampton to the hazard of destruction by a possible sudden summer squall before its salvage could be accomplished by others. So far as the evidence shows, the Master could not be sure that even with prompt notice by wireless as to the location of the place it could surely be salved by others. We find no evidence which justified an inference that the Master knew or should have known that even without intervention of a squall the plane would survive long enough to permit of salvage by others or would be without substantial value to the owner in Southampton if transported there. Clearly, we think, there was no basis for an imputation of bad faith which would preclude a recovery of salvage under the rule of the *Great Western* case, *supra*.

With these considerations in mind, upon the facts found here we hold that the Batory had a right not only to render salvage service by taking the plane aboard for removal to a place of safety but also, as an incident to the accomplishment of that proper objective, to remove the plane to Southampton, without imputation of negligence effective as a forfeiture of its salvage claim.

Note: Right of Owner to Reject Salvage Services

A salvage award may be denied if the salvor forces its services on a vessel despite rejection of them by a person with authority over the vessel. *The Indian*, 159 F. 20, 25 (5th Cir. 1908); Norris, *supra*, §§ 114-16; *see Legnos v. M/V Olga Jacob*, 498 F.2d 666, 672 (5th Cir. 1974); *Fort Myers Shell & Dredging Co. v. The Barge NBC 512*, 404 F.2d 137, 139 (5th Cir. 1968). In this case, Texas argues that it rejected the salvage services by having two laws that were then on its books: Tex. Penal Code art. 147b(3) (Vernon 1952) (repealed 1969), which required nonresidents to get a permit from the state before engaging in "any exploration or excavation in or on any ... archaeological ... site in Texas"; and Tex. Rev. Civ. Stat. Ann. art. 5421 (Vernon 1962) (repealed 1977), which authorized the Attorney General to sue anyone who had "appropriated ... any minerals or other property of value" from state lands.

We note at the outset that we can find no case where a salvage award was denied because of a constructive rejection of salvage services. The cases involve direct and unequivocal rejection, usually by the master of the distressed ship. *See, e.g., The Indian, supra*; Norris, *supra*, §§ 114-16. At the very least, constructive rejection of salvage services should bar an award only if the rejection must reasonably have been understood by the salvor.

Platoro Ltd., Inc. v. Unidentified Remains, Etc., 695 F. 2d 893, 901 (5th Cir. 1983).

---

[4] The evidence included in the appendix to appellant's brief do not show these values. However, Lambros in its libel alleges that the value of the seaplane plus the value of its loss of use thereof was $6,200. Any Gdynia in its cross-libel alleges that the value of the Batory was in excess of $7,000,000 and that in addition to 500 passengers she was heavily laden with a general cargo.

C. Property Subject to Salvage

PROVOST v. HUBER

594 F.2d 717, 1981 AMC 2999 (8th Cir. 1979)

Before GIBSON, Chief Judge, ROSS, Circuit Judge, and VAN SICKLE, District Judge

The Appellant Provost brings this timely appeal from an order of the district court which dismissed his complaint and first amended complaint for lack of subject matter jurisdiction. The action was brought under the admiralty or maritime jurisdiction of the federal courts, and sought a salvage award. The district court, in ruling upon Appellee Huber's Rule 12(b)(1) motion, found lacking a nexus with traditional maritime activity and dismissed the action upon that ground.[2]

The basic facts of this novel case are undisputed. From the allegations of the complaints (original and amended) and the affidavits submitted by the parties in connection with the motion to dismiss, it appears that Huber purchased a two-story frame house in Bayfield County, Wisconsin, with the purpose in mind of moving the structure from the mainland to a lot on Madeline Island situated in Lake Superior. Huber hired a housemover to transport the building and contents by truck-trailer over the frozen surface of Lake Superior. The move was attempted in March of 1977 and, at a point approximately three-fourths of the way to the island, the truck, trailer, house and contents broke through the ice.

While the house was partially submerged in the waters of Lake Superior, Huber was approached by an individual who represented himself to be an underwater contractor and who suggested that the structure be sunk to the bottom of the lake to preserve and protect it from ice damage until such time that it could be raised when weather permitted. Huber and his insurer agreed to the plan and the house was thereupon lowered to the lake bottom by placing sandbags on the floor.

In May of 1977 the Plaintiff and a second diver (not a party to this litigation) were approached by Mr. Edward Erickson (the underwater contractor who had lowered the structure to the lake bed). After the situation concerning the submerged house was discussed, the Plaintiff and his fellow diver agreed to assist in retrieving the building, although no specific terms of compensation were reached. Plaintiff spent about sixty hours of underwater work removing sandbags from the floor of the house. While Plaintiff was recharging his air tanks and absent from the jobsite, Erickson commenced to raise the structure. That attempt resulted in the house breaking up to the point of total destruction. Erickson retrieved substantially all of the pieces and disposed of them in a landfill at a cost of $500.00 to the Defendant and his insurer.

Prior to the move in March of 1977, the Defendant secured insurance on the structure (but not the contents) in the sum of $20,000.00. It is unclear from the record, but we may safely assume for purposes of this decision, that the insurer paid the full amount of the policy limits.

Some time after the unsuccessful attempt to retrieve the house intact from the bottom of Lake Superior, the Plaintiff billed the Defendant for $500.00 for his services rendered. The bill remains unpaid, and this suit claiming a maritime salvage of $10,000.00 followed.

As stated above, the district court dismissed Plaintiff's action for lack of a nexus with traditional maritime activity. This Court recently, in *Shows v. Harber*, 575 F.2d 1253 (1978) determined the necessity of such nexus in maritime cases. The Supreme Court has established that proposition in tort actions brought under the admiralty jurisdiction, *Executive Jet Aviation, Inc. v. Cleveland*, 409 U.S. 249, 93 S. Ct. 493, 34 L. Ed. 2d 454 (1972), and the same has been fixed for salvage cases, *Cope v. Vallette Dry Dock Co.*, 119 U.S. 625, 7 S. Ct. 336, 30 L. Ed. 501 (1887).

In *Cope* the Supreme Court, at page 627, 7 S. Ct. at page 337, rejected a salvage claim in connection with a floating drydock on the basis that "no structure that is not a ship or vessel is a subject of salvage." "Vessel" is defined at 1 U.S.C., Section 3, as "every description of water craft or other artificial contrivance used, or capable of being

---

[2] The district court, in considering the Defendant's Rule 12(b)(1) motion to dismiss, reached his decision after "... a full review of the record of the case, including the Amended Complaint, the accompanying affidavits, and the memoranda and arguments of counsel,..."

used, as a means of transportation on water." The short answer to Appellant's assertion that the tractor-trailer being used to carry the house was a vessel within the meaning of maritime law because it was transporting the structure over water is that such transportation was on ice, not water, and that immediately upon the transporter breaking through the ice, it sank to the bottom of the lake. By no stretch of the imagination can we equate a multi-wheeled device, designed and built for the purpose of transportation over a hard, defined surface such as roads, highways, and even ice with a vessel or ship as those terms are used in maritime law.

The Appellant argues that even if the transporter cannot be considered a vessel, the house is still the proper subject of salvage, thereby bringing this action with the admiralty jurisdiction of the federal courts. In support of this assertion the Appellant cites, *Inter alia, Broere v. Two Thousand One Hundred Thirty-Three Dollars*, 72 F. Supp. 115 (E.D.N.Y. 1947), wherein the court found that money found on a human body floating on navigable waters was a proper subject of salvage. The distinguishing feature found in *Broere*, however, and the determinant for finding admiralty jurisdiction, was the fact that, prior to his death, the individual concerned had embarked upon a maritime adventure. In the instant case we do not and cannot find that, prior to breaking through the ice and submerging, the house had embarked upon a "maritime" adventure. In other words, circumstances attending the placement of property in or upon navigable waters must be considered and are decisive when dealing with the question of admiralty jurisdiction and salvage. The fact that certain property may be the proper subject of salvage, standing alone, does not confer admiralty jurisdiction upon the federal courts. A nexus with traditional maritime activities must still be shown.

We recognize that cases decided since *Cope, supra*, have broadened the somewhat restrictive view therein enunciated by the Supreme Court as to what may properly be the subject of maritime salvage. For example, the Second Circuit concluded in *Lambros Seaplane Base v. The Batory*, 215 F.2d 228 (1954), that a seaplane down at sea is subject to the maritime law of salvage. *Lambros* is distinguishable on the ground that a seaplane as opposed to a wheeled land vehicle is designed and used for taking off of, flying over, and landing upon a water surface. Also, the district court in *Colby v. Todd Packing Co.*, 77 F. Supp. 956, 12 Alaska 1 (D. Alaska, 1948), allowed a salvage claim involving floating fish trap frames found adrift. The distinguishing feature in *Colby* is obvious: Fish trap frames are designed to float upon and be transported across a water surface.

We conclude, upon the facts present in this case, that the district court was correct in dismissing the action for lack of a nexus with traditional maritime activities.

Affirmed.

Note

G. Gilmore & C. Black, The Law of Admiralty 538-540 (2d ed. 1975) take a contrary position.

E. Salvage Awards

THE BLACKWALL
77 U.S. 1, 19 L. Ed. 870 (1870)

APPEAL from the Circuit Court of the United States for California; the case as it appeared from the opinion of the District Court, from which it had been taken to the court below was this:

About 4 o'clock on the morning of the 24th of August, 1867, the British ship Blackwall, then at anchor in the harbor of San Francisco, was discovered to be on fire. Shortly afterwards the alarm was communicated to the shore, and the fire department of the city called out. As soon as the cause of the alarm was ascertained, the chief engineer of the fire department, with an officer of the harbor police, proceeded to the steam-tug Goliah, then lying at one of the city's wharves, and belonging to an incorporated towing company of San Francisco, and having aroused the person in charge, requested him to "fire up" without delay, in order that the engines might be conveyed on the tug to the burning vessel. This, after a few moments' hesitation, arising it was plain from reluctance to act without orders, he proceeded to do. Messengers were despatched to the captain and engineer of the tug, who were asleep at their homes on shore, and every effort made to get steam on the tug as quickly as possible. The captain and engineer were aroused, and at once repaired to the wharf. It being found impracticable for the tug to go into the slip where the fire engines lay, two of the latter were brought around to the wharf where the tug was, and taken across the deck of a steamboat which lay between the wharf and the tug, and so on to the tug with promptitude and skill. About 6 o'clock the tug, with two engines on board, together with the firemen, &c., attached to them, moved from the wharf, and in a few minutes were alongside the ship. The fire had by this time made considerable progress. The house on deck between the fore and mizzen masts was on fire, and the flames were mounting nearly half way to the tops. The ship was also burning between decks, where the fire first originated. The officers and crew, though assisted by a party from the United States ship Lawrence, *having found all attempts to subdue the flames abortive, had desisted from further efforts, and had a few moments before the Goliah arrived, left the vessel with their effects in small boats.* Without speedy assistance the total destruction of the ship and cargo was inevitable. The measures of the firemen and officers of the tug were taken with great skill and energy. The hose of the engines was charged, as the tug approached the vessel, and as soon as she was near enough, four streams were directed upon her. The tug, without hesitation or delay, was made fast alongside the Blackwall. The firemen almost instantly mounted her rails, went thence to her forecastle, and from thence to her deck, sweeping the latter with four powerful streams, by which the fire was speedily controlled. They then descended to her between decks, and in a little more than half an hour the flames were entirely extinguished. Her anchor was then weighed by the advice of the captain of the tug, and the vessel was towed to certain flats near one of the city's wharves. The tug was then dismissed, and the engines were taken to the shore and landed.

As to the degree of danger incurred by the tug there was some conflict of testimony. That she was promptly and boldly laid alongside the burning vessel was undisputed. That she caught fire once or twice was proved, although this fire was instantly extinguished, and with the powerful appliances she had on board the danger from this cause was perhaps not great.

The chief risk incurred by her was from the falling of the masts or spars of the vessel. An accident of this kind, had it occurred, might have proved disastrous to the tug, and perhaps to many on board. The danger was not supposed to arise from the burning of the shrouds, for they were of wire, but from the fact of the mast seeming consumed by the fire, which had been burning between decks for several hours. As a matter of fact, it was found on subsequent examination that the mast was but little burnt, and was in no danger of falling. And the chief engineer of the fire department testified that he became convinced very soon after getting on board, that all fears of the masts falling were groundless. These fears were, however, entertained and expressed, not only by the officers of the tug, but by the pilot, and by the mate of the ship, so much so that axes were got in readiness to cut away the shrouds on the portside of the vessel, in order that the mast might fall to the other side.

It is also to be observed that the tug encountered the risk of the possible existence of explosive substances on board the vessel, and also, though this risk was slight, that of her own machinery or that of the fire engines becoming unserviceable, while she lay alongside the vessel.

The tug, however, was not the sole salvor. Without her assistance indeed the fire engines would have been powerless to save the ship, but without these engines on the other hand, the tug's aid would have been just as ineffectual.

In this state of facts the towing corporation, which was owner of the tug, *and* one Clark, her master, filed a libel against the ship and cargo, in the District Court at San Francisco, for salvage. The libel alleged that the ship was on fire; that the cargo as well as the ship was in great danger, and that both would have been destroyed had it not been for the exertions of the steamtug, her master and crew; that the master and crew went with the steamtug to the assistance of the ship, and that they succeeded, after great trouble and great risk to the tug, in quelling and subduing the flames, and that they then towed the ship to a place of safety. *The fire department was no party to the libel*: and in his testimony the master stated that his name was used in the libel only for the company owning the tug, and that he himself claimed no interest. The value of the ship and cargo, so far as saved, was $100,000; the value of the tug about $50,000. The District Court decreed "that libellants do have and recover of the claimants $10,000 with their costs;" and this decree having been affirmed in the Circuit Court, the owners of the Blackwall now appealed to this court.

* * *

Mr. Justice CLIFFORD delivered the opinion of the court

Salvage is claimed by the libellants, as owners of the steamtug Goliah, for services rendered by the steamtug, her master and crew, on the twenty-fourth of August, 1867, in saving the ship Blackwall and her cargo, then lying at anchor in the harbor of San Francisco. They allege that the ship was on fire; that the cargo as well as the ship was in great danger, and that both would have been destroyed had it not been for the exertions of the steamtug, her master and crew; that the master and crew went with the steamtug to the assistance of the ship, and that they succeeded, after great trouble and great risk to the tug, in quelling and subduing the flames, and that they then towed the ship to a place of safety.

Information that the ship was on fire was communicated to the master of the steamtug by one of the deck-hands of the tug, and he went immediately to the slip where she was lying, in order to give directions to the men on board to kindle up the fires and put on steam; but he found, on arriving there, that one of the harbor police had been there before him, and that he had made a similar request, and that the firemen of the tug had started the fires for the purpose of putting on steam.

Two persons were sent to the ship, which was lying at anchor in the harbor, some seven or eight hundred yards from the wharves, to see if there was any chance to extinguish the flames, and they reported that the ship might be saved. She was an English ship of twelve hundred tons burden, and she was ready to sail for her port of destination with a cargo consisting of thirty-eight thousand five hundred and one sacks of wheat, valued at sixty-thousand dollars, and she was lying at anchor where the water was eight or ten fathoms in depth. They discovered the fire at four o'clock in the morning, and at six o'clock, or a quarter past that hour, they proceeded to the ship in the steamtug, having previously taken on board two steam fire-engines, each weighing five tons, with the engineer and several firemen belonging to each engine, and the chief engineer of the fire department, making twenty persons, including the master and crew of the steamtug. Both engines were well supplied with hose, and they had on board a considerable supply of fresh water. When the steamtug reached the ship those on board had become discouraged, and there were ten or twelve boats around the ship taking off the crew, but the boats were utterly unable to do anything towards extinguishing the fire.

Commanded, as all on board the steamtug were, by her master, their first act, after running alongside, was to fasten a stern-line to the main-chains of the ship, so as to lie across the tide on the port side of the ship. At that time the fire seemed to be between decks, but the houses of the ship on deck were also on fire. Great apprehension was felt lest the foremast should fall, as it was on fire between decks, and the flames had extended to the deck and twenty feet up the mast. Her bulwarks were also on fire, and the master of the tug deemed it necessary to cut away the port-rigging attached to that mast to prevent it from falling across the steamtug. They put the engines in operation promptly, putting four streams of water on to the ship, and by those means extinguished the fire in an hour, the firemen working the engines under the command of their respective engineers. Some of the persons present advised the master of the steamtug to unshackle and slip the anchor; but he insisted that it could be saved, and it was hoisted on board the ship by the windlass.

Promptness and efficiency characterized the conduct of all engaged in performing the service throughout the transaction, and the steamtug, as soon as the fire was subdued and extinguished, took the ship in tow and proceeded with her to the adjacent flats, and left her there in safety in charge of her master and crew.

I.

Certain preliminary objections are made by the appellants to the maintenance of the suit, which will be first considered before proceeding to examine the merits. Those objections are as follows: (1.) That the master, having no interest in the claim, is improperly joined in the suit. (2.) That the libellants have no just claim to compensation, as the salvage service was performed by the members of the fire department. (3.) That the service having been performed by the members of the fire department, in pursuance of a public duty, they are not entitled to any compensation as salvage. (4.) That the decree, inasmuch as it is joint, in favor of the master as well as the owners of the steamtug, is erroneous, because the master makes no claim to recover any compensation for his services.

1. Salvage suits are frequently promoted by the master alone, in behalf of himself and the owners and crew, or in behalf of the owners and crew, or the owners alone, without making any claim in his own behalf, and the practice has never led to any practical difficulty, as the whole subject, in case of controversy, is within the control of the court. Much examination was given to the question as to proper parties, in a salvage suit decided at the last term, in a case where the owners of the steamer rendering the service were an incorporated company, and by reference to the authorities cited in the opinion of the court in that case it will be found that the suit is frequently promoted in the name of the master, or of the company and master, as in this case.[a]

Many other cases of like import might be referred to, but it must suffice to say that the court is of the opinion that the suit is well brought.[b]

2. Service undoubtedly was performed by the members of the fire department; but it is a mistake to suppose that service was not also performed by the steamtug, as it is clear that without the aid of the steamtug and the services of her master and crew the members of the fire company would never have been able to reach the ship with their engines and necessary apparatus, or to have subdued the flames and extinguished the fire. Useful services of any kind rendered to a vessel or her cargo, exposed to any impending danger and imminent peril of loss or damage, may entitle those who render such services to salvage reward.

Persons assisting to extinguish a fire on board a ship, or assisting to tow a ship from a dock where she is in imminent danger of catching fire, are as much entitled to salvage compensation as persons who render assistance to prevent a ship from being wrecked, or in securing a wreck, or protecting the cargo of a stranded vessel.[c]

Salvage is the compensation allowed to persons by whose assistance a ship or her cargo has been saved, in whole or in part, from impending peril on the sea, or in recovering such property from actual loss, as in cases of shipwreck, derelict, or recapture. Success is essential to the claim; as if the property is not saved, or if it perish, or in case of capture if it is not retaken, no compensation can be allowed. More than one set of salvors, however, may contribute to the result, and in such cases all who engaged in the enterprise and materially contributed to the saving of the property, are entitled to share in the reward which the law allows for such meritorious service, and in proportion to the nature, duration, risk, and value of the service rendered.[d]

Salvors are not deprived of a remedy because another set of salvors neglect or refuse to join in the suit, nor will such neglect or refusal benefit the libellants by giving them any claim to a larger compensation, as the non-prosecution by one set of salvors enures, not to the libellants prosecuting the claim, but to the owners of the property saved.[e]

Cases may also be found where co-salvors who neglected to appear and become parties to the suit until the decree was pronounced, were allowed to petition the court for such compensation out of the fund in the registry of the court, and where their claim received a favorable adjudication.[f]

3. Important service unquestionably was performed by the members of the fire department, but as they are not parties to this suit it is not necessary of determine whether they would, under the circumstances of this case, be entitled to a salvage reward. Pilots, under some circumstances, may become salvors, and cases may be imagined

---

[a] *The Camanche*, 8 Wallace, 470.

[b] *The Commander-in-Chief*, 1 Wallace, 51; *Houseman v. The Schooner North Carolina*, 15 Paters, 49; *The Propeller Commerce*, 1 Black, 574; *McKinlay v. Morrish*, 21 Howard, 343; 2 Parsons on Shipping, 370.

[c] *The Rosalie*, 1 Spink, 188; *Eastern Monarch*, Lushington, 81; *The Tees, Ib.* 505; Williams & Bruce, Admiralty Practice, 92.

[d] *Norris v. Island City*, 1 Clifford, 220; *The Bartley*, Swabey, 198; *Pride of Canada*, Browning & Lushington, 209; 2 Parsons on Shipping, 279.

[e] *Ship Charles Newberry*, 329; 2 Parsons on Shipping, 301.

[f] *Henry Ewbank*, 1 Sumner, 400; Roberts on Admiralty, 85; *The Camanche*, 8 Wallace, 476.

where firemen perhaps might come within the same rule, but the question not being before the court no opinion is expressed upon the subject.

* * *

5. Objection is also made that the owners of a vessel cannot promote a salvage suit unless they participate in the salvage service; or if they may promote such a suit, that they cannot participate in the reward decreed for the salvage service except for the risk and damage to which their property was exposed in rendering the salvage service. Such an objection was made in the case of *The Camanche*, before cited, but the court overruled the objection, and that ruling is adopted and applied in this case.

Beyond doubt remuneration for salvage service is awarded to the owners of vessels on account of the danger to which the service exposes their property, and the risk which they run of loss in suffering their vessels to engage in such perilous undertakings, but it is not admitted that the amount of the allowance must be reduced on that ground. Corporations, as the owners of vessels, whether sail-vessels or steamers, may promote a salvage suit, and it makes no difference in that respect whether they were present or absent, provided it appears that the vessel employed was well manned and equipped for the service.[g]

II.

Nothing remains to be considered but the question whether the amount awarded in the court below to the libellants was correct. Steam vessels are always considered as entitled to a liberal reward, not only because the service is usually rendered by a costly instrumentality, but because the service is in general rendered with greater promptitude and is of a more effectual character. Courts of admiralty usually consider the following circumstances as the main ingredients in determining the amount of the reward to be decreed for a salvage service: (1.) The labor expended by the salvors in rendering the salvage service. (2.) The promptitude, skill, and energy displayed in rendering the service and saving the property. (3.) The value of the property employed by the salvors in rendering the service, and the danger to which such property was exposed. (4.) The risk incurred by the salvors in securing the property from the impending peril. (5.) The value of the property saved. (6.) The degree of danger from which the property was rescued.

Compensation as salvage is not viewed by the admiralty courts merely as pay, on the principle of a quantum meruit, or as a remuneration PRO OPERE ET LABORE, but as a reward given for perilous services, voluntarily rendered, and as an inducement to seamen and others to embark in such undertakings to save life and property.[h]

Public policy encourages the hardy and adventurous mariner to engage in these laborious and sometimes dangerous enterprises, and with a view to withdraw from him every temptation to embezzlement and dishonesty, the law allows him, in case he is successful, a liberal compensation.[i]

Minute description of the circumstances attending the service rendered by the libellants is given in the opinion of the district judge, which is exhibited in full in the record, and we refer to that as a satisfactory statement of all the material facts in the case, and we concur with him in the conclusion, that without speedy assistance the total destruction of the ship and cargo was inevitable; that the measures for relief taken by the officers of the steamtug, and by the firemen, were characterized by great skill and energy, but the repetition of the details of those measures beyond what has already been stated, is unnecessary. Suffice it to say the flames were extinguished in an hour or less, and the property to the value of one hundred thousand dollars, including vessel and cargo, was saved. Success attended their efforts, and it is evident that the services were in a high degree meritorious, as a total loss of the ship and cargo must have been the consequence of any considerable additional delay. Those who embarked in the enterprise incurred considerable danger from the fire, in laying alongside of the burning vessel, and also from the risk that the mast would fall in consequence of the fire between decks. Dangers of the kind were apparent, and there were others apprehended which proved not to be real.

---

[g] *Island City*, 1 Black, 121; S.C., 1 Clifford, 210, 219, 221; Roberts's Admiralty, 104.
[h] Williams & Bruce, Admiralty Practice, 116; 2 Parsons on Shipping, 292.
[i] *Island City*, 1 Clifford, 228.

Viewed in the light of all the circumstances, as they are exhibited in the record, our conclusion is that the amount allowed is no more than a just salvage compensation for the entire service performed by the firemen and the steamtug, her officers and crew, but it must be remembered that the libellants, to wit, the steamtug, her officers and crew, were not the sole salvors, and it is clear that the sum decreed is for the whole service. Whether the fire department might or might not have been joined in the libel is not a question in this case. They were not made parties to the libel, and consequently their claim, if any, was not before the court, and the decree must be reversed on that ground.

Our conclusion is that a moiety of the amount allowed as salvage belongs to the libellants, and we express no opinion whether the other moiety may or may not be claimed by the fire department; but if not, then it enures to the shipowners.

DECREE REVERSED, and the cause REMANDED, with directions to enter a decree for the libellants in the sum of five thousand dollars, with costs, in the District and Circuit Courts, and with interest from the date of the former decree.

MARGATE SHIPPING COMPANY v. M/V J.A. ORGERON

143 F.3d 976 (5th Cir. 1998)

[During a severe tropical storm off the Florida coast, the M/V Cherry Valley, an oil tanker belonging to Margate Shipping Co., rescued a barge, the Poseidon, containing a valuable external fuel tank (ET-70) for NASA's space shuttle. The district court awarded Margate approximately $6.4 million in salvage. The United States appeals only as to the amount of the award.]

E. GRADY JOLLY, Circuit Judge:

* * *

II

* * *

On July 9, after a brief bench trial, Judge Duval read his findings of fact and conclusions of law into the record. In a reasoned oral ruling, he found that, based on the entirety of the evidence, Margate was entitled to a salvage award equal to 12.5% of the value of the salved property, Poseidon and ET-70.

In reaching this figure, Judge Duval relied on the six traditional salvage factors first announced[8] in *The Blackwall*, 77 U.S. (10 Wall.) 1, 14, 19 L.Ed. 870 (1869). He determined that the facts of the case pointed to the highest possible award under each of the factors, and chose what he considered to be a high percentage of a high salved value to reflect this circumstance. Judge Duval also considered the application of a seventh factor, the "salvors' skill and effort in preventing or minimizing damage to the environment," as announced in *Trico Marine Operators, Inc. v. Dow Chemical Co.*, 809 F.Supp. 440, 443 (E.D.La.1992), but ultimately concluded that it was not applicable to the case. He did consider the risk of environmental liability incurred by Cherry Valley under the rubric of the traditional factors, however.

With regard to ET-70, Judge Duval determined that it was specialized property without a market value, and therefore most appropriately appraised at its "replacement cost." This value, he found, was the production cost of ET-71, $51,387,000, because ET-71 was the likely "replacement" of ET-70. In making this finding, Judge Duval explicitly rejected the government's argument for a $19 million replacement cost based on the withdrawn 1992 option, calling it "much too speculative." He also rejected Margate's argument for a $92 million "cost-accounting" valuation.

---

[8] And, interestingly, last announced as well. *The Blackwall* contains the most recent bit of guidance that the Supreme Court has deigned to give on the subject of the calculation of salvage awards.

Combining this $51 million value for ET-70 with the $2 million stipulated value of Poseidon, Judge Duval declared a total award of $6,406,440 based on the 12.5% figure. He noted in the alternative that, even if the value of ET-70 were only $19 million as the United States claimed, the award would be the same as he would adjust the percentage accordingly. On July 12, final judgment was entered for Margate in the amount of $6,406,440. The United States appeals the amount of this award.

III

Because of the fact-specific nature of the calculation of a salvage award, "the amount allowed is to be decided by the district court in its sound discretion." *Allseas Maritime, S.A. v. M/V Mimosa*, 812 F.2d 243, 246 (5th Cir.1987). "[A]n award will be altered only if it was based upon incorrect principles of law or misapprehension of the facts or it is either so excessive or so inadequate as to indicate an abuse of discretion." *Id.* This standard of appellate review is a time-honored and integral part of American maritime law, and has changed little since its infancy. *See, e.g., Hobart v. Drogan*, 35 U.S. (10 Pet.) 108, 119, 9 L.Ed. 363 (1836) (Story, J.) ("[T]his court is not in the habit of revising such decrees as to the amount of salvage, unless upon some clear and palpable mistake or gross over-allowance of the court below."); *Oelwerke Teutonia v. Erlanger & Galinger*, 248 U.S. 521, 524, 39 S.Ct. 180, 180, 63 L.Ed. 399 (1919) (Holmes, J.) ("Unless there has been some violation of principle or clear mistake, appeals to this Court concerning the amount of the allowance are not encouraged."); 3A MARTIN J. NORRIS, BENEDICT ON ADMIRALTY § 311 (7th ed. 1997) ("An appellate court is, generally speaking, loath to change a salvage award."). We keep this well-hewn principle firmly in mind as we embark upon the somewhat more intensive investigations necessitated by the instant case.

IV

An award of salvage is generally appropriate when property is successfully and voluntarily rescued from marine peril. *The Sabine*, 101 U.S. 384, 25 L.Ed. 982 (1880). As Justice Marshall noted long ago, this rule is peculiar to maritime law, and utterly at variance with terrene common law. *Mason v. The Blaireau*, 6 U.S. (2 Cranch) 240, 266, 2 L.Ed. 266 (1804) (Marshall, J.) (although it is true that, when property on land exposed to grave peril is saved by a volunteer, no remuneration is given, "[l]et precisely the same service, at precisely the same hazard, [b]e rendered at sea, and a very ample reward will be bestowed in the courts of justice"). Because of the peculiar dangers of sea travel, public policy has long been held to favor a legally enforced reward in this limited setting, to promote commerce and encourage the preservation of valuable resources for the good of society. *See B.V. Bureau Wijsmuller v. United States*, 702 F.2d 333, 337 (2d Cir.1983) ("The law of salvage originated to preserve property and promote commerce.") (citing *Seven Coal Barges*, 21 F. Cas. 1096, 1097 (C.C.D.Ind.1870) (No. 12,677) ("The very object of the law of salvage is to promote commerce and trade, and the general interests of the country, by preventing the destruction of property.")).

In this case, there can obviously be no dispute that the basic elements supporting a salvage award are present, and the United States has expressly conceded that Margate is entitled to some award. As noted, the question for this court is simply how high that award should be.

The district court traditionally determines the amount of a salvage award according to the six *Blackwall* factors.[9] *Allseas*, 812 F.2d at 246 & n. 2. They are (in order of original listing):

1. The labor expended by the salvors in rendering the salvage service.
2. The promptitude, skill, and energy displayed in rendering the service and saving the property.
3. The value of the property employed by the salvors in rendering the service, and the danger to which such property was exposed.
4. The risk incurred by the salvors in securing the property from the impending peril.
5. The value of the property saved.
6. The degree of danger from which the property was rescued.

---

[9] At least in theory. Some commentators have said that the district court traditionally "pull[s] an arbitrary figure out of the air." GRANT GILMORE & CHARLES L. BLACK, JR., THE LAW OF ADMIRALTY 563 (Foundation 2d ed.1975).

The Blackwall, 77 U.S. (10 Wall.) 1, 14, 19 L.Ed. 870 (1869) (Clifford, J.). Although old, "[t]hese guidelines have weathered the storms of the past century." *St. Paul Marine Transport Corp. v. Cerro Sales Corp.*, 505 F.2d 1115, 1120 (9th Cir.1974).

In this case, the district court made the following findings under the factors, listed here in order of the court's assessment of their importance to the calculation of an award:

1. (*Blackwall* 6.) Poseidon and ET-70 were in imminent danger of complete loss.
2. (*Blackwall* 5.) The combined value of Poseidon and ET-70 was $53,387,000.
3. (*Blackwall* 4.) The salvors incurred extremely high risk in securing Poseidon and ET-70, both as to loss of their ship and lives and as to the creation of substantial environmental liability in the event of an oil spill.
4. (*Blackwall* 2.) The salvors displayed extremely high promptitude, skill, and energy in rescuing Poseidon and ET-70 by virtue of their daring and successful seamanship under very difficult conditions.
5. (*Blackwall* 3.) The value of Cherry Valley was $7.5 million.
6. (*Blackwall* 1.) The salvors expended two and one-third days of labor in rendering the salvage service.

As noted, the district court determined that each factor indicated the highest possible award, and it chose 12.5% of the salved value as an appropriate figure.

The United States makes three basic challenges to the district court's analysis. First, it argues that the court erred in its general application of the *Blackwall* factors, by giving too much weight to the value of the salved property, by counting the potential for environmental liability as risk to the salvors, and by using a percentage of the salved value ultimately to fix the award. Second, even assuming that the district court made a correct legal interpretation of the factors, the United States argues that the district court clearly erred in its valuation of ET-70. Finally, even assuming that the district court made a correct legal interpretation of the *Blackwall* factors and properly valued ET-70, the United States argues that the court nonetheless abused its discretion in picking such a high percentage and generally making such a large award in this case. We address each argument in turn.

A

To address properly the United States's first contention, it is necessary to excavate the somewhat obscure foundations of the *Blackwall* rule. As many commentators have noted, the sense and contours of the factors are less than plainly engraved upon their face.[10] In this case, however, the United States squarely asks us to decide whether the particular interpretation and application adopted by the district court comports with the factors' essential meaning. In order for us to answer this question, we must first ascertain what purpose the factors serve.

1

Maritime salvage is as old and hoary a doctrine as may be found in the Anglo-American law. Since time immemorial, the mariner who acted voluntarily to save property from peril on the high seas has been entitled to a reward. This simple rule has been an integral part of maritime commerce in the western world since the western world was civilized.

Simple in principle, in the many centuries of its existence, the law of salvage has become encrusted with a multitude of court-created doctrinal complexities; the *Blackwall* factors are merely the most prominent example of this phenomenon. As modern scholarship has taught us, these legal barnacles are the natural and desirable results of the common law process. Court by court and case by case, the law of salvage has been steadily honed to ever greater levels of efficiency over the years, with the resultant rules serving as a convenient shorthand for the complex calculations of compiled

---

[10] *See, e.g.*, GILMORE & BLACK at 559 (noting that the traditional "recitation of Justice Clifford's six 'ingredients' [really just] serves the useful purpose of indicating that the variables are so many and so incapable of exact measurement that it will probably be fruitless for either party to take an appeal merely on the ground that the award was incorrectly computed"). As we shall see, we ultimately take a somewhat more sanguine view of the rationality of the factors as a legal rule.

experience. In examining the underlying logic of the *Blackwall* factors, we do not take lightly their role in summarizing this most succinct and practical of legal processes. Still, in the light of the United States's challenge in the instant case, we think that this is an appropriate time for the underlying rationale of Justice Clifford's venerable factors to be formally recognized.

2

Fortunately, the principles underlying the *Blackwall* factors have not escaped the attention of our most prominent modern scholars. *See* William M. Landes & Richard A. Posner, *Salvors, Finders, Good Samaritans, and Other Rescuers: An Economic Study of Law and Altruism*, 7 J. Leg. Stud. 83 (1978). Beginning with our first principle that the law of salvage seeks to preserve society's resources, they explain that "the purpose of [court-granted] salvage awards is to encourage rescues in settings of high transaction costs by simulating the conditions and outcomes of a competitive market." *Id.* at 100. In an ideal world, every meeting of salvor and salvee would result in a freely negotiated contract for salvage services priced at a competitive level. *Id.* at 89. In the real world, however, most meetings of salvor and salvee cannot be resolved in this fashion.

To accommodate this reality, the law of salvage aims to create a post- hoc solution that will induce the parties to save the ship without first agreeing on terms. *Id.* at 100. As Justice Clifford himself noted, "[c]ompensation as salvage is ... viewed by the admiralty courts ... as a reward given for perilous services, voluntarily rendered, and as an inducement to seamen and others to embark in such undertakings to save life and property." *The Blackwall*, 77 U.S. at 14 (emphasis added).

In order properly to induce the salvor (and salvee) to act, however, the law must provide for a proper and reasonable salvage award, one that gives neither the salvor too little incentive to do the salvage properly, nor the salvee too little reason to care if his property is saved. Landes & Posner, 7 J. Leg. Stud. at 102. By definition, this "efficient" fee is the one that would have been reached by the parties through voluntary negotiation in an open and competitive market, and its value will depend on a number of factual considerations. *Id.* By far the most important of these considerations, however, will be the cost to potential salvors of performing the service and the benefit to the salvee of it being performed; obviously, no voluntary salvor would be willing to perform a salvage for less than it would cost him to do it, just as no salvee would agree to pay more for a salvage than the loss he could thereby avoid. *Id.* In a voluntary agreement between salvor and salvee, therefore, as in any agreement between arm's-length parties in any context, the twin considerations of cost and benefit will form the poles of negotiation between which any fair bargain must be struck. Should the gap between cost and benefit prove illusory, as when the costs of the service outweigh the benefits to be derived, then no agreement will be possible, and the parties must go their separate ways.

With this background in mind, it becomes immediately apparent that the *Blackwall* factors represent an explicit guide for the court to use in measuring these two most significant considerations for voluntary negotiation in the salvage context. *Id.* at 101-04; *see also Allseas*, 812 F.2d at 246 ("the[ ] factors guide the trial court in fulfilling the public policy behind salvage awards"). Labor expended by the salvors (1.), their promptitude and skill (2.), value of the salving property (3.), risk to the salvors (4.), and risk to the salved property (6.)[14] are all direct or indirect measures of the actual cost to the salvor of performing the salvage in question, which should in turn be at least indicative of the costs that would have prevailed. Correspondingly, value of the salved property (5.) and risk to the salved property (6.) are measures of the benefit that the salvage has conferred on the salvee. By giving the court a framework in which to analyze cost and benefit in the salvage context, the *Blackwall* factors plainly intend to guide it in a rational process of determining and weighing the costs and benefits of the particular transaction so that the award chosen will give the proper inducement to the saving of life and property.

---

[14] Because the salvor gets nothing for an unsuccessful rescue, *see The Sabine*, 101 U.S. at 384, one of his legitimate costs is that risk. To even things out, the salvor will want to receive a premium in the instances where he is successful. *See* Landes & Posner, 7 J. Leg. Stud. at 101. Although not of particular relevance to this case, this circumstance is reflected in Justice Clifford's well known statement that salvage is not to be calculated "merely as pay, on the principle of a quantum meruit, or as a remuneration pro opere et labore." *The Blackwall*, 77 U.S. at 14.

3

With this rationale in mind, we turn to the specifics of the United States's initial argument. There are three parts, all revolving around a core contention that the district court erred in its general assessment and application of the *Blackwall* factors. Essentially, the United States argues that the court erred: (a) by giving too much weight to the value of the salved property; (b) by counting the potential for environmental liability as risk to the salvors; and (c) by using a percentage of the salved value ultimately to fix the award. We address each point in turn.

(a)

The United States first complains that the district court gave too much weight to the fifth factor—value of the salved property—by ranking it second in its assessment of the considerations bearing upon an award. In the light of our just-concluded explication of the function of that factor, this contention is readily seen to be wholly lacking in merit.

As the principal measure of the benefit of the salvage to the salvee, the fifth is clearly one of the most important of the *Blackwall* factors, and must be accorded substantial deference in the calculation of any award. As our above discussion begins to clarify, salvage awards are not based on the altruistic principle of good samaritanism—that virtue is its own inducement and its own reward. To paraphrase and distill its many distinguished commentators, the very object of the law of salvage is to provide an economic inducement to seamen and others to save property for the good of society by bestowing a fitting reward for their services in the courts of justice. It is profit, not principle, that is the driving force behind the law of salvage, and the question for the court is simply what amount of profit is fitting in the case before it. The general economic reality is simply that, the greater the value of the threatened property, the greater the potential loss, and, consequently, the more the salvee would be willing to pay to save that property from destruction. To approximate properly the incentive that the salvee himself would offer, it follows that the law of salvage must generally grant its highest awards where the property has highest value (assuming the other factors remain constant).[15] *See* Landes & Posner, 7 J. Leg. Stud. at 103-04.[16]

In setting the price for the salvage service, therefore, the court must consider—and consider primarily—the benefit that the service conferred on the recipient. In a case like the one before us, where the benefits of the salvage are numerically so far in excess of the costs—that is, the value of the property so high and the risk of loss so great—this primary consideration becomes dispositive. We are therefore confident that the district court did not overly emphasize the fifth factor in its analysis in this case, and are skeptical that an overemphasis would have been possible. *See also Plataro Ltd. v. The Unidentified Remains of a Vessel, Her Cargo, Tackle, and Furniture, in Cause of Salvage, Civil and Maritime,* 695 F.2d 893, 904 n. 16 (5th Cir.1983); Norris § 237; Gilmore & Black at 560 (all ranking the factors as the district court did here, with the sixth and fifth factors being the first and second most important, respectively).

(b)

The United States next argues that the district court erred by counting the risk of environmental liability as risk to the salvors under the fourth factor, when it should more properly have counted against them in some way. There is no merit to this contention either.

---

[15] Indeed, the only one of the factors that can arguably be said to carry greater weight in this analysis is, as the district court correctly concluded, the sixth—risk to the salved property—for it is the other component of benefit conferred (i.e., the greater or lesser the threat of loss, the greater or lesser the benefit, and, consequently, the greater or lesser the price for the salvage service). Where, as here, the risk is essentially conceded to have been a 100 percent chance of total loss, the value of the salved property obviously takes on added significance in measuring benefit.

[16] To those who would generally emphasize the cost factors over benefit, we can only respond that no seller truly operates on the principle of selling at cost; a seller is induced to provide his goods or services by the opportunity for profit. The strong influence of benefit (as determined by the value of the property and the risk of loss) will often allow the salvor to extract a significant amount of profit in a voluntary transaction, and the law of salvage must reflect this circumstance, because it serves the very purpose of the law of salvage to provide the correct amount of incentive for the saving of property in every instance.

As just discussed, the fourth factor is intended to provide a direct measure of some of the salvor's actual salvage costs. In this context, there is no principled reason to distinguish between the costs imposed by the risk of injury or death, and those costs imposed by the risk of negligence liability or strict environmental damage liability. All are actual costs to the salvor, and he would presumably be unwilling to perform the salvage service without their recompense. For this reason, the risk of environmental liability was properly counted under the rubric of the fourth factor.[17]

This analysis is not altered by the fact that the district court did briefly consider the extra-*Blackwall* environmental protection factor announced in Trico. That case announced an additional factor, general protection of the environment by the salvors, *see* 809 F.Supp. at 443, which has never been endorsed by this court. In this case, the district court concluded that the salvors did not achieve any significant protection of the environment, and therefore it did not apply the factor. That decision did not preclude the court from properly considering all of the legal risks that Margate incurred, environmental or otherwise, under the rubric of the traditional factors.

(c)

Finally, and most significantly, the United States also complains that the district court erred by using a percentage of the salved value in its ultimate calculation of the salvage award. There is no merit to this contention either.

We note at the outset that this court itself applied a percentage-based calculation in modifying an award in our most recent salvage case. *See Allseas*, 812 F.2d at 247. Furthermore, and as we just stated above, our analysis of the economic foundations of the *Blackwall* rule indicates that the value of the salved property is one of the most important of the factors. The most natural way to effectuate its salient character is simply to make the award a function of that value. *See* Landes & Posner, 7 J. Leg. Stud. at 103-04 (concluding that this is what courts have correctly done); *accord* Gilmore & Black at 563. Indeed, since the era of the Rhodian law itself, courts have applied percentages of salved value in calculating awards. Although Justice Clifford's opinion in *The Blackwall* itself heralded an end to the earlier practice of using a fixed percentage or "moiety" across all situations, *see* Gilmore & Black at 563; *Jones v. Sea Tow Services Freeport N.Y. Inc.*, 30 F.3d 360, 364 (2d Cir.1994); *The Kia Ora*, 252 F. 507, 511 (4th Cir.1918), we see no reason why the district court may not use the other five factors to set a customized percentage to be applied to the salved value for purposes of calculating an award in the case before it. *See Compagnie Commerciale de Transport a Vapeur Francaise v. Charente Steamship Co.*, 60 F. 921 (5th Cir.1893) (acknowledging the incorrectness of the fixed percentage method, yet upholding a customized percentage award). Based on our interpretation of the purpose of the *Blackwall* factors, we can indeed think of no more appropriate way to effectuate their goals.

Consistent with our earlier analysis of the factors, we therefore expressly state (to the extent that the issue may have been in doubt) that an approved method for calculating salvage awards is to use the first, second, third, fourth, and sixth factors to arrive at a percentage to be applied to the fifth factor, salved value, for purposes of establishing the award. In setting the percentage, some care should of course be taken to stay within the bounds of historical practice, see Section C, *supra*, and to account for all of the relevant circumstances of the specific salvage at issue. The predominant consideration, however, should always be to arrive at an award that reasonably reflects the price upon which the parties would have agreed. To the extent that the district court merely applied this formula and adopted a calculation based upon a percentage of salved value, it committed no abuse of discretion in this case.

---

[17] To the extent the United States is actually arguing that maritime law be altered to reduce the incentive for overeager salvors to wreck environmental havoc in pursuit of their prize, we note that there is no need for such a change in the law. As the United States itself admits, applicable law already made Margate strictly and completely liable for any oil spill that might have resulted from the salvage operation. *See, e.g.*, 33 U.S.C. § 2702(a) ("Notwithstanding any other provision or rule of law ..., each responsible party for a vessel or a facility from which oil is discharged ... into or upon the navigable waters or adjoining shorelines ... is liable for the removal costs and damages ... that result from such incident."); *see also* 33 U.S.C. § 2718(c). As such, the environment was and is adequately protected, and there is no need to conscript admiralty law for that purpose. Putting this concern to one side, Margate was entitled to the benefit of all the calculated risks it ran in the determination of its award. This is not to say, of course, that any amount of environmental risk could justify an award for more than the value of the salved property. The maximum limitations and general principles of salvage apply regardless.

(d)

Although none of the United States's own arguments with regard to interpretation of the factors bears any fruit, we feel compelled to raise one additional concern that has been fairly implicated, even if not squarely addressed.

For what the district court did in this case goes just a bit beyond the approach that we have outlined and approved. The court first held that the *Blackwall* factors indicated an award of 12.5% of the salved value in this case. So far, so good. After determining that the salved value was $53 million, however, the court also noted that, even if the value were actually lower, as the United States argued, the dollar amount of the award would remain the same, as the court would adjust the percentage accordingly.

Based on our above interpretation of the *Blackwall* factors, we cannot approve this alternate holding. To do so would completely vitiate the effect of the fifth factor, and it is clear that such a holding would exceed the district court's discretion. Under our longstanding precedent, the district court is bound to apply all of the factors. *Allseas*, 812 F.2d at 246; *Platoro*, 695 F.2d at 903. Furthermore, as the often critical measure of the arm's-length salvage price that the *Blackwall* rule attempts to ascertain, it is clear that value of the salved property is one of the most important of the factors, and the one that truly cannot be ignored. To the extent that the district court attempted to evade the fifth factor by tying the percentage to a fixed dollar amount, we reverse that portion of its ruling. For the remainder of this opinion, we may therefore restrict our discussion to the district court's primary holding that an award of 12.5% of the salved value was appropriate, and that this figure was approximately $6.4 million.

To determine whether that holding may be allowed to stand, we must consider the United States's two remaining major complaints, *i.e.*, that the value assigned to ET-70 was a clear error, and that the overall award was excessive both as to percentage and total dollar value. We address each in turn.

B

The United States's second major contention is that the district court clearly erred in its valuation of ET-70. In this complaint, we must agree.

1

* * *

Generally, the value of property for salvage purposes is its market value as salved. *See* Norris § 263; Gilmore & Black at 561 n. 89a; *Nolan v. A.H. Basse Rederiaktieselskab*, 267 F.2d 584, 588 (3d Cir.1959). In the case of a unique good like a space shuttle fuel tank, however, this measure is clearly inapposite; as there is no market of any kind for space shuttle fuel tanks, there can be no market value.

In this situation, and bearing in mind that ET-70 remained in perfect condition despite the trials of the storm, the parties now agree that the most appropriate measure of value is "replacement cost." This conclusion accords with this circuit's decisions in other areas of maritime law. *See, e.g., E.I. DuPont de Nemours & Co.*, 899 F.2d at 380 (in maritime tort context, "[w]hen no market value exists for a vessel, 'other evidence such as replacement cost ... can also be considered' ") (quoting *King Fisher Marine Service, Inc. v. NP Sunbonnet*, 724 F.2d 1181, 1185 (5th Cir.1984)); *cf. The F.I. Robinson*, 2 F.Supp. 644, 645 (E.D.N.Y.1933) (market value preeminent, but reproduction cost may be considered in its absence). The question becomes how replacement cost is to be determined.

The United States argues that the district court erred by using the DD-250 cost of ET-71 to measure the replacement cost of ET-70. It contends that the court should have based its valuation on what it would actually have cost NASA to purchase a replacement tank, and that this figure was conclusively established to be $19 million by the 1992 option.

2

Based on our earlier discussion of the purposes of salvage law, we are convinced that the United States is quite correct, at least in part. The purpose of establishing the value of the salved property is to ascertain what benefit the salvage service conferred on the salvee; what we wish to know, in the end, is what the salvee was saved from so that we may establish what he reasonably would have paid for the benefit of the saving. Where the benefit to the salvee must be measured by the replacement cost of the salved property, that figure should reflect the contemporary price to the salvee of actual replacement. In this case, that price would simply be the amount that NASA would actually have had to pay Martin Marietta for them to make a new ET-70.

* * *

On this point, the evidence was absolutely undisputed that NASA could have purchased an additional tank for approximately $19 million in out of pocket expense at the time of the salvage. Martin Marietta had made a binding offer to produce up to four additional tanks for this price, and although the offer had been recently withdrawn, there was no evidence to suggest that it no longer accurately reflected what Martin Marietta would charge. True, the district court held that the "option" was too "speculative" to be relied on. This finding, however, was completely at odds with the record. In the light of all the evidence, we are convinced that it was in clear error.

* * *

3

Unfortunately for the United States, this holding does not quite end our inquiry. For although the "option" price was conclusive as to NASA's probable out of pocket expense in obtaining a replacement for ET-70, it did not address all of the probable replacement costs.

Any calculation of replacement cost must be based on a replacement that is comparable to the lost item in all material respects. *E.I. DuPont de Nemours & Co.*, 899 F.2d at 382. In order truly to replace ET-70, Martin Marietta would have had to provide NASA with a new tank that incorporated all of the material features of the old one, both physical and temporal. Although payment of the option price would have been sufficient to obtain a new tank with all the requisite physical characteristics, that tank would have been somewhat faulty as a temporal matter in that it would only have become available for use three years after ET-70's designated mission. In a very real sense, ET-70's value to NASA was enhanced by the fact that it was a completed tank, available for immediate use. Although the record is clear that no mission need necessarily have been postponed by a delay in ET-70's replacement, it is also clear that for three years' time NASA would have had three usable tanks in circulation instead of its desired minimum of four. Because ET-70's existence avoided this three-year shortfall, any acceptable replacement plan would have had to address it as well. Because the tank available under the option could not have done so, it would have been partially defective.

* * *

Combining this additional $12 million [The Courts reasoning and basis for constructing this amount are omitted. (Eds.)] with the $19,014,479 figure from the option, we arrive at a total replacement cost for ET-70 of approximately $31 million. We therefore hold that the district court was clearly in error in valuing ET-70 at $51,387,000, and that the correct value was $31 million. Adding the $2 million stipulated value of Poseidon, this leaves a total value for the salved property of $33 million.[26] Applying the district court's 12.5% salvage percentage, *see Compagnie Commerciale*, 60 F. at 924 (applying the district court's choice of customized salvage percentage to a corrected salved value in computing the ultimate modified award), we are left with a new salvage award of $4.125 million.

C

With this new figure in hand, we may address the United States's final complaint. Essentially, the United States argues that, even assuming a correct and error-free assessment of the *Blackwall* factors, any award in excess of either $2.5 million or 10% of the salved value constitutes an abuse of discretion in this case. The United States made this

---

[26] In making this admittedly rough-and-ready valuation, we rely on the fact that the value of the salved property need not be determined with great precision in order to calculate an appropriate award, even under the customized percentage method. *See Compagnie Commerciale*, 60 F. at 924.

argument originally with respect to the district court's $6.4 million/12.5% award. As it is equally applicable to our amended $4.125 million/12.5% figure, we must briefly address it before we can bring this case to a close. For the reasons that follow, we hold that a $4.125 million/12.5% award is not so excessive as to constitute an abuse of discretion in the context of this case.

* * *

After some fairly extensive research, we have compiled a list of the nine largest federal salvage awards in comparable high-value, high-order cases since the advent of the *Blackwall* rule. All amounts have been adjusted to 1994 dollars on the basis of the relevant U.S. Consumer Price Index deflator. See John J. McCusker, *How Much Is That in Real Money? A Historical Price Index for Use as a Deflator of Money Values in the Economy of the United States* (American Antiquarian Society 1992).

* * *

In the context of these past awards, it is difficult to say that the reduced $4.125 million/12.5% award here is wrong, much less an abuse of discretion. The range of percentages appears to run from about 4% to 25%,[28] and the percentage here is smack in the middle of that range. Furthermore, as the district court noted, it is rare that a salvage action would involve such high ratings on each of the factors as was the case here. The only case in the list that is fairly comparable in this respect is *The Omaha*, and there the salvors did not incur great risk to themselves. Furthermore, that case resulted in a higher award in percentage terms. Although the dollar amount of the award in this case would still appear to be the highest ever, even after our modification, in the light of all its factors, it simply does not look out of place in the context of high-value, high-order salvage cases. For this reason, it is not so excessive as to constitute an abuse of discretion.

V

Conclusion

In conclusion, we AFFIRM the district court's interpretation of the *Blackwall* factors and choice of salvage percentage. In particular, we AFFIRM and sanction the district court's decision to use the first, second, third, fourth, and sixth factors to calculate a percentage to be applied to the fifth factor, salved value, for purposes of fixing an award, because this practice is inherently consistent with the underlying purpose of salvage awards and the *Blackwall* factors (*i.e.*, to simulate the price that the parties would have agreed to in a competitive negotiated setting). We also AFFIRM the district court's assessment of environmental liability as a risk properly considered under the rubric of the fourth factor. Finally, we also AFFIRM the district court's specific choice of percentage in this case, because it is consistent with the historical pattern in cases of similar nature, and therefore is not so excessive as to constitute an abuse of discretion. We REVERSE the judgment of the district court as to the value of the salved property, however, and must therefore MODIFY its ultimate salvage award. For the stated reasons, we REDUCE Margate's salvage award from $6,406,440 to 4,125,000 and direct that judgment be entered in that amount.

AFFIRMED in part, REVERSED in part, award REDUCED, and RENDERED.

Notes

1. *Contrast Margate Shipping Co., supra,* with *Hernandez v. Roberts,* 675 F. Supp. 1329, 1988 AMC 1843 (S.D. Fla. 1988), where the plaintiff made unsuccessful attempts to tow and anchor a vessel that he had found floating unmanned while he was out fishing. Eventually, "[a]fter all the plaintiff's attempts at towing and anchoring, he finally did the most obvious and logical act, he radioed the Coast Guard". Id. at 1332. The Coast

---

[28] Which is consistent with the judgment of most modern commentators, *see, e.g., Gilmore & Black* at 563 (finding an upper limit of about 20% in high-value cases), and the practice of courts since the time of the Rhodian law itself, *see* note 11, *supra*.

Guard then towed the vessel to safety. The court said that the plaintiff had "exercised little skill and only self-imposed energy" and had "placed his family and himself unnecessarily at risk, through his poor judgment", which had produced "self created dangers". Id. Applying the Blackwall factors, the court determined that the plaintiff was entitled to an award of $500 for his salvage efforts.

2. In *Platoro Ltd., Inc. v. Unidentified Remains Of A Vessel*, 695 F.2d 893, 1984 AMC 2288 (5th Cir. 1984), the plaintiff sought unsuccessfully to be allowed to keep the salved res itself (artifacts from a sunken Spanish galleon) as its salvage reward, rather than being paid a sum of money to reward it for salving the res. Even if the salvor's expenses had exceeded the value of the res, the maximum allowable total reward would be the value of the res, but it would not be the res itself.

F. Misconduct of Salvors

BASIC BOATS, INC. v. UNITED STATES
352 F. Supp. 44, 1973 AMC 522 (E.D. Va. 1972)

Memorandum

Walter E. HOFFMAN, Chief Judge

This action was commenced by Basic Boats, Inc., suing by its insurance carrier, for damages allegedly caused to the sailing yacht CONJUR MAN. The United States is a proper party defendant having consented to be sued by virtue of the Suits in Admiralty Act, 46 U.S.C.A., §§ 741-752, and the Public Vessels Act, 46 U.S.C.A., §§ 781-790. The defendant asserts a claim for salvage by way of recoupment, the propriety of which was previously decided by this court. See *Basic Boats, Inc. v. United States*, 311 F. Supp. 596 (E.D. Va., 1970).

The CONJUR MAN is a 34-foot, steel-hulled ketch designed for coastal and ocean cruising and was on a return voyage from Bermuda to Annapolis, Maryland, during the month of July 1967. Leonard C. Rennie was master of the yacht and was aided by Leonard B. Tennyson and his young son as crewmen. During this return voyage, the CONJUR MAN lost its mainmast and, shortly thereafter, its mizzenmast. Rennie made a concerted effort to attract assistance since the gasoline auxiliary engine was also inoperable. Contact was finally made with a Navy helicopter and Rennie requested the pilot to inform the Coast Guard of the position and condition.

The helicopter notified a Navy convoy which was conducting exercises nearby, and the destroyer WALLACE L. LIND arrived sometime later. While approaching the yacht, the captain of the LIND prepared to provide fuel, food, technical, and medical assistance as the exact nature of distress was unknown to him. The destroyer approached the yacht upwind, and stopped dead in the water some four to five hundred yards away. Since the destroyer had a greater sail area, it drifted down on the yacht at a relative speed of one knot. Voice contact was attempted but, due to the 15 to 25 knot wind, such communication was impracticable until the vessels were extremely close. As the vessels neared contact, fenders were put out by the destroyer and an attempt was made to throw a heaving line to the CONJUR MAN, which attempt failed because of the movement of the yacht in the five to eight-foot seas.

The LIND continued to close on the CONJUR MAN until finally, at a distance of 200 yards, Rennie confirmed the fact that he required assistance but still failed to state exactly what was and what was not desired. The decision was made to make contact with the yacht amidships on the lee side since boarding the yacht might be necessary and, if merely a tow was required, it would be necessary to obtain authorization to do so since the destroyer had been ordered only to find out what assistance was required. Ten men were deployed to make ready for contact—six for handling lines and four to handle fenders. Contact was finally made with the vessels in a port-to-port relation.

A one-inch nylon line was passed up from the CONJUR MAN to the LIND which kept the yacht stationary relative to the destroyer. Lines from the destroyer were not used at this point because they were located in another part of the ship and the time sequence and temporary nature of the proceedings at that stage did not justify producing them. The yacht had other lines below, its own fenders and a boat hook, none of which was made ready by the three members on board since they were awaiting instructions. Shortly after the line from the CONJUR MAN was attached to the destroyer, a large ground swell swept down the side of the LIND causing the yacht to rise fairly high relative to the destroyer and then drop suddenly. This sudden strain on the line caused it to part and the CONJUR MAN began to move aft. A boat hook was given to Rennie with which to fend off, but the two crew members decided to abandon ship. The Navy personnel then became concerned primarily with the safety of the individuals.

The CONJUR MAN struck the screw guard, damaging the cabin structure. It then floated off and, by means of a lyle gun, a heaving line was passed to the yacht, eventually getting a tow line to it and having it attached. Rennie then got off the yacht and a crew from the destroyer went aboard for the night. The next day the yacht was turned over to a Coast Guard cutter which completed the tow to Norfolk.

Throughout the transcript references are made to the singular request on the part of Rennie for a tow. Before deciding the applicable standard of care, it must be determined whether these facts amount to a contract for towage or a salvage situation. Although the only assistance requested was a tow to Norfolk, the totality of the circumstances compels a finding of an operation in the nature of a salvage. The distinction between the two has been clearly drawn. Towage is undertaken for the sole purpose of expediting the voyage. Salvage is a service rendered to a vessel which removes it from some distress. *McConnochie v. Kerr*, 9 Fed. 50 (S.D.N.Y., 1881). Without either mast or the use of its auxiliary motor, the CONJUR MAN was in a position of anticipating some danger. Though it was not in eminent danger, the actions of the LIND were in the nature of a salvage operation as immediacy of harm is not essential to salvage.

The next question is the appropriate standard of care with respect to a Navy ship acting as a salvor. The United States would never be liable but for the waiver of its sovereign immunity, so the statutes creating liability would also indicate the standard of care imposed. Suits in Admiralty Act, 46 U.S.C.A., §§ 741-752; Public Vessels Act, 46 U.S.C.A., §§ 781-790. The Supreme Court has interpreted these statutes together to impose liability upon the government where the principles of admiralty law would impose liability on private individuals. *Canadian Aviator, Ltd. v. United States*, 324 U.S. 215, 65 S. Ct. 639, 89 L. Ed. 901 (1945). It has been argued that at least the Coast Guard should be held to a higher standard in salvage cases, since one of its functions is to aid distressed vessels, 14 U.S.C.A., §§ 2 and 88(b). However, even in light of this "duty," the liability of the Coast Guard rises no higher than that of private parties. *Frank v. United States*, 250 F.2d 178 (3 Cir., 1957), *cert. denied*, 356 U.S. 962, 78 S. Ct. 1000, 2 L. Ed. 2d 1069 (1958). *A fortiori*, the Navy cannot be held to any higher standard.[1] While one case has indicated that, for policy reasons, the United States should not be liable for its Coast Guard at sea, *P. Dougherty Co. v. United States*, 207 F.2d 626 (3 Cir., 1953), this court is of the opinion that the rule announced in Canadian Aviator, Ltd., *supra*, is controlling in a salvage situation.

For these reasons, the standard imposed on private individuals will be applicable to this case. The rule generally seems to be that a salvor must act in good faith and exercise reasonable skill and prudent seamanship. *The Laura*, 14 Wall. (81 U.S.) 336, 20 L. Ed. 813 (1871). A salvor whose conduct falls below this standard must be held accountable "as does negligence in the performance of any other assumed or imposed duty." *The Cape Race*, 18 F.2d 79, 81 (2 Cir., 1927). The difficulty arises as to the manner in which a negligent salvor will be held accountable.

The consequences of a negligent salvage will vary depending on the type damage caused thereby. If the misconduct prevents a successful salvage, generally there will be no affirmative damages awarded against the salvor unless there is a finding of gross negligence or willful misconduct. The *S.C. Schenk*, 158 F. 54 (6 Cir., 1907), *Chesapeake Bay Bridge & Tunnel Dist. v. Oil Screw Prince*, 298 F. Supp. 881 (E.D. Va., 1968). Conversely, there will be no award made to the voluntary salvor, since the operation was unsuccessful. *The Blackwall*, 10 Wall. (77 U.S.) 1, 19 L. Ed. 870 (1869).

The more difficult situation is when the distressed vessel is removed from its peril, but in the process suffers some distinguishable injury—that is, a type of damage other than that which could have been suffered had not salvage efforts been undertaken. *The Noah's Ark v. Bentley & Felton Corp.*, 292 F.2d 437 (5 Cir., 1961). The cases seem to hold the salvor liable for ordinary negligence. *See The Noah's Ark, supra; The Cape Race, supra; The Jean L. Somerville*, 286 F. 35 (5 Cir., 1923). While this seems harsh, it should be remembered that an award for salvage is much larger than if based on *quantum meruit*, thus a salvor is being paid to exercise care over the property in his control.

---

[1] *See also* exclusion of warships from provisions of salvage treaty adopted in 1910. 46 U.S.C.A. § 731. *Cf.* NORRIS, THE LAW OF SALVAGE § 79.

Some authorities draw a distinction between conduct undertaken while both ships are subjected to the peril, and conduct during the disposition of the salved vessel after removal from peril. In the former instance, courts should be reluctant to find negligence. *The Henry Steers, Jr.*, 110 F. 578 (E.D.N.Y., 1901). This is not to say that, in the proper case, the salvor should not be held accountable in damages for negligence in the act of salvage. *The Cape Race, supra*.

The rule seems to be that for a distinguishable injury, if there is negligent conduct which is the proximate cause thereof, the salvor shall be held accountable. It likewise seems to be the rule that the salvor's recovery may not only be diminished, *The Jean L. Somerville, supra*, it may be forfeited entirely, or in the proper case he may be liable by way of affirmative damages. *The Noah's Ark, supra*; *The Cape Race, supra*. An award of damages to the salved vessel seems to be contingent upon the degree of culpability and lack of care shown by the salvor. *The Minnie E. Kelton*, 181 F. 237 (D. Ore. 1910).

The CONJUR MAN suffered a distinguishable injury, since a crushed cabin was not a peril it faced absent a salvage attempt. The LIND would be accountable for any negligent conduct which was the proximate cause of the injury sustained. The negligence will have to be a matter of proof, as the mere fact of an accident creates no presumption of negligence. The plaintiff bears the burden to prove misfeasance. *The Daniel Kern*, 27 F.2d 920 (W.D. Wash. 1928).

Under the circumstances as revealed at trial, this court must find that the actions of the WALLACE L. LIND did not fall below the standard of ordinary care. It is claimed that the destroyer should not have made contact with the CONJUR MAN amidship on the lee side. Evidence revealed this to be a normal procedure with respect to boats to be taken aboard, and also for an eventual tow if the smaller craft had any power. The crew on the LIND attempted to ascertain exactly what assistance was required, but to no avail. In light of the fact that medical or technical personnel might need to board the CONJUR MAN, or that the crew members might need to abandon the yacht, or that lengthy repairs might be required, taking the yacht in its lee was proper.

Another complaint concerns the lack of the proper lines to secure the CONJUR MAN to the side of the LIND. The law imposes no duty on the Navy to have any salvage equipment on deck. *United States v. Sandra & Dennis Fishing Corp.*, 372 F.2d 189 (1 Cir., 1967); *Foltting v. Kaevando*, 324 F. Supp. 585 (S.D. Tex., 1971). The facts disclose heavy towing lines on the fantail of the destroyer, but the time sequence did not allow for their being brought forward. It is also important to note that there were sufficient lines aboard the CONJUR MAN, none of which were produced by the crew. The line which was used came from the yacht and its particular strength was within the knowledge of Rennie. This same type line is used by the destroyer crew to make their twenty-six foot whaleboats fast to the side.

Once the line parted, fault is contended with the Navy personnel for not taking action to prevent the collision with the screw guard. The destroyer did pass a boat hook to Rennie with which he unsuccessfully attempted to fend the yacht off. The crew did move the fenders down toward the stern to keep the two ships from rubbing. The fact that it was at this point that two crew members decided to abandon the CONJUR MAN also influences the finding of no negligence.

Even assuming the LIND was negligent under the circumstances confronting it, this would not be a proper case to allow affirmative damages. The negligence of the LIND is slight, if at all, and the CONJUR MAN is not wholly without fault. Both Rennie, who had sailed single-handedly to Bermuda, and Tennyson, who had four years' experience in the Coast Guard, were seasoned seamen, but neither did anything to improve the position of the CONJUR MAN or to aid in its salvage. Useful equipment aboard the CONJUR MAN was not utilized; no suggestions were made; and most significantly no information was imported as to the nature of the required assistance until after contact had been made.

For the reasons stated above, the relief sought by the plaintiff is denied. Since the issue involving recoupment is now moot, counsel may present a final judgment order.

THE NOAH'S ARK v. BENTLEY & FELTON CORP.

292 F.2d 437, 1961 AMC 1641 (5th Cir. 1961)

John R. BROWN, Circuit Judge

Growing out of the salvage of the Noah's Ark, three principal questions are raised by this appeal and cross appeal. The first is the nature of the legal liability of the salvor, the Shrimper Cudjoe, for damage sustained by the Noah's Ark as a result of the salvor's negligence.

The second is the extent of the damage attributable to the fault of the salvor. And the third is whether the salvage award, reduced because of the salvor's negligence, was inadequate.

Giving it perhaps even more of a scriptural flavor, the decree was an unusual one with Solomonic overtones. The Court held, first, that the salvage award should be reduced markedly because of negligence of the salvor Cudjoe in releasing the Noah's Ark without warning after arrival in the port of refuge. Despite this, on the Noah's Ark cross-libel for affirmative recovery of damages, it then held that this claim should be dismissed since the extensive damage sustained by her pounding on the rocks after negligent release was due to the sole fault of her own crew and in no sense the proximate result of negligence of the salvor. No one is satisfied and all appeal. When we say "all appeal," we mean it literally. For not the least of the complications in what otherwise appears to be a pretty simple case is the array of counsel nominally on the same side, but each having separate interests. One proctor appeared for the Cudjoe's salvage claim, another to defend the damage cross-libel. And, as might have been expected for one bearing the name of the Noah's Ark, her counsel came by twos apparently under a similar division on her behalf. Reacting to this, the Court added to the troubles by attempting to keep the trial of the salvage libel, with its answer of negligent damage to the Noah's Ark as a defense or set-off, separate from that of her cross-libel for the same damages to which defense was made by the Cudjoe. The result was that the Judge had to listen to frequent repetitious reading of the same depositions or extended colloquy of counsel as to just what was then being tried, offered or determined. We stress this because in reality it was one case. And it is this failure—through the influence of these extraneous factors—to recognize it as substantially one case which, we feel, is in large part responsible for the contradictory conclusions of the Trial Court.

The Noah's Ark is a small shrimper 57 feet long. On January 1, 1958, when about 70 miles west of Key West, Florida, her engine broke down. She attempted to get help from the Coast Guard but this was declined. By exchange of radio messages the Cudjoe, also a shrimper, advised she would help. The tow started about 10:00 p.m. January 1. The seas were calm and weather good, but warnings were out for impending heavy weather. Early in the morning on January 2 winds and seas whipped up. The nylon anchor line of the Noah's Ark being used for a tow line parted. Increased seas caused it to part again. A seacock was damaged and the Noah's Ark started taking on water. The auxiliary pump became inoperative so that there was a considerable amount of water in the engine space over the bilges from sea water and melting ice. The tow line parted again. Finally the Noah's Ark rigged a new tow line by using one of her steel trawl cables.

Approaching Key West Harbor the Coast Guard again was unable to render assistance. Radio communications still existed between the Cudjoe and Noah's Ark and while the evidence and terms of it was somewhat vague, the Judge found that the two masters agreed that on arrival in Key West Harbor, the Noah's Ark would make fast to the cable vessel Western Union regularly anchored in the Bight. About 6:00 p.m. January 2 the vessels entered Key West Harbor. The winds were then 60 to 72 mph varying from NE to NNW. The weather was nasty, cold and with intermittent downpours of rain. The Noah's Ark was still on the towing cable some 450 feet long. The Cudjoe heading into the wind made a line fast from her bow to a Navy finger pier on the north side of the harbor. The Noah's Ark streaming on the trawl cable was parallel to and close by the Western Union. The time was estimated from three to four minutes to as much as fifteen to twenty minutes. But the Court found that the wind held the Noah's Ark alongside for "several moments." One crew member of the Noah's Ark may have momentarily been aboard the Western Union but with wind and waves affecting both, it was not possible to secure.

At this point, and with no explanation whatsoever which would withstand even the slightest cross-examination, the Cudjoe cast off the trawl tow line. A faint claim is made that Navy guards were seen approaching and the

Cudjoe's master was apprehensive that they would make him cast off the line from the pier. Of like weight was the suggestion that the long tow line presented a danger to vessels between the Cudjoe's stern and the bow of the Noah's Ark. The District Court paid these scant heed, as do we. It found categorically that while the master of the Cudjoe believed that the Noah's Ark "was fast to the Western Union" the Cudjoe cast the line loose "without any warning to the Noah's Ark." At this time the Cudjoe knew that the Noah's Ark's radio was no longer serviceable. With neither radio nor any other means by those aboard the Noah's Ark to communicate essential information to the Cudjoe, the Cudjoe made a baseless assumption and cast off.

The Noah's Ark, a helpless, powerless derelict, was adrift in 60-70 mph winds. She was caused "to drift with the high wind several hundred yards across the harbor, where she came alongside of and in contact with a sand dredge ... tied to the seawall" on the south side of Key West Bight.

While we defer for a moment the discussion of the legal principles concerning the duty of salvors, it simplifies the problem to assay the conduct of the Noah's Ark and the Cudjoe on the assumption that ordinary prudence was the standard of care with respect to this initial occurrence. On that inquiry it is plain that this was palpable and glaring fault on the part of the Cudjoe. The District Court held as much in the formal conclusions of law that the "salvors ... were guilty of negligence in releasing the [Noah's Ark] without any warning and without ascertaining ... whether ... the Noah's Ark was fast to the Western Union."

Equally plain to us is the freedom from fault of the Noah's Ark in her drifting southward and thereafter until she fetched up along the cement seawall. The first stage from the position alongside the Western Union to the sand dredge was one of helplessness. Many theories were advanced to place blame on the Noah's Ark, principally for not dropping an anchor. She had two anchors, but no anchor line. Her anchor line had parted several times in the salvage operations. There is no evidence that had the crew in this emergency attempted to rig the anchor to the remnant anchor line the anchor in this short time and distance would have been effective in the teeth of this driving gale. As the Noah's Ark came alongside the sand dredge, one line was put out but soon parted. A crew member tried hard to throw a line on a nearby dolphin but without success. Much was made by the Cudjoe of the Noah's Ark's failure to put out more lines to the dredge including the unshipping of the remaining steel trawl cable to use it as mooring lines to make fast. But the Court did not find this a fault, nor do we. The position of the Noah's Ark was at that moment extremely precarious as the owner of the Cudjoe, the late tortfeasor, well knew. Those ashore, which included the principal stockholders of the corporate owner of the Cudjoe (the salvor claimant) observing the situation, recognized that if the Noah's Ark slipped off the sand dredge, the wind and water would force her into a small U-shaped slip along the concrete seawall. That happened shortly so that "at approximately 6:30 p.m." she was "alongside the seawall ... in an upright position but touching bottom in the shallow water." And what happened in this manner was certainly within the range of likely consequence, including the element that in the emergency conditions created by the Cudjoe's cutting her adrift, the Noah's Ark might make mistakes in her responsive efforts to overcome the faultmade hazards. RESTATEMENT OF TORTS, § 449; *Slattery v. Marra Brothers*, 2 Cir., 1951, 186 F.2d 134, at page 136, 1951 A.M.C. 183.

It is at this spot, and beginning with this time, but not before, that the Court held the Noah's Ark at fault. The Court's findings of fact show that culpable fault commenced after the Noah's Ark fetched up. This began, the Court found, when the "captain of the Noah's Ark stepped ashore and ... made a long distance telephone call ... to the owner." The Court condemned her for actions subsequent to that occurrence. The Court found that "At no time during the evening did the captain or crew of the Noah's Ark seek any assistance which was available from bystanders or from local marine facilities, or try to borrow lines to secure the vessel, or attempt to borrow a bilge pump from other vessels.... Nor did the captain ... contact the local commercial salvor, Ray Gladding, owner of a tug who was at the scene and available, to tow the Noah's Ark to deeper waters and prevent the damage to her from the bay bottom and from contact with the Lobster House." The vessel pounded against the rocky bottom and seawall and about 3:00 a.m. January 3, capsized and sunk.

On those findings the Court concluded that the subsequent sinking of the Noah's Ark was "caused by the sole negligence of her captain and crew" in their "failure to seek assistance from professional salvors or from bystanders, when such assistance was readily available, and their complete failure to discharge their duties owed to their own vessel."

The Court, after finding the Noah's Ark to have been of the value of $20,000 the moment before the Cudjoe cast off the line, found that valuable salvage services had been rendered. But then, as pointed out earlier, the Court fixed the award at $2,000 because the salvage "award must be diminished due to negligence" on the part of the Cudjoe. Simultaneously the Court denied the Noah's Ark's affirmative claim for damages on the ground that these very same damages were due to the sole negligence of her own crew.

Just how the Judge could say that the salvors had been guilty of negligence requiring diminution of the award and at the same time hold that all damage done after arrival in Key West Harbor was due to the sole negligence of the Noah's Ark crew remains a mystery. An explanation certainly cannot be found in the legal conclusion that the "negligence of the salvors did not amount to gross negligence or wilful misconduct producing a distinguishable and separate injury to the salved vessel...."

We think, however, that this finding pinpoints the basic error in the Court's approach. In stating that, we accept the conclusion that the actions of the Cudjoe "did not amount to gross negligence or wilful misconduct" because that is actually irrelevant. The Court tied this to a further conclusion that the non-gross negligence, non-wilful misconduct did not produce a "distinguishable and separate injury to the salved vessel." Without at this time attempting to fix or specify exactly what items of damage were thereby caused, it is plain to us that whatever damages were suffered by the Noah's Ark after the Cudjoe cut loose the line were distinguishable and independent.

This is important since for distinguishable independent damages done by the salvor, we are of like opinion that the maritime law holds the salvor to the usual standard of ordinary prudence. Norris, a well regarded text writer, in the Law of Salvage (1958) draws these conclusions from all of the American cases which he cites and discusses. "The salvors who undertake a service to distressed property obligate themselves to take reasonable care of the property in their charge and they may be responsible for damages which they inflict on that property.... This duty has been defined as binding them 'to take the same kind of care, and exercise the same degree of diligence in keeping the property placed in their custody, that a prudent man ordinarily takes and exercises in keeping his own property.'" § 120 at 205-6. The basic principle is then succinctly stated. "When a distinguishable injury to the salved property has resulted from the negligence of persons undertaking a salvage service, it may result not only in a diminution of the award or of a total forfeiture, but in an affirmative award of damages against the salving vessel or the salvors." Norris, *supra* at 206.

Because of obvious policy considerations to encourage the human response of men of the sea to the saving of life and property, it is true that mistaken action of the salvor in the efforts to effectuate salvage is treated with considerable lenience. But the Second Circuit has pointed out that while "negligence in a would be salvor is perhaps viewed with a benevolent eye" nevertheless when it is "plainly proved, it entails responsibility, as does negligence in the performance of any other assumed or imposed duty." *The Cape Race*, 2 Cir., 1927, 18 F.2d 79, at page 81, 1927 A.M.C. 628. Years before that Court in *Serviss v. Ferguson*, 2 Cir., 1897, 84 F. 202, had affirmed per curiam "on opinion of district judge" the decision of Judge Addison Brown. The salvor was held liable for simple non-wanton, non-wilful, nongross negligence for failure to mark the presence of the salved vessel which sunk at the pier after completion of the salvage. This distinguished Judge who did so much to mold and develop American maritime law had this to say. "If it seems a hardship to require the defendant to pay for a boat they have rescued, possibly from complete destruction, it must be remembered that the compensation which the court awards for salvage services includes the recompense for all the necessary care of the salved property; and that the seeming hardship is no other or different than that in which any other negligent loss involves every ordinary bailment for hire." Norris, *supra*, § 123 at 210-12.

All of the significant American and English cases were painstakingly considered by Chief Judge Biggs (joined by Judges Goodrich and Staley) dissenting in *P. Dougherty Co. v. United States*, 3 Cir., 1953, 207 F.2d 626, 637, 1953 A.M.C. 1541, *certiorari denied*, 347 U.S. 912, 74 S. Ct. 476, 98 L. Ed. 1068, characterized by us as "an exhaustive and penetrating analysis," *United States v. Gavagan*, 5 Cir., 1960, 280 F.2d 319, at page 326, note 14.

The key to the correct legal principle is the character of the injury inflicted—*i.e.*, distinguishable or, as sometimes called, independent. The requirement for wilful or gross negligence as an element of salvor liability relates to injuries of a non-distinguishable, non-independent kind. In a very broad sense the latter covers errors that made the salvage ineffectual. A distinguishable injury, on the other hand, is some type of damage sustained by the salved vessel other than that which she would have suffered had not salvage efforts been undertaken to extricate her from the perils to which she was exposed. *See* note 17, 207 F.2d 626, at page 644. In other words it is a harm distinct from that from which the vessel is being saved.

Here there is no effort to hold the Cudjoe liable for ineffectual salvage. On the contrary, this was performed and performed well. The disabled Noah's Ark was brought safely to the port of refuge. The Cudjoe is not pursued because had she taken this rather than that particular course of action the Noah's Ark would have been rescued. To the contrary, she is cast because having performed salvage diligently and successfully, she failed to exercise ordinary care for the property then in her actual control. Norris, *supra*, § 121 at 207.

The contradictory conclusions of the District Court did seem at first to hold the Cudjoe accountable to a degree for her obvious negligence. But in view of the categorical conclusions that this "did not amount to gross negligence or wilful conduct producing a distinguishable and separate injury" the Court's error permeated all that was to follow.

This is so because on this theory of the District Court, mistaken as it was, the predicament of the Noah's Ark from the time she slipped off the sand dredge until her final sinking was entirely of her own making and in no way attributable to any negligence for which the Cudjoe was legally responsible. That, as we have pointed out, is an indefensible conclusion.

Once it is recognized that the predicament of the Noah's Ark was due in fact and law solely to the flagrant fault of the Cudjoe, the whole case concerning conduct thereafter takes on a different complexion. That brings into play the principles of—or akin to—the doctrine of avoidable consequences which we discussed at great length in *Southport Transit Co. v. Avondale Marine Ways*, 5 Cir., 1956, 234 F.2d 947, at pages 951-954, 1956 A.M.C. 1498. What we there said has considerable operative significance in the light of our conclusion on the legal fault of the Cudjoe. "On the remand, however, the Court must regard carefully that the tug owner is the innocent party whose property was damaged, to some extent at least, by negligent performance of its contract by the shipyard. Under the teaching of the doctrine of avoidable consequence, a substantial burden is therefore heavy on the wrongdoer to establish that prudence ... for action by the tug owner at one or more of these stages; and, that had it been taken, the resulting damage would have been substantially different. Nor will inability satisfactorily to differentiate between the consequences of the tortfeasor's conduct and the innocent injured party's inaction be measured or its significance determined by common law notions which might deny recovery altogether." 234 F.2d 947, at page 954.

Additionally the circumstances of high wind, wave and water in which this occurred may well require that the law regard this as a situation in which the negligence of the Cudjoe was still at work, *i.e.*, in a continuing sense. 234 F.2d 947, at page 955. A few factors pointing in that direction may be briefly mentioned. The Noah's Ark fetched up alongside the seawall adjacent to the pier of the owner of the Cudjoe. The Cudjoe under her own power was able to moor safely not too far away. Help, in the way of lines, fenders, and pumps, was tendered to the Noah's Ark by stockholder representatives of the owner of the Cudjoe who happened to be nearby, but these were declined. An earlier assurance made by radio to the Noah's Ark by the Cudjoe's master shortly before arriving in the Harbor to seek out a salvor went unfulfilled, apparently due to apprehension over who would be responsible under such circumstances for the salvor's bill. Both the offer and the assurance were looked upon by the Cudjoe and the Court as acts of the Good Samaritan. But Bentley & Felton Corporation could claim no such status after the Noah's Ark was cast adrift by the Cudjoe. It was a tortfeasor whose wrong had put the victim in this hapless state.

Next, from the standpoint of physical forces, it is obvious that the real damage was due to the continual pounding of the Noah's Ark against the bottom and the seawall. Fenders would not have prevented that. And with the strong backwash current in this U-shaped slip described and acknowledged by all, the evidence does not yet show how additional lines from the Noah's Ark to the seawall could have overcome this terrific pounding on a vessel known to be taking water. Relief from this devastating stress on the wooden hull would come only from her being pulled out of the slip. A commercial salvor did testify that he was there about 9:00 p.m. and observed the situation of the Noah's Ark. He expressed the opinion that with his salvage tug, had he been hired at that time, he could have pulled her free to a safe mooring. But by this time considerable damage must already have occurred from the vessel's pounding. And more would occur until such salvage operations were concluded. The testimony was vague indeed on just what time the commercial salvage operations could have commenced had the master of the Noah's Ark requested them. Quite obviously so much damage as had, or would have, occurred cannot be attributed to the Noah's Ark. That likewise has to be measured against the real probability of success. The commercial salvor was optimistic, but the representatives of Cudjoe's owners expressed strong doubts that with the backwash the Noah's Ark could have been pulled out under those weather conditions. As put by one of these Feltons who was a witness to the incident, "with the seas raging in on her, and the backwash driving ... when she got" against the concrete dock "there was no use." His brother, likewise a stockholder in the organization, was more emphatic. Once the Noah's Ark was in this position, to move her under these circumstances was in his opinion "utterly impossible."

We do not express a final view now on how these factors are to be evaluated. But the facts should be developed and then evaluated in the light of the proper legal standard. *Henderson v. Flemming*, 5 Cir., 1960, 283 F.2d 882, at page 884; *United States v. Williamson*, 5 Cir., 1958, 255 F.2d 512, at page 515; *Mitchell v. Raines*, 5 Cir., 1956, 238 F.2d 186, at page 187; *Galena Oaks Co. v. Scofield*, 5 Cir., 1954, 218 F.2d 217, at page 219. The result is that the case must be remanded for a further trial on these crucial matters occurring after the Noah's Ark slipped off the sand dredge. Established by the Trial Court's findings and action by us are two things requiring no further inquiry: (1) valuable salvage services were rendered by the Cudjoe to the Noah's Ark; and (2) the salvor was guilty of negligence for which it is legally responsible in casting off the Noah's Ark without warning. The amount of the salvage award, the extent to which it should be diminished if at all, the extent and nature of damage sustained by the Noah's Ark for which the salvor is legally responsible under the applicable standards are all matters which are for a new trial and determination by the Court. Each may bear upon the other. Thus in determining the value of the salved vessel the portion vicariously restored to her value through a decree for damages may be relevant. Similarly, the amount, nature and extent of damages sustained may affect the problem of diminution or forfeiture of an award and the allowance of affirmative relief. Without undertaking to blueprint the trial or to intrude upon the considered discretion of the District Court in determining in the first instance the extent to which, or what, evidence is to be received, we would make clear that the entire present record is available for use on remand without the necessity of reproducing the witnesses or retaking depositions.

For a retrial and other consistent proceeding, the case must be reversed and remanded.

Reversed and remanded.

[For proceedings on appeal after remand *see* 322 F.2d 3 (5th Cir. 1963). Eds.]

Note

The care or lack thereof which a salvor uses in conducting the salvage operation is considered in determining the amount of the award. Thus in considering "the promptitude, skill and energy displayed by the salvors in rendering service and saving property," the court in *Beach Salvage Corp. of Florida v. The Cap't. Tom*, 201 F. Supp. 479 (S.D. Fla. 1961) found "that the Libelant (salvor) was both energetic and prompt but that its knowledge of salvage proceedings was lacking and that the skill exhibited by the salvors was of a minimal degree, even though the salvage operation was a success." The owner of the vessels filed a cross-libel claiming that the salvors negligence damaged its vessels. The court found that "Libelant used little skill in its operations," but since the damage to the vessels will be considered in making any award for salvage and allowance for costs, it was unnecessary to give judgment in the cross-libel.

JACKSON MARINE CORP. v. BLUE FOX

845 F.2d 1307, 1988 AMC 2740 (5th Cir. 1988)

W. Eugene DAVIS, Circuit Judge

Jackson Marine, the owner of the M/V MISTER JEAN, together with the vessel's captain and crew, appeal the district court's dismissal of their salvage claim on the ground that the fraud of the captain of MISTER JEAN bars their recovery for salvage. We affirm the district court's denial of a salvage award to the captain and owner of the MISTER JEAN and reverse the denial of an award to the crew.

I.

On July 14, 1981, the M/V BLUE FOX, carrying an explosive mid-deck cargo of dozens of oxygen-acetylene bottles, caught fire, some sixty miles off of Sabine Pass, Texas, in the Gulf of Mexico. After unsuccessfully attempting to extinguish the fire, the crew abandoned ship and were rescued by a nearby boat. The crew was eventually transferred to the M/V VIGILANTE FORCE on which they radioed for help. The MISTER JEAN, owned by Jackson Marine Company (Jackson Marine), answered the distress signal and extinguished the fire.

This is the second time these parties have been before this court. In *Black Gold Marine, Inc. v. Jackson Marine Co.*, 759 F.2d 466 (5th Cir. 1985), we upheld the district court's determination that Captain Trudell of the MISTER JEAN had fraudulently procured a salvage contract from Captain Totten of the BLUE FOX. Because the facts determined in *Black Gold Marine* bear significantly on this appeal, we set forth below facts important to that opinion.

After extinguishing the fire on the BLUE FOX, Captain Trudell offered to tow the BLUE FOX (whose engines were inoperative) to a safe port if Captain Totten would agree to sign an instrument that would protect the MISTER JEAN from any liability incurred as a result of the tow. In reality, the form contract that Captain Trudell presented to Captain Totten permitted Jackson Marine to recover for all of the services it performed for the BLUE FOX, including extinguishing the fire. The contract also bound Black Gold Marine, Inc., the owner of the BLUE FOX, to arbitrate with Lloyds Salvage Arbitration Board in London, England, to determine the value of those services. Relying on Captain Trudell's misrepresentations, Captain Totten signed the form instrument only to learn later that he had agreed to a potentially large salvage award in favor of Jackson Marine.

In a declaratory judgment action instituted by Black Gold Marine, the district court declared the salvage contract void due to fraud in the procurement. The district court also found that "Trudell, a captain of twenty years, was intimately familiar with the terms and effect of the salvage agreement, whereas Captain Totten had neither seen nor heard of the document before and that Trudell dishonestly mischaracterized the document to secure Totten's signature." *Black Gold Marine*, 759 F.2d at 469. On appeal, we concluded that the district court's finding of fraud was not clearly erroneous while noting that "[o]ur decision, affirming the district court's invalidation of the salvage contract, in no way limits or affects Jackson's undertaking to vindicate its 'pure salvage' rights against the M/V BLUE FOX in the absence of a salvage contract." *Id.* at 471. In the subsequent trial on the appellants' pure salvage rights the district court concluded that the fraudulent misconduct of Captain Trudell precluded any salvage award to the owner, captain, or crew of the MISTER JEAN. We now turn to a consideration of the salvage rights of the captain, the owners, and the crew of the MISTER JEAN, respectively.

II.

A determination of the salvage rights of Captain Trudell is quite straightforward: did the district court err in determining that Trudell's fraudulent misconduct bars his salvage award?

Admiralty courts have traditionally been vigilant in protecting mariners from unscrupulous and dishonest salvors. *The Bello Corrunes*, 19 U.S. (6 Wheat.) 152, 5 L. Ed. 229 (1821); *The Albany*, 44 F. 431 (D. Mich. 1890). Because of the heightened vulnerability of a distressed ship and crew to exploitation by salvors, "[t]he law cannot ... tolerate salvors [sic] dishonesty, corruption, fraud, falsehood, either in rendering the service, or in their proceedings to recover the salvage." *Church v. Seventeen Hundred and Twelve Dollars*, 5 F. Cas. 669 (S.D. Fla. 1853) (No. 2713).

While the appropriate response to a finding of fraud or misrepresentation will depend on the facts of the particular case, the district court had good reason to bar Trudell from any recovery in this case. Trudell, who served as a captain for twenty years, was "intimately familiar with the terms and effect of the salvage agreement." *Black Gold Marine*, 759 F.2d at 469. The district court found that Trudell intentionally took advantage of Totten, who had "neither seen nor heard of the document before." *Id.* The district court did not err in barring Trudell's recovery.

III.

We next consider whether Trudell's fraudulent conduct and misrepresentations should be imputed to Jackson Marine and bar the owner from any salvage recovery.

It is well established in the general maritime law that the master of a vessel is the agent and representative of the owner and as such can bind the owner by acts performed within the scope of the agency. *Massachusetts Lobstermen's Ass'n, Inc. v. United States*, 554 F. Supp. 740, 742 (D. Mass. 1982); *Farmer v. The O/S Fluffy D*, 220 F. Supp. 917, 920 (S.D. Tex. 1963); 3A M. NORRIS, BENEDICT ON ADMIRALTY, § 178 (7th ed. rev. 1987). This agency relationship makes the owner responsible both for contracts made by the captain as well as the captain's torts, so long as the torts are committed within the scope of the captain's normal duties and employment.[1] *Domar Ocean Transp. v. Independent Refining Corp.*, 783 F.2d 1185, 1190 (5th Cir. 1986); *The Rising Sun*, 20 F. Cas. 828 (D. Me. 1837) (No. 11,858); *see also* M. Norris, *supra*, § 108 n.2 (listing cases).

Consistent with general agency principles, the general maritime law imputes to the principal the servant's acts committed within the scope of a servant's employment even though "consciously criminal or tortious." RESTATEMENT (SECOND) OF AGENCY § 231 (1977); *Domar*, 783 F.2d at 1190. Intentional acts of misconduct by a servant are considered within his scope of employment when they are "so closely connected with what the servant is employed to do, and so fairly and reasonably incidental to it, that they may be regarded as methods, even though quite improper ones, of carrying out the objectives of employment." W. PROSSER AND W. KEETON, THE LAW OF TORTS 502 (5th ed. 1984); *Domar*, 783 F.2d at 1190.

In *Domar*, we considered whether the unauthorized, criminal acts of a captain could be imputed to the vessel owner. In holding the owner vicariously liable for the captain's theft of crude oil, we held that "[t]he fact that an employee engages in intentional tortious or criminal activity does not necessarily require a finding that he was acting outside the scope of his employment." *Id.*

In *Domar*, we applied a number of factors in determining that the actions of the captain were imputable to the owners. "Among the factors considered to determine whether acts are within the scope of employment are: (1) the time, place and purpose of the act; (2) its similarity to acts which the servant is authorized to perform; (3) whether the act is commonly performed by such servant; (4) the extent of departure from normal methods; (5) the previous relations between the parties; and (6) whether the master would reasonably expect that such an act would be performed." *Id.* (citing W. Prosser and W. Keeton, *supra* at 502).

These factors, when applied to this case, strongly militate in favor of imputing Trudell's actions to Jackson Marine. Trudell's actions occurred at a time and place when he was serving as captain of Jackson Marine's vessel and the main purpose of Trudell's misrepresentations was to benefit Jackson Marine. Jackson supplied Trudell with the "Lloyds form" salvage agreement to be executed by a representative of the distressed vessel. Trudell's departure from normal methods related only to his misrepresentations in this case.

In sum, Captain Trudell's misconduct was directly related to duties Jackson Marine assigned to him and the captain's fraud was committed primarily for Jackson's benefit. The district court did not err in imputing Trudell's conduct to Jackson Marine.

---

[1] Commentators are equivocal at best on when the shipowner is barred from obtaining a salvage award due to the captain's intentional misconduct. M. Norris, *supra*, § 108. Gilmore and Black are silent on the salvage rights of the owner in these circumstances.

IV.

We now turn to the rights of the crew of the MISTER JEAN to recover a salvage award. While we conclude that misconduct of Captain Trudell should be imputed to Jackson, we find no reason to bar the innocent crew from a salvage award.

Although established rules of respondeat superior operate to impute fault up the employment hierarchy, these rules do not operate in the inverse to impute fault down the employment hierarchy. Without individual knowledge or guilt, a servant is not vicariously liable for the misrepresentations of his principal. RESTATEMENT (SECOND) OF TORTS, § 348 comment b (1977). Thus, under general agency principles, the crew of the MISTER JEAN is not responsible for the actions of Trudell. This general agency rule is consistent with admiralty principles that traditionally distinguish between the rights and liability of the master and owner on one hand and the crew on the other. For example, a contract for salvage may bind the parties to the agreement but it will not bind the crew of the salving vessel if made without their sanction and concurrence. *The Neptune*, 277 F. 230 (2d Cir. 1921); *M. Norris, supra*, § 173; G. GILMORE AND C. BLACK, THE LAW OF ADMIRALTY, 567 (2d ed. 1975); *see also Waterman S.S. Corp. v. Dean*, 171 F.2d 408 (4th Cir. 1948), *cert. denied*, 337 U.S. 924, 69 S. Ct. 1168, 93 L. Ed. 1732 (1949).

The record evidence suggests no reason to impute the improper actions of Trudell to the crew. Although some members of the crew may have been present during portions of Trudell's conversation with Totten, the record evidence does not suggest, and the district court did not find, that those crewmembers knew of or participated in Trudell's misconduct. Thus, we conclude that the district court erred in denying a salvage award to the crew.

V. Conclusion

The judgment of the district court denying a salvage award to the captain and owners of the MISTER JEAN is affirmed. The judgment denying relief to the crew is reversed and the case is remanded to the district court to determine the amount of the salvage award the crew is entitled to recover.

AFFIRMED in part and REVERSED in part.

G. Contract Salvage

THE ELFRIDA

172 U.S. 186, 19 S. Ct. 146, 43 L. Ed. 413 (1898)

THIS was a libel *in rem* by the firm of Charles Clarke & Co., of Galveston, Texas, against the British steamship Elfrida, to recover the sum of $22,000, with interest and costs, claimed to be due them for services rendered in the performance of a salvage contract with the master, to release the Elfrida, then stranded near the mouth of the Brazos River.

The principal averments of the answer were, in substance, that the agreement was signed by the master under a mutual mistake of fact, or by mistake on his part, which libellants took advantage of, as to the danger in which the vessel was, and that it was improvidently made for an excessive compensation without a proper understanding by him of the vessel's alleged freedom from danger; that the master had been prevented from carrying out his instructions to accept a tender made, if lower impossible, by information of the cable being conveyed to the salvors before the master saw it; that the parties were not upon equal footing; that libellants made an unreasonable bargain with the master because of the stress of the situation and that of his vessel, and acted collusively with other salvors in obtaining from him the agreement.

On Friday, October 5, 1894, the Elfrida, a steel steamship of 1454 tons register, 290 feet long, 38 feet in width, and drawing 11 feet 10 inches, bound for the port of Velasco, Texas, in ballast, grounded on the bar between the jetties which extend from either bank of the river, about a mile into the Gulf, the outer end of these jetties for a distance of a thousand feet or more being submerged. The heel of the ship touched, there being but five inches between the bottom and the bar, and an easterly wind swung her bow against the west jetty. The captain ran out a kedge from the starboard bow, hove taut with the windlass, put the engine full speed astern, but could not move the ship. The wind and sea increased during the afternoon and evening, while the ship was straining and bumping heavily. The weather moderated somewhat on the following day, and the same efforts were continued unsuccessful until the evening, when the sea rose, carrying her over the submerged outer end of the jetty, and some distance farther shoreward on the beach. She brought up that night about a cable's length to the west of the west jetty. That part of the jetty which was above high water projected seaward beyond her stern and sheltered her from easterly winds. She lay parallel with the jetty about four or five hundred feet from the beach, head on, and about one thousand feet from water of sufficient depth to float her. The shore at this point is very flat, the bottom consisting of a layer of quicksand about ten feet deep. The steamer settled in the quicksand to her normal draft, rocking and moving in it whenever there was a high sea. She lay in nine feet of water at high tide. The weather continued generally favorable from the 7th to the 17th, with occasional gales and high seas. The ship drifted somewhat further on the beach, but efforts to relieve her by her own resources seem to have been practically abandoned.

On Tuesday, October 9, the master sent the following letter to the libellants:

VELASCO, Oct. 9, 1984.
Capt. Chas. Clarke, re S.S. Elfrida.
    DEAR SIR: Please tender for to float and place in a place of safety, say Galveston, where her bottom can be examined, furnishing diver and his apparatus. Also to furnish all material and labor in floating said steamship Elfrida, also time required. Reply at your earliest convenience under seal to Jas. Sorely, Lloyds agent, or myself.

No cure, no pay.
Yours truly,By   B. BURGESS, Master
P.S.—A convenient time to be laid to get the ship off, and if at the expiration of the time the vessel is still aground, all claim on this contract to cease and to be null and void.
                                                        B. BURGESS, Master.

In reply to this, libellants submitted a tender, offering to perform the service for the sum of $22,000, which was accepted by the advice of Lloyd's agent, who was on board the vessel at the time, and with the consent of Pyman, Bell & Co., of Newcastel-on-Tyne, owners of the Elfrida.

The following contract, which forms the basis of the present suit, was thereupon entered into:

THE STATE OF TEXAS,
COUNTY OF BRAZORIA.

    This agreement, made and entered into this 15th day of October, 1894, between the steamship Elfrida, and the owners thereof, represented herein by B. Burgess, master of said steamship, as party of the first part, and Charles Clarke & Co., of Galveston, Texas, as party of the second part,

    Witnesseth, that for and in consideration of the covenants and agreements herein contained on the part of the said party of the first part, to be kept and performed, the said party of the second part hereby agrees and binds himself, his administrators and assigns, to float and place in a safe anchorage, Quintana or Galveston, as directed, the S.S. Elfrida, which is now stranded west of and near to the west jetty at the mouth of the Brazos River, in said county and State; to furnish all labor and material at the cost of said party of the second part, and to furnish diver and necessary apparatus to survey or examine the bottom of said steamship, and to complete the same within twenty-one (21) days from date hereof.

    The said party of the first page agrees to pay to the said party of the second part for such service, *i.e.* when he shall have successfully floated said ship, as above set forth, the sum of twenty-two thousand dollars ($22,000).

The said party of the first part, however, reserving the right hereby abandon the ship to and in favor of the said second party in lieu of the amount of $22,000 agreed to be paid as aforesaid.

It is further understood and agreed by and between the parties hereto that a failure to float and place in a position of safety, as above stated, said steamship within the time herein-before specified, to wit, twenty-one days from date hereof, that said party of the second part shall receive no compensation whatever from said first party for work performed, labor, tools or appliances furnished.

Anything that may be discharged to enable vessel to float shall be replaced when she is in a position of safety. It is also agreed and understood that the use of crew and engine shall be at the use and disposal of said party.

Witness the hand of B. Burgess, master of the steamship Elfrida, for himself, said ship and the owners, party of the first part, and the hand of Charles Clarke & Co., party of the second part, this 15th day of October, 1894.

BENJ. BURGESS.
WITNESSES   CHAS. CLARKE & CO.
                          M.P. MORRISES.
                          J.H. DURKIE,
                          Master S.S. Lizzie, of Whitby.

The day before the contract was signed, the libellants, having learned that their tender for the work had been accepted, hired the schooner Louis Dolsen of fifteen tons, for which they paid $100, to take their plant to Galveston in tow of their tug Josephine. They also hired a large force of men, procured nearly a month's supplies, cables, chains, anchors, two tugboats, two lighters and two schooners, fully manned and equipped. Some of this plant belonged to them, but the schooners and lighters and their equipments were hired. For one of the lighters they agreed to pay $6500 if she should be lost. Their entire outfit was worth from $30,000 to $50,000. On arriving at Velasco on the same or following day, they engaged a derrick lighter for use in laying the anchors, and on the two following days, the 16th and 17th, the salvors were at work planting the anchors and connecting cables from them to the winches of the ship. This work was completed during the afternoon of the 17th, the water ballast pumped out, when the Elfrida's engines, winches and windlass were started by her own steam, and in less than half an hour she began to move herself off. She went slowly for the distance of about a thousand feet when she floated clear, but was carried by the current against the west jetty. The libellants' tug then for the first time took hold of her and towed her away from the jetty, and at 7:40 P.M., four hours after the work of hauling her off was begun, she was free and clear of everything, and put to sea under control of the pilot. Subsequent examination of her bottom, in the dry dock at Newport News, showed that she was wholly uninjured except for a slight indentation about a foot long in the bilge, which was probably caused by contact with the jetty. At the time she was stranded she was insured for the sum of £18,000, subsequently reduced to £16,000.

Upon a full hearing upon pleadings and proofs, the District Court entered a final decree in favor of the libellants' for the stipulated sum of $22,000, with interest and costs. Claimants appealed to the Circuit Court of Appeals, which reversed the decree of the District Court, one judge dissenting, and remanded the case with instructions to enter a decree in favor of libellants' for the sum of $10,000, with interest at six percent. 41 U.S. App. 585. A petition for rehearing having been denied, libellant applied to this court for a writ of certiorari, which was granted.

Mr. Justice BROWN, after stating the case, delivered the opinion of the Court.

But a single question is presented by the record in this case: Was the contract with the libellants' of such a character, or made under such circumstances, as required the court to relieve the Elfrida against the payment of the stipulated compensation?

We are all of opinion that this question must be answered in the negative. Salvage services are either (1) voluntary, wherein the compensation is dependent upon success; (2) rendered under a contract for a *per diem* or *per horam* wage, payable at all events; or (3) under a contract for a compensation payable only in case of success.

The first and most ancient class comprises cases of pure salvage. The second is the most common upon the Great Lakes. The third includes the one under consideration. Obviously where the stipualated compensation is dependent upon success, and particularly of success within a limited time, it may be very much larger than a mere *quantum meruit.* Indeed, such contracts will not be set aside unless corruptly entered into, or made under fraudulent representations, a clear mistake or suppression of important facts, in immediate danger to the ship, or under other circumstances amounting to compulsion, or when their enforcement would be contrary to equity and good conscience.

* * *

These are the only cases in our reports in which the question of nullifying a salvage contract was squarely presented, although there is in the case of *Post v. Jones,* 19 How. 150, 160, an expression of the court to the effect that "courts of admiralty will enforce contracts made for salvage service and salvage compensation, where the salvor has not taken advantage of his power to make an unreasonable bargain; but they will not tolerate the doctrine that a salvor can take the advantage of his situation, and avail himself of the calamities of others to drive a bargain; nor will they permit the performance of a public duty to be turned into a traffic of profit." Indeed, it may be said in this connection that the American and English courts are in entire accord in holding that a contract which the master has been corruptly or recklessly induced to sign will be wholly disregarded. *The Theodore,* Swabey, 351; *The Crus,* V. Lush, 583; *The Generous,* L.R. 2 Ad. 57, 60.

* * *

The cases in these courts are too numerous for citation, but it is believed that in nearly all of them the distinction is preserved between such contracts as are entered into corruptly, fraudulently, compulsorily or under a clear mistake of facts, and such as merely involve a bad bargain, or are accompanied with a greater or less amount of labor, difficulty or danger than was originally expected.

* * *

We do not say that to impugn a salvage contract such duress must be shown as would require a court of law to set aside an ordinary contract; but when no such circumstances exist as amount to a moral compulsion, the contract should not be held bad simply because the price agreed to be paid turned out to be much greater than the services were actually worth. The presumptions are in favor of the validity of the contract, The *Helen & George,* Swabey, 368; *The Medina,* 2 P.D. 5, although in passing upon the question of compulsion the fact that the contract was made at sea, or under circumstances demanding immediate action, is an important consideration. If when the contract is made the price agreed to be paid appears to be just and reasonable in view of the value of the property at stake, the danger from which it is to be rescued, the risk to the salvors and the salving property, the time and labor probably necessary to effect the salvage, and the contingency of losing all in case of failure, this sum ought not to be reduced by an unexpected success in accomplishing the work, unless the compensation for the work actually done be grossly exorbitant.

While in England there has been some slight fluctuation of opinion, by the great weight of authority, and particularly of the more recent cases, it is held that if the contract has been fairly entered into, with eyes open to all the facts, and no fraud or compulsion exists, the mere fact that it is a hard bargain, or that the service was attended with greater or less difficulty than was anticipated, will not justify setting it aside. *The Mulgrave,* 2 Hagg. Ad. 77; *The True Blue,* 2 W. Rob. 176; *The Henry,* 15 Jur. 183; S.C. 2 Eng. Law and Eq. 564; *The Prinz Heinrich,* 13 P.D. 31; *The Strathgarry,* (1895) P.D. 264.

* * *

The facts in this case are somewhat peculiar, and, in entering into the contract, unusual precautions were taken. On October 5, the Elfrida in entering the river grounded by the stern about mid-channel, her bow drifting over toward the west jetty. Her crew were unable to get her off, either upon that or the following day, when, owing to the sea rising, she was carried over the jetty and a very considerable distance further on to the beach (about 600 feet), where she remained in seven or eight feet of water, gradually working inward and making a bed for herself in the sand, which had a tendency to bank up about her bows. She appears to have been at no time in imminent peril, but her situation could have been hardly without serious danger, unless she were released before a heavy storm came on, which might have broken her up or driven her so far ashore that her rescue would have been impossible. It was shown that in previous years a number of vessels had gone ashore in this neighborhood, several of which were lost by bad weather coming on. In other cases the difficulty of getting them off had been very largely increased by similar causes. The testimony shows that while the Elfrida lay there the wind was at times blowing a gale with a rough sea, in which the ship strained and bumped heavily. On Saturday the 6th, the day of her final stranding, the master having given up his idea of getting her off with her own anchors, telegraphed his owners and also Lloyd's agent at Galveston, who appear to have sent Mr. Clarke, one of the libellants, down on Sunday evening. He offered to undertake the relief of the ship for what the court would allow him. This offer the master declined. About the same time Mr. Sorley, Lloyd's agent, came down to the vessel, saw her situation, remained there two days, and advised the master to invite bids for her relief. He obtained two bids, one for $24,000 and one made by the libellants for $22,000, and on the advice of Sorley and of his owners, Pynam, Bell & Co., of Newcastle-on Tyne, with whom he kept in constant communication by cable, he accepted libellants' bid, and a contract was entered into, whereby they agreed to float the Elfrida and place her in a safe anchorage, and to complete the job within twenty-one days from date. The master agreed to pay therefor the sum of $22,000, but reserved the right to abandon the ship in lieu of this amount. At the request of the owners he also inserted a further stipulation that if the libellants should fail to float the ship and place her in a position of safety within twenty-one days, they should receive no compensation whatever for the work performed, or the labor, tools or appliances furnished. This contract was made at Velasco on October 15. Clarke proceeded at once to get ready a wrecking outfit, consisting of a tugboat and schooner, with fifteen or sixteen men, went to the wreck, and spent about two days planting anchors and connecting cables from them to the winches of the ship. The tugboat took no part in the actual relief of the vessel, which was effected by the aid of the anchors and the steamer's engines, although after the Elfrida was afloat she drifted against the west jetty and the tug hauled her off.

For the work actually done the stipulated compensation was undoubtedly very large, and if the validity of the contract depended alone upon this consideration, we should have no hesitation in affirming the decree of the Circuit Court of Appeals; but the circumstances under which the contract was made put the case in a very different light. In the first place, the libellants offered to get the vessel off for such salvage as the court should award, but the master declined the proposition, and, acting under the advice of Lloyd's agent and of Moller & Co., the owners' agents at Galveston, invited bids for the service. This certainly was a very proper step upon his part, and there is no evidence showing any collusion between the bidders to charge an exorbitant sum. The conditions imposed upon the libellants were unusual and somewhat severe. Their ability to get her off must have depended largely upon the continuance of good weather. Their ability to get her off within the time limited was even more doubtful, and yet under their contract they were to receive nothing—not even a *quantum meruit*—unless they released her and put her in a place of safety within twenty-one days. Further than this, if in getting her off, or after she had been gotten off, she proved to be so much damaged that she was not worth the stipulated compensation, the master reserved the right to abandon her.

We give no weight to the advice of Pynam, Bell & Co., her owners, to enter into the contract, since in the nature of things they could have no personal knowledge of her situation, or of the possibility of relieving her; but it shows that her master, though a young man and making his first voyage as master, acted with commendable prudence. He took no step without the advice of his owners and that of the underwriters' agent at Galveston, Mr. Sorley, who was a man over seventy years of age, perfectly honest, and of large experience in these matters. Sorley visited the vessel, saw her situation, and advised an acceptance of the bid. The value of the ship is variously estimated at from $70,000 to $110,000, but the sum for which she was insured, £18,000 or $90,000, may be taken as her approximate value. Under the stringent circumstances of this contract, we do not think it could be said that an agreement to pay one quarter of her value if released could be considered unconscionable, or even exorbitant, and unless the fact that it proved to be exceedingly profitable for the libellants is decisive that it was unreasonable, it ought to be sustained. For the reasons above stated we think that the disproportion of the compensation to the work done is not the sole criterion. Very few cases are presented showing a contract entered into with more care and prudence than this, and we are clear in our opinion that is should be sustained.

BLACK GOLD MARINE, INC. v. JACKSON MARINE CO., INC.

759 F.2d 466, 1986 AMC 137 (5th Cir. 1985)

Jerre S. WILLIAMS, Circuit Judge

Appellee Black Gold Marine, Inc. instituted this declaratory judgment action to determine the validity of a contract between it and appellant Jackson Marine Co. which required, among other things, Black Gold to arbitrate in London, England, a salvage claim made by Jackson. At the conclusion of the bench trial, the district court found that Jackson had fraudulently procured the contract and that Black Gold had not ratified the contract. The court accordingly declared the agreement null and void and entered judgment for Black Gold. We hold that the findings of the district court of fraud and nonratification are not clearly erroneous, and we therefor affirm.

I.

The following recital of the facts is taken from both the district court's findings of facts and the testimony adduced at trial. At about 6:45 p.m. on July 14, 1981, a fire erupted in the engine room of one of Black Gold's ships, the M/V BLUE FOX, while the vessel was operating in the Gulf of Mexico near the Texas coast. The BLUE FOX was carrying canisters of compressed acetylene and oxygen that presented a high risk of a serious explosion. The crew was unsuccessful in extinguishing the fire, and they abandoned ship and were rescued by a nearby boat. Eventually, they reached another nearby boat, the M/V VIGALANTE FORCE, and they began radioing for help.

A vessel owned by Jackson Marine, the M/V MISTER JEAN, received the distress signals and came to the scene. At around 10:30 p.m., the crew of the MISTER JEAN began extinguishing the fire. Because of the MISTER JEAN's enormous fire-fighting capabilities, the crew had the fire under control by around 11:00 p.m. After the fire was under control, the captain of the MISTER JEAN, Captain Trudell, notified the captain of the VIGALANTE FORCE that he wished to speak with the captain of the BLUE FOX, Captain Totten. Captain Totten made his way to the MISTER JEAN and reported to the wheelhouse where he met Captain Trudell. Captains Trudell and Totten then exchanged pleasantries for approximately fifteen minutes. At this point, the version of the events becomes disputed.

Captain Totten testified that Captain Trudell offered to tow the BLUE FOX, since the BLUE FOX's engines were inoperable, and that he accepted Trudell's offer. Captain Trudell then presented Captain Totten with a four-page document entitled: "Standard Form of Salvage Agreement (Approved and Published by the Committee of Lloyd's) No Cure-No Pay," and described the document as a standard towing form. The document actually provided in less than clear language that Jackson Marine would be entitled to recover the value of the MISTER JEAN's services in extinguishing the fire and that the value of these services would be determined by the Lloyd's Salvage Arbitration Board in London, England. Although he had served as a captain for about two years, Captain Totten had never before seen this type of document. He read the first page and scanned the remaining three pages, but he could not understanding the language in the document because it was written in "lawyer talk". Trudell expressly assured him that the document was designed to limit Jackson's liability for any damage to the BLUE FOX that resulted from the tow. Trudell never mentioned either that he expected to be paid for the services rendered in saving the BLUE FOX or that he intended to file a salvage claim in London against the BLUE FOX for these services.

Captain Totten then used the radio on board the MISTER JEAN and contacted the captains of nearby vessels to learn if any had knowledge of the purpose or significance of the document. All of the captains told him that they had not heard of the document but that it seemed reasonable for a rescuing ship to seek to limit its liability when it aided another ship in peril. After speaking with these other captains, Totten signed the document with the understanding that the document merely would relieve Trudell and Jackson Marine of liability during towing. Totten returned the only copy of the document to Trudell, and Totten and Trudell never mentioned the document again.

About an hour after Trudell and Totten signed the document, Trudell received word from his superiors denying him permission to tow the BLUE FOX. He was instructed, instead, to proceed to his original destination. Another vessel then towed the BLUE FOX to safety. Captain Totten assumed that the document he had signed was a nullity because Trudell did not provide the towing service he had promised. Other disinterested witnesses who testified at trial and were privy to some of the conversations between Totten and Trudell corroborated those aspects of Totten's testimony which asserted that the contract discussions involved merely towing the BLUE FOX and holding Jackson Marine harmless for any damage the BLUE FOX sustained during towage.

Naturally, Trudell's version of the facts differs. Trudell testified that he handed Totten the document and said: "This is a Lloyd's open form salvage agreement," and that Totten accepted the document and asked no questions about it. Captain Trudell departed from the wheelhouse to supervise his crew while Totten remained inside and examined the document for about fifteen to twenty minutes. When Trudell returned to the wheelhouse, Totten asked Trudell whether the MISTER JEAN could tow the BLUE FOX to safety, and if so whether Jackson Marine would be liable for any damage to the BLUE FOX during towage. Trudell responded that the document would relieve Jackson of any such liability. At another point in his trial testimony, however, Trudell conceded that Totten had asked him what the document covered and that he reiterated that the document, in part, was designed to absolve Jackson of liability for damages to either the vessel during towage or the cargo if the fire flared up again. Trudell explained at trial that he said this because at that time he was particularly concerned about the prospect of throwing the acetylene and oxygen canisters overboard if the fire burst out again. Finally, Trudell testified that before Totten signed the document, he told Totten that Jackson would expect remuneration for the services performed by the crew of the MISTER JEAN for the BLUE FOX. There was no testimony from other witnesses corroborating the critical aspects of Captain Trudell' testimony, especially Trudell's claim that he had told Totten that Jackson would expect to receive compensation for the services of the MISTER JEAN and her crew.

Approximately two weeks after the fire, in late-July 1981, Black Gold received notice from the Lloyd's Salvage Arbitration Board that Jackson Marine asserted a substantial salvage claim against it under the salvage contract. In late August, Captain Totten met with Black Gold attorneys and related his version of the facts to them. On October 5, 1981, Black Gold instituted this action in Eastern District of Louisiana, seeking to declare the salvage contract void.

In the meantime, however, between September 10, 1981, and September 16, 1981, the parties exchanged a series of telexes concerning a security bond. Prior to the exchange of the telexes, Jackson apparently had contacted Black Gold and threatened to exercise its right under general maritime law to arrest the BLUE FOX pending resolution of its salvage claim. Understandably, Black Gold was concerned about Jackson's contemplated seizure of the BLUE FOX, since seizure would have resulted in substantial income loss to Black Gold. On September 10, 1981, Black Gold's New Orleans counsel telexed Jackson's counsel in London and informed them that Jackson need not consider arresting the BLUE FOX, since Black Gold was willing to post a security bond. Black Gold's counsel also indicated that Black Gold's insurer desired to be heard in the arbitration matter. During the next few days, the parties exchanged additional telexes. Black Gold emphasized its desire and intent to post a security bond in lieu of seizure, and it continued to request that Jackson inform it of the amount of security Jackson desired. On September 16, 1981, Jackson demanded from Black Gold a $500,000 security bond. Black Gold did not undertake the security bond, and explained to the district court below that it considered such a demand to be outrageous. Shortly thereafter, Black Gold instituted this suit.

In the proceeding below, the district court concluded that Trudell fraudulently procured the salvage contract by misstating the nature, purpose, and effect of that document. The district court also found that Trudell, a captain of twenty years, was intimately familiar with the terms and effect of the salvage agreement, whereas Captain Totten had neither seen nor heard of the document before, and that Trudell dishonestly mischaracterized the document to secure Totten's signature. The district court also rejected Jackson's claim that Black Gold ratified the contract because it failed timely to rescind and because it continued proceeding with the arbitration matter in London.

II.

A. Fraudulent Procurement of the Salvage Contract

It is well-settled that an admiralty court possesses authority to set aside a salvage contract that was procured through the salvor's misrepresentations or because of a mutual mistake of a material fact. *See THE ELFRIDA*, 172 (15 Pet.) U.S. 186, 192, 19 S. Ct. 146, 148, 43 L. Ed. 413 (1898); *Houseman v. THE NORTH CAROLINA*, 40 U.S. 40, 47, 10 L. Ed. 653 (1841); *THE THORNLEY*, 98 F. 735, 741 (5th Cir. 1899); *THE CLANDEBOYNE*, 70 F. 631, 636 & 637 (4th Cir. 1895); *Treasurer Salvors, Inc. v. Unidentified Wrecked and Abandoned Sailing Vessel*, 459 F. Supp. 507, 522 (S.D. Fla. 1978), *aff'd on other grounds*, 621 F.2d 1352 (5th Cir. 1980), *aff'd in part, rev'd in part*, 458 U.S. 670, 102 S. Ct. 3304, 73 L. Ed. 2d 1057 (1982). Admiralty courts traditionally have applied common law factors to determine if fraud has been perpetrated in consummating a salvage contract. *See THE CLANDEBOYNE, supra*, 70 Fed. at 634; *see also* 3A M. NORRIS, BENEDICT ON ADMIRALTY § 166, at 12-11 (6th ed. 1983). To prevail on a claim that a contract was fraudulently procured, the party that was deceived must show that (1) the deceiving party made a material misrepresentation or nondisclosure, (2) the representation was false or the nondisclosure implied that the facts were different from what the deceived party understood them to be, (3) the deceiving party knew that the representation was false or that the nondisclosure implied the existence of false facts, (4) the deceiving party intended the deceived party to rely on the misrepresentation or nondisclosure, and (5) the deceived party detrimentally relied upon the misrepresentation or nondisclosure. *See South Hampton Co. v. Stinnes Corp.*, 733 F.2d 1108, 1120 (5th Cir. 1984); *Shores v. Sklar*, 647 F.2d 462, 468 (5th Cir. 1981), *cert. denied*, 459 U.S. 1102, 103 S. Ct. 722, 74 L. Ed. 2d 949 (1983); *Hauben v. Harmon*, 605 F.2d 920, 923 & 924 (5th Cir. 1979); *see also* RESTATEMENT (SECOND) OF CONTRACTS §§ 159-164 (1981).

* * *

To address Jackson's contentions, we need not detail all of the district court's factual findings related to the fraudulent procurement issue. Suffice it to say, the district court obviously credited Captain Totten's partially corroborated testimony and accepted Totten's version of the facts.

* * *

B. Ratification of the Salvage Contract

In an attempt to salvage the contract, Jackson argues that Black Gold ratified the voidable contract by corresponding with Jackson's London counsel after Jackson initiated the arbitration proceeding with the Lloyd's Salvage Arbitration Board. To establish ratification, Jackson must show that Black Gold, while possessing knowledge of all of the facts related to Trudell's misrepresentation, delayed unreasonably in asserting its right to rescind the contract or exhibited other conduct indicating its intent to accept the "benefits" of that contract. *See* RESTATEMENT (SECOND) OF CONTRACTS §§ 7, 380 & 381 (1981); 1 & 1A A. CORBIN, CORBIN ON CONTRACTS §§ 6 & 228 (1963). As the district court found, no ratification occurred in this case. Black Gold did not delay seeking to rescind the salvage contract, since it instituted proceedings to declare the contract null and void only five weeks after it learned Captain Totten's version of the facts. Nor did any other act by Black Gold demonstrate any intent to ratify the salvage contract. Efforts by Black Gold to prevent Jackson from seizing the BLUE FOX, including Black Gold's correspondence with Jackson's London counsel, obviously were undertaken to protect Black Gold and preserve the status quo. They hardly constituted actions exhibiting a knowing attempt to ratify a voidable contract.[2] The district court correctly concluded that no ratification occurred in this case.

---

[2] The messages between the parties reveal that Black Gold's lawyers were trying to avoid the arrest of the vessel by Jackson Marine, and Black Gold was exploring its rights, obligations, and options under a voidable contract. These messages neither exhibit an intent to ratify a voidable contract nor indicate that Black Gold sought to dupe Jackson into forfeiting its noncontractual salvage rights. Black Gold endeavored to maintain the status quo. It repeatedly offered to post a security bond in order to prevent the seize of the BLUE FOX, and it asked Jackson to quote an acceptable security bond. Black Gold clearly remained non-committed in any way until it learned the amount of security that Jackson would demand.

* * *

III.

Our decision is limited narrowly to the validity of the Jackson Marine-Black Gold salvage contract. At oral argument, the Court was informed that in a separate action Jackson has asserted a noncontractual, general maritime law salvage claim against the M/V BLUE FOX. That case is pending in the United States District Court for the Eastern District of Louisiana. Our decision, affirming the district court's invalidation of the salvage contract, in no way limits or affects Jackson's undertaking to vindicate its "pure salvage" rights against the M/V BLUE FOX in the absence of a salvage contract. *See, e.g.,* 3A M. NORRIS, BENEDICT ON ADMIRALTY § 159 (6th ed. 1983).

AFFIRMED.

H. Life Salvage

IN RE YAMASHITA-SHINNIHON KISEN

305 F. Supp. 796, 1969 AMC 2102 (D.C. Or. 1969)

Memorandum Decision

BEEKS, District Judge

These consolidated petitions for limitation of liability present many issues. This memorandum decision resolves two of them.

The first involves claims by Hudson Waterways Corp., (Hudson) owner, the master and the thirty man crew of the American steam tanker TRANSONEIDA for a salvage award against (1) Yamashita-Shinnihon Kisen, (Yamashita) the owner of the Japanese motor ship SUWAHARU MARU (SUWAHARU); (2) Iwai & Co., Ltd., (Iwai) the owner of the cargo of logs laden on said vessel; (3) Hellenic International Shipping, S.A., (Hellenic) owner of the Liberian steam tanker MANDOIL II (MANDOIL), and (4) U.S. Oil & Refining Company (U.S.), owner of a crude oil cargo laden in said vessel, for the saving of property, and for the saving of life against Yamashita and Iwai.

At 1450[1] February 28, 1968 the SUWAHARU, bound from Coos Bay, Oregon, to Nagoya, Japan, was in collision with MANDOIL, bound from Sumatra, Indonesia, to Tacoma, Washington, at a point approximately 300 miles west of the mouth of the Columbia River. At the time of the collision TRANSONEIDA was enroute from San Pedro, California, to Whittier, Alaska, and approximately 95 miles southeasterly of the point of collision.

At 1550 TRANSONEIDA received the distress signal of SUWAHARU that she was on fire forward and needed immediate help. Whereupon TRANSONEIDA proceeded to the position of the distressed vessel.

At 2056 TRANSONEIDA arrived in the collision area and hove to at the request of the KURE MARU, the first vessel to arrive in the collision area, and hence the "control vessel." At this time there was heavy fog.

At 2102 the KURE MARU requested that TRANSONEIDA proceed on her course as her assistance was not needed and the fog presented a danger of collision.

At 2105 TRANSONEIDA resumed its course but at 2140 received a request from the Thirteenth Coast Guard District at Seattle requesting it to remain on the scene for the purpose of providing radio-telephone assistance in an air drop of medical personnel to provide attention for the master of MANDOIL who was badly burned and in need of medical assistance.

At 2221 the KURE MARU advised TRANSONEIDA that it was proceeding to Wistport, Washington with the crew of MANDOIL and asked that TRANSONEIDA watch SUWAHARU as the latter could not move. TRANSONEIDA replied in the affirmative. The survivors of MANDOIL were eventually taken to Astoria, Oregon.

At 0046 February 29th the Coast Guard requested TRANSONEIDA to remain on the scene to coordinate.

---

[1] All times are approximate.

At 0125 SUWAHARU requested permission to transfer its crew to TRANSONEIDA while the sea was calm as her master did not believe SUWAHARU could withstand heavy weather. SUWAHARU further requested TRANSONEIDA to watch until arrival of the Coast Guard cutter which was expected the evening of March 1st.

During the early morning of February 29th the master and crew of SUWAHARU transferred to TRANSONEIDA by the use of her own lifeboat and ascended to the deck of TRANSONEIDA by use of a Jacobs ladder. None of the crew of TRANSONEIDA left TRANSONEIDA during this operation. TRANSONEIDA gave food and blankets to the crew of SUWAHARU. Between 2150 and 2302 twenty-nine members of the crew transferred to the Coast Guard cutter IVY by means of the latter's motor lifeboat.

At 0708 March 1st the remaining eight members of the crew of SUWAHARU were transferred to the IVY by the same method.

At 0738 March 1st TRANSONEIDA resumed her voyage to Whittier, Alaska.

* * *

The salvage service rendered by TRANSONEIDA, as it relates to property, was of a low order, sometimes characterized as a "standby service." TRANSONEIDA at all times during obscured visibility maintained a lookout as well as a radar watch for the purpose of ascertaining the presence of and giving warning to other vessels in the area, and TRANSONEIDA was equipped with both wireless and radio telephone for use in giving aid and comfort to the distressed vessels.

In addition to an award for assistance in the saving of property claimants contend they are entitled to an award for life salvage service rendered to the master and crew of SUWAHARU. In this connection they urge that in fixing the award the Court should consider the agreed fee of $30,050.00 paid to Foss for towing SUWAHARU to Victoria, B.C.

The Life Salvage Act[2] does not provide compensation for life salvage, it only allows salvors of life who have participated in the services rendered on the occasion of the accident giving rise to salvage, a fair share of the property salvage award. Thus, whatever may be the social injustice involved, life salvors are entitled to only a fair share of the compensation awarded to property salvors. Their share must come out of the property award and they have no cause of action against the beneficiaries of their service. It would serve no useful purpose to discuss the right of claimants to participate in an award for the standby service aforesaid. The claimants who participated in each service are identical and a life salvage award would be nothing more than a participation by each in his own property award. Accordingly, the question is—are claimants entitled to an award based upon the contract salvage towage paid Foss? I think not. The life salvage statute was intended to apply only to "reward" or "pure" salvage, and not to contract salvage. Furthermore, the statute contemplates that the saving of life must have been performed substantially at the time and while both lives and property were in distress and danger of loss. The EASTLAND, 262 F. 535 (7th Cir. 1919). Here it was not. The service performed by Foss was substantially after the master and crew of SUWAHARU were transferred to the Coast Guard cutter IVY and by said cutter transported to the mainland.

* * *

Note

The court in *Markakis v. Volendem, supra,* expressed a similar view at 486 F. Supp 1103 n.28:

There are no grounds upon which to grant a life salvage award in the instant case. Although such an award is sometimes appropriate, *see Peninsular & Oriental Steam Navigation Co. v. Overseas Oil Carriers,* 553 F.2d 830, 836 n.6 (2d Cir.), *cert. denied,* 434 U.S. 859, 98 S. Ct. 183, 54 L. Ed. 2d 131 (1977), 46 U.S.C. § 729 (1975); it can be granted only to those who have forgone the opportunity to engage in the more profitable work of property salvage. *Saint Paul Marine Trans. Corp. v. Cerro Sales Corp.,* 313 F. Supp. 377, 379 (D. Hawaii 1970), *aff'd,* 505 F.2d 1115 (9th Cir. 1974); *In re Yamashita-Shinnihon Kisen,* 305 F. Supp. 796, 800 (D. Or. 1969). Here those who participated in the property

---

[2] 46 U.S.C. § 729.

salvage (*i.e.*, all of the crew of the Sun) are identical with those who aided in the life salvage. No opportunity was foregone. Under these circumstances, a life salvage award "would be nothing more than a participation by each [salvor] in his own property award." *In re Yamashita-Shinnihon Kisen, supra*, 305 F. Supp. at 800.

PENINSULAR & ORIENTAL, ETC. v. OVERSEAS OIL CARRIERS

553 F.2d 830, 1977 AMC 283 (2d Cir.), *cert. denied*, 434 U.S. 859, 98 S. Ct. 183, 54 L. Ed. 2d 131 (1977)

Irving R. KAUFMAN, Chief Judge

The perils and hardships of the sea have been notorious since the voyages of Odysseus. Although the age of sirens and cyclopes is past, the isolation and uncertainty of maritime life continue to create unique problems for sailors and courts of admiralty. In this case, we must decide whether the owner of a vessel that alters course to come to the aid of a stricken seaman aboard a ship without medical staff, may recover additional fuel costs caused by the diversion. Under the circumstances of this case, we believe application of equitable principles requires reimbursement of such expenses. Accordingly, we reverse the district court's decision to the contrary.

I.

A brief discussion of the facts, which were stipulated below, will facilitate understanding the issues raised on this appeal. The S.T. OVERSEAS PROGRESS is an American flag tanker of approximately 13,030 gross tons and a maximum speed of about 13.8 knots (15.9 mph). Her owner, Overseas Oil Carriers, is an American corporation with its principal place of business in New York. On July 4, 1973, the OVERSEAS PROGRESS was traveling in the mid-Atlantic Ocean, en route from Haifa, Israel to Baltimore. Suddenly, the ship's fireman, William Turpin, was stricken with severe chest pains. The OVERSEAS PROGRESS did not have a doctor aboard. Her officers, suspecting that the 63-year-old seaman had suffered a heart attack, aided Turpin as best they could. Guided by the ship's medical books and radio advice from the Public Health Service, they administered several morphine injections to relieve Turpin's severe pain and gave him glycerin nitrate tablets. Nonetheless, Turpin's condition did not improve. During the evening of July 5, 1973, he suffered another attack, again accompanied by severe chest pains.

Realizing that his vessel's resources were inadequate to deal with Turpin's increasingly serious condition, the Captain of the OVERSEAS PROGRESS, W.J. Lidwin, sent out a radio message calling for responses from all ships in the vicinity with doctors aboard. Three vessels answered the call. The nearest was the S.S. CANBERRA, a British flag passenger vessel.[1] The CANBERRA, with a maximum speed of 25 knots (approx. 28.8 mph) was considerably faster than the OVERSEAS PROGRESS, and was consequently able to convey Turpin more quickly to shore facilities. Moreover, the CANBERRA itself carried a hospital with a fully equipped operating room and medical personnel able to provide Turpin with immediate attention. At the time she received the OVERSEAS PROGRESS's call, the CANBERRA was en route to New York from Dakar, Senegal, traveling at 23 knots.

Realizing that the CANBERRA's position and equipment rendered it uniquely able to help the stricken seaman, the OVERSEAS PROGRESS directed a second radio message to the British liner, explaining that one of her crew members was in critical condition after suffering an apparent heart attack. The CANBERRA was requested to rendezvous with the OVERSEAS PROGRESS and provide treatment for the ailing seaman. In response to the distress call, the CANBERRA changed course and increased her speed to 25 knots. The OVERSEAS PROGRESS, which was already traveling at maximum speed, altered course to intercept the CANBERRA.

At that time the OVERSEAS PROGRESS was 740 miles from the nearest shore hospital, at St. John's Newfoundland. It would have taken the tanker, traveling at close to maximum speed, 57 hours to reach that destination. By contrast, the meeting of the CANBERRA and the OVERSEAS PROGRESS was achieved in 6 1/2 hours.

---

[1] The CANBERRA was owned by The Peninsular & Oriental Steam Navigation Company, (P & O), an English limited liability company with its principal place of business in London.

In the course of their radio communications, the masters of the CANBERRA and the OVERSEAS PROGRESS briefly considered the allocation of the rescue effort's costs. Captain Snowden of the CANBERRA informed Captain Lidwin that the CANBERRA's owner, the Peninsular & Oriental Steam Navigation Co. (P & O), "may look" to the owner of the OVERSEAS PROGRESS for "reimbursement of diversion costs, medical and out of pocket expenses." Captain Lidwin did not in any way indicate that such compensation would be refused. When the two ships met, Captain Snowden presented a letter reiterating the likelihood that P & O would seek reimbursement. This letter was then countersigned by Captain Lidwin. The parties have stipulated that this document was neither a demand for payment nor an agreement to reimburse the CANBERRA; rather, the ships' masters indicated an awareness of the problem and simply left open the question of payment for subsequent determination by the vessels' owners.

Upon encountering the OVERSEAS PROGRESS, the CANBERRA lowered one of her lifeboats and transferred William Turpin aboard. He was examined by the CANBERRA's surgeon, who diagnosed his illness as a myocardial infarction, a form of heart attack that results in the partial destruction of the central heart muscle. After taking Turpin aboard, the CANBERRA resumed her course to New York at maximum speed, 25 knots. Despite the fact that she had traveled an additional 232 miles to aid Turpin, the increased velocity enabled the CANBERRA to arrive in New York only 2½ hours later than her scheduled arrival time. Turpin was rushed by ambulance to the United States Public Health Hospital on Staten Island. Eventually, he recovered and was discharged.

Overseas Oil Carriers, the owner of the OVERSEAS PROGRESS, promptly paid $248 to the CANBERRA's surgeon for medical expenses rendered to Turpin. But it was far less generous in responding to P & O's request for reimbursement. In response to P & O's letter of September 26, 1973, seeking $12,108.95 for Turpin's accommodation and nursing while on the CANBERRA and, principally, for the additional fuel consumed by the liner as a result of the extra distance traveled and the increased speed the CANBERRA had required to reach New York without serious delay, Overseas Oil Carriers's agent, in a letter dated October 3, declined to pay any part of this amount. Although, the agent wrote, "we are extremely grateful for the kind assistance you have rendered Mr. Turpin", he continued to assert that payment of the claim would be out of keeping with the "traditional concept of rescue at sea."

On April 26, 1974, P & O filed a complaint in the Southern District of New York, seeking recovery of the $12,108.95 it had requested previously. The parties each moved for summary judgment on stipulated facts. In an opinion dated August 20, 1976, Judge Goettel granted recovery of $500 for nursing services but denied any reimbursement for the CANBERRA's additional fuel expenses. He noted that under traditional admiralty doctrines of "salvage", there could be no reward for "pure life salvage", *i.e.* a rescue at sea where men's lives are saved but property is not simultaneously recovered. Judge Goettel also rejected any claim based on "quasi-contract" because he failed to find "misconduct or fault" by Overseas Oil Carriers. He did, however, grant recovery for nursing services since Overseas would have been obliged to pay such costs if Turpin had been placed in a shore hospital. We believe, that the CANBERRA, in saving the life of Seaman Turpin, did more than uphold the great traditions of the sea. In discharging the OVERSEAS PROGRESS's request, the CANBERRA earned the right to recover the fair value of the services rendered. We accordingly reverse the judgment below.

II.

When Turpin fell ill, the Captain of the S.T. OVERSEAS PROGRESS became obligated to make reasonable efforts to provide him with swift medical care, pursuant to the ship's responsibility for "maintenance and cure". This ancient admiralty doctrine has been described as a preindustrial analogue to modern "workman's compensation" statutes.[2] If a sailor is stricken with injury or illness at sea, not caused by the seaman's own willful misconduct, his employer must assume responsibility for his medical care, food, lodging and wages for a reasonable period. *The*

---

[2] NORRIS, LAW OF SEAMEN (1970) § 538 *et seq.* The history of this doctrine may be traced to the Laws of Oleron, (Roll D'Oleron). This maritime code, which originated in Gascony, is believed to have been introduced in England by Richard I after his return from the Holy Land. It enunciated a

Bouker No. 2, 241 F. 831 (2d Cir.), *cert. den.*, 245 U.S. 647 (1917), 2 Norris, The Law of Seamen § 542-544 (1970).

On vessels that do not carry a surgical staff, the ship's master has a duty, in the sound exercise of his judgment and depending on the circumstances, to have the seaman taken speedily to a hospital or the nearest port where surgical care may be obtained. *The Iroquis*, 194 U.S. 240, 243 (1904); *The Cuzco*, 154 F. 177 (2d Cir. 1907); Norris, *supra* § 584. Without the assistance of the S.S. CANBERRA, or a vessel with similar facilities, performance of this duty would have required the OVERSEAS PROGRESS to travel to the shore hospital at St. John's, Newfoundland, entailing a considerable expenditure of time and additional fuel. The CANBERRA, by agreeing to rendezvous, provided Turpin with swifter medical attention and saved the OVERSEAS PROGRESS considerable costs. Through her expeditious intervention, the CANBERRA performed the OVERSEAS PROGRESS's duty to Turpin, far more swiftly and more efficiently than it could have been carried out by the OVERSEAS PROGRESS. In such circumstances, the principles of "quasi-contract" require recovery.

Although the law ordinarily frowns on the claims of a "mere volunteer", there is a class of cases where it is imperative that a duty be performed swiftly and efficiently for the protection of the public or an innocent third party, in which a "good Samaritan" who voluntarily intervenes to perform the duty may receive restitution for his services. This rule has become crystallized in the doctrine that performance of another's duty to a third person, if rendered by one qualified to provide such services with intent to charge for them, is a ground for recovery in quasi-contract. This principle is limited to cases where the services are immediately necessary to prevent injury or suffering. *Greenspan v. Slate*, 97 A.2d 390, 397 (N.J. 1953) (Vanderbilt, C.J.); Restatement of Restitution § 114. *Cf. Wyandotte Trans. Co. v. United States*, 389 U.S. 191, 204 (1967).

The circumstances of this case compel application of the rule. The OVERSEAS PROGRESS had a manifest duty to provide Turpin with speedy medical attention. Her Captain, in the exercise of his reasonable discretion, asked the CANBERRA to perform that duty in her stead. It is undisputed that the CANBERRA, with her fully equipped hospital and greater speed, was a proper party to provide such services, and the countersigned letter from the CANBERRA's Captain suffices to demonstrate the liner's intent to charge.[3]

Moreover, this is not a case in which a "good Samaritan" volunteered his services without the knowledge or consent of the person whose duty was discharged. OVERSEAS PROGRESS actually requested the CANBERRA to come to Turpin's aid. This decision was made after full consideration of the seaman's condition and other available sources of medical assistance.[4]

---

doctrine remarkably similar to the present rules of maintenance and cure, providing, *inter alia*:

If it happens that sickness seizes on any one of the mariners, while in the service of the ship, the master ought to set him ashore, to provide lodging and candelight for him, and also spare him one of the ship-boys, or hire a woman to attend him, and likewise to afford him such diet as is usual in the ship....

The Code, however, was far less solicitous of injuries obtained through "willful misconduct", particularly while on land. It stated:

If any of the mariners hired by the master of any vessel, go out of the ship without his leave, and get themselves drunk, and thereby happens contempt to their master, debates, or fighting and quarreling among themselves; whereby some happen to be wounded: in this case the master shall not be obliged to get them cured.... Norris, *supra* § 540.

[3] Although the parties have stipulated that the letter was not a demand for payment, it was sufficient to put Overseas on notice that the services were not intended as a gratuity.

[4] Moreover, the CANBERRA's actions represented a tangible pecuniary benefit to the OVERSEAS PROGRESS. Without her assistance, or that of a similar ship, the OVERSEAS PROGRESS would have incurred much greater delay and fuel expenses in transporting Turpin to a shore hospital. It is not necessary, in cases of this character, that the "benefit" conferred be of a monetary nature. The value rendered in performing another's duty is sufficient to permit recovery. Thus, if the OVERSEAS PROGRESS had been totally unable to reach a shore hospital and the CANBERRA had been Turpin's only source of aid, it might be argued that her intervention, although vital to Turpin, did not save OVERSEAS PROGRESS from incurring any additional expense. CANBERRA could nonetheless have recovered for providing such assistance. In this case, however, where performance of another's duty and traditional "unjust enrichment" are present, both rules clearly require recovery. Judge Goettel followed a similar analysis in awarding P & O restitution for Turpin's nursing and accommodation aboard the CANBERRA, noting that these were expenses normally borne by the shipowner. The costs of swiftly bringing a disabled seaman to a surgeon are also part of the shipowner's duty of maintenance and cure, and there seems no reason to grant recovery of one expense and not the other.

III.

Overseas contends that the principles of quasi-contract, though presumably reflecting our sense of fair and orderly arrangement of affairs on *terra firma*, should not be applied to occurrences on the sea. We fail to perceive any reason for this distinction. Although it is true that the fortuitousness of jurisdiction in eighteenth century English courts long left the application of restitutionary principles to admiralty in doubt, today the law is clear that quasi-contractual claims may be considered by the federal courts in admiralty if they arise out of maritime contracts, *see Archawski v. Hanioti*, 350 U.S. 532, 536 (1956), or other inherently maritime transactions, *see Sword Line Inc. v. United States.*[5] It is difficult to imagine a transaction more maritime in nature than the one presented here, where two ships arranged a rendezvous on the high seas in order to save the life of a sailor for whom, by ancient admiralty doctrine, one of the ships was responsible.

Overseas urges that quasi-contractual recovery under these circumstances would, in effect, subvert the long established rule in admiralty that prohibits recovery for "pure life salvage". In admiralty, a person who rescues property at sea may obtain an award based not merely on the costs he incurs but on the value of the property saved and the degree of danger encountered. These rules are designed to encourage seamen to render valorous service in the salvage of property, and remuneration has accordingly been liberal. *The Clarita and the Clara*, 90 U.S. 1, 17 (1874); GILMORE AND BLACK, *supra*, LAW OF ADMIRALTY, § 8-1. Yet it seems to have been admiralty law that rescuing lives at sea, rather than property, merited moral approbation, but no pecuniary reward.[6]

Overseas bids us to ignore the sound reasons that warrant recovery in this case, and to defer instead to this hoary, and almost universally condemned, rule of the sea. But, we do not find the rule on pure life salvage, regardless of its dubious vitality, relevant to the facts. P & O is not seeking a reward; it merely requests reimbursement for its expenses. And, we do not confront a daring "rescue at sea", but the transfer of an ailing seaman from one seaworthy vessel to another. Under these circumstances we do not believe the questionable doctrine of "pure life salvage" bars recovery.

Finally, Overseas contends that the rule we announce today will disrupt traditional maritime practices, making assistance to an ailing seaman a matter of negotiation rather than moral duty. On the contrary, we believe this rule will encourage seamen aboard large vessels to perform their moral obligation to their brethren on smaller ships without fear their benevolence will result in unreasonable expenses to their ship's owners.

Overseas also predicts that masters of small ships will be reluctant to call for aid, knowing their actions may result in the imposition of sizable fuel costs. But, masters are already under a legal obligation to make reasonable efforts to secure medical care for their stricken crewmen. In determining the proper course of action, they must consider the seriousness of the seaman's illness, the availability and adequacy of medical facilities and the costs that will be incurred in securing aid. Once it is established that the fuel expenses of a ship rendering assistance is one of these costs, it will simply become another factor to be considered in the master's calculation. With radiotelegraphy, it is a simple matter for him to ascertain the size and location of ships in the vicinity, just as the OVERSEAS PROGRESS did, and to determine which vessel can be reached with minimum expense and delay. Thus, we believe the rule we announce today will result both in greater willingness of large vessels to render assistance and in the utilization of the medical facilities of those vessels in the most efficient and productive manner.

IV.

Although we believe the masters of both vessels acted admirably and, as Judge Goettel noted, "in keeping with the finest traditions of the sea", the OVERSEAS PROGRESS was in a far better position to evaluate the relevant

---

[5] 288 F.2d 244 (2d Cir. 1955) *on rehearing* 230 F.2d 75, 77 (2d Cir.), *aff'd* 351 U.S. 976 (1956).

[6] This rule was modified by the enactment of 46 U.S.C. § 729 in 1912. That statute allowed life salvors to receive a fair share of a property salvage award arising out of the same maritime accident. It was intended to remove the disincentive to life salvage that resulted from the traditional rule, which encouraged sailors to rescue property rather than aid fellow seamen in jeopardy.

The irrationality of providing rewards for property salvage but not requiring payment for rescuing lives has been under attack for many years. L. Jarett, *The Life Salvor Problem in Admiralty*, 63 YALE L.J. 779 (1954). Under British statutory law, a person who saves a life on a British vessel anywhere in the world, or on a foreign vessel in British waters, may claim a life salvage award. *Jarett, supra*, p. 782-83.

costs and benefits of seeking various forms of aid for Turpin. It was her master's decision to summon the CANBERRA that entailed the fuel expenses at issue here. Since vessels such as OVERSEAS PROGRESS are best able to avoid unnecessary costs in obtaining medical aid for their crewmen, we conclude that the owners of such ships are liable for the reasonable value of services rendered by other vessels at their request, regardless of the value of the benefit actually conferred.

In many circumstances, reasonable value may be determined by the market price for obtaining comparable services. But here, the CANBERRA's assistance was sui generis, since no other vessel could have reached Turpin as swiftly, and thus, none could have provided comparable medical care to a man in his critical condition. Under these circumstances, the only possible measure of "reasonable value" is the reasonable expense incurred by CANBERRA as a result of her assistance to Turpin. The parties have agreed that such expenses represent $8,500 of P & O's claim. Accordingly, we reverse and order judgment entered for Peninsular and Oriental Steam Navigation Co. in the amount of $8,500.

I. Remedies

In *Lombros Seaplane Base, Inc. v. The Batory*, 215 F.2d 228 (2d cir. 1954), *supra*, the seaplane which had been placed aboard the ship and taken to England. It was never returned to the United States. Suit to recover a salvage award had been commenced in federal court in New York.

It does not follow, however that the decree dismissing the cross-libel should be reversed. For the plane was never brought into the jurisdiction of the court below; it has never been arrested on a libel *in rem*; and Lambros, the owner, is before the court only on Gdynia's libel served against it *in personam*. The law applicable to such a situation was well stated in *The Emblem*, 8 Fed. Cas. 611, at pages 613, 614, No. 4,434. There the court, after comment on the power of the Admiralty Court to satisfy a claim for salvage by the sale of property saved when libelled *in rem*, spoke as follows:

> But he [owner] is under no obligation to assert his right, by intervening with a claim. He may abandon his property if he pleases, and if he does so, and declines to make himself a party to the suit, no decree can be made against him.... If the owner wishes to receive his goods, before proceedings at law are instituted and the salvor delivers them to him, a personal libel may be maintained for the salvage.... But this is solely on the ground of his possession of the property. All the authorities speak of the right of the salvor as attaching to the thing, and not as the foundation of any personal claim against the owner, independent of the goods saved.... But the saving of property, from the perils of the sea, creates no personal obligation against the owner, independent of his interest in the property saved.

It is true that the statement in *The Emblem* opinion that a personal libel will lie against the owner of salved property "solely on the ground of his possession" thereof, was dictum for purposes of that case. But the *dictum* was approved by the Supreme Court in *The Sabine*, 101 U.S. 384, 390, 25 L. Ed. 982, in which *The Emblem*, Fed. Cas. No. 4,434 was cited (as reported in 2 Ware 61) for the proposition that if "the property saved is destroyed *after having been restored* or is clandestinely removed from the jurisdiction[5] ... no doubt is entertained that they (the salvors) may proceed *in personam* against the owners of the salvaged property." (emphasis supplied.)

United States v. Cornell Steamboat Co., 202 U.S. 184, 26 S. Ct. 648, 50 L. Ed. 987, on which the appellant chiefly relies, is not in conflict with *the Emblem* rule. For there it was implicit in the facts that the property saved had been repossessed by the owners with the result that the government's right to the duties already collected thereon was restored, or saved, to the government: on that ground it was held that the

---

[5] Here the property was not "clandestinely removed from the jurisdiction" by the owner. It was removed by the salvor who upon its deposit in England might have libelled *in rem* in a British court.

government could be held on a libel *in personam*. The court there cited the British case of the *Five Steel Barges* (1890), 15 P.D. 142, in which salvage was allowed for the salvage of two (out of five) barges in a suit *in personam* against respondents who were under contract to build the barges and deliver them to the British government. The salvage services were rendered to the barges in the course of their travel to the government and when saved the barges were in fact delivered to the government thus perfecting the respondents' right to receive their sale price. And the holding was that although title had passed to the government under its contract with the respondent builders, the respondents, under their contract, had sufficient interest in the property saved to subject them to personal liability for the salvage.

The rule, as established by these cases, modifies *the Emblem* dictum that possession of the physical property salved is essential to a libel *in personam*: one, other than the legal owner, having an intangible interest in the physical property may be so held. And thus modified, the rule is well established both in England[6] and in this country.[7] But in all the cases applying that rule, it appeared expressly or implicitly that by the salvage of the physical property, followed by repossession by the owner, the intangible interest therein of the respondent was not only saved to him but was also availed of by him. We suggest that the rationale of the rule lies in the thought that acceptance of the benefit subjects the respondents to that personal liability which would have attached to a request by him for the service rendered. No case cited to us and none that we can find goes so far as to hold that an owner of salved property who never requested salvage service and elects not to accept and possess the salved property when made available to him by the salvor, is personally liable.

The appellant, Gdynia, seems to think its position supported by Kennedy on the Law of Civil Salvage (3rd Ed.), and refers particularly to pages 11 to 16. We think that authority looks the other way. For after referring to the case of the *Five Steel Barges*, *supra*, which, as we have seen, does not deal with the immediate point now under consideration, Lord Justice Kennedy quotes (p. 16) from Dr. Lushington's opinion in The Chieftain, a statement that a proceeding *in personam* "can only be where the property is in the possession of the proprietors themselves."

Nor is the point settled by Admiralty Rule 18, 28 U.S.C.A., whether read independently or against former Rule 19 which it superseded. For the final clause of Rule 18, on which appellee relies ("and/or *in personam* against any party liable for the salvage service") states merely a procedural rule: it does not purport to say that as a matter of substantive law an owner who has never repossessed his property is personally liable for salvage.

And so here, even if the plane was deposited with the British Receiver of Wrecks in Southampton for the owner's account so that Lambros had a right and opportunity there to repossess it, we conclude that, since Lambros did not in fact repossess, it is not personally liable for the salvage. The case here falls directly within the rule of *The Emblem* and the *Sabine* cases and not within the modification thereof recognized in *Cornell Steamship* and the *Five Steel Barges*. We know of no principle of the maritime law which fastens upon an owner of marine property personal liability to pay a reward for services to his property, whether by way of salvage, towage, repair or supply, absent both a request for the services and acceptance of the benefit thereof.

What has been said in an earlier section of this opinion as to the merits of Gdynia's claim for salvage in effect disposes of the issues raised by Lambros' libel for damages. We agree with the trial judge that a claim for conversion was not proved: if, as we have held, Batory was entitled to salvage the plane, its conduct in so doing did not constitute a wrongful interference with Lambros' dominion over the seaplane. Likewise, we held, no cause for negligence has been proved such as to constitute a forfeiture of Batory's right to claim for salvage. The facts and reasoning on which that holding was based equally require the conclusion that Batory's conduct was not such as to constitute an independent ground of negligence. We find no evidence which warrants a finding that the Master, who necessarily had to decide

---

[6] *The Cargo ex Port Victor*, 1901, P. 243 (C.A.); *The Meandros* (1925) P. 61, 68.

[7] *The G.L.* 40, 2 Cir., 66 F.2d 764.

promptly whether to salve or not to salve, acted unreasonably. To be sure, the proofs show that the plane suffered some minor damage in the process of removal. But neither the pleadings nor the proofs support a claim for negligence on that account.

Interlocutory decree on Lambros' libel reversed, with a direction that said libel be dismissed: decree dismissing Gdynia's cross libel, affirmed.

Note: Non-Salvage Damages

In *Clifford v. M/V Islander*, 751 F.2d 1 (1st Cir. 1984), the court rejected plaintiff's claim for salvage (pure or contract) because of the lack of a "peril". Therefore damages had to be calculated under ordinary contract rules. The reversal by the appellate court of the trial judge's overly generous damages, illustrates the difference between salvage awards and ordinary contract damages.

Turning to the finding of an oral maritime contract and the question of damages, we note initially that the parties appear to agree that if we conclude there was no act of pure salvage, as we do, then we must uphold the finding of an oral maritime contract. The issue that remains therefore is whether that contract called for $150,000 in damages.

The district court found that Clifford was hired to aid in the repair of the vessel, that he was being hired on a daily basis, and that he later should submit a bill to the Steamship Authority. While noting that there was considerable conflict in the testimony concerning this contract, we find ample support for the district court's description of its terms. It is clear that these did not include an agreement as to what a reasonable daily rate would be. The court therefore had to turn to extrinsic evidence to determine this rate. However, the only extrinsic evidence the district court had was Clifford's own testimony that his "act of pure salvage" entitled him to an award of approximately $1,000,000, the statement in his complaint that his secondary claim in quantum meruit was for $250,000, and evidence that he was paid $600 per day for an underwater survey of the Oak Bluffs terminal, which he performed a few days after the ISLANDER left for Boston.

Somehow, without referring to any of this extrinsic evidence or making any other findings of fact, the district court determined that the "terms and conditions" of the contract called for an award of $150,000 in damages. The explanation for this result is simply lacking. With the scant information that we have, it seems impossible to conclude that Clifford's daily rate was as high as $50,000 or $75,000. It may be that the district court implicitly determined that the contract was not simply for diving but also for conducting a survey, formulating a plan of repair, and immediately overseeing the implementation of that plan, and that such a contract would require a greater daily rate than that for diving. It may also be that the district court saw in the circumstances under which Clifford was hired, an expectation on the part of the SSA that it would have to pay much more if it ultimately asked him to remain on the scene for a long, tiring, trying period of time, which he appears to have done. So too, it may be that the district court factored in the risks which Clifford faced and which must have been obvious at the outset to Broderick and the other SSA officials.

All of these factors and a number of others may have been taken into account by the district court, but we are in no position to know that at this time. This being so, we have no choice but to remand for further findings concerning what damages should be awarded under the contract. *Cf. United States v. 20.53 Acres of Land, Etc.*, 478 F.2d 484, 486-87 (10th Cir. 1973) (case remanded for further findings as to how certain property interests had been valued).

We sympathize with the sense of justice that apparently led the district court to its damages figure: the recognition that although this operation could not quite qualify for the more liberal treatment given pure salvage, it deserved compensation far above that to be expected for a routine contract for services. Nevertheless, there must be in the record sufficient basis for a reasoned judgment for damages. In this case the court should feel free to reopen the record to receive evidence of the worth of the exceptional services that were rendered under such trying circumstances. Should this be allowed, SSA of course should be accorded similar opportunity to submit contrary evidence. At the conclusion of such reconsideration, we shall expect specific findings supporting the final award.

The 1989 Salvage Convention is to be found on the Tulane Maritime Law Center website at www.tulanemaritimelaw.net/docs/SalvageConvn1989. The United States is a party to the Convention.

Printed in the United States
101880LV00001B/5-12/A